June 8–11, 2015
Newport Beach, CA, USA

Association for Computing Machinery

Advancing Computing as a Science & Profession

ICS'15

Proceedings of the 29th ACM International Conference on Supercomputing

Sponsored by:

ACM SIGARCH

Supported by:

IBM

Association for
Computing Machinery

Advancing Computing as a Science & Profession

The Association for Computing Machinery
2 Penn Plaza, Suite 701
New York, New York 10121-0701

Notice to Past Authors of ACM-Published Articles
ACM intends to create a complete electronic archive of all articles and/or other material previously published by ACM. If you have written a work that has been previously published by ACM in any journal or conference proceedings prior to 1978, or any SIG Newsletter at any time, and you do NOT want this work to appear in the ACM Digital Library, please inform permissions@acm.org, stating the title of the work, the author(s), and where and when published.

ISBN: 978-1-4503-3559-1 (Digital)

ISBN: 978-1-4503-3869-1 (Print)

Additional copies may be ordered prepaid from:

ACM Order Department
PO Box 30777
New York, NY 10087-0777, USA

Phone: 1-800-342-6626 (USA and Canada)
+1-212-626-0500 (Global)
Fax: +1-212-944-1318
E-mail: acmhelp@acm.org
Hours of Operation: 8:30 am – 4:30 pm ET

Printed in the USA

General and Program Chairs' Message

Welcome to the 29th ACM International Conference on Supercomputing (ICS), June 8-11, 2015 at Newport Beach, CA. ICS is well known as the premier technical forum where researchers present their latest results and share with colleagues their perspectives on the state-of-the-art in the field of high-performance computing systems. ICS 2015 continues the strong tradition of excellent technical presentations, motivating keynote addresses, and a few carefully selected workshops and tutorials. This year the conference is held in the beautiful city of Newport Beach, CA, which offers ten miles of extraordinary fishing, swimming, surfing, and aquatic sports activities. Newport Beach is an intimate seaside oasis that will tempt you with its elegance, modern shopping and stunning residential landscape. We welcome you to ICS 2015, and hope that you will be able to stay over and enjoy what the city offers.

This year's program contains 40 technical papers. We would like to thank the authors of the 160 paper submissions from 27 countries, and regret that we could not accept more papers. We also want to thank the 50 members of the program committee for their hard work in producing nearly 500 paper reviews, deliberating through the review rebuttal process, and participating in a program committee meeting held at Houston, TX that resulted in the selection of this excellent set of papers.

This volume represents some of the most exciting current research in high-performance computing, including big data and large-scale systems, heterogeneous systems, GPU optimizations, algorithms and applications, green computing, emerging technologies, and much more. We are fortunate to have three visionary keynote speakers this year, and the abstracts for their talks are also included in this volume.

The success of ICS 2015 is the result of an outstanding team of volunteers. We would like to thank all of them for helping organize this conference. First, Alex Veidenbaum of University of California, Irvine (UCI), who as Steering Committee Chair has guided our efforts all throughout. Next is Mehmet Esat Belviranli at University of California, Riverside (UCR) who has worked as Web and Publications Chair. In spite of his demanding schedule as a senior Ph.D. student, he has spent considerable amount of time in developing all the web material and coordinating with all others ensuring a smooth operationWe are also immensely thankful to the Finance Chair Zizhong Chen (UCR), Tutorial and Workshop Chair Murali Annavaram, Local Arrangement Chair Brian Demsky (UCI) and Publicity Chair Arun Kejariwal (Twitter) for their efforts.

The ACM provided invaluable support to ICS 2015 throughout the process. In particular, we want to thank Ashley Cozzi for her help in conference logistics and finances, Adrienne Griscti who coordinated the ICS publication, and Lisa Tolles of ACM-Sheridan Proceedings Service.

We hope that ICS 2015 provides a stimulating and productive meeting where you can engage technically and socially with other researchers, colleagues, and friends from around the world.

Laxmi N. Bhuyan
General Chair
University of California
Riverside, CA

Fred Chong
Program Co-Chair
University of California
Santa Barbara, CA

Vivek Sarkar
Program Co-Chair
Rice University
Houston, TX

Table of Contents

Session: Green Computing

Session: Emerging Technologies

Session: Keynote Address III

Session: Microarchitecture

Session: Heterogeneous Systems

ICS 2015 Organization

General Chair: Laxmi N. Bhuyan, *University of California, Riverside*

Program Chairs: Fred Chong, *University of California, Santa Barbara*
Vivek Sarkar, *Rice University*

Workshops & Tutorials Chair: Murali Annavaram, *University of Southern California*

Local Chair: Brian Demsky, *University of California, Irvine*

Finance & Registration Chair: Zizhong Chen, *University of California, Riverside*

Publicity Chair: Arun Kejariwal, *Twitter Inc.*

Proceedings & Web Chair: Mehmet E. Belviranli, *University of California, Riverside*

Program Committee: Fred Chong (Co-Chair), *University of California, Santa Barbara*
Vivek Sarkar (Co-Chair), *Rice University*
Nael Abu-Ghazaleh, *University of California, Riverside*
Yungang Bao, *Institute of Computing Technology (ICT), CAS*
Aydın Buluç, *Lawrence Berkeley National Laboratory*
Ro Cammarota, *Qualcomm*
Brad Chamberlain, *Cray Inc.*
Lizhong Chen, *Oregon State University*
Haibo Chen, *Shanghai Jiao Tong University*
Bronis de Supinski, *Lawrence Livermore National Laboratory*
Anshu Dubey, *Lawrence Berkeley National Laboratory*
Evelyn Duesterwald, *IBM T.J. Watson Research Center*
Ian Foster, *Argonne National Laboratory & The University of Chicago*
Maria Garzaran, *University of Illinois*
Ada Gavrilovska, *Georgia Institute of Technology*
Maya Gokhale, *Lawrence Livermore National Lab*
R. Govindarajan, *Indian Institute of Science*
Sudhanva Gurumurthi, *University of Virginia and AMD Research*
Kim Hazelwood, *Yahoo! Labs*
Koji Inoue, *Kyushu University*
David Kaeli, *Northeastern University*
Arun Kejariwal, *Netflix Inc.*
John Kim, *KAIST*
Hyesoon Kim, *Georgia Institute of Technology*
Tushar Krishna, *Intel*
John Kubiatowicz, *University of California, Berkeley*
Tao Li, *University of Florida*

Program Committee (continued):

Mieszko Lis, *University of British Columbia*
Guoping Long, *Institute of Software, Chinese Academy of Sciences*
Andrew Lumsdaine, *Indiana University*
Sally McKee, *Chalmers University of Technology*
Frank Mueller, *North Carolina State University*
Walid Najjar, *University of California, Riverside*
Thu Nguyen, *Rutgers University*
Alex Nicolau, *University of California, Irvine*
Tamiya Onodera, *IBM Research*
John Owens, *University of California, Davis*
Lawrence Rauchwerger, *Texas A&M University*
Shaolei Ren, *Florida International University*
Jack Sampson, *Penn State*
Arrvindh Shriraman, *Simon Fraser University*
Yang Song, *IBM*
Tatiana Shpeisman, *Intel*
Hari Sundar, *University of Utah*
Alan Sussman, *University of Maryland*
Nathan Tallent, *Pacific Northwest National Laboratory*
Lingjia Tang, *University of Michigan*
Olivier Tardieu, *IBM*
Michela Taufer, *University of Delaware*
Antonino Tumeo, *Pacific Northwest National Laboratory*
Felix Wolf, *Technische Universitaet Darmstadt*
Rich Wolski, *University of California, Santa Barbara*

Sponsor: SIGARCH

Supporter: IBM®

Streaming Task Parallelism

Albert Cohen
Senior Research Scientist, INRIA

Abstract

Stream computing is often associated with regular, data-intensive applications, and more specifically with the family of cyclo-static data-flow models. The term also refers to bulk-synchronous data parallelism on SIMD architectures. Both interpretations are valid but incomplete: streams underline the formal definition of Kahn process networks, a foundation for deterministic concurrent languages and systems with a solid heritage. Streaming task parallelism is a semantical framework for parallel languages and a model for task-parallel execution with first-class dependences. Parallel languages with dynamic, nested task creation and first-class streams expose more parallelism and enable application-specific throttle control. These expressiveness and efficient resource utilization features address an important limitation of previous data-flow programming models. To support the class of streaming task parallel languages, we propose a new lock-free algorithm for stalling and waking-up tasks in a shared-memory, user-space scheduler according to changes in the state of streaming queues. The algorithm generalizes both work-stealing with concurrent ring buffers, and is proven correct against the C11 memory model. We show through experiments that it can serve as a common runtime for efficient parallel runtime systems. We also report on scalability-oriented extensions, with multiple optimizations leveraging the explicit flow of data conveyed by the programming model. We will report on recent experiments on large scale NUMA systems with up to 24 nodes.

ACM Classification

D.3.2 [**Software**]: Language Classifications – *Concurrent, distributed, and parallel languages, Data-flow languages*; D.3.4 [**Software**]: Processors – *Run-time environments, Compilers*

Keywords

Task parallelism; stream computing; runtime systems, relaxed memory models

ICS'15, June 8–11, 2015, Newport Beach, CA, USA.
ACM 978-1-4503-3559-1/15/06.
http://dx.doi.org/10.1145/2751205.2751208

Bio

Albert Cohen is a senior research scientist at INRIA and a part-time associate professor at École Polytechnique. He graduated from École Normale Supérieure de Lyon, and received his PhD from the University of Versailles in 1999 (awarded two national prizes). He has been a visiting scholar at the University of Illinois and an invited professor at Philips Research, both for six months. Albert Cohen works on parallelizing and optimizing compilers, parallel programming, and synchronous programming for embedded systems. He will be or has been the general or program chair of major conferences, including PLDI, PPoPP, HiPEAC, CC, and the DAC embedded software track. He coauthored more than 130 peer-reviewed papers, and has been the advisor for 22 PhD theses. Several research projects initiated by Albert Cohen resulted in effective transfer to production compilers. In particular, Albert Cohen pioneered the transfer of polyhedral compilation technology to GCC.

Automatic Parallelization of Kernels in Shared-Memory Multi-GPU Nodes

Javier Cabezas
Barcelona Supercomputing Center, Spain
javier.cabezas@bsc.es

Lluís Vilanova
Barcelona Supercomputing Center, Spain
lluis.vilanova@bsc.es

Isaac Gelado
NVIDIA Corporation
Santa Clara, CA, USA
igelado@nvidia.com

Thomas B. Jablin
University of Illinois at Urbana-Champaign
Urbana, IL, USA
jablin@illinois.edu

Nacho Navarro
Universitat Politècnica de Catalunya
Barcelona Supercomputing Center, Spain
nacho@ac.upc.edu

Wen-mei W. Hwu
University of Illinois at Urbana-Champaign
Urbana, IL, USA
w-hwu@illinois.edu

ABSTRACT

In this paper we present AMGE, a programming framework and runtime system that transparently decomposes GPU kernels and executes them on multiple GPUs in parallel. AMGE exploits the remote memory access capability in modern GPUs to ensure that data can be accessed regardless of its physical location, allowing our runtime to safely decompose and distribute arrays across GPU memories. It optionally performs a compiler analysis that detects array access patterns in GPU kernels. Using this information, the runtime can perform more efficient computation and data distribution configurations than previous works. The GPU execution model allows AMGE to hide the cost of remote accesses if they are kept below 5%. We demonstrate that a thread block scheduling policy that distributes remote accesses through the whole kernel execution further reduces their overhead. Results show 1.98× and 3.89× execution speedups for 2 and 4 GPUs for a wide range of dense computations compared to the original versions on a single GPU.

Categories and Subject Descriptors

C.1.4 [**Processor Architectures**]: Parallel Architectures; D.1.3 [**Programming Techniques**]: Parallel Programming

Keywords

Multi-GPU programming; NUMA

1. INTRODUCTION

In the race towards exascale, new node architectures are being proposed to improve both performance and energy efficiency. For example, Summit and Sierra supercomputers will include multiple GPUs and CPUs in each node connected through a high-bandwidth interconnect [3]. This interconnect will allow any CPU and GPU in the system to transparently access all the memories in the system, although with different latency and bandwidth characteristics (i.e., NUMA). Current GPU programming models, such as CUDA [24] and OpenCL [17], present GPUs as external devices with their own private memory. Programmers are in charge of splitting data and computation across GPUs and taking care of data movement, making multi-GPU programming tedious and error-prone. Programming models that allow to easily exploit all the GPUs in the node are needed.

Ideally, all GPU resources should be presented as a single virtual GPU, leaving the problem of computation and data distribution to the compiler and runtime system. Some solutions have been proposed [18, 20], but their designs exhibit fundamental limitations. (1) Large memory footprint overhead due to replication of portions of the arrays that are never accessed. For example, consider a kernel that performs n-dimensional tiling (a common pattern in dense GPU computations [26, 30, 5]) where each computation partition accesses a non-contiguous memory region of a matrix. In such a case, existing proposals transfer the whole memory address ranges accessed by each computation partition, which may include large portions of the array that are never used. This limits the size of the problems that can be handled, and imposes performance overheads due to larger data transfers. (2) High costs due to data coherence as replicated output memory regions need to be merged in the host memory after each kernel call, which often leads to higher performance degradation. (3) Applications that use atomic and global memory instructions resort to single-GPU execution.

In this paper we present AMGE (Automatic Multi-GPU Execution), a programming interface, compiler support and runtime system that automatically executes computations that are programmed for a single GPU across all the GPUs in the system. The programming interface provides a data type for multidimensional arrays that allows for robust, transparent distribution of arrays across GPU memories. The compiler extracts the dimensionality information from the type of each array, and is able to determine the access pattern in each dimension of the array. The runtime system uses the compiler-provided information to transparently choose

ICS'15, June 8–11, 2015, Newport Beach, CA, USA.

http://dx.doi.org/10.1145/2751205.2751218.

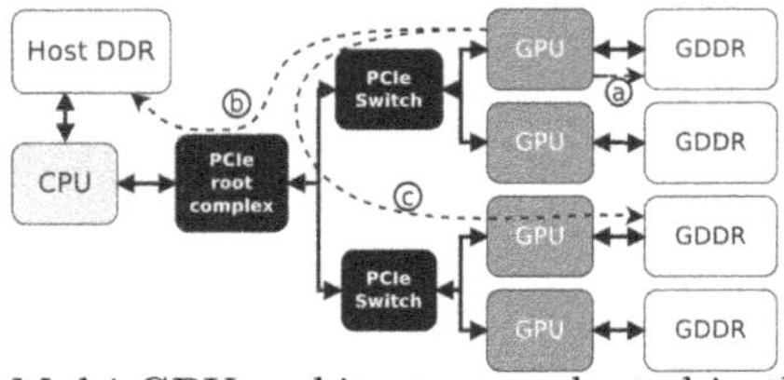

Figure 1: Multi-GPU architecture evaluated in this paper.

the best computation and data distribution configuration to minimize inter-GPU communication and memory footprint.

AMGE assumes non-coherent non-uniform shared memory accesses (NCC-NUMA) between GPUs through a relatively low-bandwidth interconnect, such that all GPUs can access and cache any partition of the arrays. Thus, we ensure that arrays can be arbitrarily decomposed, distributed and safely accessed from any GPU in the system. In current systems based on discrete GPUs, we utilize Peer-to-Peer [1] and Unified Virtual Address Space [24] technologies that enable a GPU to transparently access the memory of any other GPU connected to the same PCIe domain. While remote GPU memory accesses have been used in the past [28], this is the first work to use them as an enabling mechanism for automatic multi-GPU execution.

We also present and discuss different implementation tradeoffs for computation and data distribution across GPUs using a prototype implementation of AMGE for C++ and CUDA. The prototype includes a compiler pass that detects array access patterns in CUDA kernels and generates optimized versions of the kernels for different array decompositions. The runtime system distributes data and computation, and selects the appropriate kernel version. This prototype is evaluated using a set of GPU dense-computation benchmarks, originally developed for single-GPU execution. Results on a real system show 1.98× and 3.89× kernel execution speedups for 2 and 4 GPUs respectively, compared to the original version of the kernels running on a single GPU.

The main contributions of this paper are: (1) A multi-GPU parallelization system that performs robust space-efficient data decompositions to enable larger problem sizes. (2) A novel compiler analysis for GPU kernels that detects per-dimension array access patterns, enabling the runtime system to determine array distributions that minimize the number of remote memory accesses. (3) A simple programming interface that can be easily introduced into languages such as CUDA and OpenCL to robustly and transparently distribute computation and data across several GPUs. (4) An evaluation that shows the efficacy of the remote memory access mechanism for multi-GPU parallelization even when built on an interconnect with limited bandwidth.

2. MULTI-GPU ARCHITECTURE

AMGE targets systems that contain several CPUs and GPUs. Each processor is connected to one or more memory modules, but all CPUs and GPUs can access any memory module in the system. Accesses to remote memories have longer access latency and lower bandwidth than local accesses, thus forming a shared memory NUMA system. CPU cores access memory through a coherent cache hierarchy, while GPUs use weaker consistency models that do not require cache coherence between cores. Similar shared memory NCC-NUMA system architectures have been successfully implemented in the past (e.g., Cray T3E [25]). NVIDIA proposes a similar system architecture in the Echelon project [16]. Moreover, NVIDIA will offer single-board multi-GPU configurations in which GPUs share the memory through a non-coherent interconnect named NVLink, in the Pascal family of GPUs. AMD also implements coherent and non-coherent memory hierarchies in their APU chips [2].

We evaluate AMGE on an existing commercial system based on NVIDIA discrete GPUs (see Figure 1). In this system, GPUs access their local memory (arc a) with full-bandwidth. Accesses to CPU memories from the GPU (arc b) are routed through the PCI Express (PCIe) interconnect and the CPU memory controller. If the target address resides in a memory connected to a different CPU socket, the inter-CPU interconnect (HyperTransport/QPI) must be traversed, too. GPUs can also access the memory in another GPU through the PCIe interconnect (arc c) [1].

While the execution model provided by GPUs can hide large memory latencies, both CPU memory and the inter-GPU interconnects (e.g., PCIe 2.0/3.0) deliver a memory bandwidth which is an order of magnitude lower than the local GPU memory (GDDR5). New interconnects that provide much higher bandwidth have been announced (e.g., NVLink is projected to deliver up to 100 GB/s), but the memory technology will also keep improving, thus maintaining this gap. Therefore, minimizing remote accesses is key to maximize application performance.

2.1 GPU Programming Model

GPUs are typically programmed using a Single Program Multiple Data (SPMD) programming model, like NVIDIA CUDA [24] or OpenCL [17]. For simplicity, we adopt the CUDA terminology in the remainder of the paper. A SPMD model lets programmers spawn a large number of threads that execute the same program, although each thread can take a different control flow path. All these threads are organized into a *computation grid* of groups of *thread blocks* (i.e., groups of threads). Each thread block has an identifier and each thread has an identifier within the thread block, which can be used by programmers to map the computation to the data structures. Both CUDA and OpenCL provide weak consistency models: memory updates performed by a thread might not be perceived by others, except for atomic and memory fence instructions.

Multi-GPU Programming. In CUDA and OpenCL, GPUs are presented as external devices with their own memories. Programmers typically decompose computation and data so that each GPU only accesses its local memory. If there are regions of data that are accessed by several GPUs, programmers are responsible of replicating and keeping them coherent through explicit memory transfers. CUDA exposes a Unified Virtual Address Space (UVAS), which ensures that virtual memory addresses are unique across all memories in the system. Using UVAS, programmers can map the pages of a memory allocation on different GPU memories. However, CUDA does not provide any means to control how virtual addresses are mapped to physical memory, and allocations are bound to a single GPU.

Oftentimes, data structures need to be accessed by both CPU and GPU code, and programmers are in charge of using separate copies of the data structures and keeping them coherent through explicit memory transfers. This extra code incurs additional development time and harms maintainability. Recently, CUDA introduced UVM (Unified Virtual

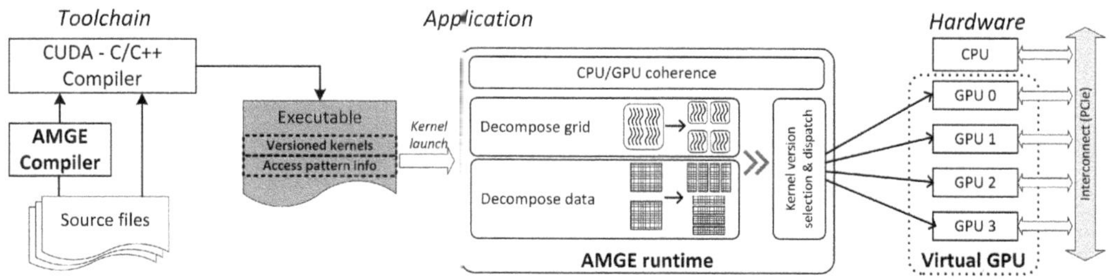

Figure 2: Overview of AMGE components. The compiler extracts array access pattern information and stores it in the program binary. It also generates optimized kernel versions for different array decompositions. The runtime system uses this information to decompose and distribute computation and data across the GPUs in the system.

Memory), which allows allocating memory that can be accessed by CPU and GPU code, but not concurrently. UVM is based on the ADSM model [13], in which the memory that is shared by CPU and GPUs is acquired/released by the GPU at kernel call boundaries. OpenCL 2.0 also exposes a Shared Virtual Memory space [17], but it does not allow programmers to specify in which memory data is actually allocated. AMGE builds on remote memory accesses, UVAS, and ADSM technologies.

3. AMGE OVERVIEW

AMGE is a programming framework that decomposes and distributes GPU kernels and data to be collaboratively executed on all the GPUs in the system. We implement AMGE using C++ and CUDA, but it can be extended to other languages. Figure 2 shows the components in AMGE and how they interact with the hardware. AMGE aggregates the GPU resources in the system and presents them as a *single virtual GPU*. Thus, programmers are relieved from the burden of decomposing the problem and explicitly managing several GPUs.

The AMGE compiler is a source-to-source compiler, that analyzes the CUDA kernels in the program to detect their array access patterns and store this information in the program executable. It also generates optimized kernel versions for the possible array decompositions. We argue that the utilization of the array dimensionality information is paramount in order to efficiently exploit multi-GPU systems. However, CUDA is an extension of the C/C++ languages, which do not provide data types with such information; programmers typically flatten the multi-dimensional arrays into 1D arrays and linearize the dimension indices in each array reference. It is practically difficult, if not infeasible, for static analysis to reliably recover the dimensionality information once the accesses have been flattened. AMGE provides a new data type for multi-dimensional arrays that makes this information available to the compiler. Details on the implementation of the data type and the generation of optimized kernel versions are discussed in Section 5.

The other key feature of AMGE is the utilization of *remote memory accesses* between GPUs [1]. On each reference to the array, the underlying implementation determines whether the element being referenced is hosted in the memory local to the GPU executing the code or on a different GPU. References from a GPU to parts of the array stored in different GPU memories are handled using remote memory accesses. This approach ensures correctness regardless of the chosen GPU computation and data distribution configuration and removes the requirement for the compiler analysis

```
void sgemm(ndarray<float, 2, cmo> C, ndarray<float, 2, cmo> A,
           ndarray<float, 2> B)
{
   float partial[SGEMM_TILE_N];
   __shared__ float b_tile_sh[SGEMM_TILE_HEIGHT][SGEMM_TILE_N];
   for (int i = 0; i < SGEMM_TILE_N; i++) partial[i] = 0.0f;

   int mid = threadIdx.y * blockDim.x + threadIdx.x;
   int row = blockIdx.x * (SGEMM_TILE_N * SGEMM_TILE_HEIGHT) + mid;
   int col = blockIdx.y *  SGEMM_TILE_N + threadIdx.x;

   for (int i = 0; i < A.get_dim(1); i += SGEMM_TILE_HEIGHT) {
      b_tile_sh[threadIdx.y][threadIdx.x] = B(i + threadIdx.y, col);
      __syncthreads();
      for (int j = 0; j < SGEMM_TILE_HEIGHT; ++j) {
         float a = A(row, i + j);
         for (int k = 0; k < SGEMM_TILE_N; ++k)
            partial[k] += a * b_tile_sh[j][k];
      }
      __syncthreads();
   }
   for (int i = 0; i < SGEMM_TILE_N; i++)
      C(row, i + by * SGEMM_TILE_N) = partial[i];
}
```

Listing 1: Multi-GPU `sgemm` GPU code with AMGE. `cmo` means *column major order*.

to unequivocally determine the bounds of the memory range accessed by a computation partition.

However, remote accesses can impose performance overheads and they must be minimized. On each kernel call, *the AMGE runtime* determines the best computation and array decompositions using the information generated by the compiler, and distributes them across all GPUs in the system.

Memory model: Arrays are transparently decomposed and/or replicated before each kernel call. Input arrays can be replicated at the cost of additional space and data transfers, but AMGE never replicates output arrays. Replicated output arrays require from additional coherence management to merge partial modifications on different GPUs. Previous works [18, 20] transfer all copies to the host memory for a merging step after every kernel call, imposing a large performance overhead in many workloads. Moreover, replicating output arrays prevents distributing codes with atomics or memory fences. AMGE always distributes output arrays across GPU memories instead, and relies on remote memory accesses to guarantee that they are available to all GPUs.

AMGE implements the ADSM model [13] to allow arrays to be used both by host and GPU code. The runtime transfers arrays between CPU and GPU memories as needed.

3.1 An example: matrix multiplication

Code programmed to run on a single GPU requires only minor modifications to use AMGE. Listing 1 shows the GPU code of a single-precision floating point matrix-matrix multiplication computation [12] (i.e., `sgemm`) using AMGE. *A* and *C* matrices are stored in *column major* order, and *B* in *row major* order, for optimal performance. The highlighted text shows the modifications performed to the original code. The

```
1   // Initialize A and B in the host code
2   ndarray<float, 2, cmo> A;
3   ndarray<float, 2>      B;
4
5   read_array("A.dat", A);
6   read_array("B.dat", B);
7
8   ndarray<float, 2, cmo> C(A.get_dim(1), B.get_dim(0));
9   // Computation grid size
10  dim3 block(MATRIXMUL_TILE_N, SGEMM_TILE_HEIGHT);
11  dim3 grid(C.get_dim(1)/(SGEMM_TILE_N * SGEMM_TILE_HEIGHT),
12            C.get_dim(0)/SGEMM_TILE_N);
13  // Kernel launch. A, B and C are used in the GPU code
14  sgemm<<<grid, block>>>(C, A, B);
15  // Write results for C into a file
16  write_array("C.dat", C);
```

Listing 2: Multi-GPU sgemm host code with AMGE.

only additional programming requirement for the kernel to be automatically decomposed is the array data type (lines 1-2), and its associated indexing routines (lines 12, 13, 16 and 23). The data type is implemented by the `ndarray<T, Dims, Storage>` C++ class template, where `T` is the type of the elements, `Dims` is the number of dimensions of the array, and `Storage` is an optional parameter that defines the storage type (by default, the C/C++ *row major* order storage convention is used). The kernel uses a 2D computation grid, in which each thread block computes a 2D tile of C by traversing A and B on their X and Y dimensions, respectively. The compiler detects these patterns and stores them in the program executable (*access pattern info* in Figure 2).

Listing 2 shows the CPU code of the `sgemm` computation. First, `float` input matrices `A` and `B` are declared in lines 2 and 3. The bounds of each dimension of the array are defined at run-time. The AMGE runtime intercepts the kernel call and uses the information generated by the compiler to decompose the matrices, and distribute both computation and data across all the GPUs. Note that `ndarray` objects can be passed both to CPU and GPU routines, making explicit data transfers between host and GPU memories unnecessary.

4. COMPUTATION/DATA DISTRIBUTION

AMGE decomposes GPU kernels at thread block boundaries. We choose this decomposition granularity because threads within a thread block share resources (e.g., shared memory), and perform barrier synchronization operations. Hence, all threads within a thread block must be executed in the same compute core of the same GPU. However, the GPU programming model guarantees that there are no data dependences across thread blocks within a kernel and, therefore, they can execute independently.

In CUDA, programmers specify a computation grid that is a multidimensional space $grid_x \times grid_y \times grid_z$ of thread blocks, similar to the iteration space in loop nests. Each thread block has a unique identifier $0 \leq block_x, block_y, block_z < grid_x, grid_y, grid_z$ within the computation grid. The AMGE runtime decomposes the computation grid so that it can be executed on several GPUs. In CUDA and OpenCL, the computation grid is canonical and rectangular. Thus, the computation grid can be uniformly decomposed into partitions along one or several of its dimensions.

AMGE uses compiler analysis to generate array access pattern information for all the GPU kernels in the program. This information is later used by the runtime system to try to place on each GPU the data accessed by the computation partition assigned to it, in order to minimize the number of remote memory accesses.

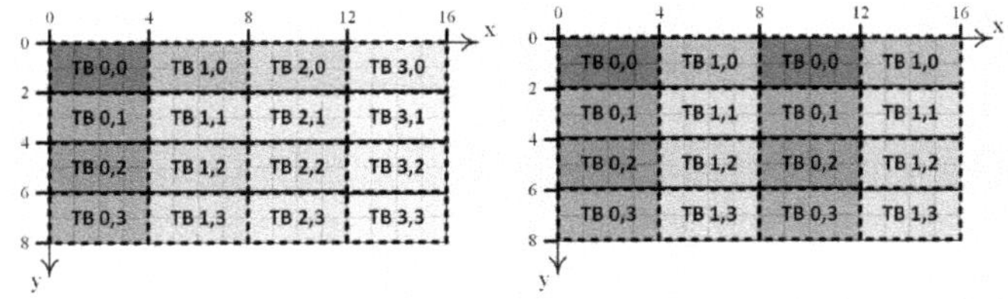

(a) BLOCK (b) BLOCK-CYCLIC

Figure 3: Computation-to-data mapping examples.

4.1 Compiler analysis

The AMGE compiler analyzes all array references in the kernel. Each reference contains one index for each of the dimensions of the array, allowing the AMGE compiler to detect the individual access pattern in each dimension. This is in contrast to previous works [18, 20] that treat all arrays as one dimensional. Kim et al. [18] compute the upper and lower memory addresses of the tiles accessed by each computation partition to distribute the arrays. This may lead to unnecessary replication of large portions of the application dataset, also imposing higher data copy costs. For example, $TB_{0,0}$ in Figure 3a accesses a 2D tile composed of elements from two different rows of a matrix: $\{(0,0)\ldots(0,3)\} \cup \{(1,0)\ldots(1,3)\}$. However, the linear memory address range defined by the upper and lower bounds of the tile also contains elements that belong to the neighboring tiles in the X dimension of the matrix: $\{(0,0)\ldots(0,15)\} \cup \{(1,0)\ldots(1,3)\}$. Moreover, for output arrays this generates additional data merging operations, as tiles might be wrongly classified as overlapping. For example, the tiles for $TB_{0,0}$ and $TB_{1,0}$ do not overlap, but the analysis in previous works uses their linear address ranges, which do overlap. The per-dimension access pattern information allows AMGE to identify multi-dimensional tiles as non-overlapping entities.

We consider three classes of access patterns: (1) as a function of thread block indices, (2) local to a thread block, and (3) data-dependent. The first class, the most commonly found in GPU applications, is produced when programmers access arrays using affine transformations of the block and thread indices. As a result, threads belonging to thread blocks with contiguous identifiers in one dimension access elements that are contiguous in a dimension of the array. In the `sgemm` example (Listing 1), $block_x$ is used to access A_y (line 16) and C_y (line 23), while $block_y$ is used to access B_x (line 13) and C_x (line 23). We use the notation A_i to refer to the ith dimension of array A. This linear relationship allows us to relate thread blocks with the portions of the arrays accessed by them.

The second access pattern type is produced when array dimensions are traversed through loop induction variables or local thread indexes. In the `sgemm` example (Listing 1), threads traverse A_x using the induction variables $i + j$ of the nested loops (line 16).

The third type of accesses cannot be determined at compile time since the indices are computed with values that are only known at kernel execution time.

Only array dimensions accessed using the first pattern class are eligible for decomposition, since the second class refers to access patterns local to a single thread or thread block, and the third class cannot be determined statically. AMGE uses a novel compiler analysis, for the dimensions that are eligible for decomposition, that identifies the thread block-to-data mappings, and classifies them into the most common distribution types: BLOCK, CYCLIC and BLOCK-CYCLIC (illustrated in Figure 3 for a 2D array)[14, 19, 6]. This analysis tries to map the index expression used in each dimension of each array reference to the following canonical form:

$$m \times t \times G + t \times B + k \qquad (1)$$

where:

- m: index of the non-contiguous array tile accessed by a thread block (an induction variable or a constant).
- t: array tile size. It is a multiple of the thread block size when threads access different elements or 1 if all threads access the same element of the array's dimension (e.g., the same row in a matrix). The actual thread block size is extracted from the kernel launch parameters at run-time.
- G: number of thread blocks in a dimension of the computation grid (e.g., $grid_x$).
- B: thread block index (e.g., $block_x$). Expressions not using this term do not belong to the first access pattern class.
- k: thread index or a constant. This value does not determine the access patterns across thread blocks.

We find that most GPU array-based computations use this form to distribute the array across thread blocks.

The most common and simple index expression is found when each thread block accesses a single contiguous array tile (i.e., $m = 0$). This expression is classified as BLOCK. Another common index expression assigns non-contiguous array tiles to each thread block (i.e., $m > 0$) using a grid-sized stride. This expression is classified as BLOCK-CYCLIC. CYCLIC is a special case of BLOCK-CYCLIC, in which $t = 1$.

Information generation for the runtime: The compiler analysis generates a record with the following information for each dimension of each array used in each GPU kernel: (1) the dimension of the computation grid whose thread block index is used to index the array dimension; (2) the access type (Read/Write); (3) the distribution type (BLOCK, CYCLIC, BLOCK-CYCLIC). This information is built by combining the values from the different references to the array in the kernel: (1) the intersection of the used computation grid dimensions; (2) the union of the access types; (3) the intersection of the distribution types. Thus, if an array dimension is indexed using block indices of different dimensions of the computation grid or different distribution types, an empty record is generated for that dimension. Array dimensions that are not indexed using the first data access pattern class, get empty records, too. Only array dimensions with non-empty records can be distributed.

4.2 Run-time distribution

On each kernel execution, the runtime identifies all possible computation grid decompositions. Then, it uses the compiler-provided information to compute the distribution configurations for each potential computation grid decomposition. Since the computation grid is limited to three dimensions, there are, at most, eight potential decompositions. Finally, the runtime ranks each distribution configuration using an analytical model (details in Section 5.3) and distributes the arrays and computation using the highest-ranked configuration.

4.2.1 *Computation grid distribution*

For a specific computation grid decomposition, the AMGE runtime defines a grid of GPUs ($gpu_0 \times gpu_1 \times \dots gpu_{N-1}$) with

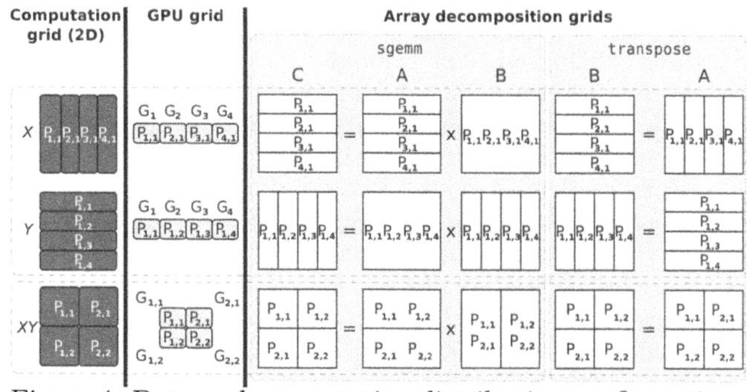

Figure 4: Data and computation distribution configurations for sgemm and transpose on a 4-GPU system. A, B, C are the arrays used in the kernels, $P_{i,j}$ is a partition of the computation grid, $G_{i,j}$ is a GPU in the GPU grid.

as many dimensions as decomposed dimensions in the computation grid. Then, the computation grid is decomposed into as many partitions as the number of GPUs in each dimension of the GPU grid, and each partition is assigned to a GPU. We refer to the mapping of the computation grid to the GPU grid as computation distribution configuration.

4.2.2 *Array distribution*

The runtime system uses the compiler-generated access pattern information to determine how arrays must be decomposed for a specific computation distribution configuration. An array is decomposed along those dimensions that are indexed with the thread block indices of the decomposed computation grid dimensions. This creates an m-dimensional grid of tiles, where m is the number of decomposed dimensions in the array. Output arrays that are not accessed with any of the thread block indexes of the decomposed computation grid dimensions, are arbitrarily decomposed along their highest-order dimension.

The size and number of tiles depend on the computation distribution configuration. If $block_i$ is used to index L_j, and $grid_i$ is mapped on the k dimension of the GPU grid, then L_j is decomposed into as many tiles as GPUs in gpu_k and distributed among them. Figure 4 shows the relationship between the computation grid, the GPU grid and the array decomposition grid in different computation distribution configurations for sgemm and transpose. In the sgemm example, C_x, C_y, A_y and B_x can be potentially decomposed, as they are indexed with thread block indices. For a configuration that decomposes the computation grid on its Y dimension ($grid_y$, second row of Figure 4), C_x and B_x are decomposed. However, since $block_x$ is used to index A_y but $grid_x$ is not decomposed, A_y is not decomposed either. In transpose, both $block_x$ and $block_y$ are used to index the two dimensions of A and B matrices and are always decomposed. The distribution of tiles among the GPU memories follows the mapping of the computation grid partitions on the GPU grid. For example, in the XY computation grid decomposition of sgemm (third row of Figure 4), neighboring tiles in C_x are distributed across neighboring GPUs in gpu_y.

Input arrays that are not decomposed are replicated in all GPU memories. Moreover, tiles from input arrays that are not indexed using the thread block indexes of all the decomposed dimensions of the computation grid, are *partially* replicated. In this case, the array tiles are only replicated in the memories of those GPUs that belong to the GPU grid dimensions on which the unused computation grid dimensions are distributed. For example, in `sgemm`, C is indexed with both $block_x$ and $block_y$ and its tiles are not replicated for any computation grid decomposition. However, A is indexed with $block_x$, and B is indexed with $block_y$, only. Thus, A and B are fully replicated in all GPUs for Y and X computation grid decompositions, respectively. In the XY configuration, the tiles in A are distributed across the GPUs in gpu_x and each tile is replicated in all GPUs in gpu_y. For example, the upper tile of A is accessed by both $P_{1,1}$ and $P_{1,2}$ computation partitions, and it is replicated in the memories of GPUs $G_{1,1}$ and $G_{1,2}$. Conversely, the tiles in B are distributed across the GPUs in gpu_y and replicated in the GPUs in gpu_x.

5. IMPLEMENTATION DETAILS

5.1 Array data type

We utilize the UVAS support to place different parts of the array in different GPU memories while having a continuous representation of the array in the virtual address space. Hence, decomposed arrays can be referenced by using regular linearization operations on the indexes: $(a_1, \cdots, a_n) \rightarrow \sum_{i=1}^{n} a_i \times \prod_{j=i+1}^{n} D_j$ where a_i is the index and D_i the number of elements in the ith dimension of the array. Indexes are ordered from the highest-order to the lowest-order dimension. We refer to this scheme as **VM** implementation.

This implementation decomposes arrays with page-size granularity which, in current GPUs, is in the order of a few kilobytes. Nevertheless, we have experimentally determined that current versions of CUDA impose a 1 MB (instead of page-size) granularity to allocate contiguous virtual memory ranges on different GPUs. This produces data distribution imbalance if partitions cannot be stored in balanced-sized groups of 1 MB chunks, resulting in an increased number of remote memory accesses. One solution to reduce the imbalance is to add padding to the lower order dimensions that are not decomposed. However, achieving perfect balancing using 1 MB chunks can impose a footprint overhead in the order of hundreds of times, especially for arrays' lowest-order dimensions, whose elements are stored contiguously in memory. Another solution is to permute the dimensions of the array to ensure that decomposed dimensions are not contiguous in memory. Unfortunately, this can break memory coalescing [27].

Therefore, we also provide an alternate implementation proposed in [4] that **reshape**s the arrays. In this implementation, each GPU contains a memory allocation that holds all the elements in a partition, and it is padded to the 1MB boundary. The array is reorganized by adding a new dimension for each decomposed one (i.e., strip-mining), that indicates the GPU in which each partition is stored. In each array reference, the original indexes are transformed into a new set of indexes. This approach allows arrays to be decomposed on any dimension as they do not have to be stored contiguously in the virtual address space. However, this flexibility comes at the cost of extra computation. For example, if a 3D volume is decomposed along its highest-order dimension using a `BLOCK` distribution, the index for this dimension a_1 is transformed as follows:

$$(a_1, a_2, a_3) \rightarrow (\left\lfloor \frac{a_1}{D_1'} \right\rfloor, a_1 \bmod D_1', a_2, a_3) \quad (2)$$

where $D_1' = \lceil \frac{D_1}{P_1} \rceil$ and P_1 is the number of tiles in the first dimension of the array's decomposition grid. The operations needed to compute the location of the element a_1, a_2, a_3, are divided into: the computations of the offset of the block in the dimension being decomposed, and the linearization of the index within the block. Therefore, an extra division and modulo operations are performed in each access to the array, compared with the regular index linearization. For `CYCLIC` and `BLOCK-CYCLIC`, similar transformations are performed.

Providing a generic indexing routine that supports all possible array decompositions can impose an unacceptable performance overhead due to the extra operations needed to transform all the indexes. In order to ensure maximum performance, our prototype provides different implementations of the indexing routines optimized for the different array decompositions and distribution types.

5.2 Source-to-source transformations

Kernel versioning: Using specialized indexing routines for each decomposition requires changes in the kernels, as (1) the kernel code must explicitly call the proper versions of the routines, and (2) the array decomposition to be used is not known at compile time. Thus, AMGE generates different kernel versions for all the possible array decompositions of the arrays used in the kernel. In each version, array references use the indexing routines that are optimized for a chosen decomposition. On each kernel execution, when the runtime system selects the distribution for all the arrays, it uses the specialized kernel version for that configuration.

Global thread block identifiers: Since computation partitions are executed independently, CUDA assigns new thread block identifiers in the kernel invocations on each GPU. In order to retain the original identifiers, we store the offsets of each computation partition in the memory of each GPU. The compiler modifies replaces `blockIdx` with code that computes the original indexes using these offsets.

Memory consistency model: Distributed kernels must honor the memory consistency of the GPU programming model. Data propagation across thread blocks in the GPU model is only guaranteed for atomic memory operations and memory fences. For atomic operations we exploit the hardware support provided by modern system architectures (e.g., atomic operations in PCIe 3.0). GPU-wide memory fences are translated to system-wide memory fences to ensure correctness. Finally, since a GPU may cache remote array partitions, GPU caches are flushed at kernel exit boundary.

AMGE toolchain: AMGE provides a toolchain based on the LLVM framework. The first pass performs the array access pattern analysis introduced in Section 4.1 on the LLVM IR generated by the CUDA compiler, and generates code to pass the information to the runtime system. The second pass handles `blockIdx` and memory fence translations. The third pass generates specialized kernel versions for the possible array decompositions, and code for the runtime system to retrieve the version for a chosen configuration. Generated code is compiled into the program executable.

5.3 Run-time distribution selection policy

As explained in Section 4.2, on a kernel call, the runtime system selects the best distribution configuration. Our prototype implements a policy that (1) favors the array implementation that imposes the least overhead, (2) minimizes the number of remote accesses. Thus, the VM implementation is preferred (since it does not impose any indexing overhead) unless it introduces *too many* remote memory accesses due to data distribution imbalance. Our policy ranks the array decompostions given by the runtime system for both VM and reshape implementations. For VM, the score is calculated using the data distribution imbalance introduced by the coarse allocation granularity. The imbalance is computed analytically by counting the bytes that belong to an array partition that should be stored in a different GPU, with respect to the total array size. The cost of this computation is negligible compared to the kernel execution time. When the imbalance exceeds a threshold, the score becomes zero (effectively choosing the reshape implementation). If several configurations get the same score, decompositions on the highest-order dimension are preferred because they allow for more efficient CPU↔GPU transfers.

6. EXPERIMENTAL METHODOLOGY

All experiments were run on a system containing a quad-core Intel i7-3820 at 3.6 GHz with 64 GB of DDR3 RAM memory, and 4 NVIDIA Tesla K40 GPU cards with 12 GB of GDDR5 each, connected through a PCIe 3.0 in x16 mode (containing two PCIe switches like in Figure 1). The machine runs a GNU/Linux system, with Linux kernel 3.12 and NVIDIA driver 340.24. Benchmarks were compiled using GCC 4.8.3 for CPU code and NVIDIA CUDA compiler 6.5 for GPU code. Execution times were measured using the CUPTI profiling library that provides support for sampling and nanosecond timing accuracy. For runs with more than one GPU, graphs show the time for the slowest GPU.

We evaluate AMGE using a number of dense scientific computations that use different computation and array access patterns. The list of benchmarks is summarized in Table 1. Some of them are found in the Parboil benchmark suite [15], some in the NVIDIA SDK, and the rest have been developed in-house. This benchmark selection provide a good variety of access patterns and thus challenges. Both CPU and GPU codes have been modified to use the `ndarray` data type instead of the flat 1D arrays which are commonly used. The benchmarks have been compiled using our toolchain and linked to our runtime system. The `ndarray` implementation has an impact on the register usage count of the kernels (columns 4-7). In the column titles, "Orig" stands for original, "VM" for virtual memory and "Re" for reshape, while "B" stands for `BLOCK`, "C" for `CYCLIC` and "B-C" for `BLOCK-CYCLIC`. `BLOCK` and `CYCLIC` are in the same column ("#Reg Re B/C") as they use the same number of registers.

Columns 8 and 9 show the array decompositions and distributions suggested by AMGE for the possible computation distribution configurations. A, B, C are the names of the arrays used in the computation. In the case of the kernels in merge sort, a suffix has been added for keys (A_k, B_k) and values (A_v, B_v). In the last column, "D" stands for distribution and "R" for replication in the GPU grid. X and Y make reference to the decomposed dimensions of the computation grid. Array decompositions are shown using the notation in HPF [19], but dimensions are ordered (left to right) from highest to lowest order as they are stored in memory. For example, the `sgemv` configuration says that for a computation decomposition on X, the A matrix is decomposed on its Y dimension and the C vector is decomposed on its X dimension. Tiles in A and C are distributed across the GPUs in the X dimension of the GPU grid while B vector is replicated.

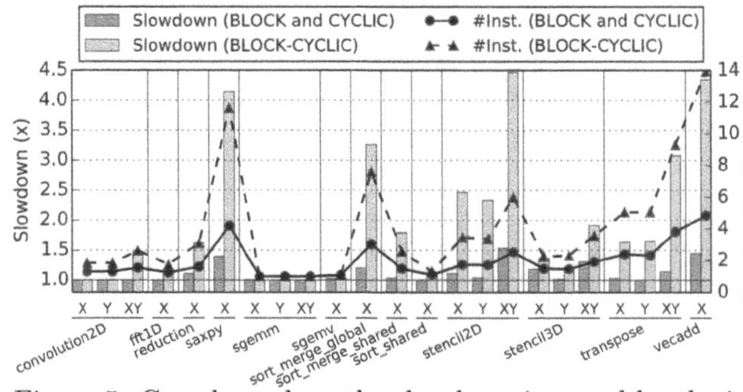

Figure 5: Grey bars show the slowdown imposed by the indexing routines for the *reshape* array implementation compared to the baseline (left axis). Lines indicate the increase in number of executed instructions (right axis).

7. PERFORMANCE EVALUATION

7.1 Indexing overhead

Table 1 shows that register utilization greatly varies depending on the used `ndarray` implementation. The *VM* implementation only performs the index linearization and the register count is similar to, or even slightly lower than the original version of the benchmarks. *reshape*, on the other hand, uses more registers in most of the kernels, especially in `BLOCK-CYCLIC` decompositions and those configurations in which arrays are decomposed along several dimensions.

Figure 5 shows the overheads imposed by the indexing routines for the *reshape* implementation on a single GPU. While AMGE suggests the utilization of the BLOCK distribution type in all kernels, we study the overhead of the routines for all the distribution types. Grey bars show the slowdown imposed by the indexing overhead of the data distributions for each computation distribution configuration (left axis). Lines represent the increase in number of executed instructions due to the extra operations performed on the indexes (right axis). `BLOCK` and `CYCLIC` are grouped (dark gray bar and solid line) as they perform very similar transformations on the indexes and the performance is virtually the same (±1%). `BLOCK-CYCLIC` (light Gray bar and dashed line) is consistently the slowest implementation (up to 4.48×) and the one that executes more instructions, too. This is caused both by the extra executed instructions and the lower achieved occupancy in the GPU due to the increased number of registers. Slowdowns are large for kernels in which thread blocks perform little work (`convolution2D`, `reduction`, `saxpy`, `sort_merge_*`, `stencil2D`, `transpose` and `vecadd`). Results for *VM* implementation are not shown because performance is within ±5% of the baseline in all kernels.

7.2 Multi-GPU performance

Figure 6 shows the speedup achieved by AMGE on our multi-GPU system for all possible distribution configurations. Results are shown for the *VM* and *reshape* implementations of the `ndarray` data type, and for an *ideal* implementation with optimal data distribution (no remote accesses). Bars labeled with "Impl" show the geometric mean for the three implementations of the speedups achieved in each kernel by the best computation distribution configuration. The *reshape* implementation exhibits linear speedups (1.91× and 3.54× on average for 2 and 4 GPUs, respectively) for all kinds of distribution configurations in most kernels. The

Kernel	Suite	Inputset	#Reg Orig	#Reg VM	#Reg Re B/C	#Reg Re B-C	Array Decompositions	Array Distribution
convolution2D	Parboil 2	16K×16K C: 9×9	17	19	19	22	X→A,B(*,BLOCK) C(*,*)	A,B:{D_x} C:{R_x}
					19	22	Y→A,B(BLOCK,*) C(*,*)	A,B:{D_x} C:{R_x}
					19	22	XY→A,B(BLOCK,BLOCK) C(*,*)	A,B:{$D_{x,y}$} C:{$R_{x,y}$}
fft1D	Parboil	256M	22	24	24	24	X→A(*) B(BLOCK)	A:{R_x} B:{D_x}
reduction	SDK	256M	12	12	11	18	X→A,B(BLOCK)	A,B:{D_x}
saxpy	-	256M	8	8	8	17	X→A,B(BLOCK)	A,B:{D_x}
sgemm	Parboil 2	4K×4K	38	33	41	41	X→A,C(*,BLOCK) B(*,*)	A,C:{D_x} B:{R_x}
					40	40	Y→A(*,*) B(*,BLOCK) C(BLOCK,*)	A:{R_x} B:{D_x} C:{D_x}
					42	42	XY→A,B(*,BLOCK) C(BLOCK,BLOCK)	A:{D_x,R_y} B:{D_y,R_x} C:{$D_{x,y}$}
sgemv	-	8K×8K	11	11	11	16	X→A(BLOCK,*) B(*) C(BLOCK)	A:{D_x} B:{R_x} C:{D_x}
sort_merge_global	SDK	256M	17	16	18	28	X→A_k,A_v,B_k,B_v(BLOCK)	A_k,A_v,B_k,B_v:{D_x}
sort_merge_shared	SDK	256M	17	16	18	27	X→A_k,A_v,B_k,B_v(BLOCK)	A_k,A_v,B_k,B_v:{D_x}
sort_shared	SDK	256M	17	18	19	28	X→A_k,A_v,B_k,B_v(BLOCK)	A_k,A_v,B_k,B_v:{D_x}
stencil2D	-	16K×16K + halos	17	18	17	23	X→A,B(*,BLOCK)	A,B:{D_x}
					17	19	Y→A,B(BLOCK,*)	A,B:{D_x}
					19	26	XY→A,B(BLOCK,BLOCK)	A,B:{$D_{x,y}$}
stencil3D	Parboil 2	1K×1K×512 + halos	24	26	30	34	X→A,B(*,*,BLOCK)	A,B:{D_x}
					29	31	Y→A,B(*,BLOCK,*)	A,B:{D_x}
					33	41	XY→A,B(*,BLOCK,BLOCK)	A,B:{$D_{x,y}$}
transpose	SDK	16K×16K	16	14	17	24	X→A(*,BLOCK) B(BLOCK,*)	A,B:{D_x}
					16	23	Y→A(BLOCK,*) B(*,BLOCK)	A,B:{D_x}
					18	26	XY→A,B(BLOCK,BLOCK)	A:{$D_{x,y}$} B:{$D_{y,x}$}
vecadd	-	256M	10	10	10	18	X→A,B,C(BLOCK)	A,B,C:{D_x}

Table 1: Benchmark description.

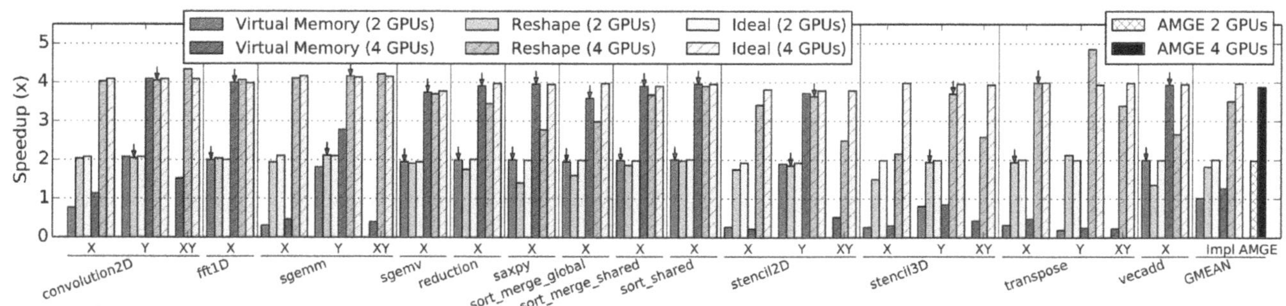

Figure 6: Speedup over baseline for different computation decomposition configurations using *reshape* and *VM* implementations. Arrows point to the configuration chosen by the runtime system for each kernel. Results shown for 2/4 GPUs.

main exceptions are X and XY configurations in `stencil3D` due to remote memory accesses, and `saxpy`, `vecadd`, `sort_merge_global` and the XY configuration in `stencil2D` due to the overhead of the indexing function. The *VM* implementation outperforms *reshape* in some configurations in which the array partitions are large enough not to suffer from imbalance due to the memory allocation granularity imposed by CUDA, but performs very poorly in the other configurations, producing lower speedups on average (1.02× and 1.27× for 2 and 4 GPUs). For example, in `transpose` at least one of the matrices must be decomposed along its X dimension, which is contiguous in memory, thus leading to an imbalanced data distribution. Therefore, performance is poor for *VM* in all configurations in `transpose`. Another example is `stencil3D`, for which the Y distribution configuration should provide reasonable performance since each plane of the volume can be distributed across GPUs. Nevertheless, the size of each plane still produces an imbalanced distribution. We study this example in more detail in Section 7.3.

On each kernel call, AMGE's runtime system tries to choose the best computation and data distribution configuration. In this evaluation, AMGE implements the policy introduced in Section 5.3, using a 5% ditribution imbalance threshold to choose between *VM* and *reshape* implementations. We choose this number because we have determined experimentally (Figure 7) that the GPUs in our evaluation system can hide the costs of up to 10% remote accesses depending on (1) how they are distributed in the kernel execution (Batch or Spread); and (2) the computational intensity of the kernel (FLOPS/load). We can see that, using this value, the policy correctly selects the best performing configuration for most of the kernels. Figure 6 highlights with an arrow the chosen configurations. The average performance across all the benchmarks (i.e., bars labeled with "AMGE") is 1.98× and 3.89× for 2 and 4 GPUs; very close to *ideal*.

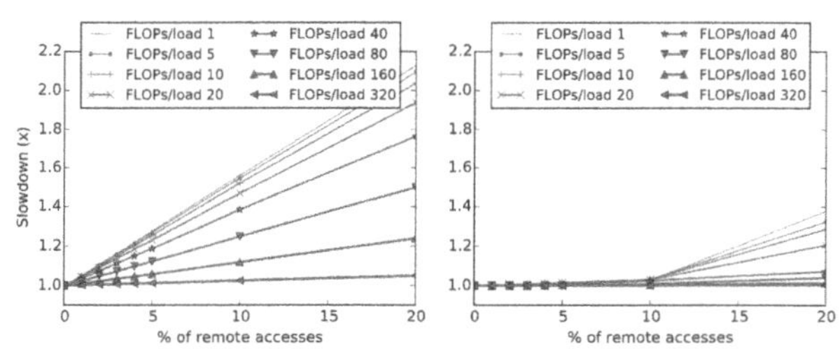

(a) Batch (b) Spread

Figure 7: Performance overhead imposed by remote accesses for different computation intensities; when they are concentrated (Batch) or evenly distributed in time (Spread).

7.3 Impact of remote accesses on performance

Figure 8 shows the percentage of accesses to RAM memory that are served by remote GPUs in all the kernels when they are distributed across 4GPUs. *reshape* eliminates the need for remote accesses in most of the configurations. Only kernels in which computation partitions share some data use them (e.g., `convolution2D`, `stencil{2,3}D`). The worst cases are the X and XY decompositions for `stencil3D` in which 17.43% and 7.61% of accesses to memory are remote, respectively. This is the reason why these configurations show poor speedups in Figure 6. In contrast, *VM* introduces a

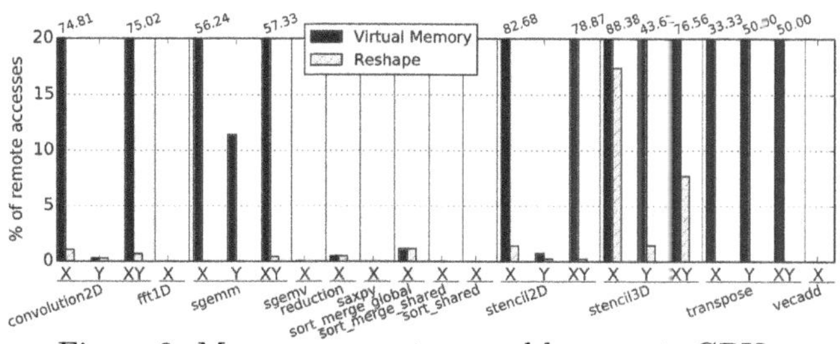

Figure 8: Memory requests served by remote GPUs.

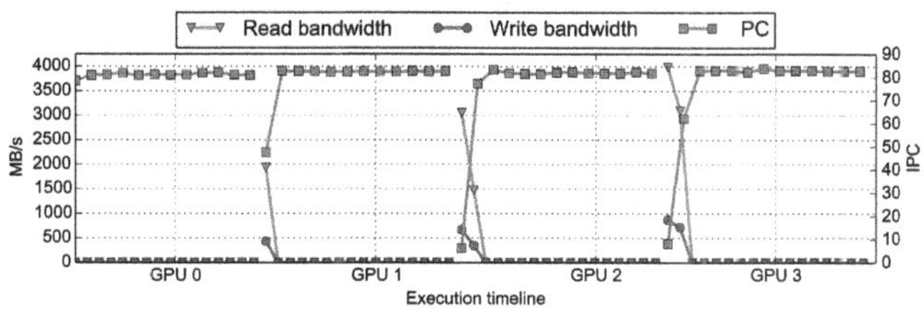

(a) Imbalanced distribution

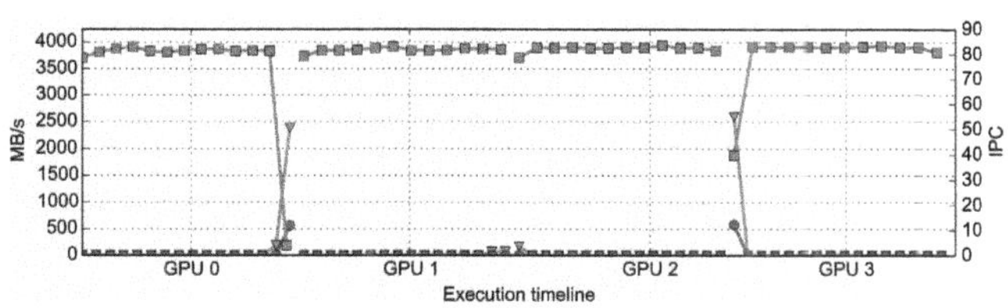

(b) Balanced distribution

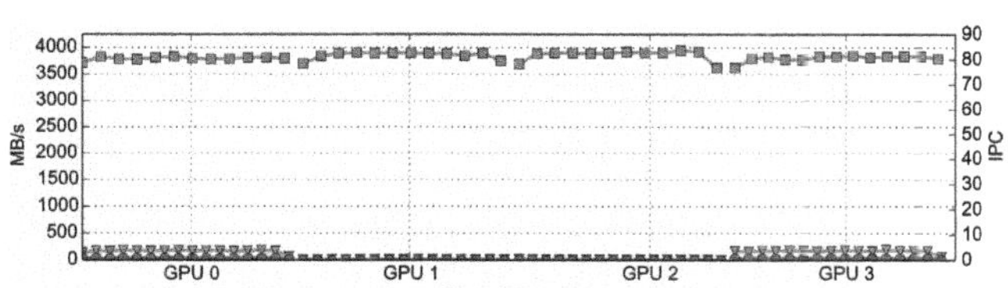

(c) Balanced distribution + transposed thread block scheduling

Figure 9: Execution timeline of `stencil2D` for 4 GPUs.

lot of remote accesses in many configurations due to the memory allocation granularity in CUDA.

Fighting data distribution imbalance in *VM*: The dimensions of the arrays in `stencil2D` and `stencil3D` kernels make it difficult to evenly split them using 1 MB granularity, causing imbalance and, therefore, remote memory accesses. The computation distribution configuration that we study is Y. Using this configuration, the volumes of `stencil3D` are distributed by allocating partitions of each plane alternatively in different GPUs. The size of each plane (1K×1K + halos) produces an imbalanced distribution (2/1/1/1MB for 4GPUs). This results in excessive communication that limits the performance (0.87× and 0.91× for 2 and 4 GPUs). Adding padding to the X dimension of the volume to obtain a balanced distribution results in a 127.01× memory footprint increment. Having a 4 KB granularity would reduce this overhead to 1.49×. Using more friendly problem sizes that do not produce imbalance results in much improved performance, reaching linear speedups of 2.08× and 3.95× for 2 and 4 GPUs.

The size (16K×16K + halos) of the plane in `stencil2D` allows for a more balanced data distribution (65/64/64/64MB for 4GPUs). However, there are still some effects on the performance. Figure 9a shows the memory bandwidth con-

Benchmark	Conf	Kim [18]	Lee [20]	AMGE
convolution2D	X	38.7K×38.7K	38.7K×38.7K	77.4K×77.4K
	Y	38.7K×38.7K	38.7K×38.7K	77.4K×77.4K
	XY	38.7K×38.7K	38.7K×38.7K	77.4K×77.4K
fft1D	X	750M	750M	3G
reduction	X	2.99G	2.99G	11.99G
saxpy	X	6G	6G	6G
sgemm	X	31.6K×31.6K	31.6K×31.6K	44.7K×44.7K
	Y	44.7K×44.7K	31.6K×31.6K	44.7K×44.7K
	XY	38.7K×38.7K	31.6K×31.6K	48.9K×48.9K
sgemv	X	77.4K×77.4K	38.7K×38.7K	77.4×77.4
sort	X	750M	750M	3G
stencil2D	X	38.7K×38.7K	38.7K×38.7K	77.4K×77.4K
	Y	48.9K×48.9K	38.7K×38.7K	77.4K×77.4K
	XY	44.7K×44.7K	38.7K×38.7K	77.4K×77.4K
stencil3D	X	$1.1K^3$	$1.1K^3$	$1.8K^3$
	Y	$1.3K^3$	$1.1K^3$	$1.8K^3$
	XY	$1.2K^3$	$1.1K^3$	$1.8K^3$
transpose	X	48.9K×48.9K	38.7K×38.7K	77.4K×77.4K
	X	48.9K×48.9K	38.7K×38.7K	77.4K×77.4K
	XY	54.7K×54.7K	38.7K×38.7K	77.4K×77.4K
vecadd	X	4G	4G	4G

Table 2: Maximum problem size for a 4-GPU system in AMGE and in the related work.

sumption due to remote loads and stores (left axis), and the number of instructions per cycle (right axis) during the execution of the `stencil2D` kernel for each GPU in the system. For the sake of clarity, we concatenate the execution timelines of the four GPUs, although they execute in parallel. GPU 0 does not perform any remote memory access and the IPC (instructions per cycle) remains stable during the kernel execution. GPUs 1, 2 and 3 perform remote memory accesses to the previous GPU memories (note that the imbalance increases with the GPU identifier). Remote accesses degrade the performance of the GPU as reflected in the lower IPC. Using padding to obtain a fully balanced array distribution would increase the memory footprint by 7.99×. Instead, we reduce the imbalance by offsetting the beginning of the array so that GPUs 0 and 3, and GPUs 1 and 2 perform the same amount of remote memory accesses (Figure 9b). The improved balancing lowers the remote memory bandwidth consumption (2.5 GBps vs 4 GBps), and the period in which remote accesses are performed is shorter. This results in a 8.2% execution speedup on the slowest GPU.

Reducing instantaneous bandwidth demands: In `stencil2D`, memory accesses concentrate at the beginning/end of the kernel execution because the default thread block scheduler in the GPU issues thread blocks that are contiguous in the X dimension in order. Thus, thread blocks that access the boundaries of the matrix partitions tend to execute concurrently, increasing the instantaneous bandwidth demands and reducing the achieved IPC. We evaluate the performance of a thread block scheduler that issues thread blocks that are contiguous in the Y dimension instead. We emulate it by transposing the mapping of thread block identifiers on the matrices. Figure 9c shows that, using this scheduler, remote accesses are distributed throughout all kernel execution, thus reducing the instantaneous bandwidth demands to 200MBps. Now the IPC is not affected, since the cost of remote accesses is hidden with the execution of other thread blocks that only perform local accesses, reducing execution time by a 5.8%.

7.4 Comparison with previous works

Memory footprint overhead. AMGE performs more space-efficient data decompositions than previous works. We quantify the benefits of AMGE over Kim et al. [18] and Lee et al. [20] by comparing the maximum problem size that can be executed by the three solutions on our 4-GPU system.

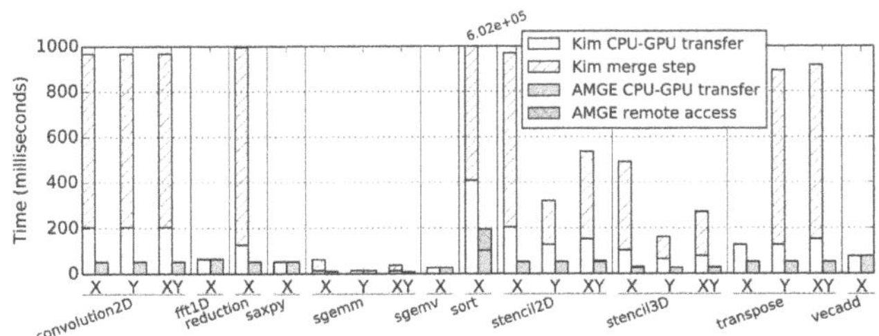

Figure 10: Overhead of the coherence mechanisms in AMGE and in the related work [18].

Table 2 shows that AMGE is able to run bigger problem sizes than previous works for most benchmarks, which is one of the major motivations for using multiple GPUs, especially on those that work on multi-dimensional arrays.

Coherence overhead: AMGE ensures coherence by not replicating output arrays and using remote memory accesses when needed. The related work relies on replication and a merge step after kernel execution. Besides, data needs to be copied from CPU to GPU memories before kernel execution. Figure 10 shows the overhead of both solutions. AMGE shows lower CPU/GPU transfer times in most cases (CPU-GPU transfer), because of the more efficient partitioning of multi-dimensional data structures, which requires smaller regions of the arrays to be resident in each GPU memory. The overhead of the merge step is even larger compared with the cost of remote accesses. The most extreme case is the `sort` benchmark, since it executes kernels iteratively and the merge step needs to be performed after each kernel call.

8. RELATED WORK

Auto-parallelization in shared memory NUMA systems: High Performance Fortran[19] provides primitives to distribute data and implements the *owner-computes rule* [8], that schedules loop iterations in such a way that communication is minimized. AMGE relieves programmers from specifying the distribution of data. Performance degradation due to remote access is much larger in GPUs than in CPU NUMA systems, and bad programmer choices might lead to large slowdowns. Therefore, providing a system that accomplishes this without programmer intervention is key for GPUs. Other proposals exploit architectural mechanisms to implement dynamic memory distribution policies (e.g., *first touch* placement) or data migration [7, 23, 21]. Nevertheless, current GPUs do not provide the necessary mechanisms (e.g., user-managed memory protection or appropriate performance counters) to implement these proposals. We rely on compiler analysis to minimize inter-GPU communication.

Compiler-based transparent multi-GPU execution: Kim et al. [18] introduce an OpenCL framework that combines multiple GPUs and treats them as a single compute device. In order to split data, they compute the array ranges accessed by computation partitions by performing sampling runs of the kernels on the CPU. The runtime system chooses the computation decomposition that minimizes the size of the data transfers between CPU and GPU memories. However, this only works for kernels in which array references are affine functions of the thread and thread block identifiers. Otherwise they fall back to replication. But even in cases where data can be decomposed, any array decomposition not performed on its highest-order dimension will produce tiles whose memory address ranges overlap, thus replicating big portions of the array in all memories. Array regions that are potentially modified from different computation partitions need to be merged after kernel execution. Lee et al. [20] extend the same idea to heterogeneous systems with CPUs and GPUs. They do not use the sampling runs on the CPU and generate a merge kernel that is more efficient than in Kim et al.; although both solutions require the merge step to be executed on the CPU, thus increasing the CPU↔GPU traffic. AMGE uses a similar approach but the compiler analysis uses the array dimensionality information by the `ndarray` type. Thanks to this information and the utilization of remote memory accesses, AMGE avoids replication in most cases, enabling bigger problem sizes and minimizing unnecessary CPU↔GPU communication. Moreover, AMGE adds support for cyclic data distributions, and exploits hardware support required by codes that use atomic operations and global memory fences.

Language/Library-based transparent multi-GPU execution: GlobalArrays [22] (GA) is a library that allows execution of computations across a distributed system using an array-like interface, and GA-GPU [29] extends GA to GPUs. The memory model in GA-GPU allows memory accesses to be ordered and, hence, it does not fit into bulk synchronous SPMD programming models such as CUDA or OpenCL. Therefore, GA-GPU recommends the utilization of GA data-parallel primitives (at the cost of lower performance due to the overhead of launching one kernel for each of the primitive operations). X10 [10] and Habanero [9] present the programmer with a single partitioned global address space. The compiler and the runtime system transparently redirect remote memory accesses to the proper memory. Sequoia [11] tries to address the problem of programming systems with different memory topologies/hierarchies. Programs are composed of two parts: (a) an algorithmic representation of the computation using a C-like programming language that decomposes data structures and defines how to map the computation on them; and (b) a mapping of the algorithm to the specific system using a declarative language. PGAS languages require a complete rewrite of the program, while AMGE requires minor code modifications.

9. CONCLUSIONS AND FUTURE WORK

Modern GPUs provide mechanisms that enable efficient auto-parallelization. In this paper we introduce AMGE, a programming interface, compiler support and runtime system that enables multi-GPU execution of computations written for a single GPU. Thanks to remote memory accesses, AMGE imposes much lower memory footprint and coherence management overheads than previous works. We also demonstrate that transparent data distribution can be efficiently implemented on current GPUs using the UVAS and compiler/runtime-assisted code versioning. Using the array data type provided in AMGE results in shorter and cleaner code, too. AMGE achieves almost linear speedups for most of the benchmarks on a real 4-GPU system with an interconnect with moderate bandwidth. Further performance improvements can be achieved by reducing the virtual memory mapping granularity exposed by CUDA and by allowing programmers to tune the thread block scheduling policy.

We believe that AMGE could be used in future systems such as NVIDIA Pascal boards to automatically scale the performance of GPU kernels to multiple GPUs. We plan to extend our evaluation to irregular computation patterns.

Acknowledgments

We would like to thank the anonymous reviewers, on their comments and help improving our work. This work is supported by NVIDIA through the UPC/BSC CUDA Center of Excellence, the Spanish Government through Programa Severo Ochoa (SEV-2011-0067), and the Spanish Ministry of Science and Technology through the TIN2012-34557 project.

10. REFERENCES

[1] NVIDIA GPUDirect. `https://developer.nvidia.com/gpudirect`, 2012.

[2] APU 101: All about AMD Fusion Accelerated Processing Units, 2013.

[3] An Inside Look at Summit and Sierra Supercomputers. `http://info.nvidianews.com/CoralWhitepapers.html`, 2014.

[4] J. M. Anderson, S. P. Amarasinghe, and M. S. Lam. Data and computation transformations for multiprocessors. PPoPP '95, 1995.

[5] M. Araya-Polo, J. Cabezas, M. Hanzich, M. Pericas, F. Rubio, I. Gelado, M. Shafiq, E. Morancho, N. Navarro, E. Ayguadé, J. Cela, and M. Valero. Assessing Accelerator-Based HPC Reverse Time Migration. *TPDS*, 22(1), 2011.

[6] L. S. Blackford, J. Choi, A. Cleary, A. Petitet, R. C. Whaley, J. Demmel, I. Dhillon, K. Stanley, J. Dongarra, S. Hammarling, G. Henry, and D. Walker. ScaLAPACK: a portable linear algebra library for distributed memory computers - design issues and performance. SC '96, 1996.

[7] W. J. Bolosky, M. L. Scott, R. P. Fitzgerald, R. J. Fowler, and A. L. Cox. NUMA policies and their relation to memory architecture. ASPLOS IV, 1991.

[8] D. Callahan and K. Kennedy. Compiling programs for distributed-memory multiprocessors. *The Journal of Supercomputing*, 2(2), 1988.

[9] V. Cavé, J. Zhao, J. Shirako, and V. Sarkar. Habanero-Java: the new adventures of old X10. PPPJ '11, 2011.

[10] P. Charles, C. Grothoff, V. Saraswat, C. Donawa, A. Kielstra, K. Ebcioglu, C. von Praun, and V. Sarkar. X10: an object-oriented approach to non-uniform cluster computing. OOPSLA '05, 2005.

[11] K. Fatahalian, D. R. Horn, T. J. Knight, L. Leem, M. Houston, J. Y. Park, M. Erez, M. Ren, A. Aiken, W. J. Dally, and P. Hanrahan. Sequoia: programming the memory hierarchy. SC '06, 2006.

[12] M. Garland, S. Le Grand, J. Nickolls, J. Anderson, J. Hardwick, S. Morton, E. Phillips, Y. Zhang, and V. Volkov. Parallel computing experiences with CUDA. *IEEE Micro*, 28(4), July 2008.

[13] I. Gelado, J. E. Stone, J. Cabezas, S. Patel, N. Navarro, and W.-m. W. Hwu. An asymmetric distributed shared memory model for heterogeneous parallel systems. ASPLOS XV, 2010.

[14] M. Gupta and P. Banerjee. Demonstration of automatic data partitioning techniques for parallelizing compilers on multicomputers. *TPDS*, 3(2), Mar. 1992.

[15] IMPACT Group. Parboil benchmark suite. `http://impact.crhc.illinois.edu/parboil.php`, 2012.

[16] S. Keckler, W. Dally, B. Khailany, M. Garland, and D. Glasco. GPUs and the future of parallel computing. *Micro, IEEE*, 31(5), 2011.

[17] The Khronos Group Inc. *The OpenCL Specification*, 2013.

[18] J. Kim, H. Kim, J. H. Lee, and J. Lee. Achieving a single compute device image in OpenCL for multiple GPUs. PPoPP '11, 2011.

[19] C. H. Koelbel, D. B. Loveman, R. S. Schreiber, G. L. Steele, Jr., and M. E. Zosel. *The high performance Fortran handbook*. 1994.

[20] J. Lee, M. Samadi, Y. Park, and S. Mahlke. Transparent CPU-GPU collaboration for data-parallel kernels on heterogeneous systems. PACT '13, 2013.

[21] J. Marathe, V. Thakkar, and F. Mueller. Feedback-directed page placement for ccNUMA via hardware-generated memory traces. *Journal of Parallel and Distributed Computing*, 70(12), 2010.

[22] J. Nieplocha, R. J. Harrison, and R. J. Littlefield. Global Arrays: A portable "shared-memory" programming model for distributed memory computers. SC '94, 1994.

[23] D. Nikolopoulos, T. Papatheodorou, C. Polychronopoulos, J. Labarta, and E. Ayguadé. User-level dynamic page migration for multiprogrammed shared-memory multiprocessors. ICPP 2000, 2000.

[24] NVIDIA Corporation. *CUDA C Programming Guide*, 2015. `http://docs.nvidia.com/cuda/cuda-c-programming-guide/`.

[25] S. L. Scott. Synchronization and communication in the T3E multiprocessor. ASPLOS VII, 1996.

[26] J. E. Stone, D. J. Hardy, I. S. Ufimtsev, and K. Schulten. GPU-accelerated molecular modeling coming of age. *Journal of Molecular Graphics and Modelling*, 29(2), 2010.

[27] J. A. Stratton, C. I. Rodrigues, I.-J. Sung, L.-W. Chang, N. Anssari, G. D. Liu, W. mei W. Hwu, and N. Obeid. Algorithm and data optimization techniques for scaling to massively threaded systems. *IEEE Computer*, 45(8), 2012.

[28] I. Tanasic, L. Vilanova, M. Jordà, J. Cabezas, I. Gelado, N. Navarro, and W.-m. W. Hwu. Comparison based sorting for systems with multiple GPUs. GPGPU-6, 2013.

[29] V. Tipparaju and J. S. Vetter. GA-GPU: extending a library-based global address space programming model for scalable heterogeneous computing systems. CF '12, 2012.

[30] J. Tölke. Implementation of a Lattice Boltzmann kernel using the Compute Unified Device Architecture developed by NVIDIA. *Computing and Visualization in Science*, 13(1), 2010.

A Stall-Aware Warp Scheduling for Dynamically Optimizing Thread-level Parallelism in GPGPUs

Yulong Yu† Weijun Xiao‡ Xubin He‡ He Guo† Yuxin Wang§ Xin Chen†

† School of Software Technology
Dalian University of Technology
Dalian, China
yuylong@acm.org
guohe@dlut.edu.cn

‡ Department of Electrical and Computer Engineering
Virginia Commonwealth University
Richmond, VA, USA
{xhe2, wxiao}@vcu.edu

§ School of Computer Science and Technology
Dalian University of Technology
Dalian, China
wyx@dlut.edu.cn

ABSTRACT

General-Purpose Graphic Processing Units (GPGPU) have been widely used in high performance computing as application accelerators due to their massive parallelism and high throughput. A GPGPU generally contains two layers of schedulers, a cooperative-thread-array (CTA) scheduler and a warp scheduler, which administer the thread level parallelism (TLP). Previous research shows the maximized TLP does not always deliver the optimal performance. Unfortunately, existing warp scheduling schemes do not optimize TLP at runtime, which is impossible to fit various access patterns for diverse applications. Dynamic TLP optimization in the warp scheduler remains a challenge to exploit the GPGPU highly-parallel compute power.

In this paper, we comprehensively investigate the TLP performance impact in the warp scheduler. Based on our analysis of the pipeline efficiency, we propose a Stall-Aware Warp Scheduling (SAWS), which optimizes the TLP according to the pipeline stalls. SAWS adds two modules to the original scheduler to dynamically adjust TLP at runtime. A trigger-based method is employed for a fast tuning response. We simulated SAWS and conducted extensive experiments on GPGPU-Sim using 21 paradigmatic benchmarks. Our numerical results show that SAWS effectively improves the pipeline efficiency by reducing the structural hazards without causing extra data hazards. SAWS achieves an average speedup of 14.7% with a geometric mean, even higher than existing Two-Level scheduling scheme with the optimal fetch group sizes over a wide range of benchmarks. More importantly, compared with the dynamic TLP optimization in the CTA scheduling, SAWS still has 9.3% performance improvement among the benchmarks, which shows that it is a competitive choice by moving dynamic TLP optimization from the CTA to warp scheduler.

ICS'15, June 8–11, 2015, Newport Beach, CA, USA.

http://dx.doi.org/10.1145/2751205.2751234.

Categories and Subject Descriptors

C.1.4 [**Computer System Organization**]: Processor Architectures—*Parallel Architectures*

General Terms

GPGPU, Thread Level Parallelism

Keywords

GPGPU; Warp Scheduler; Two-Level Scheduling; Pipeline Stall; Thread Level Parallelism

1. INTRODUCTION

General-Purpose Graphic Processing Units (GPGPUs) have been widely-used as application accelerators due to their massive parallelism and high throughput. They accelerate the performance of many applications such as image and video processing and scientific computing.

It is critical to choose optimal TLP in the GPGPU schedulers that keep high resource utility without causing too much contention. Existing warp scheduling schemes such as LRR [17] and TL [16,30] try either to maximize TLP or to select a universal TLP parameter. Previous work [16,23] shows that the maximized or a universal TLP does not always deliver the optimal performance, because it is impossible to fit various access patterns for diverse applications. Nevertheless, the dynamic TLP optimization in a cooperative-thread-array (CTA) scheduler [23] was coarse-grained and not accurate enough. Therefore, it remains a challenge to dynamically optimize TLP at runtime in the warp scheduler to exploit the performance potential.

In this paper, we comprehensively investigate the TLP performance impact in a warp scheduler. We discover that the pipeline efficiency is a main reason for various performance by tuning TLP. We propose a Stall-Aware Warp Scheduling (SAWS) upon TL with two additional modules, Stall Pending and TLP Recovery, to dynamically adjust the fetch group size at runtime. The Stall Pending employs a trigger-based method for a fast tuning response, which moves the active warps that suffer too many structural hazards into the pending group. The TLP Recovery promotes a pending warp back to be active when an insufficient TLP is detected. The warp switch policy in the original TL is retained to hide the long-latency operations. We simulate SAWS

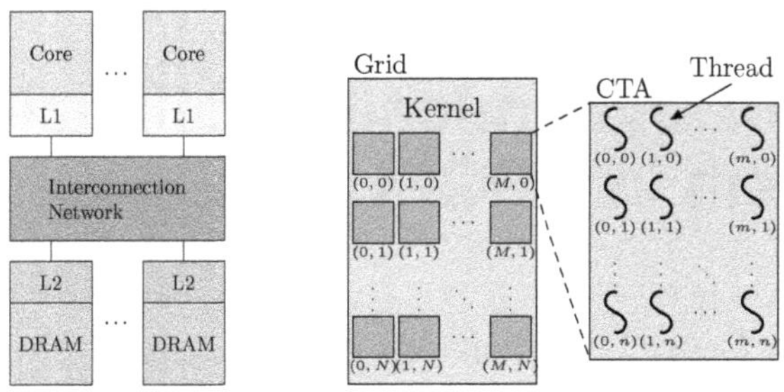

(a) Architecture (b) Programming Model

Figure 1: GPGPU baseline architecture.

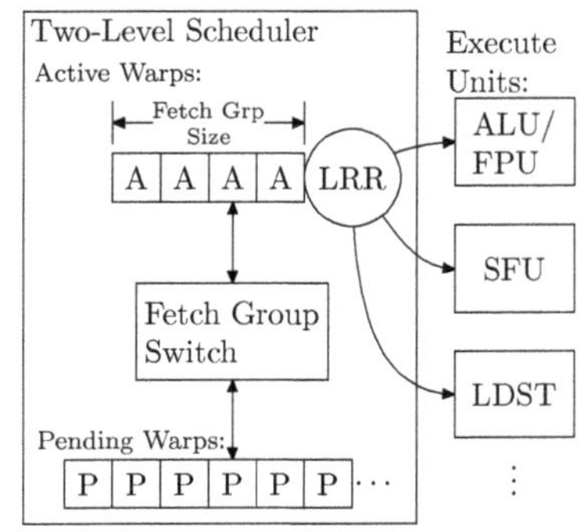

Figure 2: The design of Two-Level Scheduler [16,17].

on GPGPU-Sim [1], and evaluate its effectiveness using 21 paradigmatic benchmarks. The experimental results show that SAWS makes accurate TLP scheduling decisions. It improves the pipeline efficiency, and the geometric means of the SAWS speedups is 14.7% and the maximal speedup is up to 115.2%. Compared with the dynamic TLP optimization in the CTA scheduler, SAWS is still a competitive choice by moving the dynamic TLP optimization from the CTA to warp scheduler.

The main contributions of the paper are three-fold.

1. We give an investigation of the TLP performance impact using a fine-grained view down to the instruction execution, and discover that the pipeline efficiency is a key factor of the TLP optimization.

2. We propose a warp scheduling SAWS that dynamically adjusts TLP in the warp scheduler at runtime. A trigger-based method employed in SAWS gives a fast tuning response.

3. To the best of our knowledge, this is the first work to compare our work in the warp scheduler with the TLP optimization in a CTA scheduler. We further give an analysis of the optimization combining them together.

The rest of this paper is organized as follows. Section 2 introduces the background of GPGPU. Section 3 investigates on the TLP performance impact in warp schedulers and compares it with a CTA scheduling. Section 4 describes the detailed design of SAWS along with the hardware overhead analysis. Section 5 describes the experimental methodology and analyzes the experimental results. Section 6 discusses the related work. Section 7 concludes this paper.

2. BACKGROUND

2.1 GPGPU Baseline Architecture

A GPGPU as illustrated in Figure 1(a) is composed of many cores (also referred as streaming multiprocessors). A core executes instructions in a single-instruction-multi-thread (SIMT) way, where a group of threads referred as warps execute simultaneously on each processing lane. There are three main kinds of execution units in a core. *ALU/FPU* performs the arithmetic computation. *SFU* performs the complicated mathematical computation, whose bandwidth is lower than ALU/FPU. *LDST* performs the memory accesses that belong to long latency operations.

GPGPU applications are usually written in parallel programming interfaces such as CUDA [22] and OpenCL [14]. They organize the GPGPU compute tasks as kernels. A kernel as illustrated in Figure 1(b) is defined by a massive amount of threads. These threads are tiled into coarse-grained groups referred as blocks or CTAs. The compute tasks are allocated to cores at the CTA granularity. Multiple CTAs can be concurrently placed in the same core if there are enough resources.

2.2 GPGPU Schedulers

There are two layers of the GPGPU schedulers. A *CTA Scheduler* is the upper-layer scheduler that allocates CTAs to cores. A *Warp Scheduler* is the lower-layer scheduler equipped in each core. It issues instructions alternately from the warps of the allocated CTAs.

We focus on the warp scheduler in this work. The commonly used Loose Round Robin (LRR) [17] serves all warps as instruction issuance candidates to maximize TLP. Previous work [16, 30] has showed that LRR cannot efficiently hide the long latency operations, and causes high resource contention. A variant of LRR referred as GTO [18] employs a greedy issuance policy to optimize the resource utility, but does not essentially reduce the resource contentions.

Two-Level scheduling (TL) [16, 30] serves a partial warps as instruction issuance candidates to hide the long latency operations. Narasiman et al [30] designed TL (TL/N) by dividing the warps into several fetch groups. Gebhart et al [16] designed TL (TL/G) by dividing the warps into the active and pending groups. In this paper, we do not differentiate TL/N and TL/G due to the following two reasons. First, they both only serve the active warps as instruction issuance candidates, thus the active fetch group in TL/N is equal to the active group in TL/G, and the pending group in TL/G is equal to the union of pending fetch groups in TL/N. Second, because the active warps are executed in a round robin manner and arrive their long latency operations at nearly the same time [30], the warp switch granularity of TL/G is the same as TL/N in essence. We use a moderate design as illustrated in Figure 2, where the fetch group size is defined by the number of the active warps, and the fetch group switches at the granularity of warps, so it is not necessary to reorganize the fetch group when the TLP is changed in our proposed scheduling scheme in Section 4.

3. TLP PERFORMANCE IMPACT

In this section, we comprehensively investigate the TLP performance impact in a warp scheduler with various fetch group sizes in TL. We also analyze the TLP optimization

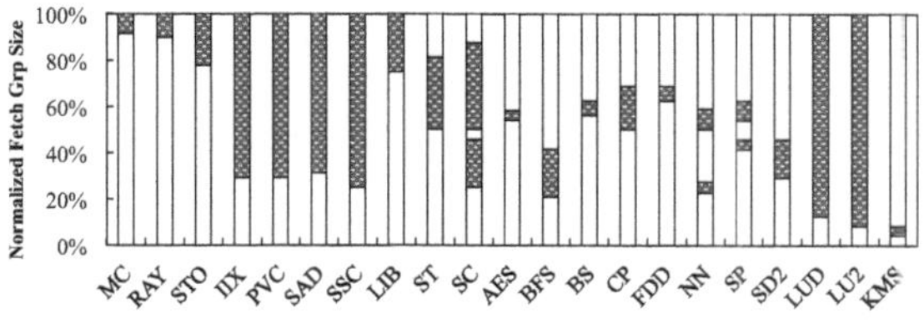

Figure 3: The normalized fetch group sizes with top-5% performance. The red blocks denote the fetch group sizes that achieves at least 95% performance of the optimal fetch group size of each benchmark.

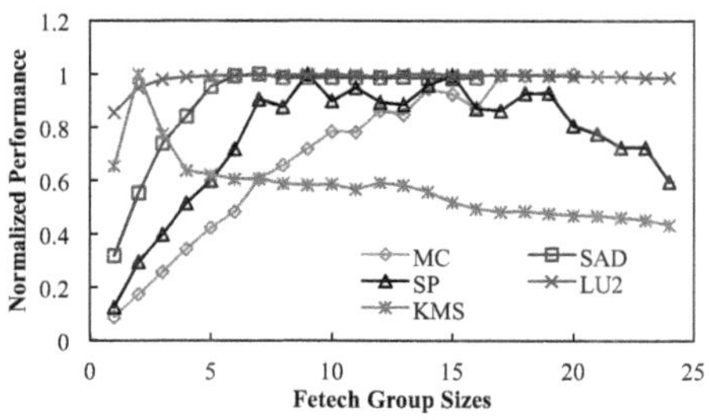

Figure 4: The normalized TL scheduling performance at various fetch group sizes. Benchmarks with different patterns have diverse optimal fetch group sizes. It is impossible to find a universal fetch group size to fit various applications.

proposed in the CTA scheduler. The experimental setup and benchmarks are described in Subsection 5.1.

3.1 Performance Impact

We obtain the optimal TL performance for each benchmark by manually changing the fetch group sizes. Figure 3 illustrates the fetch group sizes achieving at least 95% of the optimal performance. Different applications have various warp volumes in a core for the thread resource occupancy, so the results use normalized values to the warp volumes. Similar to previous observation from the CTA scheduler [18, 23], the optimal fetch group sizes vary in different benchmarks. MC and RAY reach the optimal performance at a large fetch group size, while the optimal performance of KMS appears at a small fetch group size. By considering the TLP performance impact, we categorize the benchmarks into 5 types.

1. *Type I*, such as MC, only achieves their optimal performance at the largest fetch group sizes.
2. *Type II*, such as SAD, achieves the optimal performance at medium fetch group sizes, and keeps the optimal performance in the larger fetch group sizes.
3. *Type III*, such as SP, also achieves the optimal performance at medium fetch group sizes, but their performance goes down again at the larger fetch group sizes.
4. *Type IV*, such as LU2, has a negligible performance impact by various fetch group sizes.
5. *Type V*, such as KMS, only achieves their optimal performance at small fetch group sizes.

Figure 4 illustrates the performance normalized to each optimal performance of one paradigmatic benchmark for each type. Different application types prefer various fetch group sizes. It is impossible to find a universal fetch group size to fit all applications.

(a) Fully hiding case

(b) Under hiding case

Figure 5: The TLP performance impact from fetch group switch without all other factors. In a fully hiding case, the fetch group sizes do not affect the performance. In a under hiding case, a smaller fetch group size brings better performance.

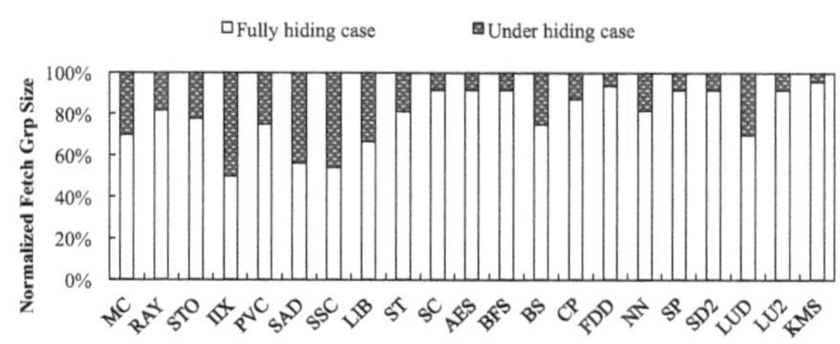

Figure 6: The fetch group sizes in the under and fully hiding cases of the benchmarks. There is no explicit correlation between the hiding case boundaries and the optimal fetch group sizes.

3.2 Fetch Group Switch

Different from the intuition, our experiments show that the fetch group switch has limited TLP performance impact. We will explain this observation shortly.

Generally, a warp in TL has three states. An *Active interval* is when a warp stays in the active group for executing a compute part. A *Busy pending interval* is when a warp waits its long latency operation in the pending group. An *Idle pending interval* is when a warp has finished its long latency operation but is still in the pending group.

Figure 5 demonstrates the TLP performance impact by the fetch group switch. Without considering all other factors, the active interval grows directly proportional to the fetch group size. A *fully hiding case* as illustrated in Figure 5(a) is the case when all the long latency operations are overlapped by computation. Its execution time is dominated by the compute part, thus there is no performance change by changing the fetch group sizes. An *under hiding case* as illustrated in Figure 5(b) is the case when the computation does not hide all long latency operations. It usually appears in large fetch group sizes, and a smaller fetch group size brings higher performance. Therefore, the optimal performance shall come up at the boundary between the under and fully hiding cases.

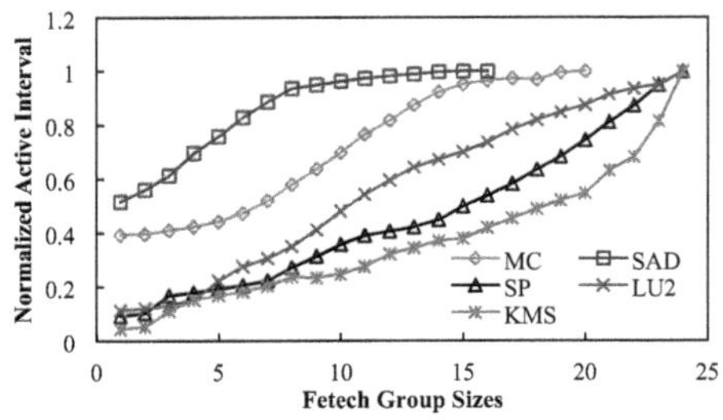

Figure 7: The average warp active intervals at various fetch group sizes. The active intervals do not grow directly proportional to the fetch group sizes.

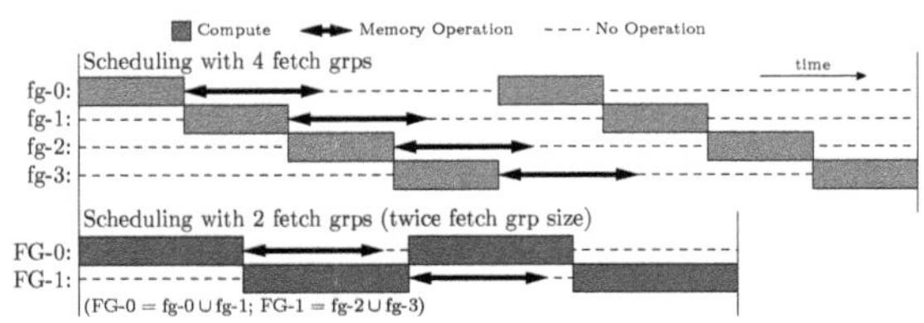

(a) The under parallel case

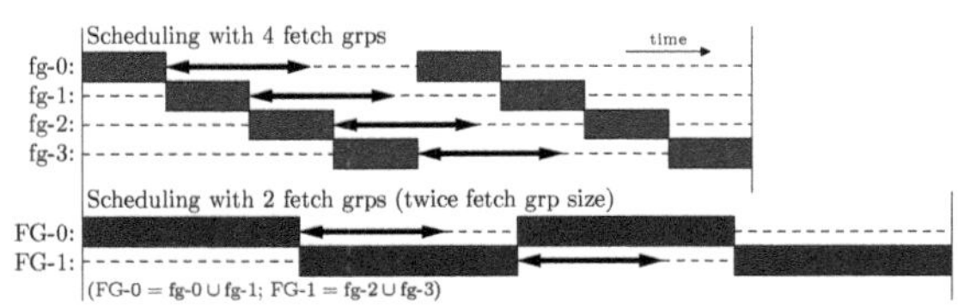

(b) The over parallel case

Figure 8: The TLP performance impact by the pipeline efficiency. In an under parallel case, the active interval grows slow, and higher performance is achieved at a larger fetch group size. In an over parallel case, the active interval grows fast, and the performance is degraded in a larger fetch group size.

We conduct an experiment to verify the assumption above. We define that an under hiding case appears if the idle pending interval is less than 1% of the active interval. Figure 6 illustrates the fetch group sizes in the fully and under hiding cases. However, compared with the optimal fetch group sizes in Figure 3, there is no explicit correlation between the hiding case boundaries and the optimal fetch group sizes.

3.3 Pipeline Efficiency

Figure 7 illustrates the normalized active intervals among fetch group sizes, which shows that they do not grow directly proportional to the fetch group sizes. We present two cases how the active interval impacts the performance at different fetch group sizes. Figure 8(a) demonstrates the *under parallel case*, such as MC, where the data hazards dominate the pipeline stalls, and the active interval grows slow, so the higher performance achieves at a larger fetch group size. In contrast, Figure 8(b) demonstrates the *over parallel case*, such as KMS, where the structural hazards dominate the pipeline stalls, and the active interval grows fast, so the performance is degraded in a larger fetch group size.

Figure 9 illustrates the pipeline stall distribution at various fetch group sizes. With increasing the fetch group sizes, more alternate warps hide more data hazards, while they bring more structural hazards for more resource competition. Because GPGPU kernels usually have simple control logic, the control hazards only hold a negligible fraction. Different application types present diverse pipeline stall patterns. The data hazards are dominant for MC at all fetch group sizes, thus it remains in the under parallel cases. In contrast, the structural hazards dominate KMS, thus it remains in the over parallel cases. Data hazards dominate SP at smaller fetch group sizes, but it changes to structural hazards at larger fetch group sizes, thus SP achieves its optimal performance at a medium fetch group size. The pipeline stalls of SAD and LU2 do not change significantly at large fetch group sizes similar to their performance shown in Figure 3.

According to above analysis, we conclude that different compute patterns require diverse optimal TLP. We need a dynamic TLP tuning technique in GPGPU schedulers. We find that the pipeline efficiency is a key factor to the TLP performance impact. Therefore, the pipeline stall is a good metric to adjust TLP at runtime.

3.4 TLP Optimization in CTA Scheduler

We look at the dynamic TLP optimization in CTA scheduler, where Dynamic CTA scheduler (DYNCTA) [23] is a pragmatic example. Figure 10 illustrates the probability distributions of the TLP decisions by DYNCTA. The TLP is measured at the warp level, which is the amount of active warps in the prioritized CTAs. The CTA scheduler is a coarse-grained scheduler, thus DYNCTA cannot reach all possible TLP parameters. For example, DYNCTA chooses the optimal number of active warps as 4 for KMS instead of 2 a better choice, because DYNCTA can only adjust TLP at a CTA granularity that contains 4 warps in KMS.

DYNCTA makes accurate decisions for most benchmarks, but wrong decisions appear in the benchmarks such as CP, BS, and FDD. DYNCTA works on the upper layer far from the pipeline, so it takes memory stalls as the optimization metric. Figure 11 illustrates the structural hazard source distributions. For more than a half of benchmarks, LDST, i.e. memory operation, is the main structural hazard source. Therefore, DYNCTA makes accurate decisions for the benchmarks such as BFS. However, ALU/FPU and SFU are the main structural hazard sources for other benchmarks, such as MC and CP. It is why DYNCTA makes wrong decisions for these benchmarks. The DYNCTA scheduling decisions are also interfered for some benchmarks with hybrid structural hazard sources, such as STO, IIX, and LIB.

Compared to the CTA scheduler, the warp scheduler can not only adjust TLP in a fine granularity, but also employ a better optimization metric for a close location to the pipeline. Therefore, the dynamic TLP optimization in the warp scheduler is a much better choice.

4. STALL-AWARE WARP SCHEDULING

In this section, we describe the detailed design of the proposed Stall-Aware Warp Scheduling (SAWS) that dynamically adjust the TLP at runtime. We also give a hardware overhead analysis in Subsection 4.3.

4.1 Trigger-based Method

SAWS employs a trigger-based method to adjust the fetch group size, which takes an action when a triggering event appears. A triggering event will be generated when an in-

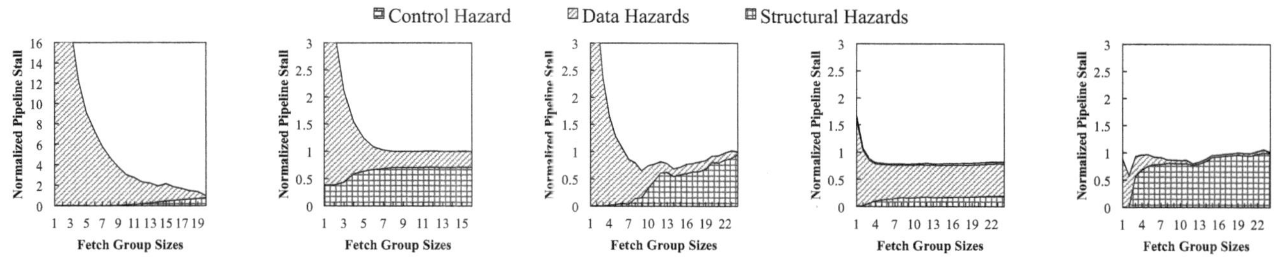

(a) MC (Type I) (b) SAD (Type II) (c) SP (Type III) (d) LU2 (Type IV) (e) KMS (Type V)

Figure 9: The pipeline stall distribution at various fetch group sizes. It increases structural hazards and decreases data hazards with increasing the fetch group size. The control hazards are negligible.

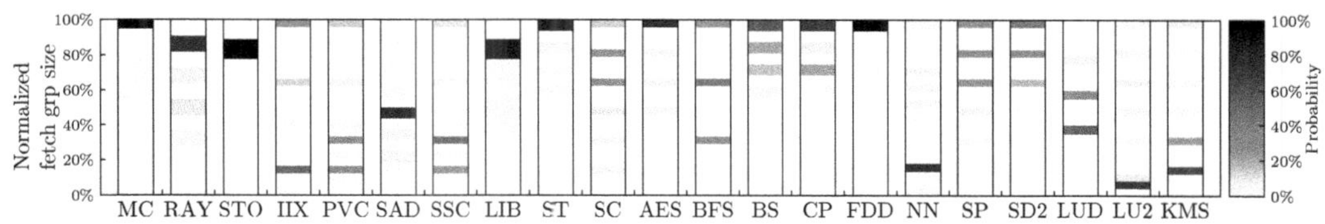

Figure 10: The scheduling decisions on TLP by DYNCTA. The colored blocks in each bar show the different probabilities that the schedulers selects a certain TLP parameter in warp i.e. the amount of active warps in a core for the benchmarks. A darker colored block means a higher probability of the corresponding TLP parameter than other TLP parameters with the lighter-colored blocks.

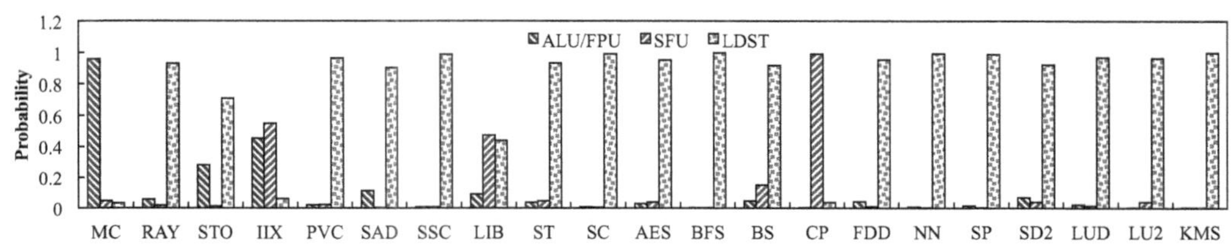

Figure 11: The structural hazard source distributions. Memory stalls (LDST) are not the only source for structural hazards. ALU/FPU and SFU are the main sources of structural hazards in MC and CP. Some benchmarks present hybrid structural hazard sources.

struction experiences too many structural hazards. SAWS monitors the structural hazards for all ready instructions, and moves the corresponding warp into the pending group if the structural hazards of this instruction exceed a threshold t_s. The threshold needs to be determined according to the GPU core configuration on the parallelism scale of the functional units through the experiments. We choose $t_s = 32$ in our experimental settings as described in Section 5. The newly pending warp is appended to the tail of the pending queue. The trigger-based method does not require to follow a sampling period, which brings a fast tuning response.

At the same time, the trigger-based method causes affordable hardware overhead. Because of the in-order instruction issuance, each warp contains at most one ready instruction each cycle. SAWS appends an extra register to each warp context as the counter of structural hazards of the current ready instruction. The counters are updated along with the warp scheduling and do not require any extra clock cycles. A counter is reset when its current ready instruction is issued. SAWS initialized a counter to zero when the corresponding warp is promoted to the active group.

Figure 12 illustrates an example to demonstrate how the trigger-based method works in SAWS. In this example, we assume that a GPGPU core contains 2 execution units E0 and E1 for compute instructions. The core executes 4 warps W0 – W3. We present the scheduling procedure of the first 4 instructions, where I0 – I2 are compute instructions which require 5, 5, and 3 cycles respectively, and I3 is a memory access. All the instructions are data dependent. We use $t_s = 4$ here. We initialize all these warps in the active group. After cycle 1, the execution units are occupied by

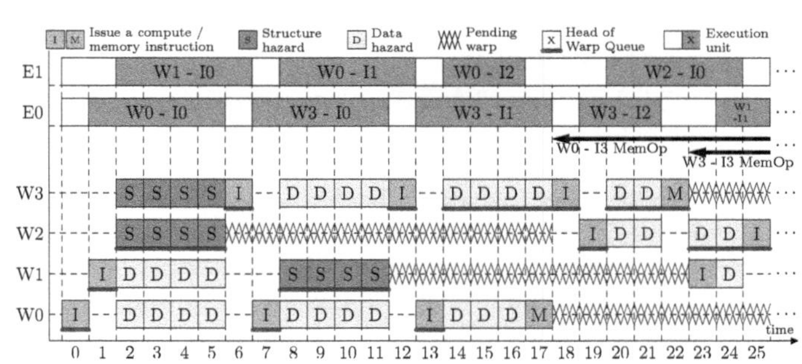

Figure 12: An example of trigger-based method. It moves a warp who suffers too many structural hazards to pending group. SAWS finds an optimal fetch group size in only 12 clock cycles.

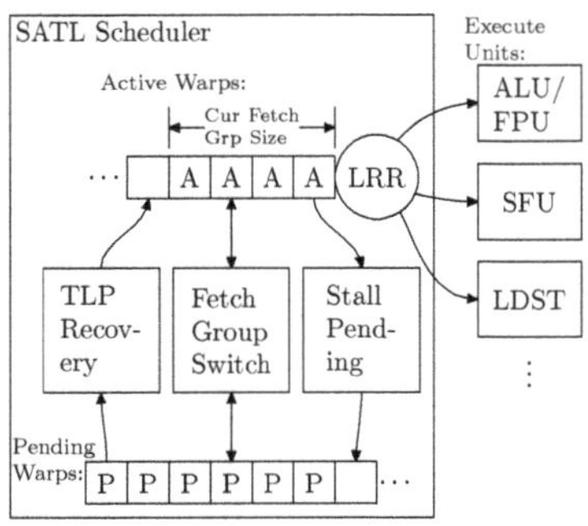

Figure 13: The design of Stall-Aware Warp Scheduling. Two modules, Stall Pending and TLP Recovery, are added on the original TL to adjust the fetch group size at runtime.

W0 and W1. In cycle 2 through 5, the warp scheduler cannot issue another instruction, because W2 and W3 suffer the structural hazards for unavailable execution units, and W0 and W1 suffer the data hazards for data dependencies. After cycle 5, W2 is moved to the pending group because there are already 4 structural hazards for its I0. The hardware usually supports only one warp movement per cycle, thus W3 still remains in the active group. At cycles 6 and 7, the warp scheduler issues another two instructions from W3 and W0. In cycle 8 through 11, W0 and W3 suffer data hazards and W1 suffers structural hazards. After only the first 11 cycles, SAWS finds the optimal fetch group size by moving W1 to the pending group without any manual configuration. It shows that the trigger-based method does bring a fast tuning response. After that, the remaining two warps execute effectively by keeping the execution units as busy as possible without any structural hazards. The fetch group switch policy swaps the pending and active warps at cycles 18 and 23 due to the memory operations, thus the long latency operations can still be hidden in SAWS.

4.2 SAWS Design

SAWS is built upon TL and adjusts the fetch group size at runtime, whose structural design is illustrated in Figure 13. SAWS adds two modules, Stall Pending and TLP Recovery. Stall Pending uses the trigger-based method as described in Subsection 4.1 to decrease the fetch group size to alleviate too much hardware contention. TLP Recovery is deployed to tolerate the compute pattern changes at runtime and to recover to a higher TLP if the hardware resource is underutilized. The Fetch Group Switch is remained in SAWS to hide the long latency operations.

Because it is hard to generate a triggering event from a pending warp, TLP Recovery employs a dynamic method. In every sampling cycle, if the structural hazards per instruction are less than a threshold T_s as well as the data hazards are larger than another threshold T_d, the execution units are considered as underutilized, then TLP Recovery promotes the head warp of the pending queue, and appends it to the tail of the active queue. T_d and T_s are chosen according to the GPGPU configurations such as the parallelism scale of the functional units. In our experimental configuration, we choose the sampling cycle as 512 clock cycles, and the thresholds $T_d = 4$ and $T_s = 3$. TLP Recovery requires 3 registers, a data hazard counter, a structural hazard counter, and an instruction counter. To simplify the hardware design, we replace the division by bit shift to approximately compute the structural hazards per instruction. These counters are reset every sampling cycle.

Table 1: GPGPU-Sim Configuration

# Cores	14
Warp Size	32
SIMD Pipeline Width	16
# Threads / Core	1024
# Registers / Core	32768
Shared Memory / Core	48KB
Constant Cache / Core	8KB, 64B line, 2-way assoc. LRU
Texture Cache / Core	12KB, 128B line, 24-way assoc. LRU
# Memory Partitions	6
L1 Data Cache	16KB, 128B line, 4-way assoc. LRU
L2 Unified Cache	128KB / Memory Partition, 128B line, 16-way assoc. LRU
Core Clock	1150 MHz
Interconnect Clock	1150 MHz
Memory Clock	750 MHz
DRAM Request Queue Size	16
Memory Scheduler	out of order (FR-FCFS)
DRAM Memory Timing	$t_{CL} = 12$, $t_{RP} = 12$, $t_{RC} = 40$, $t_{RAS} = 28$, $t_{RCD} = 12$, $t_{RRD} = 6$
DRAM Bus Width	384 bits

Since the fetch group size is not a fixed parameter in SAWS, the active and pending queues are no longer fixed-sized. The warp queue design in the original TL is not feasible in SAWS. Because the warp volume in a core is fixed, SAWS employs a ring queue with active and pending regions. To reduce the data movement, the two regions connect each head with other's tail, and a warp state change is implemented by moving the region boundaries.

4.3 Hardware Overhead

SAWS requires only small amount hardware overhead, which consumes a negligible fraction of the die area. A core whose warp volume is n_W only requires total $(n_W + 3)$ registers by SAWS as analysis in above subsections. In addition to registers, the operation logic is also simple. Only two kinds of profiling data, structural hazards per instruction and the data hazards of each core, are required by SAWS that can be collected directly from the pipeline and instruction issuance controllers. The Stall Pending and TLP Recovery modules read the counters and use comparison logic to make their tuning decisions.

5. EXPERIMENTAL EVALUATION

We simulated SAWS using a performance simulator GPGPU-Sim, and conducted extensive experiments to evaluate the effectiveness of SAWS on performance, accuracy, and pipeline efficiency. We also discussed the impact to SAWS by combining another TLP optimization in the CTA scheduler.

5.1 Methodology

Our experiments are conducted on a performance simulator GPGPU-Sim 3.2.0b [1]. GPGPU-Sim is widely used in GPGPU scheduler and architecture research. It simulates every GPU clock cycle during the kernel execution, and reports all detailed tracking and profiling data to users. We choose the default configuration of the widely used NVIDIA Tesla C2050 listed in Table 1 as the simulated GPGPU.

Table 2: Benchmarks used in Experiments

Abbr.	Src.	Applications	Type
MC	SDK [21]	Monte Carlo Reduction	I
RAY	Sim [1]	Ray Tracing	I
STO	Sim [1]	StoreGPU	I
IIX	Mars [7]	Inverted Index	II
PVC	Mars [7]	Page View Count	II
SAD	Parboil [13]	Sum of Abs. Differences	II
SSC	Mars [7]	Similarity Score	II
LIB	Sim [1]	LIBOR Monte Carlo	II
ST	Parboil [13]	Stencil	III
SC	SDK [21]	Scan of Large Arrays	III
AES	Sim [1]	AES Cryptography	III
BFS	Rodinia [26]	Breadth First Search	III
BS	SDK [21]	Blackscholes	III
CP	Sim [1]	Coulombic Potential	III
FDD	SDK [21]	Finite-Difference Time-Domain	III
NN	Sim [1]	Neural Network	III
SP	SDK [21]	Scalar Product	III
SD2	Rodinia [26]	SRAD2	III
LUD	Rodinia [26]	LU Decomposition (Incre. Ver.)	IV
LU2	Rodinia [26]	LU Decomposition	IV
KMS	Rodinia [26]	Kmeans	V

We use 21 paradigmatic benchmarks listed in Table 2 with various types to evaluate the effectiveness of SAWS. These benchmarks come from several widely used GPGPU benchmark suites including Rodinia [26], Parboil [13], Mars [7], NVIDIA Compute SDK [21], and the benchmarks in GPGPU-Sim package [1]. Most of them are executed with the default input size, but we reduce the input sizes for an acceptable simulation time.

The experiments compare SAWS with LRR [17], TL [16, 30] and GTO [18]. LRR maximizes the TLP, thus its results represent the GPGPU behavior in the highest TLP. TL uses a fixed instead of the highest TLP, thus its results represent the picture in a medium TLP. The experimental results denoted as TL-Opt is the data from the optimal fetch group sizes that are different between benchmarks. TL-Opt represents the optimal case using a fixed fetch group size. GTO also maximizes the TLP but uses a greedy policy that always issues the oldest warps. We choose two CTA scheduling schemes Greedy and DYNCTA [23] in our experiments.Greedy is a default CTA scheduling in most warp scheduling researches, which allocates a CTA to a core as soon as the resources become available and maximizes TLP. DYNCTA is a CTA scheduling scheme with dynamic TLP optimization. We choose DYNCTA to figure out the impact of the warp scheduler from another scheduler in a higher layer. To the best of our knowledge, this is the first work to investigate the impact when a warp scheduling scheme combines with DYNCTA.

5.2 Performance Evaluation

We evaluate SAWS performance compared with LRR, TL, GTO, and DYNCTA. We choose the Greedy as the CTA scheduling for LRR, TL, and GTO, and choose LRR as the warp scheduling for DYNCTA, because the maximized TLP avoids the interference with the other scheduling layer. Figure 14 illustrates the performance speedups along with a geometric mean, which are normalized to the performance of LRR. The experimental results show SAWS achieves the best geometric mean of speedup at 14.7% over LRR, which is 4.4% higher than TL-Opt, and 9.3% higher than DYNCTA. The highest speedup comes up in KMS at 115.2%. TL with a fixed fetch group size achieves small speedups, whose geometric mean of speedup is only 1.7%. In contrast, the TL-Opt achieves much better speedups (10.3%), which demonstrates the importance of the TLP optimization. Moreover, benchmarks such as RAY and SP achieve even better performance by DYNCTA and SAWS than TL-Opt, because the dynamic TLP optimization can adjust scheduling decisions to fit the various access patterns at runtime. It should be mentioned here that some benchmarks such as SC, CP, and LUD, DYNCTA achieve even lower performance than LRR. As the analysis in Subsection 3.4, the coarse granularity and the inaccurate optimization metric are two main reasons for the degraded performance. GTO reduces the actual TLP by its greedy policy where only the oldest warps are scheduled in a certain period. Because the actual TLP in GTO is determined by the issuance stalls not the pipeline stalls, GTO does not achieve the optimal TLP and performance for some benchmarks.

5.3 Scheduling Decision Accuracy

Figure 15 illustrates the scheduling decisions on TLP by SAWS. We use colors to represent the probabilities when SAWS chooses a certain fetch group size. The experimental results show that the scheduling decisions by SAWS reach all the TLP levels because of the fine-grained warp scheduling. Recalling Figure 10, the granularity is the main reason why DYNCTA achieves 58.7% speedup for KMS that is much lower than SAWS with 115.2% speedup. SAWS can flexibly choose the fetch group size as 2 or 3 for KMS.

Compared the scheduling decisions to the top-5% optimal fetch group sizes in Figure 3, we find that SAWS gives more accurate decisions than DYNCTA. Because of the optimization policies from the memory stalls, DYNCTA makes wrong decisions for the benchmarks such as CP, BS, and FDD. Such wrong decisions do not appear in SAWS because of the pipeline efficiency metric used by SAWS. In addition, the decisions for benchmarks such as RAY and SP concentrate on more than one fetch group sizes, which means SAWS is able to dynamically adjust the scheduling decisions in different execution phases.

5.4 Pipeline and Resource Efficiency

We evaluate the average structural hazards and the average data hazards per instruction, i.e. the corresponding types of pipeline stalls encountered by an instruction before its issuance, to demonstrate the pipeline effectiveness of SAWS and other scheduling schemes. Figure 16 illustrates the normalized structural hazards per instruction, and Figure 17 illustrates the normalized data hazards per instruction. The statistics here include all the stall counts of each instruction both before and after every warp pending. (It is unlike the triggering event defined in Section 4.1 where the statistics are reset when a warp becomes pended.) We choose the normalizing baseline as TL-Opt. The results show that the structural hazards in SAWS are usually less than 30% of TL-Opt for most benchmarks. Even for some benchmarks that SAWS suffers more structural hazards than TL-Opt, it is still less than DYNCTA. LRR usually suffers the most structural hazards for the maximized TLP. DYNCTA and GTO does not really reduce the structural hazards for the absent consideration on pipeline efficiency. Additionally, SAWS remains the data hazards similar to TL-Opt, and

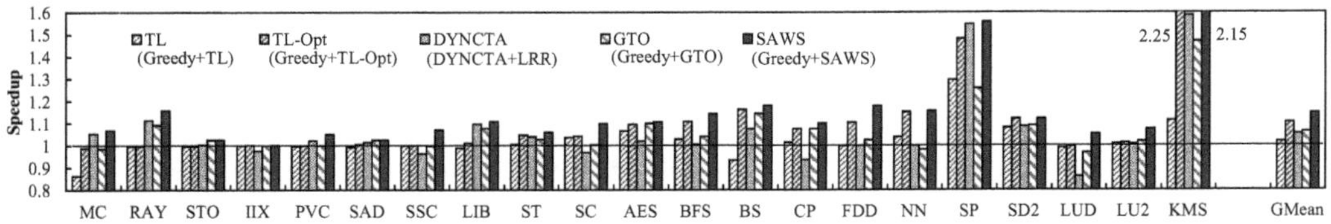

Figure 14: The performance speedups compared to LRR. SAWS achieves the best speedups even compared with TL-Opt.

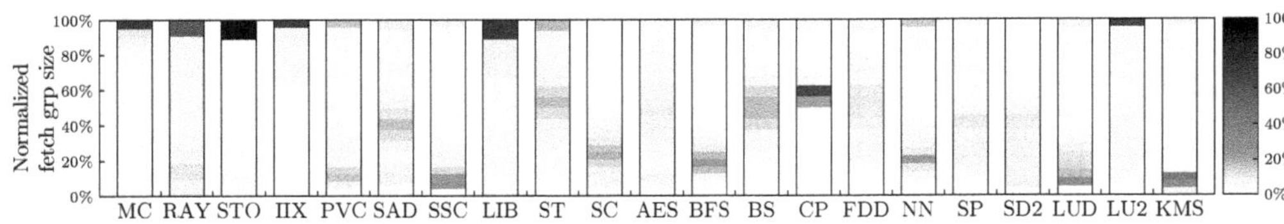

Figure 15: The TLP scheduling decisions by SAWS. The colored bars show the probabilities that SAWS chooses a certain fetch group size. SAWS makes accurate decisions for all these benchmarks.

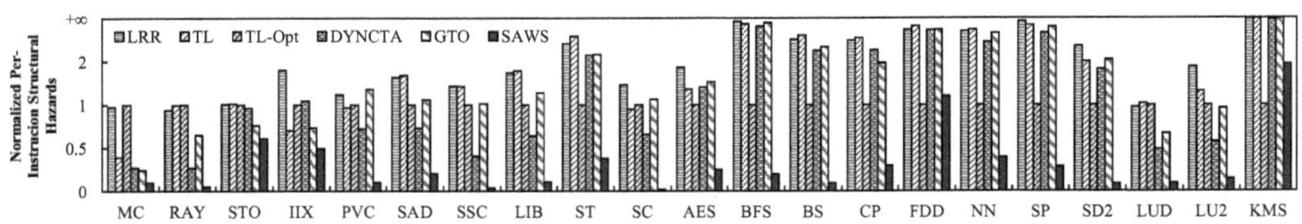

Figure 16: The structural hazards per instruction. SAWS reduces a lot of structural hazards by dynamically moving the surplus active warps to pending group.

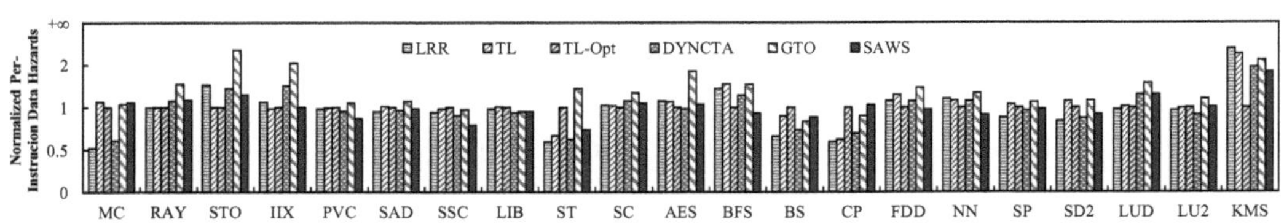

Figure 17: The data hazards per instruction. SAWS reduce the TLP but it does not significantly increase the data hazards.

does not introduce extra data hazards. Therefore, SAWS does improve the pipeline efficiency.

5.5 Combine CTA and Warp Scheduling

We evaluate the performance impact when TL, GTO, and SAWS combine with DYNCTA. In this subsection, we use $A+B$ to denote a combination of a CTA scheduling A and a warp scheduling B. Figure 18 illustrates the performance of DYNCTA+TL, DYNCTA+GTO and DYNCTA+SAWS normalized to Greedy+LRR. DYNCTA+TL brings a 3.7% higher speedup than Greedy+TL, but this performance is very close to DYNCTA+LRR. The geometric mean of speedups of DYNCTA+GTO is almost the same as Greedy+GTO, and only 1.2% higher than DYNCTA+LRR. The results indicate that TL and GTO do not further benefit the performance after the dynamic TLP optimizations at the CTA level. DYNCTA+SAWS achieves a geometric mean of speedups at 12.8%, which is much higher than DYNCTA+LRR but lower than Greedy+SAWS. It shows that SAWS helps DYNCTA making a more accurate decision, but the SAWS scheduling decisions are affected by DYNCTA.

We further analyze the scheduling decisions by DYNCTA+SAWS whose results are illustrated as in Figure 19. Compared to Figure 10, DYNCTA+SAWS makes much better scheduling decisions than DYNCTA+LRR. First, DYNCTA+SAWS avoids the granularity issue that happens in KMS, and reaches all possible TLP levels. Second, the inaccurate decisions by DYNCTA are corrected by SAWS. The manifestations are twofold. (1) If DYNCTA allocates excessive CTAs, such as CP, SAWS is able to decrease the fetch group size in the warp scheduler; (2) If DYNCTA allocates insufficient CTAs, such as NN, the high pipeline efficiency by SAWS can alleviate the memory stalls, which leads DYNCTA allocating more CTAs and corrects the original scheduling decisions. However, the fetch group sizes chosen by DYNCTA+SAWS are slightly smaller than by Greedy+SAWS. DYNCTA tends to choose a lower TLP than Greedy, which interferes with the correctness of SAWS. Therefore, moving dynamic TLP optimization from the CTA to warp scheduler is a better choice. For an optimal performance and hardware overhead, it is not necessary to combine SAWS and DYNCTA together.

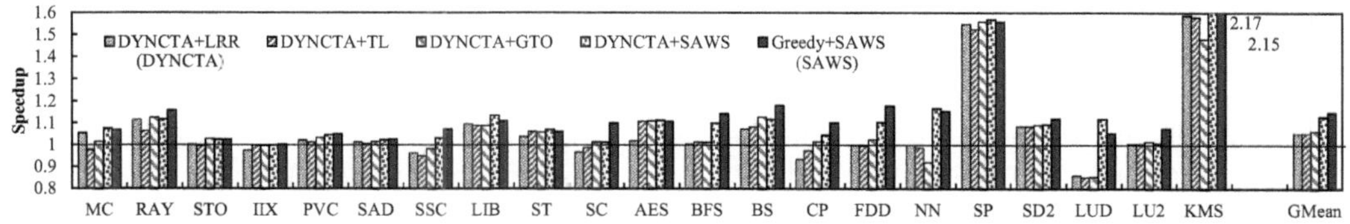

Figure 18: The speedups when TL and SAWS combined with DYNCTA. DYNCTA+SAWS achieves higher speedups than DYNCTA+LRR, but lower than Greedy+SAWS on average.

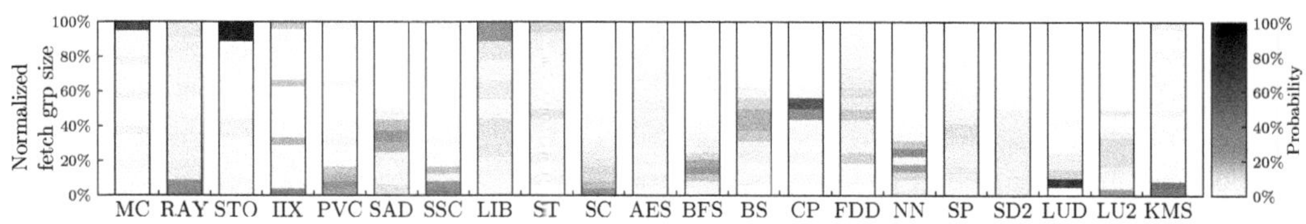

Figure 19: The TLP scheduling decisions by DYNCTA+SAWS. SAWS refines the scheduling decision by DYNCTA+LRR, but smaller fetch group sizes are chosen than Greedy+SAWS.

6. RELATED WORK

There are some GPGPU schedulers proposed to optimize TLP. Narasiman et al [30] proposed Two-Level warp scheduling (TL) using lower TLP to hide the long latency operation. Gebhart et al [16] also employed TL to reduce the register and cache pressure. Kayiran et al [23] proposed DYNCTA, which monitors the idle cycles and memory stalls, and makes CTA tuning decision every sampling period. Lee et al [18] proposed LCS using a lazy method to find out the optimal CTA capacities in a core. Nevertheless, our proposed SAWS is a fine-grain dynamic TLP optimization scheme in the warp level, which aims to improve the pipeline efficiency.

Many other warp schedulers are proposed for higher performance by improving cache and memory efficiency. Jog et al [3] proposed Prefetch-Aware warp scheduling (PA), and Jog et al [4] proposed Cooperative-Thread-Array-Aware warp scheduling (OWL) to improve the cache and memory efficiency. Chen et al [9] proposed Region-P warp scheduling to improve the overlapping efficiency between compute and memory operations. Rogers et al [29] proposed cache-conscious wavefront scheduling (CCWS) to avoid the cache thrashing. Lee et al [27] prioritized the critical warps to avoid the the warp criticality problem.

Some CTA scheduling schemes are proposed. Adriaens et al [8] demonstrated the spatial CTA scheduling in GPGPU, and analyzed some alternative CTA scheduling policies. Yu et al [35] proposed a CTA scheduling optimization scheme to improve the CTA load balance. Pai et al [28] proposed Shortest Remaining Time First (SRTF) CTA scheduler to improve performance and fairness.

There are some scheduling strategies proposed for an efficient control flow execution on GPGPUs. Meng et al [12], Fung et al [32], Fung et al [31], and Brunie et al [20] proposed several warp subdivision technologies to improve the resource utilities in the warp divergence. Huo et al [34] designed scheduling algorithms for recursive control flow on GPGPUs. Jablin et al [10] reorganized the instruction order to reduce the divergence time. Lashgar et al [5] proposed SW+ and LW+ to improve the performance for the GPGPU with various warp sizes. Xiang et al [25] and Yilmazer et al [6] exploited and eliminated the redundant computations. Chen et al [15] employed a software-assistant technology to improve the hardware utility by a task queue design.

Memory is also a critical factor to GPGPU performance. Jia et al [33] used reordering and bypassing technologies to improve the cache efficiency. Jog et al. [2] proposed an application-aware memory scheduling to avoid the unfairness on memory accesses between kernels. AlSaber et al [19] proposed a software data scheduling to reduce the CPU-GPU redundant communication.

The TLP efficiency is also investigated in other GPGPU context. For a CPU-GPU fusion architecture, Lee et al [11] proposed a TLP-aware cache management policy, and Kayiran et al [24] proposed a concurrent management technique. Yu et al [36] proposed a code transformation technique to tune the GPGPU thread granularity.

7. CONCLUSIONS

We comprehensively investigate the TLP performance impact in a warp scheduler, and discover the pipeline efficiency is a critical factor for this impact. We propose SAWS to dynamically optimize the TLP at runtime. A trigger-based method is employed to achieve a fast tuning response. We conduct experiments on a performance simulator GPGPU-Sim. The experimental results show that SAWS makes better TLP decisions and effectively reduces the structural hazards while does not cause extra data hazards. SAWS achieves significant performance improvement compare to TL, GTO, and DYNCTA, with 14.7% on a geometric mean and up to 115.2% speedups compared to LRR. For most benchmarks, SAWS even achieves higher performance than TL with the optimal fetch group sizes. Furthermore, we have compared the dynamic TLP optimizations in different scheduling layers. Our experiments demonstrate that the combination of the optimizations in different layers cannot bring extra performance improvement among the benchmarks. Considering the accuracy and hardware overhead, it is a competitive choice by using the dynamic TLP optimization in the warp scheduler.

Acknowledgments

We thank anonymous reviewers for their insightful comments. This research is sponsored in part by U.S. National

Science Foundation grants CNS-1320349 and CNS-1218960 and National Natural Science Foundation of China grant 11372067. Any opinions, findings, and conclusions or recommendations expressed in this material are those of the author(s) and do not necessarily reflect the views of the funding agencies.

8. REFERENCES

[1] A. Bakhoda, G. Yuan, W. Fung, et al. Analyzing CUDA workloads using a detailed GPU simulator. In *ISPASS*, pages 163–174, 2009.

[2] A. Jog, E. Bolotin, Z. Guz, et al. Application-aware memory system for fair and efficient execution of concurrent GPGPU applications. In *GPGPU*, pages 1–8, 2014.

[3] A. Jog, O. Kayiran, A. Mishra, et al. Orchestrated scheduling and prefetching for GPGPUs. In *ISCA*, pages 332–343, 2013.

[4] A. Jog, O. Kayiran, N. Nachiappan, et al. OWL: cooperative thread array aware scheduling techniques for improving GPGPU performance. In *ASPLOS*, pages 395–406, 2013.

[5] A. Lashgar, A. Baniasadi, and A. Khonsari. Warp size impact in GPUs: large or small? In *GPGPU*, pages 146–152, 2013.

[6] A. Yilmazer, Z. Chen, and D. Kaeli. Scalar waving: improving the efficiency of SIMD execution on GPUs. In *IPDPS*, pages 103–112, 2014.

[7] B. He, W. Fang, Q. Luo, et al. Mars: a MapReduce framework on graphics processors. In *PACT*, pages 260–269, 2008.

[8] J. Adriaens, K. Compton, N. Kim, et al. The case for GPGPU spatial multitasking. In *HPCA*, pages 1–12, 2012.

[9] J. Chen, X. Tao, Z. Yang, et al. Guided region-based GPU scheduling: utilizing multi-thread parallelism to hide memory latency. In *IPDPS*, pages 441–451, 2013.

[10] J. Jablin, T. Jablin, O. Mutlu, et al. Warp-aware trace scheduling for GPUs. In *PACT*, pages 163–174, 2014.

[11] J. Lee and H. Kim. TAP: a TLP-aware cache management policy for a CPU-GPU heterogeneous architecture. In *HPCA*, pages 1–12, 2012.

[12] J. Meng, D. Tarjan, and K. Skadron. Dynamic warp subdivision for integrated branch and memory divergence tolerance. In *ISCA*, pages 235–246, 2010.

[13] J. Stratton, C. Rodrigues, I. Sung, et al. Parboil: a revised benchmark suite for scientific and commercial throughput computing. Technical Report IMPACT-12-01, University of Illinois at Urbana-Champaign, 2012.

[14] Khronos Group. The open standard for parallel programming of heterogeneous systems, 2013.

[15] L. Chen, O. Villa, S. Krishnamoorthy, et al. Dynamic load balancing on single- and multi-GPU systems. In *IPDPS*, pages 1–12, 2010.

[16] M. Gebhart, D. Johnson, D. Tarjan, et al. Energy-efficient mechanisms for managing thread context in throughput processors. In *ISCA*, pages 235–246, 2011.

[17] M. Gebhart, D. Johnson, D. Tarjan, et al. A hierarchical thread scheduler and register file for energy-efficient throughput processors. *ACM Transactions on Computer Systems*, 30(2):1–38, 2012.

[18] M. Lee, S. Song, J. Moon, et al. Improving GPGPU resource utilization through alternative thread block scheduling. In *HPCA*, pages 263–273, 2014.

[19] N. AlSaber and M. Kulkarni. SemCache: semantics-aware caching for efficient GPU offloading. In *ICS*, pages 421–432, 2013.

[20] N. Brunie, S. Collange, and G. Diamos. Simultaneous branch and warp interweaving for sustained GPU performance. In *ISCA*, pages 49–60, 2012.

[21] NVIDIA. CUDA C/C++ SDK code samples, 2011.

[22] NVIDIA. CUDA C Programming Guide, 2012.

[23] O. Kayiran, A. Jog, M. Kandemir, et al. Neither more nor less: optimizing thread-level parallelism for GPGPUs. In *PACT*, pages 157–166, 2013.

[24] O. Kayiran, N. Nachiappan, A. Jog, et al. Managing GPU concurrency in heterogeneous architectures. In *MICRO*, pages 1–13, 2014.

[25] P. Xiang, Y. Yang, M. Mantor, et al. Exploiting uniform vector instructions for GPGPU performance, energy Efficiency, and opportunistic reliability enhancement. In *ICS*, pages 433–442, 2013.

[26] S. Che, M. Boyer, J. Meng, et al. Rodinia: a benchmark suite for heterogeneous computing. In *IISWC*, pages 44–54, 2009.

[27] S. Lee and C. Wu. CAWS: criticality-aware warp scheduling for GPGPU workloads. In *PACT*, pages 175–186, 2014.

[28] S. Pai, R. Govindarajan, and M. Thazhuthaveetil. Preemptive thread block scheduling with online structural runtime prediction for concurrent GPGPU kernels. In *PACT*, pages 483–484, 2014.

[29] T. Rogers, M. O'Connor, and T. Aamodt. Cache-conscious wavefront scheduling. In *MICRO*, pages 72–83, 2012.

[30] V. Narasiman, M. Shebanow, C. Lee, et al. Improving GPU performance via large warps and two-level warp scheduling. In *MICRO*, pages 308–317, 2011.

[31] W. Fung and T. Aamodt. Thread block compaction for efficient SIMT control flow. In *HPCA*, pages 25–36, 2011.

[32] W. Fung, I. Sham, G. Yuan, et al. Dynamic warp formation and scheduling for efficient GPU control flow. In *MICRO*, pages 407–420, 2007.

[33] W. Jia, K. Shaw, and M. Martonosi. MRPB: memory request prioritization for massively parallel processors. In *HPCA*, pages 274–285, 2014.

[34] X. Huo, S. Krishnamoorthy, and G. Agrawal. Efficient scheduling of recursive control flow on GPUs. In *ICS*, pages 409–420, 2013.

[35] Y. Yu, X. He, H. Guo, et al. A credit-based load-balance-aware CTA scheduling optimization scheme in GPGPU. *International Journal of Parallel Programming*, 42(8):1–21, 2014.

[36] Y. Yu, X. He, H. Guo, et al. APR: a novel parallel repacking algorithm for efficient GPGPU parallel code transformation. In *GPGPU*, pages 81–89, 2014.

PeerWave: Exploiting Wavefront Parallelism on GPUs with Peer-SM Synchronization*

Mehmet E. Belviranli
Computer Science Dept.
Univ. of California, Riverside
belviram@cs.ucr.edu

Peng Deng
Elec. and Comp. Eng. Dept.
Univ. of California, Riverside
pdeng002@ucr.edu

Laxmi N. Bhuyan
Computer Science Dept.
Univ. of California, Riverside
bhuyan@cs.ucr.edu

Rajiv Gupta
Computer Science Dept.
Univ. of California, Riverside
gupta@cs.ucr.edu

Qi Zhu
Elec. and Comp. Eng. Dept.
Univ. of California, Riverside
qzhu@ece.ucr.edu

ABSTRACT

Nested loops with regular iteration dependencies span a large class of applications ranging from string matching to linear system solvers. Wavefront parallelism is a well-known technique to enable concurrent processing of such applications and is widely being used on GPUs to benefit from their massively parallel computing capabilities. Wavefront parallelism on GPUs uses global barriers between processing of tiles to enforce data dependencies. However, such diagonal-wide synchronization causes load imbalance by forcing SMs to wait for the completion of the SM with longest computation. Moreover, diagonal processing causes loss of locality due to elements that border adjacent tiles.

In this paper, we propose PeerWave, an alternative GPU wavefront parallelization technique that improves inter-SM load balance by using peer-wise synchronization between SMs. and eliminating global synchronization. Our approach also increases GPU L2 cache locality through row allocation of tiles to the SMs. We further improve PeerWave performance by using flexible hyper-tiles that reduce inter-SM wait time while maximizing intra-SM utilization. We develop an analytical model for determining the optimal tile size. Finally, we present a run-time and a CUDA based API to allow users to easily implement their applications using PeerWave. We evaluate PeerWave on the NVIDIA K40c GPU using 6 different applications and achieve speedups of up to 2X compared to the most recent hyperplane transformation based GPU implementation.

Categories and Subject Descriptors

D.1.3 [**Programming Techniques**]: Concurrent Programming—*Parallel programming*; C.1.2 [**Processor Architectures**]: Multiple Data Stream Architectures (Multiprocessors)—*Single-instruction-stream, multiple-data-stream processors (SIMD)*

General Terms

Algorithms

Keywords

Wavefront parallelism; GP-GPU computing; decentralized synchronization.

1. INTRODUCTION

Since nested loops are a major source of parallelism, a great deal of research has focused on parallel execution of nested loops. Many classes of applications like time-based simulations, linear system solvers, and string matching algorithms employ a combination of DOACROSS and DOALL parallelism to process large volumes of data efficiently on massively parallel systems. Application and architecture specific challenges imposed by the data dependencies between loop iterations have lead to the development of various compile-time [5, 11], run-time[2, 12, 9], and algorithm-level [15, 3, 13] solutions.

Wavefront parallelism [16] is a well known technique for exploiting parallelism in nested loops using multiple processing units. Based on the dependency relationships across iterations along space and/or time dimensions, the computation proceeds in form of *diagonal waves* where iterations in each wave can be executed in parallel. To enforce data dependencies across consecutive waves, their execution is serialized via the use of barriers. To exploit data locality, elements are grouped into square tiles [17] and each tile is assigned to a single processor. This approach introduces a second level of parallelism where tiles can also be processed in parallel along diagonal waves with global barriers separating them.

GPUs have been used to accelerate wavefront based applications via use of their massive number of processing units. Many frequently used algorithms such as Smith-Waterman [14, 18], Cholesky Factorization [15], and SOR loop nests [4] have been adapted to run efficiently on GPUs. The two level parallelism via tile partitioning is also commonly exploited by GPU based techniques whose evaluation has been reported in several studies [5, 4, 18]. In these approaches, a thread block (TB) is created for each tiles in a diagonal and these tiles are processed in parallel by the multiple streaming multipro-

*This work is supported by the National Science Foundation, under grant CCF-0905509, CNS-1157377 and CCF-1423108

ICS'15, June 8–11, 2015, Newport Beach, CA, USA.

DOI: http://dx.doi.org/10.1145/2751205.2751243.

cessors (SMs) of the GPU (*inter-tile* parallelism). Iterations along diagonals within a tile are also executed in parallel by the SIMD computation units (i.e. CUDA cores) inside an SM (*intra-tile* parallelism). Similar to CPU based approaches, global barriers are required for both tile-level (i.e. *inter-tile*) and element-level(i.e. *intra-tile*) diagonals in order to enforce data dependencies. However, on GPUs, using global barriers for 2-level tiled wavefront execution has two major drawbacks:

1. Low utilization due to load imbalance. The use of global barriers leads to low utilization of processing units during both intra- and inter-tile parallel execution. The intra-tile imbalance causes threads utilization to be lower towards the beginning and the end of diagonal iterations. The same thing happens in processing diagonals of tiles, where the number of tiles are less at the beginning and towards the end. Moreover, inter-tile processing is also imbalanced, when other processors wait for the longest running task (i.e., processing of a tile) in a diagonal. SMs are forced to stay idle, even though new tiles are ready to execute as their dependencies have been satisfied. Intra-tile load imbalance for GPUs is addressed in [5] where tiles are transformed into polyhedral planes [8] to maximize utilization of threads processing a tile. However, this approach still uses inter-tile global barriers causing some SMs to unnecessarily wait for the longest running task.

2. Loss of data locality across tiles is another cause of performance degradation in global barriers. In CUDA, thread blocks, hence tiles, are executed in no specific order; therefore there is no guarantee that neighboring tiles will be processed by the same SM. This behavior destroys the dependency-implied locality across the border elements of adjacent tiles. Efforts have been made to overcome this drawback of global barriers. To improve data locality, [10] statically assigns row of tiles to the same processor and for shared memory multi-processors large CPU caches significantly improve data reuse between neighboring tiles. However, intra-tile operations are still carried out on a diagonal basis, which constitute most of the computations. In contrast to CPUs, both intra-tile and inter-tile locality is not exploited on GPUs since L1/L2 caches are much smaller. The effects of row or column assignments of tiles on GPU execution has not been tried before.

In this paper we address the above issues by developing PeerWave, a new GPU parallelization scheme for nested loops with data dependencies. We develop a decentralized synchronization scheme called *PeerSM* which eliminates global barriers by utilizing efficient SM-to-SM communication. PeerSM considerably reduces load imbalance by decreasing redundant idle waits and letting SMs start executing tiles independently as soon as their dependencies are satisfied. Our approach also improves cache locality across consecutive tiles by *Row-to-SM* assignment. *Flexible Hyper-Tiles* further reduces SM under utilization by allowing fine-grained control over synchronization intervals while keeping intra-tile utilization at maximum.

Our paper has the following contributions:

- We design a fast SM-to-SM peer synchronization mechanism (*PeerSM*) to eliminate load imbalance between SMs.
- We implement a row allocation scheme (*Row-to-SM*) which assigns consecutive tiles to same SM via programming of thread blocks (TBs).
- We extend hyperplane tile transformation (hyper-tile) (*Flexible Hyper-Tiles*) to further decrease idleness via adjustable synchronization intervals .
- We evaluate our scheme on the state of the art NVIDIA K40c GPU for 6 different applications and achieve speedup of up to 2X compared to approach that uses global barriers and hyper-tiles.
- We develop a generic API for CUDA to support a wide class of applications with nested loops and regular dependencies.

The rest of this paper is organized as follows. In Section 2, we give background on wavefront parallelism and related techniques. In Section 3 we describe our scheme in detail and in Section 4&5 we elaborate on the details, optimizations, our run-time and API. In Section 6 we describe the applications we use and in Section 7, we present the evaluation of our scheme. We end the paper with discussion of related work and the conclusion.

2. WAVEFRONT PARALLELISM

The wavefront technique exploits parallelism in nested loops that contain regular data dependencies across loop iterations. The main idea is to *skew* the iteration space and re-order loops to obtain a DOALL parallelism in one of the loops [16]. An example loop nest that processes a 2D array with cross iteration dependencies is given in Algorithm 1. The original loop nest is serial, and by skewing the inner j loop, DOALL parallelism is obtained across the iterations of the outer i loop. To utilize this parallelism, the two loops are swapped and their boundaries are adjusted accordingly. Figure 1(a) illustrates the iterations of this skewed&swapped loop nest. The dependencies between elements are shown via arrows and *diagonals* of elements are marked with dashed lines. Each diagonal corresponds to an iteration of the outer j loop that can be executed in parallel. An important property of such parallelism is its non-uniformity, where the parallelism first increases and then decreases along the outer diagonal iteration space.

Algorithm 1 Wavefront execution via loop skewing

```
// Original loop nest
for i=2 to n do
    for j=2 to m do
        A[i,j] = (A[i−1,j] + A[i,j−1])/2
    end for
end for

// Skewed
for i=2 to n do
    for j=i+2 to i+m do
        A[i,j−i] = (A[i−1,j−i] + A[i,j−i−1])/2
    end for
end for

// Skewed & Swapped
for j=4 to n+m do
    for i=MAX(2,j−m+2) to MIN(n,j−2) do
        A[i,j−i] = (A[i−1,j−i] + A[i,j−i−1])/2
    end for
end for
```

Tiling. In wavefront parallelism the control over granularity and locality is achieved by partitioning the iteration space into $t \times t$ square regions called *tiles* (see Figure 1(b)). Typically, tiling decreases inter-processor communication and also increases cache locality by grouping elements. Similar to the element-wise diagonal pattern, streaming multiprocessors

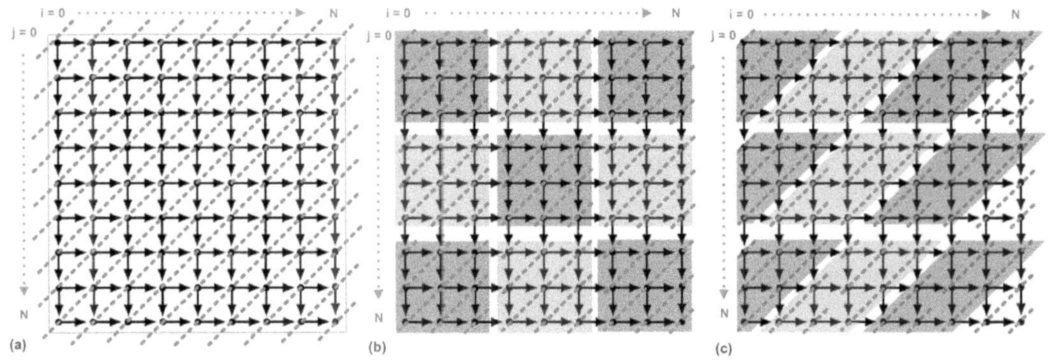

Figure 1: On the left(a), basic wavefront parallelism where dashed lines corresponds to 'waves'. In the center(b), tiling enables a second level of parallelism. On the right (c) tiles are transformed by the hyperplane technique.

(SMs) can be used to process diagonals of tiles in parallel (*inter-tile* parallelism) while diagonal elements in each tile can also be processed in parallel (*intra-tile* parallelism) by SIMD compute units (CUDA cores).

Even though GPUs enable 2-level parallelism, increased memory distance between neighboring diagonal executions combined with smaller cache sizes in GPUs reduces the possibility of cache hits and dramatically increases un-coalesced memory accesses. Moreover, due to the SIMD nature of GPGPU programming, any thread block (TB), hence a tile, can be executed on any SM, therefore voiding any possible spatial locality between neighboring tiles belonging to successive diagonals. The locality between two neighboring tiles in the same row is also lost because the data corresponding to only the last few diagonals is available in the cache. Hence straightforward allocation of two neighboring tiles to the same SM may not also benefit locality on GPUs. What we really need is the bordering data of a tile to be passed on to the same SM.

Hyperplane Transformation. An inherent drawback of using square/rectangular tiles in wavefront parallelism is the non-uniform diagonal sizes encountered during the execution of a tile. Hyperplane partitioning [8] converts square tiles into polyhedral quadrilaterals via a series of affine transformations. As shown in Figure 1(c), resulting tiles are composed of equal-sized diagonals with a total count of n, for n x n tiles whereas the square tiles end up in $2n-1$ diagonal iterations. Unlike square tiles, which limit maximum intra-tile parallelism to the minimum of tile width and height, hyper-plane partitioning allows arbitrary tile widths while keeping the diagonal size equal to the tile height. It may also be observed that the data is passed directly from the elements of a diagonal to be executed in the next iteration, hence increasing cache hits in the SM even for small cache sizes. If we allocate the next tile in the same row to the same SM, there will be cache hits for the bordering data. A technique similar to hyperplane partitioning for GPUs was proposed by [5] via compiler transformations to improve intra-tile parallelism. However, aforementioned inter-tile benefits have not been previously explored.

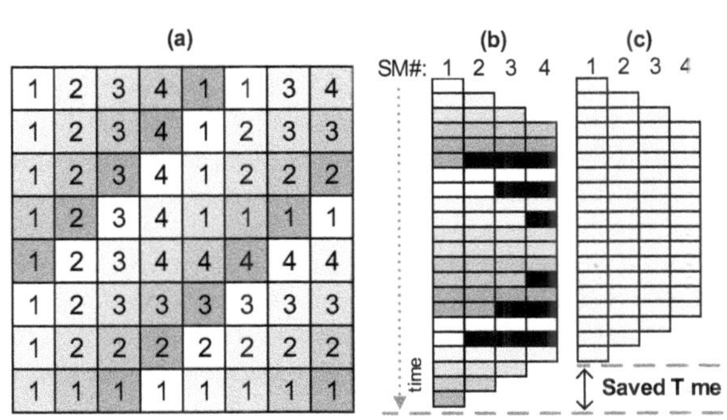

Figure 2: SM Under-utilization: On the left in (a) tiles are numbered with SMs executing them using global barriers; (b) shows the execution time-line of each SM using global barriers where dark-black slots indicate idle times; and (c) shows the ideal execution with the idle slots are eliminated.

Load Imbalance. The main drawback of using global barriers is the load imbalance caused by the diagonal-wide inter-tile synchronization. The imbalance is caused due to the varying number of tiles in each diagonal and the count is not always a multiple of an integer, hence all SMs need to wait until the SMs with the highest number of assigned tiles finish. We present an example in Figure 2 that shows the execution time line of a wavefront parallelism to demonstrate the load imbalance caused by global barriers. Figure 2(a) shows a 2D data partitioned into 8 tiles in each dimension and executed on 4 SMs using global barriers. Tiles in a diagonal are shaded with same color and numbered with the SM ids that are assigned to execute them. The scheduling is assumed to be the default round-robin TB scheduler believed to be used by NVIDIA GPUs. Figure 2(b) shows the time line for each SM where shaded rectangles correspond to busy time and dark-black slots correspond to idleness. Due to varying length of tile diagonals, some SMs are left idle for nearly all the diagonals. Figure 2(c) shows the ideal execution if global barriers are removed and SMs synchronize directly with each other to enforce dependencies. As we can see, the idleness due to inter-tile load imbalance is completely removed. Theoretically the saved time can be as high as 25% based on the total tile and SM count.

$$idle(d,p) = \begin{cases} p - |d| mod p, & \text{if } |d| > p \\ 0, & \text{otherwise} \end{cases}$$

$$n_{idle} = \sum_{d=1}^{t_x+t_y-1} idle(d,p)$$

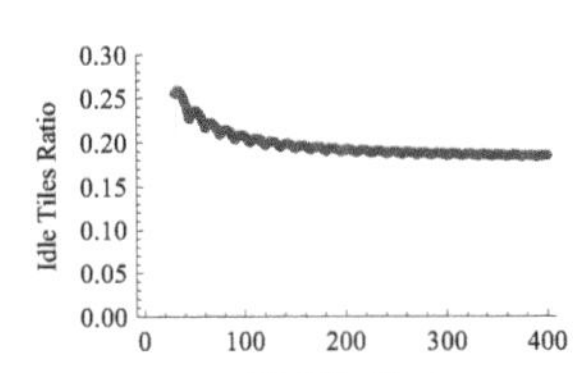

Figure 3: Number of idle tile execution slots on the left(a) and the ratio of idle slots to total tiles on the right(b).

The number of idle tile execution slots can be expressed with the equation given in Figure 3(a), where p is the number of processors and d is the diagonal iteration index. Using this equation, we have plotted the ratio of idle tile slots to the total tile count, which increases as smaller tiles are being used. As shown in Figure 3(b), even using smaller tiles to increase total tile count does not help this imbalance to be eliminated.

The rest of the paper describes PeerWave that provides the ideal execution of the rightmost Figure 2(c).

3. PEERWAVE

We propose PeerWave to employ direct SM-to-SM synchronization instead of global synchronization for wavefront parallelism to address the above drawbacks. As shown in Figure 4, PeerWave assigns a row of tiles to an SM to improve inter-tile locality and it uses decentralized synchronization to avoid barriers and load imbalance, where synchronization points are appropriately placed to maximize performance. Light triangles on the bottom-right of each tile correspond to the points where an SM writes to neighboring SM's flags after it finishes processing the tile; dark triangles on top-left of the tiles are for the places where a dependent SM reads these flags to continue execution. The rest of this section describes PeerWave in detail.

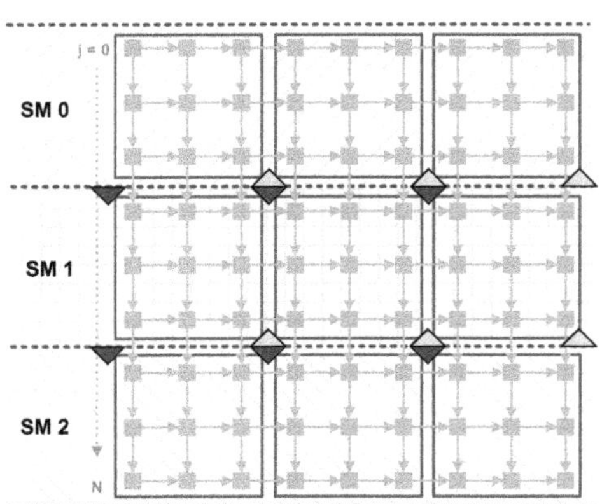

Figure 4: PeerWave: Partitioning of 2D iteration space into rows of tiles and assignment of rows to SMs. Triangles correspond to synchronization points, (light=write, dark=read).

3.1 Row-to-SM Assignment

PeerWave assigns a **tile-row**, a complete horizontal row of tiles in the 2D iteration space, to a single SM to exploit locality across tiles. In case there are more rows than SMs, the rows are distributed among the SMs in a round-robin fashion. Since CUDA does not provide any native mechanisms to manually assign thread blocks (TBs) to SMs, a TB is created for each row and *the TB-to-SM affinity* is achieved by limiting total number of TBs in a kernel launch to total number of SMs.

Row-to-SM assignment exploits locality by allowing elements close the horizontal border between tiles to remain in caches or local memory until they are accessed again. When combined with hyper-tiling, *tile-rows* further increase reuse across multiple columns with more hits on the last level cache. Moreover, this approach allows uninterrupted processing of elements across different tiles and enables two further optimizations, use of shared memory diagonal buffers and hybrid row-diagonal data storage (described in Subsection 3.4).

Algorithm 2 PeerWave main loop

```
for every row r assigned to SM i do
    for every tile t in row r do
        wait until flag[t, i] = 1
        process_tile(t, r, i)                ▷ SIMD
        flag[t, i + 1] ← 1
    end for
end for
```

Algorithm 2 shows how each SM processes its tile-rows. The outer loop iterates over the rows assigned to an SM in a round-robin fashion whereas the inner loop processes the tiles in a given row in sequence. Each SM processes its tiles one at a time while performing the major computation, i.e. processing of a tile, in parallel using SIMD computation units. In the inner loop, right before and after processing of a tile, the SM communicates with its neighboring SMs, called *Peer-SMs*, to enforce the dependencies between the tiles in adjacent rows.

3.2 Peer-SM Synchronization

Peer-SM synchronization is the key component of our method that replaces the global barrier synchronization between diagonal tiles with distributed synchronization among neighboring tiles. The decentralized nature of Peer-SM allows SMs within a GPU to work independently through synchronization points similar to CPU multithreading. Each SM processes the tiles in its row in dependence order and communicates with the SMs assigned to preceding and succeeding rows before and after processing each tile. By avoiding the redundant waits on global barriers and relying only on direct communication between neighboring SMs, Peer-SM improves load balance.

We implement inter-SM communication by using one-way *flags* located in the GPU global memory. Each SM owns a dedicated array of these flags corresponding to the tiles assigned to it. The one-way communication pattern is realized in PeerWave by having an SM read flags only from the prior row and write only to the flags for the succeeding row. Unlike the previous global-barrier based approaches, this one-way communication removes the need for atomic operations and locks, and scales well with increasing number of SMs.

When an SM is ready to process a tile, it continuously polls the corresponding flag, and begins processing once the flag is set to 1. After the SM has finished processing the tile, it sets the flag for the tile in the next SM's row that is waiting on the current tile, and then becomes ready to process the next tile in the row. When there are more rows than the number of SMs, and multiple rows are assigned to the SM, the SM resets all synchronization flags and starts processing next row immediately after the last tile of the current row has been completed. Per-SM flag arrays are created only once and then reused as the SM moves from one row to its next assigned row. Implementation details of Peer-SM synchronization are given in Section 5.

3.3 Flexible Hyper-Tiles

While tile-row assignment and peer-SM synchronization improve inter-SM load balancing with better data locality, further speedup can be achieved during intra-SM computation. Rectangular tiles result in shorter diagonals at the beginning

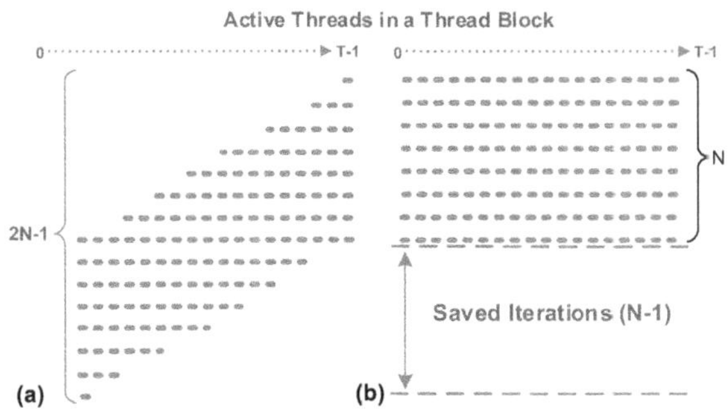

Figure 5: Intra-tile thread utilization is demonstrated for rectangular tiles on the left(a) and for hyperplane transformed tiles on the right(b)

and ending iterations within a tile and this partitioning leaves many threads (hence CUDA cores) in a TB idle. Hyperplane tile transformation improves SM utilization by maintaining a uniform diagonal size across the entire tile and thus maximizing the throughput. The number of iterations needed for intra-tile computation for square and hyperplane tiles are shown in Figure 5(a) and (b), respectively. The hyperplane tile partitioning decreases total number iterations from $2n-1$ to n in comparison to rectangular tiles. Thus, PeerWave uses hyperplane tiles (*hyper-tiles*) in addition to row-SM allocation and peer-SM synchronization. Each element in a diagonal is mapped to a thread in the TB and we iterate over diagonals until the end of the tile where inter-SM synchronization point is located. Figure 6(a) shows transformed tiles along with the synchronization points. Skewed indices change total number of tiles and shift the locations of inter-SM synchronization points. It should be noted that while [5] uses compiler level hyperplane loop transformations, unlike PeerWave, it still uses global barriers between diagonals.

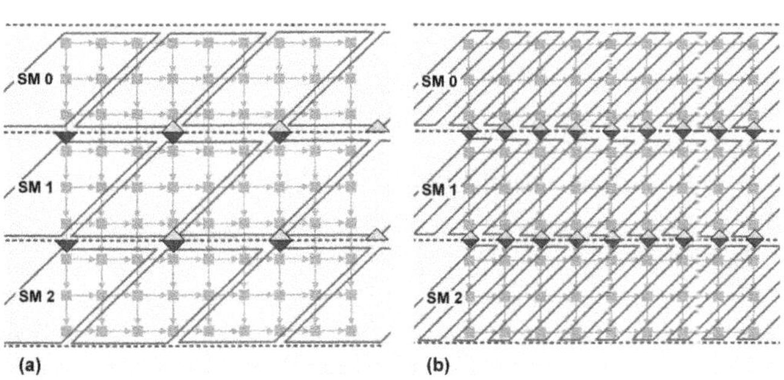

Figure 6: Hyper-Tiles on the left (a) and Flexible HT with variable synchronization intervals on the right (b)

We present *Flexible Hyper-Tiles* (FHT), an improved hyperplane transformation technique which allows us to *find* and *utilize* the optimum tile widths without changing the tile heights. Unlike the naive hyper-tiles approach with equal dimensions, FHT enables fine granular tile width adjustment for better control over the frequency of synchronization while maximizing intra-SM utilization without requiring tile heights to be changed. Smaller synchronization intervals decrease the time SMs must wait before processing their rows during the initial and final phases of execution when the parallelism is limited. Figure 6(b) shows an example of tile resizing where SM 1 can start processing tile (i=1,j=0) as soon as the diagonal corresponding to the element (i=0,j=2) has been processed by SM 0.

Different from prior studies, *Flexible Hyper-Tiles* uniquely models the optimal synchronization intervals (i.e. tile width) and finds the best trade-off between decreased load imbalance and increased synchronization cost. Optimal intervals are application and device specific and we develop an analytical model that outputs best tile width for given application/device characteristics. PeerWave runtime auto-adjusts the synchronization points based on the optimal tile width obtained from this model. Derivation of the model is presented in Section 4.

3.4 Optimizations

We further improve performance of PeerWave by employing the following optimizations.

Shared memory diagonal buffers: An important feature of PeerWave is its uninterrupted sequential processing of tiles within a row on the same SM. This enables efficient use of SM shared memory between consecutive iterations of tiles to dramatically reduce global memory accesses. Since processing a diagonal requires access to elements from preceding and succeeding diagonals, corresponding data can be stored in a sliding window of *diagonal buffers* that eliminates repetitive accesses to global memory as the diagonals are iterated upon by the same SM. When a diagonal is no longer to be accessed, it is written back to the device memory. The size of the sliding window is dependent on the length of the longest dependency vector in the transformed iteration space. FHT greatly increases the efficiency of diagonal buffers by combining accesses to partial diagonals, which are located towards the edges of neighboring tiles, into consecutively accessed 'full' diagonals.

Hybrid row/diagonal-major data layout: The diagonal access pattern during intra-tile processing requires CUDA cores inside SM to access non-consequent locations in the memory. This pattern results in highly un-coalesced memory accesses and causes significant slow down due to excessive number of memory transactions. Diagonal-major data representation [2] improves coalescing by storing elements in the same diagonal in consecutive memory locations. However, this approach does not preserve inter-tile locality, and causes the border elements to be redundantly being read and written as the processing of diagonals in one tile finishes and the next one begins. To prevent this behavior, we use a hybrid approach where the tiles in a row are continuously placed in the global memory in row-major order while the elements in the same diagonal are placed in diagonal-major order. The hybrid row-diagonal major data layout does not cause any memory space to be wasted since all diagonals in hyper-tiles have the same length.

The change in storage format requires the host data to be initialized properly. This can be done in two ways: (1) The data is converted to/from hybrid layout before and after GPU memory transfers. (2) When initializing the data from I/O resources or dynamically, the index transformation can be performed on the fly. The former method requires additional host-to-host data copy operations, therefore can be costly. The latter solution eliminates redundant copies and requires only a few additional instructions per index, whose cost are already hidden by much longer I/O instructions. We provide a simple API, whose details are given in the next section, to translate given x, y coordinates to proper data indices.

4. FINDING OPTIMAL TILE WIDTH

Next we develop an analytical model for finding the optimal tile width that will be utilized by Flexible Hyper-Tiles(FHT) to minimize the total execution time, which is a function of diagonal execution time and peer-SM synchronization cost. We compute the total execution time by identifying the critical path, i.e. the longest path through the execution. The output of our model is the optimal tile width for use in the runtime developed later.

Symbol	Definition
P	Number of SMs
W / H	2D input data width / height
w_t / h_t	Tile width / height
d	Diagonal execution time (measured)
τ_s	Peer synchronization cost (measured)
τ_e	Tile execution time

Table 1: The notation used by our model

The notation used in the derivation of the model is given in Table 2. We assume that the input is a 2D data matrix with height H and width W. The matrix is partitioned into H/h_t tile rows and P SMs are assigned to these rows in a round-robin fashion. The constants τ_s and d represent peer synchronization cost and the processing time of each intra-tile diagonal, respectively. These parameters are obtained using the *findOptimumTileWidth()* function which is provided by our API and performs an offline run on a small fraction of the input data to measure these parameters. Tile execution time τ_e is derived as a function of d, where:

$$\tau_e = w_t d \quad (1)$$

We define B to represent the time during which the processing of a row assigned to the first SM is blocked by the execution of the previous row assigned to the same SM. This case happens when there are fewer SMs than the number of tile columns. B is defined as follows:

$$B = \frac{W + h_t}{w_t}(\tau_e + \tau_s) - P(\tau_e + \tau_s) \quad (2)$$

The critical path consists of processing the first two tiles of every row and all the tiles in the last row. The point where blocking (B) occurs, marked by a dashed arrow, is where the first SM finishes processing the last tile in a row and starts the first tile in its next assigned row. Hyperplane partitioning introduces an extra tile at the beginning of each row as there is no tile on which the first tile in a row is dependent.

Using equations 1 and 2, we can formulate the critical path, hence *the total execution time*, as follows:

$$\begin{aligned} T_{total} =& \frac{H}{h_t}(\frac{h_t}{w_t} + 1)(\tau_e + \tau_s) + B(\frac{H}{h_t P} - 1) \\ &+ (\frac{W}{w_t} - 1)(\tau_e + \tau_s) \end{aligned} \quad (3)$$

According to Equation 1, enlarging h_t is always beneficial as this will lead to better intra-tile utilization and tile execution time will not increase because τ_e is invariant w.r.t h_t. On the other hand, any values w_t, s.t. $h_t \geq w_t$, will not change tile execution time. However, by analyzing equation 3 (details omitted), it can be shown that total execution time decreases as h_t increases. Thus, using maximum h_t (i.e., maximum number of threads per intra-tile diagonal) for hyper-tiles will always give best performance. With fixed h_t, total execution time becomes a function of w_t, the synchronization interval.

Equation 3 can be transformed into the form $aw_t + b/w_t + c$, where the optimal w_t that minimizes the equation is given by $\sqrt{b/a}$. Hence, the optimal synchronization interval based on the model is given by:

$$w_t = \sqrt{\frac{\tau_s(HW + Hh_t + Hh_tP - h_t^2P)}{dh_tP(P-1)}} \quad (4)$$

We use equation 4 to find the optimal synchronization interval without the need for running the application on the entire input data. We validate the above model in the Evaluation Section.

5. RUNTIME & API

We develop a runtime to handle inter-SM synchronization and an easy to use API for users to implement wavefront applications.

PeerWave runtime employs a multi-core like execution scheme with each SM acting as an independent SIMD-capable processor. It uses persistent TBs each of which runs until all corresponding tiles are processed. The run-time kernel is launched with TB count set equal to the total number of physical SMs in the GPU. The default NVIDIA TB scheduler assigns each SM in a round robin fashion, and the number of TBs per SM is determined by the resource requirements of the kernel. For this reason, in our runtime, we use large enough TBs (hence tiles) so that HW scheduler only assigns one TB per SM. A major benefit of having persistent TBs is that SMs can preserve execution state in their local memory (e.g., shared memory in CUDA) and also retain application data across iterations.

```
struct user_data{float* data; long w; long h;
    int** dependencyVectors;}
void transformIndex(int& x, int& y, int& index,
    int tile_w, int tile_h, user_data udata);
long findOptimumTileWidth(user_data udata,
    int tile_h,int nSM,float trainingRatio);
__global__ void PeerWaveKernel(user_data udata,
    int tile_w, int tile_h, int nSM, int* flags);
```

Listing 1: PeerWave kernel header and other helper functions

PeerWave runtime consists of a user-modifiable data structure, preparation functions, a main runtime kernel, and peer-SM communication functions called by this kernel. The headers for these components are given in Listing 1 and the details are elaborated in the rest of this section.

User data: *user_data* struct contains device memory pointer to the user data, dimensions of the 2D data space and the *dependencyVectors* for the stencil computation. Users are responsible for initializing the device memory via *cudaMalloc()* calls and copy initial data from host memory to GPU via *cudaMemcpy()*. *user_data* struct can be modified to add application specific pointers and parameters.

Preparation functions: We present users two optional pre-runtime functions to increase the usability of our framework. The first one is the index transformation function, *transformIndex()*, to allow users a convenient two-way index translation from/to 2D x and y coordinates to/from a data *index*. The function uses the application parameters given in *user_data* and performs the transformation to support our row/diagonal major hybrid data layout. The second function is *findOptimumTileWidth()* and it is used to find optimum tile width via the provided model. The function finds applicationarchitecture specific parameters required by the analytical model by performing an offline training run on a fraction of the input data specified by the *trainingRatio* parameter.

***PeerWave* Kernel:** PeerWave runtime, hence the user algorithm, is initiated by launching this kernel with the following parameters:

- *TB Size & Grid Size*: These two parameters are supplied to CUDA runtime while launching the kernel. The grid size (i.e., the number of TBs) is set equal to the number of SMs (*nSM*) whereas TB Size is application and architecture specific and the programmer need to determine the optimal size according to resource requirements of the wavefront application.
- *nSM*: GPU specific value denoting the total number of SMs.
- *Flags*: The communication flags which need to be preallocated on GPU memory via provided *init()* function. The size of this array is dependent on the number of SMs and the number of tiles in a row.
- *tile_h*: Height of the tiles. Since PeerWave maps each element in the vertical axis of a tile to a thread in the TB, *tile height* should be equal to the TB Size (i.e. number of threads) specified during kernel launch.
- *tile_w*: Width of the tiles (i.e. synchronization interval). As discussed in Section 3 and 4, tile width determines the synchronization interval and it is an important parameter that directly affects the performance. Users can either manually derive the optimal tile width using Equation 4 derived in Section 4 or use *transformIndex()* as described above.

```
flagRead(){
  if (threadIdx.x==0){ // Single thread only
    // check tile flag until set
    while(flags[(nTiles_x)*smID+j]==0)
      cosineSleep(); // dummy computation
    flags[(nTiles_x)*smID+j]=0;} // reset for
 future
  syncthreads(); // sync with other threads}

flagWrite(){
  if (threadIdx.x==0){ // Single thread only
    int nextSM = (smID+1)\%nSM;
    // Set flags for next row.
    flags[(nTiles_x)*nextSM+j]=1;}
  syncthreads();} // sync with other threads
```

Listing 2: Implementation of flag read (a) and write (b) operations

Once the *PeerWaveKernel* is launched, PeerWave main loop given in 2 is executed by each SM until all the data is processed. The main loop involves read of synchronization *flags*, processing of the tile and writing back to the *flags*.

Flag Read: PeerWave relies on efficient synchronization of SMs via one-way communication flags. Listing 2(a) shows the code used to ensure that the corresponding flag is set (i.e., dependencies are met) before every SM starts processing a new tile. Since NVIDIA does not provide an efficient means of inter-SM communication, we keep polling the flag corresponding to the executing SM (smID) and the current column (j) in the tile row until its value is 1. We decrease potential memory contention by idling the SM for a small short period of time using *cosineSleep()* function derived from repetitive calls to cosine function. When the flag is detected as set, we reset it for future use and move on to tile processing.

Tile Processing: Each SM processes the elements in the same diagonal in parallel using the threads in the TB. Each row of elements is mapped to a single thread and the number of columns in the tile correspond to the number of diagonals. After processing of each diagonal, threads inside the SM synchronize using *cudaThreadSync()* method, which is an efficient intra-SM HW barrier implementation provided by CUDA.

Flag Write: Once a tile is processed, SMs need to set the flag for the next SM (smID+1) in the same column (j) as well as the tile in the next column(j+1) in the same row, as shown in Listing 2(b). Border conditions are omitted for simplicity. The overhead of both flag read/write operations are measured to be minimal and reported in the evaluation section.

Element Processing: PeerWave enables users to implement their core computation by overriding the *compute_element()* function as given in Listing 3. The Listing shows an example overriding of *compute_element()* function to implement the core computation of Smith-Waterman algorithm. During tile processing, runtime performs hyper-plane transformations on border elements of each tile and calls user function with the base tile index as well as the element's global x/y coordinates. *u_data.seq1* and *u_data.seq2* are the two input data sequences added to the *user_data* struct and the *u_data.data* array corresponds to the intermediate 2D computation matrix used while calculating the similarity between the two sequences. *compute_element()* function is run in SIMD fashion where all threads in the TB are called with corresponding x and y coordinates of the elements that they are mapped to.

```
__device__ void compute_element(
    const struct user_data u_data,
    int tileRow, int tileColumn,
    int tile_w, int tile_h,
    int x, int y, int index, int nTiles){
  int upleft,left,up;
  if (u_data.seq2[y] != u_data.seq1[x])
    upleft = u_data.data[index-2*tile_height-1]-1;
  else
    upleft = u_data.data[index-2*tile_height-1]+2;
  left = u_data.data[index+tile_height]-1;
  up = u_data.data[index-tile_height-1]-1;

  int max = MAX(0,MAX(upleft, MAX(left, up)));
  udata.data[index] = max;}
```

Listing 3: An example override of *compute_element()* function.

6. WAVEFRONT APPLICATIONS

We evaluate PeerWave using 6 different wavefront parallelizable applications.

Heat 2D simulates dissipation of heat over a two dimensional surface during a specific time frame. During each simulation step, the algorithm calculates the heat of every point in the 2D surface by averaging the heats of its neighboring elements. The calculation relies on the values calculated in current and previous simulation step as follows:

$$A[i,j] = (A[i-1,j]+A[i,j-1]+A[i+1,j]"+A[i,j+1]")/4$$

SOR loops are generalized form of time based stencil computations on neighboring elements. We have considered a 2-dimensional SOR loop iteration with 5-point stencil which is similar to Heat2D but with including the self element in the average as well. The core computation is as the following:

$$A[i,j] = (A[i-1,j]+A[i,j-1]+A[i,j]" +A[i+1,j]"+A[i,j+1]")/5$$

Smith Waterman (SW) is a well known algorithm used for local sequence alignment. It takes two sequences as inputs and builds a matrix to mark and extract matching patterns. The algorithm steps backwards by one position in the three directions (i-1,j), (i, j-1), and (i-1, j-1). The related computation is shown below, where w is the penalty function that returns 2 on equality and -1 otherwise:

$$A[i,j] = \mathrm{MAX}(A[i-1,j]-1, A[i,j-1]-1, A[i,j+1]+w(i,j))$$

Dynamic Time Warping (DTW) is used to find an optimal match between two given sequences (e.g., time series). The series are "warped" in the time dimension to find a measure of their similarity without relying on certain non-linear variations in the time dimension. The pseudo code showing cost calculation across neighbors is as the following:

$$A[i,j] = |i-j|+\mathrm{MIN}(A[i-1,j]+A[i,j-1]+A[i-1,j-1])$$

Summed Area Table (SAT), also known as integral image, is used for generating the sum of values in a rectangular subset of grid. Summed area table can be computed efficiently in a single pass over the image using the equation below:

$$A[i,j] = w(i,j)+A[i-1,j]+A[i,j-1]-A[i-1,j-1])$$

Integral Histogram (INT), is another popular image processing algorithm to calculate histogram of a given bitmap. Different from SAT, it reads from the original image (i.e. bin) but writes into a separate data location used to store corresponding histogram as shown in the algorithm below:

$$A[i,j] = B[i,j]+A[i-1,j]+A[i,j-1]-A[i-1,j-1])$$

The dependencies required by above applications are illustrated in Figure 7. As shown on the left hand side of the figure, Heat2D and SOR computation on each element *(i,j)* depends on the top *(i,j-1)* and left *(i-1,j)* elements which are calculated in the previous wave, as well as bottom *(i,j+1)* and right *(i+1,j)* elements that are calculated in the previous time step (denoted with *"*) of the algorithm. Other four algorithms, SW, SAR, DTW and INT, have similar dependencies. Different from Heat2D and SOR, their computation also relies on the top-left element *(i-1,j-1)*.

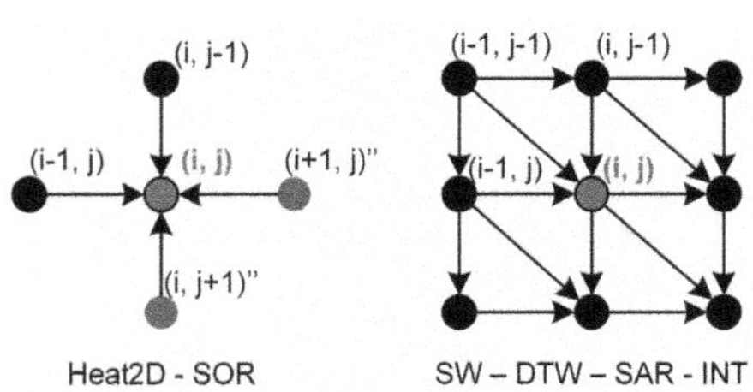

Figure 7: Computation dependencies required by Heat2D, 2D-SOR, SW, DTW, SAT and INT.

7. EVALUATION

In this section we first describe the details of our experimental setup and then present the experimental results.

Architecture. We evaluate PeerWave on NVIDIA's Tesla K40c series GPU attached to an AMD Opteron 6100 based system. The GPU has 15 SMX units each having 192 CUDA cores accessing 12GB of global DDR3 memory. K40c has a shared L2 cache size of 1.5MB and shared memory of each SMX is configured to use 16KB/48KB L1 Cache/Shared with global memory requests are not set to be cached on L1 (Kepler's default setting).

Methodology. In our evaluation, we only measure GPU kernel computation times only because our proposed technique focuses on kernel execution to improve overall execution. For all experiments, we use hybrid row/diagonal major data layout with on-the-fly index transformation as described in Section 3. Since data initialization and transfer times are observed to be similar w/ and w/o the hybrid layout, we exclude all host related operations (initialization and transfers) from our experiments to demonstrate the efficiency of our technique in more detail. Overlapping of data transfers and kernel computations for further speedup is orthogonal to our proposed method and not covered in this paper.

In all of our experiments, we fix the data size to the highest amount that fits in GPU's global memory, and set the tile height and TB size to 1024 (unless specified otherwise in the experiment). For optimal performance, we implement global barriers by using NVIDIA Kepler's dynamic parallelism that allows in-GPU *cudaDeviceSync()* calls. We compare the following wavefront execution methods:

1. *Global barriers*: The baseline global synchronization approach using square tiles.
2. *PeerWave*: Basic implementation of our proposed peer-SM synchronization based technique using square tiles.
3. *Global barriers w/ HTiles*: Global synchronization approach using hyperplane transformed tiles with equal dimensions.
4. *PeerWave w/ HTiles*: Improved version of PeerWave using hyper-tiles with equal tile dimensions.
5. *PeerWave w/ Flexible HTiles*: Optimized version of PeerWave hyper-tiles with flexible non-equal tile dimensions.

7.1 Execution Time: Equal Tile Dimensions

We first evaluate the performance of the first four techniques all of which use equal tile dimensions. Figure 8 shows execution times of each application run for varying tile sizes. TB size is set as 1024, all 15 SMs in the GPU are used and tile width and height are varied together between 256 and 1024. The first two bars correspond to rectangular (square) tiles and the last two correspond to hyper-tiles. The second and fourth bars represent improvements due to PeerWave technique.

An immediate observation is the dramatic decrease in execution time with the use of hyper-tiles. This is due to the decrease in the number of intra-tile diagonal iterations from $2n-1$ to n. PeerWave further improves the performance in both hyper-tile and square tile cases due to increased inter-tile locality and decreased SM idle times. PeerWave shows better performance when using hyper-tiles due to decreased memory contention. The details of the speedup will be analyzed throughout the remainder of this section.

The results also show that the decrease in tile sizes reduces the performance due to under-utilization of CUDA cores inside each SM. Since the maximum intra-tile parallelism is limited by the minimum dimension in the first four execution methods, tile size of 1024x1024 (hence TB of size 1024) gives maximum performance.

7.2 Execution Time: Flexible Hyper-Tiles

Flexible hyper-tiles (method 5) decreases total idle time by increasing number of synchronization points via smaller tile widths. Also, intra-tile utilization is kept maximum by using largest tile heights. The optimal tile width is determined by the provided model and then passed to PeerWave kernel as a

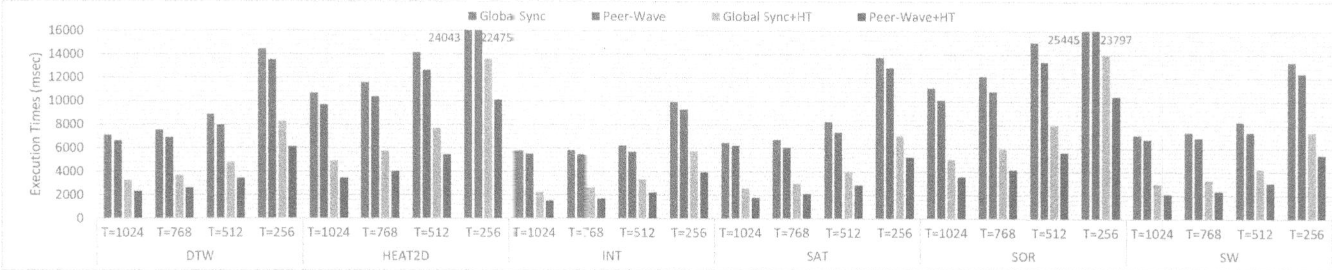

Figure 8: Kernel execution times for global barriers and PeerWave approaches with and without the use of hyper-tiles.

parameter. In this subsection, we first evaluate the accuracy of our model in finding the best synchronization intervals, and then using the optimal values, we compare Flexible hyper-tiles (FHT) method with the best performing equal tile dimension methods 3 and 4.

7.2.1 *Model Verification*

To verify the accuracy of tile width optimization model presented in Section 4, we have compared the execution time estimated by Equation 1 with the measured execution time for the FHT method. The model parameters, d and τ_s are measured in an offline run using a 0.6% of the total data. This ratio corresponds to the initial corner region which spans 135 tiles out of 2025 in total. We fix the tile height to 1024 and vary the tile width from 2 to 1024. The comparison between the estimated and measured execution times is shown in Figure 9.

Overall, our model represents the execution pattern of PeerWave approach quite well. It can be seen that both experiment and simulation curves have a U shaped pattern which points to the trade-off between synchronization overhead and idleness reduction. The slight discrepancy between the simulation and experiment is due to variation of the values d and τ_s throughout the execution. Since we are using only an initial portion of the execution, the increased memory contention towards the middle region of the input matrix affects the blocking time B and hence the critical path. Although the execution times are slightly different, the synchronization interval estimation is accurate.

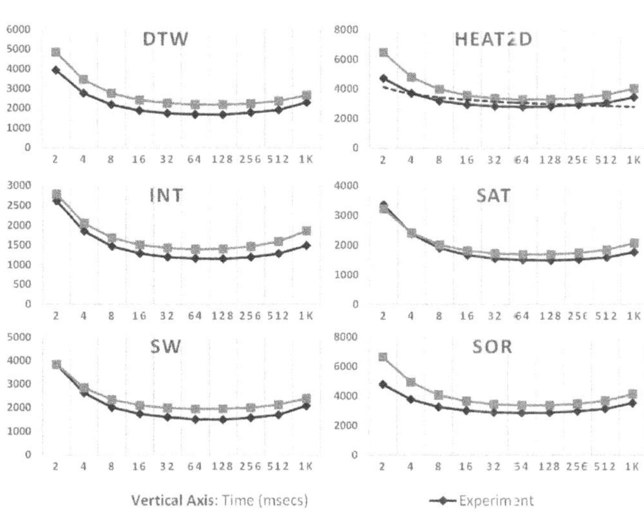

Figure 9: Comparison of numerical simulation and experimental results for Flexible hyper-tiles.

7.2.2 *Flexible Hyper-Tiles (FHT)*

To evaluate flexible hyper-tiles, we take method 3, global synchronization with hyper-tiles (GS+HT), as our baseline and compare its performance with methods 4 and 5, i.e. PeerWave w/ hyper-tiles (PW+HT) and PeerWave w/ Flexible hyper-tiles (PW+FHT). We fix both tile height and width to 1024 for GS+HT and PW+HT, as these give the best results. On the other hand, for PW+FHT, we have set tile height as 1024 and varied tile width between 64, 128, and 256, which are the most close-to-optimal values reported by our model as well as the experiments.

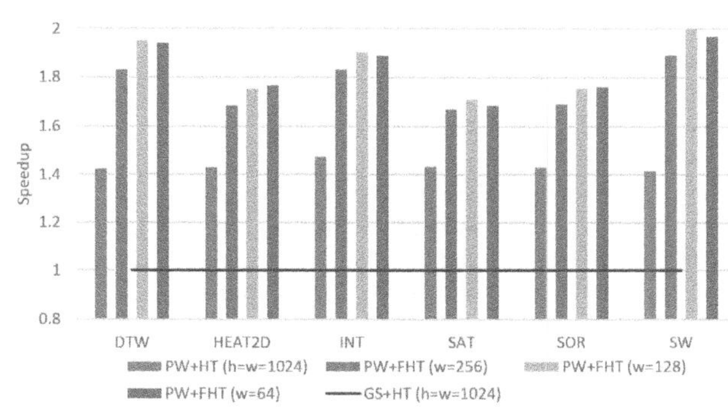

Figure 10: The speedup obtained by Flexible hyper-tiles method.

As the results given in Figure 10 show, flexible hyper-tiles approach improved upon our original PW+HT technique and increased the final speedup by up to 2x compared to the recent approach based on global barriers with hyper-tiles (GS+HT) [5]. When compared to the effects of using smaller tiles with equal dimensions shown in Figure 8, the results clearly show the benefits of changing synchronization interval without affecting utilization.

7.3 Idle Times

To further analyze the effects of peer-SM synchronization we measure the average time that an SM stays idle and compare it to the idle time spent on global barriers. As previously shown in the Figure 2 in Section 2, we classify the idle time into two categories: (a) *Corner*, the compulsory wait time spent during the beginning & end of the execution, where the parallelism is less than total number of SMs(15); and (b) *Intermediate*, where there are always more parallel tiles than SMs.

The results in Figure 11 shows the break down between border (blue) and intermediate (orange) idle times for each application and the technique. PeerWave dramatically reduces the *intermediate* idle time both with and without hyper-tiles, whereas the *corner* idle times remain similar as expected, due to limited parallelism in those regions.

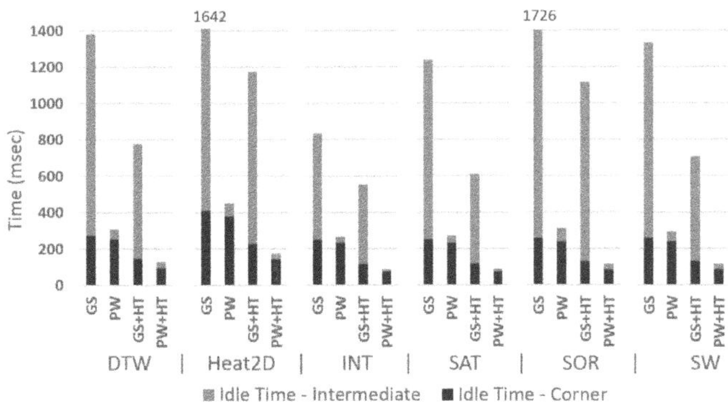

Figure 11: Breakdown of Per-SM average idle time between two phases of the execution.

Reduced idle times cause more SMs to be active hence result in increased memory throughput as shown in Figure 13. PeerWave was able to improve memory bus utilization more in both cases with and without hyper-tiles. On the other hand, use of hyper-tiles dramatically reduces total memory transactions due to reduced number of intra-tile diagonal iterations and increased coalesced accesses, therefore less throughput is needed.

7.4 Tile Locality

Another important drawback of global barriers is overcome by PeerWave via increased inter-tile locality due to row-SM assignment. To observe this, we measure average time required to execute a single tile and give the results in Figure 12(a). Tile execution times are reduced between 15% and 25% compared to global barriers.

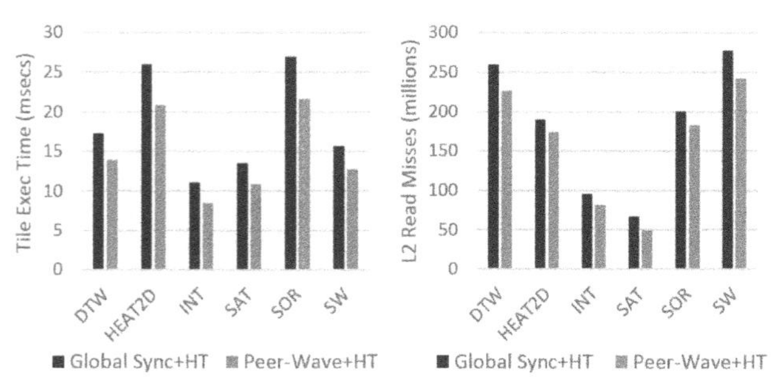

Figure 12: On the left (a) average per-tile execution times and on the right (b) total L2 read misses

We have also profiled the total number of L2 read misses using NVIDIA's profiling utility, **nvprof**, and report the results in Figure 12(b) for 32-byte transactions. As expected, PeerWave reduces the misses in both cases. Although the improvement seems to be minor, the effect on execution time is considerable due to high cost of a global memory access.

7.5 Synchronization Cost

We measured the total time spent during *flagRead()*, *flagWrite()* and global barriers using the device-side clock64() CUDA function. The cost of updating global barrier mutexes in global-synchronization with HT (GS+HT) and the communication flags in PeerWave with HT (PW+HT) is given in milliseconds in Table 2. The values correspond to the total

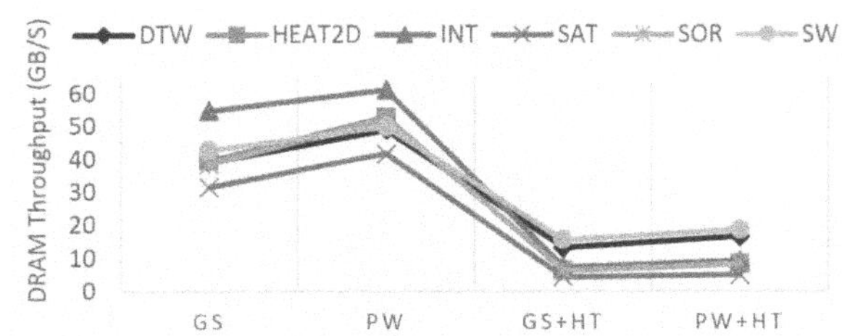

Figure 13: Total GPU global memory throughput.

time spent for synchronization . Although PeerWave improves the synchronization times by around 25%, the total sync cost in both cases is actually marginal and only corresponds to under 0.1% of the total execution times. Most of the speedup obtained by PeerWave is achieved via improved load balance and locality.

	DTW	HEAT2D	INT	SAT	SOR	SW
GS+HT	4.28	4.25	3.77	4.25	4.27	4.25
PW+HT	3.49	3.39	2.37	3.36	3.4	3.43

Table 2: SM Synchronization times in milliseconds.

8. RELATED WORK

Wavefront parallelism in the literature has drawn attention under various contexts like dynamic programming, stencil computations and time based iterations (i.e. Gauss-Seidel or Jacobi) and we discuss the GPU related sub-set of the literature in this section.

Datta et.al [3] are among the first who study the effectiveness of stencil computation on GPUs and compare the performance with multi-core architectures. They focus on data allocation and bandwidth optimizations and present a run-time that auto-tunes architecture specific parameters. [18] is another early study which employs tiling and successive placement of data on the memory for coalesced access on GPUS. They implement in-kernel global barriers using device memory, to prevent going back to CPU for ensuring diagonal dependencies and compare the performance with host-based *cudaDeviceSync()* function. Yan et al. [19] employs synchronization between different stages of parallel prefix sum to remove global barriers between reduce and scan phases.

To decrease un-coalesced memory accesses and increase locality, the study in [2] proposes a CUDA based API, Dymaxion, that remaps memory layout via on-the-fly index transformations. They implement diagonal-strip mapping which assigns tiles in the same diagonal to consecutive memory locations. Sandes et al. [14] implements Smith-Waterman algorithm on GPUs via application specific optimizations like block pruning and multi-stage algorithm execution. As an attempt to improve inter-tile load balance, the study in [9] speculatively executes tiles of Gaussi-Seidel, Jacobi and SOR loops, and tests them for accuracy as the iteration asynchronously proceeds. However, eliminating global barriers removes the need for such techniques.

Polyhedral loop transformations are commonly used to improve intra-tile utilization. The study in [5] proposes compiler-level transformations for arbitrary loop nests. Loop iteration spaces are skewed using affine transformations where the transformation matrix is determined by the dependency vectors. Grosser et al. [6] uses trapezoidal tiles and automatically generates CUDA code to transform given loop nests. Another paper [7] proposed a stencil compiler that facilitates inverted and upright split-tiling for improved parallelism. The study in [1] considers diamond tiling for time iterated computations with periodic data domains to improve parallelism and locality. However, all of these approaches still rely on global barriers between tile diagonals.

Several studies have also focused on heterogeneous execution on multi-core CPUs and multiple GPUs. Among the most notable ones, [20] automatically generates 3D stencil code for multi-GPU computing. A more recent study [12] partitions the load across multiple CPUs and GPUs while automatically adjusting tile sizes in the run-time for the best load balance across heterogeneous processors.

9. CONCLUSION

In this paper we introduced PeerWave, a new parallelization scheme for nested loops with data dependencies. Our approach eliminates inter-tile global barriers and uses SM-to-SM direct communication instead. We improve inter-tile load balance and locality that greatly reduces SM idle times. We further improve PeerWave with Flexible Hyper-Tiles which allows fine-granular synchronization interval adjustment while keeping intra-tile utilization at its maximum. We showed that PeerWave can achieve speedup of up to 2x when compared to existing global barrier based approaches.

10. REFERENCES

[1] U. Bondhugula, V. Bandishti, A. Cohen, G. Potron, and N. Vasilache. Tiling and optimizing time-iterated computations on periodic domains. In *Proceedings of the 23rd international conference on Parallel architectures and compilation (PACT)*, pages 39–50. ACM, 2014.

[2] S. Che, J. W. Sheaffer, and K. Skadron. Dymaxion: optimizing memory access patterns for heterogeneous systems. In *Proceedings of the 25th ACM international conference on Supercomputing (ICS)*, page 13, 2011.

[3] K. Datta, M. Murphy, V. Volkov, S. Williams, J. Carter, L. Oliker, D. Patterson, J. Shalf, and K. Yelick. Stencil computation optimization and auto-tuning on state-of-the-art multicore architectures. In *Proceedings of the 2008 ACM/IEEE conference on Supercomputing (ICS)*, page 4. IEEE Press, 2008.

[4] P. Di, H. Wu, J. Xue, F. Wang, and C. Yang. Parallelizing sor for gpgpus using alternate loop tiling. *Parallel Computing*, 38(6):310–328, 2012.

[5] P. Di, D. Ye, Y. Su, Y. Sui, and J. Xue. Automatic parallelization of tiled loop nests with enhanced fine-grained parallelism on gpus. In *Proceedings of the 2012 41st International Conference on Parallel Processing (ICPP)*, pages 350–359. IEEE Computer Society, 2012.

[6] T. Grosser, A. Cohen, P. H. Kelly, J. Ramanujam, P. Sadayappan, and S. Verdoolaege. Split tiling for gpus: automatic parallelization using trapezoidal tiles. In *Proceedings of the 6th Workshop on General Purpose Processor Using Graphics Processing Units (GP-GPU)*, pages 24–31. ACM, 2013.

[7] T. Henretty, R. Veras, F. Franchetti, L.-N. Pouchet, J. Ramanujam, and P. Sadayappan. A stencil compiler for short-vector simd architectures. In *Proceedings of the 27th international ACM conference on International conference on supercomputing (ICS)*, pages 13–24, 2013.

[8] F. Irigoin and R. Triolet. Supernode partitioning. In *Proceedings of the 15th ACM SIGPLAN-SIGACT symposium on Principles of programming languages*, pages 319–329. ACM, 1988.

[9] L. Liu and Z. Li. Improving parallelism and locality with asynchronous algorithms. In *Proceedings of the 15th ACM SIGPLAN Symposium on Principles and Practice of Parallel Programming (PPoPP)*, pages 213–222. ACM, 2010.

[10] N. Manjikian and T. Abdelrahman. Exploiting wavefront parallelism on large-scale shared-memory multiprocessors. *IEEE Transactions on Parallel and Distributed Systems (TPDS)*, 12(3):259–271, 2001.

[11] J. Meng and K. Skadron. Performance modeling and automatic ghost zone optimization for iterative stencil loops on gpus. In *Proceedings of the 23rd international conference on Supercomputing (ICS)*, pages 256–265. ACM, 2009.

[12] S. Mohanty and M. Cole. Autotuning wavefront applications for multicore multi-gpu hybrid architectures. In *Proceedings of Programming Models and Applications on Multicores and Manycores*, page 1. ACM, 2014.

[13] A. Nguyen, N. Satish, J. Chhugani, C. Kim, and P. Dubey. 3.5-d blocking optimization for stencil computations on modern cpus and gpus. In *Proceedings of the 24th ACM international conference on Supercomputing (ICS)*, pages 1–13, 2010.

[14] E. F. d. O. Sandes and A. C. M. de Melo. Retrieving smith-waterman alignments with optimizations for megabase biological sequences using gpu. *IEEE Transactions on Parallel and Distributed Systems (TPDS)*, 24(5):1009–1021, 2013.

[15] F. Song, S. Tomov, and J. Dongarra. Enabling and scaling matrix computations on heterogeneous multi-core and multi-gpu systems. In *Proceedings of the 26th ACM international conference on Supercomputing (ICS)*, pages 365–376. ACM, 2012.

[16] M. Wolfe. Loops skewing: The wavefront method revisited. *International Journal of Parallel Programming*, 15(4):279–293, 1986.

[17] M. Wolfe. More iteration space tiling. In *Proceedings of the 1989 ACM/IEEE conference on Supercomputing (SC)*, pages 655–664. ACM, 1989.

[18] S. Xiao, A. M. Aji, and W.-c. Feng. On the robust mapping of dynamic programming onto a graphics processing unit. In *15th International Conference on Parallel and Distributed Systems (ICPADS), 2009*, pages 26–33. IEEE, 2009.

[19] S. Yan, G. Long, and Y. Zhang. Streamscan: fast scan algorithms for gpus without global barrier synchronization. In *Proceedings of the 18th ACM SIGPLAN Symposium on Principles and Practice of Parallel Programming (PPoPP)*, volume 48, pages 229–238. ACM, 2013.

[20] Y. Zhang and F. Mueller. Autogeneration and autotuning of 3d stencil codes on homogeneous and heterogeneous gpu clusters. *IEEE Transactions on Parallel and Distributed Systems (IPDPS)*, 24(3):417–427, 2013.

PaCMap: Topology Mapping of Unstructured Communication Patterns onto Non-contiguous Allocations

Ozan Tuncer
Boston University
Boston, MA, USA
otuncer@bu.edu

Vitus J. Leung
Sandia National Laboratories
Albuquerque, NM, USA
vjleung@sandia.gov

Ayse K. Coskun
Boston University
Boston, MA, USA
acoskun@bu.edu

ABSTRACT

In high performance computing (HPC), applications usually have many parallel tasks running on multiple machine nodes. As these tasks intensively communicate with each other, the communication overhead has a significant impact on an application's execution time. This overhead is determined by the application's communication pattern as well as the network distances between communicating tasks. By mapping the tasks to the available machine nodes in a communication-aware manner, the network distances and the execution times can be significantly reduced.

Existing techniques first allocate available nodes to an application, and then map the tasks onto the allocated nodes. In this paper, we discuss the potential benefits of simultaneous allocation and mapping for applications with irregular communication patterns. We also propose a novel graph-based allocation and mapping technique to reduce the execution time in HPC machines that use non-contiguous allocation, such as Cray XK series. Simulations calibrated with real-life experiments show that our technique reduces *hop-bytes* up to 30% compared to the state-of-the-art.

Categories and Subject Descriptors

D.1.3 [**Concurrent Programming**]: Parallel Programming—*Topology Mapping*

Keywords

Topology mapping; task mapping; non-contiguous allocation; unstructured communication pattern; performance

1. INTRODUCTION

In high performance computing (HPC), highly parallel applications run on multiple machine nodes for long durations up to several days where each node typically includes multiple processing cores [15]. The size of these applications and the HPC machines have been growing exponentially in the last decade. The number of processing cores in the largest machines has increased from 65536 in 2005 to over 3 million in 2014 [2]. This growth is expected to continue in the forthcoming years, creating a need for scalable workload management solutions to reduce both the application execution times and the energy consumption [14].

One of the most important challenges in HPC workload management is topology mapping, i.e., the placement of an application's tasks to the machine nodes. Placing the highly communicating tasks close to each other can reduce the communication time significantly, and as a result, improve the overall application performance. As most of the HPC applications have a specific communication topology, the problem can be expressed as mapping an application's communication graph onto the machine's network graph.

Mapping of two graphs to each other is shown to be an NP-hard problem [17]. Thus, researchers proposed various heuristics for topology mapping such as recursive graph bisectioning [29], exploiting application's geometric information to partition the communication graph [9, 13], and graph embedding [34]. Most of these techniques focus on HPC machines with contiguous allocation, where each application is assigned to a contiguous block of machine nodes. Although contiguous allocation increases application locality, it decreases the machine utilization [24, 32]. Our work focuses on non-contiguous allocation, which is used in many HPC systems such as Cray XT, XE, and XK series [1]. Note that our technique can also be used for contiguous allocation.

We target HPC applications that have unstructured communication patterns, where each task can have an arbitrary number of neighbors and different communication weight to each neighbor. Examples for such applications include biomolecular simulations and sparse matrix multiplication. Our work is the first to propose a technique for topology mapping of unstructured applications onto machines that use non-contiguous node allocation.

To the best of our knowledge, previous work on topology mapping only considered the mapping of application tasks onto an already-selected set of nodes, which are determined by the system management software without using detailed information on the communication pattern. In this work, we explore the benefits of joint allocation and task mapping based on an application's topology. Our results indicate strong motivation to expand the job submission infrastructures to include detailed communication information.

As application and machine sizes continue to grow and computation performance continues to improve faster than communication performance, the impact of topology mapping on HPC application execution time and power con-

ICS'15, June 8–11, 2015, Newport Beach, CA, USA.

ACM 978-1-4503-3559-1/15/06 ...$15.00
http://dx.doi.org/10.1145/2751205.2751225.

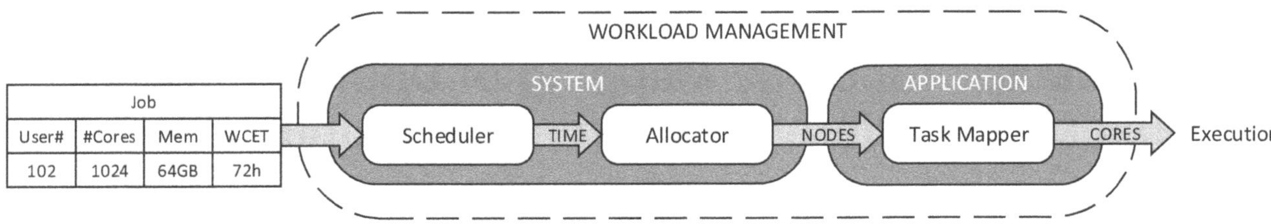

Figure 1: Workload management in conventional HPC machines.

sumption is expected to grow. Our contributions to topology mapping in this paper can be summarized as follows:

- We propose PaCMap (Partitioning And Center MAPping), a graph-based topology mapping algorithm to reduce the execution time of HPC applications with unstructured communication patterns (Section 3). Our algorithm can be used both for complete topology mapping or as a task mapping algorithm for a given set of nodes.
- Using experimental data from a Cray XE6 system, we develop a running time estimation model based on the application's communication pattern as well as the topology mapping decision (Section 4). The model is then used in simulation space to compare various topology mapping algorithms.
- We analyze the potential benefits of joint allocation and mapping (Sections 2 and 5). Simulation results show that topology-aware allocation combined with mapping can decrease *hop-bytes* (i.e., the weighted sum of the traversed network distance for all messages, weighted by the message size) by up to 30% compared to state-of-the-art.

2. TOPOLOGY MAPPING BACKGROUND

In today's HPC systems, topology mapping, i.e., the placement of application tasks onto machine nodes, includes decisions both from the system side and from the application side. The system is responsible for scheduling and allocation, whereas the application side performs task mapping.

As depicted in Figure 1, job submission in conventional HPC systems only supports sending basic requests to the system, such as number of processing cores, memory requirement, and worst case execution time (WCET), where a job refers to a specific instance of an application. Then, as part of the system software, the scheduler determines when to run the job based on the machine availability and the job queue. Once the job is scheduled, the allocator assigns a set of machine nodes for the job. Finally, the application's task mapper places its tasks to the allocated nodes. In this paper, we assume there is no space sharing, i.e., a machine node cannot be shared by multiple jobs. This is common in HPC due to ease of management and security concerns.

Due to the limitations of the job submission framework, the system is unaware of the exact communication pattern of the job for unstructured applications. For task mapping, however, programmers can specify the communication pattern through interfaces such as MPI [27]. Alternatively, the pattern can be profiled during an application's first run and used in the future runs. In addition to the communication pattern, the application side can also discover the physical network topology through system calls [33]. Based on these information, task mapping can make an efficient assignment of the application tasks to the machine nodes to minimize the communication overhead.

The rest of this section explains the problem in more detail and presents various algorithms that are currently used for topology mapping.

2.1 Job Allocation

There are two main considerations for non-contiguous allocation. First, the selected nodes should be close to each other to reduce the communication distances. Second, the allocation should not lead to fragmented machine utilization. The allocation algorithms that disregard the second issue can lead to the segmentation of large empty blocks in the machine, potentially increasing the communication overhead of future jobs. Consider the example shown in Figure 2, where two jobs are scheduled in a 6-node machine with a 2D mesh network topology. In case (a), the first job is allocated to the middle column. Thus, job 2 must be fragmented into smaller parts, increasing the communication distance. However, case (b) assigns job 1 to the side of the machine, leaving sufficient space for job 2.

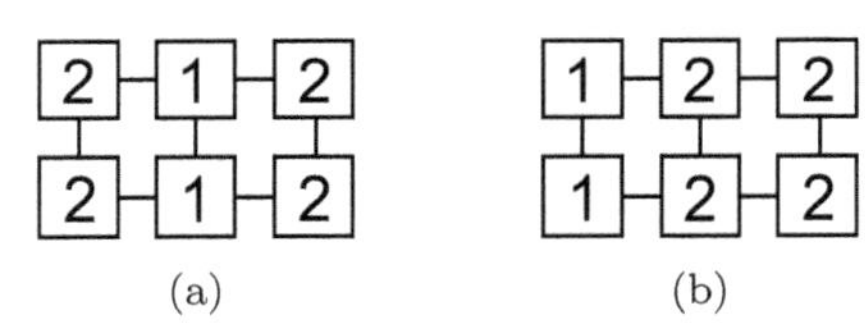

Figure 2: Example for (a) fragmented and (b) non-fragmented job allocation. The boxes represent machine nodes and the numbers represent allocated jobs.

The common techniques for non-contiguous job allocation can be classified into two categories: linear and clustered. In this paper, we use one algorithm from each category.

2.1.1 Best-fit (linear)

The best-fit strategy is a combination of the ideas proposed by Lo et al. [24] and Leung et al. [22]. The algorithm first linearly orders the machine nodes along a curve. Then, the free nodes are grouped into intervals along this curve. The job is allocated to the smallest interval that has sufficient nodes. If there is no such interval, the algorithm selects the nodes that minimize the maximum distance along the curve. This strategy is commonly used in real HPC machines due to its simplicity and its small time complexity of $O(M)$ in an M-node machine. In machines with a torus or mesh network topology, linear allocation strategies order the nodes using space-filling curves such as Hilbert curves to improve locality [5].

2.1.2 Mc1x1 (clustered)

The mc1x1 algorithm is a variant of the MC algorithm proposed by Mache et al. [26]. It is a $(2-2/k)d$ approximation to the optimal solution for minimizing the average pairwise L1 distance of tasks in a d-dimensional mesh when allocating k processors [7]. The algorithm aims to find a compact cluster of free nodes. For each free node n, mc1x1 calculates an allocation score by counting the number of free nodes in a d-dimensional hypercube centered on node n.

The size of the hypercube is started from a single node and increased until the hypercube contains sufficient free nodes for the job to be allocated. Then, the score of the center node is calculated as follows:

$$NS_{n,J} = \sum_{i=1}^{J} dist_{n,i} \tag{1}$$

where $NS_{n,J}$ is the score of node n for allocating J nodes, and $dist_{n,i}$ is the distance between nodes n and the free node i in the hypercube. The node with the least score is selected as the center node. Although mc1x1 finds clustered nodes, it does not address the fragmented allocation problem and it is not applicable in network topologies other than mesh and torus.

The time complexity of this approach depends on the machine utilization and the machine state. In the worst case, calculating the score of a free node requires checking the availability of all the nodes in the machine, whereas the best case checks only the nearest J nodes of J free nodes. Hence, depending on the machine state, allocating nodes with mc1x1 takes between $O(M^2)$ and $\Omega(J^2)$, where M is the number of nodes in the machine. Note that the node scores can be computed in parallel.

2.2 Task Mapping

Task mapping considers the assignment of the individual application tasks to the machine nodes, which are selected by the job allocation stage (Section 2.1). Unlike job allocation, task mapping is able to use information provided by the application such as the communication pattern. In this paper, we focus on three different task mapping techniques and use them as baselines for the evaluation of the proposed *PaCMap* algorithm.

2.2.1 Reverse Cuthill-Mckee (RCM)

RCM [11] reduces the bandwidth of a symmetric matrix via permutation, i.e., it reorders the matrix such that the non-zero entries that are far from the diagonal are eliminated as demonstrated in Figure 3. When applied on a task communication matrix, which shows the communication links between the tasks, this corresponds to reducing the maximum distance between the tasks when the tasks are linearly ordered.

In machines with contiguous allocation, RCM can be applied both on the network and the communication graphs with $O(JD \log D)$ complexity, where D is the maximum degree of the application graph. Then, in-order mapping of the tasks to the nodes can effectively reduce the communication distance for sparse communication patterns [8] [17].

In machines that allow non-contiguous job allocation, the machine network cannot be directly used as it results in an unconnected graph. Instead, the tasks are mapped in-order along the curve of a linear allocation algorithm.

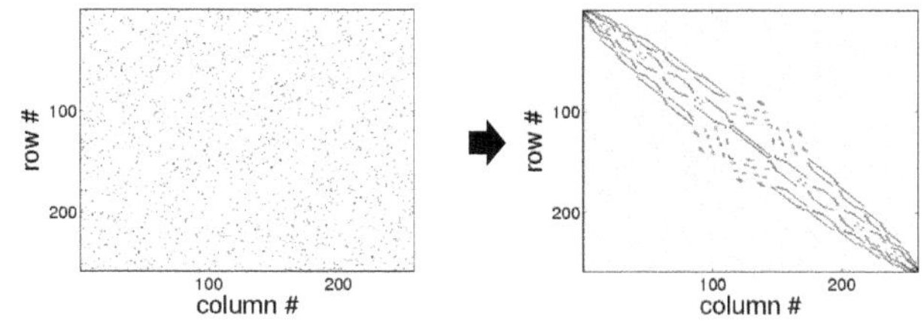

(a) Original matrix (b) RCM permutation

Figure 3: RCM applied on a sample sparse matrix

2.2.2 Recursive Graph Bisection (RGrB)

RGrB algorithm uses the task communication graph and the network topology graph. It recursively splits both graphs into equal halves using minimum weighted edge-cuts, and maps the remaining task(s) to the remaining node at the end of the recursion. This algorithm has been used for contiguous allocation by software packages such as LibTopoMap [17] and SCOTCH [29]. As there is no existing RGrB variant specific to non-contiguous allocation, we apply RGrB by building a virtual all-to-all graph for the machine network, where the edges are weighted based on the hop distance between the nodes. Due to the all-to-all graph, RGrB takes $O(J^3)$ for non-contiguous allocation for mapping J tasks [17]. Our implementation of RGrB is based on LibTopoMap, and uses the METIS library [19] for bisectioning. Although this technique demonstrated efficient mappings, it is also shown that it may result in poor p-way partitions [31].

2.2.3 Recursive Geometry Bisection (RGeoB)

Similar to the RGrB, RGeoB is based on recursive bisections. Instead of using the graphs, however, RGeoB splits the application and the machine geometries into equal halves such that the maximum dimension length is minimized [13]. The application geometry can be inherent to the application, such as the coordinates of an object in a computational fluid dynamics simulation, or it can be generated from the communication graph. Similarly, the machine geometry can be defined as x, y, z coordinates of a 3D mesh network topology. When a generic sorting algorithm with $O(J \log J)$ is used for the geometric bisectioning, the complexity of RGeoB becomes $O(J \log^2 J)$ as shown by the master theorem [10].

The effectiveness of RGeoB strictly depends on how well the communication is represented by the given application geometry. For 3D stencil computations, this technique is shown to perform better than RGrB on a Cray XE6 [13].

2.3 Interplay of Allocation and Mapping

As mentioned earlier in this section, the allocation is unaware of the application's communication pattern in current HPC systems. Hence, the allocation decision can decrease the potential efficiency of the task mapping algorithm. Consider the example in Figure 4. A communication-aware allocation algorithm will allocate a 3x3 mesh (Figure 4b) for an application with a 3x3 stencil communication pattern, so that the task mapping can reduce the average message hop distance to 1. However, if the allocation is unaware of the communication pattern, it can also select the nodes as in Figure 4c, where the minimum average message hop distance that can be achieved is 2.

Similar effects can also be observed in larger scales. Consider a 3D stencil application with dimensions 2x8x32. If

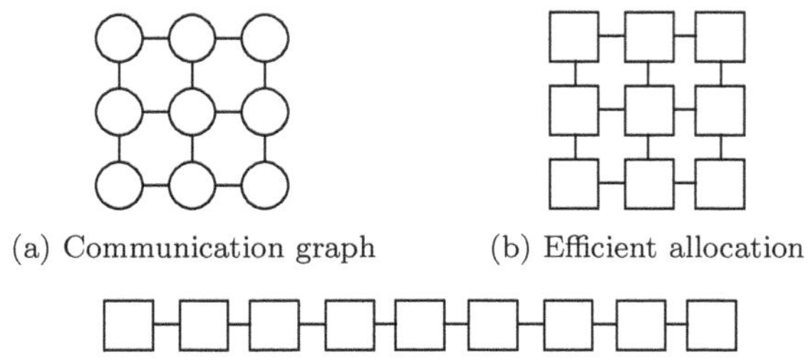

Figure 4: Communication graph of a 3x3 stencil application, and (b) communication-aware and (c) -unaware allocation examples

this application is allocated to a 2x8x32 mesh, the minimum average hop distance would be 1. However, when it is allocated to a 8x8x8 cubical mesh instead, the RGeoB task mapping algorithm, being the best task mapper for this case, results in an average hop distance of 1.92, increasing the communication overhead.

These example cases create sufficient motivation to develop algorithms that jointly consider allocation and mapping. Section 5 presents further analysis on this issue.

3. PACMAP ALGORITHM

We aim to reduce the execution time of HPC applications through communication-aware topology mapping. We propose PaCMap (partitioning and center mapping), a graph-based algorithm that simultaneously carries out job allocation and task mapping to reduce communication overhead.

As shown in Figure 5, PaCMap first partitions the communication graph into k task groups (TGs) such that each group can fit into a single node in the cluster. This step consolidates the highly-communicating tasks to be executed on the same machine node. After this step, the problem reduces to mapping the TGs into the available machine nodes. In our implementation, the partitioning is done by the multilevel k-way partitioning algorithm from the METIS library [19].

Next, PaCMap selects a *center TG* from the partitioned graph and maps it to a selected *center node* in the cluster. Then, it expands the allocation by picking a node and mapping a task to it based on the network topology and on the communication graph until all tasks are mapped.

PaCMap can also be used only for allocation by ignoring the mapping decision, or only for task mapping by limiting the nodes the algorithm can use. The rest of this section explains in detail how the center node and the center TG are selected and how the expansion is performed, along with a complexity analysis.

3.1 Center Machine Node Selection

As discussed in Section 2, the allocation determines how efficiently the cluster is utilized. The algorithm should select a collected group of nodes and should not lead to fragmented allocation of future jobs. Our solution is a heuristic that addresses both issues.

For each available node n, we look at the other available nodes in the proximity of n and calculate a node score $NS_{n,J}$, where J is the number of nodes to be allocated. To calculate the score, we first create a list of available nodes around n within a communication distance of R using breadth-first expansion. Then, we sort this list with respect to the distance to n. Starting from the closest node, we in-

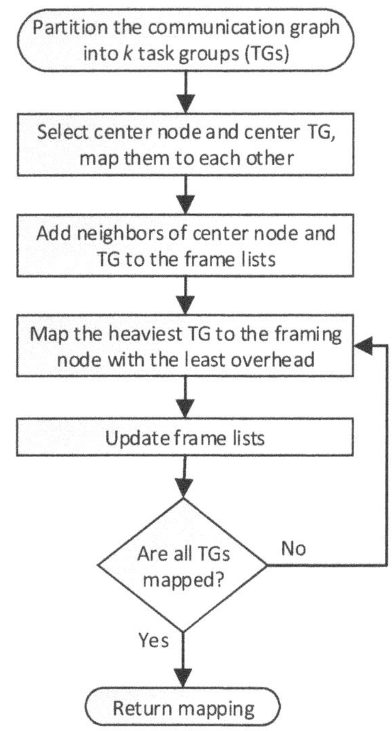

Figure 5: Flowchart of the proposed PaCMap algorithm

crease $NS_{n,J}$ for the first J nodes, and penalize it for the remaining extra nodes as follows:

$$NS_{n,J} = \sum_{i=1}^{J} f(dist_{n,i}) - \sum_{i=J+1} f(dist_{n,i}) \qquad (2)$$

where $f(dist_{n,i})$ is a function of $dist_{n,i}$, which is the communication distance between n and node i in the list. In order to avoid fragmented allocation, R should be selected such that the number of nodes within the network distance of R is larger than J. Additionally, $f(dist_{n,i})$ should prioritize the nodes that are closer to node n to improve locality.

R and $f(dist_{n,i})$ are selected based on the network topology. We use the following heuristics for 3D torus topologies: The maximum number of nodes within a network hop distance of r equals $4r^3/3 + 2r^2 + 8r/3 + 1$ in a 3D torus. Using a pre-calculated look-up table based on this formula, we first find the minimum distance r_{min} that contains J nodes. We then select $R = r_{min} + 2$ to check the excessive availability around the node n. This number can be adjusted for different machines if the above formula becomes invalid due to asymmetrical torus dimensions. We use $f(dist_{n,i}) = 1/(4dist_{n,i}^2 + 2)$ so that the maximum total impact of the nodes equidistant to n on $NS_{n,J}$ is 1. We do not observe a significant change in the allocation performance by the selection of $f(dist_{n,i})$ as long as the nodes closer to n have more impact than others. In other network topologies such as Dragonfly [20], the same methodology can be followed to select R and $f(dist_{n,i})$.

3.2 Center Task Group Selection

PaCMap expands the allocation from the center node and the center TG, while allocating nodes and mapping TGs at each expansion step. As the center machine node selection stage scores the nodes based on the availability around them without prioritizing any direction, an efficient node selection requires the expansion to be symmetric in all directions. This can be done by selecting a proper center TG.

The center TG is selected as the one with the minimum cumulative shortest-path distance to all other TGs. To find the center, we run Dijkstra's algorithm on all TGs.

3.3 Expansion

After allocating the center TG to the center node, we create two lists for the expansion: (1) a list of machine nodes that frame the current partial allocation, (2) a list of TGs that frame the currently allocated TGs. The frames are the neighboring nodes/TGs in the corresponding graphs, as demonstrated in Figure 6. The edge weights in the machine graph (the network links) are all 1, whereas the edge weights in the TG graph are given in the figure.

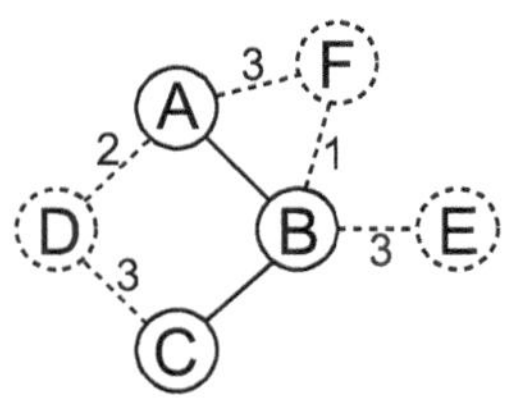

(a) Communication graph

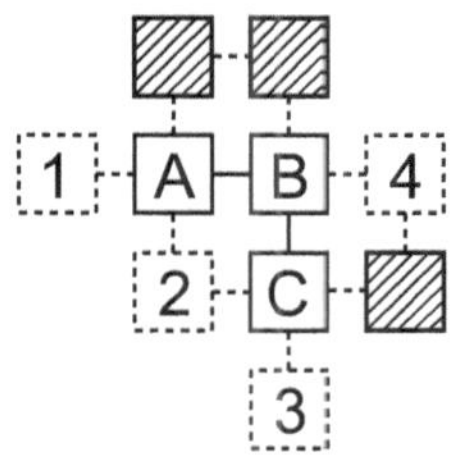

(b) Network graph

Figure 6: Partially allocated application. The solid shapes are current allocation/mapping, the dashed shapes are the frames, and striped squares are busy nodes.

For each expansion step, we select the heaviest TG, i.e., the unmapped TG that has the largest communication volume with the currently allocated tasks. In Figure 6a, D would be selected for the next step with a total weight of $2 + 3 = 5$. We map this TG to the node that leads to the least total communication overhead, calculated as follows:

$$overhead_n = \sum_i dist_{n,i} \cdot W_{n,i} \qquad (3)$$

where $W_{n,i}$ is the communication weight between the TGs mapped to nodes n and i. In Figure 6b, node #2 would be selected for task D with an overhead of $1 \cdot 2 + 1 \cdot 3 = 5$. If there is a tie between the nodes, we select the closest node to the center to maintain the symmetry of the expansion.

After mapping the heaviest TG to the selected node, we update the frames by adding the neighbors of the allocated node and the mapped TG. If there is no free node among the direct neighbors of the allocated node, we increase the search distance until a free node is found.

3.4 Complexity Analysis

The overhead of the center node selection strictly depends on the underlying network topology. In our implementation, we make use of the coordinate information of the 3D torus topology. For each free node, we check the availability of $O(R^3) = O(J)$ nodes, resulting in a total of $O(MJ)$, where M is the number of nodes in the machine. Computing the node scores is an inherently parallel operation.

Given that most HPC applications are re-run with different parameters or inputs, partitioning of the communication graph into TGs and selection of the center TG need to be done only once per application. The results can be re-used for the future submissions of the same application. Alternatively, this information can be passed to the system along with the job submission. For the sake of completeness, k-way partitioning by METIS is $O(C \log(k))$, where C is the number of edges in the communication graph [19]. This is equal to $O(C \log J)$ as the number of cores per node is bounded. Selecting the center TG by running Dijkstra's algorithm with Fibonacci heap on all TGs is $O(JC + J^2 \log(J))$ [10].

We keep the TG frame in a Fibonacci heap, and the node frame in a linked list. Hence, finding and deleting the heaviest TG for J TGs takes $O(J \log J)$. Selecting the node that leads to the least communication requires calculating the communication overhead for all neighbors of the heaviest TG and for all nodes in the frame. First, assume that there is a bounded number of nodes in the frame. During the entire mapping process, J nodes will be mapped and the communication weight of C links will be calculated, leading to $O(J + C)$ given that the node distances are known. Now, the frame size can be included in the complexity. At any time, there will be a maximum of $O(J)$ nodes in the frame as the number of ports of a router in a 3D torus network is bounded. Hence, selecting nodes during mapping takes a total of $O(J^2 + JC) = O(JC)$ for connected graphs. Note that the best node can be selected in parallel.

Updating the task frame is done by breadth-first search, where each step includes updating the weights of the unmapped neighboring TGs in the Fibonacci heap, leading to a total of $O(J + C)$. The complexity of updating the node frame depends on the machine utilization. If the utilization is close to 100%, finding the closest free node can take worst-case $O(M)$ to search all the nodes in the machine, leading to $O(MJ)$ during the entire mapping process. When the machine utilization is lower, the direct neighbors of the allocated node are likely to be free as the center node is selected with sufficient availability in its proximity. In this case, finding all closest nodes takes $\Omega(J)$ in total.

As a result, the complete allocation and mapping process has a time complexity of $O(MJ + JC)$ for a connected communication graph and for 3D torus machines, assuming that the partitioning and the center task selection is done before the job submission. This complexity is feasible in terms of real-life implementation and scalability, and it is comparable to our best-performing baselines (Section 5).

4. EXPERIMENTAL METHODOLOGY

As real HPC machines do not have the infrastructure to support combined allocation and task mapping, we use simulations for our evaluation. Hence, we also need to create realistic HPC workload traces and communication patterns. To compare allocation and task mapping algorithms, we estimate the execution time of the jobs based on their locality. This section describes our experimental framework.

4.1 Target Machine

Our target machine uses static mapping, i.e., it does not support task migration at runtime. In our evaluation, we use a 3D torus network topology. Torus topologies are commonly used in HPC due to their low cost, ease of design and installation, and high bisection bandwidth (i.e., the total bandwidth of links placed between two equal-sized node sets after partitioning). Example machines that use 3D torus include IBM BlueGene/L [3], Cray XE6 [1], and Cray XK7, which is ranked number 2 on the November 2014 Top500 list [2]. During our simulations, we use static shortest path dimension-ordered (x-y-z) routing in the network.

4.2 Workloads

In order to compare the task mapping algorithms, we need a comprehensive set of unstructured sparse communication graphs as well as application geometries. For this purpose, we use the University of Florida Sparse Matrix Collection [12] as a proxy for communication and geometry information. This collection is commonly used for the evaluation of graph algorithms such as bisectioning (e.g. [18]), and consists of data from real applications in various fields such as circuit simulations, financial modeling, and chemical process simulations. We use the applications in the collection with 2D or 3D geometry information with up to 115K tasks. We assume uniform communication between the tasks as it is the expected case for well-balanced HPC applications.

The comparison of non-contiguous allocation algorithms requires using an already populated machine. Additionally, our analysis should account for the impact of the allocation decision on the performance of future jobs. To address both issues, we use the logs provided in the Parallel Workloads Archive (PWA) [15] as inputs to our simulation, and evaluate entire workload traces. PWA logs are collected from real large scale parallel systems, and provide information on job arrival times, execution times, and job sizes, but no information on the communication. Hence, we assign communication patterns to the jobs by matching them with the proxy communication matrices in the sparse matrix collection. As the job sizes in PWA do not necessarily match with the matrix sizes in the collection, we apply *binning* to the PWA, in which the job sizes are changed to the closest available size in our application set.

Among the logs in the archive, LLNL-Atlas and CEA-Curie traces lead to the most balanced application counts after binning. LLNL-Atlas and CEA-Curie are collected from machines with 9216 CPUs (assumed to be quad-core CPUs) and 93312 cores, respectively. These are the largest machine sizes in the archive after ANL-Intrepid, which leads to an unbalanced binning and biases the results by prioritizing only a few applications in our input set. Logs from the newer and larger machines are not available in the archive due to the explosive growth of machine sizes and the lag in collecting data for research. We use the first two weeks of these two traces in our evaluation as machines like Cray Cielo [25] are usually taken down for maintenance every two weeks. Our LLNL-Atlas and CEA-Curie traces consist of 1001 and 3291 jobs, respectively.

4.3 Performance Model

During our simulations, we modify the execution time of a job based on its communication pattern and mapping. To extract the relationship between communication time and the network-related metrics, we use real-life experiments.

We conduct our real-life experiments on the Cray XE6 Cielo supercomputer located at Los Alamos National Laboratories [25]. Cielo consists of 8944 compute nodes and additional service nodes. Each compute node has a dual AMD Opteron 6136 eight-core "Magny-Cours" socket, providing a total of 16 cores. The nodes are connected using a Cray Gemini 3D torus network topology with the dimensions of 16x12x24 and two nodes per Gemini.

We use the miniGhost application [6], which is a part of the miniapps developed by the DOE community to represent the computational core of various HPC applications. MiniGhost focuses on the nearest neighbor inter-process communication strategy, with computation mainly serving to provide enough data and separation of the boundary exchanges from some computation. Its core is based on CTH, an application for modeling complex multi-dimensional problems that are characterized by large deformations and/or strong shocks [16].

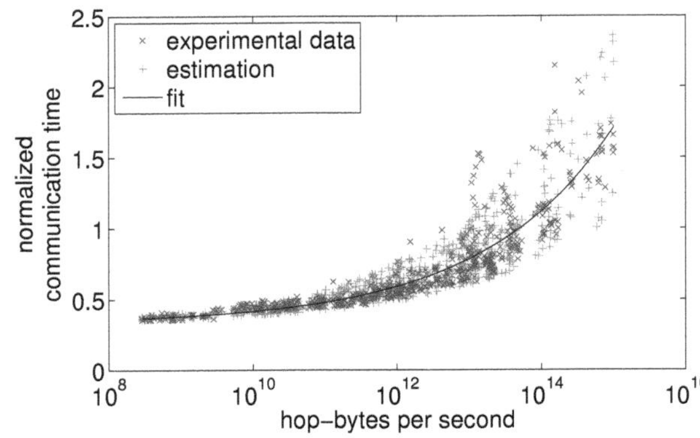

Figure 7: Relationship between communication and hop-bytes. The communication time represents the time spent in communication when the computation time equals 1.

We run miniGhost with sizes of powers of 2, from 64 to 65536. For each size, we run miniGhost under 5 allocation schemes and using 11 task mapping techniques, providing 55 executions for the same application. The task mapping techniques include all algorithms introduced in Section 2.2, all algorithms in LibTopoMap [17], and the system defaults. During the experiments, we collect time spent for communication and computation, number of bytes sent between machine nodes, maximum congestion, and message hop count.

We examine several metrics that have been associated with the communication overhead in the literature. These are maximum dilation (i.e., the maximum network hop distance a message travels), average dilation, average hops per byte, maximum network congestion, and hop-bytes as defined in Equation 4.

$$\textit{hop-bytes} = \sum_{i}^{messages} \textit{hop-distance}_i \cdot \textit{bytes}_i \tag{4}$$

Hop-bytes represents the total communication volume in the network. Our experimental results show high correlation between hop-bytes and communication time, as shown in Figure 7. Based on the experimental data, we formulate the execution time of a job as follows:

$$T_{exec} = (1 + 0.0019 \cdot \textit{hop-bytes}^{0.16+\tau}) \cdot T_{base} \tag{5}$$

where T_{base} is the execution time without considering the overhead introduced by topology mapping decision, and τ is a uniformly distributed random number between -0.013 and 0.013 that represents the variation in the experimental results. As the application tasks run on individual processing cores without consolidation, we assume that the computation time is independent of the mapping decision.

4.4 Simulation Environment

We use the Structural Simulation Toolkit (SST), which is an architectural simulation framework designed by Sandia National Laboratories to assist in the design, evaluation and

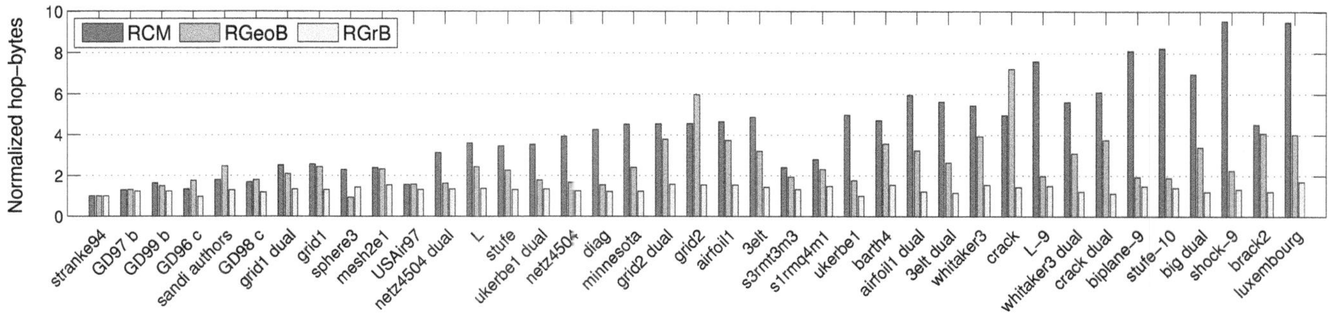

Figure 8: Hop-bytes comparison of task mappers for all applications in our input set. The values are normalized to the hop-bytes resulting from PaCMap.

optimization of HPC architectures and applications [30]. We use macro-SST simulations rather than micro-SST for speed.

For scheduling, we use the "easy scheduler" provided in SST, which is an aggressive backfilling technique that gives a guaranteed start time only to the first job in the queue [23]. We use the existing algorithms in SST for job allocation except for PaCMap. For task mapping, we implement PaCMap as well as the baseline algorithms. We calibrate the running time estimation in the simulator as described in Section 4.3.

5. EVALUATION

There are many aspects affecting the efficiency of the topology mapping algorithms, making it infeasible to perform a reliable comparison with a single series of experiments. Hence, we first start our evaluation with analyzing the task mappers independently from the allocation algorithms in Section 5.1. For this purpose, we run each application in an empty machine using the same allocation. Based on our results, we summarize how the task mappers perform for various sparse communication patterns. Then, in Section 5.2, we use long workload traces with multiple jobs to observe the impact of allocation on task mapping.

5.1 Single Job Analysis

In order to find the strengths and weaknesses of the task mappers, we run individual applications using the same allocation. We use best-fit allocator with Hilbert curves to provide a fair comparison for RCM, which maps the tasks in-order to the allocated nodes. For each application, we use the smallest empty cubical machine with single core per node, where the machine dimensions are selected as powers of 2 so that efficient Hilbert curves can be generated. We use PaCMap only as a task mapper in this analysis.

Figure 8 shows the resulting hop-bytes for all applications in our input set. The results are normalized with respect to the hop-bytes of PaCMap. The applications in the x-axis are ordered from smallest with 10 tasks (stranke94) to the largest with 115K tasks (luxembourg). Note that all cases use the same allocator so that the benefits of combined allocation and mapping is not exploited. We now present our detailed analysis on each task mapper.

RCM: In the figure, we observe that the RCM performance decreases as the application size increases. The first reason for this scalability problem is that RCM ignores the network links that are not along the curve. Second, the performance of RCM depends on the correlation between the average and the maximum distance in the communication matrix, which typically decreases with the application size. Consider the example given in Figure 9, which is the communication of the first 200 tasks of *diag*. In 9a, the maximum communication distance is 161 and the average distance is 2.37. After applying RCM, the maximum distance reduces to 33; however, the average becomes 8.84, increasing the communication overhead. Analyzing the correlation between the average and the maximum distance during topology mapping is not feasible due to its complexity. In addition to these problems, RCM assumes uniform communication between the task groups, worsening its mapping decision when a node contains multiple cores.

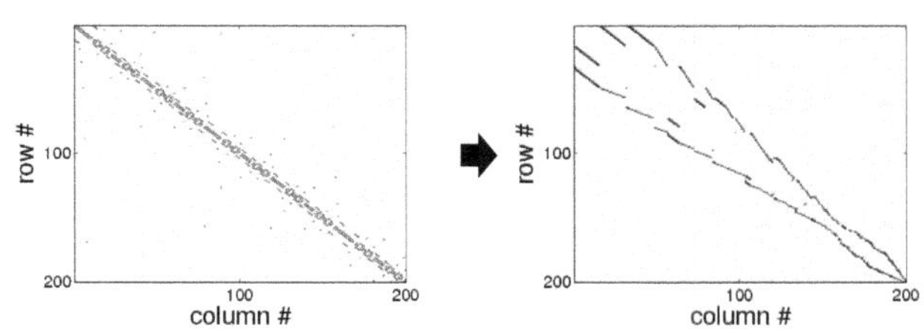

(a) Original matrix (b) RCM permutation

Figure 9: First 200 tasks of the application *diag*. RCM increases the average communication distance while decreasing the matrix bandwidth.

RGeoB: The performance of the RGeoB depends on (1) the similarity between the coordinates and the allocated node structure and (2) how well the geometry represents actual communication. For case 1, consider the example given in Figure 10. Because only coordinates are used during bisectioning, RGeoB places the tasks B and C far from each other and increases the message hop distance. This problem also occurs when the tasks have 2D coordinates but are mapped into a 3D topology. It has a significant impact on the communication overhead in larger scale, where thousands of tasks are placed far apart (e.g. *crack* in Figure 8).

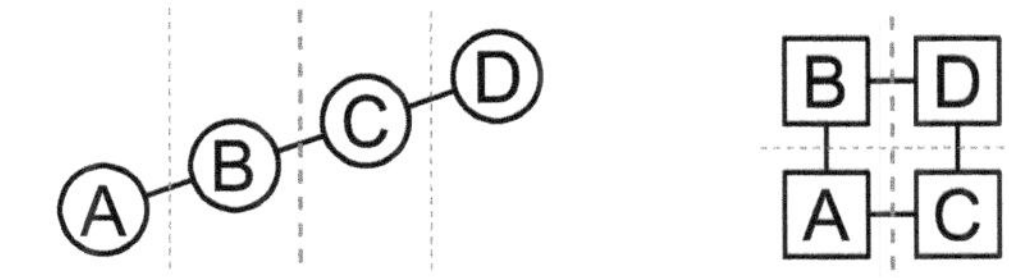

(a) Application Coordinates (b) Network Graph

Figure 10: Example for mismatching coordinates and allocation. The dashed lines represent the bisection cuts.

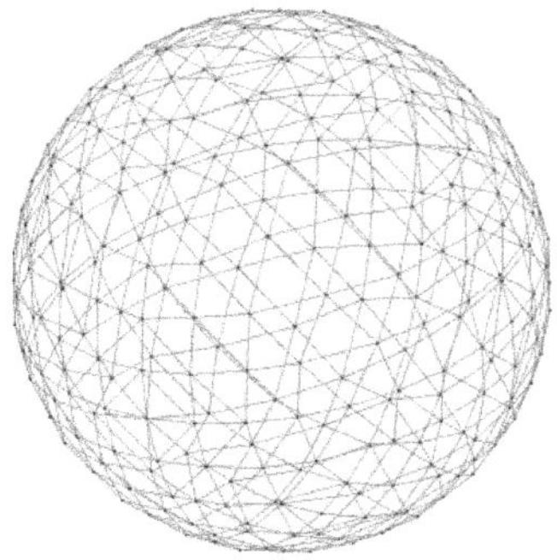

Figure 11: 3D coordinates of *sphere3* [12]. Nodes are the tasks and edges are the communication links.

To avoid this problem in torus/mesh networks for structured communication, researchers have introduced methods such as folding [8]. However, no solution exists on this issue for arbitrary communication patterns. For case 2, the most prominent example is the application *sphere3* with the coordinates given in Figure 11. In the given geometry, the communicating tasks are close to each other, meaning that the communication is represented well in 3D coordinates. As a result, RGeoB leads to the lowest hop-bytes for this application in Figure 8.

RGrB: Note that RGrB uses an all-to-all network graph as the allocation can be non-contiguous and arbitrary. One weakness of RGrB is that the heuristics used for graph bisectioning, which is also an NP-hard problem, perform poorly with all-to-all graphs. Additionally, RGrB can lead to less efficient solutions depending on the nature of the communication and machine graphs as well as how the recursive branches of these two graphs are mapped to each other [28].

PaCMap: The performance of PaCMap is reduced as the allocation is not adapted to the communication graph during this analysis. We compare our technique with others in the subsequent section.

We have performed the same analysis using average message hop distance and per-job congestion metrics to verify that our algorithm do not worsen another network metric. As we obtained very similar results to the hop-bytes metric, we do not present them due to space limitations.

RCM is not a good topology mapping solution for non-contiguous allocation due to its poor scalability. Similarly, RGeoB is preferred only for structured communication patterns. Hence, we will focus on RGrB and PaCMap in the rest of our analysis. Next, we discuss the impact of allocation algorithm on the topology mapping for unstructured communication patterns.

5.2 Workload Trace Analysis

Analyzing how the allocation decision affects the task mapping performance in a machine with non-contiguous allocation requires an already-populated machine. For this purpose, we use entire workload traces and compare the execution time of the jobs. The target HPC machine used in this analysis has 16 processing cores per node as in the real-life experiments we use for calibrations (See Section 4.3). For each input trace, the machine size is selected as the actual machine size the logs are collected from.

Figure 12 shows the cumulative execution time of all jobs that use multiple nodes (i.e., jobs with 16 or more tasks) in the traces with different allocator and task mapper pairs.

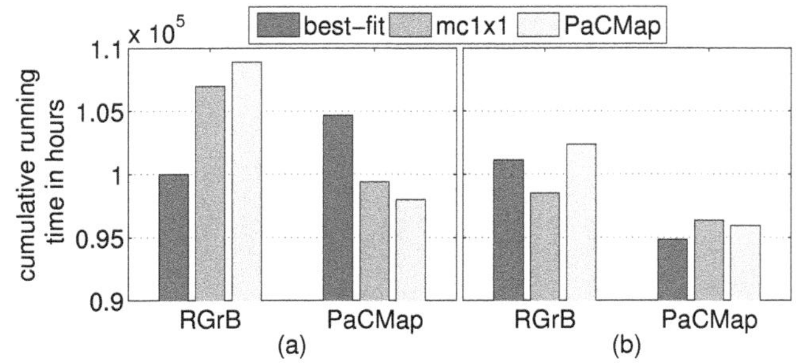

Figure 12: Cumulative running time of the jobs that use multiple nodes in (a) LLNL-Atlas and (b) CEA-Curie traces. The horizontal axis shows different task mappers; whereas bar colors are different allocators.

Each bar group uses a different task mapper, and each bar in a group uses a different allocator. Note that PaCMap can be used as an allocator and/or as a task mapper.

Although intuitively clustered allocations should be more useful for RGrB than curve-following allocations, we observe that for LLNL-Atlas, RGrB leads to 7% less cumulative execution time than mc1x1 with the best-fit allocator. This is because the Hilbert curves provide very high locality in this particular case. However, for CEA-Curie, the RGrB & mc1x1 pair leads to 3% shorter execution than with best-fit. The topology mapping performance not only depends on the allocator and the task mapper, but also on in which order the jobs arrive.

Complete topology mapping (both allocation and task mapping) with PaCMap decreases the cumulative execution time by 2% and 3% for LLNL-Atlas and CEA-Curie, respectively, compared to the best case of RGrB for each trace. Note that this reduction corresponds to 3000 hours of cumulative active node computation time in two weeks, which implies power and energy savings besides the execution time. The improvement is expected to grow with increasing application sizes based on our following analysis.

In order to verify that this difference in the execution time is not due to specific workloads, we compare the average per-application hop-bytes in Figure 13. As we generate the communication patterns by binning the job sizes in the traces to the closest available size in the sparse matrix collection, the traces do not contain all the applications. Thus, some applications are not present in the figures. The values Figure 13 are normalized with respect to the results of PaCMap.

In both traces, RGrB performs better than PaCMap for applications with less than 1K tasks. As the application size increases, however, PaCMap leads to smaller hop-bytes up to 30% compared to the best case of RGrB, excluding *sandi authors* and *mesh2e1* in the CEA-Curie trace. These two applications have very large hop-bytes because they have a few instances in the trace, which are allocated poorly in this particular case.

6. RELATED WORK

Topology mapping based on an application's communication pattern and on the network topology is a well-studied NP-hard problem. Researchers have been investigating various heuristic techniques to minimize the communication overhead of HPC applications through topology mapping. Bhatelé et al. proposed techniques such as step embedding

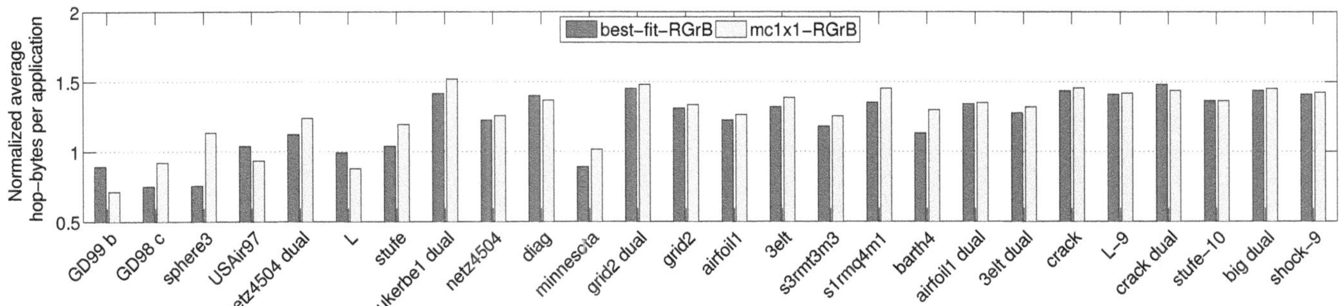

(a)

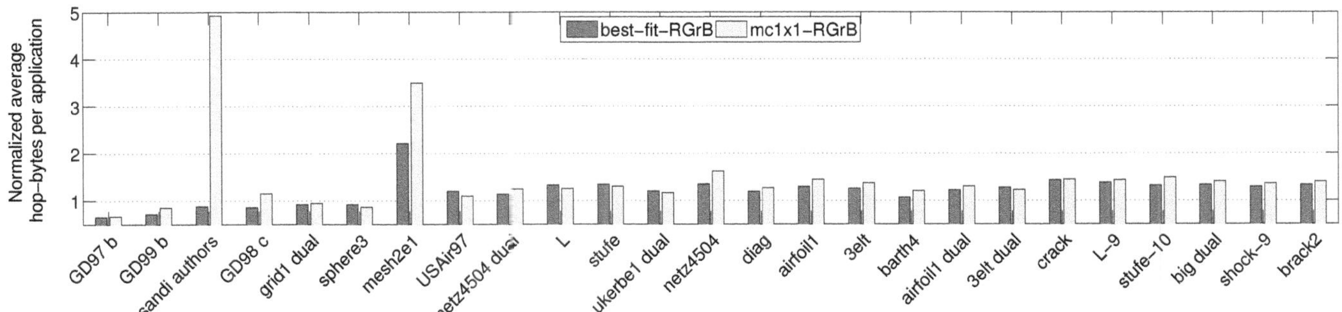

(b)

Figure 13: Average per-application hop-bytes in (a) LLNL-Atlas and (b) CEA-Curie traces with different allocator & task mapper pairs. The results are normalized with respect to PaCMap.

and folding to map 2D stencil applications into 2D and 3D mesh machines [8], as well as traversal and affine mapping algorithms to map irregular graphs into meshes [9]. Yu et al. presented graph embedding techniques for structured communication onto IBM Blue Gene/L systems [34]. Hoefler and Snir proposed mapping irregular topologies using graph similarity and graph partitioning [17]. These techniques focus on contiguous allocation, and are integrated in software packages such as LibTopoMap [17] and SCOTCH [29].

For machines with non-contiguous allocation, Krumpke et al. proposed Gen-Alg, which is a $(2 - 2/k)$-approximation allocation algorithm, to minimize the pairwise average L1 distance of the mapped tasks [21], and Lo et al. introduced various linear allocation schemes [24]. Leung et al. improved their solution by using Hilbert curves on the CPlant supercomputer [22]. Albing et al. proposed using different curves to remove the restrictions on the network topology and machine dimensions imposed by Hilbert curves [4]. These solutions limit the allocation performance by ignoring network links outside the given curve. Other researchers have introduced clustered allocation schemes to overcome such limitations. Bender et al. proposed the MM algorithm, a $(2-1/2d)$ approximation for d-dimensional grids, and the MC1x1 algorithm [7]. Their techniques are applicable only on mesh and torus topologies.

Previous work on task mapping for non-contiguous allocation has focused on stencil communication patterns. Deveci et al. considered multi-level partitioning of both the machine and application geometries [13]. It is also possible to use certain contiguous mapping algorithms for non-contiguous machines with small modifications (e.g., RCM, RGrB).

Our paper differs from prior work by focusing on the topology mapping of irregular communication patterns into non-contiguous allocation of arbitrary network topologies, including novel topologies such as Dragonfly [20]. Additionally, we analyze the potential benefits of simultaneous job allocation and task mapping.

7. CONCLUSION

Topology mapping of HPC applications have a significant impact on the execution time, especially at the macro-scale, where the applications use more than 1K machine nodes. In this paper, we have presented a novel algorithm, PaCMap, that simultaneously applies job allocation and task mapping to minimize the execution time of applications with unstructured communication patterns. PaCMap is applicable to any network topology, and it can be also used as a mere allocator or task mapper. Furthermore, we have developed an execution time estimation model based on real life experiments on a Cray XE6, which is used to calibrate the simulations of long HPC workload traces. Our results show that PaCMap reduces hop-bytes up to 30% compared to state-of-the-art approaches in HPC machines with non-contiguous allocation. This implies improvement in the machine performance as well as reduction in power and energy consumption.

Acknowledgments

This work has been partially funded by Sandia National Laboratories. Sandia National Laboratories is a multi-program laboratory managed and operated by Sandia Corporation, a wholly owned subsidiary of Lockheed Martin Corporation, for the U.S. Department of Energy's National Nuclear Security Administration under contract DE-AC04-94AL8500.

8. REFERENCES

[1] Cray Inc. http://www.cray.com/.
[2] Top 500 supercomputer sites. http://www.top500.org/.

[3] N. Adiga et al. Blue gene/l torus interconnection network. *IBM Journal of Research and Development*, 49(2.3):265–276, March 2005.

[4] C. Albing et al. Scalable node allocation for improved performance in regular and anisotropic 3d torus supercomputers. In *Proceedings of the 18th European MPI Users' Group Conference on Recent Advances in the Message Passing Interface*, EuroMPI'11, pages 61–70, 2011.

[5] D. Auble and B. Christiansen. SLURM workload manager overview. Presented at the 2014 ACM/IEEE International Conference on High Performance Computing, Networking, Storage and Analysis (SC'14).

[6] R. F. Barrett, C. T. Vaughan, and M. A. Heroux. Minighost: a miniapp for exploring boundary exchange strategies using stencil computations in scientific parallel computing. Technical report, Sandia National Laboratories, Albuquerque, NM, 2012.

[7] M. A. Bender et al. Communication-aware processor allocation for supercomputers: Finding point sets of small average distance. *Algorithmica*, 50(2):279–298, Jan. 2008.

[8] A. Bhatele et al. Automated mapping of regular communication graphs on mesh interconnects. In *International Conference on High Performance Computing (HiPC)*, pages 1–10, Dec 2010.

[9] A. Bhatelé and L. Kalé. Heuristic-based techniques for mapping irregular communication graphs to mesh topologies. In *IEEE 13th International Conference on High Performance Computing and Communications (HPCC), 2011*, pages 765–771, Sept 2011.

[10] T. H. Cormen, C. E. Leiserson, R. L. Rivest, and C. Stein. *Introduction to Algorithms.* MIT Press and McGraw-Hill, 2nd edition, 2001.

[11] E. Cuthill and J. McKee. Reducing the bandwidth of sparse symmetric matrices. In *Proceedings of the 1969 24th National Conference*, ACM '69, pages 157–172.

[12] T. A. Davis and Y. Hu. The University of Florida sparse matrix collection. *ACM Trans. Math. Softw.*, 38(1):1:1–1:25, Dec. 2011.

[13] M. Deveci et al. Exploiting geometric partitioning in task mapping for parallel computers. In *Proceedings of the IEEE International Parallel and Distributed Processing Symposium (IPDPS)*, pages 27–36, 2014.

[14] J. Dongarra et al. The international exascale software project roadmap. *Int. J. High Perform. Comput. Appl.*, 25(1):3–60, Feb. 2011.

[15] D. G. Feitelson, D. Tsafrir, and D. Krakov. Experience with the parallel workloads archive, 2012.

[16] E. S. Hertel et al. CTH: A software family for multi-dimensional shock physics analysis. In *Proceedings of the 19th International Symposium on Shock Waves*, pages 377–382, 1993.

[17] T. Hoefler and M. Snir. Generic topology mapping strategies for large-scale parallel architectures. In *Proceedings of the International Conference on Supercomputing*, ICS '11, pages 75–84, 2011.

[18] M. Holtgrewe, P. Sanders, and C. Schulz. Engineering a scalable high quality graph partitioner. IPDPS'10, pages 1–12, April 2010.

[19] G. Karypis and V. Kumar. Multilevel k-way partitioning scheme for irregular graphs. *Journal of Parallel and Distributed Computing*, 48(1):96–129, Jan. 1998.

[20] J. Kim et al. Technology-driven, highly-scalable dragonfly topology. In *35th International Symposium on Computer Architecture, 2008. ISCA '08.*, pages 77–88, June 2008.

[21] S. Krumke et al. Compact location problems. *Theoretical Computer Science*, 181:238–247, 1996.

[22] V. Leung et al. Processor allocation on cplant: achieving general processor locality using one-dimensional allocation strategies. In *IEEE International Conference on Cluster Computing (CLUSTER)*, pages 296–304, 2002.

[23] D. A. Lifka. The anl/ibm sp scheduling system. In *Proceedings of the Workshop on Job Scheduling Strategies for Parallel Processing*, IPPS '95, pages 295–303, 1995.

[24] V. Lo, K. J. Windisch, W. Liu, and B. Nitzberg. Noncontiguous processor allocation algorithms for mesh-connected multicomputers. *IEEE Trans. Parallel Distrib. Syst.*, 8(7):712–726, jul 1997.

[25] Los Alamos National Laboratory. Cielo supercomputer. http://www.lanl.gov/projects/cielo/index.php.

[26] J. Mache, V. Lo, and K. Windisch. Minimizing message-passing contention in fragmentation-free processor allocation. In *Proceedings of the 10th International Conference on Parallel and Distributed Computing Systems*, pages 120–124, 1997.

[27] MPI Forum. MPI: A message-passing interface standart. Version 3.0, Sept. 2012. http://www.mpi-forum.org/.

[28] F. Pellegrini and J. Roman. Experimental analysis of the dual recursive bipartitioning algorithm for static mapping. Technical report, TR 1038-96, LaBRI, URA CNRS 1304, Univ. Bordeaux I, 1996.

[29] F. Pellegrini and J. Roman. Scotch: A software package for static mapping by dual recursive bipartitioning of process and architecture graphs. In *Proceedings of the International Conference and Exhibition on High-Performance Computing and Networking*, HPCN Europe, pages 493–498, 1996.

[30] A. Rodrigues et al. Improvements to the structural simulation toolkit. In *Proceedings of the 5th International Conference on Simulation Tools and Techniques*, SIMUTOOLS '12, pages 190–195, 2012.

[31] H. D. Simon and S.-H. Teng. How good is recursive bisection? *SIAM J. Sci. Comput.*, 18(5):1436–1445, sep 1997.

[32] V. Subramani, R. Kettimuthu, S. Srinivasan, J. Johnston, and P. Sadayappan. Selective buddy allocation for scheduling parallel jobs on clusters. In *CLUSTER'02*, pages 107–116, 2002.

[33] H. Subramoni et al. Design of a scalable infiniband topology service to enable network topology aware placement of processes. In *SC'12*, pages 70:1–70:12, 2012.

[34] H. Yu, I.-H. Chung, and J. Moreira. Topology mapping for blue gene/l supercomputer. In *SC'06*, pages 52–52, Nov 2006.

Unique Worker Model for OpenMP

Raghesh Aloor
Dept of CSE, IIT Madras, Chennai, India
raghesh@cse.iitm.ac.in

V. Krishna Nandivada
Dept of CSE, IIT Madras, Chennai, India
nvk@iitm.ac.in

ABSTRACT

In OpenMP, because of the underlying efficient 'team of workers' model, each worker is given a chunk of *tasks* (iterations of a parallel-for-loop, or sections in a parallel-sections block), and a barrier construct is used to synchronize the workers (not the tasks). Naturally, the practitioners are discouraged from invoking barriers in these tasks; as otherwise, depending on the number of workers the behavior of the program can vary. Such a restrictive practice can adversely impact programmability and program readability. To overcome such a restrictive practice, in this paper, inspired from the more intuitive interaction of tasks and barriers found in newer task parallel languages like X10, HJ, Chapel and so on, we present an extension to OpenMP (called UW-OpenMP).

UW-OpenMP gives the programmer an impression that each parallel task has been assigned a unique worker, and importantly these parallel tasks can be synchronized using a barrier construct. Consequently, the semantics of the programs (using parallel-for-loops, sections and barriers) remains independent of the actual number of worker threads, at runtime. We argue that such a scheme allows the programmer to conveniently think and express his/her logic in parallel. We propose a source to source transformation scheme to translate UW-OpenMP C programs to equivalent OpenMP C programs that are guaranteed to not invoke barriers in any task. We have implemented our proposed translation scheme in the ROSE compiler framework. Our preliminary evaluation shows that the proposed extension leads to programs that are concise and arguably easier to understand. Importantly, the efficiency resulting from the 'team of workers' model is not compromised.

1 INTRODUCTION

The increasing popularity of multi-core systems has resulted in the advent of many task parallel languages like X10 [1], HJ [2], Chapel [3], Cilk [4], OpenMP [5] and so on. One of the mantras of parallel programming in many of these languages is that the programmer thinks in parallel and expresses the program logic in a parallel language. For instance, from a programmer's point of view, a parallel loop in HJ [2] or X10 [1] can be seen as one that creates multiple tasks, where each task will run in parallel. Figure 1a shows a sample stencil computation code (written in HJ), which creates four parallel tasks (by using the `forall` construct) and the

ICS'15, June 08 - 11, 2015, Newport Beach/Irvine, CA, USA.
Copyright 2015 ACM 978-1-4503-3559-1/15/06 ...$15.00.
http://dx.doi.org/10.1145/2751205.2751238.

```
A = new int[5];
B = new int[4];
B[0]=1;B[1]=2;
B[2]=3;B[3]=4;
D = new int[4];
void compute(){
 forall (i: 0..3) {
   workload(i);
 } }
void workload(int i){
 A[i]=B[i]-1; /*S1*/
 next; // barrier
 D[i]=A[i+1]*2;/*S2*/}
```

(a) HJ code

```
int A[5],D[4]; //zero init
int B[4]={1,2,3,4},i;
void compute(){
omp_set_num_threads(nthrds);
#pragma omp parallel
{
  #pragma omp for private(i)
  for(i=0;i<=3;i++){
   workload(i); } } }
void workload(int i){
  A[i]=B[i]-1;    /* S1 */
  #pragma omp barrier
  D[i]=A[i+1]*2; /* S2 */ }
```

(b) OpenMP code

Figure 1: Barrier inside parallel-for-loop.

goal of each task is to execute the `workload` function in parallel. Each instance of the `workload` function executes the first statement (`S1`) and then waits for the other tasks to reach the barrier (`next`). Once all the tasks reach the barrier, they continue with their execution of `S2`. The barrier (in the `workload` function) ensures that the execution of `S2` (by any task) starts only after all the instances of `S1` have been executed. The expected values in arrays `A` and `D` are [0 1 2 3 0] and [2 4 6 0], respectively.

It can be argued that the facility to place barriers inside parallel tasks (supported in many languages like X10 [1], HJ [2], Chapel [3], and so on) helps improve programmability. It helps the programmer to conveniently encode program logic such as "Create a number of tasks and each task performs a job that requires the tasks to (conditionally or unconditionally) synchronize at different points". In addition, from a programmer's point of view, it is natural to assume that the number of parallel worker threads (*workers*, for short) will match the number of parallel tasks. The HJ code shown in Figure 1a works according to this intuitive behavior, where the synchronization happens among the iterations of `forall` (parallel loop) rather than workers. However, we observe interesting challenges when a similar code is written in languages likes OpenMP C [5], PJ [6], and JOMP [7].

Figure 1b shows a code snippet (similar to that shown in Figure 1a) written in OpenMP C. OpenMP provides a simple yet powerfully efficient scheme of creating a team of workers and using them to execute various parallel tasks; in the context of OpenMP, we use 'task' to refer to either an iteration of a parallel-for-loop (specified using `#pragma omp for`) or a section (specified using `#pragma omp section`). The number of workers in a team can be set inside the code by invoking `omp_set_num_threads` (a library function). The OpenMP code in Figure 1b, compiled using GCC gives the expected output, if `nthrds=4` (= number of iterations). However, say, `nthrds=2` and the OpenMP scheduler (using static scheduling) assigns iterations 0 and 1 to worker 0, and iteration 2 and 3 to worker 1. Now worker 0 and 1 start executing iterations 0 and 2, respectively. The barrier works as a synchronization point between the workers. Once both the workers hit the barrier, they resume executing the code after the barrier. After a worker has finished executing an iteration, it continues executing the next assigned iteration. At the end of the execution of the parallel-for-loop, `D` contains [0 4 0 0], which does not match the expected value. The reason for such a mismatch is that the workers executed the statement at label `S2` (present after the barrier) of iterations 0 and 2, before they executed the statement at label `S1` (present before the barrier) of iterations 1 and 3. If `nthrds=3`, the program may not even terminate. Further, setting the number of workers to be greater than the number of tasks does not guarantee consistent results, either.

The above discussed inconsistency can be noted with all the implementations (and variations) of OpenMP we have tested (GCC [8], Cray CC [9], Clang/LLVM [10], ICC [11], PJ [6], and JOMP [7]). However, some compilers (like GCC 4.4) issue a warning to the programmer when a barrier is syntactically surrounded by a work-sharing construct (such as parallel-for-loop or parallel-sections). Similarly, GCC 4.7, Cray CC, ICC and Clang/LLVM throw an error in such a case. But if the barrier is present inside a function called within a work-sharing construct, no such warning/error is issued.

The correct way to encode the logic expressed in Figure 1a in OpenMP is to write conforming [5] OpenMP code that ensures that no barrier can execute in the body of the parallel-for-loop. A programmer can achieve this (in case of the Figure 1b) by manually inlining the function invoked in the loop-body and distributing the parallel-for-loop. In general, this leads to code bloat and arguably harder to read programs (cohesive pieces of program logic are spread across multiple parallel-for-loops). Importantly, it is not always straightforward to distribute the body of the parallel-for-loop, as the barrier may be present deep inside if-statements, or while-loops. For example, consider the illustrative iterative averaging (IA) code from [12] (modified by Shirako et al [13]) shown in Figure 2; it intends to perform iterative averaging on a one-dimensional array. Here, a simple distribution of the outer loop would not suffice, because barriers are present inside a while-loop.

To summarize, the use of barriers within parallel-for-loops and parallel-sections can improve the general programmability and readability of the OpenMP code. However, addressing the associated consistency related issues requires that such barriers are used to synchronize the iterations (or sections) of the parallel-for-loop (or parallel-sections), instead of the team of workers associated with the work-sharing construct. In this regard, we first define a runtime model called *UW* model. Note: we mainly focus on parallel-for-loops and later show that parallel-sections can be dealt similarly.

DEFINITION 1.1. *A parallel-for-loop is said to be executing in UW model if a unique worker executes each iteration therein. An OpenMP program is said to be executing in UW model if each constituent parallel-for-loop executes in UW model and each parallel-for-loop uses the same iterations to worker map.*

Any given OpenMP program may be run in UW model by setting the number of workers equal to the number of parallel tasks. To distinguish UW model from the current execution model of OpenMP (where a worker may execute one or more iterations of a parallel-for-loop), we term the latter as the *One-to-Many model* (in short OM model). To avoid the above discussed consistency related issues, we add a requirement (matching the popular advise [14]) that a program executing in OM model cannot invoke barriers inside work-sharing constructs.

```
iters = 0; delta = epsilon + 1;
#pragma omp parallel
{
 #pragma omp for
 for (j=0;j<N;j++){
   while(delta>epsilon){
     newA[j]=(oldA[j-1]+oldA[j+1])/2.0;
     diff[j]=abs(newA[j]-oldA[j]);
     #pragma omp barrier
     if(j==1){ delta=sum(diff); iters++;
               temp=newA;newA=oldA;oldA=temp;}
     #pragma omp barrier
   } if (j==0) printf("iters = %d\n",iters);
 }/*for*/ }/*parallel*/
```

Figure 2: Snippet of Iterative Averaging (IA) in OpenMP

In this paper, we propose to extend OpenMP with UW model; we call this extension UW-OpenMP. Similarly, we term the subset of OpenMP programs that can execute in OM model as OM-OpenMP programs. For the UW-OpenMP code shown in Figure 1b, an equivalent OM-OpenMP can be derived by performing function inlining and a simple loop-distribution [15] transformation across the barrier statement. However, in general, it may not be so straightforward to do the transformation, as the barrier may be present deep inside if-statements or while-loops (see for example, Figure 2). In such examples, a naive loop distribution may not lead to even syntactically correct code.

We present a source to source transformation scheme to translate UW-OpenMP C programs to equivalent OM-OpenMP C programs; the translation ensures that the semantics of the generated program is independent of the number of workers. And the generated code can still take advantage of the efficiency of the 'team of workers' model of OpenMP. Our proposed technique is inter-procedural and whole-program in nature. Another important feature induced by UW-OpenMP is that it allows OpenMP programmers to think in parallel, instead of first writing a serial program and then introducing parallelism as an afterthought.

Our Contributions:

- UW-OpenMP allows barriers to be placed inside parallel-for-loops, which helps the programmer encode the program logic in a convenient (more intuitive) way.
- A transformation scheme (based on a combination of traditional loop optimizations [15] and some novel mini-transformations) is presented that helps enforce the UW model behavior in the presence of barriers in conditional statements and loops.
- The correctness of the transformation is stated as a theorem and we present a proof thereof.
- We present a set of optimizations to generate efficient code.
- We have implemented the proposed techniques in the ROSE Compiler Framework [16].
- We present an evaluation over ten popular OpenMP kernels (taken from different benchmark suites), and show that (i) our proposed translation ensures that the generated code takes advantage of the underlying 'team of workers' model, (ii) the overheads are minimal, and (iii) the proposed optimizations are effective.

1.1 Related Work

Shirako et al [17] proposed a mechanism to adopt the concept of phasers in HJ to OpenMP. They extend the existing runtime to admit phaser related calls (e.g., registration, synchronization and drop) in OpenMP programs. In contrast, our extension does not need any modifications to the runtime, and realizes thread level synchronization by doing a source to source translation of UW-OpenMP programs to OM-OpenMP. Their proposed technique does not allow synchronization between iterations of different parallel-for-loops (or different instances of the same parallel-for-loop nested

1.	Parallel region	`#pragma omp parallel` `S`
2.	Atomic	`#pragma omp atomic` `S`
3.	Parallel-for-loop	`#pragma omp for` `for(i=0;i<N;i++) S`
4.	Parallel-sections	`#pragma omp sections` `S`
5.	Parallel section	`#pragma omp section` `S`
6.	Single	`#pragma omp single` `S`
7.	Barrier	`#pragma omp barrier`

Figure 3: Syntax of OpenMP Pragmas

inside a serial loop), or different parallel-sections, which is not the case with UW-OpenMP.

Presence of synchronization primitives inside parallel-for-loops poses interesting challenges while doing semantics preserving transformations. Nandivada et al [18] present techniques to do semantics preserving transformation of programs with task parallel loops with barriers. In this paper, we present a systematic approach to translate UW-OpenMP programs (that may contain barriers inside loops) to OM-OpenMP.

We extend many of standard loop optimizations (such as loop fusion, loop distribution) [15] in the context of OpenMP programs. Further, we propose a series of optimizations to improve the performance of the generated code. Many prior works try to optimize parallel programs [19, 20, 18, 21], by eliminating useless barriers, joins, task-creation and termination overheads. These techniques can be applied on our generated code in an orthogonal way.

2 BACKGROUND

Figure 3 lists the syntax of some of the most important pragmas supported by OpenMP C [5]. Each of the pragmas (except the one for barrier) is applied on the statement immediately after the pragma (referred to as the *body* of the pragma).

Parallel Region: A parallel region creates a team of workers, each of which executes the body `S` in parallel. For each parallel region, the number of workers is fixed (once per region) by either invoking the library routine `omp_set_numthreads`, or setting the environment variable `OMP_NUM_THREADS`.

Atomic Construct: It ensures mutual exclusion, important to concurrently update / read shared variables.

Work-sharing Constructs: OpenMP supports three types of work sharing constructs: (i) parallel-for-loop: the iterations of the enclosed for-loop are distributed among the workers of the current team. (ii) parallel-sections: This work-sharing construct distributes each section (declared using `#pragma omp section`) present in the body, among the workers of the current team. The exact distribution of the work (iterations / sections) to different workers of the team is dependent on the scheduling policy. The default policy is left to individual implementations (e.g., GCC uses a default blocked distribution). (iii) single: The body of the single construct is executed only by one of the workers in the team.

Barriers: A barrier within a parallel region acts as a synchronization point among all the workers of the current team. No worker in a team can cross a barrier, until all the workers of the team reach a barrier. There is an implicit barrier at the end of each parallel region. Each work-sharing construct (unless invoked with a special `nowait` clause) has an implicit barrier inserted at the end of it.

Memory Model: OpenMP programs support the relaxed memory consistency model [22, 23]. There is an implicit "flush" at the end of the barrier construct that ensures that all the workers crossing the barrier see a consistent view of the updates to the shared variables.

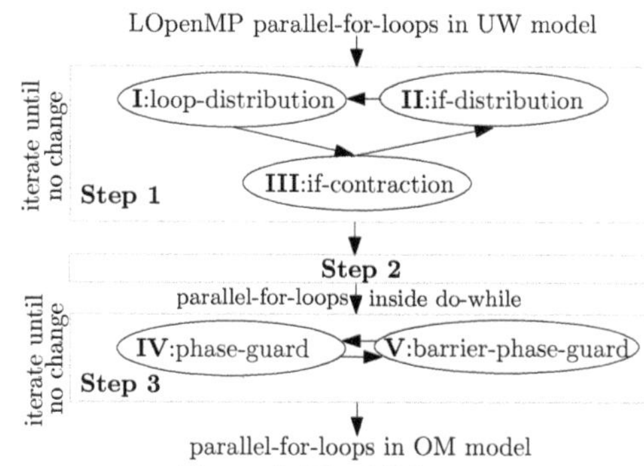

Figure 4: Block Diagram

3 FROM UW-OpenMP TO OM-OpenMP

In this section, for the ease of translation, we first define a subset of UW-OpenMP called LOpenMP and present our transformation scheme to translate LOpenMP programs to equivalent OM-OpenMP programs. Later in Section 3.3 we present a generalization.

DEFINITION 3.1. *An LOpenMP parallel region is an OpenMP parallel region which has its body comprising of one or more parallel-for-loops, each possibly nested within a sequential (while) loop. The body of a parallel-for-loop in an LOpenMP region may contain a serial loop. But the serial loop should not have further nested serial loops. An OpenMP program where each parallel region is an LOpenMP parallel region is called an LOpenMP program.*

DEFINITION 3.2. *In the execution trace of an LOpenMP parallel region in UW model, we group all the statement instances by the iteration number of the parallel-for-loop in which they execute: the sequence of statements executed by all the parallel-for-loops in their i^{th} iterations constitutes the ith UW-group. We say that the ith UW-group is generated by the ith* agent *of the LOpenMP parallel region.*

DEFINITION 3.3. *We use b_k^i to denote the $k^{th}(\geq 1)$ barrier in the ith UW-group. Let Ψ_k^i denote the set of statement instances executed before b_k^i. The kth phase (Φ_k) is defined as follows. $\Phi_1 = \bigcup_i \Psi_1^i$; and $\Phi_k = \bigcup_i \Psi_k^i \setminus \Psi_{k-1}^i$, if $k > 1$. The statement instances of any phase Φ_k are said to be executed in the kth phase of the parallel region.*

3.1 Translation Scheme

The execution of each UW-OpenMP task can be seen to be consisting of one or more phases; intuitively, a phase describes the barrier free code executed between the starting point and a barrier, between two barriers, between a barrier and the end point of the task, or between the starting and ending points. And when two or more UW-OpenMP tasks synchronize on a barrier, each one of them progresses to the next phase. Our proposed transformation scheme uses this intuition to generate equivalent OM-OpenMP code.

For ease of explanation, we introduce our transformation techniques assuming that the parallel-for-loops in the input LOpenMP program have no barriers nested inside while-loops; later in Section 3.2 we relax this requirement. We define `N` to be the maximum number of iterations present in any parallel-for-loop.

The overall block diagram of our transformation is shown in Figure 4. Our transformation consists of three steps. In *Step 1*, we repeatedly invoke loop-distribution, if-distribution, and if-contraction rules (Figure 5), till the body of each parallel-for-loop is a *simple-statement* (sequential code with no OpenMP pragmas), or a barrier, or a barrier surrounded by an `if` predicate (conditional-barrier). These rules are standard compiler transformations [24], applied in

Step 1	
I: Loop-distribution	

#pragma omp for
for(i=0;i<N;i++){
S1;S2;}
//S1 or S2 has barriers
	#pragma omp for
	for(i=0;i<N;i++){S1;}
	#pragma omp for
	for(i=0;i<N;i++){S2;}

II: If-distribution	

#pragma omp for
for(i=0;i<N;i++) {
if(e) { S1; S2; }}
//S1 or S2 has barriers
	#pragma omp for
	for(i=0;i<N;i++) {
	v = e;
	if(v) S1; if(v) S2;}

III: If-contraction	

#pragma omp for
for(i=0;i<N;i++) {
if(e1) if (e2) S1;}
//S1 has barriers
	#pragma omp for
	for(i=0;i<N;i++) {
	if(e1 && e2) S1; }

Step 2	

#pragma omp parallel
S
	H=calloc(M,
	N*sizeof(int));
	P=calloc(N,
	sizeof(int));
	cp=0;
	#pragma omp parallel
	do { S; break;
	} while (1);

Step 3	
IV: Phase-guard	

#pragma omp for
for(i=0;i<N;i++) {
S; }
	#pragma omp for
	for(i=0;i<N;i++) {
	if(P[i]==cp &&
	!H[⟦pfCnt⟧][i])
	{H[⟦pfCnt⟧][i]=1; S}}

V: Barrier-phase-guard	

#pragma omp for
for(i=0;i<N;i++) {
if(e)
#pragma omp barrier
}
	#pragma omp for
	for(i=0;i<N;i++){
	if(P[i]==cp &&
	!H[⟦pfCnt⟧][i])
	{ H[⟦pfCnt⟧][i] = 1;
	if (e) P[i]++; }
	if (P[i]!=(cp+1)){
	#pragma omp atomic
	flag=0;
	}/*end if*/}//end for
	#pragma omp single {
	tmpflag = flag;
	if(flag) cp++;
	flag = 1;}
	if(tmpflag) continue;

Figure 5: Transformation Rules

the presence of OpenMP parallel-for-loops. Note: Loop-distribution may perform scalar-expansion, if necessary.

Step 2 initializes two auxiliary variables (H and P used in Step 3) and embeds the complete body of the parallel region inside a do-while loop. This do-while loop helps avoid unstructured `goto` statements in the next step. The output from Step 2, consisting of a parallel region containing a series of parallel-for-loops (say, in total M) embedded inside a do-while loop, is given as input to *Step 3*, which in turn generates equivalent OM-OpenMP code.

Data structures: We use a shared variable `cp` (to indicate the *current phase* of the parallel region) , and a shared array `P` (to denote the *phase array*) with size equal to N. If the parallel region is in phase k, `cp` is set to k. The current phase of the ith agent is stored in `P[i]` and is incremented to emulate the behavior of the ith agent encountering a barrier. When all the agents increment the phase, we increment `cp` by 1 to indicate the change in the current phase of the parallel region. With the body of each parallel-for-loop (after Step 2), we maintain a unique identifier `pfCnt` $\in$ [0,M). We use ⟦pfCnt⟧ to indicate the value of `pfCnt` for the current parallel-for-loop. We use a two dimensional array H: M×N (to denote *statement execution history*). A statement with identifier ⟦pfCnt⟧ is executed by agent i, only if H[⟦pfCnt⟧][i]= 0 (that is, it has not already been executed). Thus, the maximum memory overhead = O(M×N).

Rules IV and V: The input to Step 3, is a parallel region containing a series of parallel-for-loops, each of whose body is either a simple-statement or a conditional-barrier; we treat unconditional-barriers also as conditional barriers, where the predicate always evaluates to true. Correspondingly, in Step 3, we present two transformation rules (IV and V) shown in Figure 5. In Rule IV, the ith instance of the simple-statement S is executed only when `P[i]` (current phase of agent i) is equal to `cp` and H[⟦pfCnt⟧][i]=0. In Rule V, the barrier inside the conditional-barrier statement is replaced by the statement `P[i]++`, which is executed only when `P[i]` (current phase of agent i) is equal to `cp` and H[⟦pfCnt⟧][i]=0. We examine the complete phase array P to check if a phase change (increment) is in the offering (happens only if all agents increment `P[i]` by 1). The phase increment is reflected by the increment of `cp` by a single thread. After the phase increment, the control goes back to the beginning of the do-while loop. This is to execute those statements which were skipped because `P[i]` was greater than the value of `cp` at that instant.

Our proposed technique ensures that we replace the abstraction of synchronization among the workers of the team (executing a parallel region) with the abstraction of synchronization among the iterations of a parallel-for-loop. This helps the programmer to code in the UW-OpenMP, ignoring the complexities arising out of the need to know the mapping of iterations to the workers at the time of placing barriers.

Correctness of Transformation

We first extend the definition of barrier given in Definition 3.3, in the context of our transformed programs: We use b^i_k to denote the $k^{th}(\geq 1)$ instance of the statement `P[`i`]++` in the ith UW-group.

The definitions of Statement instance Ψ^i_k and phase set Φ_k, in the context of the transformed program, depend on this new definition of b^i_k. The following theorem establishes the correctness of our transformation scheme.

THEOREM 1. *Let $S^{uw}_{i,n}$ denote the nth instance of statement S executed by agent i in UW model and $S^{bm}_{i,n}$ denotes the instance of statement S executed by agent i in OM model in the transformed code. If $R \rightarrow_d S$ denotes that statement S is dependent on R then*

1. *[Phase-dependence] $S^{uw}_{i,n} \in \Phi_k \Rightarrow S^{bm}_{i,n} \in \Phi_k$.*
2. *[Data-dependence] $R^{uw}_{i,m} \rightarrow_d S^{uw}_{j,n} \Rightarrow R^{bm}_{i,m} \rightarrow_d S^{bm}_{j,n}$.*

PROOF. *(Sketch)* [Phase-dependence]: The kth increment of `P[i]` in the transformed code in OM model corresponds to b^i_k in UW model. Based on the type of $S^{uw}_{i,n}$ (a simple-statement or conditional-barrier), Rules IV or V ensure that $S^{bm}_{i,n}$ executes in the phase Φ_k. This behavior is ensured by the guard `P[i]==cp`, since `cp` is incremented only when all the agents increment `P[i]`. This is equivalent to all agents executing b^i_k in the code executed in UW model.

[Data-dependence]: The phase-dependence part ensures that for each $R^{uw}_{i,m}$ and $S^{uw}_{j,n}$ there are corresponding elements in the same phase in the OM model. Since we do not add/remove any new statements and for each statement in the UW model, there is a corresponding statement in the OM model. Thus, it implies that no new statement executes in between $R^{bm}_{i,m}$ and $S^{bm}_{j,n}$; thus the dependencies are preserved. □

3.2 While Transformation

In this section, we extend the transformation rules presented in Section 3.1, to admit parallel-for-loops with a while-loop as the body;

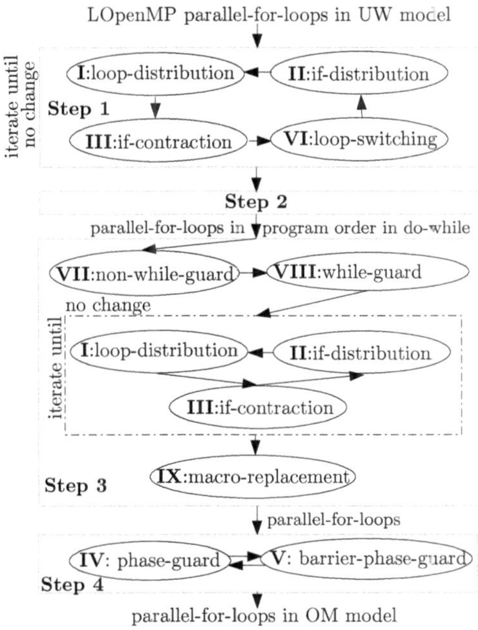

Figure 6: Block Diagram for While Transformation

the while-loop may in turn contain barriers within. Unlike a serial for-loop in normal form [24], while-loops introduce newer challenges because of the uncertainty of the number of iterations of the while-loop a priori during compilation. Note that a while-loop in LOpenMP has no nested serial loops inside.

Overall procedure: The overall block diagram for the translation of parallel-for-loops containing while-loops, carried out in four steps, is shown in Figure 6. In *Step 1*, we invoke the Rules I, II and III (Figure 5) along with the standard loop-switching rule (see Rule VI, Figure 7), till there is no change. *Step 2*: Similar to the Step 2 invoked in Section 3.1, we embed the body of the parallel region inside a do-while loop. We also initialize two new variables (`K` and `Rdy`) that are used for later bookkeeping (in some helper functions). *Step 3*: We first invoke the non-while-guard rule (Rule VII, in Figure 7), on all the parallel-for-loops whose body is not a while-loop containing barriers. We now process, in the program order, each of the parallel-for-loops that contains an immediately nested while-loop. Each such parallel-for-loop PF is processed through three sub-steps: (i) invoke the while-guard rule (Rule VIII, Figure 7) on PF, (ii) invoke Rules I, II, and III (again) on the generated code till there is no further change, and (iii) invoke the macro-replacement rule (Rule IX, Figure 7). *Step 4*: Invoke phase-guard and barrier-phase-guard (Rules IV and V, Figure 5).

We first explain the data structures and auxiliary functions used and then present an explanation of the transformation rules.

Data structures: Besides `pfCnt` (discussed in Section 3.1), we use an additional auxiliary counter `grCnt` (to indicate group-count). In Step 3, the value of `pfCnt` for a statement may change (due to the invocation of Rule I). We use ⟦`grCnt`⟧ to remember the `pfCnt` value (at the end of Step 2) for each statement. Note that the value of `grCnt` for any statement does not change in Step 3.

Consider a parallel-for-loop (PF), with an immediately nested while-loop (W); say W has statement `S` as the body and `e` as the predicate. Say, `S1` and `S2` are sequences of parallel-for-loops before and after PF, respectively. Each arbitrary iteration of PF, executes `S` until `e` evaluates to *false*, for that iteration. Thus, for any iteration `i` of PF, W contributes a sequence of statements (say, s_i) to the ith UW-group (say, denoted by G_i). In G_i, let r_i (contributed by `S1`) and t_i (contributed by `S2`) denote the sequence of statements executed before s_i and after s_i, respectively.

Step 1	

VI: Loop-switching
`#pragma omp for`
`for(i=0;i<N;i++) {`
` if(e1) {`
`  while(e2){ S;}}}`
	`#pragma omp for`
	`for(i=0;i<N;i++) {`
	`  v = e1;`
	`  while(e2){if(v){ S;}}`

Step 2	

`#pragma omp parallel`
`    S`
	`H=calloc(M,`
	`  N*sizeof(int));`
	`P=calloc(N,sizeof(int));`
	`Rdy=calloc(N,`
	`      sizeof(int));`
	`cp=0; K=0;`
	`#pragma omp parallel`
	`do { S;`
	` if(Done(0))break;`
	`} while (1);`

Step 3	

VII: Non-while-guard
`do{ S1;`
` #pragma omp for`
` for(i=0;i<N;i++) S;`
` S2;`
` if(Done(N1)) break;`
`}while (1);`
`//S has no while`
`//loop with barrier`
	`do { S1;`
	` #pragma omp for`
	` for(i=0;i<N;i++) {`
	`  if(canEnter(i,⟦grCnt⟧))`
	`   {S;iExit(i);}}`
	`  S2;`
	`  if(Done(N1+N))break;`
	`}while (1);`

VIII: While-guard:
`do { S1;`
` #pragma omp for`
` for(i=0;i<N;i++)`
`  while (e) {S}`
`  //S has barriers`
`  S2`
`  if(Done(N1))`
`   break;`
`}while (1);`
	`do { S1;`
	` #pragma omp for`
	` for(i=0;i<N;i++) {`
	`  if(canEnter(i,⟦grCnt⟧))`
	`  {v = e;`
	`   if(v) {S;`
	`    tmpreset(i,⟦pfCnt⟧);}`
	`   if (!v){iExit(i);}}}`
	`  S2`
	`  if(Done(N1+N))break;`
	`}while (1);`

IX: Macro-replacement
`#pragma omp for`
`for(i=0;i<N;i++)`
`  if(e){ S;`
`    tmpreset(i,C);}`
	`#pragma omp for`
	`for(i=0;i<N;i++)`
	` if(e) { S;`
	`  reset(i,C,⟦pfCnt⟧);}`

Figure 7: While Transformation Rules.

That is, $G_i = r_i \parallel s_i \parallel t_i$, where $\parallel$ is the concatenation operator. Our transformations ensure that the sequence of statements executed in the ith UW-group match G_i. Note that when the agent `i` has finished executing the code in r_i, statements in r_i are said to be in *done* state, the statements in s_i are considered ready to be executed (state = *ready*), and the statements in t_i are considered to be not ready (state = *ignore*).

To realize the semantics discussed above, our transformation uses two auxiliary variables: i) a zero initialized integer array `Rdy` (of size `N`, the maximum number of iterations of the parallel-for-loops). For any iteration `i` of a parallel-for-loop PF, the value of `Rdy[i]` decides if the iteration `i` is 'ready' to be executed or not, by agent `i`. Say the group-count of PF is given by ⟦`grCnt`⟧, then if the value of `Rdy[i]` $= 2 *$ ⟦`grCnt`⟧ or $2 *$ ⟦`grCnt`⟧ $+ 1$, it indicates that the ith iteration of PF, is ready to be executed, for the first time or subsequent time, respectively. ii) we use a zero initialized shared counter `K` to keep a count of the number of parallel-for-loop iterations (spread across multiple parallel-for-loops in the parallel region) that have finished executing. Say, the parallel region contains exactly two parallel-for-loops having N_1 and N_2 iterations, then the maximum value of `K` is $N_1 + N_2$.

Auxiliary procedures: The transformed code uses four auxiliary procedures, shown in Figure 8: (i) `canEnter`, (ii) `iExit`, (iii)

```
int canEnter(int i,int g){
  if(Rdy[i]==2*g){
    Rdy[i]++; return 1;}
  if(Rdy[i]==2*g+1){
    return 1;}
  return 0; }
```

```
int Done(int maxCnt){
  #pragma omp barrier
  return K == maxCnt; }
```

```
int iExit(int i){
  Rdy[i]++;
  #pragma omp atomic
  K++; return 1;}
```

```
void reset(int i,
    int l,int h){
  for (j=l;j<=h;j++)
    H[j][i]=0;
}
```

Figure 8: The Auxiliary Procedures

1. **init:** (a) ⟦`i,0`⟧=*ready* (b) $\forall g \geq 1$, ⟦`i,0`⟧=*ignore*
2. ⟦`i,g-1`⟧=*exec* $\wedge$ `iExit(i)` $\Rightarrow$ ⟦`i,g-1`⟧=*done* $\wedge$ ⟦`i,g`⟧= *ready*
3. ⟦`i,g`⟧=*ready* $\wedge$ `canEnter(i,g)` $\Rightarrow$ ⟦`i,g`⟧=*exec*
4. ⟦`i,g`⟧=*exec* $\wedge$ `canEnter(i,g)` $\Rightarrow$ ⟦`i,g`⟧=*exec*

Figure 9: State change rules for agent `i`.

`reset`, and (iv) `Done`. The ith iteration of the parallel-for-loop with `grCnt=g` will execute the body of the parallel-for-loop, only if `canEnter(i,g)` returns `1`. If the value of `Rdy[i]=2*g`, it increments `Rdy[i]` by 1 (indicates that the body has started executing). The function call `iExit(i)` increments `Rdy[i]` by 1 (indicates that the ith agent has finished executing the ith iteration of the current parallel-for-loop and is ready to start with the next parallel-for-loop). And the value of `K` is atomically incremented by `1`, to indicate that the body of one more parallel-for-loop has been executed by agent `i`. Note: the value of `Rdy[i]` at the end of a `iExit(i)` call is guaranteed to be even. The function `reset` is used to reset a part of statement execution history `H` (Section 3.1). The function call `reset(i,l,h)` resets the statement execution history corresponding to the ith agent, in the parallel-for-loops whose `pfCnt` values vary between `l` and `h` (both inclusive). The function `Done` checks if `K` matches its expected maximum value (passed as an argument). The barrier ensures that the routine waits for all the updates to `K`, by any parallel task, before evaluating the predicate. We now explain the Rules given in Figure 7.

Transformation rules: Rule #VII and VIII together provide an interesting mechanism to avoid the while-loop altogether. We start with Rule VIII for the ease of explanation.

In any iteration of the outer do-while loop (introduced in Step 2), the state ⟦`i,g`⟧ of an agent `i`, inside any parallel-for-loop with `grCnt=g` and body as `S`, can be one of the following: (a) *ready*: `i` is going to execute `S` for the first time, (b) *exec*: when the state changes from *ready* to *exec*, it indicates that the agent `i` will execute `S` one or more times. (c) *done*: `i` has finished executing `S`, or (d) *ignore*: `i` is in *exec* or *ready* state inside a parallel-for-loop with `grCnt=k` and `g>k`. The function `canEnter(i,g)` returns 1, only if ⟦`i,g`⟧ is *ready* or *exec*. Fig. 9 shows the state change rules.

In the transformation shown for Rule VIII, we can execute `e` and `S` only if `canEnter(i,g)` returns `1`. After the first invocation of `canEnter`, the element `Rdy[i]` gets incremented by 1 and ⟦`i,g`⟧ changes to *exec*. In this *exec* state, agent `i` executes the statements in the parallel-for-loop with `grCnt=g`, and not execute any other statements in any other parallel-for-loop with `grCnt`$\neq$ `g` (as their state is *done* or *ignore*). Once the predicate `e` becomes *false* for the agent `i`, the function `iExit(i)` is called to increment `Rdy[i]` by 1. As a result, ⟦`i,g`⟧ changes from *exec* to *done* and ⟦`i,g+1`⟧ changes from *ignore* to *ready*. Thus, the parallel-for-loops with `grCnt=g+1` are now ready to execute. And this process continues till all the states are set to *done*.

As discussed in Section 3.1, the statement execution history map `H` ensures that there are no duplicate executions of any statement. However, in case of the body `S` of a while-loop nested inside a parallel-for-loop, `S` may have to be executed multiple times. Thus, at the end of one iteration of the while-loop, by a parallel iteration `i`, we have to reset the corresponding `H` value entries for `i`. Considering the possibility that the code generated in Rule VIII, may be distributed in later transformations (leading to a sequence of parallel-for-loops), we use a temporary function `tmpreset` to remember the starting index (`pfCnt`) of the sequence and replace it with the auxiliary function `reset` and supply the value of the last index in Rule IX.

Rule VIII also increments the argument to the `Done` function by `N`, to indicate that `N` parallel-iterations are executed as part of the current parallel-for-loop.

Rule VII: It handles the case when the body `S` does not contain a while-loop with a barrier inside. In the transformed code, agent `i` executes `S` when `canEnter(i,`⟦`grCnt`⟧`)` returns 1. Note that the agent `i` executes `S` only once. And once executed, in the future iterations of the outer do-while loop, agent `i` will never execute `S`. This is ensured by the call to `iExit(i)` after the execution of `S`.

Phase-guard rules: Similar to the Step 3 in Section 3.1, we invoke the rules IV and V (Figure 5). Note: this may lead to multiple invocations of the `canEnter` function (max 2 times) for the same statement. This does not alter the semantics (as `canEnter` has no side effects), and is optimized away by a later pass (Section 4).

In the transformed code, the body of the do-while loop may have different parallel-for-loops. The technique explained above ensures that the statements which were part of a while-loop in the original code, repeat as many number of times as executed by the original while-loop in UW model, and the statements which are not part of any while-loop (in the original code) are executed only once.

Example Translation: Figure 10a shows a simplified version of the code discussed in Figure 2. Figures 10b–10g show the impact of applying our transformation rules on the input UW-OpenMP code (Figure 10a), along with the sequence of the rules applied to obtain the code in the figure. For brevity, we show the code generated after some of the important transformations only.

We use a sample execution to show how the semantics of Figure 10g (executing in OM-OpenMP) matches that of Figure 10a (executing in UW-OpenMP). Say, the while-loop in the latter executes its body twice. Statement `S3` is executed only after all the iterations finish the execution of the while-loop.

In Figure 10g, the arrays `H` and `P`, and the variable `cp` are initialized to 0. Similarly, the variable `flag` is initialized to 1. We term the predicate guarding the body of each of the six parallel-for-loops (L0-L5), within the do-while loop, as the *guarding-predicate*.

In Figure 10g, during the first iteration of the do-while loop, the guarding-predicate will evaluate to true for L0, L1 and L2. In L0, `v[i]` will be evaluated to true by all the iterations. In L1, `S1` will be executed by all the iterations. In L2, all the iterations increment `P[i]` to 1 and as a result the predicate `P[i]!=(cp+1)` evaluates to false (as `cp=0`). Next, `cp` is incremented to 1, by a single thread. This indicates a phase increment; it is equivalent to finishing the execution of the barrier statement by all the agents during the first iteration of the while-loop in Figure 10a. Now, in Figure 10g, all the workers execute the `continue` statement and jump to the start of the do-while loop.

During the second iteration of the do-while loop, the last term in the guarding-predicate evaluates to false for L0, L1 and L2. And the control reaches L3. In L3, `S2` and the function `reset(i,0,3)` is called by all the iterations, which resets the value of all `H` array elements corresponding to the parallel-for-loops generated because of while-loop. In L4, since the predicate `!v[i]` evaluates to false, `iExit(i)` is not executed which keeps `canEnter(i,0)` as true. In L5, `S3` will not be executed because `canEnter(i,1)` evaluates to false. The execution of the do-while loop continues because `Done(N+N)` evaluates to false.

```
// Input code
#pragma omp parallel
{
 #pragma omp for
 for(i=0;i<N;i++)
 {
  while(delta>epsilon)
  {
   S1;
   #pragma omp barrier
   S2;
  }
  S3;
 }
}
```
(a)

```
//after Rule I
#pragma omp parallel
{
 #pragma omp for
 for(i=0;i<N;i++){
  while(delta>epsilon)
  {
   S1;
   #pragma omp barrier
   S2;
  }
 }
 #pragma omp for
 for(i=0;i<N;i++) S3;
}
```
(b)

```
//after Step 2
#pragma omp parallel
 do {
 #pragma omp for
 for(i=0;i<N;i++){
  while(delta>epsilon){
   S1;
   #pragma omp barrier
   S2;
  }
 }
 #pragma omp for
 for(i=0;i<N;i++) S3;
  if(Done(0)) break;
 } while(1);
```
(c)

```
//after Rule VII
#pragma omp parallel
do{
 #pragma omp for
 for(i=0;i<N;i++){
  while(delta>epsilon){
   S1;
   #pragma omp barrier
   S2; }}
  #pragma omp for
  for(i=0;i<N;i++)
   if(canEnter(i,1)) {
    S3;iExit(i);}
 if(Done(N)) break;
}while(1);
```
(d)

```
//after Rule VIII
#pragma omp parallel
do {
 #pragma omp for
 for(i=0;i<N;i++){
  if(canEnter(i,0)){
   v=delta>epsilon;
   if(v){
    S1;
    #pragma omp barrier
    S2;
    tmpreset(i,0);}
   if(!v)iExit(i);
  }}
 #pragma omp for
 for(i=0;i<N;i++)
  if(canEnter(i,1)){
   S3;iExit(i);}
 if(Done(N)) break;
}while(1);
```
(e)

```
//Rules II,I,II,I,III
#pragma omp parallel
do {
 #pragma omp for
 for(i=0;i<N;i++){
  v1[i]=canEnter(i,0);
  if(v1[i]) {
   v[i]=delta>epsilon;}}
 #pragma omp for
 for(i=0;i<N;i++){
  if(v1[i] && v[i]){S1;
   #pragma omp barrier
   S2; tmpreset(i,0);}}
 #pragma omp for
 for(i=0;i<N;i++){
  if(v1[i] && !v[i])
   iExit(i);}
 #pragma omp for
 for(i=0;i<N;i++)
  if(canEnter(i,1)){
   S3;iExit(i);}
 if(Done(N+N)) break;
}while(1);
```
(f)

```
//Rules I,II,IX,IV,V
#pragma omp parallel
do{
 #pragma omp for // L0
 for(i=0;i<N;i++){
  if (canEnter(i,0) &&
   P[i]==cp&&!H[0][i]){
   H[0][i]=1;
   v1[i]=canEnter(i,0);
   if(v1[i])
    v[i]=delta>epsilon;
 }}
 #pragma omp for // L1
 for(i=0;i<N;i++)
  if (canEnter(i,0) &&
   P[i]==cp&&!H[1][i]){
   H[1][i]=1;
  if(v1[i] && v[i]) S1;}
 #pragma omp for // L2
 for(i=0;i<N;i++){
  if (canEnter(i,0) &&
   P[i]==cp&&!H[2][i]){
   H[2][i]=1;
   if(v1[i]&&v[i])P[i]++;}
   if(P[i]!=(cp+1)) {
    #pragma omp atomic
     flag=0;  }}
//contd.  in the next col
//contd.  from the prev col
 #pragma omp single {
  tmpflag = flag;
  if(flag) cp++;
  flag = 1;}
 if(tmpflag) continue;
 #pragma omp for // L3
 for(i=0;i<N;i++)
  if (canEnter(i,0) &&
   P[i]==cp&&!H[3][i]){
    H[3][i]=1;
    S2;  reset(i,0,3);}
 #pragma omp for // L4
 for(i=0;i<N;i++)
  if (canEnter(i,0) &&
   P[i]==cp&&!H[4][i]){
    H[4][i]=1;
    if(v1[i] && !v[i])
      iExit(i);}
  #pragma omp for // L5
  for(i=0;i<N;i++)
  if (canEnter(i,1) &&
   P[i]==cp&&!H[5][i]){
    H[5][i]=1;
    if(canEnter(i,1)){
     S3;iExit(i);}}
if(Done(N+N)) break;
}while(1);
```
(g)

Figure 10: Effect of our transformation rules shown in Figures 5 and 7. (a) input UW-OpenMP code. (b)-(g) code after applying different rules.

The third and fourth iterations of the do-while loop execute similar to that of the first and second iterations respectively. In the fifth iteration of the do-while loop, the predicate `v[i]` will be set to false. Hence in L4, `iExit(i)` will be executed. As a result, in L5, `canEnter(i,1)` evaluates to true and consequently, `S3` and `iExit(i)` are executed. Now `Done(N+N)` evaluates to true and the control comes out of the do-while loop.

3.3 Generalizing the Translation

Given any general UW-OpenMP program, we first translate it to LOpenMP and then invoke the transformations discussed in Section 3 that deal with programs written in LOpenMP.

OpenMP sections: Each parallel-section inside a `#pragma omp sections` is executed by a worker available in the parallel region. We can translate it to an equivalent parallel-for-loop (number of iterations equal to the number of sections) such that its ith iteration executes the ith section.

Statements outside parallel-for-loop: Figure 11 shows a simple scheme to handle statements, in an OpenMP parallel region, not nested inside any work-sharing construct.

#pragma omp parallel	T=omp_get_numthreads(); #pragma omp parallel
{ ... S ... }	{... #pragma omp for for(i=0;i<T;++i){S} ...}

Figure 11: Statement outside parallel for

while(e1){
 S1;
 while(e2)
  S2;
 S3;}
	inInnner=0;
	while((!inInner&&e1)||(inInner)){
	 if(!inInner) S1;
	 inInner=e2;
	 if(inInner) S2; if(!inInner) S3;}

Figure 12: Nested while loops

Nested while loops: Figure 12 shows a simple transformation to convert a nested while-loop to a non-nested one. It uses an additional variable (`inInner`) to execute the correct code.

Barriers inside functions: If a non-recursive function containing a barrier is called from a work-sharing construct, it is first inlined (as a pre-processing step). In case of a recursive function, it is specialized to take additional arguments for the auxiliary data structures. We skip the details for lack of space.

#pragma omp for	#pragma omp for
for(i=0;i<N;i++) {	for(i=0;i<N;i++) {
if(P[i]==cp&&!**H[C][i]**){	if(P[i]==cp&&
H[C][i] = 1; S1;}}	!**H[C][i]**){
#pragma omp for	**H[C][i] = 1;**
for(i=0;i<N;i++) {	S1;
if(P[i]==cp&&!**H[C+1][i]**){	S2;}}
H[C+1][i] = 1; S2;}}	

Figure 13: Loop fusion

Scheduling policies: One of the advantages of our proposed translation scheme is that the semantics of the generated code is independent of the scheduling policy [5] used in the program (static, dynamic, guided, auto, or runtime). This is because the generated code (in OM-OpenMP) never invokes barriers inside any worksharing construct. Note that to handle the possible issues arising due to multiple invocations of `omp_get_thread_num`, for each iteration, we cache the returned value of this function in a local data structure and use it in future invocations.

4 CLEANUP OPTIMIZATIONS

We now briefly describe a few optimizations to help generate efficient code; these optmizations mainly target reducing the overheads (in space and time) resulting from our translation scheme.

Direct loop distribution: In the context of the rules discussed in Section 3.1, if there exists a sequence of unconditional barriers inside a parallel-for-loop (may be interspersed with serial code in between), before any conditional barrier: we can apply loop-distribution around those unconditional barriers (incurs no overhead) and then apply the techniques of Section 3.1 on the rest of the parallel-for-loop starting with the conditional statement enclosing the barrier. We extend this logic further, to include conditional barriers guarded by single-valued expressions [25]. In such a case, we can apply the if-distribution rule, followed by the loop-distribution rule (Figure 5) and avoid any overhead, whatsoever.

Loop fusion: Figure 13 shows an extension to the standard loop fusion [15] technique to fuse some of the consecutive parallel-for-loops generated by our transformation. This helps in eliding the implicit barrier after the first parallel-for-loop, avoiding a predicate check. As shown in the text in **bold**, we are able to fuse the two loops even though the predicates are different. The underlying semantics of the `H` array guarantees the semantics preservation.

Removing avoidable atomic operations: We eliminate the atomic construct introduced for the write to the shared variable `flag` (in Rule V, Figure 5). Though this optimization may lead to non-conforming OpenMP code, we argue that it is acceptable, as the resulting race (between multiple writes to `flag`) is a benign one [26]: all of them write the same value 0. And since at most one bit may change (the old value of `flag` may only be either 0 or 1), it does not lead to partial writes [27].

Code specialization: Considering the possible overheads associated with our generated code (due to the While-transformation, discussed in Section 3.2), we specialize the transformed code (if the transformation involves the While-transformation) such that, when the number of workers matches the number of parallel iterations, the input parallel region is executed as it is, along with an option to set the chunk-size of the parallel-for-loop to 1. Though this optmization leads to non-conforming OpenMP code, the code will run according to the semantics of UW-OpenMP.

Barrier elimination: We make a pass over the generated code to check if there are two consecutive barrier statements (implicit or explicit), and eliminate one of them.

Redundant `canEnter` elimination: We make a simple pass over the code to eliminate calls to the `canEnter` function, nested within an if-statement whose predicate includes a call to `canEnter`.

```
#pragma omp for
for (i=0;i<n;++i)
  S1;
#pragma omp for
for (i=0;i<n;++i)
  S2;
```

(a)

```
#pragma omp for
for (i=0;i<n;++i){
  S1;
  #pragma omp barrier
  S2; }
```

(b)

```
while (cond) {
#pragma omp parallel
{
 #pragma omp for
 for (i=0;i<n;++i)
   S1;
 #pragma omp for
 for (i=0;i<n;++i)
  S2; } }
```

(c)

```
#pragma omp parallel
{
#pragma omp for
for (i=0;i<n;++i)
 while (cond) {
   S1;
   #pragma omp barrier
   S2; } }
```

(d)

Figure 14: (a) and (b) (and, similarly (c) and (d)) encode different program logics.

5 DISCUSSION

We now present a brief discussion on the expressiveness in our proposed extension UW-OpenMP. Depending on the specific problem under consideration, the intuitive mechanism to encode the solution may vary. Consider two typical solutions: i) Create `n` parallel tasks to execute `S1`; wait till all the tasks are completed; create `n` parallel tasks to execute `S2`. ii) Create `n` parallel tasks to compute `S1`, followed by `S2`, and ensure that each task waits for each other, after executing `S1`. Depending on the particular problem under consideration the programmer may find it convenient to encode the program logic using the first solution or the second. Unlike OM-OpenMP, where only the first solution can be coded (Figure 14a), UW-OpenMP allows the encoding of both the solutions (Figure 14a, and Figure 14b).

Similarly, consider two solutions typically applicable in many iterative computations (e.g., iterated averaging [12], Jacobi kernels from the polybench suite [28]): i) Repeat the following till convergence: in each iteration create `n` tasks to execute `S1`; wait till all the tasks are completed; and then create `n` tasks to execute `S2`; wait till all the tasks are completed. ii) Create `n` tasks, where each task executes the following code till convergence: execute `S1` followed by `S2`, and ensure that the tasks wait for each other after every execution of S_i (lock step synchrony). These two solutions are encoded in Figure 14c and Figure 14d, respectively. As has been argued in Section 1, unlike OM-OpenMP, where only the first solution can be coded (Figure 14c), UW-OpenMP allows the coding of both the solutions (Figure 14c, and Figure 14d).

In general, we see that UW-OpenMP is more expressive than OM-OpenMP, and gives the programmer more choices to encode the program logic.

6 IMPLEMENTATION AND EVALUATION

We implemented our proposed techniques as an AST to AST transformation in the ROSE compiler framework [16], which supports OpenMP 3.0 specifications. It takes as input UW-OpenMP programs and outputs equivalent OM-OpenMP code. We use the GCC 4.4 compiler to compile any of these OpenMP programs. To understand the impact of our transformations on varying hardware configurations, we conducted experiments on two different machines: an Intel 16 core system (two E5-2670 processors, 64GB RAM, hyper threading disabled), and an AMD 64 core system (four AMD 6376 processors, 512GB RAM, no hyper threading). We found that the compilation time overheads were negligible.

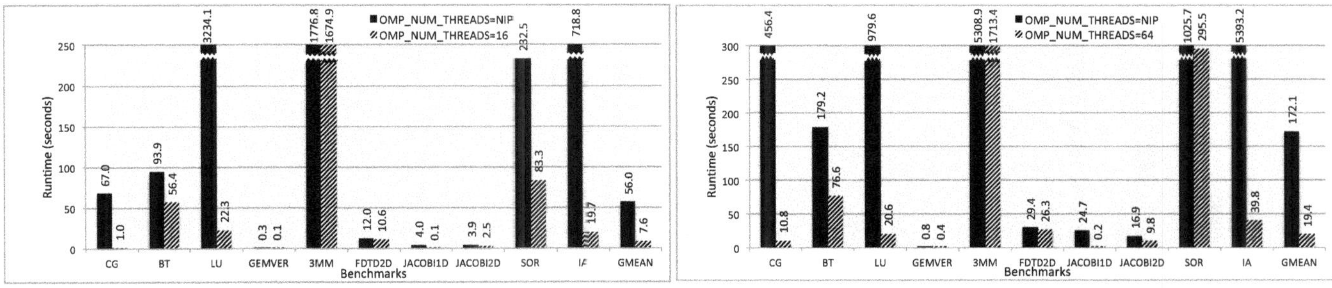

(a) 16 core Intel system, #H/W cores = 16. (b) 64 core AMD system, #H/W cores = 64.

Figure 16: Performance comparison of the input UW-OpenMP code (executed by setting OMP_NUM_THREADS to NIP) with the translated code (executed by setting OMP_NUM_THREADS to #cores).

	Bench	Source	#LOC			Input class
			UW	OMP	%less	and size
1	CG	NPB [29]	851	868	1.2	A=14k
2	BT	NPB [29]	3607	3616	0.2	B=102
3	LU	NPB [29]	3470	3481	0.3	B=102
4	GEMVER	PB [28]	177	181	2.2	L=8000
5	3MM	PB [28]	100	102	1.96	EL=8000
6	FDTD2D	PB [28]	152	154	1.2	EL=4000
7	JACOBI1D	PB [28]	116	117	0.8	ST=10000
8	JACOBI2D	PB [28]	123	124	0.8	EL=4000
9	SOR	[30]	75	77	2.6	3000
10	IA	[12]	78	80	2.5	500

Figure 15: Characteristics of the benchmark kernels.

For our evaluation, we first created UW-OpenMP versions (UW) of ten popular benchmark kernels (see Figure 15). This involved, parallelizing five kernels (3MM, GEMVER, FDTD2D, JACOBI1D and JACOBI2D) from the PolyBench [28] suite (to UW-OpenMP), rewriting CG, BT, LU and SOR in UW-OpenMP, and designing a standalone kernel for IA (based on [12]). One common feature of all these kernels is that each kernel contains at least one parallel-for-loop with at least one nested barrier within; in case of IA, JACOBI1D, and JACOBI2D the barrier is nested inside a serial loop, which in turn is nested inside the parallel-for-loop. For all of the ten kernels, we also considered their equivalent OM-OpenMP variants (OMP). The main difference between these two versions is the way in which parallelism is expressed in the programs (see Section 5).

Since the OpenMP versions distribute the code to perform certain coherent computation across multiple parallel-for-loops, it led to codes that are lengthy (marginally higher – around 1-17 lines) and arguably more complex (less readable – related parts of the parallel-for-loop are not together). For NPB and PolyBench (PB) kernels, we chose the largest class of input for which we could run the kernels. In case of SOR and IA, we chose input sizes such that the code generated by our transformation technique (from the input UW-OpenMP kernels) took at least a few tens of seconds (on the Intel system, by setting the environment variable OMP_NUM_THREADS to 16). In all these ten kernels the input size also matches the number of iterations of the main parallel-for-loop (abbreviated as NIP).

The first part of our evaluation is to address a naive argument that instead of following the elaborate translation scheme, we could let the programmer write programs in UW-OpenMP and we just set the OMP_NUM_THREADS to NIP at runtime (guarantees a consistent behavior). Figure 16 presents a comparison of the input UW-OpenMP code (executed by setting OMP_NUM_THREADS = NIP) and the translated code (executed by setting OMP_NUM_THREADS = #cores).

Figure 16a shows that on the Intel system, the execution times of our translated code are clearly lower than that of the UW-OpenMP code; a geometric mean % difference of $100\times(1-\frac{7.6}{56.0}) = 86.4\%$. The exact difference for any particular benchmark depends on the value of NIP and the work done in each iteration. Figure 16b shows

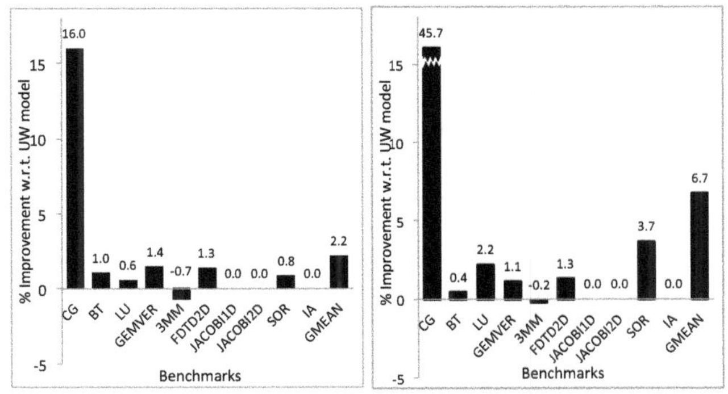

(a) 16 core Intel system. (b) 64 core AMD system.

Figure 17: Performance comparison of the generated and input code, both executed by setting OMP_NUM_THREADS=NIP.

the corresponding comparison on the 64 core AMD system. On the AMD system the geometric mean % difference is 88.7%.

This behavior is consistent with the common knowledge that setting OMP_NUM_THREADS to a large number will lead to significant performance degradation. And we show that use of our proposed scheme is definitely better than using such a naive scheme.

To explain the impact of the overheads resulting from our generated code, Figure 17 shows the comparison of the performance of the generated code (α) and the input code (β), both executed by setting OMP_NUM_THREADS set to NIP. Figure 17a shows the performance improvement on the 16 core Intel system (% improvement = $100\times$(1 - exec time of α / exec time of β). Except for 3MM, it can be seen that most of our generated codes ran faster than the input codes, even though OMP_NUM_THREADS was set to NIP. This indicates that the effects of the overheads is eclipsed by the proposed optimizations. Interestingly, in case of 3MM the performance gains actually show a dip due to some of the overheads introduced by our transformations. Overall, we observe that the impact of the overheads in our proposed transformation is more than nullified by the optimizations discussed in Section 4. We note that in case of the 64 core AMD system (Figure 17b), the performance of our generated code is similar to that seen on the 16 core Intel system.

Effect of the Optimizations: We studied the effect of the proposed optimizations (Section 4) on the generated code. In this regard, we invoked our transformation phase, with and without the optimizations, on each of the benchmark kernels.

Figure 18a shows the effect of the optimizations on the Intel system: the gains varied between 1.2% (CG) to 40.6% (IA), and geometric mean gain = 11.7%. The significant gains in IA and JACOBI1D are due to the optimizations which reduced the number of redundant barriers. The gains due to optimizations on the AMD system (Figure 18b) are similar to the ones shown in Figure 18a: the gains varied between 2.2% (3MM) to 74.9% (IA), and geomet-

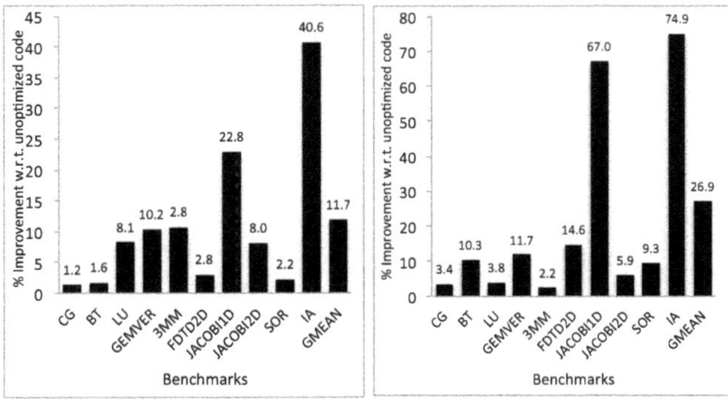

(a) Intel system, #cores=16. (b) AMD system, #cores=64.

Figure 18: Comparison of unoptimized and optimized codes (both executed by setting `OMP_NUM_THREADS` = #cores).

ric mean gain = 26.9%. Note that the gains on the AMD system are a bit more pronounced because of the increased number of cores.

Impact of code specialization: This optimization is applicable only when `OMP_NUM_THREADS`=number of iterations of the main parallel-for-loop, that has a while loop. For the evaluation shown in Figure 17, code specialization was applicable for JACOBI1D, JACOBI2D and IA. The percentage improvement varied between 51-91% on the AMD system and 43-65% on the Intel system.

7 CONCLUSION AND FUTURE WORK

In this paper, we propose UW-OpenMP (an extension to OpenMP) that allows the placement of barriers anywhere inside the OpenMP work-sharing constructs (parallel-for-loop and parallel-sections), and helps the programmer to realize synchronization among the different parallel tasks (instead of the workers), which is arguably a natural way to express parallel algorithms. Our proposed method results in concise and simpler programs, without compromising on the efficiency resulting from the underlying team of workers model of OpenMP. We validate the same by presenting an evaluation on two different hardware systems.

Extending UW-OpenMP to support OpenMP 3.0 [5] tasks (defined using `#pragma omp task`) would be an interesting future work. Further, extending UW-OpenMP to guarantee deadlock freedom would be another interesting challenge.

Acknowledgments: The authors would like to acknowledge Indu K, Aman Nougrahiya, Manas Thakur, and Jyothi Krishna V S for their valuable comments on an initial draft of this manuscript. We also thank Babu Viswanath (@ IIT Madras) and Dave Strenski (@ Cray Inc) for making available the Cray based compiler tool chains for our experiments. This research is partially supported by the New Faculty Seed Grant, funded by IIT Madras CSE/11-12/567/NFSC/NANV, DAE research grant CSE/13-14/139/BRNS/NANV and DST Fasttrack grant CSE/13-14/140/DSTX/NANV.

8 References

[1] P. Charles, C. Grothoff, V. Saraswat, C. Donawa, A. Kielstra, K. Ebcioglu, C. von Praun, and V. Sarkar. X10: An Object-oriented Approach to Non-uniform Cluster Computing. In *OOPSLA*, pages 519–538. ACM, 2005.

[2] V. Cavé, J. Zhao, J. Shirako, and V. Sarkar. Habanero-Java: The New Adventures of Old X10. In *PPPJ*, pages 51–61, 2011.

[3] Cray Inc. The Chapel Language Specification. Technical report, Feb 2013. http://chapel.cray.com.

[4] Intel Cilk Plus. https://www.cilkplus.org/.

[5] OpenMP Application Program Interface, Version 4.0. http://www.openmp.org/mp-documents/OpenMP4.0.0.pdf.

[6] K. Alan. Parallel Java: A Unified API for Shared Memory and Cluster Parallel Programming in 100% Java. In *IPDPS*, pages 1–8, 2007.

[7] J. M. Bull and M. E. Kambites. JOMP-an OpenMP-like Interface for Java. In *Java Grande*, pages 44–53. ACM, 2000.

[8] GCC Compiler. https://gcc.gnu.org/.

[9] CRAY CC Compiler. https://www.nersc.gov/users/software/compilers/.

[10] OpenMP C/C++ Language Extensions in Clang/LLVM Compiler. http://clang-omp.github.io/.

[11] ICC Compiler. https://software.intel.com/en-us/c-compilers.

[12] S. Deitz. A Comparison of a 1D Stencil Code in Co-Array Fortran, Unified Parallel C, X10, and Chapel. In *IDRIS*, 2010. http://chapel.cray.com/presentations/Stencil1D.pdf.

[13] J. Shirako, J. Zhao, V. K. Nandivada, and V. Sarkar. Chunking Parallel Loops in the Presence of Synchronization. In *ICS*, pages 181–192. ACM, 2009.

[14] OpenMP discussion forum. http://openmp.org/forum/viewtopic.php?f=3&t=945/.

[15] K. Kennedy and J. R. Allen. *Optimizing Compilers for Modern Architectures: A Dependence-based Approach.* Morgan Kaufmann Publishers Inc., 2002.

[16] D. J. Quinlan. ROSE: Compiler Support for Object-Oriented Frameworks. *Parallel Proc. Letters*, 10(2/3):215–226, 2000.

[17] J. Shirako, K. Sharma, and V. Sarkar. Unifying Barrier and Point-to-point Synchronization in OpenMP with Phasers. In *IWOMP*, pages 122–137. Springer-Verlag, 2011.

[18] V. K. Nandivada, J. Shirako, J. Zhao, and V. Sarkar. A Transformation Framework for Optimizing Task-Parallel Programs. *ACM Trans. Program. Lang. Syst.*, 35(1):3:1–3:48, April 2013.

[19] A. Nicolau, G. Li, A. V. Veidenbaum, and A. Kejariwal. Synchronization Optimizations for Efficient Execution on Multi-cores. In *ICS*, pages 169–180. ACM, 2009.

[20] C. Tseng. Compiler Optimizations for Eliminating Barrier Synchronization. In *PPoPP*, pages 144–155. ACM, 1995.

[21] S. Satoh, K. Kusano, and M. Sato. Compiler Optimization Techniques for OpenMP Programs. *Sci. Program.*, pages 131–142, 2001.

[22] G. Bronevetsky and B. R. de Supinski. Complete Formal Specification of the OpenMP Memory Model. *Int. J. Parallel Program.*, 35(4):335–392, August 2007.

[23] J. P. Hoeflinger and B. R. De Supinski. The OpenMP Memory Model. In *IWOMP*, pages 167–177, 2008.

[24] S. S. Muchnick. *Advanced Compiler Design and Implementation*. Morgan Kaufmann, 1997.

[25] A. Aiken and D. Gay. Barrier inference. In *POPL*, pages 342–354, 1998.

[26] S. Narayanasamy, Z. Wang, J. Tigani, A. Edwards, and B. Calder. Automatically Classifying Benign and Harmful Data Races Using Replay Analysis. In *PLDI*, pages 22–31. ACM, 2007.

[27] H. Boehm. How to Miscompile Programs with "Benign" Data Races. HotPar. USENIX Association, 2011.

[28] PolyBench/C Suite. http://www.cs.ucla.edu/ pouchet/software/polybench/.

[29] NAS Parallel Benchmarks. http://www.nas.nasa.gov/publications/npb.html.

[30] R. K. Karmani, N. Chen, B. Su, A. Shali, and R. Johnson. Barrier Synchronization Pattern. In *ParaPLOP*, 2009.

Exploiting Process Imbalance to Improve MPI Collective Operations in Hierarchical Systems

Benjamin S. Parsons
Purdue University*
West Lafayette, IN
bsparson@purdue.edu

Viajy S. Pai
Purdue University†
West Lafayette, IN
vpai@purdue.edu

ABSTRACT

This work improves the performance of MPI collective communication operations in the presence of imbalanced process arrival times. High performance collective communications are crucial for the performance and scalability of applications, and imbalanced process arrival times are common in these applications. A micro-benchmark is used to investigate the nature of process imbalance with perfectly balanced workloads, and understand the nature of inter- versus intra-node imbalance. These insights are then used to develop imbalance-tolerant reduction, broadcast, and all-to-all algorithms, which minimize the synchronization delay observed by early arriving processes. These algorithms have been implemented and tested on a Cray XE6 using up to 32k cores with varying buffer sizes and levels of imbalance. Results show speedups over MPICH averaging 18.9x for reduce, 5.3x for broadcast, and 6.9x for all-to-all in the presence of high, but not unreasonable, imbalance.

1. INTRODUCTION

Reducing the latency of collective communications is an important consideration for maximizing the performance of MPI systems moving into the exascale era [4]. Collective communications involve all processes in a system, and have been shown to suffer from scalability problems [18].

As system architecture has changed and multicore processors have become the standard for clusters, optimizing collective communications to target these hierarchical architectures has become a major research focus. Algorithms have been developed that utilize shared memory to optimize several collectives [10, 17, 8, 13, 9]. These algorithms can provide large speedups over their traditional counterparts, but do not address the issue of process imbalance, which has specifically been identified as an area of improvement for MPI on exascale machines [4].

*Current affiliation: USACE Engineer Research and Development Center (ERDC)

†Current affiliation: Google Inc.

ICS'15, June 8–11, 2015, Newport Beach, CA, USA.

ACM 978-1-4503-3559-1/15/06 ...$15.00.
DOI: http://dx.doi.org/10.1145/2751205.2751242.

Faraj et al. demonstrate that distributed memory systems suffer from large process imbalance, relative to collective latency, even with balanced applications [6]. This imbalance creates large synchronization delays for collective communications.

The first contribution of our work is a study of process imbalance, revealing the nature of the imbalance in more detail than past works. The imbalance is examined on an inter- and intra-node level to understand how this imbalance impacts hierarchical collectives. This understanding of the arrival pattern is then used to develop imbalance-tolerant hierarchical algorithms. Because of the large speedup provided by hierarchical collectives, they are a natural starting point for imbalance-tolerant collectives. Reduce, broadcast, and all-to-all are chosen for optimization because they represent all-to-one, one-to-all, and all-to-all communication patterns. Expanding the principles of these algorithms to other collectives would be straightforward.

The reduction and broadcast algorithms utilize a novel method known as *dynamic leader selection* to opportunistically select each node leader based on the imbalance pattern at every invocation of a collective. This method allows the early arriving processes to perform as much communication as possible before the later processes arrive. The all-to-all algorithm utilizes multiple senders to avoid delays from late arriving leaders, and utilizes *opportunistic message fragmentation* to pre-send data from early arriving processes, without delaying for later ones.

These algorithms are tested on a Cray XE6 running up to 32k cores and show speedups over the corresponding MPICH algorithms of 18.9x for reduce, 5.3x for broadcast, and 6.9x for all-to-all when averaged across all buffer sizes, levels of imbalance, and number of processes. These algorithms also outperform the default algorithms on the Cray system, with speedups averaging 35x for reduce, 5.3x for broadcast, and 2.1x for all-to-all.

The following section will explain the background regarding process imbalance and MPI collective operations, including prior work in the area. While MPI collectives have been well studied, only a few works have considered imbalanced process arrival patterns. Section 3 will investigate process imbalance on hierarchical systems, giving background information on imbalance as well as measurements from our system. Using this information Section 4 will describe several algorithms designed operate in the presence of imbalanced process arrival. Then Section 5 will outline the test system with Section 6 providing results on the developed algorithms.

2. BACKGROUND

Several works have looked to optimize collective communications on hierarchical systems without taking process imbalance into account [10, 17, 8, 13, 9]. These works develop algorithms that utilize fast shared memory within a node to reduce communication latency. These algorithms provide high speedups and are well positioned to take advantage of the increasing numbers of cores per node. Because of the clear advantage of these algorithms they will serve as a basis for our imbalance-tolerant algorithms.

Mamidala et al. was one of the first works to create MPI collective routines that performed well in the presence of process imbalance [11]. This work created Barrier and Allreduce algorithms for Infiniband using a binomial tree to collect the information, and a hardware multi-cast to disseminate it. An adaptive version of both algorithms exists to deal with process imbalance. In this algorithm the root holds a token, but can pass the token to an adjacent process in the tree, moving the root closer the slowest process. The root, which is ideally the last process to arrive, is then responsible for performing the hardware multi-cast.

Faraj et al. produce a comprehensive study that investigated imbalance in distributed memory systems [6]. This work introduced several key ideas in the study of process imbalance, including the idea of the process arrival pattern and delay factor, terms that will be described in Section 3. The process arrival patterns of several macro benchmarks were studied on two machines, showing that the synchronization latency of a collective could often outweigh the communication latency of that collective. This work also created a micro benchmark that produced an *imbalanced* process arrival pattern with a *balanced* loop of array operations. This showed that the imbalanced arrival was not due to the network or any specialized libraries, but could be created with a *balanced* program. A variation of the micro benchmark will be used in this work as well, and is given in Listing 1.

Faraj et al. found that in the macro benchmarks the imbalance of a particular collective remained temporally correlated, and proposed a scheme that enabled them to change collective algorithms for future iterations based on the imbalance of past calls. Using the STAR-MPI framework, Faraj et al analyzed the performance of a variety of collectives when called with varying imbalance patterns. They found that particular collectives were more or less effective based on the amount of imbalance, as well as the message size. STAR-MPI's run-time system was modified to take the imbalance pattern of a particular call-site into account when choosing a collective, and use that as a criteria for selecting a collective algorithm [7].

Patarasuk and Yaun continued this work and developed an efficient broadcast algorithm when used with an imbalanced arrival pattern [14]. This algorithm used control messages to notify the root when other processes had arrived at the collective. If multiple processes arrive simultaneously the root directs one of the processes to forward the data to the rest of the sub-group. This helps avoid serialization at the root if multiple processes arrive simultaneously.

Qian and Afsahi created process arrival pattern aware all-to-all and allgather algorithms for RDMA over Infiniband [15, 16]. They use direct all-to-all and allgather algorithms, where each process directly communicates its data to one other process. This makes all phases of communication independent from one another. In order to notify one process of another's arrival, the RDMA control registers are monitored, so no additional messages need to be sent. The direct algorithms then simply schedule their RDMA accesses to ensure that they are communicating with processes that have already arrived at the collective. This method works well for these direct algorithms, but would require additional messages if not using the Infiniband RDMA.

While these past works achieve good performance in the presence of imbalance, they do not build on the hierarchical algorithms mentioned in the first paragraph. This is a major disadvantage on modern systems with hierarchical algorithms becoming standard. Any imbalance tolerant algorithms will need to build on hierarchical collectives, as the algorithms developed in this paper will. Several works also utilized Infiniband specific features [15, 16, 11]. These algorithms are not general to any MPI system, and cannot be evaluate on our test platform. The algorithms developed in this paper will utilize only MPI primitives, and thus be portable.

3. PROCESS IMBALANCE

Our study of process imbalance will utilize a micro-benchmark given in Listing 1. Originally proposed by Faraj et al., our version follows Patarasuk and Yaun utilizing a barrier before the two inner loops [6, 14]. This prevents the collective algorithms from propagating process imbalance between iterations. While this produces smaller imbalance than seen in applications, but is useful for allowing the imbalance to manifest in a reliable manner. This micro-benchmark can also be thought of as the minimum imbalance that programs will reasonably see, if their synchronization points are separated in time by an amount equal to the run time of the micro-benchmark. The benchmark has each process performing an equal amount of work on private arrays. Actual applications demonstrate more complex behavior, with network IO, library calls, and memory contention all contributing to the imbalance.

Listing 1: Micro-Benchmark, note that the work load is balanced for all processes

```
for (i=0; i < test_iters; i++){
  MPI_Barrier(MPI_COMM_WORLD);
  for(m=0; m<xtime; m++){
    for (k=1; k <999; k++){
      a[k] = b[k+1] - a[k-1] * 2;
    }
  }
  //Take PAP timing here
  arrival[i] = MPI_Wtime();
  //If evaluating with imbalance
  MPI_Collective()
}
```

The imbalance can be described with two metrics, the *average* and *worst-case* imbalance. The worst-case imbalance is the difference in time between the earliest arriving process and the latest, $ArrivalTime_{last} - ArrivalTime_{first}$. The average imbalance is the average time difference between any process arrival time and the mean arrival time, for P processes: $\frac{\sum_{i=0}^{P} |ArrivalTime_i - \overline{ArrivalTime}|}{P}$.

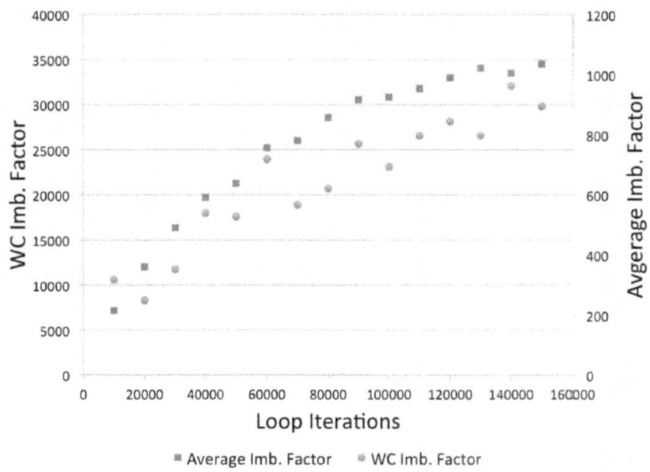

Figure 1: The average and worst-case imbalance times for the micro-benchmark on a Cray XE6 running 8192 cores

These metrics can also be described in relation to network speed with the *imbalance factor*. This is the original metric, divided by the minimum system latency for an MPI message ($2.5\mu S$ on our system). This represents the *theoretical maximum* number of *minimum length* MPI messages that can be sent within that time, and gives an idea of the magnitude of the imbalance relative to the network latency.

Figure 1 shows the worst-case and average imbalance factors for the micro-benchmark when run on a Cray XE6 with 8192 processes. The amount of time that the micro-benchmark runs is regulated by the *xtime* variable. This variable controls the number of iterations for the outer loop in the micro-benchmark. It is important to note that the *xtime* is the same for all processes, and is not the source of the imbalance. In the results section this micro-benchmark will be used to generate imbalance for testing imbalance-tolerant algorithms. The results will specify imbalance as the number of loop iterations, because it is a proxy for process imbalance. These results confirm the imbalance seen by Faraj et al., which is quite high for a balanced benchmark [6].

Figure 2 shows the heat map of the normalized process arrival times for 2048 processes run on a Cray XE6 with 32 core nodes. It can be seen that the imbalance pattern is random between nodes and within nodes. The imbalance is also distributed among all processes, with no particular process lagging from an issue such as unbalanced OS interference. Figure 3 shows the histogram of the arrival times, normalized to each node's average arrival time. This pattern shows that most processes arrive in a group, with a longer tail of late arrivals. This histogram is produced with an *xtime* value of 40000. Smaller values produce a histogram with a similar shape, but with a shorter tail and higher peak, and larger values produce a similar shape with a longer tail and shorter peak.

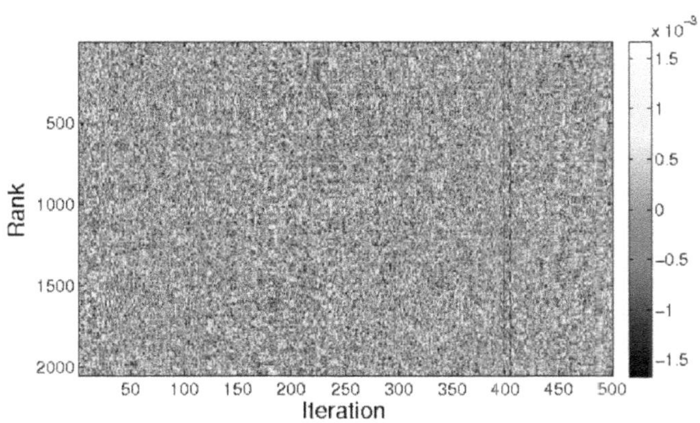

Figure 2: Normalized arrival times on a Cray XE6 running 2048 cores

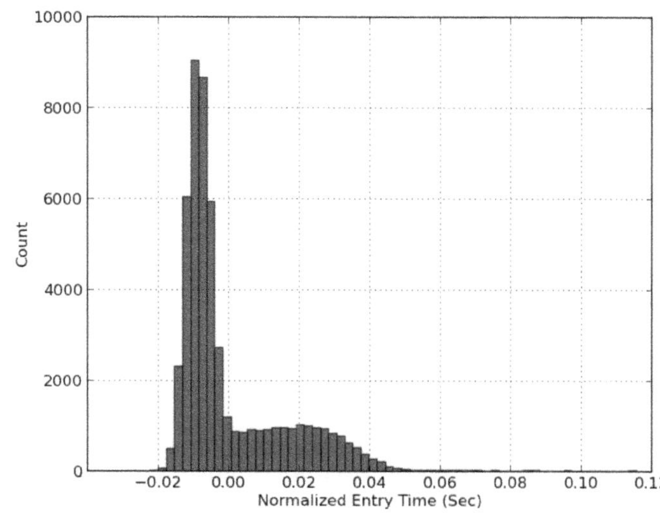

Figure 3: Normalized intra-node arrival time on a Cray XE6, 40k imbalance

This imbalance pattern is important to understand when designing imbalance-tolerant collective algorithms. The observation that processes on the *same node* are just as likely to be imbalanced as processes on *other nodes* is a new and unintuitive observation. This means that algorithms must deal with intra- and inter-node imbalance. If one process was routinely late, this history could be used to shape the communication algorithms for future invocations, but algorithms must tolerate any process arriving late.

This also means that our imbalance-tolerant algorithms can focus on minimizing the average time processes spend in a collective, instead of being forced to focus on the latency of the slowest process. Due to this, our results will measure the average time that processes spend in the collective, instead of the latency of any given process.

In order to understand the cause of the imbalance, performance counters were monitored for each process during the execution of the micro-benchmark using PAPI [12]. Counters included events such as hardware interrupts, cache misses, stall cycles, and the number of kernel instructions. The counter values were then compared to the arrival time of the process, in an attempt to find a correlation between a particular counter and the process arrival time. Figure 4 demonstrates this, showing the number of hardware interrupts that occurred for each process during a run of the micro-benchmark, versus the normalized arrival time for the process. None of the counters produced any clear correlation. If a specific event was the cause of the imbalance, i.e. the number of kernel instructions, it could be possible

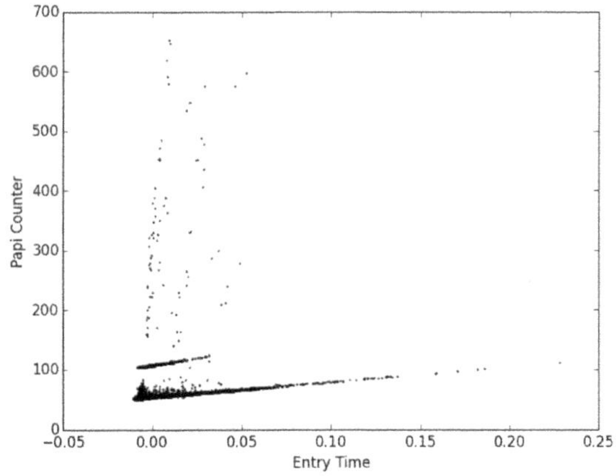

Figure 4: Hardware interrupts vs normalized arrival time on a Cray XE6, 40k imbalance

to distribute that event's impact among all processes. Instead the imbalance seems to be caused by multiple system components, with no direct correlation to any one.

4. ALGORITHMS

The following section outlines several algorithms that are designed to perform well in the presence of imbalance. The characteristic of the imbalance is important in shaping the design of these algorithms. Because processes arrive at a given call site in a random order, there is no way to predict the arrival pattern from one collective invocation to another. If predictable early or late arrivers were known from past imbalance patterns, these algorithms would be designed to take advantage of that.

The principle of these imbalance-aware algorithms is to tolerate imbalance by letting early arriving processes communicate before the later ones arrive, and leave the collective call site as soon as possible. The goal is to reduce the mean time all processes spend in the collective, minimizing the impact of the call.

4.1 Reduction

This section will discuss our novel imbalance-tolerant algorithm as well as several intermediate variations that will be evaluated. The imbalance-aware reduction algorithm is based on the binomial tree algorithm from MPICH [1]. This algorithm was chosen because it had the best performance on our system for a wide range of message sizes, and in its default form does well in the presence of process imbalance. In MPICH, a reduce-scatter followed by a gather is the default for large messages, but this creates an all-to-all data dependency that is not necessary, and our tests show the performance suffered in the presence of imbalance. The fan-in communication pattern of the binomial tree has a reduced number of processes that depend on data from one another.

The MPICH binomial tree algorithm is also evaluated in a hierarchical fashion, with shared memory buffers used for intra-node communication and a single leader performing the inter-node communication. The intra and inter-node communications are separated with a node-level barrier. This naive implementation performs well with no imbalance, using the default optimized MPI_Barrier, instead of implementing shared memory structures.

The intra-node barrier in the naive implementation adds a temporal dependency between every process on a node, when the dependency is really only needed between the leader and all other processes. This extra dependency leads to unnecessary synchronization in the presence of imbalance. To reduce this, an intra-node optimized binomial tree algorithm is developed. This version uses the binomial tree pattern between nodes and optimized intra-node communication. A single buffer version is evaluated to utilize a shared memory buffer protected by locks, with large buffer sizes utilizing multiple locks to allow for a parallel reduction. To avoid contention a multiple buffer version is also evaluated, that utilizes multiple shared memory buffers for intermediate reductions. Both versions allow early arriving processes to reduce their data into the buffer and exit the collective without waiting for later arriving processes. Further discussion will reference the multi-buffer version, but the performance difference was minimal when compared to the overall latency of the collective, which is dominated by inter-node communication. Our implementation does not preserve the order of operations in order to reduce the size of the shared memory buffers, but the order could be maintained by utilizing multiple buffers to store the data until the leader process performs the reduction in order.

In order to avoid delays while the node leader waits for all processes on a node, a method called *dynamic leader selection* is employed. When a process enters the collective, its buffer is immediately reduced into the shared memory buffer. Unless the process is the root or the last process to arrive on its node, it can exit the collective. The last process per node and the root are responsible for the inter-node communication. This results in lower synchronization cost than traditional hierarchical collectives that use fixed leaders, which must block waiting for slow processes. The dynamic leaders, due to control messages used to discover other leaders, incur extra overhead. The node-to-node communication pattern remains the same as static leaders, a binomial tree in this case, but at each invocation a different set of leaders performs the reduction. This algorithm is given in Figure 5.

The control messages are needed for the parent nodes to identify the node leader on the child nodes, with parent and child referring to the position in the binomial tree. Theses algorithms are implemented entirely on MPI primitives, requiring the leader on the child node to identify a Rank for the MPI_Send. If an MPI implementation were to im-

```
function
    LOCAL_REDUCE(Shared_Buff, Private_Buff)
    if (Last_Process or Root) then
        SEND_ID_MESG(Children)
        for all (children) do
            RECV(Temp_Buff)
            LOCAL_REDUCE(Shared_Buff, Temp_Buff)
        end for
        RECV(Parent_ID_Mesg)
        SEND(Shared_Buff)
        CANCEL(Extra_ID_Mesgs)
    end if
end function
```

Figure 5: Dynamic leader reduction algorithm, outputs in bold

```
function
    if (First_Process or Root) then
        if (!Root) then
            SEND_ID_MESG(Parent)
            RECV(Shared_Buff)
        end if
        for all (children) do
            RECV(Child_ID_Mesg)
            SEND(Shared_Buff)
        end for
    else
        RECV(Child_ID_Mesg) //Unused message
    end if
    WAIT_FOR(Shared_Buff_Valid)
    MEM_COPY(Shared_Buff, Private_Buff)
end function
```

Figure 6: Dynamic leader broadcast algorithm, outputs in bold

plement these algorithms at a lower level, special primitives could be envisioned that send a message to a particular node, and allow any process on that node to match the send. The leaders of the parent nodes do not suffer this problem, thanks to MPI_ANY_SOURCE, which allows a receive to match a send from an unknown source.

Maintaining the binomial tree pattern between nodes is done to maintain performance under low imbalance situations, but leaves an unnecessary dependency between non-root nodes. This could be eliminated using a serial inter-node reduction. While this would perform well in high imbalance cases it would lead to contention at the root when the imbalance is low.

Figure 5 uses MPI_Cancel calls to remove extra control messages from the system, which is the version is evaluated in the results section. The MPI_Cancel calls can be eliminated by leaving the control messages unreceived until the next function invocation, at which point they are matched before the collective starts. This version is used in the macro-benchmarks.

The control messages can be eliminated altogether by using the one-sided communication interface. To do this the one-sided communication window is created on top of shared memory, so that any process can access the memory region. Then the dynamic leader uses an MPI_Accumulate to place the data onto the receiving node, and mark a data ready flag. The leader on the receiving node can spin on the flag, because it is in shared memory, without the sender knowing who the receiver is.

4.2 Broadcast

The broadcast algorithm is again based on the binomial tree algorithm from MPICH. MPICH also uses a scatter followed by an allgather for large messages, but this suffers the same drawbacks as the reduce-scatter/gather reduce described in Section 4.1. The binomial tree algorithm is also evaluated in a naive hierarchical fashion using intra-node barriers to separate the inter and intra-node communication. To avoid this unnecessary synchronization an *intra-node optimized* version is evaluated, similar to reduce. This version uses a shared memory structure that tracks which processes have arrived and allows early arriving processes to copy out the data and leave the collective before later arriving processes.

The broadcast algorithm using dynamic leader selection is given in Figure 6. In this collective all processes must wait for the root, which has the potential to incur a high synchronization cost if the root arrives late, which was not a problem for reductions. For all other nodes, the **first** process to arrive at the collective call site on a particular node is selected as the leader, opposite of the reduction algorithm. This allows communication to take place before any of the other processes on a node arrive, moving the data onto nodes faster than would otherwise be possible.

Once the data is received on a given node, then the data is placed into a shared memory buffer. This allows early processes to copy out the data and leave the collective call site before later ones even arrive, reducing the synchronization delay. Unlike the reduction algorithm the extra control messages can be received by the non-leader processes, because these processes arrive after the leader, thus eliminating the need for MPI_Cancel. For this collective the control messages are used in the reverse direction, with child nodes sending ID messages to the parents. This is due to the reverse direction of the data flow, and the need for the parents to have a MPI_Send destination. Like the reduction, these messages could be eliminated with a lower level primitive to send a message to a certain node, or using the one-sided communication interface.

The intra-node potion of the algorithm is simply a memory copy from a single shared memory buffer. A NUMA or architecture optimized version like past hierarchical works was avoided due to potential synchronization delays from late processes. A NUMA optimized version could be created using a per NUMA leader for the intra-node portion of the algorithm, but because the intra-node latency is much less than the inter-node it would have little effect on the total collective latency.

4.3 All-to-All

The imbalance-aware all-to-all algorithm is approached differently than the broadcast and reduce because there is an inherent all-to-all data dependency among the processes. Unlike the prior algorithms, there is complete synchronization so removing excess synchronization is not an option. There is also no opportunity for early arriving processes to exit the collective before late arriving ones enter, no process can exit until all processes have reached the call site.

The starting point for the imbalance-aware algorithm will be the MPICH Isend all-to-all algorithm. This algorithm uses a series on non-blocking sends and receives which send messages starting at the next higher rank. The pairwise-exchange algorithm was also evaluated, but only had better performance on a few test cases. Bruck's algorithm performed better than the Isend algorithm for small messages, but when a hierarchical version of the Isend algorithm was used, the performance difference was eliminated. Bruck's algorithm is a store and forward algorithm that sends data to process $rank + 2^i$ in the *ith* communication round, and therefore maps very well to clusters whose node size is a power of 2, much like the binomial tree algorithm. Because of this Bruck's algorithm does not see the same speedups when used hierarchically.

The imbalance-aware all-to-all algorithms deal with process imbalance in two different ways, one for the imbalanced processes arriving within a node and another for communicating with processes on other nodes. The dynamic leader algorithms used control messages between nodes in order to establish the leader identity. This was found to have a higher overhead for all-to-all due to the increased paths of communication, needing $NumNodes(NumNodes - 1)$ control messages as opposed to $NumNodes - 1$ for the binomial tree. Our experimentation found this overhead to be high enough that sending control messages was not a feasible solution. Instead of using control messages, different processes within a node were statically assigned to communicate with processes on other nodes. If multiple processes on a given node can communicate, having several of those processes arrive late would still allow the others to communicate data early. Only one process from a given node communicates with any other node, so the benefits of message aggregation from hierarchical algorithms is preserved. Figure 7 shows how this method still allows communication with nodes that have late processes. In the actual implementation the senders and receivers are separate processes, to avoid cache contention with the send and receive buffers.

There is also imbalance involving the data being copied into the intra-node shared memory buffers, caused by imbalanced process arrival within a node. With the multi-sender method described above, one process is responsible for sending all the data from its node to another. If all the data is sent in one message, no data can be sent until all processes have arrived. This severely limits the amount of data that can be pre-sent. In order to avoid this limitation we introduce a method called *opportunistic message fragmentation.* When the intra-node processes copy data into the shared memory buffers they mark a flag for each segment of data. These flags are monitored by the sending processes and used to select the largest available blocks of data to send. The following preferences, outlined below, are used to send subsets of the total buffer.

1. Maximum length blocks
   (a) The entire buffer
   (b) A piece of the buffer between blocks that have already been sent or the buffer edge
   (c) Blocks going to the lowest node number higher than sender's
2. Largest available block
   (a) Blocks adjacent to sent blocks or buffer edge
   (b) Blocks going to the lowest node number higher than sender's

These preferences are used to select the largest blocks of available data, and in the event of equal amounts of data, blocks are selected in a way that reduces the fragmentation of the buffer. If multiple blocks fit that criteria the lowest numbered node higher than the sender's node number is chosen. Parameters can also limit the minimum message sizes, to avoid sending many small messages, which in the worse case would revert to the same message pattern as the Isend algorithm.

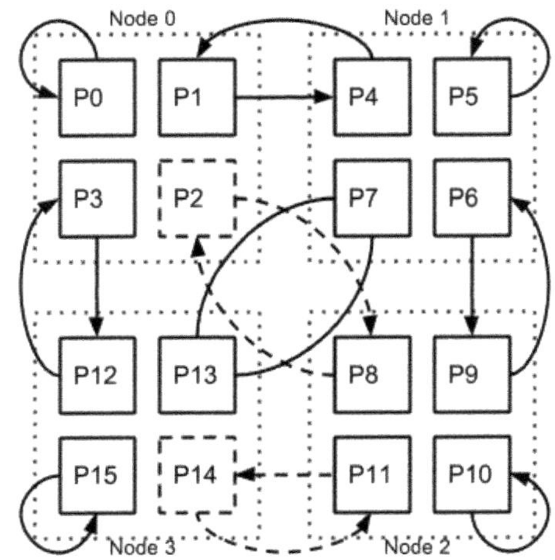

Figure 7: All-to-all communication example, arrows represent messages, dashed processors and arrows represent messages that cannot yet be sent because the process is delayed

5. EXPERIMENTAL TESTBED

All tests were run on a Cray XE6 with a dedicated Cray Gemini network. Each node on the system has two 16 core 2.5 GHz AMD 6200 Opteron processors and 64 GB of DDR3 memory. Jobs are scheduled using PBS Pro 10.4.7. Runs with different job placements seemed to have minimal impact on the results. For all test sizes, multiple iterations were run, varying from fifty to several thousand, depending on the latency of the collective. This ensured that the small-sized tests received an adequate number of iterations for repeatable results, while still making large sized tests feasible.

The Cray-mpich/6.3.0 module was used for all MPI communication. It is the default MPI implementation for the Cray XE6, and is built upon MPICH. MPICH collective algorithms are built on point-to-point operations, so a minimally modified version of the MPICH 3.0.4 source code was run on the Cray system, which is what this paper refers to as the *MPICH* algorithms. Asynchronous communication is enabled for all tests, though it seemed to have a minimal impact on collective latency. It was originally speculated that this feature might help imbalance-unaware collectives communicate before all processes arrived.

The buffer sizes for all results are given as the total buffer size. For broadcast and reduce all input and output buffers are the same size and equal to the message size. For all-to-all the per process message size is the total buffer divided by the number of processes. The smallest buffer size we report for all-to-all tests is the minimum size for each particular number of processes. Integers were used as the data type for all collectives, and the reduction operation was a summation. The results are also analyzed with different levels of imbalance, which is given in units of loop iterations. This is a reference to the micro-benchmark given in Listing 1, and described in Section 3.

In order to measure the process imbalance as well as the latency of collectives, the mpiP profiler was modified to used high-resolution timers to record information about the entry and exit times of all processes [2]. In order to record the imbalance patterns across all processes a globally syn-

Number Cores	Hier. MPICH	Intra-Opt. H. MPICH	Dyn. Leader	D.L. One-Sided
512	0.34	5.67	18.72	23.95
1024	0.34	5.70	20.13	27.08
2048	0.34	5.73	21.13	28.98
4096	0.33	5.67	20.89	30.33
8192	0.34	5.71	20.40	29.11
16384	0.34	5.68	18.21	25.75
32768	0.34	5.66	13.35	22.47

Table 1: Reduction mean latency speedups over Bi-Tree from MPICH, averaged over all buffer sizes and levels of imbalance

chronized clock is needed. Cristian's algorithm was used to compute the local clock offsets, with resynchronization every second to prevent clock drift [5]. To reduce the run-time of the testing program, imbalance was generated and recorded with high-resolution timers. This trace was then used to reproduce the imbalanced arrival with high-resolution sleep calls. The modified profiler showed that this produced identical imbalance as the micro-benchmark, but saved run-time by eliminating the need to run the micro-benchmark to generate imbalance for every collective call.

The test system uses XPMEM to optimize intra-node communication with memory copies. This allows, direct memory copies from one private address space to another, eliminating extra copies. When running the binomial tree algorithm a root of zero is always used. This makes the binomial tree ideally map to the shared memory nodes, because the cores per node is a power of two. The combination of XPMEM and ideal tree mapping results in the point-to-point implementation performing nearly identically to shared memory hierarchical implementations when used without imbalance, explaining the high performance of the MPICH implementations of these two collectives. If the MPICH binomial tree was naively run with a different root, or if the test system did not have highly optimized intra-node point-to-point communication, the latency would be higher.

6. RESULTS

6.1 Reduction

Table 1 gives the speedups for the reduction variations over the MPICH Isend algorithm for various numbers of processes. Figure 8 shows the mean latency of the reduction variations versus the loop iterations used in the micro-benchmarks which is a proxy for the process imbalance, as discussed in Section 3. The hierarchical version of MPICH does worse than the original in the presence of imbalance due to the intra-node barriers between the intra and inter-node communication. This added synchronization causes the drastic increase in latency when the imbalance is greater than zero. Because the synchronization delay is the majority of the total latency, the mean speedup numbers as the cores increase remains similar. Using intra-node optimization to remove these barriers produces speed-ups over the original version.

The dynamic leader version further reduces the latency, more so as the imbalance increases. This shows that the speedup from utilizing the *dynamic leader selection* provides additional improvements over simply optimizing the intra-node portion of the algorithm. The dynamic leader with one-

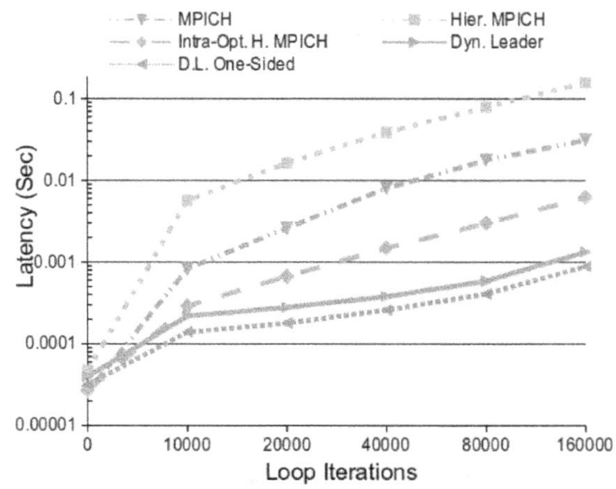

Figure 8: Mean latency for reduce vs loop iterations, 8192 cores, 2048 Byte buffer

Number Cores	Hier. MPICH	Intra-Opt. H. MPICH	Dyn. Leader
512	0.49	1.66	7.53
1024	0.49	1.53	7.12
2048	0.51	1.43	6.15
4096	0.50	1.35	5.34
8192	0.57	1.27	4.72
16384	0.57	1.24	3.64
32768	0.54	1.16	2.52

Table 2: Broadcast mean latency speedups over Bi-Tree from MPICH, averaged over all buffer sizes and levels of imbalance

sided communication version further reduces latency. This version eliminates control messages, but speedups could also be due to difference in the underlying one-sided vs point-to-point implementations.

The default Cray algorithms were omitted from the reduction results. For buffer sizes less than 2048 the results were within 5% of MPICH, and larger buffer sizes showed a slowdown. All tests were run with rank 0 as the root, leading to the binomial tree mapping ideally to the 32 core nodes. If an arbitrary root was used the performance of the MPICH algorithms would be much worse, because it would naively send unnecessary messages across node boundaries. This is discussed further in Section 5.

6.2 Broadcast

The speedups for broadcast over the MPICH algorithm are given in Table 2 and the mean latency for 8192 cores vs the micro-benchmark loop iterations is given in Figure 9. The hierarchical MPICH algorithm again is slower than the default, especially in the presence of imbalance. Like the reduction this is due to the extra synchronization caused by the node-level barriers. Removing these barriers in the intra-node optimized version leads to speedups over the original. Adding the dynamic leader algorithm to these intra-node optimization gives even higher speedup in the presence of imbalance, but causes a slowdown in the zero imbalance case due to the extra control messages. In both cases the speedups are lower when the number of processes increases,

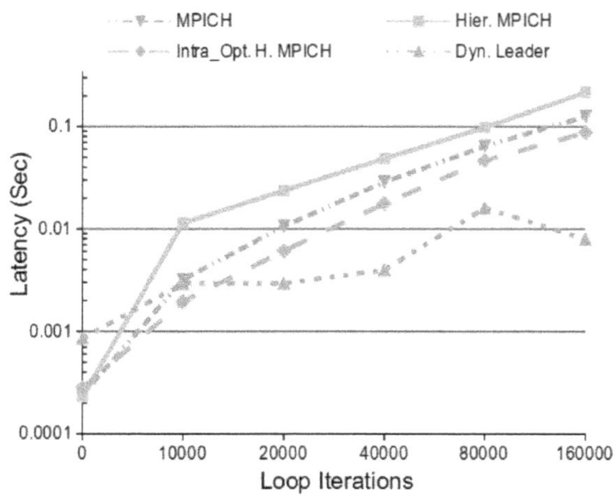

Figure 9: Mean latency for broadcast vs loop iterations, 8192 cores, 32k Byte buffer

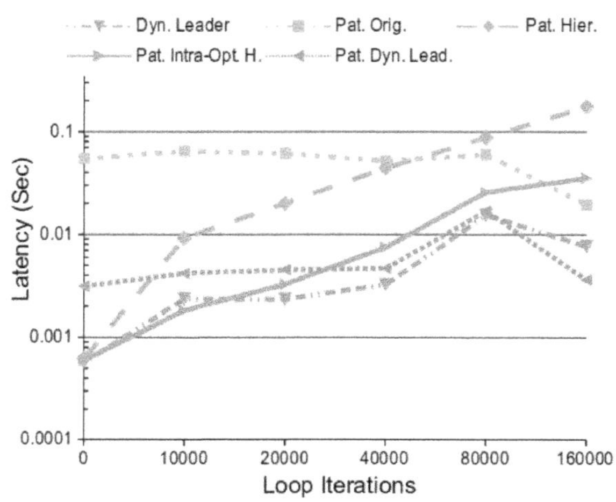

Figure 10: Mean latency for broadcast vs loop iterations, comparing to prior work, 8192 cores, 2k Byte buffer

due to the communication cost increasing while the imbalance remains constant.

A one-sided communication version of the dynamic leader algorithm was tested but performed poorly. It is suspected that the one-sided communication system handles multiple simultaneous messages out of the same node poorly. This would explain why the one-sided version did well for the reduction, since one message is sent from a node at a time. The Cray default algorithms were omitted from these graphs and tables because in all tests the results were within 5% of the MPICH algorithm.

Figure 10 compares the dynamic leader broadcast algorithms to the imbalance-aware broadcast developed by Patarasuk and Yuan discussed in Section 2 [14], as well as some improvements to it. This is the only prior work to develop an algorithm with special network features. This algorithm sends control message to the root, which then responds with the data, or directs other processes to forward the data in the case of simultaneous arrival. *Pat. Original* is our implementation of the original version of this algorithm. It uses the variation with a serial subgroup broadcast, but with the

Number Cores	Cray (default)	MPICH Isend Hier.	Hier. aware
512	1.5	1.5	2.8
1024	1.9	1.8	3.3
2048	3.0	2.1	4.7
4096	2.9	2.4	6.3
8192	4.0	3.6	8.4
16384	4.1	3.7	7.0
32768	10.4	6.7	15.4

Table 3: All-to-all mean latency speedups over MPICH, averaged over all buffer sizes and levels of imbalance

group size limited, in order to prevent complete serialization at low imbalance. It performs poorly for most cases on our large scale system, due to contention at the root, which is eased at higher imbalances. Using the Patarasuk algorithm on top of a hierarchical intra-node algorithm leads to better performance at low contention, but the extra synchronization from the intra-node barrier hurts high imbalance cases, as show by *Pat. Hier.* Using the intra-node optimization helps the high imbalance cases, but further improvement can be had by using the Patarasuk algorithm for the inter-node communication with dynamic leader selection, given as *Pat. Dyn. Lead.* This performs worse than our dynamic leader algorithms, which uses a binomial tree pattern between nodes, at low imbalance. As the imbalance increases the performance gap narrows until the highest imbalance case where the Patarasuk algorithm with dynamic leaders performs the best. This demonstrates how the dynamic leader algorithms can be used with various inter-node algorithms, which is useful in adapting the algorithms to different situations. It also highlights the importance of maintaining the binomial tree communication pattern between the nodes, even though it creates some unnecessary dependencies.

6.3 All-to-All

Table 3 gives the speedups for all-to-all over the MPICH Isend algorithm. Unlike the broadcast and reduce, the hierarchical versions do not produce a slowdown. Due to the all-to-all data dependency of the collective, the intra-node barriers do not add to the synchronization costs of the hierarchical algorithms. The speed-up for the Cray version of the collective is also given. Though the exact implementation is unknown, a store and forward algorithm is used for small messages, and all versions use an *automatically balanced injection* feature. There is no reason to think that this feature could not also be used on our hierarchical aware version.

The hierarchical aware version outperforms the other versions, because of its ability to pre-send data from early arriving processes using *opportunistic message fragmentation.* This is highlighted in Figure 11 which shows the latency of the collective *after* the arrival of the last process, which essentially removes the synchronization delay from the latency. The decreasing latency of the hierarchical aware version as the imbalance increases is caused by the ability to pre-send data from the early arriving processes. With extremely high imbalance, this latency would be equal to the latency of one process (the slowest) sending one message to all others, and receiving one message from all others. It should be noted

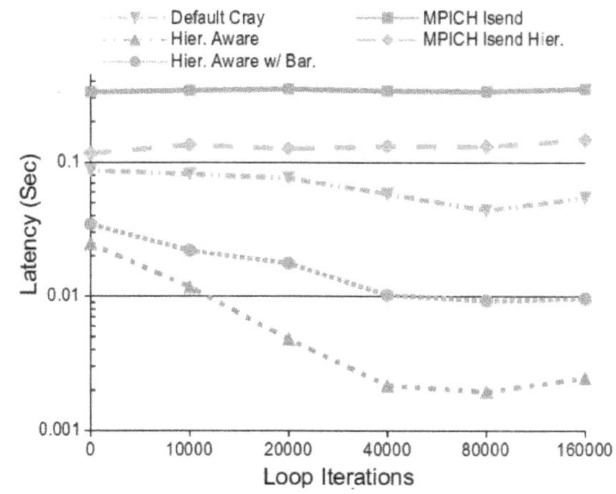

Figure 11: Mean latency after last arriving process for all-to-all vs loop iterations, 8192 cores, 131k Byte buffer

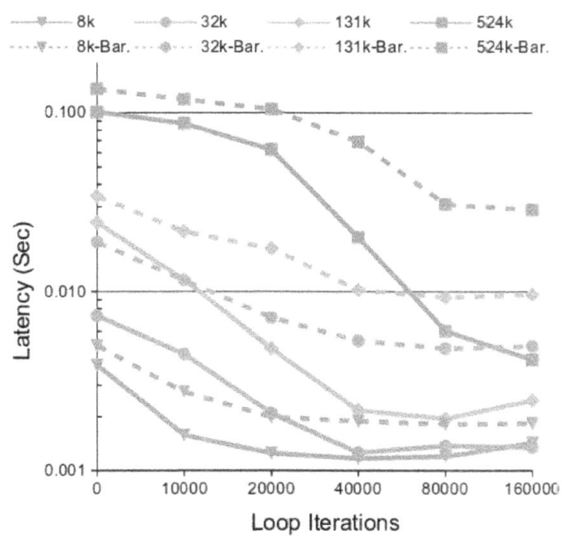

Figure 12: Mean latency after last arriving process vs loop iterations for all-to-all aware and aware with barrier, 8192 cores, multiple buffer sizes

that the speedups given in Table 3 use the entire collective latency, not the latency after the last arriving process.

The hierarchical aware algorithm also produces a speedup in the zero imbalance case. As mentioned in Section 4.3, using multiple senders on the same node provides a speedup due to better network utilization. To isolate this affect the hierarchical aware with barrier version was tested. This version adds a intra-node barrier to prevent the pre-sending of any data, but retains the multiple senders of the hierarchical aware version. Having multiple receivers still provides some means for early arriving nodes to avoid late arriving leaders, but this effect cannot be completely eliminated. Figure 12 show the imbalance-aware version as well as the imbalance aware with barrier version for several buffer sizes over various level of imbalance. In all cases the barrier version prevents the algorithm from pre-sending data, leading the gap in latency as the imbalance increases.

6.4 Macro Benchmarks

One macro benchmark was run for each collective that isolated that collective in a simple application. These tests show that the extra control messages being sent in the dynamic leader algorithm, and the fragmented messages in the all-to-all algorithm do not negatively effect the performance of an application when collectives are being called repeatedly. These benchmarks were chosen to isolate each of the collectives, and do not scale as far as the micro-benchmark tests. For broadcast, an implementation of the Floyd-Warshall all-pairs shortest path algorithm was used, with results given in Table 4. The reduction was tested with a series of inner-products with a rotating root for each iteration. This uses minimal message sizes leading to shorter collective latency, so the overhead from the control messages will be higher in comparison. These results are given in Table 5. All-to-all was tested with the the FT benchmark from the NAS Parallel Benchmark suite [3]. Unfortunately this benchmark switches the processor decomposition as the number of processors increases, leading to a true all-to-all only occurring with smaller numbers of processes. The results in Table 6 are reported for the largest numbers of processes before this switch for several test sizes. The other benchmarks are run on increasing processes until the scaling stops.

Processes	Binomial Tree	Dyn. Leader	Speedup
128	19.1	18.2	1.3
256	10.2	7.9	1.25
512	8.6	6.8	1.1

Table 4: Floyd-Warshall benchmark run-time and speedup

Processes	Binomial Tree	Dyn. Leader	Speedup
256	8.4	8.5	1.0
512	4.5	4.7	0.9
1024	2.5	2.9	0.9
2048	2.1	2.1	1.0
4096	3.4	1.7	2.0
8192	5.8	1.3	4.4

Table 5: Inner product benchmark run-time and speedup

Test	Speed-up
A-128	1.8
B-256	2.0
C-512	1.8

Table 6: FT benchmark speedup, for given test size and number of processes

7. FUTURE SYSTEMS

These algorithms are also well positioned to be effective in future systems. As the number of cores per node increases, the *dynamic leader selection* will have more opportunity to utilize early arriving processes, and need fewer leaders as well as control messages. The *opportunistic message fragmentation* employed by all-to-all will also have more data potentially available for early communication. New high performance systems that utilize intelligent network interfaces to offload communication can also take advantage of these ideas. Fan-in and Fan-out algorithms could utilize the network interface as a persistent leader, so long as careful consideration was taken to ensure minimal dependence on the process arrival pattern. This could allow for the communication of data to and from a node before *any* processes arrive. The all-to-all algorithm could also be employed with the network interface tasked with managing message fragments and pre-sending data. This would remove the need for multiple senders, but also guarantee all other nodes are available to receive message fragments.

8. CONCLUSION

In this work, we offer three major contributions that help exploit process imbalance to improve MPI collective operations in hierarchical systems. Our first contribution is a detailed examination of the nature of process imbalance in a hierarchical system. Using a custom modified profiler and hardware performance counters we describe this imbalance in greater detail than prior works. Our next contribution is developing the method of *dynamic leader selection* to create imbalance-tolerant algorithms for fan-in and fan-out collectives. Finally we introduce the idea of *opportunistic message fragmentation* as a method for pre-sending data in all-to-all collectives. Using these contributions we implement reduce, broadcast, and all-to-all algorithms, which achieve speedups over MPICH of 18.9x, 5.3x, and 6.9x respectively.

9. ACKNOWLEDGMENTS

The authors would like to thank the Information Technology Laboratory of the Army Corps of Engineers' Engineering Research and Development Center. They both granted generous access to their advanced infrastructure as well as aided in its use. Benjamin Parsons is supported by the Science, Mathematics, and Research for Transformation (SMART) Scholarship. This work was supported by the NSF under grants CNS-0751153, CNS-1117726, and OCI-1216809, and the DOE under contract DE-FC02-12ER26104.

10. REFERENCES

[1] MPICH, a high-performance and portable implementation of the MPI. `http://www.mpich.org/`. Accessed 1/2014.

[2] mpiP: Lightweight, scalable MPI profiling. `http://mpip.sourceforge.net/`. Accessed 4/21/2014.

[3] NAS parallel benchmarks. `https://www.nas.nasa.gov/publications/npb.html`. Accessed 4/21/2014.

[4] P. Balaji, D. Buntinas, D. Goodell, W. Gropp, S. Kumar, E. Lusk, R. Thakur, and J. Träff. MPI on a million processors. Lecture Notes in Computer Science. Springer Berlin Heidelberg, 2009.

[5] F. Cristian. Probabilistic clock synchronization. *Distributed Computing*, 3(3):146–158, 1989.

[6] A. Faraj, P. Patarasuk, and X. Yuan. A study of process arrival patterns for MPI collective operations. *International Journal of Parallel Programming*, 36(6):543–570, 2008.

[7] A. Faraj, X. Yuan, and D. Lowenthal. STAR-MPI: Self tuned adaptive routines for MPI collective operations. In *Proceedings of the 20th Annual International Conference on Supercomputing*, ICS '06, pages 199–208, New York, NY, USA, 2006. ACM.

[8] R. Graham, M. Venkata, J. Ladd, P. Shamis, I. Rabinovitz, V. Filipov, and G. Shainer. Cheetah: A framework for scalable hierarchical collective operations. In *Cluster, Cloud and Grid Computing, 2011 11th IEEE/ACM Int. Symp. on*, 2011.

[9] R. Kumar, A. Mamidala, and D. Panda. Scaling alltoall collective on multi-core systems. In *Parallel and Distributed Processing, 2008. IPDPS 2008. IEEE International Symposium on*, pages 1–8, April 2008.

[10] A. R. Mamidala, R. Kumar, D. De, and D. K. Panda. MPI collectives on modern multicore clusters: Performance optimizations and communication characteristics. In *Proc. 2008 8th IEEE Int. Symp. Cluster Computing and Grid*, 2008.

[11] A. R. Mamidala, J. Liu, and D. K. Panda. Efficient barrier and allreduce infiniband clusters using hardware multicast and adaptive algorithms. In *In Proceedings of Cluster Computing*, 2004.

[12] P. J. Mucci, S. Browne, C. Deane, and G. Ho. PAPI: A portable interface to hardware performance counters. In *In Proceedings of the Department of Defense HPCMP Users Group Conference*, pages 7–10, 1999.

[13] B. S. Parsons and V. S. Pai. Accelerating MPI collective communications through hierarchical algorithms without sacrificing inter-node communication flexibility. In *Parallel and Distributed Processing Symposium, IEEE 28th International*, May 2014.

[14] P. Patarasuk and X. Yuan. Efficient MPI bcast across different process arrival patterns. In *Parallel and Distributed Processing, 2008. IPDPS 2008. IEEE International Symposium on*, pages 1–11, April 2008.

[15] Y. Qian and A. Afsahi. Process arrival pattern and shared memory aware alltoall on Infiniband. In *Proceedings of the 16th European PVM/MPI Users' Group Meeting on Recent Advances in Parallel Virtual Machine and Message Passing Interface*, pages 250–260, Berlin, Heidelberg, 2009. Springer-Verlag.

[16] Y. Qian and A. Afsahi. Process arrival pattern aware alltoall and allgather on Infiniband clusters. *International Journal of Parallel Programming*, 39(4):473–493, 2011.

[17] S. Sistare, R. vandeVaart, and E. Loh. Optimization of MPI collectives on clusters of large-scale SMP's. In *Proc. of the 1999 ACM/IEEE Conf. on Supercomputing*. ACM, 1999.

[18] J. S. Vetter and F. Mueller. Communication characteristics of large-scale scientific applications for contemporary cluster architectures. *J. Parallel Distrib. Comput.*, 63(9):853–865, Sept. 2003.

Locality-Driven Dynamic GPU Cache Bypassing

Chao Li *
North Carolina State University
cli17@ncsu.edu

Shuaiwen Leon Song
Pacific Northwest National Lab
Shuaiwen.Song@pnnl.gov

Hongwen Dai
North Carolina State University
hdai3@ncsu.edu

Albert Sidelnik
NVIDIA Research
asidelnik@nvidia.com

Siva Kumar Sastry Hari
NVIDIA Research
shari@nvidia.com

Huiyang Zhou
North Carolina State University
hzhou@ncsu.edu

ABSTRACT

This paper presents novel cache optimizations for massively parallel, throughput-oriented architectures like GPUs. L1 data caches (L1 D-caches) are critical resources for providing high-bandwidth and low-latency data accesses. However, the high number of simultaneous requests from single-instruction multiple-thread (SIMT) cores makes the limited capacity of L1 D-caches a performance and energy bottleneck, especially for memory-intensive applications. We observe that the memory access streams to L1 D-caches for many applications contain a significant amount of requests with low reuse, which greatly reduce the cache efficacy. Existing GPU cache management schemes are either based on conditional/reactive solutions or hit-rate based designs specifically developed for CPU last level caches, which can limit overall performance.

To overcome these challenges, we propose an efficient locality monitoring mechanism to dynamically filter the access stream on cache insertion such that only the data with high reuse and short reuse distances are stored in the L1 D-cache. Specifically, we present a design that integrates locality filtering based on reuse characteristics of GPU workloads into the decoupled tag store of the existing L1 D-cache through simple and cost-effective hardware extensions. Results show that our proposed design can dramatically reduce cache contention and achieve up to 56.8% and an average of 30.3% performance improvement over the baseline architecture, for a range of highly-optimized cache-unfriendly applications with minor area overhead and better energy efficiency. Our design also significantly outperforms the state-of-the-art CPU and GPU bypassing schemes (especially for irregular applications), without generating extra L2 and DRAM level contention.

*A large portion of this work was done when Chao Li was an intern at PNNL. This work is supported by NSF grant #1216569 and DOE ASCR Beyond Standard Modeling (BSM) project. The Pacific Northwest National Laboratory is operated by Battelle for the U.S. Department of Energy under contract DE-AC05-76RL01830.

ICS '2015, Newport Beach, California USA

http://dx.doi.org/10.1145/2751205.2751237 .

Categories and Subject Descriptors

C.1.2 [**Multiple Data Stream Architecture**]: Single-Instruction, Multiple-Data processors (SIMD)

General Terms

Design, Experimentation, Performance, Energy Efficiency

Keywords

GPU architecture Optimization; Locality; Cache Bypassing

1. INTRODUCTION

Massively parallel, throughput-oriented processors such as graphics processing units (GPUs) leverage high thread-level parallelism to overlap long latency memory accesses with computation. On-chip caches, especially L1 data caches (L1 D-caches) which were designed to improve the performance of irregular workloads without programming scratchpads [2, 5, 4], remain critical to provide high-bandwidth low-latency data accesses. However, the limited L1 D-cache capacity becomes a performance bottleneck as the working set of the massively threaded applications often exceeds the L1 D-cache capacity, causing severe *thrashing* [24, 15]. More importantly, large number of the incoming memory requests with no or low reuse may evict cache lines with high reuse, resulting in *cache pollution*. In this case, even advanced cache replacement policies (e.g. RRIP [14] and SHiP [29]) are ineffective to address such contention problems on GPUs [24]. Furthermore, the massive multithreading on GPUs can cause the unpredictability of cache locality and various resource congestion (e.g. MSHR allocation failures) [5, 16].

To alleviate contention and avoid early eviction, cache bypassing schemes have been proposed for CPUs [19, 12, 13, 18] and GPUs [15, 30, 31, 27]. The CPU-based approaches are usually designed for last level caches (LLCs), where data locality is already filtered by previous level(s) of caches. But the poor locality of GPU workloads and resource congestion impose difficulty for them to make robust predictions and they often increase L2 and DRAM level traffic [11] (Section 6.1(a)). GPU-based bypassing schemes are generally conditional/reactive bypassing (e.g., bypass upon unavailable resources [15] or coarse-grained bypassing on warps or thread-blocks [30, 31, 27]) which can incorrectly bypass accesses with good reuse and cause memory pipeline stalls (Section 6.1(a)). None of the above approaches is a *preventive* scheme considering the uniqueness of the *data locality* of GPU access streams, which often contain a non-trivial number of requests with no/low reuse and/or distant re-reference intervals caused by frequent bursts of references (Section 3.2).

Moreover, a fully-adaptive bypassing scheme is required to maintain the efficiency of workloads with good caching behavior, which is often neglected by previous approaches [24, 15, 12, 11] (Section 6.1(b)).

In this paper, we propose a locality-driven dynamic bypassing design that automatically filters the access stream on cache insertions based on reuse frequency of accesses, so that only the data with high reuse and short reuse distances [12] are stored in the L1 D-cache. For area and energy efficiency, we propose to *decouple the tag and data stores* of the existing L1 D-cache and integrate the locality filtering capability into the tag store through simple and cost-effective hardware extensions. Our design uses separate replacement policies to manage the decoupled tag and data store, such that the reuse information of the program and temporal locality of the data lines can be preserved. Overall, this paper makes the following contributions:

(1) Through a detailed analysis on the reuse characteristics of GPU workloads, we identify the key inefficiency of the conventional thrashing and stall-prone GPU cache design: *irregular cache-unfriendly* memory accesses resulting in contention at various cache levels.

(2) We propose a locality-driven dynamic bypassing solution that is cost-effective and requires no profiling or runtime prediction. We demonstrate that our design can significantly improve the performance and energy efficiency of *irregular cache-unfriendly* workloads, while maintaining the efficiency for regular workloads with favorable caching behavior.

(3) Our design achieves significant performance improvements over the baseline caches and outperforms the state-of-the-art CPU (*PDP-best* [12]) and GPU (*MRPB* [15]) cache bypassing schemes, by dramatically reducing various types of cache contention without generating extra L2 and DRAM traffic.

The remainder of the paper is organized as follows: Section 2 discusses the background, the GPU memory hierarchy in particular. Section 3 dissects the effectiveness of L1 D-caches for various workloads. Section 4 details our new design. Section 5 presents the experimental methodology. The evaluation of our design is shown in Section 6. Section 7 discusses the related work and Section 8 concludes.

2. BACKGROUND

2.1 Baseline Architecture

This work proposes microarchitectural improvements to a massively parallel processor such as GPU architectures. Such processor consists of multiple SIMD cores, also known as streaming multiprocessors[1] (SMs) in NVIDIA GPUs or Computing Units in AMD GPUs. As shown in Figure 1, each SM follows the single instruction-multiple threads (SIMT) execution model by fetching and decoding each instruction for a group of threads called a warp. All threads in a warp execute in lock-step in the SIMT backend. In the issue stage, a warp scheduler will select one of the ready warps to issue into the computing/memory pipeline stage. GPUs provide multiple types of memory units to improve the memory bandwidth such as L1 D-caches and shared memory (or scratchpads). Global memory and scratchpad accesses are served through L1 D-cache and shared memory respectively. Both L1 D-cache and shared memory utilize the same hardware structure and the capacity can be configured through a run-time API. While shared memory can be explicitly managed by programmers, L1 D-cache is implicitly controlled by

[1]Without specified mention, NVIDIA terminology will be used throughout the paper to illustrate our work. However, the idea applies to a wide range of massively parallel architectures.

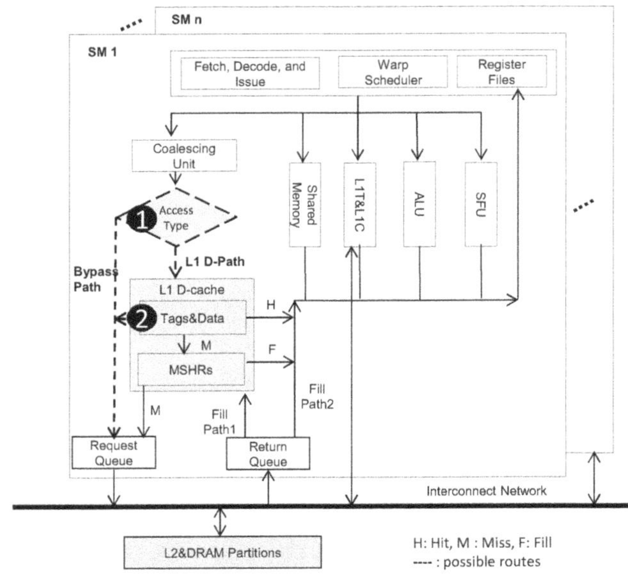

Figure 1: Memory request handling in the baseline architecture.

hardware to exploit data locality. As GPU workloads with irregular memory access patterns are becoming prevalent, effective utilization of explicitly managed memory becomes difficult. This in turn increases the importance of efficient L1 D-cache designs. All the SMs are connected by an interconnected network to the partitioned memory module, each with its own L2 data cache and DRAM partition. To save bandwidth [25], L1 is typically write through, with either write-allocate [2] or write-no-allocate [5, 4], while L2 is write back with write-allocate. Victim caches and hardware prefetching are traditionally not enabled in GPUs [6].

2.2 Baseline Memory Request Handling

When a memory instruction is dispatched into the memory pipeline, the load_store (LD_ST) units will identify the memory access type and dispatch it into different memory units (shared memory, L1 D-cache, etc.). The requests for global and local memory data from threads in the same warp will go through the coalescing unit to generate as few L1 D-cache line-sized requests as possible. Then for these requests, there are two possible paths depending on whether an access is cacheable, as shown in Figure 1. For cacheable accesses, the first path, which sends the memory requests into L1 D-cache and is labeled as '**L1 D-path**', is used. On a cache hit, a request will be served by sending data to the register file immediately. On a cache miss, the miss handling logic will first check the miss status holding register (MSHR) to see if the same request is currently pending from prior ones. If so, this request will be merged into the same entry and no new data request needs to be issued. Otherwise, a new MSHR entry and cache line will be reserved for this data request. A cache status handler may fail on resource unavailability events such as when there are no free MSHR entries, all cache blocks in that set have been reserved but still haven't been filled, the miss queue is full, etc. If any of these events occurs, the memory pipeline will stall and this request will retry every cycle until needed resources are freed. Considering the small number of cache lines and MSHR entries, these resources can be quickly occupied if all memory requests are diverted into **L1 D-Path**.

The second path is for un-cacheable accesses, such as global memory accesses in NVIDIA's Kepler architecture [4]

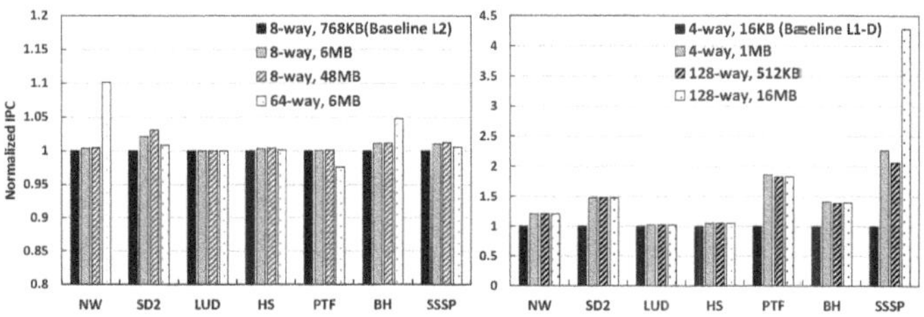

Figure 2: L1 (right) and L2 (left) level contention study by increasing their associativity and capacity. It clearly shows that the major performance bottleneck resides at the L1 D-cache level for CNF workloads.

(not cached in Kepler's L1). It diverts the memory requests to bypass the L1 D-cache (labeled as '**Bypass Path**' in Figure 1) and directly sends requests through an interconnect into the next level memory hierarchy. On the response fill from the return queue, there are two paths to fill the data correspondingly. If the original memory request follows the **L1 D-Path**, then the response data will be filled into the reserved cache line in L1 D-cache and the corresponding MSHR entry is marked as filled ('**Fill Path 1**'). Otherwise, the data will directly write back into the register file ('**Fill Path 2**').

Compared to the **Bypass Path**, the **L1 D-Path** lowers access latencies if requested data already resides in the cache. However, memory accesses following this path may incur high stall cycles for resource contention due to massive parallelism, and also thrash the cache by evicting out the data lines that may be reused shortly. Ideally, an efficient locality monitoring mechanism should exist to divert memory requests with high data reuse into the L1 D-cache, while other requests that have no or low data reuse will be directed to the **Bypass Path** instead of contending on the cache resources.

3. GPU CACHE INEFFICIENCY AND WORKLOAD ANALYSIS

App Name	N-IPC	Num Dynamic Insts	Type	Suite
PTF	1.36	7022693	CNF	[9]
SD2	1.36	740966400	CNF	[9]
NW	1.24	1617408	CNF	[9]
SSSP	1.21	385881828	CNF	[8]
LUD	1.17	5875200	CNF	[9]
HS	1.05	109686484	CNF	[9]
BH	1.04	7909748	CNF	[8]
CFD	1.00	9308160	CI	[9]
LFK	1.00	7516393326	CI	[9]
GS	1.00	12648	CI	[9]
FFT	1.00	104005632	CI	[33]
MYC	1.00	26986736	CI	[9]
PF	1.00	649231040	CI	[9]
SD1	0.97	8281816	CF	[9]
HT	0.55	8811310884	CF	[9]
MM	0.54	58851328	CF	[21]
BT	0.41	542310058	CF	[9]
BP	0.23	190054784	CF	[9]

Table 1: Application categorization based on cache bypassing impact. CNF: Cache Unfriendly, CI: Cache Insensitive, CF: Cache Friendly. IPC is normalized to the case of all taking L1 D-Path (N-IPC). The selected applications include Particular Filter (PTF), Srad2 (SD2), Needleman-Wunsch (NW), Single-Source Shortest Path (SSSP), LU Decomposition (LUD), Hotspot (HS), Barnes-Hut (BH), CFD Solver (CFD), Leukocyte (LFK), Gaussian Elimination (GS), Fourier Transformation (FFT), Myocyte (MYC), PathFinder (PF), Srad1 (SD1), Heartwall (HT), Matrix Multiplication (MM), B+Tree (BT), and Back Propagation (BP).

To evaluate the efficacy of the GPU caches, we first characterize a wide range of GPU applications (shown in Table 1) covering various cache sensitivity and memory access patterns (e.g., applications with *highly irregular access patterns* such as BH and SSSP). These applications are selected from multiple widely used benchmark suites (including GPGPUsim benchmarks [7], CUDA SDK [3], AMD SDK [1], Rodinia [9], and Lonestar suites [8], etc) and represent production GPU codes which are optimized and hand-tuned using explicitly managed scratchpad memory extensively. We quantify how much performance improvement, which is measured using normalized instruction per cycle (N-IPC), each application can gain if all memory requests have taken the **Bypass Path** compared to all taking the **L1 D-Path** in Figure 1. This IPC improvement is shown in Table 1, where the eighteen applications are sorted in descending order. Applications whose IPC improvement is greater than 1 are classified as *Cache Unfriendly* (**CNF**), indicating the current L1 D-cache management has detrimental impact on their performance. Applications whose IPC values are not impacted are classified as *Cache Insensitive* (**CI**), as whether having a L1 D-cache or not has negligible effects on their performance. The remaining applications whose IPC improvement is less than 1 are *Cache Friendly* (**CF**): workloads that perform better if all accesses go through L1 D-cache. Section 5 provides a detailed description of these applications and the baseline architecture the results from this section were collected from.

3.1 GPU Cache Inefficiency

The memory access stream of GPU workloads has two characteristics: a mix of data requests with different reuse frequencies and different reuse distances [12]. For instance, in the Fermi architecture [5], incoming accesses will enter into the L1 D-cache without being checked on whether they have future reuse. All data accesses contend with each other for limited cache resources, resulting in memory pipeline stalls. To the other extreme, similar to the bypassing approach used in Table 1, Kepler [4] will bypass all global memory accesses from L1, only handling register spills to the local memory.

In general, there are three types of contention at the L1 D-cache level: **(a) Inter-warp contention: capacity misses**. Current GPU architectures (e.g. Fermi and Kepler) commonly have 16~48 KB capacity of L1 D-cache [5, 4], but the memory footprint of the applications is typically one to two orders of magnitude larger, which causes severe thrashing. Data blocks get evicted out frequently before any reuse happens, especially when the reuse distance is long. More importantly, memory requests with no reuse may evict cache lines that have high reuse, resulting in cache pollution. **(b) Intra-warp contention: conflict misses**. This is caused by the concurrent threads within the same warp (32 threads) accessing to the same cache set (current GPU L1 has much lower set-associativity than 32). **(c) Other resource congestion**. They include resource allocation failures from limited MSHRs and miss queue entires. These resources can be quickly occupied and cause stalls if data requests come into L1 without being filtered based on their reuse patterns.

To reduce the contention described above, we apply the most direct optimization, which is increasing the capacity and associativity of the L1 and L2 caches, and observe how it affects overall performance. We intentionally increase the cache associativity and capacity to a large value, which is expensive and impractical to implement in real GPU cache designs due to increased access latency, area, and power consumption. Figure 2 shows several observations for the CNF

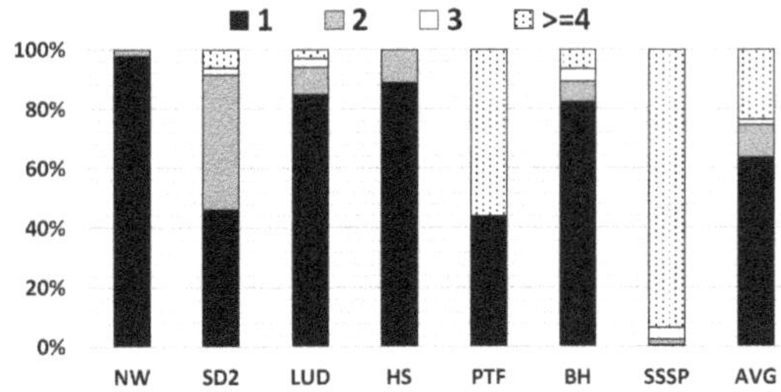

Figure 3: Reuse breakdown for CNF applications. It shows the percentage of addresses in L1 D-cache have been referenced by m number of times. The values of m are shown in the legend.

applications, which encountered the most cache contention: (1) Compared to the L1 D-cache, CNF's performance is insensitive to the capacity and associativity increase of L2, which indicates that L2 is not the major performance bottleneck. (2) CNF's performance can be improved by increasing L1 D-cache's size and associativity (to full associativity), but it is mainly bounded by cache capacity. (3) Even with these impractical cache configurations, the performance improvements for some CNF applications are still not significant, including NW, LUD, HS, and BH. These findings motivate us to develop a cost-effective cache bypassing mechanism for GPUs to maximally reduce the contention by only letting the most useful data into the L1 D-cache.

The state-of-the-art bypass policy, *protection distance prediction (PDP)* [12], has been proposed for CPU LLCs. This technique applies a *protection distance (PD)* counter to each cache line and uses it to time how many accesses are left for this line to be protected. If $PD = 0$, this line is marked as *unprotected* and can be replaced by the incoming accesses. If there are no *unprotected* lines left, cache is bypassed. However, applying PDP-based approaches (static or dynamic) to a GPU L1 D-cache can encounter several problems [11]. First, due to warp interleaving and resource congestion in GPUs, as a hit-rate based scheme designed for single thread processors, PDP may not improve the performance of CNF applications because the hit rate does not directly correlate to performance in GPUs (see Section 6.1(c)). Second, by augmenting a cache line with a protecting distance, PDP is susceptible to bypass the blocks with frequent data reuse and short reuse distances, but keeps the staled blocks with very long reuse distances for a protection interval (see Section 6.1(d)), causing cache pollution. Third, many of the CF applications shown in Table 1 have been optimized for cache performance. Therefore, any request bypassing caused by inaccurate PDP prediction can result in a significant performance degradation (see Section 6.1(b)). Finally, it is difficult for PDP to predict applications with irregular memory accesses, such as BH and SSSP (see Section 5 and 6.1(a)).

3.2 Impact of Applications On Performance

An application's intrinsic memory access and reuse pattern can also affect its performance. In this section, we use the application characterizations from Table 1 to provide insights in making design decisions for our proposed approach.

In Table 1, the CI Category contains of six applications where enabling the L1 D-cache has no performance impact. We categorize the reasons behind such insensitivity into four typical scenarios: (1) workloads have no read access from the global memory, such as LEK and CFD; (2) workloads have the characteristics of intensive branching and very little memory access, such as MYC and GS, which also have very low IPC due to branch divergences; (3) streaming work-

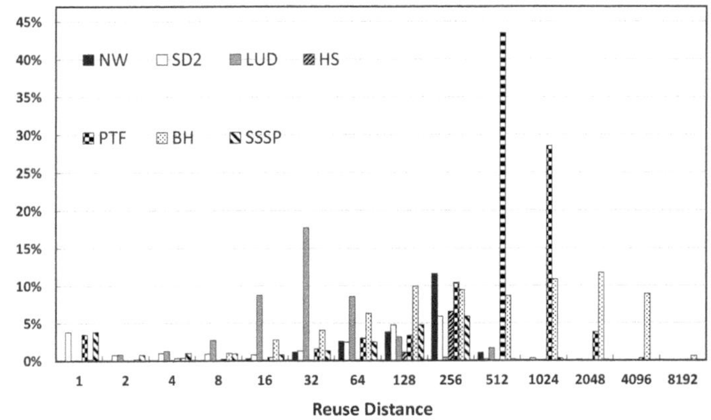

Figure 4: The reuse distance histograms of L1 D-cache access stream of the CNF applications. The reuse distance is computed at cache access level instead of cache structure level (e.g. the reuse distance for access pattern ABCA is 2).

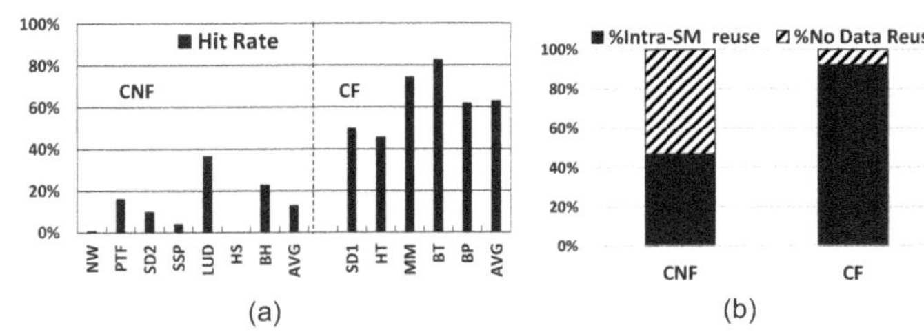

Figure 5: Hit rates and data reuse characteristics of GPU workloads: (a) Hit rates of CNF and CF applications; (b) The percentage of data accesses with and without data reuse.

loads, such as FFT, in which the global memory access happens only for loading the input signal sets into the shared memory; (4) workloads have high memory level parallelism, such as PF, where the critical path is determined by the first memory access miss. Because of their performance insensitivity to the L1 D-cache, the CI applications are not the focus of our study. However, we include them to prove the robustness of our proposed design.

The cache sensitive workloads include both CNF and CF applications. For CNF workloads, bypassing all memory requests from L1 D-cache improves the performance of NW, PTF, and SD2 by 24.2%, 36.8% and 36.6%, respectively. This is a direct result of the low cache performance across the CNF workloads, as shown in Figure 5(a). Compared with the CF applications, the overall cache hit rate in CNF is much worse. For example, the hit rates for NW and HS are smaller than 1%. LUD has the highest hit rate in CNF (36.8%). However, 62.8% of its hits are write hits, which are useless due to the write evict policy in baseline GPUs [5, 4]. On average, the cache hit rate for CNF workloads is only 8.9%, while the average for the CF workloads is as high as 55.4%. To understand why CNF workloads have such low cache performance, we evaluate the data locality of each application and quantify the data reuse rate of their memory stream in each SM. As shown in Figure 5(b), CNF workloads have a larger portion of data requests without any reuse, 53.2% on average compared to only 7.9% in the CF category. To analyze the characteristics of the reuse in the CNF workloads, we present the reuse distance histograms of these workloads in Figure 4. As shown in Figure 4, the reuse distances are relatively high when the cache block size is 128 bytes (baseline architecture). Such large reuse distances (>128) present a challenge for the limited number of blocks

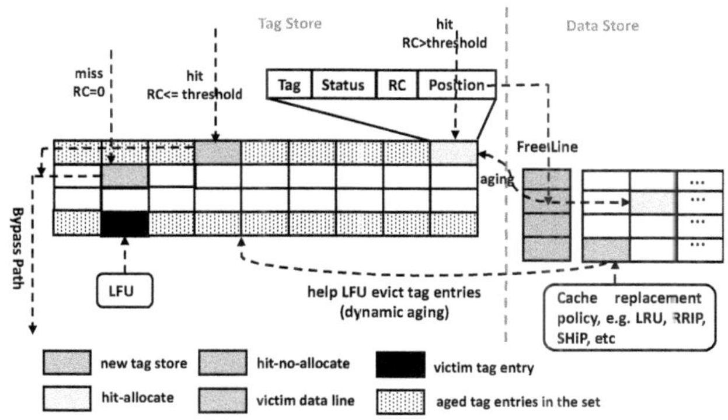

Figure 6: Decoupled L1D cache design diagram.

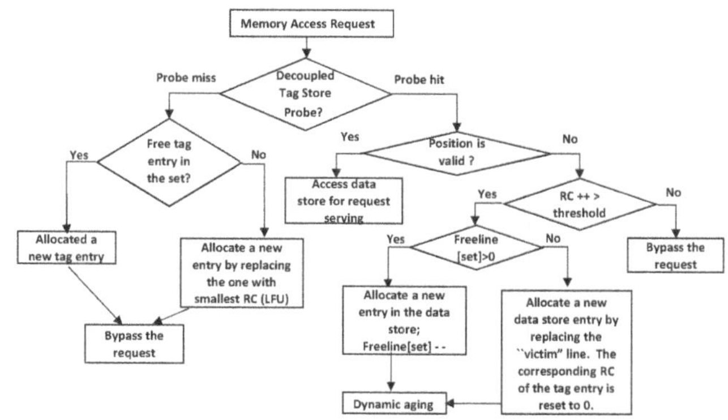

Figure 7: Operation flow chart of the Decoupled L1D.

(i.e., limited capacity) in the L1 D-cache. Also, Figure 3 shows that memory requests for the majority of CNF applications (other than PTF and SSSP) are only reused less than three times. These data accesses with no or low reuse cause two problems: (1) they will contend with accesses with high reuse for resources and resulting in the average stall time for CNF workloads as high as 48.04% of the total execution time; (2) such accesses without any reuse are scattered inside the memory access stream, which indirectly increases the reuse distance of accesses with reuse. Finally, without accurate locality information, deciding which memory requests should enter L1 D-cache is difficult for applications with irregular access patterns (e.g. SSSP), which has been neglected by the previous studies [11, 15, 24, 30].

4. DESIGN METHODOLOGY

The focus of this work is to design efficient bypassing for a GPU L1 D-cache that can dynamically divert memory requests based on reuse patterns. As shown in Figure 1, there are two design points available to implement such mechanism: an independent hardware component between the coalescing unit and L1 D-cache (❶ in Figure 1), and the existing L1 D-cache integrated with the locality filtering capability (❷ in Figure 1). We choose ❷ over ❶ because both structures consist of entries that can be identified as tags (e.g. L1 tag store) so such redundancy in ❶ will increase access latency by performing additional tag checks per access. Also, ❷ will likely have smaller area and higher energy efficiency. Accordingly, we propose to decouple the tag and data stores of the existing L1 D-cache and integrate the locality filtering capability into the tag store through minor hardware expansions. In this way, we can leverage the management of the independent tag store to control which memory requests can allocate data lines in the data store. By taking advantage of the tag store's smaller entry size (8~9 bytes) compared to that of the data store (128 bytes per line), additional entries in each set can be added in the tag store with lower overhead such that it can capture the locality information of a working set larger than the data store size. We name our new design "**Decoupled L1D**" and its diagram is shown in **Figure 6**.

4.1 Decoupled L1D: Structure

As shown in Figure 6, the tag and data store in the Decoupled L1D cache are independent structures although we choose to let them have the same number of sets to simplify the management. The decoupled tag store has expanded the original tag store with more entries in each set, and each tag entry has also been padded with more fields. In addition to the original fields, including the address tag, a status field, and a LRU counter, the new tag store entry now contains a *Reference Count (RC)* field and a *Position* field. The *RC* field (6-bit) holds the reference frequency (reuse) accumulated for the address. The *Position* field (2-bit) connects a tag store entry with a data line in the data store using a pointer to record the data line's position. Once a data line in the data store is allocated, the corresponding tag store entry needs to set the *Position* field accordingly. The new data store in our Decoupled L1D has the same structure as the original one, except that each set has added one field named *Free_Line*, indicating how many free lines are available for use in the set. This field will be updated upon a new data line allocation or an eviction.

4.2 Decoupled L1D: Operations

Instead of having uniform operations in the current L1 D-cache design, our Decoupled L1D enables separate sets of update and replacement logic for the tag and data stores. Also, we add a new cache request status *bypass* into the existing four statuses, i.e., *hit, hit pending, miss, and reservation failed*, of a L1 D-cache request. Figure 6 and 7 describe how the Decoupled L1D operates.

In the initial architectural status, each tag-store entry and data line is cleared (*Position* field is set to invalid). The *Free_Line* field is initialized with the associativity size of each set in the data store. **On a probe miss of the tag store**, a new tag entry is allocated, and a bypass status is returned, as shown in Figure 7. A bypass will not trigger the cache miss handler but instead it will directly take the **Bypass Path** (Figure 6) without allocating a line in the data store. If there are no free tag entries in that set, the entry with the smallest *RC* is taken as the replacement victim. In other words, the LFU (Least Frequently Used) replacement policy is used for the decoupled tag store. Since the way to update *RC* can significantly impact the lifetime of a tag entry, we apply a customized dynamic aging[2] scheme to the *RC* fields of the tag entries in the following scenarios: upon an allocation or eviction in the **data store**, the *RC* values of all the corresponding **tag entries** in that set (not including the allocated or evicted tag entry) are reduced by 1. Thus, the *RC* values of **stale entries** (i.e. entries with no future reference or long re-reference interval that still remain in the tag store) are reduced and eventually become small enough to be evicted out of the tag store.

On a probe hit in the decoupled tag store, there are two different operations depending on whether the *Position*

[2]We have explored several aging schemes (e.g. bit-shifting RC only upon evictions in the data store) but do not report them here due to space limitations.

field has pointed to an allocated data line. If the field has been set with a data-store line position, this memory request will proceed as a cache hit or cache hit-pending, similar to the original L1 D-cache. Otherwise, it will increase the *RC* value of the tag entry and then compare it with a *locality threshold*, which is pre-defined based on workload characteristics so that the data blocks with no or low reuse will not be inserted into the L1 D-cache. The subsequent program flow after the comparison is shown in Figure 7. If there are no free data lines in a selected set upon a data-line allocation, the data store's replacement policy (e.g. LRU, SHiP, RRIP, etc) will be triggered to find the victim line for eviction. Then, the RC value of the corresponding tag entry is set to 0 and the rest of the tag entries in the set will be aged. This ensures that the temporal locality of the data lines is preserved in our design by using the replacement policy from the original L1 D-cache. The associated parameters introduced in this section (including the number of tag entries, the set associativity, and the locality threshold) have direct impact on the area, power and performance of our design. We explore them in Section 6.2.

Fairness: For a fair system, the decision on allocating and replacing tag entries must **closely match the data reuse frequency and distance**. In our design, the locality of the program is preserved. If a data block has high reuse, its *RC* will continue to accumulate and eventually pass the threshold to allocate a new line in the data store for capturing subsequent reuses. Also, the state-of-the-art cache replacement policies (e.g. LRU, RRIP, etc) are used in the data store to help evict the tag entries (dynamic aging) that exhibit a distant re-reference interval caused by frequent bursts of references. In this way, the tag and data stores are circulated in a sustainable way with minimum number of stale tag entires generated.

4.3 SM Dueling

Our proposed design aims to improve performance of CNF applications. For CF applications, whose performance benefits greatly from utilizing the L1 D-cache, a locality threshold on *RC* may delay the data to be stored in the cache for reuse. Therefore, we can disable the *RC* checking for CF workloads by setting the locality threshold to zero, i.e., all accesses go to the L1 D-cache. For our decoupled tag store, the newly added tag entries can be power gated to reduce the energy overhead. To decide which mechanism to use for an application during execution, we employ a simple, but effective SM dueling technique [23] based on the insights from Figure 5a. Assume that we have a GPU with N SMs ($N \geq 2$). Initially, we assign *SM_0* to use our new design and *SM_1* to use the original L1 D-cache. The remaining SMs can choose to use either type. At a pre-defined time interval (see Table 3), *SM_0* and *SM_1* will compare their cache miss rates: if *SM_0* has a higher cache miss rate than *SM_1*, then all the SMs will start using the original L1 D-cache; otherwise all the SMs will enable the new design.

5. EXPERIMENTAL METHODOLOGY

Simulation Environment: Our proposed design is evaluated using GPGPUsim V3.2.2 [7], which is a widely used cycle-accurate simulator for GPU architecture research. The baseline architecture is modeled based on a generic NVIDIA Fermi GPU [5] and its configuration is shown in Table 2. Our new design can be similarly applied to other recent GPU architectures as well, such as NVIDIA Kepler and Maxwell [4]. The design choices for our Decoupled L1D (based on a 16KB

SIMT Core (SM)	15 cores, SIMD width=32, 1.4GHz, 5-stage pipeline
Max/SM	1536 threads, 32768 registers, 48 warps, 32 MSHRs with 256 entries
L1 Cache/SM	16KB/core, 128B line, 4-way assoc, 1-cycle hit latency
Shared Mem/SM	48 KB; 32 banks; 3-cycle latency; 1 access per cycle
Unified L2 Cache	768 KB, 128KB/bank, 6 banks, 128B line, 16-way assoc
DRAM	6 memory channels, BW: 48 bytes/cycle, 1.4 GHz
DRAM Schedule Queue	Size = 16 and Out of order (FR-RCFS)
Warp Scheduling Policy	Greedy then oldest (GTO)

Table 2: Baseline architecture configuration.

<table>
<tr><td rowspan="5">Decoupled L1D</td><td colspan="2">Tag Store</td><td colspan="2">Data Store</td></tr>
<tr><td>#entries</td><td>256</td><td>#lines</td><td>128</td></tr>
<tr><td>structure</td><td>32 set, 8-way</td><td colspan="2">32 set, 4-way</td></tr>
<tr><td>replacement policy</td><td>LFU dynamic aging</td><td colspan="2">LRU, SHiP, RRIP, etc.</td></tr>
<tr><td>threshold</td><td>2</td><td colspan="2">N/A</td></tr>
<tr><td>SM Dueling</td><td colspan="4">Initially, SM0– new design; SM1–baseline cache; the rest SMs follow SM1.
Time interval: 500 cycles.
Miss rate difference threshold: 10%.</td></tr>
</table>

Table 3: Configurations of our proposed Decoupled L1D.

L1 D-cache) is shown in Table 3, which will be validated in Section 6.2 (design space exploration).

Benchmarks: All 18 applications used in this study are shown in Table 1, which represents a wide range of optimized real-world GPU applications. Since shared memory is extensively used, the performance tends to be less sensitive to the L1 D-cache, which makes them the perfect candidates to show whether our proposed design can still improve performance over optimized codes. We evaluate 14 workloads from Rodinia Benchmark [9] with their default inputs. We include two additional applications: Matrix Multiplication (MM), a highly efficient version using tiled cache [21]; and Fast Fourier Transformation (FFT), an optimized version fully utilizing on-chip memory [33]. We also include two widely-used workloads: Barnes Hut N_body Simulation (BH) and Single-Source Shortest Paths (SSSP) from Lonestar GPU suite [8], both of which exhibit irregular memory access patterns. BH exhibits memory irregularity from data-dependent memory accesses, and SSSP has access irregularity from the memory traversing in a recursive iteration. In our experiments, all workloads run to completion on the simulator.

6. RESULTS AND ANALYSIS

6.1 Overall Performance Evaluation

To evaluate the performance of our proposed Decoupled L1D cache design, we compare it with several related schemes and show the results and detailed analysis. As discussed previously, Decoupled L1D uses state-of-the-art replacement policies (e.g. LRU, RRIP [14], etc.) in the data store to preserve data lines' temporal locality. To make a fair comparison, we use the same cache replacement policy (a version of LRU implemented in GPGPUsim) as the basis for all the following schemes:

BL: Baseline Architecture. This configuration is shown in Table 2. All the global/local memory accesses will be inserted into the L1 D-cache. If resources are unavailable, the memory pipeline is stalled. This architecture favors CF workloads (Table 1).

BALL: Bypass all memory accesses from the L1 D-cache. All the global/local memory accesses will be diverted into

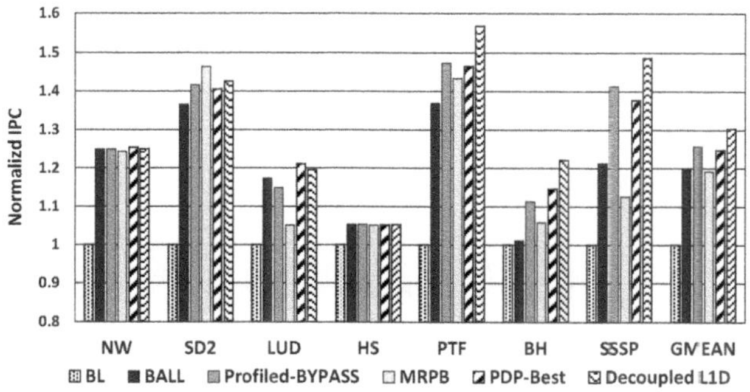

Figure 8: Performance comparisons of various cache management and bypassing schemes for the CNF workloads.

the Bypass Path (Figure 1). L1 D-cache is disabled. *BALL* favors CNF workloads (Table 1).

Profiled-BYPASS: During a profiling run, we record the reference frequency for each data block by going through every coalesced memory request before they hit L1 D-cache. This profiled information is then used to direct fine-grained L1 bypassing (acted as a software filter) in a new run. This static approach is used to evaluate performance benefits that can be achieved when the reuse information of a workload is already available. Applying such an approach for bypassing has three major downsides: (1) it is dependent on the input and thread-configuration; (2) memory traces could be non-deterministic for each run; and (3) applying bypassing in a new run based on the previous profiling information may change the completion time of different thread blocks (TBs) and their associated dispatch order.

We implemented three types of profiling-based filters: (1) a per SM local filter recording the intra-SM data reuse (local), (2) a kernel-level global filter recording the inter-SM data reuse (global), and (3) a combined local+global filter. All three filters have unlimited entries to store workloads' memory addresses and their reference counts. Different locality thresholds from 1 to 16 were tested for the best performance. Among them, the global+local filter achieved the best average performance over BL. The reason is that with bypassing enabled, the thread block execution order is altered from the profiling run and the inter-SM reuses may become intra-SM reuse. From this point on, we will only use the global+local filter (named "**Profiled-BYPASS**") for comparisons with other mechanisms. The profiling costs are ***not*** included in the figures of this section.

MRPB: The *state-of-the-art* GPU dynamic bypassing approach [15]. When any of the resource unavailable events happens that may lead to a pipeline stall, the memory requests are bypassed from the L1 D-cache until resources are available. MRPB includes memory request reordering queues, which are also modeled in our experiment.

PDP-best: The *state-of-the-art* CPU bypassing approach for LLCs, as discussed in Section 3.1. Both static and dynamic PDP approaches have been proposed in [12], in which the performance upper bound of PDP is achieved by the static PDP approach. Thus we compare our design to PDP-best, which is the best performed static PDP-bypass with the optimal PD specific to each workload (by exhaustively searching all possible PDs).

Decoupled L1D: Our design as described in Section 4.

Based on the experimental results, we make the following observations and analysis:

(a) Performance Comparisons For CNF Workloads: Figure 8 shows that for CNF workloads our proposed Decoupled L1D achieves the highest performance, up to 56.8% and an average of 30.3% performance improvement (using the geometric mean) over *BL*. The performance comparisons among the different schemes highlights the importance of cache bypassing for GPUs. *BL* (all memory accesses go into the L1 D-cache) performs the worst because without any cache insertion management, memory requests with little to no reuse are diverted into the L1 D-cache, causing cache pollution and congesting the memory pipeline. *BALL* (all memory accesses bypass L1 D-cache) improves the performance for CNF workloads due to fewer memory pipeline stalls, however this mechanism completely disables the cache and overlooks data reuse in the memory access stream. As shown in Figure 5b, there are still over 40% of the data accesses that have reuse for the CNF workloads. *MRPB* improves CNF's performance over *BL* by a geometric mean of 19.2%, only bypassing when a resource (cache lines, MSHR, miss queue entry, etc.) unavailable event occurs, in order to reduce resource contention. The disadvantage of *MRPB* is that it does not consider any data reuse pattern in the access stream. In other words, *MRPB* could still let data with no or low reuse be cached and bypass data with high reuse. In comparison, our proposed *Decoupled L1D* enables a fine-grained and effective bypassing based on reference count, which can better capture the data reuse in an access stream. Figure 8 shows that our design outperforms *MRPB* by up to 36% and an average of 11% for CNF workloads. On average, our dynamic approach also achieves better performance than the *Profiled-BYPASS*. For some CNF workloads like BH, we even observe an up to 11% performance improvement, without even counting the profiling overhead in *Profiled-BYPASS*. This proves that our dynamic method is more flexible and practical than the profiling-based bypass, without encountering profiling overheads, inaccurate requests diverting, and the potential nondeterministic effects.

Comparing with PDP-best, for the irregular CNF workloads like BH and SSSP, our *Decoupled L1D* outperforms *PDP-best* by 8% and 11%. For PTF, which has long reuse distances and burst access patterns, *Decoupled L1D* outperforms *PDP-best* by 10.33%. For the regular CNF applications with very low reuse such as HS, NW, and LUD (Figure 3), our design performs as well as *PDP-best*. Based on [5, 4], the primary reason for creating a GPU L1 D-cache is for improving the efficiency of irregular workloads processing, since shared memory cannot address the irregularities at runtime. We argue that the **essential goal** of our design is to explore the potential efficiency improvement for irregular workloads using bypassing. Unlike the hit-rate based PDP approaches constrained by the protection distance (discussed in Section 3.1), our *Decoupled L1D* monitors the dynamic reuse frequency and reuse distances using the decoupled tag store, which better captures the reuse patterns for irregular applications. Additionally, with the customized dynamic aging, stale tag entries in the tag store can be evicted out timely to avoid cache pollution.

(b) Performance Comparisons For CF and CI Workloads: CF applications, which have favorable caching behavior and regular control, can suffer greatly from inaccurate bypassing due to disrupted data locality. In Figure 9, significant performance loss compared to *BL* has been observed for *BALL* (up to 77%), *MRPB* (up to 19%), and *PDP-best* (up to 30%). On the contrary, we do not observe performance loss for our design because *SM Dueling* determines if the new management scheme fits well with the workload pattern and dynamically turns bypassing on or off in all SMs (see Section 4.3). For CI workloads, as expected, our design

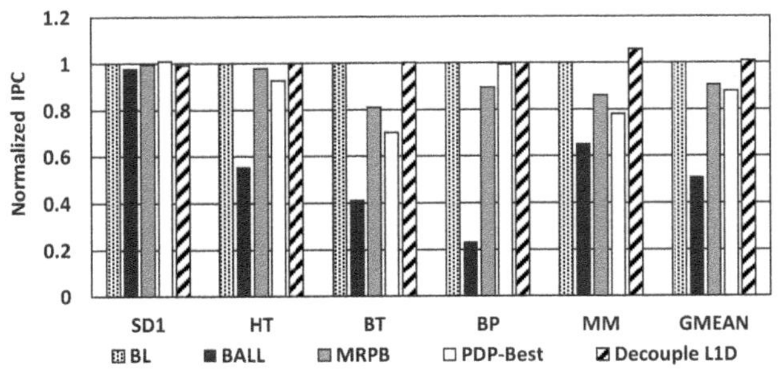

Figure 9: Performance comparisons of various cache management and bypassing schemes for the CF workloads.

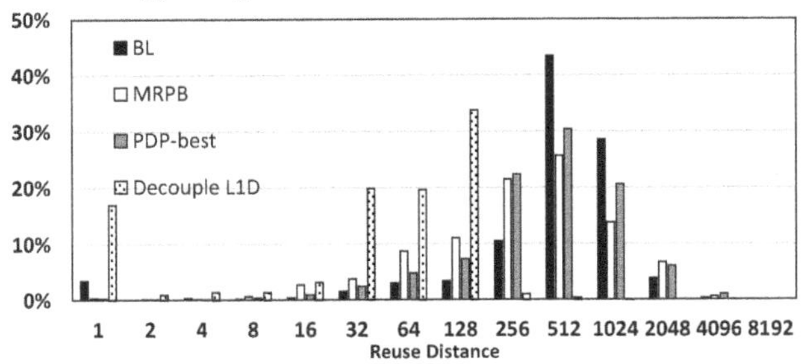

Figure 11: The reuse distance histogram of L1 access stream of PTF (a case with long reuse distance shown in Figure 4) shaped by different designs. The reuse distance is computed at the cache access level instead of cache structure level (e.g., the reuse distance for access pattern ABCA is 2).

along with other L1 D-cache management schemes has no effect on performance (with an average variance of 0.03% over the baseline performance).

(c) Hit Rate Improvement: Figure 10a shows that *Decoupled L1D* can significantly improve the L1 D-cache hit rate for CNF workloads over *BL* by an average of 38.5%. Our design also outperforms the hit-rate based scheme *PDP-best*, with significant improvements for SD2 (71%), LUD (24%) and SSP (13%). This also confirms that hit rate is not directly correlated to performance (Figure 8) on GPUs due to warp interleaving and resource congestion. Meanwhile, *MRPB* only achieves a 17.4% average hit rate due to its coarse-grained bypassing and lack of consideration for data locality. Furthermore, both NW and HS have negligible hit rates (<1%) across different mechanisms, caused by low reference counts (*RC*) for their memory requests (either 1 or 2 according to Figure 3).

(d) Shaping Cache-Friendly Memory Access: Using the CNF workload PTF as an example, Figure 11 shows that our design can shape a more cache-friendly memory access stream than other approaches. First, the data accesses that have a long reuse distance and therefore low reuse frequency will not be inserted into the L1 D-cache. As shown in Figure 11, the accesses with reuse distances of 512, 1024, and 2048 (such reuses require a cache with the capacity of 2048*the 128 cache line size = 256kB) will be bypassed in our design to avoid cache pollution. Second, our design can reduce the reuse distance of data accesses by filtering out unfriendly memory accesses. For instance, the percentage of the reuse distance '1' has been significantly increased by our design and the overall reuse distance range is shrunk to better fit the limited cache capacity.

(e) Alleviating Various Contention: Through our *Decoupled L1D*, the footprint of the filtered L1 access stream for CNF applications is dramatically reduced by an average of 63.4% compared to the baseline. This in turn reduces

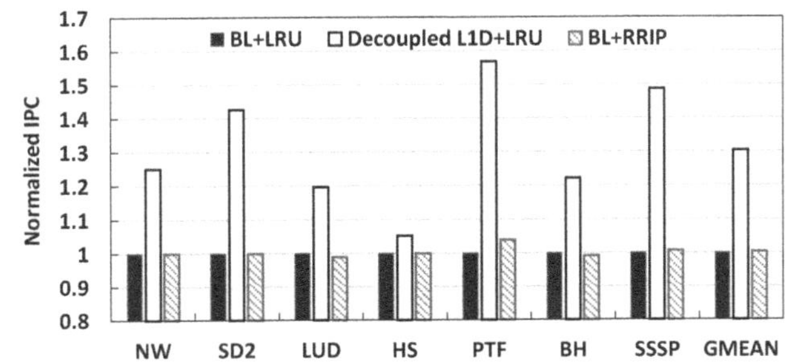

Figure 12: Impact of cache replacement policies on performance of CNF workloads on GPUs.

L1 capacity and conflict contention. Since the bypassed requests do not compete for L1 MSHRs and miss queues (Figure 1), the stall cycles due to reservation fails have also been significantly reduced by an average of 84.5% for CNF workloads.

(f) DRAM And L2 Level Traffic After Bypassing: Figure 10b and 10c show the L2 and DRAM traffic after using various bypassing mechanisms. In Figure 10b, our dynamic bypassing mechanism encounters the least amount of traffic to L2 (least pressure to NoC). The same observation can be made for DRAM traffic, shown in Figure 10c. Also, for the two irregular applications BH and SSSP, DRAM traffic from PDP-best is much higher than our design, which can result in resource congestion. This makes applying PDP approaches on GPUs less attractive because it requires warp throttling techniques to accompany PDP bypassing (e.g., the design in [11]) to be effective for irregular workloads. However, warp throttling can significantly reduce parallelism and subsequently reduce overall performance, which our design does not suffer from.

(g) Impact of Cache Replacement Policies On Performance: Advanced replacement policies such as RRIP [14] and SHiP [29] have been proposed to amortize cache contention in CPU LLCs. Although RRIP and SHiP can reduce cache contention, the blocks with long reuse distances are still brought into the cache albeit in the LRU position. This is less a problem in CPU LLCs but is problematic for GPU L1 D-cache. Figure 12 shows the performance comparison of CNF workloads running on Baseline+LRU, Baseline+RRIP, and Decoupled L1D+ LRU. We can easily observe that the replacement policies have little performance impact on CNF workloads. This is because unlike the CPU LLCs, GPU L1 D-cache has a much smaller cache associativity and capacity. Bringing in data with long reuse distances may evict more data with good locality. More importantly, without bypassing, all the L1 D-cache misses compete for limited cache resources (e.g. MSHRs and miss queue), resulting in serious resource congestion. Therefore, an efficient bypassing strategy such as ours is very necessary for GPUs, no matter which cache replacement policy is applied.

6.2 Design Space Exploration

Decoupled L1D tag store's entry size: In the decoupled tag store, there are two types of entries based on their *Position* field (Figure 6 in Section 4). The entries with their *Position* set to *valid* are those that have already been connected with a data-store line position (named committed entries) and the rest are those that are competing for allocating a data line in the data store (named candidate entries). The lower bound number of the tag entries should be larger than the number of cache lines. Otherwise, some data cache lines are wasted. A larger size of tag entries can

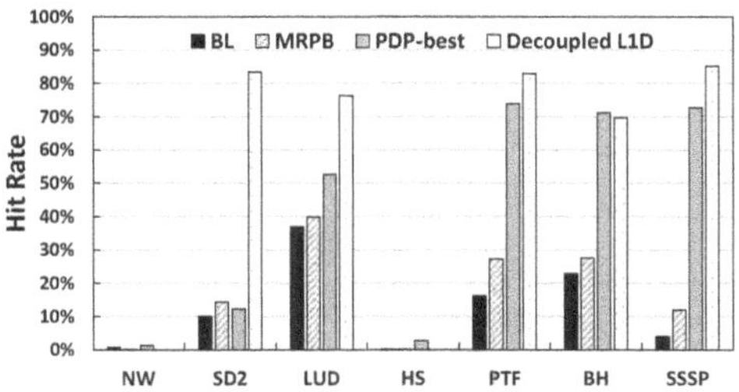

(a) L1 D-cache performance (based on hit rate) for various designs. This is the average hit rate for the overall kernel lifetime.

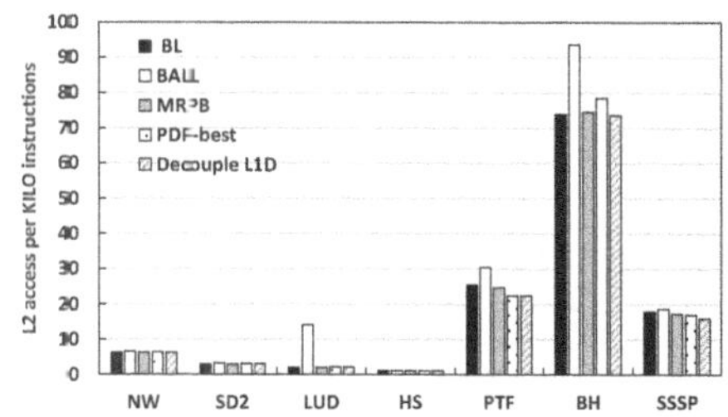

(b) Off-chip L2 accesses per thousand instructions for various designs, representing L2 level traffic.

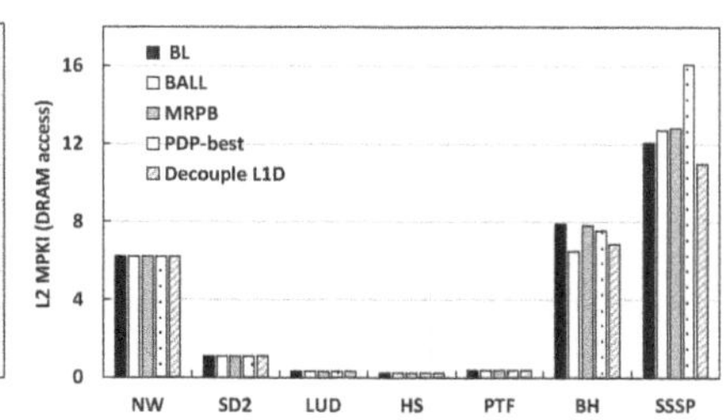

(c) L2 misses per thousand instructions (MPKI) for various designs, representing DRAM level traffic.

Figure 10: Cache performance (hit rate) and memory traffic caused by bypassing in various designs.

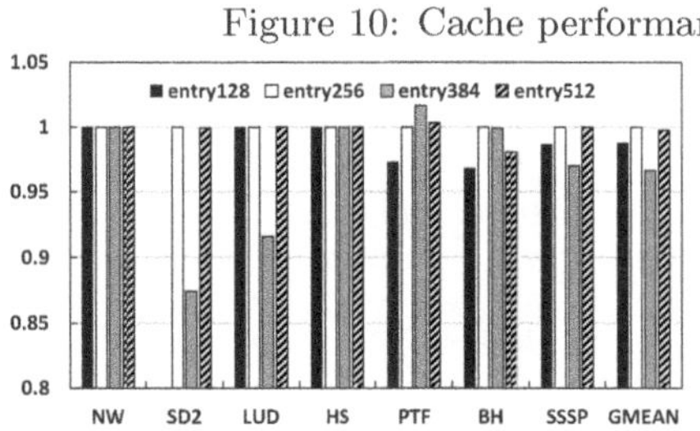

(a) The performance impact (IPC) of the entry number for the decoupled tag stores. All are normalized to the one with 256 entries. All are fully associative.

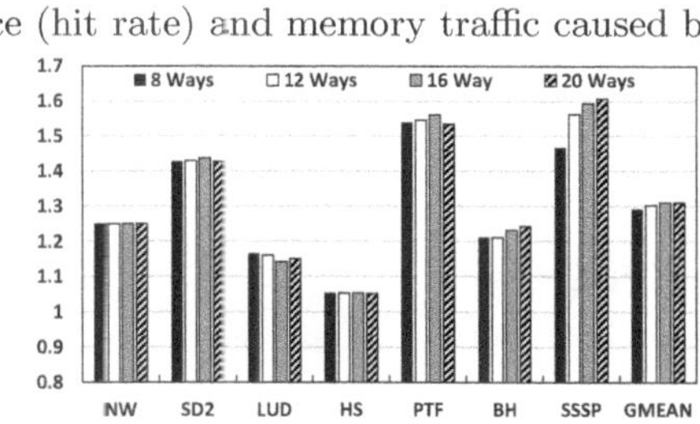

(b) The performance impact (IPC) of the set associativity of the decoupled tag store. The performance is normalized to the baseline 4-way associativity cache.

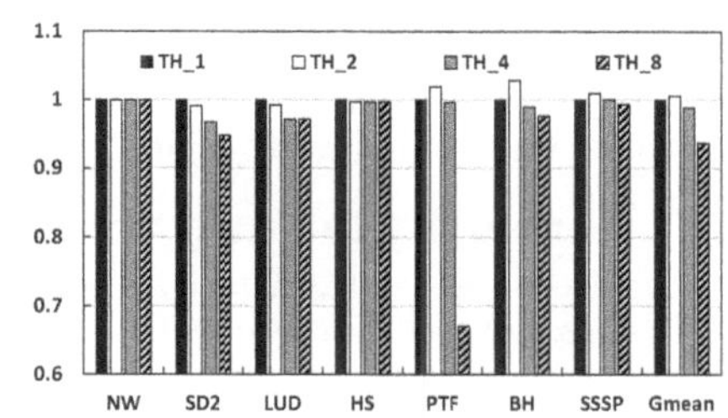

(c) Performance impact (IPC) of different locality thresholds, normalized to threshold=1.

Figure 13: Design space exploration for our proposed decoupled L1 D-cache for GPUs. The design choices match Table 3.

accommodate more candidate entries with a longer reuse distance. However, if the size of tag entries is too large, it will lose the sensitivity on reuse distance and cause cache pollution. For example, at the entry size 384, there are at least 256 entries that can be allocated for candidate entries since there are 128 cache lines (Table 2). If an entry has burst access pattern with reuse distance longer than 128, it can still stay in the tag store and may evict out other entries with short reuse distance by allocating lines in data store, causing cache pollution. Base on the results shown in Figure 13a, 256 entries should be used as the entry size in the tag store.

Decoupled L1D tag store's associativity: Figure 13b presents the effect of varying the tag store's associativity of the decoupled L1D on performance. The expanded tag store will record the reuse frequency of the incoming memory accesses and the size of way per set will affect how long an entry can reside in the tag store. When the number of ways is small, it may thrash the tag entries (that compete for allocating data lines) frequently due to high contention. When the number of ways is large, it can preserve the entries with a longer reuse distance. Our simulation results show that the 16-way design point can achieve only a 2% performance improvement over the 8-way with doubled size of the tag entries. Therefore, we select 8-way because it provides the highest performance per unit area.

Reference Count (RC)'s locality threshold selection: The RC field and locality threshold are discussed in Section 4.2 as part of our new tag store design. Figure 13c shows the effect of varying the values of the locality threshold on performance. The majority of our CNF benchmarks achieve the highest performance at the threshold value of 2 (or near the highest) due to their low data reuse pattern shown in Figure 3. Thus, we set the locality threshold value to 2 in our design. In this work, we did not implement an online system for determining the value of the threshold for individual workloads because cache unfriendly workloads do not exhibit high variation for this design point.

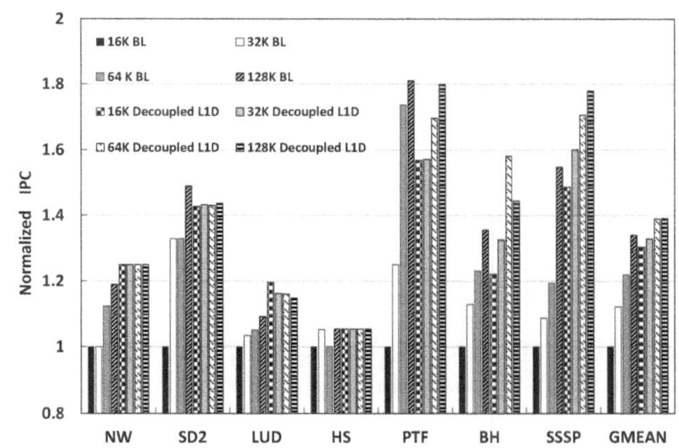

Figure 14: The effectiveness of our design on the baseline L1 D-cache with different capacities. All data is normalized to a 16KB baseline cache.

6.3 Sensitivity to L1 D-cache Sizes

Figure 14 shows the sensitivity of our design on various L1 D-cache sizes. From the performance comparisons between the baseline caches and our approach, we have two observations: (1) For every cache size we studied, our design has shown performance improvements over the baseline, even at a larger cache size (128KB). With the increasing cache size, the performance improvements of our design over the baseline do not increase as rapidly. This is because smaller cache sizes are more sensitive to contention caused by large cache footprint while bigger caches can accommodate larger working sets and accesses with longer reuse distance. Also, for a workload, if the working set fits in the cache already, fur-

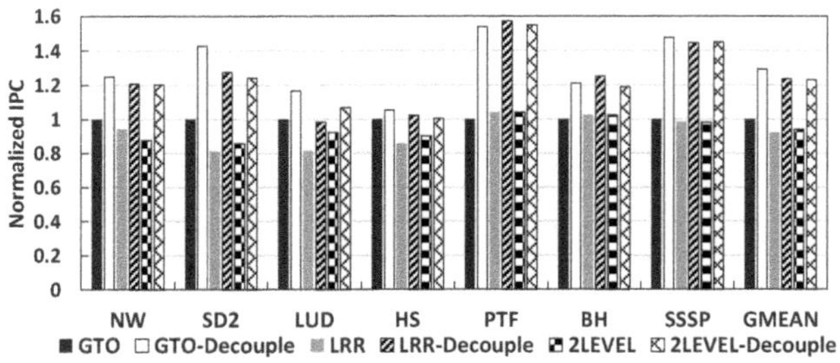

Figure 15: Performance of our design with various warp scheduling policies, normalized to pure GTO performance.

ther increasing the cache size has no performance benefit. (2) Even a 16KB Decoupled L1D can achieve the average performance close to a 128KB baseline L1 D-cache, which indicates that our design can significantly improve GPU performance without incurring higher area overhead.

6.4 Sensitivity to Warp Scheduling Policies

Prior sections use the Greedy-Then-Oldest (GTO) warp scheduling policy for experiments. Figure 15 shows the sensitivity of our design to various warp scheduling policies. Loosely Round Robin Scheduler (LRR) is oblivious to the access locality while GTO outperforms it by preserving the intra-warp data locality. The two-level scheduler (2LEVEL) proposed by Narasiman et al.[22] exploits inter-warp data locality by scheduling groups of warps (called FG) together to ensure different groups touching long-latency memory accesses at different times. However, 2LEVEL still performs worse than GTO. Rogers et al.[24] found that performing inter-FG in round-robin would destroy intra-warp locality of old warps, which however can be captured by GTO. Figure 15 highlights that improving the scheduling policy can increase performance by reducing the inter-warp contention. Our design complements it by further reducing the intra-warp contention (e.g., conflict misses & MSHR reservation fails), which cannot be addressed by any warp scheduler [15]. Therefore, our design can achieve further performance gains with different warp scheduling policies.

6.5 Hardware Cost And Energy Efficiency

We evaluate the hardware cost and energy efficiency of our Decoupled L1D design using CACTI 6.5 [28].

Hardware Cost: The major source of area overhead for supporting the SRAM-based Decoupled L1D comes from the expanded tag store. We didn't change the bandwidth and number of ports in the Decoupled L1D and we assume 1 additional cycle for the extended tag-store probe. However, this additional latency is hidden by the thread-level parallelism, similar to the additional buffer latency described in [15]. Each tag has two additional fields, one for RC (6 bit) and the other for Position field (2 bit). With the expanded tag entries (256), the total area of Decoupled L1D is estimated as 0.244 mm^2 for the entire 15-SM system using 45nm technology, which is 0.008 mm^2 more than the original L1 D-cache. Such additional area represents approximately 0.02% of the GTX480 area [5], which is also a 15-SM system implemented in a 40nm technology. Other miscellaneous overheads such as the 2-bit per set 'Free_Lines' counter in Decoupled L1D are negligible in comparison.

Energy Efficiency: Since our design is a simple tag store extension to the existing L1 D-cache, it does not require a large amount of energy-consuming cache logic circuitry. From the baseline L1 D-cache to Decoupled L1D, the *dynamic read energy per access* and *total leakage power* increases by 0.002 nJ and 1.7 mW respectively. Such small energy overhead can be disregarded compared to the substantial energy improvements from our design by significantly reducing L1 cache misses (by up to 80% for SSSP) and off-chip (L2+DRAM) memory accesses. Specifically, the three CNF workloads with the most energy reduction are PTF (10.4%), BH (14.7%) and SSSP (11.4%).

7. RELATED WORK

CPU Cache Management: Prior studies have looked into optimizing LRU-based cache replacement policies for better performance, such as PiPP[32], RRIP[14] and SHiP[29]. However, due to the small cache capacity and massive parallelism in GPUs, even the most advanced replacement policies cannot address their cache contention problems [24]. Our locality-driven dynamic bypassing design aims to decide if a memory access should even be inserted into the cache, in order to reduce cache contention. Our approach is complementary to these cache replacement optimizations and in fact they are applied to preserve the temporal locality of the cache lines in our design. There also have been some work [19, 12, 13, 18] proposed for CPUs on cache bypassing, which are usually designed for LLCs, where data locality is already filtered by previous level(s). But the poor locality of GPU workloads imposes difficulty for these approaches to make robust predictions for L1 D-cache (where locality is unfiltered). Our approach is specifically designed for throughput-oriented architectures like GPUs and it outperforms the state-of-the-art CPU bypassing approach PDP-best [12] for both CNF and CF workloads, especially for irregular applications. V-Way cache [23] manipulates data store to enable global data replacement. On the contrary, our design focuses on integrating locality filter into the L1 D-cache for bypassing by using an expanded tag store to trace the reuse frequency of accesses, with significantly different structures and operations.

GPU cache management: Previous work [22, 24, 17, 20] has made efforts on improving cache performance by changing the warp scheduling policies. For instance, CCWS [24] dynamically throttles active warps to avoid cross-warp contention by using a victim cache tag array. However, warp schedulers can neither address intra-warp contention nor eliminate cache pollution that is extensively caused by caching "unfriendly" data. Furthermore, warp throttling methods can reduce parallelism for processing memory requests and subsequently limit the resource utilization. MRPB [15] designs a FIFO queue for reordering memory requests in order to reduce intra- and inter- warp contention. It also uses a simple bypassing mechanism, which only bypasses when intra-warp contention occurs upon unavailable resources (e.g. MSHR reservation fails). More importantly, it does not consider any data locality of the access stream, which results in incorrectly bypassing accesses with good reuse. In contrast, our design aims to only store the data with high re-references and short reuse distance to maximally reduce cache pollution and resource contention. As shown in Section 6.1, for both CNF and CF workloads, our design outperforms MRPB significantly, which outperforms CCWS [24] and [22]. Work [11] directly applies a dynamic PDP approach (runtime best-effort prediction using hardware sampling) on GPUs for L1 bypassing and uses warp throttling if contention at L2 and DRAM level are generated by PDP. Our efficient design outperforms PDP-best (exhaustively search for the best PD) for both CF and irregular CNF applications without increasing L2 and DRAM level traffic. Xie et al. [31] analyzed which global-memory loads should be cached at compile time and chose a subset of thread blocks to use the cache at runtime. In [27], the program counters (PCs) of memory instructions are used to make a cache-bypassing decision. In comparison, we rely on memory address to drive our dynamic cache bypassing. As GPU kernels are relatively short, the working set of a memory access instruction can be relatively large, especially considering the same PC in all the thread blocks. Therefore, the instruction-level bypassing [31, 27] is more coarse-grain and may lose the opportunity of exploiting data reuse at memory address granularity.

Compiler [30, 16] and software level [10, 26] techniques were also proposed to improve GPU cache performance. Compiler-driven mechanisms [30, 16] depend heavily on inputs and profiling runs. Although they can be effective to optimize cache performance for regular applications, they cannot predict the runtime behaviors of irregular applications. Unlike our dynamic hardware approach, software techniques [10, 26] need to directly interact with applications for code optimization or data transformation, and can be detrimental to cross-platform performance portability [15].

8. CONCLUSIONS

In this paper, we analyze the GPU workloads to reveal the data reuse characteristics of different types of applications. For cache unfriendly (CNF) applications, their memory access stream feature accesses with low reuse and/or long reuse distances, causing severe cache contention and resource congestion. To address this challenge, we propose a locality-driven dynamic bypassing solution that integrates locality filtering functionality into the decoupled tag store of the current GPU L1 D-cache through simple and cost-effective hardware extensions. Experiment results show that our design achieves significant performance and energy improvements over the baseline caches and outperforms the state-of-the-art CPU and GPU cache bypassing schemes. It can significantly reduce various levels of contention without generating extra memory traffic and remain effective for various cache capacities and warp scheduling policies.

9. REFERENCES

[1] AMD APP SDK: http://developer.amd.com, 2015.

[2] AMD Graphics Cores Next (GCN) Architecture White paper, 2012.

[3] NVIDIA CUDA SDK: https://developer.nvidia.com/cuda-downloads. 2015.

[4] NVIDIA Kepler GK110 white paper. 2012.

[5] NVIDIA's next generation CUDA compute architecture: Fermi. 2009.

[6] S. S. Baghsorkhi et al. Efficient performance evaluation of memory hierarchy for highly multithreaded graphics processors. In *PPoPP '12*. ACM, 2012.

[7] A. Bakhoda et al. Analyzing cuda workloads using a detailed gpu simulator. In *ISPASS'09*, April 2009.

[8] M. Burtscher, R. Nasre, and K. Pingali. A quantitative study of irregular programs on gpus. In *IISWC'12*, Nov 2012.

[9] S. Che et al. Rodinia: A benchmark suite for heterogeneous computing. In *IISWC'09*, Oct 2009.

[10] S. Che et al. Dymaxion: Optimizing memory access patterns for heterogeneous systems. In *SC '11*. ACM, 2011.

[11] X. Chen et al. Adaptive cache management for energy-efficient gpu computing. In *MICRO-47*. ACM, 2014.

[12] N. Duong et al. Improving cache management policies using dynamic reuse distances. In *MICRO-45*, 2012.

[13] J. Gaur et al. Bypass and insertion algorithms for exclusive last-level caches. In *ISCA '11*. ACM, 2011.

[14] A. Jaleel et al. High performance cache replacement using re-reference interval prediction (RRIP). In *Proc of ISCA '10*. ACM, 2010.

[15] W. Jia, K. Shaw, and M. Martonosi. MRPB: Memory request prioritization for massively parallel processors. In *HPCA'14*.

[16] W. Jia, K. A. Shaw, and M. Martonosi. Characterizing and improving the use of demand-fetched caches in gpus. In *ICS '12*. ACM, 2012.

[17] A. Jog et al. OWL: Cooperative thread array aware scheduling techniques for improving gpgpu performance. In *ASPLOS '13*. ACM, 2013.

[18] T. L. Johnson and W.-m. W. Hwu. Run-time adaptive cache hierarchy management via reference analysis. In *ISCA '97*. ACM, 1997.

[19] M. Kharbutli and D. Solihin. Counter-based cache replacement and bypassing algorithms. *Computers, IEEE Transactions on*, April 2008.

[20] S.-Y. Lee and C.-J. Wu. CAWS: Criticality-aware warp scheduling for gpgpu workloads. In *PACT '14*. ACM, 2014.

[21] C. Li et al. Understanding the tradeoffs between software-managed vs. hardware-managed caches in gpus. In *ISPASS'14*, March 2014.

[22] V. Narasiman et al. Improving gpu performance via large warps and two-level warp scheduling. In *MICRO-44*, 2011.

[23] M. K. Qureshi, D. Thompson, and Y. N. Patt. The V-Way cache: Demand Based Associativity via Global Replacement. In *ISCA '05*, 2005.

[24] T. G. Rogers, M. O'Connor, and T. M. Aamodt. Cache-conscious wavefront scheduling. In *Proc of IEEE MICRO-45*, 2012.

[25] I. Singh et al. Cache coherence for GPU architectures. In *HPCA '13*. ACM, 2013.

[26] I.-J. Sung, G. Liu, and W.-M. Hwu. DL: A data layout transformation system for heterogeneous computing. In *InPar'12*, May 2012.

[27] Y. Tian et al. Adaptive gpu cache bypassing. In *GPGPU'15 workshop*. ACM, 2015.

[28] S. Wilton and N. Jouppi. CACTI: an enhanced cache access and cycle time model. *Solid-State Circuits, IEEE Journal of*, 31(5), May 1996.

[29] C.-J. Wu et al. SHiP: Signature-based hit predictor for high performance caching. In *MICRO-44*. ACM, 2011.

[30] X. Xie et al. An efficient compiler framework for cache bypassing on gpus. In *ICCAD'13*.

[31] X. Xie et al. Coordinated static and dynamic cache bypassing for gpus. In *Proc of HPCA'15*, pages 76–88. IEEE, Feb 2015.

[32] Y. Xie and G. H. Loh. PiPP: Promotion/Insertion pseudo-partitioning of multi-core shared caches. In *Proc of ISCA'09*. ACM, 2009.

[33] Y. Yang et al. Shared memory multiplexing: A novel way to improve gpgpu throughput. In *PACT '12*. ACM, 2012.

SemCache++: Semantics-Aware Caching for Efficient Multi-GPU Offloading

Nabeel Al-Saber, Milind Kulkarni
School of Electrical and Computer Engineering
Purdue University
West Lafayette, IN, USA
nalsaber, milind@purdue.edu

ABSTRACT

Offloading computations to multiple GPUs is not an easy task. It requires decomposing data, distributing computations and handling communication manually. GPU drop-in libraries (which require no program rewrite) have made it easy to offload computations to multiple GPUs by hiding this complexity inside library calls. Such encapsulation prevents the reuse of data between successive kernel invocations resulting in redundant communication. This limitation exists in multi-GPU libraries like CUBLASXT.

In this paper, we introduce SemCache++, a semantics-aware GPU cache that automatically manages communication between the CPU and multiple GPUs in addition to optimizing communication by eliminating redundant transfers using caching. SemCache++ is used to build the first multi-GPU drop-in replacement library that (a) uses the virtual memory to automatically manage and optimize multi-GPU communication and (b) requires no program rewriting or annotations. Our caching technique is efficient; it uses a two level caching directory to track matrices and sub-matrices. Experimental results show that our system can eliminate redundant communication and deliver performance improvements over multi-GPU libraries like StarPU and CUBLASXT.

Categories and Subject Descriptors

D.1.3 [**Programming Techniques**]: Concurrent Programming—*Parallel Programming*; D.4.2 [**Operating Systems**]: Storage Management—*Distributed Memories*

Keywords

Multi-GPU offloading; GPGPU; Communication optimization

1. INTRODUCTION

Graphics processing units (GPUs) offer massive, highly-efficient parallelism, making them an attractive target for computation intensive applications. Due to the difficulty of programming GPUs, a practical option for leveraging their capabilities is to *offload* computation using libraries. For example, there are many GPU implementations of linear algebra libraries [16, 11, 20, 18], which outperform CPU implementations of popular libraries such as BLAS [8] and LAPACK [3] by taking advantage of the GPU's parallel hardware. Such GPU libraries allow existing applications written against the BLAS and LAPACK APIs to easily benefit from execution on heterogeneous platforms: most computation executes on the CPU, but invocations of BLAS methods are executed on the GPU.

ICS'15, June 8–11, 2015, Newport Beach, CA, USA.

ACM 978-1-4503-3559-1/15/06 ...$15.00.
http://dx.doi.org/10.1145/2751205.2751210.

This library-based offloading approach to harnessing the power of GPUs has some drawbacks. Notably, moving data back and forth between the CPU and the GPU incurs significant expense, making optimizing this communication paramount when library calls are composed. If successive library calls operate on the same data, the data should be moved to the GPU just once, rather than separately for each call, while data should only be transferred back to the CPU if a computation requires it. Such optimization is in tension with the encapsulation objectives of library-based offloading: if a programmer has to manually manage communication between the CPU and GPU, she can no longer port her program to a heterogeneous system without modification.

To help tackle this problem, over the past several years there have been several proposals to introduce automatic memory management between the CPU and single GPU, freeing the programmer from the burden of managing data movement [13, 12, 9, 17, 2]; in fact, the newest version of CUDA [15] offers *Unified Memory (UM)*, which dynamically tracks data movement between the CPU and GPU, minimizing communication. As a result of these techniques, library-based offloading is a viable option for leveraging a GPU in a heterogeneous system.

In recent years, *Multi-GPU* systems are becoming increasingly popular, with multiple GPUs available for computation offloading. Unfortunately, handling multi-GPU systems is substantially harder than managing a single GPU, as now computation and data need to be distributed across multiple GPUs. To simplify multi-GPU offloading, libraries such as CUBLASXT [16], MAGMA [20] and CULA [11], completely encapsulate communication in their library calls: prior to invoking a method, data is transferred to the GPU(s), and upon completion, data is transferred back. Such encapsulation introduces significant overheads, as much of this data movement is redundant. However, without encapsulation, managing data movement between kernels is quite difficult in multi-GPU systems.

While there have been several attempts at developing multi-GPU frameworks that can optimize communication more thoroughly, they are not well-suited to developing library replacements. They either require adopting a new programming model such as StarPU [4] and PTask [19] or require annotating every CPU data access, including those outside the offloaded library call such as StarSs [5]. The burden of rewriting an application or annotating large numbers of data accesses makes these models hard to adopt for large applications.

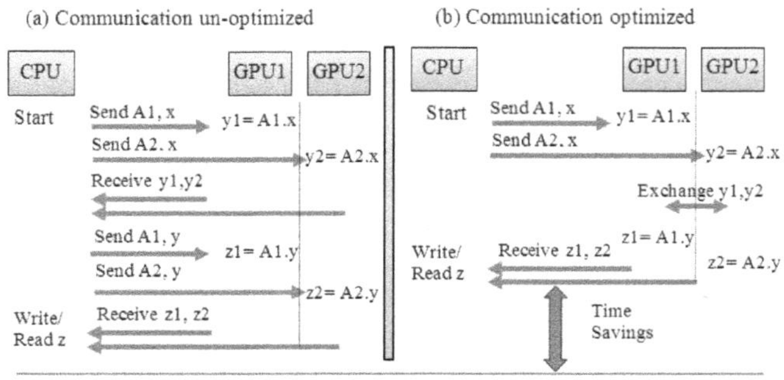

Figure 1: Communication comparison of Encapsulated Multi-GPU libraries and hand tuned communication

To understand the difficulty of managing data movement between CPUs and multiple GPUs, consider distributing a series of matrix-vector multiplications (MVMs): $y = A * x; z = A * y$. (This type of computation arises in algorithms such as Jacobi iteration.) To distribute this computation across GPUs, each operation should be decomposed. A natural decomposition is to split A horizontally into two submatrices A_1 and A_2, sending one to each GPUs. x can then be sent to both GPUs, computing $y_1 = A_1 * x$ and $y_2 = A_2 * x$.

Figure 1 demonstrates two different ways that communication could be handled for the remainder of this computation. If the MVM were fully-encapsulated, as in Figure 1(a), y_1 and y_2 would be sent back to the CPU and combined into y. When the second MVM is executed, A_1 and A_2 will be re-sent to each GPU, along with the re-composed y. A more efficient approach is to *leave* A in its decomposed form on both GPUs, as in Figure 1(b). When the second MVM is invoked, each GPU already has part of y already resident, and need only receive the portion of y they do not already have in order to complete their computation. This dramatically reduces the amount of communication. However, organizing this computation and communication correctly requires realizing that the communication of A is redundant and also that only a portion of y need be communicated. Note that the situation only becomes more complicated if the CPU requires access to the data as well: if code on the CPU (*i.e.*, not in library calls) accesses y between the two MVMs, then y must be fetched back from the GPUs, but the programmer must realize that the portions of y on the GPUs are still valid to avoid performing redundant communication for the second MVM. All in all, efficiently managing communication imposes a significant burden on the programmer.

What is needed is an *automatic* approach to managing data movement between the CPU and multiple GPUs that can *dynamically* determine whether data movement is necessary and most importantly provide a drop-in replacement library without adopting a new programming model.

In our previous work, we proposed SemCache [2], a runtime system to automatically manage and optimize communication between the CPU and a single GPU using caching. SemCache was used to build a drop-in GPU BLAS library. In this paper we propose SemCache++, an extension of SemCache that (a) enables the development of multi-GPU libraries with optimized communication by carefully tracking the coherence and matrix decomposition on multiple GPUs and (b) optimizes synchronization across library calls by continuing CPU execution past GPU library calls. This allows exploiting all devices (CPUs and GPUs) in parallel and allows to overlap communication with computation (even on a single GPU). Although both systems will have the same drop-in interface, the runtime system in SemCache++ is completely redesigned to support multiple accelerators and to allow the new features.

At a high level, SemCache++ treats the GPU memories as software caches, leaving data on the GPU even after library calls return. A SemCache++-enabled library call decomposes its computation across multiple GPUs. For example, a BLAS call will be decomposed into a series of operations over submatrices. When the computations complete, the results remain on the GPUs, rather than being transferred back to the CPU. SemCache++ tracks the location of each of the operands of the subcomputations. If another BLAS call is invoked, SemCache++ can avoid communication by directing subcomputations to GPUs that already have the necessary data. If communication is necessary, either between GPUs or because the CPU requires the results of a computation, SemCache++ can automatically perform the data transfer, updating its record of where the submatrices reside. SemCache++ exploits all GPUs in parallel. It also takes advantage of new CUDA features such as CUDA streams to overlap communication and computation, further enhancing performance. Crucially, all of SemCache++'s tracking and scheduling is encapsulated in library calls. Communication between the CPU and GPU(s) is managed transparently to the programmer, and SemCache++ libraries can be "dropped in" in place of existing linear algebra libraries without substantial program modifications.

1.1 Contributions

This paper makes the following contributions:

- The design and implementation of SemCache++, a generic multi-GPU cache that automatically manages communication between CPU and multiple GPUs at variable granularity.
- SemCache++ exploits all devices (CPUs and GPUs) in parallel, and uses CUDA streams to allow overlapping of communication and computation.
- A SemCache++-enabled multi-GPU BLAS library that provides a drop-in replacement for existing BLAS libraries.
- Experimental results showing that SemCache++ can dramatically reduce redundant communication, and deliver significant performance improvements over CUBLASXT, NVIDIA's tuned multi-GPU BLAS library.

2. BACKGROUND

2.1 Multi-GPU Drop-in Libraries

The most popular approach to leveraging multiple GPUs is to provide libraries that encapsulate the necessary decomposition and communication. CUBLASXT [16], MAGMA [20] and CULA [11] all provide subsets of BLAS and LAPACK methods that have been optimized for multiple GPUs. As described in the introduction, this encapsulation carries with it a cost: each method call is optimized in isolation, so any opportunities to identify and avoid redundant communication *across* library calls are lost. Essentially, data is "based" at the CPU, and is only distributed among GPUs for the duration of the method call, resulting in redundant communication of shared operands across method calls, and unnecessary communication of result operands when they are not necessary on the CPU.

In libraries such as CUBLASXT, this back-and-forth communication is hidden through pipelining. The computation is broken into chunks, which are distributed among the multiple GPUs. While each GPU is performing a chunk of computation, input data for the next chunk is concurrently sent to the GPU and output data from the previous chunk is retrieved from the GPU. Provided the computation is operating over sufficient data, most of the communication cost can be completely overlapped with computation. Note that the effectiveness of this overlap is dependent on properly choosing the chunk size for pipelining—CUBLASXT leaves the selection of granularity to the programmer, breaking the abstraction layer somewhat.

This pipelining strategy has a deleterious side effect: because the operands must be transferred to the GPU for *every* method call, and the implementation relies on overlapping communication with computation, the communication costs cannot be hidden for small inputs. Moreover, some linear algebra methods, such as SAXPY, simply do not contain enough computation to amortize the communication cost, regardless of how large the input data is (because communication cost grows at the same rate as computation time). Hence, such operations cannot be profitably executed on the GPU, even if there is opportunity to exploit the computation resources of multiple GPUs. As a result, CUBLASXT only provides multi-GPU implementations of BLAS Level 3 methods, while other libraries such as MAGMA also only provide a subset of LAPACK methods. The abstraction boundary imposed by the library interfaces to linear algebra routines precludes exposing communication management to programmers; the only way to support computation offloading efficiently is to automate the data management.

2.2 Multi-GPU automatic data management models

In recent years, researchers have proposed many multi-GPU frameworks to optimize communication and provide automatic data management, such as StarPU [4], FLAME [18], PTask [19], and StarSs [5]. These systems tackle the challenge of effectively managing communication between the CPU and multiple GPUs. However, they come with a different set of drawbacks than the drop-in libraries described previously. Fundamentally, these models rely on identifying all computations that operate on data that may be accessed by the GPU, allowing their runtime systems to track dependences on that data to manage communication. To support this dependence tracking, the systems either require adopting a new task-based programming model [4, 18, 19] or require annotations of all data accesses [5].

2.3 SemCache

In prior work, we proposed SemCache, a system for writing libraries suited for single-GPU offloading, backed by a variable-granularity cache to manage data movement between the CPU and GPU [2]. This section briefly summarizes SemCache's operation, as it forms the basis for SemCache++.

Like previous memory management systems for GPUs ([13, 17, 12, 9]), SemCache maintains what amounts to a distributed shared memory (DSM) between the CPU and GPU. SemCache tracks shared data at a variable granularity—as memory ranges. Memory ranges are tracked in a directory structure, along with their cache state: one of ***S***hared, ***C***PU exclusive, or ***G***PU exclusive. The granularity of a memory range is determined the first time an offloaded operation is performed on the memory. Libraries for GPU offloading use SemCache directives to register the memory ranges that are read and written by an offloaded operation. For example, in the BLAS operation DGEMM ($C += A * B$), matrices A and B are registered as read, while C is registered as read and written.

SemCache uses page protection to determine when the CPU accesses data. Although access detection is done at page granularity, SemCache tracks and transfers data at the granularity of matrices. More fined grained systems like Cuda Unified Memory transfer matrices at the granularity of pages. For large matrices, page transfers result in significant slow downs as shown in Section 5.3.

In the single-GPU case, SemCache completely avoids any redundant or unnecessary communication. Data is only transferred between the CPU and GPU when one device or the other requires the data, and caching on the GPU allows offloaded operations to reuse data transferred by earlier operations. The main limitation of SemCache is the synchronous memory transfers which blocks the CPU until the GPU communication is done. Many features can be enabled with asynchronous transfers like: hybrid CPU/GPU parallel execution, and overlapping communication with computation. The following section explains how SemCache++ builds on SemCache to work with multiple GPUs and addresses its limitations.

3. SemCache++

This section introduces SemCache++, an extension of SemCache that supports multiple GPUs. SemCache++ automatically manages data movement and synchronization across SemCache++-enabled library calls. These libraries can thus be used as direct replacements for CPU libraries, providing the performance of hand-tuned multi-GPU implementations without breaking the abstraction boundaries of the library.

3.1 High Level Overview

A SemCache++-enabled library looks, to a programmer, like a typical CPU library. SemCache++ directives (embedded in the library code, not exposed at the interface level) specify what data (matrices) are read and written by the library call. SemCache++ libraries provide multi-GPU implementations by decomposing the computation into subtasks that operate over portions of the data (submatrices). These computations are then distributed across multiple GPUs as part of the library implementation (Section 4 discusses a concrete example of how such a library might be implemented).

SemCache++ can also support hybrid CPU/GPU execution. Since each submatrix is tracked and executed separately, the CPU can be also exploited in parallel with multiple GPUs to compute part of the result.

SemCache++ manages communication by tracking the locations of the submatrices, identifying whether it is on the CPU, or on one or more GPUs, or shared between the CPU and GPUs. Data is not eagerly communicated, but instead it is only transferred if it is needed by a computation. Because the data remains distributed after a library call completes, when a future library call is issued, the subtasks of that call can be dispatched to appropriate GPUs to reduce communication.

SemCache++ then ensures that the CPU and GPU(s) maintain a consistent view of data by transferring data back from the GPU(s) whenever the CPU requires the data. As in SemCache, SemCache++ determines when a CPU reads or writes data through the use of page protection. Note that while data on the GPUs is tracked at the granularity of decomposed inputs (submatrices), data on the CPU is tracked at the granularity of entire matrices. Thus, SemCache++ uses a two-level directory structure to track data, as described next.

3.2 Cache Design and Structure

SemCache++ uses a directory structure to track the status of data that is used during offloading operations. Figure 2 illustrates the design of this directory. As mentioned above, SemCache++ uses a two-level structure: the first level of the directory tracks matrices at the granularity they are used in library calls, while the second level is used to track the submatrices that are distributed across GPUs.

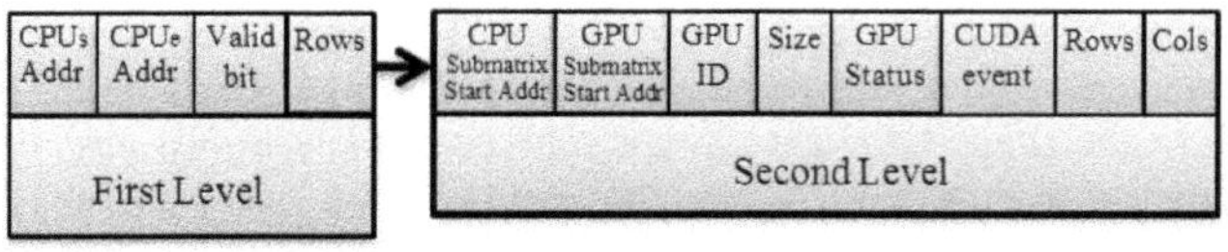

Figure 2: Structure of Caching Directory

The first level of the directory tracks the matrices that are involved in offloading operations, indexed by the CPU start address (CPU_s) and CPU end address (CPU_e). This first level also records the number of rows in the matrix (n_r), to support efficient memory transfer, as described in Section 3.2.1. Finally, the first level records whether the matrix is valid or invalid on the CPU.

SemCache++ assumes that matrices are stored contiguously in memory. When an offloadable method is invoked, the directory can be queried to see if entries exist for the matrix operands of the method. If not, an entry is created. Note that since library methods operate on entire matrices (matrices are only decomposed for distribution across multiple GPUs), lookups into the first level happen at the granularity of matrices.

The first-level entry for a matrix points to a set of *translation records* for the matrix. When a matrix is decomposed into submatrices and distributed across the GPUs, each submatrix is assigned a record in this second level. A translation record serves several purposes. First, it translates between the location of data on the CPU and the corresponding location on the GPUs, facilitating data movement between devices. Second, it keeps track of the coherence state of the data (*i.e.*, where valid copies of the submatrix reside). Finally, it tracks the ready state of the data (*i.e.*, whether the data is available for use by a task). The following sections describe these tasks in more detail.

When a task is launched to execute on a GPU, it uses SemCache++ directives to identify which submatrices are needed for the computation. If the data is already being tracked by the first level, SemCache++ checks the status of the required submatrices in the second level. If the data does not exist on the target GPU, communication is performed.

3.2.1 Translating between CPU and GPU Addresses and Transferring Data

A submatrix is a region of data within the range of a larger matrix. The submatrix may be copied to the GPU as row tiles or column tiles, the translation record stores the start address of the submatrix on the CPU as well as the number of rows and columns. The submatrices are stored contiguously on the GPU, so the translation record tracks the start address of the data on the GPU and the size of the data. Because a submatrix may be replicated on multiple GPUs, the translation record stores the GPU ID and the start address for each GPU the submatrix resides on.

This translation information is used to transfer data back and forth between the CPU and GPUs, as well as for inter-GPU transfers. Inter-GPU transfers are straightforward. If the submatrix is being moved to a GPU that does not currently have a copy of the submatrix, new space is allocated on that GPU and the translation record is updated to reflect the location of that space. When moving a submatrix from the CPU to the GPU, the row and column information stored in the translation record for the submatrix are used to generate a `cublasSetMatrix` call, which provides a single call to transfer an entire tile of a matrix to the specified GPU, allocating memory if necessary. Data tracking is done at the granularity of submatrices. When the CPU requires access to region of data computed on the GPU, only the corresponding submatrix is transferred back using a `cublasGetMatrix` call.

3.2.2 SemCache++ Coherence Protocol

SemCache++ uses a modified MSI coherence protocol to track which devices have valid copies of (sub)matrices. The states are tracked through the use of a *valid* bit in the first level entry for a matrix, as well as a *GPU Status* field for each submatrix in the second-level entry. The *CPU valid* bit in the first-level tracks whether or not the matrix is available to the CPU to speedup the lookup process. It is set when all submatrices have CPU only **C** status or shared **S** status. When the *CPU valid* bit is unset, each submatrix can have a different status and the GPU Status field in the second-level entry is used to determine the status as follows:

- **C:** Submatrix exclusive to CPU.
- **S:** Submatrix shared between CPU and GPU(s).
- **G:** Submatrix valid only on GPU(s).

The caching directory records transitions between states in the usual way, triggering communication if necessary. If a task dispatched to a GPU reads a submatrix that is not already on the GPU, then data is transferred (from the CPU if possible, as GPU-GPU communication is often slower), an entry for the submatrix is created, and the status in the second level is set to shared (**S**). SemCache++ allows multiple copies of the same submatrix to exist in the shared status; if another GPU wants the submatrix, then it receives a copy, too. However, like regular caches if a submatrix needs to be written to, all shared copies of the submatrix are discarded and only one submatrix holds a modified state (**G**).

If a matrix is *read* on the CPU while the first-level valid bit is unset, the GPU status is checked in the second level entries. If the status is **G**, submatrices are transferred from the GPU back to the CPU, the valid bit is set, and all submatrices change status to shared (**S** state). If a matrix is *written* on the CPU, then the status of the second level entries becomes **C**, with data transferred back from the GPUs if necessary.

Section 3.3 describes the CPU and GPU instrumentation that triggers the state changes in the coherence protocol.

3.2.3 Synchronization

The final purpose of the second-level translation record for a submatrix is to enable synchronization between tasks. To facilitate parallelism, and the overlap of communication and computation, tasks are launched asynchronously, using CUDA's streams. Moreover, this overlap can occur across library methods, if a second library call uses the same submatrices as the first library call.

Because tasks are launched asynchronously, and from multiple (possibly dependent) library calls, it is important that tasks do not begin to execute until their predecessor tasks complete.SemCache++ takes advantage of CUDA *events*: small kernels that can be launched to streams and act as signals. Each submatrix has an event handle associated with it, stored in the translation record. Whenever a submatrix is sent to a GPU, or when a submatrix is computed (modified) by a task, the operation is performed by dispatching the task to a stream on the target GPU. The event handle associated with the submatrix is then dispatched to the same stream using `cudaEventRecord`. The semantics of streams ensure that this event will not trigger until the previous operation (communication or computation) finishes. In other words, the event will not execute until the submatrix is up-to-date on the target GPU.

Before a communication or computation operation that needs a submatrix is dispatched, SemCache++ must make sure that the submatrix is up-to-date. The submatrix's event handle is dispatched to a stream using `cudaStreamWaitEvent`. This ensures that the operation will not commence until any previous `cudaEvent-`

`Record` events associated with the same handle have completed (even if those events were dispatched on different devices). Thus, tasks that require a submatrix will wait until operations that compute or transfer that submatrix complete. Essentially, SemCache++ uses events as full/empty bits, ensuring that consumers of a submatrix wait until producers complete.

3.3 Instrumentation

3.3.1 *Instrumenting GPU Reads and Writes*

To be able to track the status of GPU data correctly, you need to determine which data is read or written by the GPU. Prior work has used compiler analysis or programmer annotations to determine if the operation is a read or a write [13, 12, 9, 17]. Since SemCache++ focuses on libraries, it can use simple directives inserted into the library code to indicate which matrices are read and written by the GPU, as well as which submatrices are needed by tasks dispatched to various GPUs.

3.3.2 *Instrumenting CPU Reads and Writes*

Similar to SemCache, SemCache++ uses the operating system's virtual memory protection to automatically detect CPU reads and writes. Page protection can be used to limit access to the CPU data which has been sent to the GPU. For each submatrix that SemCache++ tracks on the CPU, SemCache++ sets page protection flags for all the pages the submatrix spans. The page protection flags are set according to the state of the data structure. If the submatrix is in G state, its pages are set to `NO ACCESS`; if the submatrix is in S state, its pages are set to `READ ACCESS`; and if the submatrix is in C state, the pages are set to `READ and WRITE ACCESS`.

If a CPU access triggers a page fault due to write to a no access region or a read only region, SemCache++ looks up the address that caused the page fault in the caching directory. If the translation record is found, it transfers the submatrix back from the GPU and the submatrix status becomes CPU only (C). If a CPU access triggers a page fault due to a read to a no access region, SemCache++ transfers the submatrix back from the GPU and the submatrix status becomes shared (S).

In order to avoid false sharing between matrices, memory allocation should be page-aligned and padded out to page boundaries.[1] Depending on the matrix decomposition, false sharing might also exit between submatrices which share the same page. If a single submatrix is modified by a GPU, all of the pages the submatrix spans are protected to no access. If this submatrix is invalidated, the other submatrix which shares the same page is conservatively invalidated and both submatrices are transferred back to the CPU.

Page aligned memory allocation can introduce some wasted memory which is negligible for larger data sizes. Usually, it is only profitable to offload medium to large data structures on the GPU to take advantage of the parallelism, where this overhead is minimal (<1% for 400x400 matrix). We note that this overhead is only introduced on the CPU side. On the GPUs, sub-matrices are allocated in variable sizes and do not have to be page aligned.

3.4 Managing Available GPU Memory

Using multiple GPUs increases the total available memory space. Kernels that do not fit in a single GPU memory can be executed on multiple GPUs. Although multi-GPU increases the caching space, data might occupy all of the free GPU memory. In such a situation, to allocate new data in the GPU memory, cached data must be freed. To determine which address ranges should be freed, SemCache++ uses least-recently-used (LRU) policy. Any data accessed on the GPU is added to the end of a queue. If the GPU memory is full, data at the head of the queue is removed. Note that depending on the application other polices can be used.

[1]While page aligning data requires some program modification, identifying allocations to modify is significantly easier than, for example, identifying data accesses to annotate.

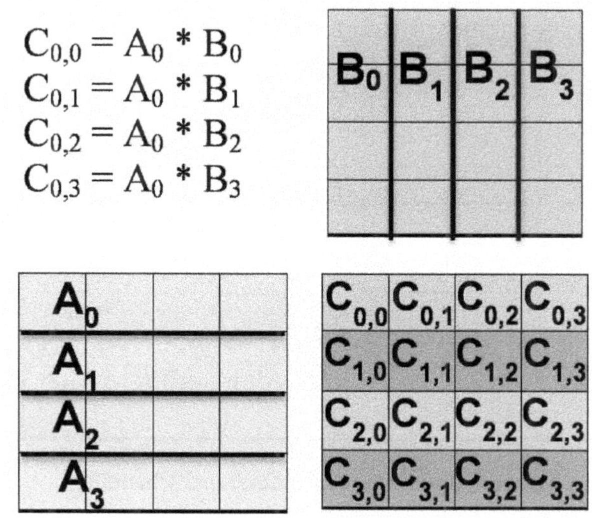

Figure 3: Matrix decomposition

4. ADAPTING A LIBRARY TO USE SemCache++

This section describes the process of building a library for multi-GPU offloading using SemCache++. First, we describe how a matrix multiply (DGEMM) call can be decomposed to distribute computations across multiple GPUs. Then we describe how SemCache++ directives can be used to perform automatic data management and synchronization.

4.1 Multi-GPU Decomposition and Scheduling

There are multiple parallel algorithms for solving matrix computations on distributed systems (*i.e.* ScaLAPACK [6]). Choosing the right algorithm depends on the underlying network and computing architecture. Many factors can be taken into consideration to determine which algorithm to use like load balancing, optimizing communication and computation-communication ratio. SemCache++ is not tied to a single algorithm, it can be used with any distribution algorithm. It can automatically cache and manage the communication with any type of these algorithms. In our implementation of DGEMM, we adopt a strategy similar to Song *et al.*, which takes advantage of locality to minimize communication [22].

DGEMM calculates $C = \alpha * A * B + \beta * C$. The distribution of the computation across N devices uses a straightforward decomposition. Each matrix is partitioned into N^2 submatrices (an $N \times N$ grid), each of which is tracked separately by SemCache++. For notational convenience, we consider that A's submatrices are grouped into N rows, $A_0, A_1, \ldots, A_{N-1}$, and B's submatrices are grouped into N columns, $B_0, B_1, \ldots, B_{N-1}$. The matrix multiplication is thus broken into N^2 tasks, with a row of A's submatrices being multiplied by a column of B's to produce a single submatrix of C. The decomposition and computation are shown pictorially in Figure 3.

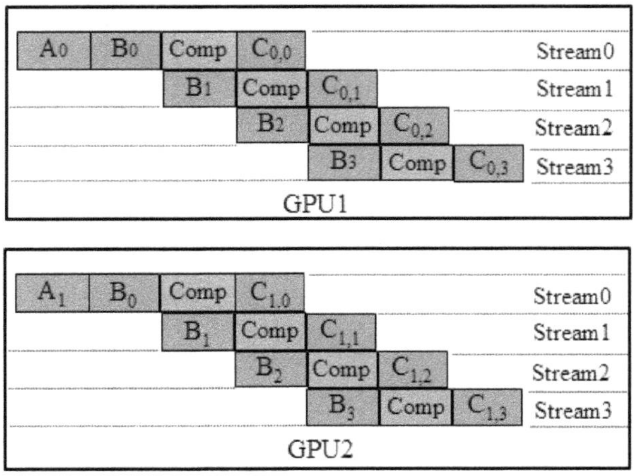

Figure 4: SemCache++ Computation scheduling

As in Song *et al.*, the computation is scheduled by (conceptually) distributing C's submatrices to the N GPUs by dividing the grid of submatrices evenly by rows. Tasks that compute each submatrix of C are then scheduled on the appropriate GPU. Independent tasks are assigned to different streams on the GPU, allowing the computation of one C submatrix to be overlapped with communicating the operands from B for the next task. Figure 4 shows how this pipelining can hide communication overheads.

Note that once the computation is completed, each GPU holds a row of A's submatrices and *all* of B. These submatrices remain on the GPUs until another device wants the data. If subsequent calls use the same matrices, mapping tasks to the appropriate GPUs can avoid communication.

For less compute intensive BLAS routines like level 1 and 2, a simple decomposition can be used. Each matrix can be split by rows into multiple sub-matrices. The number of sub-matrices is equal to the number of GPUs. Each GPU performs part of the computation. Sending the data to the GPU can be pipelined but it has little effect on the performance since the percentage of communication is much higher than the computation.

4.2 SemCache++ Directives

SemCache++'s API for identifying which computations a task needs is similar to the API defined in SemCache [2], extended to support multiple GPUs. SemCache++ requires that the programmer to specify the number of GPUs using the API method: `SemCacheDeviceSelect(devicesNumber,deviceIds)`. As in SemCache, `readGPU` is used to indicate to SemCache++ that a region of memory (in this case, a submatrix) will be read during a GPU task; the only difference is that in SemCache++, the GPU that will read the submatrix must be identified. Analogously, `writeGPU` is used to indicate that a submatrix was modified by a particular GPU after a task, potentially triggering invalidation of the submatrix on other GPUs or on the CPU.

Because it is common to distribute the entire matrices at once, SemCache++ also provides aggregate versions of `readGPU` and `writeGPU` that operate over a whole matrix, decomposing and distributing the matrix across the GPUs. These aggregate functions automatically decompose a matrix into multiple submatrices and distribute the submatrices by rows or columns to the GPUs. If the submatrix requires further decomposition, it is decomposed into N^2 submatrices. Different decomposition and distribution algorithms exist in SemCache++. Since the decomposition algorithms are not tightly coupled with SemCache++, new algorithms can be easily defined and used. `DecomposeRow` and `DecomposeCol`

```
SemCacheDgemm(TRANSA,TRANSB,M,N,K,ALPHA,
    A,LDA,B,LDB,BETA,C,LDC) {
  //A stored on CPU in memory range [A, A+(M*K*8))
  //A will be decomposed and sent to multiple GPUs, its
       state will be "S"
  entryA = readGPU(A, M, K, DecomposeRow)

  //B stored on CPU in memory range [B, B+(K*N*8))
  //B will be decomposed and sent to multiple GPUs, its
       state will be "S"
  entryB = readGPU(B, K, N, DecomposeCol)

  //C stored on CPU in memory range [C, C+(M*N*8))
  //If BETA!=0, C will be decomposed and sent to multiple
       GPUs, its state will be "S"
  entryC = readGPU(C, M, N, DecomposeRow)

  foreach GPU{
    foreach stream{
    //Perform computation on submatrix
    cublasDgemm(stream,
      TRANSA,TRANSB,Atiles,Btiles,K,ALPHA,
      entryA.subRecord.gpu_s,LDA,
      entryB.subRecord.gpu_s,LDB,BETA,
      entryC.subRecord.gpu_s,LDC)

    //Issue synchronization event for submatrix C
    cudaEventRecord(entryC.subRecord.sync_event, stream);
    }
  }
  //C was written by cublasDgemm
  //Each C block state will be updated to GPU only "G"
  writeGPU(C, M, N, DecomposeRow)
}
```

Figure 5: Pseudocode of SemCache++ matrix multiply (DGEMM)

distribute submatrices by rows and columns, respectively. Figure 5 shows how these aggregate functions can be used to manage submatrices for matrix multiply.

Inside the `readGPU` call, a lookup in the caching directory is performed using the start and end address on the CPU and the translation record is returned if found. If data does not exist on the GPU, the matrix is decomposed using the specified decomposition algorithm and sent to multiple GPUs asynchronously as described previously. If data already exist on the device, each submatrix record is inspected as follows: If a submatrix already resides on the designated GPU, no communication is necessary. If the submatrix is not valid or not on the designated GPU, a synchronization event is issued to ensure that the submatrix is up-to-date, communication is performed and the directory state is updated appropriately. `readGPU` also page-protects the CPU page(s) containing the matrix as read-only, as discussed in Section 3.3.

Pinned memory is used to allow overlapping transfers to multiple devices in parallel, it also allows concurrent communication in both direction on Fermi GPUs. Pinned memory allocates page-locked (non-swappable) memory which enables a DMA on the GPU to request transfers to and from the host memory without the involvement of the CPU.

Once all the data is transferred, the individual tasks are executed. Note that all of these kernel invocations occur asynchronously, and hence can be executed simultaneously (there are no dependences in DGEMM). However, because subsequent library calls might use the matrix C, after each task that computes C, `cudaEventRecord` is called on the submatrix's synchronization event so that later tasks wait until the submatrix is computed.

Finally, `writeGPU` changes the state of all C submatrices to GPU modified (**G**). To ensure that CPU accesses to C wait until the computation is complete and then transfer data back from the GPUs, `writeGPU` changes the page protection on C to no access.

4.3 Using SemCache++ with Complex Data Structures

While SemCache++ provides helper methods to aid in distributed matrices across multiple GPUs, not all data structures are amenable to such predictable partitioning and distribution (*e.g.*, 3D matrices, or irregular structures such as trees and graphs). In such cases, SemCache++'s low level API (`readGPU` and `writeGPU`) can be used to distribute those data structures by invoking the appropriate methods on each address range for the data structure. It becomes the library writer's responsibility to appropriately distribute the data structure. For example, to distribute a 3D matrix, SemCache++'s methods can be called individually on the address ranges for each submatrix (multiple transfer calls are needed for non-contiguous matrices) to transfer the matrix and distribute it according to the library writer's distribution algorithm. Performing distribution using the low-level methods obviates the benefits of SemCache++'s distribution functions and multi-level state tracking, but does not preclude the use of its automatic data movement capabilities.

Distributing Sparse Matrices.

As an example of distributing more complex data structures, we have used SemCache++ to provide offloading support for sparse-matrix libraries. Sparse matrices present an interesting challenge to most systems for managing communication between the CPU and the GPU because of their complex layout: a sparse matrix in CSR form has a data array, a row sum array and a column index array. Splitting the matrix between multiple GPUs requires carefully splitting the column index array and recomputing the row sum array.

SemCache++ handles distributing sparse matrices by delegating the distribution to the library implementation. The library can split the sparse matrix representation, recalculating the row sum arrays for each submatrix as necessary. SemCache++ tracks the individual arrays representing the sparse submatrix as separate submatrices. Recall that SemCache++ tracks submatrices according to a start address, number of columns and number of rows. SemCache++'s tracking of sparse matrices hence works as for any other data structure: if a task requires accessing the sparse matrix, the library issues `readGPU` calls for each of the components of the sparse matrix, and communication is performed as necessary.

This strategy for handling sparse matrices highlights a key advantage of SemCache++'s library-integrated approach to multi-GPU offloading over other approaches. The row sum arrays that are distributed across GPUs have *different contents* than the row sum array that resides on the CPU. Nevertheless, the abstract state of the sparse array is the same: the same data is stored in two different representations, depending on whether it resides on the CPU or on the GPU. SemCache++ establishes a *semantic link* between the two representations, allowing state changes on one device (*e.g.*, changing the contents of the sparse matrix on the CPU) to be reflected on other devices (*e.g.*, by invalidating all of the sparse submatrices on the GPUs).

5. EXPERIMENTAL EVALUATION

To evaluate SemCache++, we built multi-GPU implementations of the library interfaces provided by CUBLAS and CUSPARSE (NVIDIA's single-GPU linear algebra libraries) using SemCache++ directives to manage communication and synchronization. The internal, per-GPU tasks of the SemCache++ implementations were used the single-GPU CUBLAS and CUSPARSE implementations, as described in Section 4.2.

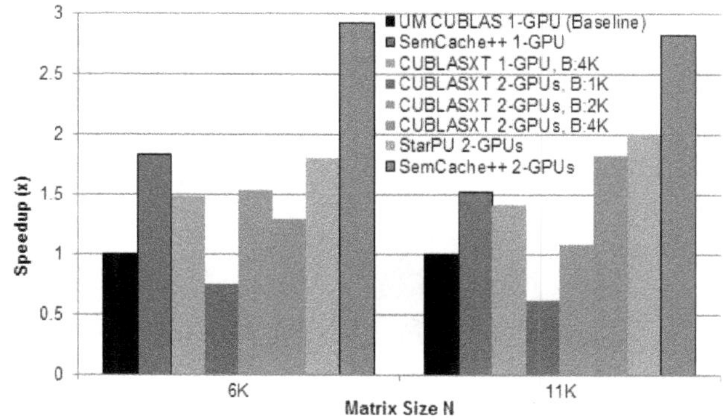

Figure 6: Speedup of microbenchmark for different matrix sizes, normalized to UM CUBLAS 1-GPU)

We evaluated three benchmarks: First, we looked at a microbenchmark that allowed us to investigate the behavior of SemCache++ as well as other multi-GPU libraries in depth. Next, we looked at two case studies of using SemCache++-enabled libraries to offload computation in two solvers: Jacobi iterative solver (which used dense matrices), and conjugate gradient (which used sparse matrices). The conjugate gradient code is taken directly from NVIDIA's CUDA benchmark suite. We compared NVIDIA's hand tuned single-GPU implementations (and UM implementations when available) with multi-GPU implementations that used SemCache++, StarPU and CUBLASXT.

We used two platforms to conduct our experiments. Most of our experiments were performed on a server with AMD Opteron Processors and 32GB memory connected via PCIe 2.0 to two NVIDIA Kepler K20 GPUs. These GPUs support compute capability 3.5 (allowing us to use NVIDIA's Unified Memory as a baseline). The second platform was used to evaluate offloading to more than two GPUs but it does not support UM. The host has AMD Opteron Processors and 64GB memory connected to eight Tesla M2090 GPUs in an external PCIe expansion chassis. While this platform let us scale to more GPUs, the external configuration of the GPUs meant that communication between the host and the GPUs was much slower. We refer to the first platform as **kepler** and the second as **tesla**.

5.1 Microbenchmark Performance Evaluation

To understand the behavior of SemCache++-enabled applications, we wrote a simple microbenchmark that performs two matrix multiplies and a DAXPY: $D = AB + AC$. Note that the two matrix multiplies share one of their operands (A), and the DAXPY operates on the results of the two multiplications. As a baseline, we used CUDA 6's unified memory along with CUBLAS to implement a communication-optimized single-GPU version of the microbenchmark. We compared this baseline to SemCache++, CUBLASXT and StarPU using one and two GPUs. Unlike SemCache++ and CUBLASXT, StarPU implementation requires rewriting the benchmark using their programming model. CUBLASXT supports multi-GPU computation by carefully overlapping communication with computation. Its performance is dependent on setting the block size for this pipelined schedule. Hence, we evaluate several different block sizes for CUBLASXT on two GPUs. These experiments were conducted on **kepler**.

Figure 6 shows the results of the microbenchmark experiment, looking at two different matrix sizes (11K×11K matrices were the largest that could fit on a single GPU for the microbenchmark). We see that even on a single GPU, both SemCache++ and CUBLASXT are faster than the baseline—this is because the baseline does not

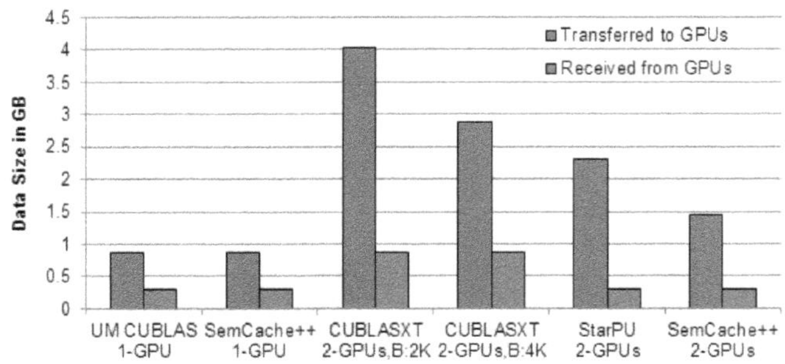

Figure 7: Microbenchmark communication results for size N=6K

overlap communication with computation, while both SemCache++ and CUBLASXT do. SemCache++ is faster than CUBLASXT because it is able to minimize communication. The A matrix is cached on both GPUs, as are the results of the DGEMMs. Hence, the DAXPY can be performed with no additional communication. In contrast, CUBLASXT, which does not leave the DGEMM results on the GPUs, must communicate the results of the DGEMMs *back* to the GPUs to perform the DAXPY.

When scaling to two GPUs, we find that SemCache++'s advantage increases: it is nearly 3× faster than the baseline, and 30-50% faster than CUBLASXT and StarPU. Although StarPU reduces redundant communication and allows overlapping communication with computation, when synchronization was used to produce correct results, overlapping was limited. Additionally, communication was not fully optimized which made it slower than SemCache++. StarPU results were similar for both: the DMDA prefetching scheduler and the eager scheduler.

We note here a further problem of CUBLASXT's reliance on computation/communication overlap: the optimal block size depends on the input matrix size. In fact, the default block size for CUBLASXT (1K) results in slower performance than a single GPU! This sort of tuning is not necessary for SemCache++, which decomposes the matrix into equal blocks regardless of input size (as described in Section 4.1). Instead, SemCache++ derives its performance improvement from avoiding redundant communication entirely.

To better understand where SemCache++'s advantages lie, we investigated two possible sources of performance improvement. First, we measured the performance of a *single* matrix multiply using SemCache++'s library and using CUBLASXT. We found that even with the optimal block size, SemCache++'s DGEMM implementation is slightly faster, about 10% for 11K matrices. We speculate this is because SemCache++ uses a simpler matrix distribution than CUBLASXT, resulting in slightly more efficient communication of the matrix operands.

The remainder of SemCache++'s performance improvement comes from optimized communication. Figure 7 shows the amount of data transferred to and from the GPU for 6K×6K matrices. SemCache++ transfers significantly less data than CUBLASXT and StarPU. Note that this figure reflects two sources of additional communication. First, StarPU's and CUBLASXT's less efficient matrix decomposition requires more communication to perform a matrix multiplication (this effect is reflected in SemCache++'s 10%-faster DGEMM than CUBLASXT). Second, in the case of CUBLASXT, matrices are re-transferred across library calls, while SemCache++ avoids this communication.

Scalability: Finally, we investigated the scalability on multiple GPUs. Figure 8 shows the microbenchmark performance on the

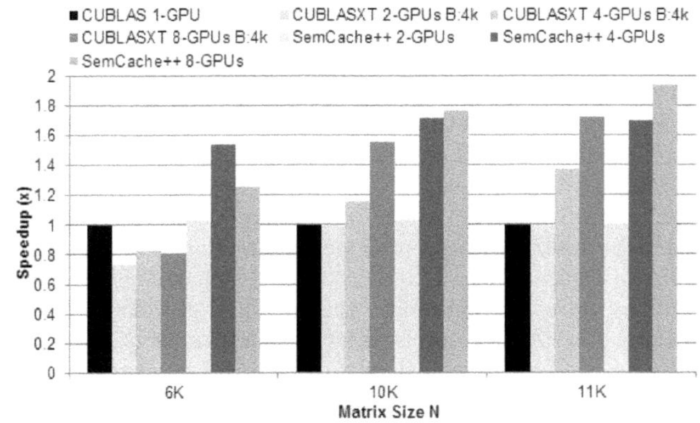

Figure 8: Microbenchmark performance on multiple GPUs for different matrix sizes, speedups with respect to CUBLAS 1-GPU)

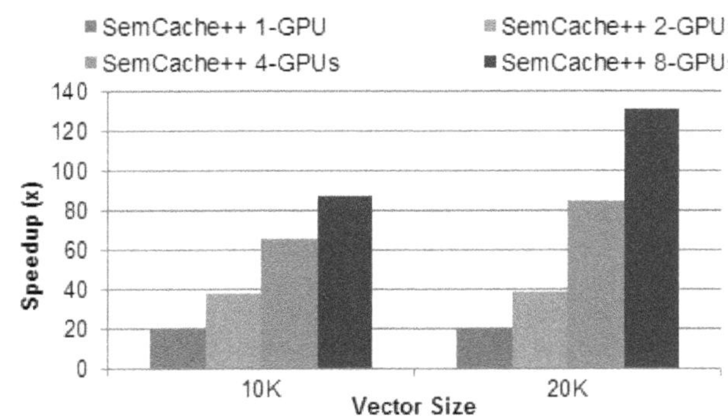

Figure 9: Speedup of Jacobi, normalized to unoptimized CUBLAS

tesla platform, running on up to 8 GPUs. For each matrix size, we show the best-performing CUBLASXT block size. Speedups are limited because communication from the host to the external GPUs is slow, and, unlike with internal GPUs that can take advantage of direct DMA transfers, with external GPUs the bandwidth is divided and hence per-GPU bandwidth decreases with scale. Nevertheless, with the largest matrices, where there is enough computation to amortize the slow communication, we see that SemCache++ is able to provide increasing performance up to 8 GPUs, and is faster than CUBLASXT running on the same number of GPUs.

5.2 Case Study(I): Jacobi Iterative Solver

The Jacobi iterative solver performs the repeated MvM computation described in the introduction. Figure 9 shows Jacobi performance for different vector sizes on the **tesla** platform. Speedups are normalized to the unoptimized CUBLAS implementation. The unoptimized version provides encapsulation; the A matrix is sent to the GPU in every iteration. Running the unoptimized CUBLAS implementation on multiple GPUs did not gain any speedups because communication cost was dominant so the results are not included in the figure. Running Jacobi using SemCache++ on a single GPU achieved 20x speedup because matrix A is cached. For large vector sizes. SemCache++ achieved linear speedups on multiple GPUs. As described in the introduction, each GPU computes part of the vector in each iteration and SemCache++ automatically sends the partial vectors to each GPU using peer to peer transfers. The communication is naturally overlapped, which minimizes the overhead. Note that unlike in our microbenchmark, the ratio of computation to communication is high enough that the slow PCIe bus does not limit scalability.

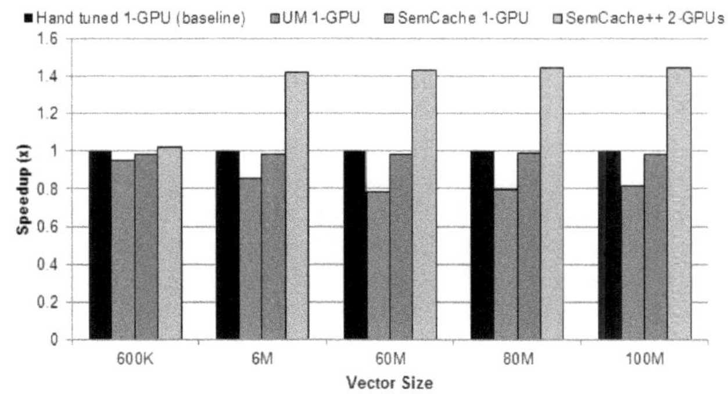

Figure 10: Speedup of CG, normalized to (Hand-tuned 1-GPU)

5.3 Case Study(II): Conjugate Gradient

NVIDIA provides two variants of conjugate gradient (CG) in its benchmark suite. In the first, communication is hand-tuned, while in the second, unified memory is used to manage communication. We use the first implementation as the baseline. Because SemCache++ enables drop-in library replacements for BLAS operations, we were able to directly use NVIDIA's unified memory code with SemCache++ to provide multi-GPU offloading.

CG uses CUBLAS and CUSPARSE libraries. Sparse matrix multiplication (SpMV) from the CUSPARSE library uses Compressed Sparse Row (CSR) format for storing matrices. The generated matrix is symmetric tridiagonal. Since the matrix is symmetric any split is balanced, we choose to split it by the number of GPUs. The rows sum is calculated per split. SpMV requires the entire vector for the matrix multiplication. Parts of the vector are computed on each GPU. SemCache++ detects from the caching directory entries that the vector is split on multiple GPUs and it automatically initiates communication to broadcast the vector to all GPUs. Each part of the vector is communicated to the other GPUs using direct GPU to GPU communication. The transfers are overlapped in both directions to double the bandwidth. It is important to note here that this is a general approach in SemCache++. It works for any SpMV kernel, there are no special optimizations done for CG.

Figure 10 shows CG performance for different vector sizes. Speedups are normalized to the hand-tuned implementation's execution time on a single GPU. SemCache performance on a single GPU is very close to hand-tuned performance, with 2% overhead due to cache lookups. Unified Memory (UM) is slower than hand-tuned because data transfers from the GPU to the CPU are done at the granularity of pages. Using SemCache++ with 2 GPUs we achieved 1.4x speedup on average over the single GPU hand-tuned baseline version for vector sizes larger than one million. Note that SemCache++ uses NVIDIA's DirectGPU capabilities when transferring data between GPUs. Nevertheless, for smaller matrix sizes, the overhead of peer-to-peer communication between GPUs limits the performance improvement. These results are consistent with the results of other multi-GPU conjugate gradient solvers [23], which found that the main limiting factor for their speedup was peer-to-peer communication.

Large problem sizes: Multi-GPU execution can not only be used to improve performance; it can also be used to run larger problem sizes than would fit on a single GPU. Splitting the matrix on 2 GPUs enabled us to run CG with sizes double the size that can fit in a single GPU. For example, we were able to run CG for a vector size of 100M on a single GPU using either single-GPU implementation, while with SemCache++ we were able to run double that size (200M) on two GPUs.

6. RELATED WORK

6.1 Programming Models

Aside from using multi-GPU enabled libraries for offloading, another approach to exploiting multiple GPUs is to use programming models that target general heterogeneous platforms. These approaches tend not to be suitable for library-based offloading, for various reasons. Kim *et al.* develop compiler tools that can automatically distribute an OpenCL kernel across multiple GPUs [14]. However, this work focuses on splitting a single kernel across GPUs, and does not consider how to optimize communication across kernels. MGPU [21] and Trilinos [10] libraries allow the programmer to specify the communication at a high level and the library automatically distributes and executes the workload on multiple GPUs. Unlike SemCache++, such libraries depends on the programmer to manually optimize communication across kernel calls.

StarPU [4], FLAME [18] and PTask [19] are task-based programming models for mapping applications to heterogeneous architectures. Such models are essentially similar: computation tasks are identified by the programmer, with dependences provided either through implicit or explicit dependence information. A runtime system then maps those tasks across the CPU and multiple GPUs, preserving dependences while trying to minimize communication. The fundamental drawback to the previous approaches is that they require writing the entire program in a task-based programming model (or using special APIs as in FLAME). Thus, these models cannot be used to provide library-based offloading, as even the non-library portions of the application must be modified to conform to the model, precluding a "drop-in" replacement for existing linear algebra libraries.

StarSs [5], OpenMP accelerator model [7] and OpenACC [1] are directive based programming languages. They require the programmer to annotate tasks with input/output information in addition to specifying the data movement. The runtime system can decompose and execute the tasks on multiple GPUs. OpenMP and OpenACC support manual caching and require the programmer to manually manage the CPU/GPU coherence. StarSs automatically caches data on the GPU for annotated tasks. Unlike drop-in replacement libraries such as those provided by SemCache++, annotations are prone to errors and they are not enough to automatically manage communication. While such models can be used to encapsulate several tasks into library calls, all computation over the data accessed during those calls must be annotated with directives, *including computations meant to execute on the CPU*. If data is cached on the GPU, any CPU access to the data needs to be annotated to maintain the coherence. Identifying such accesses for annotation is not practical for large-scale applications.

6.2 Automatic Memory Management

In the single-GPU setting, there is substantial prior work on automatic data management [13, 12, 9, 17]. Some approaches rely on compiler-assisted software coherence [13, 17], limiting applicability and scalability. Other DSM like approaches attempt to provide the appearance of a single memory space that is shared by the CPU and GPU, where data on the CPU and GPU share the same address [12, 9]. NVIDIA's Unified Memory [15] takes the same approach. Such single memory space models use the same masked address for data allocated on the CPU and the GPU to simplify address translation. If this direct address mapping is extended to multiple GPUs, each GPU needs to reserve the space for the entire matrix although only a sub-matrix is allocated on each GPU, resulting in wasted GPU memory. As a result, applications where the overall footprint is larger than a single GPU memory will not work.

Furthermore, applications where the data layout changes between the CPU and the GPU (as in the sparse matrix example) cannot be handled.

7. CONCLUSION

Multi-GPU libraries hide the complexity of decomposing data, distributing computations and handling communication manually inside library calls. Such encapsulation prevents the reuse of the data between successive kernel invocations resulting in redundant communication. In this paper, we introduced SemCache++, a semantics-aware GPU cache that automatically manages and optimizes communication between the CPU and multiple GPUs. We applied SemCache++ to the BLAS library to provide drop-in libraries that offload computation to multiple GPUs, and showed that our system can eliminate redundant communication and deliver significant performance improvements over multi-GPU libraries like CUBLASXT.

Acknowledgment: This research is supported by the Department of Energy under contract DE-FC02-12ER26104.

8. REFERENCES

[1] Openacc directives for accelerators. `http://www.openacc-standard.org`, 2011.

[2] N. AlSaber and M. Kulkarni. Semcache: Semantics-aware caching for efficient gpu offloading. In *Proceedings of the 27th International ACM Conference on International Conference on Supercomputing*, ICS '13, pages 421–432, New York, NY, USA, 2013. ACM.

[3] E. Anderson, Z. Bai, C. Bischof, S. Blackford, J. Demmel, J. Dongarra, J. Du Croz, A. Greenbaum, S. Hammarling, A. McKenney, and D. Sorensen. *LAPACK Users' Guide*. Society for Industrial and Applied Mathematics, Philadelphia, PA, third edition, 1999.

[4] C. Augonnet, S. Thibault, R. Namyst, and P.-A. Wacrenier. Starpu: A unified platform for task scheduling on heterogeneous multicore architectures. In H. Sips, D. Epema, and H.-X. Lin, editors, *Euro-Par 2009 Parallel Processing*, volume 5704 of *Lecture Notes in Computer Science*, pages 863–874. Springer Berlin Heidelberg, 2009.

[5] E. Ayguadé, R. M. Badia, F. D. Igual, J. Labarta, R. Mayo, and E. S. Quintana-Ortí. An extension of the starss programming model for platforms with multiple gpus. In *Proceedings of the 15th International Euro-Par Conference on Parallel Processing*, Euro-Par '09, pages 851–862, Berlin, Heidelberg, 2009. Springer-Verlag.

[6] O. Beaumont, V. Boudet, A. Petitet, F. Rastello, and Y. Robert. A proposal for a heterogeneous cluster scalapack (dense linear solvers). *Computers, IEEE Transactions on*, 50(10):1052–1070, Oct 2001.

[7] J. Beyer, E. Stotzer, A. Hart, and B. de Supinski. Openmp for accelerators. In B. Chapman, W. Gropp, K. Kumaran, and M. MÃijller, editors, *OpenMP in the Petascale Era*, volume 6665 of *Lecture Notes in Computer Science*, pages 108–121. Springer Berlin Heidelberg, 2011.

[8] BLAS. Basic linear algebra subprograms. `http://www.netlib.org/blas/`.

[9] I. Gelado, J. E. Stone, J. Cabezas, S. Patel, N. Navarro, and W.-m. W. Hwu. An asymmetric distributed shared memory model for heterogeneous parallel systems. In *Proceedings of the fifteenth edition of ASPLOS on Architectural support for programming languages and operating systems*, ASPLOS XV, pages 347–358, New York, NY, USA, 2010. ACM.

[10] M. A. Heroux, R. A. Bartlett, V. E. Howle, R. J. Hoekstra, J. J. Hu, T. G. Kolda, R. B. Lehoucq, K. R. Long, R. P. Pawlowski, E. T. Phipps, A. G. Salinger, H. K. Thornquist, R. S. Tuminaro, J. M. Willenbring, A. Williams, and K. S. Stanley. An overview of the trilinos project. *ACM Trans. Math. Softw.*, 31(3):397–423, 2005.

[11] J. R. Humphrey, D. K. Price, K. E. Spagnoli, A. L. Paolini, and E. J. Kelmelis. Cula: hybrid gpu accelerated linear algebra routines. *SPIE Defense and Security Symposium (DSS)*, pages 770502–770502-7, 2010.

[12] T. B. Jablin, J. A. Jablin, P. Prabhu, F. Liu, and D. I. August. Dynamically managed data for cpu-gpu architectures. In *Proceedings of the Tenth International Symposium on Code Generation and Optimization*, CGO '12, pages 165–174, New York, NY, USA, 2012. ACM.

[13] T. B. Jablin, P. Prabhu, J. A. Jablin, N. P. Johnson, S. R. Beard, and D. I. August. Automatic cpu-gpu communication management and optimization. *SIGPLAN Not.*, 47(6):142–151, June 2011.

[14] J. Kim, H. Kim, J. H. Lee, and J. Lee. Achieving a single compute device image in opencl for multiple gpus. In *Proceedings of the 16th ACM Symposium on Principles and Practice of Parallel Programming*, PPoPP '11, pages 277–288, New York, NY, USA, 2011. ACM.

[15] NVIDIA. Cuda. `https://developer.nvidia.com/cuda-toolkit`.

[16] NVIDIA. Cuda toolkit 6.0 cublas library. `http://docs.nvidia.com/cuda/cublas/index.html`, 2014.

[17] S. Pai, R. Govindarajan, and M. J. Thazhuthaveetil. Fast and efficient automatic memory management for gpus using compiler-assisted runtime coherence scheme. In *Proceedings of the 21st International Conference on Parallel Architectures and Compilation Techniques*, PACT '12, pages 33–42, New York, NY, USA, 2012. ACM.

[18] G. Quintana-Ortí, F. D. Igual, E. S. Quintana-Ortí, and R. A. van de Geijn. Solving dense linear systems on platforms with multiple hardware accelerators. In *Proceedings of the 14th ACM SIGPLAN symposium on Principles and practice of parallel programming*, PPoPP '09, pages 121–130, New York, NY, USA, 2009. ACM.

[19] C. J. Rossbach, J. Currey, M. Silberstein, B. Ray, and E. Witchel. Ptask: Operating system abstractions to manage gpus as compute devices. In *Proceedings of the Twenty-Third ACM Symposium on Operating Systems Principles*, SOSP '11, pages 233–248, New York, NY, USA, 2011. ACM.

[20] P. D. S. Tomov, R. Nath and J. Dongarra. Magma version 0.2 user guide, 2009.

[21] S. Schaetz and M. Uecker. A multi-gpu programming library for real-time applications. In *Proceedings of the 12th International Conference on Algorithms and Architectures for Parallel Processing - Volume Part I*, ICA3PP'12, pages 114–128, Berlin, Heidelberg, 2012. Springer-Verlag.

[22] F. Song, S. Tomov, and J. Dongarra. Enabling and scaling matrix computations on heterogeneous multi-core and multi-gpu systems. In *Proceedings of the 26th ACM International Conference on Supercomputing*, ICS '12, pages 365–376, New York, NY, USA, 2012. ACM.

[23] M. Verschoor and A. C. Jalba. Analysis and performance estimation of the conjugate gradient method on multiple {GPUs}. *Parallel Computing*, 38(10-11):552–575, 2012.

DaCache: Memory Divergence-Aware GPU Cache Management

Bin Wang†, Weikuan Yu†, Xian-He Sun‡, Xinning Wang†

†Department of Computer Science
Auburn University
Auburn, AL, 36849
{bwang,wkyu,xzw0033}@auburn.edu

‡Department of Computer Science
Illinois Institute of Technology
Chicago, IL 60616
sun@iit.edu

ABSTRACT

The lock-step execution model of GPU requires a warp to have the data blocks for all its threads before execution. However, there is a lack of salient cache mechanisms that can recognize the need of managing GPU cache blocks at the warp level for increasing the number of warps ready for execution. In addition, warp scheduling is very important for GPU-specific cache management to reduce both intra- and inter-warp conflicts and maximize data locality. In this paper, we propose a Divergence-Aware Cache (*DaCache*) management that can orchestrate L1D cache management and warp scheduling together for GPGPUs. In DaCache, the insertion position of an incoming data block depends on the fetching warp's scheduling priority. Blocks of warps with lower priorities are inserted closer to the LRU position of the LRU-chain so that they have shorter lifetime in cache. This fine-grained insertion policy is extended to prioritize coherent loads over divergent loads so that coherent loads are less vulnerable to both inter- and intra-warp thrashing. DaCache also adopts a constrained replacement policy with L1D bypassing to sustain a good supply of Fully Cached Warps (FCW), along with a dynamic mechanism to adjust FCW during runtime. Our experiments demonstrate that DaCache achieves 40.4% performance improvement over the baseline GPU and outperforms two state-of-the-art thrashing-resistant techniques RRIP and DIP by 40% and 24.9%, respectively.

Categories and Subject Descriptors

C.1.4 [**Computer Systems Organization**]: Processor Architectures—*Parallel Architectures*; D.1.3 [**Software**]: Programming Techniques—*Concurrent Programming*

General Terms

Design, Performance

Keywords

GPU; Caches; Memory Divergence; Warp Scheduling

ICS'15, June 8–11, 2015, Newport Beach, CA, USA.

http://dx.doi.org/10.1145/2751205.2751239 .

1. INTRODUCTION

Graphics Processing Unit (GPU) has proven itself as a viable technology for a wide variety of applications to exploit its massive computing capability. It allows an application to be programmed as thousands of threads running the same code in a lock-step manner, in which warps of 32 threads can be scheduled for execution in every cycle with zero switching overhead. The massive parallelism from these Single-Instruction Multiple Data (SIMD) threads helps GPUs achieve a dramatic improvement in computational power compared to CPUs. To reduce the latency of memory operations, GPU has employed multiple levels of data caches to save off-chip memory bandwidth when there is locality within the accesses.

Due to massive multithreading, per-thread data cache capacity often diminishes. For example, Fermi supports a maximum of 48 warps (1536 threads) on each Streaming Multiprocessor (SM), and these warps share 16KB or 48KB L1 Data Cache (L1D) [27]. Thus coalescing each warp's per-thread global memory accesses into fewer memory transactions not only minimizes the consumption of memory bandwidth, but also alleviates cache contention. But when a warp's accesses cannot be coalesced into one or two cache blocks, which is referred to as memory divergence, its cache footprint is often boosted by one order of magnitude, e.g., from 1 to 32 cache blocks. This leads to severe contention among warps, i.e., inter-warp contention, on limited L1D capacity.

Under the lock-step execution model, a warp is not ready for execution until all of its threads are ready (e.g., no thread has outstanding memory request). Meanwhile, cache-sensitive GPGPU workloads often have high intra-warp locality [32, 33], which means data blocks are re-referenced by their fetching warps. Intra-warp locality is often associated with strided accesses [19, 35], which lead to divergent memory accesses when stride size is large. The execution model, intra-warp locality, and potential memory divergence together pose a great challenge for GPU cache management, i.e., data blocks fetched by a divergent load instruction should be cached as a wholistic group. Otherwise, a warp is not ready for issuance when its blocks are partially cached. This challenge demands a GPU-specific cache management that can resist inter-warp contention and minimize partial caching. Though there are many works on thrashing-resistant cache management for multicore systems [30, 10, 17, 21], they are all divergence-oblivious, i.e., they make caching decisions at the per-thread access level rather than at the per-warp instruction level.

Recently, GPU warp scheduling has been studied to alleviate inter-warp contention from its source. Several warp scheduling techniques have been proposed based on various heuristics. For example, CCWS [32], DAWS [33], and CBWT [5] rely on detected L1D locality loss, aggregated cache footprint, and varying on-chip network latencies, respectively, to throttle concurrency at runtime.

Limiting the number of actively scheduled warps directly reduces inter-warp contention and delivers higher reductions of cache misses than the Belady [2] replacement algorithm in highly cache-sensitive GPGPU benchmarks [32]. We observe that coherent loads may also carry high intra- and inter-warp locality, but are vulnerable to the thrashing from both inter- and intra-warp divergent loads. However, warp scheduling can only be exploited to alleviate inter-warp contention at a coarse granularity, i.e., warp level. Thus there is still a need of a salient cache mechanism that can manage L1D locality at both levels and, more importantly, sustain a good supply of Fully Cached Warps (FCW) to keep warp schedulers busy.

Taken together, for a greater good on reducing cache misses and maximizing the occupancy of GPU cores, it is imperative to integrate warp scheduling with the GPU-specific cache management for a combined scheme that can overcome the inefficiency of existing GPU caches. To this end, we present a Divergence-Aware Cache (DaCache) management scheme to mitigate the impacts of memory divergence on L1D locality preservation. Based on the observation that warp scheduling shapes the locality pattern inside L1D access stream, DaCache gauges insertion positions of incoming data blocks according to the fetching warp's scheduling priority. Specifically, new blocks are inserted into L1D in an orderly manner based on their issuing warps' scheduling priorities. DaCache also prioritizes coherent loads over divergent loads in insertion to alleviate intra-warp contention. In addition, cache ways are conceptually partitioned into two regions, locality region and thrashing region, and replacement candidates are constrained within thrashing region to increase thrashing resistance. If no replacement candidate is available in thrashing region, L1D bypassing is enabled. We propose a simple mechanism to dynamically adjust the partitioning. All these features in our DaCache design need simple modifications to existing LRU caches.

In summary, this paper makes the following contributions:

- We evaluate caching effectiveness of GPU data caches for both memory-coherent and memory-divergent GPGPU benchmarks, and present the problem of partial caching in existing GPU cache management.
- We propose a Divergence-Aware Cache management technique, namely DaCache, to orchestrate warp scheduling and cache management for GPGPUs. By taking prioritization logic of warp scheduling into cache management, thrashing traffic can be quickly removed so that cache blocks of the most prioritized warps can be fully cached in L1D; in turn the increased number of fully cached loads provides more ready warps for warp schedulers to execute.
- We design a dynamic partitioning algorithm in DaCache to increase thrashing resistance and implement it in a cycle-accurate simulator. Experimental results show that it can improve caching effectiveness and improve the performance by 40.4% over baseline GPU architecture, outperform two thrashing resistance cache management, RRIP and DIP, by 40% and 24.9%, respectively.

The rest of paper is organized as follows: Section 2 introduces the baseline GPU; Section 3 summarizes the major characteristics of the evaluated GPGPU benchmarks and our motivation of DaCache; Section 4 details the design of DaCache; Experimental results and related work are presented in Section 5 and Section 6, respectively. Section 7 concludes the paper.

2. BASELINE GPU ARCHITECTURE

In this work we study modifications to a Fermi-like baseline GPU architecture as shown in Figure 1. In each Streaming Multiprocessor, two hardware warp schedulers independently manage all active warps. In each cycle, warp scheduler issues one warp among all the ready warps to execute in cores or Load/Store Unites (LD/ST) [24, 27, 28], depending on the warp's pending instruction. Once a memory instruction to global memory is issued, it's first sent to Memory Access Coalescing Unit (MACU) for access generation. MACU coalesces per-thread memory accesses to minimize off-chip memory traffic. For example, when 32 threads of a warp access 32 consecutive words in a cacheline-aligned data block, MACU will only generate one memory access to L1D. Otherwise, multiple memory accesses are generated to fetch all needed data. In the rest of this paper, the memory instructions that incur more than 2 uncoalescable memory accesses are called divergent instructions, while the others are called coherent instructions.

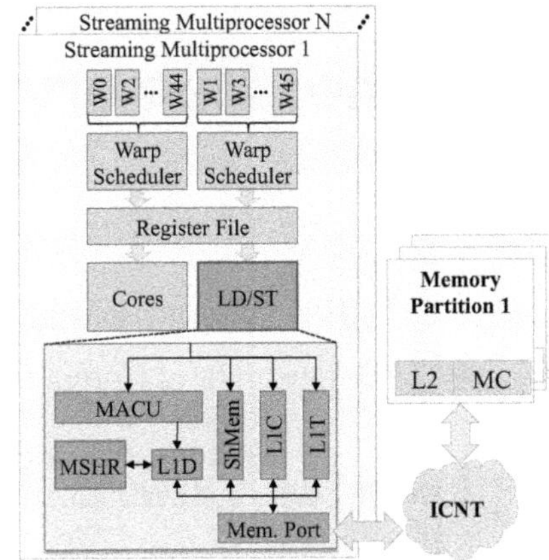

Figure 1: Baseline GPU Architecture.

The resultant memory accesses from MACU are sequentially serviced by L1D. For a load access, if there is a cache hit, requested data are sent to register file; upon cache miss, if there is Missing Status Holding Register (MSHR) entry available, a request is generated and buffered into a queue in *Memory Port*. MSHR tracks in-flight requests and merges requests to the same missing data block. An MSHR entry is reclaimed when its corresponding memory request is back and all accesses to the block are serviced. Accesses missing in L1D are replayed when no MSHR entries are available. Cache lines are reserved for outstanding requests. Without coherence support for global data, L1D writes through dirty data and evicts cache lines on write hits. Buffered memory requests are sent to target memory partitions via an interconnect (*ICNT*). Each memory partition mainly consists of a L2 data cache and a memory controller (*MC*) that manages off-chip memory devices.

3. MOTIVATION

In this section, we evaluate GPU cache performance to understand application behaviors on a cache hierarchy similar to that in current GPUs. We use memory intensive benchmarks from Rodinia [4], PolyBench/GPU [11], SHOC [7], and MapReduce [14]. For each benchmark, Table 1 lists a brief description and the input size that we use for performance evaluation. Benchmark SC repetitively invokes the same kernel 290 times with the default input size (16K points) until the computation completes. Since the simulation is several orders of magnitude slower than real hardware, we only enable two kernel invocations in SC so that the simulation time is reasonable with larger input size (256K points). All of the other benchmarks, ranging from 70 million to 6.8 billion instructions, are run to completion. The benchmarks are categorized into memory-divergent and memory-coherent ones, depending on the dynamic divergence of load instructions in these benchmarks. In general, memory-divergent benchmarks are more sensitive to cache

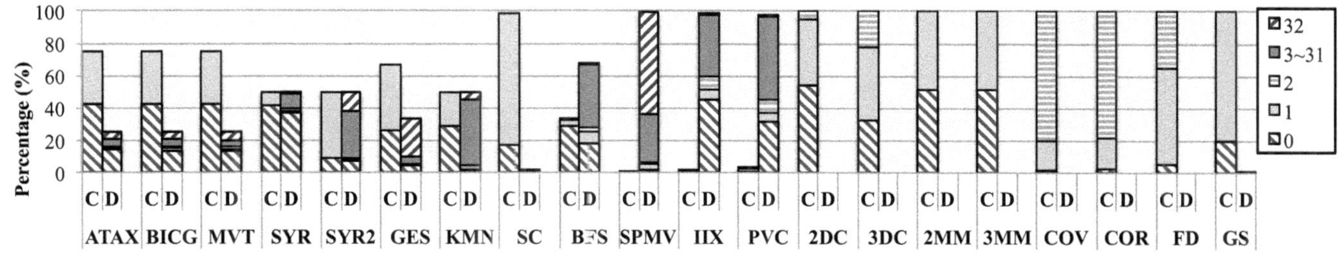

Figure 2: Distribution of Misses Per Load Instruction (MPLI) in L1 data cache. MPLIs are categorized into five groups: 0 (MPLI=0), 1 (MPLI=1), 2 (MPLI=2), 3∼31 (3⩽ MPLI ⩽ 31), and 32 (MPLI=32). MPLIs for coherent (*C*) and divergent (*D*) load instructions are accumulated separately. Each of the benchmarks on the right of the figure has only *C* bar for coherent instructions.

Table 1: GPGPU Benchmarks (CUDA)

#	Abbr.	Application	Suite	Input	Branch
		Memory Divergent Benchmarks			
1	ATAX	matrix-transpose and vector mul.	[11]	$8K \times 8K$	N
2	BICG	kernel of BiCGStab linear solver	[11]	$8K \times 8K$	N
3	MVT	Matrix-vector-product transpose	[11]	8K	N
4	SYR	Symmetric rank-K operations	[11]	512 × 512	N
5	SYR2	Symmetric rank-2K operations	[11]	256 × 256	N
6	GES	Scalar-vector-matrix mul.	[11]	4K	N
7	KMN	Kmeans Clustering	[4]	28K 4x features	N
8	SC	Stream Cluster	[4]	256K points	N
9	BFS	Breadth-First-Search	[4]	5M edges	Y
10	SPMV	Sparse matrix mul.	[7]	default	Y
11	IIX	Inverted Index	[14]	6.8M	Y
12	PVC	Page View Count	[14]	100K	Y
		Memory Coherent Benchmarks			
13	2DC	2D Convolution	[11]	default	N
14	3DC	3D Convolution	[11]	default	N
15	2MM	2 Matrix Multiply	[11]	default	N
16	3MM	3 Matrix Multiply	[11]	default	N
17	COV	Covariance Computation	[11]	default	N
18	COR	Correlation Computation	[11]	default	N
19	FD	2D Finite Difference Kernel	[11]	default	N
20	GS	Gram-Schmidt Process	[11]	default	N

capacity than memory-coherent benchmarks. Recent works [32, 33, 19, 35] report that high intra-warp L1D locality exists among these cache-sensitive workloads. In addition, BFS, SPMV, IIX, and PVC also have rich branch divergence.

3.1 Cache Misses from Divergent Accesses

Within the lock-step execution model, a warp becomes ready when all of its demanded data is available; warps that have missing data, regardless of the data size, are excluded for execution. This execution model of GPU expects that all cache blocks of each divergent load instruction are cached as a unit when there is locality. However, conventional cache management is unaware of the GPU execution model and the collective nature of divergent memory blocks. As a result, some blocks of a divergent instruction can be evicted while others are still cached, resulting in a varying number of cache misses for individual loads. Metrics, such as Miss Rate and Misses Per Kilo Instructions (MPKI), are often used to evaluate the performance of cache management. In view of the wide variation of cache misses per instruction, we use **Misses Per Load Instruction (MPLI)** to quantify such misses in GPU L1D. Divergent load instructions that have misses in the range from 1 to $\{Req(pc, w) - 1\}$ are considered as being partially cached, where $Req(pc, w)$ is the number of cache accesses that warp w incurs at memory instruction pc. If a load instruction has no cache miss, it's considered as being fully cached. MPLI can be calculated by counting the number of cache misses a load instruction experiences after all of its memory accesses are serviced by L1D.

Figure 2 shows the distribution of MPLIs across the 20 GPGPU benchmarks we have evaluated in this paper. For simplicity, MPLIs are categorized into five groups. For divergent loads, the two categories of *2* (MPLI=2) and *3∼31* (3⩽ MPLI ⩽ 31) in the figure together describe the existence of partial caching. Note that this range can only provide a close approximation for partial caching because branch divergence can reduce the number of uncoalescable memory accesses a divergent load can generate. For example, a warp with 16 threads can maximally generate 16 memory accesses for a divergent load, and an MPLI of 16 indicates full caching for this load of the warp. As we can see from the figure, coherent loads of the memory-divergent benchmarks do not experience the problem of partial caching because they all generate one memory access per instruction. However, divergent load instructions in these benchmarks greatly suffer from partial caching. Substantial amount of divergent loads in SYR2, KMN, BFS, SPMV, IIX, and PVC are partially cached. Memory-coherent benchmarks, such as 2DC, 3DC, COV, COR, and FD, also experience partial caching (MPLI=1), because their load instructions generate two memory accesses each time. Besides some cold misses and capacity misses, such prevalent cache misses due to partial caching can be caused by severe cache contention, resulting in early evictions of cache blocks after being used only once.

3.2 Warp scheduling and Cache Contention

In view of the severe cache misses as discussed in Section 3.1, we have further examined the impact of warp scheduling on L1D contention. GPU warp scheduling is often driven by a prioritization scheme. For example, in the baseline Greedy-Then-Oldest (GTO) warp scheduling, warps are dynamically prioritized by their "ages" and the oldest warps are preferentially prioritized at runtime. In order to quantify the cache contention due to aggressive warp scheduling, we measure the occupancy of warp schedulers by all active warps. Figure 3 shows the Cumulative Distribution Function (CDF) of warp scheduler occupancy when the evaluated benchmarks are scheduled under GTO prioritization. Typically these benchmarks have one fully divergent load (resulting in 32 accesses) and one coherent load (resulting in one access) in the kernel, so the cache footprint of each warp is 33 cache lines at runtime. Our baseline L1D (32 KB, 256 lines) can fully cache three warps for each warp scheduler. This means that L1D will inevitably be thrashed if the warps with GTO priorities lower than 3 are scheduled. For memory-divergent benchmarks in Figure 3(a), $58\% \sim 91\%$ of the total cycles are occupied by the top 3 prioritized warps. Since branch divergence reduces the number of accesses a divergent load can generate, as shown in Figure 3(b), the occupancy drops to $48\% \sim 63\%$ among benchmarks with both memory- and branch-divergence. Such variation in warp scheduling incurs immediate cache conflicts.

We categorize conflict misses into intra- and inter-warp misses [19]. An intra-warp miss refers to the case where a thread's data is evicted by other threads within the same warp (*misses-iwarp*); otherwise a conflict miss is referred to as inter-warp miss (*misses-xwarp*).

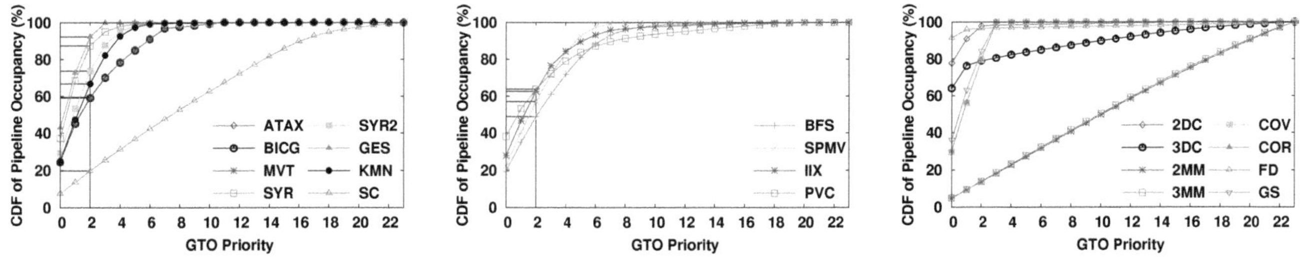

(a) Memory-Divergent (b) Memory- and Branch-Divergent (c) Memory-Coherent

Figure 3: The CDF of warp scheduler occupancy by all active warps. The percentage reflects the frequency that each warp is scheduled. *GTO priority* refers to the "age" of each warp. Since each of the two warp schedulers in an SM manages 24 warps, 0 represents the highest priority, while 23 represents the lowest priority. Our baseline L1D can typically accommodate three divergent warps for each warp scheduler.

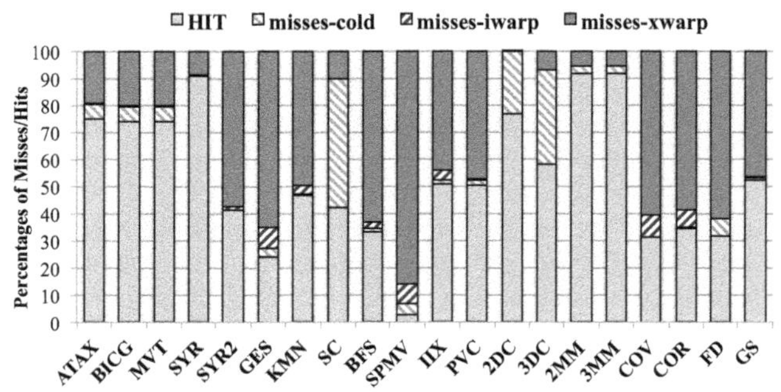

Figure 4: Categorization of L1D thrashing.

Meanwhile, we also present the percentages of cache hits (*HIT*) and cold misses (*misses-cold*). Figure 4 shows that the majority of cache misses are due to inter-warp conflicts, which in turn cause high MPLI as shown in Figure 2 and varied occupancy of warp schedulers as shown in Figure 3.

4. DIVERGENCE-AWARE GPU CACHE MANAGEMENT

As described in the previous section, divergent load instructions lead to many cache misses in L1D, especially inter-warp conflict misses. With more data blocks not being found in L1D, the number of warps that can be actively scheduled are significantly reduced. To address this problem, we propose *Divergence-Aware Cache (DaCache)* management for GPU. Based on the observation that the re-reference interval of cache blocks are shaped by warp schedulers, DaCache aims to exploit the prioritization information of warp scheduling, protect the cache blocks of highly prioritized warps from conflict-triggered eviction and maximize their chance of staying in L1D. In doing so, DaCache can alleviate the conflict misses across warps such that more warps can locate all data blocks from L1D for their load instructions. We refer to such warps as Fully Cached Warps (FCWs).

4.1 High-level Description of DaCache

Figure 5 shows a conceptual idea of DaCache in maximizing the number of FCWs. In this example, we assume four warps concurrently execute a for-loop body that has one divergent load instruction. At runtime, each warp generates four cache accesses in each loop iteration, and the fetched cache blocks are re-referenced across iterations. This is a common strided access pattern in our evaluated CUDA benchmarks. Ideally, all loads can hit in L1D due to high intra-warp locality. But severe cache contention caused by massive parallelism and scarce L1D capacity can easily thrash the locality in L1D. In order to resist thrashing, a divergence-oblivious cache management may fairly treat accesses from all warps, leading to the scenario that all warps miss one block in current iteration.

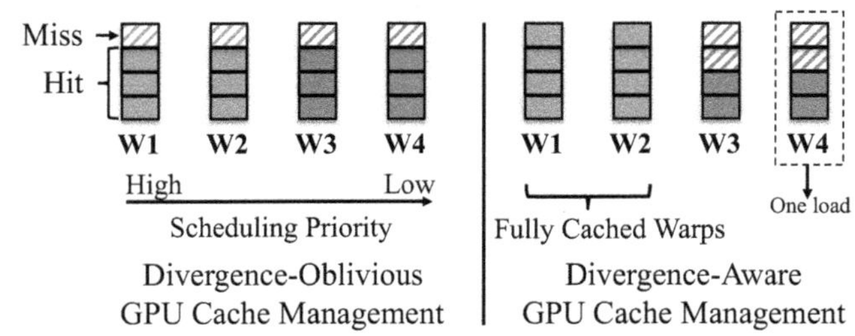

Figure 5: A conceptual example showing DaCache in maximizing the number of Fully Cache Warps.

By taking warp scheduling prioritization and memory divergence into consideration, DaCache aims at cache misses concentrated at warps that have lower scheduling priorities, such as *W3* and *W4*. Consequently, warps with higher scheduling priorities, such as *W1* and *W2*, can be fully cached so that they are immediately ready to execute the next iteration of the for-loop body.

DaCache relies on both warp scheduling-awareness and memory divergence-awareness to maximize the number of FCWs. This necessitates several innovative changes on GPU cache management policies. In general, cache management consists of three components: replacement, insertion, and promotion policies [38]. *Replacement policy* decides which block in a set should be evicted upon a conflicting cache access, *insertion policy* defines a new block's replacement priority, and *promotion policy* determines how to update the replacement priority of a re-referenced block. For example, in LRU caches, blocks at the LRU position are immediate replacing candidates; new blocks are inserted into the MRU position of the LRU chain; re-referenced blocks are promoted to the MRU position.

4.2 Gauged Insertion

In conventional LRU caches, since the replacement candidates are always selected from the LRU ends, blocks in the LRU-chains have different lifetime to stay in cache. For example, blocks at the MRU ends have the longest lifetime, while blocks at LRU ends have shortest lifetime. Based on this characteristic, locality of L1D blocks can be differentially preserved by inserting blocks at different positions in the LRU-chains according to their re-reference intervals. For example, blocks can be inserted into MRU, central, and LRU positions if they will be re-referenced in the immediate, near, and distant future, respectively. However, it is challenging for GPU caches to predict re-reference intervals of individual cache blocks from the thrashing-prone cache access streams.

Since there is often high intra-warp data locality among memory-divergent GPGPU benchmarks, the cache blocks of frequently scheduled warps have short re-reference intervals, while the blocks of infrequently warps have long re-reference intervals. Under GTO warp scheduling, old warps are prioritized over young warps and

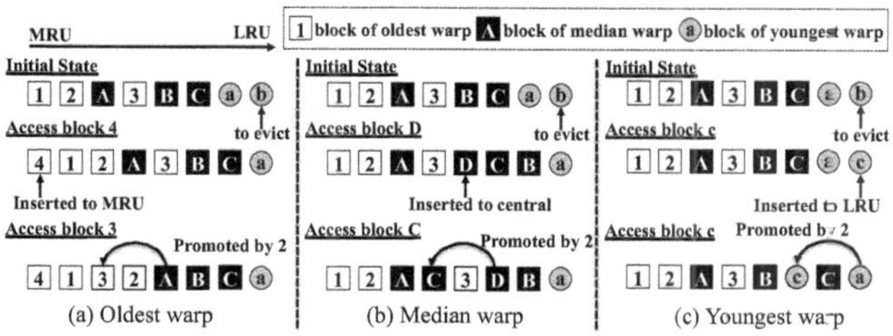

Figure 6: Illustrative example of insertion and promotion policies of DaCache.

thus are more frequently scheduled. Thus we can use each warp's GTO scheduling priority to predict its blocks' reference intervals. Based on this observation, the insertion position (*way*) in DaCache is gauged as:

$$way = min\{W_{Prio} \times N_{Sched} \times Width/N_{Set}, Asso - 1\} \quad (1)$$

where W_{Prio} is the issuing warp's scheduling priority, N_{Sched} is the number of warp schedulers in each SM, N_{Set} is the number of cache sets in L1D, $Width$ is the SIMD width, and $Asso$ is the cache associativity. Behind this gauged insertion policy, we assume the accesses from divergent loads (up-to $Width$ accesses) are equally distributed into N_{set} sets, and $Width/N_{Set}$ quantifies average intra-warp concentration in each cache set. Since L1D is shared by N_{Sched} warp schedulers, warps with the same priority but from different warp schedulers are assigned with the same insertion positions. Thus the cache blocks of consecutive warps from the same warp scheduler are dispersed by $N_{Sched} \times Width/N_{Set}$. For example, in our baseline GPU (2 warp schedulers per SM; 32 threads per warp; 32 sets per L1D), two warps with priorities of 0 and 2 are assigned insertion positions of 0 and 4, respectively. The gauged insertion policy is illustrated in Figure 6. In the figure, data blocks of "oldest warp", "median warp", and "youngest warp" are initially inserted into the MRU, central, and LRU positions, respectively. At runtime, the majority of the active warps are infrequently scheduled and share the LRU insertion position. By doing so, blocks are inserted in the LRU-chain in an orderly manner based on their issuing warps' scheduling priorities.

GPU programs often have a mix of coherent and divergent loads, which are assigned with the same insertion positions under the gauged insertion policy. Consequently, coherent loads will be interleaved with divergent loads. But interleaved insertion can make coherent loads vulnerable to thrashing from the bursty behaviors of divergent loads. The thrashing to coherent loads may not be limited to inter-warp contention. Figure 4 demonstrates the existence of intra-warp conflict misses in conventional LRU caches. We propose to explicitly prioritize coherent loads over divergent loads by inserting blocks of coherent loads into MRU positions, regardless of their issuing warps' scheduling priorities. But coherent loads may not carry any locality, and inserting their blocks into MRU positions is adversary to locality preservation. We use a victim cache to detect whether coherent loads have intra-warp locality, and then MRU insertion and LRU insertion are applied to coherent loads with and without locality, respectively. Motivated by the observation from Figure 3(b), we empirically use MRU insertion for divergent load instructions with no more than 5 memory requests.

Each entry of the victim cache has two fields, PC and data block tag. For a 48bit virtual address space, maximally the PC field needs 45 bits and the tag field needs 41 bits. Since only the mostly prioritized warp is sampled at runtime to detect the locality information of coherent loads, a 16-entry victim cache is sufficient across the evaluated benchmarks, which incurs only 172B storage overhead on each SM. The dynamic locality information of each coherent load is stored in a structure named Coherent Load Profiler (CLP). CLP entries have two fields, PC field (45 bits) and one flag field (1 bit) to indicate locality information. A 32-entry CLP incurs 184B storage overhead. Note that, when a load instruction is issued into LD/ST, memory access coalescing in MACU and CLP lookup can be executed in parallel. Once the locality information of a coherent load is determined, victim cache can be bypassed to avoid repetitive detection. Such storage overhead can be eliminated by embedding the potential locality information into PTX instructions via compiler support. We leave this as our future work.

Note that the insertion policy only gives an initial data layout in L1D to approximate re-reference intervals. During the runtime, the initial data layout can be easily disturbed because re-referenced blocks are directly promoted to the MRU positions, regardless of their current positions in the LRU-chain. In other words, this MRU promotion can invert the intention of DaCache insertion policy. Partially motivated by the incremental promotion in PIPP [38] that promotes re-referenced block by 1 position along the LRU-chain, DaCache also adopts a fine-grained promotion policy to cooperate with the insertion policy. Figure 6 illustrates a promotion granularity of 2 positions. Our experiments in Section 5.6 show that a promotion granularity of 4 achieves the best performance for the benchmarks we have evaluated.

4.3 Constrained Replacement

In general, in LRU caches, the block on the LRU end is considered as the replacement candidate. However, as we model cache contention by allocating cache block on miss and reserving blocks for outstanding requests [1], the block at the LRU position may not be replaceable. Then a replaceable block that is the closest to the LRU position is selected. Thus the replacement decision is no longer constrained on the LRU end, and any block in the set may be a replacement candidate. Such unconstrained replacement position makes inter-warp cache conflicts very unpredictable.

To protect the intention of gauged insertion, we introduce a constrained replacement policy in DaCache so that only a few blocks close to the LRU end can be replaced. This constrained replacement conceptually partitions the cache ways into two portions, locality region and thrashing region. Then replacement can only be made inside the thrashing region. This partitioning (p) can be calculated as: $p = \frac{Asso \times F}{SIMD\_Width/N_{Set}} - 1$, where F is a tuning parameter in the range between 0 and 1. Denoting the MRU and LRU ends with the way indexes of 0 and *Asso-1*, respectively, the locality region is located in the range from the 0th to the pth way of a cache set, while the thrashing region occupies the other ways. We tune the value of F to have the optimal static partitioning p. Besides, all sets in each L1D are equally partitioned.

Given the gauged insertion policy, this logical partitioning of L1D accordingly divides all active warps into two groups, locality warps and thrashing warps. If a warp's scheduling priority is higher than $(p + 1)/N_{Sched}$, it's a thrashing warp; else it is a locality warp. The cache blocks of locality warps are inserted into the locality region using the gauged insertion policy so that they can be less vulnerable to thrashing traffic. By doing so, locality warps have a better chance to be fully cached and immediately ready for re-scheduling. In order to cooperate with such a constrained replacement policy, divergent loads of thrashing warps are exclusively inserted into LRU positions so that they can not pollute existing cache blocks in L1D. Though the 3 oldest warps managed by each warp scheduler, are mostly scheduled as shown in Figure 3, i.e., p=5 in our baseline, our experiments in Section 5.4 show that maintaining 2 FCWs per warp scheduler (p=3) actually achieves the optimal performance with the extended insertion and unconstrained replacement policies.

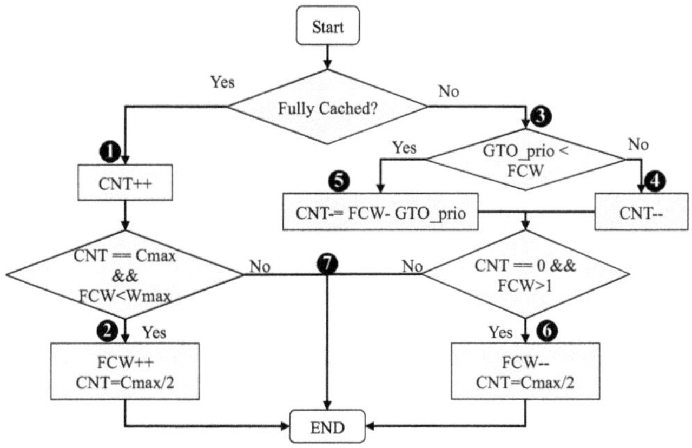

Figure 7: Flow of the proposed dynamic partitioning algorithm. *Fully Cached Warps (FCW)* is based on the number of fully cached loads (*CNT*) and each warp's GTO scheduling priority (GTO_prio).

With the constrained replacement policy, replacement candidates may not always be available. Thus we discuss two complementary approaches to enforce constrained replacement. The first approach is called **Constrained Replacement with L1D Stalling**. It's possible that a replacement candidate cannot be located within our baseline cache model, though at a very low frequency. Once this happens, the cache controller repetitively replays the missing access until one block in the thrashing region becomes replaceable. Stalling L1D is the default functionality within our cache model and then can be used with constrained replacement at no extra cost.

The second approach is called **Constrained Replacement with L1D Bypassing**. Instead of waiting for reallocating reserved cache blocks, bypassing L1D proactively forwards the thrashing traffic into lower memory hierarchy. Without touching L1D, bypassing can avoid not only L1D thrashing, but also memory pipeline stalls. When a bypassed request is back, its data is directly written to register file rather than a pre-allocated cache block [19]. In our baseline architecture, caching in L1D forces the size of missed memory requests to be cache block size. For each cache access of a divergent load instruction, only a small segment of the cache block are actually used, depending on the data size and access pattern. Without caching, the extra data in the cache block is a pure waste of memory bandwidth. Thus bypassed memory requests are further reduced to aligned 32B segments, which is the minimum coalesced segment size as discussed in [29].

4.4 Dynamic Partitioning of Warps

Our insertion and replacement policies rely on a static partitioning p, which incorporates the scheduling priorities of active warps into the cache management. However, the static choice of p is not very suitable in two important scenarios. Firstly, branch divergence reduces per-warp cache footprint so that the locality region is capable of accommodating more warps. It can be observed from Figure 3(b) that branch divergence enables more warps be actively scheduled. Secondly, kernels may have multiple divergent load instructions so that the capacity of locality region is only enough to cache one warp from each warp scheduler. For example, SYR2, GES, and SPMV have two divergent loads, while IIX and PVC have multiple divergent loads.

Thus we propose a mechanisms for dynamic partitioning of warps based on the accumulated statistics of fully cached divergent loads. Figure 7 shows the flow of dynamically adjusting *Fully Cached Warps (FCW)* based on the accumulated number of fully cached loads (*CNT*) and each warp's GTO scheduling priority (GTO_prio). At runtime, CNT is increased by 1 (❶) for each fully cached load.

Table 2: Baseline GPGPU-Sim Configuration

# of SMs	30 (15 clusters of 2)
SM Configuration	1400Mhz, Reg #: 32K, Shared Memory: 48KB, SIMD Width: 16, warp: 32 threads, max threads per SM: 1024
Caches / SM	Data: 32KB/128B-line/8-way, Constant: 8KB/64B-line/24-way, Texture: 12KB/128B-line/2-way
Branching Handling	PDOM based method [9]
Warp Scheduling	GTO
Interconnect	Butterfly, 1400Mhz, 32B channel width
L2 Unified Cache	768KB, 128B line, 16-way
Min. L2 Latency	120 cycles (compute core clock)
Cache Indexing	Pseudo-Random Hashing Function [26]
# Memory Partitions	6
# Memory Banks	16 per memory partition
Memory Controller	Out-of-Order (FR-FCFS), max request queue length: 32
GDDR5 Timing	$t_{CL} = 12, t_{RP} = 12, t_{RC} = 40, t_{RAS} = 28, t_{RCD} = 12, t_{RRD} = 6, t_{CDLR} = 5, t_{WR} = 12$

When CNT is saturated (CNT==Cmax), if FCW has not reached its maximum value (*Wmax*), FCW is increased by 1 and accordingly CNT is reset as *Cmax/2* to track fully cached divergent loads under the new partitioning (❷). For partially cached loads (❸), CNT is decreased differently depending on the issuing warp's scheduling priority. For instance, if a warp's scheduling priority is lower than FCW, CNT is decreased by 1 (❹); otherwise, CNT is decreased by FCW-GTO_prio (❺) to speed up the process of achieving the optimal FCW. When CNT reaches zero, FCW is decreased by 1 so that less warps are assigned into the locality region (❻). In our proposal, each warp scheduler has at least 1 warp in the locality region; while *Wmax* is equal to 48, which is the number of physical warps on each SM. Thus, in the corner cases when FCW is 1 or Wmax (❼), CNT will not be overflowed if it's saturated.

In order to implement the logic of dynamic partitioning, we first use one register (*Div-reg*) to mark whether a load is divergent or not, depending on the number of coalesced memory requests. *Div-reg* is populated when a new load instruction is serviced by L1D. We then use another register (*FCW-reg*) to track whether a load is fully cached or not. *FCW-reg* is reset when L1D starts to service a new load, and is set when a cache miss happens. When all the accesses of the load are serviced, *FCW-reg* being unset indicates a fully cached load. The logic of dynamic partitioning is triggered when a divergent load retires from the memory stage. We empirically use a 8-bit counter for CNT so that it can maximally record 256 consecutive occurrence of fully/partially cached loads, i.e., Cmax=256 in Figure 7. CNT is initialized as 128 while FCW is 4. This initial value of FCW is based on our experiments of static partitioning schemes showing that maintaining two FCWs for each warp scheduler has the best overall performance.

5. EXPERIMENTAL EVALUATION

We use GPGPU-Sim [1] (version 3.2.1), a cycle-accurate simulator, for the performance evaluation of DaCache. The main characteristics of our baseline GPU architecture are summarized in Table 2. The same baseline is also studied in [35, 36]. Jia et al. [19] reported that the default cache indexing method employed by this version of GPGPU-Sim can lead to severe intra-warp conflict misses, thus we use the indexing method from real Fermi GPUs, pseudo-random hashing function [26]. Actually this indexing method has been adopted in the latest versions of GPGPU-Sim. The following cache management techniques are evaluated:

LRU is the baseline cache management. Without further mentioning, all performance numbers are normalized to LRU.

DIP [30] consists of both LRU and MRU insertions. Cache misses are sampled from the sets that are dedicated to LRU and MRU insertions to determine a winning policy for all other

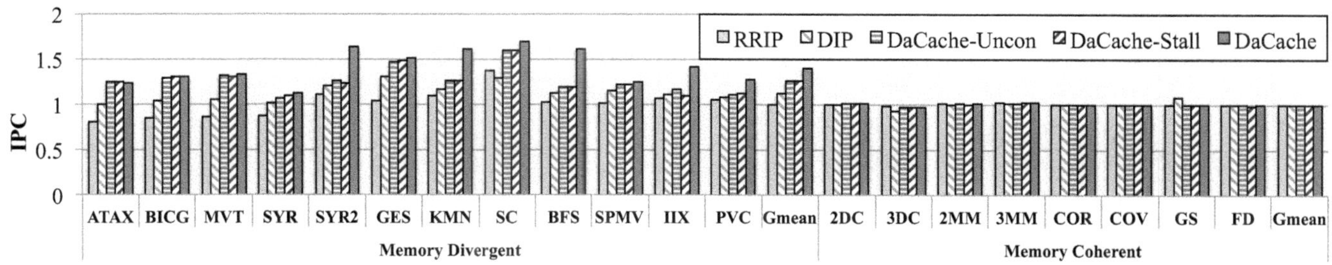

Figure 8: IPC of memory-divergent and memory-coherent benchmarks when various cache management techniques are used.

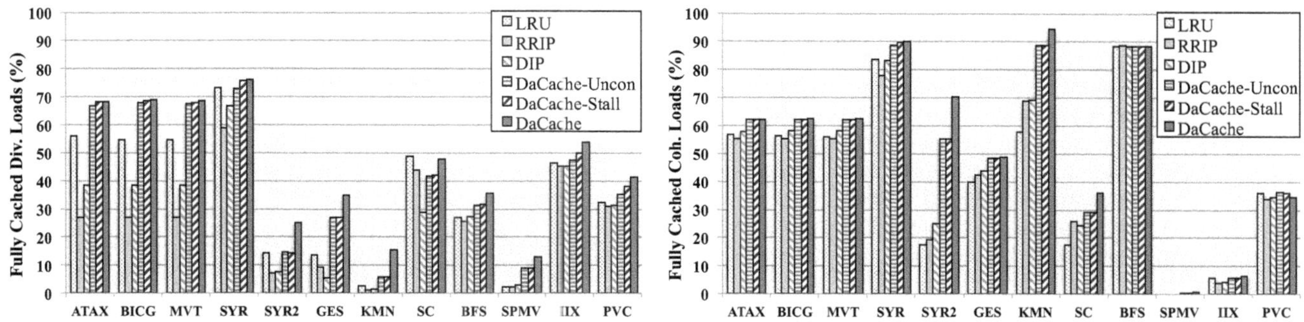

(a) Divergent Loads

(b) Coherent Loads

Figure 9: Percentages of fully cached load instructions in memory divergent benchmarks.

"follower" sets, which is referred as set-dueling. In our evaluation, 4 sets are dedicated for each insertion policy and the other 24 sets are managed by the winning policy.

RRIP [17] uses Re-Reference Prediction Values (RRPV) for insertion and replacement. With an M-bit RRPV-chain, new blocks are predicted with RRPVs of 2^M-1 or 2^M-2, depending on the winning policy from the set-dueling mechanism. We implement RRIP with a Frequency Priority based promotion and a 3-bit RRPV chain.

DaCache consists of gauged insertion and incremental promotion (Section 4.2), constrained replacement with L1D bypassing (Section 4.3), and dynamic partitioning (Section 4.4). By default, DaCache has a promotion granularity of 4 and the locality region starts with hosting 2 warps from each warp scheduler. We evaluate DaCache variants with unconstrained replacement (*DaCache-Uncon*) and constrained replacement with L1D stalling (*DaCache-Stall*) to demonstrate the importance of using warp scheduling to guide cache management.

5.1 Instructions Per Cycle (IPC)

Figure 8 compares the performance of various cache management techniques for both memory-divergent and memory-coherent benchmarks. For memory-divergent benchmarks, RRIP on average has no IPC improvement. The performance gains of RRIP are balanced out by its loss in ATAX, BICG, MVT, and SYR, which exhibit LRU-friendly accesses patterns under GTO. Because of the intra-warp locality, highly prioritized warps leave large amount of blocks in the locality region that no other warps will re-reference, i.e., dead blocks, after they retire from LD/ST units. RRIP's asymmetric processes of promotion and replacement make it slow to eliminate the dead blocks, leading to inferior performance in these LRU-friendly benchmarks. Dynamically adjusting between LRU and MRU insertions makes DIP capable of both LRU-friendly and thrashing-prone patterns, thus DIP has 12.4% IPC improvement. In contrast, *DaCache-Uncon*, *DaCache-Stall*, and *DaCache* have an improvement of 25.9%, 25.6%, and 40.4%, respectively. The performance advantage of *DaCache-Uncon* proves the effectiveness of incorporating warp scheduling into L1D cache management. Based on this warp scheduling-awareness, constrained replacement with L1D stalling (*DaCache-Stall*) has no any extra performance gain. However, enabling constrained replacement with L1D bypassing achieves another improvement of 14.5% in *DaCache*.

Among the memory-coherent benchmarks, DIP has 8% performance improvement in GS. This is because GS has inter-kernel data locality, and inserting new blocks into LRU position when detected locality is low can help to carry data locality across kernels. We believe this performance improvement will diminish when data size is large enough. For the others, all of the cache management techniques have negligible performance impact. By focusing on memory divergence, DaCache and its variants have no detrimental impacts on memory coherent workloads. We believe DaCache is applicable to a large variety of GPGPU workloads.

5.2 Fully Cached Loads

The percentages of fully cached loads (Figure 9) explain the performance impacts of various cache management techniques on these memory-divergent benchmarks. As shown in Figure 9(a), LRU outperforms DIP and RRIP in fully caching divergent loads. Since GTO warp scheduling essentially generates LRU-friendly cache access patterns, LRU cache matches the inherent pattern so that the blocks of divergent loads are inserted into the contiguous positions of the LRU-chain. In contrast, DIP and RRIP dynamically insert blocks of the same load into different positions of LRU-chain and RRPV-chain, respectively, making it hard to fully cache divergent loads. Thus the performance impacts of RRIP and DIP mainly come from their capabilities in preserving coherent loads. As shown in Figure 9(b), for ATAX, BICG, MVT, and SYR, RRIP also achieves less fully cached coherent loads than LRU, thus it has worse performance than LRU in the four benchmarks; DIP recovers more coherent loads than LRU, but these gains are offset by loss in caching divergent loads, leading to marginal performance improvement. For SYR2, GES, KMN, SC, and BFS, RRIP and DIP improve the effectiveness of caching coherent loads, leading to the performance improvement in the five benchmarks.

DaCache-Uncon, *DaCache-Stall*, and *DaCache* constantly outperform LRU, RRIP, and DIP in fully caching loads, except for benchmark SC. This advantage comes from the following three

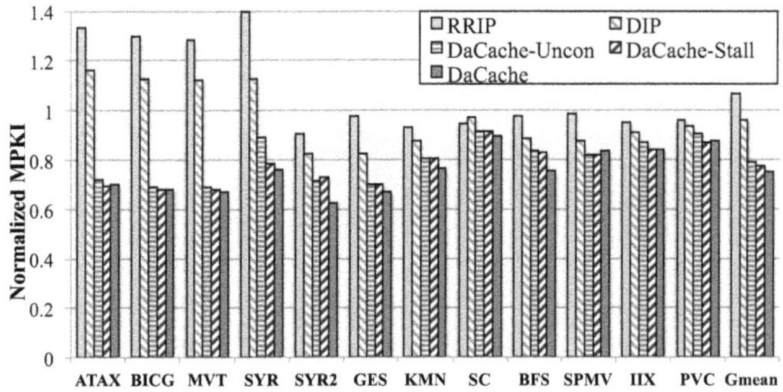

Figure 10: MPKI of various cache management techniques.

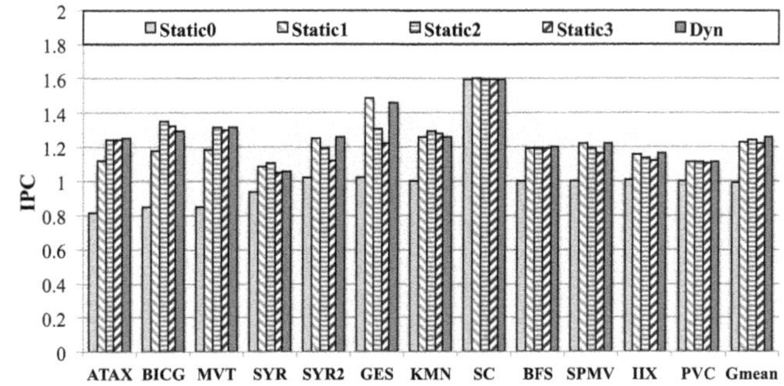

Figure 11: DaCache under static and dynamic partitioning.

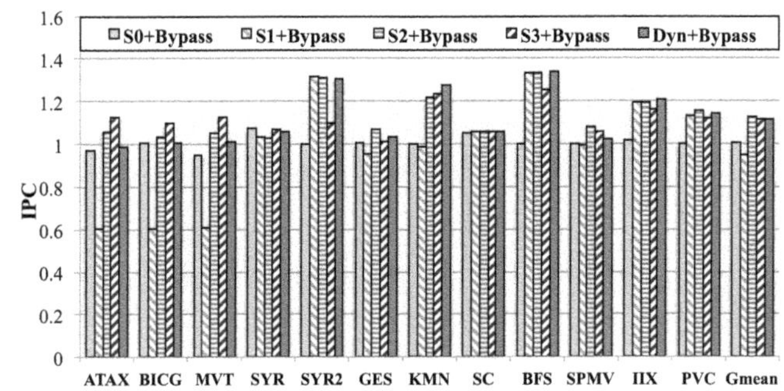

Figure 12: The impacts of using bypass to complement replacement policy under static and dynamic partitioning. Results are normalized to corresponding partitioning schemes.

factors. Firstly, guided by the warp scheduling prioritization, the gauged insertion implicitly enforces LRU-friendliness. Thus *DaCache-Uncon* achieves 35.1% more fully cached divergent loads. Secondly, deliberately prioritizing coherent loads over divergent loads alleviates the inter- and intra-warp thrashing from divergent loads. Thus *DaCache-Uncon* achieves 27.3% more fully cached coherent loads. Thirdly, constrained replacement can effectively improve the caching efficiency for highly prioritized warps. Based on *DaCache-Uncon*, constrained replacement with L1D stalling (*DaCache-Stall*) achieves 37.2% and 27.6% more fully cached divergent and coherent loads than LRU, respectively; while constrained replacement with L1D bypassing (*DaCache*) achieves 70% and 34.1% more fully cached divergent and coherent loads than LRU, respectively. In SC, the divergent loads come from the references to arrays of structs outside of a loop, and references to different members of the struct entry are sequential so that the LRU has the highest percentage of fully cached divergent loads (48.7%). But divergent loads in SC make up only a small portion of the total loads, therefore the number of fully cached coherent loads dominates the performance impacts.

5.3 Misses per Kilo Instructions (MPKI)

We also use MPKI to analyze the performance impacts of various cache management techniques on these memory-divergent benchmarks. As shown in Figure 10, except ATAX, BICG, MVT, and SYR, all of the five techniques are effective in reducing MPKIs. Because GPUs are throughput-oriented and rely on the number of fully cached warps to overlap long latency memory accesses, the significant MPKI increase of DIP in the four benchmarks is tolerated so that it doesn't have negative performance impacts. However, RRIP incurs on average a 32.5% increase in MPKIs in the four benchmarks, which leads to 14.5% performance degradation. Across the 12 benchmarks, on average, RRIP increases MPKIs by 6.4%, while DIP reduces MPKIs by 3.8%.

Meanwhile, *DaCache-Uncon*, *DaCache-Stall*, and *DaCache* consistently achieve MPKI reductions. On average, they reduce MPKIs by 20.8%, 22.4%, and 25%, respectively. Though *DaCache-Stall* reduces 1.6% more MPKIs than *DaCache-Uncon*, its potential performance advantage is compromised by adversely inserted L1D stall cycles. On the contrary, bypassing L1D in *DaCache* not only prevents L1D locality from being thrashed by warps with low scheduling priorities, but also enables these thrashing warps to directly access data cached in lower cache hierarchy. So 4.2% more MPKI reductions of *DaCache* brings 40.4% IPC improvement.

5.4 Static vs Dynamic Partitioning

Figure 11 examines the performance of DaCache when various static partitioning schemes and dynamic partitioning are enabled. For this experiment, the constrained replacement is disabled. *StaticN* means that *N* warps are cached in locality region. For example, in *Static0*, all blocks fetched by divergent loads are initially inserted into the LRU positions. Note that our baseline L1D is 8-way associative, Static3 and Static4 actually lead to identical insertion positions for all warps. Thus we only compare dynamic partition (*Dyn*) with *Static0*, *Static1*, *Static2*, and *Static3*.

Without any information from warp scheduling, *Static0* blindly inserts all blocks of divergent loads into LRU positions, thus it becomes impossible to predict which warps' cache block are more likely to be thrashed. On average, this inefficiency of *Static0* incurs 0.1% performance loss. On the contrary, by implicitly protecting 1, 2, and 3 warps for each warp scheduler, *Static1*, *Static2*, and *Static3* achieve performance improvement of 23%, 24.7%, and 21.9%, respectively. Note that *Static2* equally partitions L1D capacity into locality and thrashing regions, and the locality region is sufficient to cache two warps from each warp scheduler. Except IIX and PVC, all other benchmarks have maximally two divergent loads in each kernel, thus *Static2* has the best performance improvement. Our dynamic partitioning scheme (*Dyn*) achieves a performance improvement of 25.9%, outperforming all static partitioning schemes among the evaluated benchmarks. We expect this dynamic partitioning scheme can adapt to other L1D configurations and future GPGPU benchmarks that have diverse branch and memory divergence.

5.5 Constrained Replacement

Figure 12 explains when bypassing L1D can be an effective complement to replacement policy under static and dynamic partitioning. *SN* is equivalent to *StaticN* in Figure 11. The results are normalized to respective partitioning configurations. On average, constrained replacement with L1D bypassing incurs 0.6%, -5%, 12.8%, 11.4% and 11.6% performance improvement in *S0+Bypass*, *S1+Bypass*, *S2+Bypass*, *S3+Bypass*, and *Dyn+Bypass*, respectively. Note that these numbers are relative to partition-only configuration and are mainly used to quantify whether bypassing L1D is a viable complement to replacement policy. The performance degradation of *S1+Bypass* are mainly caused by ATAX, BICG, and MVT.

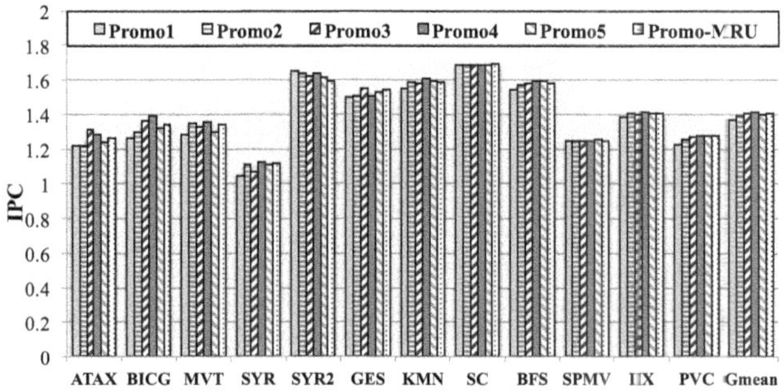

Figure 13: The impacts of promotion granularity under dynamic partitioning. *PromoN* means re-referenced blocks are promoted by *N* positions along the LRU-chain.

We observe that the three benchmarks have a large amount of dead blocks in L1D. Aggressive bypassing slows down the removal of dead blocks so that cache capacity is underutilized. We also analyzed the impact of stalling L1D as a complement to replacement policy under static and dynamic partitioning. We only observe negligible performance impacts, thus its results are not presented here due to the space limit.

5.6 Sensitivity to Promotion Granularity

Figure 13 analyzes the sensitivity of DaCache to the promotion granularity. In this experiment, *Promo-MRU* immediately promotes re-referenced blocks to the MRU positions, while *Promo1*, *Promo2*, *Promo3*, *Promo4*, and *Promo5* promote re-referenced blocks by 1, 2, 3, 4, and 5 positions respectively along the LRU-chain unless they reach the MRU position. As we can see, the majority of the benchmarks are sensitive to promotion granularity. These dead blocks are gradually demoted into thrashing region by inserting new blocks and/or promoting re-referenced blocks into locality region. Thus promotion granularity plays a critical role in eliminating dead blocks. Compared with LRU caches that directly promote re-referenced block to the MRU position, incremental promotion slowly promotes "hot" blocks towards the MRU position. The performance gap between *Promo1* (37.1%) and *Promo4* (41.6%) shows the importance of the promotion policy in DaCache.

6. RELATED WORK

There has been a large body of proposals on cache partitioning [12, 15, 16, 38, 3] and replacement policies [13, 31, 34] to increase the cache performance in CPU systems. However, these proposals do not handle the memory divergence issue within the massive parallelism of GPUs. Thus we mainly review the latest work within the context of GPU cache management.

6.1 Cache Management for GPU Architecture

L1D bypassing has been adopted by multiple proposals to improve the efficiency of GPU caches. Jia *et al.* [19] observed that certain GPGPU access patterns experience significant intra-warp conflict misses due to the pathological behaviors in conventional cache indexing methods, and thus proposed a hardware structure called Memory Request Prioritization Buffer (MRPB). MRPB reactively bypasses L1D accesses that are stalled by cache associativity conflicts. Chen *et al.* [6] used extensions in L2 cache tag to track locality loss in L1D. If a block is requested twice by the same SM, it's assumed that severe contention happens in L1D so that replacement is temporarily locked down and new requests are bypassed into L2. Chen *et al.* proposed another adaptive cache management policy, Coordinated Bypassing and Warp Throttling (CBWT) [5]. CBWT uses protection distance prediction [8] to dynamically assign each new block a protection distance (PD), which guarantees that the block will not be evicted if its PD has not reached zero. When no unprotected lines are available, bypassing is triggered and the PD values are decreased. CBWT further throttles concurrency to prevent NOC from being congested by aggressive bypassing. Different from the above three techniques, bypassing L1D in DaCache is coordinated with warp scheduling logic and a finer-grained scheme to alleviate both inter- and intra-warp contention. At runtime, bypassing is limited to the thrashing region which caches divergent loads from warps with low scheduling priorities and coherent loads with no locality.

Compiler directed bypassing techniques have been investigated to improve GPU cache performance in [18, 37], but the static bypassing decisions mainly work for regular workloads. DaCache is a hardware solution for GPU cache management and can adapt to program behavior changes at runtime. In some heterogeneous multicore processors, CPU and GPU cores share the Last Level Cache (LLC). There are also some work on cache management for this kind of heterogeneous systems [22, 25]. Although DaCache is designed for discrete GPGPUs, the idea of coordinating warp scheduling and cache management is also applicable to hybrid CPU-GPU systems.

Dong proposed an AgeLRU algorithm [23] for GPU cache management. AgeLRU uses extra fields in cache tags to track each cache line's predicted reuse distance, reuse count, and the active warp ID of the warp fetching the block, which together are used to calculate a score for replacement. The calculated score is reciprocal to each warp's age, i.e., older warps have higher scores to be protected. At runtime, the block with the lowest score is selected as replacement candidate and bypassing can be enabled when the score of the replacement victim is above a given threshold. By doing so, AgeLRU achieves the goal of preventing young warps from evicting blocks of old warps. DaCache doesn't need either storage in tag array or complicated calculation to assist replacement. By renovating the management policies, DaCache is more complexity-effective than AgeLRU to realize the same goal.

6.2 Warp Scheduling

There are several works that use warp scheduling algorithms to enable thrashing resistance in GPU data caches. Motivated by the observation that massive multithreading can increase contention in L1D for some highly cache-sensitive GPGPU benchmarks, Rogers et al. proposed a Cache Conscious Warp Scheduler (CCWS) [32] to limit the number of warps that issue load instructions when it detects loss of intra-warp locality. Following that, Rogers et al. also proposed a Divergence-Aware Warp Scheduling (DAWS) [33] to limit the number of actively scheduled warps whose aggregate cache footprint does not exceed L1D capacity. Besides, Kayiran et al. [20] proposed a dynamic Cooperative Thread Array (CTA) scheduling mechanism which throttles the number of CTAs on each core according to application characteristics. Typically, it reduces CTAs for memory-intensive applications to minimizing resource contention. By throttling concurrency, cache contention can be alleviated, and Rogers et al. reported in [32] that warp scheduling can be more effective than optimal cache replacement [2] in preserving L1D locality. However, throttling concurrency usually permits only a few warps to be active, though each warp scheduler is hosting a lot more warps that are ready for execution (maximally 24 warps in our baseline). Our work is orthogonal to these warp scheduling algorithms, because contention still exists in reduced concurrency. DaCache can be used to increase cache utilization under reduced concurrency and also uplift the resultant concurrency.

7. CONCLUSION

GPUs are throughput-oriented processors that depend on massive multithreading to tolerate long latency memory accesses. The latest GPUs all are equipped with on-chip data caches to reduce the latency of memory accesses and save the bandwidth of NOC and off-chip memory modules. But these tiny data caches are vulnerable to thrashing from massive multithreading, especially when divergent load instructions generate long bursts of cache accesses. Meanwhile, the blocks of divergent loads exhibit high intra-warp locality and are expected to be atomically cached so that the issuing warp can fully hit in L1D in the next load issuance. However, GPU caches are not designed with enough awareness of either SIMD execution model or memory divergence.

In this work, we renovate the cache management policies to design a GPU-specific data cache, *DaCache*. This design starts with the observation that warp scheduling can essentially shape the locality pattern in cache access streams. Thus we incorporate the warp scheduling logic into insertion policy so that blocks are inserted into the LRU-chain according to their issuing warp's scheduling priority. Then we deliberately prioritize coherent loads over divergent loads. In order to enable the thrashing resistance, the cache ways are partitioned by desired warp concurrency into two regions, the locality region and the thrashing region, so that replacement is constrained within the thrashing region. When no replacement candidate is available in the thrashing region, incoming requests are bypassed. We also implement a dynamic partition scheme based on the caching effectiveness that is sampled at runtime. Experiments show that DaCache achieves 40.4% performance improvement over the baseline GPU and outperform two state-of-the-art thrashing resistant cache management techniques RRIP and DIP by 40% and 24.9%, respectively.

Acknowledgments

This work is funded in part by an Alabama Innovation Award, and by National Science Foundation awards 1059376, 1320016, 1340947 and 1432892. The authors are very thankful to anonymous reviewers for their invaluable feedback.

8. REFERENCES

[1] A. Bakhoda, G. L. Yuan, W. W. L. Fung, H. Wong, and T. M. Aamodt. Analyzing CUDA Workloads Using a Detailed GPU Simulator. In *ISPASS*, 2009.

[2] L. A. Belady. A study of replacement algorithms for a virtual-storage computer. *IBM Syst. J.*, 5(2):78–101, June 1966.

[3] J. Chang and G. S. Sohi. Cooperative Cache Partitioning for Chip Multiprocessors. In *ICS*, 2007.

[4] S. Che, M. Boyer, J. Meng, D. Tarjan, J. W. Sheaffer, S.-H. Lee, and K. Skadron. Rodinia: A benchmark suite for heterogeneous computing. In *IISWC*, 2009.

[5] X. Chen, L.-W. Chang, C. I. Rodrigues, J. Lv, Z. Wang, and W.-M. W. Hwu. Adaptive Cache Management for Energy-efficient GPU Computing. In *MICRO*, 2014.

[6] X. Chen, S. Wu, L.-W. Chang, W.-S. Huang, C. Pearson, Z. Wang, and W.-M. W. Hwu. Adaptive Cache Bypass and Insertion for Many-core Accelerators. In *MES*, 2014.

[7] A. Danalis, G. Marin, C. McCurdy, J. S. Meredith, P. C. Roth, K. Spafford, V. Tipparaju, and J. S. Vetter. The Scalable Heterogeneous Computing (SHOC) benchmark suite. In *GPGPU*, 2010.

[8] N. Duong, D. Zhao, T. Kim, R. Cammarota, M. Valero, and A. V. Veidenbaum. Improving Cache Management Policies Using Dynamic Reuse Distances. In *MICRO*, 2012.

[9] W. W. L. Fung, I. Sham, G. L. Yuan, and T. M. Aamodt. Dynamic Warp Formation and Scheduling for Efficient GPU Control Flow. In *MICRO*, 2007.

[10] H. Gao and C. Wilkerson. A Dueling Segmented LRU Replacement Algorithm with Adaptive Bypassing. In J. Emer, editor, *JWAC 2010 - 1st JILP Worshop on Computer Architecture Competitions: cache replacement Championship*, Saint Malo, France, 2010.

[11] S. Grauer-Gray, L. Xu, R. Searles, S. Ayalasomayajula, and J. Cavazos. Auto-tuning a High-Level Language Targeted to GPU Codes. In *Innovative Parallel Computing*, 2012.

[12] F. Guo, Y. Solihin, L. Zhao, and R. Iyer. A Framework for Providing Quality of Service in Chip Multi-Processors. In *MICRO*, 2007.

[13] E. G. Hallnor and S. K. Reinhardt. *A fully associative software-managed cache design*, volume 28. ACM, 2000.

[14] B. He, W. Fang, Q. Luo, N. K. Govindaraju, and T. Wang. Mars: A MapReduce Framework on Graphics Processors. In *PACT*, 2008.

[15] R. Iyer. CQoS: A Framework for Enabling QoS in Shared Caches of CMP Platforms. In *ICS*, 2004.

[16] R. Iyer, L. Zhao, F. Guo, R. Illikkal, S. Makineni, D. Newell, Y. Solihin, L. Hsu, and S. Reinhardt. QoS Policies and Architecture for Cache/Memory in CMP Platforms. In *SIGMETRICS*, 2007.

[17] A. Jaleel, K. B. Theobald, S. C. Steely, Jr., and J. S. Emer. High Performance Cache Replacement Using Re-Reference Interval Prediction (RRIP). In *ISCA*, 2010.

[18] W. Jia, K. A. Shaw, and M. Martonosi. Characterizing and Improving the Use of Demand-fetched Caches in GPUs. In *ICS*, 2012.

[19] W. Jia, K. A. Shaw, and M. Martonosi. MRPB: Memory Request Prioritization for Massively Parallel Processors. In *HPCA*, 2014.

[20] O. Kayiran, A. Jog, M. T. Kandemir, and C. R. Das. Neither More Nor Less: Optimizing Thread-Level Parallelism for GPGPUs. In *PACT*, 2013.

[21] S. M. Khan, Y. Tian, and D. A. Jimenez. Sampling Dead Block Prediction for Last-Level Caches. In *MICRO*, 2010.

[22] J. Lee and H. Kim. TAP: A TLP-aware cache management policy for a CPU-GPU heterogeneous architecture. In *HPCA*, 2012.

[23] D. Li. *Orchestrating Thread Scheduling and Cache Management to Improve Memory System Throughput in Throughput Processor*. PhD thesis, University of Texas at Austin, May 2014.

[24] E. Lindholm, J. Nickolls, S. Oberman, and J. Montrym. NVIDIA Tesla: A Unified Graphics and Computing Architecture. *IEEE Micro*, 28(2):39–55, Mar. 2008.

[25] V. Mekkat, A. Holey, P.-C. Yew, and A. Zhai. Managing shared last-level cache in a heterogeneous multicore processor. In *PACT*, 2013.

[26] C. Nugteren, G.-J. van den Braak, H. Corporaal, and H. Bal. A Detailed GPU Cache Model Based on Reuse Distance Theory. In *HPCA*, 2014.

[27] NVIDIA. NVIDIA's Next Generation CUDA Compute Architecture: Fermi, 2009.

[28] NVIDIA. NVIDIA's Next Generation CUDA Compute Architecture: Kepler GK110, 2012.

[29] NVIDIA. CUDA C Programming Guide, 2013.

[30] M. K. Qureshi, A. Jaleel, Y. N. Patt, S. C. Steely, Jr., and J. S. Emer. Adaptive Insertion Policies for High Performance Caching. In *ISCA*, 2007.

[31] M. K. Qureshi, D. Thompson, and Y. N. Patt. The V-Way Cache: Demand Based Associativity via Global Replacement. In *ISCA*, 2005.

[32] T. G. Rogers, M. O'Connor, and T. M. Aamodt. Cache-Conscious Wavefront Scheduling. In *MICRO*, 2012.

[33] T. G. Rogers, M. O'Connor, and T. M. Aamodt. Divergence-aware Warp Scheduling. In *MICRO*, 2013.

[34] R. Subramanian, Y. Smaragdakis, and G. H. Loh. Adaptive Caches: Effective Shaping of Cache Behavior to Workloads. In *MICRO*, 2006.

[35] B. Wang, Z. Liu, X. Wang, and W. Yu. Eliminating Intra-Warp Conflict Misses in GPU. In *DATE*, 2015.

[36] B. Wang, B. Wu, D. Li, X. Shen, W. Yu, Y. Jiao, and J. S. Vetter. Exploring Hybrid Memory for GPU Energy Efficiency Through Software-hardware Co-design. In *PACT*, 2013.

[37] X. Xie, Y. Liang, G. Sun, and D. Chen. An Efficient Compiler Framework for Cache Bypassing on GPUs. In *ICCAD*, 2013.

[38] Y. Xie and G. H. Loh. PIPP: Promotion/Insertion Pseudo-partitioning of Multi-core Shared Caches. In *ISCA*, 2009.

Automatic Selection of Sparse Matrix Representation on GPUs

Naser Sedaghati, Te Mu, Louis-Noël Pouchet, Srinivasan Parthasarathy, P. Sadayappan
The Ohio State University
Columbus, OH, USA
{sedaghat,mut,pouchet,srini,saday}@cse.ohio-state.edu

ABSTRACT

Sparse matrix-vector multiplication (SpMV) is a core kernel in numerous applications, ranging from physics simulation and large-scale solvers to data analytics. Many GPU implementations of SpMV have been proposed, targeting several sparse representations and aiming at maximizing overall performance. No single sparse matrix representation is uniformly superior, and the best performing representation varies for sparse matrices with different sparsity patterns.

In this paper, we study the inter-relation between GPU architecture, sparse matrix representation and the sparse dataset. We perform extensive characterization of pertinent sparsity features of around 700 sparse matrices, and their SpMV performance with a number of sparse representations implemented in the NVIDIA CUSP and cuSPARSE libraries. We then build a decision model using machine learning to automatically select the best representation to use for a given sparse matrix on a given target platform, based on the sparse matrix features. Experimental results on three GPUs demonstrate that the approach is very effective in selecting the best representation.

Categories and Subject Descriptors

G.4 [**Mathematical Software**]: Efficiency

Keywords

GPU, SpMV, machine learning models

1. INTRODUCTION

Sparse Matrix-Vector Multiplication (SpMV) is a key computation at the core of many data analytics algorithms, as well as scientific computing applications [3]. Hence there has been tremendous interest in developing efficient implementations of the SpMV operation, optimized for different architectural platforms [6, 25]. A particularly challenging aspect of optimizing SpMV is that the performance profile depends not only on the characteristics of the target platform, but also on the sparsity structure of the matrix. There is a growing interest in characterizing many graph analytics applications in terms of a dataset-algorithm-platform triangle. This is a complex relationship that is not yet well characterized even for much studied core kernels like SpMV. In this paper, we make a first attempt at understanding the dataset-algorithm dependences for SpMV on GPUs.

The optimization of SpMV for GPUs has been a much researched topic over the last few years, including auto-tuning approaches to deliver very high performance [22, 11] by tuning the block size to the sparsity features of the computation. For CPUs, the compressed sparse row (CSR) – or the dual compressed sparse column – is the dominant representation, effective across domains from which the sparse matrices arise. In contrast, for GPUs no single representation has been found to be effective across a range of sparse matrices. The multiple objectives of maximizing coalesced global memory access, minimizing thread divergence, and maximizing warp occupancy often conflict with each other. Different sparse matrix representations, such as COO, ELLPACK, HYB, CSR (these representations are elaborated later in the paper), are provided by optimized libraries like SPARSKIT [22], CUSP and cuSPARSE [10] from NVIDIA because no single representation is superior in performance across different sparse matrices. But despite all the significant advances in performance of SpMV on GPUs, it remains unclear how these results apply to different kinds of sparse matrices. The question we seek to answer in this paper is the following: *Is it feasible to develop a characterization of SpMV performance corresponding to different matrix representations, as a function of simply computable metrics of sparse matrices, and further use such a characterization to effectively predict the best representation for a given sparse matrix?*

We focus on four sparse matrix representations implemented in the cuSPARSE and CUSP libraries [10] from NVIDIA: CSR [5], ELLPACK (ELL) [21], COO, and a hybrid scheme ELL-COO (HYB) [6], as well as a variant of the HYB scheme. To study the impact of sparsity features on SpMV performance, we gathered a set of 682 sparse matrices from the UFL repository [12] covering nearly all available matrices that fit in GPU global memory. We perform an extensive analysis of the performance distribution of each considered representation on three high-end NVIDIA GPUs: Tesla K20c and K40c, and a Fermi GTX 580, demonstrating the need to choose different representations based on the matrix features, library and GPU used.

We then address the problem of automatically selecting, a priori, the best performing representation using only features of the input matrix such as the average number of nonzero entries per row (the average degree of graphs). This is achieved by developing a machine learning approach using decision tree classifiers. We perform extensive characterization of the performance of our automatically generated models, achieving on average a slowdown of no more than

ICS'15, June 8–11, 2015, Newport Beach, CA, USA.

http://dx.doi.org/10.1145/2751205.2751244.

1.05x compared to an ideal oracle approach systematically selecting the best representation for every matrix. We make the following contributions:

- an extensive performance evaluation of popular SpMV schemes implemented in NVIDIA cuSPARSE and CUSP, on three high-end NVIDIA GPUs;
- the development of a fully automated approach to select the best performing sparse representation, using only simple features of the input sparse matrices;
- an extensive evaluation of numerous machine learning models to select sparse representations, leading to portable and simple-to-translate decision trees of 30 leaf nodes achieving 95% of the maximal possible performance.

The paper is organized as follows. Sec. 2 motivates our work and presents the SpMV representations considered. Sec. 3 presents and analyzes the sparse matrix dataset we use. Sec. 4 characterizes the SpMV kernel performance for all covered cases, and Sec. 5-6 presents and evaluates our machine learning method. Related work is discussed in Sec. 7.

2. BACKGROUND AND OVERVIEW

Sparse Matrix-Vector Multiplication (SpMV) is a Level-2 BLAS operation between a sparse matrix and a dense vector ($y = A \times x + y$), described (element-wise) by Equation 1.

$$\forall a_{i,j} \neq 0 : y_i = a_{i,j} \times x_j + y_i \quad (1)$$

As a low arithmetic-intensity algorithm, SpMV is typically bandwidth-bound, and due to the excellent GPU memory bandwidth relative to CPUs, it has become a good candidate for GPU implementations [11]. Sparsity in the matrix A leads to irregularity (and thus lack of locality) when accessing the matrix elements. Thus, even with optimal reuse for the elements of vectors x and y, it is the accesses to matrix A that significantly impacts the execution time of a kernel. In particular, accessing the matrix A leads to irregular and non-coalesced memory accesses and divergence among threads in a warp. A number of efforts [5, 6, 28, 17, 27, 2] have sought to address these challenges. The NVIDIA libraries, cuSPARSE [10] and CUSP [9, 5, 6], are two of the most widely-used CUDA libraries that support different sparse representations (e.g., *COO*, *ELL*, *CSR*, *HYB*). The libraries also provide a "conversion" API to convert one representation to another.

2.1 Problem Statement

From a performance perspective, for a given matrix A with a certain sparsity structure, the representation is selected based on required space (nonzero + meta-data), the conversion time, and the kernel execution time. As shown in Table 1, the required space is a factor of the number of nonzeros (nnz), matrix dimensions ($m \times n$), and other internal (matrix-specific) parameters (e.g., cut-off point k for HYB).

The representation of the sparse matrix affects SpMV performance on GPUs and none of the representations is consistently superior as shown later in Sec. 4. Table 2 shows four sparse matrices and performance of SpMV in GFLOP/s on a single Tesla K40c GPU. It can be seen that each of the four representations is the best for one of the four matrices.

The choice of "best representation" for a given matrix depends on the sparsity structure (i.e. matrix features) as well as the GPU architecture (e.g. number of SMs, size/bandwidth of global memory, etc.). However, using representative parameters from both matrix and architecture, we can develop a model to predict the best performing representation for a given input matrix, as demonstrated in this paper.

Format	Space Required
COO	$3 \times nnz$
ELL	$2 \times m \times nnz\_max$
CSR	$2 \times nnz + m + 1$
HYB	$2 \times m \times k + 3 \times (nnz - X)$

Table 1: Memory space required for every representation. (matrix A is $m \times n$ with total nnz nonzeros and nnz_max maximum nonzeros per row). k is the cut-off point for ELL/COO partitioning in HYB where X non-zero values handled by ELL.

Group	Matrix	COO	ELL	CSR	HYB
Meszaros	dbir1	**9.9**	0.9	4.4	9.4
Boeing	bcsstk39	9.9	**34.3**	18.5	25.0
GHS_indef	exdata_1	9.5	4.3	**31.5**	11.3
GHS_psdef	bmwcra_1	11.5	26.7	24.8	**35.4**

Table 2: Performance difference for sparse matrices from UFL matrix repository [12] (single-precision GFLOP/s on Tesla K40c GPU)

2.2 Sparse Matrix Representations

In this work, we do not take into account pre-processing (i.e. conversion) time and focus only on the performance of the SpMV operation but the developed approach can be extended to also account for the pre-processing time, if information about the expected number of invocations of SpMV for a given matrix is known. Some of the well-established representations (for iterative and non-iterative SpMV) are implemented and maintained in the NVIDIA cuSPARSE and CUSP libraries [10, 9].

2.2.1 Coordinate Format (COO)

COO stores a sparse matrix using three dense vectors: the nonzero values, column indices and row indices. Figure 1 demonstrates how a given matrix A can be represented using the COO.

2.2.2 Compressed Sparse Row Format (CSR)

CSR [5, 6] compresses the row index array (into row_offset) such that the non-zeros of row i, as well as their column indexes, can be found respectively in the $values$ and col_index vectors, at index r, where $row\_offset[i] \leq r \leq row\_offset[i+1]$.

2.2.3 ELLPACK Format (ELL)

ELL [21] packs the matrix into a rectangular shape by shifting the nonzeros in each row to the left and zero-padding the rows so that they all occupy the same width as the one with the largest number of nonzeros. In addition to the padded $values$ matrix, the representation requires an index matrix to store the corresponding column index for every non-zero element (as shown in Figure 1).

2.2.4 Hybrid COO-ELL Format (HYB)

HYB uses a mix of ELL and COO representations. It partitions the input matrix into a dense part and a sparse part. The "dense" part is represented and processed using the ELL representation, while the "sparse" part uses COO.

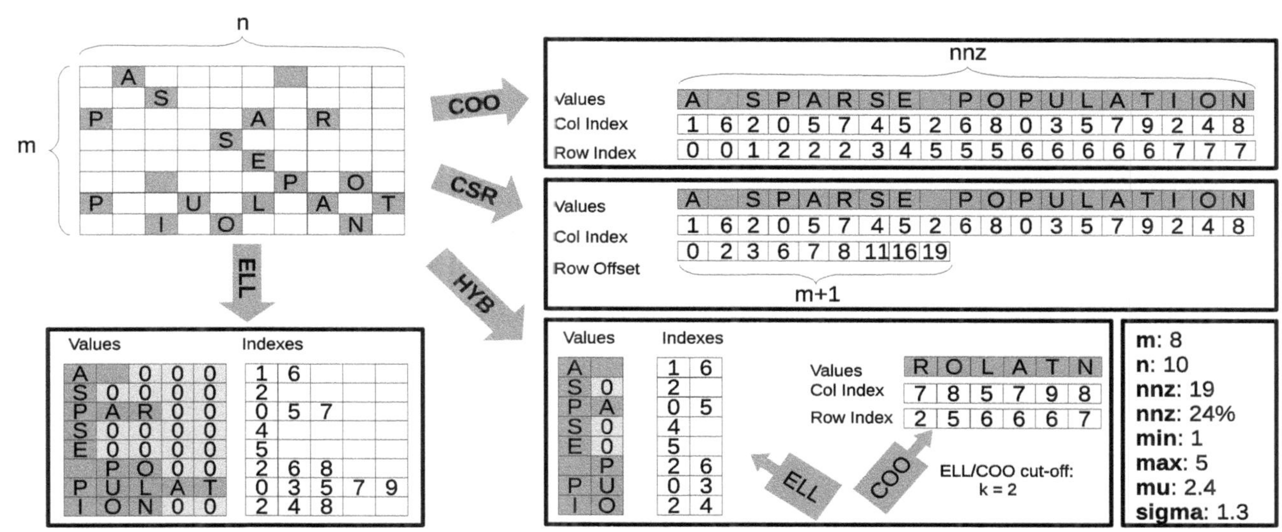

Figure 1: Sparse representations for matrix A in COO, CSR, ELL and HYB.

A parameter, k, is used to partition the first k non-zeros from each row for storiage in the ELL part, and the rest are stored in COO format. If a row has less than k non-zeros, then it is padded with zeros as shown in Figure 1. The choice of the cut-off point depends on the input matrix, and can significantly affect performance.

2.3 GPUs and Compilation

Two NVIDIA Tesla GPUs (K20c and K40c) and one Fermi GPU (GTX 580) were used for our experiments. Table 3 shows the details for each GPU. When selecting the GPUs, we have considered variety in global memory bandwidth (i.e. 192 vs 288 GB/s) as well as the compute capacity (i.e. total number of CUDA cores). The kernels were compiled using the NVIDIA C Compiler (*nvcc*) version 6.5, with the maximum compute capability supported by each device. We enabled standard optimizations using the $-O3$ switch.

GPU Model	Fermi	Tesla K20c	Tesla K40c
Chip	GTX580	GK110	GK110B
Compute Capability	2.0	3.5	3.5
Num. of SMs	16	13	15
ALUs per SM	32	192	192
Warp size	32	32	32
Threads per CTA	1024	1024	1024
Threads per SM(X)	1536	2048	2048
Sh-mem /CTA(KB)	48	48	48
L2 cache(KB)	768	1536	1536
Glob-mem (GB)	1.5	5	12
Glob-mem (GB/s)	192	208	288
Tera-FMA/s (SP/DP)	1.5/-	3.5/1.2	4.3/1.4

Table 3: GPUs hosted the experiments.

3. DATASET FEATURE ANALYSIS

3.1 Dataset Selection

We first needed a dataset of sparse matrices representative of most sparsity feature cases. For this purpose, we analyzed sparse matrices from the UFL repository [12] in Matrix Market format [18]. From more than 2650 matrices (from 177 groups of applications) in the repository, we selected 682 matrices from 114 groups. These matrices included all those used in numerous previous GPU studies [6, 8, 2, 1, 27]. While previous work using sparse matrices has usually tried to group matrices based on the domain where they arise, in this work we instead look to obtain a statistically relevant coverage among several key quantitative features describing the sparsity structure of the matrix.

Our selection mechanism applied the following constraints to set bounds on two metrics: *nnz_tot*, the total number of non-zero entries in the matrix, and *n_rows*, the number of rows:

- **C1**: the sparse matrix does not fit in the CPU LLC (8 MB for our machines). This is to focus on matrices where GPU execution is most beneficial.
- **C2**: the sparse matrix fits in the "effective" space on the global memory of the device (i.e. single-GPU execution).
- **C3**: the number of rows is large enough to guarantee minimum GPU concurrency. This is achieved by assuming that a warp works on a row; thus the minimum number of rows equals the maximum warp-level concurrency on a given device.

The size of the matrix (for **C1** and **C2**) is conservatively computed as $S = 16 \times nnz\_tot$, where a nonzero in COO, double-precision, needs 16 bytes (8 bytes for data plus two 4-byte indexes). It is also assumed that up to 80% of the global memory on the device is available to hold the sparse matrix data. In **C3**, the maximum warp-level concurrency is computed by dividing the maximum number of threads per GPU (i.e. $Threads/SMX \times \#SMXs$) by the warp size.

3.2 Feature Set

Our objective is to gather relevant information about the sparsity structure of the matrix without utilizing any domain knowledge, i.e., without considering the domain where the matrix originates. For this work, we computed a set of features as shown in Table 4.

These features were (re-)computed by doing an initial traversal of the input matrix to gather these statistics. We show later in Sec. 6 that only a small subset of these features are actually needed for effective prediction of the best

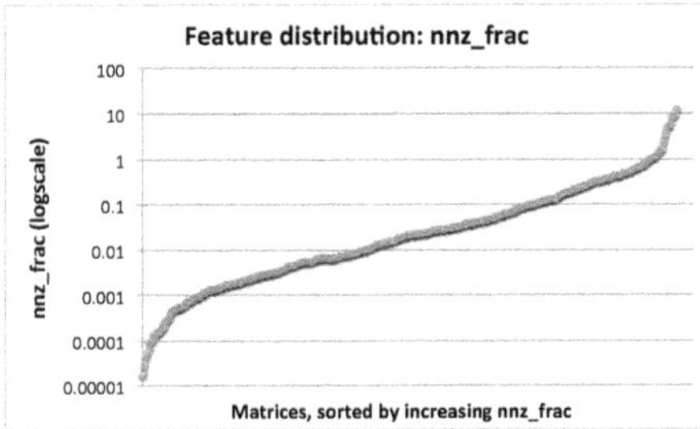

Figure 2: nnz_frac (682 matrices)

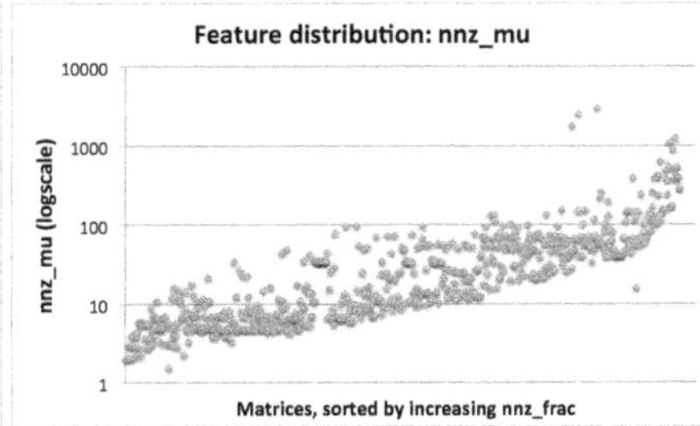

Figure 3: nnz_mu (682 matrices)

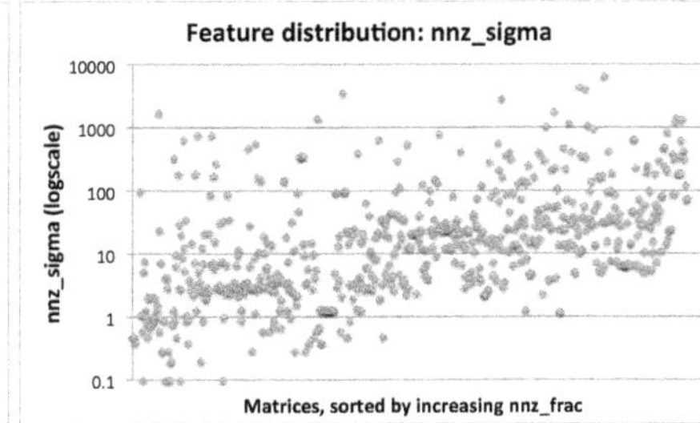

Figure 4: nnz_sigma (682 matrices)

Feature	Description
n_rows	Number of rows
n_cols	Number of columns
nnz_tot	Number of non-zeros
nnz_frac	Percentage of non-zeros
$nnz\_\{min, max, mu, sig\}$	Min, max, average (μ) and std. deviation (σ) of non-zero per row
nnzb_tot	Number of non-zero blocks
$nnzb\_\{min, max, mu, sig\}$	Min, max, average (μ) and std. deviation (σ) of number of non-zero blocks per row
$snzb\_\{min, max, mu, sig\}$	Min, max, average (μ) and std. deviation (σ) of the size of non-zero blocks per row

Table 4: Matrix features

	Min	Max	Avg.	Std. Dev.
n_rows	1301	12M	377k	118k
n_cols	2339	12M	399k	126k
nnz_tot	350k	53M	4.5M	1.7M
nnz_frac	0.000018	12.48	0.31	0.92
nnz_min	1	130	8.90	11.63
nnz_max	3	2.3M	13k	8k
nnz_mu	1.60	3098	60.46	108.73
nnz_sigma	0	6505	107.38	213.77
nnzb_tot	8256	27M	2.1M	696k
nnzb_min	1	49	2.17	2.43
nnzb_max	2	462k	2203	2580
nnzb_mu	1.5	1333	21.73	28.95
nnzb_sigma	0	2720	29.21	71.69
snzb_min	1	18	1.77	0.82
snzb_max	1	309k	1101	365.8
snzb_mu	1	126.3	5.27	6.02
snzb_sigma	0	737.4	8.45	11.09

Table 5: Statistics on main features

representation. Nevertheless, the use of more features could possibly improve the quality of the prediction. The nnz_frac feature is simply derived from the sparse data structure size and the number of matrix rows and columns, similarly for nnz_mu.

3.3 Feature Distribution

The selected matrices represent a wide range of structure (i.e. diagonal, blocked, banded-diagonal, etc.) from different application domains. We now focus on three critical features that are group/domain-independent, and discuss their distribution and correlation below.

Feature statistics. Table 5 summarizes, across the 682 matrices, the minimum, maximum, average and standard deviation of the main features considered.

We observe that the dataset covers a wide spectrum of matrix sizes, with an average of 4.5 million non-zero entries. The average block size represents the average number of contiguous columns with non-zero entries in the rows of a matrix. As shown by the snzb_mu metric of 5.27, the average block size is quite low. These statistics provide sensible information about the UFL database concerning GPU-friendly matrices, and confirm via the standard deviation values of these features (last column) that we do cover wide ranges for the various features and that our selection of matrices is effective.

Figures 2-4 show the distribution for the three critical features considered.

Fraction of non-zeros. This feature represents the fractional sparsity of the matrix, in a manner independent of the matrix size. Figure 2 plots its value for each matrix, sorted in ascending order. We observe a near perfect coverage of this feature, but with a lower density at the extremes of the range. It may be observed that this feature is an excellent discriminant between matrices in our database, from the absence of horizontal segments. This motivates its inclusion in all feature sets for prediction of the best sparse representation.

Average number of non-zeros per row. This feature is plotted in Figure 3, using the same order along the x axis as in Figure 2, i.e., it plots nnz_mu in increasing order of nnz_frac. We also observe an excellent coverage of the feature range. We observe only a mild correlation between the two features, as seen by the overall increasing trend of nnz_mu. Nevertheless there are significant outliers to this trend, indicating that nnz_mu carries complementary information to nnz_frac.

Standard deviation of number of non-zeros per row. This feature is plotted in Figure 4 in increasing order of nnz_frac. While we also observe an excellent coverage of the feature range, there is a clear decorrelation between the two features. This is indicative of different information being carried by nnz_sigma than nnz_frac, and motivates its inclusion in all feature sets.

4. PERFORMANCE ANALYSIS

We now perform a characterization of the performance of each representation tested, on all matrices in the dataset. We conducted experiments by measuring the performance of the SpMV kernel in GFLOP/s, on three GPUs (K40c, K20c and Fermi, as described in Sec. 2). The figure reports the total kernel execution time; data transfer time between

CPU and GPU is not included. This is appropriate since we particularly target iterative SpMV schemes, where the matrix is expected to be loaded once and the kernel repeated numerous times.

Best performing representations. Table 6 reports how many matrices, out of the 682 considered, are best executed (i.e., highest GFLOP/s achieved), with a given representation.[1] For cuSPARSE, we also evaluated HYB-MU, a variation of the hybrid scheme, where the cut-off point between ELL and COO is not chosen by the library, but instead set to the nnz_mu value of the matrix. Such a user-specified control is not available with CUSP.

	COO	ELL	CSR	HYB	HYB-MU
K40c-cusparse	10	**278**	104	103	185
K40c-cusp	0	168	172	**339**	N/A
K20c-cusparse	10	**269**	95	134	174
K20c-cusp	1	194	168	**318**	N/A
Fermi-cusparse	5	200	**302**	86	87

Table 6: Fastest representation statistics

First, we observe that the hybrid scheme is the best performing one in the highest number of matrices for CUSP, while for cuSPARSE ELL dominates on the Teslas. We also observe an apparent consistency between Tesla GPUs: similar trends in the distribution of the best appears for both K20c and K40c. On the older Fermi architecture, CSR actually performs consistently best, but as shown below, the true performance differences with HYB are minimal. However, care must be taken with these numbers: we conducted a more precise analysis showing that the matrices for which CSR is best for K40c are not strictly the same as the ones for K20c, and similarly between CUSP and cuSPARSE. While ELL, COO and HYB have correlation, since HYB combines the first two, we observe that CSR remains an important representation for getting the best performance for around 20% of the matrices.

Performance differences. The previous table only shows a fraction of the information. In practice, what matters is not only which representation performs best, but also the performance difference between them. Table 7 shows the average slowdown in always using the same representation for the entire dataset, compared to using the best representation found for each matrix individually. For instance, 1.97x for COO / K40c-cusparse means that we lose about 50% of the performance by always using COO for the 682 matrices, compared to using the best representation for each of them.

	COO	ELL	CSR	HYB	HYB-MU
K40c-cusparse	1.97x	1.60x	1.54x	**1.18x**	1.18x
K40c-cusp	2.21x	1.87x	1.54x	**1.14x**	N/A
K20c-cusparse	1.88x	1.60x	1.55x	**1.17x**	1.17x
K20c-cusp	2.16x	1.90x	1.52x	**1.14x**	N/A
Fermi-cusparse	2.02x	1.71x	**1.20x**	**1.20x**	**1.20x**

Table 7: Average slowdown over the 682 matrices when a fixed representation is used instead of the individual best

The HYB representation performs best overall, and there is overall consistency across libraries and GPUs. However, it also clearly demonstrates that using the popular CSR can lead to a significant average slowdown on Tesla GPUs.

[1]The latest version of CUSP did not work on the older Fermi GPU; we only report cuSPARSE results for this GPU.

Large slowdowns. While it seems from the above that HYB is a good overall representation in terms of performance, these average numbers mask very significant slowdowns on some matrices, due to the large number of matrices in the dataset. Table 8 reports the number of matrices (out of 682) for which use of a fixed representation across the entire dataset results in a slowdown greater than 2x over the best representation.

	COO	ELL	CSR	HYB	HYB-MU
K40c-cusparse	360	243	166	47	**37**
K40c-cusp	422	322	248	**50**	N/A
K20c-cusparse	339	245	134	45	**33**
K20c-cusp	410	326	231	**42**	N/A
Fermi-cusparse	404	268	68	**20**	23

Table 8: Number of > 2x slowdown cases

This table carries critical information and dismisses the one-size-fits-all strategy that might be suggested from the previous data. If HYB is always used, between 20 and 50 matrices would achieve less than 50% of the possible performance. Slowdowns of up to 10x can actually arise by always using HYB. The numbers are even more staggering for the other representations, where such loss of performance can occur for half of the matrices. *This data clearly motivates the need for an effective approach to select the best representation for each matrix* in order to achieve consistently good performance. This metric of the number of cases with 2x slowdown is a particular point of focus in the quality of our machine learning approach described in Sec. 5, where we succeed in reducing this number to no more than 6 out of 682 matrices.

Impact of ELL and CSR. Table 9 focuses on the K40c, considering the 2x-slowdown cases when using HYB, and reports which representation actually performing best, and the actual average slowdown for each of these. For example, out of the 47 cases where HYB has a 2x slowdown, for 18 of them CSR was the best representation, and a speedup of 2.36x on average can be achieved by using CSR instead of HYB for these 18 cases.

	COO	ELL	CSR	HYB-MU
(CS) > 2x slowdown	0	29	18	0
(CS) Avg. slowdown	N/A	2.36x	2.54x	N/A
(CU) > 2x slowdown	0	22	28	N/A
(CU) Avg. slowdown	N/A	2.28x	2.75x	N/A

Table 9: K40c using HYB

This shows that while the HYB-MU case does not lead to any improvement greater than 2x over HYB, both ELL and CSR are equally critical to address the cases with large slowdowns. In other words, to ensure good overall performance and avoid cases with significant loss of performance, a model must select at least between HYB, CSR and ELL.

SpMV performance breakdown. Finally Figures 5-9 plots the matrix distribution of performance (GFLOPS/s) achieved by the SpMV kernel, for all configurations. The range of GFLOP/s achieved for a configuration is split into 10 buckets, and the number of matrices achieving no more than the GFLOP/s label on the x axis (and no less than the value for the previous bucket) is reported. For example, 394 matrices achieve between 8.3 GFLOP/s and 12.4 GFLOP/s using COO with K40c/cuSPARSE in Fig. 5.

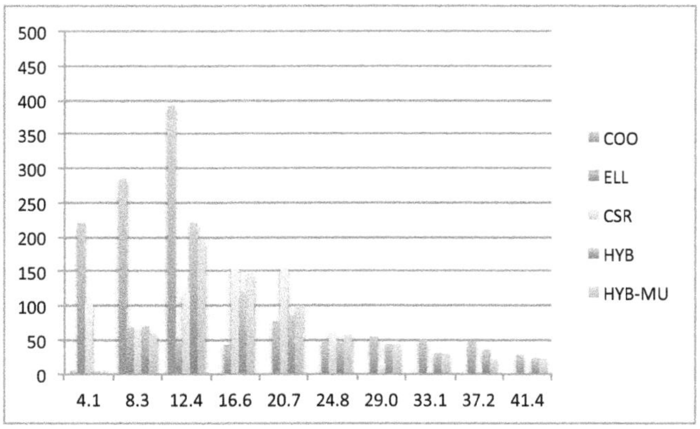

Figure 5: K40c, cuSPARSE

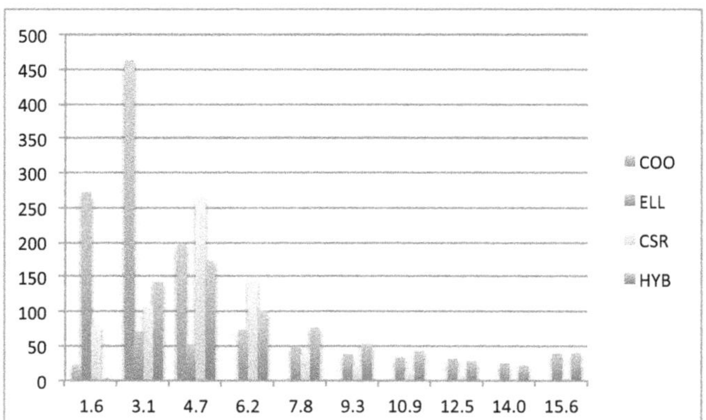

Figure 6: K40c, CUSP

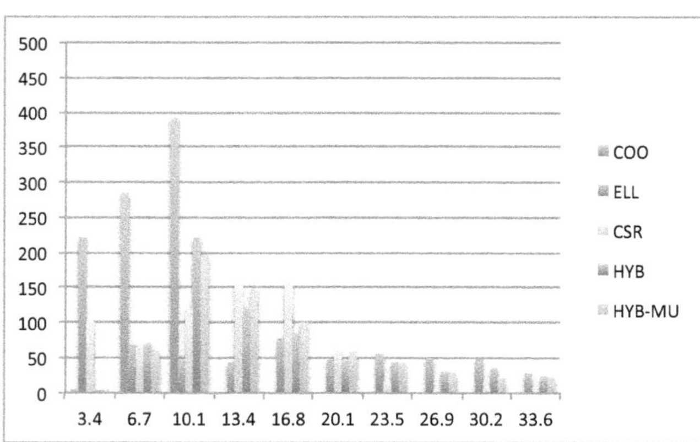

Figure 7: K20c, cuSPARSE

We observe that CSR is almost never in any of the three right-most buckets, and COO is mainly represented at the low end of the spectrum, while both HYB and ELL are spread across the entire spectrum. In other words, the GPU computing power may be better harnessed for matrices where HYB and ELL perform best. We remark that for the cases where ELL failed to convert from MatrixMarket format on

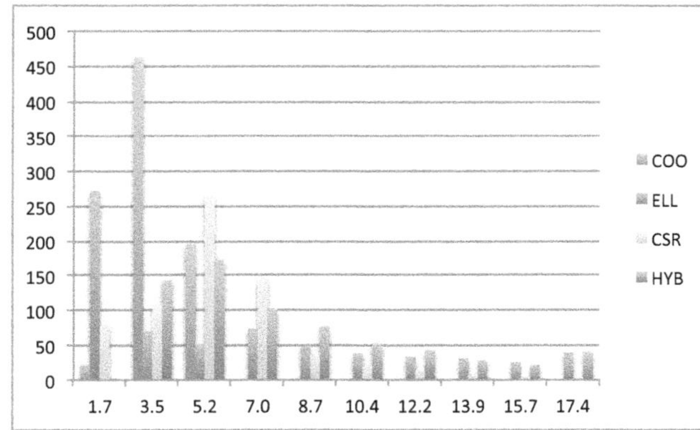

Figure 8: K20c, CUSP

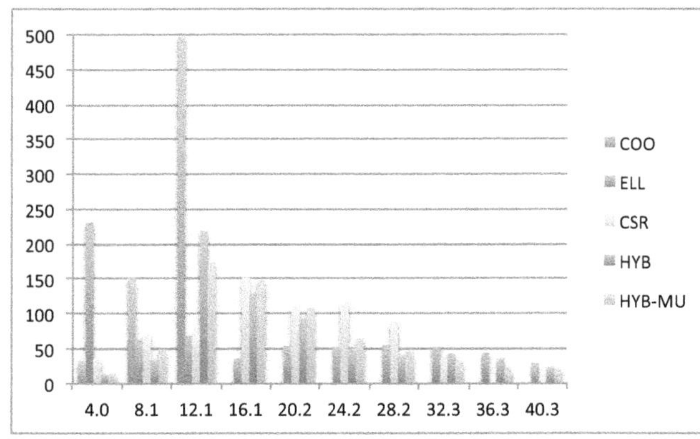

Figure 9: Fermi, cuSPARSE

the GPU, we report its GFLOP/s as 0 which artificially increases its representation in the first bucket. Such cases of failure of conversion occur typically because of very large nnz_max values, where ELL is not appropriate to use. While we could simply have removed ELL for these matrices, for consistency of the protocol, we chose to simply set their GFLOP/s to 0 (and their speedup compared to other representations also to zero).

We conducted additional study to observe if there is any correlation between the fraction of non-zero in the matrix and the GF/s achieved by each representation. We separated the set of matrices in 10 classes, by increasing range of the value of nnz_frac, and computed the average GF/s of each representation in this class. We observed that while for COO and to a more limited extent CSR the higher the nnz_frac the higher the GF/s on average, this trend is reverted for ELL and the hybrid schemes: the lower the nnz_frac the better the average GF/s. Note that there are numerous outliers to these trends: while previous results showed that, on a restricted dataset, nnz_frac was a possible predictor of the best representation [23] the extensive study we conduct in this paper showed the requirement to consider additional features to properly determine the best representation in general.

5. MACHINE LEARNING MODELING

We now elaborate on the machine learning approach we use to automatically predict the best representation, based only on efficiently computed features of the input matrix.

5.1 Problem Learned

Based on our findings presented above, we concluded on the need to develop an approach which would predict, at the very least, which of CSR, ELL or HYB is the best representation for a matrix. While this is a simpler problem instance (3 categories), in order to achieve the truly best overall performance we keep each possible representation for prediction. We build a predictor of the form:

$$Predictor(\vec{x}) = c$$

where $c \in$ { COO, ELL, CSR, HYB, HYB-MU } for cuSPARSE, and we remove HYB-MU for CUSP. $\vec{x}$ is the vector of features we consider as input; these are metrics computed for each dataset.

Learning Algorithms. A classification tree is a form of decision tree where the predicted value is a category. It takes the form of a series of conditions on the input feature values, leading to a leaf containing the predicted category when the conditions are met. Figure 10 shows an example of an excerpt of a tree built in our experiments, the number in comment (e.g., #(22)) shows the number of matrices correctly predicted by matching the input features against each conditional, until a leaf is reached. For example a matrix with nnz_sigma = 2, nnz_frac = 0.00005 is predicted as HYB here.

```
nnz_sigma < 14.9
|  nnz_mu < 5.3
|  |  nnz_sigma < 2.05
|  |  |  nnz_frac < 1.0E-4
|  |  |  |  nnz_frac < 3.0E-5: HYB-MU #(3)
|  |  |  |  nnz_frac >= 3.0E-5: HYB   #(4)
|  |  |  nnz_frac >= 1.0E-4: ELL      #(22)
```

Figure 10: Classification tree example

Tree models have numerous advantages over other algorithms, including (1) the ability for a human to read and understand them, favoring knowledge transfer; (2) their excellent evaluation speed and quick training speed, enabling use with large datasets; (3) their widespread availability in machine learning libraries and ease of implementation.

In this work we conducted an extensive study using the Weka library version 3.6.12 [19] on most of the available decision tree algorithms implemented. This included RandomTree, J48, BFTree, and SimpleCart. We determined that BFTree and SimpleCart outperformed the other algorithms and therefore focused particularly on those two. BFTree [14] is a best-first decision tree classifier, while SimpleCart [7] implements a hierarchical optimal discriminant analysis using minimal cost-complexity pruning [19]. Both these algorithms can be parameterized to control the size of the tree generated, trading off generalization and prediction quality.

5.2 Training and Testing

Our experimental protocol is as follows. First the GFLOP/s for all representations and all matrices is computed, and each matrix is given a class attribute corresponding to the actual best performing representation (c above). Then, the entire set of 682 matrices is split into two sets, following the 80%-20% rule. The training of the model is done on the largest bucket containing 80% of the dataset, while the evaluation is done on the remaining 20%. This process is repeated 5 times, each with another 80-20 split, so that each matrix is used for testing exactly once. We use a stratified cross-validation with randomization to create each case, using the available Weka tools. This seeks to approximately retain the original class (c) distribution in both sets.

In our experiments the training was completed in less than 2 seconds on a standard laptop, and the testing in less than 0.1s, for one particular machine learning algorithm instance.

6. SELECTING A REPRESENTATION

We now present the evaluation of BFTree and SimpleCart on the prediction problem.

6.1 Experimental Protocol

Feature sets. We evaluated several feature sets, described in Table 13. The Simple feature set is meant to capture features that are extremely easy to compute, only nnz_sigma needs a scan of the matrix or sampling to be obtained. The Advanced1 and Advanced2 sets on the other hand consider statistics on the number and size of blocks of non-zeros, and typically requires a scan of the matrix, or a good knowledge of the regularity in the sparsity pattern.

Name	Description
Simple	nnz_frac, nnz_mu, nnz_sigma
Advanced1	nnz_frac, nnz_mu, nnz_sigma, nnzb_mu, nnzb_sigma, snzb_mu, snzb_sigma
Advanced2	nnz_frac, nnz_max, nnz_mu, nnz_sigma, nnzb_mu, nnzb_sigma, snzb_mu, snzb_sigma

Table 13: Feature sets evaluated

Algorithm parameters. Both algorithms take two parameters as argument for the training stage, determining (1) minNum the minimal number of instances at the terminal node; and (2) numFold the number of folds used in the pruning. We have explored the Cartesian product of combinations generated with the values $minNum = \{2, 3, 4, 5\} \times numFold = \{5, 10, 15\}$.

Invalidating the random approach. We have evaluated a classical random classifier to ensure the problem cannot be addressed using a simple random selection of the best representation. As expected this approach failed, giving an average slowdown compared to the best representation of 1.7x for cuSPARSE and 4.7x for CUSP — significantly worse than always using HYB.

6.2 Evaluation of Specialized Models

We first analyze the results of a first approach of training a different model for each GPU and each library independently, before discussing the use of a single model for all cases.

Tables 10-12 presents statistics about the best performing models founds, after exploring all algorithm parameters. The criterion retained for optimality was the minimization of the number of matrices for which a 2x slowdown or more was experienced, compared to the best representation. A total of 12 configurations was tested per entry in these tables, for a grand total of 144 models trained and evaluated per GPU, from which we report the 12 best. The parameters used to train the best model are shown, along with the percentage of testing matrices that were mispredicted from the testing set, the number of matrices achieving a 2x slowdown or more compared to the best performing matrices, and the average slowdown compared to the best per-matrix representation. These tables should be put in perspective with Tables 7-8.

			minNum	numFold	misprediction	> 2x slowdown	Avg. slowdown
cuSPARSE	**BFTree**	Simple	**2**	**5**	34.8%	**6**	**1.07x**
		Advanced1	2	10	34.2%	7	1.08x
		Advanced2	**2**	**5**	20.4%	**3**	**1.04x**
	SimpleCart	Simple	2	10	35.2%	6	1.08x
		Advanced1	2	10	18.8%	3	1.04x
		Advanced2	2	10	19%	3	1.04x
CUSP	BFTree	Simple	2	10	24%	4	1.06x
		Advanced1	2	10	18.8%	3	1.04x
		Advanced2	2	5	16.2%	1	1.02x
	SimpleCart	Simple	**5**	**15**	25%	**3**	**1.05x**
		Advanced1	2	10	19%	3	1.04x
		Advanced2	**2**	**5**	16.2%	**1**	**1.02x**

Table 10: Results for K40c, training one model per library

			minNum	numFold	misprediction	> 2x slowdown	Avg. slowdown
cuSPARSE	**BFTree**	Simple	**2**	**15**	33.6%	**6**	1.08x
		Advanced1	2	15	30.2%	5	1.07x
		Advanced2	**2**	**5**	26.2%	**1**	**1.03x**
	SimpleCart	Simple	2	5	29.8%	7	1.08x
		Advanced1	3	15	24.2%	2	1.03x
		Advanced2	3	5	24%	2	1.03x
CUSP	**BFTree**	Simple	**2**	**5**	31.4%	**3**	**1.06x**
		Advanced1	2	10	24%	4	1.05x
		Advanced2	**2**	**10**	21.2%	**1**	**1.02x**
	SimpleCart	Simple	2	10	29.6%	4	1.05x
		Advanced1	2	10	24.4%	4	1.05x
		Advanced2	2	15	23.6%	2	1.03x

Table 11: Results for K20c, training one model per library

			minNum	numFold	misprediction	> 2x slowdown	Avg. slowdown
cuSPARSE	BFTree	Simple	3	5	35.4%	6	1.08x
		Advanced1	2	10	33.5%	5	1.07x
		Advanced2	2	5	26.6%	2	1.03x
	SimpleCart	Simple	**4**	**5**	35.1%	**5**	**1.08x**
		Advanced1	2	5	27.3%	2	1.03x
		Advanced2	**2**	**15**	26.6%	**2**	**1.03x**

Table 12: Results for Fermi

General observations. First and foremost, we observe the very strong gain of our approach compared to using a single representation (HYB), both in terms of average slowdown and especially in terms of number of matrices for which we use an ineffective representation. Even limiting to a simple feature set made of nnz_frac, nnz_mu and nnz_sigma, we can achieve on average 92% or more of the maximal performance and limit the number of ineffective cases to 6 or less, for both libraries and GPUs. Considering a more complicated feature set, these numbers improve to 96% and 3.

Another interesting aspect is the somewhat marginal gain that increasing the feature set provides: considering features on the block size and distribution result in a decrease of the number of ineffective cases only from 6 to 3 or less. So it appears that simple features are overall good enough for a predictor, which enhances the simplicity of the approach: such features can be computed from the size of the data structures and provided by a domain expert.

Regarding mispredictions, we observe an overall high number of matrices being mispredicted, ranging from 16% to 38% of the testing set in the worst case. We initially used this metric as the criterion to select the best parameter configuration. However, reducing this metric only led to larger trees, with no improvement in average slowdown. The reason for the lack of apparent correlation between the misprediction rate and the average slowdown is found in the performance distribution, and the overall comparable performance of different representations in numerous cases. For these, our models may not predict the absolute best representation, but at least predict a representation achieving very good performance, close to the best of the selected representations. Allowing for higher misprediction rate while preserving the average slowdown and number of ineffective cases enabled the building of simpler and smaller trees, improving generalization and knowledge transfer.

Finally, we observe that while BFTree performs overall best for the K20c GPU, SimpleCart slightly outperforms BFTree with the Fermi and K40c for CUSP. Nevertheless, with differences being so marginal, we can use either model. A more challenging observation relates to the algorithm parameters. Clearly, different parameters are needed across GPUs, and even across libraries, to achieve the best performance.

Single parameter set. Table 14 shows performance statistics for use of a single parameter configuration and classification algorithm. As no algorithm/parameter setup performs best across all configurations, we chose the one that minimizes the total number of ineffective configurations.

	> 2x slowdown	Avg. slowdown
K40c/cuSPARSE	6	1.07x
K40c/CUSP	5	1.06x
K20c/cuSPARSE	8	1.09x
K20c/CUSP	6	1.05x
Fermi/cuSPARSE	6	1.08x

Table 14: BFTree minNum=2, numFold=5, Simple features

These results show a slight degradation of the results when parameter selection is avoided, making it a good candidate for single-shot training (i.e., no auto-tuning on the parameters). We however remark that, as the training time is a matter of a few seconds per configuration, such training auto-tuning on the proposed range of parameter remains feasible at library installation time. Nevertheless, running all SpMV cases on all representations to collect the classified data for this supervised learning will remain a task-consuming task.

A trained tree for K40c. We conclude our presentation by showing the tree produced for K40c / cuSPARSE in Fig. 11. This very simple tree was trained on the entire dataset and as such can be embedded as-is as a predictor in the cuSPARSE library, to provide the user guidance on the possible fastest representation. It is particularly interesting to note how 102 (122-18) ELL cases are correctly predicted using only conditions on nnz_mu and nnz_sigma, and 34 more considering nnz_frac.

7. RELATED WORK

There is an extensive amount of work in the literature on customizing sparse matrix representations and optimizing SpMV on different platforms. This paper follows our previous work [23] and raises the question of how to choose between these representations in an automated, portable and systematic way.

In the CPU domain, Vuduc [25] studied SpMV on single-core CPUs and presented an automated system for generating efficient implementations of SpMV on these platforms. Williams et al. [26] moved toward multi-core platforms with the implementation of parallel SpMV kernels. SpMV kernels have been studied and optimized for GPUs as well. Bell and Garland implemented several sparse matrix representations in CUDA [6] and proposed HYB (hybrid of ELL and COO), that generally adapts well to a broad class of unstructured matrices.

Baskaran and Bordawekar [4] optimized CSR so that it performs about the same (modestly faster with more memory cost) as CSR-Vector [6] (in which a row is assigned to each warp, which then performs segmented reduction). Choi et al. [8] introduced blocking to CSR and ELL (BCSR and BELLPACK). These representations outperform HYB for matrices with dense block substructure but on average their auto-tuned version is not as good as HYB for general unstructured and sparse matrices.

Liu et al. [17] proposed ELLPACK Sparse Block (ESB) for the Intel Xeon Phi Co-processor, and show that on average ESB outperforms cuSPARSE on NVIDIA K20X.

Yang et al. [28] developed a representation suited for matrices with power-low characteristics, by combining Transposed Jagged Diagonal Storage (TJDS) [13] with COO and blocking. Ashari et al. [1] presented a CSR-based approach (ACSR) crafted for power-law matrices, using binning and dynamic parallelism on Kepler GPUs. Liu et. al. [16] recently proposed CSR5 (a CSR-based representation) for SpMV on different target platforms (CPU, GPU and Xeon Phi), which is insensitive to the sparsity structure of the input sparse matrix. Reguly and Giles [20] also presented a CSR-based solution with an auto-tuning algorithm to select the number of rows for a thread to work on based on available resources on the device. Additionally, there have been developments towards having a runtime to select the best-performing representation for a given matrix (e.g. Cocktail Format [24]).

As briefly summarized above, sparse storage representations have been studied extensively for GPUs. Proposed optimizations have followed changes in the GPU architecture. GPU implementation of such representations are significantly impacted by the way nonzeros are distributed across the thread-blocks and threads [6, 15, 5, 8, 27, 28, 1].

While we restricted ourselves to a set of standard representations available in NVIDIA cuSPARSE [10] and CUSP [9], our approach does not depend on the representation used and we believe it can be effectively extended to cover additional sparse matrix representations.

```
nnz_sigma < 14.9
|  nnz_mu < 5.3
|  |  nnz_sigma < 2.05
|  |  |  nnz_frac < 1.0E-4: HYB-MU #(5.0/5.0)
|  |  |  nnz_frac >= 1.0E-4: ELL #(22.0/4.0)
|  |  nnz_sigma >= 2.05
|  |  |  nnz_sigma < 2.75: HYB-MU #(7.0/6.0)
|  |  |  nnz_sigma >= 2.75: HYB-MU #(27.0/15.0)
|  nnz_mu >= 5.3
|  |  nnz_sigma < 5.95
|  |  |  nnz_mu < 34.45: ELL #(122.0/18.0)
|  |  |  nnz_mu >= 34.45: HYB #(19.0/13.0)
|  |  nnz_sigma >= 5.95
|  |  |  nnz_mu < 26.9
|  |  |  |  nnz_frac < 0.01521
|  |  |  |  |  nnz_frac < 0.00319
|  |  |  |  |  |  nnz_sigma < 6.95: HYB #(4.0/1.0)
|  |  |  |  |  |  nnz_sigma >= 6.95: HYB-MU #(5.0/5.0)
|  |  |  |  |  nnz_frac >= 0.00319: HYB-MU #(8.0/2.0)
|  |  |  |  nnz_frac >= 0.01521: ELL #(6.0/7.0)
|  |  |  nnz_mu >= 26.9
|  |  |  |  nnz_frac < 0.63702: ELL #(45.0/11.0)
|  |  |  |  nnz_frac >= 0.63702: CSR #(4.0/1.0)
nnz_sigma >= 14.9
|  nnz_frac < 0.0411
|  |  nnz_mu < 79.4
|  |  |  nnz_mu < 20.95
|  |  |  |  nnz_frac < 0.00144: HYB-MU #(14.0/1.0)
|  |  |  |  nnz_frac >= 0.00144
|  |  |  |  |  nnz_sigma < 97.3
|  |  |  |  |  |  nnz_mu < 13.7
|  |  |  |  |  |  |  nnz_mu < 8.15
|  |  |  |  |  |  |  |  nnz_sigma < 33.6: HYB #(9.0/1.0)
|  |  |  |  |  |  |  |  nnz_sigma >= 33.6: HYB-MU #(3.0/2.0)
|  |  |  |  |  |  |  nnz_mu >= 8.15: HYB-MU #(23.0/11.0)
|  |  |  |  |  |  nnz_mu >= 13.7: HYB #(9.0/1.0)
|  |  |  |  |  nnz_sigma >= 97.3: HYB-MU #(20.0/7.0)
|  |  |  nnz_mu >= 20.95: HYB-MU #(27.0/10.0)
|  |  nnz_mu >= 79.4: HYB #(5.0/0.0)
|  nnz_frac >= 0.0411
|  |  nnz_frac < 0.69183
|  |  |  nnz_sigma < 102.8
|  |  |  |  nnz_sigma < 31.45
|  |  |  |  |  nnz_mu < 21.4: HYB-MU #(3.0/3.0)
|  |  |  |  |  nnz_mu >= 21.4
|  |  |  |  |  |  nnz_sigma < 24.4
|  |  |  |  |  |  |  nnz_mu < 52.2: HYB #(4.0/5.0)
|  |  |  |  |  |  |  nnz_mu >= 52.2: ELL #(4.0/2.0)
|  |  |  |  |  |  nnz_sigma >= 24.4: ELL #(15.0/2.0)
|  |  |  |  nnz_sigma >= 31.45: CSR #(22.0/29.0)
|  |  |  nnz_sigma >= 102.8
|  |  |  |  nnz_sigma < 209.2: CSR #(9.0/5.0)
|  |  |  |  nnz_sigma >= 209.2
|  |  |  |  |  nnz_sigma < 1519.35
|  |  |  |  |  |  nnz_frac < 0.06378: HYB #(3.0/2.0)
|  |  |  |  |  |  nnz_frac >= 0.06378: HYB-MU #(12.0/9.0)
|  |  |  |  |  nnz_sigma >= 1519.35: COO #(4.0/1.0)
|  |  nnz_frac >= 0.69183: CSR #(35.0/8.0)

Size of the Tree: 59
Number of Leaf Nodes: 30
```

Figure 11: Tree trained on all input data, K40c

8. CONCLUSION

Implementing an effective SpMV algorithm on GPUs has proven to be challenging task which is only feasible in the presence of efficient sparse representation and exploitation of the matrix sparsity. NVIDIA cuSPARSE (among others) implements several such representations (e.g. CSR, ELLPACK, COO and a hybrid scheme ELL-COO). But the choice of which representation is the best for a given matrix remains mostly unknown.

In this work we have addressed the problem of automatically selecting the best sparse representation for effective SpMV execution on GPU, by using input-dependent features on the sparse matrix to be operated on. Our approach allows to achieve within 95% on average of the best performance available. We have extensively characterized the feature distribution of the popular UFL repository, selecting 682 matrices suitable for GPU acceleration. We have analyzed the performance distribution of two popular Sparse toolkits from NVIDIA, cuSPARSE and CUSP, on three high-end GPUs, GTX 580, K20c and K40c. We showed that no representation performs best across this set, and that a one-representation-fits-all approach, while providing encouraging performance, can actually result in numerous cases of very poor performance. We proposed a machine learning approach to automatically predict the best sparse representation, using classification trees. Our experiments show that, using only basic features, our approach shows no more than 6 out of 682 matrices to have poor performance using our predictor. More complex features can lead to a 98% efficiency, with only 1 matrix with poor performance using our predictor.

Acknowledgments. We thank NVIDIA Corporation for donating the K40c GPU. This work was supported in part by National Science Foundation awards CCF-0926127, CCF-1240651, CCF-1321147, CCF-1418265 and ACI-1404995.

9. REFERENCES

[1] A. Ashari, N. Sedaghati, J. Eisenlohr, S. Parthasarathy, and P. Sadayappan. Fast sparse matrix-vector multiplication on gpus for graph applications. In *SC'14*, pages 781–792, 2014.

[2] A. Ashari, N. Sedaghati, J. Eisenlohr, and P. Sadayappan. An efficient two-dimensional blocking mechanism for sparse matrix-vector multiplication on gpus. In *ICS'14*, 2014.

[3] S. Balay, J. Brown, K. Buschelman, W. D. Gropp, D. Kaushik, M. G. Knepley, L. C. McInnes, B. F. Smith, and H. Zhang. PETSc Web page, 2013. http://www.mcs.anl.gov/petsc.

[4] M. M. Baskaran and R. Bordawekar. Optimizing sparse matrix-vector multiplication on gpus. In *Technical report, IBM Research Report RC24704 (W0812-047)*, 2008.

[5] N. Bell and M. Garland. Efficient sparse matrix-vector multiplication on CUDA. NVIDIA Technical Report NVR-2008-004, NVIDIA Corporation, 2008.

[6] N. Bell and M. Garland. Implementing sparse matrix-vector multiplication on throughput-oriented processors. In *SC'09*, 2009.

[7] L. Breiman, J. H. Friedman, R. A. Olshen, and C. J. Stone. *Classification and Regression Trees.* Wadsworth International Group, Belmont, California, 1984.

[8] J. W. Choi, A. Singh, and R. W. Vuduc. Model-driven autotuning of sparse matrix-vector multiply on GPUs. In *PPoPP'10*, January 2010.

[9] CUSP. The nvidia library of generic parallel algorithms for sparse linear algebra and graph computations on cuda architecture gpus. https://developer.nvidia.com/cusp.

[10] cuSPARSE. The nvidia cuda sparse matrix library. https://developer.nvidia.com/cusparse.

[11] J. Davis and E. Chung. Spmv: A memory-bound application on the gpu stuck between a rock and a hard place. Microsoft Research Technical Report MSR-TR-2012-95, Microsoft Research, 2012.

[12] T. A. Davis and Y. Hu. The university of florida sparse matrix collection. *ACM Trans. Math. Softw.*, 38(1):1:1–1:25, Dec. 2011.

[13] A. Ekambaram and E. Montagne. An alternative compressed storage format for sparse matrices. In *ISCIS*, pages 196–203, 2003.

[14] J. Friedman, T. Hastie, and R. Tibshirani. Additive logistic regression : A statistical view of boosting. *Annals of statistics*, 28(2):337–407, 2000.

[15] J. Godwin, J. Holewinski, and P. Sadayappan. High-performance sparse matrix-vector multiplication on gpus for structured grid computations. GPGPU-5, 2012.

[16] W. Liu and B. Vinter. Csr5: An efficient storage format for cross-platform sparse matrix-vector multiplication. In *ICS'15*. ACM, 2015.

[17] X. Liu, M. Smelyanskiy, E. Chow, and P. Dubey. Efficient sparse matrix-vector multiplication on x86-based many-core processors. In *ICS'13*, pages 273–282. ACM, 2013.

[18] N. I. of Standards and Technology. The matrix market format.

[19] U. of Waikato. Weka 3: Data mining software in java. http://www.cs.waikato.ac.nz/ml/weka/.

[20] I. Reguly and M. Giles. Efficient sparse matrix-vector multiplication on cache-based gpus. In *Innovative Parallel Computing (InPar)*, pages 1–12, 2012.

[21] D. M. Y. Roger G. Grimes, David Ronald Kincaid. *ITPACK 2.0: User's Guide.* 1980.

[22] Y. Saad. Sparskit: a basic tool kit for sparse matrix computations - version 2. 1994.

[23] N. Sedaghati, A. Ashari, L.-N. Pouchet, S. Parthasarathy, and P. Sadayappan. Characterizing dataset dependence for sparse matrix-vector multiplication on gpus. In *PPAA'15*, pages 17–24. ACM, 2015.

[24] B.-Y. Su and K. Keutzer. clspmv: A cross-platform opencl spmv framework on gpus. In *ICS'12*, pages 353–364, 2012.

[25] R. W. Vuduc. *Automatic performance tuning of sparse matrix kernels.* PhD thesis, University of California, January 2004.

[26] S. Williams, L. Oliker, R. W. Vuduc, J. Shalf, K. A. Yelick, and J. Demmel. Optimization of sparse matrix-vector multiplication on emerging multicore platforms. *Parallel Computing*, 35(3):178–194, 2009.

[27] S. Yan, C. Li, Y. Zhang, and H. Zhou. yaspmv: Yet another spmv framework on gpus. In *PLDI'10*, pages 107–118. ACM, 2014.

[28] X. Yang, S. Parthasarathy, and P. Sadayappan. Fast sparse matrix-vector multiplication on gpus: implications for graph mining. *Proc. VLDB Endow.*, 4(4):231–242, January 2011.

Fine-Grained Synchronizations and Dataflow Programming on GPUs

Ang Li, Gert-Jan van den Braak, Henk Corporaal
Eindhoven University of Technology
Eindhoven, Netherlands
ang.li@tue.nl, g.j.w.v.d.braak@tue.nl, h.corporaal@tue.nl

Akash Kumar
National University of Singapore
Singapore
akash@nus.edu.sg

ABSTRACT

The last decade has witnessed the blooming emergence of many-core platforms, especially the graphic processing units (GPUs). With the exponential growth of cores in GPUs, utilizing them efficiently becomes a challenge. The data-parallel programming model assumes a single instruction stream for multiple concurrent threads (SIMT); therefore little support is offered to enforce thread ordering and fine-grained synchronizations. This becomes an obstacle when migrating algorithms which exploit fine-grained parallelism, to GPUs, such as the dataflow algorithms.

In this paper, we propose a novel approach for fine-grained inter-thread synchronizations on the shared memory of modern GPUs. We demonstrate its performance and compare it with other fine-grained and medium-grained synchronization approaches. Our method achieves 1.5x speedup over the warp-barrier based approach and 4.0x speedup over the atomic spin-lock based approach on average. To further explore the possibility of realizing fine-grained dataflow algorithms on GPUs, we apply the proposed synchronization scheme to *Needleman-Wunsch* – a 2D wavefront application involving massive cross-loop data dependencies. Our implementation achieves 3.56x speedup over the atomic spin-lock implementation and 1.15x speedup over the conventional data-parallel implementation for a basic sub-grid, which implies that the fine-grained, lock-based programming pattern could be an alternative choice for designing general-purpose GPU applications (GPGPU).

Categories and Subject Descriptors

C.1.2 [**Computer System Organization**]: Multiple Data Stream Architectures—*SIMD*; D.1.3 [**Software**]: Concurrent Programming—*Parallel programming*

Keywords

Fine-grained synchronization; Spin-lock; GPU; Dataflow

ICS'15, June 08 - 11, 2015, Newport Beach, CA, USA.

http://dx.doi.org/10.1145/2751205.2751232.

1. INTRODUCTION

To harness the unprecedented computational capacity of modern multiprocessor architectures, a program must be partitioned and executed by multiple threads that communicate via shared memory or interconnection network. To ensure correctness, however, operations from various threads must obey certain order restrictions imposed by program logic. Synchronization is the process referring to this coordination issue, during which timing information is exchanged among participant threads.

Synchronization can be further classified as *thread cooperation* and *thread contention* [1]. Thread cooperation enforces read-after-write data dependencies between cooperative threads, which is accomplished by producer-consumer primitives in general. Thread contention, on the other hand, ensures exclusive manipulation of the shared data so that program consistency is preserved. Atomic operations are provided for this purpose. The major difference between the two classifications is that thread cooperation emphasizes access order while thread contention stresses mutual exclusion. In this paper, unless stated otherwise, the word *synchronization* is specially referred to thread cooperation.

Synchronization is not free. It can consume a significant fraction of the execution time due to parallelism degradation, as threads may stall at barriers or spin at locks [2, 3]. Furthermore, the synchronization process itself induces overhead, such as the communication delay and memory traffic for enquiring and releasing locks, the operation overhead for updating mutexes, the storage cost for synchronization variables, etc.

Such overhead is particularly significant for algorithms that exploits *fine-grained parallelism* (e.g. dataflow algorithms) as the occurrence of synchronizations in these algorithms is much more frequent than in other applications [4]. As a result, numerous works have been proposed to alleviate the *fine-grained synchronization* overhead, from both architectural [5, 6, 7] and algorithmic perspectives [8, 9, 10].

Starting from the last decade, the graphics processing unit (GPU) has evolved to be applied on general purpose applications [11, 12]. However, traditional data-parallel programming models for GPUs assume single instruction stream for all concurrent threads (SIMT) and little support is offered to enable elaborate thread cooperation. This becomes an obstacle when migrating dataflow applications which exploits fine-grained parallelism to GPUs.

GPU threads are organized in a hierarchy of three levels: *thread*, *warp* and *block*. Accordingly, three different granularities are addressed for GPU synchronizations:

- *coarse-grained:* synchronizations among thread blocks.
- *medium-grained:* synchronizations among warps in thread blocks.
- *fine-grained:* synchronizations among threads in thread blocks.

GPU currently provides hardware support for medium-grained warp barriers [13]. It also offers fine-grained atomic operations on global and shared memory [14]. However, the existing atomic operation based synchronization scheme, as will be seen, exhibits poor performance; using it incurs significant overhead.

In this paper, we propose a fine-grained, highly efficient thread synchronization mechanism on the shared memory of NVIDIA Fermi GPUs [14]. Instead of seeking to reduce the occurrence of synchronizations, we look into an atomic instruction itself from a lower level standpoint. By reassembling the *micro-instructions* that comprise an atomic operation, we develop an approach that can set up a *producer-consumer* communication channel between cooperative threads in a thread block with much less overhead than the atomic spin-lock based implementation. We validate the correctness and demonstrate the effectiveness of the proposed approach through comparisons with other fine-grained and medium-grained synchronization approaches. Further, to explore the possibility of realizing thread-level dataflow algorithms on GPUs, we apply the proposed synchronization scheme in *Needleman-Wunsch* – a 2D wavefront application that contains a large amount of cross-loop data dependencies. The performance we obtained proves that the fine-grained, lock-based programming pattern could be an alternative choice for designing GPGPU applications.

This paper makes the following contributions:

- We show the inefficiency of the atomic spin-locks and propose a novel lock mechanism (called **tiny-lock**) that shows much better performance with no memory cost.
- We use the tiny-lock to build highly efficient producer-consumer primitives for fine-grained data synchronizations between cooperative threads in a thread block.
- We address two architectural factors that can lead to deadlocks: one is the structural conflicts between thread ordering and SIMD execution; one is lock alias.
- We show how to realize lock-based dataflow computing on GPUs using a wavefront application. This is the first time, to the best of our knowledge, that a fine-grained dataflow model has been reported to be efficiently implemented at the lowest *thread level* of GPUs.

2. RELATED WORK

For **coarse-grained** synchronizations on GPUs, Xiao et al. proposed three schemes [15]: a simple version, a tree-based version, and a lock-free version. The simple version leveraged a global-shared mutex via global memory atomic operations. The tree-based version improved the simple version by synchronizing progressively along the tree branches. The lock-free version allocated a monitor thread block to coordinate synchronizations among working thread blocks. Their work was later extended by Stuart et al. to build a set of course-grained synchronization primitives [16].

In terms of **medium-grained** synchronizations, although the block-wise barrier *__syncthreads()* is widely adopted, it was not until recently that a warp-to-warp synchronization approach has been developed. It relies on the *sync-arrive* barrier pair [17]: *bar.sync* is a blocking operation that suspends the current warp until all desired warps have arrived at the barrier. *bar.arrive* is a non-blocking operation that signals the arrival of the current warp to the barrier. In [18], Bauer et al. proposed a producer-consumer communication model based on this barrier-pair that could coordinate data movement from a producer warp to a consumer warp via shared memory buffers. They further applied this medium-grained synchronization approach to a chemical application [19]. The performance was demonstrated and the implementation was straightforward using the PTX embedding technique. However, for this approach, although the number of synchronization threads is parameterizable, it has to be a multiple of warp size [17] (32 for all present CUDA GPUs), meaning that the granularity is warp, not thread. Furthermore, only 16 barrier instances are available per thread block [17], making these barriers very precious and limited for frequent usage, such as in a context of dataflow programming.

Regarding **fine-grained** synchronizations, the only approach till now, to the best of our knowledge, is through the spin-locks, which are constructed using the atomic operations in global memory and shared memory. However, the performance of such atomic spin-locks is poor and their utilization is highly discouraged [20]. In fact, the lack of highly efficient, fine-grained synchronization mechanisms has already become an obstacle that disturbs the broad adoption of GPUs for general purpose applications [16, 21, 22].

3. LOCK UNIT

In this section, we briefly describe the architecture of the lock unit in GPU shared memory and the associated operations.

3.1 Architecture

The *shared memory* (i.e. *scratchpad memory*) in a GPU is a small on-chip storage shared among all processing units in a streaming multiprocessor (SM). It serves as a communication interface for fast data exchanging between different threads of a thread block. Being on-chip, the shared memory has much higher bandwidth and shorter accessing latency compared to the *global memory* (or *main memory*) of GPUs. Therefore, optimizations which can shift global memory access to shared memory access are highly advised by the CUDA programming guide [13].

The lock mechanism that enables fast atomic access is implemented in the shared memory, under the help of a module called "*lock unit*", in Fermi GPUs (see Figure 1). According to the associated patent [23], the lock bits are flags indicating the present lock status for the corresponding locations in the main storage (i.e. the Storage Resource in Figure 1). The lock bit is set so that other updating requests to that location are refused. For space concern, multiple locations in the main storage are *aliased* to a single lock bit. A hash function is implemented to perform the mapping, ensuring that successive *words* are mapped to distinct lock bits. For Fermi GPUs, a total of 1024 independent lock bits are provided for the 16KB (or 48KB based on configuration) shared

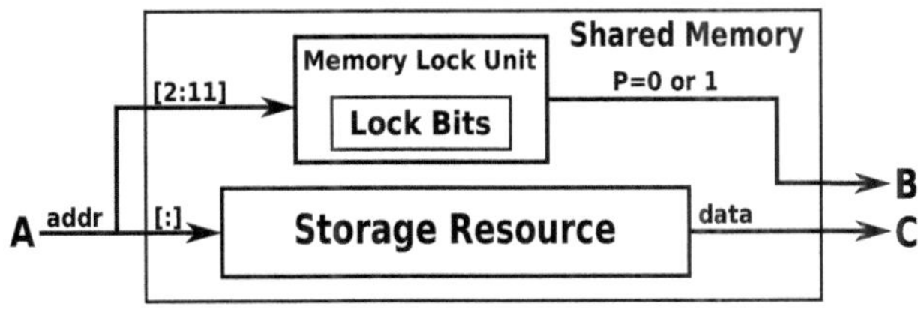

Figure 1: Shared memory lock unit. Terminal A reads the request memory address and looks it up in the storage resource The fetched data is returned to terminal C that connects to a general register. Meanwhile, the 2-to-11 bits of the data address is used to retrieve associated lock bit from the lock unit. The value of lock bit is returned to terminal C, which connects to a predicate register.

memory. Word addresses with a stride of 1024 are aliased to the same lock bit. When a memory request being delivered (to terminal A in Figure 1), the 2-to-11 bits of the data address is labeled as the lock address and redirected to the lock unit. Gomez-Luna et al. discusses this mapping mechanism exhaustively in [24] and report a number of 1024 lock bits. We confirm this value experimentally when testing deadlocks (see Section 4.4).

Regarding such a design, the following characteristics are highlighted for our proposal:

- **Efficiency:** Accessing the lock units does not require extra pipeline-stages or decision logic in the critical path because it is performed in parallel with the ordinary data access. So no extra delay is induced.
- **Flexibility:** The lock unit is not configured to track the ownership of the locks. It is the program's responsibility to honor the lock bits and to prevent illegal access to the locked locations in the main storage.

3.2 Operations

Listing 1 shows the low-level assembly sequence (SASS) generated by *cuobjdump* for the atomic instruction "*atomicAdd()*" to the shared memory of Fermi GPUs, in CUDA runtime (i.e. *atom.shared.add* instruction in PTX [17]). It indicates that the high-level *"atomic"* instruction is essentially comprised by a series of low-level SASS operations:

```
/*00a0*/  LDSLK P0, R1, [R0];
/*00a8*/  @P0 IADD R4, R1, 0x1;
/*00b0*/  @P0 STSUL [R0], R4;
/*00b8*/  @!P0 BRA 0xa0;
```

Listing 1: SASS code for atomicAdd()

- **LDSLK** loads data from address [R0] to a general register R1. It also reads the associated lock bit to a 1-bit predicate register P0. (In Figure 1, R0 is connected to A, R1 is connected to C, P0 is connected to B.) Therefore, P0 equals true implies that the target lock is successfully acquired by the current thread. Meanwhile, the lock bit in the lock unit toggles to 0, disabling subsequent locking requests. Here, "LDS" stands for loading from shared memory while "LK" means loading the lock bit simultaneously.
- Based on P0=1 (@P0), **IADD** adds 0x1 to R1 and stores the sum to R4. Note that threads in a warp may diverge here if some of them fail to acquire the locks in the present locking test (@!p0).
- Also with P0=1, **STSUL** stores R4 to [R0] and triggers the lock unit to reset the lock bit. "STS" stands for storing to shared memory while "UL" means unlocking simultaneously.
- **BRA** is the branch operation that jumps to instruction address 0xa0, which is the entry of the atomic procedure. In this way, the threads failed to obtain locks in the current test rotate back and redo the atomic process. Meanwhile, the finished threads have to wait beyond this BRA operation until all divergent threads in the warp have reached so as to continue lockstep execution.

Regarding these operations, it should be noted that:

- The default value of a lock bit is 1, indicating that it is free for fetching. LDSLK resets the lock bit to 0 while STSUL sets the lock bit to 1. It is infeasible to set the lock bit via LDSLK or reset the lock bit via STSUL. There is no alternative way to set or reset a lock bit.
- To release a lock bit, a thread **must** store a value to the corresponding memory location simultaneously. The store overwrites the original content.

4. FINE-GRAINED SYNCHRONIZATION

In this section, we present the fine-grained synchronization mechanism. We first describe our motivation and then propose the *tiny-lock*, based on which we show our fine-grained synchronization scheme.

4.1 Motivation

Our approach is motivated by the observation that an atomic instruction in the shared memory is comprised of multiple low-level SASS operations (Section III-B). Therefore, we can *reassemble these SASS operations in a different way to build other efficient synchronization procedures.*

4.2 Tiny-Lock

Fine-grained synchronization relies on fine-grained locks. Listing 2 illustrates a common implementation [25] of the fine-grained spin-locks based on atomic instructions.

```
__device__ inline void lock(int* p_mutex){
  while(atomicCAS(p_mutex,0,1)!=0);//compare and swap
}
__device__ inline void unlock(int* p_mutex){
  atomicExch(p_mutex,0);//exchange
}
```

Listing 2: Baseline implementation: atomic spin-locks [25]

In Listing 3, we show the SASS sequence of the baseline implementation. To make it more clear, we draw the corresponding control-flow-graph (CFG) in Figure 2. There are two loops in the *Lock* routine: the small loop is spinning for a lock bit. It is embedded in *atomicCAS()*. The big loop, which corresponds to the *while* statement, is the actual iteration for the user-defined mutex variable stored in the main storage of the shared memory.

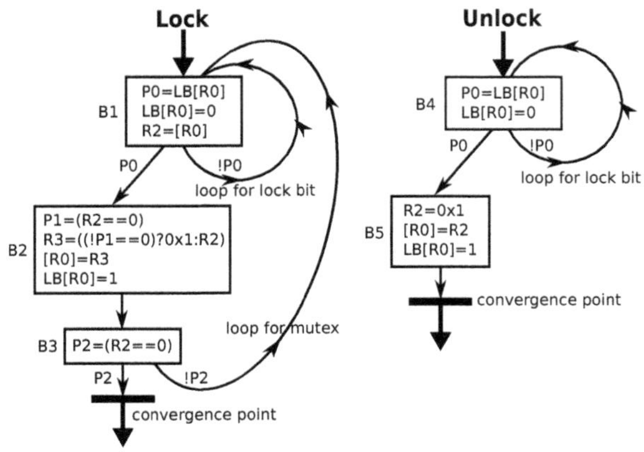

Figure 2: CFG of atomic spin-locks. LB stands for lock unit. Convergence point is the place where divergent threads of a warp rejoin to proceed lock-step execution. In the *Lock* routine, the big loop is for acquiring the user-defined mutex while the small loop is for acquiring the lock bit of the mutex. P2 being a replicate of P1 is the result of direct translation from two ptx instructions by the ptxas assembler. In the *Unlock* routine, the atomic update to the mutex (i.e. the small loop) is a must; otherwise, the updated result may be overwritten unexpectedly by another thread who acquires the lock bit but not the mutex. Since that thread needs to write a value to the mutex for releasing the lock bit, it uses a dated value obtained when fetching the lock bit as it is unaware of the latest update.

```
// ==================== Lock ====================
/*0060*/  SSY 0x98; //set convergence point
/*0068*/  LDSLK P0, R2, [R0];
/*0070*/  @P0 ISETP.EQ.U32.AND P1, pt, R2, RZ, pt;
/*0078*/  @P0 SEL R3, R2, 0x1, !P1;
/*0080*/  @P0 STSUL [R0], R3;
/*0088*/  @!P0 BRA 0x68; //atomicCAS loop
/*0090*/  ISETP.EQ.AND.S P2, pt, R2, RZ, pt;
/*0098*/  @!P2 BRA 0x60; //while loop
          //converge to proceed lockstep execution
/*00a0*/  ...
// =================== Unlock ===================
/*00b0*/  LDSLK P0, RZ, [R0];
/*00b8*/  @P0 MOV32I R2, 0x1;
/*00c0*/  @P0 STSUL [R0], R2;
/*00c8*/  @!P0 BRA 0xb0;
```

Listing 3: SASS code of atomic spin-locks

This is a recursive design: the user-defined mutex acts as an intermediate layer to realize the required locking functionality (i.e. the big loop) whereas the lock bit of the mutex is leveraged to ensure atomic updates to the mutex (i.e. small loop). Such a design behaves quite well when the mutex serves as a semaphore, but is probably redundant when only a single-bit lock is required – why not exploit the lock bit directly?

```
// ==================== Lock ====================
/*0000*/  LDSLK P0, RZ, [R0];
// ================== Waitlock ==================
/*0010*/  LDSLK P0, RZ, [R0];
/*0018*/  @!P0 BRA 0x10;
// =================== Unlock ===================
/*0020*/  STSUL [R0], RZ;
```

Listing 4: Proposed fine-grained lock

We show the novel design in Listing 4. It is called **tiny-lock**. There are two primitives for locking: *Lock* simply fetches without verifying the locking result. It is used when the programmer guarantees the acquisition of the target locks (e.g. in an initialization scenario). Otherwise, *Waitlock* has to be applied, which repeatedly fetches the lock until eventually succeeds. *Unlock* stores 1 to the lock bit for release.

Such a design completely eliminates the space cost for the user-defined mutex. It also avoids the big loop in the *Lock* routine and the small loop in the *Unlock* routine. Compared to the baseline implementation, it has the following advantages:

- **Time Delay**, the proposed design reduces the static number of SASS operations by 75% for *Lock* and *Unlock*; and by 50% for one iteration of *Waitlock* (although the dynamic number of operations executed by waitlock depends on the waiting time experienced). Meanwhile, the lock unit is accessed in parallel with the shared storage (*Efficiency* in Section 3.1), so the maximum delay for accessing locks is equal to an ordinary memory read or write. Furthermore, this delay can be completely hidden in certain scenarios, e.g. the read-after-write data synchronizations.

- **Storage Cost**, since the lock unit is isolated from the main storage, our scheme does not require any shared memory storage. In comparison, the baseline implementation has to explicitly allocate a word as an intermediate mutex. Further, since only the lock bit is of interest, in many cases (see Section 5 and Section 6) we can read the content of the memory location to the zero register in *Lock* or write the original value back in *Unlock* so that no register is used either.

- **Memory Traffic**, there is only one load transaction for *Lock* and one store transaction for *Unlock*. For *Waitlock*, unlike the baseline implementation that writes the original value back to the mutex if the lock is not obtained (B2 in Figure 2 when R2!=0), our approach does not produce any write traffic when locking. Further, it does not produce computation traffic like the baseline implementation (e.g. operations 0x0070, 0x0078 and 0x00b8 in Listing 3).

4.3 Fine-Grained Synchronization

All concurrent programming models offer programmers the ability to control the order of dataflow from different threads. However, conventional SIMT programming model assumes weak inter-dependencies among threads that relies on barriers to enforce thread ordering. However, barriers are either coarse-grained or medium-grained in GPUs, which are too coarse for thread-to-thread synchronizations. Therefore, fine-grained locks have to be used for such synchronizations.

```
void producer(){
  lock(&mutex);      //initialize
  ...
  shared_buffer = put; //store to channel
  unlock(&mutex); //signal consumer to load
}
void consumer(){
  ...
  lock(&mutex);      //wait producer to store
  get = shared_buffer; //load from channel
  unlock(&mutex); //finalize
}
```

Listing 5: Fine-grained synchronizations based on atomic spin-locks

Listing 5 illustrates how an atomic spin-lock is used for read-after-write synchronizations – *the producer thread acquires the mutex in advance and releases it after writing to the shared buffer so that when consumer thread obtains the mutex, it can read safely.*

Here, a 1-bit lock is already sufficient to accomplish the job. However, as discussed earlier and will be seen in the experiments, the atomic spin-lock incurs significant time/space/traffic overhead which makes it too costly for frequent inter-thread synchronizations. The proposed tiny-lock design significantly reduces such overheads and is therefore the ideal option upon which to construct the fine-grained synchronization scheme. Its implementation is shown in Listing 6.

```
// =============== producer ===============
/*0000*/  LDSLK P0, RZ, [R0];//initialize
...
/*0010*/  STSUL [R0], R4;//store to channel and
                        //unlock
// =============== consumer ===============
...
/*0100*/  LDSLK P0, R2, [R0];//wait and load from
                            //channel
/*0108*/  @!P0 BRA 0x100;//spinning
/*0200*/  STSUL [R0], R2;//finalize
```

Listing 6: Fine-grained synchronizations based on lock bits

This is the one-to-one synchronization scheme, which can be extended further to one-to-many and many-to-one conditions: the producer alternatively signals all its consumers or the consumer waits for all its producers.

4.4 Deadlock

Programmers must be careful when using fine-grained locks in GPUs because it is easy to generate deadlocks. Besides general causes from algorithmic aspects, there are two special scenarios that may lead to deadlocks for GPUs. We label them *SIMD Deadlock* and *Alias Deadlock*.

4.4.1 SIMD Deadlock

This kind of deadlock is due to a structural conflict between inter-thread synchronizations and SIMD-lockstep execution. Consider the following scenario: what if the producer and consumer threads are from the same warp? The answer is — a *deadlock*. The general explanation is that lockstep stresses synchronous execution whereas thread cooperation enforces consumer-after-producer (i.e. read-after-write) order, which is essentially asynchronous. Therefore, if the synchronizing threads are from the same warp, we need a divergence mechanism to separate the producer and the consumer's execution paths. In addition, for the producer, the lock and unlock operations must be within the same divergent segment, or in other words, the unlock operation must be the post-dominator for the lock operation before the next convergence point. Otherwise, the producer will wait at that convergence point for the consumer to join in order to proceed to execute the unlock instruction, whereas the consumer is waiting to acquire the lock before it can step to the convergence point. Here the inter-waiting produces a deadlock.

In fact, such deadlocks occur more often than just for synchronizations. Consider a warp executing lock function in Listing 2. The convergence point is well beyond the while loop (see the black barrier in Figure 2). If two or more threads in the warp are contending for the same mutex (not lock bit), due to atomicity, only one of them can acquire. However, this thread has to be blocked at convergence point, waiting for other threads to join. Meanwhile, the remaining threads are adversely waiting for that thread to release the mutex (via calling the unlock function) before they can proceed. Here, the same reason leads to a deadlock: *the SIMD convergence point is earlier than unlock.* To circumvent this problem, a direct implementation for the baseline scheme is shown in Listing 7. In this way, the release of the mutex (i.e. *atomicExch(p_mutex,0)*) can be performed before the warp convergence point, which is right after the while loop.

```
__device__ void producer_consumer(int* p_mutex){
  bool finished = false;
  while(!finished){
    if(atomicCAS(p_mutex,0,1)==0){
      finished=true;
      ... // critical section
      atomicExch(p_mutex,0);
} } }
```

Listing 7: Intra-warp synchronizations based on atomic spin-locks

And for our scheme in Listing 6, the predicate register can be manipulated to include unlock operation into the same divergent path, as shown in Listing 8.

```
// producer-consumer
/*00a0*/  SSY 0x110;
/*00a8*/  LDSLK P0, R2, [R0];
...       @P0 ... //critical section
/*0100*/  @P0 STSUL [R0], R2;
/*0108*/  @!P0 BRA 0xa8;
```

Listing 8: Intra-warp synchronizations based on lock bits

Although we successfully circumvent this deadlock at programming level, another problem still remains – performance degradation. As GPU adopts lane-masks to switch between divergent branches for a warp, the performance is impaired when each divergent branch has to be executed sequentially. Here, the producer lane has to wait until the consumer lane finishes. Even worse, if the consumer is in turn a producer of another synchronization also in the same warp, such as in a "scan" operation, then all the former producers have to be blocked until the final consumer finishes the synchronization. In the worst case, the performance drops by 32 folds (e.g. a propagation chain). Unless a perfect pipeline can be formed (i.e. producers start working on new data but execute in a lockstep with the consumers), some threads will be idle. The problem here is that the dispatch units only issue warp instructions, which is too coarse-grained for elaborate intra-warp coordination.

Summarizing, for synchronizations between threads of different warps, we use the lock/unlock primitives in Listing 5 and Listing 6. Both the producer and consumer can proceed immediately after the synchronization. But for synchronizations involving threads from the same warp, the critical sections in Listing 7 and Listing 8 are necessary. The producers have to wait until all their direct or indirect consumers accomplish their synchronizations and arrive at the convergence point. Although performance suffers, the fine-grained scheme is still better than a medium-grained approach as consumers from other warps can be signaled as soon as the required data is produced, instead of waiting for the whole warp that contains the consumer to be finished.

4.4.2 Alias Deadlock

This kind of deadlock is due to lock bit aliasing. There are two conditions: First, suppose a thread already holds the

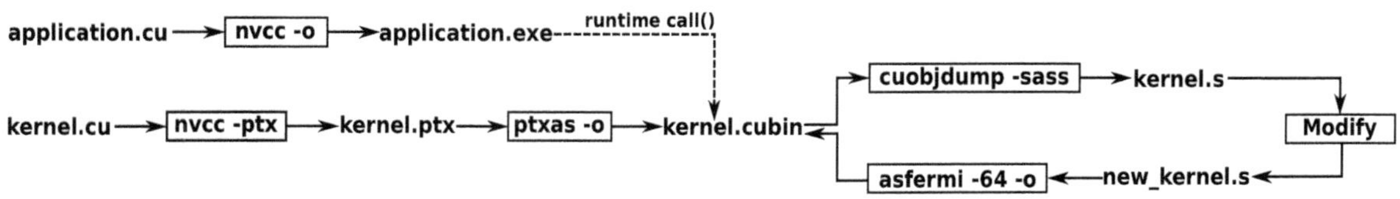

Figure 3: Experiment workflow. The application is written in CUDA driver-API that can load cubin object file at runtime. The kernel is first developed in CUDA-C and compiled to PTX code via *NVCC*. The PTX file is then assembled to a cubin binary via *ptxas* which is marked as the base binary. After that, the human-readable SASS routine is dumped from the base binary through *cuobjdump*. We modify this routine manually to insert the producer-consumer instructions, which is re-assembled to an updated cubin file for the driver-API to load.

lock bit of a memory location, say [M], but is trying to fetch from its aliased location (e.g. [M+1024], see Section 3.1). Then, the thread will trap in a circle because it is attempting to get a lock bit from itself. Based on our experiments, such a conduct immediately leads to a deadlock. However, the positive side is that such an experiment confirms the stride of lock bit alias is 1024 [24].

Second, we need to ensure the producer acquires the lock before its consumer (see Listing 5 and Listing 6). As warps are not synchronously executed in an SM, this is achieved by placing a coarse-grained barrier (i.e. *__syncthreads()*) after the initialization phase for the whole thread block. Lock-bit aliasing generates deadlock because the warp obtaining the aliased lock waits at the block-wise barrier for other warps, including the failed warp, while the failed warp is waiting for the aliased lock before it can reach the barrier.

Although alias deadlock is easy to understand, it is one of the major restrictions for the proposed synchronization scheme: *to avoid alias deadlock, only 1024 locks can be utilized safely.* This number is smaller than the allocatable threads for an SM (i.e. 1536 threads) and much smaller than the entries of the shared memory (i.e. 4096 or 12,288). Given the fact that an SM can accommodate several thread blocks, the volume of usable lock bits can significantly limit the number of thread blocks an SM could support, hence degrading the performance for a large data size (see Section 6).

4.5 Warp-shared Lock Bit

When fine-grained lock bits are exploited for the situations of medium-grained synchronizations, it is possible to share a single lock bit for the whole warp, which reduces the demand for lock bits by a factor of 32. The idea is to exploit the warp-wise voting instructions [17]. Listing 9 provides the implementations for the lock and unlock routines, based on which the readers can further construct warp synchronization primitives.

```
// ==================== Lock ====================
//R0 is the same for all threads across the warp
/*0000*/  LDSLK P0, RZ, [R0];
// ================== Waitlock ==================
//If any thread acquires the lock bit, continue
/*0010*/  LDSLK P0, RZ, [R0];
/*0018*/  VOTE.ANY RZ, P1, P0;
/*0020*/  @!P1 BRA 0x10;
// =================== Unlock ===================
//Thread 0 in the warp releases the shared lock
/*0020*/  S2R R1, SR_LaneId; //Load lane_id
/*0028*/  ISETP.EQ P0, pt, R1, RZ, pt;//lane_id=0?
/*0030*/  @P0 STSUL [R0], RZ;
```

Listing 9: Warp-shared lock bit scheme

For *Lock*, any thread in the warp may acquires the lock eventually, but we know one of them must obtain it. For *Waitlock*, after acquiring, all threads are enforced to participate in a warp-wise vote. If any thread successfully acquires the target lock (i.e. P0=1), the voting result is true (i.e. P1=1). Then the whole warp quits the spinning loop and proceeds lockstep execution. Otherwise, the warp rotates back and try again. For *Unlock*, it may be too expensive to let every thread perform the release operation since a 32-degree bank conflict and lock conflict can be generated [24]. Further, if there are multiple threads waiting for the lock, releasing it 32 times (due to conflict) may potentially violate the consistency between the waiting threads. The method here is to find a representative. Here the ISETP instruction and predicate register P0 are used to select thread 0 for releasing. Note it is not feasible to let the representative thread acquire the lock for the whole warp because the remaining 31 threads may fail to make their writings observable by other warps due to the weekly-ordered memory model [13]. However, such a design is not a problem if an atomic-spin lock is shared for the whole warp as it enforces the order in the memory.

5. VALIDATION

In this section, we validate the correctness and demonstrate the effectiveness of our fine-grained synchronization scheme. We use a NVIDIA GTX-570 GPU as the test platform. It contains 15(SM)x32 CUDA cores with compute capacity 2.0 (Fermi). The CUDA toolkit version is 4.0. In terms of tools, *cuobjdump* is employed to generate the SASS code of the target kernel. We then modify the SASS code to insert our lock operations. However, to reproduce the *cubin* binary for the updated SASS code, an SASS assembler is necessary. Since *ptxas* only accepts PTX code, we use an open-source SASS assembly tool named *asfermi* [26] instead. This is also the reason why we restrict to Fermi – *asfermi does not support other architectures right now.* The detailed workflow is depicted in Figure 3.

```
for (i=0;i<32*N;i++)
  A[i+32] = A[i] + independent_computation(i);
```

Listing 10: Validation kernel (serial version)

The loop shown in Listing 10 is used for validation. It contains a parallel independent computation phase and a serial dependent reduction phase. It is derived from the kernel developed by Tullsen et. al. [6] that represents a common map-reduce pattern. In order to compare with the medium-grained synchronization approaches (see Section 2), we extend the dependency distance from 1 to the size of a warp (i.e. 32). Meanwhile, since only 16 warp barriers are available in a thread block (see Section 2), N is set to be 16.

The whole loop is parallelized and mapped to 16 warps for concurrent execution. We compare the proposed tiny-lock implementation (i.e. *tiny_lock*, Section 4.3) with the atomic

Scheme	Shared Memory Cost	Lock Bit Used
atom_lock	2048 bytes	512 (implicit)
warp_barr	0	0
shrd_lock	128 bytes	32 (implicit)
tiny_lock	0	512 (explicit)
warp_vote	0	32 (explicit)

Table 1: Resource cost

spin-lock implementation (i.e. *atom_lock*, Section 4.2), the medium-grained sync-arrive barrier implementation (i.e. *warp_barr*, Section 2), the shared lock-bit implementation (i.e. *warp_vote*, Section 4.5) as well as a shared spin-lock implementation (a warp shares a common spin-lock, i.e. *shrd_lock*). The core of the kernels for atomic spin-lock based, sync-arrive barrier based and tiny-lock based implementations are shown in Listing 11, Listing 12 and Listing 13 respectively.

```
__shared__ int A[32*N], mutex[32*N];
  lock(mutex[tid]);//producer initially locks
  __syncthreads();//ensure producer gets lock first
  /* ============== Reduction Phase ==============*/
  if (wid > 0) lock(mutex[tid-32]); //consumer waits
  A[tid]=A[tid-32]+independent_computation(tid);
  unlock(mutex[tid]);      //producer releases
  unlock(mutex[tid-32]); //finalize
```

Listing 11: Atomic spin-lock based version (CUDA code)

```
__shared__ int A[N*32];
  int tid = threadIdx.x; int wid = tid>>5; //log32=5
  /* ============== Reduction Phase ==============*/
  if (wid>0)
    asm("bar.sync␣%0,%1;"::"r"(wid-1),"r"(64));
  A[tid+32]=A[tid]+independent_computation(tid);
  asm("bar.arrive␣%0,%1;"::"r"(wid),"r"(64));
```

Listing 12: Warp barrier based version (PTX embedded CUDA code)

```
/*0000*/ LDSLK P0,RZ,(A[tid]);//producer init locks
/*0008*/ BAR.RED.POPC RZ,RZ;  //block barrier
/* =============== Reduction Phase ===============*/
/*0100*/ ISETP.EQ P0, pt, (wid), RZ, pt;
/*0108*/ @P0 BRA 0x120; // warp_0 breaks
/*0110*/ LDSLK P1,R1,(A[tid-32]); //consumer waits
/*0118*/ !@P1 BRA 0x110;
/*0120*/ IADD R2,R1,(independent_computation(tid));
/*0128*/ STSUL (A[tid]),R2; //producer releases
/*0130*/ @!P0 STSUL (A[tid-32]),R1; //finalize
```

Listing 13: Tiny-lock based version (SASS code)

To be simple, we set *independent_computation()* to immediately return its thread index. Therefore, if we measure the elapsed time for the reduction phase, it is the *raw delay for 16 times' synchronizations and additions in sequence*. Figure 4 illustrates the measured execution time in cycles for the reduction phase for the 5 schemes. Table 1 lists the cost of resource for each scheme.

As can be seen, our tiny-lock based approach is 4.0x times faster than the atomic spin-lock based scheme and is 1.5x times faster than the warp barrier scheme. Meanwhile, warp voting is shown to be an expensive operation (it actually induces thread divergence in a warp) although the sharing saves many lock bits. Finally, picking a warp-representative thread reduces space cost at the expense of performance loss. Table 2 summarizes the 5 schemes.

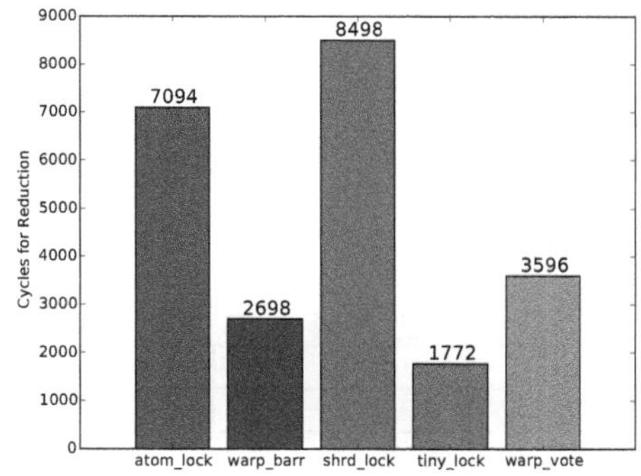

Figure 4: Execution time for the reduction phase in cycles

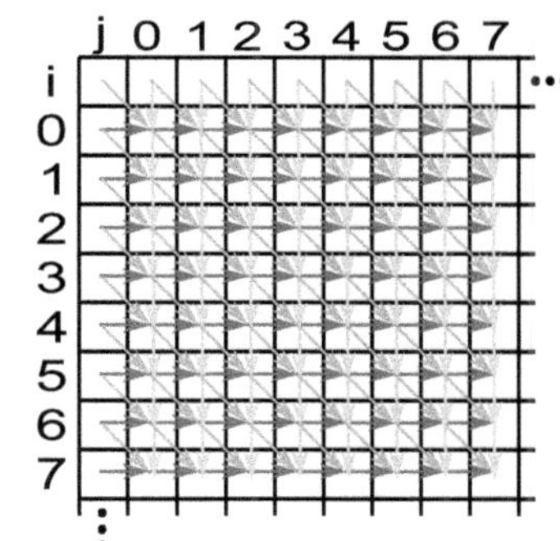

Figure 5: Dependence graph for the *Needleman-Wunsch* algorithm. The green arrows denote dependencies with the north-west neighbors. The yellow arrows refer to dependencies with north elements. The blue arrows indicate dependencies with the west grid-points. The first row and column of the grid are the initial values.

6. WAVEFRONT APPLICATION

In this section, we use the *Needleman-Wunsch* algorithm [27, 28] from the *Rodinia* benchmark [29] as an example to describe how to efficiently implement a dataflow algorithm on GPUs using the proposed fine-grained, tiny-lock based synchronization schemes. The application is to find the best alignment between protein or nucleotide sequences in bioinformatics. Its core computation is:

$$S(i,j) = max \begin{cases} S(i,j-1) - k \\ S(i-1,j-1) + p(i,j) \\ S(i-1,j) - k \end{cases} \tag{1}$$

where S is 2D grid and $p(i,j)$ is a predefined reference field. As can be seen, the computation of each grid-point has true data dependencies on its north, west and north-west neighbors. The dependence graph is shown in Figure 5.

The data-parallel model relies on wavefront propagation to resolve such dependencies. In [30], Lamport et al. show that, for a multi-dimensional volume, given a value f, all points laid in the hyperplane satisfying $i + j + ... = f$ can be processed in parallel while all their dependent points fulfill $i + j + ... = f - 1$. By stepping along the incremental direction of f and processing all elements associated, data dependencies can be respected. So far, all the existing implementations of wavefront applications on GPUs adopt this data-parallel pattern [22, 31, 32]. Figure 6 illustrates the processing trace of this pattern for the *Needleman-Wunsch* algorithm.

Scheme	Granularity	Performance	Memory Cost	Resource	Programmability
atom_lock	fine	x1.0	128 bytes/warp	4096/12,288 locations per SM	CUDA runtime
warp_barr	medium	x2.6	0	16 barriers per thread_block	PTX/embedded_PTX
shrd_lock	medium	x0.8	4 bytes/warp	4096/12,288 locations per SM	CUDA runtime
tiny_lock	fine	x4.0	0	1024 lock bits per SM	assembly
warp_vote	medium	x2.0	4 bytes/warp	1024 lock bits per SM	assembly

Table 2: Summary of synchronization schemes

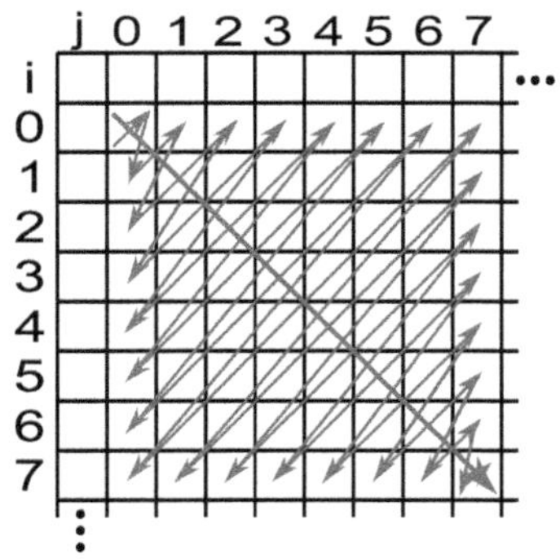

Figure 6: Working trace for wavefront parallel pattern. The wavefront direction coincides with the diagonal of the grid. In each wavefront step, the points along the anti-diagonal can be processed in parallel.

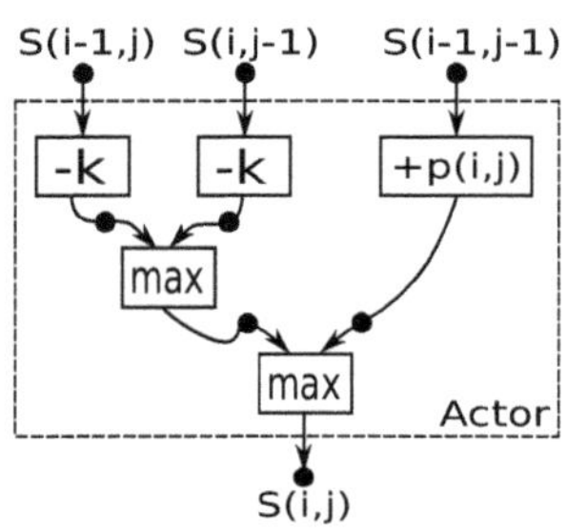

Figure 7: Dataflow graph. The actor is the computation shown in Equation.1. When the required operands $S(i-1,j)$, $S(i,j-1)$ and $S(i-1,j-1)$ are ready, the actor can fire. The arcs across the dashed box denote the dependencies with other actors, which are also the places that require synchronization.

However, the data-parallel propagation approach confronts two problems: first, as the points that can be processed in parallel are along the line that is perpendicular to the diagonal, the computation workload for each propagation step is quite unbalanced, especially for SIMD processing. Second, since the grid-points are normally sequentially stored along the axises of the gird in memory, data access in each step is cache unfriendly and cannot be coalesced for effective global memory fetch.

The major factor leading to the irregular computation and memory access is the rigorous 2D data-dependencies, which can be naturally and effectively resolved by a static dataflow model. A dataflow model describes the computation of each point as an *actor* which is executed by a GPU thread. The actor *fires* when all the operands it requires are available. Many actors may fire simultaneously, thus achieving high-level asynchronous concurrency. The dataflow graph for the application is shown in Figure 7. Since the computation of an actor is relatively simple, we concentrate on the communication part: *how to effectively synchronize between actors.*

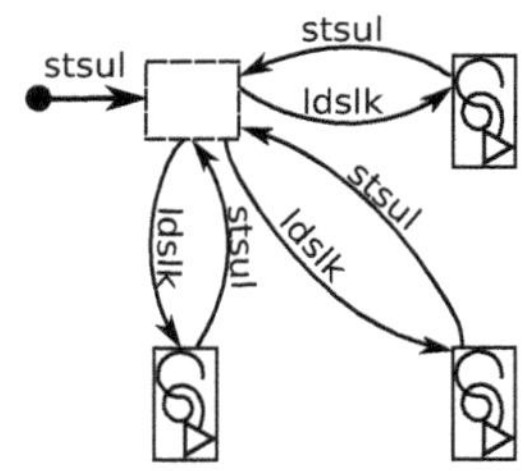

Figure 8: Using shared channel for synchronization.

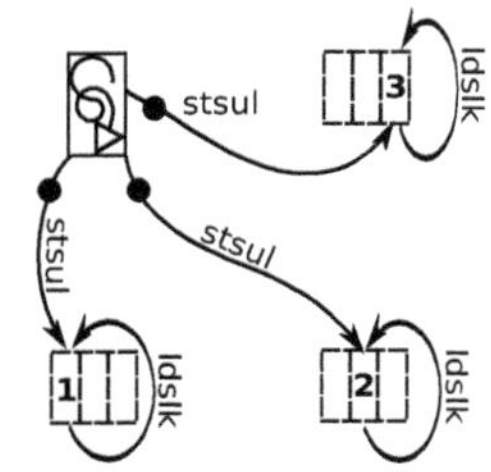

Figure 9: Using private channel for synchronization.

There are two approaches: One is *resource-preferred*, which means a common synchronization channel is shared among the three consumers of a producer (Figure 8). Recall the synchronization process in Listing 5 and Listing 6, the producer thread acquires the lock of the channel buffer first. Then, its three consumers (south, east and south-east neighbors) spin at the channel (it is also possible that they spin at other channels). When the producer fires, it releases a token to the channel. An arbitrary waiting consumer may acquire the token, but as other consumers may still wait for the token, it must restore the token back to the channel after usage. Since three consumers share one synchronization channel, a single lock is enough. However, due to the sharing of the token, a consumer may false-wait for other consumer(s) to restore the token before can fire (In fact, it only has to wait for the producer, but there is no way for it to distinguish).

The other approach is *performance preferred*, meaning that each synchronization uses an isolated channel so that the consumers are independent of each other (Figure 9). So it is possible that the consumers can start firing earlier and they do not have to restore the token afterwards, which may benefit performance. The expense is three times the lock resource cost.

```
if (ty!=0 && tx!=0){
  lock(&mutex[ty][tx]);
  __syncthreads();
  while(!finished){
    if(!north_sync &&
        atomicExch(&mutex[ty-1][tx],1)==0){
      north = s[ty-1][tx];//get north operand
      north_sync = true;
      atomicExch(&mutex[ty-1][tx],0);}
    if(!west_sync &&
         atomicExch(&mutex[ty][tx-1],1)==0){
      west = s[ty][tx-1];//get west operand
      west_sync = true;
      atomicExch(&mutex[ty][tx-1],0);}
    finished = north_sync && west_sync;//all ready?
    if(finished){//fire
      s[ty][tx]=MAX(s[ty-1][tx-1]+p[ty][tx],
                                 north-k,west-k);
      unlock(&mutex[ty][tx]);}//put self
} }
```

Listing 14: Atomic-based lock version

```
/*00e8*/   LDSLK P0, RZ, [R7];//lock self
/*00f0*/   BAR.RED.POPC RZ, RZ;
/*00f8*/   SSY 0x170;
/*0100*/   @!P1 LDSLK P1, R11, [R7+-0x4];//get west
/*0108*/   @P1 STSUL [R7+-0x4], R11;//restore token
/*0110*/   @!P3 LDSLK P3, R10, [R7+-0x80];//get north
/*0118*/   @P3 STSUL [R7+-0x80], R10;//restore token
/*0120*/   PSETP.AND.AND P2, pt, P3, P1, pt;//ready?
/*0128*/   @P2 LDS R12, [R7+-0x84];//fire
/*0130*/   @P2 ISETP.GE.AND P4, pt, R10, R11, pt;
/*0138*/   @P2 IADD R12, R12, R4;
/*0140*/   @P2 SEL R13, R10, R11, P4;
/*0148*/   @P2 IADD R13, R13, -R15;
/*0150*/   @P2 ISETP.GE.AND P5, pt, R13, R12, pt;
/*0158*/   @P2 SEL R8, R13, R12, P5;
/*0160*/   @P2 STSUL [R7], R8;//put self
/*0168*/   @!P2 BRA 0x100;
```

Listing 15: Fine-grained lock naive version

In our implementation, concerning the lock bits are limited and a shortage of locks may restrict the volume of actors, we adopt the resource-preferred approach. Meanwhile, for a point $S(i,j)$, it depends on $S(i-1,j-1)$, but as $S(i-1,j)$ and $S(i,j-1)$ also depend on $S(i-1,j-1)$, if any token(s) from $S(i-1,j)$ or $S(i,j-1)$ acquired, $S(i-1,j-1)$ can be safely loaded. The core part of the implementations based on atomic spin-locks and tiny-locks are shown in Listing 14 and Listing 15. To avoid intra-warp synchronization deadlocks (Section 4.4.1), the critical section scheme is used. Furthermore, the thread block configuration is set to be 32x32 to fully leverage the 1024 lock bits of an SM (also to avoid deadlocks due to alias, see Section 4.4.2).

We use the same outer framework as the original code and test the three implementations (data-parallel, atomic spin-lock dataflow, tiny-lock dataflow) on the GTX-570 platform.

The execution time of the kernels are listed in Table 3. As can be seen, our tiny-lock based implementation is far more efficient than the atomic spin-lock approach, with as much as 296x speedup for the 1984x1984 data grid. Compared with the original data-parallel implementation, our tiny-lock method achieves more than 1.15x speedup on small size data grid (less than 248x248), but is slower for larger sizes.

The scalability problem here is incurred by the restrictions on the number of threads and lock bits in an SM. In the data-parallel design, one warp is already sufficient to process a sub-grid, so one thread block contains only 32 threads. However, for the dataflow design, this number is 1024. Consequently, for a large grid size, more sub-grids can be processed simultaneously in the data-parallel approach, as an SM can sustain 8 thread blocks at a time for Fermi. For the dataflow approaches, however, an SM can only support one thread block (In fact, the maximum number of resident threads per SM is 1536 for Fermi, but there are only 1024 lock bits), which severely limits the exploitable parallelism at the thread block level.

If the new generation GPUs integrate more lock bits and allow more threads for a SM, the data-flow scheme could achieve superior performance than the data-parallel scheme, even for large grid sizes.

7. LIMITATIONS

Here we evaluate the limitations of the proposed synchronization scheme. First, in order to use it, one has to do low-level **SASS assembly programming**, which requires significant efforts. The coding process is error-prone and can easily lead to deadlocks, while debugging is almost impossible. However, this situation can be significantly improved if NVIDIA provides specific PTX instructions or CUDA functions to manipulate lock bits. This can also resolve the second limitation – **portability**. As no official SASS assembler is available, although the idea is general, our real hardware testing has to rely on the open-source *asfermi* that only functions smoothly for a portion of instructions for Fermi architecture. Since Kepler has dramatically improved the atomic functionality, we expect the proposed scheme can work more efficiently on the Kepler architecture. The third limitation is the **number of usable lock bits**, which restricts the parallelism and scalability that can be achieved on GPUs.

Grid Size	Atomic-Lock	Data-Parallel	Tiny-Lock
31x31	175 μs	57 μs	49 μs
62x62	466 μs	58 μs	49 μs
124x124	1050 μs	58 μs	50 μs
248x248	2285 μs	59 μs	51 μs
496x496	5052 μs	72 μs	79 μs
992x992	14757 μs	79 μs	109 μs
1984x1984	48808 μs	80 μs	165 μs

Table 3: Execution time for atomic-lock, data-parallel and tiny-lock based Implementations.

8. CONCLUSION

In this paper we proposed a highly efficient lock mechanism on the shared memory of NVIDIA Fermi GPUs. By reassembling the SASS micro-operations that comprise an atomic instruction, we developed a highly efficient, low cost lock approach that can be leveraged to set up a fine-grained producer-consumer synchronization channel between cooperative threads in a thread block. This is the first time that the SASS instructions comprising an atomic operation are used independently to form new synchronization primitives. Furthermore, we showed how to implement a dataflow algorithm on GPUs using a real 2D-wavefront application. This is the first work that explores the possibility of applying lock-based dataflow-style programming model on GPUs.

Although programming with locks for the current platform/assembler is low-level and deadlock-prone, our work is already sufficient to show the possibility and potential of lock-based dataflow programming for GPUs. We expect more developers, especially architects and library writers to see such potential and participate in exploring and simplifying the programmability of this new design pattern.

9. ACKNOWLEDGMENTS

This work was supported by Singapore Ministry of Education Academic Research Fund Tier 1 (No.R263-000-B02-112). The authors would like to thank all the anonymous reviewers for their insightful suggestions and feedback.

10. REFERENCES

[1] Gadi Taubenfeld. *Synchronization algorithms and concurrent programming.* Pearson Education, 2006.

[2] Thomas E. Anderson. The performance of spin lock alternatives for shared-money multiprocessors. *Parallel and Distributed Systems, IEEE Transactions on*, 1(1), 1990.

[3] Thomas E Anderson, Edward D Lazowska, and Henry M Levy. The performance implications of thread management alternatives for shared-memory multiprocessors. *Computers, IEEE Transactions on*, 38(12), 1989.

[4] Ding-Kai Chen, Hong-Men Su, and Pen-Chung Yew. *The impact of synchronization and granularity on parallel systems*, volume 18. ACM, 1990.

[5] Weirong Zhu, Vugranam C Sreedhar, Ziang Hu, and Guang R Gao. Synchronization state buffer: supporting efficient fine-grain synchronization on many-core architectures. In *ACM SIGARCH Computer Architecture News*, volume 35, pages 35–45. ACM, 2007.

[6] Dean M Tullsen, Jack L Lo, Susan J Eggers, and Henry M Levy. Supporting fine-grained synchronization on a simultaneous multithreading processor. In *High-Performance Computer Architecture. Proceedings. Fifth International Symposium On*, pages 54–58. IEEE, 1999.

[7] William E Cohen, Henry G Dietz, and JB Sponaugle. Dynamic barrier architecture for multi-mode fine-grain parallelism using conventional processors. In *Parallel Processing. International Conference on*, volume 1. IEEE, 1994.

[8] Alexandru Nicolau, Guangqiang Li, and Arun Kejariwal. Techniques for efficient placement of synchronization primitives. In *ACM Sigplan Notices*, volume 44, pages 199–208. ACM, 2009.

[9] Samuel P. Midkiff and David A. Padua. Compiler algorithms for synchronization. *Computers, IEEE Transactions on*, 36(12), 1987.

[10] Martin C Rinard. Effective fine-grain synchronization for automatically parallelized programs using optimistic synchronization primitives. *ACM Transactions on Computer Systems*, 17(4), 1999.

[11] W Hwu Wen-Mei. *GPU Computing Gems Emerald Edition*. Elsevier, 2011.

[12] John D Owens, Mike Houston, David Luebke, Simon Green, John E Stone, and James C Phillips. GPU computing. *Proceedings of the IEEE*, 96(5), 2008.

[13] NVIDIA. CUDA C Programming Guide. `http://docs.nvidia.com/cuda/cuda-c-programming-guide/`.

[14] Nikolaj Leischner, Vitaly Osipov, and Peter Sanders. Fermi architecture white paper. `http://www.nvidia.com/content/pdf/fermi_white_papers/nvidia_fermi_compute_architecture_whitepaper.pdf`.

[15] Shucai Xiao and Wu-Chun Feng. Inter-block GPU communication via fast barrier synchronization. In *Parallel and Distributed Processing, IEEE International Symposium on*, pages 1–12. IEEE, 2010.

[16] Jeff A Stuart and John D Owens. Efficient synchronization primitives for GPUs. *arXiv preprint arXiv:1110.4623*, 2011.

[17] NVIDIA. PTX: Parallel Thread Execution ISA Version 4.0. `http://docs.nvidia.com/cuda/parallel-thread-execution/index.html`.

[18] Michael Bauer, Henry Cook, and Brucek Khailany. Cudadma: optimizing gpu memory bandwidth via warp specialization. In *Proceedings of 2011 International Conference for High Performance Computing, Networking, Storage and Analysis*, page 12. ACM, 2011.

[19] Michael Bauer, Sean Treichler, and Alex Aiken. Singe: leveraging warp specialization for high performance on GPUs. In *Proceedings of the 19th ACM SIGPLAN symposium on Principles and practice of parallel programming*. ACM, 2014.

[20] Rupesh Nasre, Martin Burtscher, and Keshav Pingali. Atomic-free irregular computations on GPUs. In *Proceedings of the 6th Workshop on General Purpose Processor Using Graphics Processing Units*. ACM, 2013.

[21] Feng Ji and Xiaosong Ma. Using shared memory to accelerate mapreduce on graphics processing units. In *Parallel and Distributed Processing Symposium, IEEE International*, pages 805–816. IEEE, 2011.

[22] Ashwin M Aji and Wu-Chun Feng. Accelerating data-serial applications on data-parallel GPGPUs: a systems approach. Technical report, TR-08-24, Computer Science, Virginia Tech, 2008.

[23] Brett W Coon, Peter C Mills, John R Nickolls, and Lars Nyland. Lock mechanism to enable atomic updates to shared memory, November 8 2011. US Patent 8,055,856.

[24] Juan Gomez-Luna, José Marıa González-Linares, Jose Ignacio Benavides Benitez, and Nicolas Guil Mata. Performance modeling of atomic additions on GPU scratchpad memory. *Parallel and Distributed Systems, IEEE Transactions on*, 24(11), 2013.

[25] Jason Sanders and Edward Kandrot. *CUDA by example: an introduction to general-purpose GPU programming*. Addison-Wesley Professional, 2010.

[26] Yunqing Hou. Asfermi: An assembler for the NVIDIA Fermi instruction set. `http://code.google.com/p/asfermi/`, 2011.

[27] Carlos ER Alves, Edson Norberto Cáceres, Frank Dehne, and Siang W Song. A parallel wavefront algorithm for efficient biological sequence comparison. In *Computational Science and Its Applications*, pages 249–258. Springer, 2003.

[28] Hsien-Yu Liao, Meng-Lai Yin, and Yi Cheng. A parallel implementation of the smith-waterman algorithm for massive sequences searching. In *Engineering in Medicine and Biology Society. 26th Annual International Conference of the IEEE*, volume 2, pages 2817–2820. IEEE, 2004.

[29] Shuai Che, Michael Boyer, Jiayuan Meng, David Tarjan, Jeremy W Sheaffer, Sang-Ha Lee, and Kevin Skadron. Rodinia: A benchmark suite for heterogeneous computing. In *Workload Characterization. IEEE International Symposium on*, pages 44–54. IEEE, 2009.

[30] Leslie Lamport. The parallel execution of DO loops. *Communications of the ACM*, 17(2), 1974.

[31] Simon J Pennycook, Gihan R Mudalige, Simon D Hammond, and Stephen A Jarvis. Parallelising wavefront applications on general-purpose GPU devices, 2010.

[32] George Teodoro, Tony Pan, Tahsin M Kurc, Jun Kong, Lee AD Cooper, and Joel H Saltz. Efficient irregular wavefront propagation algorithms on hybrid CPU–GPU machines. *Parallel computing*, 39(4), 2013.

Enabling and Exploiting Flexible Task Assignment on GPU through SM-Centric Program Transformations

Bo Wu[◇], Guoyang Chen[⋆], Dong Li[+], Xipeng Shen[⋆], Jeffrey Vetter[†]
[◇]Department of Electrical Engineering and Computer Science, Colorado School of Mines, USA
[⋆]Department of Computer Science, North Carolina State University, USA
[+]Department of Computer Science, University of California, Merced, USA
[†]Oak Ridge National Laboratory, USA
[◇]bwu@mines.edu,[⋆]{gchen11,xshen5}@ncsu.edu,[+]dli35@ucmerced.edu,[†]vetter@ornl.gov

ABSTRACT

A GPU's computing power lies in its abundant memory bandwidth and massive parallelism. However, its hardware thread schedulers, despite being able to quickly distribute computation to processors, often fail to capitalize on program characteristics effectively, achieving only a fraction of the GPU's full potential. Moreover, current GPUs do not allow programmers or compilers to control this thread scheduling, forfeiting important optimization opportunities at the program level. This paper presents a transformation centered on Streaming Multiprocessors (SM); this software approach to circumventing the limitations of the hardware scheduler allows flexible program-level control of scheduling. By permitting precise control of job locality on SMs, the transformation overcomes inherent limitations in prior methods.

With this technique, flexible control of GPU scheduling at the program level becomes feasible, which opens up new opportunities for GPU program optimizations. The second part of the paper explores how the new opportunities could be leveraged for GPU performance enhancement, what complexities there are, and how to address them. We show that some simple optimization techniques can enhance co-runs of multiple kernels and improve data locality of irregular applications, producing 20-33% average increase in performance, system throughput, and average turnaround time.

Categories and Subject Descriptors

D.3.4 [**Programming Languages**]: Processors—*optimization, compilers*

General Terms

Performance, Experimentation

ICS'15, June 8–11, 2015, Newport Beach, CA, USA.

http://dx.doi.org/10.1145/2751205.2751213.

Keywords

GPGPU, Scheduling, Compiler Transformation, Data Affinity, Program Co-Run

1. INTRODUCTION

Recent years have seen increasing popularity of Graphics Processing Units (GPUs) in general-purpose computing, thanks to massive parallelism provided by GPUs. With hundreds of cores integrated, the GPU often creates tens of thousands of threads for an application. The massive parallelism produces large potential throughput, but also imposes grand challenges for thread management, or scheduling.

Scheduling determines when and where a task is processed. It is essential for matching communication and memory access patterns with underlying architecture, in order to fully tap into the power of a parallel system. Scheduling is usually controlled by thread schedulers. On CPU, the thread scheduling is implemented through system APIs. But on GPUs, there is no such software API; the scheduling on GPUs has been controlled by hardware and runtime. Such a design is demanded by the scale of parallelism: Hundreds of thousands of threads need to be scheduled in very short time. However, the lack of software-level control of scheduling forms a major barrier for software to leverage scheduling to optimize program executions. What increases the barrier is that the scheduling algorithms employed by GPU hardware and runtime have remained non-disclosed; the schedulers vary substantially across generations and have exhibited some obscure and non-deterministic behaviors (detailed in the next section).

The restrictions have drawn some recent attentions from researchers in various domains. A number of studies independently invented the method of *persistent threads* to go around the hardware scheduling problem [3,9,13,41,44]. The idea is to create only a small number of threads that can simultaneously run actively on a GPU. Unlike in traditional kernels where a thread terminates as it finishes a task, these threads stay alive throughout the execution of a kernel function. They continuously fetch and execute tasks from one or more task queues. By controlling the order of the tasks in the queues, one can match the executions with some communication patterns among tasks—for example, putting a producer and its consumer into the same queue.

Although persistent threads offers some support to task scheduling on the GPU, the support is restrictive. It only decides which tasks map to which persistent thread and their execution order; it gives no support for deciding *where or on which processor a task should run.* Such location control is still up to the hardware and proprietary runtime, which decide the placement of persistent threads, and hence the placement of tasks associated with those threads.

Lack of such scheduling control at the spatial dimension hinders persistent threads in supporting optimizations that are related with non-uniformity in processors. For instance, a modern GPU consists of multiple streaming multiprocessors (SM), with each containing tens of cores. Cores on one SM usually share some on-chip storage on that SM (e.g., L1 cache and texture cache). As a result, one task may be able to read the data in a cache brought by another task that concurrently runs on the same SM. With location control, one could make two tasks that share lots of data run concurrently on the same SM[1]. Such optimizations are especially beneficial for tasks with non-uniform data sharing, which include tasks of many irregular applications (e.g., N-body simulations), as well as tasks coming from different kernels (or applications) that are deployed concurrently on a GPU. Besides for data sharing, the spatial control is critical when there are architectural variations among SMs. Unintentional variations among SMs in a GPU already widely exist today [16]; with frequency scaling [21] possibly implemented in future GPUs, even more substantial (intentional) variations (e.g., different SMs could be reconfigured to different clock frequencies to balance energy and performance) are possible. In these scenarios, spatial control of scheduling is important for matching tasks with the suitable SMs.

In this work, we show that spatial scheduling control actually can be enabled through a simple program transformation, called *SM-centric transformation.*

SM-centric transformation includes two essential techniques. The first is *SM-based task selection.* In a traditional GPU kernel execution, with or without persistent threads, what tasks a thread executes are usually based on the ID of the thread (or determined randomly in a dynamic task management). While with SM-based task selection, what tasks a thread executes is based on the ID of the SM that the thread runs on. By replacing the binding between tasks and threads with the binding between tasks and SMs, the scheme enables a direct, precise control of task placement on SM.

The second technique is *filling-retreating scheme*, which offers a flexible control of the amount of active threads on an SM. Importantly, the control is resilient to the randomness and obscuration in GPU hardware thread scheduling. It helps SM-centric transformation in two aspects. First, it ensures an even distribution of active threads on SMs, which is vital for guaranteeing the correctness of SM-centric transformations. Second, it facilitates online determination of the parallelism level suitable for a kernel, which is especially important for the performance of multiple-kernel co-runs, a scenario benefiting significantly from SM-centric transformation.

SM-centric transformation, by enabling flexible program-level control of task scheduling, opens up many new opportunities for optimizations. The second part of the paper explores how the new opportunities could be leveraged for GPU performance enhancement, what complexities there are, and how to address them. Specifically, we explore the use of the scheduling flexibility to enable affinity-oriented task scheduling and SM partition for co-runs of multiple kernels. In our experiments on 72 co-runs of kernels, it helps produce on average 33% improvement in system throughput and turnaround time. When applied to locality enhancement, the enabled spatial scheduling shortens the execution times of four irregular applications by 20% on average. In both cases, it significantly outperforms the support that persistent threads provide. These results indicate that SM-centric transformation, by complementing prior methods, provides a critical missing piece of the puzzle for enabling and exploiting flexible control of task scheduling on the GPU.

In summary, this work makes following contributions.

- It proposes SM-centric transformation, which, for the first time enables precise spatial scheduling of GPU tasks. It offers the missing piece of the puzzle for circumventing GPU hardware restrictions to implement a flexible control of task scheduling.

- It uncovers the potential of the enabled scheduling control for both single-kernel runs and multi-kernel co-runs.

- It reveals some major challenges for leveraging spatial scheduling on the GPU, and develops a set of practical solutions; experiments demonstrate their effectiveness and the tangible and substantial benefits with the proposed program-level schedule control.

In the rest of this paper, Section 2 provides some necessary background on GPU scheduling, Section 3 describes SM-centric transformation, Section 4 discusses the uses of the enabled spatial scheduling for both locality enhancement in single-kernel runs and throughput improvement in multi-kernel co-runs, and discusses some major challenges. Section 5 presents some simple solutions to those challenges, through which, we are able to examine the practical benefits of the spatial scheduling. Section 6 reports experimental results, followed by related work and conclusions.

2. BACKGROUND

We base our discussions on terms in NVIDIA CUDA [1]; but the technique could be applied to other GPU programming models.

Organization of Cores and Threads.

As a massively parallel architecture, a GPU consists of a number of *streaming multiprocessors (SM)*, with each containing tens of cores. A GPU usually creates a large number of threads at the launch of a *kernel* (i.e., a CPU-invoked function that runs on GPU). These threads are typically organized in a hierarchy: 32 compose a *warp*, many warps compose a *thread block* or called a *cooperative thread array (CTA)* and many CTAs compose a *grid.*

Spatial Scheduling.

A CTA is the unit for spatial scheduling: At a kernel launch, the GPU hardware scheduler named GigaThread [32] assigns each CTA to one of its SMs. The assignment algorithm has not been disclosed to the public. It differs from

[1]Mapping two tasks to the same persistent thread can also make them map to the same SM, but the tasks have to run serially by that thread, throttling the benefits of synergistic data fetching.

one generation of GPUs to another, and exhibits lots of irregularity. For example, our experiments on Tesla M2075, a type of widely used workstation GPUs, show different CTA-to-SM assignments in two repeated invocations of the same kernel on the same input, and neither is in a round-robin or other regular predictable pattern.

Temporal Scheduling.

A warp is the unit for temporal scheduling: All threads in a warp proceed in lockstep. Many CTAs may be assigned to an SM, but at one time point, only a limited number of them can be active—meaning that they attain enough registers and other hardware resources and are ready to run. All other CTAs have to wait until some active CTA finishes executing the entire kernel function and releases some hardware resources.

Non-Uniformity on GPU.

Spatial scheduling is potentially beneficial to the GPU, as non-uniformity exists on both GPU resource sharing and its workload.

On the resource sharing aspect, modern GPU features non-uniform cache sharing. In Tesla M2075, for instance, there are 14 SMs, with each containing some cache—such as, instruction cache, L1 data cache, constant cache, and texture cache—that is shared by all cores on that SM but is not accessible by other SMs.

On the workload aspect, non-uniformity shows in two levels. For a single GPU kernel, a CTA may share different amounts of data with different CTAs. Molecular Dynamics (MD) simulation is such an example. It simulates interactions among neighbor atoms. The atoms simulated by two CTAs may have many or few neighbors, depending on the distances among them in the simulated space. That naturally leads to non-uniform data sharing among CTAs. Meanwhile, recent generations of GPUs start to support concurrent executions of multiple kernels on a single GPU. Although currently the kernels have to be launched from a single CUDA context, a more general support for concurrent executions of multiple GPU applications is expected to come in the near future. In these co-run scenario's, non-uniformity becomes even more common: CTAs from the same kernel often share more instructions and data than CTAs from different kernels do.

The non-uniformity suggests the potential of spatial scheduling. As Section 6 quantitatively confirms, a good spatial scheduling may bring an over 30% speedup on average.

3. SM-CENTRIC TRANSFORMATION

At the center of SM-centric transformation are two techniques: SM-centric task selection, and a filling-retreating scheme. In this section, we first explain the basic ideas of the two techniques and how they complement each other to form a single solution to circumvent the limitation from the hardware scheduler. As the techniques are generally applicable to various GPU programming models, we use high-level pseudo-code for description and skip detailed complexities in implementation so that the ideas can be easily grasped by general readers. We then use CUDA as an example programming model to explain the detailed implementation of the techniques, including some subtle considerations that are critical for the techniques to work efficiently. We show that the entire SM-centric transformation can be conducted through a simple pass by compilers. At the end, we give some discussions on the soundness of the transformation and its applicable conditions.

3.1 SM-Centric Task Selection

Basic Idea.

SM-centric task selection associates tasks with SMs. We explain it based on the following abstract model of GPU kernel executions.

Commonly, an invocation of a GPU kernel causes many GPU threads to create, which are often organized in a hierarchical structure. At an abstract level, the execution of a GPU kernel can be regarded as consisting of many jobs[2] conducted in parallel by a number of workers on some SMs. Here, a worker corresponds to a group of GPU threads (e.g., a CTA), and a job corresponds to the operations conducted by such a thread group, including all their data accesses. There is a unique ID number associated with each job, worker, and SM.

In traditional GPU programs, which job a worker does has been determined by the worker's ID, as the pseudo code in Figure 1 (a) shows. The technique of *Persistent threads* maps multiple jobs to a single worker, but the set of jobs for a worker is still determined by the worker's ID, as shown in Figure 1 (b). Since the placement of workers on SMs is controlled by the hardware schedulers, the job-worker binding makes the placement of jobs on SMs solely depend on the hardware schedulers.

The idea behind SM-centric task selection is to replace the job-worker binding with a binding established between jobs and SMs. As Figure 1 (c) shows, a job queue is built for every SM before the invocation of a kernel function. Inside the kernel function, each worker first figures out on what SM it resides, and then uses the SM ID to fetch the next job in the corresponding job queue to execute. In this way, controlling the placement of a job on a specific SM becomes simple: Just putting that job's ID into the job queue of that SM.

The idea is straightforward. But some complexities must be addressed to implement the idea soundly and efficiently.

Correctness Issues by Hardware Schedulers.

Through a close look at the pseudocode in Figure 1 (c), one will see that for it to work correctly on a GPU program, the number of workers assigned to an SM must be no fewer than the number of jobs assigned to the SM. It is because in that code, one worker on an SM processes only one job assigned to that SM. Some jobs on that SM would be left unprocessed if the number of workers is less than the number of jobs.

However, how many workers are assigned to an SM is determined by the GPU hardware scheduler. Our experiments indicate that the assignment by hardware schedulers is often unpredictable. On a Tesla M2075 with 14 SMs, for instance, when running a kernel with 1400 workers (i.e., CTAs), we observe an uneven distribution of workers: the number of workers per SM varies from 92 to 110. And when running the kernel with 14 workers, some SMs get multiple workers

[2]In this paper, "job" and "task" are interchangeable terms, although we tend to use "job" more often when referring to entities in this abstract kernel execution model.

```
kernel_org()
  jobID = f (workerID);
  processJob (jobID);
```

(a) original kernel

```
createJobQ4workers(); // on CPU

kernel_persist()
  while (jobID = JobQ[workerID].next() != null)
    processJob (jobID);
```

(b) with persistent thread

```
createJobQ4sms(); // on CPU

kernel_smc()
  smID = getSMID();
  jobID = JobQ[smID].next();
  if (jobID != null)
    processJob (jobID);
```

(c) with SM-centric task selection

Figure 1: Conceptual relations among jobs, workers, and SMs.

while others get none. Moreover, the worker distribution varies from run to run, displaying lots of randomness.

Such non-determinism jeopardizes the soundness of the basic SM-centric task selection. An option is to allow dynamic job stealing such that workers on one SM can steal jobs left on another SM. It requires more complicated code to be inserted into the GPU kernel to implement the job stealing logic, and hence increases register pressure and reduces parallelism. More importantly, the stealing changes the intended job-to-SM mapping.

3.2 Filling-Retreating Scheme

We address the complexity through a *filling-retreating scheme.* This scheme offers a simple way to precisely control the number of active workers on each SM.

The scheme works hand-in-hand with the concept of persistent threads. Similar to persistent threads, with this scheme, a small number of workers are kept alive for each SM throughout the kernel execution. These workers continuously fetch and process the jobs assigned to the SM until the queue gets empty. The tricky part is on how to precisely control the number of active persistent threads (or in our term, active workers) for each SM.

Filling-retreating offers a simple solution. It leverages a common property of GPU schedulers. On GPUs, each SM can only support a limited number of active workers at the same time due to hardware limitation. On all GPUs we tested, despite the differences in their schedulers, one common property is that they always try to assign a worker to an SM that can still accommodate some active workers if there is any (rather than putting the worker into a waiting queue of an SM).

Suppose that one SM can support at most m active workers at the same time. In the filling-retreating scheme, a total of $m * M$ workers are created at a kernel launch, where M is the number of SMs in the GPU. Due to the aforementioned common property, each SM gets m workers assigned. This step is the "filling" part of the scheme.

Although the "filling" step ensures every SM gets m workers, as multiple studies have shown [20,25], having the largest number of workers on an SM is not always the best for maximizing the computing efficiency due to cache and bus contention. This phenomenon is also confirmed in Section 6. The "retreating" part of our scheme facilitates flexible adjustment of the number of active workers on an SM. Suppose one wants to have n_{target} active workers per SM. A counter is created for each SM to record the number of workers that have started processing jobs on that SM. Each worker, before starting working on a job, first atomically increases the corresponding counter and then checks whether the counter

```
createJobQ4sms(); // on CPU

kernel_smc()
  smID = getSMID();
  workers = workerCounters[smID]++; // atomic
  if (workers > wantedNumPerSM)
    return;
  while (jobID = JobQ[smID].next() != null)
    processJob (jobID);
```

Figure 2: Psuedo code of a GPU kernel in a *filling-retreating* scheme.

value already exceeds n_{target}. If so, the worker exits immediately. Figure 2 shows the pseudo code.

The correctness of the filling-retreating scheme relies on the fast distribution of thread blocks by the hardware scheduler. That is, the filling phase should finish before any thread block retreats (i.e., exiting its execution). Otherwise, the hardware scheduler could assign totally more than m workers onto an SM because of the vacancy on that SM formed by the early retreat of some workers on it. Correspondingly, some other SMs would get less than m workers assigned. Fortunately, our experiments show that such cases have never happened, plausibly due to the extreme speed of the hardware-based assignment of workers. A check put into the runtime driver could further ensure the condition to hold, the necessity of which is not shown in our experiments.

The benefits of the precise control of the number of active workers on an SM goes beyond helping with the correctness of SM-centric task selection. It also enables a precise control of parallelism on GPU, which facilitates flexible partitions of SMs among co-running kernels shown in Section 5.

3.3 Implementation

The SM-centric transformation can be easily applied either manually or through a compiler. For proof of concept, we build a prototype source-to-source compiler based on Cetus [22], in which the transformation is implemented as a pass over the input code. The experience taught us the importance of several subtle considerations in the design, which we highlight next before showing the full details of the implementation.

First, the dequeue operation in the while loop in Figure 2 is good for illustrating the basic idea but poor for performance. An atomic operation could cause substantial overhead especially when the work in the loop body is small. When implementing the transformation, it is important to avoid such atomic operations in the while loop.

In our design, we circumvent the needs for atomic job fetching by leveraging a property offered by the filling-retreating scheme: There are precisely N_{target} active workers on an SM. With that property, each active worker only needs to process W/N_{target} jobs, where W is the total number of jobs assigned to the SM. So if we put the job IDs of an SM into an array, the set of jobs for a worker just corresponds to a segment of the array. The starting and ending indices of the segment can be easily attained before the worker enters the job fetching and processing loop. With this improvement, the while loop in Figure 2 can be converted into a simple for loop, iterating the elements in the segment assigned to the worker, and the atomic operation can be hence removed from the loop. In our implementation, we actually use a single array to store the IDs of all jobs. The set of jobs of an SM corresponds to just one section of the array. The position of a job ID in the array hence determines on which SM it will be processed. (Lines 9 to 16 in Listing 1 implement this design; explained later.)

Second, the ID of an SM can be obtained efficiently. CUDA, like the C programming language, allows programmers to insert assembly code, which is designed by NVIDIA as an intermediate representation named Parallel Thread Execution (PTX) [34]. It has a special register, %smid, which stores the SM identifier. One "mov" instruction can copy the value in %smid to an integer variable. Line 27 in Listing 1 shows the code.

Details.

In this part, we describe some low-level complexities that our description has skipped. The discussion is based on CUDA, but the implementation can be done for other GPU programming models, such as OpenCL.

On GPU, the spatial scheduling unit is not a thread but a CTA, an array of threads. Correspondingly, the job assignments to processors in our design is in the unit of *job chunks*—the set of jobs executed by a CTA in the original GPU program. In a typical GPU program, the thread ID is used to distinguish jobs, and one CTA handles one job chunk; the ID of a CTA in the original program is hence treated as the ID of the job chunk that CTA processes.

To minimize changes needed to the original GPU program, we encapsulate most parts of the code for SM-centric transformation into four macros. With them, applying SM-centric transformation involves only several minor changes to the original GPU program. As Listing 2 shows, on the CPU-side code, it inserts one macro, *__SMC_init*, before the invocation of a GPU kernel, and appends three arguments to the kernel call. On the GPU-side code, it inserts the calls to two other macros, *__SMC_Begin* and *__SMC_End*, and replaces the appearances of the ID of CTA in the kernel with *__SMC_chunkID*. These can be done easily by the compiler in one pass over the original GPU program.

The above four macros are defined in Listing 1. The first, *__SMC_init*, initiates the three variables with the number of workers needed, the array of the desired sequence of IDs of job chunks, and an all-zero counter array to count active workers. The functions used to initiate the first two variables can be provided by the programmer or the optimizing compiler; their definitions depend on the purpose of the specific application of the SM-centric transformation, as Section 5 will illustrate. The second macro, *__SMC_Begin*, first calls the fourth macro to get the ID of the SM by reading the

Listing 1: Macros that materialize SM-centric transformation (N jobs; M SMs).

```
1  #define __SMC_init \
2  unsigned int * __SMC_workersNeeded = __SMC_numNeeded(); \
3  unsigned int * __SMC_newChunkSeq = __SMC_buildChunkSeq(); \
4  unsigned int * __SMC_workerCount= __SMC_initiateArray();
5
6  #define __SMC_Begin \
7  __shared int __SMC_workingCTAs; \
8  __SMC_getSMid; \
9  if(offsetInCTA == 0) \
10   __SMC_workingCTAs = \
11      atomicInc (&__SMC_workerCount[__SMC_smid], INT_MAX); \
12 synchthreads(); \
13 if(__SMCS_workingCTAs >= __SMC_workersNeeded) return; \
14 int __SMC_chunksPerCTA = \
15     __SMC_chunksPerSM / __SMC_workersNeeded; \
16 int __SMC_startChunkIDidx = __SMC_smid * __SMC_chunksPerSM + \
17     __SMC_workingCTAs * __SMC_chunksPerCTA;\
18 for (int __SMC_chunkIDidx = __SMC_startChunkIDidx; \
19     __SMC_chunkIDidx < __SMC_startChunkIDidx+\
20                    __SMC_chunksPerCTA ; \
21     __SMC_chunkIDidx++) { \
22     __SMC_chunkID = __SMC_newChunkSeq[__SMC_chunkIDidx];
23
24 #define __SMC_End }
25
26 // get the ID of the current SM
27 #define __SMC_getSMid \
28 uint __SMC_smid;\
29 asm("mov.u32 %0, %smid;" : "=r"(__SMC_smid) )
```

particular register, then checks whether the SM already has enough active CTAs. If not, it computes the starting and ending positions of the sets of jobs it should work on, gets into the for loop to process them one by one. The third macro, *__SMC_End*, is trivial, just putting in the ending bracket of the "for" loop in the second macro.

3.4 Soundness

At a high level, SM-centric transformation manipulates the association between jobs and processors, and hence alters the mapping between jobs and threads and possibly the execution order of the jobs. As a kind of remapping transformation as persistent threads is, for SM-centric transformation to work soundly, the GPU program needs to meet the same conditions as in the case of persistent threads [9, 13]:

(1) The operations by different threads are discriminated only by the global thread ID; (2) The execution order of the CTAs does not disturb the correctness of the kernel.

The first condition ensures that SM-centric transformation does not change integrity of a job even though *all* appearances of the CTA ID in a kernel are replaced with the *__SMC_chunkId*. We note that even though current GPUs do not migrate CTAs across SMs, the job integrity holds even if CTA migrates—given that the attainment of *__SMC_chunkId* is atomic. The second condition ensures that the new order of execution maintains the meaning of the program.

The two conditions hold for well-formed GPU programs, due to the nature of GPU execution models. At a high level, they are Single-Program-Multiple-Data (SPMD) models; all GPU threads at a kernel launch execute the same function, while their specific operations are determined only by the thread ID. Meanwhile, for a GPU program to work properly,

Listing 2: GPU program after SM-centric transformation (N vector elements; K job chunks; M SMs).

```
/**** CPU-side code ****/
main (){
  ...
  __SMC_init;
  invoke original kernel with three extra arguments:
      __SMC_chunkCount, __SMC_newChunkSeq, K/M
  ...
}

/**** GPU-side code ****/
__global__ kernel (...,
unsigned int *__SMC_chunkCount,
unsigned int *__SMC_newChunkSeq,
unsigned int __SMC_chunksPerSM)
{
  __SMC_Begin
  // the original kernel with the ID of CTA
  // replaced with __SMC_chunkID
  ... ...
  __SMC_End
}
```

it should not rely on the execution order of CTAs, because due to the non-determinism in CTA scheduling on the GPU, it is hard to know what order would be taken in a run. Free from data race helps ensure the conditions hold. Recent years have seen a number of studies on data race detection for GPUs [5,47], which could serve as part of the automatic check of the applicability of SM-centric transformation.

4. USES AND COMPLEXITIES

By enabling program-level spatial scheduling, SM-centric transformation opens up some new opportunities for GPU optimizations. This section discusses some of them, and examines the main complexities associated with these new opportunities.

4.1 Example Uses

SM Partition for Multi-kernel Co-runs.

It has been observed that many GPU kernels exhibit sublinear speedups when the number of SMs used for the kernel increases [2,33]. As a result, simulations have shown that if the set of SMs in a GPU can be partitioned such that different subsets of SMs work for different kernels concurrently, the system often gives higher throughput and the kernels manifest better overall responsiveness [2]. However, such partitions have not been feasible in practice for lack of scheduler controllability. On NVIDIA GPUs, for instance, when two kernels are launched concurrently (each usually has many CTAs), their CTAs are assigned to all SMs. And if the threads by one kernel already use too much register or shared memory on an SM, before its completion, the other kernel cannot start, hence resulting in a serial execution of the two kernels.

With minor extension to the SM-centric transformation, partitions of SMs among concurrent kernels becomes possible. For instance, if we want the first 6 SMs to work for kernel f_1, and the remaining 8 SMs for kernel f_2, we can set the mapping array used in SM-centric transformation such that all jobs of f_1 map to the first 6 SMs and those of f_2 to the other 8 SMs. When the two kernels get launched, the GPU scheduler still assigns CTAs of both kernels to every SM. However, a statement is inserted in each kernel after obtaining the SM ID, which checks whether the ID of this SM is one of the SMs supposed to work for this kernel. If not, the CTA returns immediately so that the SM can work for the other kernel.

Affinity-Based Scheduling.

Many GPU applications have inherent non-uniform data interactions, such as the MD example mentioned in Section 2. It causes non-uniform data sharing among job chunks. Following the concepts on traditional CPU [49], we state that two job chunks have good reference affinity if they share lots of data. As Section 2 mentions, each SM has an on-chip cache. So, if we can manage to assign onto the same SM the job chunks with good affinity, we may enhance the performance of the cache. SM-centric transformation makes this affinity-based scheduling possible.

4.2 Complexities

There are some complexities for applying SM-centric transformation to the use cases mentioned earlier.

For SM partition for co-runs, the key is to decide the best partition. For affinity-based scheduling, the key is to compute the affinity among job chunks and then group job chunks accordingly.

Additionally, there is a common complexity existed in both use cases: determining the suitable number of active CTAs for a kernel. As some studies have shown [20], creating the maximum number of CTAs that an SM can hold often gives suboptimal performance, because of cache and bus contention among them. The CTA aggregation employed in SM-centric transformation allows flexible control of the number of active CTAs for a kernel.

However, determining the suitable numbers of active CTAs is challenging. It depends on many factors, including the interaction between SM partitioning and data locality, program inputs, kernels' resource requirement and so on. Moreover, when coupling with the various methods to partition SMs (for co-runs), they could result in a large search space. For 2 kernels on a 14-SM GPU, if an SM can support at most 6 active CTAs, the search space contains $6 \times 6 \times 14 = 504$ cases.

5. DESIGNS FOR VALIDATION

In this section, we describe our design to address the complexities listed in the previous section. Our goal is to validate the practical value of the spatial scheduling enabled by SM-centric transformation, rather than to find the best solution to those complexities. Simplicity and practicality are the principles in our design. The rationale is that if the enabled spatial scheduling could bring substantial benefits with minimum support, the promise of the technique is validated.

5.1 Optimal Configuration Search

We first discuss the challenges for determining the best number of active CTAs (i.e., the n_{target} mentioned in Section 3.2, which is also called parallelism control) for a kernel and for finding the best partition of SMs between co-running kernels. We call these parameters together as a configuration in our discussion. The difficulty is that the space of the configuration values is large and the best configuration depends on many factors. It is often too costly to try every possible configuration at runtime. We employ the standard sampling method to efficiently approximate the best configuration. When a kernel is inside a loop, the sampling may happen during the first several iterations; otherwise, the sampling may happen offline or across runs.

Because SM partition mainly affects interactions across SMs, while the parallelism control is mainly related with resource usage inside an SM, we observe that the optimal level of parallelism for a kernel is only loosely connected with how we partition SMs. Hence our search scheme first evenly partitions the SMs among kernels, and tries to find the appropriate numbers of active CTAs for each kernel. It starts with the maximum CTAs supported by an SM for the kernel (no larger than 8), and decreases the number by 1 in each iteration until it observes decreased performance or the number reaches 1. This is a typical process of hill climbing. After that, our search scheme fixes the CTA numbers but adjusts SM partition by setting the number of SMs assigned to a co-run kernel from 1 to the maximum-1 (in a step size of three) while the rest SMs are used for the other co-running kernel. As a prior study [33] does, this work considers only co-runs of two kernels. Based on the sampled data, the optimal partition is approximated through interpolation.

Like other online sampling-based approaches, our search scheme cannot work well when different iterations behave dramatically differently. Combining the sampling approach with domain knowledge about the behavior patterns of the program may help, which is out of the scope of this paper. In our experiment, we encountered only one such program, *reduction*. We did not give special treatment to it. The results in Section 6 show that even though the sampling method finds only suboptimal configurations for some programs, the overall benefits are still substantial, confirming the value of the SM-centric transformation.

5.2 Affinity-Based Scheduling

To implement the affinity-based scheduling, we model the scheduling problem as a graph partitioning problem. The modeling consists of two steps: graph construction and graph partitioning.

Graph Construction.

This step establishes a set of graphs named *affinity graphs*, in which, each vertex represents a job chunk and each edge weight represents the affinity score between two job chunks. Affinity score is defined as follows. Let S_1 and S_2 be the set of data blocks assessed by two job chunks J_1 and J_2 respectively. Their affinity score is $\frac{|S1 \cap S2|}{|S1 \cup S2|}$. There is no edge between two vertices when their affinity score is less than a threshold (0.05 in our experiment). If the affinity score is too small, there is only a small amount of data sharing and its effects on performance is negligible; ignoring them often breaks one affinity graph into multiple smaller graphs, allowing efficient graph partitioning in the next step.

Compiler techniques exist for analyzing working sets [35] for regular applications. On irregular applications, it is challenging as data access patterns may be unknown until run time. Runtime inspection techniques have been proposed to analyze data access patterns [27]. For GPU programs, prior work has shown the feasibility to employ CPU to implement the inspection asynchronously when the GPU is executing the kernel [45]. In this work, we used simple synchronous parallel inspection for irregular programs. But the asynchronous method may further reduce the overhead.

Graph Partitioning.

Given M SMs, this step partitions the set of vertices into M equal-size clusters. The job chunks corresponding to a cluster are scheduled to one single SM. This problem is known to be NP-hard. There are some existing heuristic algorithms, but we find them costly. Instead, we design a random, lightweight and highly parallelizable algorithm. Its basic idea is to select a seed vertex for each cluster and greedily enlarge each cluster to include the vertices that have high affinity scores with the selected vertices. The algorithm has three steps. (1) *Seeds selection.* Selecting the seed vertices is important for the partitioning quality; we try to minimize the affinity among them. The initial seed set is formed by randomly selecting a vertex from each of the affinity graphs. If the number of affinity graphs is no less than M, only M of them are randomly selected. If there are less than M seeds in the set, we iterate over the remaining vertices until we find one, whose affinity scores with all current seeds are smaller than a threshold (initialized to 0) and add it to the seed set. This step stops once we get M seeds. After iterating all vertices if we still need more seeds, we increase the threshold by 0.1 and start the next round of search. Ten rounds are needed at most as the threshold would grow to 1, the largest possible affinity score. In practice, we have not seen the need for more than 1 round. After the seeds selection, we have M clusters, each containing 1 vertex. (2) *Sorted lists construction.* For each seed vertex T_i, we create a descending list of all the vertices that fall into the same affinity graph as T_i. (3) *Cluster enlargement.* This step repetitively iterates through all clusters until all vertices are partitioned. In each iteration, it randomly selects a vertex from the current cluster, and includes the vertex that, among all remaining vertices, has the largest affinity score with this vertex, which can be determined in constant time with the sorted lists produced in step 2.

In our implementation, this graph partitioning happens in parallel on CPU. Its time complexity, in the worst case when all vertices fall into one graph, is $O(N^2 logN)$ (N for number of job chunks). But in practice, as graphs are never very large, the algorithm terminates quickly shown in the next section.

6. EVALUATIONS

We focus our experiments on answering the following main questions:
(1) How much potential does spatial scheduling enabled by SM-centric transformation have?
(2) How much overhead does SM-centric transformation have?
(3) How much benefit can it bring in practice with the simple support outlined in the previous section?

To that end, we implement the two use cases of SM-centric transformation as described in Section 4: One is SM partition for multi-kernel co-runs, and the other is affinity-based scheduling for single-kernel runs. The implementation integrates the solutions described in Section 5. For comparison, we also implement the persistent threads with the best efforts to support these two use cases.

6.1 Methodology

Benchmarks.

Given that the focus of our use cases are on enhancing memory performance, we need a set of memory intensive programs for the validation. Meanwhile, for a comprehensive assessment of the applicability of our techniques, the benchmark set should consist of programs of a broad range of domains, and have a good coverage of both regular and irregular programs. For these reasons, we select nine benchmarks to form our test set. As Table 1 shows, these programs come from four benchmark suites, cover a broad set of domains, and include a similar number of regular and irregular programs. Those irregular benchmarks impose special challenges for GPGPU optimization, and have drawn a lot of attention from the community recently [6, 24, 29, 30, 43, 45].

We give a brief description for these benchmarks. IRREG (a partial differential solver kernel) and NBF (a molecular dynamics kernel) were rewritten to CUDA from C benchmarks [15]. These two benchmarks were studied heavily by previous work [11, 14, 39, 42]. MD and SPMV are both from the SHOC benchmark suite developed by Oak Ridge National Laboratory [10]. CFD from Rodinia benchmark suite [7] simulates fluid dynamics. MM and REDUCE taken from the CUDA SDK samples represent two compute-intensive applications used widely in real-world. We also take NN and PF from the popular Rodinia benchmark suite for a broader coverage.

Co-runs of Kernels.

As current GPUs cannot support the co-existence of two different contexts yet, following prior work [33], we combine two programs into one and use two separate CUDA streams to execute the kernels of the two original programs. Since which kernels run together depends on the practical context, we co-run each pair of the benchmarks for a comprehensive coverage. We use two metrics, System Throughput (STP) and Average Normalized Turnaround Time (ANTT), proposed in [12] and used in [33]. STP shows overall throughput of the whole system, and ANTT shows programs' responsiveness. We measure the execution time of kernel executions and the extra overhead introduced by the transformation (if any) for the calculation of STP and ANTT. Since we are only interested in the overlapped execution, we modify the approach proposed by Tuck and Tullsen [40] and immediately invoke a kernel after it finishes until both kernels are invoked at least 7 times. The last instance of the kernel invocation that finishes later than the other co-run kernel is discarded, because the execution of the last instance of the kernel invocation is not fully overlapped.

Versions based on Persistent Threads.

We compare SM-centric transformation with persistent threads using both SM partition and affinity-based scheduling. As aforementioned, persistent threads by itself cannot directly dictate mappings between jobs and SMs. But with careful designs, it could still support SM partition and affinity-based scheduling, although the support is very limited and requires an awkward implementation. Our specific implementations are as follows.

For SM partition between two co-running kernels, we generate $N_1 (1 \leq N_1 \leq M)$ persistent CTAs for kernel 1, and $(M - N_1)$ persistent CTAs for kernel 2 (where M is the number of SMs in the GPU). In this way, if the hardware scheduler happens to assign one CTA onto each SM, the two kernels would run on different sets of SMs, and the SM partition is materialized. Given that an even distribution is not guaranteed by hardware schedulers, in our experiments, we repeat the experiments many times and use only the results when the distribution happens to be even (performance under uneven distributions is much worse as some SMs are left idle). In order to maintain a good amount of parallelism, each CTA is set to the largest allowable size for the particular kernel, as prior usage of persistent threads often does [9, 44]. Our experiments enumerate all possible partitions (i.e., all values of N_1), and the best performance in these settings is used to compare with the performance of SM-centric transformation results.

We employ a similar idea to let persistent threads support affinity-based scheduling of single-kernel runs. The launch of a kernel creates M (i.e., number of SMs) persistent CTAs. We again use the performance measured only in the runs where the CTAs are evenly distributed on the SMs. When creating the job queue for a persistent CTA, we try to put into the queue the jobs from the same affinity group as identified with the method in Section 5.2. We again make each persistent CTA as large as allowed such that the maximum number of jobs from the CTA queue could get concurrently executed by the CTA. This method, in effect, makes the jobs run concurrently on the same SM, just as what affinity-based scheduling aims to achieve—but only to a limited degree, subject to the number of jobs a CTA can concurrently execute.

Machine Environment.

We run all workloads on an NVIDIA M2075 GPU with CUDA runtime 4.2, compiled by NVCC with the highest optimization level. The host machine has an Intel 8-core Xeon X5672 CPU and 48 GB main memory and runs 64-bit Redhat enterprise 6.2. Without notice, each reported timing result is an average of 10 repeated measurements, and includes all overhead incurred by the transformed code.

6.2 Results in Co-Runs

Figure 3 shows the speedup in terms of ANTT brought by the optimized co-runs respectively supported with SM-centric transformation and persistent threads. The baseline is the traditional and default way to concurrently execute the original kernels. The speedup is defined as the ratio of the optimized ANTT to the original ANTT. "SMC Predicted" and "SMC Optimal" represent the speedups from the SM-centric transformation with, respectively, the parameters predicted by the online model and the best parameters found through offline exhaustive search. We observe the potential speedup because of SM-centric transformation 1.36X. Our prediction model successfully exploits most of the potential by providing 1.33X speedup on average. Three co-runs benefit from the SM-centric transformation substantially with a potential of more than 1.8X speedup. The results validate that SM-centric transformation with the prediction model better exploits the SM and cache resources than the default co-runs. We also observe that the improvement of ANTTs varies across benchmarks. In some cases (e.g., the co-run of mm and reduce), the optimized co-runs have around 2% slowdown. There are two plausible rea-

Table 1: Benchmarks

Benchmark	Source	Description	Irregular
irreg	Maryland [15]	partial diff. solver	Y
nbf	Maryland [15]	force field	Y
md	SHOC [10]	molecular dynamics	Y
spmv	SHOC [10]	sparse matrix vector multi.	Y
cfd	Rodinia [7]	finite volume solver	Y
nn	Rodinia [7]	nearest neighbor	N
pf	Rodinia [7]	dynamic programming	N
mm	CUDA SDK [31]	dense matrix multiplication	N
reduce	CUDASDK [31]	reduction	N

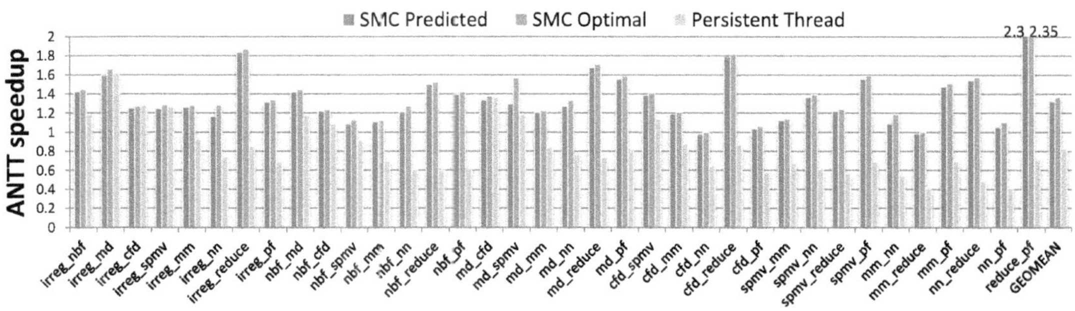

Figure 3: Speedup of average normalized turnaround time.

sons. First, the kernels already have good scalability and hence reducing the number of SMs allocated to them significantly degrades their performance. Second, since those kernels efficiently use shared memory, they do not heavily rely on L1 cache's performance. For example, when MM's thread blocks size is 256, one matrix element is reused 16 times after being loaded into shared memory.

Persistent threads perform much worse than SM-centric transformation. Its best partition leads to more than 50% ANTT degradation for 3 co-run programs. On average, we observe 17% slowdown. The main reason comes from the rigid control of parallelism in persistent threads. As the previous subsection describes, without the capability for a direct control of the job-to-SM mapping, the design of persistent threads support is subject to some restrictions on the number of a CTAs and their size, which cause suboptimal performance on the kernels.

Figure 4 provides the results on system throughput. The baseline is of the same case in Figure 3. SM-centric transformation offers up to 71% (an average of 37%) improvement on STP. The predicted configurations exploit the potential well by providing an average improvement of 33%. We did not observe any throughput degradation for the optimized co-runs, but some co-runs (e.g., cfd and mm) have trivial throughput improvement due to the same reasons as explained for the worsened ANTTs. As known [12], ANTT and STP measure different aspects of a co-run execution; a better ANTT does not always mean a better STP. For instance, the co-run of reduce and pf has the largest ANTT speedup of 2.3X, but its STP improvement is below the average.

Different from the results on ANTT, persistent threads produce an average of 11% STP improvement. The influence of persistent threads on ANTT varies greatly across co-run programs, yielding results between 63% slowdown and 64% improvement. As explained for the increased ANTT, We observe non-trivial throughput loss for some programs be-

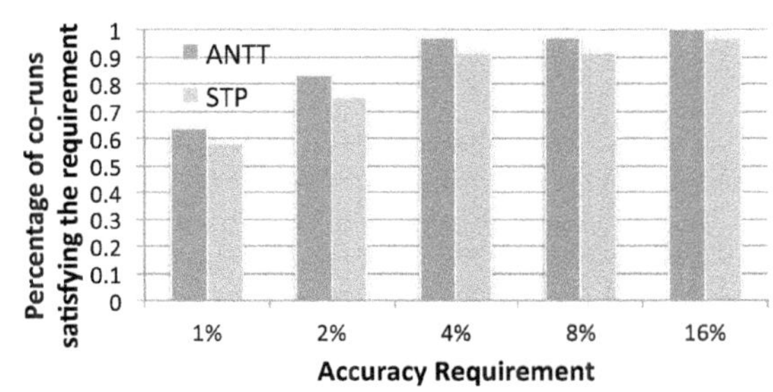

Figure 5: Prediction accuracy.

cause of the suboptimal level of parallelism. Overall, the results showed that SM-centric transformation is a much better choice for SM partitioning than persistent threads.

The SM-centric results also indicate that the simple method for predicting configurations outlined in Section 5.1 is sufficient for SM-centric transformation to effectively support SM partition. To get a direct measure of the method's effectiveness, we report in Figure 5 its accuracy in predicting the suitable configurations. The percentage on the X axis shows the accuracy requirement of the predicted configuration. To be more specific, $P\%$ means that the predicted configuration outperforms at least $N \times (1 - P\%)$ configurations, where $N (N = 36$ in this evaluation) is the total number of configurations. The bar height shows the percentage of co-runs whose predicted configuration satisfies the accuracy requirement. So the bars on the right should be higher than the bars on the left, because a larger percentage on the X axis indicates a more relaxed requirement. For ANTT, when the accuracy requirement is 1%, 63% of co-runs satisfy it. Note that 1% is a harsh requirement, as only the optimal configuration can satisfy it in a limited configuration space. If we relax the requirement to 2%, 83% of co-runs satisfy it, showing a high prediction accuracy. When the requirement

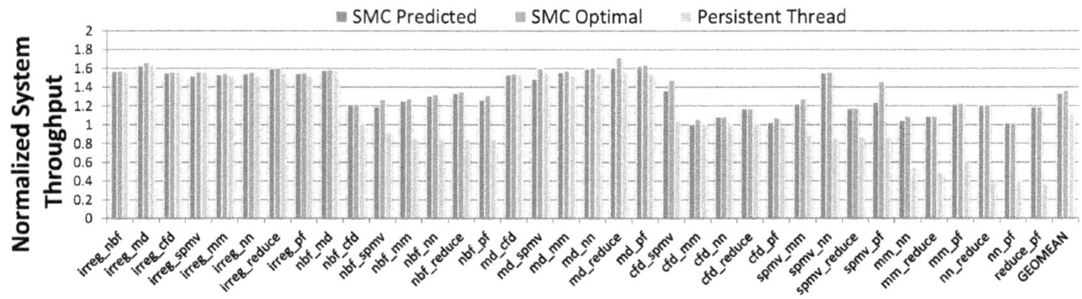

Figure 4: Improvement on system throughput.

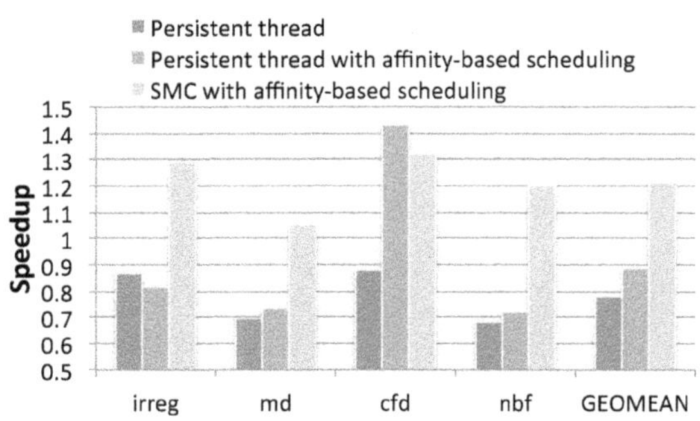

Figure 6: Speedups of single-kernel runs.

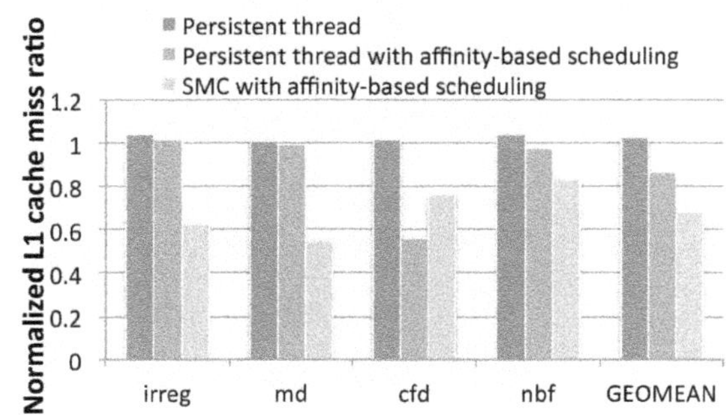

Figure 7: Normalized L1 miss ratios.

is 16%, we notice that the predicted configuration of every co-run satisfies the requirement. For STP, the prediction accuracy is a bit lower, but over 90% of co-runs satisfy the accuracy requirement of 4%. The results echo our improvement on ANTT and STP and show that a simple online model suffices to yield reasonably good configurations.

6.3 Results in Single-Kernel Runs

We also evaluate persistent threads and SM-centric transformations on single-kernel runs. We consider 4 programs (md, irreg, cfd and nbf), as they show a significant level of non-uniform data sharing and rely heavily on the data cache's performance due to their irregular memory access pattern.

Figure 6 provides the speedup results for single-kernel runs of four benchmarks over the original code. Without affinity-based scheduling, persistent threads suffer from insufficient parallelism and produce 22% performance degradation. Affinity-based scheduling improves its performance and reduces the average degradation to 15%. The results indicate that persistent threads, unlike SM-centric transformation, fails to achieve a good balance between parallelism and locality: Keeping one active thread block on each SM enables scheduling jobs with lots of data sharing to one SM, but due to the limitation of the block size, does not have enough concurrent active threads to fully explore the computing power. On the contrary, SM-centric transformation's precise control enables us to find a better trade-off between parallelism and locality, leading to an average of 21% speedup.

Figure 7 shows the L1 cache performance improvement obtained through CUDA hardware performance monitors. The reduction of the cache miss ratios shows the trends largely aligning with the speedup trends. It confirms that L1 cache performance is critical to irregular applications, and the parallelism control and affinity-based scheduling enabled by SM-centric transformation exploit L1 data cache more effectively than the default scheduling does. CFD is an exception, on which, the SM-centric approach performs less well than the persistent threads with affinity-based scheduling. A plausible reason is the effects of warp scheduling, which is out of the control of SM-centric scheduling but could sometimes affect the cache performance substantially.

6.4 Overhead from the SM-centric Transformation

SM-centric transformation adds extra code to the kernels. To quantify the overhead, for each benchmark we run the transformed kernel (with the same number of active threads as the default runs of the original kernels have) but without affinity-based scheduling, whose execution time is denoted as T_{trans}. The overhead is defined as $(T_{trans} - T_{org})/T_{org}$, where T_{org} is the execution time of the original kernel. Figure 8 provides the overhead results. We notice that the overhead can be non-trivial for some benchmarks (e.g., 6.5% for pf) due to two reasons. First, the transformation introduces atomic operations and extra memory accesses to obtain the mapping decision data. Second, the aggregation (i.e., the enhanced version of the transformation) introduces a loop, which does not exist in the original kernels. On average, the overhead from the transformation is 2.8%, but as the previous results show, the overhead is substantially outweighed by the overall benefits.

7. DISCUSSION

Currently, the SM-centric optimization works only on CUDA programs. The reason is that other GPU programming models, such as OpenCL, do not yet support run-time retrieval of

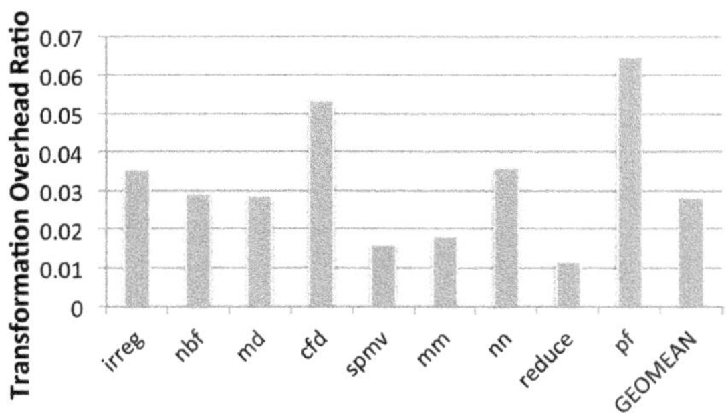

Figure 8: The percentage of overhead from SM-centric transformation.

compute unit identifier. It is our hope that with the evidence provided in this work, OpenCL community will add such a functionality in the near future. Once OpenCL provides a similar interface, the proposed optimization techniques can be easily extended to cover OpenCL programs.

OpenCL has introduced the concept of sub-device, in order to allow partitions of computing units by wrapping a subset of computing unites into a sub-device. It is however supported on only multicore CPUs. Moreover, the partitioning is at the level of OpenCL kernels or applications rather than threads, making it hard to use to manage scheduling of threads or tasks within the same kernel (e.g., the affinity-based scheduling mentioned in Section 4). SM-centric transformation offers a simple, unified solution that supports both scheduling and resource partition, and is ready to use on all GPUs that allows SM ID retrieval.

Although it might be risky to say that future GPUs will never offer interface to allow software control of thread scheduling, there is no evidence showing that such support is coming anytime soon. As a simple pure-software solution that requires no extra hardware cost and complexity, the SM-centric method has its special appeal and practical value.

The job selection component determines the job-to-SM mapping before the kernel is invoked. This fixed mapping could incur load-unbalance due to the non-uniformity in SM processing capability and jobs. It is possible to detect the load-unbalance during the sampling phase. The framework can then invoke the original kernel if load-unbalance happens. Some kernels may change dramatically across invocations in terms of execution time and memory access intensity, creating challenges to sampling-based approaches. Combination with program phase detection and prediction [36, 37] could help address such complexities.

8. RELATED WORK

Prior software methods for task scheduling on GPU mainly concentrate on persistent threads with either static or dynamic (e.g., job stealing) partition of task sets [3, 9, 13, 38, 41, 44]. As aforementioned, although persistent threads and task queues together facilitate task scheduling to a certain degree, they cannot precisely control which tasks run on which SM. It is because tasks are assigned to threads rather than SMs, and the mapping between threads and SMs is determined by hardware (with randomness). As our experiments have shown, for the precise control of task assignment to SMs, the SM-centric transformation offers new opportunities for enhancing data locality and multi-kernel co-run performance, outperforming persistent threads-based optimizations significantly.

There are some studies on changing hardware schedulers for performance, such as the large warp architecture by Narasiman and others [28], the two-level warp scheduler by Jog and his colleagues [18, 19], and the thread block scheduler by Kayiran and others [20]. The SM-centric scheduling is a software solution to the restrictions of hardware schedulers, orthogonal to these hardware approaches. There are some software scheduling works published before, the focus of which have been dealing with the load balance between CPUs and GPUs through task scheduling [4, 26].

Recent years have seen an increasing interest in supporting concurrent executions of GPU kernels. Pai et al. [33] observed significant resource under-utilization during concurrent kernel executions. They proposed elastic kernels to balance resource usage among concurrent kernels through fine-grained resource control. According to the authors of elastic kernels, the technique does not control SM partitions, and cannot be applied to kernels that use shared memory [33]. The spatial scheduling enabled in this work is complementary to elastic kernels, in the sense that it is not subject to the shared-memory limitation, and it improves co-run performance from a different angle, spatial scheduling. These two techniques can be used together. Adriaens and others [2] proposed hardware extensions to partition SMs to different applications for more efficient resource utilization, and evaluated it on a simulator. Zhong and He [48] proposed a runtime system, named Kernelet, which slices kernels into sub-kernels and schedule them for better resource control. It does not enable spatial scheduling of the GPU. CTA aggregation itself is not new. Earlier work has used a similar idea to control resources a kernel uses [33]. It is for the first time used for supporting spatial scheduling.

Many studies have been proposed to improve GPU memory performance, including data placement in memory [8] or on chip [23], streamlining irregular memory accesses or control flows at runtime [43, 45, 46], bypassing L1 cache [17] and so on. The precise control of task-SM affinity enabled by SM-centric transformation opens new opportunities, as illustrated by the affinity-based scheduling.

9. CONCLUSION

This paper presents SM-centric transformation, a simple method that for the first time offers a systematic solution to enable program-level spatial scheduling on the GPU. It reveals the potential of the enabled scheduling control for executions of both single-kernel runs and multi-kernel co-runs. It lists some main challenges for leveraging spatial scheduling on the GPU, and develops a set of practical solutions. It opens up opportunities for leveraging scheduling for optimizing GPU executions.

Acknowledgement This material is based upon work supported by DOE Early Career Award and the National Science Foundation (NSF) under Grant No. 1464216, No. 1320796 and CAREER Award. Any opinions, findings, and conclusions or recommendations expressed in this material are those of the authors and do not necessarily reflect the views of DOE or NSF.

10. REFERENCES

[1] NVIDIA CUDA. `http://www.nvidia.com/cuda`.

[2] J. T. Adriaens, K. Compton, N. S. Kim, and M. J. Schulte. The Case for GPGPU Spatial Multitasking. In *Proceedings of HPCA*, 2012.

[3] T. Aila and S. Laine. Understanding the efficiency of ray traversal on gpus. In *Proceedings of the Conference on High Performance Graphics 2009*, HPG '09, 2009.

[4] M. E. Belviranli, L. N. Bhuyan, and R. Gupta. A dynamic self-scheduling scheme for heterogeneous multiprocessor architectures. *ACM Trans. Archit. Code Optim.*, 9(4), Jan. 2013.

[5] A. Betts, N. Chong, A. Donaldson, S. Qadeer, and P. Thomson. Gpuverify: A verifier for gpu kernels. In *OOPSLA*, 2012.

[6] M. Burtscher, R. Nasre, and K. Pingali. A quantitative study of irregular programs on gpus. In *IISWC*, 2012.

[7] S. Che, M. Boyer, J. Meng, D. Tarjan, J. W. Sheaffer, S.-H. Lee, and K. Skadron. Rodinia: A benchmark suite for heterogeneous computing. In *IISWC*, 2009.

[8] G. Chen, B. Wu, D. Li, and X. Shen. Porple: An extensible optimizer for portable data placement on gpu. In *Proceedings of MICRO*, 2014.

[9] L. Chen, O. Villa, S. Krishnamoorthy, and G. Gao. Dynamic load balancing on single-and multi-gpu systems. In *IPDPS*, 2010.

[10] A. Danalis, G. Marin, C. McCurdy, J. S. Meredith, P. C. Roth, K. Spafford, V. Tipparaju, and J. S. Vetter. The scalable heterogeneous computing (shoc) benchmark suite. In *GPGPU*, 2010.

[11] C. Ding and K. Kennedy. Improving cache performance in dynamic applications through data and computation reorganization at run time. In *PLDI*, 1999.

[12] S. Eyerman and L. Eeckhout. System-level performance metrics for multiprogram workloads. *IEEE Micro*, 28(3), May 2008.

[13] K. Gupta, J. A. Stuart, and J. D. Owens. A study of persistent threads style gpu programming for gpgpu workloads. In *Innovative Parallel Computing*, 2012.

[14] H. Han and C. W. Tseng. Improving locality for adaptive irregular scientific codes. In *LCPC*, 2000.

[15] H. Han and C.-W. Tseng. Exploiting locality for irregular scientific codes. *TPDS*, 17(7):606–618, 2006.

[16] S. Herbert and D. Marculescu. Characterizing chip-multiprocessor variability-tolerance. In *DAC*, 2008.

[17] W. Jia, K. A. Shaw, and M. Martonosi. Characterizing and improving the use of demand-fetched caches in gpus. In *ICS*, 2012.

[18] A. Jog, O. Kayiran, A. K. Mishra, M. T. Kandemir, O. Mutlu, R. Iyer, and C. R. Das. Orchestrated scheduling and prefetching for gpgpus. In *ISCA*, 2013.

[19] A. Jog, O. Kayiran, N. Nachiappan, A. K. Mishra, M. T. Kandemir, O. Mutlu, R. Iyer, and C. R. Das. OWL: Cooperative Thread Array Aware Scheduling Techniques for Improving GPGPU performance. In *ASPLOS*, 2013.

[20] O. Kayiran, A. Jog, M. T. Kandemir, and C. R. Das. Neither More Nor Less: Optimizing Thread-level Parallelism for GPGPUs. In *PACT*, 2013.

[21] J. Lee, V. Sathisha, M. J. Schulte, K. Compton, and N. S. Kim. Improving throughput of power-constrained gpus using dynamic voltage/frequency and core scaling. In *PACT*, 2011.

[22] S. Lee, T. Johnson, and R. Eigenmann. Cetus - an extensible compiler infrastructure for source-to-source transformation. In *LCPC*, pages 539–553, 2003.

[23] C. Li, Y. Yang, Z. Lin, and H. Zhou. Automatic data placement into gpu on-chip memory resources. In *Proceedings of CGO*, 2015.

[24] J. Li, G. Tan, M. Chen, and N. Sun. Smat: an input adaptive auto-tuner for sparse matrix-vector multiplication. In *PLDI*, 2013.

[25] Y. Liu, E. Z. Zhang, and X. Shen. A cross-input adaptive framework for gpu programs optimization. In *IPDPS*, pages 1–10, 2009.

[26] C. Luk, S. Hong, and H. Kim. Qilin: Exploiting parallelism on heterogeneous multiprocessors with adaptive mapping. In *MICRO*, 2009.

[27] N. Mitchell, L. Carter, and J. Ferrante. Localizing non-affine array references. In *PACT*, 1999.

[28] V. Narasiman, M. Shebanow, C. J. Lee, R. Miftakhutdinov, O. Mutlu, and Y. N. Patt. Improving gpu performance via large warps and two-level warp scheduling. In *MICRO*, 2011.

[29] R. Nasre, M. Burtscher, and K. Pingali. Data-driven versus topology-driven irregular computations on gpus. In *IPDPS*, 2013.

[30] R. Nasre, M. Burtscher, and K. Pingali. Morph algorithms on gpus. In *PPOPP*, 2013.

[31] NVIDIA. Cuda software development toolkit v4.2. https://developer.nvidia.com/cuda-toolkit-42-archive.

[32] NVIDIA. Nvidia's next generation cuda computer architecture: Fermi.

[33] S. Pai, M. J. Thazhuthaveetil, and R. Govindarajan. Improving GPGPU Concurrency with Elastic Kernels. In *ASPLOS*, 2013.

[34] NVIDIA Parallel Thread Execution. http://docs.nvidia.com/cuda/parallel-thread-execution/index.html.

[35] X. Shen, Y. Gao, C. Ding, and R. Archambault. Lightweight reference affinity analysis. In *ICS*, Cambridge, MA, June 2005.

[36] X. Shen, Y. Zhong, and C. Ding. Locality phase prediction. In *Proceedings of the International Conference on Architectural Support for Programming Languages and Operating Systems*, pages 165–176, 2004.

[37] T. Sherwood, S. Sair, and B. Calder. Phase tracking and prediction. In *Proceedings of International Symposium on Computer Architecture*, pages 336–349, San Diego, CA, June 2003.

[38] M. Steinberger, M. Kenzel, P. Boechat, B. Kerbl, M. Dokter, and D. Schmalstieg. Whippletree: Task-based scheduling of dynamic workloads on the gpu. *ACM Transactions on Computer Systems*, 33(6), 2014.

[39] M. M. Strout, L. Carter, and J. Ferrante. Compile-time composition of run-time data and iteration reorderings. In *PLDI*, 2003.

[40] N. Tuck and D. M. Tullsen. Initial observations of the simultaneous multithreading pentium 4 processor. In *PACT*, 2003.

[41] S. Tzeng, A. Patney, and J. D. Owens. Task management for irregular-parallel workloads on the gpu. In *Proceedings of the Conference on High Performance Graphics*, 2010.

[42] B. Wu, E. Zhang, and X. Shen. Enhancing data locality for dynamic simulations through asynchronous data transformations and adaptive control. In *PACT*, 2011.

[43] B. Wu, Z. Zhao, E. Z. Zhang, Y. Jiang, and X. Shen. Complexity analysis and algorithm design for reorganizing data to minimize non-coalesced memory accesses on gpu. In *PPoPP*, 2013.

[44] S. Xiao and W. chun Feng. Inter-block gpu communication via fast barrier synchronization. In *IPDPS*, 2010.

[45] E. Zhang, Y. Jiang, Z. Guo, K. Tian, and X. Shen. On-the-fly elimination of dynamic irregularities for gpu computing. In *ASPLOS*, 2011.

[46] E. Z. Zhang, Y. Jiang, Z. Guo, and X. Shen. Streamlining gpu applications on the fly. In *ICS*, pages 115–125, 2010.

[47] M. Zheng, V. T. Ravi, F. Qin, and G. Agrawal. Grace: A low-overhead mechanism for detecting data races in gpu programs. In *PPoPP*, 2011.

[48] J. Zhong and B. He. Kernelet: High-throughput gpu kernel executions with dynamic slicing and scheduling. *CoRR*, abs/1303.5164, 2013.

[49] Y. Zhong, M. Orlovich, X. Shen, and C. Ding. Array regrouping and structure splitting using whole-program reference affinity. In *PLDI*, 2004.

Datacenter Efficiency – What's Next?

Ricardo Bianchini
Professor, Rutgers University and Chief Efficiency Strategist, Microsoft Research

Abstract
Over the last 10+ years, large datacenters have benefited from computer technology and physical infrastructure advances that substantially improved their efficiency. However, there is still much room for improvement, as the datacenters' computational resources are often poorly utilized and technology advances are starting to falter. In this talk, I will discuss some interesting avenues for continued efficiency improvement driven by smarter software, including greater use of parallelism and predictive workload scheduling.

ACM Classification
C.m [*Computer Systems Organizations*]: Miscellaneous

Keywords
Datacenters; performance and energy management; parallelism; scheduling; total cost of ownership

BIO

Dr. Ricardo Bianchini received his PhD degree in Computer Science from the University of Rochester. He is a Professor of Computer Science at Rutgers University, but is currently on leave working as Microsoft's Chief Efficiency Strategist. His main interests include cloud computing, and power/energy/thermal management of datacenters. In fact, Dr. Bianchini is a pioneer in datacenter energy management, energy-aware storage systems, energy-aware load distribution across datacenters, and leveraging renewable energy in datacenters. He has published eight award papers, and has received the CAREER award from the National Science Foundation. He is currently an ACM Distinguished Scientist and an IEEE Fellow.

ICS'15, June 8-11, 2015, Newport Beach/Irvine, CA, USA.
ACM 978-1-4503-3559-1/15/06.
http://dx.doi.org/10.1145/2751205.2751207

Towards Lightweight and Swift Storage Resource Management in Big Data Cloud Era

Ruijin Zhou
University of Florida
Gainesville, Florida, USA
zhourj@ufl.edu

Huixiang Chen
University of Florida
Gainesville, Florida, USA
stanley.chen@ufl.edu

Tao Li
University of Florida
Gainesville, Florida, USA
taoli@ece.ufl.edu

ABSTRACT

Workload IO behavior in modern data centers is fluctuating and unpredictable due to the rapidly adopted, public cloud environment. Nevertheless, existing storage resource management systems, such as *VMware SDRS*, are incapable of performing real time policy-based storage management due to the high cost of migrating large size virtual disks. Hence, the traditional storage management schemes become ineffective due to the lack of quick response to the frequent IO bursts and the inaccurate storage latency prediction in the light of a highly fluctuating environment.

To address the aforementioned issues, we propose *LightSRM*, which can work properly in a time-variant cloud environment. To mitigate the storage migration cost, we leverage copy-on-write/read snapshots to redirect the IO requests without moving the virtual disk. To support snapshots in storage management, we also build a performance model specifically for snapshots. We employ exponentially weighted moving average with adjustable sliding window to provide quick and accurate performance prediction. Furthermore, we propose a hybrid management scheme, which can dynamically choose either snapshot or migration for fastest performance tuning.

We build our prototype in a QEMU/KVM based virtualized environment. Our empirical evaluation results show that snapshot can redirect IO requests in a faster manner than migration can do when the virtual disk size is large. Besides, snapshot method has less disk performance impact on the applications. By employing hybrid snapshot/migration method, *LightSRM* yields less overall latency, better load balance, and less IO traffic overhead.

Categories and Subject Descriptors

D.4.2 [**Operating Systems**]: Storage Management; D.4.8 [**Operating Systems**]: Performance

General Terms

Management, Performance, Design

Keywords

Distributed Storage Management; Snapshot; Storage Migration; Storage Virtualization

1. INTRODUCTION

Automatic storage resource management in virtualized data centers has been introduced to lower the maintenance labor costs for several years. The key idea is to automatically rearrange and migrate virtual disks so that the performance of storage pools can meet specific IT requirements (e.g. performance load balancing and capacity planning). Commercial software, such as *VMware SDRS* [1, 2], has been deployed in real data centers for many years. However, due to the large size of virtual disks, virtual storage migration takes a long time and causes high IO traffic overhead to the system. To mitigate the overhead, existing storage management schemes have to avoid frequent virtual storage migration. Typically, a storage management system monitors performance characteristics during the daytime while only performs the storage migration at late night [1, 5].

ICS'15, June 8–11, 2015, Newport Beach, CA, USA.

http://dx.doi.org/10.1145/2751205.2751230

In the era of public/hybrid cloud and big data analytics, modern data centers usually host multi-tenant cloud platforms [24] and run big data applications [18, 25]. Unlike the traditional server applications, big data and cloud workloads exhibit highly fluctuating and unpredictable IO behaviors. On one hand, any user/tenant on the cloud platform can submit jobs at any time, which introduces unexpected workload surges. On the other hand, the big data applications manifest distinct IO behaviors across different execution phases [26, 27]. These workload surges occur within a couple of hours or even minutes, leading to unexpected storage load imbalance.

Although the traditional storage resource management schemes [3, 4, 5] works fine in a private data center that executes most of the jobs at daytime and keeps idle at night, they often fail to respond to the real-time IO burst in a public/hybrid cloud due to the large size of virtual disks. Moving a virtual disk from one storage pool to another can take tens of minutes or hours, during which the workload behavior may have already changed. Worse, the current load-balancing interval (i.e. 8~16 hours) is too long for detecting and responding to workload surges. These limitations can lead to: 1) high average latency of the entire storage system; 2) extremely unbalanced storage resource utilization; and 3) low quality of service (QoS) and frequently breaking service level agreement (SLA).

To solve these issues, we propose a lightweight and fast storage management scheme, *LightSRM*, which can quickly respond to workload surges. To free storage management from large virtual disks and lengthy migration duration, we use copy-on-write/read snapshots as basic units to tune the IO performance. The overhead of creating and merging a snapshot is much smaller than that of migrating the entire virtual disk. Since the introduction of snapshot changes the storage IO behavior, we build a performance model for the copy-on-write/read snapshot. With the help of quick performance tuning, we can deploy a real-time performance tracking mechanism, exponentially weighted moving average with adjustable sliding window, to provide an accurate latency prediction. In the end, based on our characterization of both snapshots and migration, we propose a hybrid method in *LightSRM*, which can dynamically decide to use either snapshot or migration to achieve the fastest performance tuning.

We implement our prototype in a *QEMU/KVM* [12, 13] based virtualized environment. We adopt libvirt [15] as our communication framework to obtain the information of virtual machines and send commands to virtualized servers. We also implement the traditional storage resource management scheme [4] in our environment for comparison purpose. Our experiments show that snapshot has less transition time when the virtual disk size is large whereas migration is faster when the virtual disk size is small enough. In our tests, snapshot yields 90% less performance impact on the running applications. Equipped with hybrid snapshot/migration method, *LightSRM* can provide lower average storage latency (91% lower in our tests) and better-balanced storage environment (93% better) than the traditional method. Besides, hybrid method generates 44% and 91% less disk IO traffic than snapshot-only and migration-only methods respectively.

Note that all prior proposals [3, 4, 5] take the assumption of large virtual disks and long storage migration time. The focus is on improving performance prediction to lower the chance of making incorrect migration decisions. Our *LightSRM*, however, tackles the root cause of the clumsy storage management by leveraging lightweight snapshot. The technical contributions of this paper are the following: 1) a snapshot-based performance tuning method, 2) a performance model for copy-on-write/read snapshot, 3) a quick and simplified storage performance tracking and modeling scheme, and 4) a hybrid mechanism that chooses snapshot or migration online for faster performance tuning.

The rest of this paper is organized as follows. Section 2 describes the background and related works. Section 3 analyzes the system behaviors and shows the motivation of this paper. Section 4 describes our design in detail. Sections 5 and 6 present the evaluation on *LightSRM*. Section 7 concludes the paper.

2. BACKGROUND AND RELATED WORK

Storage management has been intensively studied in more than a decade. Prior works mainly focused on physical devices [8, 19, 20, 21, 22, 23]. As virtualization has been widely adopted in data centers, efforts of managing storage resources via virtual machines have emerged. Singh et al. [9] proposed HARMONY system along with VectorDot algorithm to minimize performance degradation. However, VectorDot algorithm only considers the storage system utilization and ignores the workload behaviors. Related works that consider both the device and workload behaviors include Basil [3], Pesto [4], and Romano [5]. They leverage workload and device characteristics reported by the virtual machine monitor and rearrange storage resources by migrating virtual disks across different storage pools.

Gulati et al. [3] proposed Basil system, which can automatically balance IO load across storage devices. Both workload and device models are developed in this work. Based on these models, storage latency can be predicted and the load-balancing algorithm is performed accordingly. However, the storage model in this work is built offline, which limits its usability in a real system.

To address this issue, Gulati et al. [4] proposed Pesto system, which incorporates an online storage model (*L-Q* model). A workload injector is implemented to proactively adjust the storage model online when the system is not busy. Besides, a cost benefit function and the congestion management are also introduced in this work. A commercial product [1] is based on Pesto scheme.

Park et al. [5] found that both Basil and Pesto make improper balance decisions at some corner cases due to the limitation of their models. The authors proposed Romano, which makes multiple load-balancing decisions before actually migrating the virtual disks. Simulated annealing algorithm is used to filter out the potentially incorrect decisions.

All existing storage management schemes share several common drawbacks. The basic unit of these management schemes is a virtual disk, whose size can range from several hundreds of GBs to even several TBs. However, migrating large size virtual disk may result in long migration time and high performance impact. Although there have been efforts [6, 29] to improve the efficiency of storage migration, the cost of migrating large size virtual disks is still significant. The lengthy migration process hinders the current storage management from being used in real time. Instead of tracking and migrating virtual disks frequently, existing systems usually monitor and collect performance characteristics during the entire daytime, then uses 95% percentile of the sampled data to predict the average latency of next day. The actual load balancing decisions and storage migrations are made at night when no application is running. Traditional methods can achieve desirable load balancing effect in the light of a private data center that has steady IO behavior.

Nevertheless, for modern data centers that host public cloud platforms (e.g. Amazon AWS [16], Microsoft Azure [17]) and run big data applications [18], workload IO behavior can heavily fluctuate even within one day. Basak et al. [7] built a dynamic performance model for multi-tenant cloud. However, no resource-scheduling algorithm is proposed. Alvarez et al. [30] presented an approach to select cloud storage services from a cloud tenant's perspective. In a multi-tenant cloud environment, highly varying IO behavior leads to frequent storage load imbalance, which cannot be handled in a timely manner using existing storage management schemes. Worse, public cloud usually requires 24/7 services, which has no idle time at night for the traditional management scheme to perform storage migration.

3. SYSTEM BEHAVIOR ANALYSIS

This section analyzes performance fluctuation of the storage system in the light of multi-tenant cloud workloads and big data applications [10, 11]. Based on the observations, we are motivated to propose a new performance tuning method: snapshot. We then explain the benefits and new challenges of using snapshot.

3.1. Storage Performance Fluctuation

Traditional server applications, including file servers, mail servers, and database servers, have relatively stable IO behaviors. Therefore, the storage pools that host these types of applications yield predictable latency on a daily basis.

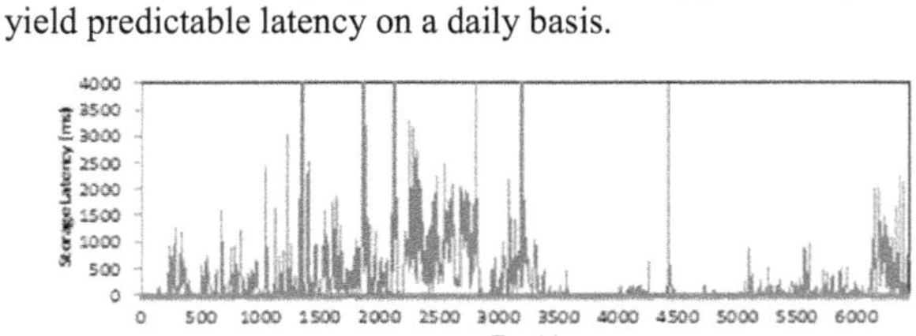

Figure 1. Average storage latency when running five hadoop virtual machines (VMs) on two storage pools

However, modern datacenters also host the multi-tenant public cloud environments and run big data workloads. In a multi-tenant cloud environment, the tenants' behaviors can vary from day to day. For big data workloads, even the application itself manifests frequent IO bursts, which leads to highly fluctuating storage latency. In Figure 1, we create five virtual machines in two storage pools and use them as hadoop nodes. The hardware platform configuration can be found in Section 5.1. We iteratively run applications of *hibench suite* [11]. As can be seen, the average storage latency of the two storage pools is high with a large variance.

Table 1. Storage latency (ms) when running big data workloads

	Average Latency	Standard Deviation
PageRank	35.6	119.3
Bayes	24.4	102.2
HiveBench	2.0	6.4
Kmeans	29.3	71.1
Nutchindex	41.9	77.5
Sort	133.9	121.8
TeraSort	43.1	55.3
Wordcount	52.7	111.6

We further analyze two types of performance variance that can occur in data centers.

1) Workload itself has a time-variant IO behavior. Table 1 shows the storage latency with its standard deviation during the execution of our big data workloads. In this experiment, we create five virtual machines, each of which is placed in a separated storage pool to avoid any resource contention. During the application execution, we measure the storage latency and its standard deviation of one storage pool. As can be seen in Table 1, the standard deviation of the storage latency is much larger than the average value. This indicates that big data workloads exhibit highly fluctuating IO behaviors even in one virtual disk. The large standard deviation also reveals the bias of using single average value to represent the storage latency for the entire execution period. A further investigation of application behaviors reveals that they all have highly varying IO characteristics (e.g. OIO, Read/Write Ratio, Randomness, IO size). Therefore, using the IO characteristics of the entire daytime to predict the storage latency of the next day is inaccurate.

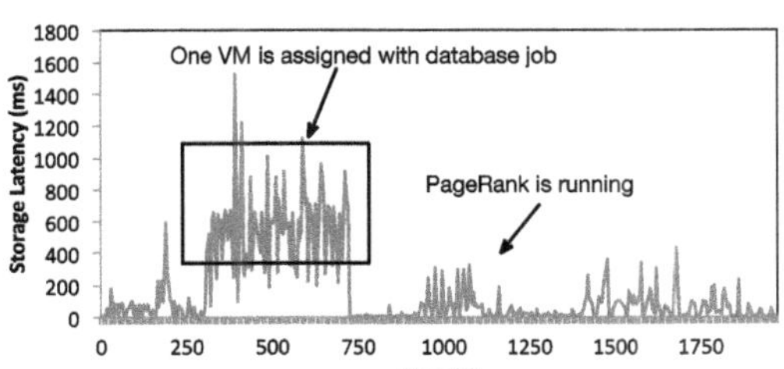

Figure 2. Average storage latency when running five hadoop VMs (during the execution, the idle VM is scheduled to run a database job)

2) New tasks can run at any time. In a multi-tenant public cloud environment, each tenant can activate his/her rented virtual machines to run applications at any time. Therefore, it is not possible to predict the tenant behaviors. Even with a strict job scheduling policy, it is challenging to predict what type of application the tenant is going to execute (IO intensive or not). In Figure 2, we create six virtual machines on six storage pools. The *PageRank* application using five virtual machines runs in the background. At a certain time, the remaining virtual machine (VM) is assigned with database job and runs for a period of time. In this experiment, we measure the average storage latency of the six storage pools. As shown in Figure 2, the average latency bumps up once the idle VM is activated to run. In real datacenters, this type of latency jump can occur more frequently. The uncertainty of when a new application is going to be scheduled makes the storage latency prediction even harder.

To sum up, the system's performance behavior is very difficult to predict if not impossible. The datacenter administrator has no idea what type of application is going to run at which time. Even under a strict scheduling policy, the application itself has time-variant IO behaviors. Traditional storage management systems yield inaccurate performance prediction because they use the performance statistics of one day to predict the storage latency of next day.

3.2. Motivations and Challenges

Based on the experiments above, we find that storage latency is highly fluctuating and unpredictable. To ensure the policy-based storage management works properly, virtual disks have to be migrated frequently to tune the IO performance. However, the size of virtual disk is usually too large to move quickly, hence making the real-time storage management impossible. Worse, a multi-tenant public cloud environment requires 24/7 service. The conventional way that performs migration at night will not work in this situation. To implement a real time storage performance management, we have to tackle the root cause: the large size virtual disk.

Snapshot technology, which is usually used to make backups/checkpoints, can almost instantly redirect IO requests to a new location (the snapshot file). Once a snapshot is made, all the upcoming write requests will be issued to the new location immediately. The read requests will be issued to wherever the latest data is. If copy-on-read technology is enabled, the data blocks will only be fetched once from the old location to the new location. Then, all the following reads will be issued to the new location. Simply put, we can leverage snapshot as sort of cache, which will be gradually filled in the destination storage. Theoretically, snapshot can change the IO load more quickly than migration.

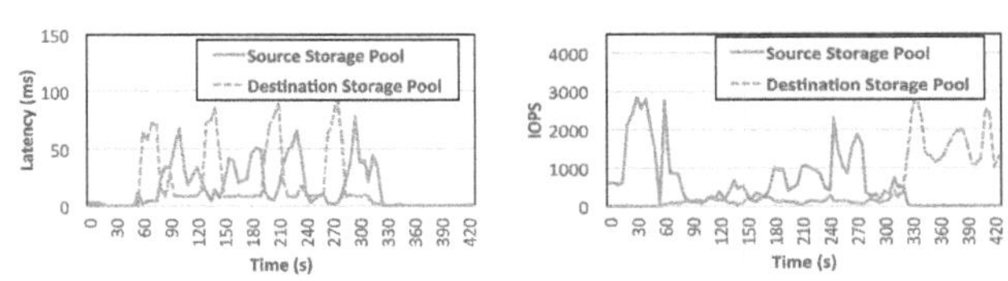

(a) Storage Latency (b) Storage IOPS

Figure 3. Performance when using storage migration

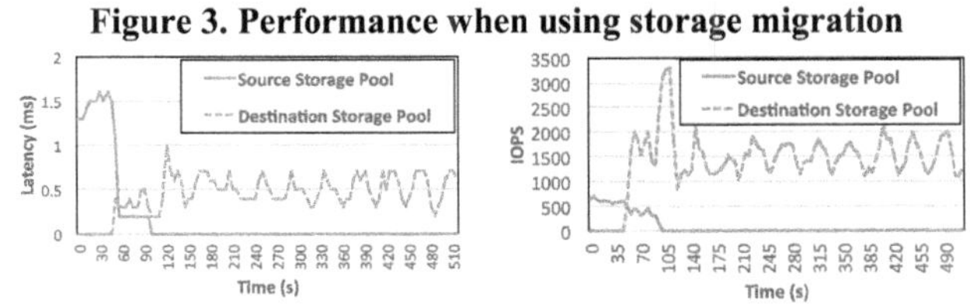

(a) Storage Latency (b) Storage IOPS

Figure 4. Performance when using snapshot

To prove the above theory, we perform a simple experiment as shown in Figures 3 and 4. At the beginning, a disk workload running inside one virtual disk is placed at source storage pool. The storage latency is around 1.5ms. We plan to move the workload to the destination storage pool and lower the latency to below 1ms. In Figure 3, we migrate the virtual disk from source to destination via the default QEMU migration method. We find that the migration takes a long time and the storage latency jumps to a much higher value in both source (around 70ms) and destination (around 60ms) storage pool as shown in Figure 3 (a). Consequently, the storage throughput (IOPS shown in Figure 3 (b)) drops to a lower value. In Figure 4, we take a snapshot and place it on the destination pool. As can be seen in Figure 4 (a), immediately, the latency of source storage pool drops and the latency of destination pool increases. The reason is that the write requests are served by destination storage instantly. The latency of the source storage maintains at a low level to serve the read requests. After all the needed data blocks are fetched to the snapshot, the latency of source storage further drops to zero and the workloads completely runs on the destination storage. Same trend can be found for the throughput (Figure 4 (b)). Therefore, using snapshot to tune IO performance is faster and has lower impact on the storage performance.

Despite the fact that snapshot can swiftly tune IO performance, using snapshot also poses several new challenges to existing storage management systems: 1) how to implement copy-on-write/read snapshot in real systems, 2) how to build a performance model for snapshot, 3) how to quickly track the storage performance, and 4) how to deal with small size virtual disks, which can be migrated quickly.

Therefore, we are motivated to build *LightSRM*, a lightweight storage management system that is based on the foundation of snapshot. In *LightSRM,* snapshot is responsible for the performance tuning while virtual disk is just used to guarantee the functional correctness. Besides, *LightSRM* redesign the entire management stack to address the above new challenges.

4. DESIGN AND IMPLEMENTATION

Figure 5 shows the design overview of *LightSRM.* On each virtualized server, we implement a copy-on-write/read snapshot on top of the original virtual disk to hold the working set of the running applications. On a centralized datacenter management server, a storage manager is implemented to perform performance load balancing and capacity planning. The performance tracking and balancing only operate on the snapshots while the capacity prediction and planning only manage the base virtual disks. Performance load balancing is triggered more frequently (every 5 minutes) than capacity planning (every 16 hours). In this paper, we redesign the performance management while still using the traditional way to do capacity planning. They do not interfere with each other.

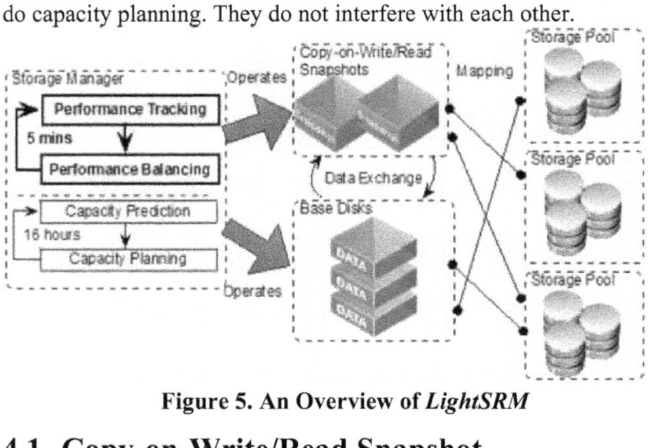

Figure 5. An Overview of *LightSRM*

4.1. Copy-on-Write/Read Snapshot

Snapshot is a common technology for backups and checkpoints. In the instance of failure, the virtual disk can be easily reverted to the previously consistent state. In original snapshot design, copy-on-write technology is leveraged to copy data from source disk to new disk only when the workload issues writes. Since the block size of snapshot usually is not larger than the IO size, there is no need to fetch data from old disks. The read requests, on the other hand, will be issued to wherever the latest data is. Therefore, making an original snapshot only redirects the write requests not the read requests.

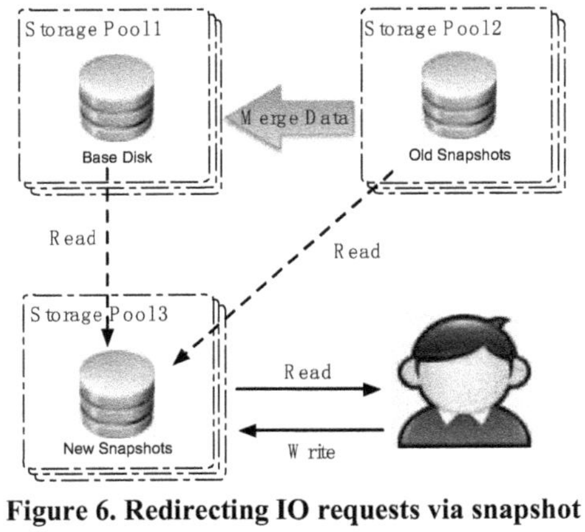

Figure 6. Redirecting IO requests via snapshot

In order to redirect the real requests as well, we add copy-on-read into snapshot design as shown in Figure 6. With copy-on-read technology, the read request will trigger the new snapshot to fetch the latest data from the old snapshot or the base virtual disk. After the data blocks are fetched to the new snapshot, the following reads to those data blocks will be served by the new snapshot, thereby redirecting the read requests to the new storage pool. Depending on the workload behavior, the time for the fetching process varies. Typically, it is much less than migration time since the working set size of a certain application is smaller than the virtual disk size. We will cover the cases when the fetching process takes longer time than the migration time in Section 4.4.

Combining both copy-on-write and copy-on-read enables snapshots to quickly divert IO requests to the destination storage. The only unsolved puzzle left is the old snapshot. If we keep it, we save the IO traffic and the time of transferring the old snapshot. However, as time goes, there will be a lot of snapshots scattered around the storage pools, which will yield high level of fragmentation. Worse, a long chain of snapshots not only makes the management even harder but also adds high indexing overhead to each IO request. Therefore, *LightSRM* merges the old snapshot to the base virtual disk at the moment the new snapshot is created as shown in Figure 6. Since the size of old snapshot (the workload working set size) is much smaller than the virtual disk size, the merging time is also shorter than migration time.

In sum, there are two phases of using copy-on-write /read snapshot to redirect IO requests:

Phase #1: *Merging and Fetching.* In this phase, *LightSRM* merges the old snapshot to base virtual disk while fetching the needed data to the new snapshot. As shown in Figure 6, additional IO traffic will be generated on storage pools 1, 2, and 3.

Phase #2: *Merging or Fetching.* In this phase, either merging or fetching process finishes. The unfinished process will continue transmitting the data.

After Phase #2, workload will completely run on destination storage. Therefore, we define the time used for Phases #1 and #2 as the *transition time* for snapshot. Similarly, the transition time for migration is the migration time.

4.2. Storage Latency Prediction

Now that we can quickly rebalance the performance load by just taking a snapshot, we need a new, fast, and accurate way to track the storage latency. In our experiments, we find out that the IO behaviors are not entirely random. For a certain period of time, the workload exhibits stable behaviors, which results in relatively stable storage latency (shown as dot line in Figure 7). The length of the stable period is workload dependent. In those periods, the average value can represent the storage latency. Similar issues have been identified and tackled in memory usage tracking [32] and network traffic estimation [33]. We tailor and customize their exponentially weighted moving average methods (*EWMA*) in our storage latency prediction.

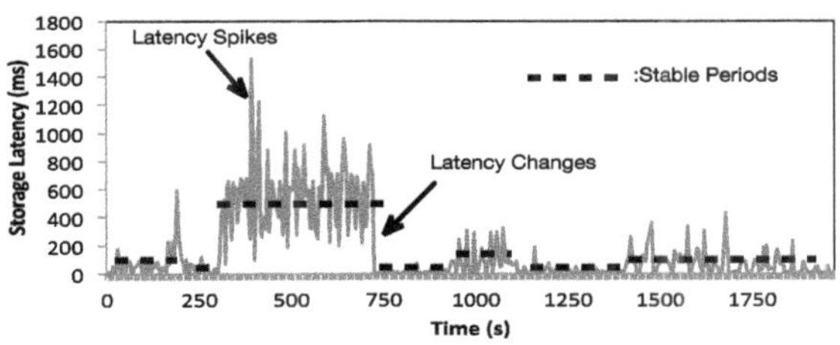

Figure 7. Latency stable period, latency changes, and latency spikes in storage latency

LightSRM employs a self-adjustable sliding window tracking mechanism. Initially, the sliding window size is set as q. In the sliding window, *LightSRM* will sample the latency of each storage pool for q times. Then, we apply *EWMA* to those q samples. The equation is as below:

$$L_t = \alpha * (L_{t-1} + (1-\alpha)L_{t-2} + \cdots + (1-\alpha)^{i-1}L_{t-i}) \quad (1)$$

where L_i means the i_{th} sample of latency and $0 < \alpha < 1$. In our system, we set α to 0.5. We calculate the L_t for all the storage pools in the system. These values will be used for the load balancing schemes.

As time elapses, new sample points will be added to the sliding window while the oldest point will be left out. In the stable periods, this method can predict the storage latency accurately. However, in the case of the sudden latency change as shown in Figure 7, the weighted average value is not able to quickly detect it in a few sample points. In order to address this issue, we keep comparing the deviation of the latest sample point with the standard deviation of the entire sampling window. If the deviation of latest sample point is much higher than the standard deviation in the sliding window, we mark the point as *deviant*. If the *deviants* keep appearing in the most recent sample points, it is highly possible that the storage latency changes to another value for the next several periods. We will intentionally set the weights of previous samples to 0 so that only the *deviant* determines the latency of next period.

A fast *EWMA* (short sliding window) can quickly detect latency changes. However, it can be easily misled by *deviant* (latency spike as shown in Figure 7). A slow *EWMA* (long sliding window) can provide smooth estimation. However, it might cover two different IO behaviors and report inaccurate latency value. In Carl's work on memory tracking [32], both *EWMA*s are maintained and the maximum value is chosen as the memory working set size. However, in latency prediction, always choosing maximum value is not accurate. Therefore, *LightSRM* leverages a self-adjustable sliding window. We increase the length of the sliding window by Δq if the reported latency value keeps flipping and decrease the length by Δq if the reported latency does not change for a long time. In our prototypes, Δq is set to be one sample point.

Storage latency tracking is part of the storage manger, running on a control server. The latency of the storage pools is reported by *pt-diskstats* [14] and sent to the storage manager. As can be seen in Figure 8, our latency tracking mechanism can successfully track the latency changes and report accurate latency value for the next period.

In the realm of time series analysis, many prediction methods are proposed, such as exponentially smoothing, moving average with different sizes of sliding window, and auto regression. They all serve the same purpose: predict the future value by the history value. We compare all of them in Section 6.3.

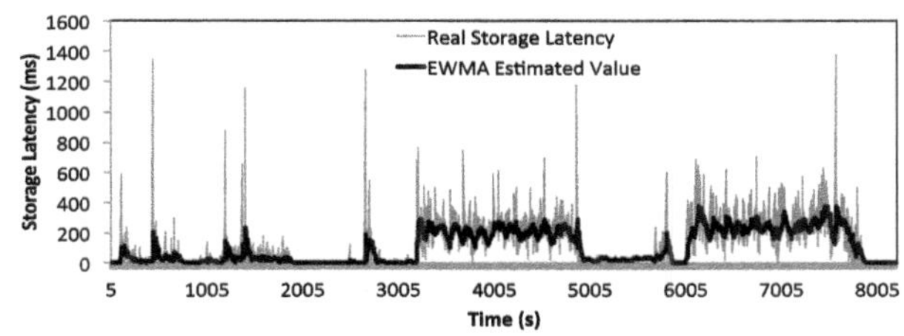

Figure 8. *EWMA* tracking for the storage latency

4.3. Performance Modeling

Performance modeling consists of two parts: workload modeling and storage device modeling. For the workload modeling, we find that the workload model can be constructed using its outstanding IOs (OIOs), IO size, Read/Write Ratio, and Randomness. This is also verified in prior research work [3, 4, 5]. Their workload model is built as below.

$$WL_i = f(OIO, IOsize, Read\ Ratio, Randomness) \quad (2)$$

The total workload on one storage pool is the summation of every WL_i on that storage pool. To convert the total workload to storage latency, the following equation is used by prior work [3, 4].

$$L_{predict} = \frac{\sum WL_i}{\rho} \quad (3)$$

where ρ is calculated via the storage device model (*L-Q* model [4]). They use a workload injector to proactively test the storage pool and build the *L-Q* model when there is no job running in the system.

For workload modeling, *LightSRM* leverages the same model as prior works except that we build performance models to support snapshot. According to the phases in Section 4.1, we build the model as follows:

Phase #1: *Merging and Fetching*: In this phase, additional IO loads are generated to all three storage pools as shown in Figure 6.

For storage pool 1, which hosts the base virtual disks, the additional workload *WLA* can be modeled as:

$$WLA_{sp1} = WLA_{Merge} + WLA_{Fetch}$$
$$= f(1, 512KB, 0\%, 0\%) + f(OIO, IOsize, 100\%, Randomness) \quad (4)$$

For storage pool 2, which hosts the old snapshot, the additional workload *WLA* can be modeled as:

$$WLA_{sp2} = WLA_{Merge} + WLA_{Fetch}$$
$$= f(1, 512KB, 100\%, 0\%) + f(OIO, IOsize, 100\%, Randomness) \quad (5)$$

For storage pool 3, which hosts the new snapshot, the additional workload *WLA* can be modeled as:

$$WLA_{sp3} = WLA_{Workload} + WLA_{Fetch}$$
$$= f(OIO, IOsize, Read\ Ratio, Randomness)$$
$$+ f(OIO, IOsize, 0\%, Randomness) \quad (6)$$

As can be seen in equations (4) (5) (6), modeling the merging process is relatively easy because the data copy operation has fixed values of OIO, IOsize, Read Ratio, and Randomness for a given platform. On the other hand, the behavior of the fetch process totally depends on the workload behavior (OIO, IOsize, and Randomness). Read Ratio is 100% for storages 1, 2 (the sender) while 0% for storage 3 (the receiver).

Phase #2: *Merging or Fetching:* In this phase, one of the merging and fetching process finishes. If merging process finishes, we simply set WLA_{Merge} to 0. Otherwise, WLA_{Fetch} is set to 0.

In both Phases #1 and #2, additional IO workload will be added to the workload model WL_i in equation (2). After Phase #2, workload completely runs on destination, in which case equation (2) itself is adequate.

For the storage device modeling, we reverse the equation (3) to compute the device characteristics ρ as below:

$$\rho = \frac{\sum WL_i}{L} \quad (7)$$

where $\sum WL_i$ is computed using the IO characteristic (OIO, IOsize, R/W Ratio, Randomness) and L is obtained from the last latency tracking period. Since the sampling period is short (5 minutes in our prototype), the chance that ρ changes in the next period is low. Besides, the storage latency and the workload IO characteristics in equation (7) will be monitored in every sampling period. Therefore, device characteristic ρ can adjust itself in every sampling period if the underlying device characteristics change.
In a traditional storage management system, ρ is initially obtained from offline device modeling. The workload injector only adjusts ρ when the system is idle. *LightSRM*, however, uses the runtime performance data to recalibrate ρ online even when the system is busy running applications.

To briefly sum up, *LightSRM* uses the performance data monitored in the last tracking period to calculate the device characteristics. It is simple but reasonable because the chance that ρ changes in such short period is low. In addition, ρ is recalibrated in each period so that the device characteristics change can be captured in a timely manner. Now that we have both workload model for snapshots and storage device characteristics, we can predict the latency changes if we rearrange the workloads among the storage pools. This is important for the load balance algorithm described in Section 4.4.

4.4. Swift IO Load Balancing with the Combination of Migration and Snapshot

The goal of load balancing is to optimize resource utilization, minimize storage latency by distributing workloads across storage pools. LightSRM pursues the same goal but in a fine-grained way. Figure 9 shows a visual view of how our LightSRM performs in real time. In monitoring period (T), we sample all performance characteristics and storage latency. In decision point (D), we have the latency prediction for next period computed in Section 4.2. We also have all the performance data (e.g. OIO, IOsize, etc.) in the monitoring period. Performance models in Section 4.3 are used to predict the possible performance if a certain workload is moved to another storage pool. Based on the performance data, policy based storage management algorithm (load balancing in this paper) is executed. In the LB period, we actually move the workload.

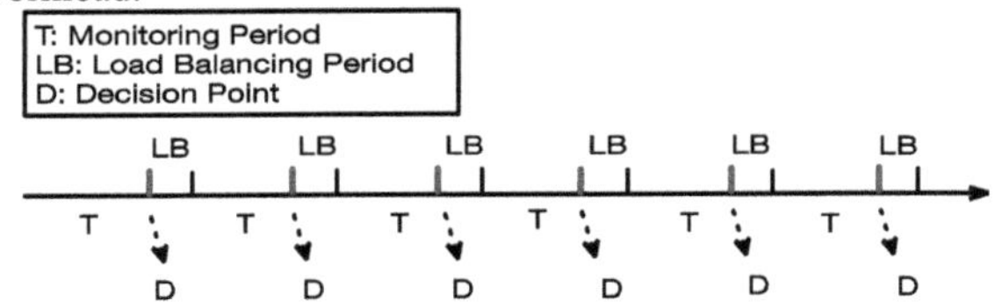

Figure 9. Time sequence of *LightSRM* load balancing

For load balancing, *LightSRM* iteratively performs the following 3 steps: 1) find the storage pool with the maximum latency (*max_storage*) and the storage pool with minimum latency (*min_storage*) in our sliding window; 2) use the performance model (in Section 4.3) to check if one of the virtual disks moved from *max_storage* to *min_storage* will lower the average storage latency and the latency difference across storage pools; and 3) if yes, add this move to migration list and update our internal database to record this movement. If no, quit the iteration and output the migration list. The iteration will continue until we cannot find a move to further lower the storage latency.

When the load balance algorithm finishes, we will have a list of migration suggestions. Although we can apply snapshot to all of them, we notice that the transition time of migration could actually be shorter than that of snapshot for some small virtual disks. Therefore, we propose a hybrid method, which uses migration if the migration time is shorter and uses snapshot if the snapshot transition time is shorter. To estimate the transition time of snapshot and migration, we develop the following functions:

$$TransitionTime_{Snapshot}$$
$$= max\{Time_{Fetching}, Time_{Merging}\}$$
$$= max\{\frac{SnapshotSize}{Throughput_{AppRead}}, \frac{SnapshotSize}{Throughput_{Merge}}\} \quad (8)$$

where $SnapshotSize$ is the size of snapshot file, $Throughput_{Merge}$ is the throughput that merge process can achieve, and $Throughput_{AppRead}$ is the throughput that workload generates. Note that the behavior of fetch process depends on the workload. Only when workload reads data will the fetch process read data from old storage pool.

$$TransitionTime_{migration} = \frac{VirtualDiskSize + WorkingSetSize}{Throughput_{Migration}} \quad (9)$$

where $VirtualDiskSize$ is the size of entire virtual disk; $Throughput_{Migration}$ is the throughput that migration process can get. According to the implementation of migration, it will also copy the data that is changed by the application during the migration (working set data). Thus, $WorkingSetSize$ is also considered.

For each suggestion on the migration list, *LightSRM* calculates the transition time of both migration and snapshot. Then, *LightSRM* selects the method that has a shorter transition time. By doing this, *LightSRM* can always choose the fastest way to perform load balance.

5. EVALUATION METHODOLOGY

5.1. Experimental Setup

To evaluate our *LightSRM*, we build a testbed consisting of six storage pools, each of which has a different configuration as shown in Table 3. They are connected to servers through Fiber

Channels. All the six storage pools are shared by Dell Power Edge r710 servers, which are equipped with 2.4GHz Intel(R) Xeon(R) CPU and 24 GB memory. The operating system on the hosts is Ubuntu 13.04. The kernel version is 3.11.0-12 with KVM modules enabled. We use the latest QEMU version 1.7.50. We also create up to 16 virtual machines, each of which has 1vCPUs and 1GB memory. Their virtual disks are placed across the six storage pools. The size of the virtual disks ranges from 16 GBs to 1TBs. The storage manager of *LightSRM* is running on a Dell Desktop Optiplex 980 with 2.7GHz Intel Core i7 and 8GB memory. The communication between the storage manager and the QEMU/KVM servers is supported by libvirt version 1.2.1 [15].

Table 3. Storage pool configurations

	No. of disks	Interface	RAID Level	Disk Size	Vendor
Storage_1	2	FC	1	2TB	IBM
Storage_2	3	FC	5	2TB	IBM
Storage_3	2	FC	0	1.3TB	IBM
Storage_4	2	FC	1	0.7TB	IBM
Storage_5	5	FC	5	2.7TB	IBM
Storage_6	4	FC	10	2TB	IBM

5.2. Prototype Implementation

The prototype of *LightSRM* has two parts: copy-on-write/read snapshot and storage manager. We modify QEMU block device driver (qemu/block.c) to support both copy-on-write and copy-on-read at the same time. To monitor the virtual machine IO characteristics (e.g. Outstanding IOs, IO Size, Read/Write Ratio, and Randomness), we instrument several performance counters in QEMU block device driver. These characteristics can be obtained via either QEMU command line interface (qmp) or libvirt API. In order to track the storage performance, we use *pt-diskstats* tool [14], which can report the real time storage latency and throughput. Our storage manager, including performance modeling and load balancing, is implemented in C. It runs on a separated machine and leverages the libvirt API to communicate with QEMU hosts and storage pools. For comparison, we also implement the Pesto scheme [4] on our QEMU/KVM platform.

5.3. Workloads and Metrics

On our testbed, we deploy two hadoop platforms, which occupy up to ten virtual machines in total. On the hadoop platform, we run hibench suite [11] as big data applications. We also create six virtual machines with IOmeter [31] installed to mimic the IO behavior of traditional server applications. The behaviors are summarized in Table 4, which are also used and verified in several prior studies [3, 4, 5, 28]. In general, we mimic a multi-tenant cloud environment with two hadoop clusters running regularly. The cloud tenant can also schedule their server applications to run at any time. In our evaluation section, we create several execution scenarios based on this setup.

Table 4. *IOmeter* settings for simulated workloads

Type	OIO	IO Size	Read Ratio	Randomness
Workstation	8	8	80%	80%
OLTP	12	8	70%	100%
Exchange	8	4	67%	100%

In order to compare *LightSRM* with other alternative designs, we evaluate the following metrics: 1) transition time, which is the time between the workload is scheduled to move and the workload completely runs on destination; 2) application observed latency, which is used to measure the performance impact of performing storage management; 3) distribution of errors/residuals, which is used to measure the accuracy of the prediction and modeling; 4) storage latency of each storage pool, which is used to show how well our design can rebalance the storage performance.

6. RESULTS AND ANALYSIS

6.1. Transition Time

As discussed in Section 4.4, the transition time of snapshot can be longer than the migration time when the virtual disk size is small enough. This section analyzes the factors that determine the transition time.

For snapshot, the transition time is the maximum value of merging time and fetching time. Since the merging process copied the data from old snapshot to the base virtual disk, the merging time is determined by the working set size of the workload. As for the fetching time, it is determined by both the working set size and the read throughput of the workload. Higher read throughput leads to more data to be fetched.

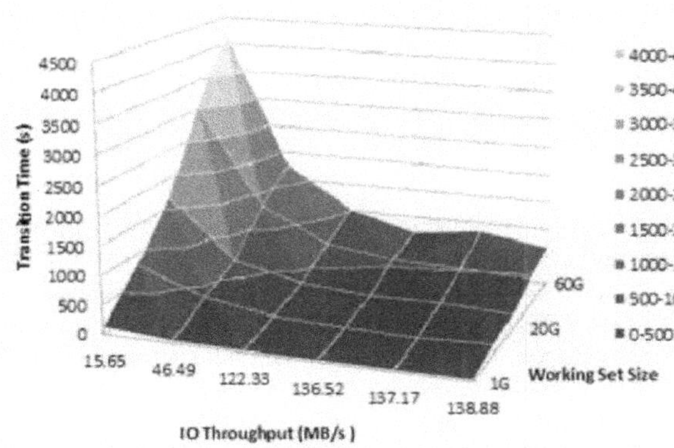

Figure 10. Transition time when using snapshot

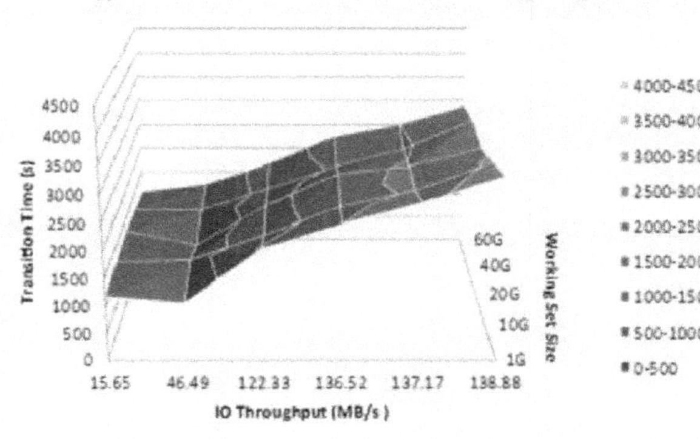

Figure 11. Transition time when using migration

In Figure 10, we measure the transition time of snapshot with different working set sizes and throughputs. On one hand, the larger the read throughput, the shorter the transition time at a given working set size. With larger read throughput, the volume of data that is driven to the new snapshot per second is larger, which inevitably leads to faster fetching process. On the other hand, the larger the working set size, the longer the transition time. Both merging and fetching process need more time to copy a larger size of working set data.

For migration, the transition time depends on the virtual disk size and size of the data that is modified during the copy process. As can be seen in Figure 11, larger throughput leads to longer migration time. With larger throughput, the volume of modified data is larger during the copy process. The migration process has to retransmit those modified data. Therefore, the higher the workload write throughput, the longer the transition time.

Cross-examining Figures 10 and 11, we find that snapshot method is preferable when workload exhibits higher read throughput and has smaller working set size. However, migration method is more efficient than snapshot method when the workload exhibits lower write throughput. In modern data centers, which host multi-tenant public clouds, the workload exhibits variable working set sizes and different IO behaviors. Therefore, a hybrid method that can dynamically choose a faster method (snapshot or migration) online as we proposed in Section 4.4 will be beneficial.

6.2. Performance Impact on Workloads

Both snapshot and migration technology have impact on the workload performance. They both generate additional disk traffic, which will compete the storage resources with the currently running workloads. In this section, we measure the observed latency changes of the workloads when we perform snapshot and migration. We run three different types of workloads (e.g. OLTP, Workstation, and Exchange). At the beginning, they are running on a slow storage pool. We plan to move them to a faster storage pool.

Figure 12 (a) shows the latency changes when we move the workload by storage migration. As can be seen, the workload latency jumps as much as 4X during the migration although eventually the latency drops as the migration finishes. The copy process of the migration occupies the disk resources on both source and destination storage, which inevitably leads to low performance of the running application.

Figure 12 (b) shows the latency changes when we move the workload by snapshot. The latency observed by the workload during the transition is between the latency of the slow and fast storage pool. The moment the snapshot is taken, all the write requests of the workload are served by new storage pool. The new storage pool will serve the read requests after the first batch of read requests. Besides, the merging time is much shorter than the migration time so that the impact on the workload latency is smaller (on average, 90% less overhead in our experiments).

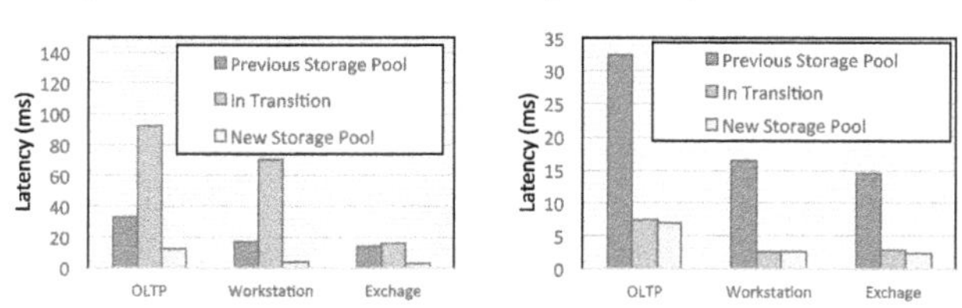

(a) Migration (b) Snapshots

Figure 12. Performance impact on workloads

6.3. Accuracy of Latency Prediction

There are two predictions in *LightSRM*:

1) Latency prediction for next period. The traditional method uses the *95-percentile* of the latency samples as the latency value of next period. Our *LightSRM* uses exponentially weighted moving average (*EWMA*) with adjustable window size to predict the storage latency. In time series analysis, exponential smoothing (*ExpoS*), moving average with different lags (*MA_xL*), and auto regression (*AR*) are also proposed to do prediction. Figure 13 shows the distribution of residuals when different prediction methods are used. An accurate prediction will have a distribution graph that is close to 0. In Figure 13, *MA_xL* means weighted moving average is used with a window length of *x*. As can be seen, the traditional way of prediction (*95-percentile*) yields the most inaccurate prediction results, whose residuals are mostly far away from 0. *MA_xL, AR and ExpoS* yield similar results. *EWMA* with adjustable window shows the most accurate results as most of the residuals are around 0.

2) Latency prediction when a certain virtual disk is moved. Figure 14 shows the prediction residuals when a snapshot is created on the new storage pool. As can be seen, without snapshot modeling, most of the residuals are negative, which means most of the prediction value is lower than the actual latency. When the snapshot model is used to capture the additional traffic generated by snapshots, the residuals are closer to 0. Therefore, *LightSRM* can accurately capture the system performance by modeling the snapshots.

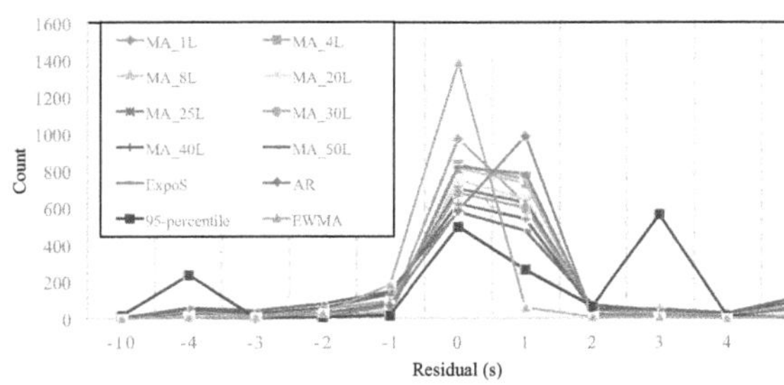

Figure 13. Distribution of residuals

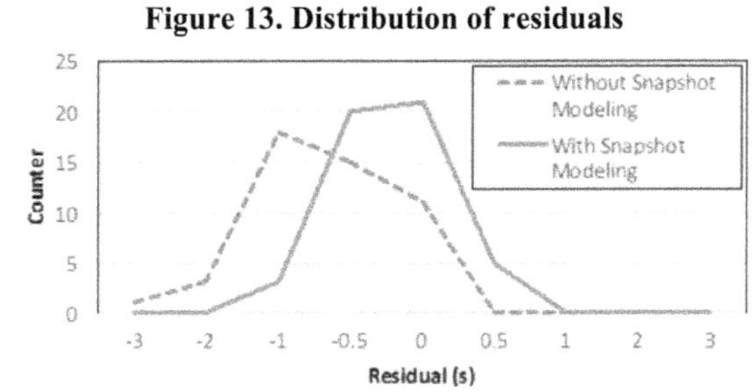

Figure 14. Distribution of residuals

6.4. Storage Policy-based Management for Big Data Workloads

In this section, we deploy *LightSRM* in a big data cloud environment. And we create two execution scenarios to test how well *LightSRM* performs.

Case #1: Performance Imbalance at Beginning

In a storage system with four storage devices (storage 1~4 in Table 3), we place one VM on storage 1, two VMs on storage 2, one VM on storage 3, and no VM on storage 4. The size of virtual disks ranges from 400GB to 1TB. We run PageRank from hibench suite in the virtual machines. So, at the beginning, the system is imbalanced (storage 2 is overloaded while storage 4 is idle).

As can be seen in Figure 15 (a), *LightSRM* detects the imbalance at the beginning and decides to move one of the VMs from storage 2 to storage 4. Since the virtual disk size is too large, taking snapshots will be faster. *LightSRM* makes a snapshot on storage 4 so that the performance is quickly balanced as shown in Figure 15 (a). Here, we found another fact that most of big data workloads tend to read the data at the beginning of execution. Therefore, the transition time of snapshot is very short because the workload fetches the data it needs quickly to the new location. If migration method is used as in the traditional method in Figure 15 (b), the migration time is very long due to the large size of virtual disk. As can be seen, the migration cannot even finish within the workload execution. The performance of storage pools remains imbalance to the end of workload execution.

Further investigating the application behavior, we find that big data workloads tend to have large IO size and different IO pattern among computing nodes (virtual machines). Assuming network bandwidth is not saturated, large IO size usually leads to high disk throughput, which helps to copy the data to new location when using snapshots. Therefore, in general using snapshot to tune performance is preferable in the light of big data workloads. However, as can be seen in the PageRank example (shown in Figure 16), the IO behavior of big data application varies across different virtual machines during the execution process. Therefore, it is desirable to introduce the hybrid method as in *LightSRM*, which can dynamically choose a faster tuning method based on the workload behavior.

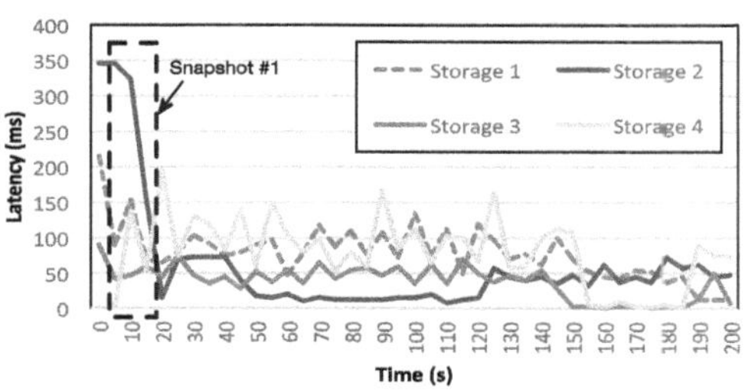

(a) *LigthSRM* (snapshot)

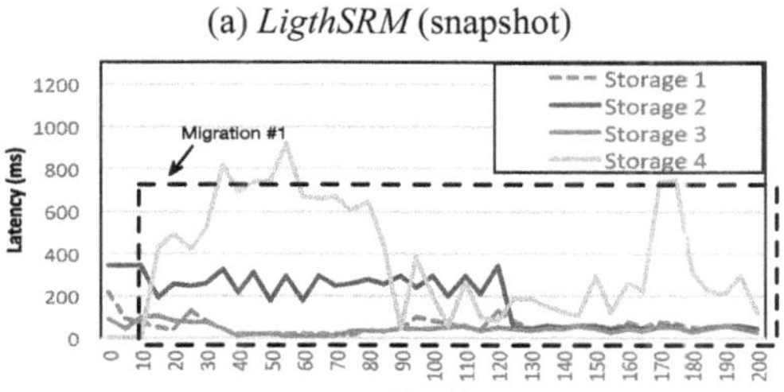

(b) Traditional Method (migration)

Figure 15. Storage performance load balance

Figure 16. IO size of PageRank during the execution

Case #2: Unexpected Scheduled Jobs

As shown in Figure 17, we deploy two sets of hadoop platform (VMh11 ~ VMh15, VMh21 ~VMh25) on six storage pools. There are also six VMs (VMinj1 ~VMinj6) installed with *IOmeter*. Initially, there are all idle and balanced. In our experiments, we run *hibench* suite on both hadoop platforms. At a certain time during the execution, we randomly select three VMs from VMinj1 ~ VMinj6 to run *IOmeter* with traditional server application configurations as shown in Table 4. The virtual disk sizes for VMh1x and VMh2x range from 200GB to 1TB while the size for VMinjx is only 16GB. Therefore, we intentionally create a scenario that some VMs are potentially suitable for migration while others are not.

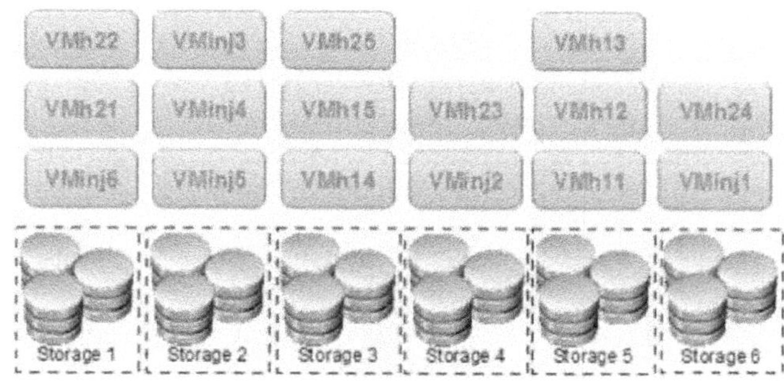

Figure 17. Initial virtual disk placement

As known, traditional management scheme uses migration for every data movement even if the virtual disk is very large such as VMhx. Our *LightSRM* can dynamically choose a suitable way to relocate virtual disks. Figure 18 (a) shows the average latency of the six storage pools, which will exhibit spikes if suddenly scheduled job is not handled in time. Figure 18 (b) shows the standard deviation for the latency of the six storage pools, which reflects how well the storage pools are balanced. As can be seen, *LightSRM* has 91% lower average storage latency (28ms) than that of the traditional method (312ms). Besides, *LightSRM* shows 93% lower standard deviation (49ms) across storage pools. Further looking into the reason behind those numbers, we find that *LightSRM* takes two snapshots for the large size VMs and three migrations for small size VMs as shown in Table 5. As can be seen in Table 5, the transition time of making those moves are relatively short. However, the traditional method takes around 1hr to migrate the large size virtual disk (VMh21, VMh22). These lengthy migrations yield high IO traffic in the system, which leads to high latency in the system (as shown in Figure 18 (a)). Worse, the randomly scheduled VMs are not handled timely, which results in highly imbalanced storage system as shown in Figure 18 (b). Therefore, *LightSRM* is more capable in handling situations with both large and small size virtual disks.

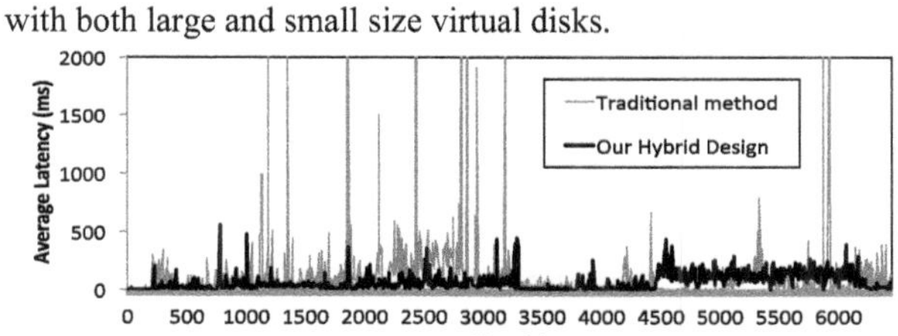

Figure 18 (a). Average latency of the storage pools

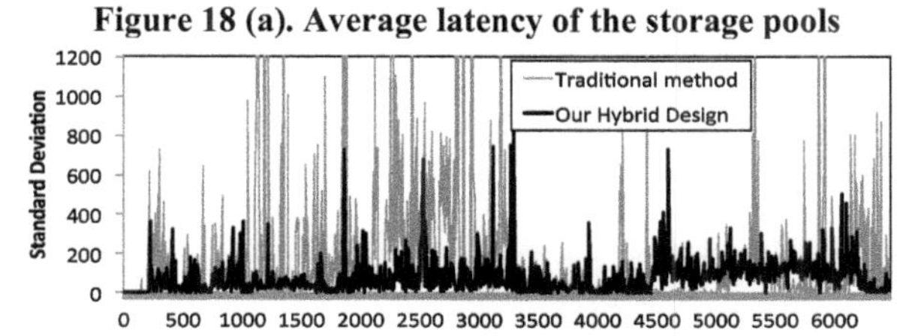

Figure 18 (b). Standard deviation of the latency across all the storage pools

Table 5. Load balance suggestions

Round	Balancing Decisions	Time
2	Snapshot VMh22 from Storage 1 to 2	12s
4	Migrate VMinj3 from Storage 2 to 5	85s
	Migrate VMinj4 from Storage 2 to 6	70s
9	Snapshot VMh21 from Storage 1 to 3	39s
15	Migrate VMinj1 from Storage 6 to 1	71s

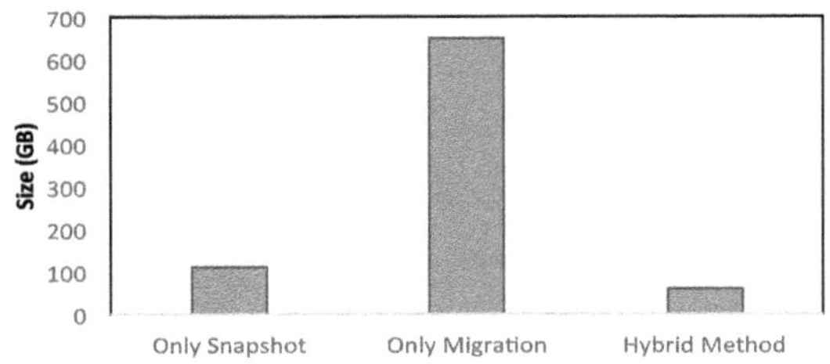

Figure 19. Data traffic generated by load balancing

Figure 19 shows the additional data traffic that is generated by the load balancing management. If only migration is used, the additional data traffic will be roughly equal to the sum of sizes of migrated virtual disks. If only snapshot is used, the additional data traffic is twice of the workload working set size (one for merging process, one for fetching process). If virtual disk size is smaller than double working set size, migration actually yields less additional traffic. Therefore, using hybrid methods as shown in Figure 19 can achieve much less data traffic than other methods (44% less than only snapshot method and 91% less than only migration method in our experiments).

7. CONCLUSIONS

Modern data centers host not only private cloud but also public/hybrid cloud, which exhibits highly fluctuated IO behavior and requires 24/7 service. Traditional storage management system cannot work properly due to the large size virtual disk. In this paper, we propose *LightSRM*, a storage resource management system that can quickly respond to unexpected IO load imbalance. The foundation of *LightSRM* is the copy-on-write/read snapshot, which only contains the data blocks that matters to the storage performance. Thanks to the snapshot, *LightSRM* can redirect the IO requests quickly. A real-time tracking (*EWMA* with adjustable window length) is used to accelerate the performance monitoring process. To support snapshot in performance management, we also develop the performance model for snapshots. Based on our characterization, we further propose to use a hybrid method to dynamically choose either snapshot or migration to achieve optimal transition time. Our experiment results show that *LightSRM* with hybrid design performs better than only snapshot and only migration design.

8. ACKNOWLEDGMENTS

This work is supported in part by NSF grants 1423090, 1320100,1117261, 0937869, 0916384, 0845721(CAREER), 0834288, 0811611, 0720476, by SRC grants 2008-HJ-1798, 2007-RJ-1651G, by Microsoft Research Trustworthy Computing, Safe and Scalable Multi-core Computing Awards, and by three IBM Faculty Awards.

9. REFERENCES

[1] Understanding VMware vSphere® 5.1 Storage DRS, VMware Technical white paper, March 2013.

[2] VMware Distributed Resource Scheduler, White Paper.

[3] Ajay Gulati, Chethan Kumar, Irfan Ahmad, and Karan Kumar, BASIL: Automated IO Load Balancing across Storage Devices. USENIX FAST, 2010.

[4] Ajay Gulati, et al., Pesto: Online Storage Performance Management in Virtualized Datacenters. SOCC, 2011.

[5] Nohhyun Park, Irfan Ahmad, and David Lilja, Romano: Autonomous Storage Management using Performance Prediction in Multi-Tenant Datacenters, SOCC, 2012.

[6] Ali Mashtizadeh, Emre Celebi, Tal Garfinkel, and Min Cai, The Design and Evolution of Live Storage Migration in VMware ESX, USENIX ATC, 2011.

[7] Jayanta Basak, et al., Model Building for Dynamic Multi-tenant Provider Environments, ACM SIGOPS Operating Systems Review, 2012.

[8] Mengzhi Wang, et al., Storage Device Performance Prediction with CART Models, MASCOT, 2014.

[9] Aameek Singh, Madhukar Korupolu, and Dushmanta Mohapatra, Server-Storage Virtualization: Integration and Load Balancing in Data Centers, SC, 2008.

[10] Hadoop, http://hadoop.apache.org.

[11] Hibench, https://github.com/intel-hadoop/HiBench.

[12] QEMU, http://wiki.qemu.org.

[13] KVM, http://www.linux-kvm.org/page/Main_Page.

[14] pt-diskstats, http://www.percona.com/doc/percona-toolkit/2.1/pt-diskstats.html.

[15] Libvirt 1.2.1, http://libvirt.org.

[16] Amazon AWS, http://aws.amazon.com.

[17] Azure, http://www.azure.microsoft.com/en-us/.

[18] Oracle Information Architecture: An Architect's Guide to Big Data, Oracle White Paper, 2012.

[19] Swaroop Kavalanekar, Bruce Worthington, Qi Zhang, and Vishal Sharda, Characterization of Storage Workload Traces from Production Windows Servers, IISWC 2008.

[20] Ajay Gulati, Chethan Kumar, and Irfan Ahmad, Storage Workload Characterization and Consolidation in Virtualized Environments, VPACT, 2009.

[21] Eric Anderson, et al., Hippodrome: Running Circles around Storage Administration, FAST, 2002.

[22] George Alvarez, et al., MINERVA: An Automated Resource Provisioning Tool for Large-Scale Storage Systems, ACM Transactions on Computer Systems, 2001.

[23] Chenyang Lu, et al., Aqueduct: Online Data Migration with Performance Guarantees, USENIX FAST, 2002.

[24] Bhaskar Prasad Rimal, Eunmi Choi, and Ian Lumb, A Taxonomy and Survery of Cloud Computing System, Fifth International Joint Conference on INC, IMS and IDC, 2009.

[25] Divyakant Agrawal, et al., Big data and cloud computing: current state and future opportunities, EDBT/ICDT, 2011.

[26] Xuelian Lin, et al., A Practical Performance Model for Hadoop MapReduce, Cluster Computing Workshops, 2012.

[27] Herodotos Herodotou, Hadoop Performance Models, Technical Report, Duke University, CS-2011-05.

[28] Irfan Ahmad, et al., Storage Workload Characterization and Consolidation in Virtualized Environments, VPACT, 2009.

[29] Ruijin Zhou, et al., Optimizing Virtual Machine Live Storage Migration in Heterogeneous Storage Environment, VEE, 2013.

[30] Arkaitz Ruiz-Alvarez, et al., An Automated Approach to Cloud Storage Service Selection, ScienceCloud, 2011.

[31] IOmeter, http://www.iometer.org

[32] Carl A. Waldspurger, Memory Resource Management in VMware ESX Server, OSDI, 2002.

[33] Minkyong Kim, and Brian Noble, Mobile Network Estimation, MobiCom, 2001.

Hadoop+: Modeling and Evaluating the Heterogeneity for MapReduce Applications in Heterogeneous Clusters

Wenting He *†, Huimin Cui *, Binbin Lu *, Jiacheng Zhao *†, Shengmei Li *, Gong Ruan *†, Jingling Xue ¶, Xiaobing Feng *, Wensen Yang +, Youliang Yan +

*SKL Computer Architecture, Institute of Computing Technology, CAS, China
†University of Chinese Academy of Sciences, China
¶School of Computer Science and Engineering, University of New South Wales, Australia
+Shannon Laboratory, Huawei Technologies Co., Ltd., Shenzhen, China
{hewenting, cuihm, lubinbin, zhaojiacheng, lishengmei, ruangong, fxb}@ict.ac.cn
jingling@cse.unsw.edu.au
{yangwensen, yanyouliang}@huawei.com

ABSTRACT

Despite the widespread adoption of heterogeneous clusters in modern data centers, modeling heterogeneity is still a big challenge, especially for large-scale MapReduce applications. In a CPU/GPU hybrid heterogeneous cluster, allocating more computing resources to a MapReduce application does not always mean better performance, since simultaneously running CPU and GPU tasks will contend for shared resources.

This paper proposes a heterogeneity model to predict the shared resource contention between the simultaneously running tasks of a MapReduce application when heterogeneous computing resources (e.g. CPUs and GPUs) are allocated. To support the approach, we present a heterogeneous MapReduce framework, Hadoop+, which enables CPUs and GPUs to process big data coordinately, and leverages the heterogeneity model to assist users in selecting the computing resources for different purposes.

Our experimental results show three benefits. First, Hadoop+ exploits GPU capability, and achieves 1.4x to 16.1x speedups over Hadoop for 5 real applications when running individually. Second, the heterogeneity model can be used to allocate GPUs among multiple simultaneously running MapReduce applications, bringing up to 36.9% (17.6% in average) speedup when multiple applications are running simultaneously. Third, the model is verified to be able to select the optimal or most cost-effective resource consumption.

1. INTRODUCTION

MapReduce is emerging as an important programming model in data centers for large-scale data-parallel applications, due to the ease of development and deployment in large-scale clusters. It has been widely used in a number of domains, including non-compute-intensive domains, such as log analysis, and compute-intensive domains, such as deep learning. To efficiently support these diverse applications, heterogeneous clusters are being widely adopted in data centers, to gain advantages in performance and energy consumption. In such heterogeneous clusters, for a MapReduce application, both of its performance and cost would vary with the consumed resources. Therefore, two questions arise. First, how to select computing resources for a MapReduce application under different user purposes, e.g., performance or cost-efficiency? Second, how to allocate computing resources across multiple simultaneously running MapReduce applications? To answer the above two questions, a heterogeneity model is required to model the behaviors of MapReduce applications in heterogeneous clusters.

MapReduce was originally proposed by Google in 2004 [14], which automatically divides large input data into multiple splits for parallel processing in distributed environments. Since then, a number of researchers have made great efforts on implementing MapReduce on modern architectures. As the *multi-core CPU* has become mainstream, Phoenix is proposed to automatically distribute map and reduce tasks on multiple cores in a single shared-memory machine [30]. Based on Phoenix, Ostrich partitions a MapReduce job into a number of small sub-jobs, and iteratively processes one at a time to use resources efficiently [9]. As *GPUs* are emerging, Mars [20] and MapCG [21] are proposed, which utilize a large number of GPU threads for map and reduce tasks and assign each thread a small number of (key, value) pairs to process. As *heterogeneous CPU/GPU clusters* are emerging, HAPI [29] and HadoopCL [19] are proposed to integrate OpenCL codes into MapReduce to enable the use of accelerators in heterogeneous clusters.

Despite the efforts on MapReduce framework on a variety of architectures, modeling heterogeneity is still a big challenge for MapReduce applications. Consider a representative GPGPU platform, a six-core Intel Xeon E5-2620 configured with two NVIDIA Tesla C2050 GPUs. The memory controller and I/O resource are shared by the CPU cores and GPUs (via corresponding host threads on the CPU).

ICS'15, June 08 – 11, 2015, Newport Beach, CA, USA.

DOI: http://dx.doi.org/10.1145/2751205.2751236.

When CPU and GPU tasks are running simultaneously, the resource contention would bring unexpected performance interference. We take KNN as an example to demonstrate the problem. When only one GPU task is running, the data processing speed of 60MB/s can be attained, however, when we launch a CPU task to work with the GPU task, the overall data processing speed (CPU+GPU) would decrease to 53MB/s. The reason is that resource contention slows the GPU task down. It demonstrates that more resources do not always bring performance gain (More details in Section 2). **Therefore it is challenging to model the performance against different resource consumptions.**

In this paper, we propose an approach to model the heterogeneity for MapReduce applications in heterogeneous clusters. To this end, we introduce a heterogeneous MapReduce framework, Hadoop+, which enables user-provided CUDA/OpenCL functions to be integrated as plug-ins into Hadoop. Moreover, Hadoop+ enables users to tune and control the simultaneously running GPU and CPU tasks flexibly in order to maximize data processing speed or select a most cost-effective configuration.

This paper makes the following contributions:

- We present a Hadoop+ framework, which enables user-provided CUDA/OpenCL Map and(or) Reduce functions to be embedded into Hadoop as plug-ins, thereby enabling CPUs and GPUs to process big data coordinately. Our experimental results show that Hadoop+ exploits the capability of GPUs, and achieves speedups ranging from 1.4x to 16.1x over Hadoop for 5 real applications when running individually.

- We create a heterogeneity model to predict the shared resource contention among simultaneously running heterogeneous tasks (CPU and GPU, and further predict the performance gain when allocating a computing resource to an application.). Using the model to allocate GPUs among applications achieves up to 36.9% (17.6% in average) performance improvement when multiple MapReduce applications are running simultaneously.

- Our approach can assist users to select an optimal or most cost-effective resource allocation strategy for an application, with no need of running the application under all possible resource allocation strategies.

The rest of the paper is organized as follows. Section 2 introduces the background and our motivation. Section 3 presents our Hadoop+ framework. Section 4 discusses our methodology for modeling heterogeneity. Section 5 describes our experimental validation. Section 6 discusses the related work. Section 7 concludes.

2. BACKGROUND AND MOTIVATION

2.1 MapReduce

MapReduce [14] is a data-parallel programming model for processing big data in data centers. Programmers are only required to specify a *Map* function which takes a (key, value) pair as input and generates a list of intermediate (key, value) pairs, and a *Reduce* function which takes all values associated with the same key and produces a list of (key, value) pairs as output. The Apache Hadoop [5] is a Java-based open-source implementation of MapReduce programming model, built based on a distributed file system (HDFS).

Algorithm 1 The KNN program in Hadoop

```
function MAP(train, TEST)
    Compute_All_Distances(train, TEST)
end function
function REDUCE(test, DistanceOf(test, TRAIN))
    Select_TopK(Distance(test, TRAIN))
end function
```

Algorithm 1 shows the pseudo-code of K-nearest neighbors (KNN) algorithm [11] written in Hadoop. KNN is a widely used algorithm in classification. Given a set of training examples and a number of testing samples, it computes the K nearest neighbors in the training set for each testing sample.

The programmer only needs to implement the two functions of MapReduce primitive *Map* and *Reduce*. In particular, *Map* takes one train sample (denoted as $train$) and the test set (denoted as $TEST$) as input, calculates the distance of $train$ to every item in the test set $TEST$, and *Reduce* gets a list of distances attaching to the same test sample, selects the topK nearest neighbors for each test sample.

The MapReduce framework automatically divides the input data into multiple splits, which will be processed in parallel. Each split is processed by a map task, also called a mapper. The outputs of the map tasks are grouped by key, and the outputs with the same key are shuffled to one reduce task (also called a reducer) for processing.

2.2 Motivation Example

2.2.1 Experimental Methodology

To examine the behavior of a MapReduce application in heterogeneous clusters, we implement the above KNN in the Hadoop+ framework, and more details of the framework will be discussed in Section 3. Here, we only highlight some features for discussing the motivation example:

- Hadoop+ will launch a user-provided map/reduce task written with CUDA/OpenCL on a GPU, when a GPU resource is available.

- Hadoop+ will also launch a traditional map/reduce task on one or more CPU cores, in the same way with Hadoop. The Hadoop *Mapper* or *MultithreadedMapper* can be used to issue single-threaded or multi-threaded map tasks.

The platform we use is an Intel six-core Xeon E5-2620 chip, configured with two NVIDIA Tesla C2050 GPUs. Other hardware parameters and the parameters for KNN are listed in Section 5. In this paper, we use the metric of *data processing speed* to represent the performance of an application, which is calculated with the equation:

$$dps = V/T \tag{1}$$

where V represents the total data volume processed on the cluster and T represents the time for processing the data.

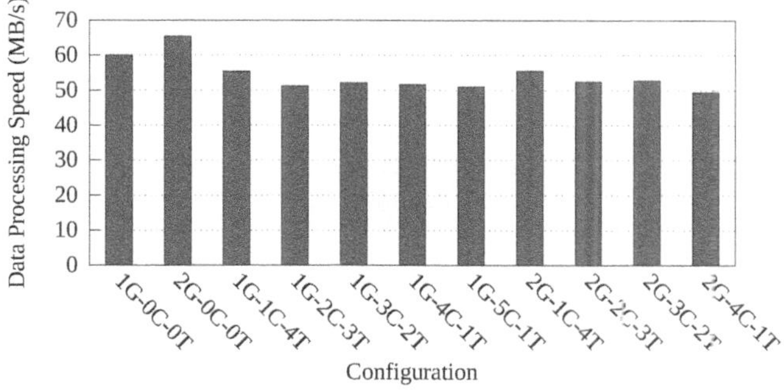

Figure 1: KNN's data processing speed.

2.2.2 *Key Observations*

We evaluate 11 computing resource configurations, as shown by the horizontal axis in Figure 1. Each configuration is denoted as gG-cC-tT, where g represents for the number of simultaneously running GPU map tasks, c for the number of simultaneously running CPU tasks, and t for the number of threads inside each CPU map task. Figure 1 shows the performance, with the vertical axis representing the data processing speed. We make two significant observations from the results:

- *Using two GPUs only brings very slight performance gain over one GPU.* When only one GPU is used, the data processing speed is 60MB/s (the first bar in Figure 1). However, when another GPU is exploited simultaneously, the data processing speed is only slightly increased to 65MB/s (the second bar in Figure 1).
- *Coordinating CPUs together with one GPU leads to worse performance than that of only using one GPU.* When only one GPU is used, the data processing speed is 60MB/s (the first bar). However, When one or more CPU tasks are running simultaneously with one GPU task (bars 3-7), the overall performance would decrease unexpectedly, varying from 58MB/s to 51MB/s. A similar observation can be found for the configurations containing two GPU tasks.

2.2.3 *Analysis*

First we demonstrate the different behaviors of a CPU task and a GPU task in Hadoop+, as shown in Figure 2. As the red line shows, the I/O traffic of a CPU task keeps almost unchanged during the task execution. The reason is that Hadoop+ leverages the execution mechanism in Hadoop for CPU tasks, which iteratively reads only a small piece of data and processes them quickly, thus the I/O traffic keeps low. However, the behavior of the GPU task is different, as shown by the blue line. To obtain high GPU occupancy, the GPU task reads a chunk of data, transfers it to the GPU, and launches the GPU kernel to process it, thus it exhibits obvious phase behavior. In particular, the I/O traffic is high when the GPU task is reading data from HDFS (via its host thread), and low when the GPU task is executing the kernel.

To analyze the reason for the observations in Section 2.2.2, we take one GPU task, denoted x, and examine its performance under the 11 configurations. We find that the key reason is shared I/O resource contention among CPU and GPU tasks. To demonstrate this, we comment out the computation in x and run it under the 11 configurations. In

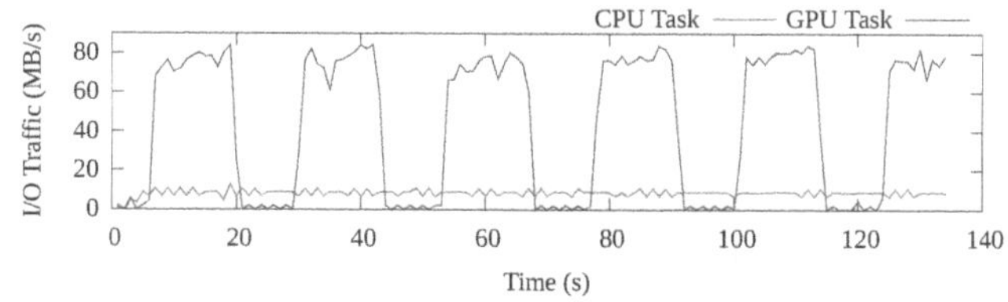

Figure 2: Behaviors of CPU/GPU tasks.

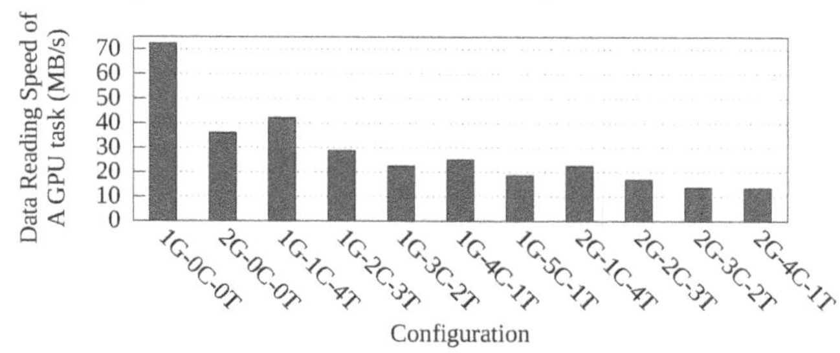

Figure 3: KNN's data reading speed.

this way, each GPU task reads a split from HDFS without any following computations. Figure 3 shows the data reading speed of x. When only x is running, the data reading speed can reach 72MB/s (the first bar 1G-0C-0T), while it drops to 36MB/s when another GPU task is running simultaneously (the second bar 2G-0C-0T). Furthermore, when 4 single-threaded CPU tasks and another GPU task are running together with x, its data reading speed would decrease to only 14MB/s (the last bar 2G-4C-1T).

2.2.4 *Summary - The Challenge*

The observations and our analyses demonstrate that it is a challenge to model the heterogeneity for MapReduce applications running in heterogeneous clusters. In particular, the challenge can be summarized into the following questions:

- What factors would affect the performance gain when allocating a computing resource to an application?
- How will the performance contribution of one computing resource, e.g., GPU, vary with applications?
- How to select a resource configuration for an application for different purposes, e.g., to obtain best performance, or to be most cost-effective?

3. HADOOP+ FRAMEWORK

Figure 4 gives an overview of our Hadoop+ framework. Besides the *Map* and *Reduce* primitives in Hadoop, Hadoop+ provides another two primitives, *PMap* and *PReduce*, to programmers. The difference is that the *PMap* and *PReduce* in Hadoop+ enable programmers to write explicit parallel CUDA/OpenCL functions running on GPUs as plug-ins, as shown by the box of "User-Provided PMap/PReduce Function" in Figure 4. Meanwhile, users can also use the *Map* and *Reduce* functions in Hadoop. In Hadoop+, users can provide *Map*, *PMap* or both, and *Reduce*, *PReduce* or both.

To support explicit parallel Map functions, Hadoop+ provides different input parameters for *Map* and *PMap*. In particular, the input of *Map* is $(key, value)$, while the input

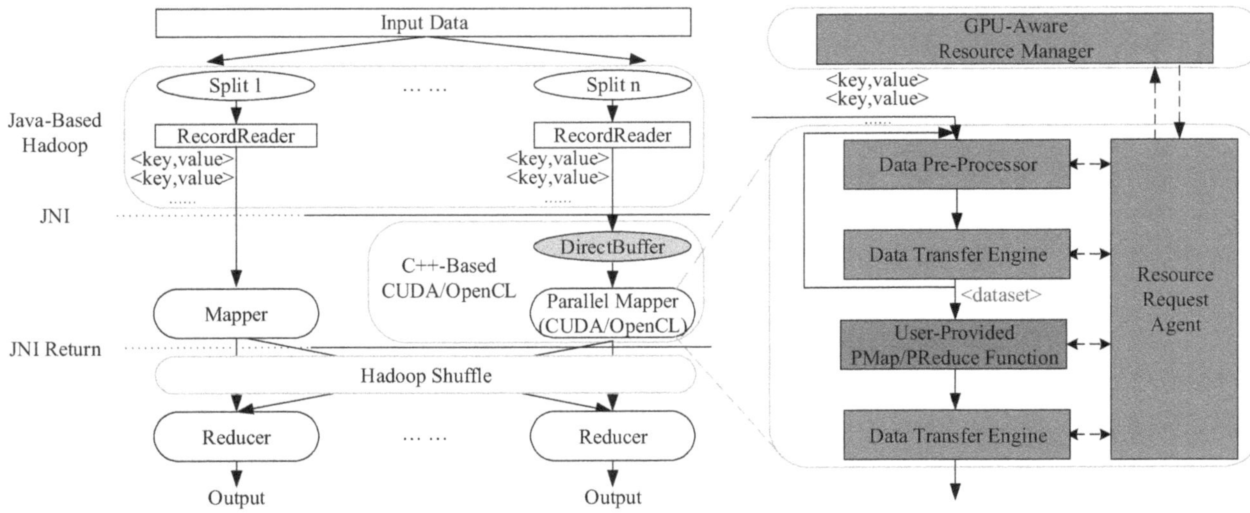

Figure 4: Overview of Hadoop+ framework. (Only parallel mapper is shown for clarity.)

of *PMap* is *dataset*, i.e., a list of $(key, value)$. Meanwhile, the input parameters for *Reduce* and *PReduce* are identical, which are the outputs with the same key from all map tasks. The *PMap* and *PReduce* functions are defined as follows:

$PMap : (k1, v1) * -> (k2, v2) *$.

$PReduce : (k2, v2*) -> (k2, v3) *$.

We continue to use the example of KNN to illustrate Hadoop+. Algorithm 2 shows the pseudo code, with the CUDA kernel omitted. Comparing with Algorithm 1, the function takes a *train_dataset* rather than an individual *train* as the input, and writes explicitly parallel CUDA code in *PMap*.

Algorithm 2 The KNN program in Hadoop+

```
function PMAP(train_dataset, TEST)
    for all train in train_dataset do
        Compute_Distances_CUDA(train, TEST)
        Insert_Distance_CUDA(train, TEST) to TopK(TEST)
    end for
end function
function REDUCE(test, DistanceOf(test, TRAIN))
    Select_TopK(Distance(test, TRAIN))
end function
```

3.1 Overall Workflow

As Figure 4 shows, Hadoop+ also divides the input data into multiple splits, which will be processed in parallel, with each split being processed by a mapper. If a mapper does not include *PMap*, the split is processed in the same way as Hadoop, which processes the $(key, value)$ pairs sequentially. Otherwise, if a mapper includes *PMap*, each split is parsed into a "dataset" before processing, which combines a list of $(key, value)$ pairs, together with the meta data describing the format of the dataset. Programmers take the dataset as the input of the *PMap* function, and Hadoop+ leverages JNI (Jave Native Interface) to invoke the native functions.

Hadoop+ extends the resource manager in Hadoop for managing the non-preemptible GPU resources, as shown by the "GPU-Aware Resource Manager" in Figure 4. At runtime, each map task has a "Resource Request Agent", which is responsible for requesting computing resources from the "GPU-Aware Resource Manager". For clarity, we denote the map task which successfully obtains a GPU as a *GPU mapper*. If a mapper does not successfully obtain a GPU, it would be a CPU mapper and be processed in the same way with Hadoop, so we discuss only the GPU mapper in this section.

As in Hadoop, the input split is first read from HDFS (Hadoop Distributed File System) and parsed into $(key, value)$ pairs by the RecordReader. To enable the $(key, value)$ pairs to be accessible and further processed by native functions, we need to put them into a buffer that can be accessed by both the Java and native codes. Therefore, we take advantage of the *DirectBuffer* mechanism in Java, which resides outside of the garbage-collected heap. In particular, the Java code allocates a DirectBuffer and sequentially puts $(key, value)$ pairs into the buffer, and the native code reads the buffer for processing. To assist the native code to correctly parse the buffer, Hadoop+ automatically generates the meta data from the input file format description, which is provided by users in an XML format. In particular, the meta data serve to instruct the native code how to parse the input file, as the RecordReader for Hadoop.

With the data in the *DirectBuffer*, the GPU mapper processes the data with four steps. First, the data are preprocessed with some built-in or user-defined functions by the "Data Pre-Processor", e.g., text parsing, byte order conversion, etc. Second, the "Data Transfer Engine" accumulates a chunk of data and transfers the data to the target device, according to the obtained computing resource via "Resource Request Agent". Third, the "User-Provided PMap Function" would be invoked, and finally the output $(key, value)$ pairs are transferred back to Hadoop+ for shuffling. Thus the mapper task terminates.

Afterwards, the output of the mappers with the same *key* would be shuffled to one reducer, and the same workflow in Figure 4 applies for parallel reducers. If no *PReduce* is provided, the reducer would be processed in the same way with Hadoop.

3.2 Resource Management

In Hadoop+, there are two components responsible for resource management. The "GPU-Aware Resource Manager" is global and maintains all the resources in the cluster, serving all map and reduce tasks. The resource manager is located on a preset node denoted as RM in Hadoop scheduler, YARN [3]. And there is a "Resource Request Agent" for an individual map or reduce task, to communicate with the resource manager.

The resource manager maintains a pool for available GPUs, to ensure that one GPU would not be allocated to multiple tasks simultaneously. Each machine in the cluster updates its own available GPUs to the resource manager per heartbeat, which allows the resource manager to know the status of all machines. The resource manager processes GPU resource requests from all tasks in an FIFO order by default.

For each task, the resource request agent automatically detects user-provided native functions. If CUDA or OpenCL functions are detected, it would request a GPU resource from the resource manager. When the resource manager receives the request, it seeks for a GPU on that machine. Once the request is responded as success, the resource request agent would get the allocated GPU, and launch CUDA or OpenCL kernels to the corresponding GPU.

Meanwhile, the resource manager maintains a model to determine the resource configuration, i.e., the number of simultaneously running CPU and GPU tasks, together with the number of threads for each CPU task. The model is obtained using the approach in Section 4. It can assist users to determine the resource configuration for an application for different purposes, e.g., to obtain the best performance, or the most cost-effective. Furthermore, it can be used to allocate GPUs across multiple simultaneously running applications.

4. MODELING THE HETEROGENEITY

In this section, we continue to take KNN as our example to answer the questions raised in Section 2.2.

4.1 Problem Formulation

The problem of modeling the resource heterogeneity per node can be formulated as:

On a GPGPU platform with n GPUs, with the host CPU having p cores, given a resource configuration, i.e., the number of GPU tasks (g), the number of CPU tasks (c), together with the number of threads per CPU task (t), how to determine the data processing speed under the configuration for any given MapReduce application?

We will continue to use the metric of data processing speed introduced in Section 2. In particular, for the GPGPU platform in the problem formulation, the data processing speed of the platform is:

$$dps = \frac{c}{tc} + \frac{g}{tg} \quad (2)$$

where tc is the time for processing a split using a CPU mapper, and tg for a GPU mapper. $\frac{1}{tc}$ and $\frac{1}{tg}$ are the data processing speeds of one CPU and GPU task respectively. Therefore, the data processing speed of the platform is the accumulated processing speed of the simultaneously running c CPU tasks and g GPU tasks.

If a user aims to obtain the best-performing configuration, we can use the model to maximize the *dps*. Alternatively, users can also define other objectives, e.g., cost-efficiency, which will be discussed in Section 5.

4.2 Characterizing A Task

In Equation 2, tc and tg would vary with the resource configurations due to resource contention. It is impractical to profile the processing time under all configurations. Therefore, we model *dps* using the behavior of a single-threaded CPU and a GPU task running individually on the platform, to avoid profile space explosion. We call the two tasks as the **CPU_base** and **GPU_base** of a MapReduce application on the platform, denoted as β_{CPU} and β_{GPU} respectively.

Table 1: List of parameters for modeling the *dps*.

Platform	p	number of CPU hardware threads
	n	number of GPUs
App.	tdc_0	time of reading a split into CPU memory for CPU_base
	tpc_0	time of processing a split on CPU for CPU_base
	tdg_0	time of reading a split into CPU memory for GPU_base
	tpg_0	time of processing a split on GPU for GPU_base
	$tdcg_0$	time of transferring a split from CPU into GPU memory
Conf.	g	number of concurrent GPU tasks
	c	number of concurrent CPU tasks
	t	number of threads per CPU task

First, we characterize β_{CPU} and β_{GPU} into two feature vectors, one for CPU and the other for GPU.

$$\begin{cases} fv_{cpu}(task) = (tdc_0, tpc_0) \\ fv_{gpu}(task) = (tdg_0, tdcg_0, tpg_0) \end{cases} \quad (3)$$

where the meanings of tdc_0, tpc_0, tdg_0, tpg_0 and $tdcg_0$ are listed in Table 1. We introduce a 0 in the subscript to emphasize that these features are collected *only* for the base tasks. Therefore, the feature vectors are determined only by the application and the platform, and do not vary with configurations.

Note that the data reading time for β_{CPU} and β_{GPU} may differ, due to the different data processing patterns on CPUs and GPUs, as shown in Figure 2.

4.3 Modeling Data Processing Speed

For the problem in Section 4.1, given a configuration k, we model the $dps(k)$. In particular, a configuration k includes: the number of GPU tasks running simultaneously (g), the number of CPU tasks running simultaneously (c), and the number of threads per CPU task (t). For clarity, we list the parameters in our model in Table 1.

In this paper we focus only on data-local tasks, i.e., for a task, its data are located on where the task is executed. Modeling non-local tasks would introduce network cost and is beyond the scope of this paper.

For a given task configuration k, the execution time of one task can be computed using:

$$T_k = \begin{cases} tdc(k) + tpc(k), \ for\ CPU\ task \\ tdg(k) + tpg(k) + tdcg(k), \ for\ GPU\ task \end{cases} \quad (4)$$

where tdc, tpc, tdg, tpg and $tdcg$ are the same as in Table 1, except that these variables represent the corresponding time under a given configuration k. We observed that the time of transferring data from CPU to GPU memory is much less than the time spent on reading data from disk, i.e., 0.2 seconds vs 14.1 seconds for 1GB data. Therefore, we omit the item of $tdcg$ in Equation 4.

In particular, a map/reduce task can be divided into two phases: data reading and computing. For GPU tasks, its computation time $tpg(k)$ does not change with configurations. For multi-threaded CPU tasks, we assume the performance would be perfectly scaled up with the number of threads. The assumption is reasonable since MapReduce applications are data parallel and do not include synchronization inside a task, and the performance interference across multiple threads caused by shared cache and bandwidth contentions can be predicted using the approach in [39], which is ignored in this paper. So the data processing time under a given configuration k can be computed using Equation 5, and the data reading time will be discussed in Section 4.4.

$$\begin{cases} tpc(k) = tpc_0/t \\ tpg(k) = tpg_0 \end{cases} \tag{5}$$

4.4 Modeling Data Reading Time

In Hadoop+, the CPU and GPU tasks would contend for the shared I/O resource, and we use map tasks for discussion. As discussed in Section 2, the simultaneously running tasks would cause shared I/O resource contention and increase the data reading time for each task. Therefore for the configuration parameters in Table 1, the number of simultaneously running CPU and GPU tasks (c and g) would affect the data reading time.

We empirically observe that the data reading time is affected by two factors: the total I/O traffic, and the number of applications issuing I/O requests. Our methodology is based on the observation as follows. First, we construct a HDFS reader benchmark *base* which continuously reads data from a HDFS file and includes no computation. We launch *base* to run individually and record the data reading time $d0$. Second, we create another HDFS reader benchmark *hreader*, which reads some bytes from a HDFS file periodically. By adjusting the reading interval, we can vary its I/O traffic. Then we co-run the *hreader* with *base*, and record the data reading time of *base*. Third, we launch 2-5 *hreader* and vary their I/O traffic, co-run with *base*, and record the data reading time of *base*. Finally, we plot these points into Figures 5 and 6.

Figure 5 shows *base*'s data reading time varying with co-runners. In particular, the vertical axis shows the data reading time normalized to $d0$. Each color represents the data for one fixed number of co-runners. It gives two observations: 1) For a given number of co-runners, *base*'s data reading time increases linearly with I/O traffic, until an upper bound is reached. 2) The upper bound is determined by the number of co-runners, which can be represented as a linear function, as shown in Figure 6. In particular, when n tasks are reading a file from HDFS simultaneously, the maximal data reading time is n times of base task, since only $1/n$ of the I/O resource can be obtained for each task.

Thus, the data reading time can be represented as

$$\begin{aligned} tdc(k) &= min(a * sumio + b, fmax(g + c * t)) * tdc0 \\ tdg(k) &= min(a * sumio + b, fmax(g + c * t)) * tdg0 \end{aligned} \tag{6}$$

where

$$fmax(n) = n, \quad sumio = \frac{VS}{tdc_0 + tpc_0} * (c * t) + \frac{VS}{tdg_0} * g \tag{7}$$

In Equation 7, VS is the data volume of one split, therefore $\frac{VS}{tdg_0}$ is the I/O traffic for a GPU task. For a CPU task, due to the pattern of alternating data reading and computing, the exhibited average I/O traffic of each working thread would be $\frac{VS}{tdc_0+tpc_0}$. As a result, $(\frac{VS}{tdc_0+tpc_0} * (c*t) + \frac{VS}{tdg_0} * g)$ is the aggregated I/O traffic for all simultaneously running tasks. The min function in Equation 6 means that the maximal data reading time would not exceed the maximum shown in Figure 6.

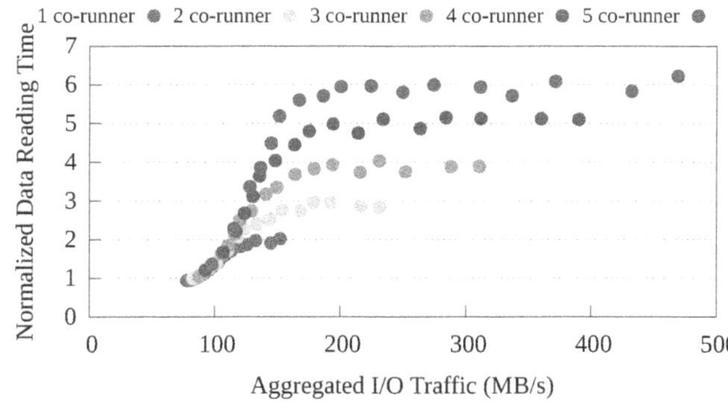

Figure 5: Data reading time with co-runners.

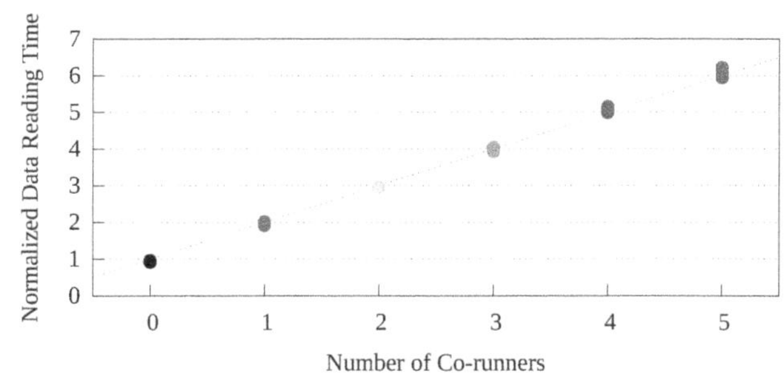

Figure 6: Maximal data reading time.

Note that the data reading model only depends on the platform and does not depend on applications. We will demonstrate this in Section 5.

4.5 Understanding the Motivation Example

Now we use KNN to answer the three questions raised in Section 2.2.4.

Q:What factors would affect the performance gain when allocating a computing resource to an application?

A:The performance is determined by the application's feature vectors, i.e., the data reading time and computation time. In other words, the performance gain is relevant to the ratio between data reading and computation, and the speedup of GPU computation over CPU computation for the application.

Q:How will the performance contribution of one computing resource, i.e., GPU, vary with applications?

A:If an application's data reading time makes up a high proportion of the processing, more computing resources would cause shared I/O resource contention, thereby resulting in little performance gain. Contrarily, if an application's computation time dominates the processing, more computing resources would bring significant performance gain.

For KNN, its feature vectors are $fv_{cpu}(KNN) = (14.1, 120.2)$, and $fv_{gpu}(KNN) = (14.1, 0.2, 2.9)$. For the GPU base task, the data reading time is 14.1 seconds while the processing time is only 2.9 seconds. Therefore KNN cannot obtain a significant speedup when more computing resources are allocated to it, as discussed in Section 2.

Q:How to select a resource configuration for an application for different purposes, e.g., to obtain the best performance, or to be the most cost-effective to satisfy some performance requirement?

A:We can use our model to predict the data processing speed under different resource configurations, as illustrated in Figure 1, and select the resource configuration under different objectives. For KNN, the configuration of 2G-0C-0T would exhibit the best performance, and the configuration of 0G-6C-1T is the most cost-effective, as discussed in Section 5.

4.6 Summary and Discussion

For an application, we run its GPU_base and CPU_base independently and obtain its feature vectors. Then we use our heterogeneity model to compute the data processing speeds under different configurations, and determine the resource configuration for different purposes. In particular, we leverage the data reading model in Equation 6 to predict the data reading time, and Equation 5 to predict the data processing time under different resource configurations.

So far our model does not consider the following issues, which will be our future work. First, the model does not include the resource contention for network communication. Second, the model does not enable multiple GPU tasks to run simultaneously on one GPU card. Third, the model does not enable multiple tasks running simultaneously on one hardware core.

5. EVALUATION

5.1 Platform and Benchmark

The heterogeneous cluster we use includes 8 nodes, with each node being an Intel 2.00GHz six-core Xeon E5-2620 chip configured with two NVIDIA Tesla C2050 GPUs, and each GPU has a 3GB global memory and 14 SMs, each containing 32 Streaming Processors(SPs). Each SM has 32768 registers and a 48KB shared memory.

Our Hadoop+ is implemented based on Hadoop 2.1.0 beta. We use the following big data applications for evaluation:

- *K-nearest neighbors (KNN)*. Details of the algorithm have been discussed in Section 2.

  The base Hadoop version for comparison is implemented using the algorithm presented in [11]. For fairness, we also introduced a maximum heap in the version to select the top-K training examples before shuffling.

  The input data size is 960GB. The dimension of input is 128, the number of training examples is 977,054,400, the number of testing examples is 448, and K is 4. The split size is 1GB.

- *K-Means Clustering (Kmeans)*. Kmeans partitions a number of objects into k clusters such that similar objects belong to the same cluster [12].

  The base Hadoop version for comparison is mahout-0.7.0 [1].

  The data set consists of 3,932,280,000 four-dimension vectors. The number of clusters (K) is set to 100. The split size is set as 1GB.

- *Row Similarity (RS)*. The algorithm is typically used in recommendation systems. It takes a number of vectors as input, and computes the similarity between two vectors of the inner product space.

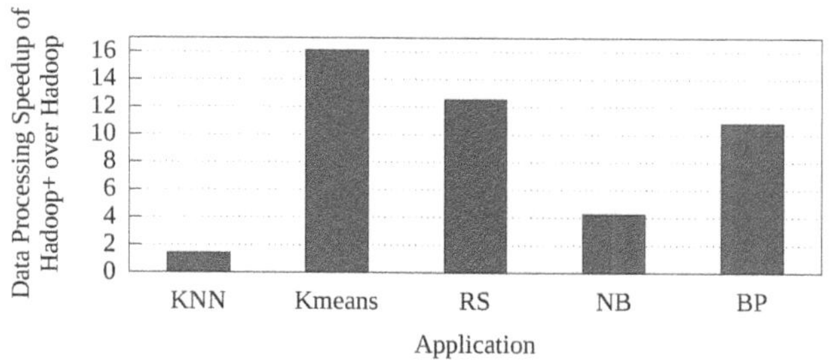

Figure 7: Speedup of Hadoop+ over Hadoop.

  The base Hadoop version for comparison is mahout-0.7.0 [1].

  The dimension of vectors is 16,777,216, the number of vectors is 8192, the sparsity is set to 0.0625, and the split size is set as 1GB.

- *Naive Bayes Classifier (NB)*. This is a popular method for text categorization. It uses word frequencies as the features, and judges documents as belonging to one category of the other.

  The base Hadoop version for comparison is mahout-0.7.0 [1].

  The size of the input data is 96GB, and the number of classes is 20, and the split size is set as 1GB.

- *Back Propagation (BP)*. This is a classical algorithm for training artificial neural networks. It calculates the gradient of a loss function with respects to all the weights in the network, and iteratively updates the weights to minimize the loss function.

  We implement the Hadoop version and Hadoop+ version using the approach in [25].

  The training data are 1,024,000 48-dimension vectors. The number of nodes in hidden layer and output layer is set to 65536 and 48 respectively, and the split size is set as 4MB.

For all the five applications we used, the map phase dominates the execution. Therefore, we write the *PMap* functions with CUDA using the Hadoop+ interface for GPU acceleration, and keep using original *Reduce* functions for the reduce phase. Meanwhile, the original *Map* functions are also included for CPU tasks.

We evaluate Hadoop+ in two scenarios. First, the five applications are executed one by one in single-application scenario and we evaluate the performance for each application. Second, two of the five applications are launched simultaneously to emulate the multi-application scenario, and we evaluate the completion time for the two applications. Sections 5.2 and 5.3 present the performance results for the two scenarios respectively, Section 5.4 discusses the experimental results case by case, Section 5.5 verifies our performance prediction model, and Section 5.6 demonstrates how to find a cost-efficient resource consumption using our model.

5.2 Results in Single-App Scenario

In this section, we present the overall performance speedup for the five application implemented in Hadoop+ over Hadoop. To make a fair comparison, we also tune the optimal configuration for Hadoop applications, which is identical for all the five applications, i.e., 6 single-threaded CPU tasks.

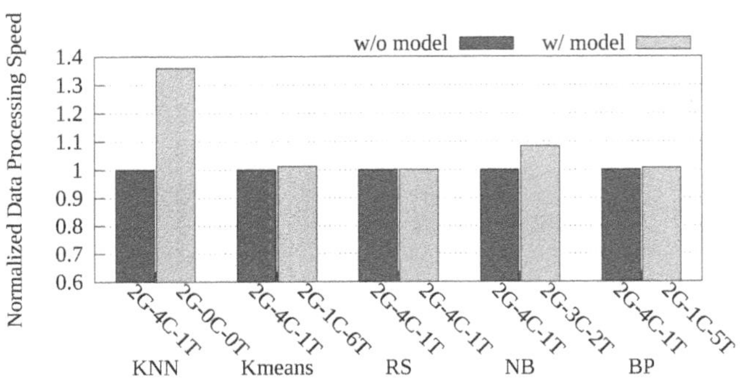

Figure 8: Performance improvement of configuration selection using the heterogeneity model.

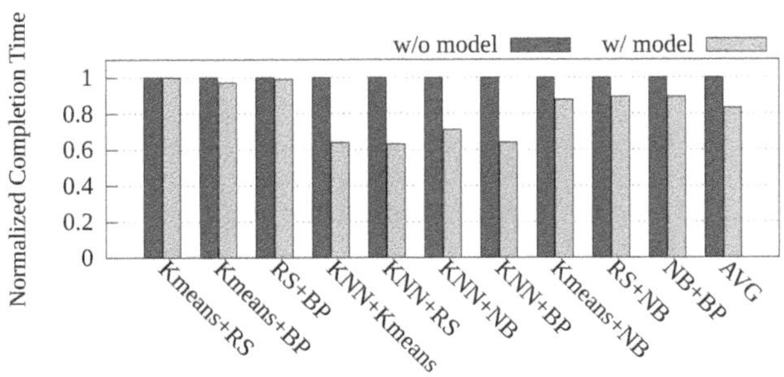

Figure 9: Results in a multi-app scenario.

Figure 7 shows that Hadoop+ can achieve 1.4x to 16.1x speedups over Hadoop. The benefit depends on the features of applications, and we will further discuss it in Section 5.4.

Figure 8 shows the performance contribution of our heterogeneity model, with the obtained optimal task configurations annotated on the horizontal axis. For each application, the left bar shows the performance (normalized to 1) of the default configuration, i.e., 2G-4C-1T, and the right bar shows the normalized performance with the optimal configuration obtained using our heterogeneity model. For RS, the obtained optimal configuration is identical to the default value. For Kmeans and BP, the optimal configuration brings only 1.1% and 0.7% performance improvement. However, for KNN and NB, the optimal configuration would bring 36.0% and 8.3% performance improvement respectively.

5.3 Results in Multi-App Scenario

Using the 5 applications, we generate $C_5^2 = 10$ pair-wise combinations to evaluate the multi-application scenario. Without our heterogeneity model, FIFO scheduler is used to allocate GPUs among the simultaneously running applications. With the heterogeneity model, we can allocate GPUs to the applications for which GPU can bring more performance gain. In particular, for two simultaneously running applications A and B, if A is predicted to be able to get more performance gain from GPUs than B, A would be given high priority to obtain GPUs.

Figure 9 shows the normalized completion time for each combination, with each group representing for one combination. For each combination, the first bar represents the completion time when FIFO scheduler is used without the heterogeneity model, and the second bar represents the completion time when GPUs are allocated using the heterogeneity model. As shown in Figure 9, for the 10 combinations,

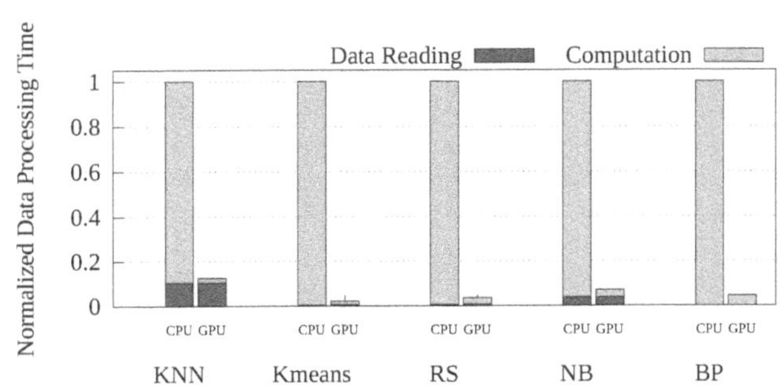

Figure 10: Normalized data processing time.

our performance model would reduce the completion time up to 36.9%, with the average of 17.6%.

From Figure 9, we make the following observations:

- For a given pair-wise combination, if each application can get significant benefit from GPUs, the GPU allocation strategy would not bring significant performance improvement for the combination. In particular, the combinations of Kmeans+RS, Kmeans+BP, and RS+BP belong to this category.
- For a given pair-wise combination, if one application can get significant benefit from GPUs while the other cannot, the GPU allocation strategy would bring significant performance improvement. The other 7 combinations belong to this category.

5.4 Case Study

As we discussed earlier, the performance gain from leveraging GPUs depends on two issues: the ratio between data reading and computation, and the speedup of GPU computation over CPU computation. In this section, we use experimental results to demonstrate the analysis.

To analyze the application features, we use Figure 10 to break down the data reading time and computation time for GPU and CPU tasks. For each application, the left bar shows the execution time of a CPU_base task, which is normalized to 1, and the right bar shows the execution of a GPU_base task, normalized by the CPU_base's execution time. Furthermore, both bars are broken down into data reading time (the dark blue section on the bottom) and computation time (the light blue section on the top).

We take KNN for the first case study, the speedup of Hadoop+ with GPU over Hadoop is 1.4x, since the data reading time dominates the data processing time for the GPU task, i.e., the data reading takes 14.1 seconds while the computation takes only 2.9 seconds. Even if the GPU task exhibits a significant speedup over CPU computation (2.9 seconds vs 120.2 seconds), the high proportion of I/O reading time makes the GPU speedup concealed from the perspective of the whole application execution. In particular, Hadoop issues 6 CPU single-threaded tasks to run simultaneously, and can complete 6 splits in 138.9 seconds, while Hadoop+ can process one split in 17.0 seconds. Thus the overall speedup is only 1.4x.

Kmeans, RS and BP exhibit different behaviors in Figure 10, for which the GPU task spends very little time on data reading, thus the tasks are dominated by GPU computations. For Kmeans, RS and BP, the data reading time occupies less than 0.6% of the total execution time. Meanwhile, the computation on GPU obtains significant speedups

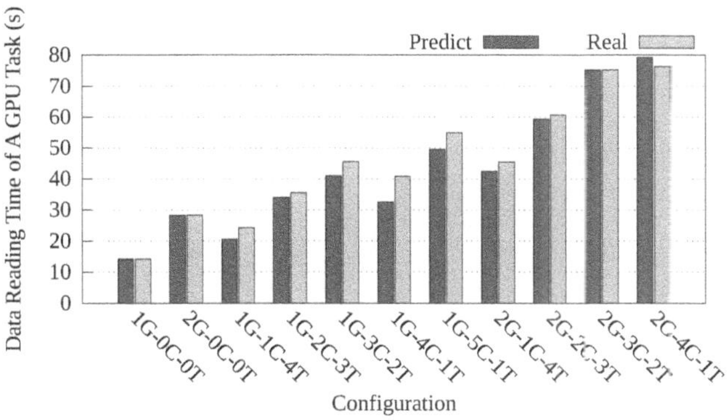

Figure 11: KNN's predicted data reading time.

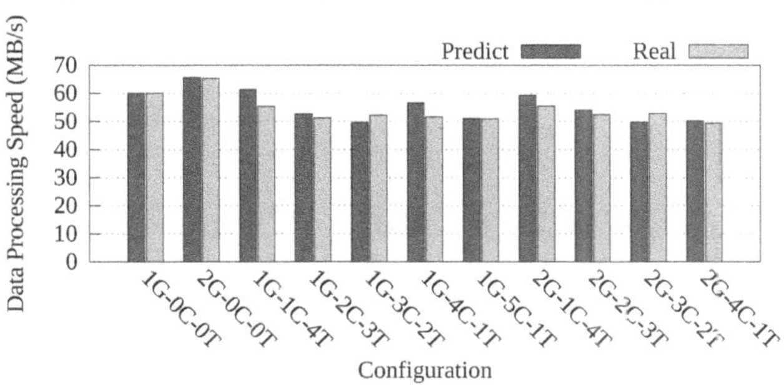

Figure 12: KNN's predicted processing speed.

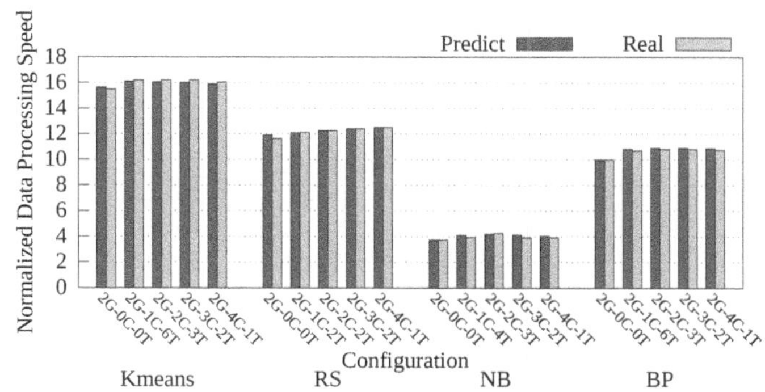

Figure 13: Predicted vs. measured data processing speeds. (Normalized to dps on Hadoop.)

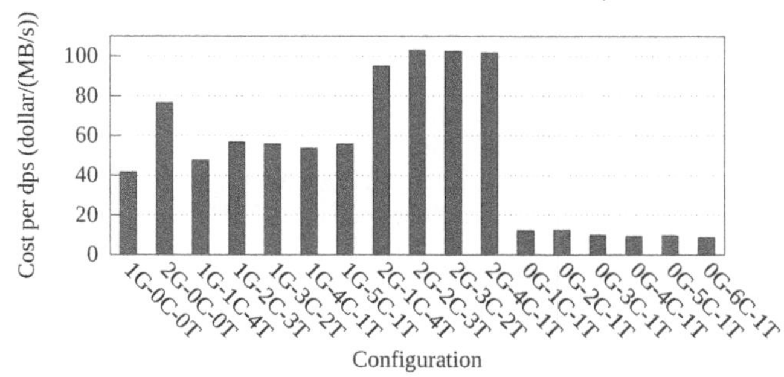

Figure 14: Cost efficiency for KNN.

over CPU, i.e., 61.6x, 34.0x, and 22.6x for Kmeans, RS and BP respectively. Therefore, they obtain 16.1x, 12.5x and 10.8x speedups over Hadoop respectively.

NB is an application in between the above two types. Its data reading time occupies 53.9% of the total execution time for GPU tasks, and the computation of GPU obtains 26.7x speedup. Therefore, its performance is also in between the above two types, i.e., 4.2x over Hadoop.

5.5 Model Verification

We use the configuration schemes in Figure 1 for our model verification. Figure 11 shows the predicted and real data reading time under different resource configurations for KNN, with the left bars representing the predicted values, and the right for the real values. The average error is only 5.9%. Furthermore, our model can accurately predict KNN's overall data processing speed of the whole cluster under different resource configurations (For clarity, each node in the cluster shares the same resource configuration). Figure 12 shows the predicted and real data processing speed of the cluster, with an average error of 3.8%.

Using the same approach, we can create the data processing model for the other 4 applications. Due to space limitations, we select five 2-GPU configurations to verify our model. Figure 13 presents the experimental results for these applications, and it shows that our model can accurately predict the data processing speed under different resource configurations, with an average error of 2.5%.

5.6 Cost Efficiency

In this section, we leverage our model to help users select the most cost-effective resource configuration. We use the official price of our CPU and GPU card to define the cost per time unit [4, 28]. In particular, the price of a CPU is \$408, with each core priced \$68, and the price of a GPU card is \$2499. Therefore, if the cost per time unit of one CPU core is normalized to 1, the cost per time unit of one GPU card would be \$36.8. To evaluate the cost efficiency, we use the 11 configurations in Figure 1, together with 6 extra configurations with GPUs disabled.

Now we seek for the most cost-effective resource configuration for each application. Given a MapReduce application and a platform with p CPU cores and n GPUs, for a given resource configuration, its cost-efficiency is defined as the cost divided by the performance:

$$\begin{aligned} cost\_efficiency(k) &= cost(k)/performance(k) \\ &= (G * g + C * c * t) * (V/dps)/dps \end{aligned} \tag{8}$$

where G and C represent the cost per time unit for a GPU card and a CPU core respectively. For a given configuration k, it uses g GPUs and $c * t$ CPU cores, thus $G * g + C * c * t$ is the accumulated cost per time unit of the configuration k, and V/dps is the execution time. So $(G*g+C*c*t)*(V/dps)$ represents the total cost for completing the application, and dps is used for representing the performance.

Figure 14 presents the cost efficiency for KNN, which shows that the most cost-effective configuration is using only CPUs (0G-6C-1T). Table 2 lists the most cost-effective configurations obtained using our model for the 5 applications. NB is similar to KNN, with the 0-GPU configuration being the most cost-effective. For Kmeans, BP and RS, leveraging GPU would increase the cost efficiency, with Kmeans and BP using 1 GPU, and RS using 2 GPUs.

Table 2: The most cost-effective configurations.

Benchmark	g	c	t
KNN	0	6	1
Kmeans	1	0	0
RS	2	0	0
NB	0	4	1
BP	1	2	3

6. RELATED WORK

There has been a lot of work on developing MapReduce frameworks on modern architectures, especially for GPU-involved heterogeneous platforms/clusters.

On single-node GPGPU platform, Catanzaro et al presented a MapReduce framework which executes user-provided mapper and reducer CUDA kernels on a GPU [7]. He et al proposed Mars, which provides a similar MapReduce programming API and introduces a sort stage to sort the intermediate (key, value) pairs [20]. Hong et al proposed MapCG, another framework which can port user-provided MapReduce programs to either CPU or GPU [21]. Comparing with Mars, MapCG proposed a GPU-based hash table, to avoid sorting intermediate (key, value) pairs before reduce [21]. Furthermore, Ji et al, Chen et al proposed to use shared memory to optimize MapReduce framework on GPUs [22, 8]. All these related work are single-node MapReduce frameworks, requiring the data to be processed can fit into a single GPU's memory.

On GPU clusters, Stuart and Owen proposed GPMR, a stand-alone C++-based MapReduce framework, which enables user-written CUDA kernels. Meanwhile, GPMR introduced a number of intermediate stages, such as partial reduction and accumulation to minimize inter-node communication. Furthermore, GPMR also supports multiple GPUs per node with dedicated processes for each GPU [32].

On CPU/GPGPU hybrid clusters, HAPI [29] and HadoopCL [19] are representative work. Both of them use APARAPI [18] to automatically generate GPU OpenCL kernels from Java code. In particular, HAPI provides a heterogeneous mapper class, including preprocess, gpu and gpuprocess, which are provided by users. After users provide these class implementations in Hadoop, HAPI can automatically generate the corresponding OpenCL mapper kernel on GPU using APARAPI. At runtime, the HAPI would invoke the generated OpenCL kernel via JNI. HadoopCL further enhances HAPI to provide more friendly programming interface for programmers. Glasswing [16] is another MapReduce framework using OpenCL to exploit multi-core CPUs and accelerators. It uses pipeline to overlap computation, communication, memory transfer and disk access, and exploits fine-grained parallelism within each stage by taking advantage of a variety of devices.

HAPI and HadoopCL are most closely related to our work. However, our work has the following differences: 1) Hadoop+ takes the shared resource contention into consideration and provides a heterogeneity model, to guide users to select their desired resource utilization for the purposes of improving performance or cost-efficiency, or to guide the GPU allocation across multiple simultaneously running MapReduce applications. Thus users can select specific computing resources under different purposes. 2) Hadoop+ enables users to provide explicitly parallel functions as plug-ins, thus it can easily integrate existing high-performance libraries into a large-scale data-processing framework, thus facilitating exploitations of GPUs in the Hadoop framework. 3) Hadoop+ enables the original *Map* and *Reduce* functions in Hadoop to co-exist with user-provided explicitly parallel *PMap* and *PReduce* functions. Thus users can take existing CUDA/ OpenCL codes, plug it into existing Hadoop programs, to make the applications coordinately run on both CPUs and GPUs. For example, in our evaluation, we directly download the CUDA code of K-means from [2] and plug it into the Hadoop implementation of K-means in mahout [1], thus facilitating programming for heterogeneous clusters.

Performance degradation caused by shared resource contention is another related area of our work. There has been a lot of work addressing contentions on shared cache [10, 23, 38], memory bandwidth [15, 37, 36], memory subsystem [26, 27, 40, 17, 33, 34, 39], and I/O resource [6, 35, 24]. Meanwhile, GPUPerf [31] has been developed to predict the performance and understand bottlenecks of GPGPU applications. Our work focuses on MapReduce applications and models their behaviors in heterogeneous clusters.

7. CONCLUSION AND FUTURE WORK

This paper presents a heterogeneous MapReduce framework, Hadoop+, which enables user-provided explicit parallel functions written in native languages to be embedded in Hadoop as plug-ins. Furthermore, we leverage Hadoop+ to model the heterogeneity for a MapReduce application, thus determining the optimal or most cost-effective resource configuration for an application. We evaluate the model by using 5 real-world big data applications and demonstrate that Hadoop+ enables users to exploit GPU capability, thus achieving 1.4x–16.1x speedups over Hadoop for the 5 real applications. Moreover, the heterogeneity model can be used to allocate GPUs among multiple simultaneously running MapReduce applications, bringing up to 36.9% (17.6% in average) performance improvement.

In future work, we plan to take the non-data-local tasks into consideration. And we will extend this work to model the heterogeneous resource contention for more distributed computing applications, e.g., MPI applications, and for more architectures, e.g., closely integrated on-chip GPUs. Furthermore, we will consider to automatically generate CUDA codes for MapReduce applications [13].

Acknowledgment

This research is supported by the National High Technology Research and Development Program of China under grant No. 2012AA010902 and 2015AA011505; the NSFC under grants No. 61202055, 61221062,61303053, 61432016 and 61402445; and the National Basic Research Program of China under grant No. 2011CB302504; Australian Council Research (ARC) Grants, DP110104628 and DP130101970. We would like to thank all the reviewers for their valuable comments and suggestions.

8. REFERENCES

[1] Apache mahout. http://mahout.apache.org/.

[2] Efficient algorithms for k-means clustering. http://www.cs.umd.edu/ mount/Projects/KMeans/.

[3] Hadoop Yarn. In *http://hadoop.apache.org/docs/r2.3.0/ hadoop-yarn/hadoop-yarn-site/YARN.html.*

[4] Official Price for Intel Xeon E5-2620. http://ark.intel.com/products/64594/Intel-Xeon-Processor-E5-2620-15M-Cache-2_00-GHz-7_20-GTs-Intel-QPI.

[5] Apache Hadoop. In *http://lucene.apache.org/hadoop/*, 2006.

[6] P. Carns, K. Harms, W. Allcock, C. Bacon, S. Lang, R. Latham, and R. Ross. Understanding and improving computational science storage access through continuous characterization. In *MSST*, 2011.

[7] B. Catanzaro, N. Sundaram, and K. K. A map reduce framework for programming graphics processors. In *Workshop on Software Tools for MultiCore Systems*, 2008.

[8] L. Chen and G. Agrawal. Optimizing mapreduce for gpus with effective shared memory usage. In *HPDC*, 2012.

[9] R. Chen, H. Chen, and B. Zang. Tiled-mapreduce: Optimizing resource usages of data-parallel applications on multicore with tiling. In *PACT*, pages 523–534, 2010.

[10] S. Cho and L. Jin. Managing distributed, shared L2 caches through OS-level page allocation. In *MICRO*, 2006.

[11] T. Cover and P. Hart. Nearest neighbor pattern classification. *IEEE Trans. Inf. Theor.*, 13(1):21–27, Sept. 2006.

[12] H. Cui, G. Ruan, J. Xue, R. Xie, L. Wang, and X. Feng. A collaborative divide-and-conquer k-means clustering algorithm for processing large data. In *CF*, 2014.

[13] H. Cui, L. Wang, J. Xue, Y. Yang, and X. Feng. Automatic library generation for blas3 on gpus. In *IPDPS*, 2011.

[14] J. Dean and S. Ghemawat. "mapreduce: simplified data processing on large clusters". In *OSDI*, 2004.

[15] D. Eklov, N. Nikoleris, D. Black-Schaffer, and E. Hagersten. Bandwidth Bandit: Quantitative characterization of memory contention. In *CGO*, 2013.

[16] I. El-Helw, R. Hofman, and H. E. Bal. Scaling mapreduce vertically and horizontally. In *SC'14*, pages 525–535, 2014.

[17] A. Fedorova, M. Seltzer, and M. Smith. Improving performance isolation on chip multiprocessors via an operating system scheduler. In *PACT*, 2007.

[18] G. Frost. Aparapi in amd developer websize. In *"http://developer.amd.com/tools/heterogeneous-computing/aparapi/"*.

[19] M. Grossman, M. Breternitz, and V. Sarkar. "hadoopcl: Mapreduce on distributed heterogeneous platforms through seamless integration of hadoop and opencl". In *IPDPSW*, 2013.

[20] B. He, W. Fang, Q. Luo, N. K. Govindaraju, and T. Wang. "mars: A mapreduce framework on graphics processors". In *PACT*, 2008.

[21] C. Hong, D. Chen, W. Chen, W. Zheng, and H. Lin. Mapcg: writing parallel program portable between cpu and gpu. In *PACT*, 2010.

[22] F. Ji and X. Ma. Using shared memory to accelerate mapreduce on graphics processing units. In *IPDPS*, 2011.

[23] J. Lin, Q. Lu, X. Ding, Z. Zhang, X. Zhang, and P. Sadayappan. Gaining insights into multicore cache partitioning: Bridging the gap between simulation and real systems. In *HPCA*, 2008.

[24] Y. Liu, R. Gunasekarany, X. Ma, and S. S. Vazhkudai. Automatic Identification of Application I/O Signatures from Noisy Server-Side Traces. In *FAST*, 2014.

[25] Z. Liu, H. Li, and G. Miao. Mapreduce-based backpropagation neural network over large scale mobile data. In *ICNC*, 2010.

[26] J. Mars, L. Tang, R. Hundt, K. Skadron, and M. L. Soffa. Bubble-Up: Increasing Utilization in Modern Warehouse Scale Computers via Sensible Co-locations. In *MICRO*, 2011.

[27] J. Mars, L. Tang, and M. L. Soffa. Directly characterizing cross-core interference through contention synthesis. In *HiPEAC*, 2011.

[28] NVIDIA. Official Price for Tesla C2050. In *http://www.nvidia.com/object/io_1258360868914.html*.

[29] S. Okur, C. Radio, and Y. Lin. "hadoop+aparapi: Making heterogeneous mapreduce programming easier". In *"https://netfiles.uiuc.edu/okur2"*.

[30] C. Ranger, R. Raghuraman, A. Penmetsa, G. Bradski, and C. Kozyrakis. "evaluating mapreduce for multi-core and multiprocessor systems". In *HPCA*, 2007.

[31] J. Sim, A. Dasgupta, H. Kim, and R. Vuduc. A performance analysis framework for identifying potential benefits in gpgpu applications. In *PPoPP*, 2012.

[32] J. A. Stuart and J. D. Owens. Multi-gpu mapreduce on gpu clusters. In *IPDPS*, 2011.

[33] L. Tang, J. Mars, and M. L. Soffa. Compiling For Niceness Mitigating Contention for QoS in Warehouse Scale Computers. In *CGO*, 2012.

[34] L. Tang, J. Mars, N. Vachharajani, R. Hundt, and M. L. Soffa. The Impact of Memory Subsystem Resource Sharing on Datacenter Applications. In *ISCA*, 2011.

[35] A. Uselton, M. Howison, N. Wright, D. Skinner, N. Keen, J. Shalf, K. Karavanic, and L. Oliker. Parallel I/O performance: From events to ensembles. In *IPDPS*, 2010.

[36] D. Xu, C. Wu, P. Yew, J. Li, and Z. Wang. Providing Fairness on Shared-Memory Multiprocessors via Process Scheduling. In *SIGMETRICS*, 2012.

[37] D. Xu, C. Wu, and P.-C. Yew. On mitigating memory bandwidth contention through bandwidth-aware scheduling. In *PACT*, 2010.

[38] X. Zhang, S. Dwarkadas, and K. Shen. Towards practical page coloring-based multicore cache management. In *EuroSys*, 2009.

[39] J. Zhao, H. Cui, J. Xue, X. Feng, Y. Yan, and W. Yang. An empirical model for predicting cross-core performance interference on multicore processors. In *PACT*, 2013.

[40] S. Zhuravlev, S. Blagodurov, and A. Fedorova. Addressing shared resource contention in multicore processors via scheduling. In *ASPLOS*, 2010.

Active Access: A Mechanism for High-Performance Distributed Data-Centric Computations

Maciej Besta
Department of Computer Science
ETH Zurich
maciej.besta@inf.ethz.ch

Torsten Hoefler
Department of Computer Science
ETH Zurich
htor@inf.ethz.ch

ABSTRACT

Remote memory access (RMA) is an emerging high-performance programming model that uses RDMA hardware directly. Yet, accessing remote memories cannot invoke activities at the target which complicates implementation and limits performance of data-centric algorithms. We propose Active Access (AA), a mechanism that integrates well-known active messaging (AM) semantics with RMA to enable high-performance distributed data-centric computations. AA supports a new programming model where the user specifies handlers that are triggered when incoming puts and gets reference designated addresses. AA is based on a set of extensions to the Input/Output Memory Management Unit (IOMMU), a unit that provides high-performance hardware support for remapping I/O accesses to memory. We illustrate that AA outperforms existing AM and RMA designs, accelerates various codes such as distributed hashtables or logging schemes, and enables new protocols such as incremental checkpointing for RMA. We also discuss how extended IOMMUs can support a virtualized global address space in a distributed system that offers features known from on-node memory virtualization. We expect that AA and other IOMMU features can enhance the design of HPC operating and runtime systems in large computing centers.

1. INTRODUCTION

Scaling on-chip parallelism alone cannot satisfy growing computational demands of datacenters and HPC centers with tens of thousands of nodes [15]. Remote direct memory access (RDMA) [35], a technology that completely removes the CPU and the OS from the messaging path, enhances performance in such systems. RDMA networking hardware gave rise to a new class of Remote Memory Access (RMA) programming models that offer a Partitioned Global Address Space (PGAS) abstraction to the programmer. Languages such as Unified Parallel C (UPC) [38] or Fortran 2008 [23], and libraries such as MPI-3 [26] or SHMEM implement the RMA principles and enable direct *one-sided* low-overhead *put* and *get* access to the memories of remote nodes, outperforming Message Passing (MP) routines [19].

Active Messages (AMs) [40] are another scheme for improving performance in distributed environments. An active message invokes a handler at the receiver's side and thus AMs can be viewed as lightweight remote procedure calls (RPC). AMs are widely used in a number of different areas (example libraries include IBM's DCMF, IBM's PAMI, Myrinet Express (MX), GASNet [11], and AM++ [41]). Unfortunately, AMs are limited to message passing and cannot be directly used in RMA programming.

In this work we propose *Active Access* (AA), a mechanism that enhances RMA with AM semantics. The core idea is that a remote memory access triggers a user-definable CPU handler at the target. As we explain in § 1.1, AA eliminates some of the performance problems specific to RMA.

Intercepting and processing puts or gets requires control logic to identify memory accesses, to decide when to run a handler, and to buffer necessary data. To preserve all RDMA benefits (OS-bypass, zero-copy, etc.) in AA, we propose a hardware-based design that extends the input/output memory management unit (IOMMU), a hardware unit that supports I/O virtualization. IOMMUs evolved from simple DMA remapping devices to units offering advanced hardware virtualization [8]. Still, AA shows that many potential benefits of IOMMUs are yet to be explored. For example, as we will later show (§ 3.5), moving the notification functionality from the NIC to the IOMMU enables high performance communication with the CPU for AA. Moreover, AA based on IOMMUs can generalize the concept of virtual memory and enable hardware-supported virtualization of networked memories with enhanced data-centric paging capabilities.

In summary, our key contributions are as follows:

- We propose *Active Access* (AA), a mechanism that combines active messages and RMA to improve the performance of RMA-based applications and systems.
- We illustrate a detailed hardware design of simple extensions to IOMMUs to construct AA.
- We show that AA enables a new data-centric programming model that facilitates developing RMA applications.
- We evaluate AA using microbenchmarks and four large-scale use-cases (a distributed hashtable, an access counter, a logging system, and fault-tolerant parallel sort). We show that AA outperforms other communication schemes.
- We discuss how the IOMMU could enable hardware-based virtualization of remote memories.

ICS'15, June 8–11, 2015, Newport Beach, CA, USA.

ACM 978-1-4503-3559-1/15/06 ...$15.00.
http://dx.doi.org/10.1145/2751205.2751219.

1.1 Motivation

Consider a distributed hashtable (DHT): RMA programming improves its performance in comparison to MP 2-10 times [19]. Yet, hash collisions impact performance as handling them requires to issue many expensive remote atomics (see § 4). Figure 1 shows how the performance varies by a factor of ≈10 with different collision rates.

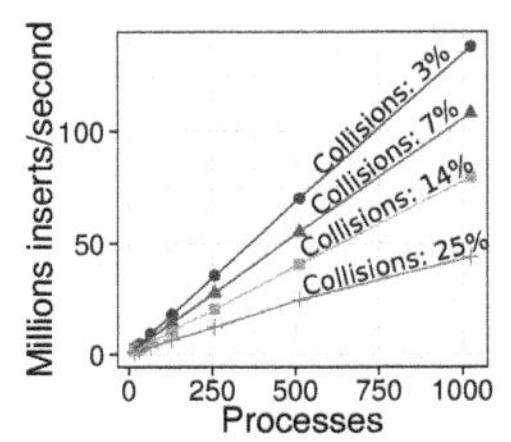

Figure 1: Inserts/s in our RMA hashtable (§ 1.1)

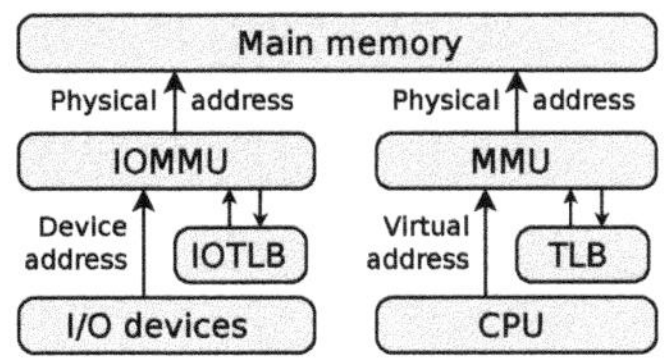

Figure 2: Comparison of the IOMMU and the MMU (§ 2.2)

We will show later (§ 4) how AA reduces the number of remote accesses from six to *one*. Intuitively, the design of AA, based on IOMMU remapping logic, intercepts memory requests and passes them for direct processing to the local CPU. Thus, AA combines the benefits of AMs and OS-bypass in RMA communications.

2. BACKGROUND

We now briefly outline RMA programming. Then, we discuss the parts of the IOMMU design (DMA remapping, IOMMU paging) that we later use to design Active Access.

2.1 RMA Programming Models

RMA is a programming model in which processes communicate by directly accessing one another's memories. RMA is typically built on OS-bypass RDMA hardware to achieve highest performance. Thus, RMA *put* (writes to remote memories) and *get* (reads from remote memories) have very low latencies, and significantly improve performance over MP [19]. RDMA is available in virtually all modern networks (e.g., IBM's Cell on-chip network, InfiniBand [37], IBM PERCS, iWARP, and RoCE). In addition, numerous existing languages and libraries based on RMA such as UPC, Titanium, Fortran 2008, X10, Chapel, or MPI-3.0 RMA are actively developed and offer unique features for parallel programming. Consequently, the number of applications in the RMA model is growing rapidly.

Here, we use *source* or *target* to refer to a process that issues or is targeted by an RMA access. We always use *sender* and *receiver* to refer to processes that exchange messages.

2.2 IOMMUs

IOMMUs are located between peripheral devices and main memory and can thus intercept any I/O traffic. Like the well-known memory management units (MMUs), they can be programmed to translate device addresses to physical host addresses. Figure 2 shows the similarities between MMUs and IOMMUs. An IOMMU can virtualize the view of I/O devices and control access rights to memory pages.

All major hardware vendors such as IBM, Intel, AMD, Sun, and ARM offer IOMMU implementations to support virtualized environments; Table 1 provides an overview. We conclude that IOMMUs are a standard part of modern computer architecture and the recent growth in virtualization for cloud computing ensures that they will remain important in

Vendor	IOMMU and its application
AMD	GART [1]: address translation for the use by AGP
	DEV [8]: memory protection
	AMD IOMMU [2]: address translation & memory protection
IBM	Calgary PCI-X bridge [8]: address translation, isolation
	DART [8]: address translation, validity tracking
	IOMMU in Cell processors [8]: address translation, isolation
	IOMMU in POWER5 [5]: hardware enhanced I/O virtualization
	TCE [21]: enhancing I/O virtualization in pSeries 690 servers
Intel	VT-d [22]: memory protection, address translation
ARM	CoreLink SMMU [25]: memory management in System-on-Chip (SoC) bus masters, memory protection, address translation
PCI-SIG	IOV & ATS [33]: address translation, memory protection
Sun	IOMMU in SPARC [29]: address translation, memory protection
SolarFlare	IOMMU in SF NICs [34]: address translation, memory protection

Table 1: An overview of existing IOMMUs (§ 2.2).

the future. However, IOMMUs are a relatively new concept with many unexplored opportunities. Their ability to intercept any memory access and provide full address space virtualization can be the basis for many novel mechanisms for managing global (RDMA) address spaces.

To be as specific as possible, we selected Intel's IOMMU technology [22] to explain concepts of generic IOMMUs. Other implementations vary in some details but share the core features (per-page protection, DMA remapping, etc.).

DMA Remapping DMA remapping is the IOMMU function that we use extensively to design AA. The IOMMU remapping logic allows any I/O device to be assigned to its own private subset of host physical memory that is isolated from accesses by other devices. To achieve this, IOMMUs utilize three types of remapping structures (all located in main memory): *root-entry* tables, *context-entry* tables, and IOMMU *page tables*. The first two are used to map I/O devices to device-specific page tables. To improve the access time, the remapping hardware maintains several caches such as the *context-cache* (device-to-page-table mappings) and the *I/O Translation Lookaside Buffer* (IOTLB) (translations from device addresses to host physical addresses).

Page Tables & Page Faults IOMMU page tables allow to manage host physical memory in a hierarchical way; they are similar to standard MMU page tables (still, MMU and IOMMU page tables are set up independently). A 4-level table allows 4KB page granularity on 64 bit machines (superpages of various sizes are also supported).

IOMMU page tables implement a page fault mechanism similar to MMUs. Every page table entry (PTE) contains two protection bits, W and R, which indicate whether the page is writable and readable, respectively. Any access that violates the protection conditions is blocked by the hardware and a *page fault* is generated, logged, and reported to the OS. The IOMMU logs the fault information using special registers and in-memory *fault logs*. The OS is notified using Message Signal Interrupts (MSI). Every page fault is logged as a fixed-sized *fault entry* that contains the fault metadata (the address of the targeted page, etc.); the data being transferred is discarded. We will later extend this mechanism to log active accesses and their data and to bypass the OS.

3. THE ACTIVE ACCESS MECHANISM

Active Access combines the benefits of RMA and AMs. AMs enhance the message passing model by allowing messages to actively integrate into the computation on the re-

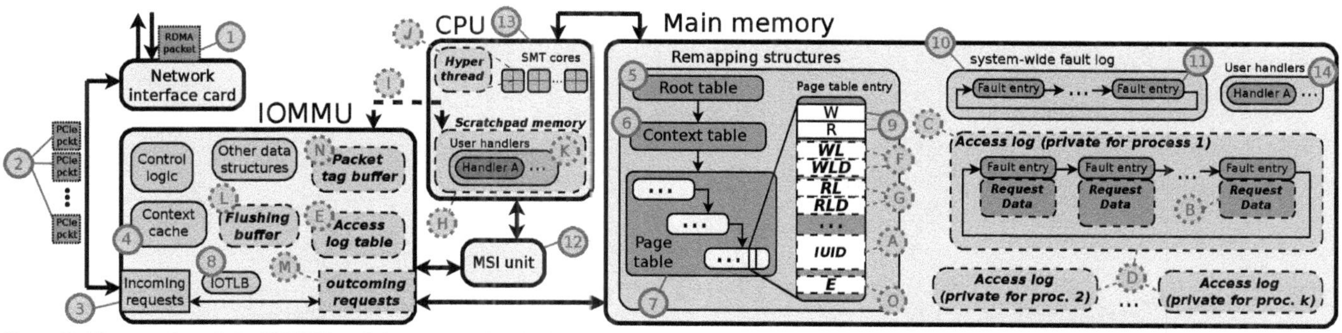

Figure 3: The overview of the IOMMU and the cooperating devices. The proposed extensions are marked with dashed edges and bold-italic text. Solid circles with numbers (①-⑭) indicate the specific steps discussed in detail in § 3.1. Dashed circles (Ⓐ-Ⓞ) are extensions pointed out in § 3.1-§ 3.7.

ceiver side. In RMA, processes communicate by accessing remote memories instead of sending messages. Thus, an analogous scheme for RMA has to provide the *active* semantics for both types of remote operations; puts and gets become *active puts* (AP) and *active gets* (AG), respectively.

Listing 1 shows the interface of AM and AA. An active message sent to a process `receiver_id` carries `arguments` and `payload` that will be used by a handler identified by a pointer `hlr_addr`. In AA, the user issues puts and gets at `trgt_addr` in the address space of a process `trgt_id`. No handler address is specified. Instead, we enable the user to associate an arbitrary page of data with a selected handler and with a set of additional actions (discussed in § 3.3 and § 3.4). When a put or a get touches such a page, it becomes *active*: first, it may or may not finalize its default memory effects (depending on the specified actions); second, *both* its metadata *and* data are ultimately processed by the associated handler. AA is fully transparent to RMA and, as Listing 1 shows, it entails no changes to the traditional interface.

```
/***************** interface of AM ***************/
void send_active_message(ptr hlr_addr, void* arguments,
      void* payload, int receiver_id) { ... }
/***************** interface of AA ***************/
void put(void* trgt_addr, void* data, int trgt_id) {
  /* Attempt to copy data from the local memory into
  the memory location trgt_addr of a process trgt_id.*/
}
void get(void* trgt_addr, void* l_addr, int trgt_id) {
  /* Attempt to fetch the data from the memory location
  trgt_addr of a process trgt_id to l_addr.*/
}
void assoc_page(void* addr, void* act, int hlr_id) {
  /* Associate a page at addr with actions act and
  with a handler identified by the id hlr_id. */
```

Listing 1: Interface of Active Messages and Active Access (§ 3)

We now show how to extend IOMMUs to implement the above AA interface and to enable active puts and gets. From now on, we will focus on designs based on PCI Express (PCIe) [32]. We first describe the interactions between an RDMA request and current IOMMUs. The numbers in circles (① - ⑭) refer to the corresponding numbers in Figure 3.

3.1 State-of-the-art IOMMU Processing Path

Consider an RDMA put or a get that is issued by a remote process. First, the local NIC receives the RDMA packet ①. The NIC attempts to access the main memory with DMA and thus it generates appropriate PCIe packets (one or more depending on the type of the PCIe transaction [32]) ②. Each packet is intercepted by the IOMMU ③. First, the IOMMU resolves the mapping from the device to its page table (using the packet header [22]). Here, the IOMMU uses the context cache ④ or, in case of a cache miss, it walks the remapping tables ⑤-⑥. Finally, the IOMMU obtains the location of the specific page-table ⑦. The IOMMU then resolves the mapping from a device address to a physical address using the IOTLB ⑧ or, in the event of a miss, the page-table ⑦. When it finds the target PTE, it checks its protection bits `W` and `R` ⑨. The next steps depend on the request type. For puts, if `W=1`, the value is simply written to the target location. If `W=0`, the IOMMU raises a page fault and does not modify the page. For gets, if `R=1`, the request returns the accessed value to the NIC. If `R=0`, the IOMMU raises a page fault and does not return the value.

Upon a page fault, the IOMMU tries to record the fault information (fault entry) in the system-wide fault log ⑩ (implemented as an in-memory ring buffer). In case of an overflow (e.g., if the OS does not process the recorded entries fast enough) the fault entry is not recorded. If the fault entry is logged ⑪, the IOMMU interrupts the CPU ⑬ with MSI ⑫ to run one of the specified handlers ⑭.

We now analyze the extensions that enable active puts/gets (symbols Ⓐ - Ⓞ refer to the related symbols in Figure 3). Our goal is to enable the IOMMU to multiplex intercepted accesses among processes, buffer them in designated memory locations, and pass them for processing to a CPU.

3.2 Processing the Intercepted Data

In the original IOMMU design the fault log ⑩ is shared by all the processes running on the node where the IOMMU resides; a potential performance bottleneck. In addition, the IOMMU does not enable multiplexing the data coming from the NIC across the processes and handlers, limiting performance in multi/manycore environments. Finally, the data of a blocked RDMA put is lost as the fault log entry only records the address (see steps ⑨-⑩). To alleviate these issues, we propose to enhance the design of the IOMMU and its page tables to enable a data-centric multiplexing mechanism in which *the PTEs themselves guide the incoming requests to be recorded in the specified logging data structures and processed by the designated user-space handlers.*

We first add a programmable field *IOMMU User Domain ID* (IUID) to every IOMMU PTE Ⓐ. This field enables *associating* pages with user domains. The OS and the NIC can ensure that one IUID is associated with at most one local process, similarly to Protection Domains in RDMA [35]. To add IUID we use bits 52-61 of IOMMU PTEs (ignored by the current IOMMU hardware [22]). We can store 2^{10} domains on each node; enough to fully utilize, e.g., BlueGene/Q (64 hardware threads/node) or Intel Xeon Phi (256 hardware threads/chip). Second, our extended IOMMU logs *both* the generated fault entry *and* the carried data Ⓑ to the *access log*, a new in-memory circular ring buffer Ⓒ. A process can have multiple private IUIDs/access logs located in its address space Ⓓ. Third, the IOMMU maintains the *access log*

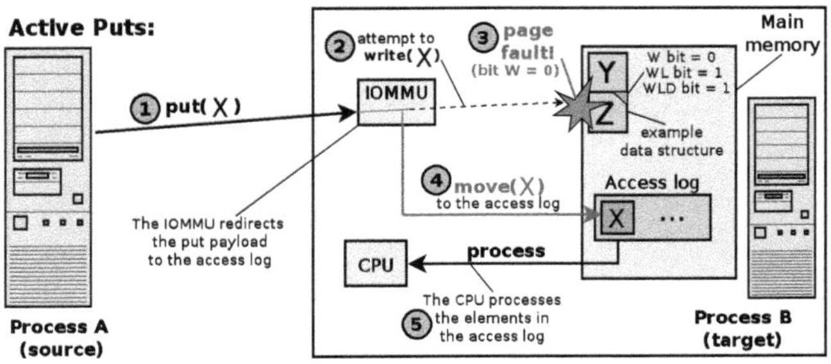

(a) An active put (§ 3.3)

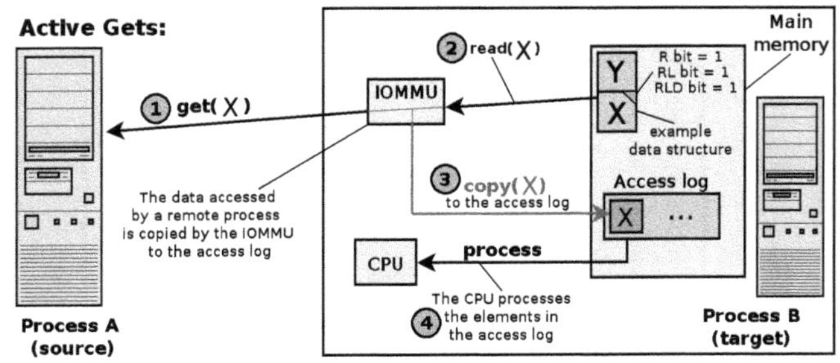

(b) An active get (§ 3.4)

Figure 4: Active puts and gets. Here, the numbers in circles are independent of the numbering in Figure 3.

table (E), a simple internal associative data structure with tuples (`IUID,base,head,tail,size`). One entry maps an IUID to three physical addresses (the base, the head, and the tail pointer) and the size of the respective access log ring buffer. The access log table is implemented as content addressable memory (CAM) for rapid access and it can be programmed in the same way as other Intel IOMMU structures [22].

3.3 Controlling Active Puts (APs)

Active puts enable redirecting data coming from the NIC and/or related metadata to a specified access log. Figure 4a illustrates active puts in more detail. Two additional PTE bits control the logging of fault entry and data: `WL` (Write Log) and `WLD` (Write Log Data) (F). If `WL=1` then the IOMMU logs the fault entry for the written page and if `WLD=1` then the IOMMU logs both the fault entry and the data. The flags `W`, `WL` and `WLD` are independent. For example, an active put page is marked as `W=0, WL=1, WLD=1`. The standard way, in which IOMMUs manage faults triggered by writes, is defined by the values `W=0, WL=1, WLD=0`.

3.4 Controlling Active Gets (AGs)

Active gets enable the IOMMU to log a copy of the remotely accessed data locally. When a get succeeds and the returned data is flowing from the main memory to the NIC, it is replicated by the IOMMU and saved in the access log (see Figure 4b). Similar to active puts, two additional PTE bits control the logging behavior of such accesses: `RL` (Read Log) and `RLD` (Read Log Data) (G). If `RL=1` then the IOMMU logs the fault entry for the read page and if `RLD=1` then the IOMMU logs the fault entry and the returned data.

The proposed control bit extensions for active puts and active gets can easily be implemented in practice. For example, bits 7-10 in the Intel IOMMU PTEs are ignored [22]. These bits can be used to store `WL`, `WLD`, `RL`, and `RLD`.

3.5 Interactions with the Local CPU

Finally, the IOMMU has to notify the CPU to run a handler to process the logs. Here, we discuss interrupts/polling and we propose a new scheme where the IOMMU directly accesses the CPU, bypassing the main memory.

Interrupts Here, one could use a high-performance MSI wakeup mechanism analogous to the scheme in InfiniBand [37]. The developer specifies conditions for triggering interrupts (when the amount of free space in an access log is below a certain threshold, or at pre-determined intervals). If the access log is sufficiently large and messages are pipelined then the interrupt latency may not influence the overall performance significantly (cf. § 5.2).

Polling As the IOMMU inserts data directly into a user address space, processes can monitor the access log head/-tail pointers and begin processing the data when required. Polling can be done either directly by the user, or by a runtime system that runs the handlers transparently to the user.

Direct CPU Access This mechanism is motivated by the architectural trends to place scratchpad memories on processing units, a common practice in today's NVIDIA GPUs [31] and several multicore architectures [24]. One could add a scratchpad to the CPU (H), connect it directly with the IOMMU (I), and place the head/tail pointers in it. A dedicated hyperthread (J) polls the pointers and runs the handlers if a free entry is available (14). If the size of the handler code is small, it can also be placed in the scratchpad, further reducing the number of memory accesses (K).

The IOMMU and the CPU also have to synchronize while processing the access log. This can be done with a simple lock for mutual access. The IOMMU and the CPU could also synchronize with the pointers from the access log table.

3.6 Consistency Model

We now enhance AA to enable a weak consistency model similar to MPI-3 RMA [20]. In RMA, a blocking flush synchronizes nonblocking puts/gets. In AA, we use an *active flush* (`flush(int target_id)`) to enforce the completion of active accesses issued by the calling process and targeted at `target_id`. One way to implement active flushes could be to issue an active `get` targeted at a special designated *flushing page* in the address space of `target_id`. The IOMMU, upon intercepting this get, would wait until the CPU processes the related access log and then it would finish the `get` to notify the source that the accesses have been committed.

Extending the IOMMU We add an IOMMU internal data structure called the *flushing buffer* (L) to store tuples (`address,IUID,active,requester-ID,tag`), where `address` is the address of the flushing page, `active` is a binary value initially set to `false`, and `requester-ID,tag` are values of two PCIe packet fields with identical names; they are initially zeroed and we discuss them later in this section. The flushing buffer is implemented as CAM for rapid access.

Selecting a Flushing Page Here, the system could reserve a high virtual address for this purpose. We then add a respective entry (with the selected address and the related IUID) to the flushing buffer.

Finalizing an Active Flush The IOMMU intercepts the issued get, finds the matching entry in the flushing buffer, sets `active=true`, copies the values of the `tag` and `requester-ID` PCIe fields to the matching entry, and discards the get. Processing of the targeted access log is then initiated with any mechanism from § 3.5, depending on user's choice.

Alternative Mechanism The proposed consistency mechanism sacrifices one page from the user virtual address space. To alleviate this issue, we propose a second scheme similar to the semantics offered by, e.g., GASNet [11]. Here, AA does not guarantee any consistency. Instead, it allows the user to develop the necessary consistency by issuing a *reply* (implemented as an active put) from within the handler. This reply informs which elements from the access log have been processed. To save bandwidth, replies can be batched. The reply would be targeted at a designated page (with bits `W=0`, `WL`=1, `WLD`=1) with an `IUID` pointing to a designated access log. The user would poll the log and use the replies to enforce an arbitrary consistency.

Mixing AA/RMA Accesses At times, mixing AA and RMA puts/gets may be desirable (see § 4.1). The consistency of such a mixed scheme can be managed with active and traditional RMA flushes as these two calls are orthogonal. The completion of pending AA/RMA accesses is enforced with AA/RMA flushes, respectively.

3.7 Hardware Implementation Issues

We now describe solutions to several PCIe and RDMA control flow, ordering, and backward compatibility issues in the proposed extensions. If the reader is not interested in these details then they may skip this part and proceed to § 4. Numbers and capitals in circles refer to Figure 3.

Logging Data of PCIe Write Requests Every RDMA put is translated into one or more PCIe write requests flowing from NIC to main memory. The ordering rules for *Posted Requests* from the PCIe specification (§ 2.4.1 in [32], entry A2a) ensure that the packets for the same request arrive in order and may thus be simply appended to the log.

Logging Data of PCIe Read Requests A PCIe read transaction consists of one read request (issued by the NIC) and one or more read replies (issued by the memory controller). The IOMMU has to properly match the incoming and outgoing PCIe packets. For this, we first enable the IOMMU to intercept PCIe packets flowing back to the NIC (M) (standard IOMMUs process only incoming memory accesses). Second, we add the *packet tag buffer* (N) (implemented as CAM) to the IOMMU to temporarily maintain information about PCIe packets. The IOMMU would add the transaction tags of incoming PCIe read requests that access a page where `RLD=1` to the tag buffer. PCIe read reply packets are then matched against the buffer and logged if needed.

We require the tag buffer as PCIe read replies only contain seven lower bits of the address of the accessed memory region (see § 2.2.9 in [32]), preventing the IOMMU from matching incoming requests with replies. The PCIe standard also ensures ordering of read replies (see § 2.3.1.1 in [32]).

Order of PCIe Packets from Multiple Devices The final ordering issue concerns multiple RMA puts or gets concurrently targeted at the same IOMMU. If several multi-packet accesses originate from different devices then the IOMMU may observe an arbitrary interleaving of PCIe packets. To correctly reassemble the packets in the access log, we extend the tag buffer so that it also stores pointers into the access log. Upon intercepting the first PCIe packet of a new PCIe transaction, the IOMMU inserts a tuple (`transaction-tag`, `tail`) into the tag buffer, records the packet in the access log, and adds the size of the *whole* PCIe transaction to the tail pointer. Thus, if some transactions interleave, the IOMMU leaves "holes" in the access log and fill these holes when appropriate PCIe packets arrive[1]. The IOMMU removes an entry from the buffer after processing the last transaction packet. To ensure that the CPU only processes packets with no holes, the IOMMU increments `tail` or sets appropriate synchronization variables only when each PCIe packet of the next transaction is recorded in the respective access log.

Control Flow IOMMUs, unlike MMUs, cannot suspend a remote process and thus buffers may overflow if they are not emptied fast enough. To avoid data loss, we utilize the back-pressure mechanism of the PCIe transaction layer protocol (TLP) as described in § 2.6.1. in [32]. This will eventually propagate through a reliable network and block the sending process(es). Issues such as head of line blocking and deadlocks are similar to existing reliable network technologies and require efficient programming at the application layer (regular emptying of the queues). Head of line blocking can also be avoided by dropping packets and retransmission [6].

Support for Legacy Codes Some codes may rely on the default IOMMU behavior to buffer the metadata in the default fault log (10). To cover such cases, we add the `E` bit (O) to IOMMU PTEs to determine if the page fault is recorded in the fault log (`E=0`) or in one of the access logs (`E=1`).

4. ACTIVE ACCESS PROGRAMMING

We now discuss example RMA-based codes that leverage AA. AA improves the application performance by reducing the amount of communication and remote synchronization. First, it reduces the number of puts, gets, and remote atomic operations in distributed data structures and other codes that perform complex remote memory accesses. For example, enqueueing an element into a remote queue costs at least two remote accesses (atomically get and increment the tail pointer and put the element). With AA, this would be a simple put to the list address and a handler that inserts the element; our DHT example is very similar. Second, since handlers are executed by local cores, the usual on-node synchronization mechanisms are utilized with no need to issue expensive remote synchronization calls such as remote locks.

4.1 Designing Distributed Hash Tables

DHTs are basic data structures that are used to construct distributed key-value stores such as Memcached [17]. In our design, the DHT is open and each process manages its part called the local *volume*. The volume consists of a table of elements and an overflow heap for elements with hash collisions. Both the table and the heap are implemented as fixed-size arrays. To avoid costly array traversals, pointers to most recently inserted items and to the next free cells are stored along with the remaining data in each local volume.

Due to space constraints we discuss inserts and only briefly lookups and deletes. In RMA, inserts are based on atomics (Compare-and-Swap and Fetch-and-Op, denoted as `cas` and `fao`), RMA puts (`rma_put`) and RMA flushes (`rma_flush`); see Listing 2. For simplicity we assume that atomics are blocking. The semantics of CAS are as follows: `int cas(elem, compare, target, owner)`; if `compare` == `target` then `target` is changed to `elem` and its previous value is returned. For FAO we have `int fao(op, value, target, owner)`; it applies an atomic operation `op` to `target` using a parameter `value`, and returns `target`'s previous value. In both `cas` and `fao`, `owner` is the id of the process that owns the targeted address space. The semantics for `rma_put` and `rma_flush` are the same as for AA puts and flushes (cf. § 3, § 3.6). $\emptyset$ indicates that the specific array cell is empty. To insert `elem` we first issue a `cas` (line 9). Upon a

[1]PCI Express 3.0 Specification limits the PCIe transaction size to 4KB. Thus, the maximum size of an active put or get also amounts to 4 KB. This limitation can be easily overcome in future PCIe systems.

```
1 /* Volume is a structure that contains the fields:
2 owner: the id of the volume owner; vol_size: volume size,
3 elems[]: the table + the overflow heap; each cell contains
      two subfields: elem (the actual value) and ptr (the
      pointer to the next element),
4 next_free_cell: a ptr to the next free cell in the heap,
5 last_ptr[]: pointers to the most recent elements */
6
7 void insert(int elem, Volume v) {//put elem into volume v
8   int pos = hash(elem); //get the position of elem in v
9   if(cas(elem,∅,v.elems[pos].elem,v.owner) != ∅) {
10    int free_cell = fao(SUM,1,v.next_free_cell,v.owner);
11    if(free_cell>=v.vol_size) {/*an overflow - resize*/}
12    rma_put(elem,v.elems[free_cell].elem,v.owner);
13    rma_flush(v.owner);
14    int prev_ptr=fao(REPLACE,free_cell,v.last_ptr[pos],
        v.owner);
15    if(cas(free_cell,∅,v.elems[pos].ptr,v.owner) != ∅) {
16      rma_put(free_cell,v.elems[prev_ptr].ptr,v.owner);
17      rma_flush(v.owner); } } }
```

Listing 2: Insert in the traditional RMA-based DHT

```
1 void insert(int elem, Volume v) {
2   put(elem, v.elems[hash(elem)].elem, v.owner);
3 }
4
5 void insert_handler(Access_log log) {
6   while(log.tail != log.head) {
7     local_insert(*log.tail); log.tail += sizeof(int);
8       if(log.tail == log.base + log.size) {
9           log.tail = log.base;
10 } } }
11
12 void local_insert(int elem) {//lv is the local DHT volume
13   int pos = hash(elem); //get the position of elem in lv
14   if(cas(elem,∅,lv.elems[pos].elem) != ∅) {
15     int free_cell = fao(SUM,1,lv.next_free_cell);
16     if(free_cell>=lv.vol_size) {/*an overflow - resize*/}
17     lv.elems[free_cell].elem = elem;
18     int prev_ptr=fao(REPLACE,free_cell,lv.last_ptr[pos]);
19     if(cas(free_cell,∅,lv.elems[pos].ptr) != ∅) {
20       lv.elems[prev_ptr].ptr = free_cell; } } }
```

Listing 3: Insert in the AA-based DHT

collision we acquire a new element in the overflow heap (line 10). We then insert `elem` into the new position (lines 12-13), update the respective last pointer and the next pointer of the previous element in the heap (lines 14-17).

Implementation of Inserts with Active Puts We now accelerate inserts with AA. We present the multi-threaded code in Listing 3. The inserting process calls `insert` (lines 1-3). The PTEs of the hash table data are marked with `W=0`, `WL=1`, `WLD=1`; thus, the metadata and the data from the put is placed in the access log. The CPU then (after being interrupted or by polling the memory/scratchpad) executes `insert_handler` to insert the elements into the local volume (lines 5-10). Here, we assume that a thread owns one access log and that the size of the access log is divisible by the size of `int`. Elements are inserted with `local_insert`, a function similar to `insert` from Listing 2. The difference is that each call is local (we thus skip the `lv.owner` argument).

Synchronization AA handlers are executed by the local CPU, thus, `local_insert` requires no synchronization with remote processes. In our code we use local atomics, however, other simple local synchronization mechanisms (e.g., locks or hardware transactional memory) may also be utilized.

Consistency The proposed DHT is loosely consistent. For implementing any other consistency (e.g., sequential consistency) one can use either active flushes or enforce the required consistency using replies from within the handler.

Lookups Contrary to inserts, lookups do not generate hash collisions that entail multiple memory accesses. Thus, we propose to implement a lookup as a single *traditional* RMA get, similarly to [14]. For this, we mark the PTEs associated with the hashtable data as `R=1`, `RL=0`, `RLD=0`. Here, we assume that DMA is cache coherent (true on, e.g., Intel x86 [14]) and that RMA gets are aligned. As the DHT elements are word-size integers, a get is atomic with respect to any concurrent accesses from Listing 3. Consistency with other lookups and with inserts can be achieved with RMA and active flushes, respectively. More complicated schemes that fetch the data from the overflow heap are possible; the details are outside the scope of the paper.

Deletes A simple protocol built over active puts performs deletes. Here, we use a designated page P marked as `W=0`, `WL=1`, `WLD=1`. The implementation of the delete issues an active put. This put is targeted at P and it contains a key of the element(s) to be deleted. The IOMMU moves the keys to a designated access log and a specified handler uses them to remove the elements from the local volume.

4.2 Collecting Statistics on Memory Accesses

Recent work [18] presents an *active* key-value store "Comet", where automated gathering of statistics is one of the key functionalities. Such systems are usually implemented in the application layer, which significantly limits their performance. Architectures based on traditional RMA suffer from issues similar to the ones described in § 4.1.

AA enables hardware-based gathering statistics. For example, to count the number of puts or gets to a data structure, one has to appropriately set the control bits in the PTEs that point to the memory region where this structure is located: `W=1`, `WL=1`, `WLD=0` (for puts), and `R=1`, `RL=1`, `RLD=0` (for gets). Thus, the IOMMU ignores the data and logs only metadata that is later processed in a handler to generate statistics; the processing can be enforced with active flushes. This mechanism would also improve the performance of cache eviction schemes in memcached applications.

AA enables gathering separate statistics for each page of data. Yet, sometimes a finer granularity could be required to count accesses to elements of smaller sizes. In such cases one could place the respective elements in separate pages.

4.3 Enabling Incremental Checkpointing

Recent predictions about mean time between failures (MTBF) of large-scale systems indicate failures every few hours [9]. Fault tolerance can be achieved with various mechanisms. In *checkpoint/restart* [9] all processes synchronize and record their state to memories or disks. Traditional checkpointing schemes record the same amount of data during every checkpoint. However, often only a small subset of the application state changes between two consecutive checkpoints [39]. Thus, saving all the data wastes time, energy, and bandwidth. In *incremental checkpointing* only the modified data is recorded. A popular scheme [39] tracks data modifications at the granularity of pages and uses the dirty bit (DB) to detect if a given page requires checkpointing. This scheme cannot be directly applied to RMA because memory accesses performed by remote processes are not tracked by the MMU paging hierarchy [35].

AA enables incremental checkpointing in RMA codes. The combination `W=1`, `WL=1`, `WLD=0` (set to the data that requires checkpointing) enables tracking the modified pages. To take a checkpoint all the processes synchronize and process the access logs to find and record the modified data. Our incremental checkpointing mechanism for tracking data modifications is orthogonal to the details of synchronization and recording; one could use any available scheme [9].

Most often both remote and local accesses modify the memory. The latter can be tracked by the MMU and any existing method (e.g., the DB scheme [39]) can be used. While checkpointing, every process parses both the access log and the MMU page table to track both types of memory writes.

4.4 Reducing the Overheads of Logging

Another fault tolerance mechanism for RMA is uncoordinated checkpointing combined with *logging of puts and gets* where the crashed processes repeat their work and replay puts and gets that modified their state before the failure; these puts and gets are logged during the application runtime [9]. While logging puts is simple and does not impact performance, logging gets wastes network bandwidth because it requires transferring additional data [9]. We now describe this issue and propose a solution based on AA.

Logging Gets in Traditional RMA A get issued by process A and targeted at B fetches data from B's memory and impacts the state of A. Thus, if A fails and begins recovery, it has to replay this get. Still, A cannot log this get locally because the contents of its memory are lost after the crash (see Fig. 5, part 1). Thus, B can log the get [9].

The core problem in RMA is that B knows nothing of gets issued by A, and cannot actively perform any logging action. It means that A has to wait for the data to be fetched from B and only then can it *send this data back to B*. This naive scheme comes from the fundamental rules of one-sided RMA communication: B is completely oblivious to any remote accesses to its memory [9] (cf. Fig. 5, part 2).

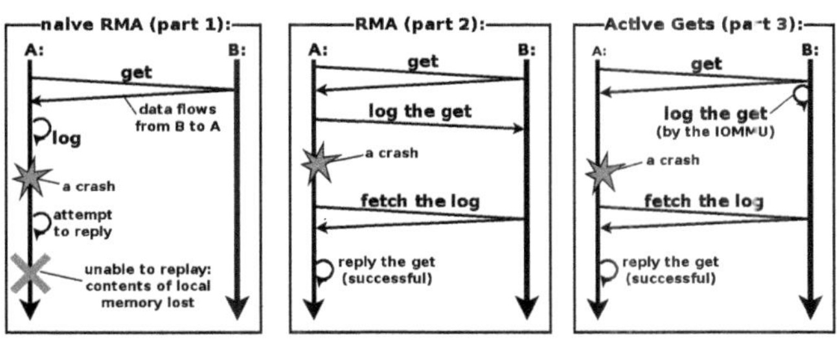

Figure 5: Logging and replaying issued operations in RMA and AA.

Improving the Performance with Active Gets In AA, the IOMMU can intercept incoming gets and log the accessed data locally. First, we set up PTEs in the IOMMU page table that point to the part of memory that is targeted by gets. We set the control bits (`R=1,RL=1,RLD=1`) in these PTEs to make each get touching this page active. Every such get triggers the IOMMU to copy the accessed data into the access log annihilating the need for the source to send the same data back (see Figure 5, part 3). During the recovery a crashed process fetches the logs and then uses them to recover to the state before the failure. We omit further details of this scheme as this is outside the scope of this paper; example protocols (e.g., for clearing the logs or replaying puts and gets preserving the RMA consistency order) can be found in the literature [9].

5. EVALUATION

To evaluate AA we first conduct cycle-accurate simulations to cover the details of the interaction between the NIC, the IOMMU, the CPU, and the memory system. Second, we perform simplified large-scale simulations to illustrate how AA impacts the performance of large-scale codes.

5.1 Microbenchmarks

We first perform cycle-accurate microbenchmarks that evaluate the performance of data transfer between two machines connected with an Ethernet link. We compare system configurations without the IOMMU (`no-iommu`) and with the extended IOMMU presented in this paper (`e-iommu`). We use the gem5 cycle-accurate full-system simulator [10] and a standard testbed that allows for modeling two networked machines with in-order CPUs, Intel 8254x 1GbE NICs with Intel e1000 driver, a full operating system, TCP/IP stack, and PCIe buses. The utilized OS is Ubuntu 11.04 with precompiled 3.3.0-rc3 Linux kernel that supports 2047MB memory. We modify the simulated system by splitting the PCIe bus and inserting an IOMMU in between the two parts. We model the IOMMU as a bridge with an attached PTE cache (IOTLB). The bridge provides buffering and a fixed delay for passing packets; we set the delay to be $70ns$ for each additional memory access. We also use a $5ns$ delay for simulating IOMMU internal processing. We base these values on the L1/memory latencies of the simulated system.

We first measure the performance of data transfer with PktGen [28] (a high-speed packet generator) enhanced with netmap [36] (a framework for fast packet I/O). Second, we evaluate the performance of a TCP and a UDP stream with netperf, a popular benchmark for measuring network performance. We show the results in Figures 6a-6b. The IOMMU presence only marginally affects the data transfer bandwidth (the difference between the `no-iommu` and `e-iommu` is 1-5% with `no-iommu`, as expected, being marginally faster).

We also simulate a hashtable workload of one process inserting new elements at full link bandwidth into the memory of the remote machine; the results are presented in Figure 6c. Here, we compare AA with a traditional RMA design of the DHT. As the collision rate increases, the performance of both designs drops due to a higher number of memory accesses. Still, AA is $\approx$3 times more performant than RMA.

5.2 Evaluation of Large-Scale Applications

The second performance-related question is how the AA semantics, implemented using the proposed IOMMU design, impacts the performance of *large-scale* codes. To be able to run large-scale benchmarks on a real supercomputer we simplify the simulation infrastructure. We simulate one-sided RMA calls with MPI point-to-point messages. We replace one-directional RMA puts with a single message and two-directional RMA calls (gets and atomics) with a pair of messages exchanged by the source and target, just like packets in hardware. We then emulate extended IOMMUs by appropriately stalling message handlers. As the IOMMU performs data replication and redirection bypassing the CPU, there are four possible sources of such overheads: interrupts, memory accesses due to the logging, IOMMU page table lookups, and accesses to the scratchpads on the CPU.

First, we determine the interrupt and memory access latencies on our system to be $3\mu s$ and $\approx 70ns$, respectively. Second, we simulate the IOTLB and page table lookups varying several parameters (PTE size, associativity, eviction policy). Finally, we assume that an access to the scratchpad to notify a polling hyperthread is equal to the cost of an L3 access and we evaluate it to $\approx 15ns$.

All the experiments are executed on the CSCS Monte Rosa Cray XE6 system. Each node contains four 8-core AMD processors (Opteron 6276 Interlagos 2.3 GHz) and is

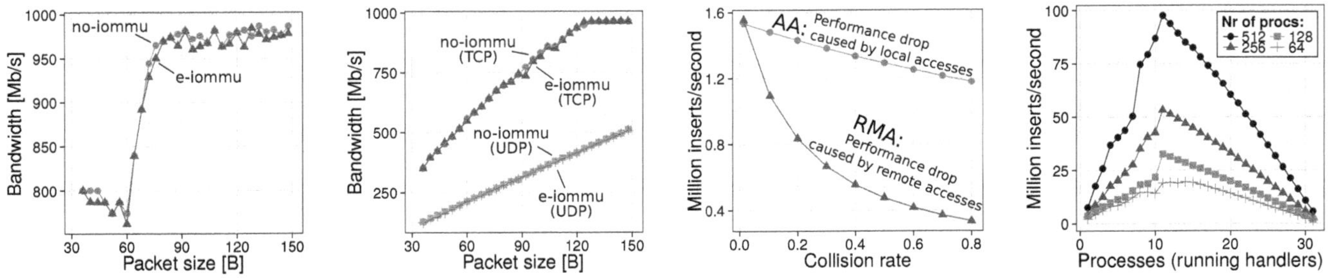

(a) Performance of Netmap (§ 5.1) (b) Performance of Netperf (§ 5.1) (c) Performance of the DHT (§ 5.1) (d) Finding the best C (§ 5.2.1)

Figure 6: Microbenchmarks (Figures 6a-6c) and finding optimum configuration for AA-Onload (Figure 6d).

connected to a 3D-Torus Gemini network. We use 32 processes/node and the GNU Environment 4.1.46 for compiling.

We compare the following communication schemes:

AA-Int, AA-Poll, AA-SP: AA based on the IOMMU communicating with the CPU using: interrupts, polling the main memory, and accessing the scratchpad, respectively.

RMA: traditional RMA representing RDMA architectures.

AM: an AM scheme in which processes poll at regular intervals to check for messages. Note that this protocol is equivalent to traditional message passing.

AM-Exp: an AM variant based on exponential backoff to reduce polling overhead. If there is no incoming message, we double the interval after which a process will poll.

AM-Onload: an AM scheme where several cores are only dedicated to running AM handlers and constantly poll on flags that indicate whether new AMs have to be processed.

AM-Ints: an AM mechanism based on interrupts generated by the NIC that signal to the CPU it has to run the handler.

5.2.1 Distributed Hashtable

We implement eight hashtable variants using each of the schemes above. Here, processes insert random elements with random keys (delete evaluation gives similar performance and is skipped due to space constraints). Each DHT volume can contain 2^{21} elements. We vary different parameters to cover a broad spectrum of possible scenarios. First, we study the scalability by changing the number of inserting processes P. Second, we evaluate benchmarks with different numbers of hash collisions (R_{cols}, the ratio between the number of hash collisions and the total number of inserts). Third, we simulate different applications by varying computation ratios (R_{comp}, the ratio between the time spent on local computation and the total experiment runtime). We also vary the IOTLB parameters: IOTLB size, associativity, and the eviction policy. Finally, we analyzed two variants of AA-Ints/AM-Ints in which an interrupt is issued every 10^1 and 10^2 inserts (the differences in performance were negligible (<5%); we only report numbers for the former).

AM-Onload depends on the number of cores (C) per node that are dedicated to processing AM requests. Thus, to make the comparison fair, we run AM-Onload for every C between 1 and 31 in order to find the most advantageous configuration for every experiment. Figure 6d shows that $C = 11$ delivers maximum performance. If $C < 11$ the cores become congested and the performance decreases. $C > 11$ limits performance as receiving cores become underutilized.

Varying P and R_{cols} Figure 7a shows the results for $R_{cols} = 5\%$ and Figure 7b for $R_{cols} = 25\%$. Here, both AA-SC and AA-Poll outperform all other schemes by a factor of ≈2. As expected, AA-SC is slightly (≈1%) more performant than AA-Poll. AA-Ints is comparable to AM-Ints; both mechanisms suffer from interrupt latency overheads. The reasons for performance differences in the remaining schemes are as follows: in AM-Exp and AM the computing processes have to poll on the receive buffer and, upon active message arrival, extract the payload. In AA this part is managed by the IOMMU and the computing processes only have to insert the elements into the local hashtable. AM-Onload devotes smaller number of processes to compute and thus, even in its best configuration, cannot outperform AA. RMA issues costly atomics for every insert and 6 more remote operations for every collision, degrading performance.

Varying R_{comp} Increasing R_{comp} from 0% to 95% did not significantly influence the performance patterns between evaluated schemes. The only noticeable effect was that the differences between the results of respective schemes were smaller (which is expected as scaling R_{comp} reduces appropriately the amount of communication per time unit).

Varying the IOTLB Parameters We now analyze the influence of various IOTLB parameters on the performance of DHT; the results are presented in Figure 7c. The name of each plot encodes the used eviction policy (lru: least recently used, rnd: random) and associativity (a1: direct-mapped, a2: 2-way, a4: 4-way, af: fully-mapped). For plot clarity we only analyze AA-Poll; both AA-SP and AA-Ints follow similar performance patterns. For a given associativity, lru is always better than rnd as it entails fewer IOTLB misses. Increasing associativity and IOTLB size improves the performance, for example, using lru_af instead of lru_a4 allows for an up to 16% higher insert rate.

5.2.2 Access Counter

We now test the performance of a simple tool that counts accesses to an arbitrary data structure. We compare AA-Poll (counting done by the IOMMU), RMA (increasing counters with remote atomics), and two additional designs: an approach based on the "active key-value" store [18] (A-KV), and a scheme where counting is done at the source and the final sums are computed with the Allreduce collective operation [26] (Allreduce). Finally, we test a scenario with no counting (No-Cnt). The number of accesses per second is presented in Figure 7d. AA-Poll outperforms A-KV (overheads caused by the application-level design), RMA (issuing costly atomics), and All-Reduce (expensive synchronization).

5.2.3 Performant Logging of Gets

In the next step we evaluate the performance of active gets by testing the implementation of the mechanism that logs RMA gets. Here, processes issue remote gets targeted at random processes. Every get transfers one 8-byte integer value. In this benchmark we do not compare to AM-Exp, AM-Onload, and AM-Ints because these schemes were not suitable for implementing this type of application. Instead,

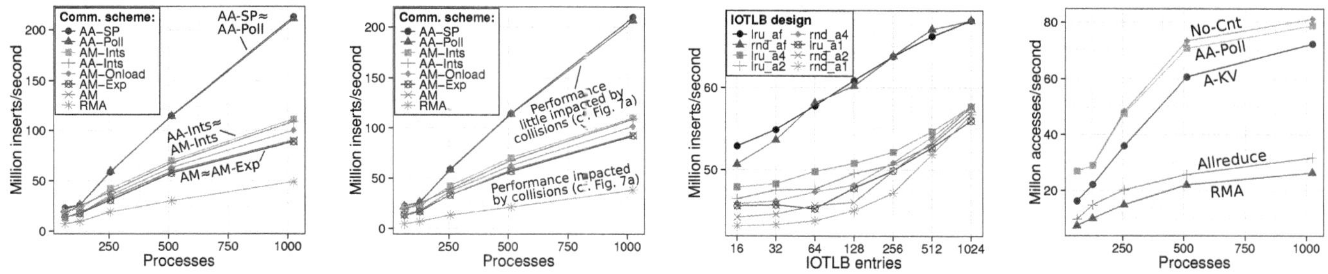

(a) DHT, R_{cols} ≈5% (§ 5.2.1) (b) DHT, R_{cols} ≈25% (§ 5.2.1) (c) DHT, IOTLB analysis (§ 5.2.1) (d) Access Counter results (§ 5.2.2)

Figure 7: The performance of the DHT (Figures 7a, 7b, 7c) and the access counter (Figure 7d). We use 32 processes/node.

we compare to No-FT: a variant with no logging (no fault-tolerance overhead) that constitutes the best-case baseline. We illustrate the scalability of AA in Figure 8a. AA achieves the best performance, close to No-FT. In all the remaining protocols the data to be logged has to be transferred back to a remote storage using a put (RMA) or a send (AM), which incurs significant overheads. Varying the remaining parameters (R_{comp}, IOTLB parameters) follows the same performance pattern as in the hashtable evaluation.

5.2.4 *Fault-Tolerant Performant Sort*

To evaluate the performance of active gets we also implemented an RMA-based version of the parallel sort Coral Benchmark [13] that utilizes gets instead of messages and made it fault-tolerant. We present the total time required to communicate the results of sorting 1GB of data between processes in Figure 8b. Again, AA is close to No-FT (< 1%) and reduces communication time by ≈50% and ≈80% in comparison to AM and RMA, respectively.

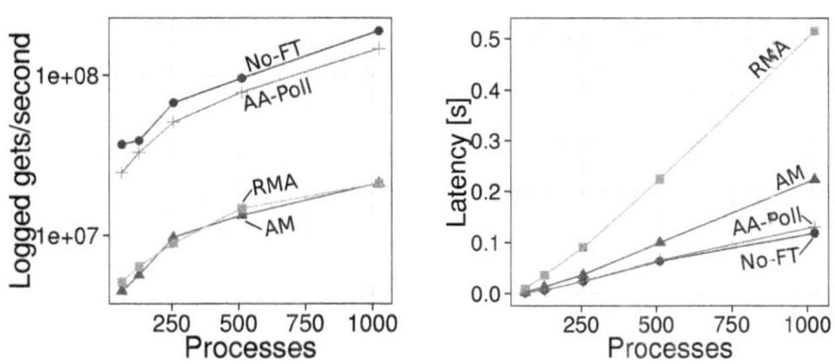

(a) Logging gets (§ 5.2.3) (b) Sort Time (§ 5.2.4)

Figure 8: The performance of the AA-based fault tolerance scheme.

6. RELATED WORK AND DISCUSSION

Not all possible use cases for IOMMUs have been studied so far. Ben-Yehuda et al. [8] discuss IOMMUs for virtualization in Linux. Other works target efficient IOMMU emulation [4], reducing IOTLB miss rates [3], isolating Linux device drivers [12], and mitigating IOMMUs' overheads [7]. There are also vendors' white papers and specifications [1,2,5,21,22,25,33]. Our work goes beyond these studies by proposing a new a mechanism and a programming model that combines AM with RMA and uses IOMMUs for high-performance distributed data-centric computations.

There are several mechanisms that extend the memory subsystem to improve the performance of various codes. Active Pages [30] enable the memory to perform some simple operations allowing the CPU to operate at peak computational bandwidth. Active Memory [16] and in-memory computing [42] add simple compute logic to the memory controller and the memory itself, respectively. AA differs from these schemes as it targets distributed RMA computations and its implementation does not modify the memory subsystem requiring minor extensions to the commodity IOMMUs.

Scale-Out NUMA [27] is an architecture, programming model, and communication protocol that offers low latency of remote memory accesses. It differs from AA as it does not provide the active semantics for both puts and gets and it introduces significant changes to the memory subsystem.

Active messages were introduced by von Eicken et al [40]. Scalable programming for RMA was discussed by Gerstenberger et al [19]. Some of AA's functionalities could be achieved using existing RMA/AM interfaces such as Portals [6], InfiniBand [37], or GASNet [11]. However, Portals would introduce additional memory overheads per NIC because it requires descriptors for every memory region. These overheads may grow prohibitively for multiple NICs. Contrarily, AA uses a single centralized IOMMU with existing paging structures, ensuring no additional memory overheads. Furthermore, AA offers notifications on gets and it enables various novel schemes such as incremental checkpointing for RMA and performant logging of gets.

AA could also be implemented in the NIC. Still, using IOMMUs provides several advantages. Modern IOMMUs are integrated with the memory controller/CPU and thus can be directly connected with CPU stratchpads for a high-performance notification mechanism (see § 3.5). This way, all I/O devices could take advantage of this functionality (e.g., Ethernet RoCE NICs). Moreover, we envision other future mechanisms that would enable even further integration with the CPU. For example, the IOMMU could be directly connected to the CPU instruction pipeline to directly feed the CPU with handler code.

Finally, AA's potential can be further explored to provide hardware virtualization of remote memories. There are three major advantages of virtual memory: it enables an OS to swap memory blocks into disk, it facilitates the application development by providing processes with separate address spaces, and it enables useful features such as memory protection or dirty bits. Some schemes (e.g., PGAS languages) emulate a part of these functionalities for networked memories. Extending AA with features specific to MMU PTEs (e.g., invalid bits) would enable a hardware-based *virtual global address space* (V-GAS) with novel enhanced paging capabilities and data-centric handlers running transparently to any code accessing the memory; see Fig. 9.

The IOMMUs could also become the basis of V-GAS for Ethernet. All the described IOMMU extensions are generic and do not rely on any specific NIC features, leaving the possibility of moving the V-GAS potential into commodity machines that do not provide native RDMA support. For example, by utilizing Single Root I/O Virtualization (SR/IOV), a standard support for hardware virtualization

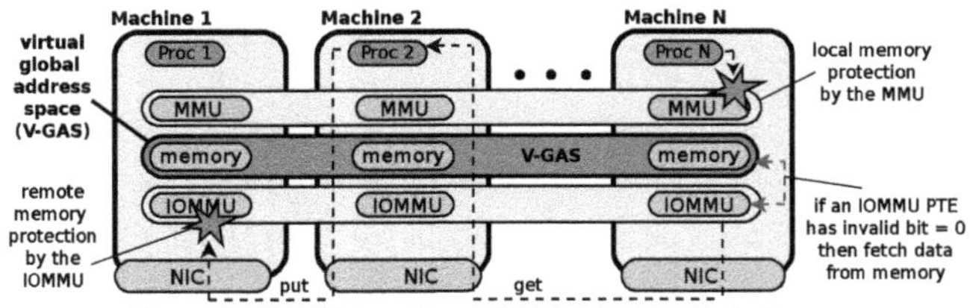

Figure 9: V-GAS together with some example features.

combined with multiple receive and transmit rings, one can utilize IOMMUs to safely divert traffic right into userspace.

7. CONCLUSION

RMA is becoming more popular for programming datacenters and HPC computers. However, its traditional one-sided model of communication may incur performance penalties in several types of applications such as DHT.

To alleviate this issue we propose the Active Access scheme that utilizes IOMMUs to provide hardware support for *active* semantics in RMA. For example, our AA-based DHT implementation offers a speedup of two over optimized AMs. The novel AA-based fault tolerance protocol enables performant logging of gets and adds negligible (1-5%) overheads to the application runtime. Furthermore, AA enables new schemes such as incremental checkpointing in RMA. Finally, our design bypasses the OS and enables more effective programming of datacenters and HPC centers.

AA enables a new programming model that combines the benefits of one-sided communication and active messages. AA is *data-centric* as it enables triggering handlers when certain data is accessed. Thus, it could be useful for future data processing and analysis schemes and protocols.

The proposed AA design, based on IOMMUs, shows the potential behind currently available off-the-shelf hardware for developing novel mechanisms. By moving the notification functionality from the NIC to the IOMMU we adopt the existing IOMMU paging structures and we eliminate the need for expensive memory descriptors present in, e.g., Portals, thus reducing memory overheads. The IOMMU-based design may enable even more performant notification mechanisms such as direct access from the IOMMU to the CPU pipeline. Thus, AA may play an important role in designing efficient codes and OS/runtime systems in large datacenters, HPC computers, and highly parallel manycore environments which are becoming commonplace even in commodity off-the-shelf computers.

Acknowledgements

We thank the CSCS team granting access to the Monte Rosa machine, and for their excellent technical support. We thank Greg Bronevetsky (LLNL) for inspiring comments and Ali Saidi for help with the gem5 simulator. MB is supported by the 2013 Google European Doctoral Fellowship in Parallel Computing.

8. REFERENCES

[1] AMD. Software Optimization Guide for the AMD64 Processors, 2005.

[2] AMD. AMD I/O Virtualization Technology (IOMMU) Spec., 2011.

[3] N. Amit, M. Ben-Yehuda, and B.-A. Yassour. IOMMU: strategies for mitigating the IOTLB bottleneck. In *Proc. of Intl. Conf. on Comp. Arch.*, ISCA'10, pages 256–274, 2010.

[4] N. Amit et al. vIOMMU: efficient IOMMU emulation. In *USENIX Ann. Tech. Conf.*, USENIXATC'11, pages 6–6, 2011.

[5] W. J. Armstrong et al. Advanced virtualization capabilities of POWER5 systems. *IBM J. Res. Dev.*, 49(4/5):523–532, 2005.

[6] B. W. Barrett et al. The Portals 4.0 network programming interface, 2012. Sandia National Laboratories.

[7] Ben-Yehuda et al. The price of safety: Evaluating IOMMU performance. In *Ottawa Linux Symp.(OLS)*, pages 9–20, 2007.

[8] M. Ben-Yehuda et al. Utilizing IOMMUs for virtualization in Linux and Xen. In *In Proc. of the Linux Symp.*, 2006.

[9] M. Besta and T. Hoefler. Fault Tolerance for Remote Memory Access Programming Models. In *Proc. of the 23rd Intl Symp. on High-perf. Par. and Dist. Comp.*, HPDC '14, pages 37–48, 2014.

[10] N. Binkert et al. The gem5 simulator. *SIGARCH Comput. Archit. News*, 39(2):1–7, Aug. 2011.

[11] D. Bonachea. GASNet Spec., v1. *Tech. Rep. UCB/CSD-02-1207*, 2002.

[12] S. Boyd-Wickizer and N. Zeldovich. Tolerating malicious device drivers in Linux. In *USENIX Ann. Tech. Conf.*, USENIXATC'10, pages 9–9, 2010.

[13] Coral Collaboration. Coral Procurement Benchmarks. In *Coral Vendor Meeting*, 2013.

[14] A. Dragojević et al. FaRM: fast remote memory. In *Proc. of the 11th USENIX Symp. on Net. Syst. Des. and Impl. (NSDI 14)*. USENIX, 2014.

[15] H. Esmaeilzadeh et al. Dark silicon and the end of multicore scaling. In *Proc. of Intl. Symp. Comp. Arch.*, ISCA '11, pages 365–376, 2011.

[16] Z. Fang et al. Active Memory Operations. In *Proc. of the 21st Ann. Intl Conf. on Supercomp.*, ICS '07, pages 232–241, 2007.

[17] B. Fitzpatrick. Distributed caching with memcached. *Linux journal*, 2004(124):5, 2004.

[18] R. Geambasu et al. Comet: An Active Distributed Key-value Store. In *USENIX Conf. on Op. Sys. Des. and Impl.*, OSDI'10, pages 1–13, 2010.

[19] R. Gerstenberger, M. Besta, and T. Hoefler. Enabling Highly-scalable Remote Memory Access Programming with MPI-3 One Sided. In *Proc. of ACM/IEEE Supercomputing*, SC '13, pages 53:1–53:12, 2013.

[20] T. Hoefler et al. Remote Memory Access Programming in MPI-3. *ACM Trans. Par. Comp. (TOPC)*, 2015. accepted for publication on Dec. 4th.

[21] IBM. *Logical Partition Security in the IBM @server pSeries 690.* 2002.

[22] Intel. Intel Virtualization Technology for Directed I/O (VT-d) Architecture Specification, September 2013.

[23] ISO Fortran Committee. Fortran 2008 Standard (ISO/IEC 1539-1:2010). 2010.

[24] Y. Kim, D. Broman, J. Cai, and A. Shrivastaval. WCET-aware dynamic code management on scratchpads for software-managed multicores. In *IEEE Real-Time and Emb. Tech. and App. Symp. (RTAS)*, 2014.

[25] R. Mijat and A. Nightingale. The ARM Architecture Virtualization Extensions and the importance of System MMU for virtualized solutions and beyond, 2011. ARM White Paper.

[26] MPI Forum. MPI: A Message-Passing Interface Standard. Ver. 3, 2012.

[27] S. Novakovic et al. Scale-out NUMA. In *Intl. Conf. on Arch. Sup. for Prog. Lang. and Op. Sys.*, ASPLOS '14, pages 3–18, 2014.

[28] R. Olsson. PktGen the linux packet generator. In *Proc. of the Linux Symp., Ottawa, Canada*, volume 2, pages 11–24, 2005.

[29] Oracle. *UltraSPARC Virtual Machine Spec.* 2010.

[30] M. Oskin, F. T. Chong, and T. Sherwood. Active Pages: A Computation Model for Intelligent Memory. In *Proc. of the 25th Ann. Intl Symp. on Comp. Arch.*, ISCA '98, pages 192–203, 1998.

[31] D. Patterson. The top 10 innovations in the new NVIDIA Fermi architecture, and the top 3 next challenges. *NVIDIA Whitepaper*, 2009.

[32] PCI-SIG. *PCI Express Base Spec. Rev. 3.0.* 2010.

[33] PCI-SIG. PCI-SIG I/O Virtualization (IOV) Specifications, 2013.

[34] S. Pope and D. Riddoch. Introduction to OpenOnload, 2011. SolarFlare White Paper.

[35] R. Recio, B. Metzler, P. Culley, J. Hilland, and D. Garcia. A remote direct memory access protocol specification, Oct 2007. RFC 5040.

[36] L. Rizzo. netmap: A novel framework for fast packet i/o. In *USENIX Annual Technical Conference*, pages 101–112, 2012.

[37] The InfiniBand Trade Association. *Infiniband Architecture Spec. Vol. 1-2, Rel. 1.3.* InfiniBand Trade Association, 2004.

[38] UPC Consortium. UPC language spec., v1.2. Technical report, Lawrence Berkeley National Laboratory, 2005. LBNL-59208.

[39] M. Vasavada, F. Mueller, P. H. Hargrove, and E. Roman. Comparing different approaches for incremental checkpointing: The showdown. In *Linux'11: The 13th Annual Linux Symposium*, pages 69–79, 2011.

[40] T. von Eicken, D. E. Culler, S. C. Goldstein, and K. E. Schauser. Active messages: a mechanism for integrated communication and computation. In *Proc. of Intl. Symp. Comp. Arch.*, ISCA '92, pages 256–266, 1992.

[41] J. Willcock et al. AM++: A Generalized Active Message Framework. In *Intl. Conf. on Par. Arch. and Comp. Tech.*, pages 401–410, 2010.

[42] Q. Zhu et al. Accelerating sparse matrix-matrix multiplication with 3D-stacked logic-in-memory hardware. In *High Perf. Ext. Comp. Conf. (HPEC)*, pages 1–6. IEEE, 2013.

Exascaling Your Library: Will Your Implementation Meet Your Expectations?

Sergei Shudler
TU Darmstadt
Darmstadt, Germany
shudler@cs.tu-darmstadt.de

Alexandru Calotoiu
TU Darmstadt
Darmstadt, Germany
calotoiu@cs.tu-darmstadt.de

Torsten Hoefler
ETH Zurich
Zürich, Switzerland
htor@inf.ethz.ch

Alexandre Strube
Jülich Supercomputing Centre
Jülich, Germany
a.strube@fz-juelich.de

Felix Wolf
TU Darmstadt
Darmstadt, Germany
wolf@cs.tu-darmstadt.de

ABSTRACT

Many libraries in the HPC field encapsulate sophisticated algorithms with clear theoretical scalability expectations. However, hardware constraints or programming bugs may sometimes render these expectations inaccurate or even plainly wrong. While algorithm engineers have already been advocating the systematic combination of analytical performance models with practical measurements for a very long time, we go one step further and show how this comparison can become part of automated testing procedures. The most important applications of our method include initial validation, regression testing, and benchmarking to compare implementation and platform alternatives. Advancing the concept of performance assertions, we verify asymptotic scaling trends rather than precise analytical expressions, relieving the developer from the burden of having to specify and maintain very fine-grained and potentially non-portable expectations. In this way, scalability validation can be continuously applied throughout the whole development cycle with very little effort. Using MPI as an example, we show how our method can help uncover non-obvious limitations of both libraries and underlying platforms.

Categories and Subject Descriptors

D.2.5 [**Software Engineering**]: Testing and Debugging—*testing tools*; D.4.8 [**Performance**]: Modeling and prediction; C.4 [**Performance of Systems**]: Modeling techniques; D.1.3 [**Concurrent Programming**]: Parallel programming

Keywords

software engineering; high performance computing; parallel programming; performance analysis

ICS'15, June 8–11, 2015, Newport Beach, CA, USA.

http://dx.doi.org/10.1145/2751205.2751216.

1. INTRODUCTION

The most powerful supercomputers today allow computations to be run on millions of cores and in the not-so-distant future this number may grow to tens of millions and billions of cores. Since many applications critically depend on parallel libraries such as MPI, PETSc, ScaLAPACK and HDF5, the scalability of these libraries is of utmost importance for reaching performance targets at scale. This becomes even clearer considering that application developers may be able to remove performance bottlenecks from their own code, but may encounter more challenges removing these bottlenecks in the libraries they are using.

Library developers, on the other hand, are confronted with the challenge of continuous scalability validation as their code base evolves. In the past, they often did this by scaling the library to the full extent of the largest machine available to them, after which they manually compared the results with theoretical expectations. This is expensive in terms of both machine time and manpower. In cases where the library encapsulates complex algorithms that are the product of years of research, such expectations often exist in the form of analytical performance models [7, 19, 22]. However, translating such abstract models into concrete verifiable expressions is hard because it requires knowing all constants and restricts function domains to performance metrics that are effectively measurable on the target system. If only the asymptotic complexity is known, as is very commonly the case, this is in fact impossible. And if such a verifiable expression exists, it must be adapted every time the test platform is replaced and performance metrics and constants change.

To mitigate this situation, we combine automated performance modeling with performance expectations in a novel scalability test framework. Similar to performance assertions [21], our framework supports the user in the specification and validation of performance expectations. However, rather than formulating precise analytical expressions involving measurable metrics, the user need only provide the asymptotic growth rate of the function/metric pair in question, making this a simple but effective solution for future exascale library development. We generate performance models similar to Calotoiu et al. [6]. However, instead of creating scaling models independently from the expected

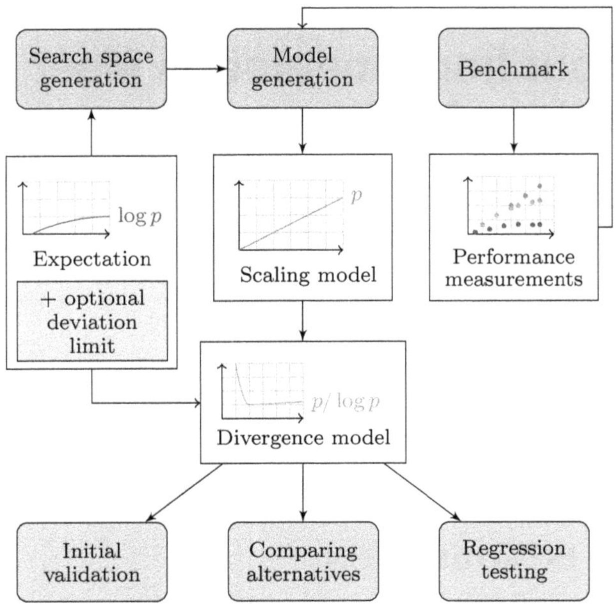

Figure 1: Framework overview including use cases.

behavior as they do, we tailor the model search spaces to expectations and also generate divergence models that help in understanding how the difference between expected and actual behavior would evolve as the number of processes increases. Moreover, in the absence of a clear expectation, the framework is able to supply the status quo as a substitute. This is especially useful during regression testing when the main task is to prevent later modifications from reducing scalability. A performance model generator combined with an automated workflow manager makes sure that the actual and expected behavior can be continuously compared.

Use cases of our framework include initial validation, regression testing, and benchmarking to compare implementation and platform alternatives. Although our work is not restricted to a specific type of software, we focus on library development because of its high impact and the greater availability of theoretical performance models. In comparison to the state of the art, we make the following specific contributions:

- Scalability validation based on simple asymptotic growth rates, which are often easier to obtain than fully evaluable analytical expressions
- Generation of divergence models to characterize deviation as a function of the number of processes
- Targeted model search through expectation-driven construction of the search space
- Automatic workflow including execution of performance experiments and generation of performance models
- Testing whether the scaling behavior of the library is consistent across different functions

In the first case study involving several MPI implementations, we demonstrate how our framework can be applied to (i) uncover growing memory consumption, (ii) reveal architectural constraints that limit the performance of a wide range of collective operations, and (iii) predict the violation of MPI performance guidelines. In the second case study involving the MAFIA (Merging of Adaptive Finite IntervAls) code [3], we demonstrate that our approach is also applicable to algorithmic modeling. In this case, the model is a function of algorithm parameters.

The remainder of the paper is organized as follows: in Section 2, we provide an overview of our approach. Section 3 outlines how the framework must be instantiated for the MPI example and Section 4 then shows the experimental results. Since the MAFIA study relies largely on the same infrastructure, we chose to present it in the same section immediately after the MPI study. Finally, we review related work in Section 5, before drawing our conclusions in Section 6.

2. APPROACH

The objective of our approach, which is illustrated in Figure 1, is to provide insights into the scaling behavior of a library with as little effort as possible. It includes the following four steps: (i) *define expectations*; (ii) *design benchmark*; (iii) *generate scaling models*; (iv) *validate expectations*. The first two are manual because they involve user decisions, while the second two are automatic. We describe each of them in detail below.

2.1 Define Expectations

We aim to keep our method simple and effective: it has to be usable in various settings with only an approximate idea of the expected result. For example, it is very unlikely that a programmer of a matrix-matrix multiplication can tell the floating-point rate or the achieved memory bandwidth for a given matrix size N. Thus, these metrics may be less useful in practice. However, every programmer will know whether he used the simple $\mathcal{O}(N^3)$ algorithm or Strassen's $\mathcal{O}(N^{2.8074})$ algorithm. Therefore, we let the user define expectations in big O notation (aka Landau notation). For some functions, one could even formulate a black-box hypothesis. A library call `sort(int *array, int N)`, for example, that sorts an integer array should perform the sorting in $\mathcal{O}(N \log N)$ rather than in $\mathcal{O}(N^2)$ steps.

In our expectation-centric performance modeling approach we assume that the user is a domain expert capable of providing initial expectations. However, before being able to define expectations, a user has to choose the library functions that will be subjected to the scaling analysis and the relevant scaling metrics. The more functions a user selects the more expensive it will become to construct the benchmark, which is why it can make sense to restrict the selection to those deemed most relevant. On the other hand, making too narrow a choice poses the risk of overlooking hidden scalability issues. Another important decision concerns the selection of scaling metrics. For some rarely called functions, memory consumption might be the primary concern, but for many others it will probably be runtime or floating-point operations. Very often, countable metrics such as floating-point operations yield better empirical scaling models because they are less prone to jitter. If only a hypothetical expectation is available, the model generator can use it to generate a model which better describes the current behavior. This model can then become the new expectation. This is especially useful when the user has little knowledge of the library or during regression testing when the main task is to prevent later modifications from introducing scalability bugs.

Sometimes, the functionality offered by one library function is a subset or a superset of the functionality offered by another library function. Or a library API may offer convenience functions with functionality that can be regarded as a short cut for a combination of other API functions. In such cases, it is possible to define optional *cross-function rules* that specify relationships between the scaling behavior of different functions. For example, a short cut should not scale worse than the spelled-out implementation.

2.2 Design Benchmark

The benchmark must provide or generate valid library inputs and measure the selected performance metrics for the selected functions in various execution configurations (e.g., different numbers of processes or input sizes).

Occasionally, unexpected architectural constraints such as the network topology may increase the observable complexity of an implementation – without such factors, the software could be blamed in the sense of a performance bug that requires a fix. To help distinguish such effects from programming bugs, it is advisable to manually re-implement one or more representative library functions in a way that has been proven to show the expected behavior under ideal conditions - for example, using a known optimal algorithm from the literature. The difference between this *performance litmus test* and the original library functions is that the tester can usually trust the replica more than the original function because he thoroughly knows its internals. Should the original library function now show performance deviations, they can be compared with the results obtained for the litmus test. A similar deviation observed for the replica could then be seen as a strong indicator of architectural constraints that might also influence the behavior of other regular library functions. We discuss an example as part of our first case study in Section 3.2.

2.3 Generate Scaling Models

Our expectation-centric performance modeling approach assumes that the user provides an initial expectation function $E(x)$. Together with this expectation the user either provides a deviation limit $D(x)$ or a default deviation is chosen automatically. Looking at how most computer algorithms are designed and their complexity, we can identify a number of function classes with distinct rates of growth.

$$F_1(x) = \left\{\log_2^{i_1} x\right\}$$

$$F_2(x) = \left\{x^{i_2}\right\}$$

$$F_3(x) = \left\{2^{i_3 x}\right\}$$

This division into classes provides the foundation of our performance-modeling technique; however, we do not claim that the above classes are exhaustive, and new ones can be added on demand to reflect changes in algorithms and applications. The basic modeling technique will nevertheless be the same. We first classify the leading-order term of the expectation $E(x)$ according to our scheme. Since we assume that $E(x)$ is sound and our goal is to validate it, we are not interested in a wide deviation limit. Therefore, if the user provides no such limit we choose a default deviation $D(x)$ from the same class. In other words, if $E(x)$ was classified as belonging to $F_k(x)$ we define $D(x)$ by halving the leading-order term exponent i_k of $E(x)$. The lower deviation limit is then defined as $D_l(x) = E(x)/D(x)$, and the upper deviation limit is defined as $D_u(x) = E(x) \cdot D(x)$. By default, the model search space boundaries extend beyond the deviation limits $D_l(x)$ and $D_u(x)$, thus the lower boundary is defined as $B_l(x) = 1$ and the upper boundary as $B_u(x) = E^2(x)$. These boundaries limit the growth of generated performance models. The deviation limits $D_l(x)$ and $D_u(x)$, on the other hand, define our bug criteria; if a model falls outside these limits, we classify this as a scalability bug.

The next step is to choose the functions inside the model search space, and thus define its resolution. The user can provide his own search space or let it be generated automatically using the expectation $E(x)$. The construction of the search space is analogous to placing ticks on a ruler. The bigger ticks (e.g., centimeters) are the terms from class $F_k(x)$ to which $E(x)$ belongs. The outermost ticks are by default B_l and B_u; while the inner ticks are constructed by recursively halving the intervals between existing ticks. Each new tick corresponds to a new term and is added to the search space. Practically, this is achieved by averaging the exponents of adjacent terms that are already in the search space. We denote the set of exponents of the terms already in the search space as $I_k \subset \mathbb{Q}$, which means we can define the search space up to this point as $\{f(x) \in F_k(x) | i_k \in I_k\}$. By introducing smaller ticks (e.g., millimeters), we can increase the resolution even further. In contrast to the bigger ticks, smaller ticks are constructed by multiplying the terms from class $F_k(x)$ that are already elements of the search space with terms from $F_{k-1}(x)$. As a rule of thumb and a default choice, the first term we select from $F_{k-1}(x)$ has an exponent of 1. We can then expand this selection as needed by incrementing and decrementing the exponent by a step of 1, 1/2, 1/3, and so on. Selecting more terms from $F_{k-1}(x)$ increases the search space resolution which incurs more overhead and is not always needed. We do not consider any terms from a class lower than $F_{k-1}(x)$ because the ticks this would create are too fine-grained to characterize significant deviations. Finally, we multiply each term in the search space with a coefficient placeholder that will be instantiated when fitting the functions in the search space to actual measurements.

We offer both simplicity and flexibility to the user. The only input that the user has to provide is the expectation. The deviation limit and the search space can then be generated automatically, thus relieving the user of the complexity of too many choices. However, if more flexibility is required, the user has the option of providing the deviation limit and modifying the search space. It means either refining the resolution by placing further exponents in gaps between existing terms or expanding the space beyond the default boundaries of B_l and B_u. However, there is a trade-off between accuracy and speed; therefore, applying these modifications will increase the model-generation time. As an approximate point of orientation, the entire modeling process in our case studies never took more than a few seconds per library.

As an example, let us consider the expectation $E(p) = p$. In this case, the default deviation limit is $D(p) = \sqrt{p}$ since it is exactly half of the power of p. The default lower and upper search space boundaries are respectively 1 and p^2. By averaging the exponents of adjacent terms in our search space we first construct the models $\sqrt{p}$ and $p\sqrt{p}$, and in the next step we add $\{p^j \mid j = \frac{1}{4}, \frac{3}{4}, \frac{5}{4}, \frac{7}{4}\}$. We then select a term with exponent 1 from the next lower class, $\log p$ in this case, and multiply it by the terms that are already inside the search space. Note that we skip the upper boundary p^2 in order to keep the search space within our defined boundaries:

$$\left\{1,\ \log p,\ p^{\frac{1}{4}}, p^{\frac{1}{4}} \log p,\ \sqrt{p},\ ...,\ p,\ p \log p,\ ...,\ p^{\frac{7}{4}} \log p,\ p^2\right\}$$

The model generator now needs a set of measurements as input whose precise nature depends on the scaling objective (e.g., number of processes vs. input size, weak vs. strong). As a rule of thumb derived from our experience, the generator needs at least five different settings of the model parameter (e.g., five different numbers of processes). It then starts searching the search space for the model that best fits the measurements and uses the adjusted coefficient of determination as an accuracy metric. The adjusted coefficient of determination is a standard statistical fit factor $\in [0, 1]$, with 1 indicating optimal fit.

2.4 Validate Expectations

Since we accept expectations in big O notation, we first need to transform the generated models accordingly. This involves isolating the leading-order term in a model and stripping off its coefficient.

Unfortunately, run-to-run variation, which affects almost any system, may introduce a certain degree of noise into the measurement data. This means that we are confronted with a trade-off decision. On the one hand, if we increase the search space resolution, we have to accept that the model would not only reflect the behavior we are interested in but potentially also the noise. On the other hand, if we restrict the resolution too much, we have to accept models that do not fit the data precisely, increasing the likelihood that they will misguide the user. Since according to our experience the latter option is more dangerous, we decided to allow more fine-grained model choices.

To assist the user in understanding the results we define the *divergence model* to be $\delta(x) = G(x)/E(x)$, where $G(x)$ is the generated model and $E(x)$ is the expectation provided by the user. This model characterizes the degree of divergence between the expectation and the observed behavior. It can also be used to visualize the severity of the deviation. Thus, the output we present to the user consists of $G(x)$, $\delta(x)$, and a match rank with three possible indications: total match (meaning $G(x)$ corresponds to $E(x)$), approximate match ($G(x)$ is within the deviation limits), and no match ($G(x)$ is outside the deviation limits).

Severe divergence can either point to a bug in the algorithm, a bug in its implementation, a constraint of the underlying architecture, an unrealistic expectation, or a combination of several factors. The root cause is not always obvious. For example, even if the implementation seems correct at the first glance, it is always possible that bugs such as false sharing, unnecessary synchronization, or poor communication schedules increase the actual complexity of the implementation. Nonetheless, the performance litmus test introduced earlier can help separate architectural from implementation constraints. Based on the generated models, we can now also verify the compliance of the actual behavior with the optional cross-function rules. For this purpose, we combine the models involved in such rules before transforming them into their asymptotic form. Finally, if the generated models fall within the deviation limit (i.e. match the expectations either exactly or approximately) the user may instantiate them to predict the scaling limits of selected library functions at specific target scales.

3. CASE STUDY: MPI

MPI is a fundamental building block in most HPC applications, and previous work identified the runtime of collective operations and memory consumption as two potential scalability obstacles [4]. This makes MPI an ideal case study for testing our approach. We now present the instantiation of each step in our test framework. The benchmark design is discussed in more detail as it is important to understand how we benchmark and measure our target functions and metrics. This case study can be used as a guideline for applying the test framework to other libraries.

3.1 Expectations

We chose to focus on the most common MPI collective functions and latency-oriented runtimes (message sizes in the order of hundreds of bytes). Specifically, we looked at: *Barrier*, *Bcast*, *Reduce*, *Allreduce*, *Gather*, *Allgather*, and *Alltoall*. By focusing on latency, we limit ourselves to only one aspect of performance. It is sufficient for the initial study, but the message size is a changeable parameter and the study could be extended to include bandwidth as well. We also focus on the memory requirements of communicators, and measure the memory overhead of the *Comm_create*, *Comm_dup*, *Win_create*, and *Cart_create* functions. Lastly, we also chose to analyze the MPI memory consumption by estimating the process memory allocated during the benchmark execution.

The expectations for the runtime of collective operations in our MPI case study come from either the analysis of Chan et al. [7] or MPICH [19]. These particular cost models incorporate years of research and optimizations that make them a good reference for comparison. They are configurable, and can be changed as needed to reflect more specialized requirements. Table 2 presents these expectations for each collective operation. Many implementations of MPI collective functions (including MPICH) use different algorithms depending on the message size and the number of processes. Since we use a small message and numbers of processes equal to a power of two, we selected the expected models such that they reflect this setup. The expectations for communicator memory overheads are taken from the analysis by Balaji et al. [4]. The memory overhead of communicator creation, either from a group or for a new Cartesian topology, is expected to be linear in its number of processes. Communicator duplication, on the other hand, requires only constant overhead and is therefore expected to remain constant as the number of processes grows. The creation of an RMA window (`MPI_Win_create`) is expected to be linear in the number of processes. In general, a scalable MPI library should consume a fixed amount of memory, independent of the number of processes [4]. Some libraries, however, require translation tables for ranks in MPI_COMM_WORLD to network ranks (e.g., IP addresses). However, this is suboptimal and should not consume more than a few bytes per MPI process in order to support highly scalable systems.

MPI performance guidelines specify internal performance consistency rules between MPI functions [20]. These rules define consistency expectations, and we specifically evaluate two guidelines: *Allreduce* $\preceq$ *Reduce* + *Bcast* and *Allgather* $\preceq$ *Gather* + *Bcast*. These define the cross-function rules that we focus on. The first guideline states that, since semantically it is the same operation, it is reasonable to expect from a correct and optimized MPI implementation that the execution time of MPI_Allreduce is not greater than the execution time of a combination of MPI_Reduce and MPI_Bcast. The same logic is also applied to the second guideline.

3.2 Benchmark Design

Although the benchmark we designed focuses on MPI, the general structure and principles can be adapted in other libraries as well. It consists of a series of smaller micro-benchmarks which evaluate different collective functions, either in terms of execution time or memory consumption. Each one produces results that are later used as input to the model generation phase of the framework. To obtain timings for collectives, we adopted the approach by Hoefler et al. [10], which first lets all processes start a collective operation at the same time, and then takes the maximum runtime across all processes. According to this method, we first calculate clock differences relative to the first process, and then set a time window relative to this process in which every process should start the operation.

A micro-benchmark starts with a number of warm-up runs and continues to execute the collective function R times. We measure the memory overhead by wrapping malloc and free and, for operations that create a new communicator, it gives us exactly the memory overhead of the new communicator. The results of each repetition (both the runtime and the memory overhead) are reduced to a maximum value across all processes. To strike a balance between the number of repetitions and the total runtime of the benchmark, we empirically chose $R = 400$ for all the machines we used.

The memory allocated to a process on Linux and Unix-like systems is measured by analyzing the mapped memory regions in a */proc/self/smaps* file. We count either the shared and the private regions, or the proportional set size (PSS) of the process. On Blue Gene/Q the compute nodes run a special minimal version of the Linux kernel (CNK) that pre-allocates the memory for the process in advance and does not provide the actual status of the memory in */proc/self/maps*. As an alternative, we use the Kernel_GetMemorySize function to obtain the desired value. To isolate the part which is used by MPI we first measure the allocated memory before MPI is initialized, and then subtract it from the measurement after all MPI functions have been executed and all user-created MPI data objects been freed, but before MPI is finalized. The additional memory for buffers and variables that were allocated by the micro-benchmarks is also subtracted from the estimate.

To help identify architectural constraints, or negative effects of neighbor network activity, we calibrate the benchmark by running a manually implemented binary-tree broadcast [7] as our performance litmus test. It is implemented using point-to-point MPI functions and we understand the precise behavior of this implementation under ideal conditions. If its generated performance model does not correspond to the expected analytical model, it suggests that other factors, e.g., network contention or neighbor activity are influencing the runtime. After this calibration, we can attribute unexpected behavior with greater confidence to either problematic implementations or to machine-related overheads.

The benchmark runs are orchestrated by the Jülich Benchmarking Environment (JuBE) [1], which allows the user to configure a wide choice of execution parameters and specify ranges for some of them. For example, the user specifies the number of processes per node and a range for the requested nodes. JuBE then iterates over these ranges independently and creates a batch job for each combination.

Table 1: Machine specifications (cores and memory size are given per node).

	Juqueen	Juropa	Piz Daint
Platform	Blue Gene/Q	Intel, IB	Cray-XC30
Topology	5D torus	Fat tree	Dragonfly
Nodes	28,672	3,288	5,272
CPU	PPC A2	Xeon X5570	Xeon E5-2670
Clock	1.6 GHz	2.93 GHz	2.6 GHz
Cores	16	8	8
Memory	16 GB	24 GB	32 GB
MPI	PAMI	ParaStation	Cray

3.3 Generation of Scaling Models

The inputs of the model generation phase are runtimes of collective functions, communicator memory overheads, and the estimate of the memory allocated by MPI, measured for an increasing number of processes. Many benchmarks reduce the results of multiple iterations to a single value by using an average. In our case, however, to mitigate significant noise we use the first quartile. By choosing this approach, we shift our focus from the average case toward the best case and reduce the risk of false positives that can occur when the levels of noise are very high. In any case, the divergence model in the average case is as big as in the best case.

As depicted in Tables 2 and 3, there were four different expectations in this case study: $\mathcal{O}(1)$, $\mathcal{O}(\log p)$, $\mathcal{O}(p)$, and $\mathcal{O}(p \log p)$. The first two were classified as belonging to the class $F_1(x)$, and the other two as belonging to $F_2(x)$. Note that $\mathcal{O}(1)$ is a special case; it can be assigned to any one of the classes by choosing the exponent of 0. The default choice, therefore, is to classify it as belonging to $F_1(x)$, thus also expanding the default search space boundaries. For more consistency, we decided to refine the largest default search space we had, which was the search space of expectation $\mathcal{O}(p \log p)$. In other words, the search space in all the cases was defined by logarithms with powers of 0 and 1, and powers of 0, $\frac{1}{4}$, $\frac{1}{3}$ and all their multiples up to 2 for p. We also used the same deviation of $\sqrt{p}$ for all the expectations.

3.4 Validation of Expectations

In this step, we automatically validate the generated performance models against our expectations. We compute the divergence models and evaluate the cross-function consistency expectations. The final output is a list of generated models, in which each model has an adjusted coefficient of determination, a divergence model, and a match indicator. Table 2 is an example of such a list. The divergence model and the match indicator were already discussed in Section 2.4.

4. EVALUATION

In this section, we analyze the results of our experiments. We used three different machines and MPI implementations, and, as already explained, measured the runtime of collective functions, the memory overhead of communicators, and the memory allocated by the process during the benchmark execution. We first present the machines and the experimental setup and then discuss the results.

4.1 Experimental Setup

Table 1 presents the specifications of the three machines on which we conducted our experiments and tested our approach. Juqueen is a Blue Gene/Q machine built by IBM and it is the capability supercomputer at Forschungszentrum Jülich (FZJ). It is specifically designed for highly scalable codes and features improved energy efficiency. The specialized CNK kernel on the compute nodes reduces jitter and allows for reproducible measurements. Juropa, on the other hand, is the capacity machine at FZJ and is based on an Intel architecture. Piz Daint, an x86-based Cray-XC30 machine at the Swiss National Supercomputing Centre (CSCS), was built by Cray, and therefore has both a different network topology and a different MPI implementation. We believe the differences between these machines make them good choices for our case study and allow us to evaluate the scalability of different MPI implementations.

Table 2: Generated (empirical) runtime models of collective functions on Juqueen, Juropa, and Piz Daint alongside their theoretical expectations.

	Juqueen	Juropa	Piz Daint
Barrier			Expectation: $\mathcal{O}(\log p)$
Model	$\mathcal{O}(\log p)$	$\mathcal{O}(p^{0.67}\log p)$	$\mathcal{O}(p^{0.33})$
$\bar{R}^2$	0.99	0.99	0.99
$\delta(p)$	$\mathcal{O}(1)$	$\mathcal{O}(p^{0.67})$	$\mathcal{O}(p^{0.33}/\log p)$
Match	✓	x	≈
Bcast			Expectation: $\mathcal{O}(\log p)$
Model	$\mathcal{O}(\log p)$	$\mathcal{O}(p^{0.5})$	$\mathcal{O}(p^{0.5})$
$\bar{R}^2$	0.86	0.98	0.94
$\delta(p)$	$\mathcal{O}(1)$	$\mathcal{O}(p^{0.5}/\log p)$	$\mathcal{O}(p^{0.5}/\log p)$
Match	✓	≈	≈
Reduce			Expectation: $\mathcal{O}(\log p)$
Model	$\mathcal{O}(\log p)$	$\mathcal{O}(p^{0.5}\log p)$	$\mathcal{O}(p^{0.5}\log p)$
$\bar{R}^2$	0.93	0.99	0.94
$\delta(p)$	$\mathcal{O}(1)$	$\mathcal{O}(p^{0.5})$	$\mathcal{O}(p^{0.5})$
Match	✓	≈	≈
Allreduce			Expectation: $\mathcal{O}(\log p)$
Model	$\mathcal{O}(\log p)$	$\mathcal{O}(p^{0.5})$	$\mathcal{O}(p^{0.67}\log p)$
$\bar{R}^2$	0.87	0.99	0.99
$\delta(p)$	$\mathcal{O}(1)$	$\mathcal{O}(p^{0.5}/\log p)$	$\mathcal{O}(p^{0.67})$
Match	✓	≈	x ⚠
Gather			Expectation: $\mathcal{O}(p)$
Model	$\mathcal{O}(p)$	$\mathcal{O}(p)$	$\mathcal{O}(p)$
$\bar{R}^2$	0.99	0.99	0.99
$\delta(p)$	$\mathcal{O}(1)$	$\mathcal{O}(1)$	$\mathcal{O}(1)$
Match	✓	✓	✓
Allgather			Expectation: $\mathcal{O}(p)$
Model	$\mathcal{O}(p)$	$\mathcal{O}(p)$	$\mathcal{O}(p^{1.25})$
$\bar{R}^2$	0.99	0.98	0.99
$\delta(p)$	$\mathcal{O}(1)$	$\mathcal{O}(1)$	$\mathcal{O}(p^{0.25})$
Match	✓	✓	≈
Alltoall			Expectation: $\mathcal{O}(p\log p)$
Model	$\mathcal{O}(p)$	$\mathcal{O}(p^{1.25})$	$\mathcal{O}(p^{1.33})$
$\bar{R}^2$	0.99	0.99	0.99
$\delta(p)$	$\mathcal{O}(1/\log p)$	$\mathcal{O}(p^{0.25}/\log p)$	$\mathcal{O}(p^{0.33}/\log p)$
Match	≈	≈	≈
Bcast (BT)			Expectation: $\mathcal{O}(\log p)$
Model	$\mathcal{O}(\log p)$	$\mathcal{O}(p^{1.25}\log p)$	$\mathcal{O}(p\log p)$
$\bar{R}^2$	0.99	0.99	0.99
$\delta(p)$	$\mathcal{O}(1)$	$\mathcal{O}(p^{1.25})$	$\mathcal{O}(p)$
Match	✓	x	x

The MPI implementation on Juqueen is based on the PAMI interface [13] and uses special hardware components to accelerate collective functions [8]. Users have a choice of various protocols for some of the frequently used collective functions, e.g., binary-tree or binomial for `MPI_Allreduce`. They also have the option to revert to the plain MPICH implementation from which the Blue Gene version was derived. For some numbers of processes and message sizes, the special hardware components have no tangible benefits; in these cases, the implementation might revert automatically to the original MPICH algorithm. Juqueen provides an extension of MPI that makes it possible to query which algorithm was actually used during the execution of the collective function. Piz Daint is a Cray machine and uses Cray MPI, which is a vendor implementation of MPI and is quite closely coupled to the machine itself. In these cases, support for non-native implementations, such as Open MPI, is quite limited. Therefore, we chose to focus our study on supported implementations, that is, PAMI on Juqueen, ParaStation MPI on Juropa, and CrayMPI on Piz Daint. We chose to set the number of MPI processes per node to be the same as the number of cores in the node. The reason is that oversubscribing, namely running more processes than the number of cores, can cause network contention at the node level. On the other hand, undersubscribing, namely having fewer processes, can potentially cause insufficient utilization of the node's computational resources and means that the application would need to have more threads.

All three machines in our experiments provide highly accurate, high-resolution hardware timers in the form of registers that can be read very quickly with an atomic instruction: MFTB on PowerPC, and RDTSC on x86. They allow individual runtimes to be measured instead of executing a function N times in a loop, measuring the total runtime, and then dividing it by N to get an average. The latter approach suffers from pipeline effects and tends to underestimate the latency [10]. As mentioned before, each run of the benchmark performs R iterations. In order to capture performance fluctuations due to topology and network noise, we repeated the runs 10 times. Each run was submitted separately to the batch system and thus was given a different node allocation. We note that the experiments on Piz Daint were performed with default Cray MPI library optimizations. The newer version of Cray MPI has additional algorithms that may improve scaling, and can be used by setting appropriate environment variables.

4.2 Result Analysis

In this subsection, we present the results of our analysis. Tables 2 and 3 present the models as formulae next to our expectations. Table 2 refers to runtime and Table 3 to memory metrics. Since the size of the memory growth coefficients may be significant, we show full models of memory overheads and estimated memory consumption by MPI. The $\bar{R}^2$ row lists the adjusted coefficient of determination, which indicates how well the data fits a statistical model. It is used in the model generation phase to create models that fit the data better [6]. Note that $\bar{R}^2$ is not applicable to constant models. Then follows the δ row with the divergence models as defined in Section 2.4. Finally, the match row specifies whether the generated model meets our expectations. If the two are in agreement, a checkmark ✓ is shown. If the match is approximate according to the definition in Section 2.4, a $\approx$ is shown. A solid x represents an unquestionable mismatch. A warning sign ⚠ indicates the violation of a performance guideline. Figure 2 presents the runtime models for the collective functions we benchmarked plus the estimation of memory consumption as graphs. The circles, squares, and triangles depict the actual measurements, whereas the lines are the predictions. Each curve is annotated with the corresponding model which sits on top of the curve. Since we focus on the scalability behavior of the models, we chose not to show the constant terms. The discussion below starts with Juqueen, on which almost all the generated models correspond almost fully to expectations. We then continue to Juropa and Piz Daint, on which the results differed from our expectations to some degree.

Juqueen

On Juqueen, the performance of collective functions was generally better than on the other machines and we found that almost all of our expectations were met. All the models on Juqueen are either logarithmic or linear with respect to the number of processes p. As can be seen in Table 2, all the generated models on Juqueen correspond exactly to the expected models with the exception of `MPI_Alltoall`, which is identified as linear when, in fact, the expectation would be $\mathcal{O}(p \log p)$. The difference between reality and expectation is small enough to be explained by noise and other system effects. The manually implemented binary-tree (BT) version of the broadcast is shown at the bottom of Table 2. The expected cost of this algorithm for small messages is: $(\alpha + \beta) \log p$; and though it is slower in absolute terms than the native `MPI_Bcast`, the generated model is still logarithmic. It serves as a strong indicator that other factors have minimal influence on the runtime. Table 3 presents the models for the communicator memory overheads and the estimated fraction of the memory allocated by the process that is consumed by MPI. Although the generated models on Juqueen correspond to the expectations, the linear growth of some of the communicator constructors can still become an issue at very large scale.

Juropa and Piz Daint

On Juropa and Piz Daint, the predicted performance models of some collective functions did not fully match their expectations. These discrepancies between predicted and expected behavior suggest potential scalability issues. Almost all the generated models, including the ones for `MPI_Barrier`, `MPI_Bcast`, and `MPI_Reduce`, did not correspond to the expected logarithmic models. It is important to note that `MPI_Barrier` can have both logarithmic and linear implementations [15]. However, since the optimized MPICH implementation is logarithmic [19], we expect it to behave logarithmically on Juropa as well. The generated model of the binary-tree (BT) broadcast falls outside the deviation limits and clearly fails to match the expected logarithmic model. Since we have a clear understanding of this algorithm and its complexity, we can point to a number of external factors as potential causes of this discrepancy:

1. The network model which was used to calculate the expected cost of the binary-tree broadcast algorithm is simpler than the IB fat-tree interconnect on Juropa.

2. On some machines, the performance of communication-heavy applications strongly depends on the node allocation they receive and the neighborhood of each node [5]. An application which runs on a neighbor node and produces heavy network load creates more perturbation for our benchmark.

3. Network hardware and topology can influence the runtime of various collective functions and make them slower than expected [11,12].

The above factors can also offer an explanation for the discrepancies between the generated models and the expectations on Piz Daint. The performance models of `MPI_Gather` on both Juropa and Piz Daint, as well as the `MPI_Allgather` model on Juropa, are linear as expected. On Piz Daint, however, the performance model of the latter does not match the expectation but still falls within the deviation limits. In Table 2, the warning sign under *Match* signals that a performance guideline violation was detected. As discussed in Section 3.4, the automatic validation evaluates two performance guidelines, one for *Allreduce* and one for *Allgather*. Although the actual measurements on Piz Daint do not violate the *Allreduce* guideline, the generated models predict

Table 3: Generated (empirical) runtime models of memory overhead on Juqueen, Juropa, and Piz Daint alongside their theoretical expectations.

	Juqueen	Juropa	Piz Daint
MPI memory [MB]			Expectation: $\mathcal{O}(\log p)$
Model	$10.7 \cdot 10^{-3} \cdot \log p$	$16 + 0.56 \cdot p$	$46 + 1.35 \cdot \log p$
$\bar{R}^2$	0.72	1	0.23
$\delta(p)$	$\mathcal{O}(1)$	$\mathcal{O}(p/\log p)$	$\mathcal{O}(1)$
Match	✓	x	✓
Comm_create [B]			Expectation: $\mathcal{O}(p)$
Model	$2.2 \cdot 10^5 + 24 \cdot p$	$264 + 28 \cdot p$	$3770 + 46 \cdot p$
$\bar{R}^2$	1	1	0.99
$\delta(p)$	$\mathcal{O}(1)$	$\mathcal{O}(1)$	$\mathcal{O}(1)$
Match	✓	✓	✓
Comm_dup [B]			Expectation: $\mathcal{O}(1)$
Model	$2.2 \cdot 10^5$	256	$3770 + 18 \cdot p$
$\bar{R}^2$	-	-	0.99
$\delta(p)$	$\mathcal{O}(1)$	$\mathcal{O}(1)$	$\mathcal{O}(p)$
Match	✓	✓	x
Win_create [B]			Expectation: $\mathcal{O}(p)$
Model	$96 \cdot p$	$256 + 60 \cdot p$	$3287 + 118 \cdot p$
$\bar{R}^2$	1	1	0.99
$\delta(p)$	$\mathcal{O}(1)$	$\mathcal{O}(1)$	$\mathcal{O}(1)$
Match	✓	✓	✓
Cart_create [B]			Expectation: $\mathcal{O}(p)$
Model	$2.2 \cdot 10^5 + 52 \cdot p$	$356 + 24 \cdot p$	$2545 + 63 \cdot p$
$\bar{R}^2$	0.99	1	0.99
$\delta(p)$	$\mathcal{O}(1)$	$\mathcal{O}(1)$	$\mathcal{O}(1)$
Match	✓	✓	✓

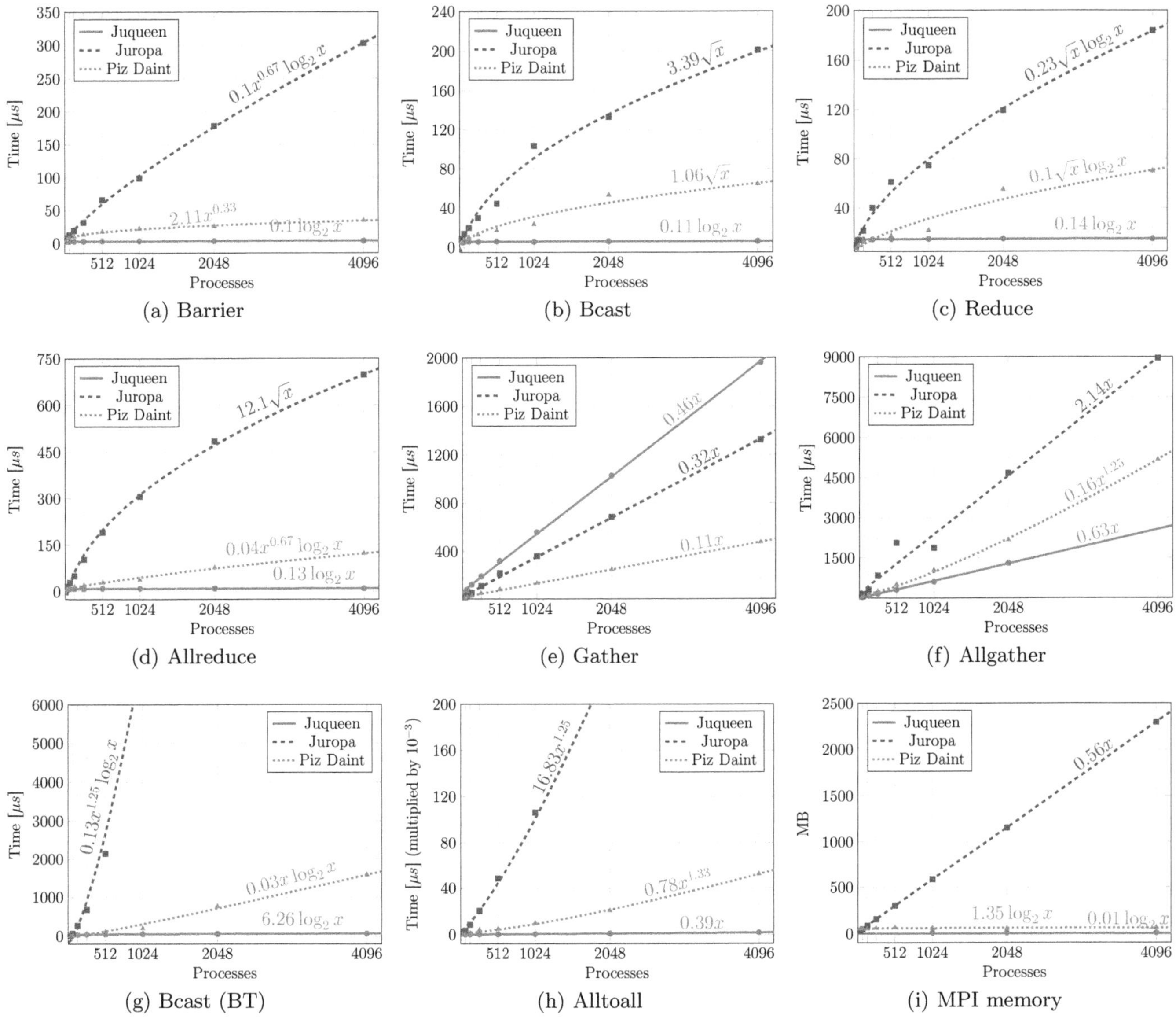

Figure 2: Measurements (circles, squares, triangles) and generated runtime models (plot lines) on Juqueen, Juropa, and Piz Daint.

that the guideline would be violated at larger scales. However, whether this is indeed the case must be verified in future experiments.

The communicator memory overheads on Juropa and Piz Daint are presented in Table 3. On Juropa, the generated models correspond to expectations, and it is interesting to note that the initial overheads (the constants) are very small. This is in direct contrast to Juqueen, on which these constants are much higher. The model for communicator duplication on Piz Daint is linear, although it is expected to be constant. The development team at Cray confirmed that the implementation of `MPI_Comm_dup` is taken from MPICH 3.1.2, and that the MPICH version behaves in the same manner. This result clearly shows that there might be a scalability bug in this function; further study is required to find ways to fix it.

Figure 2i presents the models for the estimated fraction of the process memory that is consumed by MPI on all three machines. In the case of Juropa, the generated model reveals a severe scalability problem. Even with smaller values of p, it is non-scalable. Starting with 1024 nodes, it is impossible to have 8 MPI processes per node since all the processes would require 35 GB in total and the node's memory is just 24 GB. Our experiments confirmed this memory wall: memory allocation failed when the total number of processes was 8192 (with 8 processes per node). Our findings are confirmed by the documentation; the reason for the linear increase in allocated memory is that ParaStation MPI uses by default the Reliable Connected (RC) InfiniBand service, which needs 0.55 MB of memory for each MPI connection [2]. When using `MPI_Alltoall` each process will allocate $0.55p$ MB of memory, which is exactly the linear behavior we discovered through our experiments.

Table 4: Generated (empirical) runtime models of MAFIA functions alongside their theoretical expectations.

	gen	dedup	pcount	unjoin
Expectation	$\mathcal{O}(k^3 2^k)$	$\mathcal{O}(k^4 2^k)$	$\mathcal{O}(k 2^k)$	$\mathcal{O}(k^3 2^k)$
Model	$\mathcal{O}(k^4 2^k)$	$\mathcal{O}(k^4 2^k)$	$\mathcal{O}(k 2^k)$	$\mathcal{O}(k^2 2^k)$
$\delta(k)$	$\mathcal{O}(k)$	$\mathcal{O}(1)$	$\mathcal{O}(1)$	$\mathcal{O}(1/k)$
Match	$\approx$	✓	✓	$\approx$

4.3 MAFIA

No matter how large the degree of parallelism, optimizing sequential code is still essential to achieve good performance. The subject of our second case is therefore MAFIA (Merging of Adaptive Finite IntervAls), a sequential data-mining program utilizing a collection of key routines. One of the basic problems in data mining is identifying regions of similarity in a multi-dimensional data set. Many applications, however, exhibit a high degree of dimensionality in the data, which makes traditional approaches of all-attribute clustering problematic. A possible solution is to use subspace clustering methods to identify clusters in a subset of dimensions. MAFIA is one example of such a method. It is a serial algorithm for subspace clustering based on adaptive grid methods [3]. The cluster dimensionality k is a critical parameter in this algorithm since the ultimate goal is to identify clusters across all dimensions. Users of MAFIA will start with a smaller k but will be interested in increasing it to catch all the dimensions. We are interested in applying our framework to see whether our scaling expectations as a function of k are valid. This use case is an example of algorithmic modeling since the model parameter k is a parameter of the algorithm itself.

Following the four steps of our approach, we start by defining the expectations. Along with k, the parameters of MAFIA are the number of data points n, the dimensionality of the points d, and the number of clusters m. We further identify four main functions (i.e., kernels) in the main computation phase of MAFIA, *gen*, *dedup*, *pcount*, and *unjoin*. They correspond to the generation of candidate sets, de-duplication of them, identifying dense sets, and checking whether lower dimensional sets were not already absorbed by the higher ones [16] respectively. Table 4 presents the expectations for these functions provided by Adinetz et al. [3] in their effort to optimize MAFIA.

The benchmarking process was much simpler in this case since MAFIA is a serial code and we were not modeling scalability on an increasing number of cores. The focus in this use case was the runtime of the algorithm as k increases; therefore we set the other parameters as follows: $n = 10^5$, $d = 20$, and $m = 3$. The experiments were conducted on one node of Juropa and repeated for $k = 3, 4, ..., 13$. In contrast to the MPI study, all the expectations were exponential: $\mathcal{O}(k2^k)$, $\mathcal{O}(k^3 2^k)$, and $\mathcal{O}(k^4 2^k)$. In all of these cases we did not change the default deviation limits or the search space boundaries. As Table 4 shows, all the generated models matched our expectations completely or were inside the deviation limits.

This example illustrates the flexibility of our approach, which can be adapted to different scalability problems with different expectations.

5. RELATED WORK

Our approach combines two earlier ideas, performance assertions [21] and automated empirical performance modeling [6], into a new approach for practical performance-centric code design. Performance assertions are source-code annotations that specify performance requirements in terms of conditional expressions consisting of performance metrics, program variables, and constants. At runtime, the expressions are instantiated with measurements and subsequently evaluated. Violations are reported. If the number of processes is included in such an expression, performance assertions can be used to verify the compliance with scalability requirements as long as these can be specified in terms of performance data acquired during a single run. Even though assertions support tolerance thresholds, their design necessitates a rather precise notion of how the application should perform at a given number of processes. Because of the detailed understanding of the code and/or the underlying system this requires, it is often unrealistic to expect such a precise notion. Furthermore, it is rarely portable. Our approach, in contrast, specifies scalability expectations in terms of the more prevalent asymptotic complexities, ignoring platform-dependent coefficients. Rather than looking at a single run, we determine and evaluate the growth rate of a given metric across multiple runs with an increasing number of processes. Thus, our approach would be more practical in the common scenario where the developer has only a vague idea of how the code scales.

The model generator we apply to create our performance models is similar in spirit to the one used by Calotoiu et al. [6]. While their generator uses a manually configured search space, our extended generator builds the search space automatically around an expected performance model, leveraging the user's available knowledge. It means that it can also find exponential models - something which is not supported by their generator. Another difference is that we compute divergence models as an indicator of how the deviation would grow as the scale increases. We expect that our methodology integrates well with other performance modeling frameworks such as PALM [18] or the PMaC tools [14].

Our case study, the scalability analysis of MPI implementations, was inspired by various MPI benchmarking efforts. Notably, *SKaMPI* [17] defined a way to accurately measure collective operations [23], which was later extended in *NBCBench* [9,10] and which we adapted for our work. Our idea of comparing the scalability of different parts of the target library was motivated by *mpicroscope* [20]. Instead of giving the users direct time metrics, the benchmark searches for violations of performance guidelines. One guideline, for example, states that `MPI_Allreduce` should take a smaller or equal amount of time when compared to `MPI_Reduce` followed by `MPI_Bcast`. A violation of this guideline suggests that there is some optimization flaw in an MPI implementation. However, our approach offers a different perspective since it automatically evaluates the guidelines using the generated models, and thus can predict violations for a large number of processes.

6. CONCLUSION

In this paper, we propose a new software engineering discipline for extreme-scale systems. With our scheme, we identify scalability issues in libraries which are thought to be scalable and pinpoint possible performance bugs and room for improvement. In contrast to previous approaches, our technique only requires the performance engineer to have a vague (asymptotic) idea of the scalability, although the accuracy improves if more information is available (e.g., a performance litmus test or more precise expectations). We also supply a tool chain that automates large parts of our four-step process and is ready for immediate use by performance engineers.

To achieve this, our tool chain utilizes automated performance modeling to generate analytical models of the runtime and memory overheads of selected library functions. Divergence models derived from the generated models show how the actual behavior differs when increasing the number of processes, revealing potential performance problems in the implementation.

We demonstrate the effectiveness of our mechanism using what is probably the most important library interface in HPC: the Message Passing Interface. We chose it as a use case because many commercially mature and well-tested implementations are available and clear performance expectations exist in the literature. We show how our approach enables MPI developers to spot scalability bugs early on, before commencing full-scale tests on the target supercomputer. For this, we used automated experiments on three different machines with three different MPI libraries, and our tool discovered a number of scalability issues that can be grouped into the following cases: (a) key collective functions on Juropa and Piz Daint display unexpected behavior; (b) the performance guideline $Allreduce \preceq Reduce + Bcast$ is potentially violated on Piz Daint; (c) memory consumption on Juropa limits the number of possible processes; (d) communicator duplication on Piz Daint consumes more memory than necessary. We conclude that our approach is a viable technique that can both point to limitations of the systems and provide MPI developers with important hints for improving the scalability of their implementations. We also expect that this will motivate the development of clear performance expectations for other parallel libraries such as ScaLAPACK or the parallel BLAS.

7. ACKNOWLEDGMENTS

This work was supported in part by the German Research Foundation (DFG) and the Swiss National Science Foundation (SNSF) through the DFG Priority Programme 1648 *Software for Exascale Computing* (SPPEXA). We would like to thank Andrew Adinetz and Marius Poke for their contribution to the MAFIA study. We would also like to acknowledge Jülich Supercomputing Centre (JSC) and Swiss National Supercomputing Centre (CSCS), which gave us access to their supercomputers. Finally, we would like to express our gratitude to the Cray software development team, and specifically Mark Pagel, for their help and support.

8. REFERENCES

[1] JuBE: Jülich Benchmarking Environment. `http://www.fz-juelich.de/jsc/jube`.

[2] ParaStation MPI User's Guide. `http://docs.par-tec.com/html/psmpi-userguide/index.html`.

[3] A. Adinetz, J. Kraus, J. Meinke, and D. Pleiter. GPUMAFIA: Efficient Subspace Clustering with MAFIA on GPUs. In *Proc of the 19th International Conference on Parallel Processing*, Euro-Par'13, pages 838–849. Springer-Verlag, 2013.

[4] P. Balaji, D. Buntinas, D. Goodell, W. Gropp, T. Hoefler, S. Kumar, E. Lusk, R. Thakur, and J. L. Traeff. MPI on Millions of Cores. *Parallel Processing Letters (PPL)*, 21(1):45–60, Mar. 2011.

[5] A. Bhatele, K. Mohror, S. H. Langer, and K. E. Isaacs. There Goes the Neighborhood: Performance Degradation Due to Nearby Jobs. In *Proc. of the ACM/IEEE Conference on Supercomputing*, SC '13, pages 41:1–41:12. ACM, 2013.

[6] A. Calotoiu, T. Hoefler, M. Poke, and F. Wolf. Using Automated Performance Modeling to Find Scalability Bugs in Complex Codes. In *Proc. of the ACM/IEEE Conference on Supercomputing*, SC '13, pages 45:1–45:12. ACM, 2013.

[7] E. Chan, M. Heimlich, A. Purkayastha, and R. van de Geijn. Collective Communication: Theory, Practice, and Experience. *Concurr. Comput. : Pract. Exper.*, 19(13):1749–1783, Sep 2007.

[8] D. Chen, N. A. Eisley, P. Heidelberger, R. M. Senger, Y. Sugawara, S. Kumar, V. Salapura, D. L. Satterfield, B. Steinmacher-Burow, and J. J. Parker. The IBM Blue Gene/Q Interconnection Network and Message Unit. In *Proc. of the ACM/IEEE Conference on Supercomputing*, SC '11, pages 26:1–26:10. ACM, 2011.

[9] T. Hoefler, A. Lumsdaine, and W. Rehm. Implementation and Performance Analysis of Non-Blocking Collective Operations for MPI. In *Proc. of the ACM/IEEE Conference on Supercomputing*, SC '07, pages 52:1–52:10. IEEE Computer Society/ACM, 2007.

[10] T. Hoefler, T. Schneider, and A. Lumsdaine. Accurately Measuring Collective Operations at Massive Scale. In *Proc. of the IEEE International Parallel & Distributed Processing Symp.*, IPDPS '08, pages 1–8, 2008.

[11] T. Hoefler, T. Schneider, and A. Lumsdaine. The Impact of Network Noise at Large-Scale Communication Performance. In *Proc. of the IEEE International Parallel & Distributed Processing Symp.*, IPDPS '09, pages 1–8, 2009.

[12] T. Hoefler and M. Snir. Generic Topology Mapping Strategies for Large-scale Parallel Architectures. In *Proc. of the ACM International Conference on Supercomputing*, ICS '11, pages 75–84. ACM, 2011.

[13] S. Kumar, A. R. Mamidala, D. A. Faraj, B. Smith, M. Blocksome, B. Cernohous, D. Miller, J. Parker, J. Ratterman, P. Heidelberger, D. Chen, and B. Steinmacher-Burrow. PAMI: A Parallel Active Message Interface for the Blue Gene/Q Supercomputer. In *Proc. of the IEEE International Parallel & Distributed Processing Symp.*, IPDPS '12, pages 763–773. IEEE Computer Society, 2012.

[14] M. R. Meswani, L. Carrington, D. Unat, A. Snavely, S. Baden, and S. Poole. Modeling and Predicting Performance of High Performance Computing Applications on Hardware Accelerators. *Int. J. High Perform. Comput. Appl.*, 27(2):89–108, May 2013.

[15] J. Pješivac-Grbović, T. Angskun, G. Bosilca, G. E. Fagg, E. Gabriel, and J. J. Dongarra. Performance

Analysis of MPI Collective Operations. *Cluster Computing*, 10(2):127–143, 2007.

[16] M. Poke. SymPtOM: Informed Automatic Performance Modeling. Master's thesis, German Research School for Simulation Sciences, Aachen, Germany, Oct 2013.

[17] R. Reussner, P. Sanders, and J. L. Träff. SKaMPI: a comprehensive benchmark for public benchmarking of MPI. *Scientific Programming*, 10(1):55–65, 2002.

[18] N. R. Tallent and A. Hoisie. Palm: Easing the Burden of Analytical Performance Modeling. In *Proc. of the ACM International Conference on Supercomputing*, ICS '14, pages 221–230. ACM, 2014.

[19] R. Thakur, R. Rabenseifner, and W. Gropp. Optimization of Collective Communication Operations in MPICH. *International Journal of High Performance Computing Applications*, 19(1):49–66, 2005.

[20] J. L. Träff. mpicroscope: Towards an MPI Benchmark Tool for Performance Guideline Verification. In *Proc. of the European MPI Users' Group Meeting*, EuroMPI '12, pages 100–109. Springer-Verlag, 2012.

[21] J. S. Vetter and P. H. Worley. Asserting Performance Expectations. In *Proc. of the ACM/IEEE Conference on Supercomputing*, SC '02, pages 1–13. IEEE Computer Society Press, 2002.

[22] C. Vömel. ScaLAPACK's MRRR algorithm. *ACM Transactions on Mathematical Software (TOMS)*, 37(1), 2010.

[23] T. Worsch, R. Reussner, and W. Augustin. On Benchmarking Collective MPI Operations. In *Proc. of the European PVM/MPI Users' Group Meeting*, pages 271–279. Springer-Verlag, 2002.

MODESTO: Data-centric Analytic Optimization of Complex Stencil Programs on Heterogeneous Architectures

Tobias Gysi
Dep. of Computer Science
ETH Zurich
tobias.gysi@inf.ethz.ch

Tobias Grosser
Dep. of Computer Science
ETH Zurich
tobias.grosser@inf.ethz.ch

Torsten Hoefler
Dep. of Computer Science
ETH Zurich
htor@inf.ethz.ch

ABSTRACT

Code transformations, such as loop tiling and loop fusion, are of key importance for the efficient implementation of stencil computations. However, their direct application to a large code base is costly and severely impacts program maintainability. While recently introduced domain-specific languages facilitate the application of such transformations, they typically still require manual tuning or auto-tuning techniques to select the transformations that yield optimal performance. In this paper, we introduce MODESTO, a model-driven stencil optimization framework, that for a stencil program suggests program transformations optimized for a given target architecture. Initially, we review and categorize data locality transformations for stencil programs and introduce a stencil algebra that allows the expression and enumeration of different stencil program implementation variants. Combining this algebra with a compile-time performance model, we show how to automatically tune stencil programs. We use our framework to model the STELLA library and optimize kernels used by the COSMO atmospheric model on multi-core and hybrid CPU-GPU architectures. Compared to naive and expert-tuned variants, the automatically tuned kernels attain a 2.0–3.1x and a 1.0–1.8x speedup respectively.

Categories and Subject Descriptors

D.3.4 [**Processors**]: Optimization

Keywords

stencil; tiling; fusion; performance model; heterogeneous systems

1. INTRODUCTION

Stencil computations on regular domains are one of the most important algorithmic motifs in embedded, high-performance, and scientific computing. Applications range from climate modeling [4], seismic imaging [8], fluid dynamics, heat diffusion and electromagnetic simulations [14] through image processing [11] to machine learning. Given their importance, numerous optimization strategies [1, 5, 10] and domain-specific languages [2, 11, 15] exist. Yet, most of these schemes consider the optimization of a single stencil in isolation. Many applications, however, require nested stencils [18] that are applied in succession. The data dependencies of these nestings can form complex directed acyclic *stencil graphs* where multiple stencils need to be optimized in tandem to achieve highest performance.

Stencils programs perform element-wise computations on a fixed neighborhood called the stencil. Such stencils often have low arithmetic intensity because they have a fixed number of operations per loaded value. The biggest challenge is to map stencil programs to modern architectures with a growing gap between memory and compute bandwidth. Such architectures require *data-centric optimizations* that arrange data accesses to efficiently use the available memory bandwidth. Complex stencil graphs can be optimized using various techniques such as loop fusion, tiling, and various communication strategies on subgraphs. We model all possible combinations of optimizations for a particular stencil program (graph) as an *application algebra* and apply mathematical optimization techniques to find the best combination specific to an abstract hierarchical machine model.

Since typical stencil programs contain hundreds of stencils arranged in paths with dozens of stages and several input arrays, manual tuning of all options is infeasible. In fact, the number of stencil program variants is usually exponential in the number of stencils. In addition, the optimal stencil program variant is specific to each architecture. We show how to fully automate the optimization and implement it in our open-source[1] tool MODESTO, a **MO**del **D**riv**E**n **ST**encil **O**ptimization framework.

We demonstrate the efficacy of our method using the real-world application COSMO [4], a numerical weather prediction and regional climate model used by more than 10 national weather services and many other institutions. The dynamical core of COSMO, a central part of its implementation, applies more than 150 stencils, each operating on 13 arrays on average. This most performance-critical code has been rewritten using the STELLA library and was carefully tuned by experts for optimal performance. MODESTO-optimized stencil graphs match or improve upon the expert-tuned code by a factor of 1.0-1.8x. This demonstrates how our technique enables next generation stencil libraries that completely abstract optimizations from the library interface. Hence, we are able to improve usability as well as performance portability compared to state-of-the-art stencil libraries such as STELLA [6] or Halide [11]. In summary, we make the following contributions:

- We introduce a set of data-centric code transformations, an algebraic formulation of the transformation space, and a compile-time performance model that facilitate the automatic optimization of complex stencil programs.

ICS'15, June 8–11, 2015, Newport Beach, CA, USA.

ACM 978-1-4503-3559-1/15/06 ...$15.00.
DOI: http://dx.doi.org/10.1145/2751205.2751223.

[1] http://spcl.inf.ethz.ch/Research/Parallel_Programming/MODESTO/

- We evaluate our approach by modeling the optimization of stencil codes written using the STELLA library and successfully tune kernels of a real-world application.
- We formulate the automatic tuning of stencil programs as a mathematical optimization problem and solve it using dynamic programming techniques.

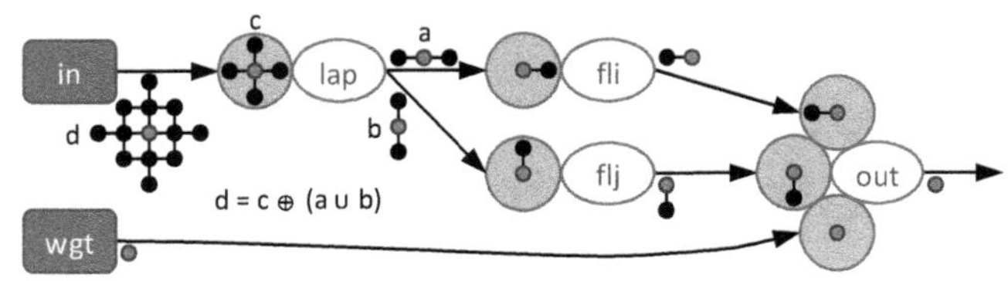

Figure 1: Horizontal diffusion dependency graph annotated with stencil (c) and stencil program (a, b, and d) access patterns

```
// Allocate temporary storage
Field[double] lap(ibegin,iend),
  fli(ibegin,iend), flj(ibegin,iend);
// Apply the lap stencil
for(int i=ibegin-1; i<iend+1; ++i)
  for(int j=jbegin-1; j<jend+1; ++j)
    lap(i,j) = -4.0 * in(i,j) +
      in(i-1,j) + in(i+1,j) + in(i,j-1) + in(i,j+1);
// Apply the fli stencil
for(int i=ibegin-1; i<iend; ++i)
  for(int j=jbegin; j<jend; ++j)
    fli(i,j) = lap(i+1,j) - lap(i,j);
// Apply the flj stencil
for(int i=ibegin; i<iend; ++i)
  for(int j=jbegin-1; j<jend; ++j)
    flj(i,j) = lap(i,j+1) - lap(i,j);
// Apply the out stencil
for(int i=ibegin; i<iend; ++i)
  for(int j=jbegin; j<jend; ++j)
    out(i,j) = wgt(i,j) *
      (fli(i-1,j) - fli(i,j) + flj(i,j-1) - flj(i,j));
```

Figure 2: Naive implementation of the simplified horizontal diffusion example used by the COSMO [4] atmospheric model

2. STENCIL ALGEBRA

Although the stencil motif appears in a wide range of codes from various application domains, common patterns can be identified. Using them, we introduce a stencil algebra that formalizes stencil computations and facilitates their analysis and optimization.

2.1 Definition of a Stencil Program

The following core elements describe a stencil program:

A **field** F defines a dense, multi-dimensional and commonly hyperrectangular set of data values, which can be read and modified.

A **stencil** S is a computation that derives a value located in an output field from a set of input field values located within bounded distance to the output value. It is described by the triple (ops, out, in). The first element, ops, specifies the (possibly approximated) computational cost of executing this stencil. The second element, out, is the output field of the stencil. The third element, in, is a set that defines the input elements of the stencil. The elements of the input set are so-called "named vectors" that are named according to the field the input is read from and the vector itself describes the location of the input element as a relative offset to the position of the element the stencil computes. The set of input elements in is not allowed to contain elements of the output field. We define an example stencil s that computes the value $F_0(i,j)$ from the inputs $F_1(i,j)$, $F_1(i,j+1)$ and $F_2(i,j)$ with 5 computational operations using the following notation: $s := (5, F_0, \{F_1(0,0), F_1(0,1), F_2(0,0)\})$

A **stencil program** $P = T \cup O$ consists of a set of temporary stencils T as well as a set of output stencils O, where the results computed by the output stencils form the result of the stencil program, but the results of the temporary stencils are not made available outside of the stencil program. All stencils and fields have the same dimensionality.

The program definition just introduced is formulated minimalistically and with a strong focus on stencil graphs. As a consequence, it omits aspects that in the context of our article are of limited importance, e.g., boundary conditions, variable input field dimensionality, as well as complex dynamic control flow. However, programs which use such concepts can in many cases still be modeled. For example, stencils with varying input sets, due to the use of special boundary conditions, can often be modeled with an over-approximated input set and iterative stencil computations can be modeled by (partially) unrolling the relevant time loop.

2.2 Example

We now present an example stencil program which is derived from a horizontal diffusion kernel used by the COSMO atmospheric model [4]. We define the stencil program P_{hd} in terms of the temporary stencils s_{lap}, s_{fli}, and s_{flj} necessary to evaluate the output stencil s_{out}. A data dependency either refers to an input field loaded by the stencil program, such as in or wgt, or to a temporary field computed by the corresponding temporary stencil, such as fli, flj, or lap:

$$s_{lap} := (5, lap, \{in(-1,0), in(1,0), in(0,-1), in(0,1), in(0,0)\})$$
$$s_{fli} := (1, fli, \{lap(1,0), lap(0,0)\})$$
$$s_{flj} := (1, flj, \{lap(0,1), lap(0,0)\})$$
$$s_{out} := (5, out, \{fli(-1,0), fli(0,0), flj(0,-1), flj(0,0), wgt(0,0)\})$$
$$P_{hd} := \{s_{lap}, s_{fli}, s_{flj}\} \cup \{s_{out}\}$$

Figure 1 illustrates the data flow of the stencil program using a directed graph, whose black and white nodes represent input fields and stencils respectively. Arrows that do not point to a node and consequently exit the stencil graph model the outputs of the stencil program. A directed edge in the graph corresponds to a flow dependency between two nodes. We annotate each incoming edge of a stencil with the access pattern necessary for a single stencil evaluation. For instance, a single evaluation of the lap stencil accesses the in field at the five offsets shown by c. In addition, we annotate all outgoing edges of a stencil or an input field with the accumulated access pattern necessary to evaluate the out stencil at a single position. E.g., the lap stencil is evaluated at the positions defined by the union of the sets a and b. We compute the accumulated in field access pattern d as the Minkowski sum $d = (a \cup b) \oplus c$, with $a \oplus b = \{a' + b' \mid a' \in a, b' \in b\}$. Figure 2 shows a naive implementation of the horizontal diffusion kernel, which executes each stencil using a separate loop nest. While such an implementation may be straightforward to write, it is not efficient in terms of data locality, memory usage, or parallelism.

2.3 Data Locality Transformations

To improve the data locality of stencil programs, we discuss code transformations that combine loop tiling and loop fusion. While tiling sub-divides the loop domain into typically hyperrectangular tiles of limited size, fusion substitutes a sequence of loops by a sin-

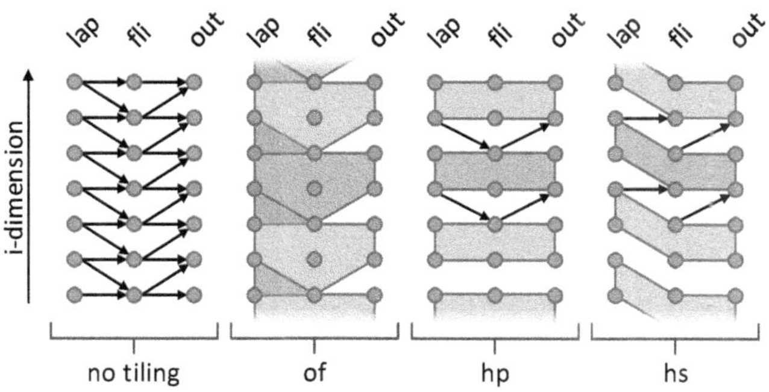

Figure 3: Tile shapes (shaded) for different tilings applied to a subset of the horizontal diffusion example projected to the i-dimension

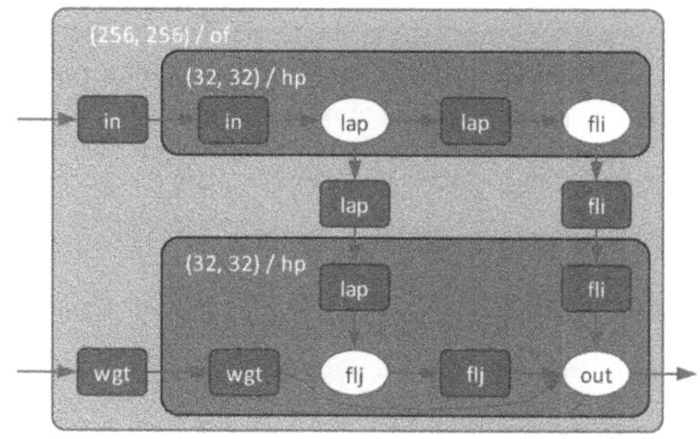

Figure 4: Stencil dependency graph of the horizontal diffusion example annotated with two tiling hierarchy levels.

gle loop. Applied to stencil codes, we divide the stencil evaluation domain into tiles and apply multiple stencils tile-by-tile. Consequently, we can store temporary values in smaller buffers that hold the working set of a single tile instead of the full evaluation domain.

While tiling increases the data locality, it causes additional synchronization efforts at the tile boundaries. As shown in Figure 1, a single stencil evaluation depends on one or more input or temporary fields accessed in a local neighborhood. When combining multiple stencils the neighborhoods grow depending on the stencil access patterns and the longest path in the dependency graph. We call all dependencies outside of the tile domain the **halo points** of a tile. In addition, we suggest three halo strategies that trade off parallelism against computation. Figure 3 shows the iteration space of one dependency path in the horizontal diffusion example. once without any tiling and then with different tiles as they result from the suggested halo strategies. Shaded regions mark the points that belong to a specific tile.

Computation on-the-fly (of) satisfies all halo point dependencies using redundant computation at the tile boundaries. Hence, we load input fields and evaluate temporary stencils in an extended domain covering the tile itself as well as its halo points. Using computation on-the-fly, we can update different tiles independently postponing synchronization at the cost of additional computation. As shown by Figure 3, computation on-the-fly results in overlapping tiles and is therefore often referred to as overlapped tiling [7, 21, 11].

Halo exchange parallel (hp) satisfies all halo point dependencies using communication with neighboring tiles. More precisely, we update all tiles in parallel and perform at least one halo exchange communication per edge in the longest dependency chain of the stencil dependency graph. Hence, halo exchange parallel avoids redundant computation at the cost of additional synchronizations.

Halo exchange sequential (hs) modifies the tile shape such that all unsatisfied halo point dependencies point in one direction. By iterating over the tiles in reverse dependency direction, we can update all tiles sequentially using a single sweep. While halo exchange sequential in general applies to one-dimensional tilings only, we can complement it with other halo strategies to support higher dimensional tilings. In summary, halo exchange sequential avoids redundant computation and synchronizations at the cost of being sequential.

As the surface to volume ratio decreases with increasing tile size, we preferably update small tiles using halo exchange communication and large tiles using computation on-the-fly. Depending on the hardware architecture high synchronization costs make computation on-the-fly attractive. Overall, choosing the optimal data locality transformations is not straight forward and motivates the use of a performance model.

2.4 Stencil Algebra Definition

Using the data locality transformations introduced in the previous section, we are able to generate a large number of stencil program implementation variants. In particular, we can repeatedly apply our tiling transformations to obtain a hierarchical tiling that leverages multiple levels of the memory hierarchy. By combining our data locality transformations, we are therefore able to cover most of the established stencil implementation techniques. Next, we formally define a stencil algebra whose elements express different stencil program implementation variants and show how to enumerate them. Figure 4 shows an implementation variant of the horizontal diffusion example, introduced in Section 2.2, annotated with two tiling hierarchy levels. Each white node corresponds to a stencil and each black node to a storage region that buffers either an input or a temporary field. We extend the dependency graph with boxes that represent the tiling hierarchy. More precisely, the boxes form a tiling tree where each box corresponds to a tiling that executes all contained boxes respectively stencils. Finally, we annotate each box with the tile size and the halo strategy of the tiling. In Figure 4 we employ an on-the-fly tiling at the bottom of the tiling hierarchy with two nested halo exchange parallel tilings.

In order to specify an element of our stencil algebra, we initially define a tiling hierarchy. More precisely, we define a tile size $t^l \in \mathbb{Z}^n$ for each level l of the tiling hierarchy. In case of the horizontal diffusion example we define two tiling hierarchy levels:

$$t^1_{hd} = (256, 256) \qquad t^2_{hd} = (32, 32)$$

Next, we specify a stencil program implementation variant as a bracket expression. We put all stencils that correspond to a specific tiling hierarchy level into brackets. Therefore, a hierarchical tiling results in a nested bracket expression with the outermost bracket term representing the bottom of the tiling hierarchy. We can define the horizontal diffusion implementation variant shown by Figure 4 using a twofold nested bracket expression.

$$[[s_{lap}, s_{fli}], [s_{flj}, s_{out}]]$$

In the following, we call each bracket term representing a tiling hierarchy a stencil group. A stencil group can be seen as a node of the tiling tree containing nested stencils or stencil groups that as a whole define the stencil program implementation variant.

Let g be a stencil group, then $g.child$ is the set of all children of the stencil group g, where a child is either a stencil or a nested stencil group. In addition, $g.sten$ is the set of all stencils in the subtree defined by the stencil group g. Finally, $g.in$ and $g.out$ define the input and output sets of a stencil group g, where an input and an output correspond to an incoming respectively to an outgoing data dependency. As an example, we provide the stencil properties of the horizontal diffusion example shown in Figure 4.

$$g_0 = [g_1, g_2] \qquad g_1 = [s_{lap}, s_{fli}] \qquad g_2 = [s_{flj}, s_{out}]$$

First, we define the tree properties.

$$g_0.child = \{g_1, g_2\} \qquad g_0.sten = \{s_{lap}, s_{fli}, s_{flj}, s_{out}\}$$

Next, we define the external data dependencies.

$$g_0.in = \{in, wgt\} \qquad g_0.out = \{out\}$$

We enumerate all stencil program implementation variants using two operations: 1) shuffle the stencils respecting their topological order and 2) group stencils on different tiling hierarchy levels.

2.5 Performance Modeling

In order to understand the performance characteristic of a stencil program implementation variant, we next introduce a performance model. Similar to the Roofline model [19], we estimate the execution time based on the peak compute and communication throughput of the target hardware. In addition, we do not only distinguish between cached and global memory accesses but model additional memory hierarchy levels.

To model our target hardware we use an abstract machine that is built around a processing unit that performs computations on a limited set of local registers. All data is by default stored in a global memory (e.g., DRAM) with limited bandwidth to the processing unit. Data is transferred from global memory to local registers before any computation is performed and the results of a computation are transferred back to global memory before becoming externally visible. Between global memory and local registers there is a set of additional hierarchically organized memory levels, each with limited size, but increasing bandwidth to the processing unit.

When mapping a parallel hardware architecture to our model, the bandwidth of a given memory hierarchy level is the combined bandwidth of all (possibly multiple) memories at this level. The size of a memory hierarchy level is not the combined size, but the size of an individual memory at this level. E.g., assuming there are multiple L1 caches, we consider the size of a single L1 cache. Finally, assuming sufficient parallelism to simultaneously use all processing resources, the compute throughput of our model is the combined peak compute throughput of the hardware architecture.

We now consider again Figure 4, an illustration of a stencil program implementation variant with two tiling hierarchy levels that was introduced in the previous section. Each tiling hierarchy targets one specific level of the memory hierarchy, such as the DDR memory or the L1 cache of a CPU. We assume all input and temporary values of a stencil group are stored in the associated memory hierarchy level. Whenever a stencil program communicates data from one tiling hierarchy level to the next higher one, we model the communication time using the bandwidth of the associated memory hierarchy level. Therefore, we define a communication bandwidth $V^l \in \mathbb{R}$ as well as a memory capacity $M^l \in \mathbb{Z}$ for each level l of the tiling hierarchy. In addition to this vertical communication, a stencil code might also perform lateral halo exchange communication between neighboring tiles of the tiling hierarchy. Hence, we define a lateral communication bandwidth $L^l \in \mathbb{R}$ for each level l of the tiling hierarchy. Typical representatives of lateral communication links are interconnect networks or the scratch pad memory of a GPU. Finally, we define the compute throughput $C \in \mathbb{Z}$ of the target architecture. Thereby, we define storage sizes in terms of floating point values instead of bytes. In case two nested tiling hierarchy levels are associated to the same memory hierarchy level,

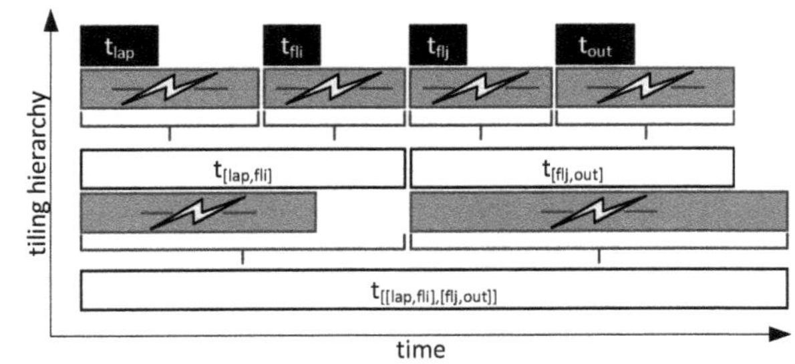

Figure 5: The time estimation for the horizontal diffusion example

we set the vertical communication bandwidth to infinity. Like the Roofline model, we assume that we can overlap communication and computation on all communication links respectively compute units of the system.

When modeling the performance of a stencil program, we assume that the arithmetic intensity remains constant during the execution of a single stencil. On the other hand, the arithmetic intensities of different stencils might vary. Figure 5 illustrates the time estimation for the horizontal diffusion implementation variant shown by Figure 4. At the top of the tiling hierarchy, black boxes denote the stencil execution times. Below, gray boxes (with flashes) denote the communication times between parents and children in the tiling hierarchy. Furthermore, white boxes denote the stencil group execution times computed as the sum of the maximum between stencil execution times and communication times.

In particular, we estimate the execution time t_s of a stencil s that performs c_s floating point operations as the time needed to compute the stencil without considering any communication cost.

$$t_s = c_s / C$$

Using the child execution time t_c of a child stencil or stencil group c that causes v_c vertical and $l_c^1, \ldots, l_c^l$ lateral data movements, we compute the execution time t_g of a stencil group g that corresponds to level l of the tiling hierarchy as the sum of the maximum of the child execution times, the vertical communication between the stencil group and its children, and the lateral communication necessary to update the halo points of the temporary fields. We thereby optimistically assume the lateral communication overlaps with the child execution, which assumes the later communication is sufficiently balanced over the stencil group execution.

$$t_g = \sum_{c \in g.child} \max(t_c, v_c/V^l, l_c^1/L^1, \ldots, l_c^l/L^l)$$

We model the performance of an entire stencil program as the estimated execution time of the stencil group at the bottom of the tiling hierarchy. Furthermore, we complement the performance estimation with a feasibility check that compares the storage requirements of the stencil program to the available memory capacity on all tiling hierarchy levels.

2.6 Stencil Program Analysis

In order to evaluate our performance model, we analyze stencil programs using the mathematical concept of affine sets and affine maps. In particular, we show how to count the number of floating point operations, data movements, and storage locations required during the stencil program execution. Using the performance model introduced in Section 2.5, our analysis finally allows estimating execution time and feasibility of a stencil program.

2.6.1 Affine Sets and Maps

An affine set $S = \{\vec{i} \mid \vec{i} \in \mathbb{Z}^n \wedge \text{cons}(\vec{i})\}$ is a set of n-dimensional integer vectors, where the elements of the set are constrained by a Presburger formula cons$(\vec{i})$. Presburger formulas consist of comparisons ($<, \leq, =, \neq, \geq, >$) between expressions (quasi-)affine in vector dimensions and external parameters that are combined by Boolean operations ($\wedge, \vee, \neg$). For affine sets set operations such as union, intersection, subtraction, projection as well as cardinality are defined.

An affine map $M = \{\vec{i} \to \vec{j} \mid \vec{i} \in \mathbb{Z}^n, \vec{j} \in \mathbb{Z}^m \wedge \text{cons}(\vec{i}, \vec{j})\}$ is a relation, that relates n-dimensional input (domain) vectors with m-dimensional output (range) vectors. The elements are again constraint by a Presburger formula cons$(\vec{i}, \vec{j})$. Besides the normal set operations, there exist map-specific operations such as the application of a map m on a set s ($m(s)$), the composition of two maps ($m_0 \circ m_1$), or the inverse of a map (m^{-1}), which switches input and output of a map. We define the following set of important map operations in more detail.

The range product of two maps R_1 and R_2 is defined as:

$$R_1 \times_{\text{ran}} R_2 = \{\, \vec{i} \to (\vec{j}_1, \vec{j}_2) \mid \vec{i} \to \vec{j}_1 \in R_1 \wedge \vec{i} \to \vec{j}_2 \in R_2\}$$

The range intersection of a map R with a set S is:

$$R \cap_{\text{ran}} S = \{\vec{i} \to \vec{j} \mid \vec{i} \to \vec{j} \in R \wedge \vec{j} \in S\}$$

The range-projection of a map R projects the n output dimensions of a map onto the first $k+1$ output dimensions:

$$\mathcal{P}^{\text{ran}}_{[0-k]}(R) = \{\vec{i} \to (j_0, \ldots, j_k) \mid \exists x_{k+1}, \ldots, x_{n-1} \in \mathbb{Z} : \vec{i} \to (j_0, \ldots, j_k, x_{k+1}, \ldots, x_{n-1}) \in R\}$$

R^+ is the transitive closure of R:

$$R^+ = \{\vec{i} \to \vec{j} \mid \exists m \geq 0 : \vec{j} = (\underbrace{R \circ \cdots \circ R}_{m \text{ times}})(\vec{i})\}$$

We use $|S|$ to specify the cardinality of a set and $|R|$ to specify the cardinality of a map, where the cardinality of a map is defined as the number of related domain and range pairs.

We also define named sets and named maps as affine sets and maps that contain so-called "named vectors". The elements of these sets can either be written as tuples of a string and a vector, for example $\{(\text{“}A\text{”}, \vec{i}), (\text{“}B\text{”}, \vec{j}) \mid \vec{i} \in \mathbb{Z}^n, \vec{j} \in \mathbb{Z}^m\}$, or as named vectors $\{A(\vec{i}), B(\vec{j}) \mid \vec{i} \in \mathbb{Z}^n, \vec{j} \in \mathbb{Z}^m\}$. Named sets (maps) allow differently named elements to have vectors of different dimensionality. On named sets and maps the operations introduced above are applied individually to subsets or submaps that share the same name and dimensionality. To extract a set from a named set S, we define a bracket operator $S[\text{“}x\text{”}] = \{(\text{“}x\text{”}, \vec{i}) \mid (\text{“}x\text{”}, \vec{i}) \in S\}$. The bracket operator applied on a map, filters the maps according to the name of their domains $R[\text{“}x\text{”}] = \{(\text{“}x\text{”}, \vec{i}) \to (name, \vec{j}) \mid (\text{“}x\text{”}, \vec{i}) \to (name, \vec{j}) \in R\}$.

Computations on integer sets can be performed with isl [16] and counting of integer sets is possible with barvinok [17].

2.6.2 Data Dependencies

Given a stencil program P the set of flow dependencies in P can be derived from the stencil data dependencies. To obtain them, we define for each stencil $s \in P$ a map D_s that associates the stencil evaluations to the corresponding input data dependencies.

$$D_s = \{s.out(\vec{u}) \to d(\vec{u} + \vec{v}) \mid d(\vec{v}) \in s.in\}$$

Next, we define the union of all stencil data dependencies.

$$D = \bigcup_{s \in P} D_s$$

2.6.3 Stencil Tiling Maps

We model the tiling transformations discussed in Section 2.3 using affine maps that relate the stencil evaluation domain to the tile domain. More precisely, we define for each stencil a tiling map that maps each point in the n-dimensional stencil evaluation domain to an n-dimensional tile identifier, such that all points that belong to the same tile are associated with a common tile identifier. We initially consider only a single tiling level and later generalize the concept to nested tilings.

Given a multi-dimensional tile size vector $\vec{t} = (t_0, \ldots, t_{n-1}) \in \mathbb{Z}^n$, we define a hyperrectangular tiling of a single stencil s as a named map $T_s^{\square}$ that associates each point $\vec{i} = (i_0, \ldots, i_{n-1}) \in \mathbb{Z}^n$ of the stencil evaluation domain with exactly one tile identifier.

$$T_s^{\square} = \{(s, \vec{i}) \to (\lfloor i_0/t_0 \rfloor, \ldots, \lfloor i_{n-1}/t_{n-1} \rfloor)\}$$

Depending on size and alignment of tiles and stencil evaluation domains, such a tiling may yield truncated tiles at the stencil evaluation domain boundaries. In case a given dimension of the stencil evaluation domain should not be tiled (indicated by tile size ∞), the corresponding dimension of the tile identifiers is set to zero.

We represent the tiling of a stencil group g by computing a named map that contains a tiling map for each stencil of the stencil group. We distinguish here between the three halo strategies introduced in Section 2.3.

Computation on-the-fly satisfies halo point dependencies using redundant computation. The corresponding tiling map is therefore a relation which maps the halo point stencil evaluations at the tile boundaries to multiple overlapping tiles. Given a stencil group g, we construct a tile map T_g in two steps. First, all output stencils of g are tiled with a rectangular tiling map. This does not yet introduce any redundant computation. Next, we compute for each tile all stencil evaluations that are required to compute the output points already assign to this tile. We do this by first defining the set of data dependencies D_g that are local to g and then composing the inverse transitive hull of D_g with the tiling map already defined for the output stencils. The resulting map connects the temporary stencil evaluations via the dependent output stencil evaluation to the corresponding tile identifier. This map may now possibly relate one temporary stencil evaluation to multiple tiles and can consequently introduce redundant computation.

$$T_g = \bigcup_{s \in g.out} T_s^{\square} \circ (D_g^{+})^{-1}$$

Halo exchange parallel satisfies halo point dependencies using communication. We therefore assign each point in the stencil evaluation domain to exactly one tile and use tiles of identical size, shape and alignment for all stencils in our stencil group. The tiling map T_g describes such a tiling for a stencil group g.

$$T_g = \bigcup_{s \in g.sten} T_s^{\square}$$

Halo exchange sequential is a variant of halo exchange parallel, whose tiling map is constructed accordingly. In contrast to halo exchange parallel, we shift the stencil tiling maps such that all unsatisfied halo point dependencies between tiles point in one direction. Figure 3 illustrates the tile shape of shifted stencil tiling maps and their halo point dependencies. We define a shifted tiling map by subtracting the shift offset form the stencil evaluation domain before computing the associated tile identifiers.

Nested Tilings.

We now describe the construction of nested tilings, tilings that result from recursively applying the previously introduced tiling

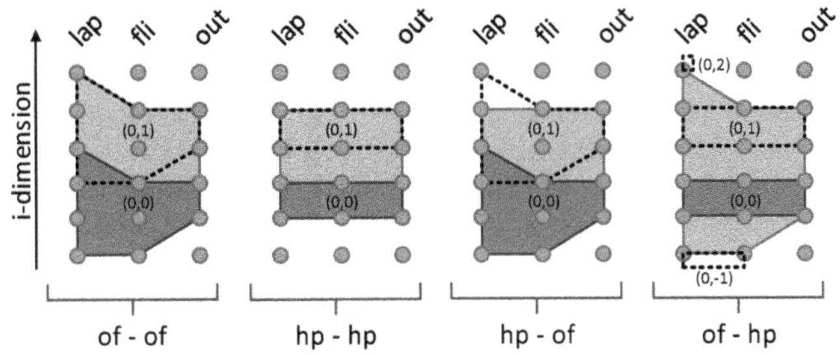

Figure 6: Tile shapes (shaded) for a nested tiling applied to a subset of the horizontal diffusion example projected to the i-dimension

transformations. To give a first intuition of such tilings, Figure 6 shows the different nested tilings that can be constructed from combining on-the-fly and halo exchange parallel tiling on two tiling levels. It shows for each combination one full outer tile, one full inner tile, and, using dashed lines, the remaining inner tiles placed inside the outer tile. Most combinations are rather straightforward, but it is interesting to note, that in case of on-the-fly tiling being nested inside halo exchange parallel tiling, the redundant computation of the on-the-fly tiles may require the computation of points located outside of the surrounding tile.

As visible in the illustration just discussed, we identify each nested tile with a tile vector whose first and second entry correspond to the tile identifiers of the first and second tiling level respectively. Hence, we can model a nested tiling with l tiling hierarchy levels with a tiling map that relates each point in the n-dimensional stencil evaluation domain to a tile identifier with $n \cdot l$ dimensions. To construct such a map for a given stencil group g nested in another stencil group p we first define tiling maps for the output stencils of g. These tiling maps are formed by combining for each stencil the tiling map $T_p[s]$ that we derive for this stencil from p (not considering any nested groups) with an additional hyperrectangular tiling that uses the tile sizes specified for g. We define the tiling map $T_{g,s}$ of such a stencil s as the range product of the tiling map $T_s^{\square}$ with the recursively computed parent tiling map $T_p[s]$.

$$T_{g,s} = T_p[s] \times_{\text{ran}} T_s^{\square}$$

When computing the tiling map of a nested stencil group T_g, we adapt the previously introduced on-the-fly and halo exchange tiling maps to use $T_{g,s}$ instead of $T_s^{\square}$. The resulting tiling maps for halo exchange parallel and on-the-fly tiling are

$$T_g = \bigcup_{s \in g.sten} T_{g,s} \quad \text{and} \quad T_g = \bigcup_{s \in g.out} T_{g,s} \circ (D_g^{+})^{-1}.$$

We can now define for each stencil a tiling map T_s that maps each evaluation of this stencil to a tile identifier with $l \cdot n$ dimensions, that identifies for all levels of the tiling hierarchy the tiles the stencil evaluation is assigned to. We obtain T_s by extracting the tile map that corresponds to s from the tile map of the stencil group g at the top of the tiling hierarchy that contains s.

$$T_s = T_g[s]$$

When constructing hierarchical tilings that involve halo exchange sequential, we inherit the shift offsets introduced by the sequential execution to all nested tiling hierarchy levels. Thereby, we align the nested tiles to the parent tile boundaries.

2.6.4 I/O Maps

While the tiling maps alone allow the analysis of computational aspects, we introduce auxiliary maps that support the analysis of data movements and storage usage.

First, we define for each stencil s an input map I_s that relates a set of inputs (stencil evaluations or input fields) used by a certain evaluation of s to the tile(s) this evaluation is assigned to. The construction of I_s is similar to the construction of the on-the-fly tiling. We compose the stencil tiling map T_s with the reversed stencil data dependencies D_s^{-1}. Furthermore, we define the input map of an entire stencil group g as the union of all nested stencil input maps.

$$I_s = T_s \circ D_s^{-1} \qquad I_g = \bigcup_{s \in g.sten} I_s$$

Second, we define for each child stencil or stencil group c an output map O_c that relates the set of outputs written by the child to the tiles they are assigned to. In case the parent stencil group applies halo exchange communication, we define the output map O_c as the union of the child output stencil tiling maps.

$$O_c = \bigcup_{s \in c.out} T_s$$

In case the parent stencil group applies computation on-the-fly, we compute the output map by following the data dependencies starting from the parent stencil group output stencils. While this construction is similar to the computation of the on-the-fly stencil evaluation tiling map, it differs by the fact that we only consider the data dependencies of the stencils executed after the child stencil or stencil group. Thereby, we make sure we do not consider internal dependencies between the output stencils of the child stencil group. Initially, we define the partial input map $I_{p,c}$ of a parent stencil group p and a child stencil or stencil group c considering all input dependencies of children executed after the child c.

$$I_{p,c} = \bigcup_{\substack{c_i \in p.child \\ c < c_i}} I_{c_i}$$

Then the output map O_c of a child stencil or stencil group is the union of all partial input and parent output dependencies.

$$O_c = \bigcup_{s \in c.out} \left(I_{p,c}[s] \cup \left(\bigcup_{o \in p.out} T_{p,o}\right)[s]\right)$$

2.6.5 Tile Selection

We analyze the characteristics of a stencil program by counting stencil evaluations, data movements, or storage requirements on a limited domain. As we are interested in the relative rather than the absolute performance and as our performance model does not consider low hardware utilization due to strong scaling, we can choose an arbitrary but limited domain size. We therefore perform our analysis on the origin tile of the lowest tiling hierarchy level. Assuming m tiling hierarchy levels, we select the origin tile of the lowest tiling hierarchy level using the tile selection set S that contains all tile identifiers with the first n-dimensions fixed to zero.

$$S = \{(x_0, \ldots, x_{n-1}, y_n, \ldots, y_{nm}) \mid x_i = 0 \wedge y_j \in \mathbb{Z}\}$$

When analyzing the storage requirements, we want to make sure a single tile fits the memory capacity of the corresponding memory hierarchy level. We therefore define an additional tile selection set S^* that selects the origin tile on all levels of the tiling hierarchy.

$$S^* = \{(x_0, \ldots, x_{nm}) \mid x_i = 0\}$$

In order to limit the domain of a tiling map, we finally intersect the range of the tiling map with a selection set.

2.6.6 *Analysis*

Relying on the previously introduced stencil program formulation, we now discuss the analyses we use to obtain the program properties needed for evaluating the performance model introduced in Section 2.5. Using the previously introduced maps, we count the points that correspond to the number of stencils evaluations, the amount of data moved, and the amount of storage used when evaluating a given stencil program on a limited domain.

Computation.

In order to analyze the amount of computation performed by a stencil program, we count the stencil evaluations associated to the origin tile of the lowest tiling hierarchy level. We obtain these evaluations by intersecting the range of the stencil evaluation tiling map with the origin tile selection set S. We then count all stencil evaluations associated to the remaining tile identifiers. Hence, we define the amount of computation c_s performed by a stencil s as the cardinality of the constraint tiling map times the number of floating point operations performed by a single stencil evaluation.

$$c_s = |T_s \cap_{\text{ran}} S| \cdot s.ops$$

Vertical Communication.

As discussed in Section 2.5, vertical communication refers to the data movements between a parent stencil group and its child stencils or stencil groups. We therefore analyze the number of loads and stores performed by a child stencil or stencil group when executed by a parent stencil group. We analyze the vertical communication on a restricted domain that corresponds to the origin tile of the lowest tiling hierarchy level.

In order to compute the number of loads performed by a stencil or stencil group c, we count the elements in the constraint input map of c. More precisely, we intersect the range with the origin tile selection set and project out any dimension above the parent stencil group tiling hierarchy level l. Due to the projection, the points in the resulting map describe all elements loaded by the child stencil or stencil group not considering redundant stencil evaluations on nested tiling hierarchy levels. Hence, we define the number of loads l_c performed by a child stencil or stencil group c as the cardinality of the constraint and projected child input map.

$$l_c = \sum_{s \in c.in} |\mathcal{P}^{\text{ran}}_{[0-nl]}(I_c[s] \cap_{\text{ran}} S)|$$

Accordingly, we define the number of stores s_c performed by a child stencil or stencil group c as the cardinality of the constraint and projected child output map.

$$s_c = \sum_{s \in c.out} |\mathcal{P}^{\text{ran}}_{[0-nl]}(O_c[s] \cap_{\text{ran}} S)|$$

Finally, we define the total amount of vertical communication of a child stencil or stencil group c as the sum of its loads and stores.

$$v_c = l_c + s_c$$

Lateral Communication.

Lateral communication refers to the halo exchange communication between neighboring tiles of the same tiling hierarchy level. We therefore compute the lateral communication performed by a stencil group as the difference between the amount of computed and the amount of consumed temporary values, which corresponds to the unsatisfied halo point dependencies between the children of the stencil group. We analyze the lateral communication on a restricted domain that corresponds to the origin tile of the lowest tiling hierarchy level.

We compute the amount of lateral communication necessary to update the outputs of a child stencil or stencil group, as the difference of the elements used by subsequent children and the elements written by the child itself. Therefore, we intersect the range of the partial input map and output maps with the origin tile selection set and project out any dimensions above the parent stencil group tiling hierarchy level l. Hence, we define the amount of halo points l_c communicated by a child stencil or stencil group c as the cardinality of the difference between the projected and constraint partial input and output maps.

$$l_c = \sum_{s \in c.out} |\mathcal{P}^{\text{ran}}_{[0-nl]}((I_{p,c}[s] \setminus O_c[s]) \cap_{\text{ran}} S)|$$

In case multiple nested tiling hierarchy levels employ halo exchange communication, we possibly run lateral communication on all these levels. By projecting out one level after the other, we assign the lateral communication to the different levels of the tiling hierarchy. Thereby, we get the sum of the lateral communication on the remaining tiling hierarchy levels not yet projected out. By computing the difference of adjacent levels, we finally get the lateral communication assigned to exactly one level.

Storage Requirements.

We analyze the feasibility of a stencil program by computing an upper bound for the storage necessary in order to execute a single tile on each level of the tiling hierarchy. We therefore analyze the storage requirements on a restricted domain that corresponds to the origin tile on all levels of the tiling hierarchy. In case the upper bound exceeds the capacity of one memory hierarchy level, we say a stencil program is infeasible.

We compute the storage requirement of a stencil group as the amount of storage necessary to evaluate the stencil group on a single tile. As shown by Figure 4, we reserve storage for each input and temporary field used during the evaluation of the stencil group. In contrast, output fields are immediately written to storage managed outside of the stencil group. Thereby, we overestimate the storage requirement as the limited life time of some fields might allow sharing a common buffer. We evaluate the storage requirements using the input map intersected with the tile selection set S^*. Furthermore, we project out any dimension above the parent stencil group tiling hierarchy level l. Hence, we define the amount of storage m_p required by a parent stencil group p as the cardinality of the constraint and projected input maps.

$$m_p = \sum_{c \in p.child} \sum_{s \in c.in} |\mathcal{P}^{\text{ran}}_{[0-nl]}(I_p[s] \cap_{\text{ran}} S^*)|$$

In order to determine the feasibility of a stencil program, we compare the memory requirements of each stencil group to the available memory capacity.

3. CASE STUDY

We evaluate our approach using the real-world application COSMO. Its dynamical core was recently rewritten using the STELLA [6] stencil library, which exposes the possibility to manually fuse or split stencils on multiple tiling hierarchy levels. In this case study we show how to automatically tune STELLA programs.

3.1 STELLA

STELLA is a domain specific embedded language for finite difference methods that is designed to separate the stencil specifica-

Hierarchy	Vertical	Tile Size	Strategy
1	DDR	$(256, 256, 64)$	of
2	L2	$(8, 8, 64)$	of

Table 1: CPU tiling hierarchy

Hierarchy	Vertical/Lateral	Tile Size	Strategy
1	GDDR/-	$(256, 256, 64)$	of
2	GDDR/-	$(64, 4, 64)$	of
3	Register/Register	$(\infty, \infty, 1)$	hs
4	Register/Shared	$(1, 1, 1)$	hp

Table 2: GPU tiling hierarchy

tion from the hardware architecture specific implementation strategy. When executing a stencil program STELLA uses two levels of parallelism: 1) coarse grained parallelization that decomposes the stencil evaluation domain into blocks executed on different processing units and 2) fine grained parallelization that executes the individual blocks on a single processing unit possibly using vectorization and hardware threads. STELLA supports stencil fusion on three different tiling hierarchy levels. We can apply consecutive stencils using a single loop over a block, using multiple separate loops over a block, or using multiple separate loops over the full domain.

At compile-time, STELLA generates target architecture specific loop code using C++ template meta-programming. With two available backends, STELLA can currently target CPU and GPU architectures using the OpenMP and CUDA programming models respectively. Thereby, STELLA employs a fixed but platform specific tiling hierarchy, which we will model using our stencil algebra.

We model the CPU backend of STELLA using the two tiling hierarchy levels shown by Table 1. As discussed in Section 2.6, we compute all stencil program performance characteristics for the origin tile of the base tiling hierarchy level. Therefore, we introduce a first tiling hierarchy level that represents the stencil program evaluation domain. A second tiling hierarchy level models the coarse grained parallelism of STELLA. Currently, the CPU backend does not implement fine grained parallelism. Hence, there is no need to model the third tiling hierarchy level of STELLA.

We model the GPU backend of STELLA using the four tiling hierarchy levels shown by Table 2. Just as in case of the CPU backend, we introduce two tiling hierarchy levels to model the stencil program evaluation domain and the coarse grained parallelism. Furthermore, we introduce two additional tiling hierarchy levels that represent the fine grained parallelism. The GPU backend allocates one thread per ij-position (tiling hierarchy level 4) that iterates over all points in the k-dimension (tiling hierarchy level 3). Thereby, different threads communicate via shared memory, while different loop iterations communicate via registers. Moreover, tile size infinity denotes no tiling in the corresponding dimension.

3.2 Stencil Program Optimization

When implementing a stencil program using STELLA, we have multiple degrees of freedom. As discussed in Section 2.4, we can change the stencil evaluation order and fuse or split the execution of successive stencils on multiple levels of the tiling hierarchy. We therefore split the optimization in two steps and apply different optimization methods: 1) we optimize the stencil evaluation order using brute force search 2) we optimize the tiling for a given stencil evaluation order using dynamic programming. During our optimization we do not consider tile size choices, but rely on the tile sizes that are used by COSMO and have proven robust for a wide range of stencil programs and their implementation variants.

In order to optimize the stencil evaluation order, we enumerate all topological sorts of the stencil dependency graph using brute force search. In general, a graph may have up to $\mathcal{O}(n!)$ valid topological orders. However, due to its data dependency chains a typical stencil dependency graph has less topological orders resulting in a much smaller search space.

In a second step, we search the optimal tiling given a stencil evaluation order. Using a tiling hierarchy and an abstract machine model, we search for a tiling with minimal estimated execution time and a storage requirement that fits all levels of the memory hierarchy. We estimate execution time and storage requirements using the analysis introduced in Section 2.6. In order to enumerate the search space, we fuse all pairs of subsequent stencils on all levels of the tiling hierarchy. Thereby, we assume the subsequent stencils are executed by nested stencil groups that represent the full tiling hierarchy. Given m tiling hierarchy levels and n stencils, up to m tiling hierarchies can be split between each pair of neighboring stencils. Overall, this means there are $\mathcal{O}(m^n)$ ways to split the stencil program. Assuming we have a set of all stencil program implementation variants I and the functions $t(x)$ and $m^l(x)$ that estimate the execution time and the maximal storage requirement at the level l of the tiling hierarchy respectively, we define the following optimization problem:

$$\begin{aligned} &\underset{x \in I}{\text{minimize}} && t(x) \\ &\text{subject to} && m^l(x) \leq M^l \qquad l = 1, \dots, m \end{aligned}$$

We can either solve the optimization problem using brute force search or employ our dynamic programming approach reducing the search space from $\mathcal{O}(m^n)$ to $\mathcal{O}(mn^4)$ elements. We can apply dynamic programming as the problem has optimal substructure. In particular, we compute for each tiling hierarchy level an n^2 matrix that contains the optimal stencil group executing a continuous subset of the stencil program. Thereby, one matrix dimension corresponds to the start index and the other matrix dimension to the stop index of the subset. We compute a matrix entry using a second dynamic programming algorithm that constructs the optimal stencil group using a combination of the previously computed optimal child stencil groups. More precisely, we compute the optimum for a given start and stop index either using the optimal child stencil group containing all stencils or using a child stencil group containing all stencils from an intermediate index to the stop index plus the recursively computed optimum from the start index to the intermediate index. By increasing the intermediate index step-by-step and storing partial solutions, we compute a single entry of our n^2 matrix using $\mathcal{O}(n^2)$ steps.

4. EVALUATION

We evaluated our framework using three example kernels from the COSMO atmospheric model. In addition to the horizontal diffusion kernel "hd" introduced in Section 2.2, we use two kernels that are part of the most time-consuming component in COSMO, the sound wave forward integration. More precisely, the "uv" kernel updates the horizontal wind velocity components by computing the horizontal pressure gradient, whereas the "div" kernel computes the divergence of the three-dimensional wind field. Figure 7 illustrates all kernels used during the evaluation including a combination of the "uv" and "div" kernels.

We perform our experiments using adapted standalone kernels: 1) we replace divisions by multiplications to increase the numerical stability on random input data and 2) we replace one-dimensional

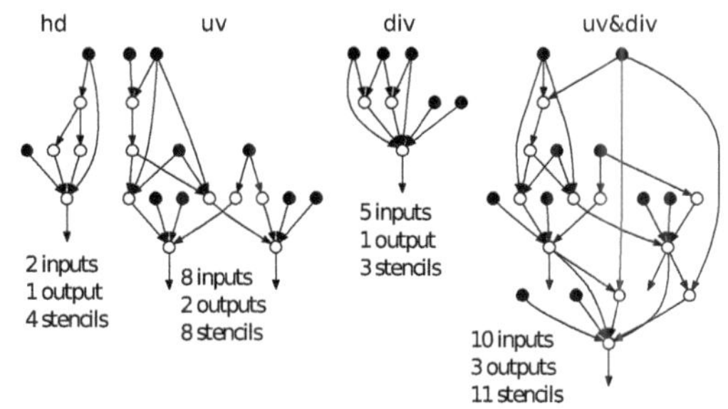

Figure 7: Example kernel stencil dependency graphs

Hierarchy	Vertical (V)	Memory (M)
1	26 GB/s	∞
2	768 GB/s	512 KB

Table 3: Intel Core i5-3330

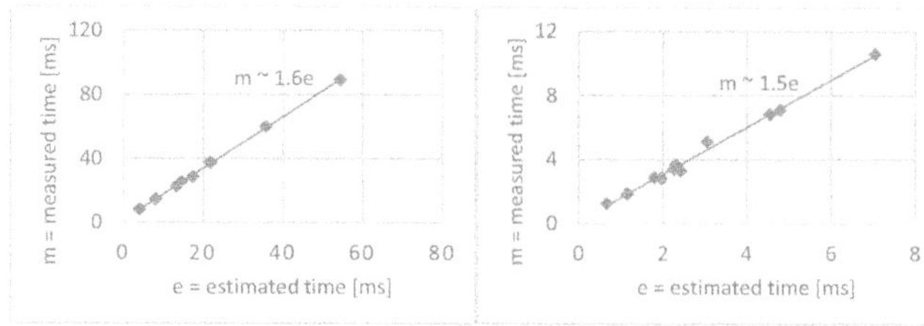

(a) Accuracy CPU (b) Accuracy GPU

Figure 8: Comparison of measured and estimated execution time

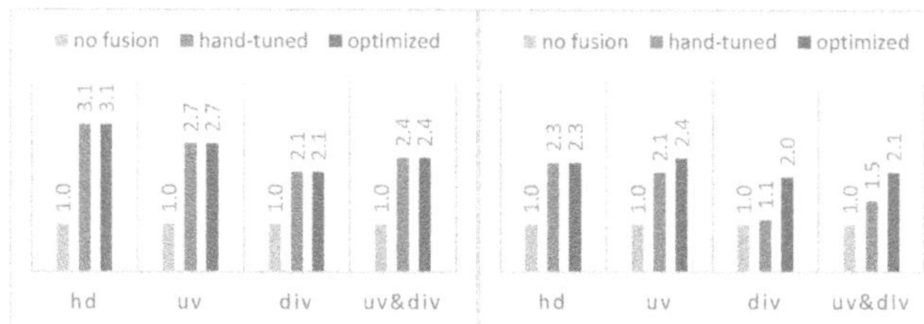

(a) Speedup CPU (b) Speedup GPU

Figure 9: Speedup of hand-tuned and optimized kernels

constant fields by scalar constants as our framework does only support n-dimensional fields. We implement for each kernel three different variants: 1) "no fusion" refers to a naive implementation without loop fusion, 2) "hand-tuned" refers to a manually tuned implementation as used in production by COSMO, and 3) "optimized" refers to an automatically tuned version using MODESTO. All kernel variants are written using STELLA and therefore are parallel and employ tiling. Similar to the production configuration, we run our experiments using a $(256, 256, 64)$ point domain that provides sufficient parallelism to fully utilize the hardware.

We measure the performance of our example kernels using two target architectures: 1) an Intel Core i5-3330 CPU with a dual channel DDR3-1600 memory interface and 2) a Nvidia Tesla K20c GPU. Table 3 and Table 4 define the machine model of the target architectures for the STELLA tiling hierarchy discussed in Section 3.1. Thereby, we use the peak bandwidth of the individual memory hierarchy levels, except for the register file and shared memory where we assume infinite bandwidth and one half of the peak bandwidth respectively. More precisely, we divide the peak bandwidth of memories used for lateral communication by two as each communication corresponds to a write and a read access. Furthermore, we underestimate the capacity of the GPU register file as it is used for additional tasks such as index computations. Finally, we set the peak performance C of the target architectures to 48 Gflops and 585 Gflops respectively (without fused multiply add).

To evaluate the accuracy of our performance model, we compare the measured execution time of our example kernels to the modeled execution time. Figure 8 shows the accuracy of the model for both target architectures. Using linear regression, we fit trend lines that show a close correlation of modeled and measured performance. Hence, the relative performance of modeled and measured execution times for different kernels are in accordance, which is of key importance for our approach. However, we consistently overestimate the absolute performance as the kernels can not leverage the peak performance of both target architectures. Our performance model shows that our kernels, like most stencil computations, are heavily memory bandwidth limited. Consequently, the correlation factors of 1.5x respectively 1.6x can be attributed to the fact that the kernels attain only a fraction of the peak main memory bandwidth.

Hierarchy	Vertical (V)	Lateral (L)	Memory (M)
1	208 GB/s	-	∞
2	208 GB/s	-	∞
3	∞	1174 GB/s	4096 Registers
4	∞	∞	32 Registers

Table 4: Nvidia Tesla K20c

Figure 9 shows the speedup of hand-tuned and automatically tuned implementation variants for both target architectures. As discussed in Section 3.2, MODESTO optimizes topological order and stencil fusion. Overall, MODESTO achieves the same or better performance compared to the hand-tuned kernels used by COSMO. Starting from a naive STELLA implementation, we are able to improve the performance by a factor 2.0x–3.1x. The first three experiments achieve optimal performance by fusing all stencils on the highest level of the tiling hierarchy. In contrast, for the last experiment fusing all stencils exceeds the memory capacity. Hence, the optimization splits the stencils in two separate groups. To verify this decision, we implemented an additional variant of the last experiment that fuses all stencils. On CPU and GPU fusing all stencils results in a 10% and 8% performance reduction respectively.

5. RELATED WORK

Optimal and close-to-optimal stencil arrangements have been investigated for several decades. Many approaches rely on empirical methods to derive efficient implementations. Datta et al. [3] optimize an example stencil for a wide range of hardware architectures using autotuning. Patus [2] is a DSL autotuning framework for single stencil computations on multi-core CPUs and single GPUs. Zhang et al. [20] present an iterative compilation approach for single stencil computations on single and multi GPU systems which focuses on deriving optimal block sizes.

Overtile [7] is a DSL code generator for iterative stencils that uses overlap tiling to generate efficient GPU code also relying on iterative compilation. There is also a cache-oblivious tiling strategy for iterative stencil computations [5] for which the number of expected cache misses has been analytically computed and empirically evaluated for single CPU systems and one caching level.

For stencil graphs, there is Halide [11], a DSL based approach focused on image processing. Halide uses again compilation based autotuning to choose stencil program implementation variants considering a set of tiling strategies and further optimizations. PolyMage [9] is an image processing DSL that guides the optimization using a model-driven heuristic. Basu et. al [1] perform loop fusion, overlapped tiling and wave front execution for optimizing a geometric multigrid stencil graph. They do not consider hierarchical tiling and do not use any analytical model. Olschanowsky et al. [10] optimize an iterative, but multi-kernel stencil computation resulting from solving partial differential equations and study different inter-loop optimizations using empirically evaluation on multi-core CPUs.

There has also been work that discusses analytical performance models. There is work not limited to stencil computations that provides lower bounds for tile sizes selection [13]. Renganarayana et al. [12] use geometric optimization to model tiling and related problems on one and multiple levels and to derive optimal tile sizes. Zhou et al. [21] present work on hierarchical overlapped tiling and optimize OpenCL programs for multi-core CPUs. They provide basic performance models for the number of stencils to fuse into one tile focusing on (possibly unrolled) kernels that process only one stencil repeatedly and do not consider varying tiling and fusion strategies. Finally, Wahib et al. [18] take arbitrary stencil graphs from larger scientific applications and present an analytical performance model for choosing an optimal execution strategy. Even though closely related, they limit themselves to kernel fusion using computation on-the-fly only considering shared memory and apply their work on NVIDIA GPUs only.

6. CONCLUSION

With MODESTO we have presented an approach for modeling and automatically selecting efficient implementation strategies for stencil programs. Focusing not only on single, possibly iterative applications of stencils, but on directed acyclic graphs of stencils we consider the effects of three different tiling strategies in combination with different fusion choices, all applied on possibly multiple hierarchy levels. We model the effects of these implementation strategies on the use of both lateral and vertical memory bandwidth, and estimate the cost of possibly redundant computation by using a analytical model that allows to predict the amount of data transfer and computation for a given stencil program implementation variant. In combination with a given CPU or GPU model we estimate the relative performance of the different implementation variants and show using a combination of exhaustive search and dynamic programming how to choose the best implementation variant.

We evaluated MODESTO by means of the STELLA stencil library that implements different stencil program transformations for CPU and GPU architectures. In particular, we successfully model the tiling hierarchy of STELLA and automatically tune kernels of the COSMO atmospheric model. Thereby, we achieve speedups of 2.0–3.1x against naive and speedups of 1.0–1.8x against expert-tuned implementation variants.

Acknowledgments

This publication has been funded by Swissuniversities through the Platform for Advanced Computing Initiative (PASC). We thank Oliver Fuhrer (MeteoSwiss) and Carlos Osuna Escamilla (ETH) for helpful discussions, Armin Größlinger (University of Passau) for providing isl bindings for Java, as well as the Swiss National Supercomputing Center (CSCS) for their continuous support.

7. REFERENCES

[1] P. Basu, A. Venkat, M. Hall, S. Williams, B. Van Straalen, and L. Oliker. Compiler generation and autotuning of communication-avoiding operators for geometric multigrid. In *High Performance Computing (HiPC), Int. Conf. on*, pages 452–461. IEEE, 2013.

[2] M. Christen, O. Schenk, and H. Burkhart. Patus: A code generation and autotuning framework for parallel iterative stencil computations on modern microarchitectures. In *Parallel Distributed Processing Symposium (IPDPS), 2011 IEEE Int.*, pages 676–687, May 2011.

[3] K. Datta, M. Murphy, V. Volkov, S. Williams, J. Carter, L. Oliker, D. Patterson, J. Shalf, and K. Yelick. Stencil computation optimization and auto-tuning on state-of-the-art multicore architectures. In *Proc. of the 2008 ACM/IEEE Conf. on Supercomputing*, SC '08, pages 4:1–4:12. IEEE Press, 2008.

[4] G. Doms and U. Schättler. The nonhydrostatic limited-area model LM (lokal-model) of the DWD. Part I: Scientific documentation. Technical report, German Weather Service (DWD), Germany, 1999.

[5] M. Frigo and V. Strumpen. The memory behavior of cache oblivious stencil computations. *The J. of Supercomputing*, 39(2):93–112, 2007.

[6] O. Fuhrer, C. Osuna, X. Lapillonne, T. Gysi, B. Cumming, M. Bianco, A. Arteaga, and T. Schulthess. Towards a performance portable, architecture agnostic implementation strategy for weather and climate models. *Supercomputing frontiers and innovations*, 2014.

[7] J. Holewinski, L.-N. Pouchet, and P. Sadayappan. High-performance code generation for stencil computations on GPU architectures. In *Int. Conf. on Supercomputing, Proc. of*, pages 311–320. ACM, 2012.

[8] G. A. McMECHAN. Migration by extrapolation of time-dependent boundary values*. *Geophysical Prospecting*, 31(3):413–420, 1983.

[9] R. T. Mullapudi, V. Vasista, and U. Bondhugula. Polymage: Automatic optimization for image processing pipelines. In *Proc. of the Twentieth Int. Conf. on Architectural Support for Programming Languages and Operating Systems*, ASPLOS '15, pages 429–443, New York, NY, USA, 2015. ACM.

[10] C. Olschanowsky, M. M. Strout, S. Guzik, J. Loffeld, and J. Hittinger. A study on balancing parallelism, data locality, and recomputation in existing PDE solvers. In *Proc. of the Int. Conf. for High Performance Computing, Networking, Storage and Analysis*, SC '14, pages 793–804, NJ, USA, 2014. IEEE Press.

[11] J. Ragan-Kelley, C. Barnes, A. Adams, S. Paris, F. Durand, and S. Amarasinghe. Halide: A language and compiler for optimizing parallelism, locality, and recomputation in image processing pipelines. In *Proc. of the ACM Conf. on Programming Language Design and Implementation*, PLDI '13, pages 519–530. ACM, 2013.

[12] L. Renganarayana and S. Rajopadhye. Positivity, posynomials and tile size selection. In *ACM/IEEE Conf. on Supercomputing, Proc. of*, SC '08, pages 55:1–55:12, NJ, USA, 2008. IEEE Press.

[13] J. Shirako, K. Sharma, N. Fauzia, L.-N. Pouchet, J. Ramanujam, P. Sadayappan, and V. Sarkar. Analytical bounds for optimal tile size selection. In *Compiler Construction*, pages 101–121. Springer, 2012.

[14] A. Taflove. Review of the formulation and applications of the finite-difference time-domain method for numerical modeling of electromagnetic wave interactions with arbitrary structures. *Wave Motion*, 10(6):547 – 582, 1988. Special Issue on Numerical Methods for Electromagnetic Wave Interactions.

[15] Y. Tang, R. A. Chowdhury, B. C. Kuszmaul, C.-K. Luk, and C. E. Leiserson. The Pochoir stencil compiler. In *Proc. of the Twenty-third Annual ACM Symp. on Parallelism in Algorithms and Architectures*, SPAA '11, pages 117–128, New York, NY, USA, 2011. ACM.

[16] S. Verdoolaege. isl: An integer set library for the polyhedral model. In *Mathematical Software–ICMS'10*, pages 299–302. Springer, 2010.

[17] S. Verdoolaege, R. Seghir, K. Beyls, V. Loechner, and M. Bruynooghe. Counting integer points in parametric polytopes using barvinok's rational functions. *Algorithmica*, 48(1):37–66, 2007.

[18] M. Wahib and N. Maruyama. Scalable kernel fusion for memory-bound GPU applications. In *Proc. of the Int. Conf. for High Performance Computing, Networking, Storage and Analysis*, SC '14, pages 191–202, Piscataway, NJ, USA, 2014. IEEE Press.

[19] S. Williams, A. Waterman, and D. Patterson. Roofline: An insightful visual performance model for multicore architectures. *Commun. ACM*, 52(4):65–76, Apr. 2009.

[20] Y. Zhang and F. Mueller. Autogeneration and autotuning of 3d stencil codes on homogeneous and heterogeneous gpu clusters. *Parallel and Distributed Systems, IEEE Transactions on*, 24(3):417–427, 2013.

[21] X. Zhou, J.-P. Giacalone, M. J. Garzarán, R. H. Kuhn, Y. Ni, and D. Padua. Hierarchical overlapped tiling. In *Proc. of the Inter. Symp. on Code Generation and Optimization*, CGO '12, pages 207–218, New York, NY, USA, 2012. ACM.

FAST: A Fast Stencil Autotuning Framework Based on an Optimal-solution Space Model

Yulong Luo†, Guangming Tan†, Zeyao Mo‡, Ninghui Sun†
†State Key Laboratory of Computer Architecture, Institute of Computing Technology
‡Institute of Applied Physics and Computational Mathematics
Beijing, China
{luoyulong,tgm,snh}@ncic.ac.cn, zeyao_ mo@iapcm.ac.cn

ABSTRACT

Stencil computations comprise an important class of kernels in many scientific computing applications. As the diversity of both architectures and programming models grow, autotuning is emerging as a critical strategy for achieving portable performance across a broad range of execution contexts for stencil computations. However, costly tuning overhead is a major obstacle to its popularity. In this work, we propose a fast stencil autotuning framework FAST based on an Optimal-Solution Space (OSS) model to significantly improve tuning speed. It leverages a feature extractor that comprehensively characterizes stencil computation. Using the extracted features, FAST constructs an OSS database to train an off-line model which provides an on-line prediction. We evaluate FAST with five important stencil computation applications on both an Intel Xeon multicore CPU and an NVIDIA Tesla K20c GPU. Compared with state-of-the-art stencil autotuners like Patus and SDSL, FAST improves autotuning speed by 10 – 2697 times without any user annotation, while achieving comparable performance.

Categories and Subject Descriptors

D.1.3 [**Programming techniques**]: Concurrent programming—*Parallel Programming*; D.3.4 [**Programming Languages**]: Processors—*Code Generation, Compilers*

General Terms

Algorithms, Performance, Languages

Keywords

Stencil; Autotuning; OSS

1. INTRODUCTION

Stencil computations are of critical importance for scientific computing, engineering, image processing, particle simulation, and geometric modeling. For example, grand challenge applications including climate, weather, and ocean modeling use explicit time-integration methods of partial differential equations that require Exascale stencil computations. Other important examples include computational electromagnetics and quantum dynamics codes using the finite-difference time-domain (FDTD) method, medical and image-processing applications that perform smoothing and other neighbor pixel-based computations, and certain cellular automata and seismic simulations. Due to the importance of stencil computations, it has resulted in extensive programming model research efforts, as well as architectural support.

ICS'15, June 8–11, 2015, Newport Beach, CA, USA.
Copyright © 2015 ACM 978-1-4503-3559-1/15/06 ...$15.00.
http://dx.doi.org/10.1145/2751205.2751214.

Table 1: The reported autotuning speed in existing stencil autotuning systems.

Autotuner	Search Time	Search Strategy
PATUS [35]	8 hours	Greedy
SDSL [20]	>33 hours	Exhaustive
Halide [41]	2 hours - 2 days	Stochastic
PARTANS [31]	2.5 hours - 32 days	Hill climbing

The advent of multi/many-core processors brings more complexity and diversity in architectures and programming models. As a consequence, it increases the difficulty of developing high performance programs with reasonable efficiency. Recently, a critical technology to deal with the significant changes is autotuning [4] that acts as either an auto-tuning library [51, 50] or adaptive performance tuning framework [12, 35, 7] for some specific domain. In general, autotuning explores a search space of possible optimization solutions, which reflect functional equivalence but employ different algorithms or implementations, and optimization parameters. A core problem addressed by recent technical approaches is to tune optimization strategies considering program and execution context together. The term ***running instance*** is used within autotuning to refer to the combination of program code, input, target platform, and back-end compiler. It encapsulates the program code and execution context as a whole, and directly determines actual performance of an application.

Two major approaches to autotuning are empirical search-based and prediction-based. Search-based autotuning is a universal but time consuming approach which measures the runtime of all the candidate optimization solutions. For most stencil autotuners, the search-based approach is employed to select a suitable optimization solution from a huge optimization space. A number of pruning strategies and search heuristics are adopted to reduce optimization space and speed up the tuning process[43, 35, 12, 31, 27, 10, 11, 40,

8, 52, 36]. In addition, analytical models derived by composing analysis of code with architectural models are also used to reduce an optimization space to more profitable solutions. However, for some complicated tuning problems, these techniques may still result in unacceptable overhead. Table 1 surveys the autotuning search time reported by existing stencil autotuning systems. In contrast to search-based approaches, prediction-based autotuning gives suitable optimization solutions directly and shows very low overhead, relatively. This approach relies on building a machine learning model that maps from a feature space to an optimal solution space and is usually applied to algorithm selection. However, for stencil autotuning, there are three challenges preventing prediction-based techniques from being applied: i) the optimal optimization solutions are affected by the input data, platform, and stencil itself, and vary a lot when these features are changing. ii) the number of optimization solutions is extremely large, and a prohibitive amount of training data is required. iii) the performance gap between the optimal and a near-optimal solution is not always distinct, resulting in low accuracy of the model.

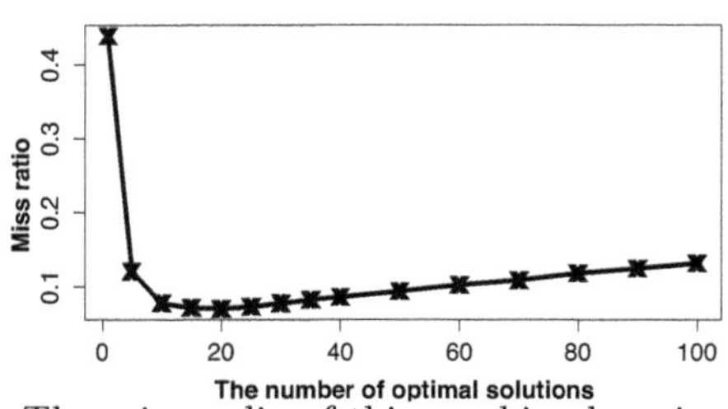

Figure 1: The miss radio of this machine learning model is related to the number of predicted optimal solutions.

In this paper, we propose a *Framework based on optimAl-solution Space modeling for sTencil autotuning* (FAST), integrating techniques of static analysis, domain-specific languages, and machine learning methods to overcome these challenges above. First, FAST adopts static analysis and domain-specific techniques to extract inherent features from target running instances to assist autotuning. Second, a self-learning database is set up to collect training data during either training or tuning phases, lowering the requirement for initial training data. Furthermore, Figure 1 presents the average miss ratio of a machine learning model that predicts a set of optimal solutions, where a smaller miss ratio means higher accuracy. When the number of predicted optimal solutions equals 1, it indicates an approach directly predicting the best solution, and the miss ratio is about 50%. When the number of predicted optimal solutions grows, the miss ratio decreases until the number is 25, where a minimum point is reached. Instead of predicting the best solution directly, it is more feasible to predict a set of optimal solutions (or near-optimal). According to this observation, FAST uses a prediction-based approach to generate highly-tuned solutions by predicting a set of optimal solutions (refer to as an ***optimal-solution space***), thereby it significantly improves the tuning speed.

More specifically, we make the following contributions:

- We develop a feature extractor that extracts inherent features of a running instance, including aspects of algorithm, architecture and input, to characterize stencil computation. Afterwards, an embedded domain-specific language for stencil is proposed to facilitate feature extraction, which is implemented using the ROSE compiler infrastructure (Section 4).
- We formulate a machine learning model to correlate features with an optimal-solution space. The core of this model is that the OSSs of two running instances are similar if their features are of high similarity (Section 5).
- We set up a self-learning database to train the model and generate OSSs. It automatically records optimization recipes and constructs OSSs during either training or tuning phases (Section 5).
- We implement a code generator that supports C/Fortran/CUDA back-end code generation and optimization. It performs code translation and transformation according to the back-end compiler and selected optimization solution (Section 6).

Compared with state-of-the-art stencil autotuning systems like Patus and SDSL, FAST accomplishes the autotuning process in minutes and the tuning step is reduced by $10-2697$ times without any user annotations while achieving comparable performance.

2. MOTIVATION

A stencil is a geometric structure and defines the value of a grid point $v(R)$ in a d-dimensional spatial grid R at time t as a function of neighboring grid points at recent times before t. A stencil computation sweeps over R to update $v(R)$ as a mapping function f of its neighbors $v(R')$, where $R' \in neighbor(R)$. It computes the stencil repeatedly for each grid point over many time steps. Stencil order H is defined as the distance between the central grid point R and the farthest grid points R' in $neighbor(R)$ along a certain axis. Stencil size N is defined as the cardinality $|neighbor(R)|$, that is the number of grid points R' in $neighbor(R)$ including R itself. The definition of a stencil computation doesn't specify how the map function f exactly performs, its concrete implementation depends on a physical model in practice. Therefore, it is impossible to define a common library like BLAS routines for stencil computation. In other words, optimization solutions applied to stencil computations are either input-sensitive or application-specific.

The design principle of our autotuning framework is motived by observations on the relationship between algorithm features and optimization solutions. Figure 2 demonstrates an example of four stencil computation kernels in two groups. Intuitively, it is obvious that the difference between $kernel1$ and $kernel2$ in $GroupA$ is less than that between $kernel3$ and $kernel4$ in $GroupB$. In fact, we can characterize their algorithm features using some quantitative metrics. As an illustrative instance, we simply use several metrics including *array number*(AN), *flop density*(FD), and *reference density*(RD), to characterize the four kernels. For this example, it is easy to calculate these metrics by hand. The values are summarized in the tables of Figure 2. The differences of all metrics in $GroupA$ are extremely low while the difference in $GroupB$ are much higher. A straightforward conclusion from the feature difference is that there is a high probability of applying the same optimization solutions to all kernels in $GroupA$, but different optimization solutions should be applied to each kernel in $GroupB$.

Group A

//kernel1: 2 array, 6 flops, and 28 bytes data reference

$$a_{i,j,k}=\alpha b_{i,j,k-1}+b_{i,j,k+1}+b_{i,j-1,k}+b_{i,j+1,k}+b_{i-1,j,k}+b_{i+1,j,k}$$

//kernel2: 2 array, 8 flops, and 32 bytes data reference

$$a_{i,j,k}=\alpha b_{i,j,k-1}+\beta b_{i,j,k+1}+b_{i,j-1,k}+b_{i,j+1,k}+b_{i-1,j,k}+b_{i+1,j,k}+b_{i,j,k}$$

Group B

//kernel3: 4 array, 14 flops, and 116 bytes data reference

$$a^1_{i,j,k}=\alpha b^1_{i,j,k-1}+b1_{i,j,k+1}+b^1_{i,j-1,k}+b^1_{i,j+1,k}+b^1_{i-1,j,k}+b^1_{i+1,j,k}+b_{i,j,k}$$

$$a^2_{i,j,k}=\alpha b^2_{i,j,k-1}+b^2_{i,j,k+1}+b^2_{i,j-1,k}+b^2_{i,j+1,k}+b^2_{i-1,j,k}+b^2_{i+1,j,k}+b^2_{i,j,k}$$

//kernel4: 2 array, 28 flops, and 60 bytes data reference

$$\begin{aligned}a_{i,j,k}=\alpha b_{i-1,j-1,k-1}&+b_{i,j-1,k-1}+b_{i+1,j-1,k-1}+b_{i-1,j,k-1}+b_{i,j,k-1}+\\ &b_{i+1,j,k-1}+b_{i-1,j+1,k-1}+b_{i,j+1,k-1}+b_{i+1,j+1,k-1}+b_{i-1,j-1,k}+\\ &b_{i,j-1,k}+b_{i+1,j-1,k}+b_{i-1,j,k}+b_{i,j,k}+b_{i+1,j,k}+b_{i-1,j+1,k}+\\ &b_{i,j+1,k}+b_{i+1,j+1,k}+b_{i-1,j-1,k+1}+b_{i,j-1,k+1}+b_{i+1,j-1,k+1}+\\ &b_{i-1,j,k+1}+b_{i,j,k+1}+b_{i+1,j,k+1}+b_{i-1,j+1,k+1}+b_{i,j+1,k+1}+b_{i+1,j+1,k+1}\end{aligned}$$

feature	AN	FD	RD
kernel1	2	6	28
kernel2	2	8	32
diff	**0**	**2**	**4**
kernel3	4	14	116
kernel4	2	28	60
diff	**2**	**14**	**56**

Figure 2: An example of four stencil computation kernels and several typical computing features. AN: the number of arrays. FD: the number of floating-point operations per stencil point. RD: the number of data references per stencil point.

Group A				Group B	
kernel1			kernel2	kernel3	kernel4
tiling	unrolling	simd	...	...	...
127,15,64...	1	Y	....	....	....
127,15,24...	1	Y	....	....	....
127,15,32...	1	Y	....	....	....
127,15,18...	1	Y	....	....	....
127,15,19...	1	Y	....	....	....
		⋮			
127,64,14...	1	Y	....	....	....

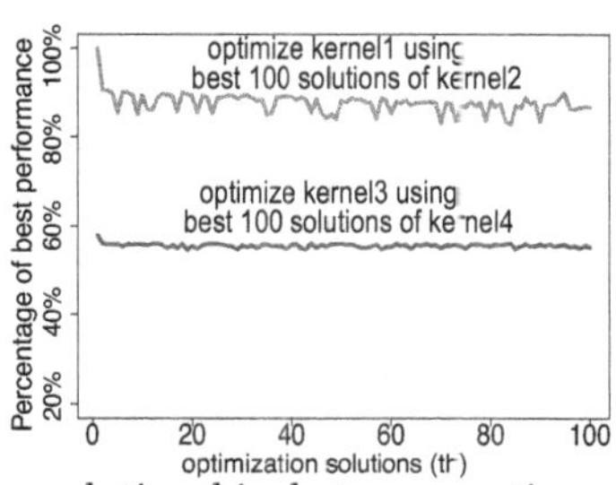

Figure 3: An illustration of the relationship between optimization solution and similarity of computing feature for the two groups of stencil kernels.

In our experiments, we first construct the best 100 optimization solutions for *kernel*2 and *kernel*4 by brute-force search, then apply these optimization solutions to *kernel*1 and *kernel*3, respectively. For this motivating example we adopt three optimization strategies— *tiling*, *unrolling*, and *SIMD* to search optimal solutions (the table in the left of Figure 3). The right picture in Figure 3 plots performance normalized to the best solution [1] for *kernel*1 and *kernel*3. For *GroupA*, *kernel*1 reaches more than 90% of its best performance when using the same optimization solutions as *kernel*2. For *GroupB*, *kernel*3 reaches only 60% of its best performance when using the same optimization with *kernel*4. The experimental result indicates a key attribute where two stencil computations share the same (near-)optimal solutions if they have high similarity in computing features. Further, an autotuning system can leverage this attribute to quickly find optimal solutions based on a priori knowledge instead of a time-consuming empirical search-based approach.

3. AUTOTUNING FRAMEWORK

Figure 4 highlights the major constituent parts of FAST, including (1) a feature extractor that characterizes inherent features of an incoming running instance with the support of a domain specific language, (2) an OSS module used to find optimal solutions that is comprised of a model and a database, (3) a code generator applying translation and optimization according to the back-end compiler and selected optimization solution. We give a brief introduction to each component by going through the autotuning process.

[1]It's achieved by brute-force search.

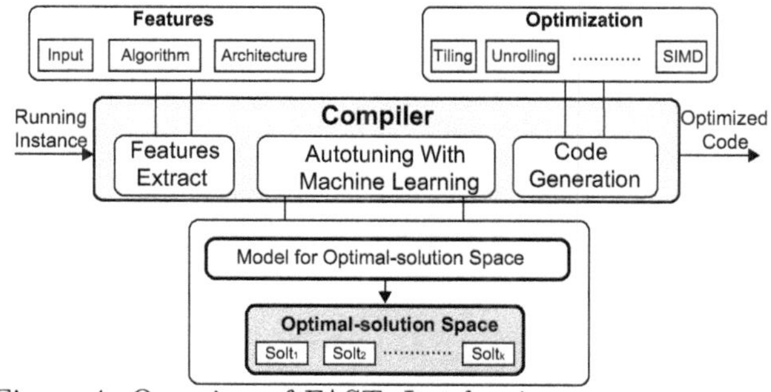

Figure 4: Overview of FAST. It takes in a program source written in domain-specific language, input data and architecture description, outputs an optimized program binary for target architecture.

At the first step, the feature extractor performs an analysis on an incoming running instance comprised of input data, program code and architectural description. In order to comprehensively characterize a running instance, we develop an embedded domain-specific language (eDSL) for stencil computations. The extracted features are then formed as a feature vector.

With the extracted feature vector, the next step is to obtain the optimal solution. FAST first sets up a self-learning database that saves optimization recipes and forms an OSS. Then it builds a model that correlates the behavior of a new running instance with previous knowledge. The model takes the difference of the feature vector from the new running instance and each saved feature vector as the input and predicts the similarity of their OSSs. With the model, an OSS that has maximum similarity with that of the incoming case is picked out from the OSS database. According to a preset threshold, the chosen OSS is validated through an empirical approach, and the first optimization solution satisfying the threshold is returned as the result.

Finally, the code generator performs source-to-source translation according to the detected programming model and the resulting optimization solution. This step is comprised of two phases. In the first phase, a naive implementation without optimization is generated in the form of a high-level language (C or CUDA) according to the back-end compiler. In the second phase, optimization strategies are applied to the naive implementation based on the resulting optimization solution, and binary code is generated for a given execution context.

4. FEATURE ANALYSIS

4.1 Features

The feature extractor focuses on three feature types— *architecture*, *algorithm* and *input*. Table 2 summarizes these features. The architecture features include several basic configurations like processor core (e.g., frequency and vector length.) and memory hierarchy (e.g., cache/shared memory, bandwidth). The programming model is also considered as an architecture feature, where tuning is a combination of compiler options in a back-end compiler [13, 35, 3]. Although the target of our autotuing system is stencil computations, the algorithm feature is independent of stencils and

Table 2: Features extracted by FAST.

Feature Name	Optimization solution
Architecture	
Cores number	parallelism
Frequency	computing upper bound
L1/L2/L3 cache size	blocking
Shared memory (CUDA)	blocking & parallelism
Global memory	data layout
Register number	unrolling & parallelism
Memory bandwidth	blocking
Memory access latency	parallelism
Programing model	compiler options
Algorithm	
Operational intensity	parallelism
Flop density	instruction pipeline
Reference density	unrolling & blocking & texture (CUDA)
Array number	blocking & data layout
Loop radius	blocking & data reuse
Active cache lines	data reuse
Data type	data alignment & blocking
Input	
Problem size	all
Problem shape	loop transformation
Step/iteration time	tradeoff optimization overhead

can be used to characterize any program or problem. These algorithm features mixed with the architecture and input features are used to explore optimization solutions listed in Table 4. For example, the loop radius together with cache parameters is related to cache blocking. The input features are specific to stencil computations. These feature types include problem size, shape and iterations. To some extent, the problem size is related to all optimization solutions.

4.2 Compiler Support

In order to facilitate feature extraction, we design and implement a stencil embedded domain-specific language (eDSL) that is similar to other stencil DSLs [35, 20, 43, 34]. It is a minimal extension of the C/C++/Fortran high-level language, which expresses stencil domain information, such as the grid array referenced in sweeping, and the domain area that determines the range of sweeping. The extension structures are listed in Table 3, and we give a example of 3D 7-point in Figure 5.

```
void 7P_stencil(float*** a,float*** b,float alpha,float beta,int t)
{ RegisterGridData (a,N,N,N);
  RegisterGridData (b,N,N,N);
  RegisterDomain ("dom",1,N−1,1,N−1,1,N−1);
  STENCIL("dom",t)
   b[0][0][0]=(a[0][0][−1]+a[0][0][1]+a[0][−1][0]+a[0][1][0]+
                 a[−1][0][0]+a[1][0[0])*beta+a[0][0][0]*alpha;
}
```

Figure 5: An example of 3D 7-point stencil.

During feature extraction, the DSL code is first translated to an AST (Abstraction Syntax Tree) through front-end compiling. The functions *RegisterGridData()* and *RegisterDomain()* in the AST are identified to construct internal objects of **GridData** and **Domain**. Each internal object is inserted into a global table to finish "registration". The structure *STENCIL(domain, T)* is transformed to a **stencil** object using the previous global table, which represents a stencil computation. Then, a feature analysis pass is performed on **stencil** and outputs formatted feature data.

Table 3: The eDSL extends C/C++/Fortran with two data types, two intrinsic functions and one special structure to facilitate stencil representation and feature extraction.

Specification	Description
GridData	It wraps the array address, dimension and dimensionality into a stencil data object, and enables the compiler to do array index overflow checks and code generation on multiple platforms.
Domain	It expresses a grid area that the stencil computation is sweeping on and wraps N pairs of boundary arguments that specify the upper boundary and the lower boundary for each dimension of the grid area.
RegisterGridData **(source,n1...)**	It registers an array as a **GridData** object to be identified in the **STENCIL** body. The function has $N+1$ arguments, where the first one determines the data source of **GridData**, and the next N arguments describe the shape of the n-dimensional grid.
RegisterDomain **(id,l1,u1...)**	It registers a grid area as a **Domain** object with a unique id that identifies the **Domain** object and $2*N$ arguments to describe the shape of the sweeping domain for their upper boundaries and lower boundaries.
STENCIL **(domain,T)** **{..}**	It is composed of three parts: (i) a unique **Domain**; (ii) a integer variable T representing the number of repeated stencil computations; (iii) the shape of the stencil defining the actual computations. A language restriction is that every referenced point is an element of one registered **GridData**. The array indices represent offsets away from the central point of the stencil.

5. OPTIMAL-SOLUTION SPACE MODULE

5.1 Optimal-Solution Space

Formally, given an optimization space $R = \{v_1, v_2, ..., v_N\}$ of N optimization solutions v_i $(i = 1..N)$, let $M(v_i)$ be a metric to evaluate an optimization solution v_i. An *optimal-solution space* containing K solutions can be expressed as:

$$OSS^K = \{v | M(v) \geq M(v_K^*), v, v_K^* \in R\} \quad (1)$$

where v_K^* is the K-th best optimization solution in R and each v in OSS^K is not worse than v_k^*. In other words, OSS^K is a subset containing the best K optimization solutions. Further, we define a notion of *Overlapping Ratio* OR to measure the similarity of two OSS^Ks:

$$OR = \frac{|OSS_x^K \cap OSS_y^K|}{K} \quad (2)$$

It represents the ratio of the similar part between two OSSs. Our aim is to build a module that provides a mechanism leveraging feature vector $\vec{f}$ =<*architecture, algorithm, input*> to generate an OSS. We approach this problem by learning mapping (Section 5.2) from the feature vector difference of two running instance, $\vec{x} = \Delta\vec{f}$, to a probability distribution over OR of their OSS, $y = OR$. Once this distribution has been trained, to predict the OSS for a new running instance is achieved by traversing a OSS database (Section 5.3) and returning an OSS with a maximum predicted overlap ratio OR^*,

$$OR^* = \operatorname*{argmax}_{x} q(y|\vec{x})$$

To provide a design principle to this machine learning model, we use a set of analytical experiments to study three key attributes of the OSS, including:

Overlapping ratio: We conduct experiments on 288 running instances (details in Section7.1) on both CPU and GPU platforms and achieve their OSSs by evaluating and ranking the optimization solutions listed in Table 4. Figure 6 presents the average ORs of these OSSs, and the x-axis presents their sizes (K). On both platforms, the average ORs drop when K decreases. For the CPU instance, when the size is 2100, the average OR is 78%. When the size becomes 100, the average OR drops to 20%. The GPU platform is the same. This result indicates a straightforward observation that *larger OSSs have higher OR they share more optimal (near-optimal) solutions with each other*. However, this leads to a dilemma that a larger OSS requires higher overhead for its empirical validation.

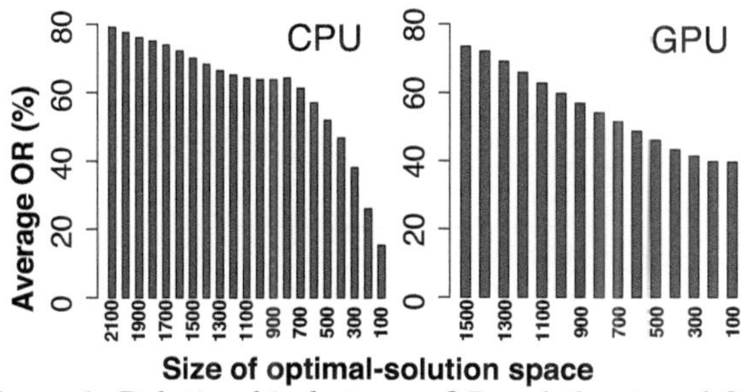

Figure 6: Relationship between OR and the size of OSSs.

Performance coverage: In an OSS^K, the performance lower bound is determined by the *K-th* best optimization solution p_K,

$$p_{lower}(OSS^K) = p_K$$

To study the performance coverage of OSSs, we construct the OSSs with different sizes (K) for 288 running instances and evaluate their average performance lower bound $\mathcal{D}_K$ by computing,

$$\mathcal{D}_K = \frac{\sum_{m=1}^{N} \frac{p_{m_K}}{p_m^*}}{N}$$

For a running instance m, p_m^* is its best optimization solution, and p_{m_K} is its *K-th* best optimization solution. We normalize the p_{m_k} value to p_m^*, and calculate the average value. As Figure 7 shows, $\mathcal{D}_K$ slowly degrades when K grows. More specifically, the $\mathcal{D}_K$ decreases 10% in performance compared to the best optimization solutions on the CPU when K is 100. On the GPU, a 10% performance slowdown occurs when K is 20. This observation indicates that *a small OSS covers most of the solutions with the highest performance.*

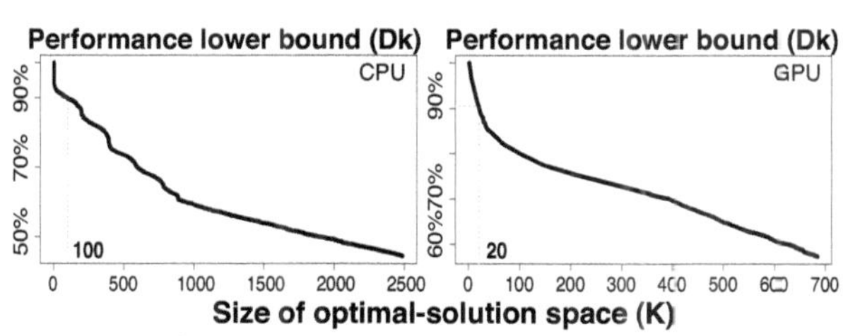

Figure 7: Performance lower bound of OSSs with different size.

Sensitivity to features: For two running instances with different features, their OSSs are different. To evaluate sensitivity of OSS to feature difference, we conduct two experiments by varying features of *flop density* and *problem size*, respectively. In each experiment, one feature is fixed and the other one varies. We measure the variability of features in each group by computing their coefficient of variation:

$$c_v = \frac{\sigma}{\mu} = \frac{\sqrt{\frac{1}{N}\sum_{i=1}^{N}(x_i - \overline{x})^2}}{\overline{x}}$$

c_v is a normalized measure of the dispersion of a probability distribution. It is defined as the ratio of the standard deviation σ to the mean μ. Figure 8 presents the average OR for four groups of kernels with c_v from 80% to 3%. The result shows that when the coefficient of variation is smaller, the OR between two OSSs is higher. This observation indicates that *the OSSs of two running instances have a high OR if their features are of high similarity*. Therefore, it is reasonable that we can achieve an OSS having high OR with incoming running instances using a recorded running instance that has similar features.

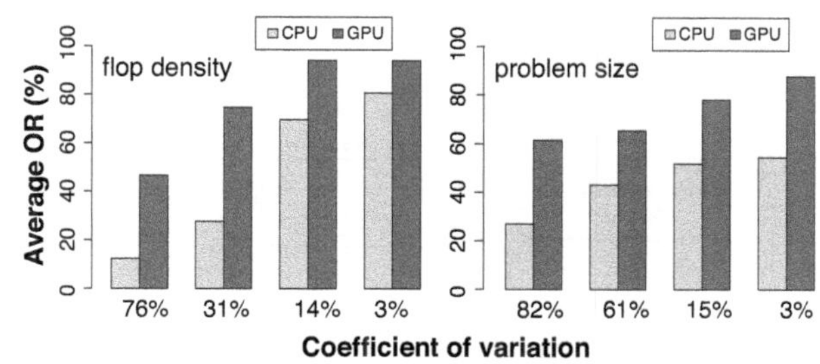

Figure 8: Averaged OR of OSS^{100}s for the four groups of example kernels. Stencils in each group have different features of *flop density*(left) and *problem size*(right) , and use c_v to denote extent of variability.

5.2 Build a Model

Based on the previous observations, we construct an optimal-space model inputting feature vector difference of two running instances, $\vec{x} = \Delta\vec{f}$, and predicting a probability distribution over OR of their OSS, $y = OR$. We let the feature vector difference $\vec{x}$ be the result of subtracting two given feature vectors,

$$x_i = \begin{cases} f_i - f_i' & numeric \\ 0/1 & non-numeric \end{cases}$$

where x_i is vector components of $\vec{x}$. For the numeric feature f_i, we perform a subtraction on them. For non-numeric f_i, x_i is 1 if the two features are the same. Otherwise x_i is 0. For each vector component x_i, the difference of two running instances in the *i-th* feature is a predictor variable and the OR is a response variable. To fit a machine learning model, we make use of the training records stored in a relational database to generate a training set $< \mathcal{X}, \mathcal{Y} >$ where each vector $\vec{x} \in \mathcal{X}$ is a feature vector difference $(x_1, x_2.., x_D)$ and each target $y \in \mathcal{Y}$ denotes the OR of the OSS of two running instances. Because there is more than one predictor variable in our model, we have used multiple linear regression and assumed the form of the model as:

$$y = \sum_{i=1}^{D} \mathcal{F}(x_i)$$

D is the dimensionality of the feature vector difference, and it equals to number of features. For each vector component x_i, the $\mathcal{F}(x_i)$ denotes the effect of the feature difference x_i on OR. Considering the nonlinear relationship between feature vector differences and OR, we employ a polynomial regression and represent each $\mathcal{F}(x_i)$ as a three-order regression function:

$$\mathcal{F}(x_i) = \alpha_i \Delta x_i + \beta_i \Delta x_i^2 + \gamma_i \Delta x_i^3 + \delta_i$$

The α_i, β_i, γ_i are partial regression coefficients of x_i, and δ_i is its intercept.

$$y = \sum_{i=1}^{D} (\alpha_i \Delta x_i + \beta_i \Delta x_i^2 + \gamma_i \Delta x_i^3 + \delta_i)$$

It is easy to build the model with a solver in the R language, assuming that $\hat{\alpha}$, $\hat{\beta}$, $\hat{\gamma}$ are estimations for the parameters, and $\epsilon_i = y' - y$ are residuals between estimations and real values. We can get $\hat{\alpha}$, $\hat{\beta}$, $\hat{\gamma}$ by minimizing residuals for each ϵ_i.

5.3 OSS Database

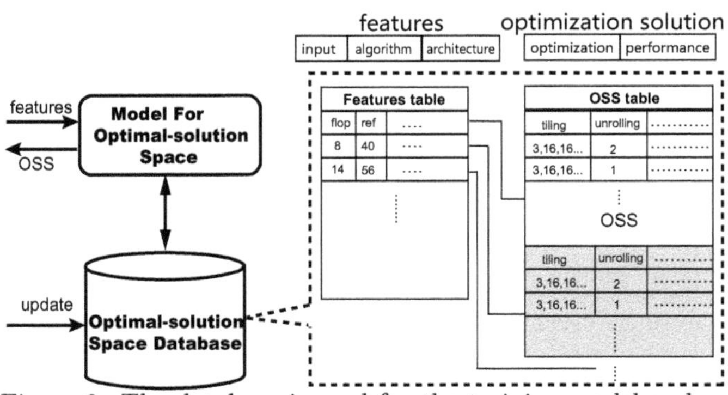

Figure 9: The database is used for the training model and for generating OSSs. It is indexed by the feature vector, and returns the corresponding OSS.

Figure 9 illustrates the structure of the OSS database and its workflow. It is indexed by the feature vector, and returns the corresponding OSS if it exists. The feature vectors and OSS are stored in two tables, and are connected by a foreign key, i.e., `feature.id` equals to `optimalspace.featureid`.

During the training phase, the OSS database stores and updates the OSS for each training instance. Once a training running instance finishes executing, an **Update** function is invoked to update its running record in the database. For each running record, there is one feature vector that is extracted by the feature analysis module, and one solution vector containing optimization parameters as well as the corresponding performance results collected by TAU [32]. If either one of the two tables has no matched record, **Update** adds the corresponding feature vector or solution vector. Otherwise, the new training record is updated in the OSS database.

5.4 Generate And Validate OSS

During the autotuning phase, the module is responsible for inputting the feature vector of the incoming case and returning its OSS. For an incoming test case, its feature vector is compared with that of running instances in the OSS database. The module calculates their differences and uses the OSS model to predict the OR of their OSSs. Then, the OSS with maximum OR is returned as the result. The result contains near-optimal solutions and we validate these solutions using an empirical approach. In addition, we provide an option to set a performance threshold, and validation is stopped when reaching the threshold. Considering the rationale of this model, the optimization solutions of high quality accomplish the empirical validation rapidly and make the whole autotuning overhead much lower than with other strategies.

If the performance threshold is not satisfying after finishing validation, a traditional search-based approach will be performed as a backup. One thing to note is that the traditional autotuning procedure also updates the OSS database with its running record. As a consequence, the iteration may generate a self-learning database that trains a more powerful model.

6. CODE GENERATION

Table 4: The parameterized optimization space.

Optimization		Parameter	Range
Technology	Description		
Cache Blocking	blocking for Level 1	L_{1i} L_{1j} L_{1k}	{1,2..N} {1,2..N} {1,2..N}
	blocking for Level 2	L_{2i} L_{2j} L_{2k}	{1,2..N} {1,2..N} {1,2..N}
	blocking for Level 3	L_{3i} L_{3j} L_{3k}	{1,2..N} {1,2..N} {1,2..N}
CUDA Blocking	blocking for CUDA threads	t_x t_y t_z	{1,2..N} {1,2..N} {1,2..N}
	blocking for CUDA blocks	b_x b_y b_z	{1,2..N} {1,2..N} {1,2..N}
OpenMP	thread-level parallelism	*number*	{1,2..16}
Unrolling	unrolling stencil loop	*factor*	{1,2..8}
SIMDization	data-level parallelism	*dosimd*	{0,1}
Compiler	flag for icc or nvcc	*cflag*	{O0,O1,O2,-O3,-xSSE3,-xAVX...}

According to the detected programming model or compiler back-end, the eDSL codes are translated to the corresponding high level language. For each **STENCIL** structure, the translator first acquires domain information and computation times through **Domain** and **T**, and creates a loop body for the stencil computation. Second, **GridData** variables are replaced by memory objects corresponding to an array and its iterator variables in the memory of a particular programming model. The generated code is a naive code solution and needs to be optimized. We apply optimization strategies based on previous autotuning results. Some of our optimization strategies are summarized in Table 4. Finally, a highly-tuned code solution is generated and the autotuing process finishes.

7. EVALUATION

7.1 Experimental Setup

We conduct the experiments on a 16-core SMP system integrating two Intel Xeon E5-2670 multicore CPUs (116.4 GFlops double-precision and 332.8 GFlops single-precision) and a NVIDIA Tesla K20c GPU (1.17 TFlops double-precision and 3.52 TFlops single-precision). The back-end compiler is an Intel compiler version 13.1 and an NVCC version 6.0, respectively.

Test Dataset: We evaluate FAST with a benchmark set composed of five stencil computation applications. FDTD [29] represents a 3D 5-point stencil with order-1, which is used in modeling computational electrodynamics. HEAT [20] represents a 3D 7-point stencil with order-1 which is used in chemical diffusion, WAVE [37] represents 3D 25-points stencil with order-4 which is used in fluid dynamics, POISSON [48] represents 3D 19-points stencil with order-1 that used in mechanical engineering. HIMENO [21] represents 3D 19-points with order-1.

Initializing Database: We initialize the OSS database from various stencil running instances using a Python script and generate stencil kernels by varying stencil order (n_o) from 1 to 3, parameter number (n_p) from 1 to 4 and array number (n_a) in $\{2, 4, 8, 16\}$. That is, the number of training kernels is $3 \times 4 \times 4 = 48$. The *flop density* is equal to $(1 + (6 + n_p) * o) * n_a/2 - 1$, and *reference density* is equal to $(1 + 6 * n_o) * n_a/2 * 4$ when the data type is single floating point. We use three input sizes $\{128^2 \times 256, 256^2 \times 512, 512^2 \times 1024\}$ and two target platforms {Sandy Bridge, K20}. Thus, the total number of running instances is $3 \times 2 \times 48 = 288$.

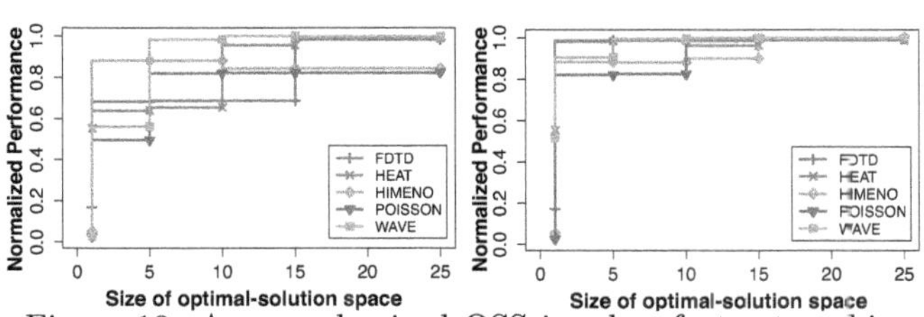

Figure 10: A properly sized OSS is a key factor to achieving high performance in FAST. The left graph shows the performance result using different OSS sizes. In the right graph, we further combine five closest OSSs as the result to improve robustness.

Training Model: An appropriate OSS size is important to FAST. As shown in the left graph in Figure 10, the performance achieved for five applications (described in the test dataset) is far away from the optimal solution when the size of the OSS is one. When increasing the size, the performance becomes better and stable once it reaches 20. However, there are still two applications whose performance is less than 90% of the optimal solution. We found that the prediction model is not so robust, where the returned OSS is not the closest one all the time. We improve FAST further by combining five closest OSSs predicted by the model and returning it as the target OSS. The right picture of Figure 10 shows that all cases achieve 99% of their best performance when the size of the OSS is larger than 15. As a result, we set the size of the OSS to be 25 in FAST's training process and combine the five closest OSSs to create each resulting OSS.

We compare *FAST* with baseline programs (*Baseline*) and two other stencil optimization frameworks (*SDSL, Patus*) with the support of the DSL compiler and autotuning techniques. For simplicity of presentation we only report experimental results for the $128 \times 128 \times 256$ problem size.

- *Baseline*: A straightforward implementation of five benchmark applications according to their stencil formulations. They are compiled by the back-end compiler with default optimization flags, i.e., `'-O3 -ipo'` for the Intel compiler, `'-O3 -Xcompiler -O3'` for CUDA.

Table 5: Autotuning running time in seconds.

Program	Feature Analysis	Tuning	Total
HIMENO	4.6	551	555.6
FDTD	4.8	99	103.8
POISSON	4.4	107	111.4
WAVE	4.6	47	51.6
HEAT	4.2	199	203.2

- *SDSL [20]*: The stencil domain specific language (SDSL) can be embedded in C/C++/MATLAB and focuses on polyhedral compiler optimization for short-vector SIMD and CUDA as well. There is a built-in autotuning module that implements an improved brute-force search with the help of tuning annotations in the language.

- *Patus [35]*: The Patus stencil optimization framework focuses on the autotuning strategy itself, which is the most similar counterpart to FAST. There is a flexible autotuner that integrates several efficient heuristic algorithms and provides language support to annotate the tuning strategy.

We evaluate the autotuning frameworks in terms of autotuning speed and performance. In summary, our framework achieves the best performance for most of the benchmark applications. The most remarkable advantage of our framework is that it generates optimized codes in minutes instead of either hours or days (Table 1). More specifically, it reduces tuning steps by $10 - 2697$ times compared with the conventional search-based strategies used extensively in the counterpart autotuning frameworks.

7.2 Autotuning Speed

Table 5 profiles the execution time of the whole autotuning process. Compared to the existing stencil computation autotuning systems, which require either hours or days to perform tuning, FAST finishes the autotuning process in minutes. A major source of this improvement comes from the significantly reduced tuning steps. Due to the brute-force-like search algorithm used in SDSL, we evaluate autotuning speed in terms of the tuning step by comparing with Patus. In fact, Patus adopts several representative auto-tuning search strategies that appeared in most of autotuners [3]. Figure 11 plots the best performance achieved at each tuning step for both CPU and GPU implementations. The blue line represents the greedy-based autotuning used in Patus and the red line represents FAST. Two dotted lines are used to mark the tuning steps' satisfying threshold, which is 95% of best performance. For Patus, the fastest one costs 225 steps in the case of FDTD and the slowest one costs 2725 steps in the case of Poisson. For FAST, the fastest one costs one step, and the slowest one only costs 23 steps in the case of FDTD. In summary, the autotuning overhead is significantly reduced by an average two orders of magnitude with FAST. The rapid convergence of FAST is due to the high quality solutions contained in the predicted OSS. Figure 12 presents normalized performance of the optimization solutions in the predicted OSS. The y-axis is the performance normalized to the best optimization solution and the x-axis presents optimization solutions in the predicted OSS. For HIMENO and WAVE, all optimization solutions fall in the interval of 90%-100% to of the best performance. For POISSON and FDTD, there are half of the optimization solutions achieved at least 90% of the best performance. For

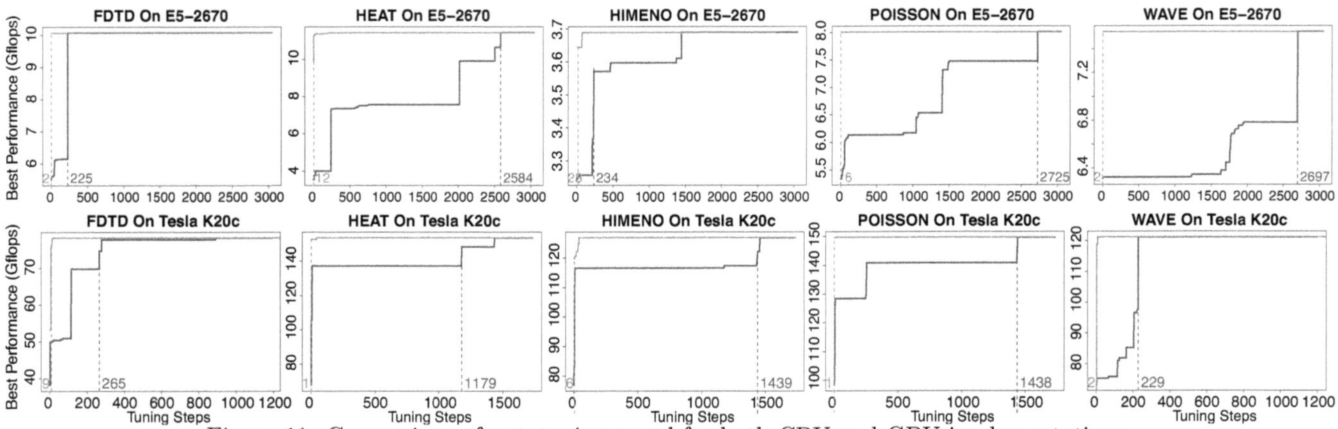

Figure 11: Comparison of autotuning speed for both CPU and GPU implementations.

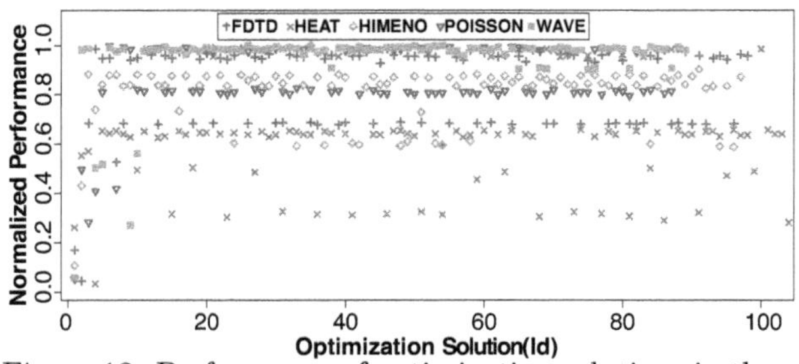

Figure 12: Performance of optimization solutions in the predicted OSS.

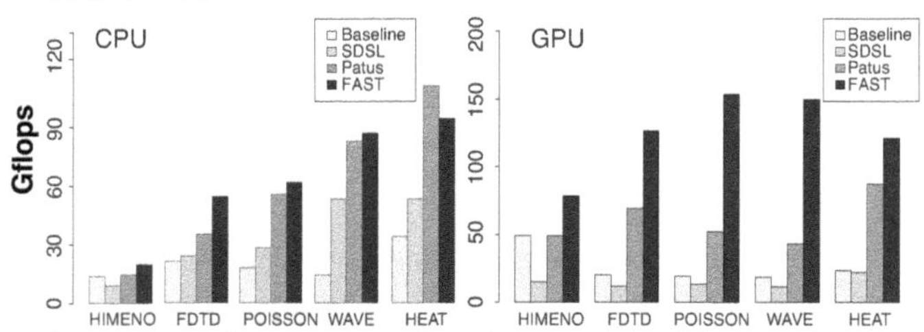

Figure 13: Comparison of performance in Gflops on for both CPU and GPU implementations.

HIMENO, only one-third of optimization solutions are better than 90% of the best performance. The behaviors of these optimization solutions are due to the differences between the applications and the running instances in initial OSS database. Obviously, WAVE is the most similar case, which shares most optimal solutions with these running instances in the OSS database. In spite of this, for all five benchmark applications, their OSS definitely contains several optimization solutions that achieve more than 95% of best performance. This verifies that FAST results in high accuracy of prediction for optimal solutions.

7.3 Performance

We report performance in Gflops for these five benchmark applications in Figure 13 on both the CPU and GPU. On average, *FAST* improves performance by 3.28 times over *Baseline*, 100% times over *SDSL* and 18% times over *Patus* on the CPU, and by 4.86 times over *Baseline*, 8.3 times over *SDSL* and 1.25 times over *Patus* on the GPU.

CPU: The left bar graph in Figure 13 shows performance comparison for the CPU implementations. First, for the CPU implementations, *FAST* improves performance by 1.4-6.2 times over *Baseline*, 64%-120% over *SDSL* and -15%-53% over *Patus*, respectively. *FAST* employs the 2.5D blocking strategy [38] to reuse data between two adjacent blocks. As a consequence, for memory bound applications, such as FDTD and HIMENO, we obtain better performance results than *Patus*. However, for applications with high operational intensity, such as HEAT, Patus surpasses *FAST* due to its explicit SIMD optimization by using intrinsic functions. *SDSL* also works well on short-vector SIMD architectures and performs tiling optimizations on temporal and spatial dimensions. However, the time-tiling used is restricted by the growing size of tiles when the dimension is larger than two. That leads to its unsatisfactory performance on five three-dimension applications. Second, the performance improvement differs with the five stencil applications. For example, *FAST* achieves higher speedups for HEAT and WAVE than for HIMENO and FDTD. The difference is related to the algorithmic feature of *Operational intensity*, which sets the performance upper bound according the roofline model [52].

GPU: The right bar graph in Figure 13 shows the performance comparison for the GPU implementations. *FAST* improves performance by 58% – 7 times over *Baseline*, 4.24 – 12.3 times over *SDSL* and 39% – 2.48 times over *Patus*, respectively. Unlike the implementations on the CPU, *FAST* outperforms the GPU counterparts. One major reason is that our optimization solutions adopt 2.5D blocking, shared memory, constant memory and texture reference optimization strategies, but both *SDSL* and *Patus* only employ straightforward parallelization and blocking strategies.

8. RELATED WORK

Autotuning has emerged as a critical strategy for achieving high performance as architectural complexity grows. A number of autotuning frameworks have been developed for building efficient, portable libraries or frameworks in specific domains. For example, PHiPAC [5] is an autotuning system for dense matrix multiplication. ATLAS [51] utilizes empirical autotuning to produce a cache-contained matrix multiply. FFTW [16] uses empirical autotuning to combine solvers for FFTs. Other autotuning systems include SPARSITY [23] for sparse matrix computations, SPIRAL [39, 49, 15] for digital signal processing, UHFFT [1] for FFT on multicore systems, and OSKI [50] for sparse matrix kernels. ActiveHarmony [44, 46] provides a general framework for tuning configurable libraries and exploring different compiler optimizations. Two major approaches of autotuning are search-based and prediction-based. Search-based autotuning is a generic but time consuming approach, which empirically evaluates candidates in the optimization space. For this reason, a number of strategies have been applied to speed up search, such as pruning, heuristics and analytical models [17, 9, 25, 52, 31, 19, 41, 20, 33, 12]. Prediction-based autotuning leverages prior knowledge to achieve the best optimization solution directly and has very low overhead. It is always applied to the problem of code solution or algorithm selection [30, 42, 45, 28, 18, 14, 24].

On the other hand, as a higher level of abstraction, DSLs are promising trend to improve usability since many application domains do not have a clear abstraction as a library interface. They leverage a specialized compiler to help application experts easily write high performance codes and facilitate optimization. Several successful attempts include graph [22], multigrid [2] and stencil [34] computations.

FAST combines techniques of DSL and autotuning for optimizing stencil computation. Recent work [10, 2, 43, 35, 12, 31, 27, 26, 20] has demonstrated their strength in automatic optimization on diverse architectures. FAST shares the same programming productivity of DSLs with these works for domain application experts and further exploits using the DSLs to extract features that help with autotuning. The features extraction is an important aspect of our autotuning approach compared to existing ones. For example, some general frameworks like Intelligent Compilers [6], CHiLL [47], Patus [35] and Orio [19] are designed for autotuning compiler or library developers instead of domain application experts. They force an experienced user to write a script for tuning configurations. Afterwards, FAST takes a prediction-based approach to deal with stencil autotuning that differs from previous work. First, previous autotuning systems employ pruning and heuristic algorithms to search the optimization space. They establish the optimization space using all configurable parameters exposed in the strategy definition and some internal default parameters (loop nest unrolling factors, padding). Then, multiple search algorithms are applied, such as Nelder-Mead simplex search, dynamic programming and stochastic optimization methods including random, evolutionary, and hill climbing. Recently, OpenTuner [3] allows many search techniques to work together and supports customizable configuration representations of a sophisticated search technique. Instead of using these search-based approaches, FAST builds a self-learning OSS database to automatically learn an OSS prediction model and predicts optimal solutions directly, which significantly decreases tuning overhead.

9. CONCLUSION

In this paper, we propose and implement a framework based on the OSS model for stencil autotuning (FAST). Compared to previous work, FAST adopts a prediction-based approach to autotune stencil computations, and greatly decreases tuning overhead. The key insight behind FAST is that that two running instances have a small OSS with high overlap ratio if their features are of high similarity. The experiments on both x86 multicore CPU and NVIDIA GPU show that FAST outperforms its counterparts in terms of both performance and autotuning speed. In particular, the autotuning speed is improved by $10 - 2697$ times over the conventional autotuning strategy.

10. ACKNOWLEDGMENTS

We would like to express our gratitude to all reviewer's constructive comments and Dr. Brad Chamberlain for helping us polishing this paper. This work is supported by National Natural Science Foundation of China, under grant no. (61272134, 31327901, 91430218, 60921002, 60925009, 61472395), National 863 Program (2009AA01A129) and 973 Program (2012CB316502 and 2011CB302502).

References

[1] A. Ali, L. Johnsson, and J. Subhlok. Scheduling fft computation on smp and multicore systems. In *Proceedings of the 21st annual international conference on Supercomputing*, pages 293–301. ACM, 2007.

[2] J. Ansel, C. Chan, Y. L. Wong, M. Olszewski, Q. Zhao, A. Edelman, and S. Amarasinghe. Petabricks: a language and compiler for algorithmic choice. In *Proceedings of the 2009 ACM SIGPLAN conference on Programming language design and implementation*, volume 44. ACM, 2009.

[3] J. Ansel, S. Kamil, K. Veeramachaneni, J. Ragan-Kelley, J. Bosboom, U.-M. O'Reilly, and S. Amarasinghe. Opentuner: An extensible framework for program autotuning. In *International Conference on Parallel Architectures and Compilation Techniques*, Edmonton, Canada, August 2014.

[4] P. Basu, M. Hall, M. Khan, S. Maindola, S. Muralidharan, S. Ramalingam, A. Rivera, M. Shantharam, and A. Venkat. Towards making autotuning mainstream. *The International Journal of High Performance Computing Applications*, 27(4):379–393, 2013.

[5] J. Bilmes, K. Asanovic, C.-W. Chin, and J. Demmel. Optimizing matrix multiply using phipac: a portable, high-performance, ansi c coding methodology. In *Proceedings of the 11th international conference on Supercomputing*, pages 340–347. ACM, 1997.

[6] J. Cavazos. Intelligent compilers. In *Cluster Computing, 2008 IEEE International Conference on*, pages 360–368. IEEE, 2008.

[7] C. Chen, J. Chame, and M. Hall. Combining models and guided empirical search to optimize for multiple levels of the memory hierarchy. In *International Symposium on Code Generation and Optimization*, pages 111–122. IEEE, 2005.

[8] J. W. Choi, A. Singh, and R. W. Vuduc. Model-driven autotuning of sparse matrix-vector multiply on gpus. In *Proceedings of the 15th ACM SIGPLAN Symposium on Principles and Practice of Parallel Programming*, volume 45, pages 115–126. ACM, 2010.

[9] M. Christen, O. Schenk, and Y. Cui. Patus for convenient high-performance stencils: evaluation in earthquake simulations. In *High Performance Computing, Networking, Storage and Analysis (SC), 2012 International Conference for*, pages 1–10. IEEE, 2012.

[10] K. D. Cooper, P. J. Schielke, and D. Subramanian. Optimizing for reduced code space using genetic algorithms. *ACM SIGPLAN Notices*, 34(7):1–9, 1999.

[11] K. Datta, S. Kamil, S. Williams, L. Oliker, J. Shalf, and K. Yelick. Optimization and performance modeling of stencil computations on modern microprocessors. *SIAM review*, 51(1):129–159, 2009.

[12] K. Datta, M. Murphy, V. Volkov, S. Williams, J. Carter, L. Oliker, D. Patterson, J. Shalf, and K. Yelick. Stencil computation optimization and auto-tuning on state-of-the-art multicore architectures. In *Proceedings of the 2008 ACM/IEEE conference on Supercomputing*, page 4. IEEE Press, 2008.

[13] C. Dubach, T. Jones, and M. O'Boyle. Microarchitectural design space exploration using an architecture-centric approach. In *Proceedings of the 40th Annual IEEE/ACM International Symposium on Microarchitecture*, pages 262–271. IEEE Computer Society, 2007.

[14] E. Fink. How to solve it automatically: Selection among problem solving methods. In *AIPS*, pages 128–136, 1998.

[15] F. Franchetti, F. de Mesmay, D. McFarlin, and M. Püschel. Operator language: A program generation framework for fast kernels. In *Domain-Specific Languages*, pages 385–409. Springer, 2009.

[16] M. Frigo and S. G. Johnson. The design and implementation of fftw3. *Proceedings of the IEEE*, 93(2):216–231, 2005.

[17] A. Ganapathi, K. Datta, A. Fox, and D. Patterson. A case for machine learning to optimize multicore performance. In *First USENIX Workshop on Hot Topics in Parallelism (HotPar'09)*, 2009.

[18] A. Guerri and M. Milano. Learning techniques for automatic algorithm portfolio selection. In *ECAI*, volume 16, page 475, 2004.

[19] A. Hartono, B. Norris, and P. Sadayappan. Annotation-based empirical performance tuning using orio. In *Parallel & Distributed Processing, 2009. IPDPS 2009. IEEE International Symposium on*, pages 1–11. IEEE, 2009.

[20] T. Henretty, R. Veras, F. Franchetti, L.-N. Pouchet, J. Ramanujam, and P. Sadayappan. A stencil compiler for short-vector simd architectures. In *Proceedings of the 27th international ACM conference on International conference on supercomputing*, pages 13–24. ACM, 2013.

[21] R. Himeno. Himeno benchmark, 2011.

[22] S. Hong, H. Chafi, E. Sedlar, and K. Olukotun. Green-marl: a dsl for easy and efficient graph analysis. In *Proceedings of the seventeenth international conference on Architectural Support for Programming Languages and Operating Systems*, volume 40, pages 349–362. ACM, 2012.

[23] E.-J. Im and K. Yelick. Optimizing sparse matrix computations for register reuse in sparsity. In *Computational ScienceâĂŤICCS 2001*, pages 127–136. Springer, 2001.

[24] N. Jain, A. Bhatele, M. P. Robson, T. Gamblin, and L. V. Kale. Predicting application performance using supervised learning on communication features. In *Proceedings of SC13: International Conference for High Performance Computing, Networking, Storage and Analysis*, page 95. ACM, 2013.

[25] S. Kamil, C. Chan, L. Oliker, J. Shalf, and S. Williams. An auto-tuning framework for parallel multicore stencil computations. In *Parallel & Distributed Processing (IPDPS), 2010 IEEE International Symposium on*, pages 1–12. IEEE, 2010.

[26] S. Kamil, D. Coetzee, and A. Fox. Bringing parallel performance to python with domain-specific selective embedded just-in-time specialization. In *Python for Scientific Computing Conference (SciPy)*, 2011.

[27] M. Khan, P. Basu, G. Rudy, M. Hall, C. Chen, and J. Chame. A script-based autotuning compiler system to generate high-performance cuda code. *ACM Transactions on Architecture and Code Optimization (TACO)*, 9(4):31, 2013.

[28] L. Kotthoff, I. P. Gent, and I. Miguel. A preliminary evaluation of machine learning in algorithm selection for search problems. In *Fourth Annual Symposium on Combinatorial Search*, 2011.

[29] K. S. Kunz and R. J. Luebbers. *The finite difference time domain method for electromagnetics*. CRC press, 1993.

[30] J. Li, G. Tan, M. Chen, and N. Sun. Smat: an input adaptive auto-tuner for sparse matrix-vector multiplication. In *ACM SIGPLAN Notices*, volume 48, pages 117–126. ACM, 2013.

[31] T. Lutz, C. Fensch, and M. Cole. Partans: An autotuning framework for stencil computation on multi-gpu systems. *ACM Transactions on Architecture and Code Optimization (TACO)*, 9(4):59, 2013.

[32] A. D. Malony, J. Cuny, and S. Shende. Tau: Tuning and analysis utilities. Technical report, LALP-99-205, Los Alamos National Laboratory Publication, 1999.

[33] A. Mametjanov, D. Lowell, C.-C. Ma, and B. Norris. Autotuning stencil-based computations on gpus. In *Cluster Computing (CLUSTER), 2012 IEEE International Conference on*, pages 266–274. IEEE, 2012.

[34] N. Maruyama, T. Nomura, K. Sato, and S. Matsuoka. Physis: an implicitly parallel programming model for stencil computations on large-scale gpu-accelerated supercomputers. In *High Performance Computing, Networking, Storage and Analysis (SC), 2011 International Conference for*, pages 1–12. IEEE, 2011.

[35] C. Matthias, S. Olaf, and B. Helmar. Patus: A code generation and autotuning framework for parallel iterative stencil computations on modern microarchitectures. In *Parallel & Distributed Processing Symposium (IPDPS), 2011 IEEE International*, pages 676–687. IEEE, 2011.

[36] J. Meng and K. Skadron. Performance modeling and automatic ghost zone optimization for iterative stencil loops on gpus. In *Proceedings of the 23rd international conference on Supercomputing*, pages 256–265. ACM, 2009.

[37] P. Micikevicius. 3d finite difference computation on gpus using cuda. In *Proceedings of 2nd Workshop on General Purpose Processing on Graphics Processing Units*, pages 79–84. ACM, 2009.

[38] A. Nguyen, N. Satish, J. Chhugani, C. Kim, and P. Dubey. 3.5-d blocking optimization for stencil computations on modern cpus and gpus. In *Proceedings of the 2010 ACM/IEEE International Conference for High Performance Computing, Networking, Storage and Analysis*, pages 1–13. IEEE Computer Society, 2010.

[39] M. Püschel, J. M. Moura, B. Singer, J. Xiong, J. Johnson, D. Padua, M. Veloso, and R. W. Johnson. Spiral: A generator for platform-adapted libraries of signal processing alogorithms. *International Journal of High Performance Computing Applications*, 18(1):21–45, 2004.

[40] A. Qasem, M. J. Cade, and D. Tamir. Improved energy efficiency for multithreaded kernels through model-based autotuning. In *Green Technologies Conference, 2012 IEEE*, pages 1–6. IEEE, 2012.

[41] J. Ragan-Kelley, C. Barnes, A. Adams, S. Paris, F. Durand, and S. Amarasinghe. Halide: a language and compiler for optimizing parallelism, locality, and recomputation in image processing pipelines. *ACM SIGPLAN Notices*, 48(6):519–530, 2013.

[42] J. R. Rice. The algorithm selection problem. 1975.

[43] Y. Tang, R. A. Chowdhury, B. C. Kuszmaul, C.-K. Luk, and C. E. Leiserson. The pochoir stencil compiler. In *Proceedings of the twenty-third annual ACM symposium on Parallelism in algorithms and architectures*, pages 117–128. ACM, 2011.

[44] C. Ţăpuş, I.-H. Chung, J. K. Hollingsworth, et al. Active harmony: Towards automated performance tuning. In *Proceedings of the 2002 ACM/IEEE conference on Supercomputing*, pages 1–11. IEEE Computer Society Press, 2002.

[45] N. Thomas, G. Tanase, O. Tkachyshyn, J. Perdue, N. M. Amato, and L. Rauchwerger. A framework for adaptive algorithm selection in stapl. In *Proceedings of the tenth ACM SIGPLAN symposium on Principles and practice of parallel programming*, pages 277–288. ACM, 2005.

[46] A. Tiwari, C. Chen, J. Chame, M. Hall, and J. K. Hollingsworth. A scalable auto-tuning framework for compiler optimization. In *Parallel & Distributed Processing, 2009. IPDPS 2009. IEEE International Symposium on*, pages 1–12. IEEE, 2009.

[47] A. Tiwari, C. Chen, J. Chame, M. Hall, and J. K. Hollingsworth. A scalable autotuning framework for compiler optimization. In *Proceedings of the International Parallel and Distributed Processing Symposium*, 2009.

[48] D. Unat, X. Cai, and S. B. Baden. Mint: realizing cuda performance in 3d stencil methods with annotated c. In *Proceedings of the international conference on Supercomputing*, pages 214–224. ACM, 2011.

[49] Y. Voronenko, F. de Mesmay, and M. Püschel. Computer generation of general size linear transform libraries. In *Proceedings of the 7th annual IEEE/ACM International Symposium on Code Generation and Optimization*, pages 102–113. IEEE Computer Society, 2009.

[50] R. Vuduc, J. W. Demmel, and K. A. Yelick. Oski: A library of automatically tuned sparse matrix kernels. In *Journal of Physics: Conference Series*, volume 16, page 521. IOP Publishing, 2005.

[51] R. C. Whaley and J. J. Dongarra. Automatically tuned linear algebra software. In *Proceedings of the 1998 ACM/IEEE conference on Supercomputing*, pages 1–27. IEEE Computer Society, 1998.

[52] S. Williams, A. Waterman, and D. Patterson. Roofline: an insightful visual performance model for multicore architectures. *Communications of the ACM*, 52(4):65–76, 2009.

Parameterized Diamond Tiling for Stencil Computations with Chapel parallel iterators

Ian J. Bertolacci
Colorado State University
Ft. Collins, Colorado
ibertola@cs.colostate.edu

Catherine Olschanowsky
Colorado State University
Ft. Collins, Colorado
cathie@cs.colostate.edu

Ben Harshbarger
Cray Inc.
Seattle, Washington
bharshbarg@cray.com

Bradford L. Chamberlain
Cray Inc.
Seattle, Washington
bradc@cray.com

David G. Wonnacott
Haverford College
Haverford, Pennsylvania
davew@cs.haverford.edu

Michelle Mills Strout
Colorado State University
Ft. Collins, Colorado
mstrout@cs.colostate.edu

ABSTRACT

Stencil computations figure prominently in the core kernels of many scientific computations, such as partial differential equation solvers. Parallel scaling of stencil computations can be significantly improved on multicore processors using advanced tiling techniques that include the time dimension, such as diamond tiling. Such techniques are difficult to include in general purpose optimizing compilers because of the need for inter-procedural pointer and array data-flow analysis, plus the need to tune scheduling strategies and tile size parameters for each pairing of stencil computation and machine.

Since a fully automatic solution is problematic, we propose to provide parameterized space and time tiling iterators through libraries. Ideally, the execution schedule or tiling code will be expressed orthogonally to the computation. This supports code reuse, easier tuning, and improved programmer productivity. Chapel iterators provide this capability implicitly. We present an advanced, parameterized tiling approach that we have implemented using Chapel parallel iterators. We show how such iterators can be used by programmers in stencil computations with multiple spatial dimensions. We also demonstrate that these new iterators provide better scaling than a traditional data parallel schedule.

Categories and Subject Descriptors

D.3.3 [**Language Constructs and Features**]: Control structures; D.3.4 [**Processors**]: Code generation, Optimization

Keywords

stencil computations, diamond tiling, Chapel, parallel iterators, separation of concerns

ICS'15, June 8–11, 2015, Newport Beach, CA, USA.

ACM 978-1-4503-3559-1/15/06 ...$15.00.
http://dx.doi.org/10.1145/2751205.275122.

1. INTRODUCTION

Stencil computations are ubiquitous in scientific simulation applications, often composing the most time-intensive kernels of the application. Advanced optimization techniques, such as *diamond tiling* [1] reduce memory bandwidth pressure, which is crucial to efficient scaling and is becoming more important as memory hierarchies deepen and the bandwidth-to-flops ratio decreases [18]. However, applying complex tiling techniques manually to application code obfuscates the core computational kernels and causes code maintenance issues by complicating the control flow. Additionally, tiling techniques require architecture-specific tile size selection, and the inclusion of such tuning parameters within the primary specification of a computational kernel thwarts performance portability. This work provides solutions to the challenges associated with diamond tiling using a framework that can be extended to other advanced tiling techniques.

Loop tiling [17] changes the execution order of the iterations of a loop nest to improve data locality, which in turn reduces memory bandwidth pressure. Tiling has been shown to improve both single-processor performance and the scalability of performance on parallel systems. Including the time dimension in the tiling takes further advantage of the available locality in stencil operations [14,24,25,30,31]. Diamond tiling further improves performance by allowing work on tiles to begin simultaneously, thus increasing available parallelism.

Most optimizing compilers do not include diamond tiling techniques. Even when a compiler can perform this optimization on a small benchmark, it may fail to do so on a larger code due to program analysis limitations. This leaves application developers no choice but to include such tiling transformations in the primary specification of the computation. This is undesirable for two reasons: (1) The tiling loop structures obfuscate the original stencil computation to the point of making them virtually unrecognizable [21]. (2) The size and shape of the tiles required varies with architecture; including this diminishes portability.

The goal of this work is to enable the quick adoption of novel tiling techniques without obfuscating application code. This is achieved by removing the execution schedule from the primary specification of the computation using Chapel

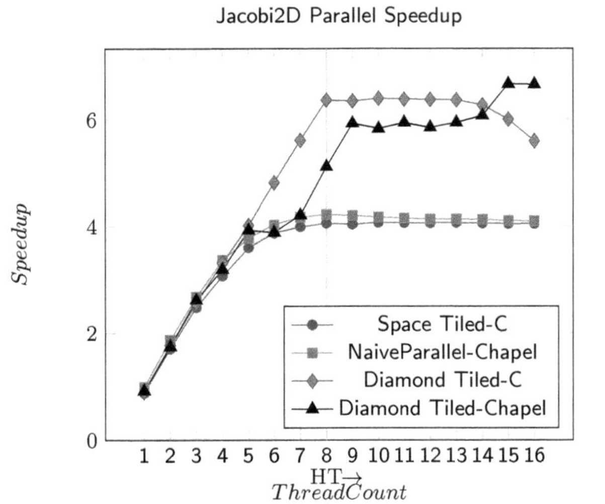

Figure 1: Speedup of the Jacobi2D benchmark with respect to a serial version of space tiling implemented in C+OpenMP. Diamond tiling clearly outperforms the parallel space tiling version, and the version implemented with a parameterized Chapel parallel iterator is competitive with the comparable C+OpenMP version when the number of threads is a multiple of the number of cores.

parallel iterators. The iterator implementation of diamond tiling is parameterized to enable performance tuning.

1.1 Motivation for Parameterizing Tiling

Currently, applying diamond tiling requires manually including the tiling loops in the primary expression of the computation. The source-to-source compiler Pluto [7] can automate diamond tiling in some cases and code generation tools can be used to aid with this process; however, they require tile sizes be specified for non-rectangular tiles [3,23].

Given a fixed tile size, the iteration space that results from diamond tiling is affine. However, adding the parameter size as a variable causes the iteration space to no longer be affine. This is because the tile size is involved in a multiplication determining the bounds of the generated loops. Current code generation tools cannot handle non-affine iteration spaces. Parameterizing the diamond tiling overcomes this challenge, thereby simplifying the development and tuning workflow.

The workflow for applying diamond tiling within a stencil computation currently involves the following steps:

1. develop the code using a standard execution schedule,
2. generate the tiling loops for a best-guess tile size,
3. manually incorporate the generated code,
4. recompile and run a performance test, and
5. improve the tile size guess and return to step 2 until satisfactory performance has been achieved.

By parameterizing the generated code, we remove the repeated manual step, prevent the need for code regeneration and recompilation, and enable auto-tuning using run-time parameters.

1.2 Motivation for Using Iterators

The loop nests necessary for a tiled execution schedule are complex and their direct use within application code leads to code duplication, challenging and error-prone incorporation, and obfuscated application code. Iterators are an increasingly common programming construct that solve these challenges by providing code modularity for the loop nests themselves. Modular code lends itself to reuse, testing, and maintenance.

An additional benefit to this approach is that parameterized iterators provide a level of performance portability. Performance portability means that the code can be optimized for various architectures without changing the primary specification of the calculations. Given that the iterator can be parameterized for tuning parameters, in this case tile size, the parameters can be changed to accommodate varying target architectures.

1.3 Technical Contributions

The technical contributions of this paper include:

- **Parameterizing diamond tiling.** We present a systematic method for creating diamond tiling code that is parameterized for tile size and specific to the tiling hyperplanes.
- **Implementing the parameterized diamond tiling using Chapel parallel iterators.** This separates the expression of the tiling schedule (the loop nest) from the expression of the computation itself (the loop body). We created a proof of concept that shows we can develop libraries of schedules that could be adopted by end-users.

We demonstrate that the parameterized diamond tiling variants perform as well as fixed-size diamond tiling variants, and reproduce results showing that diamond tiling is faster than rectangular space tiling. The Chapel parallel iterators demonstrate competitive performance while providing significant programmability benefits over the C+OpenMP implementations (see Figure 1). The results are discussed in detail in Section 5. Section 7 concludes.

2. BACKGROUND

This work makes practical the use of advanced tiling techniques, specifically diamond tiling, within stencil-based applications. This section provides background about stencil applications in general, the stencil benchmarks used in this work, standard space and time tiling techniques, and diamond tiling.

2.1 Stencil Computations/Benchmarks

A stencil computation is one in which the result, or update to each cell, depends on the values of some set of neighbors. In this paper, we use the Jacobi 1D and 2D benchmarks. These benchmarks are general representations of other Jacobi-like stencils with dependencies through time that are common in applications, such as heat and discrete wave equations. The quintessential Jacobi stencil is the average of a Von Neumann neighborhood of depth 1 over a series of time-steps.

A one-dimensional implementation of Jacobi can be set up to simulate heat dissipation through a theoretical one dimensional rod. In our implementation we set the initial conditions to 0.0 at each end and use a random number generator to assign values at each discreet point within the rod. The "dissipation" is calculated using an average of each point and its direct neighbors. It is not likely that a scientific application will use a Jacobi1D calculation on its own;

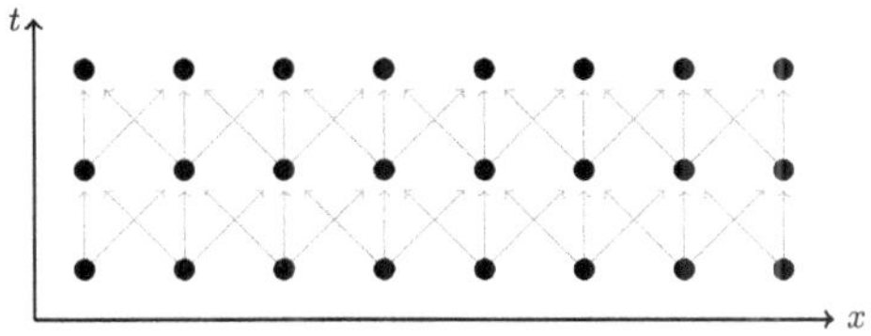

Figure 2: The dataflow pattern resulting from a 1D stencil of depth 1. The vertical axis is time.

however, this is a common case study for temporal tiling approaches.

Figure 2 illustrates the data dependency pattern in the Jacobi1D benchmark. Each cell is updated using the following statement:

```
A[t,i] = ( A[t-1, i-1]
         + A[t-1, i  ]
         + A[t-1, i+1] ) / 3 ;
```

This operation is fully parallel within a time step. In fact a naive parallelization of Jacobi1D surrounds this statement with two loops, an outer time loop, and an inner space loop. An OpenMP statement, or other programming construct for thread-level parallelism, can be used to indicate that the inner loop should be executed in parallel.

The 2D case can be thought of as simulating heat dissipation through a theoretical surface. Each cell in the surface has 4 neighbors (not using diagonal neighbors). The cell update statement is the following:

```
A[t,i,j] = ( A[t-1,i,j-1]
           + A[t-1,i,j+1]
           + A[t-1,i,j  ]
           + A[t-1,i-1,j]
           + A[t-1,i+1,j] ) / 5 ;
```

As with the Jacobi1D operation, within a single time step the loops executing this statement are fully parallel. A naive implementation executes one of the two space dimension loops in parallel. One obvious improvement to this is to collapse the space loops into a single loop and parallelize that. We refer to this as naive parallelization. Given that the problem size falls outside of last-level cache, it benefits performance to apply a simple space-only tiling using rectangular tiles laid over the plane. This implementation is referred to as a naive space tiling variant of the benchmark.

2.2 Rectangular Tiling in Space

Rectangular tiling breaks a large iteration space into a set of smaller iteration spaces [17]. The goal in doing so is to improve spatial and temporal locality. The advantages of this for 2D data are very clear. When iterating over a large 2D dataset applying a 5 point stencil (north, south, east, west, self), it is likely that the north neighbor will be pushed out of cache before the iteration comes around to the point again (this time as self). Breaking the larger iteration space into smaller tiles can prevent that cache miss.

2.3 Diamond Tiling

Diamond tiling [1] is a method of space-time tiling that provides parallelism, including concurrent startup, while maintaining data locality. The original presentation of diamond tiling demonstrated excellent performance and scaling, beating the previous state of the art [6] that required a wavefront startup, and, therefore, had less available parallelism.

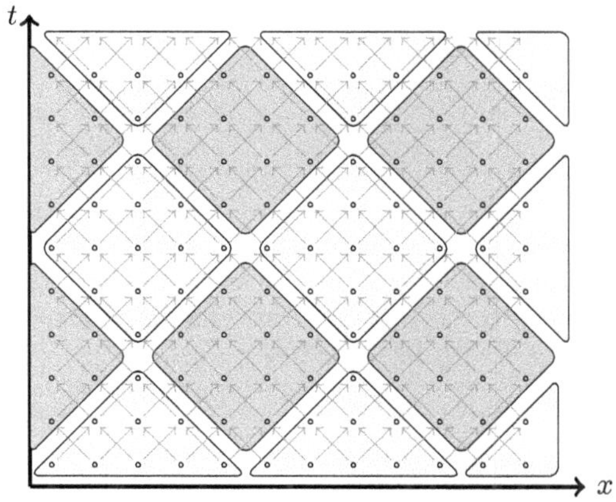

Figure 3: Diamond Tiling with 1D data and time.

Figure 3 shows a possible diamond tiling for a 1D stencil operation across many time steps. The available parallelism comes in wavefronts. The first wavefront of tiles that can be executed concurrently is the set of lower yellow tiles. This is then followed by the first row of blue tiles, the second row of yellow tiles, and so on. The number of tiles that compose the width of the problem domain determines the amount of parallelism available.

The downside of applying diamond tiling to an application is the difficulty of implementation. Diamond tiling code — the loop structures and bounds necessary to execute the schedule — is determined by the slopes and the spacing of the hyperplanes. Without a fixed procedure for creating the code it is time consuming and error-prone (see Figure 4 for a preview of the code complexity).

3. PARAMETERIZED DIAMOND TILING

In this section we describe a method to parameterize any tiling for a given set of tiling hyperplanes assuming a hyperrectangular iteration space. First, we review how tiling hyperplanes are used to specify a tiling schedule and why, if the tile sizes in those schedules are left as parameters, the schedule is non-affine. Non-affine schedules cannot be handled by existing code generators. Then, we describe a tractable process for deriving the loops over the tiles and the loops over iterations within such tiles while keeping the tile size a parameter.

3.1 Tiling Hyperplanes

Tiling hyperplanes determine the shape and, therefore, the iteration space within tiles. Figure 3 illustrates the tiles that result from two sets of hyperplanes: one set of lines with slope -1 and the other set with slope 1. Each set of tiling hyperplanes can be specified by a vector normal to the hyperplanes and the distance between hyperplanes in that set. The normal for the -1 slope hyperplanes in Figure 3 is $(1, 1)$ and for the 1 slope hyperplane is $(-1, 1)$.

Given tiling hyperplanes, it is possible to specify a tiling to a polyhedral code generator with a scattering function. A *scattering function* maps the original iteration space for a loop into a new iteration space. The code generator creates loop code that executes the computations in the new iteration space in lexicographical order.

Assume a d-dimensional rectangular iteration space $\{[i_0, i_1, ..., i_{d-1}] \mid (l_0 \leq i_0 < u_0) \wedge ... \wedge (l_{d-1} \leq i_{d-1} < u_{d-1})\}$.

The scattering function for a d-dimensional tiling with hyperplane normals $\vec{v_0}$, $\vec{v_1}$, ..., $\vec{v}_{d-1}$ is the following:

$$\{[i_0, i_1, ..., i_{d-1}] \rightarrow [k_0, k_1, ..., k_{d-1}, i_0, i_1, ..., i_{d-1}] \mid (k_0 = (\vec{v_0} \cdot \vec{i})/\tau) \wedge ... \wedge (k_{d-1} = (\vec{v_{d-1}} \cdot \vec{i})/\tau)\},$$

where k_0, k_1, ... k_{d-1} are the iterators for the new tile loops and τ is the spacing between hyperplanes for all d sets of tiling hyperplanes[1]. Using the Chinese remainder theorem, we can remove the division by introducing remainders r_0, r_1, ..., r_{d-1} to obtain the following:

$$\{[i_0, i_1, ..., i_{d-1}] \rightarrow [k_0, k_1, ..., k_{d-1}, i_0, i_1, ..., i_{d-1}] \mid \exists r_0, r_1, ..., r_{d-1}, (0 \leq r_0 < \tau) \wedge (\tau k_0 + r_0 = \vec{v_0} \cdot \vec{i}) \wedge ... \wedge (0 \leq r_{d-1} < \tau) \wedge (\tau k_{d-1} + r_{d-1} = \vec{v_{d-1}} \cdot \vec{i})\}.$$

The multiplication of the tile size τ by each of the tile iterators causes the scattering function to be non-affine.

3.2 Plan for Tile Size Parameterization

We could do a symbolic Fourier Motzkin elimination process to obtain the new loop bounds, but that results in an exponential blow-up in loop bounds. All of the extra loop bounds result in more loop overhead.

Approaches already exist to do parametric tilings when the tiles are rectangular. With rectangular tiling, developing a parameterized tiling can be split into two problems: (1) expanding the iteration space so it includes all possible tile origins for a parameterized-sized tile and having the tile loops iterate over these origins, and (2) generating parameterized tile loops that iterate over the points within a tile [16, 22, 23]. This approach of splitting the code generation problem into loops over tiles and then loops within tiles was also used by Goumas et al. [13] to generate code for fixed-sized, non-rectangular tiles. The parametric tiling techniques work with rectangular tiles and any polyhedral iteration space, but leverage the fact that with rectangular tiles the tile boundaries align with the iteration axes (although possibly in the skewed iteration space).

Diamond tilings have hyperplanes that do *not* align with the iteration space axes. It is not possible to skew the iteration space to compensate without introducing holes in the iteration space. However, since we are focused on diamond tilings in the context of stencil computations, we can leverage the fact that the iteration space is rectangular to split the problem into two similar pieces: (1) finding bounds on the tile space (i.e., bounds on the k iterators) and (2) generating parameterized tile loops that iterate over the points within a tile. Our solution to each of the sub-problems is different because the tile iterators k_j are iterating within a separate tile space instead of over the tile origins in the original iteration space.

3.3 Iterating Over Tiles

In the context of diamond tiling, the loops over tiles do not iterate over tile origins as they do in rectangular tiling. Rather, they loop over a separate, parameterized tile space. The parameterized tile loops are found by characterizing a single tile as a parameterized set and then projecting that set on the axes of the original iteration space. A single, representative tile can be characterized by the following set:

$$\{[k_0, k_1, ..., k_{d-1}, i_0, i_1, ..., i_{d-1}] \mid \exists r_0, r_1, ..., r_{d-1}, (0 \leq r_0 < \tau) \wedge (\tau k_0 + r_0 = \vec{v_0} \cdot \vec{i}) \wedge ... \wedge (0 \leq r_{d-1} < \tau) \wedge (\tau k_{d-1} + r_{d-1} = \vec{v_{d-1}} \cdot \vec{i})\}.$$

To determine the bounds on the tile iterators k_0, k_1, ..., k_{d-1}, we project the single tile, which is parameterized by tile size, on each of the canonical axes of the rectangular iteration space, i_0, i_1, ..., i_{d-1}. With the projection, we will have the min and max values for each tile on each axis. Then we can make sure that if even one point of the tile is in the iteration space, the tile is visited. The tile's lower bounds are inclusive, and therefore anytime the projected tile lower bound is less than or equal to the iteration space upper bound, the tile contains at least one iteration point that is in the iteration space.

It is possible to compute the lower and upper bounds for a single tile (i.e., setting all k_j values to 1) projected on each axis with a code generator as was done in ISCC [27], but the loop bounds generated are inclusive. We did the projection by hand to determine the real number of intersection points on the axes. We did the projection for stencils with depth 1 in two-dimensional and three-dimensional iteration spaces for use with Jacobi1D and Jacobi2D, but here we show the results for the three-dimensional iteration spaces.

For the three-dimensional diamond tiling for Jacobi2D, the hyperplanes are $v_0 = (1, 1, 0)$, $v_1 = (1, 0, 1)$, and $v_2 = (1, -1, -1)$. Given this set of hyperplanes the iteration space within a tile is defined as shown in Equation 1.

$$\begin{aligned}\{[t, i, j] \mid \exists r_0, r_1, r_2,\ & (0 \leq r_0 < \tau) \wedge (0 \leq r_1 < \tau) \wedge (0 \leq r_2 < \tau) \\ & \wedge\ k_0\tau + r_0 = t + i \\ & \wedge\ k_1\tau + r_1 = t + j \\ & \wedge\ k_2\tau + r_2 = t - i - j\}\end{aligned} \quad (1)$$

Here are the projections of the parameterized tile on the axes:

$$\begin{aligned}(k_0 + k_1 + k_2)\tau/3 \leq\ & t < (3 + k_0 + k_1 + k_2)\tau/3 \\ (2k_0 - k_1 - k_2 - 2)\tau/3 <\ & i < (2 + 2k_0 - k_1 - k_2)\tau/3 \\ (2k_1 - k_0 - k_2 - 2)\tau/3 <\ & j < (2 + 2k_1 - k_0 - k_2)\tau/3\end{aligned}$$

To find the bounds for the tile-iterator loops k_0, k_1, and k_2, we substitute the (unique) upper (or lower) bound on each dimension of the iteration space for the corresponding iteration space variable. For example, to be sure to visit every tile whose minimum t value is below the upper bound of the iteration space (T), we substitute T for t in the above lower bound on t, producing the upper bound on k_0 of $(k_0 + k_1 + k_2)\tau/3 \leq T$. Substituting 1 for t in the upper bound on t gives $(3 + k_0 + k_1 + k_2)\tau/3 > 1$. Continuing this process for i and j, we produce the following set of constraints for the tile iterators:

$$\begin{aligned}\{[k_0, k_1, k_2] \mid\ & (3 + k_0 + k_1 + k_2)\tau/3 > 1 \wedge (k_0 + k_1 + k_2)\tau/3 \leq T \\ & \wedge (2 + 2k_0 - k_1 - k_2)\tau/3 > L_i \\ & \wedge (2k_0 - k_1 - k_2 - 2)\tau/3 < U_i \\ & \wedge (2 + 2k_1 - k_0 - k_2)\tau/3 > L_j \\ & \wedge (2k_1 - k_0 - k_2 - 2)\tau/3 < U_j\}\end{aligned}$$

[1] Using different spacing per set of hyperplanes would be more general, but results in less regular parallel wavefronts of diamond tiles and causes the parameterization to be more complex.

```
// Loop over tile wavefronts.
for (kt=ceild(3,tau)-3; kt<=floord(3*T,tau); kt++) {

  // The next two loops iterate within a tile wavefront.
  int k1_lb = ceild(3*Lj+2+(kt-2)*tau,tau*3);
  int k1_ub = floord(3*Uj+(kt+2)*tau,tau*3);
  int k2_lb = floord((2*kt-2)*tau-3*Ui+2,tau*3);
  int k2_ub = floord((2+2*kt)*tau-3*Li-2,tau*3);

  //Loops over tile coordinates within a parallel wavefront of tiles.
  #pragma omp parallel for ...
  for (k1 = k1_lb; k1 <= k1_ub; k1++) {
    for (x = k2_lb; x <= k2_ub; x++) {
      k2 = x - k1;  // Removing k1 term from k2 upper and lower bounds enables collapse(2).

      // Loop over time within a tile.
      for (t =  max(1, floord(kt*tau-1, 3)); t < min(T+1, tau + floord(kt*tau, 3)); t++) {
        write = t & 1; // equivalent to t mod 2
        read = 1 - write;

        // Loops over the spatial dimensions within each tile.
        for (i =  max(Li,max((kt-k1-k2)*tau-t, 2*t-(2+k1+k2)*tau+2));
             i <= min(Ui,min((1+kt-k1-k2)*tau-t-1, 2*t-(k1+k2)*tau)); i++) {
          for (j =  max(Lj,max(tau*k1-t, t-i-(1+k2)*tau+1));
               j <= min(Uj,min((1+k1)*tau-t-1, t-i-k2*tau)); j++) {
                 A[write][x][y] = (A[read][x-1][y] + A[read][x][y-1] + ... ;
} } } } } }
```

Figure 4: Parameterized diamond tiled code for any 2D stencil of depth 1 that uses values from the previous time step only (Jacobi-like data dependencies). Note that the floord function computes the integer quotient of its operands, like C's % operation, but unlike C's % rounds any fractional part toward negative infinity rather than zero [28].

To create wavefronts of tiles that can be executed in parallel, we introduce a new tile space iterator $k_t = k_0 + k_1 + k_2$, by solving for k_0 and replacing all of the k_0s in the above bounds with $k_t - k_1 - k_2$. We then determine the bounds for the k_t, k_1, and k_2 loops to be the following:

$$\begin{aligned}
&\{[k_t, k_1, k_2] \mid k_t > 3/\tau - 3 \wedge k_t \leq 3T/\tau \\
&\wedge\ 3k_1 > (3L_j/\tau) + k_t - 2 \\
&\wedge\ 3k_1 < (3U_j/\tau) + k_t + 2 \\
&\wedge\ 3k_2 > 2k_t - 3k_1 - 2 - (3U_i/\tau)) \\
&\wedge\ 3k_2 < 2k_t - 3k_1 + 2 - (3L_i/\tau)\},
\end{aligned}$$

which can be implemented with the outer three loops shown in Figure 4.

3.4 Iterating within a Diamond Tile

After determining the loop bounds for the tile loops, the next step is to determine the bounds for the loops that iterate over points within each tile. We start with the set that specifies a single tile (see Equation 1). Then we do the wavefront substitution $k_0 = k_t - k_1 - k_2$.

The resulting loop bounds are not affine because of the multiplication of two parameters in three of the constraints: $k_0\tau$, $k_1\tau$, and $k_2\tau$. To enable code generation with ISCC, we perform a substitution. Let $x_t = k_t\tau$, $x_1 = k_1\tau$, and $x_2 = k_2\tau$. This is legal because the tuple (k_t, k_1, k_2) is constant. The resulting loop bounds over points within a tile for the three-dimensional diamond tiling of Jacobi2D are shown in Figure 4.

In summary, we can apply the tile size parameterization process to any set of tiling hyperplanes (diamond or otherwise). Therefore, other stencils that require different diamond tiling hyperplanes can also benefit from this process.

4. PROVIDING TILING IN A LIBRARY

Due to the complexity of the diamond tiling loop structure it is desirable to abstract it away from the primary specification of the algorithm. We do this by implementing the diamond tiling code within a Chapel parallel iterator. This section provides a brief overview of the Chapel language and information about our implementation.

4.1 Chapel Parallel Iterators

We use Chapel parallel iterators to explore the viability of providing advanced tiling schedules as a module. Chapel is an open-source language currently in development at Cray Inc.[2] which is designed to simplify parallel programming for the desktop and at scale via various language features [10, 11]. It represents a growing movement to design languages and compilers that abstract away the complexity of developing highly parallel programs. Sample features include: *forall loops* and a rich set of domains and arrays for data parallel computations; support for task-based concurrent programming including data-centric coordination between tasks via atomic variables and *sync variables* with full-empty semantics; and *locales* as a first-class language concept for reasoning about architectural locality. Chapel follows a *multiresolution philosophy* in which users can control low-level details like parallel loop schedules or array layout and distribution while making them available to others via high-level abstractions.

As part of its productivity-oriented features, Chapel sup-

[2]http://chapel.cray.com

```
iter DiamondTileIterator( L: int, U: int, T: int, tau: int,
                          param tag: iterKind): 4*int
                          where tag == iterKind.standalone {
  // Loop over tile wavefronts.
  for kt in ceild(3,tau) .. floord(3*T,tau) {

    // The next two loops iterate within a tile wavefront.  Assumes a square iteration space.
    var k1_lb: int = floord(3*L+2+(kt-2)*tau, tau*3);
    var k1_ub: int = floord(3*U+(kt+2)*tau-2, tau*3);
    var k2_lb: int = floord((2*kt-2)*tau-3*U+2, tau*3);
    var k2_ub: int = floord((2+2*kt)*tau-3*L-2, tau*3);

    // Loops over tile coordinates within a parallel wavefront of tiles.
    forall k1 in k1_lb .. k1_ub {
      for x in k2_lb .. k2_ub {
        var k2 = x-k1;

        // Loop over time within a tile.
        for t in max(1,floord(kt*tau,3)) .. min(T,floord((3+kt)*tau-3,3)){
          write = t & 1; // equivalent to t mod 2
          read = 1 - write;

          // Loops over the spatial dimensions within each tile.
          for i in max(L,max((kt-k1-k2)*tau-t, 2*t-(2+k1+k2)*tau+2))
                .. min(U,min((1+kt-k1-k2)*tau-t-1, 2*t-(k1+k2)*tau)) {
            for j in max(L,max(tau*k1-t,t-i-(1+k2)*tau+1))
                .. min(U,min((1+k1)*tau-t-1,t-i-k2*tau)){
              yield (read, write, i, j);
  } } } } } } }
```

Figure 5: 2D Diamond Tile Parallel Iterator in Chapel

ports *iterators* [9], inspired by those of the CLU language [19]. An iterator is a function that *yields* values back to its callsite and then continues executing rather than simply returning a single value per call like traditional functions. In this way, iterators can be used to drive loops, or to specify the elements defining a collection. Just as traditional functions can be used to parameterize common idioms and factor them away from straight-line code, iterators can provide similar software engineering benefits for loops and loop nests, improving code reuse and readability.

This effort makes use of Chapel's multiresolution philosophy by specifying complex loop schedules using the language's features for parallel iterators and then invoking them via high-level data parallel forall loops. In this way, the details of tile specification and scheduling can be factored away from the parallel stencil computation loops themselves, making it easier for application programmers to focus on their computations without tripping over the details of tiling specification and programming.

```
forall (read, write, x ,y)
       in DiamondTileIterator(L, U, T, tau) {

  A[write, x, y] =
      (A[read,x-1,y] + A[read,x,y-1] +
       A[read,x   ,y] + A[read,x,y+1] +
       A[read,x+1,y]) / 5;
}
```

Figure 6: Use of the diamond tiling iterator. Contrast the programmabilty of this with that of Figure 4.

4.2 Iterator Implementation

Figure 5 shows the iterator code for the 2D diamond tile iterator. Inside the body of the iterator, the code is much like the diamond-tiled code in C shown in Figure 4. Translation simply consists of the modification of variable declarations, the transformation from C loop bounds to range iterations, and the replacement of stencil calls with the *yield* statement. Parallel *forall* loops take the place of loops with OpenMP pragmas.

Figure 6 illustrates an invocation of the iterator. Using the diamond tile iterator written in Chapel code is simple. Most importantly, the computation specification is much cleaner than if the diamond tiling iterator code were inlined in the loop nest itself.

Consider a program that has a dozen invocations of one of these stencil loops with slight variations in the stencil computation. In the Chapel program, this amounts to 12 of these clean loop nests, potentially passing in different parameters such as tile size at each callsite. But in a language like C, C++, or Fortran, there is no good option for abstracting such parallel loop nests away from their uses. While one can create serial iterators via classes/structs and support begin()/next()/end()-style methods/functions on them, there is no clean way to abstract the OpenMP-parallelized loops into such methods and functions. One could create a helper function representing the loop nest and pass a function pointer representing the loop body into it, but this would result in a very expensive loop body without optimizations to inline the function pointer and specialize the loop nest function for each callsite. Alternatively, one could use something outside the language like pre-processor macro expansion to create the loop nests, but this is less robust than supporting parallel iterators in the language directly.

5. EXPERIMENTAL RESULTS

Our experimental results demonstrate that the parameterized, diamond-tiled code has *better* performance than code generated for specific tile sizes, and that using Chapel parallel iterators does not result in any appreciable overhead when compared with C+OpenMP code. Additionally, we reproduce results demonstrating the positive performance impact of diamond tiling on Jacobi 1D and 2D benchmarks. We focus on intranode parallelism, specifically leveraging the on-chip cache hierarchy, because stencil computations do not scale well at small core counts due to their memory bandwidth demands.

In this section we also present our methods for selecting tile sizes and a comparison of diamond tiling to spatial tiling in the context of Jacobi2D.

5.1 Experimental Setup

Hardware: Experiments were run on a 2.60GHz Intel Xeon E5-2650 v2 workstation. This machine has a single NUMA domain, one socket containing 8 cores (16 Hyper-Threads). Each core has its own 32K L1 data cache and 256K L2 cache. The L3 cache is 20Mb and shared among all cores. The memory is 32Gb.

Problem Size: We tested all benchmarks with problem sizes that exceeded L3 cache. The Jacobi1D problem size (N=5242880, footprint=2*N*sizeof(double)) is 2 times the size of L3. The Jacobi2D problem size (N=4096 X 4096) is 12.8 times the size of L3. Each benchmark ran 100 time steps.

Compilers: GCC (version 4.8.3) was used to compile all the C+OpenMP benchmarks, as well as the back-end for compiling the Chapel compiler. The Chapel compiler itself (version 1.11) was retrieved from the public download page maintained by Cray and the Chapel team[3].

Compiler Options: When building the serial C and C+OpenMP benchmarks the `-O3` flag was used to optimize. Chapel builds used the flags `-sassertNoSlicing`, which disables unnecessary array striding calculations, and `--fast`, which removes run-time safety checks and compiles generated C code with the `-O3` flag.

Baseline for Speedup: All speedup measurements are relative to a serial C version of the same stencil.

5.2 Tiling Methods Comparison

The diamond tiling variants of the code outperformed the naive parallel for both Jacobi1D and Jacobi2D. The naive parallel variant for Jacobi1D was parallelized with an OpenMP statement around the spatial loop using the default static schedule. Figure 7 shows that the naive parallel implementation stops effectively scaling at 4 threads even though this version tiles the spatial loops. The diamond tiling variant uses a dynamic schedule with the default chunk size being one row of tiles. Jacobi2D when diamond tiled maintains nearly linear speedup out to 8 cores.

5.3 Fixed Verses Parameterized Tile Size Performance

A key requirement for success with parameterized diamond tiling is that the parameterization does not result in a negative performance impact. Our experiments confirm that it does not. To measure this impact we generated a sampling of tile-size-specific variants of the code for a selection of tile sizes for Jacobi2D. The code was generated using the ISCC code generator [27], which is used as the code generator for Pluto [7], PoCC[4], and Polly [15]. Figure 8 shows a comparison of the execution times for the equivalent parameterized tiling runs. We use a tile size of $\tau = 276$ for both of the Jacobi2D diamond tiling variants in Figure 1.

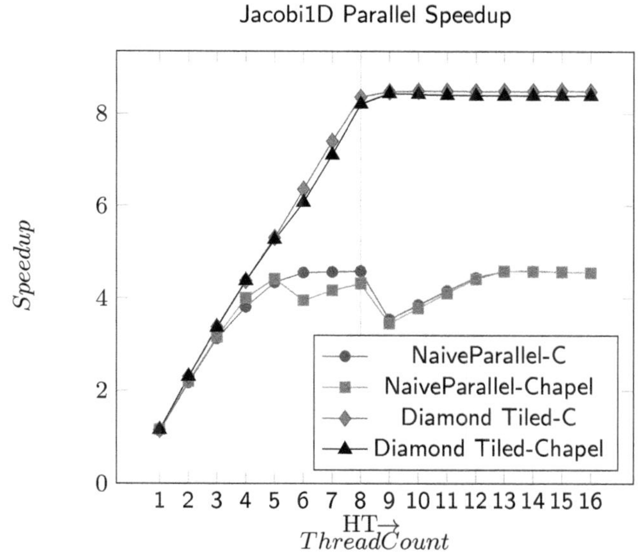

Figure 7: Speedup of Jacobi1D.

5.4 Chapel versus C Performance

There are two primary comparisons to make with respect to Chapel performance. First, the performance differences when using naive parallel scheduling techniques, and, second, the differences when using diamond tiling. In both cases Chapel's performance is competitive with C+OpenMP's.

A consistent performance variation was observed in the Chapel executions. For specific thread counts, 5-12 for diamond tiling and 5-8 for naive parallel, repeated execution revealed a multimodal distribution. This variation occurred only within the Chapel executions and for both the dynamic and static parallel schedules. The execution times in the fastest mode of the distribution were on-par or faster than the execution times of C+OpenMP. The Chapel team believes this to be due to a race in how Chapel tasks are assigned to cores resulting in an occasional load imbalance. The Chapel development team plans to address this in a future release. All times reported here are the average of all execution times, each test was repeated 32 times.

The lower two lines of data in Figure 7 show that for the Jacobi1D benchmark Chapel matches the performances of C+OpenMP except in the 5-8 thread region. Both of these implementations use a naive parallelization. Figure 1 shows the same for the Jacobi2D benchmark. In this case it is notable that the naive implementation of Chapel is outperforming the space-tiled variant of C+OpenMP. This can be attributed to the parallel schedule used by Chapel. The performance of the Chapel variants using diamond tiling is also competitive with that of the C+OpenMP variants except for the aforementioned issue in the 5-12 thread range.

[3]`https://github.com/chapel-lang/chapel`

[4]`http://www.cs.ucla.edu/~pouchet/software/pocc/`

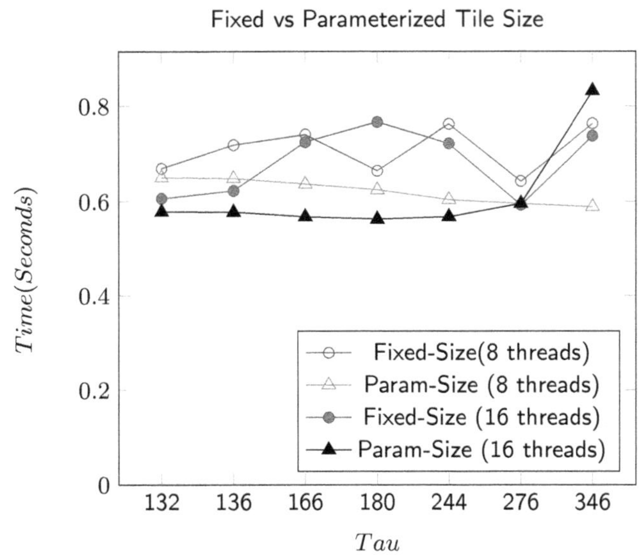

Figure 8: Fixed vs parameterized tile size performance comparison in C+OpenMP

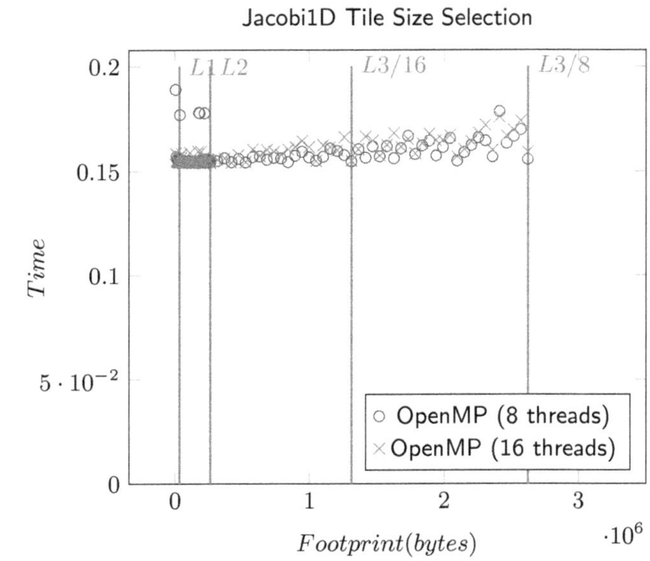

Figure 9: Tile size selection done with a sweep of tile sizes Jacobi1D.

5.5 Tile Size Selection

Tile size selection is an important factor in the performance of all tiling methods. If a tile size is too big it will fall out of cache or push another thread's tile out of cache, and if a tile is too small it will create unnecessary loop overhead and will exhibit poor cache reuse. The optimal tile size was found using an exhaustive search over the span of reasonable tile widths. The tile width is expressed as τ. The reasonable range of τ was determined by using a footprint calculation and targeting each level of cache.

The memory footprints were determined by using the single tile description for two- and three-dimensional parameterized diamond tiles and projecting them onto the spatial dimensions of the computation and using ISCC [27] to compute the cardinality of the set as a function of the tile size τ. The memory footprint in bytes of a diamond tile in 1D is

$$footprint = (\tau \cdot 2 - 1) \cdot (2) \cdot \texttt{sizeof(type)} \qquad (2)$$

In 2D, the footprint is

$$footprint = (\tau^2 - \tau - 1) \cdot (2) \cdot \texttt{sizeof(type)} \qquad (3)$$

The Jacobi benchmarks store only the previous and current time steps. Thus the multiplication by 2.

We expect that under normal operating conditions (i.e. one task/thread per processing unit with no thread migration) that the entire memory projection of a tile (maximum spatial bounds on the tile) will not be evicted from last-level cache until that tile is completely finished.

Figures 9 and 10 show execution time versus tile footprint for the Jacobi 1D and 2D benchmarks respectively. The vertical lines represent cache occupancy for L1 and L2 with no hyper-threading and then for L3 being shared among 8 threads and 16 threads. For Jacobi1D the optimal point lies just beyond L1 occupancy with a τ value of 4259. The optimal point for Jacobi2D fell within L3 (τ=276).

6. RELATED WORK

Our work extends current practice with both run-time parametrization of diamond tiling [1], and a novel approach to expressing this tiling with a Chapel parallel iterator. Related work includes various approaches to tiling through time, other work that uses iterators/generators, and previous work that has hand-tuned stencil computations in Chapel.

6.1 Tiling through Time

Loop tiling and more specifically tiling through time is a long-standing technique [17]. As it has increased in importance due to recent architecture trends, a number of variants have been explored; Wonnacott and Strout provide a description of many [31].

The recent development of diamond tiling for multi-dimensional data sets by Bandishti et al. [1] combines (we believe, for the first time) asymptotic scalability, high performance even on relatively small numbers of processors, and full implementation in the polyhedral infrastructure that underlies many automatic optimization tools such as Pluto [31]. However, the work of Bandishti et al. requires the tile size to be known at compile time. Prior work on parameterized tiling [23] has been limited to semi-oblique parallelepiped tilings, and thus is not applicable to multi-dimensional diamond tiles. We have developed a parameterized version of this tiling for the 2D Jacobi stencil, and expressed this tiling in both OpenMP and as an iterator for the Chapel language. The former provides a basis for performance comparison with other OpenMP tilings, and the latter provides a clean mechanism to give programmers control of iteration-space tiling.

6.2 Iterator Programming Constructs

Chapel's iterators are quite similar to both Python's *generator functions* [26] and the *iterator functions* of C# and Visual Basic [20, 29]. Being a parallel language, Chapel expands upon conventional approaches by adding the ability to specify iterators that can drive data parallel computations such as *forall loops*. This is done by specifying *standalone* or *leader-follower iterators* [12] which support parallel loops over multiple iterators in a simultaneous—or *zippered*—manner, similar to the NESL language [4, 5].

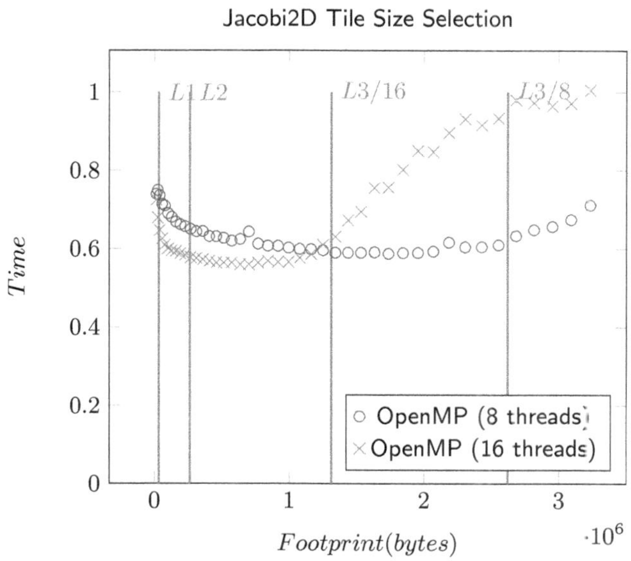

Figure 10: Tile size selection done with a sweep of tile sizes Jacobi2D.

However, in NESL zippered iterations were only supported by the compiler for a small number of built-in data types, whereas in Chapel users have the ability to author their own parallel zippered iterators.

6.3 Stencil Computations in Chapel

In Chapel's formative years, Barrett *et al.* studied different ways of expressing stencil computations in Chapel, with the eventual goal of being able to express the *sweep3d* benchmark in Chapel [2]. At this point in Chapel's history, its compiler was only just starting to generate parallel code, preventing the study from performing compelling performance studies. More recently, in [8], variants of a stencil computation were implemented in Chapel to determine which idioms generated the best performance compared to conventional programming models. Our work differs from this effort in that it studies tiling across time and space and considers the programmability benefits of using parallel iterators to factor complex loop structures away from the stencil computations themselves.

7. CONCLUSIONS

Diamond tiling is an advanced scheduling method that results in improved cache reuse and a high degree of concurrency. However, its adoption is hindered by its complexity and fixed tile-size code generation constraints. We have presented a method of generating parameterized diamond tiling and implemented it in benchmarks, showing that diamond tiling outperforms naive schedules that are simpler to develop and maintain. Additionally, we have shown that these schedules can be implemented in the Chapel language to take advantage of the parallel iterator construct and that performance is competitive with that of C+OpenMP.

We have also demonstrated that Chapel parallel iterators are an effective way to simplify the development process of stencil computations and increase the adoption of better schedules. Typically, the development of the stencil computation and the development of the iteration schedule are intertwined, although they have little to do with each other. This requires that both stencil computation and iteration schedule be modified together through the application's lifetime, impeding improvements to performance. The use of Chapel parallel iterators allows for separate development of each, creating a more agile development process. The addition of a new tiling schedule only requires that the schedule yield the appropriate values, and that new stencil codes can reuse existing high performance schedules.

The growth of high-performance computing into the Exascale era, and the creation of scientific applications requiring such computing power, poses many challenges. Among them, Exascale applications may require further advances in scheduling methods, and developers will benefit from ways to explore new schedules, or adopt those of other codes, without interfering with other aspects of their application. We have demonstrated that this separation of application code and high-performance scheduling can be achieved via Chapel iterators.

8. ACKNOWLEDGMENTS

This project is supported by a Department of Energy Early Career Grant DE-SC0003956 and a National Science Foundation Grant CCF-1422725. We thank our anonymous reviewers and Andrew Lumsdaine for their many useful suggestions for improving the paper, and Wayne Trzyna for providing us dedicated computation time.

9. REFERENCES

[1] V. Bandishti, I. Pananilath, and U. Bondhugula. Tiling stencil computations to maximize parallelism. In *Proceedings of the International Conference for High Performance Computing, Networking, Storage, and Analysis (SC)*, 2012.

[2] R. Barrett, P. Roth, and S. Poole. Finite difference stencils implemented using chapel. Technical Report TM-2007/119, Oak Ridge National Laboratory, 2007.

[3] M. M. Baskaran, A. Hartono, S. Tavarageri, T. Henretty, J. Ramanujam, and P. Sadayappan. Parameterized Tiling Revisited. In *Proceedings of the 8th Annual IEEE/ACM International Symposium on Code Generation and Optimization*, CGO '10, pages 200–209, New York, NY, USA, 2010. ACM.

[4] G. Blelloch, S. Chatterjee, J. Hardwick, J. Sipelstein, and M. Zagha. Implementation of a portable nested data-parallel language. *Journal of Parallel and Distributed Computing*, 21(1):102–111, April 1994.

[5] G. E. Blelloch. NESL: A nested data-parallel language (version 3.1). Technical Report CMU-CS-95-170, Carnegie Mellon, Pittsburgh, PA, September 1995.

[6] U. Bondhugula, M. Baskaran, S. Krishnamoorthy, J. Ramanujam, A. Rountev, and P. Sadayappan. Automatic transformations for communication-minimized parallelization and locality optimization in the polyhedral model. In L. Hendren, editor, *Compiler Construction*, volume 4959 of *Lecture Notes in Computer Science*, pages 132–146. Springer Berlin Heidelberg, 2008.

[7] U. Bondhugula, A. Hartono, J. Ramanujam, and P. Sadayappan. A practical automatic polyhedral program optimization system. In *Proceedings of the ACM SIGPLAN Conference on Programming*

Language Design and Implementation (PLDI), New York, NY, USA, June 2008. ACM.

[8] H. Burkhart, M. Sathe, M. Christen, O. Schenk, and M. Rietmann. Run, stencil, run! HPC productivity studies in the classroom. In *PGAS*, 2012.

[9] B. Chamberlain. Chapel parallel iterators: Giving programmers productivity and control. Cray Inc. blog, September 2013.

[10] B. L. Chamberlain. Chapel. In P. Balaji, editor, *A Brief Overview of Parallel Programming Models*. MIT Press, 2015 (expected).

[11] B. L. Chamberlain, D. Callahan, and H. P. Zima. Parallel programmability and the Chapel language. *International Journal of High Performance Computing Applicati ons*, 21(3):291–312, August 2007.

[12] B. L. Chamberlain, S.-E. Choi, S. J. Deitzand, and A. Navarro. User-defined parallel zippered iterators in chapel. In *Fifth Conference on Partitioned Global Address Space Programming Models (PGAS 2011)*, Galveston Island, TX, USA, October 2011.

[13] G. Goumas, M. Athanasaki, and N. Koziris. An efficient code generation technique for tiled iteration spaces. *IEEE Transactions on Parallel and Distributed Systems*, 14(10), October 2003.

[14] T. Grosser, A. Cohen, J. Holewinski, P. Sadayappan, and S. Verdoolaege. Hybrid hexagonal/classical tiling for GPUs. In *Proceedings of Annual IEEE/ACM International Symposium on Code Generation and Optimization*, CGO '14, pages 66:66–66:75, New York, NY, USA, 2014. ACM.

[15] T. Grosser, A. Groesslinger, and C. Lengauer. Polly - performing polyhedral optimizations on a low-level intermediate representation. *Parallel Processing Letters*, 22(04):1250010, 2012.

[16] A. Hartono, M. M. Baskaran, C. Bastoul, A. Cohen, S. Krishnamoorth, B. Norris, J. Ramanujam, and P. Sadayappan. PrimeTile: A parametric multi-level tiler for imperfect loop nests. In *Prioceedings of the 23rd International Conference on Supercomputing, June 8-12, 2009, IBM T. J. Watson Research Center, Yorktown Heights, NY, USA*, 2009.

[17] F. Irigoin and R. Triolet. Supernode partitioning. In *Conference Record of the Fifteenth ACM Symposium on Principles of Programming Languages*, pages 319–329, 1988.

[18] P. Kogge and D. Resnick. Yearly update: Exascale projections for 2013. Technical Report SAND2013-9229, Sandia National Laboratories, 2013.

[19] B. Liskov, A. Snyder, R. Atkinson, and C. Schaffert. Abstraction mechanisms in CLU. *Communications of the ACM*, 20(8):564–576, August 1977.

[20] Microsoft Corporation. *C# Language Specification*, version 5.0 edition, June 2013.

[21] C. Olschanowsky, S. Guzik, J. Loffeld, J. Hittinger, and M. M. Strout. A study on balancing parallelism, data locality, and recomputation in existing PDE solvers. In *The IEEE/ACM International Conference for High Performance Computing, Networking, Storage and Analysis (SC)*, November 2014.

[22] L. Renganarayana, D. Kim, M. M. Strout, and S. Rajopadhye. Parameterized loop tiling. *Transactions on Programming Languages and Systems (TOPLAS)*, 34(1), May 2012.

[23] L. Renganarayanan, D. Kim, S. Rajopadhye, and M. M. Strout. Parameterized tiled loops for free. In *Proceedings of the ACM SIGPLAN Conference on Programming Language Design and Implementation (PLDI)*, June 2007.

[24] Y. Song and Z. Li. New tiling techniques to improve cache temporal locality. In *ACM SIGPLAN '99 Conference on Programming Language Design and Implementation*, pages 215–228, May 1999.

[25] R. Strzodka, M. Shaheen, and D. Pajak. Time skewing made simple. In *PPOPP*, pages 295–296, 2011.

[26] G. van Rossum and P. J. Eby. Coroutines via enhanced generators, May 2005.

[27] S. Verdoolaege. Isl: An integer set library for the polyhedral model. In *Proceedings of the Third International Congress Conference on Mathematical Software*, ICMS'10, pages 299–302, Berlin, Heidelberg, 2010. Springer-Verlag.

[28] S. Verdoolaege and T. Grosser. Polyhedral extraction tool. In *Second International Workshop on Polyhedral Compilation Techniques (IMPACT12), Paris, France*, 2012.

[29] P. Vick and L. Wischik. *The Microsoft® Visual Basic® Language Specification*. Microsoft Corporation, version 11.0 edition, June 2013.

[30] D. Wonnacott. Achieving scalable locality with Time Skewing. *International Journal of Parallel Programming*, 30(3):181–221, June 2002.

[31] D. G. Wonnacott and M. M. Strout. On the scalability of loop tiling techniques. In *Proceedings of the 3rd International Workshop on Polyhedral Compilation Techniques (IMPACT)*, January 2013.

Quantifying Performance Bottlenecks of Stencil Computations Using the Execution-Cache-Memory Model

Holger Stengel Jan Treibig Georg Hager Gerhard Wellein
Erlangen Regional Computing Center (RRZE)
Friedrich-Alexander University of Erlangen-Nuremberg
Erlangen, Germany
{holger.stengel,jan.treibig,georg.hager,gerhard.wellein}@fau.de

ABSTRACT

Stencil algorithms on regular lattices appear in many fields of computational science, and much effort has been put into optimized implementations. Such activities are usually not guided by performance models that provide estimates of expected speedup. Understanding the performance properties and bottlenecks by performance modeling enables a clear view on promising optimization opportunities. In this work we refine the recently developed Execution-Cache-Memory (ECM) model and use it to quantify the performance bottlenecks of stencil algorithms on a contemporary Intel processor. This includes applying the model to arrive at single-core performance and scalability predictions for typical "corner case" stencil loop kernels. Guided by the ECM model we accurately quantify the significance of "layer conditions," which are required to estimate the data traffic through the memory hierarchy, and study the impact of typical optimization approaches such as spatial blocking, strength reduction, and temporal blocking for their expected benefits. We also compare the ECM model to the widely known Roofline model.

Keywords

stencils; performance model; optimization; multicore

1. INTRODUCTION AND RELATED WORK

Stencil computations on regular lattices are important in many computational science applications operating on regular lattices. The combination of low computational intensity and their iterative nature have made them a popular target for loop optimizations. Beyond established cache blocking techniques, leveraging SIMD capabilities [1] and an efficient shared memory parallelization [2] are subject to recent research. An overview about the state of the art in stencil optimizations can be found in a review by Datta et al. [3].

In the compiler community modeling approaches based on cache usage have been employed for stencil optimizations more than a decade ago [4]. Modeling was also used to estimate the optimal performance of stencil codes and to validate the effectiveness of applied optimizations. One can roughly separate those efforts into two categories: "black box" modeling, which relies on statistical methods and machine learning to describe and predict performance behavior based on observed data such as hardware performance metrics [5], and "white box" modeling, which uses simplified machine models to describe the interaction of code with the hardware from "first principles." Simple bottleneck-centric approaches based on memory bandwidth vs. computational peak performance have been in use for a long time [6, 7]. This line of thinking was popularized and refined by Williams et al. [8], and is now known as the "Roofline model." The Roofline model is tremendously useful in getting first estimates of the "light speed" of a loop on a given architecture. Its central assumption is that data transfers through the memory hierarchy overlap with code execution on the core(s). This implies that data access latencies are assumed to be hidden by prefetching mechanisms. However, the Roofline model cannot describe relevant bottlenecks beyond memory bandwidth and peak performance. Especially in long-range stencils common in seismic imaging there is no single dominating bottleneck anymore and the influence of in-cache transfers on performance is significant. The recently introduced ECM model provides an accurate single-core performance and scaling prediction. It can be seen as an extension and refinement of the Roofline model for multicore processors. Like the Roofline model it focuses on resource utilization but considers contributions from the complete memory hierarchy. The ECM model was first introduced in [2] and later refined and combined with a multicore power model in [9]. It provides clear insights into the relevant contributions of the hardware model to the performance of a given loop code and therefore allows a clear identification of optimization opportunities. Based on the single-core performance estimate it also predicts a performance saturation point. This paper refines the ECM model with clear rules for overlapping execution and data transfers and introduces an accessible notation to ease the usage and description of the model. The power of the model to validate and guide performance engineering efforts is demonstrated on the example of three relevant stencil code patterns.

The paper is structured as follows. In Sect. 2 we describe the architecture of the test machine used for measurements. Section 3 introduces and refines the ECM model on the example of simple streaming loop kernels. In Sections 4, 5, and 6 we apply the model to successively more complex stencils to show how it can identify bottlenecks, reveal optimization opportunities, and prevent misleading conclusions. The paper concludes in Sect. 7.

2. EXPERIMENTAL TESTBED

Unless noted otherwise, a standard two-socket server based on eight-core SandyBridge-EP (SNB) CPUs was used for the measurements. The core supports SSE and AVX SIMD instruction set

ICS'15, June 8–11, 2015, Newport Beach, CA, USA.

http://dx.doi.org/10.1145/2751205.2751240.

Microarchitecture	Intel SandyBridge-EP [10]
Model	Xeon E5-2680
Clock speed (fixed)	2.7 GHz
Cores/Threads	8/16
SIMD Support	SSE (128 bit), AVX (256 bit)
L1/L2/L3 Cache	8×32 kB/8×256 kB/20 MB
Main Memory Configuration	4 channels DDR3-1600
Update Benchmark Bandwidth	40 GB/s

Table 1: Test machine specifications. All information is shown for one socket. "Update" is a multi-threaded streaming benchmark that modifies an array in memory.

extensions. Using floating-point arithmetic, each core can execute one multiply and one add instruction per cycle, leading to a peak performance of eight double precision (DP) or 16 single precision (SP) flops per cycle. Memory is connected via four DDR3-1600 memory channels per socket. The SNB core can sustain one full-width AVX load and one half-width AVX store per cycle. With SSE or scalar execution, these limits are changed: In both cases the core can sustain either one load and one store, or two loads per cycle, to the effect that many loops do not show a 4× speedup of core execution when going from scalar mode to AVX. The L2 cache sustains refills and evicts to and from L1 at 256 bits per cycle (half-duplex). A full 64-B cache line transfer thus takes two cycles. The L3 cache is segmented, with one segment per core. All segments are connected by a ring bus. Each segment has the same bandwidth capabilities as the L2 cache, i.e., it can sustain 256 bits per cycle (half-duplex) to and from L2. This means that the L3 cache is usually not a bandwidth bottleneck, which is an improvement compared to previous Intel processors. An overview of the specifications is given in Table 1. In Sect. 5 we use a 3.0 GHz Intel Ivy Bridge CPU for comparison. The relevant differences will be described there.

Measurements for the vector summation example were performed with LIKWID-bench [11], and the Intel C Compiler (version 13.1.3) was used to compile the stencil codes. The clock frequency was fixed to 2.7 GHz.

3. THE ECM PERFORMANCE MODEL

The ECM model delivers a prediction of the number of CPU cycles required to execute a certain number of iterations n_{it} of a given loop on a single core. Since the smallest amount of data that can be transferred between adjacent cache levels is usually a cache line (CL), n_{it} is typically chosen to be "one cache line's worth of work." With a 64-B CL, this amounts to $n_{\text{it}} = 8$ for a streaming kernel with double precision data and stride-one data access to all arrays (such as the STREAM benchmarks). Depending on the data types and access characteristics this number may vary, however.

3.1 Model input, construction, and assumptions

Some input data is required to construct the ECM model for a loop code on a given architecture. We consider two parts of the input separately: The time to execute the instructions on the processor core, assuming that there are no cache misses, and the time to transfer data between its initial location and the L1 cache. For the sake of clarity we review and refine the model, which was first introduced in [2, 9], using simple streaming loops such as DAXPY (`A(:)=A(:)+s*B(:)`) before turning to more complex cases.

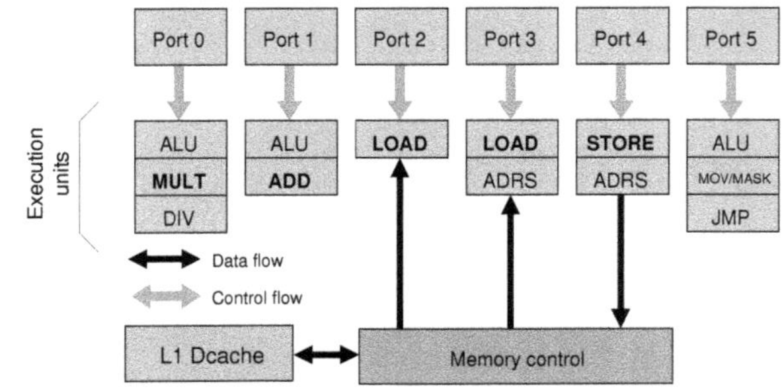

Figure 1: Simplified view of execution resources on a modern out-of-order CPU core.

3.1.1 *In-core execution time*

To determine the in-core execution time a simple model for instruction throughput capabilities of a microarchitecture is required. On Intel processors the port scheduler model can be used for this purpose. Figure 1 shows the port model for the Intel Sandy Bridge microarchitecture. We assume that all instructions in a loop are independently scheduled to the ports and executed out of program order within the execution units u_i. The execution time is then set by the unit that takes the most cycles to execute the instructions:

$$T_{\text{core}} = \max_i T_{u_i} \ . \qquad (1)$$

An additional limitation that may be relevant is the overall maximum instruction throughput of four instructions per cycle on Intel microarchitectures.[1] For example, the loop body of the DAXPY operation

```
for(i=0; i<N; ++i)
  a[i] = a[i] + s * b[i];
```

consists of two loads, one store, one add, and one multiply instruction regardless of SIMD vectorization. In addition there is typically one integer add, one integer compare, and one conditional branch in the body to implement the "loop mechanics." If the loop is unrolled, the relative share of these instructions is smaller and can usually be neglected. With AVX vectorization, one work unit (eight iterations) comprises four load, two store, two add, and two multiply instructions, which require four cycles to execute on the SNB core. In this case the load (and store) pipeline throughput is the bottleneck. In Fig. 2 we visualize this situation in a timeline diagram (cycles 1 to 4). Since there are no loop-carried dependencies in the code, the four-cycle prediction holds if the loop is sufficiently unrolled. In complex cases one can employ the *Intel Architecture Code Analyzer* (IACA) [12] to get an estimate of the loop body execution time under the throughput assumption.

3.1.2 *Data transfers through the memory hierarchy*

Data not present in the L1 cache must be fetched from lower levels of the memory hierarchy before it can be processed in CPU registers, and modified data must be evicted to make room for new cache lines. We call the time needed for these transfers the "transfer time." Again we assume the best possible case of perfect streaming, i.e., there are no latency effects and the cost for transferring one CL can be computed using the maximum bandwidth. For the SNB architecture, one CL transfer takes two cycles between adjacent cache levels. Getting a 64-B CL from memory to L3 or back takes $64\,\text{B} \cdot f/b_S$ cycles, where f is the CPU clock speed and b_S is the

[1] The term "instruction" is used in a microarchitectural context; on Intel architectures these are called "μops."

achievable memory bandwidth as measured by a suitable streaming benchmark.

Calculating the transfer times through the memory hierarchy requires an accurate account of the data volumes between all cache levels. For the DAXPY loop kernel discussed above this means that, due to the cache hierarchy being inclusive, three CLs must be transferred between each pair of adjacent memory levels: two for loading the data for a and b, and one for evicting modified data of a. This leads to transfer times of six cycles each between cache levels, and 13 cycles between memory and L3 cache (at a maximum socket bandwidth of 40 GB/s and a clock frequency of 2.7 GHz). If the "uncore" part of the chip, especially the L3 cache, has a clock speed that is set independently from the core clock, a correction factor can be applied to the L3-L2 cycle count.

3.1.3 Single-core prediction and examples

The in-core execution and transfer times described above must be put together to arrive at a prediction of single-thread execution time. Therefore we must specify which of the runtime contributions can overlap with each other. If T_{data} is the transfer time (L1 downward, as described above), T_{OL} is the part of the core execution that overlaps with the transfer time, and T_{nOL} is the part that does not, then

$$T_{\text{core}} = \max\left(T_{\text{nOL}}, T_{\text{OL}}\right) \quad (2)$$

$$T_{\text{ECM}} = \max(T_{\text{nOL}} + T_{\text{data}}, T_{\text{OL}})\,. \quad (3)$$

There are two open questions here: (i) Which components of T_{core} in (1) are overlapping? (ii) How is T_{data} composed of the different data transfer contributions along the memory hierarchy?

The ECM model makes the following fundamental assumptions for single-core performance prediction: (1) All instructions in the loop are independently scheduled to the execution ports and executed out of program order within the execution units. The unit that takes the longest time executing its instructions is the bottleneck on the core level (see Sect. 3.1.1). If dependencies lead to pipeline stalls, these appear as additional cycles on the core level and count as overlapping time in the full model (see below). The maximum throughput capabilities of the microarchitecture are a further limitation. (2) Loads (more specifically, cycles in which loads are retired) do not overlap with any other data transfer in the memory hierarchy. All other instructions, and also pipeline bubbles, overlap perfectly with data transfers. This means that only the time needed for the loads to the L1 cache contributes to T_{nOL} (store-bound loop kernels show significant overlap). (3) The transfer times up to the L1 cache are mutually non-overlapping, i.e., all cache line transfers across the memory hierarchy are serialized. Additional non-overlapping penalty cycles may be added in cases where the prefetchers cannot hide the memory latency completely.

The non-overlapping assumptions seem very pessimistic; they were motivated by the observation that the L1 cache on Intel processors can either communicate with the L2 cache *or* the registers, but not both in the same cycle. We will show below that they lead to the most accurate description of performance behavior. Due to this non-overlap assumption the ECM model does not provide an absolute upper performance bound. In contrast to the Roofline model it allows for performance measurements to exceed the model prediction.

In case of the DAXPY example on the Intel SNB core, these rules lead to the timeline diagram shown in Fig. 2. In this particular case the overall execution time is dominated by data transfers, even if the data comes from the L1 cache.

In order to be able to discuss the ECM model more efficiently we introduce a shorthand notation that summarizes the most relevant information from timeline diagrams such as Fig. 2. We write the predicted cycle counts for T_{OL} and T_{nOL}, separated by "$\|$". After T_{nOL} we attach the individual contributions for the different memory hierarchy levels (which make up T_{data}), separated by "$|$":

$$\{T_{\text{OL}} \,\|\, T_{\text{nOL}} \,|\, T_{\text{L1L2}} \,|\, T_{\text{L2L3}} \,|\, T_{\text{L3Mem}}\} \quad (4)$$

For example, the ECM model for DAXPY would be written as $\{4\,\|\,4\,|\,6\,|\,6\,|\,13\}$ cy. Cycle predictions for data sets fitting into any particular cache level can then be easily calculated from this representation by adding up the appropriate contributions from T_{data} and T_{nOL}, and finding the maximum of that number and T_{OL} according to (3). For instance, the prediction for data in L2 will be $\max(4, 4+6)$ cy $=$ 10 cy. As a shorthand notation for these predictions we use a similar format but with "$\rceil$" as the delimiter. For DAXPY this would read as $T_{\text{ECM}} = \{4\rceil 10\rceil 16\rceil 29\}$ cy.

As a further example that does not exhibit the strong data transfer dominance of DAXPY we pick a double precision vector summation:

```
for(i=0; i<N; ++i)
  s = s + a[i];
```

We construct the ECM model for this kernel in four cases: naive, scalar, SSE, and AVX vectorization on a SNB core. In all but the "naive" case we assume that appropriate modulo unrolling has been applied (at least 3-way due to the 3-cycle add latency) on top of SIMD vectorization to allow for filling the add pipeline despite the register dependency. The "naive" code is scalar and does not use modulo unrolling, so the full latency must be paid for every add instruction. The results are shown in Table 2. One can immediately see that the naive code is executing so slowly ($T_{\text{OL}} = 24$ cy/CL due to the dependency on the add pipeline) that it does not "feel" the memory hierarchy even if the data is in memory. The scalar code is dominated by core execution down to the L3 cache and starts to degrade in performance only when the data comes from mem-

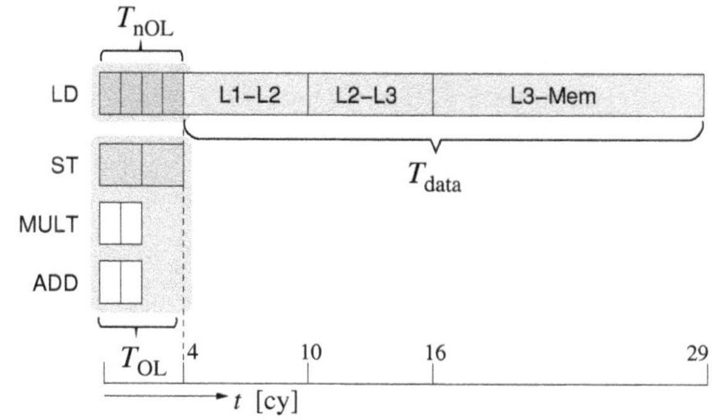

Figure 2: Single-core ECM model for the DAXPY loop kernel on Intel SNB. The predicted number of cycles per CL is 29 if the data is in memory, 16 for the L3 cache, 10 for the L2 cache, and 4 in L1 (using AVX).

case	ECM model [cy]	prediction [cy]	measurement [cy]
naive	$\{24\,\|\,4\,\|\,2\,\|\,2\,\|\,4.3\}$	$\{24\rceil 24\rceil 24\rceil 24\}$	$24\rceil 24\rceil 24\rceil 27$
scalar	$\{8\,\|\,4\,\|\,2\,\|\,2\,\|\,4.3\}$	$\{8\rceil 8\rceil 8\rceil 12\}$	$8.1\rceil 8.9\rceil 11\rceil 18$
SSE	$\{4\,\|\,2\,\|\,2\,\|\,2\,\|\,4.3\}$	$\{4\rceil 4\rceil 6\rceil 10\}$	$4.1\rceil 5\rceil 7.2\rceil 15$
AVX	$\{2\,\|\,2\,\|\,2\,\|\,2\,\|\,4.3\}$	$\{2\rceil 4\rceil 6\rceil 10\}$	$2.1\rceil 4.9\rceil 7.2\rceil 14$

Table 2: ECM model and cycle predictions on a SNB core for the vector summation loop in double precision.

ory. Furthermore, although SSE vectorization yields a significant speedup in L1 and L2 cache, the gain is only about 20% in memory. Finally, going from SSE to AVX pays off only if the data is in the L1 cache. These predictions are in line with the general observation that the performance of "slow," i.e., unoptimized code is largely independent of the position of data in the memory hierarchy.

3.1.4 Conclusions from the ECM model

The ECM model explains accurately why the theoretical bandwidth limits of all memory hierarchy levels except the L1 cache cannot be hit with a single thread. Even with a highly efficient, bandwidth-demanding loop kernel the non-overlapping contributions to T_{data} from the higher memory levels prevent full bandwidth utilization. If multiple threads are used, bandwidth saturation is possible. See Sect. 3.1.5 for scalability predictions.

Once the execution time for the basic work unit is known from the ECM model, one can calculate the single-core performance by dividing work by time: $P_{\mathrm{ECM}} = W/T$. Any appropriate unit of "work" will do, be it flops, iterations, "lattice site updates," etc. In case of the scalar summation, the performance in flop/s on a SNB core is

$$P = \frac{8\,\mathrm{flops}\cdot f}{\{8\rceil 8\rceil 8\rceil 8+4.3f/f_0\}\,\mathrm{cy}} \,. \qquad (5)$$

Here we allow for a modification of the CPU clock speed away from the base frequency f_0. At the nominal clock speed of $f_0 = 2.7\,\mathrm{GHz}$ we get $P(f_0) = \{2.7\rceil 2.7\rceil 2.7\rceil 1.8\}$ Gflop/s. The model shows clearly that the single-core performance changes with the clock frequency even if the data is in memory: $P(1.6\,\mathrm{GHz}) = \{1.6\rceil 1.6\rceil 1.6\rceil 1.2\}$ Gflop/s. The larger the relative share of T_{L3Mem} versus the other contributions, the weaker this dependence will be.

3.1.5 Chip-level scaling and comparison with Roofline

For describing the chip-level performance scaling we assume that the single-core performance scales linearly with the number of cores until a bottleneck is hit [13]. In case of the modern Intel processors the only bottleneck is the memory bandwidth, which means that an upper performance limit is given by the Roofline prediction for memory-bound execution: $P_{\mathrm{BW}} = b_{\mathrm{S}}/B_{\mathrm{C}}$, where B_{C} is the code balance (inverse computational intensity) of the loop code and b_{S} is the memory bandwidth (one may certainly consider other bottlenecks, such as a non-scalable L3 cache like on the Intel Westmere processors). The performance scaling for n cores is thus described by

$$P(n) = \min\left(nP_{\mathrm{ECM}}^{\mathrm{mem}}, \frac{b_{\mathrm{S}}}{B_{\mathrm{C}}}\right) \qquad (6)$$

if $P_{\mathrm{ECM}}^{\mathrm{mem}}$ is the ECM model prediction if the data is in main memory.

This expression allows us to draw a comparison between the ECM model and the Roofline model. The Roofline model considers only a single data transfer bottleneck. This could be main memory access but also any other memory hierarchy level. Constructing the Roofline model for any core count thus requires measured maximum bandwidth numbers for all memory levels and all core counts as input parameters, since none of these values can be predicted by the model. Due to the overlapping assumption of the Roofline model, the predicted single-core performance is then

$$P^{\mathrm{Roof}}(n) = \min_i\left(nP_{\max}^{\mathrm{core}}, \frac{b_{\mathrm{S},i}(n)}{B_{\mathrm{C},i}}\right) \,. \qquad (7)$$

Here, $P_{\max}^{\mathrm{core}}$ is the maximum in-core sequential performance, i.e., with all data coming from the L1 cache (one may use the arithmetic peak performance here and treat the L1 cache as an additional memory level). It corresponds to T_{core} as used in the ECM model. $b_{\mathrm{S},i}(n)$ and $B_{\mathrm{C},i}$ are the measured maximum bandwidth and code balance, respectively, at n cores and in memory level i (excluding L1). There are two limiting cases where the Roofline model and ECM model predictions coincide on the processor architectures considered here:

LC	ECM model [cy]	prediction [cy]	$P_{\mathrm{ECM}}^{\mathrm{mem}}$ [MLUP/s]	$N_i <$	n_{S}
L1	$\{6 \Vert 8 \vert 6 \vert 6 \vert 13\}$	$\{8\rceil 14\rceil 20\rceil 33\}$	659	683	3
L2	$\{6 \Vert 8 \vert 10 \vert 6 \vert 13\}$	$\{8\rceil 18\rceil 24\rceil 37\}$	587	5461	3
L3	$\{6 \Vert 8 \vert 10 \vert 10 \vert 13\}$	$\{8\rceil 18\rceil 28\rceil 41\}$	529	436900	4
—	$\{6 \Vert 8 \vert 10 \vert 10 \vert 22\}$	$\{8\rceil 18\rceil 28\rceil 50\}$	438	N/A	3

Table 3: ECM model, main memory code balance, predicted performance, required leading dimension, and saturation point for the 2D Jacobi kernel when the layer condition (LC) is fulfilled in different memory hierarchy levels, from L1 down to main memory on one SNB core.

- T_{core} is large compared to all contributions from data transfers. Then, if n is large enough, the memory bottleneck may become relevant, but this is described in the same way by both models. One typical example would be a kernel that is absolutely dominated by long-latency operations such as divides or square roots, like the "divide triad" kernel analyzed in [9].
- The loop code has single-core data transfer and execution characteristics that make its Roofline-based performance estimate coincide with the measured streaming benchmark performance used for obtaining the $b_{\mathrm{S},i}(n)$. We will show an example for this in Sect. 4.3.

If, however, in-core execution time and data transfer times are comparable but much larger than those of the streaming benchmark, the Roofline model is not able to describe the performance characteristics accurately. See Sect. 6 for an example.

According to (6), the performance will saturate at n_{S} cores:

$$n_{\mathrm{S}} = \left\lceil \frac{b_{\mathrm{S}}/B_{\mathrm{C}}}{P_{\mathrm{ECM}}^{\mathrm{mem}}} \right\rceil = \left\lceil \frac{T_{\mathrm{ECM}}^{\mathrm{mem}}}{T_{\mathrm{L3Mem}}} \right\rceil \,. \qquad (8)$$

The model confirms the well-known effect that "slow" loop code needs more cores to reach saturation. For example, the AVX summation code has a predicted single-core performance of $P_{\mathrm{ECM}}^{\mathrm{mem}} = 2.1\,\mathrm{Gflop/s}$ at nominal clock speed and it will saturate at three cores, while the naive, non-pipelined code with $P_{\mathrm{ECM}}^{\mathrm{mem}} = 0.9\,\mathrm{Gflop/s}$ will require six. Hence, in this case a low code quality can be "healed" by using more resources.[2] This would not be possible at a clock speed of 1.6 GHz, since the slow code would then need ten cores to saturate, but the CPU only has eight.

4. CASE STUDY: 5-POINT STENCIL

We use the arguably most simple non-trivial stencil variant to employ the ECM model in a setting that is more complex than the pure streaming kernels shown earlier. All concepts, however, are generalizable to other stencils. One sweep (complete update of all

[2]If time to solution is the only relevant metric, this attitude may be justified. However, it is not acceptable in view of energy consumption. See [9], and references therein.

points) of the 2D five-point Jacobi stencil looks as follows (double precision assumed):

```
for(j=1; j<Nj-1; ++j)
  for(i=1; i<Ni-1; ++i)
    b[j][i] = ( a[j][i-1] + a[j][i+1]
              + a[j-1][i] + a[j+1][i] ) * s;
```

Unless otherwise noted we assume that the array dimensions are large so that the arrays a and b do not fit in any cache. We adopt "lattice site updates per second" (LUP/s), i.e., scalar inner kernel iterations, as an appropriate performance metric.

4.1 Basic analysis

With AVX vectorization (4-wide vector registers in double precision), one unit of work (eight LUPs) comprises eight AVX loads, two AVX stores, six AVX adds, and two AVX multiply instructions (note that there will be no benefit from inner loop unrolling to enable re-use of data along the leading dimension). Hence, $T_{\mathrm{nOL}} = 8\,\mathrm{cy}$ and $T_{\mathrm{OL}} = 6\,\mathrm{cy}$. The code is thus limited by the LOAD pipeline throughput at the core level.

The data transfer properties of the loop nest depend on the problem size in relation to the available cache sizes. The target array b causes a traffic of two CLs across the complete memory hierarchy due to the write-allocate transfer on every store miss. The right hand side element `a[j][i-1]` can always be obtained from the L1 cache since it was loaded two inner iterations before as `a[j][i+1]`, and `a[j+1][i]` must be loaded from memory since it was not used before within the sweep. Whether `a[j-1][i]` and `a[j][i+1]` cause cache misses in a certain cache level depends on whether three successive rows of the array a fit into the cache [3]. We call this the *layer condition* (LC). If the size of cache k is C_k, it can be formulated as

$$3 \cdot N_i \cdot 8\,\mathrm{B} < \frac{C_k}{2} . \qquad (9)$$

The factor of $1/2$ is a rule of thumb: we assume that half the cache size is available for storing layers. The number of layers is connected to the *stencil radius* in the outer dimension. If r is the radius, $(2r+1)$ layers have to fit.

If the layer condition is fulfilled for cache level k, only `a[j-1][i]` causes a cache miss in this level, and is subsequently used three times from the cache. The code balance is then $24\,\mathrm{B/LUP}$ as seen from the next memory hierarchy level (cache $k+1$, or main memory), because only three data streams must be sustained. If the condition is violated, only `a[j][i-1]` comes from the cache and all other elements cause misses, leading to five data streams and a code balance of $40\,\mathrm{B/LUP}$. Columns 2–4 in Table 3 show a summary of the ECM model timing and performance predictions on a SNB core. In column 5 we give the leading dimension below which the respective layer condition is satisfied. This number was obtained by solving (9) for N_i and using the cache sizes of the SNB processor in Table 1.

4.2 Single-core performance vs. problem size

Figure 3 shows the measured performance and the ECM model prediction for a large range of memory-bound problem sizes. After the problem drops out to main memory at $N_i \approx 1145$ (quadratic domain), three phases can be distinguished. These can be attributed to the layer condition being satisfied in the L2 cache, the L3 cache, and not at all, corresponding to rows 2–4 in Table 3. An L1 layer condition would require a leading dimension of less than 683, which leads to an in-cache problem size if $N_i = N_j$. For each phase we also show the predicted code balance for different levels of the memory hierarchy. These results indicate that the Roofline

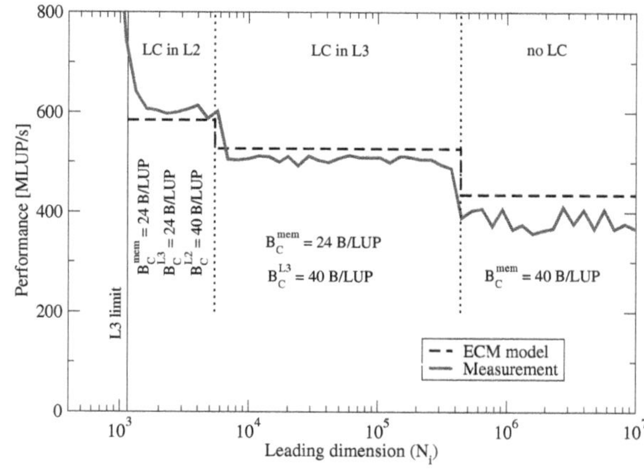

Figure 3: In-memory performance and ECM prediction vs. leading array dimension of the 2D Jacobi sweep on a SNB core. Up to a leading dimension of 2×10^4 the domain is quadratic. Beyond that, the overall problem size is kept constant.

model may not be a reliable model for the single core, because the performance changes considerably when the leading dimension grows beyond $N_i = 5461$ although B_C^{mem} stays the same. See below for more discussion on this issue.

The dashed line in Fig. 3 shows the ECM model prediction, which is in good agreement with the measurement in all three phases. The model fits well within a 10% margin, and it is even slightly below the measurement if the layer condition is fulfilled in L2 cache. We have observed this effect in many situations where the pressure on the memory hierarchy gets smaller when moving towards main memory (i.e., when the number of streams goes down). One may speculate that the non-overlapping assumption of the model is inaccurate in these cases; the deviation is generally small, however.

Despite the performance fluctuations (especially in the phase with $B_C = 40\,\mathrm{B/LUP}$), the actual memory code balance obtained by measuring the data volume with hardware performance events is within 5% of the predicted value.

4.3 Spatial blocking optimization

Spatial blocking (also called "loop tiling") is a well-known optimization for loop nests that aims at improving temporal data access locality. In the context of stencil solvers it amounts to rearranging the order of the stencil updates so that some layer condition is met, leading to a decrease in code balance. We can predict the expected gain of spatial blocking on the single core by setting up an ECM model for different blocking strategies. This is especially simple for the 2D Jacobi stencil as the layer condition (9) only depends on the leading dimension. One must conclude that it is sufficient to block the inner loop:

```
// inner block size = b_i
for(is=1; is<Ni-1; is += bi)
  for(j=1; j<Nj-1; ++j)
    for(i=is; i<min(Ni-1,is+bi-1; ++i)
      b[j][i] = ( a[j][i-1] + a[j][i+1]
                + a[j-1][i] + a[j+1][i] ) * s;
```

The layer condition (9) now takes a modified form:

$$3 \cdot b_i \cdot 8\,\mathrm{B} < \frac{C_k}{2} . \qquad (10)$$

Hence, the block size b_i determines whether the layer condition will be satisfied in cache level k, and column 5 in Table 3 again pro-

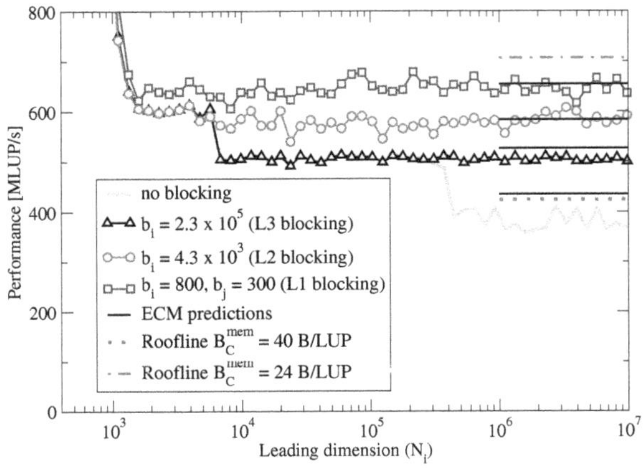

Figure 4: Performance vs. problem size for the 2D Jacobi stencil as in Fig. 3 but with spatial blocking of the leading dimension with block size b_i. The four ECM model predictions correspond to the rows of Table 3. In case of the L1 layer condition (squares) blocking in j direction is required (see also Fig. 5). The single-core Roofline predictions are shown for comparison. Roofline does not yield different predictions across different blocking strategies.

vides the relevant thresholds. Choosing b_i appropriately is called "blocking for cache level k." Figure 4 shows performance vs. leading dimension for three block sizes and no blocking. These four cases (squares, circles, triangles, gray line) correspond to the four possible layer conditions in Table 3, and the ECM models given there apply. The solid lines denote the ECM performance predictions. The dotted and dashed-dotted lines mark the Roofline model predictions derived from measured single-thread cache and memory bandwidths.[3] Since the Roofline model predicts a memory-bound situation in all cases (independent of the blocking), there are only two performance levels: a lower level for $B_C^{mem} = 40\,\text{B/LUP}$ and a higher level for $B_C^{mem} = 24\,\text{B/LUP}$. Although the Roofline model cannot distinguish between different blocking strategies, the best and worst case scenarios (L1 blocking and no blocking) are covered with useful accuracy. Note, however, that this is a coincidence: As the ECM model shows, the runtime contributions are rather evenly distributed across the memory hierarchy. The Roofline model works in this case because the benchmark used for taking the single-thread memory bandwidth limit has similar characteristics (in fact, the ECM model prediction for the STREAM COPY loop is $\{4\rceil 10\rceil 16\rceil 29\}$ cy, and the number of data streams is the same as for the Jacobi 2D kernel with L1 blocking).

The data shows that the ECM model is able to describe the performance impact of spatial blocking quite accurately, and that the gain from moving a layer condition up in the memory hierarchy (i.e., satisfying it in a higher cache level) can be leveraged also for larger leading dimensions. In case of pure L1 blocking, however, the observed performance was at first lower than expected. A measurement of the memory data traffic revealed that the actual code balance was much higher than $24\,\text{B/LUP}$, which was caused by the hardware prefetcher: If the inner block size b_i is small, the leading array dimension is only traversed partially, but the hardware prefetcher cannot foresee when the loop ends. It fetches cache lines from beyond the actual end of the short inner loop block. Those cannot be used before the next inner block is updated, they are thus

[3]STREAM COPY kernel: $b_S^{mem} = 17\,\text{GB/s}$, $b_S^{L3} = 34\,\text{GB/s}$, $b_S^{L2} = 56\,\text{GB/s}$. The in-core model was the same as for ECM.

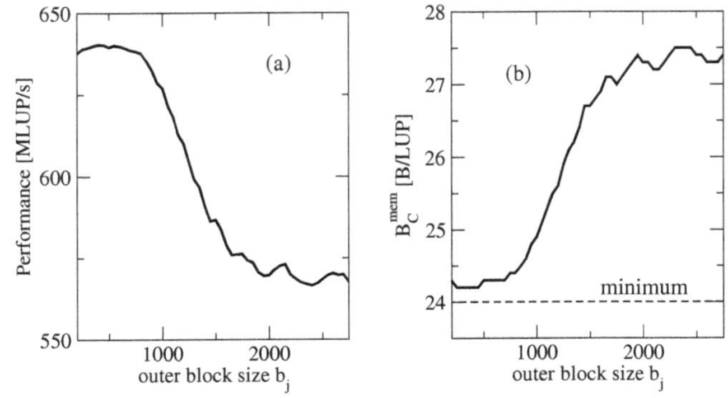

Figure 5: Influence of outer loop blocking on the 2D Jacobi stencil at a constant inner loop block size of $b_i = 800$ and a constant problem size of $N_i = 3.5 \times 10^4$ and $N_j = 1.2 \times 10^4$. (a) Performance vs. outer loop block size. (b) Measured in-memory code balance vs. outer loop block size.

evicted prematurely and cause excess memory traffic. Additional blocking in the outer dimension was added to correct this problem:

```
for(js=1; js<Nj-1; js += bj)
  for(is=1; is<Ni-1; is += bi)
    for(j=js; j<min(Nj-1,js+bj-1); ++j)
      for(i=is; i<min(Ni-1,is+bi-1); ++i)
        b[j][i] = ( a[j][i-1]+a[j][i+1]
                  + a[j-1][i]+a[j+1][i] ) * s;
```

In Fig. 5 we show the effect of the outer loop blocking with block size b_j on the performance and on the measured in-memory code balance at a constant inner block size of $b_i = 800$. It turns out that $b_j \approx 300$ alleviates the prefetcher problem: blocks of size $b_i \times b_j$ are updated consecutively along the leading dimension, and all excess cache lines can be used. Note that one can determine the excess traffic, and hence the prefetch distance, from the measured data volume at large b_j. We have calculated the prefetch distance to be about 33 CL in our case, but this result is probably not generic since the details of the prefetch mechanism are unknown. Data overheads at block boundaries (of which eager prefetching is just the most striking example) may be incorporated into the model if the corresponding data volumes are known.

Although all considered problem sizes are bigger than the L3 cache, the execution is far from memory bound. Even when blocking for the L1 cache (squares in Fig. 4), the memory bandwidth as calculated from the product of performance and code balance is barely 17 GB/s out of a maximum of over 40 GB/s.

Since the code balance is already at its possible minimum of $24\,\text{B/LUP}$ across all cache levels, spatial blocking cannot improve the single-core performance any further. The ECM model prediction in the first row of Table 3 shows that if one were able to reduce the core time by a factor of two (from 8 to 4 cycles) by some advanced optimization technique such as register blocking, single-core performance would improve by a factor of $33/(33-4) = 1.14$.

4.4 Multi-core scaling

When going from single-threaded to multi-threaded execution on a multicore chip, two architectural features impact the performance behavior: (i) the memory bandwidth bottleneck and (ii) the shared outer-level cache (if present). In Fig. 6 we show performance scaling across the cores of a SNB socket at $N_i = 1.2 \times 10^6$. Two-dimensional L1 blocking was only used where necessary. In

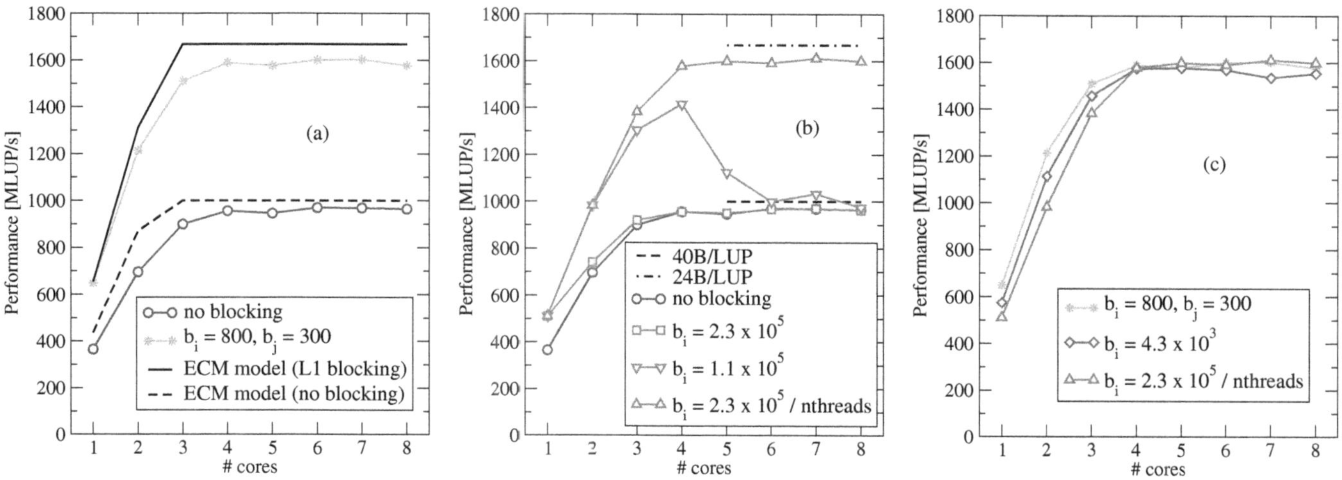

Figure 6: Scaling of the Jacobi 2D kernel across the cores of a SNB chip at $N_i = 1.2 \times 10^6$. (a) Comparison of ECM model and measurement for L1 blocking and no blocking. (b) Choosing the right block size b_i for the L3 layer condition. (c) Comparison of saturation behavior for L1, L2, and L3 blocking.

all cases (blocked or not), the *j* loop was parallelized with OpenMP and static loop scheduling. This ensures that the prefetcher problem described in the previous section remains solved, since each thread works on a consecutive string of blocks in the leading dimension.

Figure 6a compares the ECM model and scaling predictions with measurements for the two extreme cases of no blocking (circles) and L1 blocking (stars). The general scaling behavior is described well, although there is a deviation in the vicinity of the saturation point, which we attribute to changes in the prefetching strategy when the memory interface is almost fully utilized [10]: For instance, cache lines are only prefetched into L3 and the prefetch distance is smaller. This leads to an additional latency penalty, which is not part of the ECM model (but could be included). The saturation level is slightly smaller than predicted by the code balance, but the deviation is well below 10%.

In Fig. 6b we study the influence of the block size on the scalability when blocking for the L3 cache. At $b_i = 2.3 \times 10^5$ (squares) the single-core speedup versus the non-blocked version (circles) is as expected, but performance saturates at a level that indicates a code balance of 40 B/LUP. Reducing the block size to $b_i = 1.1 \times 10^5$ shows no improvement on the single core but leads to much higher performance up to four cores. Beyond four cores, however, performance degrades and settles again at the same level as before. The reason for this behavior is the shared L3 cache, which requires a modified layer condition:

$$3 \cdot b_i \cdot n \cdot 8\,\mathrm{B} < \frac{C_3}{2} \,. \tag{11}$$

The n-dependent block size ensures that three layers *per thread* fit into the cache, and leads to the saturation performance expected from a code balance of 24 B/LUP (triangles). Note that block size adaptivity is not required when blocking for core-private caches, since their aggregate size scales with the number of cores.

Finally we need to comment on the influence of the chosen blocking strategy (L1, L2, or L3) on the scalability. Technically the ECM model predicts different saturation points for L3 blocking (4 cores) and L1 or L2 blocking (3 cores), as shown in the last column of Table 3. In reality they display very similar saturation behavior for the Jacobi 2D kernel (see Fig. 6c), although the general trend to saturate earlier with faster single-core code can certainly be observed. If maximum performance is the only significant metric, it is irrelevant in practice which blocking strategy is chosen as long as the in-memory code balance is at its minimum of 24 B/LUP. Saturating earlier, however, has some advantages: "expendable" cores can be put into a low-power mode, saving energy ("concurrency throttling"), or they can be used for other tasks such as asynchronous communication.

Note that the use of non-temporal stores (also called "streaming stores") may reduce the in-memory code balance from 24 B/LUP to 16 B/LUP by ignoring the cache hierarchy on a store miss, saving the write-allocate transfers. However, their implementation on Intel processors cannot be described by a simple throughput assumption. Therefore it is unclear as yet how to incorporate the non-temporal store instructions in the ECM model.

5. CASE STUDY: UXX STENCIL

The "uxx" stencil [14] is a part of a simulation code for dynamic rupture and earthquake wave propagation. The basic loop nest without any blocking optimizations looks as follows:

```
#pragma omp parallel for schedule(static) \
                         private(d)
for(int k=2; k<=N-1; k++){
 for (int j=2; j<=N-1; j++){
  for (int i=2; i<=N-1; i++){
   d = 0.25*(d1[ k ][j][i] + d1[ k ][j-1][i]
          + d1[k-1][j][i] + d1[k-1][j-1][i]);
   u1[k][j][i] = u1[k][j][i] + (dth/d)
   *( c1*(xx[ k ][ j ][ i ]-xx[ k ][ j ][i-1])
    + c2*(xx[ k ][ j ][i+1]-xx[ k ][ j ][i-2])
    + c1*(xy[ k ][ j ][ i ]-xy[ k ][j-1][ i ])
    + c2*(xy[ k ][j+1][ i ]-xy[ k ][j-2][ i ])
    + c1*(xz[ k ][ j ][ i ]-xz[k-1][ j ][ i ])
    + c2*(xz[k+1][ j ][ i ]-xz[k-2][ j ][ i ]));
}}}}
```

The code is used with either single or double precision, and it contains a divide operation in the inner loop. Without any guidance by performance modeling one would probably try to eliminate the divide (which is non-trivial) because "divides are expensive."

5.1 Analysis and ECM model

The loop code as generated by the compiler is quite complex, so we employ the IACA tool. At double precision (DP) the through-

version	ECM model [cy]	prediction [cy]
DP	$\{84 \,\|\, 38 \,\vert\, 20 \,\vert\, 20 \,\vert\, 26\}$	$\{84 \rceil 84 \rceil 84 \rceil 104\}$
SP	$\{45 \,\|\, 38 \,\vert\, 20 \,\vert\, 20 \,\vert\, 26\}$	$\{45 \rceil 58 \rceil 78 \rceil 104\}$
DP noDIV	$\{41 \,\|\, 38 \,\vert\, 20 \,\vert\, 20 \,\vert\, 26\}$	$\{41 \rceil 58 \rceil 78 \rceil 104\}$

Table 4: ECM model and cycle predictions for the uxx stencil code in double precision (DP) and single precision (SP), respectively, with L3 blocking. The unit of work is 8 LUPs for DP and 16 LUPs for SP. The "noDIV" version performs a multiply instead of a divide in the inner loop.

put analysis reports the divider to be the bottleneck on the core, causing a core time of $T_{\mathrm{core}} = T_{\mathrm{OL}} = 84\,\mathrm{cy}$ per CL (eight iterations) due to the very slow 42-cycle throughput for the divide instruction (`vdivpd`). The non-overlapping part is $T_{\mathrm{nOL}} = 38\,\mathrm{cy}$, caused by the loads to the arrays `xx`, `xy`, `xz`, `d1`, and `u1`. With single precision (SP) the machine code does not contain any divide at all: the compiler uses the `vrcpps` instruction instead, which provides a low-precision (11 bits) but fully vectorized and pipelined reciprocal, and employs a subsequent Newton-Raphson step and a multiply to perform a 22-bit divide [10]. This results again in $T_{\mathrm{nOL}} = 38\,\mathrm{cy}$ as the load instructions are the same as with DP. The overlapping part is $T_{\mathrm{OL}} = 35\,\mathrm{cy}$, caused by add, multiply, and 16-byte move instructions. The code is close to the limit of four micro-ops per cycle on the SNB, which is why IACA reports a front-end bottleneck and an overall throughput of $T_{\mathrm{core}} = 45\,\mathrm{cy}$. Since front-end stalls overlap with the transfer time, the seven extra cycles have no significance and will be ignored in the following.

Calculating the transfer time requires an analysis of relevant layer conditions. There are two types of layers in a 3D stencil code: one-dimensional layers along the leading dimension (rows along i of size N) and layers that span the extent of the inner two-level loop nest (size $N \times N$). At relevant problem sizes only the latter will matter, and we can safely ignore the "row conditions" since they will be automatically fulfilled in the L1 cache. The only data structures which are subject to layer conditions are thus `xz` and `d1`, because their stencil radius is larger than zero in the outer (k) dimension. The cache must hold as many layers as there are distinct outer index references, i.e., two for `d1` (which is accessed in layers k and $k-1$) and four for `xz` (which is accessed in layers $k-2$ to $k+1$). Hence, the layer condition for n threads in the shared L3 cache and blocking in the j dimension is

$$(4+2)\cdot N \cdot b_j \cdot n \cdot \left\{ \begin{array}{c} 4\,\mathrm{B}\ (\mathrm{SP}) \\ 8\,\mathrm{B}\ (\mathrm{DP}) \end{array} \right\} < \frac{C_3}{2}. \qquad (12)$$

One may certainly consider higher cache levels or block the inner dimension as well, but we omit this discussion here since it would not provide new insights.

With L3 blocking, the transfer time will be independent of the precision. Six consecutive data streams hit the memory interface per thread: one each for `xx`, `xy`, `xz`, and `d1`, and two for `u1`. The code balance in memory is thus $B_{\mathrm{C}}^{\mathrm{mem}} = 24\,\mathrm{B/LUP}$ in SP and $48\,\mathrm{B/LUP}$ in DP. Assuming that the higher caches are too small to hold the layers, the L3 cache will be hit by ten streams per thread.

The analysis in the previous sections now enables us to construct the ECM model for the uxx stencil. The first two rows in Table 4 show the model and the cycle predictions for SP and DP. For comparison we also include a special DP version ("noDIV") in which the divide as substituted by a multiplication.

The ECM model yields the same cycle prediction per unit of work in main memory for all versions (104 cy), hence we expect a

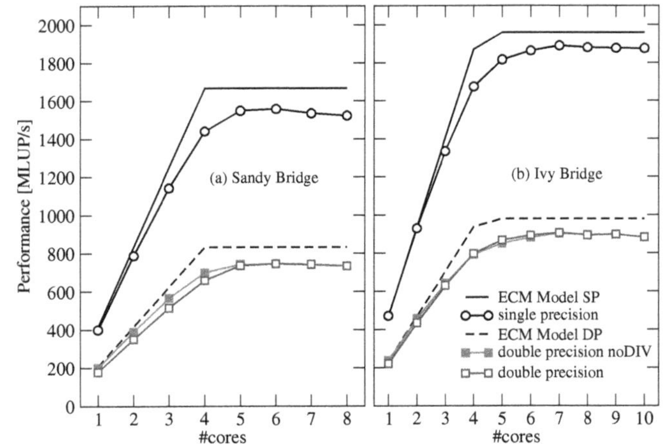

Figure 7: Performance scaling and ECM model predictions of the uxx stencil benchmark with L3 blocking at a problem size of 276^3 grid points across the cores of one SNB socket (left) and one IVB socket (right) in single and double precision.

factor of two in performance between SP and DP. Also, all versions should saturate at four cores. Probably the most striking result is that the presence or absence of the divide does not make a difference as

$$T_{\mathrm{data}} + T_{\mathrm{nOL}} > T_{\mathrm{OL}} \qquad (13)$$

despite the low-throughput divide. Going to great lengths in trying to eliminate it from the code will thus not be rewarded with performance improvements. These predictions are confirmed by the performance data shown for one SNB socket in Fig. 7a. There is actually a slight speedup for the "noDIV" version below saturation. Using the latency analysis in the IACA tool revealed that the critical code path through the loop body has a worst case execution time of 192 cy. Usually the throughput prediction is much closer to the measured runtime since the out of order logic can fill a lot of pipeline bubbles across the independent loop iterations. In this case, however, the critical path is so long that (13) is just barely satisfied (in fact there is a 10% deviation from the model on the single core). Removing the divide shortens the critical path so much that (13) can be easily met, and the ECM model prediction is very precise. For comparison we present the results on an Intel Ivy Bridge CPU (3.0 GHz, $b_S = 47\,\mathrm{GB/s}$) in Fig. 7b. This architecture is quite similar to Sandy Bridge apart from the higher memory bandwidth and the faster divide throughput (28 cy instead of 42 cy for a double precision divide with AVX). The accuracy of the model is even better here because of the shorter critical path in double precision. The ECM model in this case is $\{56 \,\|\, 38 \,\vert\, 20 \,\vert\, 20 \,\vert\, 25\}$ cy, leading to a prediction of $\{56 \rceil 58 \rceil 78 \rceil 103\}$ cy. The divide instruction has no impact if the data does not fit into the L1 cache.

5.2 Optimization opportunities

One typical stencil optimization that goes beyond spatial blocking is *temporal blocking*, which can dramatically reduce the in-memory code balance by performing multiple updates on each grid point in cache before it gets evicted. The ECM model can provide upper limits to the expected benefit of temporal blocking. In case of uxx, optimal temporal blocking for the L3 cache would completely remove the memory transfer time of $T_{\mathrm{L3Mem}} = 26\,\mathrm{cy}$, resulting in a 24% (DP) or 33% (SP) speedup on the single core. The next bottleneck will then be the divide for DP (84 cy) and the L3 transfer time for SP (78 cy), respectively, but both of these are purely core-local.

The true potential of temporal blocking is thus not in the speedup on the single core but in the removal of the memory bandwidth bottleneck, allowing for scalable performance with an upper limit of over 2000 MLUP/s even for DP and still including the divide. Even in this case the benefit from temporal blocking would by far outweigh the speedup gained from removing the divide.

See [15] for a case study of temporal blocking with a 3D Jacobi smoother supported by an ECM model analysis.

6. CASE STUDY: 3D LONG-RANGE STENCIL

A large stencil radius in the outer grid dimension leads to a high pressure on the cache levels since they have to hold a large number of layers. As an example we consider a constant coefficient long-range stencil code in single precision with a radius of four in each dimension:

```
#pragma omp parallel for
for(int k=4; k < N-4; k++) {
 for(int j=4; j < N-4; j++) {
  for(int i=4; i < N-4; i++) {
   float lap = c0 * V[k][j][i]
  + c1 * ( V[ k ][ j ][i+1]+ V[ k ][ j ][i-1])
  + c1 * ( V[ k ][j+1][ i ]+ V[ k ][j-1][ i ])
  + c1 * ( V[k+1][ j ][ i ]+ V[k-1][ j ][ i ])
  + c2 * ( V[ k ][ j ][i+2]+ V[ k ][ j ][i-2])
  + c2 * ( V[ k ][j+2][ i ]+ V[ k ][j-2][ i ])
  + c2 * ( V[k+2][ j ][ i ]+ V[k-2][ j ][ i ])
  + c3 * ( V[ k ][ j ][i+3]+ V[ k ][ j ][i-3])
  + c3 * ( V[ k ][j+3][ i ]+ V[ k ][j-3][ i ])
  + c3 * ( V[k+3][ j ][ i ]+ V[k-3][ j ][ i ])
  + c4 * ( V[ k ][ j ][i+4]+ V[ k ][ j ][i-4])
  + c4 * ( V[ k ][j+4][ i ]+ V[ k ][j-4][ i ])
  + c4 * ( V[k+4][ j ][ i ]+ V[k-4][ j ][ i ]);
   U[k][j][i] = 2.f * V[k][j][i]- U[k][j][i]
              + ROC[k][j][i] * lap;
}}}
```

The only array that is relevant for layer conditions here is V; the others (U and ROC) are accessed in linear order without potential for cache re-use.

6.1 Analysis and ECM model

The IACA tool reports an overlapping core time of $T_{\mathrm{OL}} = 68\,\mathrm{cy}$, which is mainly due to adds and frontend stalls, while the load port limitation is at $T_{\mathrm{nOL}} = 62\,\mathrm{cy}$ (there are only 27 visible loads in the loop body, but due to some integer register spilling four more cycles are required). Since the stencil radius is 4 in all directions, the block size in the j direction must be chosen so that the cache can hold nine layers. The n-thread layer condition is

$$9 \cdot N \cdot b_j \cdot n \cdot 4\mathrm{B} < \frac{C_3}{2}\,. \qquad (14)$$

In this case, four data streams per thread will hit the memory and the code balance will be $B_{\mathrm{c}}^{\mathrm{mem}} = 16\,\mathrm{B/LUP}$. If the layer condition is only satisfied in L3, this cache will be hit by twelve streams per thread, which already indicates that the transfer time is significant for this kernel and that the main contribution to it does not come from main memory. Indeed the ECM model is $\{68 \,\|\, 62 \,|\, 24 \,|\, 24 \,|\, 17\}\,\mathrm{cy}$, which leads to a cycle prediction of $\{68 \rceil 86 \rceil 110 \rceil 127\}\,\mathrm{cy}$. Hence, only $17/127 \approx 13\%$ of the execution time is attributed to T_{L3Mem}, and the code will just barely saturate at eight cores. If the layer condition is not satisfied at all, the memory code balance will rise to $B_{\mathrm{c}}^{\mathrm{mem}} = 48\,\mathrm{B/LUP}$. In Fig. 8 we show performance data on a SNB socket with and without blocking. At the chosen problem size of 480^3, the layer condition is fulfilled without blocking for a single thread, which is why

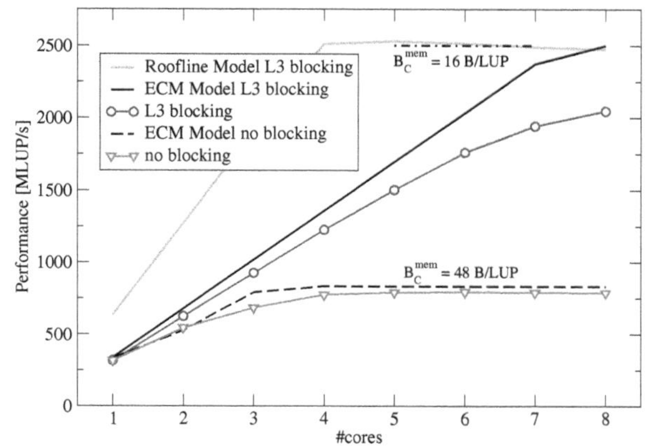

Figure 8: Performance scaling and ECM model predictions of the 3D long-range stencil benchmark with (circles) and without (triangles) L3 blocking at a problem size of 480^3 grid points across the cores of one SNB socket in single precision. The Roofline model prediction is shown for reference.

the single-core performance and prediction is the same in both cases. At two cores and above, however, blocking is required. The blocked code scales well almost up to the full socket, as predicted by the ECM model.

This stencil provides a good example for a situation where the Roofline model fails to deliver a useful performance estimate. Due to the large in-core execution time, the loop is predicted to be core-bound until the memory bandwidth is saturated, which happens at four cores (top data set in Fig. 8). However, the other data transfer contributions are far from negligible, so the Roofline model is much too optimistic here due to its overlapping assumption.

6.2 Optimization opportunities

The blocking optimization has almost removed the memory bottleneck, and the ECM model predicts that temporal blocking, which would eliminate T_{L3Mem} altogether, would only have a minor effect on the single core *and the full socket.* In order to get any performance improvement one would have to reduce the major contribution in $T_{\mathrm{mem}}^{\mathrm{ECM}}$, which is T_{nOL}. If all core contributions including T_{nOL} could be shrunk by 50%, the ECM model would be $\{34 \,\|\, 31 \,|\, 24 \,|\, 24 \,|\, 17\}\,\mathrm{cy}$ and the prediction would be $\{34 \rceil 55 \rceil 79 \rceil 96\}\,\mathrm{cy}$. The single-core code would be accelerated by 33% and saturation would set in at six cores, making temporal blocking a viable optimization. Possible code transformations leading to a substantial improvement of T_{core} would have to save on arithmetic operations as well as on loads. The semi-stencil algorithm [16] is one recent example.

7. SUMMARY

In this work we have reviewed the ECM performance model using simple streaming kernels and refined it to clearly state its assumptions regarding the overlap of different contributions to the single-core runtime of a loop kernel across the memory hierarchy. By introducing a short-hand notation we could ease the presentation of the model results and performance predictions. We have then applied the model to three stencil algorithms with different code characteristics on an Intel SandyBridge processor. Using a 2D Jacobi stencil as the initial example we were able to explain the single-core performance vs. problem size by accurately calculating the runtime contributions. The performance and scalability impact of spatial blocking for establishing "layer conditions" in different cache levels was quantified using the ECM model, and it was shown why outer loop blocking is required although the layer condition does not depend on the outer problem dimension. The performance of a more complex 3D stencil with an expensive divide operation in the inner loop was shown to be independent of the presence of the divide because of the dominance of transfer times. Temporal blocking was predicted to show a minor speedup on the single core but a major performance boost on the full chip even if the divide operation is left untouched. Finally we have used the model to show that a 3D long-range stencil cannot saturate the memory bandwidth of the CPU at minimum in-memory code balance because of in-cache contributions to the single-core runtime. Any optimization attempt would thus have to aim at reducing the in-cache runtime before more advanced techniques such as temporal blocking are applied.

It must be stressed that we have barely scratched the surface of the vast range of known stencil optimizations, but the basic line of thinking has been clearly demonstrated. We have also shown when and why Roofline model predictions fail to coincide with the ECM model. The ECM model is to our knowledge the only model that can usefully estimate the contributions to the single-core execution time of streaming loop kernels, of which stencil codes are just one example. It leads to a clear understanding of relevant bottlenecks and potential optimization approaches but can mostly be set up using "pencil and paper." Work is ongoing to build a simple tool that can construct the model from a high-level description of the code and the architecture, making it simpler to apply for the non-expert.

One basic limitation of the ECM model is its "streaming assumption:" The model is over-optimistic if the data transfers through the memory hierarchy are latency-bound, which is the case, e.g., in "pointer chasing" scenarios, or on processors for which hardware and/or software prefetch mechanisms cannot hide the latency cost. In addition, we do not know yet how to incorporate the cost of non-temporal stores. Finally we have observed the model to be too optimistic for the memory data transfer time of tight loops with low T_{core} on processors with high-frequency memory interfaces. These shortcomings may be "fixed" by introducing additional latency penalties, but we consider such an approach undesirable, since it would introduce additional parameters just for making the predictions more accurate. The main goal of the model is, however, to understand trends and bottlenecks, for which a precise performance prediction is often not required.

Acknowledgment

We thank Andrey Semin (Intel Germany) for useful discussions, Olaf Schenk (USI Lugano) for providing the "uxx" benchmark case, and Hatem Ltaief (KAUST) for providing the 3D long-range stencil case. Part of this work was supported by the DFG priority programme 1648 "SPPEXA" under the project "EXASTEEL."

8. REFERENCES

[1] T. Henretty, K. Stock, L.-N. Pouchet, F. Franchetti, J. Ramanujam, and P. Sadayappan, "Data layout transformation for stencil computations on short-vector simd architectures," in *Proceedings of the 20th International Conference on Compiler Construction: Part of the Joint European Conferences on Theory and Practice of Software*, ser. CC'11/ETAPS'11. Berlin, Heidelberg: Springer-Verlag, 2011, pp. 225–245.

[2] J. Treibig and G. Hager, "Introducing a performance model for bandwidth-limited loop kernels," in *Parallel Processing and Applied Mathematics*, ser. Lecture Notes in Computer Science, R. Wyrzykowski, J. Dongarra, K. Karczewski, and J. Wasniewski, Eds. Springer Berlin / Heidelberg, 2010, vol. 6067, pp. 615–624.

[3] K. Datta, S. Kamil, S. Williams, L. Oliker, J. Shalf, and K. Yelick, "Optimization and performance modeling of stencil computations on modern microprocessors," *SIAM Review*, vol. 51, no. 1, pp. 129–159, 2009.

[4] C. Leopold, "Tight bounds on capacity misses for 3d stencil codes," in *Proceedings of the International Conference on Computational Science-Part I*, ser. ICCS '02. London, UK, UK: Springer-Verlag, 2002, pp. 843–852.

[5] S. M. F. Rahman, Q. Yi, and A. Qasem, "Understanding stencil code performance on multicore architectures," in *Proceedings of the 8th ACM International Conference on Computing Frontiers*, ser. CF '11. New York, NY, USA: ACM, 2011, pp. 30:1–30:10.

[6] D. Callahan, J. Cocke, and K. Kennedy, "Estimating interlock and improving balance for pipelined architectures," *Journal of Parallel and Distributed Computing*, vol. 5, no. 4, pp. 334 – 358, 1988.

[7] R. W. Hockney and I. J. Curington, "$f_{1/2}$: A parameter to characterize memory and communication bottlenecks," *Parallel Computing*, vol. 10, no. 3, pp. 277–286, 1989.

[8] S. Williams, A. Waterman, and D. Patterson, "Roofline: An insightful visual performance model for multicore architectures," *Commun. ACM*, vol. 52, no. 4, pp. 65–76, 2009.

[9] G. Hager, J. Treibig, J. Habich, and G. Wellein, "Exploring performance and power properties of modern multicore chips via simple machine models," *Concurrency Computat.: Pract. Exper.*, 2013, DOI: 10.1002/cpe.3180.

[10] "Intel 64 and IA-32 architectures optimization reference manual," September 2014.

[11] J. Treibig, G. Hager, and G. Wellein, "LIKWID: A lightweight performance-oriented tool suite for x86 multicore environments," in *Proc. PSTI2010*. Los Alamitos, CA, USA: IEEE Computer Society, 2010, pp. 207–216, DOI: 10.1109/ICPPW.2010.38.

[12] "Intel architecture code analyzer." [Online]. Available: http://software.intel.com/en-us/articles/intel-architecture-code-analyzer/

[13] M. A. Suleman, M. K. Qureshi, and Y. N. Patt, "Feedback-driven threading: power-efficient and high-performance execution of multi-threaded workloads on CMPs," *SIGARCH Comput. Archit. News*, vol. 36, no. 1, pp. 277–286, Mar. 2008.

[14] M. Christen and O. Schenk, "A performance study of an anelastic wave propagation code using auto-tuned stencil computations," in *Proc. ICCS 2012, Omaha, Nebraska, USA, 4-6 June, 2012*, ser. Procedia Computer Science, H. H. Ali, Y. Shi, D. Khazanchi, M. Lees, G. D. van Albada, J. Dongarra, and P. M. A. Sloot, Eds., vol. 9. Elsevier, 2012, pp. 956–965.

[15] S. Kronawitter, H. Stengel, G. Hager, and C. Lengauer, "Domain-specific optimization of two Jacobi smoother kernels and their evaluation in the ECM performance model," *Parallel Processing Letters*, vol. 24, no. 03, p. 1441004, 2014.

[16] R. de la Cruz and M. Araya-Polo, "Algorithm 942: Semi-Stencil," *ACM Trans. Math. Softw.*, vol. 40, no. 3, pp. 23:1–23:39, Apr. 2014.

GreenPar: Scheduling Parallel High Performance Applications in Green Datacenters

Md E. Haque† Íñigo Goiri‡* Ricardo Bianchini†‡ Thu D. Nguyen†
†Rutgers University ‡Microsoft Research
{mdhaque, tdnguyen}@cs.rutgers.edu {inigog, ricardob}@microsoft.com

ABSTRACT

We propose GreenPar, a scheduler for parallel high-performance applications in datacenters partially powered by on-site generation of renewable ("green") energy. GreenPar schedules the workload to maximize the green energy consumption and minimize the grid ("brown") energy consumption, while respecting a performance service-level agreement (SLA). When green energy is available, GreenPar increases the resource allocations of active jobs to reduce runtimes. When using brown energy, GreenPar reduces resource allocations within the constraints imposed by the performance SLA to conserve energy. GreenPar makes its decisions based on the speedup profile of each job. We have implemented GreenPar in a real solar-powered datacenter. Our results show that GreenPar can increase the green energy consumption and reduce both the average job runtime and the brown energy consumption, compared to schedulers that are oblivious to on-site green energy.

Categories and Subject Descriptors

C.4 [**Computer Systems Organizations**]: Performance of Systems

Keywords

Renewable energy; energy-aware scheduling; datacenters.

1. INTRODUCTION

Datacenters consume an enormous amount of electricity, and this consumption is growing rapidly. Estimates for 2010 indicate that datacenters consumed 1.5% of the total electricity used world-wide, and that this usage increased by 56% over the previous 5 years [28]. This consumption translates into high carbon emissions, since most of the electricity is produced by burning fossil fuels.

With increasing societal awareness of emissions and climate change, there is an increasing demand for cleaner products and services. As a result, there is a rising interest in powering datacenters at least partially using on-site generation of renewable ("green") energy from sources such as wind and solar. For example, Apple and McGraw-Hill have built 40MW [6] and 14MW [10] co-located solar arrays, respectively, for their datacenters. Green House Data [19], AISO [1], and GreenQloud [20] are cloud providers that operate green datacenters mostly (or entirely) powered by wind and/or solar energy.

Such "green" datacenters hold great promise for reducing the environmental impact and electricity cost of datacenter computing. For example, Goiri et al. argue that the installed capital cost for the solar energy system of a green micro-datacenter can be recovered from electricity cost savings in less than 10 years [16]. However, an important research challenge arising in these green datacenters is that generation of green energy from sources such as solar and wind is variable. For example, photovoltaic (PV) solar energy is only available during the day and the amount produced depends on the weather and season. One approach for mitigating this variability is to store green energy in batteries or the grid via net metering. However, this approach has significant disadvantages: (1) batteries are expensive[1] and common types of batteries (e.g., lead-acid) are harmful for the environment, (2) batteries incur energy losses, (3) net metering incurs losses and is not available everywhere, and (4) where net metering is available, the power company may pay less than the retail electricity price for the green energy.

Given the above disadvantages, in this paper, we investigate how to manage the computational workload to better match the energy demand to the energy supply. Specifically, we propose and evaluate GreenPar, a scheduler for parallel high-performance computing (HPC) workloads in green datacenters. GreenPar seeks to maximize green energy consumption without the need for energy storage, thereby increasing the benefits of on-site generation.[2] GreenPar also seeks to minimize "brown" grid energy consumption (when there is insufficient green energy) while respecting a performance service-level agreement (SLA). GreenPar increases the resource allocations of active parallel jobs to reduce runtimes when green energy is available. When there is insuf-

*This work was done while Goiri was at Rutgers University.

ICS'15, June 8–11, 2015, Newport Beach, CA, USA.

http://dx.doi.org/10.1145/2751205.2751221.

[1] Goiri et al. found that the cost of batteries is currently not amortizable when they are used as a power source in a green datacenter, unless there is enough performance slack for deferring the workload [16].

[2] The datacenter still has batteries for handling grid failures, but GreenPar does not use them because that would require extra capacity and frequent charge/discharge may shorten their lifetimes.

ficient green energy, GreenPar reduces resource allocations within the constraints imposed by the performance SLA to conserve brown energy. GreenPar relies on the jobs' speedup profiles in making its decisions. A specific performance SLA that we consider in this paper is a maximum runtime slowdown percentage; for example, the SLA might state that a job's execution cannot be slowed down by more than 10% in order to conserve brown energy.

GreenPar can reduce brown energy consumption *even when it is not allowed to slow down the jobs*. It can do this by first allocating more resources than requested to a parallel job when green energy is available, increasing the job's rate of progress and thus letting it accumulate performance "slack." Subsequently, when running on brown energy, GreenPar can conserve energy by reducing the resource allocation of the job, using the accumulated performance slack to avoid lengthening its overall completion time.

We have designed four green-energy-aware scheduling policies for GreenPar, targeting solar-powered green datacenters. Each policy assumes a different amount of knowledge about future green energy production, jobs' characteristics, and the datacenter workload. We have implemented these policies in a GreenPar prototype framework, and evaluated this implementation in Parasol, a solar-powered micro-datacenter we built at Rutgers University [16]. Our evaluation uses workloads comprising jobs executing a subset of the NAS Parallel Benchmark (NBP) suite [35]. The workloads are constructed to resemble traces of real HPC workloads obtained from the Grid Workload Archive [21] and the Parallel Workload Archive [14]. The NBP applications are linked with the MPICH2 MPI implementation [8], and run inside virtual machines (VMs) executing on Xen [7]. (Prior work has demonstrated that virtualization degrades the performance of HPC applications by less than 4% [24, 26].) The virtualization layer allows GreenPar to dynamically change a job's resource allocation, i.e., the set of physical servers hosting the job's VMs, by migrating and consolidating VMs within the datacenter as appropriate, without requiring changes to the MPI implementation.

For repeatability, we also evaluate GreenPar using properly scaled-down traces of green energy production from a solar farm at Rutgers University. When allowing GreenPar to slow jobs' executions down by at most 10%, we show that GreenPar can reduce brown energy consumption by 10% while *reducing* average runtime by 13%, compared to a baseline policy not aware of on-site green energy production. In addition, GreenPar satisfied the jobs' performance SLAs in all our experiments. These results show that while GreenPar may slow down some jobs (within their performance SLAs) to increase brown energy savings, it successfully leverages green energy to speedup overall executions. If applications have good speedup profiles (e.g., close to linear speedup), GreenPar can reduce brown energy consumption by 15% while reducing average runtime by 40%.

In summary, we make the following contributions: (1) we introduce GreenPar, a scheduling framework for parallel HPC workloads in datacenters partially powered by solar energy; (2) we introduce four scheduling policies for GreenPar, each assuming a different amount of knowledge about future green energy production, job characteristics, and datacenter workloads; (3) we implement GreenPar and evaluate it on Parasol, a real solar-powered micro-datacenter; and (4) we present extensive evaluation results for GreenPar, isolating the impact of the different amounts of knowledge in the four policies, and exploring its sensitivity to various parameters.

2. RELATED WORK

As far as we know, GreenPar is the first resource scheduler for green datacenters running parallel HPC applications. Though prior works have considered moldability, malleability, and folding in these applications (e.g., [12, 42]), none of them considered green energy and using it to reduce brown energy consumption and speed up executions. Other works [16–18, 29, 32] considered green energy in the context of scheduling batch applications, but did not dynamically change server allocations of running jobs or attempted to speed up executions using green energy while considering application speedup characteristics.

We divide the other works that relate to GreenPar into two areas: brown power management in parallel applications, and green energy management in datacenters.

Brown power management in parallel applications. Researchers have used multiple techniques to minimize energy consumption or to keep power consumption within a budget when running parallel applications. A popular technique is Dynamic Voltage and Frequency Scaling [25, 38]. Researchers also addressed power measurement and/or modeling of parallel applications [15,33,37] in power-aware clusters. Other researchers [9, 36] focused on scheduling for greater efficiency, which indirectly reduces energy consumption. Unlike GreenPar, these works did not consider on-site generation of green energy, where sometimes consuming more (green) energy is a good idea. Leveraging green energy, GreenPar can conserve brown energy even when it is not allowed to trade off performance (i.e., when the SLA does not allow for any performance slowdown).

Green energy management in datacenters. Stewart and Shen [41] and Le et al. [30] have explored request distribution policies for interactive online services that span multiple datacenters to explicitly manage the consumption of green and brown energy. Aksanli et al. [3] have considered the scheduling of mixed batch and service workloads in green datacenters. Akoush et al. [2] proposed workload distribution in virtualized systems. Several efforts have investigated load migration within a datacenter to better leverage on-site green energy production [23, 27, 31, 34].

Unlike these works, GreenPar manages the green energy usage to reduce the brown energy consumption and improve the performance of parallel HPC applications. Moreover, GreenPar dynamically re-allocates resources across running jobs while considering their speedup characteristics to maximize the benefit of green energy.

3. GREENPAR

We propose GreenPar, a job scheduler for parallel HPC workloads running in green datacenters partially powered by solar energy (see Figure 1). Note that, except for the prediction of near-future production of solar energy, *GreenPar is directly applicable to wind-powered green datacenters.* In this section, we first overview GreenPar, and then discuss four specific green-energy-aware policies for it. We also present a simple green-energy-unaware policy that we use as a basis for comparison in Section 5.

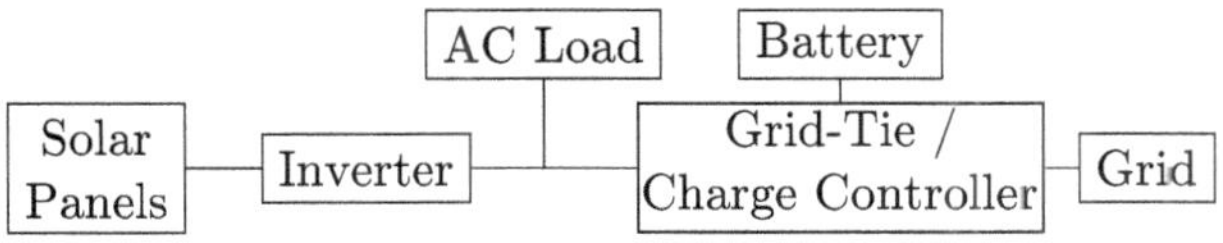

Figure 1: A possible setup for a datacenter partially powered by solar energy. The datacenter is connected to the electrical grid, which can meet the datacenter's peak power demand even when no solar energy is being produced. Batteries are only used as backup for grid outages.

3.1 Overview

GreenPar seeks to maximize green energy consumption and minimize brown energy consumption, while respecting a performance SLA. GreenPar achieves its goals by dynamically changing the resource allocations of jobs based on the availability of green energy, jobs' characteristics, and jobs' accumulated resource allocations.

We assume that each parallel job executes inside a set of VMs (one process per VM), as has been done in previous papers (e.g., [24,26]). GreenPar can dynamically change the number of physical servers assigned to run a job, migrating and consolidating VMs within the datacenter as necessary. Unused servers are put into a low-power state (e.g., ACPI S3) to conserve energy. Note that *GreenPar does not require a virtualized environment.* Rather, it only requires that jobs can adapt to dynamically changing numbers of servers. Bag-of-tasks applications, for example, are amenable to changes in the number of servers without any need for virtualization. Moreover, several papers (e.g., [12, 42]) have demonstrated moldable and malleable HPC frameworks based on MPI, again without using virtualization.

Each parallel job j is submitted to GreenPar with a requested number of servers (N_j) and a maximum acceptable slowdown factor (F_j). Three of the GreenPar policies also ask the user to supply a speedup profile $SP_j(n)$, defined as $SP_j(n) = RT_j(1)/RT_j(n)$, where $RT_j(n)$ is j's runtime when running its VMs on a constant allocation of n servers. (Two policies actually require two speedup profiles, as we explain below.) F_j is a factor ≥ 1 such as 1.1, which would allow GreenPar to slow down job execution by at most 10%. For simplicity, we assume that F_j is the same for all jobs, although our policies can easily be extended to handle different slowdown factors for different jobs.

GreenPar avoids excessively degrading execution times (i.e., degrading them by more than a factor of F) as a result of trying to conserve brown energy. To avoid potentially increasing waiting times due to brown energy conservation, GreenPar reverts back to the user-requested resource allocations when utilization becomes so high that jobs cannot be started immediately upon arrival. As Section 5 demonstrates, GreenPar tends to reduce average runtimes compared to green-energy-oblivious schedulers, which makes it less likely that jobs have to wait at all.

In our current implementation, three GreenPar policies start either twice or four times as many VMs as the requested number of servers. (The other GreenPar policy and the baseline policy always start two VMs per requested server.) The choice between these two options depends on the expected amount of green energy. For example, these policies typically start 16 VMs for $N_j = 8$ in our evaluation environment, where each server has a dual-core processor and so can efficiently host 2 VMs. But they may start 32 VMs, if they are expecting plentiful green energy, so that they are likely to allocate more than N_j servers to job j. Two of these policies use speedup profiles to make decisions, and so require two speedup profiles–one for 16 VMs and another for 32 VMs in our example–for each job, because the job's speedup depends on its number of VMs.

GreenPar then periodically computes the resource allocations for the active jobs. It dynamically increases the numbers of servers allocated to jobs that can achieve further speedups when expecting excess green energy. It dynamically decreases resource allocations of jobs that have accumulated or can be expected to accumulate performance slack (via larger resource allocations than requested when green energy was/will be available) to conserve energy when brown energy is needed.

GreenPar considers the speedup profiles of active jobs when making resource allocation decisions. For example, suppose two jobs, A and B, are each running on 10 servers, and A will not speedup if given more than 10 servers but B will until its allocation exceeds 25 servers. Then, if GreenPar expects that enough green energy will be produced to support 30 servers for a period of time, it will use the speedup profiles to increase B's server allocation to 20, while leaving A's at 10. Note that if B finishes before the green energy production decreases, GreenPar will have successfully used the excess green energy to decrease B's runtime.

However, if both A and B continue to run until a time period when no green energy is available, GreenPar will reduce both their allocations to below 10 servers to conserve brown energy. Of course, GreenPar cannot reduce the allocations so much that either A or B would take more than F times longer to complete compared to when each is running on a constant allocation of 10 servers. In this example, GreenPar may be able to reduce the allocation of B more than A, since B had accumulated some performance slack while running on 20 servers.

While the use of jobs' speedup profiles allows GreenPar to make intelligent decisions about resource allocation, it does make GreenPar reliant on having this information. Speedup information can be gathered across multiple runs of an application, and/or constructed using profiling (e.g., [15,39]). These approaches can produce very accurate speedup profiles, because HPC applications are often run many times with similar inputs. It is also possible to measure speedup at runtime with sufficient hardware and system software support [36]. Regardless, *to assess the impact on GreenPar if this information was not available, one of the GreenPar policies only uses a hint from the user on whether the submitted job would speedup if given more resources than requested.* Users that are unsure about their applications' behaviors can just supply a "no, the job will not speedup" hint.

3.2 Policies

We now present the four GreenPar policies and the baseline policy. Each GreenPar policy assumes a different amount of knowledge about future green energy production, jobs' characteristics, and future load. All policies divide time into discrete epochs for computing resource allocation schedules. All policies respond to job arrivals and completions within a time epoch.

Reactive. As its name suggests, Reactive does not assume any knowledge or prediction of future job arrivals and runtimes. Instead, it tracks the resource allocation for each job,

```
0.  For each job j, the user specifies the desired number of servers N_j and speedup profile S_j(n)

1.  For each event in {Job Arrival, Job Finish, Change in Green Energy, Reallocation Needed}
2.      For each job j,
3.          Calculate the minimum server allocation n_j for j (lines 14-20 below)
4.      Let C = sum of all n_j
5.      Let G = number of nodes that can be powered by the expected available green energy
6.      For each job j, allocate n_j servers to j
7.      While G > C:
8.          For each job j,
9.              Calculate the decrease in efficiency for further node allocation δ_j
10.         Sort the jobs in ascending order of δ_j
11.         Increase n_j by a threshold number of servers m_j to the first job j in the list
12.         C = C + m_j and update δ_j
13.         Resort the jobs in ascending order of δ_j

14. Calculate Minimum number of nodes for job j:
15.     if j is new, average speedup as_j = 0 and achieved runtime rt_j = 0
16.     Assume that j will run for another threshold time period t
18.     n_j = the minimum number of nodes such that as_j ≥ F · S_j(N_j)
19.     Schedule a Reallocation Needed event t time into the future
20.     Return n_j
```

Figure 2: Pseudocode for the Reactive scheduling algorithm.

predicts the green energy production for the next time epoch at the end of every time epoch, and reacts to the expected availability of green energy. When there is excess green energy, Reactive tries to increase the server allocation of active jobs to decrease runtimes. It greedily tries to increase the allocation of jobs with the best marginal speedups first, seeking maximum reduction in job runtimes for each additional allocated server. Subsequently, when there is insufficient green energy, Reactive tries to shrink the server allocations of active jobs that have accumulated some performance slack to conserve brown energy. It again greedily tries to reduce the allocations of jobs with the smallest marginal speedups first, seeking a minimum increase in runtimes for each removed server.

Reactive does not need to know jobs' runtimes to respect the SLA. Instead, knowing the requested number of servers and jobs' speedup profiles is sufficient since:

$$MaxRunTime = F \cdot RunTime_{j,1}/SP_j(N), \text{ and}$$
$$RunTime = RunTime_{j,1}/AverageSpeedup_j$$

implying that we can meet the performance SLA if:

$$AverageSpeedup_j \geq SP_j(N)/F$$

In our current implementation, Reactive always starts a job with twice as many VMs as the number of requested servers, so it requires only one speedup profile for each job. Figure 2 shows the pseudo-code for Reactive.

Offline optimization. For comparison, we develop an optimization-based policy with oracular knowledge of job arrivals, job speedups and runtimes, and green energy production. We call this policy Offline because GreenPar is unlikely to have the assumed information.

Table 1 lists the parameters of our optimization framework. Using them, we formulate the optimization problem shown in Figure 3. The optimization works on a scheduling horizon (e.g., 24 hours into the future) that is divided into discrete time epochs (t). Solving the optimization problem produces V_j (the number of VMs to run job j) and an epoch-based schedule of the number of servers ($S_j(t)$) assigned to each job j arriving in the scheduling horizon. Our current implementation considers starting each new job with twice or four times as many VMs as the user-requested number of servers for the job. The optimization is re-solved periodically to account for new knowledge (e.g., jobs arriving after the current 24-hour scheduling horizon).

Table 1: Framework parameters. Time epochs in the scheduling horizon are numbered from 1 to T.

Symbol	Meaning
T	Set of time epochs comprising scheduling horizon
J	Set of jobs arriving in the scheduling horizon
β	Relative weight of the average runtime vs. the brown energy cost in the objective function
F	Maximum acceptable slowdown factor
C	Number of servers in the datacenter
$GE(t)$	Predicted green energy production in epoch t
$PB(t)$	Price of the brown energy during epoch t
A_j	Epoch that job j arrives and starts running
E_j	Epoch that job j completes
N_j	Number of servers requested for job j
$RT_{j,1}$	Runtime of job j when running on 1 server
$SP_j(n,v)$	Job j's speedup when running on n servers with v VMs
$ME_j(n)$	Migration energy when job j's server allocation changes by n
$Pow_j(n)$	Power demand of job j when running on n servers
V_j	Number of VMs used to run job j
$S_j(t)$	Number of servers allocated to job j in epoch t

This optimization minimizes *Objective*, a weighted sum of the brown energy cost (*BrownCost*) and average job runtime (*AvgRuntime*).[3] The β factor allows us to adjust the relative importance of conserving brown energy versus increasing job runtimes. *BrownCost* is a function of the brown energy use ($BrownEn(t)$) over time and the brown energy price. Brown energy is consumed only when more energy ($En(t)$) is needed than the amount of green energy being produced. Energy is consumed both by jobs executing and migrations required to adapt to dynamically changing resource allocations ($MiEn_j(t)$). We use the v parameter in $SP_j(n,v)$ to represent the two user-provided speedup curves.

GreenPar solves the optimization problem under constraints formulated to ensure that the jobs' performance SLAs are met, jobs complete their executions, jobs are not preempted once they start running, and the allocated servers do not exceed the datacenter capacity.

The optimization problem can be transformed into a linear problem except for: (a) the migration energy $ME_j(n)$

[3]Previous studies have used different optimization objectives, e.g., $Energy \times Delay$ or $Energy \times Delay^2$. We choose this linear combination because it has been used successfully [4], and it allows us to formulate a linear optimization problem that can be solved efficiently.

$$
\begin{aligned}
Objective &= BrownCost + \beta \cdot AvgRuntime & (1)\\
BrownCost &= \sum_{t \in T} BrownEn(t) \cdot PB(t) & (2)\\
BrownEn(t) &= \begin{cases} En(t) - GE(t) & \text{if } En(t) > GE(t) \\ 0 & \text{otherwise} \end{cases} & (3)\\
En(t) &= \sum_{j \in J} (Pow_j(S_j(t)) \cdot |t| + MiEn_j(t)) & (4)\\
MiEn_j(t) &= ME_j(|S_j(t) - S_j(t-1)|) & (5)\\
AvgRuntime &= \frac{1}{|J|} \cdot \sum_{j \in J} \sum_{t \in T} Running_j(t) \cdot |t| & (6)\\
Running_j(t) &= \begin{cases} 1 & \text{if } S_j(t) > 0 \\ 0 & \text{otherwise} \end{cases} & (7)\\
E_j &= A_j + \sum_{t \in T} Running_j(t) & (8)\\
AvgSpeedup_j &= \sum_{t \in T} SP_j(S_j(t), V_j)/(E_j - A_j + 1) & (9)
\end{aligned}
$$

Figure 3: Optimization framework.

and the power demand of a job $Pow_j(n)$ may be non-linear functions, and (b) the speedup functions $SP_j(n, v)$ may be non-linear. We address the first issue by experimentally measuring and using approximate linear functions for both functions; in fact, we use only a single $Pow(n)$ and $ME(n)$ function for all jobs. In our evaluations, we found that this assumption introduced only small inaccuracies. We address the second issue by instantiating the speedup functions of each job as a table look-up using Integer Programming. Thus, the result is a Mixed Integer Linear Programming (MILP) problem that we can efficiently solve (at the sizes we consider) with standard solvers (e.g., [22]).

Aggressive. This policy is essentially the same as Offline except that it only assumes knowledge of jobs' runtimes and speedup profiles. It predicts future green energy production, implying that $GE(t)$ includes prediction errors. We discuss green energy predictions further in Section 4. It also solves the optimization problem only for active jobs, i.e., J only contains the jobs that have already arrived, and thus does not rely on knowledge of future arrivals.

Aggressive re-solves the optimization whenever a new job arrives. The optimization generates the number of VMs (V_j) for the new job and an epoch-based schedule of the number of servers ($S_j(t)$) assigned to each job j. Aggressive must also re-solve the optimization when there are significant changes to the predictions of green energy production. In our experiments, solving the Aggressive optimization problem takes less than 2 seconds.

Nebulous. Finally, we develop and study Nebulous, a policy that does not assume accurate knowledge of speedup profiles. Rather, it uses a user-provided hint about job speedup (excellent, good, fair, poor) and a rough estimate of job runtime. With these hints, it is impossible for Nebulous to support the same performance SLA as the previous policies. Thus, Nebulous instead seeks to ensure that the average resource allocation to each job is never less than $1/F$ times the number of requested servers.

Nebulous predicts green energy production, and, when a job arrives, it starts the job with more VMs if it expects that there will be enough green energy to run the larger number of VMs for the estimated duration of the job. This approach is conservative in that the runtime estimate is for the smaller number of VMs, so it is likely to be longer than the runtime when using the larger number of VMs.

Nebulous is then somewhat similar to Reactive. When there is excess green energy, it greedily allocates more servers to jobs with the best speedup hints and smallest average allocations thus far vs. their requested numbers of servers. Using the intuition that marginal speedup typically decreases with increased resource allocations, it only gives the smallest number of extra servers possible to each job before considering the next job. When green energy production decreases, Nebulous reduces server allocations to jobs in the reverse order (i.e., take away servers from jobs with poor speedup hints and most accumulated slack first).

Finally, since Nebulous only uses the runtime estimate to decide whether to run a job with more VMs, it can use statistics from previous runs of the application. When an application is run for the first time, Nebulous conservatively assumes that the job will run for a long time, implying that it does not start the job with more VMs. In our evaluations, we use the average of the previous runs of each application and correct speedup hints.

Baseline. We use a Baseline policy as a basis for comparison in our evaluation of the green-energy-aware policies. Baseline runs each job as it arrives, starting each job with twice the number of VMs as requested servers.

4. EVALUATION METHODOLOGY

Prototype implementation and evaluation platform. We have implemented a prototype of GreenPar comprising roughly 2200 lines of python code. The prototype includes all four policies Reactive, Aggressive, Offline, and Nebulous.

We evaluate the prototype running on Parasol. Our evaluation uses 55 servers, where each server is equipped with a dual-core 1.6GHz Atom processor, 4GB of memory, one 250GB hard disk, and one 64GB solid-state drive. This cluster uses 5 machines as NFS servers to hold VM images and application data, and the remaining 50 machines for running jobs executing inside VMs. Each server consumes between 22W to 30W, giving a peak power consumption of 1.5kW for the computing servers. The servers are interconnected with a 1Gbps Ethernet network.

The 50 compute servers run Xen 4.3 [7], using the Linux 3.11 kernel for both the host and guest OSes. Each VM image is configured with 1 virtual CPU, 384MB of memory, and a 4GB disk. Baseline always assigns two VMs to each server, giving each VM a dedicated core. The other policies can assign 1 VM to each server when a job is given extra resources, or up to 4 VMs per server when the job is consolidated to save energy. Although running a VM with just one virtual CPU on a dual-core server may seem somewhat inefficient, it can speedup execution by 66% over running 2 VMs on the server for communication-intensive applications (e.g., NAS IS). We use Xen's live migration capability to migrate VMs without interrupting job executions. The virtual disks are stored on the NFS servers, and so do not have to be migrated. Measurements show that live migrations had very little impact on job runtimes. Idle servers are placed into the ACPI S3 state to conserve energy.

Parasol allows us to measure the energy consumption of individual servers. Thus, all results below are from actual measurements of energy consumed by executing workloads.

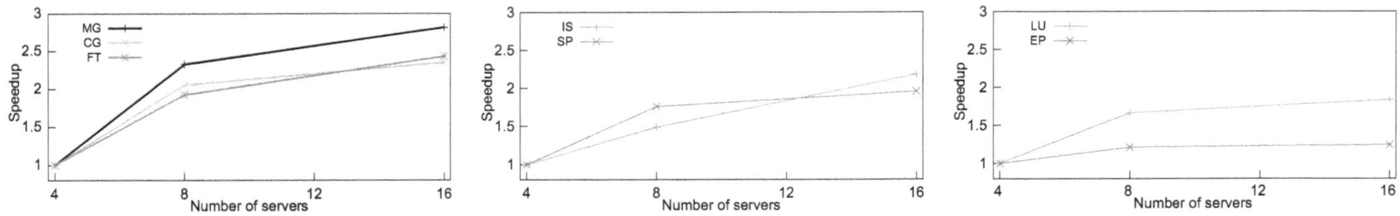

Figure 4: Speedup profiles of NPB applications running with 16 VMs on different numbers of physical servers. The speedup profile of BT is not shown because it is exactly same as SP.

Table 2: Core count mapping for Intrepid.

Intrepid core count	256, 512	1024, 2048	4096	Others
Mapped core count	4	8	16	32

Workloads. We study two workloads created to emulate two real traces. The first workload, called Grid5k, emulates a trace from the Grid Workload Archive [11]. The original trace was collected on the Grid'5000 system [21], a 2,218-node distributed system spread across 9 sites in France, from May 2004 to November 2006. We chose an arbitrary 24-hour period from this trace and filtered out short running jobs that ask for just one processor core, assuming that they are small test runs, to scale the workload to our datacenter. After filtering, the chosen sub-trace has 26 jobs, with a peak processing demand of 96 cores. Most of the results presented below were obtained using this workload trace.

The second workload, called Intrepid, emulates a trace from the Parallel Workload Archive [14]. The original trace was collected on the Intrepid system, a 40-rack, 40,960-node Blue Gene/P system deployed at Argonne National Laboratory, from January 2009 to August 2009. We selected an arbitrary 24-hour portion of the trace, and then scaled down job sizes as explained in the next paragraph to fit our datacenter. The selected period has 113 jobs, with a peak processing demand of 86 cores.

Each of the workload traces includes information on job arrival time, job runtime, and the number of cores requested. However, they do not include information about the applications nor the input data. Thus, we use a subset of applications from the NAS Parallel Benchmark (NPB) [35] to instantiate the workloads. NPB contains 8 applications with different input sizes. We use a mix of applications and input sizes to emulate the two different traces. Figure 4 shows the speedup curves for all the applications used in our workload.

Most NPB jobs require a power-of-2 number of VMs. We map each job in the Grid5k trace to the closest NPB application in terms of core count (assuming 1 VM per core) and runtime, with 2 VMs running on each dual-core server. With this mapping, the resulting Grid5k workload includes 12 FT, 6 LU, 3 MG, 2 CG, and 1 each of SP, EP and IS. In contrast, Intrepid jobs ask for large numbers of cores, with the minimum being 256. To scale these jobs to our datacenter, we map the Intrepid jobs following Table 2. The resulting workload contains 73 IS, 24 MG, 14 CG, 1 FT and 1 SP applications. Figure 5 shows the workload demand (in number of cores) of Grid5k and Intrepid, as a function of time. The workloads never require more servers than are available (50 servers with 100 cores) in our setup.

Energy prices. We use the average brown energy price for New Jersey: 10.55 cents/kWh [13]. The use of a constant price equates saving brown energy with reducing brown energy cost. However, in general, both Aggressive and Offline can leverage dynamically changing energy prices to reduce the brown energy cost. We assume self-generation of solar energy, so that green energy has zero (marginal) cost. Our framework can be easily extended to account for a non-zero green energy cost, if desired.

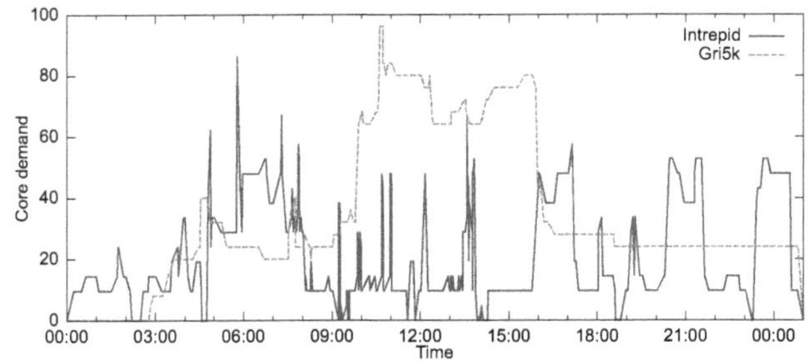

Figure 5: Workload demand in number of cores, as a function of time.

Optimization weighting factor. The outcome of the Aggressive and Offline policies is affected by the value of β. β controls the relative importance of runtime compared to electricity cost. To gauge this relationship, we first convert runtime to a cost figure (using the cost of computation in the cloud) and then compare it to the electricity cost of the same computation and for the same runtime. Specifically, we compare the per-hour cost of renting a large VM instance on Amazon's EC2 [5] (\$0.24) with the per-hour electricity cost of a server with the same specification as the instance (roughly 0.3kWh × \$0.1055/kWh). So, our chosen value for β is 8 ($= \frac{\$0.24}{0.3kWh \times \$0.1055/kWh}$).

We also ran experiments with β ranging from 0.8 to 80. We omit these results as they were as expected, and do not affect the observations in our evaluation.

Estimating migration overheads. We measured the migration time for all the applications in our environment. The measured migration time (and thus energy overhead) does not vary much among the applications. So, we use the average migration time for every application when solving the optimization problem in Aggressive and Offline.

Solar energy production and prediction. Although Parasol is partially powered by a set of solar panels, for repeatability, we used traces of solar energy production in our experiments. However, we have run many validation runs on Parasol, using real predictions and production of solar energy. We show results from one of these runs below to show that GreenPar behaves as expected under live execution.

In our experiments, we model the solar power generation as a scaled-down version of a solar farm at Rutgers that has a rated production capacity of 1.4MW. We scale the farm's production down to 8 solar panels capable of producing 1.88kW. After derating, the peak solar power production matches the peak power consumption of our datacenter.

We evaluate our scheduling policies using three days with different amounts of solar energy production: one sunny

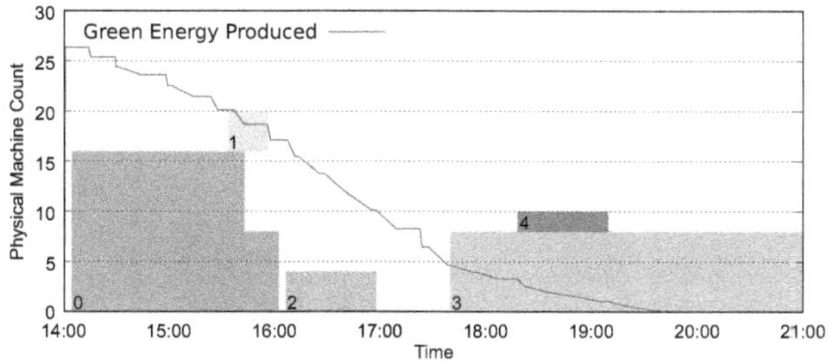

Figure 6: Green energy production and server allocations during a 7-hour validation run of Grid5k.

day (5/9/11) with high solar energy production (totaling 12kWh), one day (6/16/11) with medium solar energy production (totaling 8kWh), and one day (5/15/11) with low solar energy production (totaling 2.84kWh). We call these the "High", "Medium", and "Low" days, respectively.

We use the method from [18] (which is based on [40]) to predict solar energy production for a horizon of 48 hours. Briefly, the model relates solar energy generation to cloud cover as $E_p(t) = B(t)(1 - CloudCover)$, where $E_p(t)$ is the amount of energy predicted for time period t, $B(t)$ is the amount of energy expected under ideal sunny conditions, and $CloudCover$ is the forecasted percentage cloud cover. We use Intellicast.com's weather forecasts, which predicts $CloudCover$ for each hour of the next 48 hours. This leads to prediction granularity (i.e., t) of one hour. We set $B(t)$ for each hour of the day to the amount of energy generated during that hour on the day with the highest energy generation from the previous month.

Of course, weather forecasts are sometimes wrong. Thus, the prediction includes a technique for using recent energy production to predict future production when predictions based on weather forecasts are inaccurate [17]. The evaluation in [18] shows that one-hour ahead predictions using this method produce inaccuracies of around 11%.

Our prediction method produces different accuracies for the High, Medium, and Low days. Predictions are mostly accurate for the High day, although there are some under-predictions. They are also mostly accurate for the Low day. However, those for the Medium day contain significant errors, with periods of over- and under-predictions.

Accelerated experiments. To make it possible to run a large number of experiments, each experiment is an accelerated run of the workload. Specifically, the time frame is accelerated by a factor of 60, making 1 minute of experiment execution represent 1 hour of real time. We accelerate jobs' execution times by reducing the size of the inputs. We also constrained the system to not migrate VMs more often than once a minute (1 hour in real time). Note that this is pessimistic in two ways: (a) the migration time did not scale down linearly; thus, migration overheads would have been smaller in un-accelerated execution; and (b) lower migration overheads would have allowed our policies to adjust allocations more often (e.g., every 15 minutes). The validation experiment shown in Figure 6 was run in real time (that is, it was not accelerated).

Experimental setup. We set the scheduling horizon to 24 hours, and divide this horizon into 15-minute epochs.[4] We use the Gurobi solver [22] to solve the optimization problems for Aggressive and Offline. In our experiments, solutions of Aggressive take less than 2 seconds to execute. Offline runs completely offline to determine the best case for comparison, so we let it execute for 30 minutes in our experiments.

We use the same amount of maximum acceptable runtime slowdown for all jobs for Reactive, Offline, and Aggressive. The default is 10%, although we also study settings in the 0%–50% range. For Nebulous, we use a maximum reduced average resource allocation of 10%. In our experiments, *GreenPar is able to satisfy all performance SLAs.*

Finally, to make efficient use of resources, GreenPar only allocates powers-of-2 servers to each job, so that the number of VMs per server for a job is always the same. Also, GreenPar cannot allocate more servers to a job than the number of VMs in that job, and cannot consolidate more than 4 VMs onto a single server. All of these limit the flexibility with which GreenPar can adjust jobs' server allocations, but are limitations of our experimental setup rather than fundamental to GreenPar itself. GreenPar would perform better if jobs could dynamically adapt to arbitrary server allocations.

5. VALIDATION AND EVALUATION

In this section, we first present a validation experiment of GreenPar running on Parasol with real energy production and prediction. We then present our evaluation of the four GreenPar policies using our scaled-down solar traces.

Validation. Figure 6 shows the results from a validation experiment using Aggressive and the Grid5k workload. The experiment ran over 7 hours on Parasol, using real solar energy production and live predictions of solar energy production. In Figure 6, each box shows the server allocation of a job over its lifetime. The green line depicts the green energy available over time. The numbers in the colored boxes are the job identifiers. In this execution, jobs 0, 1, and 2 requested 8, 2, and 2 servers, respectively. However, because of the high green energy availability, GreenPar doubled the allocations of each of these jobs to reduce their runtimes. When the production of green energy decreased toward the end of job 0's execution, GreenPar adjusted by reducing job 0's server allocation to 8 servers. GreenPar was able to reduce the runtimes of these jobs by an average of 23.8%.

Evaluation. Figure 7 compares the brown energy consumption, green energy usage, total number of VMs, and average runtime reduction achieved by Baseline and the four GreenPar policies when running Grid5k for the High day. The total number of VMs is the sum of all VMs used by all the jobs; a larger number of VMs means that jobs were executed with greater parallelism. The brown energy consumption, green energy usage, and total number of VMs are normalized compared to those of Offline (Y-axis on the left). Average runtime reduction is the percentage reduction of jobs compared to when they are scheduled by Baseline (Y-axis on the right).

These results show that all four policies can reduce brown energy consumption *and* reduce job runtimes. They achieve these savings by slowing down job execution when only brown energy is available, and speeding up job execution when green energy is available. While Reactive only reduces brown energy consumption by a small amount (~2% reduction), it successfully uses more green energy to reduce average job runtimes by 5%. This means that even when the policy has

[4]The epoch duration can involve tradeoffs between scheduling overhead and faster response to changing conditions. However, our evaluation is insensitive to this parameter, since migration overheads are small and near-future prediction of green-energy is relatively accurate.

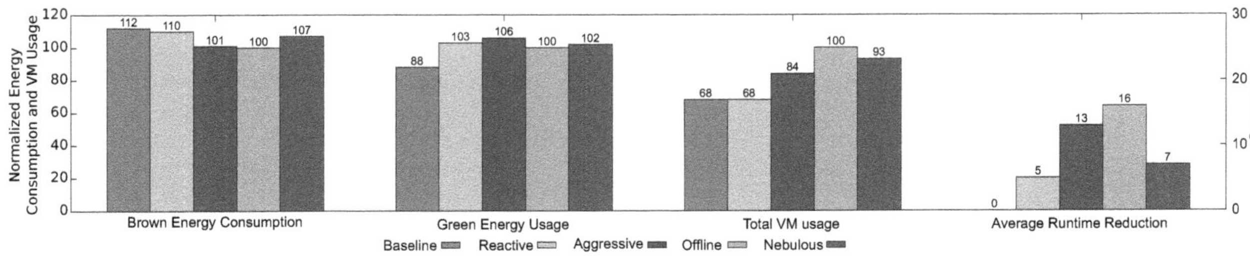

Figure 7: Comparison of policies for Grid5k workload running on the High day.

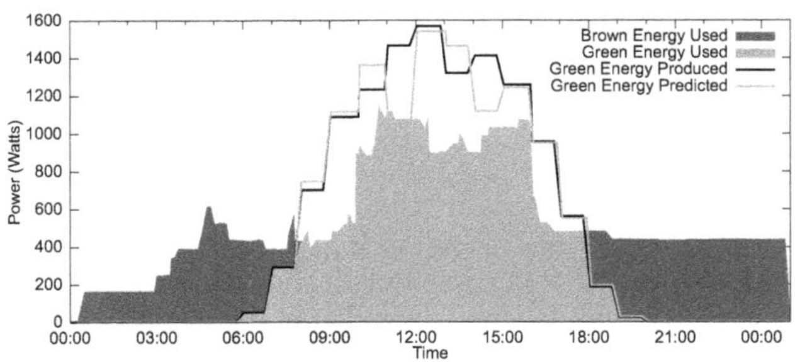

Figure 8: Behavior of Baseline, Grid5k, High day.

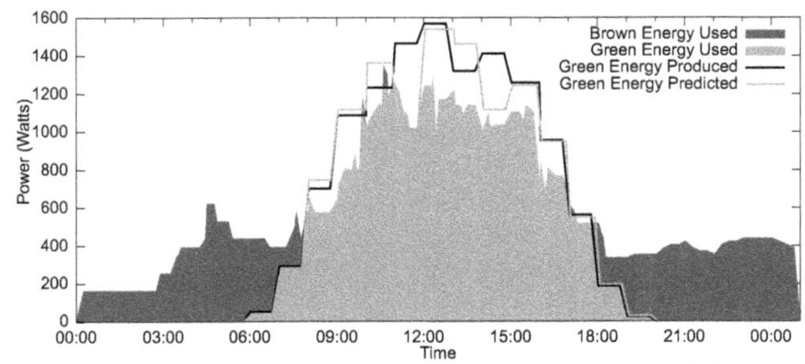

Figure 9: Behavior of Reactive, Grid5k, High day.

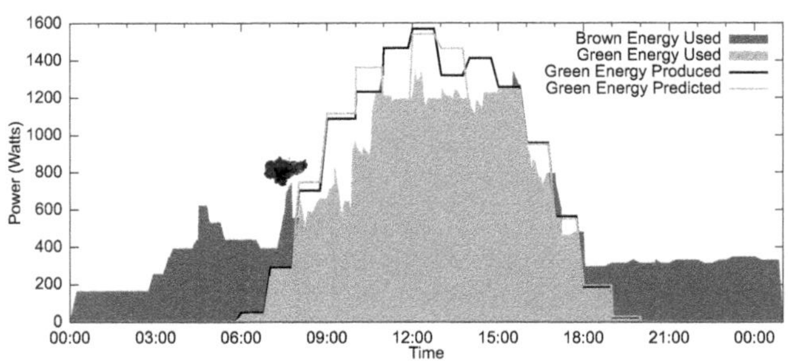

Figure 10: Behavior of Aggressive, Grid5k, High day.

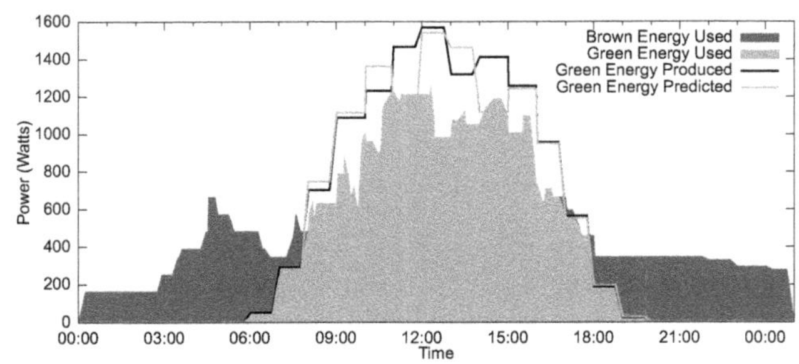

Figure 11: Behavior of Offline, Grid5k, High day.

no knowledge of job arrivals and runtimes, it can leverage green energy to improve runtimes.

Aggressive is better than Reactive because it uses knowledge of job runtimes and predictions of green energy availability in the near future to more aggressively start jobs with higher levels of parallelism; the same set of jobs is run with 84 VMs under Aggressive compared to 68 under Reactive. This allows Aggressive to successfully use more green energy, less brown energy, and achieve shorter job runtimes.

In fact, Aggressive behaves almost as well as Offline. It uses only slightly more brown energy (1% more), and almost matches Offline in the average reduction of runtimes (13% vs. 16%). The advantages of Offline arise from its oracle knowledge of the future. Aggressive immediately runs an arriving job with a larger number of VMs if it expects green energy to be available. However, this may prevent it from running the next arriving job with a large number of VMs–there may be insufficient resources left–even though the subsequent job has better speedup characteristics. Offline can make the correct choice given its knowledge of the future. Interestingly, Offline uses less green energy because it uses it more efficiently; it allocates the energy to the jobs with the best speedup, allowing these jobs to finish more quickly and stop consuming energy.

Finally, Nebulous behaves slightly better than Reactive even though it is given only hints about speedup. This is because it aggressively starts jobs with more VMs when expecting excess green energy in the future. Thus, Nebulous uses more green energy to speedup jobs than Reactive.

On the other hand, Nebulous cannot match Aggressive because its heuristic for choosing the number of VMs is less accurate. In our implementation, Nebulous only chooses the larger number of VMs (per requested server) if it expects to have excess green energy for the entire estimated runtime of a job. However, the job may finish much faster when it is given extra resources. Thus, Nebulous's decisions are often overly conservative compared to Aggressive. Also, Nebulous's allocations of extra resources between multiple jobs are often not as good as Aggressive's allocations, because it does not have accurate speedup information.

Detailed power demand profiles for the five policies when running Grid5k for the High day are shown in Figures 8–12. The first 6 hours are similar for all policies because there is no green energy production, and the jobs can only be slowed down by a maximum of 10%. In the daytime, when green energy becomes available, the green-energy-aware policies increase power consumption by either increasing the server allocations of active jobs (all four policies) and/or starting new jobs with more VMs, allowing larger than requested server allocations (Aggressive, Offline, and Nebulous). As mentioned earlier, Offline consumes less green energy even though it runs jobs with more parallelism (greater number of VMs) because it allocates the green energy to the most efficient jobs, leading to the greatest reduction in job runtimes. Finally, Aggressive and Offline can reduce brown energy consumption at night (right portion of the figures) either because jobs finished faster (they were run with more parallelism when green energy was available) or enough per-

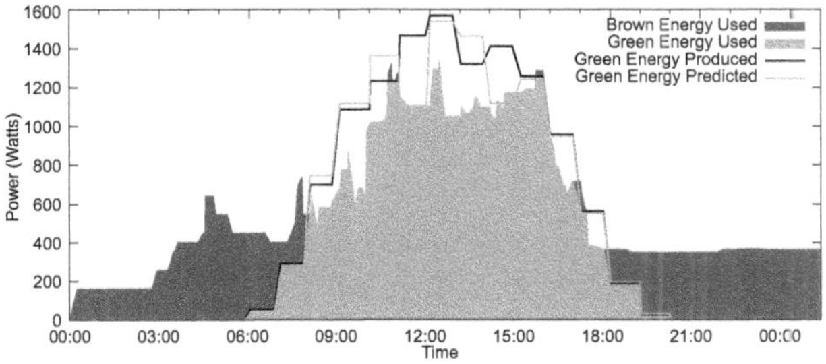

Figure 12: Behavior of Nebulous, Grid5k, High day.

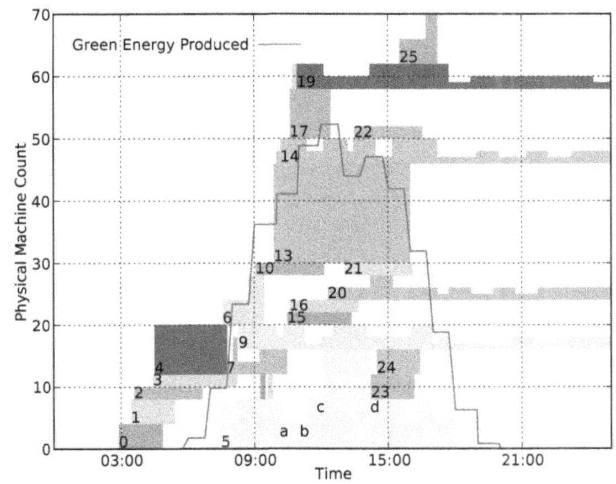

Figure 13: Aggressive's server allocation for Grid5k.

formance slack has been accumulated so that some jobs can be consolidated onto fewer physical machines compared to Baseline. Reactive and Nebulous achieve smaller savings.

For a more detailed look at the behavior of a green-energy-aware policy, Figure 13 shows the allocation of physical servers to jobs for Aggressive over time. The green line, boxes, and numerical labels are the same as for Figure 6. A closer look at job 5 reveals several interesting points. First, Aggressive starts job 5, which requested 4 servers, with 16 VMs because it is expecting to have excess green energy. This allows Aggressive to run job 5 on more servers, consuming green energy to speedup job execution. Initially, Aggressive allocates 8 servers to the job (2 VMs per dual-core machine). At point 'a', job 14 arrives with better speedup characteristics. Thus, Aggressive shrinks job 5's server allocation to 4. Later, as more green energy becomes available, Aggressive increases job 5's allocation to 8 (point 'b') and then to 16 (point 'c'). Note that, with 16 servers, job 5 is being run with only 1 VM per server. This allocation achieves limited speedup since the second core on each server is frequently idle. However, since the green energy is "free" in this case, it is beneficial to use this energy whenever some speedup is still possible. As green energy production decreases over the day, and other jobs enter the system, Aggressive again decreases job 5's allocation (point 'd' and beyond). In comparison, job 5 ran for a much longer time with a static allocation of 4 servers under Baseline (not shown here).

Impact of green energy availability. We also run Baseline and Aggressive for the Medium and Low days. Figure 14 shows the behavior of Aggressive for the Medium day. As previously mentioned, this day has significant mis-predictions of the solar energy production, including both under- and over-predictions. Over-predictions can lead Aggressive to use brown energy unnecessarily (and less effi-

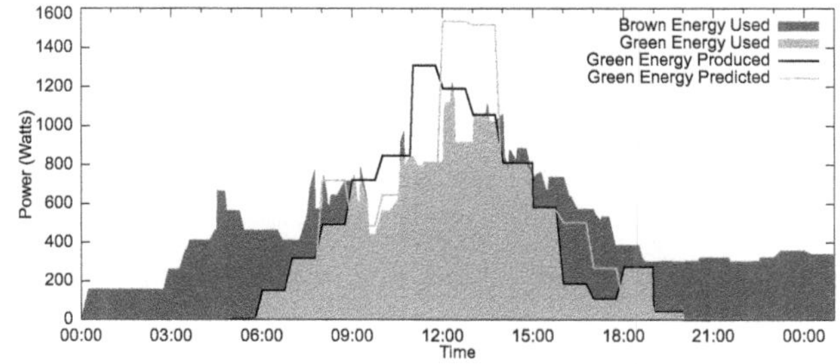

Figure 14: Behavior of Aggressive, Grid5k, Medium day.

ciently). On the other hand, under-predictions can lead it to waste green energy. Overall, Aggressive still reduces the average runtime by 27% despite the mis-predictions. However, it uses 5% more brown energy than Baseline. On the Low day, Aggressive and Baseline behave the same because there was little green energy to leverage.

We also study Aggressive and Baseline for different green energy production capacities. Scaling the solar power system does not change the overall behaviors. On the High day, a peak solar production capacity of 125% of the peak datacenter power consumption leads to an 11.3% reduction in the brown energy consumption (compared to 10% above), and a 12.9% reduction in the average runtime (compared to 12% above). Scaling down the peak solar energy production to 75% of the peak datacenter power consumption leads to an 8.6% reduction in the brown energy consumption and a 10.3% reduction in the average runtime.

Impact of application speedup. GreenPar's efficacy can be strongly affected by the speedup characteristics of jobs in the workloads. To see the impact of having jobs with better speedups, we constructed a Grid5k workload using only EP jobs. When an EP job is run with 16 VMs, it achieves much better speedup (much closer to linear) than that shown in Figure 4. When running this workload, Aggressive reduces the brown energy consumption by 15% while reducing the average runtime by 40% compared to Baseline.

Impact of performance SLA. When we disallow GreenPar to slow down job execution, i.e., set F to 1, Aggressive can still reduce the brown energy consumption by 8% and reduce the average runtime by 12%. If we instead allow a 50% slow down factor, Aggressive consumes 16% less brown energy than Baseline while reducing the average runtime by 9%. In this case, Aggressive's lack of knowledge about future job arrivals limits its performance. Specifically, before the green energy production starts to ramp up, Aggressive (aggressively) slows down the execution of active jobs, planning to use the green energy produced later on to recoup the performance loss. However, new jobs arriving later in the day will consume some of the green energy, leading Aggressive to consume brown energy instead to catch up; the catching up is typically done at lower efficiency since execution at larger server allocations is typically less efficient.

Impact of runtime mis-estimations. Aggressive outperforms Baseline but relies on knowing jobs' runtimes. We have studied their relative performance where the user provided job runtimes to Aggressive are inaccurate by ±25%. These inaccuracies did not significantly affect Aggressive since it recomputes a new schedule whenever a job completes anyways. Thus, the performance differences between Aggressive and Baseline were close to those presented above.

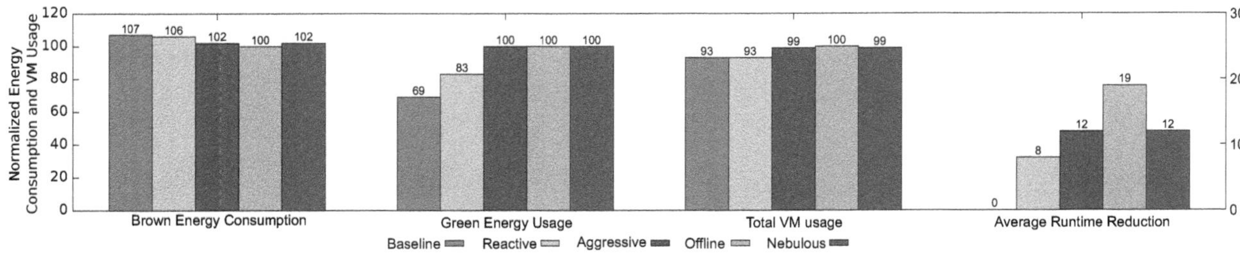

Figure 15: Comparison of policies for the Intrepid workload running on the High day.

Impact of datacenter utilization. Under Baseline, Grid5k produces a datacenter utilization of approximately 33%. The traces we use to construct our workloads exhibit similar utilizations. Nevertheless, we also run experiments with higher utilizations to gauge GreenPar's behavior under heavy load. Specifically, we doubled (2x) and tripled (3x) Grid5k, causing lengthy queue build up over time in Baseline. At 2x load, 12% more jobs complete under Aggressive than Baseline. This is because Aggressive is still occasionally able to give some jobs extra resources, allowing them to complete faster and reduce contention. At 3x load, the two policies perform the same. Thus, we conclude that GreenPar's benefits tail off as utilization becomes very high. *However, GreenPar does not harm performance even at very high loads.*

Impact of workload characteristics. Figure 15 compares the brown energy consumption, green energy usage, total number of VMs, and average runtime reduction achieved by the policies when running Intrepid for the High day. These results show the same trends as those observed for Grid5k. Interestingly however, Nebulous's performance almost matches Aggressive. This is because most jobs are short so that they easily fit within periods of high solar energy. Thus, both policies make similar decisions about the number of VMs to start per job.

6. CONCLUSIONS

In this paper, we proposed GreenPar, a scheduler for parallel HPC workloads running in datacenters partially powered by solar energy. GreenPar seeks to maximize the use of green energy to reduce job runtimes and brown energy consumption. We have implemented and evaluated it using realistic workloads, running on a real solar-powered datacenter. Our results show that GreenPar can increase green energy consumption and decrease brown energy consumption, while reducing average runtime at the same time. The results also show that an online policy using information about job speedups, runtimes, and predictions of solar energy production can come close to matching an offline policy that additionally has perfect information about future job arrivals and green energy production. Finally, GreenPar still provides benefits (albeit smaller ones) when it only has rough hints for speedup and runtime.

We conclude that GreenPar can become an important software component in green datacenters that run HPC workloads, helping to improve the sustainability of our Information Technology ecosystem.

Acknowledgments. We would like to thank William Katsak and the anonymous reviewers for their helpful comments and suggestions. This work was partially supported by NSF grant CSR-1117368 and the Rutgers Green Computing Initiative.

7. REFERENCES

[1] AISO.net. Web Hosting as Nature Intended, 2012. http://www.aiso.net.

[2] S. Akoush, R. Sohan, A. Rice, A. Moore, and A. Hopper. Free Lunch: Exploiting Renewable Energy for Computing. In *Workshop on hot topics in operating systems (HotOS)*, 2011.

[3] B. Aksanli, J. Venkatesh, L. Zhang, and T. Rosing. Utilizing Green Energy Prediction to Schedule Mixed Batch and Service Jobs in Data Centers. In *Workshop on Power-Aware Computing and Systems (HotPower)*, 2011.

[4] S. Albers and H. Fujiwara. Energy-Efficient Algorithms for Flow Time Minimization. In *Symposium on Theoretical Aspects of Computer Science (STACS)*, 2006.

[5] Amazon EC2 Pricing. http://aws.amazon.com/ec2, Retrieved on February 2013.

[6] Apple Inc. Apple Environmental Responsibility Report. https://www.apple.com/environment/reports/docs/apple_environmental_responsibility_report_0714.pdf, 2014.

[7] P. Barham, B. Dragovic, K. Fraser, S. Hand, T. Harris, A. Ho, R. Neugebauer, I. Pratt, and A. Warfield. Xen and the Art of Virtualization. In *Symposium on Operating Systems Principles (SOSP)*, 2003.

[8] A. Bouteiller, F. Cappello, T. Hérault, G. Krawezik, P. Lemarinier, and F. Magniette. MPICH-V2: a Fault Tolerant MPI for Volatile Nodes based on Pessimistic Sender Based Message Logging. In *Supercomputing (SC)*, 2003.

[9] J. Corbalan and J. Labarta. Improving Processor Allocation Through Run-time Measured Efficiency. In *International Parallel and Distributed Processing Symposium (IPDPS)*, 2001.

[10] Data Center Knowledge. Data Centers Scale Up Their Solar Power, 2012. http://www.datacenterknowledge.com/archives/2012/05/14/data-centers-scale-up-their-solarpower.

[11] Delft University of Technology. The Grid Workloads Archive. http://gwa.ewi.tudelft.nl/pmwiki/pmwiki.php?n=Workloads.Gwa-t-2.

[12] T. Desell, K. El Maghraoui, and C. A. Varela. Malleable Applications for Scalable High Performance Computing. *Cluster Computing*, 10(3), 2007.

[13] Energy Information Administration. Average Retail Price of Electricity to Ultimate Customers by End-Use Sector, by State. http://www.eia.gov/electricity/monthly/epm_table_grapher.cfm?t=epmt_5_6_b, Retrieved on January 2013.

[14] D. Feitelson. Parallel Workload Archive. `http://www.cs.huji.ac.il/labs/parallel/workload/l_anl_int/index.html`.

[15] R. Ge and K. Cameron. Power-aware Speedup. In *International Parallel and Distributed Processing Symposium (IPDPS)*, 2007.

[16] I. Goiri, W. Katsak, K. Le, T. D. Nguyen, and R. Bianchini. Parasol and GreenSwitch: Managing Datacenters Powered by Renewable Energy. In *International Conference on Architectural Support for Programming Languages and Operating System (ASPLOS)*, 2013.

[17] I. Goiri, K. Le, M. E. Haque, R. Beauchea, T. D. Nguyen, J. Guitart, J. Torres, and R. Bianchini. GreenSlot: Scheduling Energy Consumption in Green Datacenters. In *Supercomputing (SC)*, 2011.

[18] I. Goiri, K. Le, T. D. Nguyen, J. Guitart, J. Torres, and R. Bianchini. GreenHadoop: Leveraging Green Energy in Data-Processing Frameworks. In *European Conference on Computer Systems (EuroSys)*, 2012.

[19] Green House Data. An Economically Responsible Data Center, 2012. `http://www.greenhousedata.com`.

[20] GreenQloud, 2013. `http://greenqloud.com`.

[21] Grid'5000. Grid'5000 Experimentation Platform. `www.grid5000.fr`.

[22] Gurobi Optimization Inc. Gurobi Optimization. `http://www.gurobi.com`.

[23] M. E. Haque, K. Le, I. Goiri, R. Bianchini, and T. D. Nguyen. Providing Green SLAs in High Performance Computing Clouds. In *International Green Computing Conference (IGCC)*, 2013.

[24] S. Hazelhurst. Scientific Computing Using Virtual High-performance Computing: A Case Study Using the Amazon Elastic Computing Cloud. In *Annual Research Conference of the South African Institute of Computer Scientists and Information Technologists (SAICSIT)*, 2008.

[25] Q. Huang, S. Su, J. Li, P. Xu, K. Shuang, and X. Huang. Enhanced Energy-Efficient Scheduling for Parallel Applications in Cloud. In *Symposium on Cluster, Cloud, and Grid Computing (CCGRID)*, 2012.

[26] W. Huang, J. Liu, B. Abali, and D. K. Panda. A Case for High Performance Computing with Virtual Machines. In *International Conference on Supercomputing (ICS)*, 2006.

[27] K. Kant, M. Murugan, and D. H.C.Du. Willow: A Control System for Energy and Thermal Adaptive Computing. In *International Parallel and Distributed Processing Symposium (IPDPS)*, 2011.

[28] J. Koomey. Growth in Data Center Electricity Use 2005 to 2010, 2011. Analytic Press.

[29] A. Krioukov, C. Goebel, S. Alspaugh, Y. Chen, D. Culler, and R. Katz. Integrating Renewable Energy Using Data Analytics Systems: Challenges and Opportunities. *Bulletin of the IEEE Computer Society Technical Committee on Data Engineering*, March 2011.

[30] K. Le, O. Bilgir, R. Bianchini, M. Martonosi, and T. D. Nguyen. Capping the Brown Energy Consumption of Internet Services at Low Cost. In *International Green Computing Conference (IGCC)*, 2010.

[31] C. Li, A. Qouneh, and T. Li. iSwitch: Coordinating and Optimizing Renewable Energy Powered Server Clusters. In *International Symposium on Computer Architectur (ISCA)*, 2012.

[32] C. Li, R. Wang, T. Li, D. Qian, and J. Yuan. Managing green datacenters powered by hybrid renewable energy systems. In *International Conference on Autonomic Computing (ICAC)*, 2014.

[33] D. Li, B. De Supinski, M. Schulz, K. Cameron, and D. Nikolopoulos. Hybrid MPI/OpenMP power-aware computing. In *International Parallel and Distributed Processing Symposium (IPDPS)*, 2010.

[34] Z. Liu, Y. Chen, C. Bash, A. Wierman, D. Gmach, Z. Wang, M. Marwah, and C. Hyser. Renewable and Cooling Aware Workload Management for Sustainable Data Centers. In *International Conference on Measurement and Modeling of Computer Systems (SIGMETRICS)*, 2012.

[35] NASA Advanced Supercomputing Division, Retrieved on December 2013. `www.nas.nasa.gov/publications/npb.html`.

[36] T. D. Nguyen, R. Vaswani, and J. Zahorjan. Using Runtime Measured Workload Characteristics in Parallel Processor Scheduling. In *Job Scheduling Strategies for Parallel Processing (JSSPP)*, 1996.

[37] A. Porterfield, S. Olivier, S. Bhalachandra, and J. Prins. Power Measurement and Concurrency Throttling for Energy Reduction in OpenMP Programs. In *International Parallel and Distributed Processing Symposium Workshops PhD Forum (IPDPSW)*, 2013.

[38] B. Rountree, D. K. Lowenthal, S. Funk, V. W. Freeh, B. R. de Supinski, and M. Schulz. Bounding Energy Consumption in Large-Scale MPI Programs. In *Supercomputing (SC)*, 2007.

[39] M. Shantharam, Y. Youn, and P. Raghavan. Speedup-Aware Co-Schedules for Efficient Workload Management. *Parallel Processing Letters*, 23(02), 2013.

[40] N. Sharma, J. Gummeson, D. Irwin, and P. Shenoy. Cloudy Computing: Leveraging Weather Forecasts in Energy Harvesting Sensor Systems. In *International Conference on Sensor Mesh and Ad Hoc Communications and Networks (SECON)*, 2010.

[41] C. Stewart and K. Shen. Some Joules Are More Precious Than Others: Managing Renewable Energy in the Datacenter. In *Workshop on Power Aware Computing and Systems (HotPower)*, 2009.

[42] G. Utrera, J. Corbalan, and J. Labarta. Implementing Malleability on MPI Jobs. In *International Conference on Parallel Architectures and Compilation Techniques (PACT)*, 2004.

Underprovisioning the Grid Power Infrastructure for Green Datacenters

Xu Zhou[†*], Qiang Cao[†*$], Hong Jiang[‡], Changsheng Xie[†*]
[†]School of Computer, Huazhong University of Science and Technology, Wuhan, China
[*]Wuhan National Laboratory for Optoelectronics, Wuhan, China
[‡]Dept. of Computer Science and Engineering, University of Nebraska-Lincoln, Lincoln, NE, USA
[$]Corresponding Author: caoqiang@hust.edu.cn

ABSTRACT

While there have been prior studies on underprovisioning the power distribution infrastructure for a grid-based datacenter, how to save grid capital investment by means of leveraging renewable energy to underprovision the grid power infrastructure in green datacenters remains largely an unexplored, open issue. Aggressively underprovisioning grid infrastructure can trigger power emergency in which simultaneous peak power draws across the datacenter exceed the tightly budgeted grid power capacity, leading to possible serious consequences including power shutdown. The resulting power emergency mandates a graceful reaction mechanism to sustain the power requirement to avoid power overdraw. While leveraging renewable energy in a green datacenter provides a possibility to prevent power overdraw during such a power emergency, the intermittent nature of renewable energy makes it a very challenging task because of the potentially unpredictable performance impact to individual applications. This paper addresses this issue by designing a novel renewable energy delivery infrastructure and considering performance consequences to individual applications of underprovisioning the grid power infrastructure in the presence of varied renewable power and limited battery's energy capacity in a datacenter. We build an experimental prototype to demonstrate such grid power underprovisioning on a cluster of 10 servers, with a simulated solar power generator. Using representative datacenter benchmarks to evaluate the effectiveness of the renewable solution in handling power emergencies, we show that renewable energy by itself can sustain different duration lengths of power emergency when its supply is sufficient. Batteries play an important role for performance boost when the supply of the renewable energy is insufficient. Our theoretical solution, in conjunction with workload migration, provides a seamless bridge across the whole spectrum of duration lengths of power emergency.

Categories and Subject Descriptors

C.0 [**Computer Systems Organization**]: General

Keywords

Green Datacenters; Grid Power Infrastructure; Underprovision; Power Management; Battery; Renewable Energy

ICS'15, June 8–11, 2015, Newport Beach, CA, USA.

http://dx.doi.org/10.1145/2751205.2751222.

1. INTRODUCTION

To tackle the challenges brought by power consumption and carbon emissions, many datacenters have begun to seek renewable energy such as solar or wind energy, along with innovative energy-efficient technologies, to reduce the cost and environmental impact. Several IT giants such as Apple, Google, Microsoft and Yahoo! have proposed plans to build on-site "green" datacenters that will be powered by renewable energy sources. Due to the intermittent and variable nature of the renewable energy, these green datacenters have to deploy grid utilities as a backup to complement and compensate for the intermittency of the green power [1, 2].

Unlike the grid power provision in traditional datacenters that must meet the entire datacenter power demand, the grid infrastructure in green datacenters is called upon only when there is no sufficient green power. Consequently, given the backup characteristics, provisioning a cost-effective grid power infrastructure for green datacenters poses interesting research challenges. *Should we provision the grid power infrastructure to supplement the green power according to the peak power requirement of a datacenter?* In a typical datacenter, the capital cost spent on provisioning the grid utility infrastructure is between $10-$25 for each watt [3], whether that watt is actually consumed or not. Recent studies [4, 5, 6, 7, 8] also show that provisioning for the theoretical peak (using face-plate ratings of the equipment) can prove very expensive, contributing to over a third of the amortized cost of a large datacenter. A study of power consumption on a Google datacenter [3] shows that the probability of the datacenter's power demand exceeding 90% of the potential peak is less than 1%. Given the increasing incorporation of the renewable energy into green datacenters, the actual power requirement for the grid in such datacenters is likely to gradually reduce.

But *how should the grid infrastructure be underprovisioned in a green datacenter while ensuring an acceptable performance for individual applications hosted there?* In particular, underprovisioning the grid infrastructure for a green datacenter can result in power emergency when the simultaneous power draw across the datacenter exceeds the much tighter grid power budget leading to serious consequences including power shutdown. Figure 1 shows how three cases of power emergency might be coped with when underprovisioning the grid infrastructure. In Case A, the green power supply complementing the grid power can fully satisfy the surged power requirement. In Case B where the green power supply is insufficient for the power demand surge, the batteries, strategically charged when there is a surplus of power supply from either the renewable or grid source, discharge to make up for the power shortage. In Case C where all available power sources are unable to meet the power demand surge from the current workloads, certain power management knobs (e.g., DVFS, clock throttling and workload/data migration, etc.) can be adopted to relegate the power requirement to match the current power provision, potentially resulting in a performance degradation for some applications. Obviously, underprovisioning the grid infrastructure can help significantly save the capital expense, provided that the power emergencies that arise in such an underprovisioned grid infrastructure can be addressed in a seamless fashion.

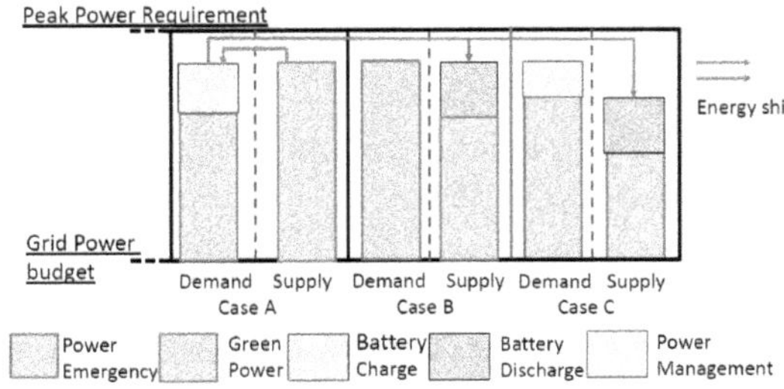

Figure 1: Power Emergency for Underprovisioned Green Datacenter.

To that end, this paper attempts to explore the interplay among the renewable energy, batteries, grid energy and power management techniques to cost-effectively and gracefully deal with the power emergencies in green datacenters with a dedicated underprovisioned grid infrastructure. When using renewable energy to underprovision the grid-based power infrastructure, we have several choices for a fixed target of underprovisioning that include (a) varying the renewable-energy provisioned power capacity, (b) varying the energy capacity of the batteries, and (c) a combination thereof. With reduced grid capacity, application performance may be impacted in case of a power emergency if the supplies of renewable power and battery are insufficient. There are different alternatives to avoiding power overdraw, such as consolidation and power throttling, etc. In this paper, we use the term availability to loosely refer to renewable energy *availability* of the datacenter during a power emergency and we quantify it in our proposed scheduling mechanism.

To the best of our knowledge, while much prior arts have focused on underprovisioing the grid power distribution infrastructure, the issues of underprovisioning the grid capacity in the presence of green energy and its cost-benefit trade-off have not been addressed. In exploring the design space trade-offs of employing renewable energy for underprovisioning grid power infrastructure, this paper makes the following contributions. (1) We propose a novel renewable power distribution architecture that enables the underprovisioning of the grid power infrastructure in green datacenters. (2) We present a theoretical framework that integrates several key power management mechanisms (e.g., renewable energy, batteries, power states, workload migration, etc.) to find a performance-optimal way of handling a power emergency for a given degree of grid power underprovisioning. (3) We develop an experimental prototype consisting of 10 servers, a simulated solar power generator, and a server-level battery provision, coupled with existing software and hardware mechanisms, to demonstrate and evaluate our proposed approach to underprovisioning the grid infrastructure for green datacenters. Using representative datacenter workloads, we evaluate the effectiveness of different mechanisms such as throttling and workload migration on suppressing power emergencies. Our renewable solution, in conjunction with batteries and workload migration, is shown to provide a seamless bridge across all duration lengths of power emergency and be able to minimize the performance impact.

2. BACKGROUND AND MOTIVATION

In this section we provide the necessary background to motivate our proposed research.

Datacenter Power Underprovisioning: The high cost of power provisioning and consumption in datacenters draws attentions to underprovision the power infrastructure [9, 10, 11, 12, 3, 13, 6, 5, 7, 14, 15, 16]. Prior studies to peak power reduction primarily rely on (a) server-level power reduction using active processor power states, inactive deep sleep states, (b) workload shaping via migration or distribution and (c) energy-storage/battery based peak shaving approaches. While sharing a common goal of reducing power consumption, leveraging *green* power to underprovision and *existing* power underprovisioning without green power are quite different in that: (i) Unlike existing underprovisioning mechanisms that do not leverage renewable energy, we focus on designing a renewable energy delivery architecture to underprovision the grid power capacity, the intermittent nature of the *green* power means that both the intrinsic characteristic of green power and the energy storage capacity must be considered simultaneously. (ii) This characteristic of green mechanism calls for power management mechanisms to handle the varied green power supply and limited energy storage capacity, as opposed to handling only limited energy capacity in the existing underprovisioning mechanisms. Efficiently utilizing green power becomes as important as capping power peaks. (iii) Green energy as a power source, as opposed to energy storage that is considered as an *energy buffer* in the state-of-art underprovisioning mechanisms, has the potential to provide a long-time power supply. This may lessen the performance impact of and ensure seamless operation for long-duration power emergencies.

Real or Prototype Implementations of Green Datacenters: The prototype of Blink [17] modulates the motherboards' duty cycles to deal with energy variability without the grid provision. HP Labs aim to build a *net-zero* datacenter with clusters of servers partially provisioned by a PV solar array [18]. The grid utility is still used to compensate for the intermittent unavailability of solar energy. In addition to focusing on workload management, attention is also paid to the cooling power. Researchers from the Rutgers University have built a solar-powered micro-datacenter called Parasol [19] whose workloads and energy sources are managed by a system called GreenSwitch. Parasol schedules non-critical and interactive workloads for renewable energy.

Since our work focuses on reducing grid capacity in the presence of renewable energy, we choose to connect the renewable energy system at the PDU level, allowing us to underprovision the grid power capacity on a per-rack basis. Parasol and *net-zero* designs focus on the datacenter-level power integration, which cannot support grid capacity underprovisioning very well because the underprovision level determine the grid capital expenditure saving. Moreover, we choose not to synchronize the renewable energy with grid power because it provides a convenient way to scale the renewable power capacity provision to be commensurate with the degree of underprovision. In contrast, Parasol and *net-zero* with central power integration, do not support fine-grained renewable power capacity provision very well.

Our work leverages both renewable energy availability and existing power management mechanisms to handle power emergencies and investigates the performance impact on different renewable energy provision schemes. The grid capacity is overprovisioned in the Parasol and *net-zero* designs and they use the grid as backup without forcing power management knobs to shave the power peaks to avoid power overload when renewable energy and battery are insufficient.

Li et al. propose a real solar-powered server-level prototype called *Oasis* [8] to ensure power capacity scale out economically and sustainably as datacenter reaches the power capacity. In contrast to *Oasis*, the underprovisioned grid power capacity calls for a novel renewable energy delivery infrastructure to exploiting the green power capacity provision to supplement the tighter grid capacity to achieve the underprovision goal while considering the varied green power generation and the potential power emergencies. Green energy and battery in our scheduling mechanisms are called upon only for occasional power peaks, unlike the totally green and power scale-out designs that have more frequent green power demands.

Scheduling for Green Energy: While some researchers have studied the scheduling of batch jobs to maximize the use of renewable energy [20, 21], others have proposed to adapt the amount of batch processing dynamically to a mix of interactive and batch workloads in datacenters [22]. SolarCore [23] leverages per core DVFS on multi-core systems to temporarily lower server power demand when solar power drops. Li et al. [24] have proposed an architecture in which two sets of servers draw power respectively from two different sources (e.g., the grid or a wind farm). In their setup, energy source management entails migrating workloads between the two sets. In [25], Li et al. investigate the benefits of load following mechanism in distributed generation powered datacenters and adjust datacenter power demand for improving load following efficiency.

By leveraging the above existing approaches to improve the efficacy of renewable energy, our contributions lie in evaluating the performance trade-offs with underprovisioning grid power infrastructure, the handling techniques used during the power emergencies, different availability of renewable energy and durations of power emergency and diverse application characteristics.

3. DESIGN PRINCIPLES

3.1 Overview of An Underprovisioned Infrastructure

Figure 2 depicts an architectural overview of an on-site green datacenter power hierarchy with an underprovisioned grid power infrastructure. To achieve the underprovisioning goal, we directly connect the on-site renewable power supplies such as photovoltaic (PV) and wind to the power distribution unit (PDU) level to provide the dual-power supply of grid and renewable power rather than integrate the renewable energy into the utility power. The PDU-level renewable energy provision allows us to underprovision the grid power capacity on a per rack basis. Moreover, the choice decreases the impacts of voltage transients, frequency distortions and harmonics on the grid utility. For power emergencies, there are servers powered only by the renewable energy with a separate green power bus while the other servers will depend on the utility power. As we aggressively push such underprovisioning to equipment at the rack level, there is potential for additional cap-ex savings compared to the higher levels. As shown in the figure, grid power capping at the server level results in capital expenditure saving at the rack, PDU, diesel-generator and utility levels of the power hierarchy.

Our design targets the three key objectives of (1) effectively utilizing the reduced grid power capacity across the entire dynamic power load range while reducing the capital expenditure (cap-ex) of the grid power infrastructure; (2) gracefully employing renewable power to sustain the power emergencies; and (3) providing a convenient way to scale the renewable power capacity provision to be commensurate with the degree of underprovision. Since the grid power capacity is underprovisioned, the renewable power can join the PDU via an inverter device, which can combine electricity produced from the provisioned green power and the underprovisioned grid power in the same circuit for power supply. Note that, the PDU connected with green power is provisioned as normal capacity (i.e., theoretical nameplate-based provision) and the capacity of the PDU allows for the infusion of the renewable energy. The DC renewable power is converted to AC to match the output level of the grid power that is routed to the rack-level power distribution strip that further feeds a cluster of server nodes. However, the PDU for the utility-dependent racks is capacity underprovisioned. We could adjust the underprovisioned PDU capacity of utility-dependent racks for the addition of more renewable power capacity as computing demand increases, since the probability of emergencies can increase as we get closer to the next upgrade, and such solutions can help relieve overload during these periods.

Since we push the underprovisioing to the PDU level, we leverage the distributed battery architecture shown in Figure 2, which is widely employed by IT companies such as Google [26] (server-level battery) and Facebook [27] (rack-level) to smooth the supply of the renewable power. In the Facebook design, a cabinet of batteries is used to provide standby power for a rack triplet to replace the centralized battery. In the Google design, a battery is attached on every server after the power supply unit (PSU). This design could achieve energy efficiency through bringing the AC distribution (green and grid) even closer to the IT load, before it is converted (we adopt this design in our solutions).

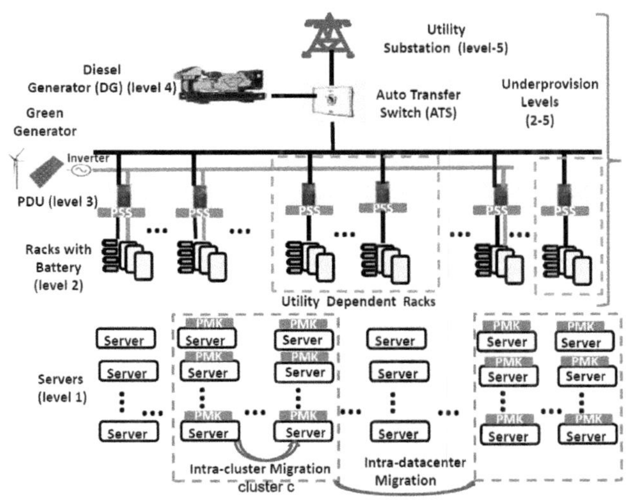

Figure 2: The Underprovisioned Power Infrastructure.

This distributed battery architecture is advantageous to the centralized battery architecture because it (i) provides a convenient way to dynamically scale the battery system with the power capacity of the renewable power provision, (ii) allows a fine-grained way for activating a battery to match the incremental power draw, thus, as each server/rack exceeds the underprovision grid capacity, a distributed battery would be brought on line and (iii) improves renewable energy efficiency by avoiding AC-DC-AC double conversion .

To cope with the time-varying, intermittent renewable power, we employ a power-source selector (PSS) to adaptively switch among different forms of power supplies (i.e., green, battery and underprovisioned grid power). PSS performs switch tuning based on the discrepancy between the workload power demand and the grid power provision. PSS is also configured to charge the battery when there is an excess of green power, and discharge it when green power is insufficient or unavailable. Once the battery is fully charged, excess green power is used for the reduction of carbon emission and electricity bills in a conventional way. PSS is able to identify the switching parameters for the inverter and charge controllers of batteries to allow for a full control of every power source. Programmable power electronics circuitry can be used to implement the PSS. However, since our experimental setup does not provide this functionality, our evaluations account for such control capability in the form of managing the underprovision decisions, which is detailed in Section 4.1. As shown in Figure 2, a server-level power management knob (PMK) that is provided receives the execution output from the PSS to control the power demand on a per-server basis. When renewable power and battery are not sufficient, PMK leverages the existing hardware/kernel/VM interfaces to keep servers within the grid power budget by considering the application's diverse characteristics. As shown in the figure, we can dynamically change the CPU power states and trigger the intra-cluster and intra-datacenter workload migration to reduce the power demand for each server to be commensurate with the reduced grid power capacity. We dynamically change the settings for these scheduling behaviors according to our power emergency handling mechanisms as elaborated in Section 4.2.

The underprovision design is orthogonal to the design consideration for operational expenses (op-ex) (e.g., cutting electricity bills), and we leave the work on op-ex reduction to our future work.

3.2 Design Space

Rather than relying on additional renewable energy and battery, we propose to use renewable energy and battery that already exists in the green datacenters. The performance of applications is impacted by how much the renewable energy and batteries are provisioned. In this paper, we consider a conservative renewable-energy provision mechanism that powers part of the datacenter using renewable energy sources. We assume that the number of renewable-energy powered servers is fewer than 40% of the overall deployed machines since a datacenter typically consumes about 60% of its actual peak power [3]. The rationale behind this assumption is fourfold. First, this choice allows the datacenters to sufficiently use the grid power capacity. For instance, when we underprovision 30% of the peak grid capacity (name-plate based provision), the overall deployed servers can be supplied by 70% of the peak grid capacity that comprises the majority of power requirement in a datacenter. Second, power emergencies can be reasonably handled since part of the servers are powered by renewable energy. For instance, the power emergency, along with the 30% grid underprovision, can be handled by the green provision since 30% of the deployed servers can draw power from renewable energy. Third, even if the green power is extremely low, there still exists a large portion of the peak grid capacity (e.g., 70% of peak grid capacity) that can be made available for all servers upon a power emergency. Finally, the conservative renewable energy provision could allow us to achieve further grid cap-ex reduction (PDU capacity) since more utility dependent racks will exist (shown in Figure 2). We conduct a preliminary investigation on the impact of allowing additional renewable energy provision and the resulting cap-ex savings achieved by grid power infrastructure underprovisioning (Section 5.5). A detailed study of such green provisioning cost-performance tradeoffs is considered as the future work.

We vary the renewable energy provision and battery energy capacity to investigate the performance impact of a given underprovision degree (e.g., 30% of peak grid capacity). Table 1 shows the various green configurations for the underprovisioning of the grid power capacity. Current green datacenters employ the provisions of renewable energy and batteries [18] merely as a mechanism to reduce the op-ex and still rely on the overprovisioned peak grid capacity as a backup and offers seamless performance during power emergencies. We use this setting as a performance baseline (*MaxPerf*) for comparison.

Renewable power capacity: We denote by $Peak_{RE}$ the peak renewable power provision for which a single photovoltaic module can sustain the associated underprovision needs. We use the value from [28] to estimate the DC-AC derate factor α (0.77) of the solar power. For example, when we provision k servers with renewable energy, theoretical maximum renewable power AC output is $k * Peak_{RE} * \alpha$. The actual available solar power output, denoted by $REPower$, is equal to the percentage of the maximum theoretical solar power production, that is actually determined by the solar irradiation, ambient temperature, and the server load connected to it.

Battery behavior: We model a server-level 12V value-regulated lead-acid battery (VRLA), similar to that used by Li et al. [25]. Battery is characterized by their supply time as approximated by Peuker's Law (Peukert's exponent is 1.15 for LA battery [7]), which shows the time taken to drain a certain capacity for different power demands. We exploit this property to force a lower draw for a longer battery supply time. Depth of discharge (DoD) is a critical parameter determining a battery's lifetime. We assume DoD=40% in our setup, which translates to a lifetime of 1300 recharge cycles [7]. If the energy used to charge a battery is higher than what can be drawn out subsequently, it implies power loss or an energy efficiency η (75% for LA [6]) of less than 100%. We choose two battery capacities to smooth the renewable energy variance as shown in Table 1, where 3.2Ah is the existing server-level battery capacity deployed in the Google datacenter as Uninterrupted Power Supply (UPS) [7].

Lifetime concerns: We need to ensure that we do not compromise on datacenter's power reliability with renewable energy provision. Recent works point out that solar panels can last for 25 years (lifetime) with a degradation rate of less than 1% loss per year [29]. Moreover, reports in different areas [30, 4, 25] reveal that batteries can help significantly improve the power availability of datacenters. As discussed above, we have to ensure that our approach does not result in replacement of batteries sooner than their expected lifetime. Using this analysis, we find that utilizing renewable energy and battery provision can handle the relatively frequent power emergencies well within the expected renewable energy and battery lifetime.

Performance implications during power emergencies: Underprovisioned grid power infrastructure has multiple performance and power availability ramifications. We use the term *availability* to loosely indicate the available renewable energy. That is, the performance of services or applications are greatly affected by: (i) the variance of the weather and environment dependent renewable energy can greatly affect the performance of service or application due to the varying *renewable peak power*, (ii) the performance of services or applications can be impacted by the *insufficient energy capacity* in batteries and the limitation of their lifetime during power emergencies.

The occurrence time of a power emergency during the execution of a workload can determine both the power source selection and the impact to the application performance for the following cases. (a) When a power emergency occurs at a time when there is no green power, i.e., the *availability* is minimum, the underprovisioning mechanism must depend solely on the batteries. The batteries have capacity limitation, which can result in performance degradation. (b) When a power emergency happens at a time when the *availability* is maximum, the renewable power can sustain the power emergency by directly supplying green power to servers without using batteries to boost the performance while simultaneously charging batteries with excess green

Configurations	RE	Batt. (Server level)
RE-Batt	30% servers	10Ah
REOnly	30% servers	0
RE-SBatt	30% servers	3.2Ah
SRE-SBatt	20% servers	3.2Ah

Table 1: Options for green provision. "RE" represents renewable energy provision. "S" stands for *small* renewable energy and battery energy capacity provisions

power. (c) Given the large variance of the renewable power, servers associated with green power cannot draw sufficient power from renewable energy (i.e., the *availability* is medium), where performance of services or applications can be impacted by both the time-varying renewable power supply and batteries energy capacity.

3.3 Problem Statement

We endeavor to answer the following research question, that is, given a grid power budget of P_{budget} with underprovision at the cluster level where the cluster c is composed of the racks shown in Figure 2 and accommodates n servers, *how can we cap the grid power under the given power budget while meeting the applications' SLA?* We denote $GridLoad^{A}_{c,t}$ as the aggregate grid power demand of cluster c in epoch t for application A, then the underprovisioning of the grid power capacity exploits property $GridLoad^{A}_{c,t} \leq P_{budget}$, $\forall t$ ($GridLoad^{A}_{c,t} = \sum_{j=1}^{n} P_{j,t}$, $P_{j,t}$ represents the grid power draw of each server j in epoch t). The underprovisioning mechanism with renewable energy can strike a tradeoff between the performance of applications and the cap-ex savings. Since renewable power is varied and the power supply of battery is constrained by their capacity, it is possible that the aggregate grid power of the n servers will not be safely accommodated by the design. As a result, we use techniques provided by PMK to deal with the power overdraw to meet the reduced power budget P_{budget}.

4. HANDLING POWER EMERGENCIES WITH RENEWABLE SOLUTIONS

In this section, we describe a theoretical framework for managing power sources and scheduling workloads. The framework is used to assist the power source selector (PSS) and power management knobs (PMK) in their decision-making process.

4.1 Power Source Selector

Goal: The power source selector enables the execution of applications with the renewable energy and/or battery to stay within the tighter grid power budget. PSS relies on the information on the power demand, renewable energy *availability*, and the amount of energy stored in the battery to produce a power-source schedule to handle the power emergency.

Figure 3 illustrates how PSS operates in general. In the figure, the period of a power emergency is divided into discrete scheduling epochs ($t_1, t_2, ..., T$) and at each epoch the tighter grid power provision is achieved by powering the cluster from renewable energy or battery. The figure shows the four distinct states of the cluster at each epoch t, namely, (i) renewable power is abundant and can be independently used for power emergency handling and the excess power can be used to charge the battery, (ii) renewable power is not sufficient but battery can be activated to supplement the green power to sustain the power emergency over a period of time, (iii) battery can be activated independently to sustain the power emergency when renewable power is untouchable, and (iv) renewable power is not available while the grid power can be used to charge the battery for handling power emergency at a later time. However, utility dependent rack only allows to charge its battery by grid power as shown in Figure 2. Next, we propose a general framework to help PSS make the right decision in each epoch t. Our PSS scheduler is inspired by a real-time energy sources switching mechanism for electricity bill reduction [19].

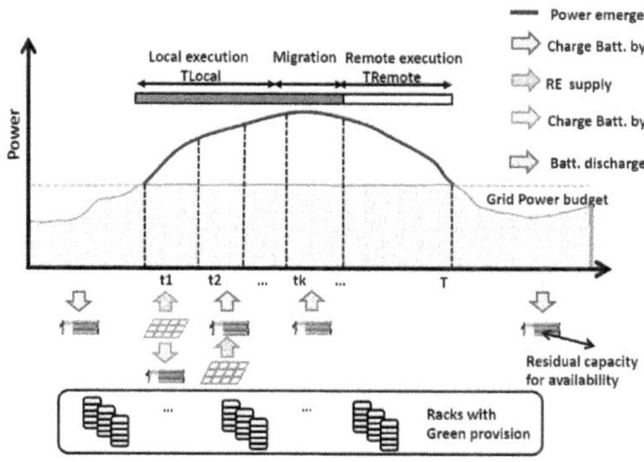

Figure 3: Renewable energy and battery provide power to the cluster to meet the cluster-level power budget requirement for each epoch t during the period of a power emergency. The shaded region indicates the grid power used. Migration happens at t_k instantaneously in this illustration as power sources do not suffice while throttling could be combined with power sources scheduling.

Power sources: Upon an emergency, three power sources can be used to meet the aggregate power demand $PoweD_{c,t}$ of cluster c for each epoch t , namely, the renewable power ($RELoad_{c,t}$), the battery power ($BattLoad_{c,t} = \sum_{j=1}^{n} BattLoad_j$, $BattLoad_j$ represents the power supply of the battery associated with server j), and the grid power ($GridLoad_{c,t}$). Thus,

$$\forall t \in T:$$
$$RELoad_{c,t} + BattLoad_{c,t} + GridLoad_{c,t} = PowerD_{c,t}$$

Recall that to meet our underprovision goal P_{budget}, we must ensure that the grid power demand of cluster c is within P_{budget}:

$$\forall t \in T: GridLoad_{c,t} \leq P_{budget}$$

The available renewable power ($REPower_c$) may be used for multiple purposes, including directly supplying for handling a power emergency ($RELoad_c$) and charging the battery associated with green provision ($Batt\_RE_{c,t}$). Thus,

$$\forall t \in T: RELoad_{c,t} + Batt\_RE_{c,t} \leq REPower_{c,t}$$

where $Batt\_RE_{c,t} = \sum_{gi=1}^{k} Batt\_RE_{gj,t}$, gj expresses the server with green provision and k is the number of servers with green provision ($k \leq n$).

Similarly, the grid ($GridLoad_c$) can be used to charge each battery j in cluster c ($Batt\_Grid_j$) during a non-emergency period.

Since, we choose not to synchronize the renewable power to the grid power line, we cannot use the grid power and renewable power simultaneously for the server gj provisioned with renewable energy:

$$\forall t \in \{T | RELoad_{gj,t} > 0\}: GridLoad_{gj,t} = 0$$

Battery behaviours: Battery charging itself during an emergency can help achieve a good performance result and we account for the battery's energy efficiency (η), i.e., only a fraction (η) of the energy we store in the battery will be available. We define the current available capacity of the battery ($BattCap_j$) at epoch t as:

$$\forall t \in T: BattCap_{j,t} = BattCap_{j,t-1} + Duration \times \eta$$
$$Batt\_RE_{j,t-1} - Duration \times BattLoad_{j,t}$$

where *Duration* is the length of each epoch t. As discussed in Section 3.2, leveraging battery as a power source should not harm their lifetime. The depth of discharge (DoD) is an important measurement for battery's lifetime,

$$\forall t \in T :$$
$$(1 - DoD) \times BattMaxCap_j \leq BattCap_{j,t} \leq BattMaxCap_j$$

where $BattMaxCap$ denotes the battery maximum capacity.

Obviously, one cannot use more energy than what is actually stored in the battery, thus,

$$\forall t \in T : Duration \times BattLoad_{j,t} \leq BattCap_{j,t}$$

Since battery charging itself with grid power is considered for adhering to P_{budget}, we restrict $Batt\_Grid_{c,t}$ to non-emergency periods,

$$\forall t \in \{T | RELoad_{c,t} > 0 \ or \ BattLoad_{j,t} > 0\} :$$
$$Batt\_Grid_{j,t} = 0$$

4.2 Power Management Knob

Goal: Upon any power emergency, the power management knobs (PMK) allow us to continue executing the applications when the combined power and energy of the renewable energy and battery sources are insufficient to meet the grid power budget, with a lower power demand to sustain within the underprovisioned grid power infrastructure. A PMK consists of the *Throttling* (local knob) and *Migration* (remote knob). We summarize the demand required by these techniques in Table 2.

Throttling: With throttling, an application may be operated in a low-performance mode using active power states, such as dynamic voltage and frequency scaling (DVFS) and clock throttling. *Throttling* mechanisms are local to a server and quite agile, since transitioning to these throttling states is almost instantaneous (within tens of μsecs), and therefore effective in reducing the power demand during a power emergency. Throttling techniques can affect the execution and degrade the performance of applications especially when the applications do not provide sufficient slack in their offered load.

Each server $j = 1, ..., n$ in cluster c can operate during an interval within a power emergency in a particular power state S_j (e.g., save-state, DVFS and Clock throttling states), ordered as S_0 where the server enters in the *save-state* (Sleep/Hibernation), to S_r which is the highest power consuming state and best in performance. We also denote the intensity of a workload during this emergency as L_j, which can be of any of the w levels between the minimum and maximum intensity levels for a given application, such as $L_1, ..., L_w$. The power reduction $P_{TH,t} = \sum_{j=1}^{n}(P_j(L_{j,t}, S_{r,t}) - P_j(L_{j,t}, S_{j,t}))$ offered by *Throttling* for each power emergency epoch t not only depends on the workload intensity level $L_{j,t}$ that is being served on server j during epoch t but also on the power state. We calculate power demand for per server $P_j(L_{j,t}, S_{j,t})$ *a priori* and obtain $S_j \in (S_0, ..., S_r)$ for different workload intensity levels $L_j \in (L_1, ..., L_w)$. Hence, an optimal *Throttling* is achievable that corresponds to the power supply of the power sources with the least performance slowdown $Perf_{TH}^{A}$ due to power throttling (where $Perf_{TH}^{A} \in [0, 1]$).

Many workloads, such as MapReduce and scientific computation, can tolerate some delays due to natural deadlines as stated in [21, 20]. Importantly, such loose deadlines provide the flexibility that allows compute workloads to be close to the *availability* of renewable energy and thus completely avoid any power emergency. In this scenario, the jobs can be suspended instead of being cancelled, where the *Sleep* state is ideally the power state for the delayed operation and $Perf_{TH}^{A}$ will be set to zero.

PMK techniques	Time overhead	Power state
Throttling	Tens of μ seconds	Throttled state
Migration	A few minutes	Consolidated state
Sleep	A few seconds	2-4W per DIMM
Hibernation	A few minutes	0W

Table 2: Impact of PMK techniques on the handling of power emergency.

Migration: An alternative approach is to consolidate applications on fewer servers, with each given a smaller fraction of the processor cycles, memory space and other resources. Immediately upon a power emergency, applications are moved to regions of the datacenter with a sufficient headroom. This can be more energy efficiency due to the lack of energy proportionality in today's servers. In workload migration, the application state is migrated to a remote server while the primary server is kept powered until migration is complete. Once all the state data is transferred, the originating server is powered down and the application is resumed at the remote server. However, migration operation is not always allowable for several reasons. First, migration can be expensive, depending on the application state that needs to be migrated. Second, the migration destination in the datacenter may not be always available, particularly if the entire datacenter is highly utilized. Third, not all applications are agreeable to migration as they may require resources on specific clusters. In this paper, we consider two migration strategies, *intra-datacenter* (outside cluster c) migration and *intra-cluster* migration. The former allows workload to be migrated from one cluster to another with sufficient headroom within the datacenter. For simplicity, we assume that a cluster with a sufficient headroom elsewhere in the datacenter can be found, and thus do not consider the problem of where to move the workload and performance interference as discussed in [4]. The latter is employed when the former is not possible, e.g., no headroom outside the cluster or administrative reasons force the application to be tied to nodes within the current cluster, and/or the locality of the application needs (frequent communication, data stored locally, etc.).

Each server j in cluster c maintains the application state D_j during epoch t within the power emergency, and the application state D_j of server j in cluster c can also be ordered from low to high. If migration is necessary, since the application's state determines the migration execution time, we start from the server with the lowest D_j and migrate one by one. The peak power demand can be decreased by $P_{Mig,t} = \sum_{j=1}^{m}(P_j(L_{j,t}, S_{j,t}, D_{j,t}) - P_j(S_{0,t}, D_{j,t}))$ for epoch t, where m ($m \leq n$) denotes the number of servers involved in migration. After migration, the servers can be put in the *save-state*. We still require *a priori* knowledge for application's memory state of each server to achieve an optimal migration operation given the power supply of power sources and the throttling techniques. After being migrated to another server or cluster, the application can also suffer from a performance slowdown $Perf_{Mig}^{A}$ (where $Perf_{Mig}^{A} \in [0, 1]$) if the destination server is highly utilized or there is severe interference from native applications.

4.3 Integration of PSS and PMK

Table 3 summarizes how the individual PSS and PMK techniques behave in handling power emergency in each of the three phases. It is obviously preferred if PSS alone could handle the emergency since the techniques provided in PMK can result in performance degradation. A power supply-demand equation can be derived as follows,

$$\forall t \in T : RELoad_{c,t} + BattLoad_{c,t} + P_{TH,t} +$$
$$P_{Mig,t} + GridLoad_{c,t} = PowerD_{c,t}$$

Technique	Start of power emergency	During power emergency	After power emergency
Renewable energy	Direct supply or Charge Battery	Direct supply or Charge Battery	Charge Battery
Battery with renewable energy	Discharge/Charge by renewable energy	Discharge/Charge by renewable energy	Charge by renewable energy
Battery with Grid	Discharge	Discharge	Charge by Grid power
Throttling	Throttled Perf.	Throttled Perf.	Restore full service
Migration	Migrate to remote memory	Consolidated service	Migrate back
Sleep	Suspend to local memory	No service	Resume from memory
Hibernation	Suspend to local disk	No service	Resume from disk

Table 3: Operational and Performance implications of the individual PSS and PMK mechanisms

Recall that we use the term *availability* to loosely indicate the available renewable energy. PMK helps control the power demand on the server with the renewable energy provision to effectively utilize the varying renewable power. Note that, even after migration, *Throttling* technique still determines the power demand. Hence, the available renewable power ($REPower_c$) has a lower bound determined by the power demand of a green provisioned server gj:

$$\forall t \in T : P_{gj}(L_{gj,t}, S_{gj,t}) \leq REPower_{c,t}$$

$P_{gj}(L_{gj}, S_{gj})$ is a *start point* for a single server gj to switch to the green power bus while determining the renewable energy *availability*. $P_{gj}(L_{gj}, S_{gj})$ is determined by the server type, application characteristics and the workload's intensity level. The renewable energy *availability* reaches its minimum ($RELoad_{c,t} = 0$) when $REPower_{c,t} < P_{gj}(L_{gj,t}, S_{gj,t})$. Similarly, renewable energy *availability* achieves its maximum when $REPower_{c,t} \geq \sum_{gj=1}^{k} P_{gj}(L_{gj,t}, S_{r,t})$, where k is the maximum number of green-powered servers in cluster c and S_r is the highest power state for server gj. In the latter case the renewable energy can self-sufficiently handle the power emergency without the support of PMK and batteries associated with green provision, and also possibly charge the batteries ($Batt\_RE_{c,t} \geq 0$).

Moreover, the migration operation for green powered server gj will not start without first fully utilizing the available renewable source:

$$\forall t \in \{T | REPower_{c,t} \geq P_{gj}(L_{gj,t}, S_{gj,t})\} : Perf_{gj,Mig} = 1$$

To reduce the migration overhead, workload migration for each server j in cluster c will not be triggered if renewable energy, batteries or their combination can offer a better performance than migration:

$$\forall t \in \{T | Perf_{j,TH} \geq Perf_{j,Mig}\} : Perf_{j,Mig} = 1$$

Performance Impact: We denote the original execution time (*MaxPerf*) for traditional grid overprovision as T_E. To continue processing during power emergencies in the underprovision design, the execution time, denoted by T_S, may be extended. Let T_{Local} denote the application's execution time with the power supply of renewable energy (*RELoad*) and battery (*BattLoad*) in conjunction with *Throttling*. When the remote knob (*Migration*) is triggered, the execution time will be adjusted to T_{Remote}. T_{Save} is the resumed time from the *save-state*. Hence, we can obtain the relationship between the execution time after employing the techniques of handling power emergency and the original execution time, as follows.

$$T_S - (T_{Local} + T_{Remote} * (1 - Perf_{Mig})) * (1 - Perf_{TH}) - T_{Save} = T_E$$

Note that the execution time is increased due to $Perf_{TH}$ and $Perf_{Mig}$ and the save states. The value of $Perf_{TH}$ is mainly governed by the renewable energy *availability* and available battery capacity. $Perf_{Mig}$ is determined by its locality properties since we assume that the destination has sufficient headroom to run the migrated workload without any power-related dampening.

From Figure 3, it is clear that when power sources are not able to meet the power demand while throttling severely degrades the performance, we must migrate the application to meet the stringent SLA requirement. On the other hand, the application would be migrated back as the power sources are sufficient. In addition, the save-state of server also impacts the performance due to the resume overhead (Table 2). We refer to the solution offered by our framework as *Green*, the solution allowing intra-cluster migration as *Green-C*, and intra-datacenter migration as *Green-D* and the solution it offers solely using local PMK knobs without migration as *Green-L*.

Scheduling Goal: We use $R_{j,t}^{sus}(L_{j,t}, S_{j,t})$, whose minimization corresponds to meeting the application's SLA, to denote a generic performance metric based on the sustain mechanisms used for handling epoch t of a power emergency. We can use this metric to express the problem of minimizing performance impact for a given power budget ($\forall t \in T : GridLoad_{c,t} \leq P_{budget}$):

$$min \sum^{t \in T} \sum^{j \in c} R_{j,t}^{sus}(L_{j,t}, S_{j,t})$$

5. PROTOTYPE EVALUATION

Experimental Setup and Methodology: Our scale-down experimental prototype uses a cluster c of $N = 10$ homogeneous servers with 6-core 2.0GHz Intel Xeon E5-2620 processors (i.e., 12 cores per server), 48GB RAM and 1Gbps Ethernet interface and run our applications hosted on the Unbantu Linux OS. Our cluster has a shared NAS box that is mounted as a NFS storage volume by all the servers. We use another cluster of 10 servers that is not underprovisioned as the destination for migrating workloads to simulate an intra-datacenter migration *Green-D*. The power consumption of each server is monitored using an external power meter [31]. The face-plate rating of these servers is 450W. Their idle power is around 90W. The dynamic power consumption can be modulated with 10 DVFS states and 15 clock throttling states.

To simulate a datacenter with renewable energy provision, we randomly choose one of the renewable power production traces with one-week duration from NREL [32], including irradiation every minute, and replay the chosen trace on our prototype. We scale the solar power production to correspond the power source configuration (Table 1) to simulate the available renewable power output ($REPower_c$ in Section 4.1). In our setup, we consider a solar panel provisioned for a server i with 275W DC output (theoretical peak power), which is in line with the existing capacities in Grapesolar [33]. Hence, we can obtain the peak renewable power AC supply for a single solar panel that corresponds $Peak_{RE} * \alpha = 275 * 0.77 = 211.75W$. Hence, as shown in Figure 4, for the *RE-Batt* configuration, we assume that 3 servers in our prototype are provided with renewable energy system that is capable of supplying the maximum green power of 635.25 W ($REPower_c$). For the configuration with *SRE* that provides 2 servers with renewable energy, the maximum green power obtainable is 423.5W ($REPower_c$). We assume that each server in the cluster is equipped with a battery unit and the battery energy capacity is shown in Table 1.

Workloads	Memory Usage	Performance Metric
Specjbb	10GB	Latency-constrained, ops/sec
Web-search	20GB	Latency-constrained, queries/sec
Memcached	20GB	Queries/sec
SpecCPU2006	24GB	Completion time

Table 4: Workload Description

We use *cpufreq* to implement *Throttling* technique, and leverage the Xen live migration [34] implementation for *Migration*. Moreover, we use the standard OS commands in Linux to implement the *save-state*.

In order to evaluate the efficacy of our design and theoretical framework, we experiment and evaluate four relevant scenarios, including (i) power emergencies lasting a duration ranging from 15 minutes to 120 minutes, (ii) underprovision degree set to 30% of the potential peak power demand. (we measure the peak power demand for each application based on our setup), (iii) power emergencies occurring given different levels of renewable energy *availability* (i.e., minimum, medium, maximum) for a duration ranging from15 minutes to 120 minutes, and (iv) a comparison among techniques, *Throttling*(*Green-L*) and *Migration* (*Green-C*,*Green-D*), of their effectiveness in handling the power emergency. Moreover, the *start point* is determined as the 70% of the potential peak power corresponding to the underprovision degree for a single green powered server and the *start point* is also determined as the power demand for *Sleep* state. Note that we are only concerned with performance of cluster *c* during a power emergency in this work. For each application, we normalize its performance to that in *MaxPerf* (recall Section 3.2). We consider *MaxPerf* in our setup as the maximum performance without allowing any power cap techniques.

We believe that the smaller setup can be used to harvest as many insights (performance impact and power sources scheduling) as that from a larger-scale platform using the following methodology. We subject each application or server to the power sources and workload schedulers described earlier and profile the power consumption per server of each workload *a priori*. We also profile the application performance per server *a priori*, when the application is subject to the mechanisms for handling power emergency provided in our theoretical framework. Power and performance data are collected at fine temporal resolutions and allow us to scale the scheduling mechanism to different system sizes and renewable power and battery energy capacities.

Workloads: We consider the following representative datacenter workloads (Table 4) that have different performance characteristics that result in different peak power demands on renewable energy and batteries. Interactive applications include the Specjbb [35], an in-memory key-value store Memcached benchmark [36], Web-search from Cloudsuite [37]. SpecCPU benchmarks [38] represent High Performance Computing (HPC) applications. We use *mcf* from SpecCPU2006 in our experiments as a representative for memory intensive scientific computation workloads. Since each mcf instance only consumes 2 GB memory, we instantiate 12 mcf instances to increase its memory usage to emulate power emergencies of HPC applications.

5.1 Effectiveness of Power Emergency Handling Mechanisms

We now compare the performance impact offered by different emergency-handling techniques provided in PMK (Section 4.2). In the interest of clarity, we first show representative results for Specjbb, and then show specific results for the other applications. Applications like Specjbb are known to experience significant temporal variations in the load. We add replicas of the workload in the cluster until all 10 servers are fully utilized. This can cause a power emergency since the aggregate draw of these servers can exceed the power budget of the underprovisioned cluster. For instance, when the workload saturates all 10 servers, the aggregate power consumption hits 1590W. If the grid power infrastructure is underprovisioned by 30%, then the corresponding P_{budget} limit is 1113W. From the renewable energy side, if renewable energy can supply 3 servers in the cluster (i.e., the RE-Batt configuration), the 30% underprovision will be satisfied for the green provision. We inject workload to deliberately induce power emergency durations of 15, 30, 60 and 120 minutes, over these provisioned limits. We use the average operations/second (ops) of cluster *c* as our performance metric for Specjbb.

Figure 4 shows the evolution of the aggregated peak power of the 3 green-provisioned servers running Specjbb given different levels of renewable energy *availability*. We see high variation of the renewable power production over time. We have evaluated such performance consequences for all the cases of medium availability over different power emergency durations. In this paper, we only present the results of the *B*1 scenario for the applications we specified above for medium renewable energy *availability* (worst case for performance) to show the performance impact of the renewable energy variation. We determine the *start point* for Specjbb to be the time point when a server with green provision starts to use renewable power as it obtains 111.3W from the green power bus.

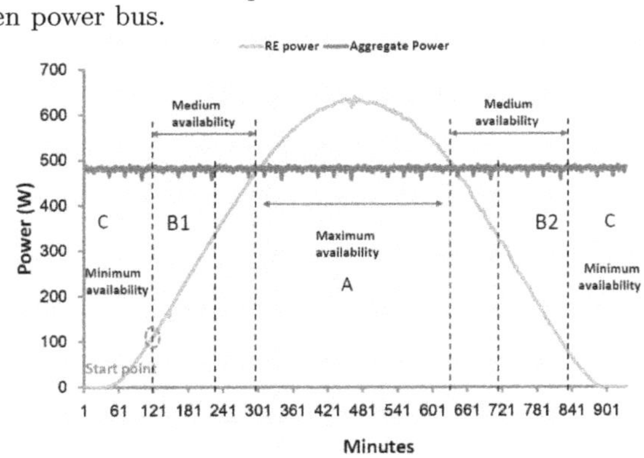

Figure 4: The Specjbb power profile as a function of the renewable energy availability over time.

Impact of renewable energy availability: Figure 5 presents the performance degradation in ops of Specjbb under the different power-emergency handling techniques given the minimum, medium, and maximum renewable energy *availability* for the emergency durations we specify above.

Green-L: For short and moderate power emergencies (15-minute and 30-minute durations), even when the renewable energy is unavailable, battery alone is able to completely handle the power emergency without degrading the performance. In fact, in such power emergencies *Green-C* and *Green-D* are never activated by our theoretical framework. However, battery incurs high performance overhead on long power emergencies since *Green-L* uses a lower power state on servers sourced from batteries, stretching the battery's runtime for the minimum renewable energy *availability*. The performance degrades to 88% of *MaxPerf* for the 60-minute duration, 73% of *MaxPerf* for the 120-minute duration with *Green-L*.

For the medium *availability* of renewable energy, 96% and 90% of *MaxPerf* can be achieved for the 60-minute and 120-minute power emergencies respectively. It is interesting to observe that the *start point* of when to utilize renewable energy determines the length of the medium *availability* of renewable energy and the battery's behavior. This shows the importance of dynamically adjusting the *start point* of switching to the green power bus to match the power emergency durations. This, however, is beyond the scope of this paper, which we plan to investigate in our future work.

As expected, in the case of the maximum *availability* of renewable energy (i.e., case A shown in Figure 4), three servers in the cluster can be directly powered by renewable power without any performance degradation. Further, the excess green power can be used to charge the battery for later use.

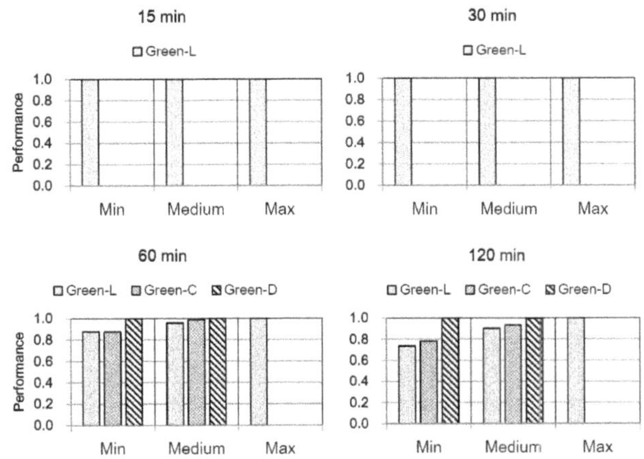

Figure 5: Performance with underprovision, normalized to *MaxPerf* (with overprovision baseline), as a function of the duration length of power emergency and renewable energy availability, for Specjbb with the *RE-Batt* configuration.

Green-D: Specifically, workload migration is only allowed when *Green-L* alone is not sufficient. Upon the minimum *availability* of renewable energy, batteries are activated first to postpone the migration action and then we migrate 3 replicas (3 servers) of Specjbb to another cluster with sufficient headroom to achieve 30% underprovisioning. *Migration* in itself does introduce a spike in power consumption (of 10%) for this workload, and the battery is also needed to temporarily keep the grid power draw under control during the process of migration. Live migration can be carried out in about 5 minutes for Specjbb with 10GB memory size. The loss of data locality suffered by the migrated VMs is negligible in this case (i.e., small impact of $Perf_{Mig}$), implying very little performance impact after the migration. The only situations where *Migration* is an unwise choice is when the power emergency lasts for 5 minutes or less, in which case the migration overhead outweighs the gain

In the case of the medium *availability* of renewable energy, the *Green-D* mechanism only allows the migration of the servers that are not currently powered by the green source and migrates such servers back from the remote nodes when renewable power production reaches the *start point*. Moreover, unlike the case of minimum *availability*, the power spikes required of carrying out the reverse migration operation can be accommodated by the green power and the energy of batteries will be reserved for boosting performance after the servers migrate back.

The results show that *Green-D* can achieve 99% of *MaxPerf* for cluster *c* upon the 120-minute power emergency. The performance impact (compared to *Green-D* of minimum *availability*) is due to *Throttling* in the green powered servers to control the power demand to match renewable power production while the associated batteries are insufficient to cover such a long duration. *Green-D* achieves *MaxPerf* for the 60-minute power emergency. Consequently, intra-datacenter migration combined with *Throttling* turns out to be the most effective mechanism and is able to handle the entire range of power emergencies with high performance regardless of the renewable energy *availability*.

Green-C: Finally, we assess the intra-cluster migration, *Green-C*. Since the 10 servers running Specjbb are operating at their peak computation-resource requirement, *Green-C* co-locates the workload that is experiencing significant resource shortage, causing performance degradation. In fact, *Green-C* fares worse than *Green-D* in that the former cannot be triggered where *Green-D* is allowed. For the minimum renewable energy *availability*, performance impact is determined by the battery energy capacity. *Green-C* chooses to drain the battery fully to postpone the migration and results in undesirable performance for longer power emergencies since the battery is not able to provide power beyond a certain period of time, thus forcing it to switch to in-cluster migration and hurt the Specjbb performance.

For the medium renewable energy *availability*, renewable energy can trigger the reverse migration when the servers can be directly powered by the green source while alleviating the resource contention in the cluster to reduce the performance impact. We find that even for long power emergencies (120 minutes) with the medium renewable energy *availability*, *Green-C* still achieves 93% of *MaxPerf*, in contrast to the 78% of *MaxPerf* achieved with the minimum renewable energy *availability*.

Save-state: After migration, we put the server into *Sleep* state where preserving application's state in memory reduces the additional performance impact after the emergency. The *Sleep* state dissipates only around 6W per server and resumes back to the normal operation for 8 seconds. The battery can satisfy the power draw of the *Sleep* state for short and moderate power emergencies (15 min - 30 min) in the case of the minimum renewable energy *availability*. However for longer power emergencies (120 min and beyond), preserving application's state may not buy much since the emergency duration far outweighs the overheads of losing state, sleep state could draw relative large energy from battery (DoD consideration, Section 4.1). *Hibernation* suffers 255 seconds for resuming service, which is negligible compared to the 120 minutes of a long power emergency while saving energy. However, for the medium *availability*, despite of the large variance of the renewable power, it still can make room for the power demand of the *Sleep* state.

We find that the most effective techniques for handling power emergencies are different for different levels of renewable energy availability. For the minimum *availability*, the battery is the only power source for handling the power emergencies. This means that the most effective techniques are determined by the energy capacity of battery. For instance, for short power emergencies of 15 or 30 minutes, *Throttling* is preferred to achieve a good performance since the battery can typically supply sufficient power for such durations. Though *Migration* (Green-D) is also able to achieve *MaxPerf* (not shown in the figure), it requires a relatively long migration time of up to 5 minutes. For longer power emergencies lasting 1 hour or more, given the minimum *availability*, *Throttling* becomes infeasible while *Migration* shows the performance advantage, since the limited battery energy capacity can hardly sustain such a long time to provide an ideal performance. For the medium *availability*, *Throttling* is able to handle long power emergencies (60 minutes - 120 minutes) with only a slight performance impact (performance degradation $\leq$ 10%). This is primarily due to renewable energy that directly powers the servers to alleviate the pressure of underprovision on the battery. For power emergencies longer than 2 hours, *Migration* (both intra-cluster and intra-datacenter migration) is able to achieve a better performance with a relatively short migration overhead (5 minutes). On the other hand, *Throttling* and *Migration* are not required irrespective of the length of a power emergency if given a larger battery energy capacity configuration with the medium *availability*.

5.2 Performance impact of different green configurations

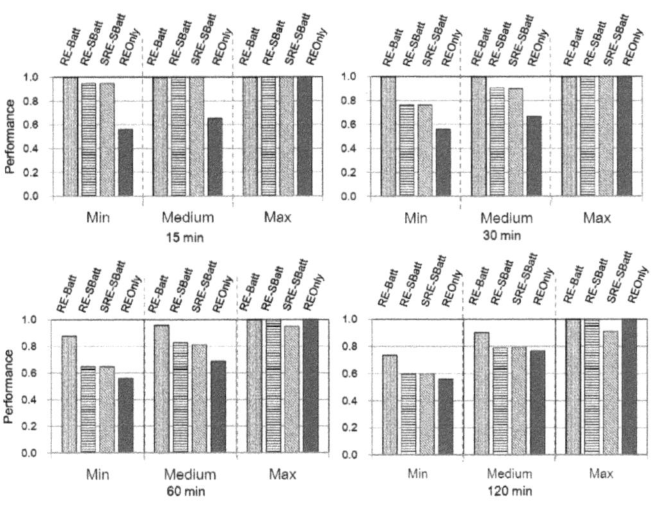

Figure 6: Performance tradeoffs among the 4 green configurations - *RE-Batt, RE-SBatt, SRE-SBatt* and *RE-Only* - under the Specjbb workload.

In this subsection, we evaluate the performance tradeoffs among different green configurations (i.e., different combinations of renewable power capacities and battery energy capacities) from Table 1. For each green configuration, we use the *Green-L* technique to show the performance impact, since *Green-C* and *Green-D* show similarity performance impacts. Figure 6 presents the performance of Specjbb with various green configurations.

Impact of renewable energy: As renewable energy could power the servers, long emergencies can be transformed into short emergencies from the perspective of performance.

In the REOnly configuration (in Table 1), the performance with the minimum renewable energy *availability* is same as that with only using *Throttling* for power capping. Renewable energy significantly improves performance, from 56% of *MaxPerf* without it (minimum *availability*) to 77% of *MaxPerf* with it for 120-minute long power emergencies with the medium renewable energy *availability*. Configurations with a small battery capacity, RE-SBatt and SRE-SBatt, can ride-out the minimum *availability* but with a significant performance penalty for 30 minutes duration (77% of *MaxPerf*). However, even with small renewable energy provision, *SRE-SBatt* achieves *MaxPerf* for up to 30 minutes with the maximum renewable energy *availability*. With the medium renewable energy *availability*, SRE-SBatt is still able to achieve 81% of *MaxPerf* for a 60-minute power emergency and 79% of *MaxPerf* for a 120-minute power emergency. RE-SBatt shows a similar performance to the SRE-SBatt configuration but achieves *MaxPerf* upon the maximum renewable energy *availability* regardless of the emergency duration.

Impact of battery: Given the minimum renewable energy *availability*, in configurations with the battery (RE-SBatt and RE-Batt) and with the minimum renewable energy *availability*, performance impact for REOnly configuration (56% of *MaxPerf*) can be reduced since the battery can supply power. The RE-SBatt configuration with limited battery energy (3.2Ah) capacity suffers a performance degradation (95% of *MaxPerf*) even during a 15-minute power emergency with the minimum renewable energy *availability* while RE-Batt can achieve *MaxPerf* up to 30 minutes.

With the medium renewable energy *availability*, battery plays an important role in boosting the performance. Even with a small battery energy capacity (3.2Ah), RE-SBatt is able to achieve *MaxPerf* for a 15-minute power emergency and sustains 83% of the (degraded) performance for a 60-minute emergency, in contrast to the REOnly configuration that achieves only 69% of *MaxPerf*. However, for power emergencies lasting 120 minutes or beyond, configurations with a small battery capacity (RE-SBatt and SRE-SBatt) show less benefit than the REOnly configuration, since the battery is not able to sustain such long-time operation for the entire emergency duration. And finally, performance can benefit more from larger battery energy capacity. For instance, RE-Batt (10Ah) achieves 96% of *MaxPerf* for a power emergency of 1 hour and maintains a 90% of (degraded) performance for a power emergency of 120 minutes. This implies that one can significantly improve the performance irrespective of renewable energy *availability* by purchasing more battery energy capacity.

5.3 Impact of application characteristics

For the rest of the evaluation, we only consider *SRE-SBatt* configuration (Table 1) and compare the effect of under-provisioning for applications with diverse performance and power peaks characteristics for the variations in the small renewable power and battery energy capacity. We mainly focus the differences.

Memcached and Web-search (Figure 7 and Figure 8): Memcached loads the memory with the necessary data from disk before handling client requests. Memcached with 20GB takes 10 minutes to migrate. Because Memcached has high memory-related CPU stalls, we find that the performance offered by *Throttling* and intra-cluster migration *Green-C* to be much better than that for Specjbb with a 20GB memory size (not shown in the figure for clarity). The performance with the medium and maximum *availability* shows a significant improvement over that with the minimum *availability* as the green power source participates in the handling of the power emergency. Intra-cluster migration (*Green-C*), combined with *Throttling*, achieves better performance than the *Throttling* mechanism (*Green-L*) alone. This implies that applications with low frequency of page modifications may benefit more from the migration mechanism as renewable energy does not suffice.

Web-search uses volatile memory as a cache for index data that are stored in persistent storage to improve query latency. Interestingly, *Throttling* for Web-search shows a better performance than that with Memcached and higher power state can outperform the *Green-C* technique for maximum *availability*. This implies a fine-grain power state of *Throttling* for Web-search may cover a larger spectrum of renewable energy availability and offered performance than the other workloads, which we plan to investigate in the future work. Moreover, we find that the *Hibernation* state for Web-search requires 4.8 minutes to resume from disk, resulting in poor query performance even the workload is available - 47% reduction in throughput - during the 3-4 minutes warm-up duration. Hence, renewable power can help achieve a good performance result and avoid prolonging the emergency duration for Web-search since it can power *Sleep* state.

SpecCPU (Figure 9): We observe that the performance of *SpecCPU* offered by *Throttling* becomes unacceptable because of the high memory contention from the 12 mcf instances. Furthermore, *Throttling* heightens the contention impact while causing a huge slowdown when all cores execute such memory-bound tasks. We choose not to migrate the HPC workload, since it can be delayed as discussed in [21] (recall Section 4.2). From the figure, we can see that the performance is improved as long as the workload can be

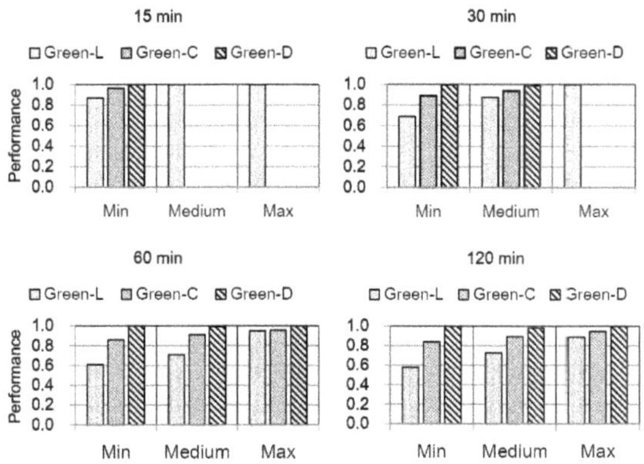

Figure 7: Performance of Memcached with the SRE-SBatt configuration.

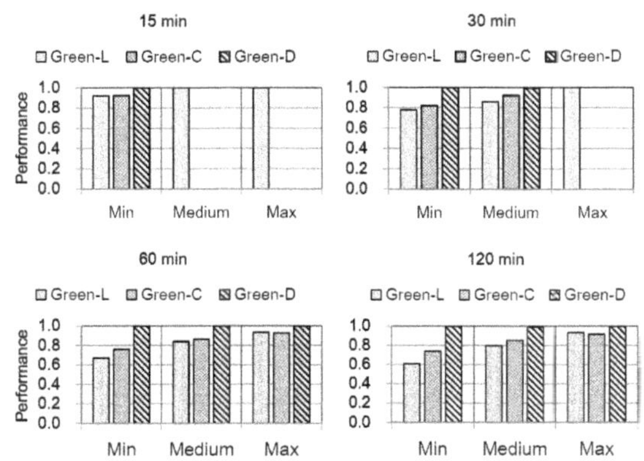

Figure 8: Performance of Web-search with the SRE-SBatt configuration.

powered by the green power. For instance, the performance reaches 94% of *MaxPerf* with the maximum *availability*, in contrast to 49% of *MaxPerf* with the minimum *availability* upon a 120-minute power emergency. Even with the medium *availability* for 2 hours duration, renewable energy helps achieve 30% performance improvement over that with the minimum *availability*.

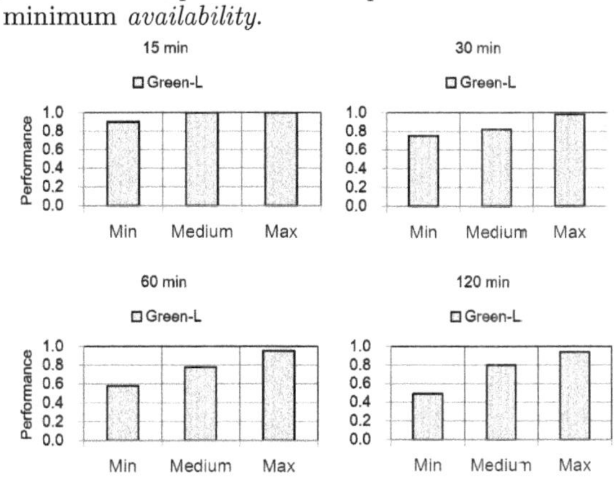

Figure 9: Performance of SpecCPU with the SRE-SBatt configuration.

5.4 Summary of Observations

In summary, we find that: (i) Though renewable energy shows large variance for power production, it plays as an important power source for emergency handling from the perspective of offered long time power supply. (ii) Renewable energy can be self sufficient regardless of the durations of emergencies for datacenters willing to delay computer loads (e.g., scientific computations) during emergencies. (iii) Renewable energy, conjunction with batteries can achieve the same performance as with today's overprovision approach for short and moderate emergencies. (iv) Renewable energy can supplement battery to reduce performance impact. (v) Throttling is infeasible at lower power supply of renewable energy and battery, though it can cover a large spectrum of the renewable energy availability for short to long emergencies for keeping within the underprovison grid power budget. (vi) Migration is preferred for longer emergency to offer a better performance compared to throttling for the power shortage of renewable energy and battery.

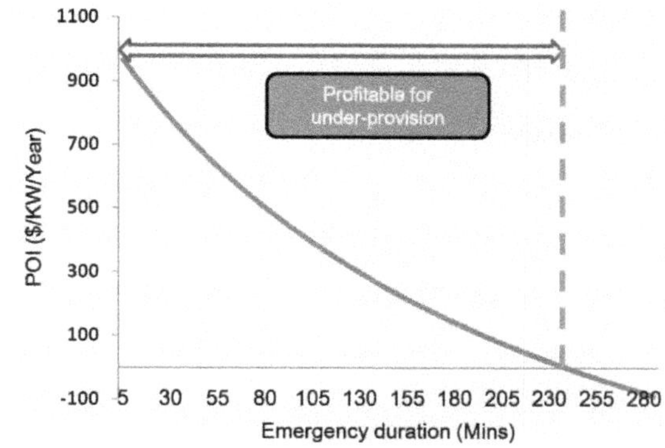

Figure 10: POI with additional renewable energy and battery investment.

5.5 TCO Consideration

Although we have considered a conservative provision of renewable energy and battery that already exist in green datacenters in our experiments, we will illustrate whether the cost of additional green provision can be justified by the potential reduction in the cost of datacenter's underprovisioned grid power infrastructure that we can obtain. We first denote the cost of procuring the additional PV module capacity as $REPowerCost$ \$/watt, the additional battery capacity to sustain T hours of power emergency as $T * BattCost$ \$/kWh and the cap-ex cost reduction of the grid power infrastructure due to underprovision as $GridCost$. We denote $REInCost$ \$/watt as the inverter cost.

We estimate our green-power capacity cost to be \$4.74/W, based on a recent report for moderate-scale PV panel (several hundred KW) [39]. In addition, we ensure that PV panels are amortized over 25 years (lifetime). The cost of central inverters at the multi-megawatt (MWs) level is around \$0.18/W and the inverter lifetime is around 10 years using the estimates of recent study [40]. The cost of the lead-acid battery is \$0.21/Wh as used in [19] while the battery's lifetime is assumed to be 4 years. We assume a grid utility cap-ex of \$5/W based on the estimate of the capital cost of the grid infrastructure for a typical 12-year datacenter from [4].

We use the measure of Profit-On-Investment (POI) to estimate the cost effectiveness of additional green infrastructure. POI is plotted in Figure 10 as a function of the length of a power emergency ($POI = \frac{GridCost}{T*BattCost+REPowerCost+REInCost} - 1$). In this calculation, we ensure that all components are amortized over their lifetime. Any length of a power emergency to the left of the crossover point (which turns out to be around 4 hours in this case) indicates a profitable investment. This suggests that investing in additional green provision may be worthwhile for most power emergencies. In fact, the result is conservative in that we do not consider the operation expense reduction (e.g., electricity cost reduction) through the green provision, which is a significant cost in datacenter.

6. CONCLUSION

We propose a novel renewable power distribution architecture that enables the underprovisioning of the grid power infrastructure in green datacenters. We have presented a framework for dealing with power emergencies arising from the aggressive underprovisioning of the grid power infrastructure in green datacenters. To avoid power overdraw, power management knobs, such as power state modulation and workload migration, can be supplemented with our new proposal of leveraging the already existing renewable energy and battery in green datacenters to gracefully deal with power emergencies. We demonstrate that, using an experimental prototype and assuming a 30% underprovision of the grid infrastructure, sufficient renewable energy by itself can sustain entire power emergencies (around 15-120 minutes on our prototype) even without the use of battery. Medium renewable energy availability, combined with battery, sustain short and moderate (15-30 minutes) power emergencies without any performance impact. Minimum renewable energy availability requires workload migration since sustained local throttling hurts performance if the limited battery energy capacity is not able to sustain the entire power emergency. Our renewable-energy solution, in conjunction with battery and workload migration, provides a graceful solution to handling power emergencies of all lengths arising from aggressive underprovisionsing of the grid power infrastructure with minimum performance impact.

7. ACKNOWLEDGMENTS

We would like to thank anonymous reviewers for their insightful comments. This research is sponsored by the National Basic Research 973 Program of China under Grant No. 2011CB302303, the National Natural Science Foundation of China under Grant No. 61300046, and the National High Technology Research and Development Program of China (863 Program) under Grant No.2013AA013203, and the Fundamental Research Funds for Central Universities, HUST, (Grant No. 2013KXYQ003).

8. REFERENCES

[1] http://www.aiso.net/technology-network-sun.html.
[2] http://www.greenhousedata.com/.
[3] X. Fan et al. Power provisioning for a warehouse-sized computer. In *ISCA*, 2007.
[4] S. Govindan et al. Leveraging Stored Energy for Handling Power Emergencies in Aggressively Provisioned Datacenters. In *ASPLOS*, 2012.
[5] D. Wang et al. Virtual Power Distribution in Datacenters. In *ISCA*, 2013.
[6] D. Wang et al. Energy Storage in Datacenters: What, Where, and How much? In *SIGMETRICS*, 2012.
[7] V. Kontorinis et al. Managing Distributed UPS Energy for Effective Power Capping in Data Centers. In *ISCA*, 2012.
[8] C. Li et al. Enabling datacenter servers to scale out economically and sustainably. In *MICRO*, 2013.
[9] Luiz André Barroso and Urs Hölzle. The case of energy-proportional computing. *Computer*, 40(12):22–40, 2007.
[10] C. Lefurgy et al. Server-level power control. In *ICAC*, 2007.
[11] S. Govindan et al. Benefits and Limitations of Tapping into Stored Energy for Datacenters. In *ISCA*, 2011.
[12] P. Bohrer et al. Energy Conservation for Servers. In *Workshop on Power Management for Real-Time and Embedded Systems*, 2001.
[13] X. Fu et al. How Much Power Oversubscription Is Safe and Allowed in Data Centers. In *ICAC*, 2011.
[14] D. Wang et al. Underprovisioning Backup Power Infrastructure for Datacenters. In *ASPLOS*, 2014.
[15] S. Govindan et al. Statistical profiling-based techniques for effective power provisioning in data centers. In *EuroSys*, 2009.
[16] W. Zheng et al. Exploiting Thermal Energy Storage to Reduce Data Center Capital and Operating Expenses. In *HPCA*, 2014.
[17] N. Sharma et al. Blink: Managing server clusters on intermittent power. In *ASPLOS*, 2011.
[18] Z. Liu et al. Renewable and Cooling Aware Workload Management for Sustainable Data Centers. In *SIGMETRICS*, 2012.
[19] I. Goiri et al. Parasol and Greenswitch: Managing Datacenters Powered by Renewable Energy. In *ASPLOS*, 2013.
[20] I. Goiri et al. GreenHadoop:Leveraging Green Energy in Data Processing Frameworks. In *EuroSys*, 2012.
[21] I. Goiri et al. GreenSlot: Scheduling Energy Consumption in Green Datacenters. In *SC*, 2011.
[22] B. Aksanli et al. Utilizing Green Energy Prediction to Schedule Mixed Batch and Service Jobs in Data Centers. In *HotPower*, 2011.
[23] C. Li et al. Solarcore: Solar energy driven multi-core architecture power management. In *HPCA*, 2011.
[24] C. Li et al. iSwitch: Coordinating and Optimizing Renewable Energy Powered Server Clusters. In *ISCA*, 2012.
[25] C. Li et al. Enabling distributed generation powered sustainable high performance data center. In *HPCA*, 2013.
[26] Google Summit. http://www.google.com/corporate/datacenter/events/dcsummit2009.html.
[27] Facebook. Hacking conventional computing infrastructure. http://opencompute.org/, 2011.
[28] http://rredc.nrel.gov/solar/calculators/pvwatts/.
[29] D. C. Jordan et al. Photovoltaic Degradation Rates - An Analytical Review. *Progress in Photovoltaics: Research and Applications*, 21:12–29, 2013.
[30] D.Manz et al. Enhanced reliability of photovoltaic systems with energy storage and controls. In *National Renewable Energy Laboratory, Report*, 2008.
[31] Zh-101 portable electric power fault recorder and analyzer, 2009.
[32] Measurement and instrumentation data center. http://www.nrel.gov/midc/.
[33] Grapesolar. www.grapesolar.com/.
[34] C. Clark et al. Live Migration of Virtual Machines. In *NSDI*, 2005.
[35] SPECJBB 2013:Java Business Benchmark. http://www.spec.org/jbb2013/.
[36] MEMCACHED:Memory-object Caching System. http://www.memcached.org.
[37] M. Ferdman et al. Clearing the clouds: A study of emerging scale-out workloads on modern hardware. In *ASPLOS*, 2012.
[38] SPECCPU. http://www.spec.org/cpu2006/.
[39] D. Feldman et al. Photovoltaic (PV) Pricing Trends: Historical, Recent, and Near-Term Projections. *Joint Technical Report*, 2012.
[40] R. Simpson. Levelized cost of energy from residential to large scale pv. In *The Applied Power Electronics Conference and Exposition*, 2012.

Building Fuel Powered Supercomputing Data Center at Low Cost

Yiqing Hua[1,2] Chao Li[1] Weichao Tang[1,2] Li Jiang[2] Xiaoyao Liang[2]

[1]Sustainable Architectures and Integration Laboratory
Department of Computer Science and Engineering
Shanghai Jiao Tong University, Shanghai, China
E-mail: lichao@cs.sjtu.edu.cn

[2]Advanced Computer Architecture Laboratory
Department of Computer Science and Engineering
Shanghai Jiao Tong University, Shanghai, China
E-mail: liang-xy@cs.sjtu.edu.cn

ABSTRACT

Distributed power generations that fed with various economical clean fuels are emerging as promising power supplies for extreme-scale computing systems. Recent years have witnessed a growing adoption of these non-conventional power supplies in data center designs due to the heightening demand for reducing IT carbon footprint and server energy cost. However, the benefits of such a fuel powered data center are often severely compromised by its high initial capital cost (CapEx). This is because most pilot designs today either rely on expensive advanced generators or employ low-performance generators with costly standby power backup.

In this study we exploit heterogeneous generation to reduce the cost of data center powered by fuel. We show that different types of power supplies, if used together, can greatly improve the cost-effectiveness of self-generation but introduce a new layer of design complexity and raise an important question of how to dispatch computing tasks on heterogeneous power supplies. Specifically, due to the non-ideal output power response speed of heterogeneous generators, servers may incur serious power budget deficiencies when dispatching large amount of jobs. We refer to this phenomenon as *power lagging,* which jeopardizes system reliability and are not economical to be handled by costly power backup systems. To overcome this barrier, we propose *μBatch*, an agile load dispatching scheme that eliminate *power lagging* at the system/software level. Other than dispatch computing tasks in bulk without considering power system behaviors, *μBatch* intelligently splits job queue into small sets and incrementally schedule jobs based on the power ramping rate constraints and total power budget constraints. Using realistic HPC datacenter load traces, we demonstrate that *μBatch* enables supercomputers to smoothly operate on heterogeneous power. Our design helps data center operators save over 80% cost while maintaining the desired workload performance.

Categories and Subject Descriptors

C.0 **[Computer Systems Organization]**: General
C.4 **[Performance of Systems]**: Design Studies

General Terms

Design, Management, Performance, Efficiency

Keywords

Data Center; Dispatching; Hybrid Generation; Fuel; Cost

ICS'15, June 8–11, 2015, Newport Beach, CA, USA.

http://dx.doi.org/10.1145/2751205.2751215

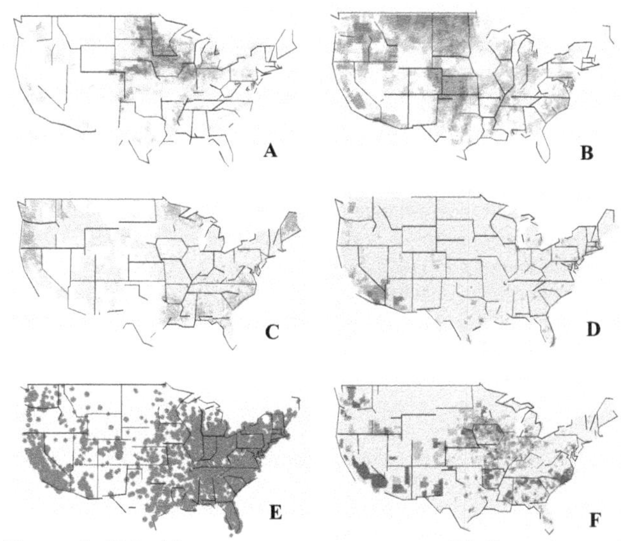

Figure 1. U.S. biomass resources maps. (A) Corn stover, (B) wheat straw, (C) forest residues, (D) wood/mil residues, (E) landfills, (F) manure. Data Source: National Renewable Energy Lab [4]

1. INTRODUCTION

With the advent of the smart grid initiative [1] and the evolution of various distributed generation (DG) systems [2], data centers today are facing new opportunities of supporting their escalating energy needs and continued capacity growth. Specifically, clean fuel based DG systems have shown great promise in offering 24×7 reliable power supply while maintaining carbon-neutral. If configured in combined heat and power mode (CHP) [3], these green generators can be over 80% efficient. Consequently, onsite fuel-based generation are expected to become the next frontier of power provisioning for server clusters and supercomputers.

In fact, there is a great potential to dramatically expand the use of clean fuel for power-hungry systems. Many fuels such as methane (natural gas), propane, ethanol, and methanol can be made from various biological materials (biomass) showing in Figure 1. The total biomass resource in the US is estimated to be 680 million dry tons per year, which can be exploited to generate about 730 billion kWh [5]. In 2010 the annual server energy demand in the US is about 135 billion kWh; in the worst case, this demand may double in 2015 [6]. Be that as it may, half of the biomass generated electricity is enough to power all the data center servers.

Many recent examples point to an increasing interest in data centers powered by various fuels. In Wyoming, Microsoft has deployed a non-conventional cluster for high-performance computing and modeling applications. Its power source is an onsite fuel cell

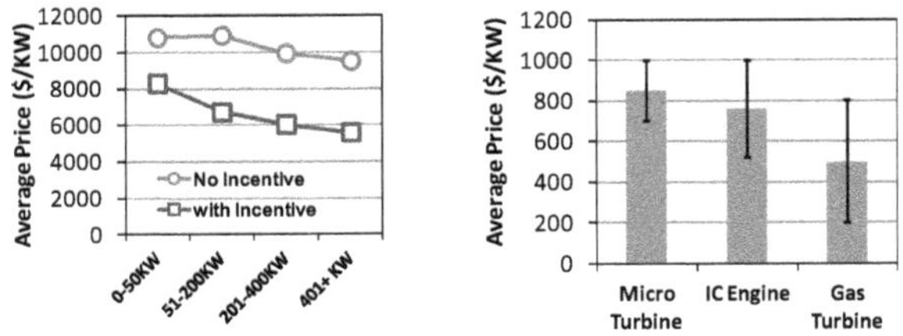

(a) Fuel cell costs (b) Heat engine costs

Figure 2. Capital cost of fuel-based generators [19-23]

system that converts methane biogas to electricity [7]. Several IT companies including Apple and eBay are also running part of their server racks on biogas-based fuel cell engine (called Energy Server [8]) developed by Bloom Energy [9, 10]. HP has investigated a data center power provisioning infrastructure that uses farm waste as primary fuel [11]. In addition, its Net-Zero data center can take advantage of various bio-gas turbines as well [12].

Given the growth in the popularity and scale of clean fuel based DG systems, this study aims to develop an understanding of fuel-powered large-scale computing facilities. We do not argue that tapping into fuel is the only design choice or the best way of delivering green high performance computing. However, the direct use of clean fuel in data center is attractive for several reasons:

1) The energy cost is usually low, particular for CHP systems (a.k.a. cogeneration) that have higher efficiency [3]. There is a favorable differential between the price of natural gas and the price of electricity, called the spark spread [13]. As a result, the annual energy cost savings can be up to $700 per kW installed capacity [3].
2) The reliability of fuel delivery system is known to be high [14]. Unlike the utility power grid, the gas system is underground and exposed to fewer natural disasters. Its delivery contracts often exhibit over 99.99%, which matches the availability of a fully fault-tolerant Tier-IV data center and is much better than the main grid (99.9% or less) [15-17].
3) Onsite fuel based generators are often dispatchable, namely, their power output can be adjusted on demand [3]. Each generation module can also be turned on or off dynamically based on the average loading of data centers. This is a key advantage over wind/solar power systems which have intermittent and time-varying output.
4) Supporting smart energy initiatives can be a wise business move as well. Given the growing awareness of climate change and energy security, companies and consumers will increasingly show preferences to a diverse generation method and smarter grid [18]. Integrating various carbon-natural fuels into a datacenter facility's structure helps attain leading market positions and strong public relations.

One of the key obstacles that could hold back the development of fuel-powered data center is high cost. Existing fuel-based DG system can be grouped into two broad categories: fuel cells (*FC*) and heat engines (*HE*). The cost of a fuel cell system is inherently high, as shown in Figure 2-a. Without incentive, a 100 kW system sold by Bloom Energy can cost $800,000 [24]. Although heat engines are about one-tenth the price of fuel cells (Figure 2-b), they have slow output response speed and often require costly standby power capacity. For example, if using utility power grid and redundant UPS capacity as backup, the power infrastructure cost is estimated to be $10~25 per watt [25]. In addition, utility companies also charge a power demand fee from $8/kW [26] to 18/kW [27] per billing cycle. Moreover, if not managed properly, UPS batteries incur frequent replacement cost at over $2,000 per kW [28]. Therefore, many potential benefits of the fuel-powered data center could be severely compromised due to high power related cost.

To build economically viable and even cost-competitive system, this paper explores mixing different power generation technologies and minimizing underutilized standby power in fuel-powered data centers. We propose a new power provisioning strategy called Phi (Φ), which stands for *provisioning in hybrid and islanded mode*. This architecture has two salient features. (1) It exploits a hybrid power infrastructure that combines fuel cells with inexpensive heat engines. The resulting system is expect to exhibit a synergism in which the data center can yield a cost-effectiveness far better than that can be offered by either power generator alone. (2) It takes advantage of the highly reliable nature of the DG systems and offloads the burden of managing power spikes onto them. This could eventually allow us to eliminate the needs of reserving large power capacity from the utility grid and onsite battery (i.e., islanded).

While the Φ architecture has great promise for reducing the CapEx of power infrastructure, applying it to a mission critical system can be challenging. The main reason is that hybrid power systems, from the viewpoint of a sensitive load, are not ideal power supplies. A homogeneous fuel cell system only take several seconds to ramp power up as load changes. Therefore, it is reasonable to completely replace backup power with fuel cell [17]. Nevertheless, most heat generators takes several minutes or more to ramp up since the change of the turbine speed takes time. With majority being inexpensive heat engines, the Φ architecture has very limited capability to handle unexpected load surges. Without careful control, existing data centers can get very sluggish power increase when schedule large amount of tasks in a short time, which we refer to as "power lagging". This phenomenon can often cause suboptimal energy efficiency and even costly power failures.

To support a graceful transition to the Φ architecture, we have developed a novel load dispatching scheme called *μBatch*. It is an agile load dispatching scheme tailored to the behaviors of hybrid power supplies. Rather than dispatch batch jobs merely based on the availability of computing resources, *μBatch* also considers various supply-side constraints. It firstly divides a large job queue into two medium job sets based on the job classification information and the available power budget of the two types of DG system (e.g., fuel cell and heat engine). It then incrementally schedule each job set based on the power ramping rate constraint of the power supply. This judicious load dispatching scheme enables fuel-powered data center to overcome the "power lagging" barrier while maintaining high performance and efficiency.

To our knowledge, this is the first extensive study of a fuel-powered supercomputing data center design at the architecture and system level. This paper makes the following contributions:

- We investigate clean fuel powered high performance data centers. We propose Phi (Φ), a new power provisioning architecture which allows a data center to maximally exploit the benefits of fuel-based generation at low cost.
- We identify the "power lagging" issue in data centers powered by hybrid DG generators. We characterize it and show that being able to adapt to the "power lagging" is the key to build a cost-effective system.
- We propose μBatch, an agile load management framework tailored for fuel-powered data centers. It is a power-driven, incremental job dispatching approach that allows one to overcome the limitations of power supply through a software and system level control.
- We evaluate the design space of μBatch using realistic job traces. We show that it can reduce over 80% TCO in a fuel-powered data center, with near-optimal (within 1% difference) performance.

The rest of this paper is organized as follows. Section 2 discusses related work. Section 3 introduces background of fuel based generation. Section 4 propose and analyze the Phi architecture. Section 5 elaborates the μBatch load dispatching scheme. Section 6 describes experimental methodology. Section 7 presents evaluation results. Finally, Section 8 concludes this paper.

2. RELATED WORK

[Data Center Powered by Fuel] Very little prior work exists on fuel-powered data center design. Similar studies are mainly carried out by several pioneers in the industry. For example, Sharma et al. [11] from HP investigate data center self-generation that uses biogas generated from livestock wastes. Their work introduces the key resource management flow but lacks quantitative analysis. [17] conducted by Microsoft is the first research study to promote fuel based data center design. Zhao et al. [29] also from Microsoft have demonstrated the feasibility of operating server racks on fuel cells. These designs choose to conservatively add battery as power backup. In contrast, our design allows the data center to further reduce the high capital cost by minimizing the needs of backup power capacity. In general, all these prior work focus on the supply-side infrastructure and power management from an electrical point of view. In this paper we propose workload-side solutions that enable us to maximally exploit fuel-powered data center.

[Load-Following Power Supply] Another representative work in the context of clean fuel powered data center is to explore the use of the load following capability of generators. For example, Liu et al. [30] formulate an energy-aware request routing problem in geographically distributed cloud data centers powered by fuel cells. Li et al. [31] exploit distributed generation for tracking the fluctuation of data center demand. Unfortunately, both designs only look at homogeneous power provisioning schemes and miss the opportunity to reduce high design cost. In addition, our power management scheme considers the power ramping rate constraints of load-following DG, while prior optimization schemes in these work overlooked this critical power supply characteristics.

[Non-Dispatchable DG System] There is a large body of work in terms of intermittent (non-dispatchable) renewable energy (solar and wind energy) powered data centers [32-38]. Sharma et al. [32] investigate the impact of power supply intermittency on the most critical memcached workloads. Goiri et al. [33] propose to leverage deferrable batch workload in HPC centers to maximally harvest the intermittent green energy. Li et al. [34], on the other hand, uses VM-based workload migration to improve the utilization of wind energy powered server cluster. Deng et al. [35] show that the profit of a green data center can be largely affected by the way they manage carbon footprint. Gao et al. [36] propose FORTE, a framework that can determine suitable expansion plan. A data center expansion strategy is also proposed in [37], which leverages modular solar panels and distributed battery systems. In [38], the author has demonstrated a scaled-down prototype of a grid-connected solar data center called Parasol. Our work differs from these studies in that we focus on another important green power supply: clean fuel-based dispatchable generators. In addition, we investigate the most effective way to cut capital cost in these systems other than merely emphasize improving green energy utilization or performance.

[Hybrid Power Provisioning] A few recent studies have focused on hybrid power supplies. For example, Li et al. [39] investigate data centers on green energy mix that combines dispatchable and non-dispatchable power. However, they still focus on homogene-

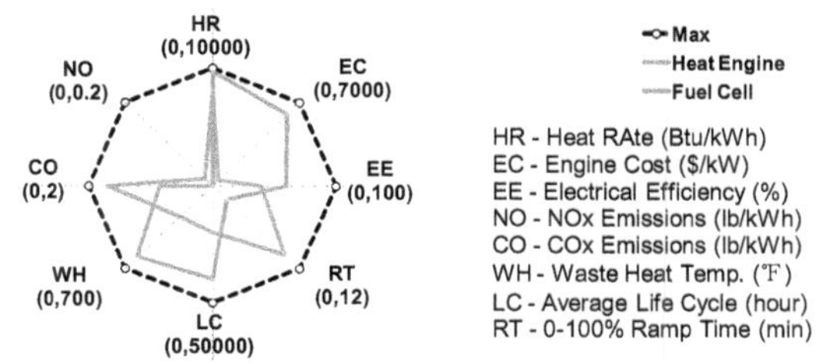

Figure 3. Comparison of fuel-based generation. Each technology has its own pros and cons [19-23, 46-48]

ous fuel-based generators and rely on bulk backup batteries. In [40], Liu et al. propose heterogeneous power provisioning. Their work is only limited to hybrid energy storage devices (i.e., batteries and super-capacitors). In other domains, fuel cell/heat engine hybrid systems have been well studied with the aim to improve generator inner efficiency [41, 42]. In this study we show that simply connecting computing loads to these systems often result in sub-optimal design tradeoffs due to a lack of supply-load coordination. When hybrid power system become part of a data center's energy portfolio, new power-aware load management schemes at the computer architecture and system level is highly desired.

[Batteries and Peak Shaving] Prior research has demonstrated the benefits of leveraging energy storage devices, such as UPS batteries, in datacenters to shave peak power demand [43-45]. This can significantly save OpEx and Cap-Ex cost. However, batteries do not generate power on their own and they can only serve as ancillary backup in distributed generation systems. To minimize the upfront cost in a fuel-powered data center, our goal is to minimize the dependency on them by leveraging smart load dispatching.

The novelty of our work is three-folded. (1) We explore powering high-performance computing data center with hybrid clean fuel based generation. (2) We follow a KISS[1] design principle when designing the Phi (Φ) architecture – minimizing unnecessary power backup makes our system more cost-effective. (3) We propose a new load dispatching scheme called μBatch to provide a system support for managing heterogeneous power supply.

3. BACKGROUND

This section briefly introduces fuel-based self-generation which has the potential to reshape the way we run data centers.

3.1 Generating Power from Fuel

Electricity can be generated from fuel in different ways. Fuel cells produce electricity through a pollution-free electrochemical process [42]. Heat engines, one the other hand, rely on various advanced combustion turbines that burn fuels [46]. Both fuel cells and heat engines generate large amount of heat, which can be recycled to yield an overall energy efficiency of over 80% [47]. Consequently, they are deemed to be among the most promising distributed generation resources in the smart grid era [47].

No generation technology totally dominates. The radar chart in Figure 3 compares several key parameters of typical fuel cells and heat engines. Heat engines offer lower acquisition cost while fuel cells have much better power ramp rate (the speed to change power output). Sudden and massive requests for computing nodes can cause significant power demand increase, which challenges the ramp rate of distributed generation systems. If this demand-supply

[1] KISS: Keep It Simple, Stupid. http://en.wikipedia.org/wiki/KISS_principle

	Generation Technology	Warm-up Time (cold start)	Ramp Rate (0-100%)
FC	Solid Oxide FC	10 min	sever seconds
	Phosphoric Acid FC	6 min	sever seconds
	Proton Exchange Membrane FC	1 min	sever seconds
HE	Micro Turbine	7 min	8 min
	Gas Turbine	7 min	8 min
	Internal Combustion Engine	1 min	6 min

Table 1. Power output response speed comparison

power gap is not well managed, the result can be significant deterioration in power quality or even costly power outages. In Table 1 we show the ramp rate of several representative technologies [46, 47]. Fuel cells can release power almost immediately and could be used to handle abrupt power changes once they are warmed up. In contrast, most heat engines need time to be committed (reach a desired engine speed). They provide a sluggish load following, which typically occurs on the timescale of several minutes.

3.2 Advantages and Limitations

The technical and economic viability of tapping into fuel largely depend on the availability of fuel supplies. Fortunately, there are a variety widely distributed biomass resources such as agricultural residuals, forests residuals, industry byproducts, and urban wastes. In addition, the extensive natural gas infrastructure also provides very convenient low-emission fuel delivery.

Clean fuel-based onsite generators are ideally suited for high-performance computing data centers for several reasons. (1) They are reliable source of power. A fuel cell generator can be expected to run continuously for over ten years [48]. In fact, the ability of an aging electric power grid to meet the soaring server power demand is at stake [49, 50]. Data center operators are increasingly challenged to rely on conventional approaches to meet their expanding power capacity needs. (2) Fuel generated from biomass is renewable energy resources which greatly reduce the carbon footprint of a supercomputing center. Although burning biofuel releases CO_2, this is offset by the CO_2 absorbed in the growth of new biomass through photosynthesis. (3) They can provide dispatchable power whenever data center have different power demand. Not like intermittent solar/wind energy, fuel-based generators produce power in a controllable fashion. Various onsite generators can be interconnected to form a low-voltage network called micro-grid [47], which further increases the manageability of onsite generation.

The major barrier to the adoption of large-scale fuel-based generation in data centers is high initial cost. In some scenarios, renewable energy certificates (carbon credits) could turn it feasible to generate energy onsite using clean fuel. Still, the price of fuel cell and the price of backup power system that is required by heat engines often make onsite generation economically less attractive. Substantial effort has been put into optimizing the inner efficiency of the generator. However, improving cost-effectiveness in fuel powered data center demands continued innovation in architecture design and system management. Our work fills this critical void.

4. THE PHI (Φ) ARCHITECTURE

To turn fuel-powered HPC data center into a competitive edge, we explore aggressively utilizing onsite generation while minimizing the needs of power backup. We propose a new power provisioning architecture Phi: power provisioning in hybrid (heterogeneous) and islanded (isolated) mode. The Φ architecture allows us to greatly reduce the cost of a fuel-powered HPC data center.

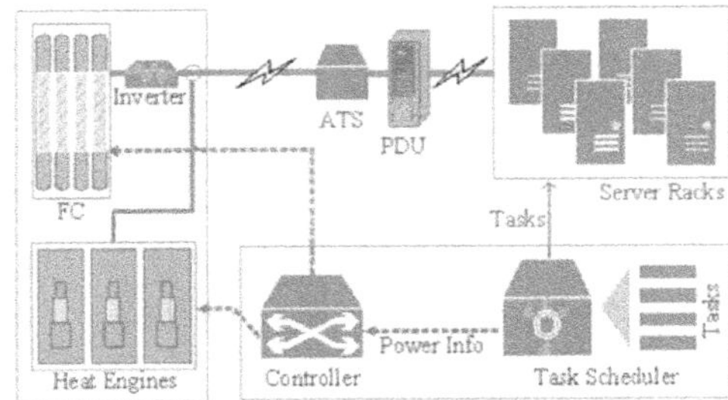

Figure 4. Schematics of the Phi architecture

In this section we first introduce the unique architecture of Phi. We than discuss its necessity and cost benefits in data center design. Finally we discuss the main limitation of this architecture from a power management point of view. We propose a system-level solution to overcome this limitation in Section 5.

4.1 Hybrid and Islanded System

The main feature of Phi is two folded. First, Phi employs heterogeneous power. Second, Phi is isolated from other standby power sources (no matter it is utility power grid or onsite batteries).

Figure 4 depicts the overall structure of Phi. The hybrid power system is the only power source that the data center is connected to. The output of fuel cells is DC power. It is first inverted to AC and then interconnected with the heat engine to form a local micro-grid system. On the data center side, a power controller is responsible for coordinating the output levels of different power supplies.

Combing fuel cells and heat engines brings unprecedented opportunity for data center power provisioning. Such a heterogeneous power system can optimize global efficiency and cost-effectiveness. The total capacity of the installed fuel cell is normally larger than that of heat engines. Fuel cells have better power ramping capability and can be used to handle the abrupt power demand change. Heat engines are inexpensive source of power and are used to provide base load power and a slower load following service.

The islanded mode of Φ is partially enlightened by the islanding state of a micro-grid. A micro-grid can disconnect itself from the main grid and enters an islanding state when the utility grid incurs power quality problems. It maintains normal operation on all of its loads in an islanding mode. In this study our goal is to enable data center to run smoothly on islanded mode to radically reduce cost.

It is not uncommon to use standalone (i.e., islanded) systems. For example, Yank [51] allows a green data center to unplug from the utility grid. Besides, iSwitch [34] also has partial of its server clusters powered only by onsite wind turbines. However, both designs have backup computing capacity. They move workloads to reserved computing systems when renewable power is inadequate or power failure happens. In this study we do not over-provisioning computing systems (with is very costly) and therefore do not have additional server racks as backup. In fact, there is no need to do so on fuel powered data center since the availability of energy supply is high (99.99%) and the power supply is stable.

4.2 The Power Lagging Problem

Although the Φ Architecture is expected to greatly reduce the design cost, current data centers are not able to benefit from it. The reason is very simple: they still need costly backup power system in order to run smoothly on the Φ Architecture.

Sluggish power ramp speed of the hybrid power system is the main challenge in directly employing Φ in data centers. Heat engines are the majority in the Φ Architecture and they have very long ramp up time. Fuel cells can increase its output in a matter of

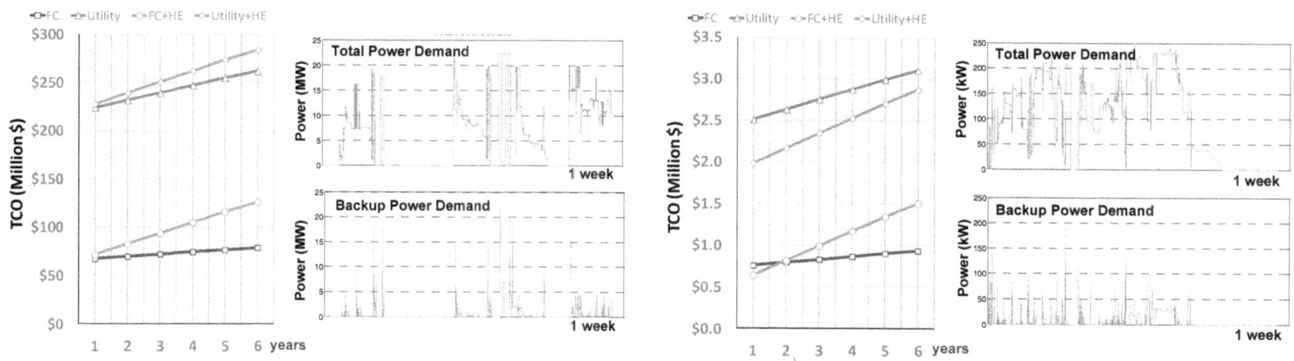

(a) Blue Gene/P system called Intrepid (b) San Diego Supercomputing Center

Figure 5. TCO analysis of different power provisioning schemes

seconds to adapt to rapid shocks in power demand, but their total capacity is very limited. In other words, the Φ Architecture itself simply lack the capability to many data center power surges.

Consequently, data centers encounter a situation in which the power supply lags behind the power demand. Existing data center load dispatchers are unaware of the power ramping behaviors of the onsite generation, and therefore release large amount of jobs upon the availability of computing resources. This can introduce a step change in data center power demand. Oftentimes, the huge power mismatch between demand and supply cannot be handled by the Φ Architecture either due to inadequate fuel cell capacity or slow power ramp rate of the heat engine. This situation is often worsened by under-provisioning fuel cells.

4.3 Understanding the Cost Overhead

Due to the power lagging issue, the cost-effectiveness can be still very low in data centers employing Φ. To understand this, we characterize the total cost of ownership (TCO) of various system configurations, as shown in Table 2. The capital cost of fuel cell is conservatively estimated to be \$3000/kW, and its O&M cost is at \$0.04/kWh [52]. The infrastructure cost of the utility backup infrastructure is \$10/W and the electricity price is \$0.13/kWh. Although the engine cost of heat engine (\$200/kW) is much lower than a fuel cell, the O&M (operating and maintenance) cost can be higher if using conventional combustion engine set (\$0.2/kWh) [53].

Strategy	Descriptions
UG	Only use the utility power grid
FC	Only use FC as power supply
HE+UG	HE with utility grid as backup
HE+FC	Φ without optimization

Table 2. Evaluated design scenarios

We use realistic HPC data center traces obtained online [54]. One trace comes from a BlueGene/L system at Lawrence Livermore National Lab. It features a massive amount of short jobs (over 90% jobs run for less than 5 seconds), resulting in heavily fluctuating power demand. The other trace is collected from the San Diego Supercomputer Center. Its average job size (requested number of CPU nodes) is about 1/50 of the BlueGene/L system, but its average job runtime is longer (almost 2X). We provision each data center in such a way that the data center power system can just satisfy the server power demand without affecting the job completion deadline. Figure 5 presents our evaluation results.

It is clear that a fuel-powered data center can exert heavy power spikes on its backup power systems. As shown in Figures 5-(a) and 5-(b), both HPC data centers can create highly bursty total power demand. Since heat engines have very limited ramp up rate, *HE+UG* has to occasionally request large amount of power for a very short period (several minutes) from the utility grid. While the total energy drawn from the utility grid in this case is negligible, the associated infrastructure cost can be skyrocketing. In addition, the utility company often installs a power demand meter onsite. A demand charge will be applied based on the highest average kW measured in a 15-minute time interval in the last billing period [26]. Therefore, the usage of heat engine as a primary power supply in the *HE+UG* does not reduce its reliance on utility power backup. Consequently, the TCO of *HE+UG* can be even higher than a conventional data center that is only powered by the utility grid.

Similarly, the TCO of the *HE+FC* configuration is also not optimistic at all if data center operators overlook the power lagging issue. As Figure 5 shows, the cost of *HE+FC* may significantly exceed a fuel-cell-only data center in a typical five-year *HE* life span. This is because server loads can create significant amount of power surges, which requires large amount of onsite fuel cells to provide transient power support. Thus, the usage of heat engine as a primary power supply in the *HE+FC* configuration does not reduce a data center's reliance on fuel cell system. On the country, the result is significantly over-provisioned onsite generators.

In addition, simply adding battery systems to the *HE+FC* configuration is not a sound solution. First, batteries can be very costly if used as transient power backup; their power capacity cost can be \$2000~4600/kW for the most widely used lead-acid batteries [28]. In addition, frequent high-current discharge greatly reduces a battery's lifetime, which further increases the depreciation cost of a battery. Moreover, batteries are essentially not power generators. They need to be charged once their stored energy level is low and they also incur a round-trip energy loss issue.

In fact, a very easy and intuitive way to reduce TCO in data centers running on Φ is to reduce the height of any abrupt power change. In Figures 5-(a) the height of power spikes exerted on the backup system is almost the same as the maximum power demand of the data center. In Figures 5-(b), however, the height of the peak backup power demand is only 87% of the peak data center power. As a result, the *HE+UG* configuration in Figure 5-(b) shows better cost effectiveness. The *HE+FC* configuration in Figure 5-(b) also becomes cheaper compared to *FC* in the first two years.

Summary: Current data centers cannot directly run on the Φ architecture due to a lack of resilience to the power lagging problem of hybrid generators. They often requires significant amount of backup power capacity, which contradicts our commitment to reduce the cost. The cost of a fuel-powered data center can be greatly affected by the way we manage the data center load.

5. INCREMENTAL LOAD DISPATCHING

We investigate how load management will help to improve a data center's resilience to the power uncertainty incurred in Φ. Rather than waiting for the power systems to be smart (i.e., better *HE* and cheaper *FC*), we instead design an intelligent load dispatching strategy. It allows data centers to develop the flexibility to run smoothly on Φ, in spite of the fact that the power supply is less-than-perfect and the power demand unavoidably fluctuating.

5.1 Overview of μBatch

We propose *μBatch*, an agile load dispatching scheme tailored to the behaviors of hybrid distributed generation. Traditional dispatchable power systems have been designed in this way that generation can follow the load power demand. To enable a data center to graceful operate on Phi, it is best to also dynamically control the job flow so that the load also follows the generation patterns to some extent. To achieve this, μBatch uses an incremental job dispatching strategy. It judiciously dispatch jobs based on the power ramp rate and power budget constraints.

Existing data center job dispatching strategies are largely workload-driven. A list of jobs are normally submitted to a scheduler that is responsible for validating job parameters, queueing jobs, allocating compute nodes, and monitoring the status of job operation. One important goal of conventional scheduling policies is to reduce ensure better resource utilization while minimizing job turnaround time. For example, backfilling policies [55] rearrange jobs instead of execute jobs in their order of arrival to minimize system fragmentation. Such a compute load oriented job scheduler typically dispatches jobs once the computational resources are available in the system. They can handle complex parallel jobs with heavily constrained computing resource but cannot efficiently adapt to the power lagging issue in hybrid power provisioning environment.

In contrast, μBatch is primarily power-driven. It takes into account the available power capacity of different types of power supplies (i.e., heat engine and fuel cell) and their power ramping speed. It then classifies the submitted jobs and evaluates all the computational resources available in the data center to decide which jobs have to be dispatched, where and when. An important goal of μBatch is to optimally exploit the available energy source while minimizing the negative impact of power lagging on job execution. Its design follows three general considerations from the view point of data center power management:

First, we do not over-generate power and energy, since electricity cannot be stored onsite for Phi. In fact, over-generating is not wise even for grid-connected data center. Although the data center owner could run *FC* and *HE* at full capacity all the time and export excess power to the utility company, the price the utility pays for the exported power does not make it economically attractive to do so. Therefore, it is best to full utilize all the energy generated.

Second, we defer workload, other than curtail workload. In other words, μBatch schedule jobs only when the power generation ramps up to a desired level. Similar to existing work [33], we take advantage of the fact that most data processing jobs are deferrable to a certain extent. Existing designs often resolve power brownout (caused by over-loading) in a rather crude way: using DVFS to place a hard power cap, or simply shut down the server (load shedding). We chose not to do so since running at less-than-ideal frequency significantly decrease the efficiency of a server. In addition, scaling node performance or shutting down servers can cause great adverse impact on all the parallel tasks that have interdependence.

Third, we manage the power usage of different types of generators at the system level. There has been prior work that divides data center into two server clusters and uses separated power provisioning paths [34]. In fact, such a hardware-based approach is not suitable for fuel-based generation since it may exacerbate the power lagging issue on the sever cluster that connect to heat engines. Workload migration may be a solution to allow power sharing between two clusters, but it incurs significant overhead.

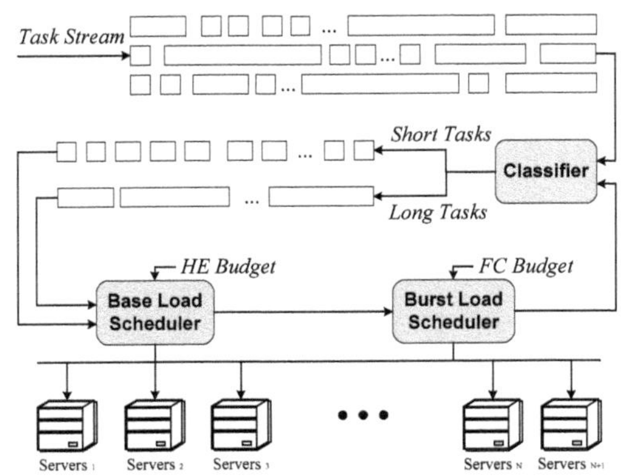

Figure 6. Schematics of the μBatch dispatching strategy

5.2 Dispatching Strategy

We formulate the job dispatching strategy on Φ as a two-fold problem. 1) Given limited power ramp speed, apply appropriate load deferring policy for jobs that have different runtime. 2) Given that the installed fuel cell capacity is very limited, appropriate power capacity management between responsive (i.e., fuel cells) and sluggish (i.e., heat engines) power supply is necessary.

Figure 6 illustrates the proposed μBatch design. Its scheduling approach takes three steps: classification of forthcoming job requests, allocation of base-load power (i.e., heat energy power capacity) for majority of the jobs, and opportunistic usage of fuel cell power capacity to manage any potential bursty loads. Thus, μBatch can be seen as a supply-load co-scheduling technique.

In the first step, μBatch requests profiling information from the job queue and classifies jobs into two types: short jobs that are expected to finish within the lead-in time (i.e., power ramp up time) of HE generators, and long jobs that maintain steady power demand for extended period of time (> than the lead-in time). Short jobs are more likely to result in transient load power demand fluctuation, while long jobs contribute less to load fluctuation.

Our dispatcher first allocates the heat engine generation. Heat engines accounts for a larger portion of the available power capacity and are inexpensive source of power. They are ideal base-load power for long-running jobs. In Figure 6, the base-load scheduler dynamically checks the newly available power budget as a result of power ramping. Once the additional power budget headroom is meet the power demands of any one job in the queue, our scheduler will dispatch it immediately no matter it is short or long.

Our dispatcher allocates the fuel cell generation after the heat engine power has been allocated. Fuel cell power capacity is limited and it is critical to judiciously utilize this precious source of responsive power supply. In Figure 6, our bursty-load scheduler gives high priority to short jobs high priority. It selects the most delayed one from short jobs that can be scheduled based on the available fuel cell power budget headroom. Instead, we never use fuel cell to power long jobs for good reasons: the impact of job deferring on long jobs is much smaller than short jobs. Since most heat engine can ramp up to full capacity in 10 minutes, the maximum job delay for a long job can be 10 minutes which may be a

Algorithm 1: Pseudo code for μBatch dispatching

```
Indicator = Maintain;
for each fine-grained timestamp
        change the power supply based on the Indicator;
        add the job to wait[];
while HE has enough power
        schedule a job from wait[];
if wait[] is not empty
        Indicator = Up;
else if Power goes down won't affect job running now
        Indicator = Down;
else Indicator = Maintain;
while FC has enough power
        schedule the most delayed short task from wait[];
```

Trace Abbr.	Short/Long	Highest Peak	
Seth	24%	1573KW	Small
BH	68%	1768KW	Small
CM5	61%	3415KW	Medium
PIK	20%	5536KW	Large
DS	52%	7124KW	Large

Table 3. Summary statistics of the selected traces

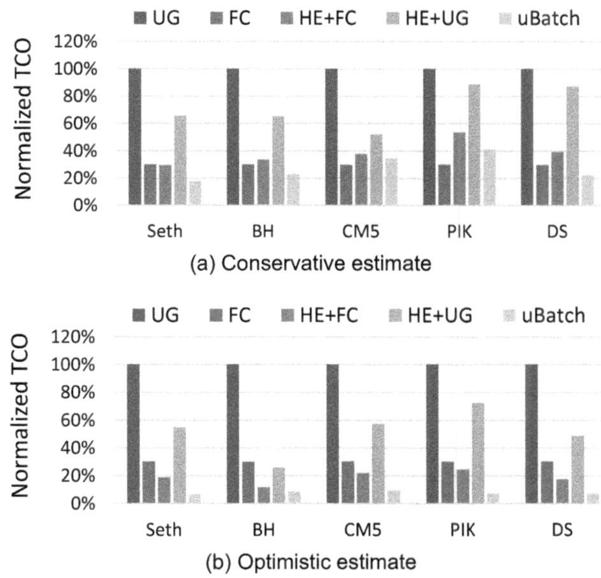

Figure 7. Normalized TCO schemes for different schemes

very small percentage of its overall all execution time (several hours or many days). In contrast, a 10-minutes delay may be too long for jobs that are expected to finish within tens of seconds.

In Algorithm 1 we show the pseudo code for the co-scheduling scheme used in μBatch. Similar to existing backfilling policy, we expect users to provide nearly accurate estimates of their job execution durations. In each round of scheduling there are two stages: base-load allocation and bursty-load allocation. Jobs that are not dispatched will remain in the job queue. The result is a series of micro/small batch of jobs and an incremental job execution flow.

We expect μBatch to reshape data center power demand. It maintains a mild power demand variation, and therefore enables data centers to run smoothly on Phi, our clean fuel-based, sustainable power provisioning architecture with very low cost.

6. EVALUATION METHODOLOGY

We use data logs from six large-scale clusters [54]. Each log provides the job arrival time, waiting time, the number of processors requested, the actual duration, average CPU time, and the start time. Our framework uses discrete-event simulation approach to process a chronological sequence of job events. For each trace we evaluate 5 million seconds of operation duration, which is about two months. We select six traces as summarized below:

- **Seth**: *This log is from a 120-node Linux cluster named Seth, which belongs to the HPC Center North (HPC2N) located in Sweden. Original job scheduler is Maui*
- **BH**: *This is the San Diego Supercomputer Center Blue Horizon log. The total machine size is 144 nodes (8-way SMP) for batch use. Jobs are collected using the LoadLeveler.*
- **CM5:** *This trace comes from a 1024-node connection machine CM-5 system deployed at the Los Alamos National Lab. Scheduling was performed by the DJM software.*
- **PIK**: *This log is collected from a 320-nodes IBM iDataPlex cluster at the Potsdam Institute for Climate Impact Research (PIK). The maximal job size observed used 128 nodes.*
- **DS**: *The San Diego Supercomputer Center DataStar log contains data comes from a 184-node machine. However only 171 nodes are used to process batch jobs.*

Two parameters affect our evaluation: 1) the ratio between short and long jobs, and 2) the highest power demand of the system. The former is closely related with the scheduling decisions of μBatch, while the latter significantly affect the total power capacity planning decision. Table 3 summarizes the statistics of the selected traces. We classify jobs according to their execution duration. The threshold that separates short jobs and long jobs is 10 minutes. Significant variability is observed in the job duration. The ratio between short and long jobs ranges from 7% to 68%. We consider both small-scale clusters and extremely large data centers.

The data center infrastructure we evaluated is based on the HP ProLiant DL 380 G6 server system (Intel Xeon L5530 processor, 2.4G). Our simulation assumes that the jobs are CPU-intensive. According to the published SPECpower_ssj2008 Results, the evaluated server system has an average power of 93 Watt per chip at 100% utilization and a minimum power of 31 Watt per chip in active idle state. The total onsite power capacity of the heat engine system is based the maximum peak power of the evaluated data center trace. We assume the worst-case ramp time is 10 minutes. The default fuel cell capacity is one-tenth of the heat engine.

7. RESULTS

In this section we discuss the benefits of applying μBatch to data centers powered by hybrid onsite green power supplies. We compare μBatch to various design approaches discussed in Table 2. We first evaluate the cost benefits of the proposed Phi architecture. We then discuss the performance impact of μBatch. Finally we evaluate the importance of capacity planning in our design.

7.1 Cost Benefits

The key motivation of the Phi architecture and μBatch is to reduce the cost of a fuel-powered data center by enabling aggressive utilization of the power provisioning systems. In Figures 7-(a) and 7-(b) we present the 5-year total cost of ownership for different data center traces under various power management schemes. We consider both conservative design estimation and optimistic design estimation (i.e., the O&M cost of heat engine is $0.2/kWh [53] and

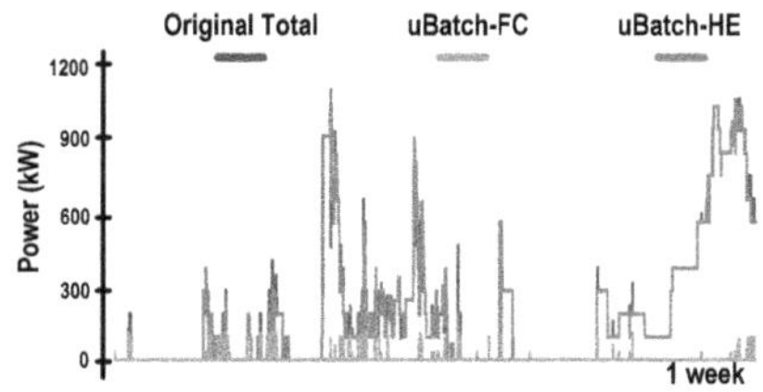

(a) High fluctuation (*Seth*)

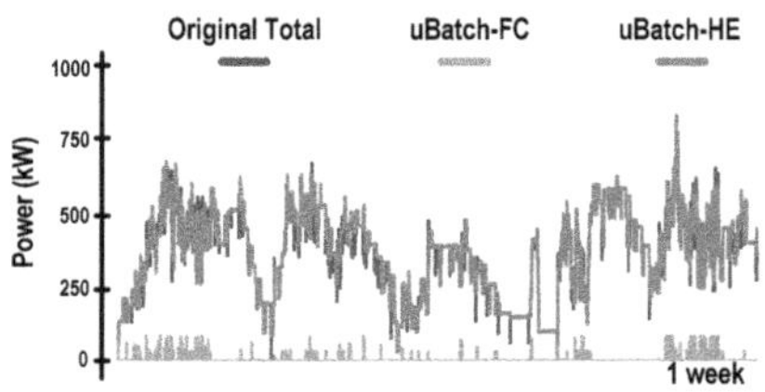

(b) Mild fluctuation (*CM5*)

Figure 8. Power re-shaping results

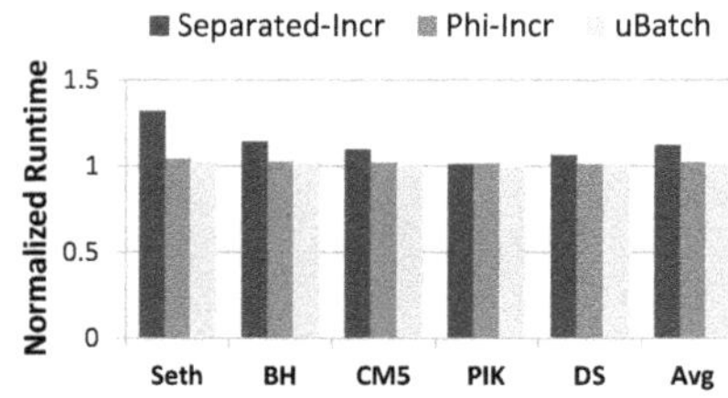

(a) Average performance

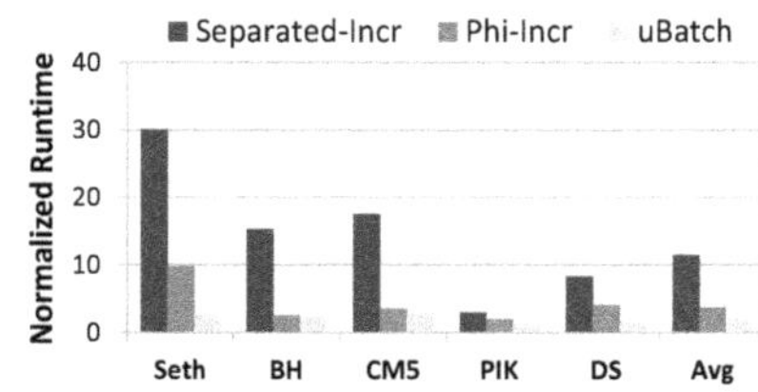

(b) Worst-case observed

Figure 9. Workload performance

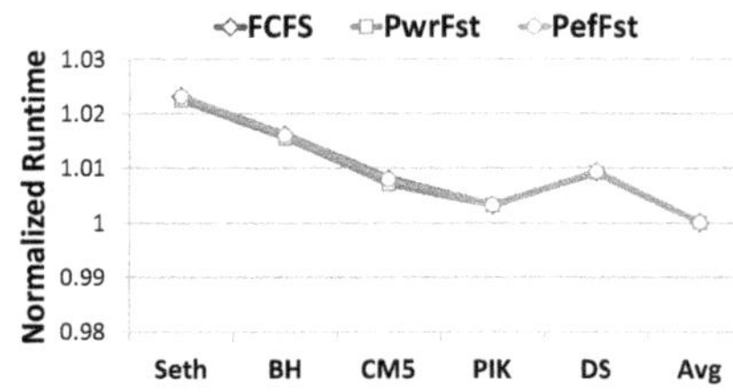

(a) Average performance

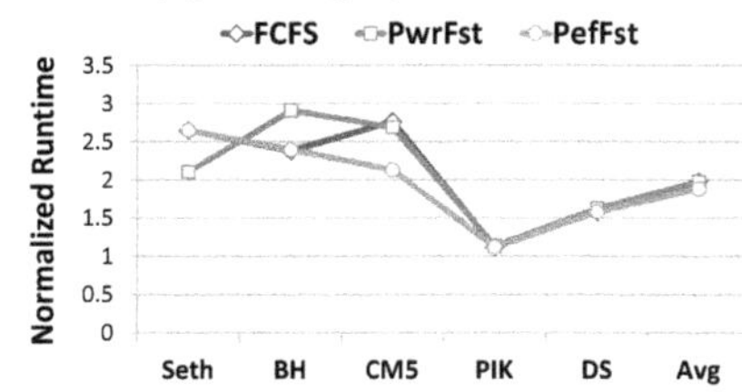

(b) Worst-case observed

Figure 10. Impact of scheduling policy

\$0.03/kWh [56], respectively). In Figure 7-(a), μBatch shows much lower cost compared to *HE+FC*, but in some cases it shows higher than a fuel-cell-only design. For CM5 and PIK in Figure 7-(a), the initial cost of μBatch is only 19% and 26% of *FC*, respectively. However, their TCO values under μBatch become larger than *FC* in the fourth year of deployment. Therefore, if the heat engine has high O&M cost (e.g., when using bio-diesel generators of low lifetime), the benefits of hybrid power system can be significantly compromised.

When factor in the low price of some heat engines, μBatch could significantly outperform other designs. In Figure 7-(b) we consider heat engines (e.g., gas turbines) that are more durable than conventional combustion engines and not sensitive to fuel quality like fuel cells [11]. If data centers can use methane biogas from a landfill or waste treatment plant (like Microsoft), the fuel cost can be even lower. In fact, even a small drop in energy cost can deliver substantial cost savings over time. On average, the TCO of the proposed fuel powered data center (i.e., Phi + μBatch) is only 7% of constructing a new utility-based data center. Its cost is only 30% of a fuel-cell-only data center (e.g., data centers running on the Bloom's Energy Server) and 19% of an non-optimized hybrid power provisioning approaches (i.e., *HE+FC*)

In Figure 7, the cost improvement of μBatch varies for different data center traces. For example, the normalize cost of *Seth* is only half of *CM5*. This is primarily becomes these data center traces have different power demand behaviors. Figures 8-(a) and 8-(b) show the power demand of the original data center traces and the actual power provisioning schemes under μBatch. It is clear that Seth has many significant, abrupt power demand changes, while CM5 has relatively smaller power variation range. As a result, the optimization effectiveness of μBatch on Seth is more noticeable.

7.2 Performance

The design of Phi and μBatch is not at the cost of workload performance. To demonstrate this, we further compare μBatch with two other important design alternatives: (1) *Separated-Incr* applies the proposed incremental load dispatching on a conventional separated power provisioning scheme similar to [34]. (2) *Phi-Incr* uses incremental load dispatching on the proposed Phi power provisioning architecture, but without the 3-step optimization of μBatch (i.e., job classification, first-round base-load scheduling, and the second-round bursty-load scheduling, detailed in Section 5.2).

Our results show that μBatch provides better performance guarantee. In Figure 9-(a) we show the average normalized job turnaround time (normalized to its original duration). On average, *Separated-Incr* yields a job turn-around time increase of 12%, while the number for *Phi-Incr* is just above 2%. In contrast, μBatch shows only 1% compared to the original job turn-around time. In fact, the most significant benefit of μBatch is to provide a better SLA even in the worst-case. The performance differences among the worst delayed job are much larger, as shown in Figure 9-(b). *Separated-Incr* could cause up to 30X increased duration on some short jobs that requires only tens of seconds to finish. In contrast, in the worst case μBatch maintains less than 10X job turn-around time increase, on average this number is less than 1X (98%).

To further under the benefits of μBatch and the impact of various job scheduling policy used in μBatch, we evaluate three variations of μBatch: *FCFS*, *PwrFst*, and *PefFst*. They affect the way we schedule jobs in the base-load scheduling and bursty-load scheduling steps (detailed in Section 5.2):

- ***FCFS**: jobs are always selected in a first-come-first-service way if multiple jobs can be scheduled based on the available power headroom*
- ***PwrFst**: jobs that have less power demand are given higher priority if multiple jobs can be scheduled based on the available power headroom*
- ***PefFst**: jobs that have the longest waiting time are selected first if multiple jobs can be scheduled based on the available power headroom. It is the default policy for μBatch*

In Figures 10-(a) and 10-(b), while the differences of the average job turn-around time are not noticeable, the differences in the worst case we observed can be large. *PefFst* always show better worst-case job turn-around time than *FCFS* (6% improvement on average). However, in some cases *PefFst* outperforms *PwrFst* while in other cases it does not (such as Seth). This is because *PefFst* may select a job that has very high power demand, and Seth happens to have many such short-and-large jobs, as indicated by Figure 8-(a). This could prevent other delayed jobs from being timely dispatched. Therefore, if users are sensitive about the worst-case performance, one might need to design a more complicated policy that considers both job power demand and waiting time. Otherwise, either *PwrFst* or *PefFst* can provide satisfactory performance guarantee (on the average job turn-around time)

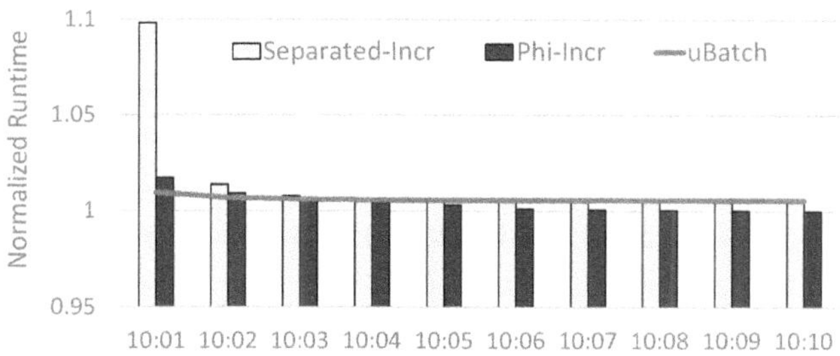

Figure 11. Average perfomance under different capacity ratio between *HE* and *FC* (the capacity of *HE* is fixed)

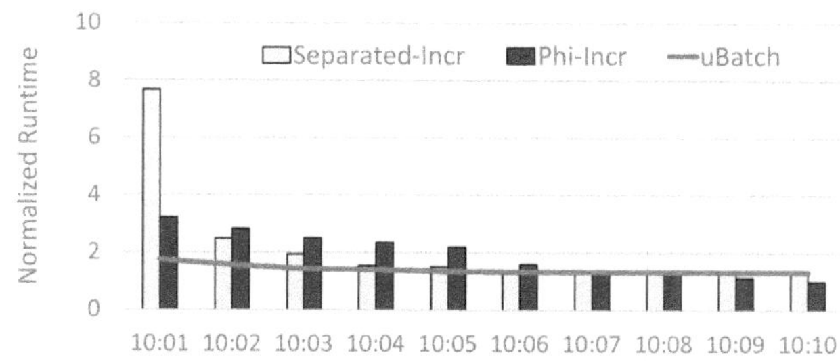

Figure 12. The worst-case perfomance under different capacity ratio between *HE* and *FC* (the capacity of *HE* is fixed)

7.3 Design Space Exploration

We further evaluate our design under different power provisioning capacities. We fix the capacity of heat engine and vary the ratio between heat engine and fuel cell (i.e., adjust the initial installed fuel cell capacity), as shown in Figures 11 and 12. The results shown are the mean value across all traces.

It's clear that over-provisioning improves workload performance. The job turn-around time gradually decreases for all three schemes as we increase the capacity of fuel cell (which increase the total cost of ownership). Due to the cost of additional fuel cell stacks, significant over-provisioning may not be economically attractive. This is especially true when the return-on-investment (ROI) of capacity expansion becomes much lower at high fuel cell capacities. In Figure 11, doubling the installed fuel cell capacity at a *HE/FC* ratio of 10:01 can reduce the job turn-around time by 8% for *Separated-Incr*, while doubling at a *HE/FC* ratio of 10:02 can only yield a further reduction of less than 1%.

Expanding onsite fuel cell generation often have greater influence on the worst-case job performance. For example, by doubling the fuel cell capacity at a *HE/FC* ratio of 10:01 (which increases the total onsite engine cost by 60%) can reduce job turn-around time by 68% for *Separated-Incr*. This number becomes much lower for *Phi-Incr* (12.5%) since *Phi-Incr* has better overall energy and power utilization even if the installed fuel cell capacity is low. The average job turn-around time increase is less than 1% for all the three evaluated designs and can actually be ignored.

Furthermore, by comparing the performance of different power provisioning schemes, we can conclude the following results. (1) μBatch could enable a fuel powered data center to perform better in an energy/power constrained environment. The job turn-around time of μBatch is normally better than both *Separated-Incr* and *Phi-Incr* when the installed fuel cell capacity is low (i.e., less than 30% of the heat engine capacity in Figures 11 and 12). This is because the less responsive power system installed onsite, the higher requirement on the system resiliency of the data center. (2) When the fuel cell is over-provisioned, the 3-step heuristic optimization of μBatch could be inefficient. In Figure 11, μBatch yields less than 1% performance difference compared to *Phi-Incr* at a HE/FC ratio of 10:10, whereas the difference can reach 33% in Figure 12. This is because our intuitive idea of μBatch design is to save the fuel cell capacity for handling power emergency, which cause less-effective utilization of fuel cell when it is over-provisioned. As new materials and power technology emerges, fuel cells could be more cost-competitive in the future. At that time, a straightforward incremental job dispatching scheme such as *Phi-Incr* may be sufficient and better. However, over-provisioning fuel cells is not likely today since they are still one of the most expensive generators.

8. CONCLUSIONS

We expect clean fuel powered data center to be a very promising design practice today and tomorrow, since the energy crisis and climate change have become a growing concern. However, several challenges need to be addressed to realize this vision. First, the cost of conventional power provisioning infrastructure is very high. Second, a coordination scheme between the computing system and smart energy system is lacking.

In this study we propose to use a hybrid and islanded power provisioning architecture, referred to as Phi, to fundamentally cut the cost of a fuel powered data center. We show that the key challenge to transition to such an unconventional design is a "power lagging" issue incurred in today's onsite generators. To solve this problem, we also propose a novel supply-/load -aware load dispatching schemes called μBatch. It allows data center to develop the resiliency to handle power lagging and greatly facilitate the deployment of fuel-based generation onsite. Using realistic data center workload traces, we show that our proposed scheme can reduce data center power provisioning cost (OpEx + CapEx) by over 90% compared to conventional utility power based design, and by over 80% compared to a non-optimized fuel-powered data center. The proposed design seeks a synergism of power generation scheduling and computing load dispatching, and therefore does not significantly affect workload performance. Our results show that the proposed design maintains a near-optimal (within 1%) performance in terms of average job turn-around time, and a significantly lowered worst-case design penalty compared to other design alternatives. The proposed design allows fuel powered data center to aggressively and efficiently utilize its onsite power system in a power/energy constrained environment.

ACKNOWLEDGEMENT

We thank the anonymous reviewers for their valuable comments. Chao Li is supported in part by Shanghai Jiao Tong University New Faculty Start-up Funding and SJTU-MSRA Faculty Award. This work is also partly supported by the National Natural Science Foundation of China (Grant No. 61202026 and No. 61332001) and Program of China National 1000 Young Talent Plan.

REFERENCES

1. The Smart Grid: An Introduction, *White Paper*, U.S. Department of Energy
2. S. Chowdhury, S.P. Chowdhury, and P. Crossley. Microgrids and Active Distribution Networks, *Institution of Engineering and Technology*, 2009
3. The Role of Distributed Generation and Combined Heat and Power (CHP) Systems in Data Centers. *Technical Report*, U.S. EPA. 2007
4. http://maps.nrel.gov/biomass

5. Biomass Holds the Promise of Clean Power and Fuel - If Handled Correctly. *White Paper*. 2012. http://www.ucsusa.org/
6. J. Koomey. Growth in Data Center Electricity Use 2005 to 2010. Analytics Press, 2009.
7. Wyoming Waste Powers Microsoft Datacenter, 2014 http://www.enterprisetech.com/2014/11/06/wyoming-waste-powers-microsoft-datacenter/
8. Energy Server Architecture. Bloom Energy Corporate http://www.bloomenergy.com/fuel-cell/energy-server-architecture/
9. Apple Data Center Does Fuel Cell Industry a Huge Favor, 2012 http://www.technologyreview.com/view/508421/apple-data-center-does-fuel-cell-industry-a-huge-favor/
10. EBAY Hosts Unveiling of Groundbreaking New "Bloom Box" Fuel Cell, 2010 http://blog.ebay.com/ebay-hosts-unveiling-of-groundbreaking-new-bloom-box-fuel-cell/
11. R. Sharma, T. Christian, M. Arlitt, C. Bash, and C. Patel. Design of Farm Waste-Driven Supply Side Infrastructure for Data Centers, *ASME 2010 the 4th Int. Conf. on Energy Sustainability*, 2010
12. P. Banerjee, C. Patel, C. Bash, A. Shah, and M. Arlitt. Towards a Net-Zero Data Center. *Journal on Emerging Technologies in Computing Systems*, 2012
13. An introduction to spark spread, U.S. Energy Information Administration, 2013, http://www.eia.gov/todayinenergy/detail.cfm?id=9911
14. Natural Gas Pipeline System: Reliability and Resiliency. *White Paper*. Bloom Energy Corporate, 2013
15. D. Chiesa and S. Zirkelbach. Microgrids Help More than They Hurt. *IEEE Electrification Magazine*, 2014
16. Schenider Electric Expands in Secured Power. *White Paper*, Schneider Electric, 2003
17. A. Riekstin, S. James, A. Kansal, J. Liu, E. Peterson. No More Electrical Infrastructure: Towards Fuel Cell Powered Data Centers. *Workshop on Power-Aware Computing (HotPower)*, 2013
18. C. Vyas and B. Gohn. Smart Grid Consumer Survey, Pike Research, 2012
19. G. Saur, J. Kurtz, C. Ainscough, and M. Peters. Stationary Fuel Cell Evaluation. Technical Report, *National Renewable Energy Lab*. 2014
20. Cost-Effectiveness of Distributed Generation Technologies. *White Paper*, *CPUC Self-Generation Incentive Program*. 2011
21. Onsite Distributed Generation Systems for Laboratories. *White Paper*, U.S. Environmental Protection Agency and U.S. Department of Energy. 2011.
22. Gas Turbine Prices per KW. http://www.gas-turbines.com/trader/kwprice.htm
23. Improving the Operating Efficiency of Microturbine-Based Distributed Generation at an Affordable Price. *White Paper*, U.S. Department of Energy. 2014 http://www.energy.gov/sites/prod/files/2014/09/f18/capstone.pdf
24. Doing the Match on Bloom Energy http://www.forbes.com/2010/02/25/fuel-cell-costs-technology-ecotech-bloom-energy.html
25. W. Turner and K. Brill, Cost Model: Dollars per kW plus Dollars per Square Foot of Computer Floor. *White Paper*. Uptime Institute, 2008
26. Understanding Electric Demand. *White Paper*, National Grid, 2012 https://www.nationalgridus.com/niagaramohawk/non_html/eff_elec-demand.pdf
27. Residential Demand Rate, http://www.georgiapower.com/pricing/residential/residential-demand.cshtml
28. Electricity Energy Storage Technology Options. *White Paper*, Electric Power Research Institute, 2010
29. L. Zhao, J. Brouwer, S. James, J. Siegler, E. Peterson, A. Kansal, and J. Liu, Servers Powered by a 10KW In-Rack Proton Exchange Membrane Fuel Cell System, *ASME 2014 the 8th Int. Conf. on Energy Sustainability*, 2014
30. Z., Zhi, F. Liu, B. Li, B. Li, H. Jin, R. Zou, and Z. Liu. Fuel Cell Generation in Geo-Distributed Cloud Services: A Quantitative Study. *Int. Conf. on Distributed Computing Systems (ICDCS)*, 2014
31. C. Li, R. Zhou, and T. Li. Enabling Distributed Generation Powered Sustainable High-Performance Data Center. *Int. Symp. on High-Performance Computer Architecture (HPCA)*, 2013
32. N. Sharma, S. Barker, D. Irwin, and P. Shenoy. Blink: Managing Server Clusters on Intermittent Power. *Int. Conf. on Architectural Support for Programming Languages and Operating Systems (ASPLOS)*, 2011
33. I. Goiri, R. Beauchea, K. Le, T.D. Nguyen, M. Haque, J. Guitart, J.Torres, and R. Bianchini. GreenSlot: Scheduling Energy Consumption in Green Datacenters. *Int. Conf. for High Performance Computing, Networking, Storage and Analysis (SC)*, 2011
34. C. Li, A. Qouneh, and T. Li. iSwitch: Coordinating and Optimizing Renewable Energy Powered Server Clusters. *Int. Symp. on Computer Architecture (ISCA)*, 2012
35. N. Deng, C. Stewart, D. Gmach, M. Arlitt, and J. Kelley. Adaptive Green Hosting. *Int. Conf. on Autonomic Computing (ICAC)*, 2012
36. P. Gao, A. Curtis, B. Wong, and S. Keshav. It's Not Easy Being Green. *ACM SIGCOMM*, 2012
37. C. Li, Y. Hu, R. Zhou, M. Liu, L. Liu, J. Yuan, T. Li. Oasis: Enabling Datacenter to Scale Out Economically and Sustainably. *Int. Symp. on Microarchitecture (MICRO)*, 2013
38. I. Goiri, W. Katsak, K. Le, T. Nguyen, and R. Bianchini. Parasol and GreenSwitch: Managing Datacenters Powered by Renewable Energy. *Int. Conf. on Architectural Support for Programming Languages and Operating Systems (ASPLOS)*, 2013
39. C. Li, R. Wang, T. Li, D. Qian, and J. Yuan. Managing Green Datacenters Powered by Hybrid Renewable Energy Systems. *Int. Conf. on Autonomic Computing (ICAC)*, 2014
40. L. Liu, C. Li, H. Sun, Y. Hu, J. Xin, N. Zheng, and T. Li. Leveraging Heterogeneous Power for Improving Datacenter Efficiency and Resiliency. *IEEE Computer Architecture Letters*, 2014
41. K. Rajashekara. Hybrid Fuel-Cell Strategies for Clean Power Generation, *IEEE Trans. on Industry Applications*, Vol. 41, Issue 3, 2005
42. A. Choudhury, H. Chandra, and A. Arora. Application of Solid Oxide Fuel Cell Technology for Power Generation—A Review. *Renewable and Sustainable Energy Reviews*, Volume 20, 2014
43. S. Govindan, D. Wang, A. Sivasubramaniam, and B. Urgaonkar. Leveraging Stored Energy for Handling Power Emergencies in Aggressively Provisioned Datacenters. *Int. Conf.on Architectural Support for Programming Languages and Operating Systems (ASPLOS)*, 2012
44. S. Govindan, A. Sivasubramaniam and B. Urgaonkar. Benefits and Limitations of Tapping into Stored Energy for Datacenters, *Int. Symp. on Computer Architecture (ISCA)*, 2011
45. V. Kontorinis, L. Zhang, B. Aksanli, J. Sampson, H. Homayoun, E. Pettis, T. Rosing and D. Tullsen, Managing Distributed UPS Energy for Effective Power Capping in Data Centers, *International Symposium on Computer Architecture* (ISCA), 2012
46. Power Generation Technologies. *Chapter 6 of the EPA Combined Heat and Power Partnership*, U.S. Environmental Protection Agency, 2007 http://www.epa.gov/chp/documents/biomass_chp_catalog_part6.pdf
47. http://www.wartsila.com/en/power-plants/learning-center/overview
48. Economics of Fuel Cell Solutions for Backup Power. *White Paper*, Ballard Power Systems Inc., 2012
49. A. Halsey III. Aging Power Grid on Overload as U.S. Demands More Electricity. *The Washington Post*, August 1, 2012.
50. L. Rhodes, US Power Grid Has Issues with Reliability. 2013 http://www.datacenterknowledge.com/archives/2013/01/16/us-power-grid-has-issues-with-reliability/
51. Yank R. Singh, D. Irwin, P. Shenoy, K. Ramakrishnan. Yank: Ena-bling Green Data Centers to Pull the Plug. *USENIX Symp. on Networked System Design and Implementation (NSDI)*, 2013
52. T. Lipman. Overview of Stationary Fuel Cell Systems. *Report*, US Department of Energy Clean Energy Application Center, 2010 http://www.ncsl.org/documents/energy/TLipman0910.pdf
53. Data Collection of Diesel Generators in South Australia. *White Paper*, IT Power (Australia) Pty Limited. 2013
54. Logs of Real Parallel Workloads from Production Systems http://www.cs.huji.ac.il/labs/parallel/workload/logs.html
55. B. Lawson, E. Smirni, and D. Puiu. Self-adapting Backfilling Scheduling for Parallel Systems. *International Conf. on Parallel Processing (ICPP)*, 2002.
56. Cost and Performance Data for Power Generation Technologies. *Technical Report*, Black & Veatch Holding Company, 2011

History-Assisted Adaptive-Granularity Caches (HAAG$) for High Performance 3D DRAM Architectures

Ke Chen† Sheng Li‡ Jung Ho Ahn§ Naveen Muralimanohar¶ Jishen Zhao# Cong Xu♭
Seongil O§ Yuan Xie♮ Jay B. Brockman⊤ Norman P. Jouppi⊥

†Oracle Corporation* ‡Intel Labs* §Seoul National University
#University of California at Santa Cruz* ¶Hewlett-Packard Labs ♭Pennsylvania State University
♮University of California at Santa Barbara ⊤University of Notre Dame ⊥Google*

†ke.c.chen@oracle.com ‡sheng.r.li@intel.com §{gajh, swdfish}@snu.ac.kr
¶naveen.muralimanohar@hp.com #jishen.zhao@ucsc.edu ♭czx102@psu.edu
♮yuanxie@ece.ucsb.edu ⊤jbb@nd.edu ⊥jouppi@acm.org

ABSTRACT

3D-stacked DRAM has the potential to provide high performance and large capacity memory for future high performance computing systems and datacenters, and the integration of a dedicated logic die opens up opportunities for architectural enhancements such as DRAM row-buffer caches. However, high performance and cost-effective row-buffer cache designs remain challenging for 3D memory systems. In this paper, we propose History-Assisted Adaptive-Granularity Cache (HAAG$) that employs an adaptive caching scheme to support full associativity at various granularities, and an intelligent history-assisted predictor to support a large number of banks in 3D memory systems. By increasing the row-buffer cache hit rate and avoiding unnecessary data caching, HAAG$ significantly reduces memory access latency and dynamic power. Our design works particularly well for manycore CPUs running (irregular) memory intensive applications where memory locality is hard to exploit. Evaluation results show that with memory-intensive CPU workloads, HAAG$ can outperform the state-of-the-art row buffer cache by 33.5%.

Categories and Subject Descriptors

B.3.1 [**Memory Structures**]: Semiconductor Memories

General Terms

Design; Performance; Experimentation

Keywords

3D DRAM; HAAG$; row buffer cache; adaptive granularity

* This work was done while Ke Chen was at the University of Notre Dame, and while Norman P. Jouppi, Sheng Li, and Jishen Zhao were with Hewlett-Packard Labs.

ICS'15, June 8–11, 2015, Newport Beach, CA, USA.

ACM 978-1-4503-3559-1/15/06 ...$15.00.
DOI: http://dx.doi.org/10.1145/2751205.2751227 .

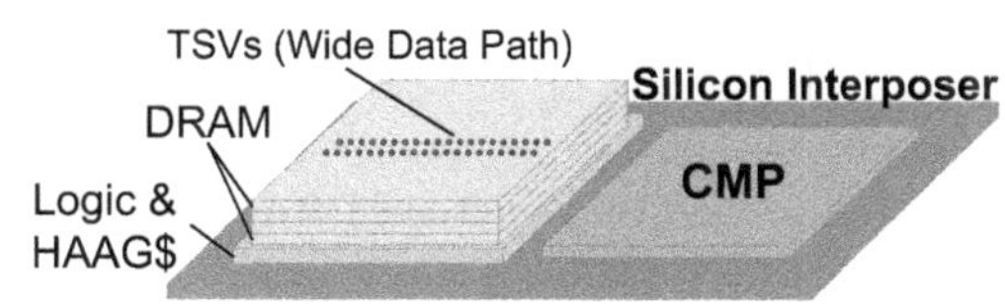

Figure 1: The target system design for integrating the HAAG$: a hybrid 3D DRAM stack and a chip multiprocessor are co-located on a silicon interposer.

1. INTRODUCTION

Future high performance computing demands high performance and large capacity memory subsystems with low cost. Existing mainstream DDR3/4 DRAM systems, however, are neither efficient nor capable of meeting these demands because of limited pin count per socket [31] and fan-out restrictions in high-speed signaling [30, 33]. Emerging 3D stacked memory [14, 17] is a promising solution to provide high bandwidth (with high bank concurrency), large memory capacity (with multiple stacked DRAM die in a package), and cost efficiency (by sharing common peripheral circuitry over the stack). Moreover, the hybrid integration of logic die into DRAM stack [29] (as shown in Figure 1) also opens up opportunities for architecture enhancements in memory.

In conventional DRAM, row buffers are employed to keep a data row open (active) so as to avoid long latency when accessing the large DRAM cell array repetitively for contiguous memory references (i.e., with adjacent addresses). With a desire to maintain multiple rows open even when there are row-buffer conflicts, a row-buffer cache (i.e., cache of row buffers) [9, 15, 19, 37] has been proposed to further improve performance. By caching memory data with high access locality on the memory side, a DRAM row-buffer cache can help lower the average memory reference latency, and reduce the number of power-hungry row-buffer activations and precharges in DRAM. Despite these potential benefits, previous row-buffer cache designs suffer from implementation challenges when being fabricated on the same DRAM die, especially due to the cost constraints such as limited metal layers, slow DRAM process, and tight area budget.

Emerging hybrid memory stacks with both memory layers and a logic layer (Figure 1) are ideally suited for DRAM row-buffer caches. First, a row-buffer cache can now be fabricated on the separate logic layer with a logic process that can be optimized for high performance and power efficiency. Second, a vertical dimensional interconnect – through silicon vias (TSVs) – is introduced to shorten the data transfer latency between the row buffers in stacked DRAM and the row-buffer cache on the logic die.

However, designing efficient row-buffer caches for 3D memory systems remains challenging, with one reason being the trade-off between cost and efficiency (performance and energy). In particular, although ideally TSVs can have a high density and bandwidth with their small size, the data bus width between the stacked die is still constrained. This is because increasing the data bus width incurs large routing logic area overhead and therefore increases the cost significantly. Figure 2 illustrates the cost increase versus data bus width (see Section 4 for our detailed methodology). As seen in the figure, the area overhead can be more than 20% higher for memory data buses that are 512b/bank or wider, which is prohibitively high for extremely cost-sensitive memory products.

As a result, existing 3D DRAM products such as Micron's Hybrid Memory Cubes (HMC) [29] (highlighted in Figure 2) and Samsung's 3D DRAM memory [14] have adopted a conservative internal data bus width, which is far smaller than the size of an entire DRAM row. The resulting limited internal memory data paths inside the 3D memory stack have made it impractical to transfer the entire DRAM row every time (e.g., 256 cycles with a 64-bit data bus for 2KB DRAM row). As also pointed out in [23], this mismatch between internal data bus width and DRAM row size leads to a limited performance benefit for a conventional row-buffer cache because of contention on the internal narrow data bus and timing constraints imposed by modern DRAM technologies, even for 3D memory systems.

The recent "register-file approach" row-buffer cache (FM-RB$) proposed by Loh [23] tries to address this challenge and achieves better performance on 3D memory systems with constrained internal/TSV channel width by selectively caching DRAM rows. However, it still caches the entire row every time regardless of the program locality and the limited TSV channel width, resulting in unnecessary performance and energy losses. Also, the FM-RB$ design uses a pending memory request queue in the memory controller as decisive information for caching. Given the large number of banks (e.g., 128 [29]) in modern high-performance 3D DRAMs, the narrow window of a per-bank memory controller request queue can suffer from limited visibility to memory access locality and leads to sub-optimal caching decisions. Because of these limitations, the demonstrated gain in performance and energy-efficiency of FM-RB$ design was mainly from GPU workloads with very regular memory access patterns and high locality, whereas supporting a wider range of applications remains an opportunity for new innovations.

In order to tackle these challenges and to fully unleash the performance and energy efficiency potential of 3D DRAM systems, especially in manycore CPU systems running memory intensive applications where memory-side access locality is hard to exploit [2], we propose a History-Assisted Adaptive-Granularity Cache (HAAG$). HAAG$ is the first attempt to design a DRAM row-buffer cache with adaptive cache line granularity and an intelligent data mapping scheme. The goal is to efficiently utilize the narrow TSV channel of a 3D DRAM memory system, and maximize performance and energy efficiency for data-intensive applications even with irregular memory access patterns (as usually found in multithreaded applications). The innovative features of our HAAG$ include:

- An intelligent predictor that decides: 1) whether to cache the corresponding DRAM row for an outstanding request, and 2) if so, how much of the DRAM row should be cached. The predictor not only increases the row-buffer hit rate with more accurate prediction, but its queue size is also scalable to keep up with the increasing number of banks in 3D stacked memory;

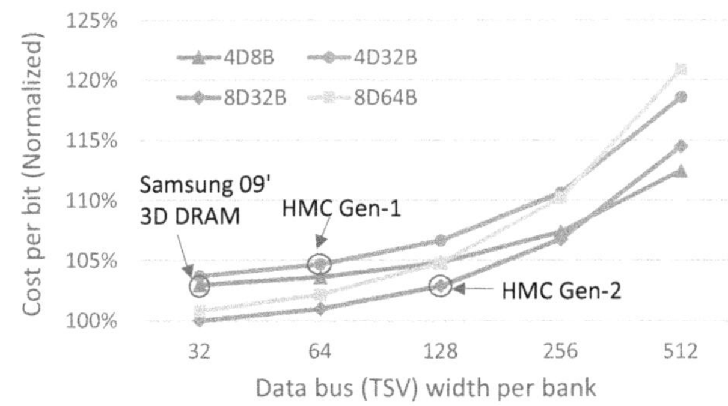

Figure 2: Cost for 3D DRAM stack configurations with different die counts in a stack ('D') , bank counts in a die ('B'), and memory bus width (or equally the TSV channel width). Several typical 3D DRAM configurations such as Samsung's 3D DRAM memory [14] and Micron's HMCs (both Gen1 and Gen2) [29] are highlighted.

- An adaptive-granularity cache that dynamically adjusts the amount of data to cache for different DRAM accesses. One novelty is a power efficient content addressable memory (CAM) design with an improved tag array that enables mapping to cache lines with variable granularities. It improves performance and power by avoiding transferring unnecessary data while increasing the data storage efficiency.

Figure 1 also shows the target system design for a 3D DRAM stack equipped with a HAAG$ which serves a manycore processor. It co-locates the stack on the same silicon interposer as the chip multiprocessor (CMP), similar to either the near-memory HMC design [29] or the JEDEC High Bandwidth Memory (HBM) standard [12][1] (with a logic layer below the HBM stack). In other words, a HAAG$ design can be flexibly incorporated into DRAM stack architecture and is compatible with multiple interfaces. Our system-level evaluation results show that our HAAG$ design outperforms the state-of-the-art by 33.5% for memory-intensive CPU applications.

2. MOTIVATION AND RELATED WORK

This section first reviews the related work on 3D memory architecture and motivates designing sophisticated DRAM row-buffer caches. Then we present 3D-stacked DRAM structures where the design and optimization of a DRAM row-buffer cache is tightly coupled with the design of the 3D DRAM.

2.1 Row-Buffer Cache in 3D Memory

While there have been recent studies on 3D memory that focus on stacking memory die directly on a processor die to enable fast access to DRAM [6,13,16,22,24,34], there is a relative absence of research on more conventional 3D memory systems. The first commercial products are 3D stacked DRAM [14,17] (from Samsung) and hybrid memory cubes [1,29] (from Micron). Although these products have shown superior performance and power efficiency compared to conventional DRAMs, further gains are possible only by fully exploring 3D memory's potential advantages at the architecture level.

The row-buffer cache is a promising architectural enhancement to leverage the integrated logic die of hybrid memory stacks. Although row-buffer caches and cached DRAM [9,15,37] have been

[1] HBM is an emerging DRAM interface standard for 3D-stacked DRAM defined by the JEDEC organization, which uses a wide-interface architecture to achieve high-speed, low-power operation.

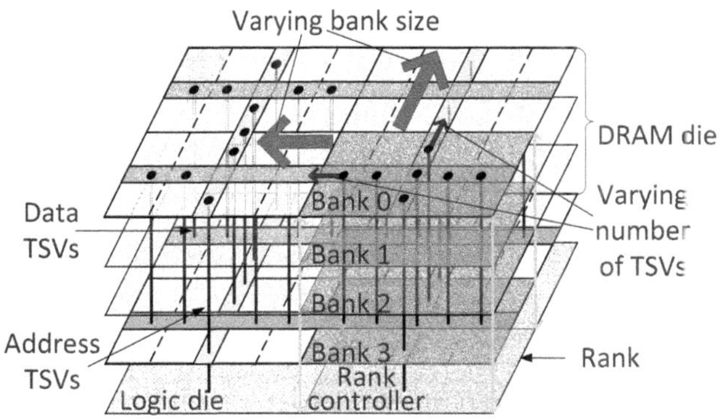

Figure 3: Illustration of hybrid DRAM stack internal structure, including rank, bank, and layout of peripheral circuitry and TSVs.

proposed to overcome the problem of row-buffer conflicts in memory, the cost of modifying the existing bank structure to support additional buffers has kept memory manufacturers from embracing this technique. With the added logic die of a hybrid memory stack and the silicon area it provides, it is now feasible to support such extensions without significantly increasing the overall memory cost.

However, a basic row-buffer cache that caches DRAM data on every memory access only results in marginal performance gain [23] because the row-buffer cache is a limited resource with high competition. In addition, the problem with deploying row-buffer caches in stacked memory is that data from DRAM cells has to be sent through cost-constrained and thus relatively narrow TSV channels (e.g., 64-bit wide [29]), which is detrimental to performance and power as every activation now requires multiple cycles to send the entire page to the row-buffer cache (e.g., 256 cycles for 2KB DRAM row).

FM-RB$ proposed by Loh [23] attempts to address the high overhead in a basic row-buffer cache design from caching every activated page. It looks ahead into the pending memory request queue in a memory controller to decide whether to allocate an entry in the row-buffer cache or to access the data directly from a bank's row buffer. However, it still caches the entire DRAM row despite the narrow TSV data bus available and the limited memory access locality over an entire DRAM page. This wastes time, power, and storage by loading and evicting unused data on the data bus, meanwhile limiting the performance and energy benefits for applications with different memory access granularity requirements. As a result, although FM-RB$ demonstrated significant performance gain on GPU workloads (with very high locality), it showed limited performance gain for CPU applications because they have low locality which requires extra efforts to leverage. Our HAAG$ is designed to solve this challenge for CPU workloads.

Our proposed HAAG$ for 3D DRAM is better in several ways than the state-of-the-art FM-RB$ design. First, the cache line granularity can vary dynamically to adapt to applications' requirements at runtime, which is especially beneficial for irregular access patterns. Second, while FM-RB$ only considers the pending memory requests to identify targets for row-buffer caches, the proposed HAAG$ deploys a decoupled predictor queue that also holds the addresses of previously served memory requests. This decoupled predictor queue not only increases the prediction accuracy with extended information of the historical memory access pattern, but is also scalable to meet prediction window size requirements at low hardware cost for 3D memory with a large number of banks.

2.2 Hybrid Memory Stack Structure

Stacking a base logic die under 3D DRAM opens up the opportunity to make the DRAM row-buffer cache achieve high performance and cost efficiency, and tightly couples the configuration of the DRAM cache design with the 3D DRAM architecture. Thus it is important to understand the 3D DRAM structure and its implications on row-buffer cache designs.

Figure 3 shows the internal structure of a typical hybrid DRAM stack that will be used in the study of HAAG$. DRAM die are stacked on top of each other, while a set of vertically overlapped banks in the stack can be grouped together and function as a rank. In a typical memory setup, a rank consists of a set of DRAM banks that share the same memory bus (in this case TSVs) to the memory controller. While each bank within a rank can operate concurrently, at any given time only one bank can communicate to the memory controller through the shared bus.

For stacked DRAM, the bank internal organization is similar to that of single-layer DRAM because of the TSV pitch mismatch with on-chip wires and a desire to avoid modifications to the basic building blocks. A bank can consist of one or multiple DRAM cell arrays. As sharing reduces the footprint of peripheral circuits of 3D DRAM, a larger number of smaller banks can be employed than conventional planar DRAM, resulting in better concurrency, reduced bank access latency, and more effective use of TSVs as internal buses. A similar design can be found in the Micron HMC [29] and Microbank [33].

TSVs are laid out on the edge of DRAM arrays of a bank, and used as the inter-die data/address/command bus to connect the circuit blocks on the base logic die to the DRAM banks above. As mentioned in Section 1, the TSV data bus width is constrained by the bank internal datapath, and further limits the internal data transfer bandwidth. This raises the question of how to best leverage the internal data bandwidth in a DRAM stack, and is a key aspect of HAAG$.

The dedicated logic die holds common peripheral circuit blocks that can be shared among DRAM die to reduce cost and energy. This includes rank control logic, input buffers, delay-locked loop (DLL), and clock circuitry. The existence of various circuit blocks limits the remaining real estate on the logic die, which should be carefully exploited for the integration of HAAG$.

3. HISTORY-ASSISTED ADAPTIVE-GRANULARITY CACHE (HAAG$)

Figure 4a shows an overview of the proposed HAAG$ architecture, where the key components are a scalable predictor with historical memory address information to assist making caching decisions and an adaptive-granularity row-buffer cache with elastic mapping. The predictor is used to decide whether to and how much to cache the corresponding DRAM row for an outstanding memory request. It is placed on the processor side to make fast cache/not-cache decisions by directly accessing existing entries in pending memory request queue and hit/miss information of an allocation table (detailed below) inside the memory controller. The predictor also has access to historical memory request addresses stored in predictor queue (detailed below) to obtain more comprehensive information on memory access locality to make more accurate caching decisions for each DRAM bank.

Meanwhile, the adaptive-granularity row-buffer cache consists of a data store and an allocation table that keeps the meta information (e.g., granularity and head address) of the rows in the data store. While both the allocation table and data store logically belong to the same row-buffer cache, they are physically separated

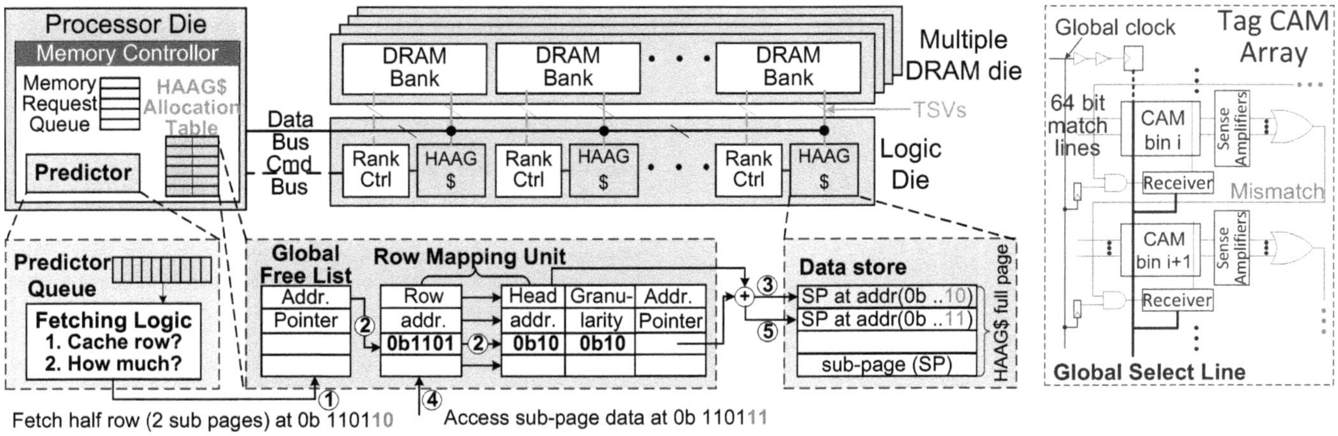

(a) Overview of the History-Assisted Adaptive-Granularity Cache (HAAG$) architecture and operation flow. (b) CAM in row mapping unit.

Figure 4: Illustration of (a) the History-Assisted Adaptive-Granularity Cache (HAAG$) architecture and an example flow of partial row caching and a subsequent hit, and (b) a specially designed CAM design for the tag portion in the row mapping unit. The HAAG$ is composed of a predictor and an allocation table in the memory controller as well as a data store on the logic die.

to maximize performance benefits and achieve easy implementation with existing memory interfaces and protocols. The allocation table (i.e., tag array) of the HAAG$ is placed close to the processor-side memory controller to avoid long round-trip latency for probing the cache status if it were implemented on the memory-side logic die. The data store of a HAAG$ is located on the logic die below the DRAM stack to directly receive/send data from/to the DRAM row buffers through TSVs, and the allocation table is placed in the processor side as part of the memory controller to help make fast caching decisions and detecting hits and misses.

The memory controller consults the allocation table and the predictor before scheduling a memory request, and then issues appropriate command sequences based on the results of hit or miss on the HAAG$, and the HAAG$ caching or not caching decision for the pending memory request. This design is easy to implement as it is compatible with the design methodology of current memory interfaces (e.g., DDR3/4) where the memory controller is the master device and maintains deterministic timing of memory commands and data replies.[2] Accordingly, the DRAM and the HAAG$ share common command/address/data buses. Note that HAAG$ is a lower level memory hierarchy than the memory controller. Thus it is a serialization point and does not need to maintain coherency. We will describe the implementation details of these hardware components, and demonstrate their function and usage through an example operation flow in the following sub-sections.

3.1 History-Assisted Scalable Predictor

The dedicated predictor shown in Figure 4a consists of two parts: a **Decoupled Predictor Queue** and **Fetching Logic**.

The Decoupled Predictor Queue: The prediction of whether to cache data to the row-buffer cache as well as what part of the row to cache is based on the memory locality. The pending memory request queue inside a memory controller could be used for prediction, and for making decisions to allocate an entry into the row-buffer cache when there are future references for that particular row. However, the memory request queue in the memory controller is a very narrow window (e.g., 32 entries), and provides very limited visibility to memory locality. While this approach works well for memories with a limited number of banks per channel (16 as assumed in previous work [23]), it is not scalable to satisfy the demands of up to hundreds of banks per channel in near-future 3D DRAM designs [29], which are employed to mitigate the notorious row-buffer conflict problems [2] and to increase parallelism. First, a large bank count leads to high bank-level parallelism, and therefore reduces the number of queued-up pending memory requests (i.e., prediction window size) per bank. As a result, there is insufficient access pattern information in the pending memory request queue, significantly lowering the prediction accuracy of the row-buffer cache data caching. Second, increasing the size of the pending memory request queue is very costly [4], because it holds all memory access information including addresses, data, and control in a complex and power-hungry content addressable memory (CAM) structure.

The Decoupled Predictor Queue is proposed to meet scalability demands, and to solve the problems of limited memory access pattern availability and large overhead of a long pending memory request queue. The Decoupled Predictor is a separate hardware queue in the memory controller that stores the addresses of both the pending memory requests *and* previously served requests. The queue size is more scalable than in previous approaches because there can be as many served memory request entries in the queue as the system demands. Further, the access pattern information is more comprehensive, not only because of a larger queue size, but also because of a combination of *future* and *historical* memory accesses in the predictor queue. Finally, the hardware overhead is much less than the pending memory request queue with the same number of entries in that it only needs to store addresses in the queue. In summary, the Decoupled Predictor Queue is much more capable to meet the demands on increasing predictor queue size for a large number of banks in 3D memory. The flexible addition of historical memory requests provides a much wider information window and thus more visibility into memory access locality than only the MC pending request queue with limited entries, and there-

[2] For systems with decoupled/disintegrated memory controllers [8] where the processor-side memory controller only packetizes memory requests and off-loads the protocol implementation (e.g., DDRx, LPDDRx) to memory-side co-controllers, both the allocation table and data store of the HAAG$ can be located at the memory side co-controller.

fore significantly increases the caching prediction accuracy as we will show in Section 5.

The Fetching Logic is implemented to make selective caching decisions with adaptive granularities based on the information stored in the predictor queue. Specifically, the fetching logic makes two decisions for each outstanding memory request based on the predictor queue: 1) whether to cache data from the same row as the outstanding request, and 2) if so, how much data on adjacent addresses needs to be cached.

The first decision, *whether* to cache a DRAM row to the HAAG$ on the logic die is made by techniques similar to [23] "Load with Modification"[3], "Few Uses"[4], and "Bank-aware Deallocation"[5]. If the fetching logic decides to fetch a DRAM row and cache it in the HAAG$, then in addition it makes a second decision as *how much* data (or what fraction) of the DRAM row should be cached. This step is unique to HAAG$ and essential for improving performance and energy efficiency in the context of limited TSV bus width in practical 3D architectures. This second decision is made by comparing all the memory requests in the predictor queue with the target row address of the outstanding request. Assuming that the size of a CPU last-level cache line is 64 bytes, the fraction of the DRAM row (i.e., how many 64 byte data blocks) to be fetched and cached is determined by the longest distance between requested cache lines (including both pending and past requests) in the same row.

Since 64-byte lines are cached in the processor LLC anyway and 128-byte data can also be cached in the processor by next line prefetching, caching data blocks smaller than 256 bytes in the HAAG$ can hardly provide a significant performance gain. Thus, the predictor chooses to cache data with adaptive granularity from a *sub-page* of size 256B to a *full page* with the size of an entire DRAM row, in increments of a sub-page. We use a simple pop count circuit to tally the number of row address matches among the requests in the predictor queue and pending request queue, and all the sub-pages with the same row address as the outstanding memory request will be cached. Here the final decision made by the fetching logic is sent via the command bus to the rank controllers in the 3D DRAM stack as shown in Figure 4a. Since the internal CPU clock is faster than an external memory transaction, this approach can be easily implemented with minimal overhead. For example, if a DRAM row has 16 CPU LLC lines and is partitioned into four sub-pages (each has four CPU cache lines), and the 1st, 4th, and 9th CPU cache line in the row are predicted as "useful", then the corresponding 1st, 2nd, and 3rd sub-pages will be fetched.

3.2 Adaptive-Granularity Row Buffer Cache

Since multithreaded and multiprogramming applications running on multi/many-core systems do not demonstrate distinct memory access granularity preferences [21, 36], a fixed row-buffer cache line size can only improve performance on a few applications while degrading performance for others. Since different cache line sizes benefit different benchmarks, only a row buffer cache with adaptive granularity can improve performance for all applications. Prior work [11] also sought to dynamically optimize cache line sizes by exploiting the memory reference locality; but the target was on-chip caches with embedded DRAM, and the scheme for determining variable sizes of cache lines is different.

Being a small and scarce resource while supporting different access granularities from a sub-page to a full page, HAAG$ gives rise to three special design requirements. First, adjacent sub-pages of a DRAM row need to be placed adjacently in the HAAG$ to enable burst block transfers between the HAAG$ and the memory stack. Otherwise, evicting a full page or several sub-pages from the HAAG$ will result in multiple row-buffer activations and precharges that are slow and power-hungry. Second, partial rows need to be placed as close as possible in the HAAG$ to eliminate fragmentation. Finally, the HAAG$ should ideally be fully associative to avoid expensive conflicts that involve lengthy and power-hungry DRAM row activations/precharges. It is challenging to design such a fully-associative adaptive granularity cache at low cost.

Our HAAG$ design is able to meet these requirements and support full associativity at various granularities at a low cost with low fragmentation. Taking a 128KB-sized HAAG$ as an example, its associativity is 512 with access granularity of a 256B sub-page, and 64 with a 2KB full page. Figure 4a illustrates the adaptive-granularity fully associative HAAG$ architecture, which consists of two main parts: the *HAAG$ allocation table* and the *data store*. To reduce the hardware cost from supporting the highest adaptive associativity, we design a special content addressable memory (CAM) as shown in Figure 4b (detailed later in this section).

HAAG$ Allocation Table is essentially a specially designed tag array of a common cache, where the HAAG$ allocation table and data store are physically separated and located on the processor-side memory controller and the memory stack respectively. On one side, the HAAG$ allocation table is implemented in the processor-side memory controller to better track which (partial) rows are currently stored in the HAAG$, and therefore accelerate HAAG$ hit and miss detection. Also, the allocation table helps the memory controller with command scheduling. On the other side, the data store of HAAG$ is placed on the logic layer and close to the 3D-stacked DRAM to directly use TSV buses for transferring data between stacked DRAM and logic die. This split cache design is reasonable particularly because DRAM accesses are less latency sensitive than the small caches on processor chips, and the miss rates are typically higher.

The HAAG$ allocation table is the heart of the adaptive-granularity fully associative cache. There are two major components in the HAAG$ allocation table: a *global free list* and a *row mapping unit*:

- *The global free list* holds occupancy information for the cache lines in the data store, and is responsible for mapping rows in the row mapping unit during cache line install or replacement.
- *The row mapping unit* is a self-contained fully associative cache. The tag portion is implemented in a specially designed CAM, and stores the row addresses of memory blocks for lookup. The data portion holds the cache line information including *head address*, *granularity*, and *address pointers* to index the data store, in addition to common cache information such as dirty bit and valid bit (not shown in the figure).

Data Store. The HAAG$ data store is distributed rather than centralized on the logic die to avoid conflicts between DRAM ranks, and to avoid the energy overhead for transferring data over the long inter-rank data lines. As shown in Figure 4a, each memory rank owns a separate data store that is shared by the stacked DRAM banks within the rank. Multiple adjacent sub-pages can be bundled to form a cache line with larger granularity up to a full page. In this

[3] A DRAM row that is loaded into a HAAG$ entry and written to will eventually be written back to the DRAM row buffer.

[4] A DRAM row with few (or no) additional pending requests in the predictor queue will simply bypass the HAAG$ and directly serve the access from the memory controller.

[5] During cache entry replacement, a victim HAAG$ entry that maps to a different bank than the incoming DRAM row is prioritized to avoid conflicts on the data bus.

process, the sub-pages must be aligned at the corresponding address boundary of the access granularity. It is not possible to have multiple sub-pages from the same DRAM row scattered in the data store. Instead they must be stored contiguously to avoid multiple evictions to the same row.

CAM Design in the Row Mapping Unit. To reduce the cost of maintaining the high associativity of HAAG$ with variable granularities (e.g., from whole row to a sub-page), we design a power efficient CAM for the tag portion of the row mapping unit as shown in Figure 4b. The two key design features are hierarchical searching and hardware supported sorting. The combination of these two techniques ensures that the tags of frequently accessed cache lines (even with different granularities) are placed near the top. Therefore, search operations will usually complete much earlier than in a traditional CAM, reducing energy and latency overhead.

Our hierarchical searching technique divides the CAM array into *bins*, where only the mismatch signal of the previous bin will trigger an access (i.e., comparison) in the next bin. The design is based on a key observation that HAAG$ is different from caches or TLBs that require low access latency and a uniform access for all entries. Essentially, only row addresses are stored in the tag CAM, and the offset information is computed after the row address lookup in the tag CAM. Since different applications usually have certain preferences for memory access granularity [21], row address tags of certain sub-pages will have a much higher hit rate than those of others.

For example, if applications prefer accessing the full page of 2KB in a 64-entry HAAG$ whose sub-page size is 256B, all tag comparisons will happen at the corresponding 64 sub-pages (those are the head of a full page) out of the total 512 in the data store. Therefore, if all these entries are placed in the first bin of the tag CAM in the row mapping unit as shown in Figure 4b, the 512-way associative row mapping unit will have comparable power and timing to a 64-entry CAM, while still covering the worst case.

The memory controller will monitor the average access granularity and periodically sort the tag store by moving the entries with preferred access granularity to upper CAM bins. This hardware sorting can ensure the tags of frequent cache lines will be placed near the top in the common case. The hardware-sorted table can be implemented using techniques in prior work [27] with a time complexity of O(n). Furthermore, the sorting of bins in the CAM can be scheduled to be performed during idle time and may be completed before new memory accesses arrive. It can also pause the sorting by giving higher priority to memory accesses.

Replacement Policy. The Least Recently Used (LRU) replacement policy is not optimal for HAAG$ management because it can cause thrashing of HAAG$ entries. Moreover, if the LRU-selected HAAG$ dirty line is mapped to a busy bank, waiting to evict this line will cause significant delay in servicing pending memory requests. Therefore, a cache line is preferred as the eviction victim if there are no future memory requests to it and it is not mapped to a busy bank. If no HAAG$ lines meet the criteria, the replacement policy naturally degrades to LRU.

In order to support adaptive granularity, we apply two extra rules (in priority order) for eviction victim selection: 1) large enough (equal to or larger than the size of the pending request) cache lines are preferred so that a single eviction will make enough room for the new request, 2) non-dirty cache lines are preferred over dirty lines. If neither of these apply, we use the rules in [23], and prefer a cache line as the eviction victim if it has no future memory requests and is not mapped to a busy bank.

Operation Flow of HAAG$. Figure 4a also demonstrates an example flow of operations in HAAG$.

- *Step 1:* When the predictor detects a new (partial) row that needs to be cached, it sends out requests to the HAAG$. In the example we assume that a full page is 2KB with four sub-pages, and the HAAG$ needs to cache a half row (two sub-pages) with the row address as 0b 1101 (0x D) and the sub-page address as 0b 1101 10.
- *Step 2:* The global free list will pick an available cache line at the 512B boundary in the data store (highlighted in Figure 4a) and insert this into the empty entries of the row mapping unit. The row address and the meta information are stored in the tag and data portions of the row mapping unit respectively. The meta information includes the head address of 0b 10 (the offset address in the DRAM row), the granularity of 0b 10 (two sub-pages), and the pointer to index the data store cache line.
- *Step 3:* The memory controller issues both a DRAM access command and a HAAG$ access command to retrieve the data from DRAM and store the half row (two sub-pages) in the data store.
- *Step 4:* With a new memory request accessing data at sub-page 0b 1101 11, the memory controller consults the HAAG$ allocation table.
- *Step 5:* A hit in the row mapping unit indicates that the (partial) row is cached. Since the granularity of the cached row is unknown at this time, the Hamming distance of this sub-page and that of the head address are compared with the granularity to further confirm whether this is a real hit. In the example, it is a real hit, and the starting address of this half row and the Hamming distance are used together to address the data store for data retrieval.

4. METHODOLOGY

To enable a thorough evaluation of HAAG$ in the context of 3D DRAM, we built a comprehensive evaluation infrastructure consisting of two major components: 1) a modeling framework (shown in Figure 5) to study, design, and optimize HAAG$ considering 3D-stacked memory system cost (including silicon area), energy, and latency; and 2) a simulation framework based on an extended McSimA+ simulator [3] combined with McPAT [20] to evaluate the system-level performance and energy efficiency of HAAG$ with standard SPLASH-2 and SPEC CPU2006 benchmarks.

The design and optimization of HAAG$ depends tightly on the architecture of the 3D DRAM. This makes the design of 3D DRAM and row-buffer cache an inseparable endeavor, and a detailed study of the stacked DRAM design space is a prerequisite for architecting HAAG$. Therefore, we first built a framework as shown in Figure 5 to study the cost, performance, and energy consumption over a large space of 3D DRAM designs to achieve a near-optimal 3D DRAM architecture that drives the final design of the HAAG$.

As memory vendors often compete in commodity markets with thin profit margins, cost takes precedence over other metrics. Thus we first built a comprehensive cost model (Figure 5) based on [7], with die area, die yield, packaging cost and other parameters collected from projections for semiconductor chips using the IC Knowledge[6] models [10], and TSV geometry parameters from ITRS [31] and industrial products [14, 17]. Our cost model covers the cost in the entire manufacturing flow attributed to DRAM fabrication, logic process, and packaging, and also accounts for yield losses

[6] A commercial tool widely used for chip cost projections.

SPLASH-2

Application	Dataset	Application	Dataset
Barnes	16K particles	Cholesky	tk17.O
FFT	1,024K points	Radiosity	room
FMM	16K particles	Raytrace	car
LU	512×512 matrix	Volrend	head
Ocean	258×258 grids		
Radix	8M integers		
Water-Sp	4K molecules		

SPEC CPU2006

Set	Applications
CINT	
high	429.mcf, 462.libquantum, 471.omnetpp, 473.astar
med	401.bzip2, 456.hmmer, 464.h264ref, 483.xalancbmk
low	400.perlbench, 403.gcc, 445.gobmk, 458.sjeng
CFP	
high	433.milc, 450.soplex, 459.GemsFDTD, 470.lbm
med	410.bwaves, 434.zeusmp, 437.leslie3d, 481.wrf
low	436.cactusADM, 447.dealII, 454.calculix, 482.sphinx3

Table 1: SPLASH-2 datasets and SPEC CPU2006 application mixes for high, medium, and low memory bandwidth.

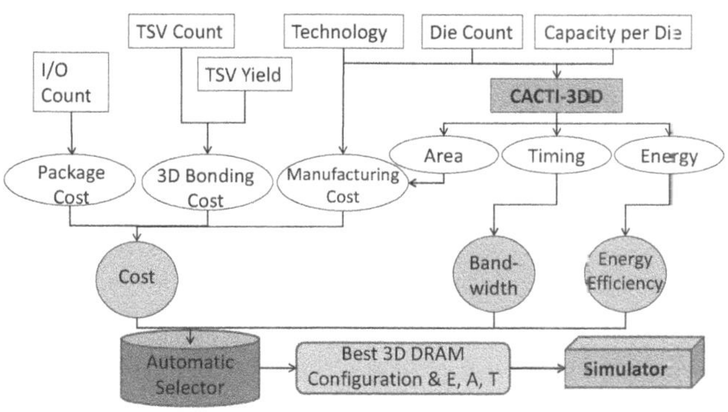

Figure 5: Modeling framework of 3D-stacked DRAM.

during die bonding and TSV fabrication. In particular, chip area and stacking yield are the two major factors that affect DRAM stack cost. We then extended CACTI-3DD [5] to simultaneously model power, area, and timing for 3D-stacked DRAM.

Using this framework (Figure 5) that includes both the extended CACTI-3DD and cost model, we performed a design space exploration for 3D DRAM, where we evaluated the cost, internal data bandwidth, and energy efficiency of the stack. Specifically, the internal data bandwidth is approximately proportional to the bank concurrency and data bus bandwidth, while the energy efficiency is the energy consumption for each memory access divided by the input/output width.

For the system performance study, our simulation infrastructure is based on McSimA+ [3], a Pin [25]-based manycore simulator that models multithreaded in-order and out-of-order cores, caches, directories, on-chip networks, and memory channels in detail. We modified McSimA+ to support HAAG$ with adaptive granularity. We used McPAT [20] to obtain power and energy parameters for our energy efficiency study. We used the SPLASH-2 benchmarks [35] with increased dataset sizes as summarized in Table 1. We also used the SPEC CPU2006 benchmark suite [26] to measure the system performance on consolidated workloads. The benchmark suite consists of both integer (CINT) and floating-point (CFP) benchmarks, all being single-threaded. We picked 12 applications from both CINT and CFP, and made three groups each, with four applications per group, based on their main memory bandwidth demand [2] as shown in Table 1. We found the representative simulation phases of each application and their weights using Simpoint 3.0 [32]. Each hardware thread runs a simulation phase and the number of instances per phase is proportional to its weight. We skipped the initialization phases of each multithreaded workload and simulate two billion instructions unless it finishes earlier.

5. EVALUATION

In this section, we evaluate the performance and energy efficiency improvements of HAAG$ integrated in hybrid 3D DRAM architecture. Figure 6 shows the target system used for evaluating our proposal, which employs a HAAG$ on the logic die of each 3D stack (Figure 6a) and connects the stack to a manycore processor with high-bandwidth interconnect on the same silicon interposer (Figure 6b). The target system closely resembles an HMC near-memory implementation [29] or the JEDEC High Bandwidth Memory (HBM) standard [12] (with an additional logic layer under the HBM stack). A multi-channel memory controller is responsible for communication between the processor and each of the hybrid DRAM stacks.

The manycore processor is organized as multiple clusters of cores interconnected by an on-chip 2D mesh network (Figure 6c). Each cluster has four multithreaded Niagara-like cores [18], and a shared four-bank 16-way L2 cache with a bank size of 256KB (Figure 6d). Each core has four hardware threads and separate 32KB 4-way set associative data and instruction L1 caches. Within a cluster, a crossbar is used for communication between cores and the L2 cache banks. A two-level hierarchical directory-based MESI protocol is used for cache coherency at both L1 and L2 cache levels.

5.1 Architecting the HAAG$ Enabled 3D Memory System

As integrated in the hybrid DRAM stack, the design specifications of a HAAG$, including the capacity, adaptive cache line granularity, and associativity are determined by the organization of the 3D stacked DRAM including the TSV channel width, stack size, and bank count. Also, the 3D DRAM determines a significant portion of the system performance and energy consumption. Thus, before evaluating system-level aspects of the HAAG$, it is necessary to get a reasonable architecture configuration for the 3D-stacked memory and row-buffer cache.

Accordingly, we performed a detailed design space exploration of 3D DRAM architecture and obtained the overall optimal design point accounting for cost, data bandwidth, and energy efficiency. Figure 2 presents a subset of the design exploration results for cost. Specifically, increasing stacked die count is beneficial in terms of area, as the more we stack, the more we will share within a stack. Meanwhile, increasing the memory datapath width causes area overhead and thus adds significantly to the cost. From the overall design space we have the best design point with 8 stacked die, 32 banks per die, and 128 IO per bank, which gives the highest bandwidth (proportional to bank count and TSV data width) and energy efficiency within the acceptable cost overhead toler-

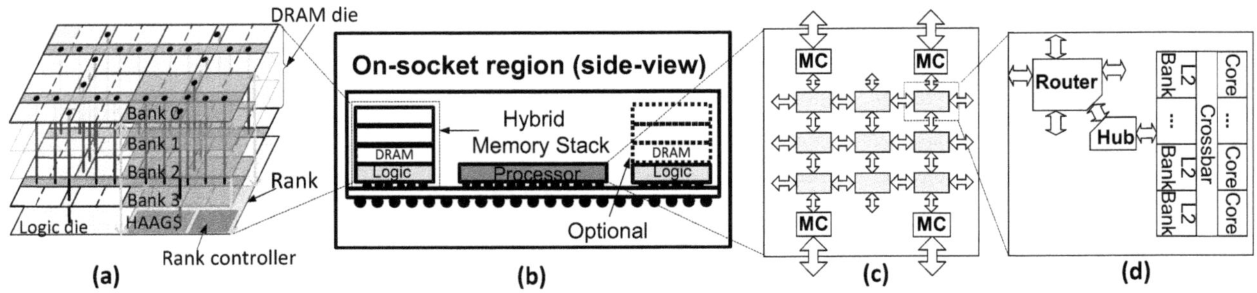

Figure 6: Illustration of our target system architecture in a package: a silicon interposer holding a manycore processor surrounded by hybrid memory stacks with a high-bandwidth interface. (a) A single 3D DRAM stack evaluated in the experiments. (b) Side view of the package. (c) The 2D mesh architecture of the manycore processor with the memory controllers (MC) at the edge. (d) Magnified core architecture.

3D DRAM	Num bank per die 32	IO width per bank 128	Page size 2KB/rank	Read latency 15 ns	Read energy 2.4 nJ	Internal BW 280 GB/s
HAAG$	Capacity per rank 64KB	Associativity* 32 to 256	IO width 512	Read latency† 0.79 ns	Read energy† 0.08 nJ	Access granularity 2KB to 256B
Manycore processor	Thread count 256	Core count 64	Clock 3GHz	L1 32KB 4 Way	L2 256KB/core 16-way	Thermal design power 107.5W

Table 2: Parameters of the manycore processor, 3D-stacked DRAM, and HAAG$ at 22 nm technology. †Worst case numbers for transferring each 64 byte data block to the processor from the HAAG$ including tag lookup and data retrieval (off-chip I/O is not included here). *Depending on access granularity.

ance range (3%). It is worth noting that the design configuration is similar to the second-generation HMC [29].

Table 2 lists the detailed system parameters and modeling results of both the 3D DRAM stack and the HAAG$ at a 22nm technology node. Specifically, the 3D DRAM has a page size of 2KB/rank, and an internal data transfer bandwidth of 280 GB/s. Also, TSVs have a latency of 0.7ns and energy per bit of 0.16 pJ based on CACTI-3DD. The HAAG$ timing and energy results are obtained from McPAT.

The major factor that limits the HAAG$ size is the available empty space in the logic die left by the shared common peripheral circuitry (input buffer, rank controller, decoder, bus, and TSVs). In our 3D DRAM configuration, the logic die has $0.34mm^2$ available for every vertical rank in the stack based on our area model. We fill this space with a 64KB SRAM-based HAAG$, which has an area of $0.27mm^2$. With the page (i.e., row) size of 2KB from the best stacked DRAM configuration, the HAAG$ in each rank can hold a maximum of 32 DRAM rows (2KB each).

Also, the HAAG$ access granularity has an upper bound of the DRAM page size and a lower bound of 256B as discussed in Section 3.1. Accordingly, the associativity is flexible from 32 to 256. In addition, the HAAG$ has a data block size and IO width of 64B (a CPU cache line). We assume there is an address controller in the HAAG$ so that a cacheline address can be incremented to assemble multiple small entries for the entire or a partial page (row). Finally, the memory controller queue and the predictor queue are assumed to have 32 and 128 entries respectively.

The total processor-to-memory bandwidth of the system is determined by the number of memory controllers and the bandwidth of each hybrid memory stack connected to the memory controller. The selected design configuration shown in Table 2 can achieve 280GB/s internal bandwidth with high bank concurrency, and we assume an external bandwidth of 128GB/s between the processor and the memory stack (Figure 6). Both these bandwidths match the HBM interface standard definition [12] and the hybrid memory cube design target by Micron [29]. The 128GB/s memory bandwidth is distributed to two memory channels of a memory controller. All internal ranks share the external memory channels and communicate to the processor on the same silicon interposer. The memory controller uses parallelism-aware batch-scheduling (PAR-BS) [28] for scheduling memory accesses. Within a request batch, it prioritizes read requests over writes as reads are typically more latency sensitive.

5.2 System Performance and Energy Efficiency

Based on all the timing and energy parameters of HAAG$, 3D DRAM, and processor obtained in Table 2, we demonstrate the improvement in performance and energy efficiency that HAAG$ brings into the system. Figure 7 demonstrates power, instructions per cycle (IPC), and system energy-delay product (EDP) of the baseline 3D DRAM architecture without row-buffer caches (RB$s), the architecture that simulates Loh's proposal (FM-RB$), and our proposed History-Assisted Adaptive-Granularity Cache (HAAG$). Because the HAAG$ explores the synergy of the inseparable history-assisted predictor in addition to the adaptive-granularity cache to achieve performance and power improvements, we evaluate the design's efficiency in its entirety.

Figure 7a shows the IPC and the dynamic power breakdown of the memory stack. As we can see, the HAAG$ memory subsystem is clearly better in terms of both performance and power consumption than the state-of-the-art FM-RB$. In particular, applications with high bandwidth demands such as RADIX, OCEAN, CFP.high, and CINT.high show up to 43.5% performance improvement (33.5% on harmonic average) and 41.3% power reduction (28.9% on average) compared to FM-RB$. Figure 7a shows normalized IPCs of all workloads so that they are at the same scale. For reference, the absolute IPC values examples of RADIX, OCEAN, CFP.high, and CINT.high running on a system with HAAG$ are 10.2, 13.1 15.2, and 15.5, respectively.

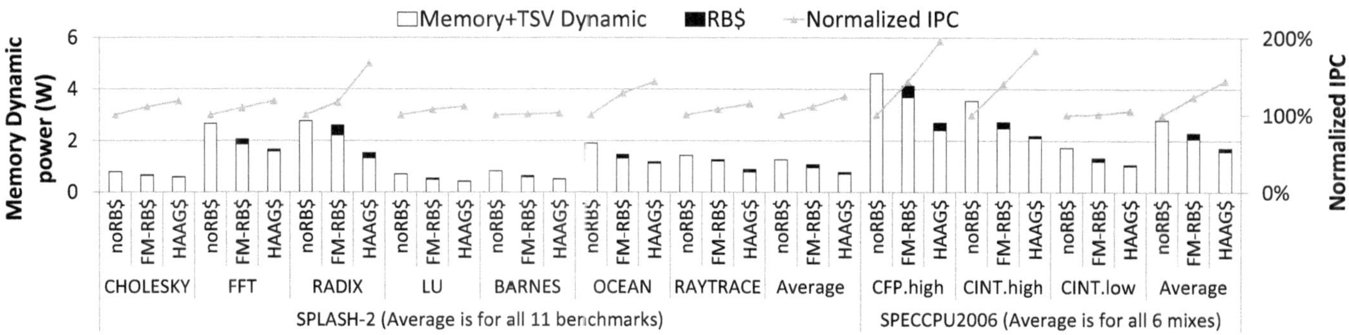

(a) Memory dynamic power and IPC (normalized against no-RB$ for each workload)

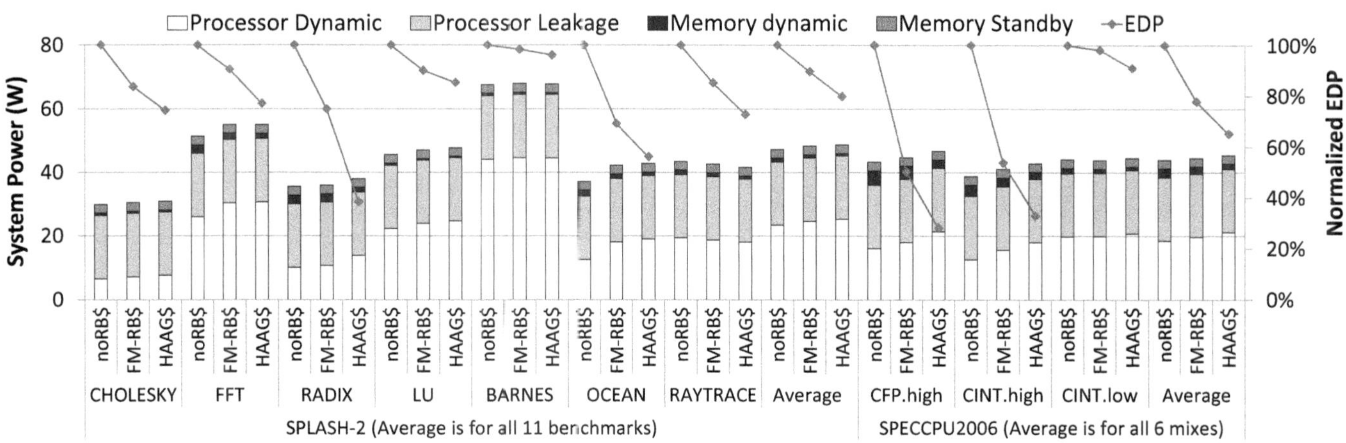

(b) Normalized EDP (normalized against no-RB$ for each workload)

Figure 7: Power, IPC (higher is better), and normalized EDP (lower is better) of the baseline, FM-RB$, and HAAG$ systems running the SPLASH-2 and SPEC CPU2006 benchmarks. 'noRB$', 'FM-RB$', and 'HAAG$' denote (single memory stack) system without row buffer cache (RB$), with 'FM-RB$', and with 'HAAG$', respectively. Note that the harmonic average numbers in the figures are over the entire benchmark suite of SPLASH-2 and SPEC CPU2006 respectively, although only a subset of benchmarks have their results shown in the figure due to limited space.

An important observation is that HAAG$ works particularly well for memory-intensive applications with irregular data access and limited locality (many memory-intensive multithreaded applications belong to this category), compared to FM-RB$. For instance, although RADIX is more memory-intensive than OCEAN, FM-RB$ performs better for OCEAN (28.2% over the baseline) than RADIX (16.3% over the baseline) due to the poor locality in RADIX. In comparison, HAAG$ performs better for RADIX (67.1% over the baseline) than OCEAN (43.2% over the baseline). Thus, HAAG$ improves performance regardless of access locality because of its ability to adapt to row-buffer cache granularity to match the behavior of applications. This is especially important for manycore CPU workloads where memory-side locality is hard to leverage [2].

Figure 7b shows normalized system EDP, where energy (E) includes dynamic and leakage parts for both the processor and the memory. The figure also illustrates the breakdown of total system power attributed to individual contributions from processor/memory and dynamic/leakage. HAAG$ has the best EDP for all the workloads with a maximum improvement of up to 48.7% and an average of 13.3% compared to FM-RB$. For memory-intensive benchmarks such as RADIX, OCEAN, CFP.high, and CINT.high, the EDP of HAAG$ improves more significantly (39.4% on harmonic average) compared to FM-RB$. This results from their higher IPC (i.e., better performance) and correspondingly much less application execution time and lower energy. Again, it proves that HAAG$ is much more effective in improving both performance and energy efficiency for memory intensive applications running on manycore systems by exploiting the hidden locality in memory accesses.

The improvement in performance and EDP results from the synergy of a higher row-buffer cache hit rate and reduced data transfers for smaller data granularity. Figure 8 shows HAAG$'s effectiveness in increasing cache hit rate. For the exemplified memory-intensive applications, the row-buffer hit rate (no-RB$) is as low as 15%-20% because the high thread count causes severe row-buffer conflicts. HAAG$ is able to increase the hit rate over the state-of-the-art FM-RB$ by an average of 24.1% for memory-intensive applications. The results in Figures 7 and 8 demonstrate the effectiveness of the adaptive-granularity scheme and the decoupled predictor.

5.3 Impact of System Memory Bandwidth

We then studied the sensitivity of HAAG$ to memory bandwidth on both in-order and out-of-order (OOO) processors by increasing the memory stack bandwidth. The results reveal the relationship of performance over bandwidth as shown in Figure 9. For OOO processors we employ 16 OOO Nehalem-like cores running at 3GHz, with a peak performance of 192 GOPS/s that matches the 64-core in-order processor. Each OOO core has a 64-entry reorder-buffer, a 128-entry instruction queue, 32KB 4-way set associative L1 I/D

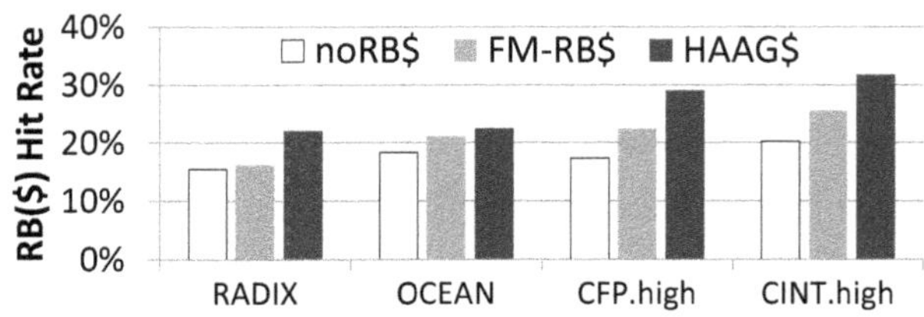

Figure 8: Comparison of row-buffer cache hit rates for RB$ designs with memory-intensive workloads (RADIX, OCEAN, CFP.high, and CINT.high). For no-RB$ case we show row-buffer hit rate.

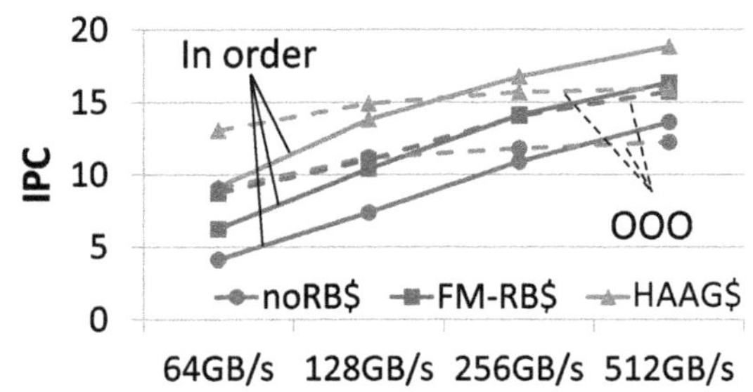

Figure 9: Comparison of IPC results averaged over memory-intensive workloads (RADIX, OCEAN, CFP.high, and CINT.high) for different external memory bandwidths on both in-order and out-of-order processors. The stack's internal to external bandwidth ratio is fixed at 2×.

caches and a 1MB 16-way set associative L2 cache. Although it has the same theoretical throughput as the in-order processor configuration, the OOO processor has better single thread performance but lower throughput than the in-order processor in practice, especially when provided sufficient memory bandwidth.

Benchmarks with relatively high memory bandwidth demands (i.e., RADIX, OCEAN, CFP.high, and CINT.high) see improvement in performance as we scale provisioned external system memory bandwidth from 64GB/s to 512GB/s for both in order and out-of-order processors. HAAG$ is more advantageous than both FM-RB$ and no-RB$ designs for all external system memory bandwidth configurations. Especially when the available system memory bandwidth is low, HAAG$ performs much better than the other two schemes. This is because with a limited available external system bandwidth, HAAG$ makes the best use of the internal memory bandwidth by caching data more judiciously.

When memory bandwidth increases, requests tend to be served faster with less contention at the memory controller. Thus, the relative performance differences among noRB$, FM-RB$, and HAAG$ become smaller. However, it is important to note that the performance of HAAG$ at a lower available external system memory bandwidth (e.g., 128GB/s) is similar to that of FM-RB$ at a higher bandwidth (e.g., 256GB/s), and that of no-RB$ at an even higher bandwidth (e.g., 512GB/s). This also further demonstrates that HAAG$ requires much less external system memory bandwidth than FM-RB$ for achieving the same performance, and thus saves cost and energy on memory and links.

6. CONCLUSION AND FUTURE WORK

3D stacked DRAM is a promising solution to the ever-increasing demands for memory capacity and bandwidth in supercomputers and datacenters. However, the limited in-stack data bus width becomes a bottleneck for fully unleashing performance and energy benefits from 3D DRAM. In this work we proposed the History-Assisted Adaptive-Granularity Cache (HAAG$) to best utilize the narrow TSV channel width in the 3D DRAM stack, and fully exploit the potential of 3D DRAM to maximize performance and energy efficiency at the system level. A HAAG$ employs an adaptive caching scheme that dynamically adjusts the amount of data to cache and an intelligent predictor that makes decisions on whether and how much data to cache from a DRAM row. With these two synergistic techniques, HAAG$ significantly improves memory access latency and memory system energy efficiency by increasing the row-buffer cache hit rate and avoiding unnecessary data transfers. For important memory-intensive SPLASH-2 and SPEC CPU-2006 workloads, HAAG$ outperforms the state-of-the-art by 33.5% on average. It is important to note that although evaluated in the context of 3D DRAM architecture, the proposal is not constrained to 3D DRAM and can be implemented in other memory systems with buffer-on-board (BoB) chips as well, such as the DDR3/4 interfaced load-reduced DIMMs (LRDIMMs) with LR-Buffers. We leave the application of HAAG$ to other memory systems as future work.

The goal of our proposed HAAG$ is making DRAM row-buffer cache designs efficient and practical so that their advantages can be well leveraged for maximizing performance and energy efficiency of memory systems in general. The innovations of adaptive granularity and history-assisted prediction work especially well for memory systems with a modest data bus width, cost-constrained cache size, and scalable memory capacity. Especially since future CPUs will get more and more cores and row locality will go down dramatically, HAAG$ with its adaptivity will become more important and will be a much needed innovation.

Acknowledgments

We thank the anonymous reviewers for their insightful comments to improve our paper. Ke Chen and Jay Brockman were partially supported by the C2S2 Focus Center, one of six research centers funded under the Focus Center Research Program (FCRP), a Semiconductor Research Corporation entity. Jung Ho Ahn was partially supported by the Future Semiconductor Device Technology Development Program (10044735) funded by MOTIE and KSRC. Cong Xu and Yuan Xie were supported in part by NSF 1500848, 1017277, and 1461698. This material was also partially based on work supported by the Department of Energy under Award Number DE - SC0005026.

7. REFERENCES

[1] "Hybrid Memory Cube Specification 1.0," Hybrid Memory Cube Consortium, Tech. Rep., Jan 2013.

[2] J. Ahn, N. P. Jouppi, C. Kozyrakis, J. Leverich, and R. S. Schreiber, "Future Scaling of Processor-Memory Interfaces," in *Supercomputing*, 2009.

[3] J. Ahn, S. Li, S. O, and N. P. Jouppi, "McSimA+: A Manycore Simulator with Application-level+ Simulation and Detailed Microarchitecture Modeling," in *ISPASS*, 2013.

[4] R. Ausavarungnirun, K. K.-W. Chang, L. Subramanian, G. H. Loh, and O. Mutlu, "Staged Memory Scheduling: Achieving High Performance and Scalability in Heterogeneous Systems," in *ISCA*, 2012.

[5] K. Chen, S. Li, N. Muralimanohar, J. B. Brockman, and N. P. Jouppi, "CACTI-3DD: Architecture-level Modeling for 3D Die-stacked DRAM Main Memory," in *DATE*, 2012.

[6] X. Dong, Y. Xie, N. Muralimanohar, N. Jouppi, and R. Kaufmann, "Simple but Effective Heterogeneous Main

Memory with On-chip Memory Controller Support," in *SC*, 2010.
[7] X. Dong and Y. Xie, "System-Level Cost Analysis and Design Exploration for Three-Dimensional Integrated Circuits (3D ICs)," in *ASP-DAC*, 2009.
[8] T. J. Ham, B. Chelepalli, N. Xue, and B. Lee, "Disintegrated Control for Energy-Efficient and Heterogeneous Memory Systems," in *HPCA*, 2013.
[9] H. Hidaka, Y. Matsuda, M. Asakura, and K. Fujishima, "The cache DRAM Architecture: A DRAM with an On-Chip Cache Memory," vol. 10, no. 2, pp. 14–25, 1990.
[10] IC Konwledge LLC, "IC Cost Model Revision 1105 http://www.icknowledge.com/," 2011.
[11] K. Inoue, K. Kai, and K. Murakami, "Dynamically Variable Line-Size Cache Exploiting High On-Chip Memory Bandwidth of Merged DRAM/Logic LSIs," in *HPCA*, 1999, pp. 218–222.
[12] JEDEC, "High Bandwidth Memory (HBM) DRAM - JESD235," Oct 2013. [Online]. Available: http://www.jedec.org/standards-documents/docs/jesd235
[13] D. Jevdjic, G. H. Loh, C. Kaynak, and B. Falsafi, "Unison Cache: A Scalable and Effective Die-Stacked DRAM Cache," in *MICRO*, 2014.
[14] U. Kang *et al.*, "8 Gb 3-D DDR3 DRAM Using Through-Silicon-Via Technology," *JSSC*, vol. 45, no. 1, pp. 111–119, 2010.
[15] G. Kedem and R. P. Koganti, "WCDRAM: A Fully Associative Integrated Cached-DRAM with Wide Cache Lines," Duke University, Tech. Rep., 1997.
[16] T. Kgil, S. D'Souza, A. Saidi, N. Binkert, R. Dreslinski, T. Mudge, S. Reinhardt, and K. Flautner, "PicoServer: Using 3D Stacking Technology to Enable a Compact Energy Efficient Chip Multiprocessor," in *ASPLOS*, 2006.
[17] J.-S. Kim *et al.*, "A 1.2V 12.8GB/s 2Gb Mobile Wide-I/O DRAM with 4x128 I/Os Using TSV-Based Stacking," in *ISSCC*, 2011.
[18] P. Kongetira, K. Aingaran, and K. Olukotun, "Niagara: A 32-Way Multithreaded Sparc Processor," *IEEE Micro*, vol. 25, no. 2, pp. 21–29, 2005.
[19] D. Lee, Y. Kim, V. Seshadri, J. Liu, L. Subramanian, and O. Mutlu, "Tiered-latency DRAM: A Low Latency and Low Cost DRAM Architecture," in *HPCA*, 2013.
[20] S. Li, J. Ahn, R. D. Strong, J. B. Brockman, D. M. Tullsen, and N. P. Jouppi, "McPAT: An Integrated Power, Area, and Timing Modeling Framework for Multicore and Manycore Architectures," in *MICRO*, 2009.
[21] S. Li, D. H. Yoon, K. Chen, J. Zhao, J. Ahn, J. B. Brockman, Y. Xie, and N. P. Jouppi, "MAGE: Adaptive Granularity and ECC for Resilient and Power Efficient Memory Systems," in *SC*, 2012.
[22] G. H. Loh, "3D-Stacked Memory Architectures for Multi-Core Processors," in *ISCA*, 2008.
[23] ——, "A Register-file Approach for Row Buffer Caches in Die-stacked DRAMs," in *MICRO*, 2011.
[24] G. Loi, B. Agrawal, N. Srivastava, S. Lin, T. Sherwood, and K. Banerjee, "A Thermally-Aware Performance Analysis of Vertically Integrated (3-D) Processor-Memory Hierarchy," in *DAC*, 2006.
[25] C.-K. Luk, R. Cohn, R. Muth, H. Patil, A. Klauser, G. Lowney, S. Wallace, V. J. Reddi, and K. Hazelwood, "Pin: Building Customized Program Analysis Tools with Dynamic Instrumentation," in *PLDI*, Jun 2005.
[26] H. McGhan, "SPEC CPU2006 Benchmark Suite," in *Microprocessor Report*, Oct 2006.
[27] S. W. Moore and B. T. Graham, "Tagged Up/Down Sorter - a Hardware Priority Queue," *The Computer Journal*, vol. 38, pp. 695–703, 1995.
[28] O. Mutlu and T. Moscibroda, "Parallelism-Aware Batch Scheduling: Enhancing both Performance and Fairness of Shared DRAM Systems," in *ISCA*, 2008.
[29] J. T. Pawlowski, "Hybrid Memory Cube (HMC)," in *Hot Chips*, 2011.
[30] Samsung Electronics, "DDR3 SDRAM Datasheet," 2002.
[31] Semiconductor Industries Association , "International Technology Roadmap for Semiconductors." 2007.
[32] T. Sherwood, E. Perelman, G. Hamerly, and B. Calder, "Automatically Characterizing Large Scale Program Behavior," in *ASPLOS*, 2002.
[33] Y. H. Son, S. O, H. Yang, D. Jung, J. Ahn, J. Kim, J. Kim, and J. W. Lee, "Microbank: Architecting Through-silicon Interposer-based Main Memory Systems," in *SC*, 2014.
[34] D. H. Woo, N. H. Seong, D. L. Lewis, and H.-H. S. Lee, "An Optimized 3D-Stacked Memory Architecture by Exploiting Excessive, High-Density TSV Bandwidth," in *HPCA*, 2010.
[35] S. C. Woo, M. Ohara, E. Torrie, J. P. Singh, and A. Gupta, "The SPLASH-2 programs: Characterization and Methodological Considerations," in *ISCA*, 1995.
[36] D. H. Yoon, M. K. Jeong, and M. Erez, "Adaptive Granularity Memory Systems: A Tradeoff between Storage Efficiency and Throughput," in *ISCA*, June 2011.
[37] Z. Zhang, Z. Zhu, and X. Zhang, "Cached DRAM for ILP Processor Memory Access Latency Reduction," in *IEEE Micro*, vol. 21, no. 4, 2001, pp. 22–32.

Real-Time In-Memory Checkpointing for Future Hybrid Memory Systems

Shen Gao[1,2] Bingsheng He[1] Jianliang Xu[2]
[1]Nanyang Technological University, Singapore
[2]Hong Kong Baptist University

ABSTRACT

In this paper, we study real-time in-memory checkpointing as an effective means to improve the reliability of future large-scale parallel processing systems. Under this context, the checkpoint overhead can become a significant performance bottleneck. Novel memory system designs with upcoming non-volatile random access memory (NVRAM) technologies are emerging to address this performance issue. However, we find that those designs can still have prohibitively high checkpoint overhead and system downtime, especially when checkpoints are taken frequently to implement a reliable system. In this paper, we propose a novel in-memory checkpointing system, named *Mona*, for reducing the checkpoint overhead of hybrid memory systems with NVRAM and DRAM. To minimize the in-memory checkpoint overhead, Mona dynamically writes partial checkpoints from DRAM to NVRAM during application execution. To reduce the interference of partial checkpointing, Mona utilizes runtime idle periods and leverages a cost model to guide partial checkpointing decisions for individual DRAM ranks. We further develop load-balancing mechanisms to balance checkpoint overheads across different DRAM ranks. Simulation results demonstrate the efficiency and effectiveness of Mona in reducing the checkpoint overhead, downtime and restarting time.

Categories and Subject Descriptors

D.4.5 [**Reliability**]: Checkpoint/restart; C.4.1 [**Computer Systems Organization**]: Performance of Systems–design studies

General Terms

Design, Performance

Keywords

NVRAM; Phase Change Memory; Checkpointing; Parallel Computing

ICS'15, June 8–11, 2015, Newport Beach, CA, USA.

http://dx.doi.org/10.1145/2751205.2751212.

1. INTRODUCTION

The increasing scale of parallel processing systems is being severely challenged by high failure rates. It is predicted that transient errors in CPUs and memories will increase by 32 times in the next decade [3]. On the other hand, increasingly large memory capacities cause a higher chance of memory failures [28]. As a result, the upcoming large-scale system will have the severe problem of frequent crashes, which can degrade the system performance dramatically. Real-time in-memory checkpointing offers a fine-grained checkpointing, which can be an effective means to improve the reliability of future large-scale parallel processing systems. In the event a failure occurs, the application is restarted from the latest checkpoint, thus minimizing repeated computation. But, due to potential high failure rates in large-scale parallel processing systems, checkpoints should be taken in a real-time and fine-grained manner. Obviously, high checkpointing frequency poses significant challenges on novel checkpoint mechanism designs. Thus, this paper investigates whether and how we can reduce the overhead of checkpointing-restart mechanisms to enable real-time in-memory checkpointing in large-scale systems.

Traditionally, hard disk-based checkpoint systems have been adopted. Since hard disks are over two orders (even three orders) of magnitude slower than main memory, checkpoint/restart mechanisms can cause significant overhead to the overall system performance. A large-scale system may suffer more than 50% performance degradation and spend up to 80% of extra I/O traffic, because of frequent checkpointing operations [22, 11, 10]. Even worse, during checkpointing, the application execution may suffer from a period of downtime for writing checkpoints. This downtime is exaggerated for applications with large memory footprint.

More recently, emerging NVRAM technologies such as phase-change memory (PCM) have been exploited to reduce the checkpoint overhead (i.e., NVRAM-assisted checkpoint) [6, 7, 33]. Those studies have demonstrated promising results in reducing the checkpoint overhead of large-scale systems. However, existing NVRAM-assisted checkpoint techniques [6, 7, 33] have the following three limitations towards real-time in-memory checkpointing. First, even with NVRAM, they still cause a long downtime. This is partly because the low latency feature of PCM is not exploited to reduce the total checkpoint overhead (details are presented in Section 3.1). Second, while asynchronous or non-blocking checkpointing can reduce the downtime to a certain degree, the mechanism is complicated and the runtime overhead can be high in practice [27]. Third, most previous studies (such as [6, 7, 33, 14, 16]) target at a sole optimization goal. Some applications may simply require minimizing the checkpoint overhead so that the total expected execution time is minimized. Other critical applications might have rigid requirements on the restarting time or downtime. System re-design/re-implementation is required for a different optimization goal.

In this paper, we propose a novel hybrid memory design, named *Mona*, towards enabling real-time in-memory checkpointing. Particularly, Mona uses PCM, one of the promising NVRAM technologies, to store checkpointing files. Mona has the following novel designs to address the aforesaid limitations of the existing techniques:

- To support efficient checkpointing-restart mechanisms, we develop a PCM-assisted dynamic checkpointing approach to perform partial checkpointing from DRAM to PCM. Additionally, our design takes advantage of memory rank parallelism. Inspired by speculative checkpointing [18], partial checkpointing is performed at application runtime.
- To minimize the interference, we write dirty pages from DRAM to PCM *only when* there are sufficiently lengthy idle periods in a DRAM rank. Instead of determining the length of each idle period, we estimate the idle period distributions and determine a *write threshold* on the idle period length: only when the current idle period exceeds the write threshold, we trigger the dirty-page writing from DRAM to PCM. That can avoid the penalty caused by checkpointing in very short idle periods. Also, we carefully select the dirty pages to be written to PCM.
- Balancing the checkpoint overhead across different memory ranks is another important performance issue for Mona, since writes to PCM are often a performance bottleneck in hybrid memory systems [25]. We propose load-balancing strategies to minimize the worst checkpoint overhead among all DRAM ranks. Both PCM-assisted dynamic checkpointing and load-balancing strategies are guided by our cost model for adapting idle period distributions and page access patterns. With the cost model, Mona can optimize the system for different goals such as the total checkpoint overhead or the restarting time.

We implement our design into a cycle-accurate simulator and evaluate the efficiency and effectiveness of Mona with both micro and macro benchmarks. Overall, Mona significantly reduces the checkpoint overhead, downtime and restarting time. Particularly, compared with the state-of-the-art PCM-based checkpointing method [6], Mona reduces the total checkpointing cost by 65%, and the restarting time by 80%. We extend Mona to support multi-level checkpointing and demonstrate the effectiveness of our approach in multi-level checkpointing for larger-scale applications.

Organization. The rest of the paper is organized as follows. We briefly introduce the background on NVRAM and checkpointing in Section 2. Section 3 describes an overview of Mona, followed by detailed design and implementations in Section 4. The experimental results are presented in Section 5. We review the related work in Section 6 and conclude this paper in Section 7.

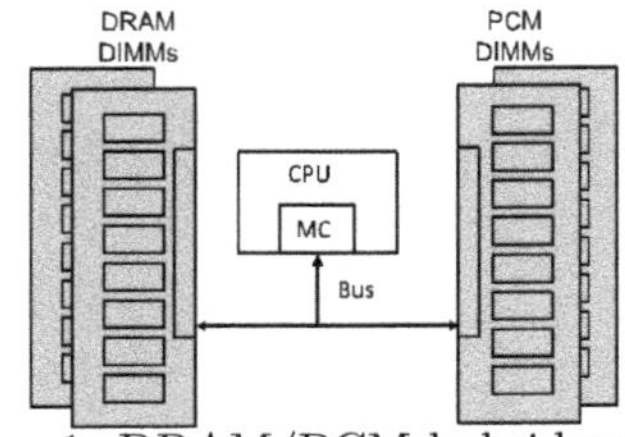

Figure 1: DRAM/PCM hybrid system.

2. PRELIMINARY AND BACKGROUND ON NVRAM

Since conventional DRAM technologies encounter scaling difficulties and power issues, NVRAM technologies such as PCM and memristors have been developed. This paper focuses on PCM, which has gained much attention in the research community [6, 34, 15, 12]. The read latency of PCM is close to that of DRAM and two orders of magnitude shorter than that of flash memory. The write latency of PCM is in between those of DRAM and flash memory. Without erase-before-write constraints, its random-write performance is much better than that of flash memory. Moreover, PCM is likely to be cheaper than DRAM when produced in mass market quantities. It is feasible that PCM will be integrated into future computer systems.

Recent studies have proposed three major methods of integrating PCM into the memory hierarchy. The first approach is to use PCM as a replacement of DRAM [15, 2]. The second approach is to use PCM as an external storage like a hard disk [5]. The third approach is to integrate PCM into DIMMs and the main memory system becomes a hybrid system [25, 6, 8]. This paper adopts the third approach. PCM is allocated on separate DIMMs for a better bandwidth and ease-of-integration, as illustrated in Figure 1. In this study, we assume a DDR3 memory system, where PCM and DRAM are allocated on DDR3 DIMMs. Each DIMM contains multiple ranks to transmit data independently.

Our design is inspired by NVDIMM [20], which is commercially available and is a combination of DRAM and NAND flash. During normal operations, NVDIMM is working as DRAM while flash is invisible to the host. However, upon power failure, NVDIMM saves all the data from DRAM to flash by using supercapacitor to make the data persistent. In contrast, our design leverages PCM to replace NAND flash in NVIDIMM, eliminating supercapacitors. Moreover, since PCM is much faster than NAND flash, our design enables real-time in-memory checkpointing.

3. SYSTEM DESIGN

In this section, we discuss design motivations and give a design overview of Mona.

3.1 Design Motivations

Existing NVRAM-assisted checkpoint techniques [6, 7, 33] all use synchronous and incremental checkpointing. At each checkpointing stage, the application execution is temporarily suspended, and all the dirty pages in DRAM are written to PCM. The role of PCM is similar to that of hard disks in the sense that both of them are used as persistent storage for storing checkpointing files, and little modifications are required for the conventional checkpointing-restart algorithm. However, such a simple approach has several obstacles/deficiencies:

- First, during the checkpointing process, it has to write many dirty pages from DRAM to PCM, still causing a significant overhead and downtime especially on large-memory machines. Another issue is on memory ranks. To fully utilize the memory bandwidth, all memory ranks should perform checkpointing in parallel. The checkpoint overhead is thus bounded by the longest writing latency of all the ranks. Uneven loads among the ranks would magnify the checkpointing cost.

- Second, it may underutilize the PCM bandwidth. On one hand, PCM is only used in checkpointing, and is idle during application execution. On the other hand, memory-intensive workloads still have many idle periods with reasonable lengths (e.g., hundreds of cycles) [13, 31, 17]. It is desirable to take advantage of those idle periods.
- Finally, as architectures and applications vary, we should provide the flexibility to achieve different optimization goals, such as minimizing either the total checkpointing cost or the restarting time.

3.2 Overview of Mona

To address the aforementioned obstacles, we propose a novel in-memory checkpointing design Mona with *dynamic partial checkpointing* and cost models. Using incremental checkpointing, Mona divides the application execution into a series of *checkpointing intervals*. Each checkpointing interval is further divided into two phases: partial checkpointing (during application execution) and final checkpointing. In partial checkpointing, we dynamically select the *cold* dirty pages that are less likely to be written by the application in the future and write them to PCM. In final checkpointing, we use a synchronous scheme and the application execution is temporarily suspended until the next checkpointing interval. With the dynamic partial checkpointing, Mona is able to reduce the downtime in the final checkpointing. Based on the access pattern of each dirty page, we develop a *coldness threshold* to identify the pages for partial checkpointing. When the elapsed time of a page since its last write access in DRAM is longer than the coldness threshold, the page becomes a candidate cold page.

To fully utilize the memory bandwidth, we propose to leverage the idle period during application execution to perform the partial checkpointing writes to PCM. However, those writes may pose interference to the application execution. Ideally, we should identify the lengthy idle periods that can accommodate the PCM writes. However, it is impossible or impractical to predict the length of the next idle period without a *prior* knowledge. Inspired by the previous study [31], we periodically estimate the idle period distribution and determine a *write threshold* for individual DRAM ranks according to the distribution. During the non-checkpointing period, only if the current idle period exceeds the write threshold, Mona performs a PCM write.

We further develop mechanisms of load balancing across DRAM ranks for both partial checkpointing and final checkpointing. In partial checkpointing, we consider the number of pages to write and the idle periods of all ranks, and periodically migrate the pages among them or tune the parameters (write threshold and coldness threshold) for each rank so that the partial checkpointing cost is balanced among DRAM ranks. In final checkpointing, we even up the number of dirty pages in each DRAM rank prior to perform PCM writes. Specifically, we perform page migration among DRAM ranks, because the cost of a page migration in DRAM is much lower than that of a PCM write.

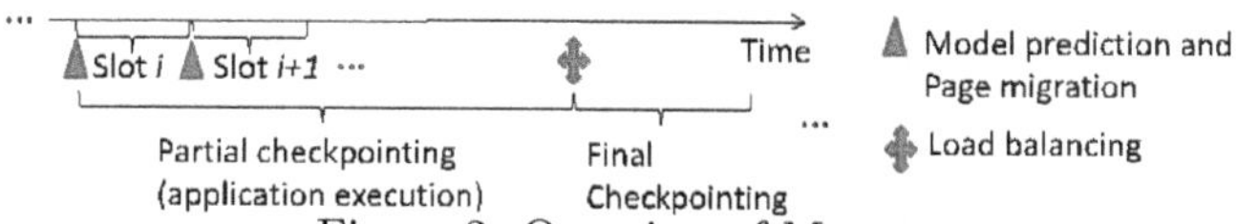

Figure 2: Overview of Mona.

To support the flexibility of different optimization goals, Mona develops a cost model to guide its decision, by estimating the checkpoint overhead or checkpointing interval. In this paper, we use two common scenarios as examples: first, minimize the checkpointing overhead given a checkpointing interval; second, minimize the checkpointing interval given a penalty budget on the application execution. Since these two scenarios are dual problems, this paper mainly focuses on the first scenario, and evaluates the second scenario in the experiment.

Algorithm 1 The workflow of Mona for a checkpoint interval

```
/*Partial checkpointing*/
for each idle period e do
   Update histogram information;
   According to the write threshold configuration, Mona performs
   PCM writes with the dirty pages satisfying coldness thresh-
   old;/*Section 4.1.1*/
for each memory access r do
   if r is a write then
      Update page access pattern information;
for the beginning of a new slot do
   Perform model prediction and load balancing among DRAM
   ranks; /*Sections 4.1.2*/
/*Final checkpointing*/
Balance the dirty pages among DRAM ranks; /*Section 4.2*/
Write all the dirty pages to PCM;
```

The overall workflow of Mona on a checkpointing interval is given in Algorithm 1. In partial checkpointing, we use a histogram to represent the idle period distribution. For each idle period, we update the histogram. For each write request, we need to update access pattern information. The details of the update procedures will be presented in Sections 4.1.1 and 4.1.2. In final checkpointing, we first perform load balancing among DRAM ranks, and then write all the dirty pages to PCM. Note that our load balancing is guided by the cost model and, hence, it adapts to memory architectures and configurations. Afterwards, an incremental checkpoint is created and the next checkpointing interval starts. Figure 2 illustrates a checkpointing interval. We further divide a partial checkpointing period into multiple equal-sized *slots*. At the beginning of each slot, we perform the cost estimation and load balancing across DRAM ranks. The cost estimation is performed with a sliding history window, and the window length is equal to the checkpointing interval.

Finally, upon a system failure, Mona constructs the latest checkpoint and restarts the execution. In the event of failures during transferring a partial checkpoint from DRAM to PCM, we can choose to retry the checkpointing writes or adopt other existing failure recovery methods. Since the restarting process is not the main focus of this paper, Mona uses the classic recovery algorithm [23] for incremental checkpointing.

4. DESIGN AND IMPLEMENTATIONS

We describe the implementation details for key components in Mona, including the cost model and the load balancing module. The cost model guides the optimization for individual DRAM ranks, and load balancing aims at evening up the checkpointing cost of all DRAM ranks.

4.1 Cost Model

The cost model guides Mona to determine the threshold values of individual ranks including coldness threshold and write threshold under different optimization goals. As a case study, we mainly focus on the goal of minimizing the total checkpoint overhead given the checkpointing interval. Thus, in this section, we present the cost model of determining the threshold values under this optimization goal.

In a checkpointing interval, the total checkpoint overhead is the sum of the performance penalty caused by PCM writes in partial checkpointing and the cost of PCM writes in final checkpointing, denoted as $C_{partial}$ and C_{final}, respectively. The notations for the cost model are summarized in Table 1. Thus, the total checkpoint overhead is given by:

$$C_{total} = C_{partial} + C_{final}. \quad (1)$$

We further derive each cost component with the unit cost multiplying the number of PCM writes:

$$C_{total} = N_{partial} \times W_{partial} + N_{final} \times W_{PCM}. \quad (2)$$

In final checkpointing, the unit cost is simply the cost of a normal PCM write (W_{PCM}), which can be a constant obtained from specification or calibration. In partial checkpointing, Mona leverages the idle period to perform the PCM write. We present the detailed algorithm of determining the optimal $W_{partial}$ given the number of partial writes ($N_{partial}$) in Section 4.1.2.

Table 1: Notations in this paper

Notations	Description
R_{dram}	Number of DRAM ranks in Mona
R_{pcm}	Number of PCM ranks in Mona
C_{total}	Total checkpointing cost of a checkpointing interval
$C_{partial}/C_{final}$	Total cost of partial/final checkpointing
$N_{partial}$	Number of PCM writes in partial checkpointing
$W_{partial}$	Average cost of a PCM write in partial checkpointing
N_{final}	Number of PCM writes in final checkpointing
W_{PCM}	Average cost of a PCM write in final checkpointing
T_C	*Coldness threshold*
$\vec{t}$	*Write threshold* vector

Since we can determine the optimal $W_{partial}$ given $N_{partial}$, our task is to find $N_{partial}$ and N_{final} so that C_{total} is minimized. There is a tradeoff between $N_{partial}$ and N_{final}. If more pages are written to PCM during partial checkpointing ($N_{partial}$ is larger), N_{final} tends to be smaller. On the other hand, some pages may be written to PCM for multiple times in one checkpointing interval. Thus, we should determine a suitable coldness threshold to ensure the effectiveness of partial checkpointing. Given a coldness threshold T_C, we develop the algorithm to estimate $N_{partial}$ and N_{final} (described in Section 4.1.1).

To put them all together, the cost model determines the threshold values in Algorithm 2. We iterate all the possible values for T_C, and find the best C_{total}. To reduce the number of iterations, we iterate T_C with a unit of δ cycles (δ is set to be 1% of the checkpointing interval in our experiments). Additionally, in practice, we observe that C_{total} is usually a concave function to T_C. Thus, we can stop the iterations right after reaching the minimum T_C.

Algorithm 2 The workflow of determining suitable threshold values with the cost model

```
1: Initialize curCost = 0, C_total = +∞, I to be the length of the
   checkpointing interval;
2: for T_C = 0, δ, 2δ, ..., I do
3:     According to T_C, determine N_partial and N_final;
       /*Section 4.1.1*/
4:     According to N_partial in Line 3, determine W_partial;
       /*Section 4.1.2*/
5:     Based on the results of Lines 3 and 4, calculate the total
       checkpointing cost to be curCost;
6:     if curCost < C_total then
7:         C_total = curCost;
8:         Update threshold values with the new obtained setting;
9: Return threshold values that result in the smallest C_total;
```

4.1.1 *Estimating $N_{partial}$ and N_{final}*

We now discuss how to estimate $N_{partial}$ and N_{final}, given a coldness threshold T_C. The estimation is based on a history window with length equal to one checkpointing interval. We derive $N_{partial}$ and N_{final} based on the historical memory access statistics. Specifically, the coldness of a page is indicated by the elapsed time since its last write access. We record each page's first write access time, last write access time and the total number of write accesses, denoted as T_{first}, T_{last} and N_{write}, respectively.

We model the problem as a sweeping line on a plane. An example is given in Figure 3. Each page P_i is represented as an interval or a dot $<T_{first}, T_{last}, addr>$ on the plane, where *addr* is the starting address of P_i (such as P_1 through P_4 in Figure 3). Assuming line l at time T_l is sweeping from the plane's right boundary to its left boundary. Each time line l sweeps a distance of δ. The time difference between l and the right boundary is thus viewed as the *coldness threshold* T_C. That is, as line l sweeps to the left, we essentially increase T_C as in Line 2 of Algorithm 2. Depending on a page's access span $T_{span} = T_{last} - T_{first}$ and its N_{write}, the sweeping line l divides all the pages into the following three categories:

- *Category 1:* If P_i's T_{first} is larger than T_l (e.g., P_4), this page is not cold and should be written to PCM only once in final checkpointing.
- *Category 2:* If P_i's T_{last} is smaller than T_l (e.g., P_1), it has been written to PCM in partial checkpointing. To predict the number of writes to PCM, we further compare its T_{span} and N_{write} in two cases: 1) If P_i's N_{write} is larger than $\lceil T_{span}/T_C \rceil$, P_i is frequently written. We will only write it once after its last write access, since P_i will never be cold enough during its T_{span}. 2) Otherwise, P_i will be written to PCM at most N_{write} times under the assumption that each of the time span between two successive write accesses is long enough that P_i has to be written once.
- *Category 3:* For P_i's T_{span} is stabbed by line l (e.g., P_2 and P_3), we apply the same idea as in the second category: 1) If P_i's N_{write} is larger than $\lceil T_{span}/T_C \rceil$, we will only write it once during final checkpointing. 2) Otherwise, P_i will be written at least once. Moreover, it may also be written at most $N_{write} - 1$ times during partial checkpointing.

Given the three categories, we calculate $N_{partial}$ and N_{final} as in Algorithm 3 by counting all the pages in each category.

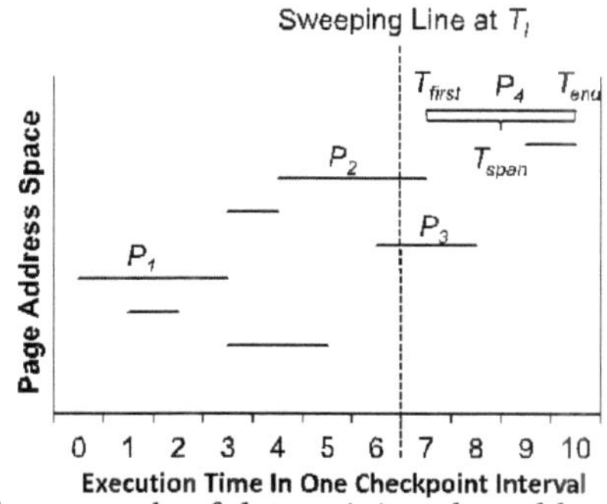

Figure 3: An example of determining the coldness threshold

Algorithm 3 Finding $N_{partial}$ and N_{final} given a coldness threshold T_C at sweeping line T_l

```
Initialize N_partial = 0, N_final = 0;
for each page P_i do
    if T_first > T_l then
        N_final ++;
    else if T_last < T_l then
        if N_write > ⌈T_span/T_C⌉ then
            N_partial ++;
        else
            N_partial += N_write;
    else
        N_final ++;
        if N_write <= ⌈T_span/T_C⌉ then
            N_partial += N_write − 1;
```

The estimation is light-weight. For each page, Mona maintains three metadata (T_{start}, T_{end} and N_{access}) in the form of three integers. They are kept in the page-header, which requires no hardware cost. The maintenance can be piggy-backed into the page-header update process of the virtual-memory system of the operating system. We adopt a similar approach proposed by Zhou et al. [38]. After each DRAM write operation, we update the coldness information. Noted that this update cost is very small, as we only need to update one piece of information.

4.1.2 *Estimating* $W_{partial}$

After getting $N_{partial}$ and N_{final}, we now estimate the average cost of a PCM write ($W_{partial}$) during partial checkpointing. Recall that, during partial checkpointing, we take advantage of idle periods to perform PCM writes. Thus, the actual cost of a PCM write on the application execution is affected by the length of an idle period. If the idle period is too short, the PCM write can cause significant penalty, because the PCM write is much slower than the DRAM access. On the other hand, if the idle period is lengthy, there are opportunities of performing multiple PCM writes. However, it is impossible to predict the length of the current idle period without a priori knowledge. Thus, we estimate the idle period length distribution in a slot. Then, we adopt a simple approach to determine whether to perform a PCM write: if the current idle period is longer than the *write threshold*, we perform the PCM write.

We use a histogram to represent the distribution of idle lengths. Particularly, the histogram is used to hold the frequency counts of the idle period lengths. Suppose the histogram has $T+1$ buckets denoted as $Hist[i]$, $i = 0, 1, ..., T$, where $Hist[i]$ denotes the frequency count for the idle period with a length of i cycles. $Hist[0]$ simply represents the number of memory access cycles. Given a write threshold of t cycles, a memory access delay of $(t + W_{PCM} - i)$ will happen for an idle period of i cycles.

Algorithm 4 Obtain the optimal write threshold vector $\vec{t}$ for an idle period

```
1: Initialize t⃗ = null, curWrite = 0, curCost = 0, minCost = +∞;
2: FindTI(t, curWrite, curCost, minCost, Hist);
Procedure FindTI (t⃗, curWrite, curCost, minCost, Hist)
1: for t = 0, 1, ..., T do
2:     for i = t + 1, 2, ..., t + W_PCM do
3:         curCost+ = (t + W_PCM − i) × Hist[i];
4:         curWrite+ = Hist[i];
5:         if curWrite ≥ N_partial then
6:             break;
7:         else
8:             if i = t + W_PCM then
9:                 for i = t + W_PCM, ..., T do
10:                    Hist'[i]=Hist[i − (t + W_PCM)];
11:                FindTI(t⃗, curWrite, curCost, minCost, Hist');
12:    if curCost < minCost then
13:        minCost = curCost
14:        T_I = t;
15:    else
16:        add T_I to t⃗;
```

To support multiple PCM writes in a lengthy idle period, we use a vector $\vec{t}$ to represent the write threshold values within the same idle period. $\vec{t}[i]$ is the write threshold value for the ith PCM write. Consider the scenario that an idle period starts. We perform the first PCM write if the idle period reaches $\vec{t}[0]$ cycle. After the PCM write finishes, if we are still in the same idle period, we will perform the second PCM write if the idle period lasts for $\vec{t}[1]$ cycles more. Thus, we perform a recursive algorithm to find the vector, as illustrated in Algorithm 4. When the number of PCM writes that have been performed is smaller than $N_{partial}$, we need to find one more level of PCM writes in the relatively long idle periods. We derive this process as a subproblem of the original problem (Line 11), with the updated histogram as input to Procedure *FindTI*.

Previous studies [13, 31, 17] have shown that the idle periods usually demonstrate a "long tail" phenomenon, where there are many short idle periods and very few long idle periods. Thus, as we increase the write threshold value t, the optimal cost first decreases as we can skip the short idle periods, and then increases as we miss those sufficiently long idle periods. We take advantage of this property to reduce the computation for Procedure *FindTI* (Lines 12–16).

4.2 Load Balancing

The cost model guides the configuration parameters for an individual DRAM rank. However, the total page migration time is bounded by the longest migration time among all DRAM ranks. There are two kinds of skews among DRAM ranks. First, in partial checkpointing, a DRAM rank may consist of many dirty pages and too few lengthy idle periods. This causes the imbalance in the cost of partial checkpointing. Second, in final checkpointing, a DRAM rank may consist of a much larger number of dirty pages than other ranks. This causes the imbalance in final checkpointing. In the following, we present algorithms for addressing the cost imbalance caused by these two kinds of skews.

Balancing final checkpointing. In final checkpointing, the set of dirty pages to be written from DRAM to PCM is already known. The goal is to balance the dirty pages among DRAM ranks. Since DRAM accesses are much faster than PCM writes, one simple approach is to perform page migrations among DRAM ranks before starting PCM writes. The page migration moves the dirty pages from the DRAM rank that has more dirty pages (denoted as H) to another DRAM rank with fewer dirty pages (denoted as L). If L does not have sufficient free space for the migrated dirty pages, we move clean pages from L to H. Particularly, we choose a dirty page from H to L and randomly choose a clean page from L to H as appropriate. We further adopt the parallel page migration approach of the previous study [31] to better utilize the memory bandwidth. The migration ends when the dirty pages are even among the DRAM ranks.

Balancing partial checkpointing. We have developed two approaches to balance partial checkpointing: one with page migrations and the other with parameter tuning (namely LB-PM and LB-PT, respectively). With the cost model, Mona is able to compare the estimated cost of these two approaches, and choose the one with the smaller cost.

In LB-PM, we attempt to balance the partial checkpoint overhead among DRAM ranks through page migrations. Here, we only need to balance the partial checkpointing cost, since the final checkpointing cost among ranks will be balanced later. The basic idea is to migrate pages from the rank with the highest cost to the rank with the lowest cost.

The page migration is performed in an iterative manner. In each iteration, we first run the cost model and get the total cost of partial checkpointing for each rank. If the cost is almost even among DRAM ranks (the difference is smaller than 3% in our experiments), we end the page migration process. Otherwise, we adopt a greedy method to choose the rank with the highest cost as $Rank_S$ and the rank with the lowest delay as $Rank_T$. We migrate pages from $Rank_S$ to $Rank_T$. The number of pages migrated at a time is a tuning parameter, which affects the overhead of running the cost model and the evenness of the migration cost among DRAM ranks. We have experimentally evaluated its impact and choose eight pages at a time as the default setting.

The page chosen to be migrated needs careful consideration. To reduce the number of page migrations, we should choose those pages that affect the checkpointing cost more significantly. Thus, we choose the dirty pages with the least write localities in $Rank_S$. In LRU, we choose the page from the least recent accessed position in the LRU queue. If $Rank_T$ does not have sufficient free space, we choose the clean pages with the least read localities in $Rank_T$ and move them to $Rank_S$. Since the selected pages are the least recent accessed ones, we ignore their impact on the histogram of idle periods for simplicity.

Unlike LB-PM resulting in the page migration overhead, LB-PT simply adjusts the *write threshold* values and *coldness threshold* to balance the cost of partial checkpointing. Specifically, through parameter tuning on T_C and $\vec{t}$, we adjust the $C_{partial}$ and C_{final} for each rank so that all ranks have similar $C_{partial}$. Meanwhile, the largest total checkpointing cost of all ranks is minimized. Please note, LB-PT considers the load balancing for final checkpointing as well. LB-PT relies on the intermediate output in the cost model (Algorithm 2) to find the threshold values when adjusting $C_{partial}$ and C_{final}. Particularly, the computation process of the cost model gives different mappings from (T_C, $\vec{t}$) to ($C_{partial}$, C_{final}). Originally, we choose the lowest total cost for each rank. Now, we need to choose T_C and $\vec{t}$ that can balance the cost across different ranks.

We briefly describe the load balancing algorithm of LB-PT as follows. For Rank i ($1 \leq i \leq R_{dram}$), we maintain a sorted queue Q_i to hold all pairs of $C_{partial}$ and C_{final}, in the ascending order of $C_{partial}$. Initially, we pop the head of each Q_i and form a set of possible cost combinations, $Set_{candidate}$. We calculate the total cost among all ranks (denoted as $\mathfrak{C}$) after balancing final checkpointing. After that, we remove one pair of $C_{partial}$ and C_{final} with the highest $C_{partial}$ from $Set_{candidate}$ and add a new pair of $C_{partial}$ and C_{final} from the corresponding queue. We repeat this process until we find the minimal $\mathfrak{C}$. Then, we can find the corresponding thresholds for each rank based on $Set_{candidate}$.

4.3 Other Implementation Details

Mona adds a few new components to the memory controller and operating system. Our design and implementations balance the issues on simplicity and efficiency. For example, the memory requests from page migrations are designed off the critical path of memory accesses, giving the priority to the memory accesses from other logics. In the following, we briefly present the following issues for Mona.

Multi-level checkpointing. We extend Mona to handle multi-level checkpointing in two steps, following the design of previous NVRAM-assisted multi-level checkpoint designs [6, 7]. First, each node performs local checkpointing according to Mona. Second, after several local checkpoint intervals, a global checkpoint is initiated. A new global checkpoint is created from the latest local checkpoints and stored in the parallel file system.

Runtime and storage overhead. The structure complexity and storage overhead of Mona are similar to the previous proposals, e.g., [25, 31]. For example, our design has small DRAM space requirement (less than 2% of the total amount of DRAM), and an acceptable runtime overhead in maintaining the cost model and page access statistics (less than 3% of the total application execution time). For page migrations, only page descriptors and their mapping tables are stored. For the histogram in the cost model, we use the two-array storage method of the previous study [31] to reduce the storage overhead.

Limitations. Compared with existing NVRAM-assisted checkpoint designs, Mona has the following limitations. First, Mona relies on the history of memory accesses for cost estimation. More advanced workload prediction mechanisms are helpful to improve the robustness. Second, Mona has more PCM writes, which decrease PCM's lifetime. Our on-going work is to integrate/adapt the wear-leveling techniques to extend the lifetime of PCM (e.g., [24, 4]). Also, another possible solution is to leverage write consolidation techniques [32] to reduce the number of writes. We leave it as future work. Nevertheless, the predictions [25] for future PCM cells suggest significant endurance improvement (from 10^9 in 2012 to 10^{15} writes by 2022).

5. EVALUATION

5.1 Experiment Setup

We have developed a cycle-accurate simulator based on PTLSim v3.0 simulator [36]. Our simulator models all relevant aspects of the OS, memory controller, DRAM and PCM devices. In the simulator, the DRAM can be configured with different capacities (64GB to 512GB). For

Table 2: Mixed workload: memory footprint (FP), memory accesses statistics per 5×10^8 cycles ($Mean$ and $\frac{Stdev}{Mean}$).

Name	FP (MB)	$Mean$ (10^6)	$\frac{Stdev}{Mean}$	Applications
M1	661	0.6	1.02	gromacs, gobmk, hmmer, bzip
M2	1477	1.7	1.11	bzip, soplex, sjeng, cactusADM
M3	626	2.9	0.59	soplex, sjeng, gcc, zeusmp

a fair comparison, we adopt the configurations from the previous study [6]. We simulate multiple CPUs, each running at 2.667 GHz, L1 I/D cache of 48 KB each and L2/L3 shared cache 256KB/4MB. The cache line and page size are set at 64B and 4KB, respectively. We use the DDR3-1333 architecture from Micron's configuration[1]. By default, we assume a 16-rank hybrid memory system, with 128GB DRAM in 8 homogeneous ranks and with 256GB PCM in another 8 homogeneous ranks. The PCM can be configured with different PCM write delays. By default, we assume the write delay of PCM is 10 times of that of DRAM. The average latencies of DRAM and PCM are 100 and 1000 cycles, respectively.

Workloads. Since it is hard to mimic the memory trace of a real large-scale parallel processing system, we use both micro and macro benchmarks for performance evaluation. Micro benchmarks are used to perform detailed evaluation on using Mona as a local checkpoint design of each machine in a large-scale system. In contrast, macro benchmarks are used to assess multi-level checkpointing in a parallel processing system. Particularly, we execute the NAS Parallel Benchmark (NPB) [29] on our local cluster.

Micro benchmark. The micro benchmark include real workloads as well as synthetic workloads on a single machine. For real workloads, we selected 12 applications from SPEC 2006. These applications have widely different memory footprints and localities. To evaluate our techniques under the context of multi-core CPUs, we study 3 mixed workloads (denoted by M1, M2, and M3), each with four different applications (see Table 2) as one batch. Each mixed workload is generated by starting the four applications at the same time as one batch. In order to scale the memory footprint and accesses, we run 50 batches of each workload simultaneously in the system. The memory access statistics of these workloads, including the average number of memory accesses ($Mean$) and the standard deviation ($\frac{Stdev}{Mean}$) per 5×10^8 cycles, is shown in Table 2. We report the results of three particular applications, i.e., cactusADM, gcc, and gemsFDTD (denoted by S1, S2, and S3, respectively). Also, we run 50 instances each of the workload for scaling the memory footprint and memory accesses. We set the number of CPU cores according to the number of applications.

Synthetic workloads allow us to extensively evaluate different memory access patterns. For synthetic workloads, we assume that the arrival of page accesses follows a Poisson distribution, and thus the idle periods follow an exponential distribution with an expected value σ. The default value of σ is set at 2,000 cycles. We assume that the accesses over different pages follow a Zipf distribution with 1.5 as the skewness parameter. The read-write ratio is set at 3:1.

For each micro benchmark workload, we measure the performance after system warm-up (i.e., DRAM is filled up). For Mona, the initial *coldness threshold* and *write threshold* are derived based on the system statistics collected during the warm-up period. Each measurement lasts for 15×10^9 cycles in the original PTLSim simulation, which represents a stable and sufficiently long execution behavior [31]. The default checkpointing interval is 1×10^9 cycles, and the prediction slot is 2×10^8 cycles. Such fine-grained checkpointing intervals are specifically designed for the rigid requirement of critical jobs. We observed similar performance improvement when varying the interval and slot in a reasonable domain.

[1]http://download.micron.com/pdf/datasheets/dram/ddr3/1Gb DDR3 SDRAM.pdf

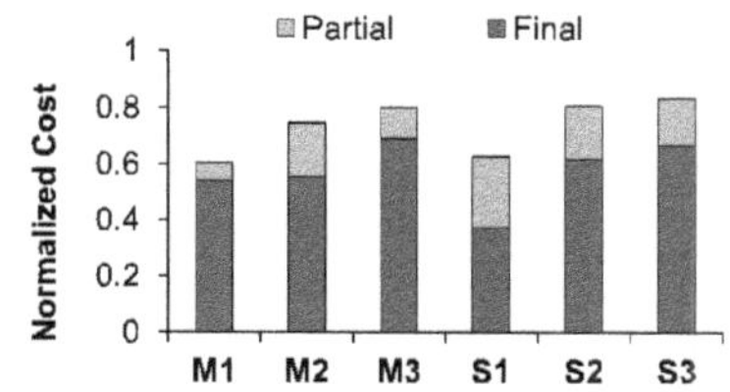

Figure 4: Performance of real workloads

Marco benchmark. We run NPB [29] in a local cluster. NPB includes eight benchmark programs derived from computational fluid dynamics (CFD) applications. We run both class B and class C for each of the NPB programs. The number of processes is 64 by default. We focus on the results in class C. The cluster has 16 nodes, each with CentOS 5.0, two Intel Xeon E5430 4-core processors and 24GB DRAM. They are interconnected via QDR InfiniBand network. NFS is used as the shared file system. The MPI library is Intel MPI 4.0.1. We adopt a hybrid approach of simulation/execution: the local checkpointing process is simulated by our simulator, and the other operations like MPI communications and global checkpointing are performed on the real environments. We focus on total checkpoint overhead by summing all local checkpoint overhead from each simulator.

Comparisons. We compare the state-of-the-art NVRAM-assisted checkpointing method [6, 7] (denoted as **baseline**) with Mona. In the baseline method, the system is suspended and then incremental checkpointing is performed. Its cost is the elapsed time in writing all dirty pages from memory ranks to PCM. To minimize the elapsed time in concurrent writing, like Mona, we also perform page migrations so as to even out the write workloads across different ranks. For clarity of presentation, we normalize the partial and final checkpointing cost of Mona to the total cost of the baseline method.

5.2 Overall Micro Benchmark Results

We first present the overall comparison results in Figure 4, where the cost of Mona is normalized by that of the baseline checkpointing method. For real workloads, Mona achieves 16% to 39% of performance improvement against the baseline method on the overall checkpointing cost. Mona can adjust the costs between partial and final checkpointings for different workloads. In Figure 5, we plot the results of synthetic workloads. We vary the PCM write delay per page with 500, 1000 (default), and 2000 cycles (denoted as PCM1, PCM2, and PCM3, respectively). We also vary the expected idle period with 1000, 2000 (default), and 4000 cycles (denoted as Idle1, Idle2, and Idle3, respectively). Mona achieves an improvement of up to 65% over the baseline method. The improvement is relatively higher for short PCM write delays and long idle periods.

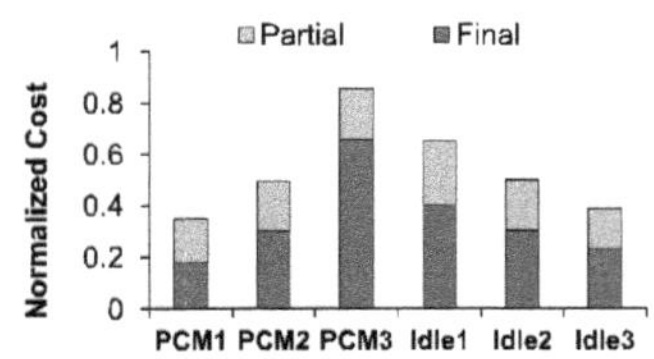

Figure 5: Performance of synthetic workloads

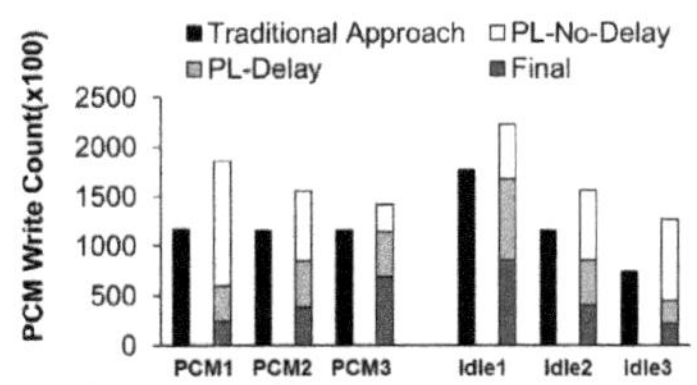

Figure 6: Number of PCM writes in synthetic workloads

To further understand the improvement, we plot the actual number of PCM writes of the synthetic workloads in Figure 6. For Mona, we show the counts for three kinds of PCM writes: PCM writes in final checkpointing, PCM writes with and without causing a delay during partial checkpointing. Mona has a large portion of PCM writes in partial checkpointing that cause no penalty under a short PCM write delay or a long idle period. That suggests our cost model is able to adapt to the system parameters and reduce the cost of partial checkpointing. Although Mona performs more partial checkpointing, the overall cost still becomes less. This phenomenon can also be observed by comparing the cost ratio of partial checkpointing to total checkpointing. Under the shortest PCM write delay, the ratio of partial checkpointing increases to about 47% of the total cost. On average, Mona has 28% more PCM writes than the baseline approach on all workloads.

To better understand the performance of Mona, in the following sections, we show more detailed results with the synthetic workloads (PCM2 by default).

5.3 Cost Model Evaluation

To reveal the effectiveness of our cost model, we present the prediction results for a memory rank during one checkpointing interval. In Figure 7, we plot the predicted write counts of partial and final checkpointings for DRAM Rank 1, under different coldness thresholds. We observe similar results on other DRAM ranks. With a larger threshold, more pages are written during final checkpointing, since they are not "cold" enough to be written to PCM during partial checkpointing. Thus, the dominant portion of the total cost changes from partial checkpointing to final checkpointing. As a result, the total cost decreases at first, and then

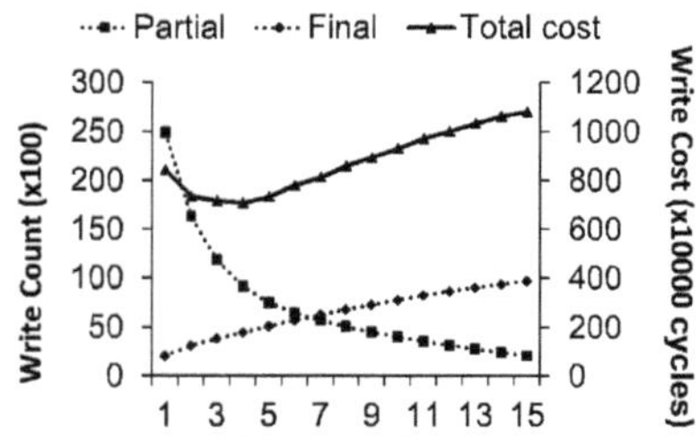

Figure 7: Number of PCM writes and cost estimation (on PCM2)

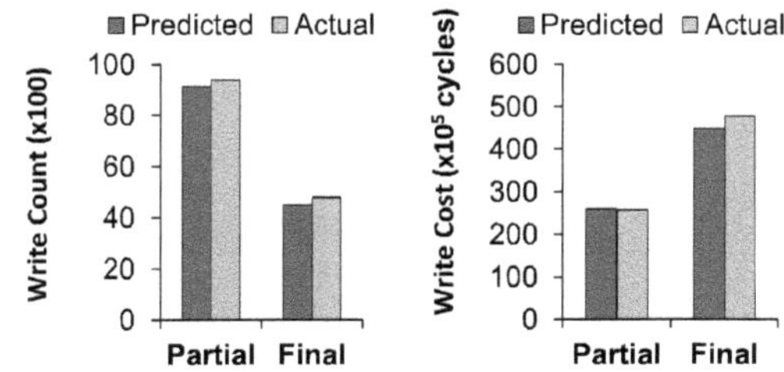

(a) Write counts (b) Write costs

Figure 8: Comparison between estimation and actual

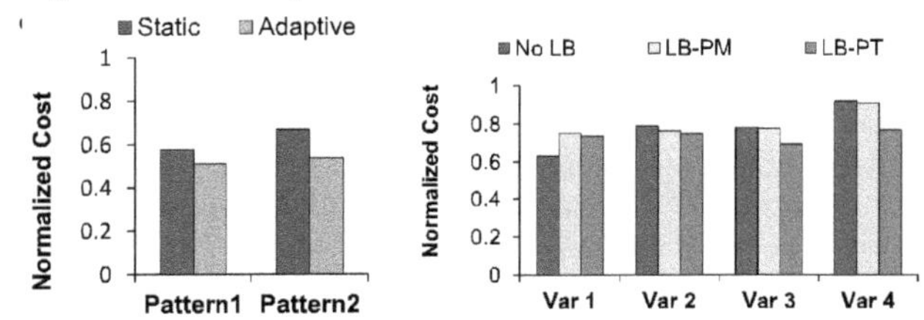

(a) (b)

Figure 9: Individual techniques: a) adaptive cost estimation, b) load-balancing methods.

increases as the threshold continues to enlarge. Through this cost model, we can find the minimal cost and its corresponding *coldness threshold* and *write threshold*.

Figure 8 validates our prediction by comparing the predicted and the actual write counts and costs. The error is only at most 6% for both predictions. We observed similar results on other DRAM ranks. This implies that our model can guide the checkpointing process with an accurately predicted cost.

5.4 Impacts of Individual Techniques

Adaptive Cost Estimation. We now compare the results between dynamic and static predictions in Figure 9a. For the dynamic method, we keep a sliding window and tune the system parameters at every slot. For the static method, we only use the initial predicted thresholds. We show the results on two dynamic page access patterns: (Pattern 1) $w_i = 0.95w_0 \cdot (i \bmod 2) + w_0 \cdot ((i+1) \bmod 2)$ and (Pattern 2) $w_i = w_0(1 + i\%)$, where w_i is the write ratio within the $(i+1)$-th checkpoint, and w_0 is the default setting (0.25). Pattern 1 simulates the case where the workload periodically changes. Pattern 2 simulates the case where write requests gradually become dominant in the workload. As shown in Figure 9a, our adaptive prediction achieves 6% to 13% better performance than the static method. A higher improvement is observed for Pattern 2, because there are more write requests in Pattern 2, incurring more performance penalty in the static cost model.

Load balancing methods. To investigate the performance advantage of load balancing, we compare three approaches in Figure 9b: Mona without load balancing, the page-migration method, and the parameter-tuning method. We set the variations of mean idle period and read-write ratio between different ranks as 200 and 0.1 (Var1), 400 and 0.2 (Var2), 600 and 0.3 (Var3), to 800 and 0.4 (Var4). Under small variations, both migration methods do not perform well, because the migration cost or the parameter tuning cost may exceed the benefits on the overall checkpointing process. Under large variations, both methods outperform the method without any load balancing. Specifically, the parameter-tuning method achieves the best result and out-

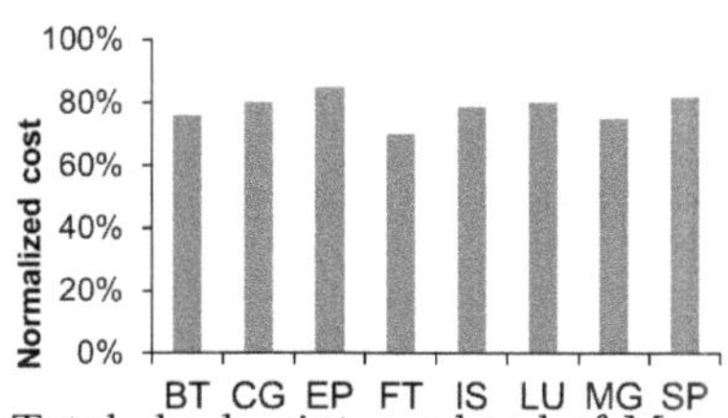

Figure 10: Total checkpoint overhead of Mona (normalized to the baseline approach). Local and global checkpointing intervals are 40 and 400 seconds, respectively.

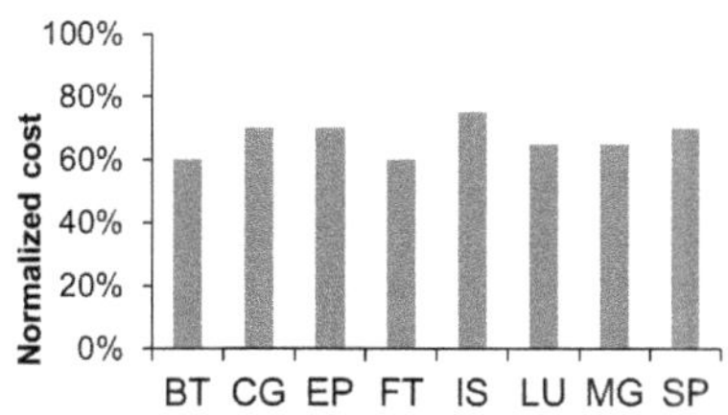

Figure 11: Total checkpoint overhead of Mona (normalized to the baseline approach). Local and global checkpointing intervals are 1 and 10 seconds, respectively.

performs the page-migration method by about 10% with the largest variation. This is because the page-migration method involves a relatively high migration overhead. For the parameter-tuning method, the overhead of not choosing the optimal settings for individual ranks is worthy to achieve a better overall performance. In experiments, Mona chooses the best policy to be the one with the smallest estimated cost (Section 4.2).

5.5 Macro Benchmark Results

We now present the macro benchmark results on multi-level checkpointing. Overall, we have observed that Mona significantly improves the performance of multi-level checkpointing, thanks to the efficiency in the local checkpointing of each machine. More frequent checkpoints increase system availability, but degrades the baseline approach significantly.

Figure 10 reports the normalized total checkpoint overhead on coarse-grained checkpointing when the local and global checkpointing intervals are 40 and 400 seconds, respectively. The average checkpoint overhead reduction of Mona is 22% over the baseline approach. The performance improvement of Mona is slightly smaller for coarse-grained checkpointing than those reported in the paper, since some pages need to be written for multiple times.

Figure 11 shows the comparison with fine-grained checkpointing when the local and global checkpointing intervals are 1 and 10 seconds, respectively. The average checkpoint overhead reduction of Mona is 33% over the baseline approach. The improvement is much more significant than those observed in Figure 10. Mona achieves a much lower overhead while also delivering fine-grained checkpointing for critical jobs. The findings with the hybrid local/global checkpointing algorithm are consistent with the results in a single node.

5.6 Sensitivity Studies

We present our sensitivity studies in Figure 12. First, we vary the DRAM size to be 64GB, 128GB (default), 256GB, and 512GB. A higher performance improvement is observed as the DRAM size increases. Second, we vary the number of DRAM ranks to be 2, 4 and 8 (default), and keep the number

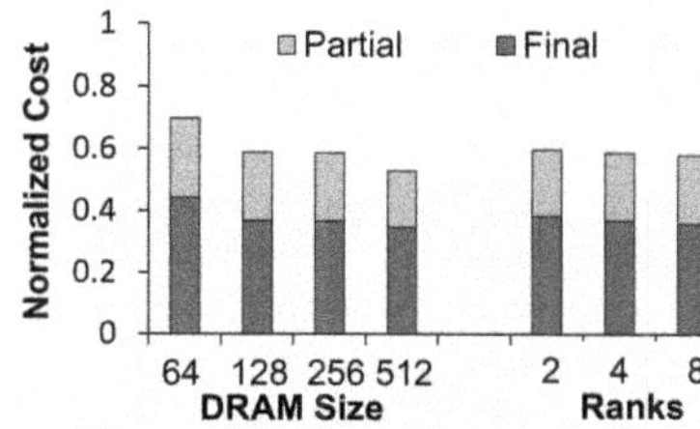

Figure 12: Sensitivity studies

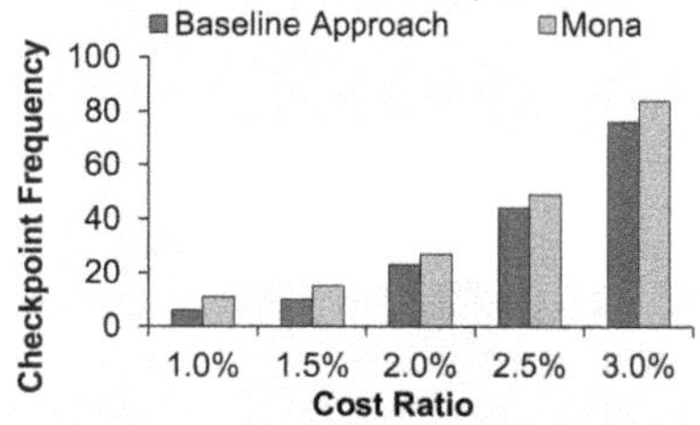

Figure 13: Results on optimizing checkpoint interval

of DRAM ranks equal to the number of PCM ranks. The performance improvement slightly improves for more ranks in the memory system. We also vary the read ratio from 0.6 to 0.9, and have observed similar performance improvement.

5.7 Optimizing Checkpointing Interval

Finally, we present the results when Mona's optimization goal is set to minimize the checkpoint interval. This goal also means minimizing the restart time (i.e., the total time of loading the lastest checkpoint and re-execution till the point of failure). We vary the ratio of total allowed cost budget from 1% to 3% to the application execution time and compare the total checkpointing count. As shown in Figure 13, Mona achieves 10% to 80% of improvement on the checkpoint frequency. The improvement generally decreases as the allowed cost ratio increases. This is because as the interval becomes smaller, Mona tends to behave like the baseline method. In the extreme case where the allowed cost ratio is very large, Mona and the baseline method will have the same checkpointing cost, which writes out every page right after it becomes dirty.

6. RELATED WORK

There have been decades of research on checkpointing-restart mechanisms. More related works can be found in a recent survey [9]. Incremental checkpointing [1] can reduce the checkpoint file size, and speculative checkpointing [18] can reduce the downtime. Mona adopts page-level incremental checkpointing, and the partial checkpointing of Mona is inspired by speculative checkpointing. Differently, our checkpointing leverages idle period distributions, and relies on a cost model to minimize the interference to the application execution.

Similar to our study, Dong et al. [6] proposed a hybrid checkpoint model by investigating different architectural design options for PCM-based checkpointing systems. Zhou et al. [37] used writeback information to partition bandwidth for hybrid memory. Essen et al. [30] developed PerMA NVRAM simulator to study different roles of NVRAM in data-intensive architectures. Li et al. [16] studied the opportunities of NVRAM for extreme-scale scientifc applications. Our study further enables the real-time checkpointing for extreme-scale applications. Mona addresses the limitation of the previous work [6, 7, 14] with two novel techniques. First, Mona has a model-guided dynamic partial checkpointing during application execution, which can accurately write back the more valuable pages. Second, Mona develops finer-grained load balancing mechanisms among memory ranks.

NVRAM has been used for checkpointing in other scenarios. UniFI [26] aims at energy saving and fault tolerance by exploiting NVRAM in both CPU caches and main memory. Yoon et at. [35] proposed a new architecture for Multilevel-cell phase change memory to cope with the problem of resistance drift. However, this work focus on the hardware design, instead of new checkpoint system. In [21], Oikawa proposed a checkpointing mechanism for operating system kernel rejuvenation. In our study, we target at a hybrid memory system, since the low access latency of PCM make it infeasible to independently serve as the main memory.

As for multi-level checkpointing, Moody et al. [19] performed extensive modeling and evaluations and showed that the benefits of multi-level checkpointing increase as the system size increases. Sato et al. [27] studied a non-blocking checkpoint system to reduce the I/O contention on PFS. This paper demonstrates that a novel NVRAM-assisted design can further improve multi-level checkpointing.

7. CONCLUSION

Real-time in-memory checkpointing is essential for reliable large-scale parallel processing systems. This paper optimizes the runtime overhead of in-memory checkpointing in a hybrid memory system with PCM and DRAM. It embraces dynamic partial checkpointing during application execution with optimizations on reducing the interference and load balancing among ranks to reduce the checkpoint overhead. Those decisions are guided by a cost model. We conduct simulation-based experiments to evaluate the performance of Mona under various workloads. Compared to the state-of-the-art checkpointing method, Mona reduces the total checkpointing cost by up to 65% under the goal of minimizing the checkpointing cost.

8. ACKNOWLEDGMENTS

Shen's work was done when he was a visiting student at NTU Singapore. This work is supported by a MoE AcRF Tier 2 grant (MOE2012-T2-1-126) in Singapore.

9. REFERENCES

[1] S. Agarwal and et al. Adaptive incremental checkpointing for massively parallel systems. In *ICS*, 2004.

[2] K. Bailey and et al. Operating system implications of fast, cheap, non-volatile memory. In *HotOS*, 2011.

[3] S. Borkar. Designing reliable systems from unreliable components: The challenges of transistor variability and degradation. *IEEE Micro*, 2005.

[4] C.-H. Chen and et al. Age-based PCM wear leveling with nearly zero search cost. In *DAC*, 2012.

[5] J. Condit and et al. Better I/O through byte-addressable, persistent memory. In *SOSP*, 2009.

[6] X. Dong and et al. Leveraging 3D PCRAM technologies to reduce checkpoint overhead for future exascale systems. In *SC*, 2009.

[7] X. Dong and et al. Hybrid checkpointing using emerging nonvolatile memories for future exascale systems. *ACM TACO*, 2011.

[8] Y. Du and et al. Delta-compressed caching for overcoming the write bandwidth limitation of hybrid main memory. *ACM TACO*, 2013.

[9] I. Egwutuoha and et al. A survey of fault tolerance mechanisms and checkpoint/restart implementations for high performance computing systems. *The Journal of Supercomputing*, 2013.

[10] E. N. Elnozahy and et al. Checkpointing for peta-scale systems: A look into the future of practical rollback-recovery. *IEEE TDSC*, 2004.

[11] E. N. M. Elnozahy and et al. A survey of rollback-recovery protocols in message-passing systems. *ACM Comput. Surv.*, 2002.

[12] S. Gao and et al. Pcmlogging: Reducing transaction logging overhead with pcm. CIKM, 2011.

[13] H. Huang, K. G. Shin, C. Lefurgy, and T. Keller. Improving energy efficiency by making dram less randomly accessed. In *ISLPED*, 2005.

[14] S. Kannan and et al. Optimizing checkpoints using nvm as virtual memory. In *IPDPS*, 2013.

[15] B. C. Lee and et al. Phase-change technology and the future of main memory. *IEEE Micro*, 2010.

[16] D. Li and et al. Identifying opportunities for byte-addressable non-volatile memory in extreme-scale scientific applications. In *IPDPS*, 2012.

[17] K. T. Malladi and et al. Towards energy-proportional datacenter memory with mobile dram. In *ISCA*, 2012.

[18] S. Matsuoka and et al. Speculative checkpointing: Exploiting temporal affinity of memory operations. In *HPC Asia*, 2009.

[19] A. Moody and et al. Design, modeling, and evaluation of a scalable multi-level checkpointing system. In *SC*, 2010.

[20] D. Narayanan and O. Hodson. Whole-system persistence with non-volatile memories. In *ASPLOS*, 2012.

[21] S. Oikawa. Independent kernel/process checkpointing on non-volatile main memory for quick kernel rejuvenation. In *ARCS*, 2014.

[22] F. Petrini. Scaling to thousands of processors with buffered coscheduling. In *Scaling to New Heights Workshop*, 2002.

[23] J. S. Plank and et al. Libckpt: Transparent checkpointing under Unix. In *Usenix Winter Technical Conference*, 1995.

[24] M. K. Qureshi and et al. Enhancing lifetime and security of PCM-based main memory with start-gap wear leveling. In *MICRO*, 2009.

[25] L. E. Ramos and et al. Page placement in hybrid memory systems. In *ICS*, 2011.

[26] S. Sardashti and et al. UniFI: leveraging non-volatile memories for a unified fault tolerance and idle power management technique. In *ICS*, 2012.

[27] K. Sato and et al. Design and modeling of a non-blocking checkpointing system. In *SC*, 2012.

[28] B. Schroeder and et al. Dram errors in the wild: a large-scale field study. In *SIGMETRICS*, 2009.

[29] The NAS Parallel Benchmarks. http://www.nas.nasa.gov/resources/software/npb.html, 2013.

[30] B. Van Essen and et al. On the role of nvram in data-intensive architectures: An evaluation. In *IPDPS*, 2012.

[31] D. Wu and et al. RAMZzz: rank-aware dram power management with dynamic migrations and demotions. In *SC*, 2012.

[32] F. Xia and et al. Dwc: Dynamic write consolidation for phase change memory systems. In *ICS*, 2014.

[33] J. Xie and et al. 3D memory stacking for fast checkpointing/restore applications. In *IEEE 3DIC*, 2010.

[34] J. Yang and et al. Nv-tree: Reducing consistency cost for nvm-based single level systems. USENIX FAST, 2015.

[35] D. H. Yoon and et al. Practical nonvolatile multilevel-cell phase change memory. SC, 2013.

[36] M. T. Yourst. PTLsim: A cycle accurate full system x86-64 microarchitectural simulator. In *ISPASS*, 2007.

[37] M. Zhou and et al. Writeback-aware bandwidth partitioning for multi-core systems with pcm. In *PACT*, 2013.

[38] P. Zhou and et al. Dynamic tracking of page miss ratio curve for memory management. In *ASPLOS XI*, 2004.

Leveraging Silicon-Photonic NoC for Designing Scalable GPUs

Amir Kavyan Ziabari[†], José L. Abellán [‡], Rafael Ubal[†], Chao Chen[§]
Ajay Joshi[♮], David Kaeli[†]

[†]Electrical and Computer Engineering Dept.
Northeastern University
{aziabari,ubal,kaeli}@ece.neu.edu

[‡]Computer Science Dept.
Universidad Católica San Antonio de Murcia
jlabellan@ucam.edu

[§]Digital Networking Group Dept.
Freescale Semiconductor, Inc.
chen9810@gmail.com

[♮]Electrical and Computer Engineering Dept.
Boston University
joshi@bu.edu

ABSTRACT

Silicon-photonic link technology promises to satisfy the growing need for high bandwidth, low-latency and energy-efficient network-on-chip (NoC) architectures. While silicon-photonic NoC designs have been extensively studied for future many-core systems, their use in massively-threaded GPUs has received little attention to date. In this paper, we first analyze an electrical NoC which connects different cache levels (L1 to L2) in a contemporary GPU memory hierarchy. Evaluating workloads from the AMD SDK run on the Multi2sim GPU simulator finds that, apart from limits in memory bandwidth, an electrical NoC can significantly hamper performance and impede scalability, especially as the number of compute units grows in future GPU systems.

To address this issue, we advocate using silicon-photonic link technology for on-chip communication in GPUs, and we present the first GPU-specific analysis of a cost-effective hybrid photonic crossbar NoC. Our baseline is based on an AMD Southern Islands GPU with 32 compute units (CUs) and we compare this design to our proposed hybrid silicon-photonic NoC. Our proposed photonic hybrid NoC increases performance by up to 6× (2.7× on average) and reduces the energy-delay^2 product (ED^{2}P) by up to 99% (79% on average) as compared to conventional electrical crossbars. For future GPU systems, we study an electrical 2D-mesh topology since it scales better than an electrical crossbar. For a 128-CU GPU, the proposed hybrid silicon-photonic NoC can improve performance by up to 1.9× (43% on average) and achieve up to 62% reduction in ED^{2}P (3% on average) in comparison to mesh design with best performance.

ICS'15, June 8–11, 2015, Newport Beach, CA, USA.

http://dx.doi.org/10.1145/2751205.2751229 .

Categories and Subject Descriptors

B.4.3 [**Input/Output and Data Communications**]: Interconnections (subsystems)—*fiber optics, physical structures, topology*; C.1.2 [**Processor Architectures**]: Multiple Data Stream Architectures—*Single-Instruction Stream, Multiple-Data Processors (SIMD)*

Keywords

Network-on-Chip, Photonics Technology, GPUs

1. INTRODUCTION

A little over a decade ago, GPUs were fixed-function processors built around a pipeline that was dedicated to rendering 3-D graphics. In the past decade, as the potential for GPUs to provide massive compute parallelism became apparent, the software community developed programming environments to leverage these massively-parallel architectures. Vendors facilitated this move toward massive parallelism by incorporating programmable graphics pipelines. Parallel programming frameworks such as OpenCL [12] were introduced, and tools were developed to explore GPU architectures. NVIDIA and AMD, two of the leading graphics vendors today, tailor their GPU designs for general purpose high-performance computing by providing higher compute throughput and memory bandwidth [3, 4]. Contemporary GPUs are composed of tens of compute units (CUs). CUs are composed of separate scalar and vector pipelines designed to execute a massive number of concurrent threads (e.g., 2048 threads on the AMD Radeon HD 7970) in a single instruction, multiple data (SIMD) fashion [20].

Multi-threaded applications running on multi-core CPUs exhibit coherence traffic and data sharing which leads to significant L1-to-L1 traffic (between cores) on the interconnection network. GPU applications, on the other hand, are executed as thread blocks (workgroups) on multiple compute units. There is limited communication between different workgroups. Since GPU applications generally exhibit little L1 temporal locality [9], the communication between the L1 and L2 caches becomes the main source of traffic on the GPU's on-chip interconnection network. As the number

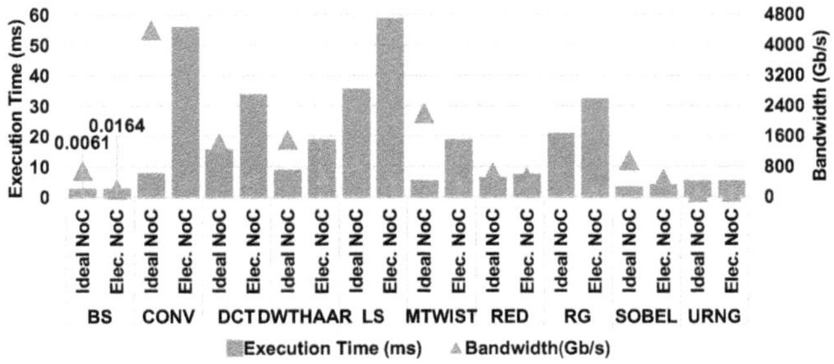

Figure 1: Potential improvements for various workloads running on a 32-CU GPU, with an ideal crossbar NoC against an electrical NoC.

of CUs increases in each future generation of GPU systems, latency in the on-chip interconnection network becomes a major performance bottleneck on the GPU [6].

To evaluate the potential benefits of employing a low-latency Network-on-Chip (NoC) for GPUs, we evaluate a 32-compute unit GPU system (see a more detailed description in Section 3). We compare a system with an electrical Multi-Write-Single-Read crossbar network against a system deploying an ideal NoC, with a fixed 3-cycle latency between source and destination nodes. To evaluate the GPU system performance when using these NoCs, we utilize applications from the AMD Accelerated Parallel Processing (APP) Software Development Kit (SDK) [1]. The ideal NoC offers up to 90% (51% on average) reduction in execution time, and up to 10.3× (3.38× on average) higher bandwidth (see Figure 1). These results clearly motivate the need to explore novel link technologies and architectures to design low-latency high-bandwidth NoCs that can significantly improve performance in current and future GPUs.

Silicon-photonic link technology has been proposed as a potential replacement for electrical link technology for the design of NoC architectures for future manycore systems [10, 16, 17, 27, 34]. Silicon-photonic links have the potential to provide significantly lower latency and an order of magnitude higher bandwidth density for global communication in comparison to electrical links. We take advantage of photonic link technology in designing a NoC for GPU systems.

The main contributions of the paper are as follows:

- We explore the design of Multiple-Write, Single-Read (MWSR), and Single-Write, Multiple-Read (SWMR) electrical and photonic crossbar NoCs for communication between L1 and L2 of a GPU with 32 CUs.
- We propose the design of a GPU-specific hybrid NoC with reduced channel count based on the traffic patterns observed in the communications between L1 and L2 cache units in the GPU systems. We compare the electrical and silicon-photonic implementations of this hybrid NoC architecture in a GPU with 32 CUs running standard GPU benchmarks.
- We evaluate the scalability of a silicon-photonic NoC on a larger GPU system with 128 CUs, comparing our proposed hybrid photonic crossbar against a competitive electrical 2D-mesh NoC.

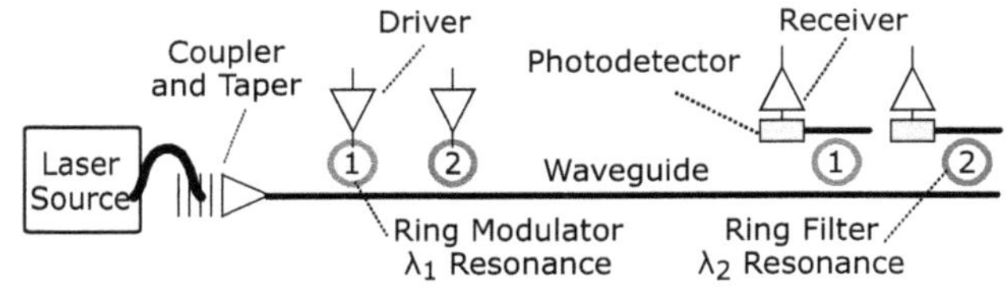

Figure 2: Photonic Link Components – Two point-to-point photonic links implemented with Wavelength-Devision Multiplexing (WDM).

2. SILICON-PHOTONIC TECHNOLOGY

Figure 2 shows a generic silicon-photonic channel with two links multiplexed onto the same waveguide. These two silicon-photonic links are powered using a laser source. The output of the laser source is coupled into the planar waveguides using vertical grating couplers. Each light wave is modulated by the respective ring modulator that is controlled by a modulator driver. During this modulation step, the data is converted from the electrical domain to the photonic domain. The modulated light waves propagate along the waveguide and can pass through zero or more ring filters. On the receiver side, the ring filter whose resonant wavelength matches with the wavelength of the light wave "drops" the light wave onto a photodetector. The resulting photodetector current is sensed by an electrical receiver. At this stage, data is converted back into the electrical domain from the photonic domain.

Each Electrical-to-Optical (E/O) and Optical-to-Electrical (O/E) conversion stages introduce a 1-cycle latency. The time-of-flight for the data on the photonic link is 1 cycle. The serialization latency, on the other hand, depends on the bandwidth of the photonic link. Contention and queuing delays are other contributing factors to the overall latency of transmissions. We consider all these forms of latency in our simulation framework.

For our silicon-photonic NoCs, we consider monolithically-integrated links [13,25,26]. Monolithic integration of silicon-photonic links use the existing layers in the process technology to design photonic devices. Working prototypes of links designed using monolithic integration have been presented in previous work [13,25,26]. We consider a next-generation link design [16] that uses double-ring filters with a 4 THz free-spectral range. For our analysis we project the E-O-E conversion cost, thermal tuning, and photonic device losses for this next generation link using the measurements results in previous works [13,25,26]. This design supports up to 128 wavelengths (λ) modulated at 10 Gbps on each waveguide (64λ in each direction, which are interleaved to alleviate filter roll-off requirements and crosstalk). A non-linearity limit of 30 mW at 1 dB loss is assumed for the waveguides. The waveguides are single mode and have a pitch of 4 μm to minimize the crosstalk between neighboring waveguides. The modulator ring and filter ring diameters are ~10 μm (further details in Tables 4 and 5). The silicon-photonic links are driven by an off-chip laser source.

3. TARGET GPU SYSTEMS

3.1 32-CU GPU Architecture

To explore the NoC design in the memory hierarchy of a GPU, we leverage an existing simulation model of a high

Table 1: **AMD Radeon HD 7970 GPU specification.**

Processor Cores		Memory System	
Fabrication process	28nm	Size of L1 Vector Cache	16KB
Clock Frequency	925	Size of L1 Scalar Cache	16KB
Compute Units	32	L2 Caches/Mem. Cntrls.	6B
MSHR per Compute Unit	16	Block Size	64B
SIMD Width	16	Size of L2 Cache	128KB
Threads per Core	256	Memory Page Size	4KB
Wavefront Size	64	LDS Size	64KB

performance GPU. We target an AMD Radeon HD 7970, a state-of-the-art GPU of AMD's Southern Islands family. CUs are clocked at 925 MHz, are manufactured in a 28 nm CMOS technology node, and are tailored for general purpose workloads [3]. The die size for this GPU is reported to be 352 mm^2 and its maximum power draw is 250 watts [21].

The layout of the AMD Radeon HD 7970 GPU chip is shown in Figure 3a [22]. Table 1 outlines the details of the different GPU components. The Radeon HD 7970 has 32 CUs. Each CU has a shared front-end and multiple execution units, where instructions are classified in computational categories and scheduled appropriately to a special-purpose execution units. Four execution units are SIMD, formed of 16 SIMD lanes, which run integer and floating-point operations in parallel.

Each CU is equipped with a L1 vector data cache unit (vL1), known as a vector cache, which provides the data for vector-memory operations. The vector cache is 16KB and 4-way set associative, with a 64B line size. The vector cache is coherent with the L2 and other cache units in the GPU system. The vector cache has a write-through, write-allocate design. Scalar operations (i.e., computations shared by all threads running as one SIMD unit) use a dedicated set of L1 scalar data cache units (sL1s), known as scalar caches, shared by 4 CUs. The scalar cache units are also connected to L2 cache units through the NoC [3].

The L2 cache in the Southern Islands architecture is physically partitioned into banks that are coupled with separate memory controllers. Similar to the L2 cache units, memory controllers are partitioned into different memory address spaces. Each L2 cache unit is associated with only one memory controller. Sequential 4KB memory pages are distributed across L2 banks, which reduces the load on any single memory controller while maximizing spatial locality [3].

Two types of messages are transmitted between L1 and L2 cache units in the memory hierarchy. The first type is an 8 bytes control message. Cache requests such as reads, writes, and invalidations generate and transmit control messages. These control messages contain information on the destination cache unit. The second type of the message is a cache line which has a size of 64 bytes. Since cache line does not contain any information on type of requests or the unit which should receive the cache-line, it should always follow a control message that contains this information.

3.2 128-CU GPU Architecture

We consider a forward-looking GPU design that uses the 32-CU Radeon HD 7970 GPU as a building block, and increases the number of CUs. In this new architecture, we quadruple the number of CUs to 128 while keeping the same CU design as in the 32-CU GPU for individual CUs. The 128-CU GPU also quadruples the number of memory components in the HD 7970 GPU chip: 128 L1 vector caches, 32 L1 scalar caches, and 24 shared L2 Caches. We assume that the 128-CU GPU is designed using 14 nm CMOS technology, which results in a reasonable floorplan area of 402.2 mm^2.

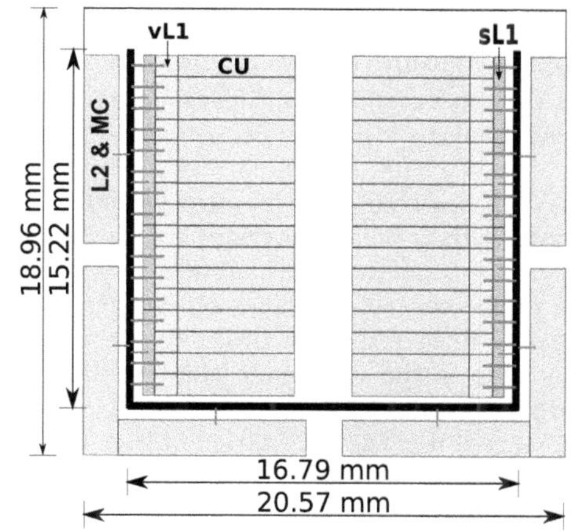

(a) Crossbar for the 32-CU GPU (28 nm).

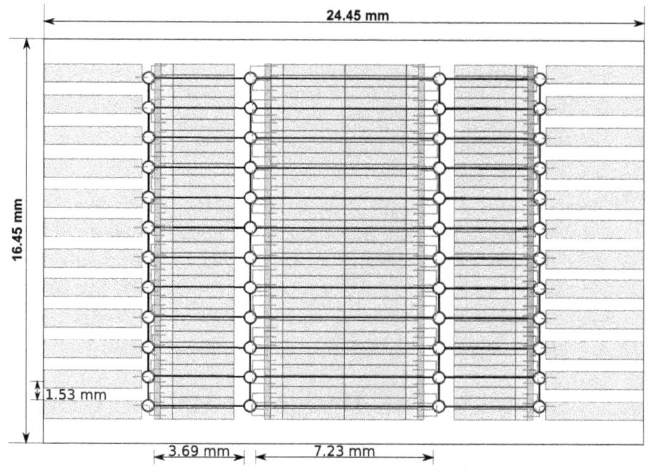

(b) 4x12 2D-mesh for the 128-CU GPU (14 nm).

Figure 3: Physical layouts of the electrical NoCs for the two GPU chips.

4. NOC DESIGN FOR GPU SYSTEMS

In this section, we discuss the electrical and photonic NoC designs used in our evaluation of the 32-CU GPU (described in Section 3.1), and the scaled-up 128-CU GPU (described in Section 3.2).

4.1 Electrical NoC Design for 32-CU GPU

Although not every detail of the interconnect used in the AMD Radeon HD 7970 chip has been publicly disclosed, online resources suggest that the crossbar topology is in fact used between the L1 and L2 caches [3, 23]. Therefore, we model a crossbar NoC for the baseline 32-CU GPU to provide communication between its 40 L1 caches and 6 L2 caches.

The crossbar is a low-diameter high-radix topology that supports a strict non-blocking connectivity, and can provide high throughput. The crossbar network topology can be implemented as a multi-bus topology, where each node in the network has a dedicated bus. Different buses of the crossbar topology can be routed around the GPU chip to form a U-shaped layout (Figure 3a). We consider two main designs for the bus crossbar – a Single-Write-Multiple-Read (SWMR) design and a Multiple-Write-Single-Read (MWSR) design.

In the SWMR crossbar, each transmitting node has a designated channel to transfer messages. All receiving nodes are able to *listen* to all sending channels. All nodes decode the header of the control messages on the channel and decide whether to receive the rest of the message or not. The destination node is the only node that receives the cache line that directly follows the control message. A node receives a message if it is the destination of that message. The message is received and buffered in the destination node's input buffer. The destination node applies Round-Robin (RR) arbitration between messages it receives from multiple transmitting nodes at the same time. In the MWSR crossbar, each transmitting node needs to acquire access to the receiver's dedicated bus to transmit a message. An access is granted in a RR fashion between nodes that have a message to transmit. The channels in both designs utilize credit-based flow control for buffer management, with acknowledgments in the reverse direction being piggybacked on control messages.

Each L1 and L2 cache unit in the GPU system acts as a node in the network. For example, in the design of the SWMR crossbar NoC in the 32-CU GPU there are 40 dedicated SWMR buses (32 for vector caches and 8 for scalar caches) required for L1 units, and 6 dedicated SWMR buses for L2 units to send information to all the other units.

4.2 Electrical NoC Design for 128-CU GPUs

As the number of CUs in a GPU grows, the number of L1 and L2 units that need to communicate also grows. This means that additional SWMR/MWSR buses are required in the crossbar to support this communication. A larger number of buses, implemented using electrical link technology, translates to large die area and higher power dissipation. Moreover, in a MWSR, the transmitting units need to acquire access to one of the buses in the crossbar via arbitration. Also, if each node holds on to the bus for a large number of cycles (due to serialization and transmission delays), this will result in very long wait times for other nodes. Large number of SWMR buses impose pressure on the receiving cache unit which has limited number of ports. Therefore, for GPUs with large CU counts, we propose to use an electrical 2D-mesh network. The mesh is a low-radix high-diameter topology that uses decentralized flow control. An electrical mesh network is easy to design from a hardware perspective due to its short wires and low-radix routers. While a mesh avoids the long arbitration delays present within a crossbar, it has higher zero-load latency, as each packet has to traverse multiple routers (hops) to reach its destination.

A typical 2D-mesh is constructed using radix-5 routers connected neighboring routers and sender/receiver end-nodes. The main drawback of using a 2D-mesh with a large number of nodes is the high hop count, which results in longer latencies. To alleviate this issue, we propose using a concentrated 2D-mesh, where each router has a larger radix. As shown in Figure 3b, for the 128-CU GPU, we use routers with radix 7 and radix 8.

In our baseline 2D-mesh designs for a 128-CU GPU, a single router is connected to L1 vector and scalar cache units,

Table 2: Number of global buses required for topologies in 32- and 128-CUs GPU – HYB = The proposed hybrid, DOWN = L1 to L2 traffic, and UP = L2 to L1 traffic.

	32-CU GPU		128-CU GPU	
Design	DOWN	UP	DOWN	UP
MWSR	6	40	24	160
SWMR	40	6	160	24
HYB	6	6	24	24

depending on the location of the router on the layout. While various configurations are possible for placement of L2 units [6], we chose to connect L2 units to the mesh through the routers placed along the periphery of the mesh to follow a similar layout to the AMD Radeon 7970 for our 128-CU GPUs. In the AMD Radeon 7970 the L2 banks are placed on the periphery of the die [22]

The mesh design is modeled using state-of-the-art single-cycle routers [28], each having room for 8 cache lines in the input buffers and no virtual channels. The routers use a standard matrix-based crossbar that implements round-robin arbitration. We use an X-Y routing scheme with credit-based flow control.

4.3 Hybrid NoC Design for GPU

As mentioned earlier, there are considerable drawbacks in terms of area and power dissipation with both the SWMR and MWSR crossbars, due to the large number of global channels. To address this problem, we design a NoC with a significantly lower number of channels, by taking advantage of the asymmetry in the L1-to-L2 versus L2-to-L1 network traffic, and by analyzing the communication between L1 units.

We propose to use SWMR buses for L2-to-L1 communication and MWSR buses for L2-to-L1 communication for our hybrid design. The choice of a SWMR bus in the L2-to-L1 network is easy to justify. The data from L2 cache units to L1 cache units is latency sensitive since this data is needed for the work-items to start their execution. In SWMR, there is no arbitration latency in the transmitting side (L1 cache). Additionally, the number of buses is low, equal to the number of L2 caches.

Using the MWSR buses in the L1-to-L2 direction requires few buses (equal to the number of L2 caches), at the expense of introducing additional arbitration latency—hardware must deal with the worst case where all L1 caches attempt to access the same bus simultaneously. However, this has minimal impact on the overall performance because the latency of L1-to-L2 traffic is typically not critical as the GPU programming model enforces that no other CU should be stalled awaiting completion of a write-back transfer. At the same time, GPU workloads exhibit light traffic for L1-to-L2 accesses. Our analysis of the GPU applications in the AMD APP SDK benchmark reveals that on average, 80.5% of the traffic generated from L1-to-L2 is due to control messages (8 byte messages). This means any bus with a bandwidth wider than 8B would have a 0-cycle serialization latency for 80% of the messages from L1 to L2. Thus, scaling down the L1-to-L2 network causes no noticeable increase in contention.

A crossbar topology provides point-to-point connections between all the L1 and L2 units. Therefore, any L1-to-L1

Table 3: The main elements in the photonic crossbars. The channel width is 72 Bytes. WG = Waveguides, MD = Modulators, FL = Filters, TL = MD+FL. The columns are for the 32-CU GPU if not stated otherwise. HYB128 uses concentration through access points (AP) to reduce the number of rings (4 vL1s and 1 sL1 share an AP).

	SWMR	MWSR	HYB	HYB128
WG	63	63	26	186
MD	2668	27840	14268	45936
FL	27840	2668	14268	45936
TL	30508	30508	28536	91872

communication has a dedicated path. As mentioned in Section 1, the GPU applications causes a very small amount of L1-to-L1 communication. This is while modern GPU designs all provide coherency between L1 units. We evaluated many memory-intensive applications in the AMD APP SDK benchmark suite in order to calculate the amount of traffic between L1 units. As expected, all applications in the suite exhibit close to zero transactions between L1 units, except for two applications *conv* and *dct* (for these two applications, 16% and 12% of all the traffic on the network are L1-to-L1 transactions, respectively – see Table 6 for further details on applications).

So in our hybrid design, in order to reduce the power consumption of the NoC, we also removed the connections between L1 units. So any L1-to-L1 transaction will be replaced with two transactions: one from L1-to-L2 and a second one from L2-to-L1. By this change we would also reduce any latency that might be introduced by arbitration due to small amount of communications between L1 units.

Overall, the hybrid design reduces the number of buses in the crossbar for the 32-CU GPU from 46 to 12. Similarly, using the hybrid design reduces the number of buses from 184 to 48 for the 128-CU GPU (see Table 2 for details).

4.4 Photonic NoC Designs

The link length-independent data-dependent energy of silicon-photonic links makes this technology more appropriate for designing low-diameter high-radix topologies such as a crossbar, clos or butterfly. In this work, we consider crossbar since it provides strictly non-blocking connectivity, and is easy to program. A photonic crossbar provides relatively lower latency in comparison to an electrical crossbar. We use silicon-photonic link technology to design a crossbar NoC for the GPU, as discussed in Section 4.1.

The photonic MWSR implementation uses an optical token channel with fast-forwarding, which provides the same RR arbitration as the electrical crossbars [35]. The photonic SWMR implementation avoids the need for arbitration. At every transmission, the source node sends the control message, and its head flit is decoded by all the receiving nodes. All nodes except the destination node turn off their receiver ring detector after the decode process [27]. Similar to our electrical hybrid NoC, our photonic hybrid design also utilizes SWMR buses for L2-to-L1 and MWSR for L1-to-L2 communications.

Table 3 shows the number of photonic components required for the different crossbars for the maximum bus width (72 bytes). If we compare the three topologies for the 32-CU GPU, our proposed hybrid scheme requires fewer waveguides due to the lower number of buses (see Table 2) and a correspondingly lower number of total rings (modulators and filters), which results in lower NoC power. As a result, we will only consider this hybrid design for the photonic NoC for larger 128-CU GPU. To further minimize static NoC power, the hybrid crossbar utilizes concentration through Access Points (AP). In particular, 4 vector L1 caches and 1 shared L1 cache use the same AP to access their corresponding crossbar's bus on a time-division multiplexing basis (see Figure 4b).

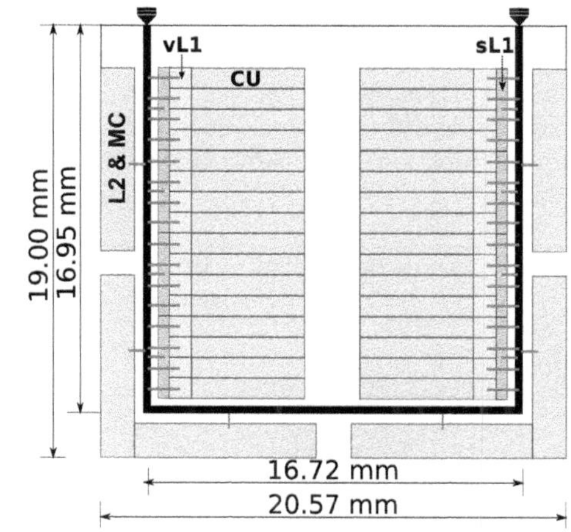

(a) Crossbar for the 32-CU GPU (28 nm).

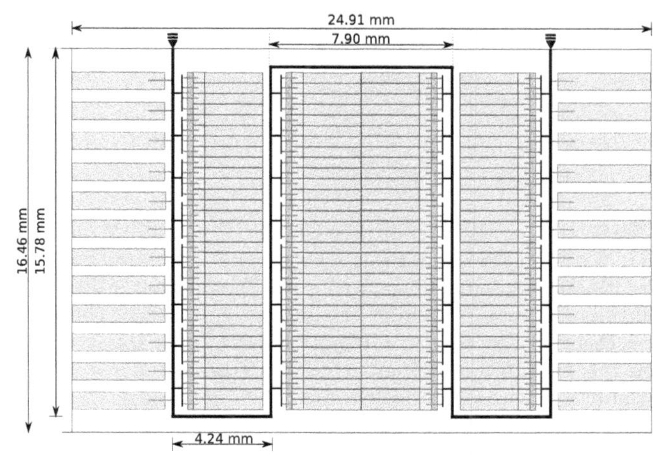

(b) 32×24 Crossbar for the 128-CU GPU (14 nm).

Figure 4: Physical layout of the silicon-photonic NoCs for the two GPU chips. We use 4 μm-pitch waveguides and 10 μm-diameter rings.

Photonic topologies can be mapped onto the U-shaped and serpentine physical layouts illustrated in Figure 4a and Figure 4b, respectively, for the two GPUs under study. Note that the Figures show the GPU chip dimensions. As explained in Section 3, to obtain the 128-CU floorplan area, we scale down the dimensions of the 32-CU chip components (CUs, vL1s, sL1s, L2s and MCs) from 28 nm (the technology node of the 32-CU GPU) to 14 nm technology node. Monolithic integration of a photonic crossbar would slightly increase the area of the GPU chip. We use 4 μm-pitch waveguides and 10 μm-diameter rings. When comparing the total area of the GPU chips with the electrical NoCs and the photonic NoCs, we obtain floorplan areas of

Table 4: **Energy Projections for Photonic links based on [13, 25, 26].** - Tx = Modulator driver circuits, Rx = Receiver circuits, Dynamic energy = Data-traffic dependent energy, Fixed energy = clock and leakage We consider 20% (conservative projection) and 30% (aggressive projection) laser efficiency.

Circuit	Data-dependent energy	Fixed energy	Thermal tuning
Tx (fJ/bt)	20	5	16
Rx (fJ/bt)	20	5	16

Table 5: **Projected/Measured Optical Loss per Component** [13, 25, 26]. We consider -17 dBm (conservative projection) and -20 dBm (aggressive projection) for the photodetector sensitivity.

Device	Loss (dB)	Device	Loss (dB)
Optical Fiber (per cm)	5e-6	Coupler	1
Non-linearity (at 30 mW)	1	Splitter	0.2
Modulator Insertion	1	Filter through	1e-3
Waveguide crossing	0.05	Filter drop	1.5
Waveguide (per cm)	2	Photodetector	0.1

390.0 mm^2 vs. 390.8 mm^2 (32-CU GPU) and 402.2 mm^2 vs 410.0 mm^2 (128-CU GPU), respectively. Photonic components are not scalable (contrary to CMOS transistors) and that is the main reason for this increase in area. The area overhead in the 128-CU GPU is 7.8mm^2. This area is equal to the area of approximately 2 CUs (the area for a CU is 4 mm^2). Increasing the number of CUs from 128 to 130 results in a very small performance improvement.

Energy and loss projections for photonic crossbars are presented in Tables 4 and 5, respectively [13,25,26]. We use conservative choices for the 32-CU GPU and aggressive choices for the 128-CU GPU. Conservative and aggressive designs employ different parameters for the photodetector sensitivity and laser efficiency (-17 dBm vs. -20 dBm in the former, and 20% vs. 30% in the latter, respectively).

5. EVALUATION METHODOLOGY

We conducted experiments to evaluate the potential for silicon-photonic NoC in GPUs using the Multi2sim 4.2 simulation framework [31]. The simulator has a configurable model for commercial AMD and NVIDIA GPU architectures. Multi2sim integrates an emulator for the AMD Southern Islands instruction set. The emulator provides traces of instructions at the ISA level, which are fed to an architectural simulation featuring a detailed timing model of the GPU pipelines and memory system.

We have extended Multi2sim to include models for both electrical and photonic buses, as well as packet processing and flitting support for NoCs. To validate the updated Multi2sim simulation framework, we leveraged the standalone network simulation mode of Multi2sim that can inject random traffic in various network topologies. We compared and verified the reported latencies and performance numbers in our cycle-based model against previous research [7, 11].

The applications evaluated in this work are taken from the AMD APP SDK [1], which AMD has provided to highlight efficient use of the AMD Southern Islands family of GPUs. For each application, we can change program inputs to specify the workload intensity. We chose large input sizes for our benchmarks to show how current GPUs are unable to support the growth in data set sizes we expect to see in future workloads. We made sure that the selected subset of applications include a diversity of workload features and varying intensities for creating a range of traffic behaviors. Table 6 lists the set of applications selected from this benchmark suite, and includes a brief description for each application.

The power for the electrical network is estimated using a detailed transistor-level circuit model. The power dissipated by the network is calculated based on the physical layout, the flow control mechanism and network traffic workloads. For the 32-CU GPU, the wires in the crossbar are designed in the global metal layers using pipelining and repeater insertion in 28 nm technology [2]. All of inter-router channels in the 2D mesh are implemented in semi-global metal layers with standard repeater wires. We use the 14 *nm* technology node [2] for the 128-CU GPU systems. The power dissipated in the SRAM array and crossbar of the routers is calculated using the methodology described in [19] and [36], respectively. We use the photonic technology described in Sections 2 and 4.3 to calculate laser power, Tx/Rx power and thermal tuning power in the NoC.

6. EXPERIMENTAL RESULTS

6.1 Electrical vs. Photonic Designs of Crossbar Topologies for a 32-CU GPU

As described in Section 3.1, 64B cache line should immediately follow an 8B control message. This means the biggest message in the network is 72B. For any channel with a bandwidth smaller than 72B (e.g., 32B), the control signal will be transfered in a separate cycle first, and the cache line is packeted and transfered immediately in the next cycles (2 cycles for 32B). In our evaluation, we considered MWSR and SWMR electrical buses with channel widths of 16, 32 (divisors of 64), and 72B (packing control signals and the cache line in 1 message) for the 32-CU GPU system. For the photonic NoC, due to the bandwidth density advantage of silicon-photonic link technology versus electrical link technology, we considered SWMR and MWSR buses with a channel width of 72B.

In Figure 5a, we compare the electrical and photonic MWSR and SWMR crossbars in terms of performance (top plot) and network traffic (bottom plot). To calculate the performance improvement (i.e., speed up) for each application, we divided the application execution time when using the MWSR electrical crossbar NoC with a 32B channel width (E-MWSR-32) by the execution time for the other NoC designs. As shown in the corresponding plot, the photonic SWMR crossbar (P-SWMR-72) achieves an average 2.60× speedup, and the photonic MWSR crossbar (P-MWSR-72) achieves an average 2.64× speedup compared to E-MWSR-32. A similar performance improvement is observed if we compare P-MWSR-72 and P-SWMR-72 with E-SWMR-72. The magnitude of speedups directly correlate to the network bandwidth required by the applications (see the bottom plot in the Figure 5a). Applications with a higher number of memory transactions (i.e., larger offered bandwidth) exhibit larger benefits (i.e. 6.3× for *mtwist* and 5.2× for *conv*). The benefits we observe are a result of the low latency nature of photonic NoCs. As can be seen in the figure, increasing the channel bandwidth of the electrical crossbars results in very

Table 6: **The workloads selected from the AMD APP SDK.**

Application	Description
BS	It finds the position of a given element in a sorted array of size 1048576.
CONV	Convolution filtering on each element of an input matrix of 4096 × 4096 with blur mask of 5 × 5
DCT	Discrete Cosine Transforms on an input matrix of size 8192 × 8192
DWTHAAR	One-dimensional Haar wavelet transform on a one-dimensional matrix of size 8388608
LARGSCAN-LS	Performs scan on a large default array of 134217728 elements
MTWIST	SIMD-oriented Fast Mersenne Twister (SFMT) generates 4194304 random numbers and uses Box-Muller to convert these numbers to Gaussian random numbers.
RED	Performs reduction by dividing an array of 33554432 into blocks, calculating the sum of blocks and calculating the sum of block sums.
RG	Performs recursive Gaussian filter on an image of size 1536 × 1536.
SOBEL	Performs Sobel Edge detection algorithm on an image of size 1536 × 1536.
URNG	Generates unifrom noise on an input image of size 1536 × 1536.

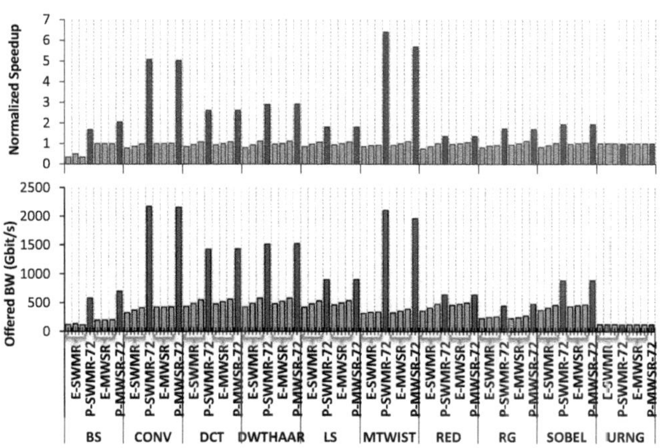

(a) Speedup and offered bandwidth results for a 32-CU GPU with different crossbars.

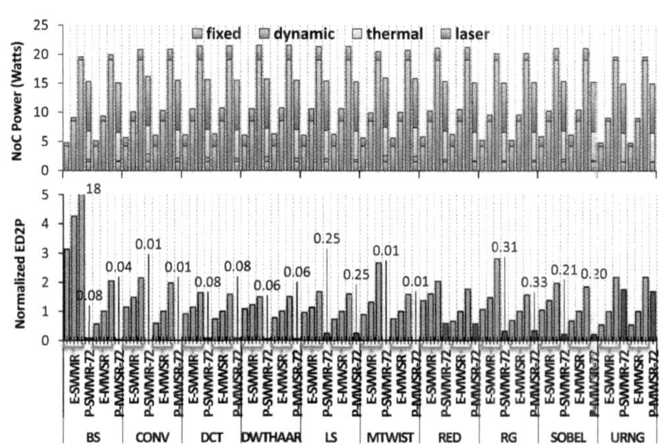

(b) Breakdown of the total power and energy-delay^2 product of NoCs in a 32-CU GPU.

Figure 5: Evaluation of a current 32-CU GPU with electrical and photonic MWSR and SWMR crossbar NoCs – Ticks in the x-axis follow the pattern *T-X-N*, where *T* refers to the type of technology (electrical = E; photonic = P), *X* is the type of crossbar (MWSR or SWMR), and *N* refers to the channel width in bytes. For electrical NoCs three different link bandwidths (from left to right 16, 32 and 72) are considered. The performance speedup and ED^{2}P are normalized to an electrical MWSR crossbar NoC with a 32-byte channel width ($E - MWSR - 32$).

small performance improvements in memory intensive applications (such as *conv*), since transmission latency of the electrical channel (4 cycles on average) masks any benefit of reduction in serialization latency through increase in bandwidth.

Compute intensive applications (such as *urng*), and applications with a small number of thread blocks (such as *bs*), can store their entire dataset in L1 data caches (generating very few memory accesses to the L2 banks). Therefore, these applications do not benefit from high bandwidth NoC designs since the NoC is not utilized.

Figure 5b compares the E-MWSR, E-SWMR, P-MWSR and P-SWMR crossbars using NoC power (see top plot) and the energy-delay^2-product (ED^{2}P) metrics (see bottom plot) across the different benchmarks. For all benchmarks, the static power of electrical crossbars is dominant and increases from 2.1 Watts to 19 Watts when the channel width is increased from 8 to 72 bytes. A 72B link requires 72 × 8 wires, and each wire is 46.71 mm long. We have 46 buses in the network. This means 26,496 wires are required. If we assume 4 segments comprise a wire, running at a frequency of 1 GHz, the wire consumes roughly 180 fJ/bit in 28 nm technology. This leads to a 19 Watts power dissipation for the NoC, which is too high so commercial GPUs do not use the electrical networks that have links with 72B bandwidth.

The P-MWSR-72 and P-SWMR-72 crossbars consume 29% lower power on average as compared to E-MWSR-72 and E-SWMR-72, but they consume 32% more power on average as compared to E-MWSR-32 and E-SWMR-32. Note that the static power values for both the P-MWSR and P-SWMR crossbars (fixed, thermal and laser components) are very similar. The reason for their similar power dissipation is that both P-MWSR and P-SWMR crossbars utilize the same number of photonic rings and waveguides (see Table 3). To reduce this large fraction of static power, a NoC layout using concentration can be adopted. For instance, access points can be used to attach 4 vL1s and 1 sL1 through a single link to the bus. By adding access points, we can reduce the total number of rings by a factor of 4.78 (30,508 vs. 6,380) and the number of waveguides by 3.5 (63 vs. 18). As explained in Section 4.4, we apply this technique to reduce NoC power for scaled-up GPU system (128 CUs) with a hybrid NoC.

In any case, the bottom plot of Figure 5b still shows that the photonic NoCs achieve the lowest ED^{2}P for all the benchmarks, except *urng*. The *urng* application is insensitive to NoC channel bandwidths, so the electrical crossbar NoC with the smallest channel width reports the best ED^{2}P,

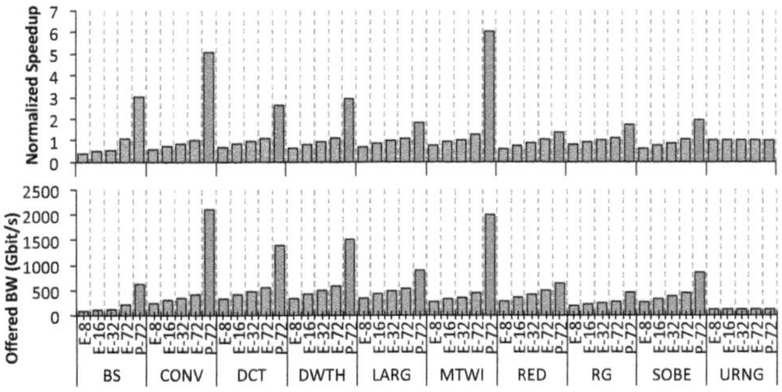

(a) Speedup and offered bandwidth of benchmarks running on 32-CU GPU systems with a hybrid NoC topology.

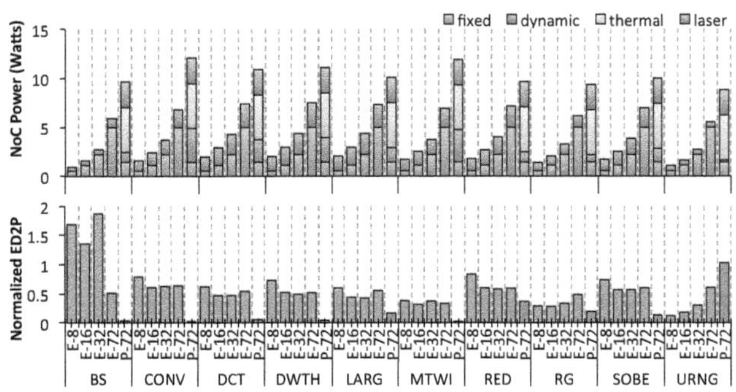

(b) Breakdown of total power and energy-delay^2 product of the hybrid NoCs in a 32-CU GPU.

Figure 6: Evaluation of a 32-CU GPU with electrical and photonic hybrid NoCs – The Speed up and ED^{2}P are normalized to E-MWSR-32 (not shown for clarity). Captions in x-axis follows the pattern *T*-*N*, where *T* refers to type of technology (electrical = E; photonic = P) and *N* refers to channel width in bytes (8, 16, 32 and 72).

as its power is lower than its electrical counterpart, and its performance equals the performance of the crossbar with the largest bus bandwidth. Note that the ED^{2}P is significantly improved when considering our photonic NoCs (the average reduction across all benchmarks in terms of ED^{2}P is 66.5% for P-SWMR and 67.7% for P-MWSR, when compared to E-MWSR-32).

6.2 Photonic vs. Electrical Design of a Hybrid Topology for 32-CU GPUs

Figure 6 presents results of the electrical and photonic implementations of our proposed hybrid design (see Section 4.3). By comparing Figures 6 and 5 (results in both Figures are normalized to E-MWSR-32), we can observe that our electrical implementation of the hybrid design, E-HYB-72, does not show any performance improvement over its crossbar counterparts, E-MWSR-32 and E-MWSR-72. But this implementation reduces the power consumption of the electrical crossbar on average by 68% (due to less hardware), while providing the same performance. On the other hand, our photonic hybrid design, P-HYB-72 provides higher speedup than E-MWSR-32 and E-MWSR-72 (2.7× for both). Increasing the bandwidth of the electrical crossbar did not affect GPU's performance due to high electrical link latency, as shown in Section 6.1.

The P-HYB-72 consumes 51% less power than both E-MWSR-72 and E-SWMR-72. It also has a marginally higher power dissipation (2%) than E-MWSR-32 and E-SWMR-32. This makes our hybrid design a very good contender compared to any electrical crossbar design.

The P-HYB-72, achieves higher performance than P-MWSR-72 (1.05×) and P-SWMR-72 (1.03×) on average, by slightly reducing the latency (See Section 4.3 for details) and achieves 32% and 33% lower power dissipation on average, by using less hardware resources. Therefore P-HYB-72 achieves 34% and 30% reduction in the ED^{2}P in comparison to P-MWSR-72 and P-SWMR-72, respectively.

The comparison between photonic hybrid design and electrical hybrid design (E-HYB) (Figure 6a) in terms of performance (top plot of Figure 6a) and network bandwidth (bottom plot of Figure 6a) reveals the clear benefits of using low latency photonics technology. P-HYB-72 exhibits, on average, a 2.5× speedup and offers 0.6 Tbit/s more bandwidth versus E-HYB with the highest bandwidth (E-HYB-72).

Figure 6b compares the electrical hybrid (E-HYB) and photonic hybrid (P-HYB) designs in terms of power (top plot) and the ED^{2}P metric (bottom plot). P-HYB-72 reports 51% higher power than the E-HYB-72 NoC due to higher static power consumption (laser, thermal tuning and fixed power). One solution is to adapt a run-time management mechanism based on the workload on compute units. Using run-time management, we can deactivate photonic links when they are not being used [8]. We leave run-time management mechanisms as an area for future work.

Nonetheless, when analyzing the ED^{2}P metric in the bottom plot of the Figure 6b, we can see that our P-HYB-72 produces on average 82% lower ED^{2}P as compared to the E-HYB-72 NoC.

6.3 Electrical Mesh vs Photonic Hybrid Designs for 128-CU GPUs

In this section, we consider future GPUs with 128 CUs, to study the scalability of electrical and photonic NoC designs presented in Section 4. For comparison, we consider an electrical mesh design and photonic hybrid design with channel widths of 16, 32 and 72 bytes. Here, all comparison metrics are normalized to an electrical 2D-mesh with 16-byte channel widths (E-MESH-16).

Figure 7a compares performance (top plot) and bandwidth (bottom plot) of the E-MESH design with our P-HYB, for 128-CU GPU, assuming the same set of channel widths as the previous evaluation. The performance speedup reported for P-HYB-72 is 82% better than the speedup for E-MESH-72 (with maximum 3.43× speedup for *mtwist*). The E-MESH-72 offers increased bandwidth up to 2.81 Tbit/s (*dct*), whereas P-HYB-72 achieves up to 7.28 Tbit/s bandwidth (*mtwist*).

Figure 7b compares E-MESH and P-HYB in terms of power (top plot) and ED^{2}P (bottom plot). P-HYB NoCs generally consume more power than an E-MESH counterpart. This leads to 19% higher ED^{2}P for P-HYB-72, in comparison to E-MESH-72.

We can reduce the bandwidth of the channel to reduce power dissipation of the P-HYB. Reduction in the P-HYB channel bandwidth from 72 bytes to 32 and 16 bytes, reduces this power dissipation by 39% and 60%, respectively. The average speedup observed for all the applications in our study for P-HYB-32 is 43%, and for P-HYB-16 is 17%, when

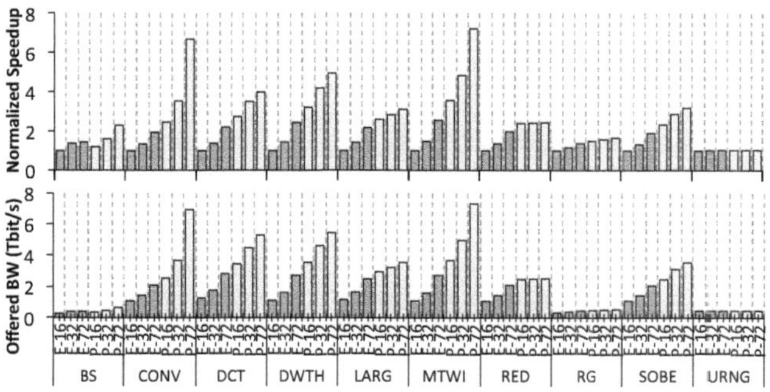

(a) Speedup and bandwidth of benchmarks running on a 128-CU GPU system with varying hybrid NoCs.

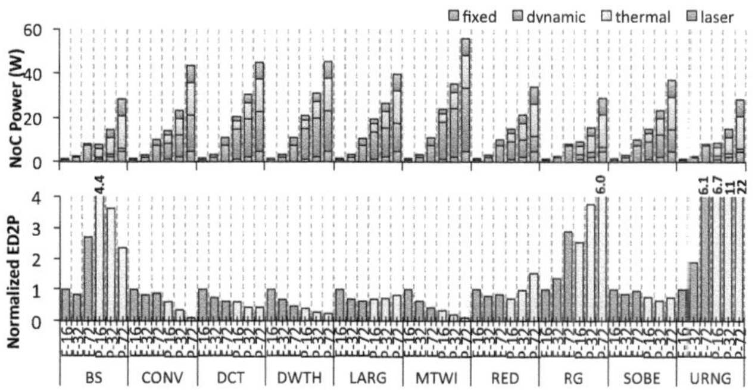

(b) Breakdown of the total power and energy-delay^2 product of GPU's NoC.

Figure 7: Evaluation of 128-CU GPUs with an electrical 2D-mesh NoC and a photonic hybrid NoC. - Captions along the x-axis follow the pattern T-N, where T refers to type of technology and topology (electrical 2D-mesh = E; photonic hybrid = P) and N refers to channel width in bytes (16, 32 and 72). Speedup and ED^{2}P results are normalized to $E-16$.

compared to E-MESH-72. By reducing the channel width to 32B or 16B, we reduce the power consumption, and therefore ED^{2}P in our hybrid designs. Therefore the ED^{2}P for P-HYB-32 and P-HYB-16 is reduced by 3% (for both) when compared to E-MESH-72. This means both P-HYB-32 and P-HYB-16 are marginally better than the 2D-mesh.

One important feature of the hybrid design is its effect on memory intensive applications. If applications utilize the memory hierarchy (such as *conv*, *dct*, *dwthaar*, *mtwist*, *largescan* and *sobel*), this will favor the photonic hybrid design. For these memory intensive applications, P-HYB-16 enjoys, on average, a 26% performance speedup and a reduction of 13%, on average, in ED^{2}P as compared to E-MESH-72.

Since these applications scale well with the number of GPU units, P-HYB-32 and P-HYB-72 provides significant reductions in ED^{2}P against E-MESH-72 (34% and 40% respectively). The reported speedups for P-HYB-32 and P-HYB-72, for these memory-intensive applications, are on average 1.6× and 2.2× in comparison to E-MESH-72, respectively.

Our results clearly show that for future GPU systems that will execute memory intensive workloads, a photonic hybrid design provides the best ED^{2}P solution.

7. RELATED WORK

A large amount of work has been done in the area of NoC design for manycore architectures, with the goal of providing energy-efficient on-chip communication. The maturity of electrical NoCs for manycore systems is evidenced by the availability of commercial designs (80-tile, Sub-100W TeraFLOPS processor introduced by Vangal et al. [33], or Tilera's 64-core TILE64 chip [37]), On the photonic NoC front, there are no working prototypes, but researchers have explored the entire spectrum of network topologies – from low-radix high-diameter mesh/torus topologies [10,17,30] to medium-radix medium-diameter butterfly/crossbar topologies [15,16,27] to high-radix low-diameter bus/crossbar topologies [29,34] to multilayer topologies [24,32,38].

The area of GPU NoCs has not been widely explored. Bakhoda et al. [6] exploit the many-to-few traffic patterns in manycore accelerators by alternating full routers in congested areas with half routers. In a related work [5], the same authors evaluate GPU performance degradation due to NoC router latencies. Both [5] and our work corroborate the motivation for low-latency networks to mitigate their impact on GPU performance.

Lee et al. [18] identify a novel trade-off in CPU-GPU heterogeneous systems concerning the NoC design. CPUs run highly latency-sensitive threads, while coexisting GPUs demand high bandwidth. They thoroughly survey the impact of primary network design parameters on the CPU-GPU system performance, including routing algorithms, cache partitioning, arbitration policies, link heterogeneity, and node placement.

In [14], Goswami et al. explore a 3D-stacked GPU microarchitecture that uses an optical on-chip crossbar to connect shader cores and memory controllers in the GPU memory hierarchy. The main difference between our work and [14] is that we present our own tailored monolithically-integrated photonic NoCs for communication between L1 cache and L2 cache and evaluate them against different electrical designs for current and future scaled-up GPUs.

8. CONCLUSIONS

In this paper, we combine our knowledge of silicon-photonic link technology and GPU architecture to present a GPU-specific photonic hybrid NoC (used for communication between L1 and L2) that is more energy efficient than the electrical NoC. Our proposed hybrid design uses MWSR for L1-to-L2 communication and SWMR for L2-to-L1 communication. Our simulation-based analysis shows that applications that are bandwidth sensitive can take advantage of a photonic hybrid NoC to achieve better performance, while achieving an energy-delay^2 value that is lower than the traditional electrical NoC. In the AMD Southern Islands GPU chip with 32 CUs, our proposed photonic hybrid NoC increases application performance by up to 6× (2.7× on average) while reducing ED^{2}P by up to 99% (79% on average). We also evaluated the scalability of the photonic hybrid NoC to a GPU system with 128 CUs. For the 128-CU GPU system running memory intensive applications, we can achieve up to 3.43× (2.2× on average) performance speedup, while reducing ED^{2}P by up to 99% (82% on average), compared to electrical mesh NoC. Moving forward, we plan to explore techniques for run-time power management of photonic NoCs to extend this improvement to all applications.

Here, depending on the application requirements, the photonic NoC bandwidth (and hence the photonic NoC power) will be appropriately scaled up/down to achieve energy efficient operation in the photonic NoC, as well as in the system as whole for the entire spectrum of applications.

9. ACKNOWLEDGMENT

This work was supported in part by DARPA Contract No. W911NF-12-1-0211 and NSF CISE grant CNS-1319501.

10. REFERENCES

[1] AMD Accelerated Parallel Processing (APP) Software Development Kit (SDK). http://developer.amd.com/sdks/amdappsdk/.

[2] Predictive Technology Model. http://ptm.asu.edu/.

[3] AMD Graphics Cores Next (GCN) Architecture, June 2012. White paper.

[4] NVIDIA's Next Generation CUDA Compute Architecture: Kepler GK110, 2012. http://www.nvidia.com/content/PDF/kepler/NVIDIA-Kepler-GK110-Architecture-Whitepaper.pdf.

[5] A. Bakhoda et al. Analyzing CUDA Workloads Using a Detailed GPU Simulator. In *Proc. Int'l Symposium on Performance Analysis of Systems and Software*, April 2009.

[6] A. Bakhoda, J. Kim, and T. M. Aamodt. On-Chip Network Design Considerations for Compute Accelerators. In *Proc. of the 19th Int'l Conference on Parallel Architectures and Compilation Techniques*, Sept. 2010.

[7] C. Batten et al. Building manycore processor-to-dram networks with monolithic silicon photonics. In *High Performance Interconnects, 2008. HOTI'08. 16th IEEE Symposium on.* IEEE, 2008.

[8] C. Chen and A. Joshi. Runtime management of laser power in silicon-photonic multibus noc architecture. *IEEE Journal of Selected Topics in Quantum Electronics*, 19(2):338–350, 2013.

[9] X. Chen et al. Adaptive cache management for energy-efficient gpu computing. In *Proceedings of the 47th Annual IEEE/ACM International Symposium on Microarchitecture, December 2014.*

[10] M. J. Cianchetti, J. C. Kerekes, and D. H. Albonesi. Phastlane: A Rapid Transit Optical Routing Network. *SIGARCH Computer Architecture News*, 37(3), June 2009.

[11] W. Dally. Virtual-Channel Flow Control. *IEEE Transactions on Parallel and Distributed Systems*, 3(2), March 1992.

[12] B. R. Gaster, L. W. Howes, D. R. Kaeli, P. Mistry, and D. Schaa. *Heterogeneous Computing with OpenCL - Revised OpenCL 1.2 Edition*, volume 2. Morgan Kaufmann, 2013.

[13] M. Georgas et al. A Monolithically-Integrated Optical Receiver in Standard 45-nm SOI. *IEEE Journal of Solid-State Circuits*, 47, July 2012.

[14] N. Goswami, Z. Li, R. Shankar, and T. Li. Exploring silicon nanophotonics in throughput architecture. *Design & Test, IEEE*, 31(5):18–27, 2014.

[15] H. Gu, J. Xu, and W. Zhang. A low-power fat tree-based optical network-on-chip for multiprocessor system-on-chip. In *Proceedings of the Conference on Design, Automation and Test in Europe*, DATE '09, pages 3–8, 2009.

[16] A. Joshi et al. Silicon-Photonic Clos Networks for Global On-Chip Communication. In *3rd AMC/IEEE Int'l Symposium on Networks on Chip*, May 2009.

[17] N. Kirman and J. F. Martínez. A Power-efficient All-Optical On-Chip Interconnect Using Wavelength-Based Oblivious Routing. In *Proc. of the 15th Int'l Conference on Architectural Support for Programming Languages and Operating Systems*, Mar. 2010.

[18] J. Lee et al. Design Space Exploration of On-chip Ring Interconnection for a CPU-GPU Architecture. *Journal of Parallel and Distributed Computing*, 73(12), Dec. 2012.

[19] X. Liang, K. Turgay, and D. Brooks. Architectural power models for sram and cam structures based on hybrid analytical/empirical techniques. In *Proc. of the Int'l Conference on Computer Aided Design*, 2007.

[20] E. Lindholm et al. NVIDIA Tesla: A Unified Graphics and Computing Architecture. *IEEE Micro*, 28(2), March 2008.

[21] L. Mah. The AMD GCN Architecture, a Crash Course. *AMD Fusion Developer Summit*, 2013.

[22] M. Mantor. Amd hd7970 graphics core next (gcn) architecture. In *HOT Chips, A Symposium on High Performance Chips*, 2012.

[23] M. Mantor and M. Houston. AMD Graphics Core Next: Low-Power High-Performance Graphics and Parallel Compute. *AMD Fusion Developer Summit*, 2011.

[24] R. Morris, A. Kodi, and A. Louri. Dynamic Reconfiguration of 3D Photonic Networks-on-Chip for Maximizing Performance and Improving Fault Tolerance. In *Proc. of the 45th Int'l Symposium on Microarchitecture*, Dec. 2012.

[25] B. Moss et al. A 1.23pj/b 2.5gb/s monolithically integrated optical carrier-injection ring modulator and all-digital driver circuit in commercial 45nm soi. In *Solid-State Circuits Conference Digest of Technical Papers (ISSCC), 2013 IEEE International*, pages 126–127, Feb 2013.

[26] J. S. Orcutt et al. Nanophotonic integration in state-of-the-art cmos foundries. *Opt. Express*, 19(3):2335–2346, Jan 2011.

[27] Y. Pan et al. Firefly: Illuminating Future Network-on-chip with Nanophotonics. *SIGARCH Computuer Architecture News*, 37(3), June 2009.

[28] S. Park et al. Approaching the Theoretical Limits of a Mesh NoC with a 16-Node Chip Prototype in 45nm SOI. In *Proc. of the 49th Design Automation Conference*, June 2012.

[29] J. Psota et al. ATAC: Improving Performance and Programmability with On-Chip Optical Networks. In *Proc. Int'l Symposium on Circuits and Systems*, 2010.

[30] A. Shacham, K. Bergman, and L. P. Carloni. On the design of a photonic network-on-chip. In *Proceedings of the First International Symposium on Networks-on-Chip*, NOCS '07, pages 53–64, 2007.

[31] R. Ubal et al. Multi2Sim: A Simulation Framework for CPU-GPU Computing. In *Proc. of the 21st Int'l Conference on Parallel Architectures and Compilation Techniques*, Sept. 2012.

[32] A. N. Udipi et al. Combining Memory and a Controller with Photonics Through 3D-Stacking to Enable Scalable and Energy-Efficient Systems. In *Proc. of the 38th Int'l Symposium on Computer Architecture*, June 2011.

[33] S. R. Vangal et al. An 80-Tile Sub-100W TeraFLOPS Processor in 65nm CMOS. *IEEE Journal of Solid-State Circuits*, 43(1), Jan. 2008.

[34] D. Vantrease et al. Corona: System Implications of Emerging Nanophotonic Technology. In *Proc. of the 35th Int'l Symposium on Computer Architecture*, June 2008.

[35] D. Vantrease et al. Light speed arbitration and flow control for nanophotonic interconnects. In *Microarchitecture, 2009. MICRO-42. 42nd Annual IEEE/ACM International Symposium on*, pages 304–315. IEEE, 2009.

[36] H. Wang, L.-S. Peh, and S. Malik. Power-Driven Design of Router Microarchitectures in On-Chip Networks. In *Proc. of the 36th Int'l Symposium on Microarchitecture*, 2003.

[37] D. Wentzlaff et al. On-Chip Interconnection Architecture of the Tile Processor. *IEEE Micro*, 27(5), Sept. 2007.

[38] X. Zhang and A. Louri. A Multilayer Nanophotonic Interconnection Network for On-Chip Many-Core Communications. In *Proc. of the 47th Design Automation Conference*, June 2010.

Automatically Scalable Computation

Margo Seltzer
Herchel Smith Professor of Computer Science,
Harvard School of Engineering and Applied Sciences

Abstract

As our computational infrastructure races gracefully forward into increasingly parallel multi-core and clustered systems, our ability to easily produce software that can successfully exploit such systems continues to stumble. For years, we've fantasized about the world in which we'd write simple, sequential programs, add magic sauce, and suddenly have scalable, parallel executions. We're not there. We're not even close. I'll present a radical, potentially crazy approach to automatic scalability, combining learning, prediction, and speculation. To date, we've achieved surprisingly good speedup in limited domains, but the potential is tantalizingly enormous.

ACM Classification

C.0 [*Computer Systems Organization*]: General -- System architectures

Keywords

Speculation; prediction; parallelization; deep learning.

BIO

Margo Seltzer is a Herchel Smith Professor of Computer Science in the Harvard School of Engineering and Applied Sciences. Her research interests include architecture, provenance, file systems, databases, transaction processing systems, and applying technology to problems in healthcare. She is the author of several widely-used software packages including database and transaction libraries and the 4.4BSD log-structured file system. Dr. Seltzer was a founder and CTO of Sleepycat Software, the makers of Berkeley DB, and is now an Architect at Oracle Corp. She is currently the President of the USENIX Association and a member of the Computing Research Association Board. She is a Sloan Foundation Fellow in Computer Science, an ACM Fellow, a Bunting Fellow, and was the recipient of the 1996 Radcliffe Junior Faculty Fellowship.

She is recognized as an outstanding teacher and mentor, having received the Phi Beta Kappa teaching award in 1996, the Abrahmson Teaching Award in 1999, and the Capers and Marion McDonald Award for Excellence in Mentoring and Advising in 2010.

Dr. Seltzer received an A.B. degree in Applied Mathematics from Harvard/Radcliffe College in 1983 and a Ph. D. in Computer Science from the University of California, Berkeley, in 1992.

ICS'15, June 08-11, 2015, Newport Beach/Irvine, CA, USA
ACM 978-1-4503-3559-1/15/06.
http://dx.doi.org/10.1145/2751205.2751206

Mower : A New Design for Non-blocking Misprediction Recovery *

Zhaoxiang Jin
Department of Computer Science
Michigan Technological University, USA
zjin3@mtu.edu

Görkem Aşılıoğlu
Department of Computer Science
Michigan Technological University, USA
galolu@mtu.edu

Soner Önder
Department of Computer Science
Michigan Technological University, USA
soner@mtu.edu

ABSTRACT

Mower is a micro-architecture technique which targets the branch misprediction penalty in superscalar processors. It speeds-up the misprediction recovery process by dynamically evicting stale instructions and correcting the Register Alias Table (RAT) using explicit control dependency tracking. Tracking control dependencies is accomplished by using simple bit matrices. This low-overhead technique allows overlapping of the recovery process with instruction fetching, renaming and scheduling from the correct path. Our evaluation of the mechanism indicates that it yields performance very close to ideal recovery and provides up to 5% speed-up and 2% reduction in power consumption compared to a recovery mechanism using a reorder buffer and a walker. The simplicity of the mechanism should permit easy implementation of Mower in an actual processor.

1. INTRODUCTION

Branch prediction is a vital component in any contemporary processor. Today, most superscalar processors are organized in the form of decoupled architectures where an in-program-order front-end chases the instruction stream by relying on accurate branch prediction and an out-of-program-order back-end schedules and executes these instructions based on operand availability. The performance of such an architecture is dependent on not only the accuracy of branch prediction, but also the cost of control misspeculation. A branch misprediction leaves the two halves of the processor in an incorrect state which needs to be corrected before instruction fetch and execution can resume.

When a particular branch is detected to be mispredicted, the processor needs to do the following: (1) Eliminate all the instructions which follow the mispredicted branch; (2) Restore the processor structures, such as rename map tables which are frequently referred to as *Register Alias Table* (*RAT*) to their correct values; (3) Resume fetching from the correct branch target.

Each of these tasks contribute to the branch misprediction penalty and each must be targeted individually to reduce its impact on processor performance. In other words, to be effective, any technique which targets branch misprediction penalty must reduce both the duration of each task and permit overlapping of individual tasks to the maximum extent possible. Eliminating instructions following the mispredicted branch requires knowledge of where in the processor these instructions are and a mechanism to nullify them. Restoring the processor structures requires knowledge of what constitutes the correct processor state [13]. Resuming the fetching from the correct target requires knowledge of the correct target and the resources necessary to store the new instructions. Provision of resources is particularly important if fetching is to resume before the invalidation is complete as newly fetched instructions cannot be mixed with those already in the pipeline. As a result, either a separate set of locations must be provided to store the correct instructions or a mechanism should exist to distinguish the two. As we will discuss shortly, Mower accomplishes a reduction in the duration of all three tasks and maximises their overlap, in essence reducing the overall branch misprediction penalty.

In order to understand the issues involved, revisiting a commonly used basic recovery mechanism [19] will be helpful. This simple recovery scheme incorporates a *reorder buffer* (ROB) into which instructions are fed in program-order as they are fetched. A *front-end* register alias table (F-RAT) is used to speculatively rename the incoming instruction stream and a *retirement* register alias table (R-RAT) is used to record the in-order state as the instructions complete and retire. The F-RAT is updated when instructions are being renamed and the R-RAT is updated when an instruction *commits*, i.e., it is determined to be part of the in-order state. Once a branch misprediction is detected, instruction fetching is halted and the execution of existing instructions continues until the mispredicted branch arrives at the head of the reorder buffer. Waiting for the completion of prior instructions leaves only invalid instructions in the pipeline and hence promotes the development of simple and fast mechanisms to squash invalid instructions by making the identification of invalid instructions trivial and restoring the correct state easy. When the branch reaches the head of ROB, the retirement map table R-RAT contains the correct state which can simply be copied over F-RAT. On the other hand, this simple mechanism does not permit overlapping of

*This work is supported in part by NSF grants CCF-1116551 and CCF-1450062.

ICS'15, June 8–11, 2015, Newport Beach, CA, USA.

http://dx.doi.org/10.1145/2751205.2751228.

subtasks involved in the recovery process and accomodates a highly variable misprediction penalty that is strongly correlated with the position of the mispredicted branch in the ROB. When the branch is close to the ROB head, it takes less time for the rear-end to retire the instructions preceding the mispredicted branch. However, if the mispredicted branch is far from the ROB head, or, if the rear-end is waiting for a long latency operation ahead of the branch (such as a missed load), the time to recover from the misprediction may increase significantly.

Branch misprediction penalty has been the target of several techniques which can be broadly classified into two groups: those which target the pipeline fill delay after a misprediction and those concerned mainly with state maintenance. Techniques which target the pipeline fill delay are orthogonal to Mower and we do not discuss them further except in related work. Existing state maintenance techniques can be grouped into *checkpointing* and (ROB) *walking*. Checkpointing is a technique where a copy of the RAT is made for each potential misprediction. When a misprediction is detected, the correct copy of the RAT is restored immediately from one of the available checkpoints. The technique also permits fast invalidation of instructions within the processor as the required information is readily available and is part of the checkpoint. Since checkpointing requires a copy of the RAT per checkpoint, each checkpoint may require a significant amount of space. As a result, taking a checkpoint at every branch may be prohibitively expensive. Several modifications to the base checkpointing technique are available to address this. An example of these modifications is to take checkpoints only on low confidence branches and using the basic recovery technique outlined above to recover from branches that do not have checkpoints [1].

Walking is a technique where the RAT is corrected by *walking* over the ROB. *Walking* over the ROB from the ROB head up to the mispredicted branch while pseudo-retiring each instruction in between will construct the correct R-RAT, which can then be used to restore the front-end state as well. Since the processor does not actually have to wait for instructions to complete to construct the alias table, this technique fetches instructions from the correct path faster than waiting. Alternatively, we can forego the use of a retirement alias table and store the previous mapping values in ROB entries. Then, we can walk over the ROB starting from the tail up to the mispredicted branch and undo each change that was made in error [19].

Mower attempts to combine several concepts from the basic recovery techniques checkpointing and walking, and provides complete overlapping of the recovery tasks. It accomplishes rapid elimination of invalid instructions by explicitly keeping track of control dependencies by means of simple bit matrices. It also permits immediate fetching of instructions from the correct path upon a misspeculation detection by (1) selectively blocking entries in the F-RAT while the recovery process is continuing; (2) by relying on a novel walking mechanism which rapidly restores the state and provides space where new instructions can be stored by *mowing* the invalid instructions.

The rest of the paper is organized as follows: In section 2, we review the recent techniques and compare them with Mower. In Section 3, we give an overview of the technique we propose. Section 4 provides the detailed design. In Section 5 we present our experimental evaluation and analysis. Finally, we summarize our critical findings in Section 6.

2. RELATED WORK

In this section, we give an overview of relevant misprediction recovery techniques to Mower.

Smith et. al. [19] show recovery mechanisms using ROB in their study to set the stage for the majority of non-checkpointing based recovery techniques. Hwu et. al. [12] propose a checkpointed recovery system to repair processor state. A checkpoint of the processor state is taken at every branch and recovery happens from these checkpoints on a misprediction. This is the technique Mower is tested against in this paper. Variations and improvements using checkpoints have been proposed by other authors. Akkary et. al. [1] propose Checkpoint Processing and Recovery (CPR). The major contribution of CPR is selective checkpointing (only low confidence branches are checkpointed). Both the original chekpointing algorithm as well as CPR do not use an ROB.

Zhou et. al. [22] propose Eager Misprediction Recovery (EMR), which is the second technique we compare with Mower. EMR creates checkpoints of the front-end mapping tables. However, when a misprediction occurs, instructions from the new path are immediately fetched and decoded. Misprediction recovery allows each new instructions to reach up to the reservation station but incorrect front-end mappings are marked as damaged. Unlike Mower, which restores the correct mappings before instructions are renamed, EMR instead restores the correct values of damaged mappings into the damaged physical registers by utilizing functional units.

Amit et. al. [8] propose Selective Branch Recovery which is another technique which does not necessarily discard all instructions from the incorrect path immediately. SBR attempts to detect if the mispredicted path will converge back on to the correct path. If such a convergence is detected, some results from the incorrect path may still be useful.

Akl et. al. [3] propose Turbo-ROB, which is an ROB based recovery design that only allocates ROB entries at certain points determined to be repair points. Turbo-ROB gives the illusion of a larger ROB while using fewer entries at the cost of not being able to restore the state to any instruction. Latorre et. al. [15] provide a similar improvement with CROB but handle misprediction recovery by copying over a checkpoint of relevant processor structures per branch.

Hilton et. al. [11] propose a checkpointing scheme with an ROB called CPROB. CPROB switches to an ROB based recovery scheme if mispredictions are frequent and uses a smaller window. If predictions are going well, the window size is dynamically expanded and the misprediction recovery scheme switches to using checkpoints. Golander et. al. [9] propose a similar checkpointing scheme. They take checkpoints more frequently when mispredictions are frequent, and vice versa.

BranchTap [2] by Akl et. al. is a technique that allows a processor to stop fetching instructions when a threshold of low confidence branches are in the processor. This threshold is dynamically calculated during execution. BranchTap can work with or without checkpointing. BranchTap is orthogonal to Mower - not fetching many incorrect instructions would speed up Mower's recovery.

Another technique orthogonal to Mower is WPE [5] by Armstrong et. al. WPE detects so called Wrong Path

Events which include unusual or illegal behaviour such as a NULL pointer access or a divide by zero. These events are then used to speculate that we are on the wrong path of execution. WPE would allow Mower to start recovery early.

Several techniques have been proposed that fetch instructions from both paths on low confidence branches. Such techniques target the pipeline fill delay, which is not targeted by Mower. Use of these techniques alongside Mower could further improve Mower's performance. Disjoint Eager Execution (DEE) by Uht et. al. [20] is one of the earlier examples. Code paths that are likely to be executed are taken, meaning both paths on a branch that is likely to mispredict will be executed. Heil et. al. [10] propose Selective Dual Path Execution (SPDE) which selectively executes two (and only two) branch paths at the same time based on prediction confidence. SPDE is implemented in a regular superscalar processor with the addition of confidence predictors and an additional register alias table. Another work in this area is Selective Eager Execution (SEE) by Klauser et. al. [14] SEE is similar to SPDE but uses a novel instruction tagging and register renaming to avoid including a second RAT. Wallace et. al. [21] apply a similar technique to simultaneous multithreading processors to allow the SMT processor to execute two paths from the same process called Threaded Multiple Path Execution (TMPE). TMPE introduces the Mapping Synchronization Bus which allows a new thread to be forked when a low confidence branch is encountered. TMPE also deals with resource use between the multiple paths. Dual Path Instruction Processing (DPIP) is proposed by Aragon et. al. [4]. DPIP specifically targets the window fill penalty where it fetches, decodes and renames instructions from the alternate path but does not execute them. An extension to DPIP gets pre-fetched instructions in an estimated schedule for rapid issue into execution units.

3. MOWER

3.1 General overview

Mower is a novel technique which aims for complete overlapping of new instruction fetching with state restoration after a branch misprediction. This approach implies that the front-end will be fetching and processing instructions even if the back-end has not yet been drained of incorrect instructions. Mixing invalid instructions with valid instructions in the pipeline requires several concepts to be realized in the processor. In the front-end, renaming must be delayed for new instructions if they are referencing invalid mappings that have not yet been restored. Mower must therefore know if each RAT mapping is valid or not. In the back-end, Mower must release resources occupied by invalid instructions precisely to restore the state without damaging the current state created by valid instructions. More specifically, the RAT mappings must be restored to their previous values and invalid instructions must be evicted or otherwise made ineffectual in reservation stations, execution units as well as the load/store queue.

Figure 1 shows the overall additions required by Mower on a typical out-of-order superscalar pipeline. In the figure, darker colored sections show Mower components. Overall, the pipeline stages for the traditional superscalar are kept the same. Branches and jumps are resolved in the jump unit (separated from execution units for clarity).

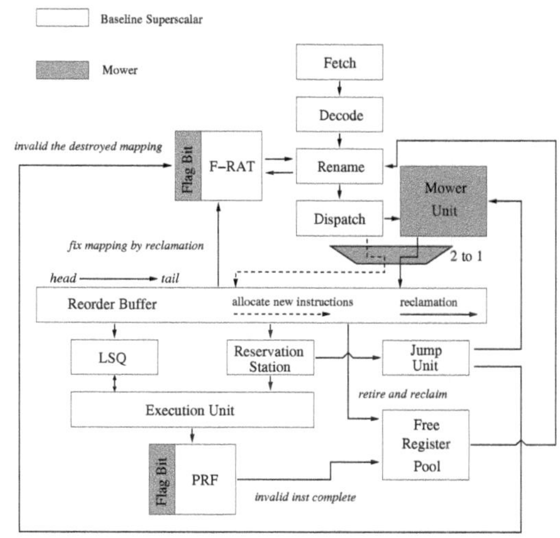

Figure 1: Block Diagram

Examining the figure in pipeline flow order, the first change we notice is the additional bits which are attached to RAT. Mower uses these bits to identify whether a mapping has been damaged by a previous misprediction or not. All mapping bits start out valid. They are selectively invalidated when a branch instruction mispredicts. Note that there is no R-RAT under Mower, as the front RAT is incrementally updated to reflect the correct mapping after a misprediction.

Next, the *Mover Unit* (Figure 1, top-right) is responsible for maintaining and generating the mapping bits for RAT, walking over the ROB entries for rapid state recovery and releasing the resources kept by invalid instructions as well as making sure that invalid instructions still located in deep execution pipelines do not modify the state upon completion. Mower uses a single bit attached to each register in the Physical Register File (PRF) (Figure 1, bottom-left) to selectively disable writes for a particular register so that invalid instructions in deep pipelines can be allowed to complete without changing the state.

The operation of the Mower Unit involves its interaction with the jump unit, the reorder buffer and the renamer. The jump unit consults the Mower Unit, which provides a list of all mappings control dependent on the mispredicting branch. These valid bits therefore allow the front-end to delay the renaming of those instructions which reference to invalid mappings until the correct mapping is restored. In addition, during rename each jump or branch instruction is assigned a unique tag used by the Mower Unit. Since each branch is allocated a tag, the total number of in-flight branch instructions is equal to the number of available tags.

Although the Mower algorithm uses *walking* to reclaim resources, it is quite different. Mower walks sequentially from the mispredicted branch towards the ROB tail as opposed to existing algorithms, such as the walking technique which scans from the head of ROB towards the mispredicted branch and the history-buffer which starts from the tail of the buffer towards the mispredicted branch. Both of these techniques have to complete the entire scan before a usable, correct state is restored. In contrast, in case of Mower, due to its ability to identify damaged set of registers through a separate mechanism, scanning starts at the mispredicted branch and each register needs to be corrected only once

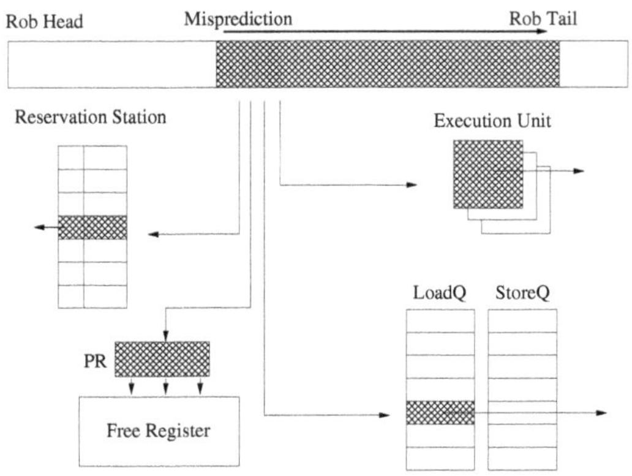

Figure 2: Mow all the invalid instructions through ROB, release all the relative resources.

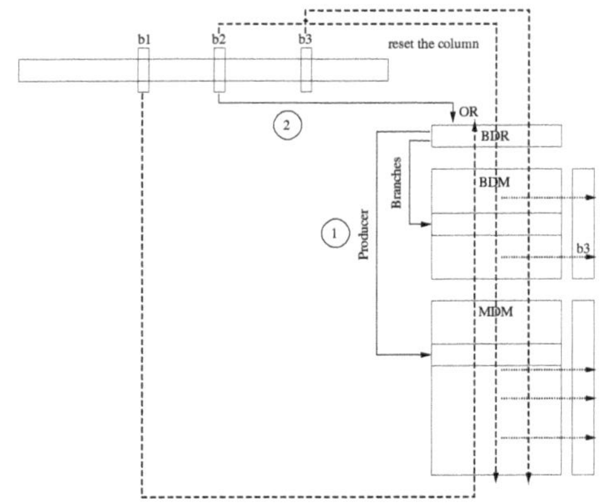

Figure 3: Explicit Control Dependency Tracking

each step it is clearly known which part of the state is valid and which part of the state is still damaged. During Mower's walking process, each visited ROB entry undoes any changes it made to the processor structures. Visited invalid instructions are evicted from the reservation stations, load/store queues; release physical registers and restore their previous mappings in the RAT. Instructions which are still in deep pipelines are permitted to continue their execution as discussed above. When such an instruction completes, it frees the register instead of writing its result in that register. The walker then *mows* away all invalid instructions until the position of the ROB tail at the time of misprediction is reached. Newly fetched instructions are stored in the freshly *mowed* area. Figure 2 illustrates resources released from the back-end by Mower.

3.2 Explicit Control Dependency Tracking and Out-of-order Branch Resolution

In order to accomplish full overlap of instruction fetching and state restoration as outlined, there are two problems which needs to be addressed. First, we need to keep track of control dependency information for each instruction so that the required information is readily available as soon as a branch is mispredicted. In this respect, we are particularly interested to know which registers had been redefined after a mispredicted branch so that the front-end map table validity information can be immediately updated. Second, due to the out-of-order nature of branch completion, branch mispredictions may be detected in an out-of-order manner, which means additional mispredictions may come from those branches which follow as well as precede the branch which is in the process of state recovery. Obviously, mispredictions which come from later branches need to be ignored and mispredictions from prior branches should take over.

We address these issues by relying on two simple bit matrices, called the Mapping Dependency Matrix (MDM) and the Branch Dependency Matrix (BDM). The operation of both matrices are identical; if a given resource (branch for BDM or register mapping for MDM) assigned to row i is dependent on a branch assigned to column j, the location $[i, j]$ is set to one. This organization permits easy extraction of the set of branches a particular resource is dependent on as well as the set of branches which are dependent on a particular resource.

Tracking Rename Map Validity

The organization of the MDM, which tracks rename map validity bits is shown together with the BDM which tracks in-flight branches in Figure 3. Each line in the MDM corresponds to a logical register number. Each column represents a dependency to a given branch tag. Therefore the MDM has a size of $L \times B$ where L is the number of logical registers and B is the number of in-flight branches. When Mower recovery starts, the column corresponding to the mispredicted branch is checked. If a given logical register has a dependency on the mispredicted branch, i.e., it was redefined after the branch, it will have a 1 in the mispredicted branch id's column. Consequently, it is flagged as invalid. An invalid mapping can't be used to rename new instructions until corrected.

To populate the MDM, the Mower Unit must keep track of what branches a register should be dependent on at rename-time. A register called the Branch Dependency Register (BDR) of size B is maintained in the unit. Each time a branch is assigned a tag (decoded), the bit corresponding to the assigned tag is set in the register. BDR therefore provides an accurate representation of active control dependencies at rename time. Each time an instruction is renamed, the BDR is inserted into the corresponding mapping line in the MDM, as shown in the figure.

When a branch instruction completes, there are two possible outcomes. If the branch has been correctly predicted, we should release the branch tag so new branches can use it. Since the branch is now complete, new instructions shouldn't be control dependent on it either. Therefore we reset the corresponding bit in the BDR. Pre-existing physical registers should also clear their control dependency on the recently completed branch since the tag could now be re-used for a later branch instruction. Dependency clearing is accomplished by resetting the column corresponding to the branch tag in the MDM. In the case where the branch is mispredicted, the BDR and the MDM are handled in the same manner. Before clearing the MDM column, each register's dependency on the mipsredicted branch is checked. If it is dependent on the mispredicted branch, the register is marked as invalid.

The MDM covers invalidation of instructions that have a physical register mapping. Store and branch instructions do not have such a mapping. Handling invalid store instructions is simple. Stores do not affect processor state until they commit but they will not be allowed to write to memory since they are behind the mispredicted branch. All that needs to be done is to wait for the walker. Branch instructions are handled as discussed below.

Tracking Branch Dependencies

Branch exception ordering requires identification of which branch instructions are dependent on one another. Clearly, a branch instruction which was fetched after another branch instruction is dependent on that instruction. In order to track B in-flight branches, a $B \times B$ BDM matrix is used. When a branch is decoded, the BDR is copied into the BDM before being modified. When a branch is completed, the corresponding columns in the BDM, MDM, and BDR are cleared regardless of prediction accuracy. It is easy to see that the BDM is functionally identical to the MDM and provides a similar information with respect to branch instructions.

Let's now see an example of these matrices in action. Considering Figure 3, let us assume the branches *b1*, *b2* and *b3* are in program order, but they are resolved in the order *b2*, *b3* and *b1*. *b2* and *b3* are mispredicted. When *b2* resolves, the Mower Unit will check the BDM and MDM to discover branch instructions and mappings affected by *b2*'s misprediction, and supply these flags to external structures if necessary. Following that, the bit columns corresponding to *b2*'s tag from the BDM and MDM will be cleared, as well as the bit corresponding to the tag in the BDR. When *b3* resolves, the BDM's flag register will inform the Mower Unit that it is an invalid branch. Thus, all columns corresponding to *b3*'s tag will still be cleared but no recovery will be triggered even though *b3* is a mispredicted branch. Finally, when *b1* resolves, the columns and the bit corresponding to *b1*'s tag will be cleared, but no additional action will be taken since *b1* has been predicted correctly.

3.3 Recovery Timing and Details

Mower precisely recovers resources by walking over the ROB starting from the mispredicted instruction while allowing new instructions to be fetched and inserted into the ROB as soon as possible. Considering the corrections required in the ROB, the correct location for the first instruction from the correct path in the ROB should be at the tail pointer, which should be reset to the mispredicting branch for recovery. In Mower, at the time of misprediction detection, these ROB slots are occupied by invalid instructions and may contain data crucial to precise state recovery. Therefore Mower must walk over several ROB entries before these entries could be allocated.

Walking over the ROB requires entries to be read and written to the ROB. If Mower had to accomplish this in the same cycle as it is fetching instructions, we would be required to double the number of ports on the ROB. We clearly can't start fetching new instructions before doing at least some recovery since the slots in the ROB are occupied.

We observe that it will take several cycles, based on pipeline depth, for newly fetched instructions to make it to the rename stage in the pipeline. Mower would like to overlap this time with recovery time. We use an interleaved reclamation scheme where the ROB ports are split in half. The first half are used to walk over and recover some ROB entries. The next half is used to insert new instructions into ROB. Note that instructions are not inserted into the ROB until several cycles into the pipeline. During these cycles, Mower uses

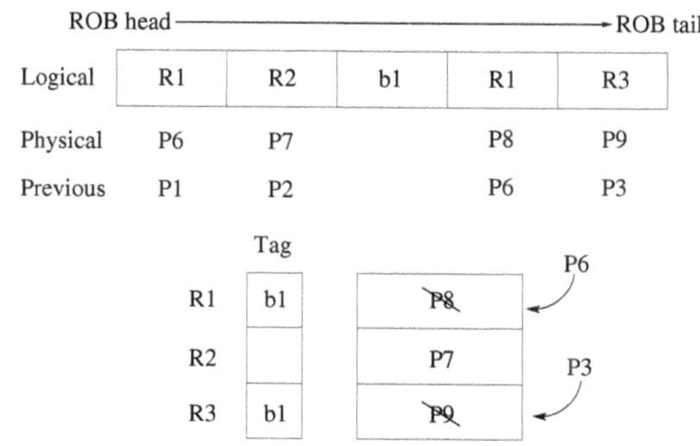

Figure 4: Fix the RAT by the reclamation

the full ROB port bandwidth available to recover resources. Using this interleaved technique, Mower can walk over the ROB as it is being populated by new instructions without adding much extra hardware. Most notably, Mower does not require extra ports for the ROB. While new instructions dependent on damaged mapping will need to be stalled at the rename stage, we observe that by the time instructions make it to the rename stage, most mappings will have been recovered.

Figure 4 shows an example of RAT recovery in Mower. *b1* is a mispredicted branch. When *b1* is confirmed to be mispredicted, R1 and R3 mappings are marked as invalid. As Mower walks over these entries, the previous entry in the RAT is replaced with the previous mapping entry stored in the ROB. The register mapped to the invalid instruction is returned to the free pool (P8, in R1's case), and the register re-written into the table is marked as valid (P6, in R1's case). Note that walking in this direction, only one fix per RAT entry is applied. Once a RAT entry is fixed, further mappings to that logical register during walking is ignored and only physical register release is performed.

4. HARDWARE DESIGN

In this section we discuss the hardware design of the structures required to implement Mower, shown in Figure 1.

4.1 Renaming Branches

As discussed in Section 3.1, Mower assigns unique physical tags to each branch from a free pool of tags when a branch is decoded. If there are no free tags available (i.e. processor has reached the limit of in-flight branches), that branch is stalled until more tags become available. In-use branch tags are released when the related branch instruction is completed or reclaimed from invalid branch instructions during recovery. Branch tags are encoded differently compared to regular rename identifiers. If there are B in-flight branches allowed in the processor, each tag will be B bits long. The tag contents will be the same as a $2^{log(B)}$-to-B decoder. For example, for $B = 4$, the branch tags will be 0001, 0010, 0100 and 1000.

4.2 Bit Matrices

Mower uses a $B \times B$ BDM as well as a $L \times B$ MDM. One possible hardware implementation of bit matrices can be found in [18].

Both matrices require updates on certain events. When a relevant instruction (a branch for the BDM, a result producing instruction for the MDM) is decoded, a new line is

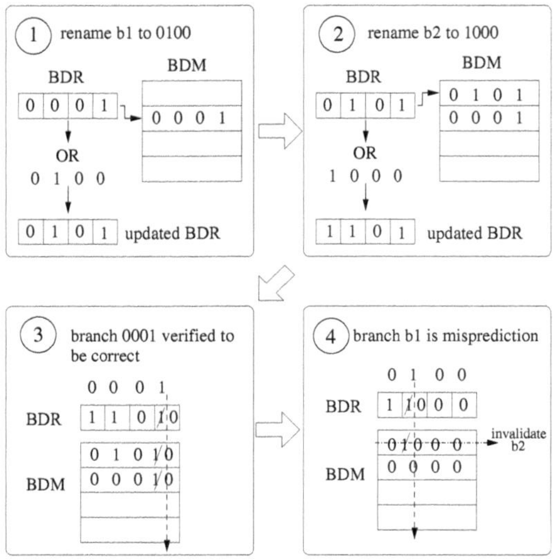

Figure 5: Branch Dependency Matrix

inserted into the matrices. When a branch completes, it clears the corresponding columns it was renamed to in both matrices. Each line in the matrix indicates if it has a dependency on a certain branch.

To facilitate insertions into the matrices, a Branch Dependency Register is located near the matrices. This branch dependency register contains the logical OR of all current in flight branch tags. This operation constructs a B bit register which has the value 1 for branches that are currently in-flight and 0 for unassigned branches. Each time a new entry is inserted into either matrix at the appropriate position, the BDR is copied into the line instead, to simplify acquiring new entries.

Figure 5 illustrates all the possible operations on a BDM in a processor which only allows 4 in-flight branches. Before the start of the example, a branch renamed to 0001 has entered the processor and is yet unresolved - any further branches will be dependent on 0001. In the figure ① *b1* is renamed to 0100 and the current BDR value is copied to the 2nd row of the BDM. The BDR is updated to 0101 by setting the 2nd most significant bit. Then in figure ② we rename another branch *b2* to 1000, the BDR is copied to the 1st row of BDM and we can see that the 2nd most significant bit is set which means *b2* is dependent on *b1*. Both *b1* and *b2* are dependent on branch 0001. In figure ③, branch 0001 is resolved and has been correctly predicted. Thus we reset its corresponding column in both the BDR and the BDM. All future branches will be independent from this cleared branch until a new branch is renamed to that value. Finally in figure ④ *b1* is resolved and is mispredicted. We still reset its column as before. However, we also invalidate all younger branches in flight by invalidating all the entries which have a dependency on the physical tag of *b1* (which is 0100 in this example). Updates to the MDM are handled similarly.

4.3 Correcting the RAT

As with the BDM, the MDM is updated by copying the BDR into the line which corresponds to the register that was just renamed. On a misprediction on a given branch b, entries which have a 1 in column b correspond to damaged mapping entries.

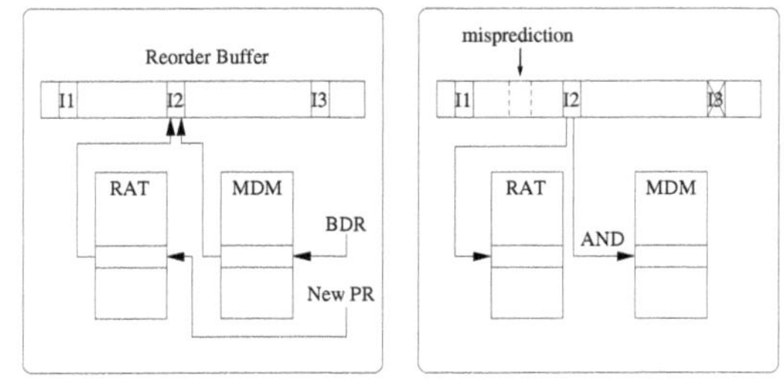

Figure 6: Recovering RAT from MDM

Processor Configuration	
Physical Register size	128
LSQ size	32
Fetch width	8
Decode width	8
Issue width	8
Int adder/subtractor	1 cycle
Int multiplier	3 cycles
Int divider	7 cycles
Float adder/sutractor	7 cycles
Float multiplier	7 cycles
Branch Predictor	4KB GShare 14 bits global branch history shift register

Figure 6 demonstrates the procedure to correct the alias table as well as updating the MDM.

The figure on the left shows I2 being renamed, where I1 is an instruction older than I2 and I3 is younger than I2. All three instructions write to the same logical register. When I2 is renamed, its previous mapping and branch information is stored in the ROB. At this point, we update both the RAT and the MDM with current information. The figure on the left shows the state of the structures after a misprediction is detected between I1 and I2. When walking back over the ROB, if the RAT entry corresponding to the instruction's logical destination is damaged, the previous mapping stored in ROB is restored and the RAT entry is marked clean. In the example, we can see that when walking over I2, we will correct the RAT to I1's mapping (since I2 stored that as it was being renamed), but not when we walk over I3 since the mapping table entry is marked as clean at that time. In the MDM, we unfortunately can't simply restore the entry from the ROB. A branch the mapping was depended on may have completed, making the archived entry invalid. In essence, we want the intersection of the archived branch dependencies and the current branch dependencies. We can achieve this by ANDing the archived entry with the entry currently in the MDM. This concludes everything necessary to restore the RAT mappings and maintain MDM state while walking back over the ROB after a misprediction.

5. EVALUATION

5.1 Methodology

We use MIPS I ISA to evaluate Mower. Mower is modeled in ADL [17], an architecture description language used to generate cycle-accurate simulators. We incorporated power models and estimated the power consumption for both Mower and the baseline. Power values have been obtained by adapting Wattch[6] to the ADL simulator framework. The power results have been validated against the McPAT[16] tool tested with a very similar superscalar pipeline to ensure correctness. Additionally, the non-ideal clock gating option is enabled in Wattch (causes only 10% power use when a particular port is not in use) as well as the dynamic activity factors (only precharges memory lines if they previously contained 0). The BDM and MDM matrices are implemented as CAM-like structures in Wattch for power evaluation purposes.

We use Spec2006 benchmark suite for performance and power evaluations. The suite was compiled using gcc version 4.3 with the highest optimization setting (-O3). Binutils 2.22 was used as the software environment. uClibC 0.9.33 was used to link the benchmarks and was simulated along with benchmark code. O/S kernel was not simulated. The ref inputs for the given benchmarks were ran for 500 million instructions to warm up the branch predictor and the cache, and an additional 1 billion instructions were simulated to gather the data.

The baseline implementation is an 8-wide conventional superscalar processor. A GShare branch predictor is used in the front end.

Aside from the baseline superscalar implementation, we also compared Mower with EMR (Eager Misprediction Recovery)[22] and CR (Checkpoint Recovery) [12] algorithms. For sanity checking, a perfect recovery technique is also tested against Mower.

The tested EMR implementation is implemented with 4 in-flight checkpoints which are used per misprediction recovery. Invalid instructions are eliminated immediately once detected. The CR utilizes 8 checkpoints. Each decoded branch will occupy one checkpoint until all instructions dependent on that branch complete. Checkpoints are released out-of-order. 8 checkpoints were chosen since it is expensive to implement a large number of checkpoints. The perfect recovery technique is an ROB based technique which recovers from a misprediction in the same cycle with no delays and resources being occupied.

5.2 Performance Results

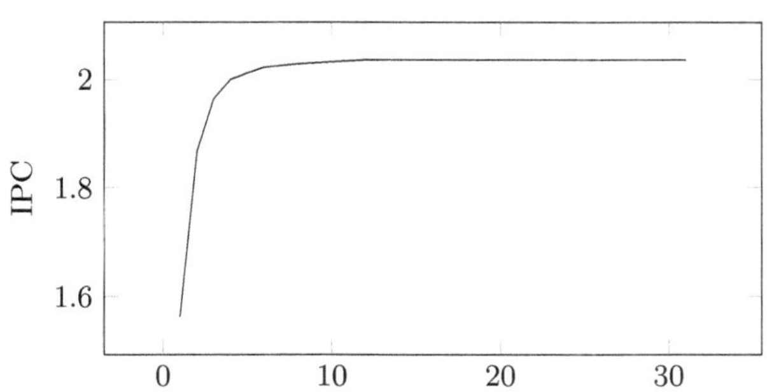

Figure 7: IPC vs In-flight Branches

We first explored the Mower design space to figure out what the in-flight branch limit should be. Figure 7 shows the average IPC value of Mower with different in-flight branch numbers. Even with only 4 in-flight branches, Mower can extract 98.2% of performance available to a processor with access to unlimited in-flight branches. In our experiments, we set the in-flight branch number to 12 which puts our Mower implementation at 99.99% performance of a Mower processor with unlimited in-flight branches.

Next, we show the number of damaged mappings throughout the recovery procedure. In figure 8, the values identified

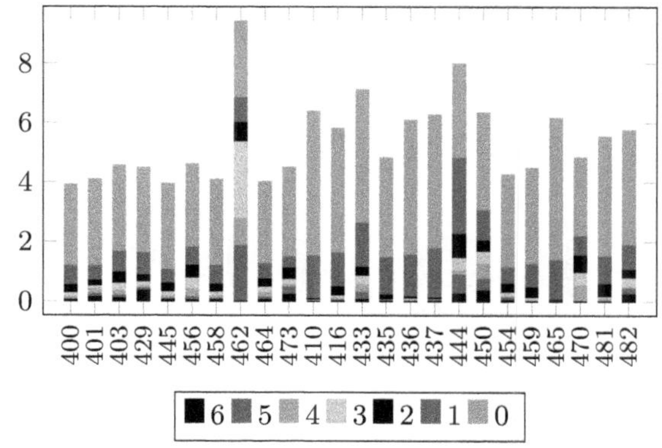

Figure 8: The Damaged F-RAT through the recovery process

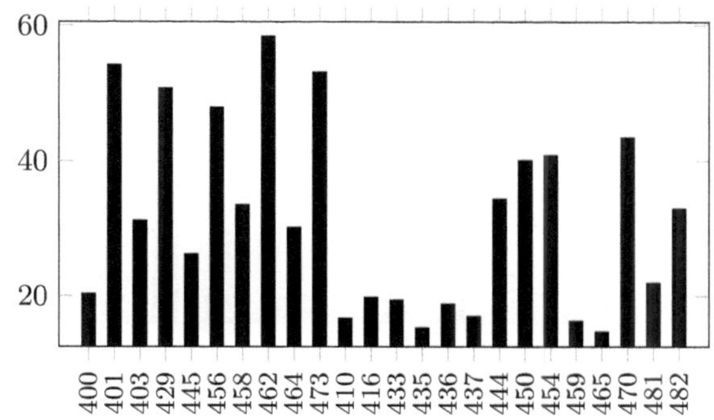

Figure 9: The average number of invalid instructions left in the pipeline when misprediction is detected

by 0 show the number of damaged mappings when misprediction is first indicated. Index 1 shows damaged mappings after one cycle of recovery. Index 2 shows damaged mappings after two cycles of recovery and so on. Our data shows that after 6 cycles, Mower recovers nearly as much as the perfect recovery baseline, and no delays will be incurred by instructions arriving at the rename stage at this point.

We also measured the number of invalid instructions left in the processor after misprediction. This data is presented in Figure 9. Looking at Figure 9 and Figure 8 together, we see invalid instructions reach almost to 60 after a misprediction, yet the number of invalid mappings never exceeds 8. This is partly due to store and branch instructions within the invalid instructions which do not have mappings, and partly due to register overrides. Having very few invalid mappings makes the recovery job easier.

Figure 10 and 11 show the geometric mean of the speed up over the baseline system in all Spec2006 Integer and Float bechmarks. Different shades of color indicate different configurations. The first number in the configuration is the number of front-end pipeline stages (up to where an instruction would be inserted into the reservation stations) and the second number indicates the number of stages before retirement but after execution. These graphs show that having a shorter front-end pipeline is better for faster recovery. This is expected since a shorter pipeline fill delay will benefit all techniques implemented here. Another observation is that performance increase jumps up when retiring an instruction takes more than one cycle after completion. The baseline

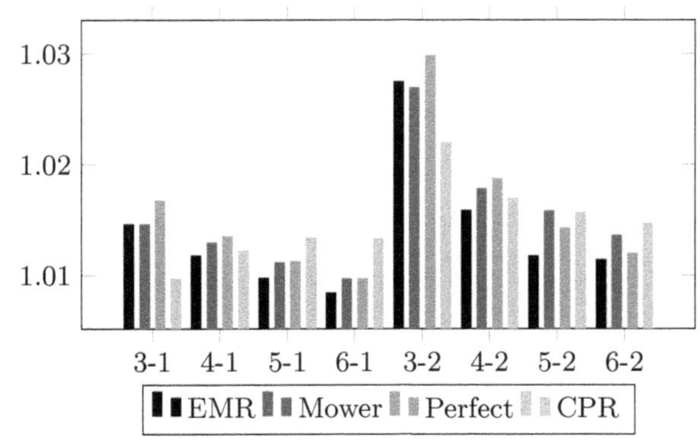

Figure 10: Spec2006 Integer Speedup (Normalized to Baseline)

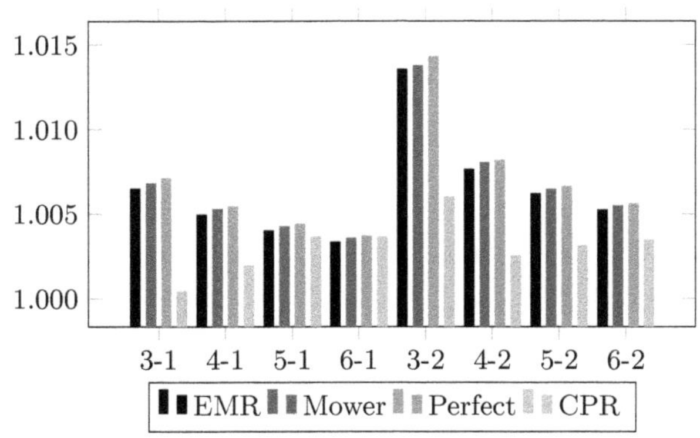

Figure 11: Spec2006 Float Speedup (Normalized to Baseline)

Spec2006	Mispred. Per 10k	Mower Speedup
401.bzip2	30.0	1%
403.gcc	66.9	3%
429.mcf	59.9	2%
445.gobmk	89.4	5%
458.sjeng	52.4	4%
462.libquantum	11.9	0%
464.h264ref	31.5	1%
473.astar	88.8	4%

Table 1: Misprediction Rates for Spec2006INT

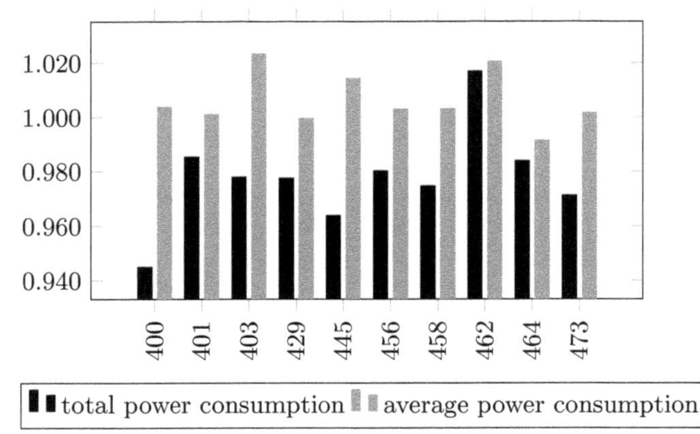

Figure 12: Power Evaluation Spec2006 Integer (Normalized to Baseline)

implementation has to wait for the misprediction to retire, but Mower moves ahead with the fetching during the same time frame. Most notably, we can see that Mower performs very close to perfect misprediction recovery in every case.

Looking at Table 1 lets us examine the speedups provided by Mower. In general, we can see a correlation between the misprediction rate and performance increase in the integer benchmarks. There are some outliers, for instance the 429.mcf benchmark shows a smaller speedup while having a greater misprediction rate than 458.sjeng. A more telling example is the comparison of the gcc benchmarks for Spec2000 and Spec2006 suites. 176.gcc from Spec2000 shows 132.9 mispredictions per 10k instructions, which is roughly double the number of mispredictions from the Spec2006 version. The performance is similarly impacted: 176.gcc shows close to 6% performance increase using the same parameters. Since Mower is a technique that targets branch misprediction recovery delays, if many mispredictions do not occur in the base case, not much performance will be extracted since there are no delays in the first place.

5.3 Power Estimation

In Figure 12, we illustrate the power consumption of Mower for all integer benchmarks. The data is normalized to the baseline superscalar. The lighter bar is the average power consumption and the darker bar is the total power consumption for a given benchmark. Mower saves close to 2% of total power in most integer benchmarks (462.libquantum is an exception). All power savings come from early reclamation.

Looking at performance results, we can also see an association between performance increase and power savings. Reclaiming more invalid instructions for mispredictions translates to power savings.

Unfortunately, Figure 13 shows a poorer picture for total power dissipation. This is due to the smaller number of branches in floating point benchmarks. Fewer branches mean even fewer mispredictions, and fewer mispredictions mean the additional structures employed by Mower are being used without providing a major advantage. 465.tonto has more branches than any other floating point benchmark, explaining the power difference.

It should be noted that the average power consumption is always worse for Mower since additional structures are involved. However, since Mower completes workloads faster, total power per workload is lower when Mower structures are being taken advantage of.

Detailed power numbers can be seen in Table 2. MDM dominates the additional power use of Mower due to it's large size compared to the BDM. Additionally, all instructions which produce a value update the MDM while this is only true for branch instructions in the case of BDM. A possible solution for this issue would be to bank the MDM as described in [7].

Figure 14 displays the EDP of Mower normalized to the baseline configuration. It is not surprising that a benchmark which saves more energy will be more power efficient since it reduces the total execution time at the same time. Mower helps to reclaim the invalid instructions early by which more energy is saved and misprediction penalty is reduced. In this manner, Mower is more power efficient in most benchmarks except 462.libquantum and 470.lbm. Even in these two benchmarks Mower is only 1% worse than the baseline.

	Mower				Baseline	
	total power	average power	average BDM	average MDM	total power	average power
400.perlbench	39414282.82	23.0847	0.0178	0.3418	41711982.94	22.9941
401.bzip2	19912545881	36.5107	0.0099	0.4674	20209901773	36.4707
403.gcc	20577678552	31.064	0.0177	0.4205	21044400878	30.3547
429.mcf	24399551282	23.9638	0.0125	0.2964	24962176205	23.9732
445.gobmk	21246144709	30.1403	0.0116	0.4082	22043497993	29.7116
456.hmmer	20169386181	52.1055	0.0108	0.7009	20578874932	51.9498
458.sjeng	20952348479	45.881	0.0243	0.5581	21498326343	45.7369
462.libquantum	18367126463	56.8546	0.014	0.7518	18062344589	55.7114
464.h264ref	19009792993	44.2755	0.015	0.5757	19321361564	44.6614
473.astar	25288238076	47.5951	0.0157	0.6439	26039881396	47.5177
410.bwaves	23545019645	49.1315	0.0012	0.5251	23570556909	49.1887
416.gamess	20683416431	53.3552	0.0097	0.6136	20859995597	52.8809
433.milc	22033327175	40.0966	0.004	0.4567	22017599284	39.7845
435.gromacs	20251109581	41.9003	0.0329	0.5177	20689221337	40.9992
436.cactusADM	24119700357	28.5811	0.0018	0.3049	24181298377	28.62
437.leslie3d	22490620504	44.733	0.0043	0.5086	22515068357	44.3398
444.namd	19011620317	47.6229	0.0348	0.5776	19297024881	47.6767
450.soplex	3531370375	42.2901	0.0134	0.5432	3558493095	41.6645
454.calculix	10508899197	51.8637	0.0172	0.6256	10344855160	45.8328
459.GemsFDTD	18450836352	42.359	0.0428	0.5504	18700506380	40.4183
465.tonto	21579146650	45.8823	0.022	0.605	23147948645	47.7491
470.lbm	21052658006	34.911	0.003	0.3709	20799850538	34.4426
481.wrf	23438584264	56.3007	0.015	0.5877	23322660370	55.017
482.sphinx3	20007152673	45.5453	0.0387	0.5723	20354623969	45.564

Table 2: Power distribution in Spec2006

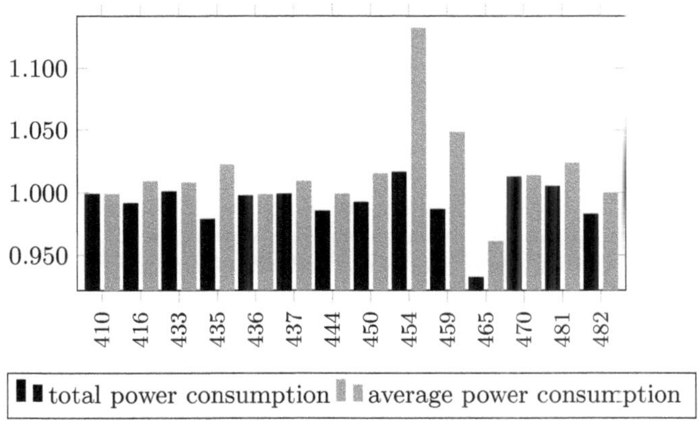

Figure 13: Power Evaluation Spec2006 Float (Normalized to Baseline)

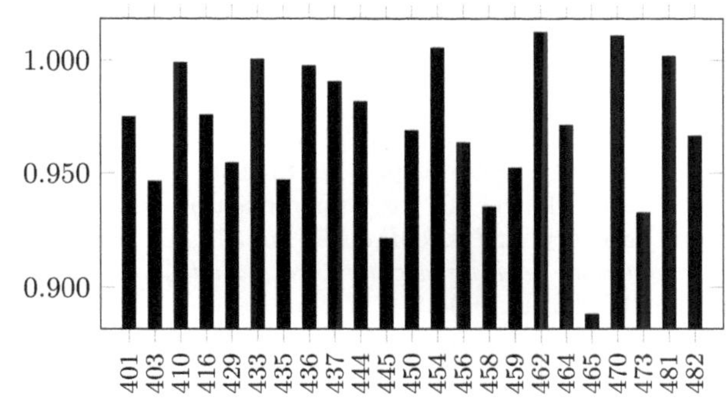

Figure 14: EDP normalized to baseline configuration

In other benchmarks, Mower performs much better than our baseline configuration in power efficiency. For example in 465.tonto Mower is 13% more power efficient.

We will now consider the area overhead of Mower. Mower uses a maximum of 12 in-flight branches and requires two major bit matrices called BDM and MDM. BDM's size is $12x12$ bits (18 bytes) and MDM's size is $68x12$ (102 bytes) (68 is the number of logical registers). The overhead of the two bit matrices total a size of 120 bytes. Mower also needs to keep track of the previous MDM row for each ROB entry, creating an overhead of 12 bits (number of in-flight branches) per ROB entry. Assuming an ROB size of 128, this creates 192 bytes of overhead. For CPR, with 68 logical registers, 128 physical registers and 8 checkpoints, we will need 476 bytes of overhead. Mower has significantly less overhead compared to CPR. Additionally, Mower does not use a back-end RAT which is extra saved space compared to the baseline.

6. CONCLUSION

Mower is an innovative mechanism to provide better branch misprediction recovery for superscalar processors. we believe there are several important contributions made by the Mower algorithm. These are 1) ability to dynamically release the stale resources while keeping correct dependencies; 2) Fixing the frontend RAT at the same time in order to make an expedited channel to the backend. 3) sharing ROB access ports during reclaim process to maximize the utilization.

In most recovery algorithms, the recovery process is limited by hardware resources which are predetermined. We believe Mower is the first approach to do it dynamically so that there are no predetermined limitations in the sense that it can deal with any number of mispredictions which can happen. Mower is also a low-cost solution. Added structures are small in size, providing reasonable power consumption while improving performance. Our evaluation indicates that Mower eliminates nearly all of state restoration penalty component of branch mispredictions. We believe the proposed technique is an effective technique, particularly for integer programs which contain a large number of high penalty branch mispredictions.

7. REFERENCES

[1] H. Akkary, R. Rajwar, and S. T. Srinivasan. Checkpoint processing and recovery: Towards scalable large instruction window processors. In *Proceedings of the 36th Annual IEEE/ACM International Symposium on Microarchitecture (MICRO-36)*, pages 423–434. IEEE, 2003.

[2] P. Akl and A. Moshovos. Branchtap: Improving performance with very few checkpoints through adaptive speculation control. In *Proceedings of the 20th Annual International Conference on Supercomputing*, ICS '06, pages 36–45, New York, NY, USA, 2006. ACM.

[3] P. Akl and A. Moshovos. Turbo-rob: a low cost checkpoint/restore accelerator. In *High Performance Embedded Architectures and Compilers*, pages 258–272. Springer, 2008.

[4] J. L. Aragón, J. González, A. González, and J. E. Smith. Dual path instruction processing. In *Proceedings of the 16th international conference on Supercomputing*, pages 220–229. ACM, 2002.

[5] D. N. Armstrong, H. Kim, O. Mutlu, and Y. N. Patt. Wrong path events: Exploiting unusual and illegal program behavior for early misprediction detection and recovery. In *Proceedings of the 37th International Symposium on Microarchitecture (MICRO-37)*, pages 119–128. IEEE, 2004.

[6] D. Brooks, V. Tiwari, and M. Martonosi. Wattch: A framework for architectural-level power analysis and optimizations. In *Proceedings of the 27th Annual International Symposium on Computer Architecture*, ISCA '00, pages 83–94, New York, NY, USA, 2000. ACM.

[7] J.-L. Cruz, A. Gonzalez, M. Valero, and N. Topham. Multiple-banked register file architectures. In *Proceedings of the 27th International Symposium on Computer Architecture*, pages 316–325, June 2000.

[8] A. Gandhi, H. Akkary, and S. T. Srinivasan. Reducing branch misprediction penalty via selective branch recovery. In *10th International Symposium on High Performance Computer Architecture (HPCA)*, pages 254–264. IEEE Computer Society, 2004.

[9] A. Golander and S. Weiss. Checkpoint allocation and release. *ACM Trans. Archit. Code Optim.*, 6(3):10:1–10:27, Oct. 2009.

[10] T. H. Heil and J. E. Smith. Selective dual path execution. Technical report, University of Wisconsin-Madison, 1996.

[11] A. Hilton, N. Eswaran, and A. Roth. Cprob: Checkpoint processing with opportunistic minimal recovery. In *Proceedings of the 18th International Conference on Parallel Architectures and Compilation Techniques (PACT)*, pages 159–168. IEEE, 2009.

[12] W.-m. W. Hwu and Y. N. Patt. Checkpoint repair for out-of-order execution machines. In *Proceedings of the 14th annual international symposium on Computer architecture*, pages 18–26. ACM, 1987.

[13] M. Johnson. *Superscalar Microprocessor Design.* Prentice Hall, 1991.

[14] A. Klauser, A. Paithankar, and D. Grunwald. Selective eager execution on the polypath architecture. In *ACM SIGARCH Computer Architecture News*, volume 26, pages 250–259. IEEE Computer Society, 1998.

[15] F. Latorre, G. Magklis, J. González, P. Chaparro, and A. González. Crob: implementing a large instruction window through compression. In *Transactions on high-performance embedded architectures and compilers III*, pages 115–134. Springer, 2011.

[16] S. Li, J. H. Ahn, R. D. Strong, J. B. Brockman, D. M. Tullsen, and N. P. Jouppi. Mcpat: an integrated power, area, and timing modeling framework for multicore and manycore architectures. In *MICRO-42. 42nd Annual IEEE/ACM International Symposium on Microarchitecture*, pages 469–480. IEEE, 2009.

[17] S. Önder and R. Gupta. Automatic generation of microarchitecture simulators. In *IEEE International Conference on Computer Languages*, pages 80–89, Chicago, May 1998.

[18] P. G. Sassone, J. Rupley, II, E. Brekelbaum, G. H. Loh, and B. Black. Matrix scheduler reloaded. In *Proceedings of the 34th Annual International Symposium on Computer Architecture*, ISCA '07, pages 335–346, New York, NY, USA, 2007. ACM.

[19] J. E. Smith and A. R. Pleszkun. Implementing precise interrupts in pipelined processors. *IEEE Transactions on Computers*, 37(5):562–573, 1988.

[20] A. K. Uht, V. Sindagi, and K. Hall. Disjoint eager execution: An optimal form of speculative execution. In *Proceedings of the 28th annual international symposium on Microarchitecture*, pages 313–325. IEEE Computer Society Press, 1995.

[21] S. Wallace, B. Calder, and D. M. Tullsen. Threaded multiple path execution. In *ACM SIGARCH Computer Architecture News*, volume 26, pages 238–249. IEEE Computer Society, 1998.

[22] P. Zhou, S. Önder, and S. Carr. Fast branch misprediction recovery in out-of-order superscalar processors. In *Proceedings of the 19th Annual International Conference on Supercomputing*, ICS '05, pages 41–50, New York, NY, USA, 2005. ACM.

zFENCE: Data-less Coherence for Efficient Fences

Shaizeen Aga Abhayendra Singh Satish Narayanasamy

University of Michigan, Ann Arbor
{shaizeen, ansingh, nsatish}@umich.edu

ABSTRACT

Efficient fences will not only help improve the performance of today's concurrent algorithms, but could also pave the way for the adoption of stronger memory models such as Sequential consistency (SC). However, the cost of fences in commodity processors remains prohibitively expensive.

A hardware fence only requires that all memory accesses preceding a fence in the program order are performed *before the fence and its following memory accesses are performed. But, it does not require that these operations are* completed *in that order.*

In this work we observe that a significant fraction of fence overhead is caused by stores that are waiting for data from memory. We propose the zFENCE *architecture that exploits this observation for efficiently implementing a fence by introducing the capability to grant coherence permission for a store much earlier than servicing its data from memory. We show that* zFENCE *eliminates fence overhead in a majority of scenarios, and helps bridge the performance gap between SC and TSO runtime memory models for a low design cost.*

Categories and Subject Descriptors

C.1.4 [**Computer Systems Organization**]: PROCESSOR ARCHITECTURES—*Parallel Architectures*

Keywords

Memory Consistency; Sequential Consistency; Fences; Data Less Coherence; Parallel Programming

1. INTRODUCTION

While the merits of the sequentially consistent (SC) memory model are well known, the concern for its performance overhead has prevented its adoption in mainstream languages. To guarantee language-level SC, both compiler and hardware optimizations need to be restricted to be SC-preserving. Recent studies have produced encouraging results showing that it is indeed possible to preserve SC during compiler optimizations for a fairly low performance cost (less than 4% on average) [32]. However, preserving SC at runtime in the presence of hardware optimizations continues to be a challenge.

Today's mainstream concurrent programming languages, including C++ [8], Java [31] and OpenCL [25], have adopted variants of the data-race-free (DRF) memory model [2]. While these languages guarantee SC for correctly written data-race-free programs, they guarantee either no semantics [8] or weak and complex semantics for programs with data races [31].

While existing hardware does not guarantee SC, in order to support the DRF-0 model, their ISAs provide support for a full *fence*. Fences are used by a DRF-0 compliant compiler to implement memory accesses to synchronization variables (annotated as `volatile` in Java or `atomic` in C++). Completion of a full fence instruction in hardware guarantees that all the instructions in the same thread that precede the fence in the program order have been *performed*, before performing any instruction after the fence.

Compiler can guarantee SC on relaxed DRF-0 compliant hardware by conservatively inserting a fence for each memory access [13]. Memory model constraints enforced on hardware by these compiler-inserted fences are equivalent to the constraints that a hardware would have to anyway honor to guarantee SC.

Unfortunately, fences are prohibitively expensive in today's commodity hardware (about 20 cycles even when store-buffer is empty, and an order of magnitude higher when it contains store misses). We believe that if fences become inexpensive, language developers would be more willing to adopt stronger memory model standards, such as SC. Therefore, instead of asking for SC hardware, proponents of a language-level SC memory model should simply ask for efficient hardware support for fences. As efficient fences are useful to improve the performance of existing DRF-0 compliant concurrent programs, processor industry has a clear short-term incentive to optimize fences.

In this paper, we present *z*FENCE, a simple optimization that can provide near zero overhead hardware fences. We believe that *z*FENCE can remove the remaining performance hurdle that is holding back language designers from adopting SC, without requiring complex changes to commodity hardware designs.

Past solutions for realizing efficient SC hardware and fences employed complex out-of-window speculation [7, 4, 18, 34, 24, 20, 10, 37], global mechanisms that continuously

ICS'15, June 8–11, 2015, Newport Beach, CA, USA.

http://dx.doi.org/10.1145/2751205.2751211.

check and prevent memory ordering violations while reordering memory accesses [30, 13, 22], or additional hardware and system support that identify and optimize safe data-race-free accesses [35].

We observe that *long latency store misses serviced by main memory* are by far the dominant cost of fences in a modern TSO multi-core processor. This cost can be easily optimized using hardware mechanisms that are much simpler than past solutions for efficient fences and SC.

In an efficiently implemented out-of-order processor with in-window speculation [18], the only intrinsic performance cost due to a fence is the cost of draining the store buffer before completing a fence. Furthermore, a huge fraction of the cost of draining the store buffer is due to long latency store misses serviced by main memory. It is less critical to optimize the low-latency store misses that are serviced either by an on-chip second-level cache or by another processor core's cache. Multi-processor SC designs proposed before the multi-core era perhaps did not consider this cost-benefit trade-off, as off-chip communication between multiple processors could be as expensive as fetching data from main memory.

We discuss a simple hardware design, zFENCE, which significantly reduces the impact of store misses serviced by main memory in enforcing fence constraints. zFENCE enables the directory to grant the exclusive coherence permission for a store before servicing the data. As we show in this paper, the coherence permission to a cache block can be serviced much faster than data for critical long latency store misses. A fence can be completed as long as all stores in the store buffer have acquired and retain their exclusive permission [16]. It is not necessary for those stores to have completed by writing their new values to data in cache or memory.

zFENCE optimization is fairly simple. On receiving a store miss request that needs to be serviced by the slow main memory, instead of waiting for the data fetch from the memory to complete, the on-chip directory cache responds immediately by sending a message granting coherence permission (but without data) for the requested block to the requester. Fences stall at the head of the re-order buffer only if there are pending stores in the store-buffer without the coherence permission. The only additional constraint that zFENCE needs to enforce to guarantee fence semantics is that a processor core does not relinquish the coherence permission to a cache block before any pending store in the store buffer to that cache block is completed. Fortunately, holding coherence permissions for pending stores cannot cause a deadlock, because they are not waiting for other processor cores but simply waiting for the data fetch from the main memory to complete.

Our optimization exceeds or equals most of the benefits of the optimizations that targets relaxing the memory ordering constraint for the private data [35], because, zFENCE optimizes any L2 store miss to private data, without relying on conservative compiler analysis or page-level tracking of private locations [35]. In addition, any store misses to shared data serviced by memory are also optimized. However, zFENCE does not optimize relatively low-latency store misses to cache blocks owned by other processor cores. We show that this is a worthy trade-off for realizing a complexity-effective design.

Unlike single-socket architectures, in a multi-socket architecture, coherence permissions cannot always be obtained through on-chip communication. Nevertheless, we find that zFENCE is still effective for multi-socket architectures for at least two reasons. First, a significant fraction of stores misses are to private data, whose home directory tends to be located on the same chip as the requesting core. Second, even when a store miss is serviced by a remote memory, zFENCE can be effective as the off-chip directory could grant the permission without waiting for the data fetch from memory to complete.

We study the use of zFENCE in guaranteeing SC at runtime for several x86 macro-benchmarks (SPLASH-2 [38], PARSEC [6], and Apache). We use our compiler to conservatively insert fences for all memory accesses to guarantee SC at runtime on an RMO processor. We show that the performance of this SC system is only 1.54% slower than TSO and 2.93% slower than RMO without the additional fences we insert. zFENCE based SC system also outperforms a recent SC hardware proposal [35], which is also more complex than zFENCE, as it requires store-to-load forwarding from two store buffers and hardware to determine safe accesses (private and shared read-only accesses).

This paper makes the following contributions:

- In modern multi-core processors, we observe that store misses serviced by main memory constitute the dominant cost of fence overhead. Optimizing this cost is largely adequate in eliminating memory ordering costs of fences.
- We propose zFENCE, which enables the directory to grant coherence permission before servicing data from main memory. This capability allows a fence to complete without waiting for data for stores to be fetched from main memory.
- We show that zFENCE optimization eliminates most of the fence overhead. We study both single and multi-socket systems, and compare SC implemented using zFENCE with TSO and RMO processors. We also show that our SC system outperforms a recent SC hardware design [35].

2. BACKGROUND AND MOTIVATION

In this section, we discuss the motivation for SC and the challenges in supporting efficient fences.

2.1 Need for SC

Programmers commonly take two programming abstractions for granted when analyzing a program snippet: *program order*, which requires that instructions in a thread execute one after the other in the order they appear in the program text; and *shared memory* that behaves as a map from addresses to values with each memory operation taking effect immediately. The memory model that preserves this intuitive program behavior for multithreaded programs is formally known as *sequential consistency* (SC) [26].

Before the arrival of commodity multi-core processors, the issue of memory models was mostly delegated to processor architects and assembly-level programmers. Ubiquitous adoption of parallel programming made it essential to standardize concurrency semantics at the language-level. Unfortunately, memory models of mainstream languages such as

C++ and Java chose to provide SC only for data-race-free programs [2, 31, 8]. For racy programs, these languages either provide no semantics or a weak semantics, which permit obscure thread interleavings that are hard for a programmer to reason about. Furthermore, proving the correctness and safety of various compiler and hardware optimizations under these weak memory models continues to be a challenge [36, 9].

2.2 Processor Actions

We clarify a few common terms that describe events in a processor core. An *in-flight* instruction is one that has been fetched into the processor pipeline but has not yet been committed. In an out-of-order processor, instructions may *execute* out-of-order but must *commit* from the reorder buffer (ROB) in the program order. Two memory operations in different threads are said to *conflict* if they access the same memory location and at least one of them is a write.

A load or a store is *performed* if its actions are observable to all the processors [14]. In most processors, a load is performed when it is committed from the ROB. In SC, stores are performed at commit. In TSO or RMO, a store may commit from the ROB and be placed in a store buffer *without* being performed. A store is *completed* when it eventually *retires* from the store buffer and its value is written to cache or memory.

2.3 Challenges in Realizing Efficient Fences

Compilers can guarantee SC on commodity processors by inserting fences between stores and loads. Thus, efficient fences can allow us realize efficient SC. However, realizing an efficient hardware fence design remains a challenge. It is not only sufficient to produce an efficient design but the modifications needed to a commodity processor should be simple enough that hardware vendors would be willing to adopt it in practice.

Though there are various flavors of fences in modern processors, we consider a full fence. A full fence requires that all the preceding stores and loads in the program order are performed before that fence and its following accesses (all in the same thread) are performed.

In-window speculation [18] allows in-flight loads to speculatively execute (i.e., read from memory) out-of-order ahead of preceding memory operations and fences, while still guaranteeing that they appear to perform at the time of their commit. Since TSO disallows load-load reordering, most modern x86 processors also implement in-window speculation to allow out-of-order execution of loads. In-window speculation is also useful in a relaxed memory-order (RMO) processor as it would allow loads to execute ahead of memory fences in the pipeline. Hence, we assume support for in-window speculation in all the hardware designs we study.

In window speculation, however, does not help us hide the overhead of fence constraint for stores, as stores have to be performed before performing a fence. To guarantee this fence constraint, a conservative hardware stalls the commit of a fence from the ROB when the store buffer is not empty. This store buffer drain is the primary overhead in enforcing fence constraint.

3. *z*FENCE OVERVIEW

As we described in the previous Section 2, waiting for the store buffer drain is the primary cost associated with a fence. We present an overview of the *z*FENCE optimization that addresses this cost.

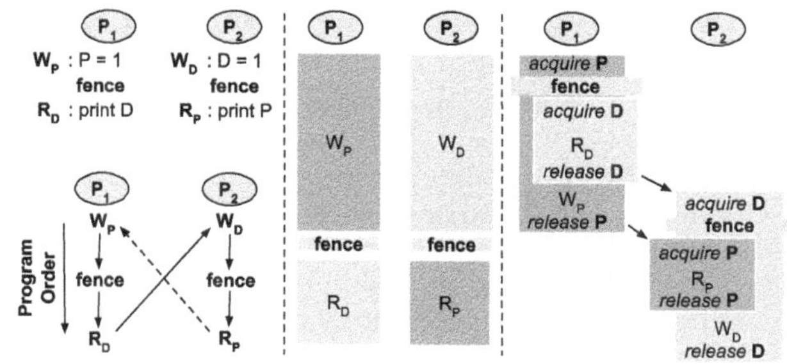

Figure 1: Performing a store before completing it.

3.1 Store Buffer Drain is not Necessary to Preserve Fence Semantics

To implement fences efficiently, we exploit the crucial observation [16]: it is not necessary to *complete* a store in order to *perform* it. A store is performed at an instant when a load issued to the same address by any processor returns that store's new value. To perform a store, it is not necessary to have completed the store actions by merging its new value to the architectural memory state. In past this observation has been used to reduce the latency of store by sending eager acknowledgments [19] for invalidation requests. However, past approaches do not optimize for the case where stores go to main memory.

In *z*FENCE we propose to exploit the above observation for stores that do not require any invalidation and receive data from memory. To perform a store, it is sufficient to acquire the coherence permission for that store's address, provided it is not released until its actions are completed.

Figure 1 provides an example to clarify the above observation. In a conventional fence implementation (middle figure in 1), processors P1 and P2 each have to *complete* their respective stores before their fences can be committed. This overly constrained fence implementation unnecessarily stalls the pipeline, delaying the commit of instructions following the fence (loads in our example).

In *z*FENCE, as shown in the rightmost figure in 1, a processor stalls a fence commit only till the pending stores in the store-buffer acquire their coherence permissions (without waiting for data). While stores are waiting for the data fetch from memory to complete, later fence and loads are allowed to complete out-of-order.

Even though the completion of write W_P is delayed, fence semantics are not violated. Once W_P is performed by acquiring its coherence permission, any later read to P is guaranteed to observe the new value of W_P, as it would have to wait for W_P to complete and release the coherence permission. This is ensured as we do not relinquish the coherence permission acquired for W_P until it is completed. This will not cause a deadlock as pending stores are waiting for data fetch from memory and not on an action by any other processor. In summary, once W_P is performed, the dotted edge in Figure 1 representing the execution order that is necessary to violate fence semantics can never happen.

3.2 Decoupling Coherence Permission from Data Fetch

For zFENCE to commit fences faster, acquiring coherence permissions should be faster. We observe that most fence overhead is caused by pending stores serviced by main memory. zFENCE specifically targets such long latency stores and expedites acquisition of their coherence permission by decoupling coherence permission acquisition from data fetch.

To accomplish this, when a directory receives an exclusive coherence request to a cache block that needs to be serviced by the main memory (i.e., the cache block is in `Invalid` state), the directory immediately responds back with a special coherence reply, zMESSAGE, which grants exclusive coherence permission to the requester without sending the data. Simultaneously, it instructs the memory controller to fetch the required data from memory and forwards it to the requester once it is fetched. Thus, coherence permission acquisition is a magnitude faster since we take off-chip data access off the critical path.

We did not attempt to decouple the coherence permission from data for store misses that are serviced by either the on-chip L2 cache or by another processor core's private cache. Coherence transactions necessary to service these stores are relatively low latency operations as they do not involve a main memory access. As a result, the coherence permissions for a large fraction of these store misses is acquired even before the store reaches the head of the ROB due to the coherence prefetch request optimization [18]. Modern x86 TSO processors commonly support this optimization where a processor core issues a coherence read-exclusive prefetch request as soon as a store's address is resolved in the processor pipeline.

4. zFENCE ARCHITECTURE

In this section, we describe our proposed zFENCE architecture that enables fences to commit without requiring expensive store buffer drain. zFENCE mostly relies on the directory based coherence infrastructure of a commodity processor.

4.1 Baseline Fence Design

We assume a single-socket processor that supports MOESI coherence protocol using distributed directories (we describe multi-socket design in Section 4.5). We assume directory caches are inclusive [12]. That is, a directory cache miss to a cache block implies that it is not cached by any processor core (i.e., cache block is in `Invalid` state).

Each processor core contains a private L1 cache and a private L2 cache. We also assume two optimizations that are commonly supported in TSO processors. The first optimization is in-window speculation [18] that enables out-of-order execution of loads across fences, while providing an illusion that they are performed in the program order (Section 2.3). The second optimization is issuing a coherence read-exclusive prefetch request [18] for stores as soon as a store's address is resolved in the processor pipeline, which helps hide some part of the store miss latency.

In our baseline architecture, we assume that a fence is committed from ROB only when all preceding stores are completed. This is achieved by draining the store buffer. This may incur an expensive pipeline stall, especially if stores in the store buffer have missed in on-chip caches and are waiting for data to be fetched from the slow main memory. This overhead constitutes the bulk of the performance cost associated with fences.

4.2 Directory Controller Extensions

The directory controller is responsible for decoupling coherence permission from data only while servicing exclusive permission request to a cache block whose data resides in the main memory (that is, when the cache block is in the `Invalid` state). For the reasons described in Section 3.2, zFENCE directory does not decouple coherence permission from data while handling any other coherence request to blocks in any other state, and hence its actions to service them remain the same as in the baseline.

On receiving an exclusive coherence request to a cache block in the `Invalid` state, the zFENCE directory controller immediately responds with a special zMESSAGE granting exclusive coherence permission to the requester. This is the only addition to the baseline directory controller. Rest of the actions are the same as in the baseline, which includes sending a message to the memory controller instructing it to fetch the appropriate data, and blocking all later coherence requests to the same block till the data is fetched and sent to the requester.

4.3 Processor Core Extensions

In order to commit a fence in zFENCE, we need to test if all preceding stores have their coherence permissions. In zFENCE, we expedite coherence permission acquisition for long latency stores by decoupling coherence permission from data. Thus, processors could acquire coherence permission without data and as an effect we need to provision to track this state.

Modern out-of-order processor cores use a content addressable store queue (different from store buffer) to keep track of all in-flight stores. The store queue is used to enable store-to-load forwarding. In zFENCE, we propose to add an additional bit, zBIT, to each store queue entry as well as to each store buffer entry. On receiving the zMESSAGE or the coherence permission with data for a cache block, processor core searches the store queue and store buffer for the stores to that cache block. Matching store entries get their zBIT set to remember that the exclusive coherence permissions have been acquired.

When a store reaches the head of the ROB, it is committed to an unordered coalescing store buffer and its zBIT is copied over to the corresponding store buffer entry. The store waits here for its cache block data to arrive and then it completes.

A fence is allowed to commit from the head of ROB only when all stores in the store buffer have their zBIT set. Otherwise, the fence is stalled.

It is also necessary to ensure that exclusive permission to a cache block is not lost when there is a pending store to that block in the store buffer with its zBIT set, as that could violate fence semantics. Note that in zFENCE we would commit a fence only when all pending stores have their zBIT set and thus it is safe to relinquish coherence permissions for pending stores if their zBIT is not set. A processor core could have to relinquish coherence permission either to service an incoming coherence invalidation request or to allocate space for a cache block requested by a later memory operation. Even in a blocking directory protocol, it is possible for a processor to get a forwarded request while there it has a pending store to same location as stores to same location could prefetch permissions for subsequent stores. *z*FENCE forces these two actions to a cache block to stall until the pending store to that cache block is completed.

Stalling the above two actions causes insignificant performance overhead. Stalling the eviction of a recently accessed cache block for which there is a pending store is an insignificant performance issue (and perhaps could be a performance win). Stalling a cache invalidation could potentially delay the operation in the requesting processor but in practice we observe that this case is not common.

Before evicting a cache block from L1 or downgrading its exclusive permission, it is necessary to search the store queue. The *z*BIT for any matching entry in the store queue needs to be reset to indicate that the coherence permission for the corresponding store is no longer available. Note that stores in store queue are *in-flight* and resetting of their *z*BIT does not effect their completion. When the store reaches the head of ROB, a binding cache coherence request will be issued for it.

4.4 Correctness and Deadlock Freedom

In this section, we provide an informal proof sketch for correctness and deadlock-freedom for *z*FENCE.

Loads preceding a fence are always committed before the fence. A load that follows a fence, even though could execute out-of-order with respect to the fence, in-window speculation [18] guarantees that it appears to have performed at the time of its commit. For stores, *z*FENCE guarantees fence semantics by ensuring that all stores preceding a fence in the program order acquire their coherence permissions before we commit that fence. Furthermore, coherence permissions to pending stores in the store buffer with their *z*BIT set are not relinquished before they are completed. These are sufficient constraints to guarantee full fence semantics.

*z*FENCE is deadlock-free. The only stall it introduces is stalling the actions that cause a processor core to relinquish the exclusive coherence permission to a cache block for which there is a pending store in the store buffer. Having already acquired the coherence permission, a pending store in the store buffer is either waiting for the data response or cache write port access in order to complete its actions. When these pending stores complete, any actions stalled on their behalf can be allowed to proceed.

4.5 Multi-Socket Systems

*z*FENCE is also effective in reducing the overhead of fences in a multi-socket architecture, though to a lesser degree. We study the multi-socket architecture shown in Figure 2. Each processor chip is a chip-multiprocessor (CMP). We assume two-level coherence for such systems: intra-cmp coherence and inter-cmp coherence. Intra-cmp coherence manages permissions between cores within a processor chip. This is supported by the first-level directories. In *z*FENCE, this remains unchanged.

Inter-cmp coherence is involved while managing coherence for cache blocks serviced by the main memory or by a remote processor core on another chip. This is supported by the second-level directories. Since the second-level directories are responsible for granting coherence permissions for cache blocks residing in main memory, we extend it to support *z*FENCE. That is, when a second-level directory receives request to a cache block that resides in the local memory it manages, it immediately responds back to the requester with the *z*MESSAGE.

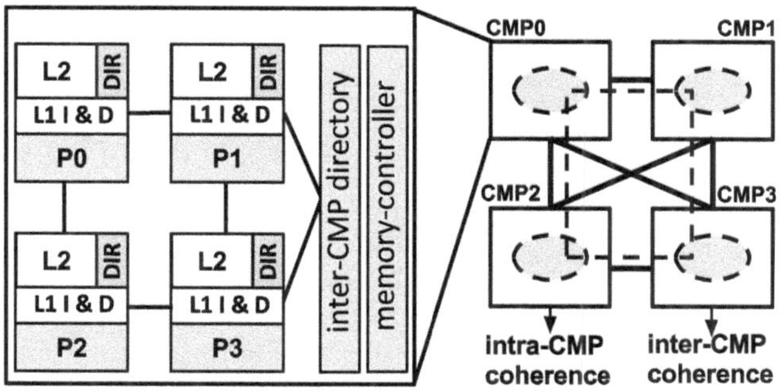

Figure 2: Multi-chip system overview

We assume that the operating system allocates pages in the memory that is local to the first processor that requests it. This ensures that a significant fraction of the private data accessed by threads executing in a processor are allocated in the local memory. Any store miss to a private cache block stored in a processor's local memory would enjoy all the performance benefits in *z*FENCE discussed before.

If a store miss request is serviced by a remote memory, it would entail off-chip communication with the second-level directory located in a remote processor chip. Nevertheless, *z*FENCE is still effective in reducing the fence overhead caused by such stores as the remote directory can respond with the *z*MESSAGE much faster when compared to servicing data from the remote memory.

One limitation of *z*FENCE is that it does not help reduce the overhead of store misses that are serviced by other processor cores, as we do not decouple data from coherence for servicing such stores. Coherence prefetch optimization is largely effective in fetching permissions before the stores get to the head of the ROB in single-socket systems where the permissions are serviced by on-chip cores. However, in multi-socket systems, when permission to a store is serviced by remote off-chip cores, it may result in some overhead as it requires off-chip communication.

4.6 Illustration

Figure 3 (b) illustrates the program execution shown in Figure 3 (a) under two different architectures: baseline RMO with traditional fences, and RMO with *z*FENCE. In this example, a program executes two threads on two processor cores `P1` and `P2` as shown in Figure 3. The initial state of all three variables `P`, `D` and `F` is zero. Under fence semantics, it is not possible for loads in `P2` for `P` and `D` to have values `0` and `1` respectively. Fence semantics are violated only if both conflict orders shown in Figure 3 are observed in an execution. A memory operation that results in a cache miss is represented using a gray shade.

RMO using baseline fences conservatively stalls the commit of a fence due to pending store miss $\texttt{ST}_P$ and consecutively all its following operations in `P1` (❶). Though required to preserve fence semantics, this enforces an unnecessarily strict constraint, which could result in long pipeline stalls, especially if $\texttt{ST}_P$ is serviced by the main memory.

*z*FENCE, on the other, hand commits the fence after ensuring that `P1` owns the exclusive coherence permission for the cache block `P` which is the only pending store. While

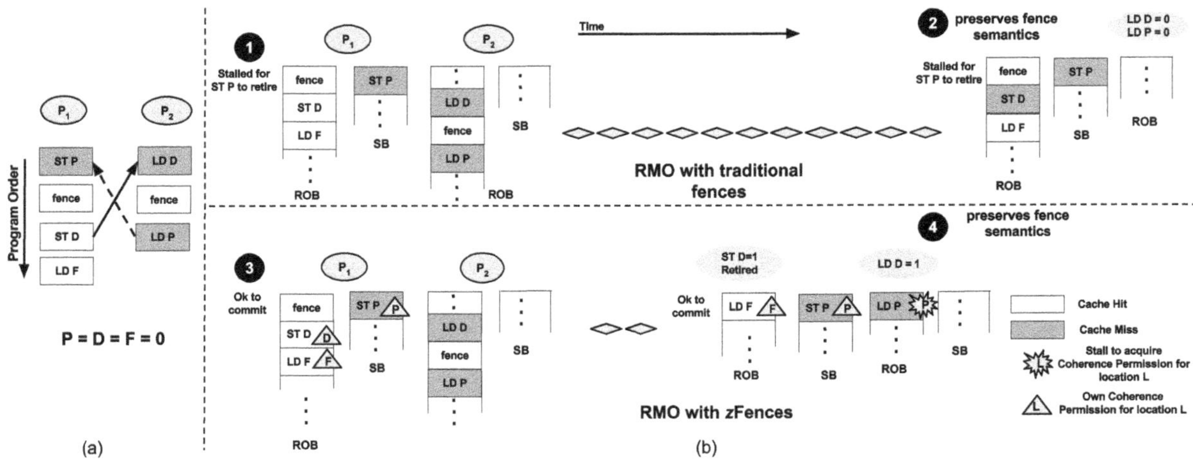

Figure 3: (a) A program's execution. (b) RMO with *z*Fence compared to RMO with baseline fence.

ST_P is waiting for its block to be fetched from memory, later operations in P1 are allowed to commit from the ROB (❸). This allows P1 to commit and complete ST_D whose value is then observed by LD_D in P2. Thus, solid conflict edge in Figure 3 (a) is observed in this execution. However, *z*FENCE preserves fence semantics by ensuring that the dotted conflict edge is not observed. This is ensured by enforcing a constraint that P1 does not release its coherence permission for P when there is a pending store to P. When P1 receives a coherence request for P from P2, it simply stalls the response till ST_P is completed, which in turn stalls LD_P in P2 (❹). When P1 eventually releases the coherence permission for P, P2 is guaranteed to see the new value written by ST_P, preserving fence semantics.

5. STRONGER MEMORY MODELS USING *Z*FENCE

In this section we highlight the performance benefits that *z*FENCE enables for stronger memory models.

A compiler can preserve SC at runtime on RMO hardware by conservatively inserting a fence after every memory access. Note that this does not necessarily imply addition of more instructions. With the shift to 64-bit ISA we expect more freedom in finding unused bits in the ISA to convey that an instruction has fence semantics. Only if this is not an option, we can resort to adding fence instructions, which all DRF0-compliant ISAs (ARM, x86, PowerPC) support.

Compared to using traditional fences, *z*FENCE based SC system enjoys the following performance benefits:

- A load can commit even if there are pending stores in the store buffer waiting for the data response from the main memory. The fence associated with a load only needs to wait for the pending stores to acquire their coherence permissions.
- Stores can be committed to unordered coalescing store buffer as soon as preceding stores have acquired their coherence permissions.
- Pending stores in *z*FENCE's unordered store buffer can be completed and retired from the store buffer out-of-order.
- Pending stores in the store buffer can be coalesced.

Notice that the last two benefits listed above are an advantage over a TSO processor, which needs to ensure in-order retirement of stores from its FIFO store buffer.

Relaxed memory model like TSO can also benefit from *z*FENCE. TSO mandates ordered store retirement. This can be accomplished with a fence between every two consecutive stores. *z*FENCE helps TSO as it enables an unordered coalescing store buffer for TSO which would let stores complete out-of-order while still honoring TSO constraints.

6. EXPERIMENTAL EVALUATION

We study in this section the efficiency of *z*FENCE and its use in supporting stronger memory model.

6.1 Configurations Studied

Our end goal is to enable a language-level SC memory model. Therefore, in all of our experiments we use the binaries compiled using the publicly available SC-preserving version of LLVM compiler [32]. This compiler preserves SC across compiler optimizations but does not guarantee SC on relaxed memory models such as TSO or RMO.

The goal of our experiments is to understand the performance overhead of enforcing SC at runtime and compare it to the performance of more relaxed Total Store Order (TSO) (similar to x86 model) and RMO. To evaluate the performance overhead of SC, we studied three configurations. The first configuration is a baseline SC processor design, where each load requires a store-buffer drain and stores are retired in the program order. We refer to this design simply as *SC*. The second design assumes an RMO processor with *z*FENCE support. We use the compiler to generate fences for each memory access in order to guarantee SC on this processor. Note that this does not require adding extra instructions as a single bit (lock-prefix like bit in x86) suffices to convey that a memory instruction is to be treated as a fence. Original fences produced by the baseline compiler (e.g., for atomic accesses) are also inserted. We refer to this system as *z*SC. We also compared against a recent non-speculative SC design [35] which we refer as `type-SC`. Type-SC delivers high SC performance without employing complex out-of-window speculation by relaxing SC constraints for safe memory op-

Table 1: Simulator Parameters

Configuration	CMP: 16 cores on chip
	Multi-chip: 4 CMPs each with 4 cores on chip
Processor	4GHz core with 96 entry ROB
Fetch, Execute, Commit	4 instructions (max 2 loads and 1 store) per cycle per core
Store Buffer	SC, TSO: 8-byte 64-entry FIFO buffer RMO: 64-byte 8-entry unordered coalescing buffer
L1 Cache	64 KB per-core private, 4-way set associative, 64B block size, 2-cycle hit latency, write-back
L2 Cache	512KB per-core private, 4-way set associative, 64B block size, 10 cycle hit latency
Coherence	CMP: MOESI directory protocol
	Multi-chip: Hierarchical MOESI directory protocol
Directory	Distributed, 10-cycle lookup latency
Interconnect	CMP: Torus-2D topology, 256-bit link width, 1ns link latency
	Multi-chip: On-chip Ring, 256-bit link width, 1ns latency Off-chip all-to-all, 32-bit link width, 20ns cycle latency
Memory	160-cycle DRAM lookup latency

erations (accesses to private and read-only shared locations). It requires an additional safe store buffer that is used to accelerate safe stores. In addition, it requires hardware and operating system support for tracking safe pages.

We also evaluated the performance of TSO and RMO memory models with *z*FENCE optimization, but did not observe any significant performance improvement, as our baseline TSO/RMO designs and their fence implementations are aggressively optimized using known techniques. We leave these results in the current submission due to space constraints.

6.2 Simulation Model

We modeled the hardware designs using a Simics based execution driven, cycle-level x86 simulator FeS2 [15]. Table 1 lists the parameters assumed in our experiments.

To model a single-socket chip-multiprocessor (CMP), we study a 16-core processor with 2D-Torus interconnect. For baseline SC and TSO processors, we assume a 64-entry FIFO store buffer with 8-byte (one word) entries. For RMO, we assume an 8-entry unordered coalescing store buffer with 64-byte wide entries (size of an L1 cache block). Thus, across all configurations we are area neutral in terms of store buffer size. For all configurations we implemented in-window load speculation and read-exclusive prefetches for stores [17]. We modeled a directory based MOESI coherence protocol.

We also model a multi-socket system with four CMPs, each with four processor cores as shown in Figure 2. Structures in each CMP are modeled similar to the CMP in our single-socket configuration. We configure an all-to-all off-chip interconnect and a ring based on-chip interconnect network. Since a multi-socket system requires caches to be kept coherent across different chips, we employ an hierarchical directory based coherence protocol modeled along the lines of [33]. Such an hierarchical coherence protocol is composed of an intra-cmp coherence protocol for caches on chip, which is then coupled with an inter-cmp coherence protocol for coherence amongst different chips as depicted in Figure 2.

In both single and multi socket configurations we model an inclusive directory cache not backed by main memory. We target a coverage ratio of 1.6X for our directory caches. If the cache block of an entry that is evicted from the directory cache is *not* in `Invalid` state, a recall [12] is issued to invalidate its permissions in processor's private caches to ensure inclusivity.

6.3 Benchmarks

We study applications from PARSEC [6], SPLASH-2 [38] and a commercial web server benchmark, `Apache`. For the applications in PARSEC we used `simlarge` inputs. For `barnes` in SPLASH-2, we used 65536 n-body simulation, and for `Apache` we used the SURGE [5] benchmark.

For `Apache`, we warmed up the caches and micro architectural state for 10000 transactions and then collected simulation statistics over another 10000 transactions. For `barnes`, we simulated the entire parallel section after warming the L2 cache with an execution that produced at least as many L2 cache misses as the number of L2 cache lines per core.

For benchmarks in PARSEC, due to long simulation time it was not feasible to simulate the entire parallel section and hence sampling was employed. We took checkpoints for five samples spanned across most of the parallel section. In each simulation run we warmed up the caches by restoring cache state at the end of the last checkpoint. To warm-up rest of the micro-architectural state we also ran each checkpoint in the warm-up phase for 1 million user stores per core. After the warm-up, we measured the performance by simulating 160 million user stores across all cores.

6.4 *z*SC compares favorably to TSO and RMO

We evaluate the *z*SC system (RMO processor with *z*FENCE) and demonstrate how it effectively eliminates most of the performance penalties incurred by a conventional SC machine.

Figures 6 and 4 compare the performance of *z*SC system to baseline SC (labeled as SC), type-SC [35], and the relaxed processors TSO and RMO for the single-socket and multi-socket systems respectively. Performance overhead is reported with respect to RMO.

When compared to RMO, on average, baseline SC incurs overhead of about 8.88% for a single-socket system and this overhead goes up to 9.46% for the multi-socket system. For certain benchmarks like `barnes`, SC exhibits considerable overhead when compared to RMO. By enabling un-ordered coalescing store buffer, *z*SC reduces SC overhead to about 0.95% on average for single-socket and 2.93% for multi-socket system. This demonstrates that even if coherence permission is off-chip, *z*SC can successfully eliminate overhead of fences in SC. Also, this supports our hypothesis that majority of fence overhead is attributable to stores serviced by main memory for it is only this cost that we optimize in *z*SC. The maximum overheads we observe are for `apache` and `swaptions`. Section 6.6 analyzes the overhead in these two benchmarks in depth.

TSO is more constrained than RMO, for RMO employs an unordered coalescing store buffer, but TSO requires a FIFO store buffer. This advantage is also present in *z*SC as it too employs an unordered coalescing buffer like RMO. Performance gap between TSO and *z*SC is as low 1.37% on average for multi chip system.

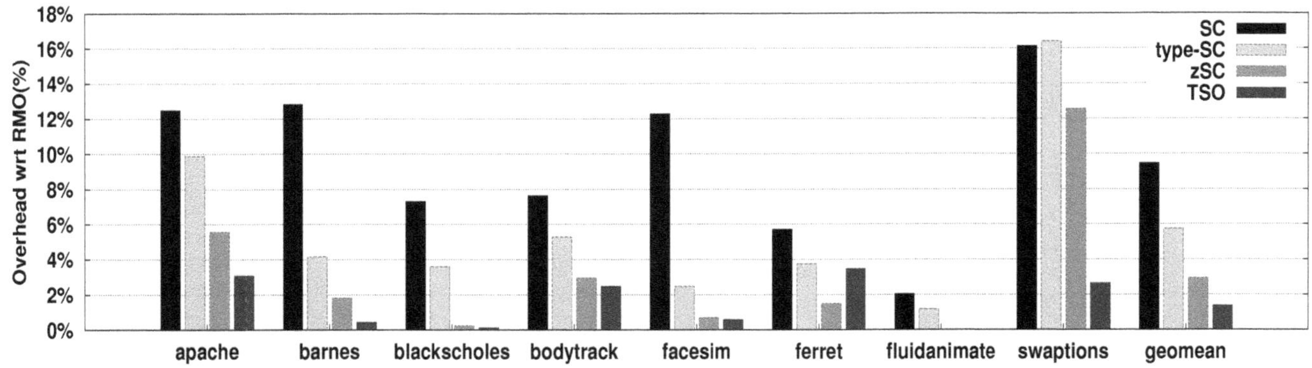

Figure 4: SC performance overhead with respect to RMO in Multi-Socket System

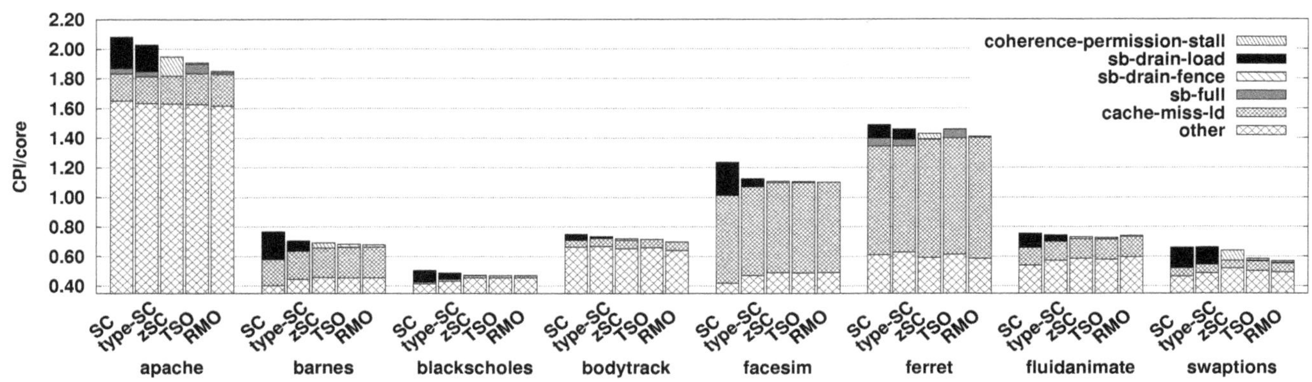

Figure 5: CPI stack depicting commit stage stall reasons in Multi-Socket System

6.5 Comparison to Type-SC

Figure 6 also shows that *z*SC outperforms a recent non-speculative SC design [35] (type-SC). Average overhead of type-SC is about 4.91% on average for single-socket and 5.74% for multi-socket; which is brought down by *z*SC. The overhead in type-SC is slightly higher than the reported result in [35]. We believe this is due to longer samples in our simulations, and also we carry over the unsafe state for pages across different samples. As a program executes longer, more and more pages would be classified as shared unsafe locations. While this overhead could be optimized by resetting classifications periodically, it would entail additional complexity.

*z*SC compares favorably with type-SC not only with respect to performance but also in terms of complexity. Type-SC requires two store buffers (one each for safe and unsafe stores) which introduces complexities in the store-to-load forwarding logic. Also, additional software and hardware support is needed for statically and dynamically classifying memory operations as safe and unsafe.

6.6 Detailed Analysis of Memory Ordering Overhead

In Figure 5, we analyze various sources of memory ordering overhead for different processor designs we studied for the multi-socket system. We attribute each processor core's cycle to one of the following categories and calculate their contributions to average CPI per core. Since we model a commit-width of four instructions, a cycle in which all four instructions at the head of the ROB are committed or commit is stalled for a reason other than ones being considered here is classified under *other*. Otherwise, the cycle is attributed to one of the following reasons that caused the commit stall. The first instruction in the program order that caused the stall is referred to as the `Head`. At the end of each stall category we indicate the processor configurations that could incur the stall.

- *cache-miss-ld*: `Head` is a load miss waiting for the data. (All configurations)
- *sb-full*: `Head` is a store and the store buffer is full. (All configurations)
- *sb-drain-fence*: `Head` is a fence waiting for the store buffer to drain. (TSO and RMO)
- *sb-drain-load*: `Head` is a load. It is ready to perform, but stalled for store buffer drain. (Baseline SC and Type-SC)
- *coherence-permission-stall*: `Head` is a lock-prefixed store waiting to acquire coherence permission as explained in Section 6.4. (*z*SC).
- *other*: None of the above or core committed commit-width instructions.

In Figure 5 the cycles attributed to the *other* categories varies across different contributions. This is due to an artifact of our classification strategy. A load stalled for store buffer drain will contribute to *sb-drain-load* in baseline SC and will mask any potential stalls contributing to *other*

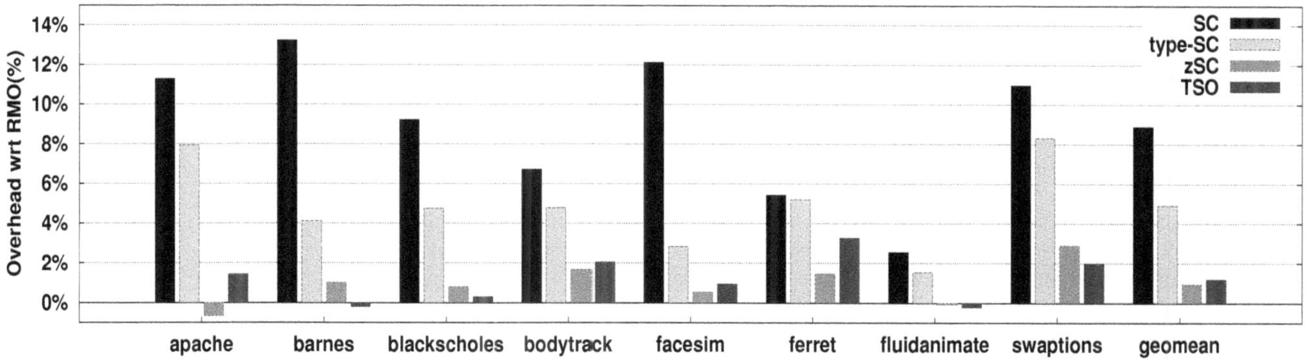

Figure 6: SC performance overhead with respect to RMO in Single-Socket System

bucket. Since loads do not contribute stall cycles to *sb-drain-load* in RMO or *z*SC configurations, we could have higher *other* stall cycles that were masked in SC.

Stalls caused by *sb-drain-load* dominate the commit stage stalls in both baseline SC and *type*-SC configurations. We see considerable *sb-drain-load* stalls in `facesim`, `barnes` and `apache` in baseline SC which *type*-SC helps eliminate to certain extent, while *z*SC eliminates this overhead completely.

Since baseline SC, *type*-SC, and TSO employ a FIFO store buffer, they suffer from commit stalls due to FIFO store buffer being full. On the other hand RMO and *z*SC employ unordered coalescing store buffers, and thus they do not incur these *sb-full* stalls significantly.

While *z*SC is successful in reducing the overhead of ensuring SC in most benchmarks, `apache` and `swaptions` are still left with considerable overhead. The factor which limits the performance of *z*SC as compared to RMO and TSO is *coherence-permission-stall.* For benchmarks under consideration this overhead tends to be negligible except for apache and swaptions where this overhead is considerable, about 6.59% and 10.82% of total execution time respectively.

7. RELATED WORK

For the set of benchmarks under study, even though a small percentage of total store misses get serviced by main memory, they are primary contributors to memory ordering overhead. Our proposed technique helps eliminate precisely this overhead by granting coherence permission without data for requests serviced by main memory. To our knowledge, earlier designs for efficient fences did not employ this optimization to amortize the overhead of enforcing fence constraints.

7.1 Store Miss Optimizations

A store miss waits for all sharers to acknowledge invalidation request. Store wait time can be reduced by *early acknowledgment* [3, 16, 27, 1] of an invalidation request as soon as it is queued at the recipient processor. The AlphaServer GS320 [19] exploits this optimization to perform stores faster. Early acknowledgment only targets store misses already cached in other processors, but not long latency off-chip store misses. We observe that store misses to blocks cached in other cores contribute far less to fence overhead as compared to off-chip store misses.

To address the overhead of off-chip store misses in a TSO processor, Chou *et al.* proposed a victim-cache-like structure (named SMAC) for the last-level L2 [11]. SMAC stores the addresses of evicted L2 blocks that had exclusive permission. If a store miss hits in SMAC, and if it is at the head of the FIFO store buffer, it is allowed to retire. SMAC optimization is complementary to ours in that it can help optimize store miss latency to cache blocks mapped to remote processors in a multi-socket system. While *z*FENCE can reduce store miss latency to any block managed by the directory, SMAC optimizes only for those that were recently evicted.

7.2 Efficient fences

There have been several proposals directed at making fences efficient. Techniques like Invisifence [7, 37] use out-of-window speculation to bring down the overhead of fences. Note that these proposals not only rely on checkpointing of large amount of processor state but also demand non-trivial amount of storage. Our proposed technique does not rely on any form of speculation and is thus free of any concomitant overheads of checkpointing or rollback.

There have also been non-speculative proposals to bring down fence overhead. Lin *et al.* [28] proposed conditional fences in which compiler communicates to the hardware about set of fences (called associate fences) for which fence ordering must be ensured. In other words, they ensure that all memory operations prior to a fence must be completed before its associate fence is issued. To keep track of associate fences, they propose to use a global table that maintains information about currently active fences in the system that have outstanding store misses. In contrast, our proposal does not need hardware support for tracking pending stores globally.

More recently, WeeFence [13] also uses global information about pending conflicting stores to allow memory accesses to skip fences. In contrast, our technique does not require keeping track of pending accesses at other cores and hence does not incur the additional complexity and storage overhead associated with it. SFence [29] aims to reduce fence overhead by letting programmers convey which memory operations need ordering guarantees provided by fences. and as such is orthogonal to our technique. SFence could use our optimization to further bring down the fence overhead and also we could use SFence to limit the stores whose coherence permission need to be waited on before committing a fence.

7.3 Efficient SC Designs

In this section we describe prior work on efficient SC hardware. Techniques proposed in these prior work can be potentially used to reduce the cost of fences.

To enable store buffer optimization while preserving SC, past work proposed aggressive out-of-window speculation [34, 21, 20, 23, 10]. These designs allowed loads to speculatively commit even when the store buffer is not empty. To detect a memory ordering violation, incoming coherence invalidations need to be compared with addresses of all the loads committed after the oldest pending store. When a violation is detected for a speculatively committed load, execution needs to be rolled back to that load, which requires that the hardware checkpoints the program state at each speculatively committed store. Thus, out-of-window speculation requires fairly complex hardware to detect and recover from memory ordering violations.

Non-speculative SC hardware designs like Afek et al.'s "lazy caching" [3] and Landin et al.'s "race-free networks" [27] achieve SC but rely on special properties such as bus based ordering or race-freedom in the network. More recently, Lin et al. [30] proposed "conflict-ordering". Their key insight is that a processor is allowed to perform a memory access as long as there are no pending conflicting accesses preceding it in the global total order. Thus, correctness in [30] was contingent on efficient conflict detection mechanism: a core has to be apprised of all pending conflicting memory operations at any other core before a memory operation could be committed from ROB. This constraint requires an augmented write buffer to track every memory operation until all preceding memory operations in global total order are complete. It further requires elaborate changes to coherence protocol for cores to communicate presence of pending memory operations to other cores.

Singh *et al.* proposed the End-to-End SC that supports SC efficiently by not enforcing SC constraints on provably safe accesses. We have discussed this design in Section 6.4. Recently, Gope *et al.* proposed Atomic-SC [22] a non speculative SC design for in-order multi-core systems. They implement another layer of functionality which they term as mutexes. Cores acquire mutex for every miss and for all hits under the shadow of a miss. Cores release acquired mutex for an operation only when all preceding operations in program order are *complete*. Thus, using mutexes they attain the net effect of obtaining a lock on a memory location and all subsequent operations before moving past a memory operation and keeping it pending. While implementing this technique for out-of-order multi-core systems is non-trivial, our proposed technique avoids the complexities of an additional mutex layer by harnessing the existing coherence infrastructure.

8. CONCLUSION

We observed that a significant fraction of fence overhead could be amortized simply by introducing a capability where the directory is able to grant the coherence permission before servicing the data. The only micro-architectural state that is added to a baseline hardware to take advantage of these early coherence permissions without data is a bit per store queue entry and store buffer entry. These early coherence permissions enable an effective fence design we term *z*FENCE that does not wait for long latency stores to be serviced by the main memory.

Our SC realization using *z*FENCE, *z*SC successfully eliminates most of the runtime SC overhead in single-socket systems by reducing it to 0.95% performance cost when compared to RMO hardware. Even for multi-socket systems, *z*SC is shown to be effective for a majority of programs. We also demonstrated that *z*SC outperforms a recently proposed SC hardware design.

9. ACKNOWLEDGMENTS

We thank the anonymous reviewers for their comments which helped improve this paper. This work is supported by the National Science Foundation under the CAREER-1149773 award.

10. REFERENCES

[1] S. V. Adve and M. D. Hill. Implementing sequential consistency in cache-based systems. In *Proc. of the 1990 International Conference on Parallel Processing*, 1990.

[2] S. V. Adve and M. D. Hill. Weak Ordering—A New Definition. In *Proc. of the 17th Annual International Symposium on Computer Architecture*, 1990.

[3] Y. Afek, G. Brown, and M. Merritt. A lazy cache algorithm. In *SPAA '89: Proc. of the ACM Symposium on Parallel Algorithms and Architectures*, pages 209–222, 1989.

[4] W. Ahn, S. Qi, J.-W. Lee, M. Nicolaides, X. Fang, J. Torrellas, D. Wong, and S. Midkiff. BulkCompiler: High-Performance Sequential Consistency through Cooperative Compiler and Hardware Support. In *Proc. of the 42nd Annual International Symposium on Microarchitecture*, 2009.

[5] P. Barford and M. Crovella. Generating Representative Web Workloads for Network and Server Performance Evaluation. In *Proc. of the 1998 ACM SIGMETRICS Conference on Measurement and Modeling of Computer Systems*, 1998.

[6] C. Bienia, S. Kumar, J. P. Singh, and K. Li. The PARSEC Benchmark Suite: Characterization and Architectural Implications. In *Proc. of the 17th International Conference on Parallel Architectures and Compilation Techniques*, 2008.

[7] C. Blundell, M. Martin, and T. Wenisch. InvisiFence: Performance-Transparent Memory Ordering in Conventional Multiprocessors. In *Proc. of the 36th Annual International Symposium on Computer Architecture*, 2009.

[8] H. J. Boehm and S. V. Adve. Foundations of the C++ Concurrency Memory Model. In *Proc. of the 2008 ACM SIGPLAN Conference on Programming Language Design and Implementation*, pages 68–78, 2008.

[9] P. Cenciarelli, A. Knapp, and E. Sibilio. The java memory model: Operationally, denotationally, axiomatically. In *16th European Symposium on Programming*, pages 331–346, 2007.

[10] L. Ceze, J. Tuck, P. Montesinos, and J. Torrellas. BulkSC: Bulk Enforcement of Sequential Consistency.

In *Proc. of the 34th Annual International Symposium on Computer Architecture*, 2007.

[11] Y. Chou, L. Spracklen, and S. Abraham. Store memory-level parallelism optimizations for commercial applications. In *Proc. of the 38th Annual International Symposium on Microarchitecture*, 2005.

[12] P. Conway, N. Kalyanasundharam, G. Donley, K. Lepak, and B. Hughes. Cache hierarchy and memory subsystem of the amd opteron processor. *Micro, IEEE*, 2010.

[13] Y. Duan, A. Muzahid, and J. Torrellas. Weefence: toward making fences free in tso. In *Proc. of the 40th Annual International Symposium on Computer Architecture*, pages 213–224, 2013.

[14] M. Dubois, C. Scheurich, and F. A. Briggs. Memory access buffering in multiprocessors. In *Proc. of the 13th Annual International Symposium on Computer Architecture*, pages 434–442, 1986.

[15] The FeS2 simulator. `http://fes2.cs.uiuc.edu/`.

[16] K. Gharachorloo. *Memory Consistency Models for Shared-memory Multiprocessors*. PhD thesis, Stanford, CA, USA, 1996. UMI Order No. GAX96-20480.

[17] K. Gharachorloo and P. Gibbons. Detecting violations of sequential consistency. In *SPAA '90: 2nd Annual ACM Symposium on Parallel Algorithms and Architectures*, pages 316–326, 1991.

[18] K. Gharachorloo, A. Gupta, and J. Hennessy. Two Techniques to Enhance the Performance of Memory Consistency Models. In *Proc. of the International Conference on Parallel Processing*, 1991.

[19] K. Gharachorloo, M. Sharma, S. Steely, and S. Van Doren. Architecture and design of alphaserver gs320. In *Ninth International Conference on Architectural Support for Programming Languages and Operating Systems*, 2000.

[20] C. Gniady and B. Falsafi. Speculative Sequential Consistency with Little Custom Storage. In *Proc. of the 11th International Conference on Parallel Architectures and Compilation Techniques*, 2002.

[21] C. Gniady, B. Falsafi, and T. N. Vijaykumar. Is SC + ILP=RC? In *Proc. of the 26th Annual International Symposium on Computer Architecture*, 1999.

[22] D. Gope and M. Lipasti. Atomic sc for simple in-order processors. In *Proc. of the 20th International Symposium on High-Performance Computer Architecture*, 2014.

[23] L. Hammond, B. D. Carlstrom, V. Wong, B. Hertzberg, M. Chen, C. Kozyrakis, and K. Olukotun. Programming with Transactional Coherence and Consistency (TCC). In *12th International Conference on Architectural Support for Programming Languages and Operating Systems*, 2004.

[24] M. D. Hill. Multiprocessors Should Support Simple Memory-Consistency Models. *IEEE Computer*, 31:28–34, 1998.

[25] Khronos. The opencl specification. version 2.0. 2014.

[26] L. Lamport. How to Make a Multiprocessor Computer that Correctly Executes Multiprocess Programs. *IEEE Computer*, 1979.

[27] A. Landin, E. Hagersten, and S. Haridi. Race-free Interconnection Networks and Multiprocessor Consistency. *Proc. of the 18th Annual International Symposium on Computer Architecture*, 1991.

[28] C. Lin, V. Nagarajan, and R. Gupta. Efficient Sequential Consistency using Conditional Fences. In *Proc. of the 19th International Conference on Parallel Architectures and Compilation Techniques*, 2010.

[29] C. Lin, V. Nagarajan, and R. Gupta. Fence scoping. In *SC'14*, 2014.

[30] C. Lin, V. Nagarajan, R. Gupta, and B. Rajaram. Efficient Sequential Consistency via Conflict Ordering. In *20th International Conference on Architectural Support for Programming Languages and Operating Systems*, 2012.

[31] J. Manson, W. Pugh, and S. V. Adve. The Java Memory Model. In *Proc. of the 32nd ACM SIGPLAN-SIGACT symposium on Principles of Programming Languages*, 2005.

[32] D. Marino, A. Singh, T. Millstein, M. Musuvathi, and S. Narayanasamy. A Case for an SC-Preserving Compiler. In *Proc. of the 32nd ACM SIGPLAN Conference on Programming Language Design and Implementation*, 2011.

[33] M. R. Marty, J. D. Bingham, M. D. Hill, A. J. Hu, M. M. K. Martin, and D. A. Wood. Improving multiple-cmp systems using token coherence. In *Proc. of the 11th International Symposium on High-Performance Computer Architecture*, 2005.

[34] P. Ranganathan, V. Pai, and S. Adve. Using Speculative Retirement and Larger Instruction Windows to Narrow the Performance Gap between Memory Consistency Models. In *Proc. of the ninth Annual ACM Symposium on Parallel Algorithms and Architectures*, 1997.

[35] A. Singh, S. Narayanasamy, D. Marino, T. Millstein, and M. Musuvathi. End-to-end Sequential Consistency. In *Proc. of the 39th Annual International Symposium on Computer Architecture*, 2012.

[36] J. Ševčík and D. Aspinall. On validity of program transformations in the Java memory model. In *Proc. of the 22nd European Conference on Object-Oriented Programming*, pages 27–51, 2008.

[37] T. Wenisch, A. Ailamaki, B. Falsafi, and A. Moshovos. Mechanisms for Store-wait-free Multiprocessors. In *Proc. of the 34th Annual International Symposium on Computer Architecture*, 2007.

[38] S. C. Woo, M. Ohara, E. Torrie, J. P. Singh, and A. Gupta. The SPLASH-2 Programs: Characterization and Methodological Considerations. In *Proc. of the 22nd Annual International Symposium on Computer Architecture*, 1995.

PALMOS: A Transparent, Multi-tasking Acceleration Layer for Parallel Heterogeneous Systems

Christos Margiolas
University of Edinburgh
c.margiolas@ed.ac.uk

Michael F.P. O'Boyle
University of Edinburgh
mob@inf.ed.ac.uk

ABSTRACT

Accelerators, such as Graphic Processing Units (GPUs), are increasingly popular components of modern parallel systems. This move towards heterogeneity, however, has not progressed through all layers of system software. There is no transparent Operating System (OS) support for the management and sharing of accelerators between users and applications. Consequently, there is also no support for OS-level virtualization (containers) targeting heterogeneous software. This paper presents a secure, user-space virtualization layer that integrates the accelerator resources of a system with the standard multi-tasking and user-space virtualization facilities of commodity Linux OS. It targets heterogeneous commodity systems found in data center nodes and requires no modification to the OS, OpenCL or application. It eliminates high setup overhead, enables fine-grained sharing of mixed-vendor accelerator resources and provides resource and platform aware scheduling. The average throughput improvement across workloads and mixed-vendor platform configurations varies from 1.29x to 3.87x speedup over existing schemes. Our approach outperforms both vendor accelerator sharing facilities and message passing solutions.

Categories and Subject Descriptors

D.3.4 [**Software**]: Programming Languages—*Processors, Runtime environments, Optimization*

Keywords

heterogeneity; heterogeneous computing; virtualization; resource management; OpenCL; GPU; data placement

1. INTRODUCTION

Accelerators, such as Graphic Processing Units (GPUs), have proved to be popular components of modern heterogeneous systems. They provide the potential for low-cost, high-performance computing for highly parallel workloads. This move towards heterogeneity has been mirrored by the development of parallel programming languages such as CUDA[38] and OpenCL[25] which is portable across accelerators and standard multi-cores.

However, there is no further integration across the system software stack. Each accelerator is still viewed as a co-processor managed by the application; there is no transparent Operating System (OS) support for sharing accelerator resources between applications and users. There is no scheduling control for multi-accelerator systems. Currently, an accelerator is either exclusively dedicated to an application or supports limited sharing via vendor drivers where the sharing preconditions are non-obvious and lack fine-grained control. Such an approach may be sufficient for traditional HPC and single application systems, but introduces significant issues for multi-tasking systems.

There are a number of issues that are barriers to general use of heterogeneous systems. Firstly, accelerator sharing is either limited or not supported depending on the vendor. There is no support for mixed-vendor accelerator sharing between applications. Secondly, there is no OS-level resource isolation support for heterogeneous software using accelerators. Applications ignore the presence and activity of other applications and their accelerator usage which leads to resource contention. Thirdly, application setup times for heterogeneous software are currently prohibitive. This introduces a significant overhead for multi-tasking and virtualized environments where multiple applications co-exist. Finally, as applications run on shared memory platforms with multiple physical nodes, data placement and the selection of appropriate CPUs and accelerators can significantly affect the performance of an application or the system.

In this paper, we introduce PALMOS[1], a user-space virtualization layer that integrates the accelerator resources of a system with standard OS multi-tasking and enables OS-level virtualization for heterogeneous software. Our design reduces setup overhead, enables inter-vendor accelerator sharing and provides resource aware scheduling for heterogeneous applications. Our approach exclusively relies on the interfaces of OpenCL and standard system libraries. It remains compatible with existing software and systems. It does not require **any** modification of the OS, OpenCL library or application.

PALMOS targets standard heterogeneous systems found in data center nodes. Datacenter nodes support large numbers of diverse user tasks which need both performance and secure execution. While there is support for communica-

ICS'15, June 8–11, 2015, Newport Beach, CA, USA.

http://dx.doi.org/10.1145/2751205.2751217 .

[1]PALMOS stands for Parallel Acceleration Layer for Multi-tasking Operating Systems.

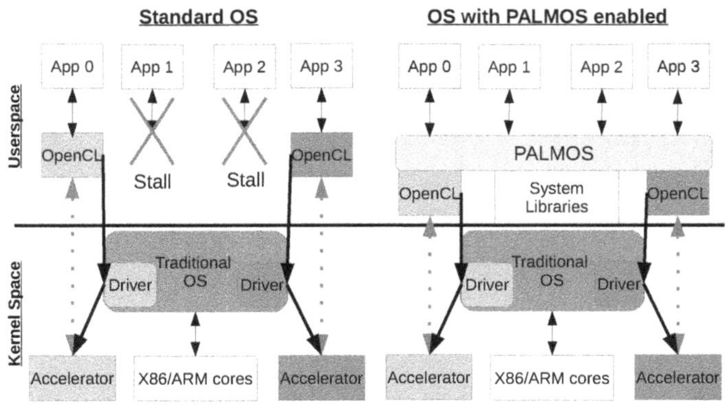

Figure 1: Motivation for PALMOS. Standard OpenCL accesses directly accelerator resources, suffers from large setup times and there is no resource sharing control. PALMOS enables fine-grained and inter-vendor accelerator sharing between multi-user applications, reduces setup overhead and performs resource aware scheduling.

tion and task scheduling between nodes such as Quasar[14], or Whare-Map[31], there is no appropriate support on node level, specially for systems with accelerators.

Hypervisors such as Xen[5]or Kvm[27] efficiently support OS virtualization but there is an upcoming need for more lightweight approaches [4][44][2][48] which provide virtualization and resource isolation for individual processes at user-space instead of full OS virtualization. Production technologies such as Docker [15] and OpenVZ [41] enable user-space virtualization but they focus on traditional applications and not on heterogeneous software. NVIDIA supports accelerator sharing between Virtual Machines [39]. However, it does not provide scheduling and resource sharing control or user-space virtualization. It is also vendor specific.

PALMOS performs accelerator management and sharing at user-space level, enabling virtualization for heterogeneous software. To summarize, this paper makes the following contributions:

- A lightweight and secure virtualization layer for multi-user heterogeneous computing.
- Seamless system integration requiring no modification to existing applications, OS or accelerators.
- Fine-grain sharing and control of inter-vendor accelerator resources between applications and users.
- Resource and NUMA aware multi-tasking and scheduling on host and accelerators.

We evaluate PALMOS across different, mixed-vendor platform configurations and workloads. It improves average throughput from 2.1x to 3.87x speedup over existing schemes.

The remainder of the paper is organized as follows. Section 2 describes our motivation for PALMOS. Section 3 provides a high-level overview of PALMOS. Sections 4, 5 and 6 present the key components and features of PALMOS. Section 7 describes our security control. We present our experimental setup and evaluation in sections 8 and 9. Sections 10 and 11 discuss the related work and conclusions.

2. MOTIVATION

This section provides a motivational example for this work. Consider figure 1 which shows the execution of four heterogeneous applications on a system with two accelerators.

On current systems, as shown in the left hand side of the figure 1, applications directly access the accelerators. Depending on the capabilities of the accelerators, some applications may fail to execute, stall or execute concurrently[37]. The OS has no knowledge about the accelerators and their capabilities and completely ignores memory transfers and scheduling on them. Everything is controlled by the application and there is no handling from a system perspective.

PALMOS, as shown in the right side of the figure, operates transparently as a user-space virtualization layer between the application and OS. Here, the applications do not directly access the accelerator resources. Instead, PALMOS controls scheduling on CPUs and accelerators and enforces fine grained inter-vendor sharing between the applications. Furthermore, it integrates smoothly with OS-level virtualization facilities. It operates transparently with standard application processes and applications running as part of containers built on the top of Linux namespaces[33].

3. PALMOS OVERVIEW

In this section, we provide a high-level overview of PALMOS, our user-space virtualization layer that integrates accelerator resources with commodity OS components. The design of the layer is portable, built on top of OpenCL and standard system libraries. The layer is transparent to both the OS and applications, requiring no modifications. It operates as a high priority user-space process which collects and manages computation and communication requests from different applications and users. It then schedules them on accelerator resources.

PALMOS builds an environment where each application can safely assume that it exclusively uses the host and accelerator resources. The application performs ordinary operations, computes on the host, allocates memory and makes the ususal calls to OpenCL functions for accelerator use. However, these function calls are forwarded to PALMOS which decides, for each application, which host CPUs to use, how to allocate memory and which accelerator to exploit.

3.1 Key Design Choices

One of the primary goals of PALMOS is portability and transparency i.e. no change to existing applications, libraries or OS. This means that the APIs that connect an OpenCL application to hardware, OpenCL library calls and standard memory management, must be preserved.

The next design goal is to support efficient heterogeneous multi-tasking and accelerator sharing. PALMOS is a separate layer between the applications and OS that manages all the system resources and controls scheduling to improve system throughput. These design decisions, however, introduce two problems: *communication overhead* and *security.*

Both PALMOS and the applications are ordinary processes that reside in different address spaces. This preserves compatibility as no piece of software has to be changed or recompiled. In addition, each application executes in a secure, isolated environment. A new challenge is therefore, how to achieve efficient inter-process communication and data sharing between PALMOS and its attached applications.

We solve this by using POSIX shared memory segments[40], segments of memory that are allocated independently of a single process and that are later mapped to the address spaces of the associated processes. This solution dramat-

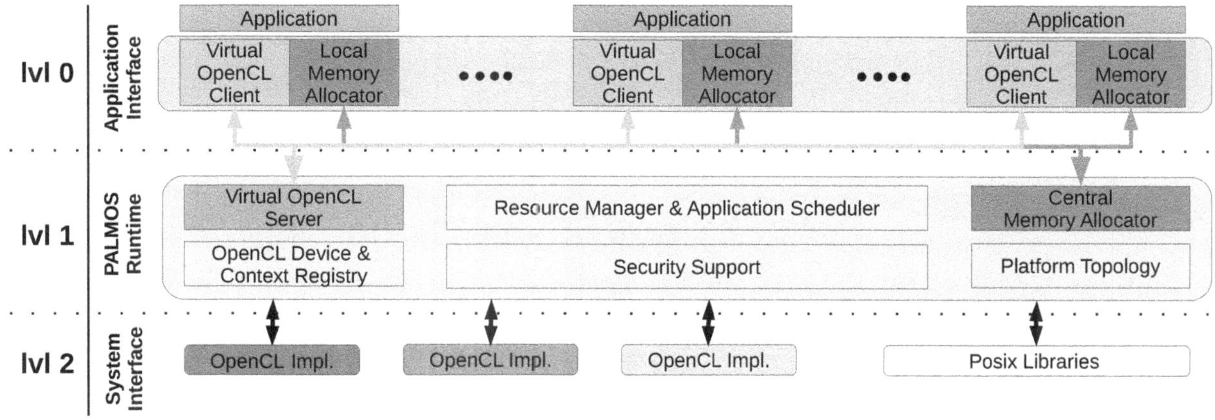

Figure 2: Overview of PALMOS. The layer design consists of three levels, the Application Interface (level 0), the PALMOS Runtime (level 1) and the System Interface (level 2), its connection to existing OS and runtimes. PALMOS operates transparently between existing applications, OS and OpenCL runtimes.

ically reduces overheads but raises security concerns that we address below and in more detail in section 7.

3.2 PALMOS Structured Design

Figure 2 gives an overview of PALMOS. The design consists of three levels. The Application Interface, level 0, enables the communication of application with PALMOS and guarantees transparency and portability. The APIs provided to applications are identical to those of OpenCL and system libraries. Level 1 is the heart of PALMOS; it provides inter-vendor accelerator sharing, scheduling control, environment setup, memory allocation and security. At level 2, the System Interface connects PALMOS with the existing OS and runtime libraries.

3.2.1 Level 0: The Application Interface

Applications are attached to PALMOS and interact with it without modifications. This is done via two interfaces (a) a Virtual OpenCL client that replaces the standard OpenCL library and (b) a Local Memory Allocator, provided by PALMOS, that replaces the standard memory allocator. Both interfaces are supplied as dynamic libraries that are preloaded.

Virtual OpenCL Client: It supports all OpenCL 1.2 functions and redirects any application call to them to the *Virtual OpenCL Server* of PALMOS instead of the actual OpenCL library. Virtual OpenCL is built on the top of shared memory for efficiency. We provide a detailed description of this mechanism in section 4.

Local Memory Allocator: This serves the memory allocation requests of the application. It is part of a two-level *"Inter-Space" Memory Allocator* which enables data sharing between the application and PALMOS, which are two distinct processes with distinct address spaces. The allocator leverages shared memory segments and an *Address Space Translation* mechanism to enable zero copy data sharing. Section 5 provides a detailed description.

3.2.2 Level 1: The PALMOS Runtime

This layer provides the core functionality of PALMOS including accelerator management, resource sharing control and improved scheduling.

Resource Manager & Application Scheduler: This monitors the execution of all applications and makes decisions about their scheduling on host and accelerators. It also takes care of data placement in multi-node shared memory, NUMA platforms. The scheduler receives operation requests via Virtual OpenCL and dispatches OpenCL operations to an accelerator based on its scheduling decisions. Section 6 provides further details.

Virtual OpenCL Server, Central Memory Manager: These are the PALMOS-side counterparts of the *Virtual OpenCL* and *Inter-Space Memory Allocator*. Sections 4 and 5 provide further details.

OpenCL Device & Context Registry: It stores accelerator specific information and OpenCL contexts. OpenCL contexts are now part of the PALMOS runtime relieving applications of high setup overheads.

Security Support: This addresses security within PALMOS. The PALMOS process and the application processes communicate through shared memory segments. In the absence of security control, there are potential threats. An application could send an invalid OpenCL call or attempt to communicate through a Virtual OpenCL Client it does not own. An application may also attempt to access data of a different application. This component prevents this by controlling the access to shared memory segments. Our security scheme integrates with the existing system security mechanisms for safe resource sharing and process protection. Further details are provided in section 7.

Platform Topology: This detects the topology of multi-node systems including the number of nodes, the size of local memories, the processor and accelerator locations.

3.2.3 Level 2: The System Interface

PALMOS exclusively depends on OpenCL, POSIX[40] and Linux system[30] libraries. OpenCL provides access and management of the accelerator resources while POSIX and Linux libraries are used for the management of standard CPU and memory resources, scheduling of application host code, data placement and security control.

4. VIRTUAL OPENCL

Virtual OpenCL forwards OpenCL operation requests to PALMOS. It is available to the application as a dynamic library that replaces standard OpenCL. It ensures transparency for the application, which operates as before with-

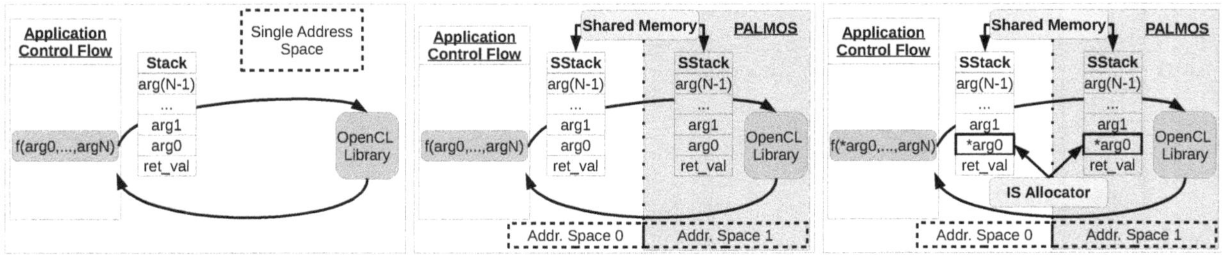

(a) Standard OpenCL Call (b) RPC OpenCL Call (c) RPC OpenCL Call (IS M. Allocator)

Figure 3: Comparison of the function call convention of the standard OpenCL environment (a) against our Virtual OpenCL mechanism that supports function calling across distinct processes. It supports function calling with arguments passed by value (b) and reference (c). Virtual OpenCL permits the efficient interaction of OpenCL applications with PALMOS.

out any modification or re-compilation. Virtual OpenCL consists of (a) a client that is loaded by the application process and (b) a server which is part of the PALMOS runtime process. The key issue is how the client and server communicate in an efficient manner that eliminates data coping between the different address spaces. We achieve this by using a *Shared Stack* which relies on POSIX shared memory.

4.1 Shared Stack

Figure 3a shows a function call made by the application to the OpenCL library. The application places the call arguments on the stack and then performs the call. The called function reads the arguments, executes and returns control.

In our scheme, each call to an OpenCL function is forwarded to the PALMOS runtime. The call cannot be performed directly as PALMOS and the application are in different address spaces. Instead there is a *Shared Stack* where the function arguments and return values are stored in a shared memory segment, which is mapped onto the address spaces of both PALMOS and the application. We handle the call as a Remote Process Call (RPC)[11], where the application makes the call request and PALMOS is the remote process that performs it. To illustrate this, see figure 3b which shows a function call using the Shared Stack. The application operates in address space 0 and performs an OpenCL call that is served by an OpenCL library that operates in a different address space, address space 1, owned by PALMOS. The application and library share the function call data via the Shared Stack. As shown in section 9.3, the use of Shared Stack leads to negligible overhead in comparison to standard OpenCL and other RPC approaches that use system message passing services or MPI[35].

4.2 Shared Data

The above approach works if the arguments are passed by value. If arguments are passed by reference[21] and pointers are used, then this approach is not sufficient. Pointers refer to arbitrary addresses of application memory which are not directly accessible to PALMOS. Our *Inter-Space Memory Allocator* (Section 5) enables data sharing between the application and PALMOS runtime without data copying. The application uses memory allocated through a custom allocator, which is accessible by the PALMOS runtime.

The RPC OpenCL call is now enhanced as shown in figure 3c. Here arg0 of the function call is a pointer referring to an address in the application address space. The memory it points to has been allocated by the Inter-Space Memory Allocator. PALMOS now can access the application data but the RPC call needs to translate the address value of arg0, which is valid in address space 0 of the application, to a valid address in address space 1 of PALMOS runtime. This is done by the *Address Space Translator* mechanism of the Inter-Space Allocator with negligible overhead.

Virtual OpenCL is built on the top of tuned *shared stack* and synchronization primitives that exploit shared memory segments. Both client and server sides of Virtual OpenCL rely on those primitives and they are automatically generated by our library code generator, which is implemented as an LLVM[28] compiler pass.

5. INTER-SPACE MEMORY ALLOCATOR

The Inter-Space Memory Allocator operates exclusively in user-space and enables zero copy, data sharing between the applications and PALMOS by operating across multiple address spaces. It also supports data placement control for multi-node NUMA platforms directed by the Resource Manager & Application Scheduler. Although it is used concurrently by multiple processes and threads, its operation remains lock free by design.

5.1 Two-Level Memory Allocator

Figure 4 shows the structure of our two-level custom allocator [9]. The Central Memory Allocator (CMA) allocates memory chunks from system memory and grants them for use to Local Memory Allocators (LMA). An LMA is instantiated per application thread.

Each chunk is granted exclusively to a single LMA. The LMA manages its chunks as allocation heaps and serves memory allocation requests made by the application. When the allocation heaps of an LMA run out of free memory, the LMA requests a new chunk from CMA. The LMA also yields unused chunks back to CMA. The chunk size is adaptive to the size of memory allocation requests.

The two level design of our allocator guarantees high performance and responsiveness[9]. Each application thread has its own LMA that manages its own local heaps and its operation is decoupled from other LMAs and the CMA. It contacts CMA rarely, only when new chunks are required.

5.2 Address Space Translator

The Inter-Space Memory Allocator uses shared memory segments as chunks. The key issue here is that for each process a shared segment is mapped onto a local address range that is valid only in the address space of the process.

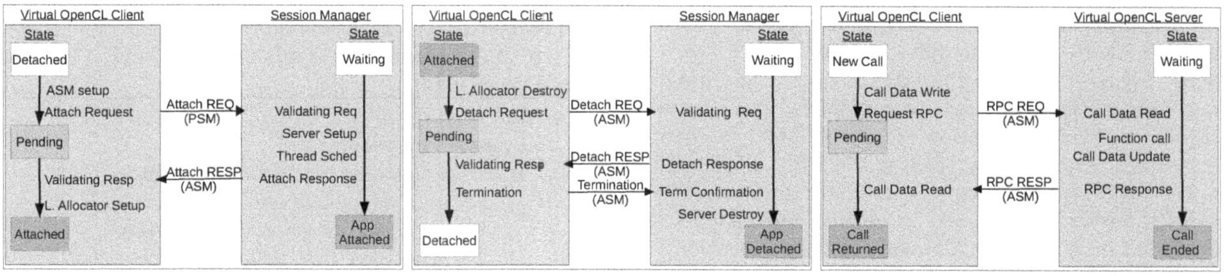

(a) Attach (b) Detach (c) Interaction

Figure 5: PALMOS Session Protocol. It enables the handshaking of an application with PALMOS and their further interaction. The protocol operations take place in the background via the Virtual OpenCL mechanism and no application modification is required. The design of the protocol is part of our security mechanisms found in section 7.

However, PALMOS requires access to application data and a mechanism that translates addresses across the different address spaces is required. We introduce the *Address Space Translator* that converts local addresses to a *global representation* and vice-versa. The global representation is valid across the address spaces and Address Space Translator converts it to valid local addresses for each process.

The global representation has the same size with pointer data types, which is equal to the architecture word size. The most significant half word represents a unique ID given by the CMA, which uniquely identifies a chunk. The least significant half word represents an address offset in the chunk. The translation overhead is negligible. It exclusively involves simple arithmetic operations and a data structure lookup. Section 9.3 presents real application scenarios and compares against standard OpenCL. As figure 4 shows, address translation takes place in both application and PALMOS.

5.3 Lock-free design

Our memory allocator enables data sharing between PALMOS and applications without the need for mutual exclusion as PALMOS and applications interact in a specific manner. An application allocates memory and passes a reference to PALMOS with function calls performed via Virtual OpenCL. While PALMOS processes a call, the application is blocked waiting for the response guaranteeing that the application code neither reads nor updates its data.

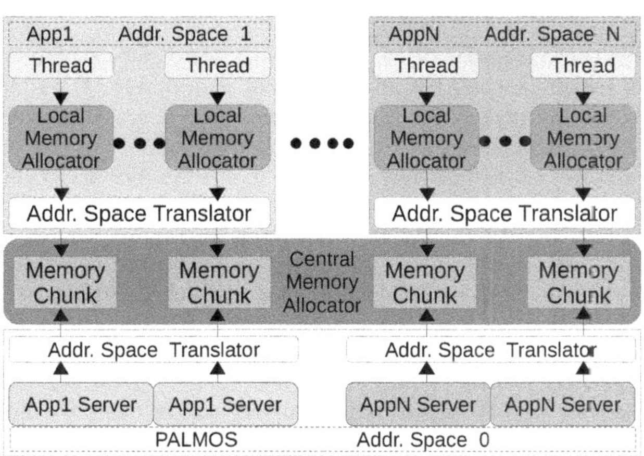

Figure 4: Data Sharing with Inter-Space Memory Allocator. Inter-Space memory allocator enables zero copy data sharing between the applications and PALMOS. Each application thread owns a Local Memory Allocator that uses memory chunks, provided by the Central Allocator, as heaps. A special component, called Address Space Translator, is used for the translation of data addresses between the address spaces of applications and PALMOS.

Furthermore, PALMOS only reads or updates data in application memory locations specified by the application function calls. It does not allocate new memory that is accessed by the application. An OpenCL implementation may allocate memory internally for its operation but this memory resides only in PALMOS and no sharing is required.

6. RESOURCE MANAGER & APPLICATION SCHEDULER

This section describes the Resource Manager & Application Scheduler (RMAS), the core component of PALMOS. It manages the system resources, monitors application execution and performs efficient scheduling on both host and accelerators. Furthermore, it controls data placement and location aware scheduling for multi-node shared memory systems. RMAS decides which accelerator is used based on its availability. It also reduces the application setup overhead; expensive operations such as accelerator reservation and OpenCL context creation are now done during PALMOS initialization instead of application setup.

6.1 PALMOS Session

PALMOS requires that each application is attached to it via a *session*. This session is used by RMAS to monitor and control the application execution and by our Security component (section 7) to build a secure environment for both the application and PALMOS. The session is managed by a protocol with three operations, *Attach*, *Detach* and *Interaction*. Those operations run in the background via the Virtual OpenCL mechanism, no application modification is required or API changes.

The protocol operations exchange messages between the Virtual OpenCL client of the application and the Virtual OpenCL server of PALMOS runtime via shared memory segments. PALMOS maintains a shared memory segment, named PALMOS Shared Memory (PSM), where it receives attach requests from Virtual OpenCL clients. The Virtual OpenCL client of an application maintains a shared memory segment, named Application Shared Memory (ASM) which is used as the *Shared Stack* (Section 4) and by the attach and detach operations of the PALMOS Session protocol. ASM access is restricted to the application and PALMOS while PSM is accessible by all applications (section 7).

Attach: Figure 5a shows the Attach operation. PALMOS has created PSM and awaits new requests. The Virtual OpenCL client of the application creates ASM. The client sends an *Attach Request* to PALMOS via PSM. PALMOS receives the request, validates it and instantiates a Virtual OpenCL Server which sends an *Attach Response* back via ASM. The Local Memory Allocator of the application is then instantiated by the Virtual OpenCL client.

Detach: Detach operation, shown in figure 5b, takes place just before the application termination. The Virtual OpenCL client destroys the Local Memory Allocator and sends a *Detach Request* to PALMOS. PALMOS validates the request and sends a *Detach Response* back. The client then sends a *Termination* message and application terminates. PALMOS then destroys the corresponding Virtual OpenCL Server. All the communication is done over ASM.

Interaction: Figure 5c shows the interaction of application with PALMOS while the session is established. ASM is used as *Shared Stack* for Virtual OpenCL (section 4) where the application performs RPC calls to PALMOS.

6.2 Application Scheduling

PALMOS has a unified scheduling approach for both CPU and accelerators. It controls the scheduling of host code on CPUs and the scheduling of OpenCL communication and computation operations on accelerators. We deploy a *First In First Out (FIFO)* scheduling policy which follows the same priority semantics with the FIFO scheduling policy of the modern Linux kernel. However, our system is modular and new policies can be added.

Thread Scheduling on Host: RMAS manages multi-threaded applications. Each application thread is attached separately, has its own session and a distinct Virtual OpenCL Server. That choice guarantees high responsiveness. An application thread along with its Server thread are scheduled on the same CPU core to increase data locality.

Operation Scheduling on Accelerators: RMAS manages all the accelerators and schedules operations of host-device communication and kernel computation on them. The application has no direct access to accelerators as it uses Virtual OpenCL, our OpenCL implementation that gives control to PALMOS. RMAS decides which accelerator is used at runtime and performs the actual OpenCL calls.

Operation Multiplexing on Accelerators: A scheduling policy may demand the suspension of an application and the allocation of its computational resources to another application. In the case of host code that runs on CPUs, OS *preemption* takes care of this.

For accelerators, however, the OS has no control over operation ordering or preemption. Accelerators may not support resource sharing and preemption. We solve this by enabling *Operation Multiplexing* that provides operation scheduling control at the granularity of OpenCL operations. OpenCL operations requested by the application are managed by our scheduler which decides which accelerator to use, and the time and order they will be sent to that accelerator. If an application is Paused, its pending operations will not be sent to the accelerator until the application is active again. This is provided by our OpenCL Command Queue implementation.

Algorithm 1: FIFO Scheduling. We provide a First In First Out, priority aware scheduling policy on both host and accelerators.

```
while True do
    event=wait_event();
    if event is a new app (attach) then
        priority_queue.enqueue(app);
        if an accelerator is available then
            accel=get_first_available_accelerator();
            app.set_state(Running);
            run_application(app,accel);
        else
            running_app=
            running_app_with_lowest_prio();
            if app.priority > running_app.priority then
                running_app.set_state(Paused);
                app.set_state(app,Running);
                multiplex(app,running_app);
            else
                app.set_state(app,Waiting);
    else if event is app completion (detach) then
        app.set_state(Completed);
        release_accelerator_of(app);
        priority_queue.remove(app);
        if priority_queue is not empty then
            app=nextWaitingOrPausedApp(priority_queue)
            accel=get_first_available_accelerator();
            app.set_state(app,Running);
            run_application(app,accel);
```

FIFO Scheduling Policy: Algorithm 1 presents the unified scheduling policy we use for the evaluation of PALMOS in this paper. When an application starts its execution, a new entry is added in a *Scheduling Priority Queue*. Each entry contains the application state and its priority. We develop a First In First Out (FIFO) scheduling policy with full priority support on both host and accelerators. The scheduling algorithm is driven by two events: the *Attach* and *Detach* of an application.

Attach Event: When a new application gets attached, the scheduler checks if an accelerator is available. If yes, it assigns the accelerator to the application, sets its state to Running and starts its execution. If there is no accelerator available two things may happen. The scheduler picks the running application with the lowest priority. If its priority is lower than the newly attached application, preemption is performed on the host and operation multiplexing on the accelerator. If the priority is higher, the scheduler sets the state of the newly attached application to Waiting and the application waits for its execution.

Detach Event: When an application gets detached, the scheduler sets its state to Completed and releases the accelerator. Then, it checks the *Scheduling Priority Queue* for waiting or paused applications. If there is one, the scheduler sets its state to Running and starts its execution.

6.3 NUMA AWARENESS

PALMOS provides improved scheduling and data placement for multi-node Non Uniform Memory Access (NUMA) platforms. Here the system resources are distributed among multiple nodes. Each node owns part of the system processors/cores and maintains its own physical memory. The nodes communicate and share data through interconnects.

Host Code: The scheduling of application threads and the placement of its data on the same node improves application performance [32]. It reduces the inter-node communication for data sharing or synchronization. Inter-node interconnects typically have lower bandwidth than the node memory.

Accelerator Use: Another factor that affects performance is the location of accelerators. An accelerator is typically attached to a single node and its use by code running on remote nodes requires additional communication through the inter-node interconnects. It is highly preferable for an application to exclusively run and use memory from the node where the accelerator is attached[45][36].

7. SECURITY

PALMOS is a user-space virtualization layer for heterogeneous applications that uses shared memory for efficient inter-process communication. While this design choice guarantees high performance, it raises security concerns. Security is key part of our design and we provide a safe environment to both applications and PALMOS.

Secure PALMOS - application interaction: An application interacts with PALMOS through Virtual OpenCL (section 4), Inter-Space Memory Allocator (section 5) and Session Protocol (section 6.1) which all use shared memory segments. Our approach for safety is to restrict the access to shared memory segments only to processes that actually should access them. OS provides permission control over shared memory segments in the same manner it does for filesystem access. A shared segment can be read or written only by users and processes that have permissions for those actions. We build a secure environment by enforcing user and group ownership and the corresponding permissions.

Protection of Application Process: Virtual OpenCL forwards computation and communication requests to PALMOS while Session Protocol handles the handshaking between application and PALMOS. Both Virtual OpenCL and Session Protocol access Application Shared Memory (ASM, section 6.1), which is created by the application and needs to be accessed by PALMOS. We set the permission of ASM to be accessible only by the application and PALMOS processes. The use of two shared memory segments in attach operation of Session Protocol enables communication security. PALMOS accepts attach requests through its "public" shared memory, the PALMOS Shared Memory (PSM) which is accessible to any process. Then, further message exchanging takes place over ASM, which is accessible only by the application and PALMOS. By following that approach we block spoofing attacks and data corruption made by malicious or faulty applications.

Data Privacy: Inter-Space Memory Allocator operates across multiple address spaces and enables data sharing between the application and PALMOS. We ensure data privacy by ensuring that application memory is only accessible by the application and PALMOS. The Inter-Space Memory Allocator uses memory chunks which are allocated as shared memory segments. Each chunk is granted to a Local Memory Allocator (LMA) of an application and needs to be accessed by the application and PALMOS runtime. We set read and write permissions for that chunk only to the processes of the application and PALMOS. Under these permissions the application data is shared safely between the application and PALMOS. During system operation, a chunk may be recycled by the allocator and used by different applications at different times. We handle that by updating chunk's owner and group. This is done by PALMOS runtime that has the necessary privilege capabilities[20].

Buffer Overflow & Illegal Memory Access: We avoid Buffer Overflow attacks in Virtual OpenCL by perfoming address range and function type checks in both application and PALMOS. The memory chunks used by Inter-Space Memory Allocator are aligned to page size and have sizes multiples of page size. Any application access outside their address ranges causes immediately application segmentation fault. If there is a misuse, PALMOS terminates the application execution, while it continues serving the other applications.

Special User: For the protection of PALMOS from malicious attacks that can happen through the user environment, the PALMOS process is executed by a special account.

8. EXPERIMENTAL SETUP

We evaluate PALMOS using a wide range of workloads on 6 platform configurations. Here, we describe how the workloads are selected and present the platform configurations.

8.1 Workloads

The workloads considered, consist of between 1 and 64 concurrently running OpenCL programs selected from the Parboil benchmark suite[46] and the largest available dataset is used. Initially, we consider each program in isolation and investigate its performance. Each benchmark was executed 20 times with the average time taken recorded. This is performed in every experiment reported in this paper to reduce the impact of noise. We then generate multi-program workloads by selecting multiple benchmarks from Parboil. We looked at workload groups containing 1, 4, 16, 32 and 64 programs to investigate scaling. We randomly selected 50 distinct combinations of benchmarks for each workload group and report the gmean execution time. Our baseline is the standard OpenCL environment provided by the vendors.

8.2 Platform

Our evaluation platform is a NUMA x86 system with two nodes. Each node has an Intel Xeon E5-2620 CPU running at 2.00GHz and 8 Gigabytes of DDR3 memory running at 1333MHz. The system bus is a QPI interconnect. We have attached two NVIDIA and one AMD GPUs. One NVIDIA and one AMD GPUs are attached on the first node through its local PCI-Express interface. The second NVIDIA GPU is attached on the second node through its local interface. Both NVIDIA GPUs are Tesla K20c[37] and the AMD GPU is Tahiti 7970[3]. The Operating System is Linux with kernel version 3.7 and three OpenCL implementations, Intel OpenCL 1.2 (Build 67279), NVIDIA OpenCL 1.1 (CUDA 6.0.1) and AMD OpenCL 1.2 (Build 1348.5). Both CPUs are treated as a single accelerator.

We define distinct platform configurations by making different number of accelerators available for use. Our configurations are (a) *Single NVIDIA GPU*, (b) *Single AMD GPU*, (c) *Intel CPU*, (d) *Two NVIDIA GPUs*, (e) *Two NVIDIA and one AMD GPUs*, (f) *One NVIDIA GPU and Intel CPU*, (g) *Two NVIDIA GPUs and Intel CPU*, (h) *Two NVIDIA GPUs, one AMD GPU and Intel CPU*.

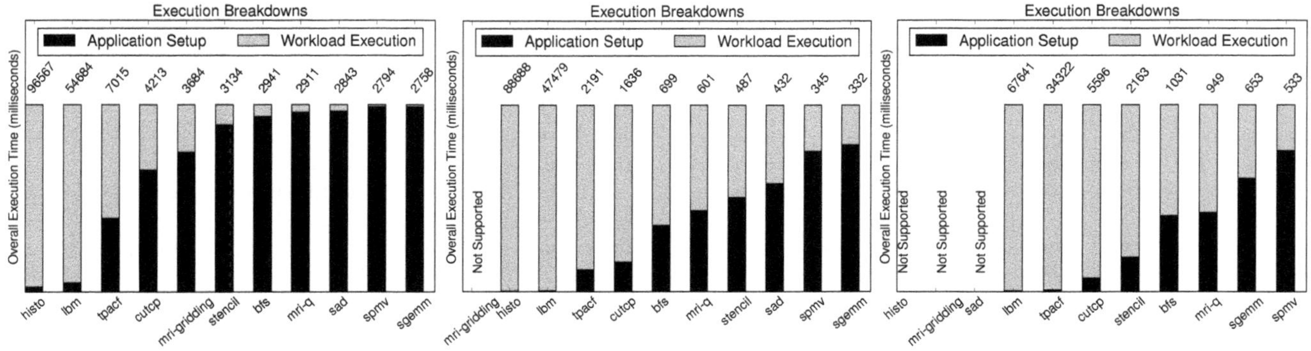

(a) NVIDIA GPU as Accelerator **(b)** AMD GPU as Accelerator **(c)** CPU as Accelerator

Figure 7: Normalized Execution Time Breakdowns of benchmarks on Standard OpenCL environment. The stacks present the time spent on application setup and on actual workload execution. Setup times can be prohibitive regardless the accelerator vendor. PALMOS design reduces this overhead dramatically.

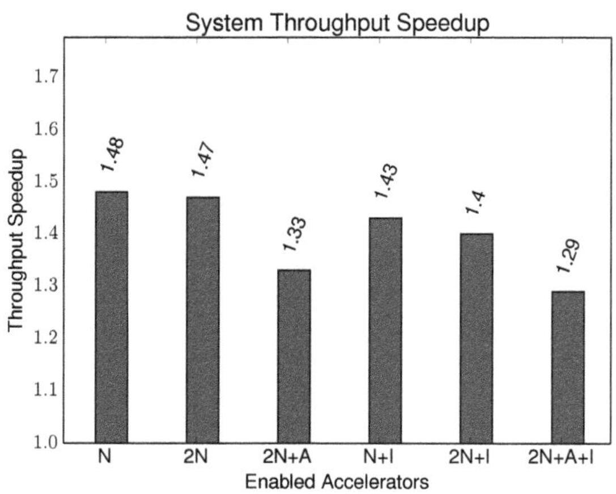

Figure 6: Representative of throughput speedup results delived by PALMOS for multi-program workloads of 64 benchmark instances. We consider the following 6 platform configurations: **N**: 1 NVIDIA GPU, **2N**: 2 NVIDIA GPUs, **2N+A**: 2 NVIDIA and 1 AMD GPUS, **2N+I**: 2 NVIDIA GPUS and Intel CPU, **2N+A+I**: 2 NVIDIA and 1 AMD GPUs and Intel CPU.

Three benchmarks, `histo`, `mri-gridding` and `sad`, fail to run if the CPU is used as the accelerator. In case of AMD GPU, `mri-gridding` fails too. The PALMOS scheduler handles this situation. The benchmarks that fail with one accelerator type are not scheduled on it. These benchmarks are not fully compatible with OpenCL standard.

8.3 Comparison to existing approaches

Vendor Solutions The NVIDIA Kepler architecture enables multi-program execution and supports concurrent kernel executions that overlap with host-accelerator communication. We have modified our FIFO scheduling policy to enable concurrent execution of multiple programs on NVIDIA GPUs. There is, however, limited space for performance improvement because benchmarks tend to consume all the GPU resources leaving no space for concurrent execution[42].

Message Passing Based Solutions There have been a number of message passing based schemes that allow sharing of accelerators. As these require extensive development and modification of the OpenCL benchmarks to use an extended API, our evaluation is more limited. We implemented the best performing scheme described in [8] and evaluated a small number of task scenarios. We compare PALMOS against it on our shared memory platform.

Bench	N(%)	NP(%)	A(%)	AP(%)	I(%)	IP(%)
histo	3	0.2	0.2	0.1	N/A	N/A
lbm	5	0.3	0.5	0.2	0.6	0.2
tpacf	39.1	5	11	2	1.1	0.7
cutcp	65	7	16	2.4	7	1.5
mri-gr	74.6	8.5	N/A	N/A	N/A	N/A
stencil	89	10.1	50	8.3	18	4.7
bfs	93.2	11.4	35	7.0	40	7.9
mri-q	95.7	12.1	43	7.6	42	7
sad	96.5	12.2	58	8.7	N/A	N/A
spvm	97	12.2	75.2	8.6	76.2	8.6
sgemm	97.6	12.2	79.6	8.9	61	8.2

Table 1: Comparison of Setup Overhead on Standard OpenCL and PALMOS environment. The results present the proportion (%) of total execution time spent on setup per benchmark. **N**: NVIDIA GPU, **NP**: NVIDIA GPU with PALMOS, **A**: AMD GPU, **AP**: AMD GPU with PALMOS, **I**: Intel CPU, **IP**: Intel CPU with PALMOS.

9. RESULTS

The main goal of our work is improving multi-program system throughput. A summary of the results is shown in figure 6 for multi-program workloads consisting of 64 programs on each of the 6 platform configurations. Overall, PALMOS delivers significant speedups ranging from from 1.29x to 1.48x. The remainder of this section examines in greater detail the performance of our approach. Section 9.1 examines individual benchmark performance improvement. Section 9.2 then evaluates performance for varying sized multi-program workloads on each platform configuration. Our evaluation baseline is the performance provided by the standard OpenCL environments. Section 9.3 provides a direct performance comparison against the Standard OpenCL environment and an alternate, state-of-the-art message passing based approach.

9.1 Single application performance

Here, we evaluate the performance of each application running in isolation. We examine (a) reduction of application setup overhead and (b) NUMA aware scheduling and data placement.

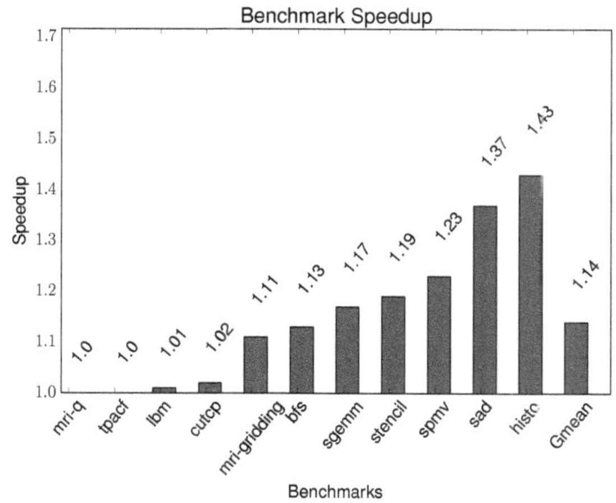

(a) NVIDIA GPU

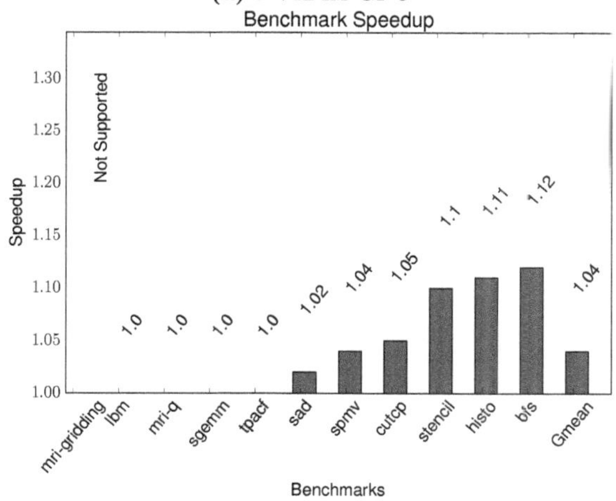

(b) AMD GPU

Figure 8: Execution speedups for individual benchmarks delivered by the NUMA mode of PALMOS. The baseline here is the standard PALMOS environment. Logarithmic scale. This is applicable to GPUs only.

9.1.1 Reduced Setup Overhead

In standard OpenCL, an application has significant setup overhead as it must reserve an accelerator and create an OpenCL context. In the PALMOS environment, those operations happen once at initialization and overhead is significantly reduced.

NVIDIA GPU: Figure 7a shows the total execution times of benchmarks with an NVIDIA GPU as accelerator and the percentage time spent in setup and execution. Benchmarks, such as `histo` and `lbm` spend as little as 3% and 5% of their execution on setup, which are reduced by PALMOS to 0.2% and 0.3% as shown in table 1, rows 1 and 2. In contrast, benchmarks such as `spmv` and `sgemm` spend 97% and 97.6% of their execution on setup, values that are significantly reduced to 12.2% and 12.2% (table 1, rows 10 and 11).

AMD GPU: Figure 7b shows execution time breakdown for the AMD GPU. While AMD kernel execution times are approximately the same as NVIDIA, setup overhead is approximately an order of magnitude faster, 328ms compared to 2630ms. Benchmarks `histo` and `lbm` now spend 0.2% and 0.5% of their execution on setup, values that are reduced by PALMOS to 0.1% and 0.2% as shown in table 1. Benchmarks such as `spmv` and `sgemm` spend the 75.2% and 79.6% of their execution on setup, those values get reduced to 8.6% and 8.9%.

Intel CPU: Figure 7c shows the total execution times when the CPUs are used as a single accelerator. The executions of OpenCL kernels on CPUs are slower and Intel OpenCL has lower setup times. Benchmarks such as `lbm` and `tpacf` spend 0.6% and 1.1% of their execution on setup, those values get reduced by PALMOS to 0.2% and 0.7%, as shown in table 1. Benchmarks such as `sgemm` and `spmv` spend 61% and 76.2% of their execution on setup and PALMOS reduces those values to 8.2% and 8.6%.

Benchmark Classification: Based on the proportion of the total execution time benchmarks spend on setup we classify them in two groups for later evaluation. The first includes the benchmarks with **High** workload that have low setup overhead, which are `histo, lbm, tpacf, cutcp` and `mri-gridding`. The second group includes benchmarks with **Low** workloads that have high setup overhead, which are `stencil, bfs, mri-q, sad, spmv` and `sgemm`.

9.1.2 NUMA Aware Scheduling and Data Placement

Here, we report the additional speedups delivered by the enhanced NUMA aware mode of PALMOS. This applies only when GPUs are used as accelerators because both CPUs are treated as a single accelerator.

NVIDIA GPU: Figure 8a shows the speedups for NVIDIA GPUs when PALMOS is NUMA aware which range from 1.0x to 1.43x with a geometric average of 1.14x. Benchmarks that perform significant host-accelerator communication such as `sad` and `histo` present notably higher speedups than benchmarks with reduced communication such as `tpacf` and `cutcp`.

AMD GPU: Figure 8b shows the speedups for AMD GPU. The reported speedup values are now lower and range from 1.0x to 1.12x. However, benchmarks with significant host-accelerator communication, such as `histo` and `bfs` still present the highest speedups of 1.11x and 1.12x.

9.2 Multi-program performance

This section evaluates multi-user, multi-program performance in more detail. We consider three benchmark groups: **High**, **Low** and finally **All** which contains all the benchmarks of the previous two groups.

To evaluate multi-tasking, we randomly generate sets of benchmarks that run concurrently on the system. We consider sets of 4, 16, 32 and 64 benchmark instances. For each benchmark group and set size we randomly generate 50 permutations of the benchmarks belonging to that group. We run each of these permutations 20 times to eliminate noise. We present a geomean throughput speedup for each benchmark group and set size as shown in figure 9.

Single NVIDA GPU: Figure 9a shows the throughput speedup when a single NVIDIA GPU is available. Here, for **High** workloads as the size of the workload increases from 4 to 64, the improvement gains level to around a 1.36x speedup as resource contention begins to increase. For **Low** workloadsour improvements are actually more significant, ranging from 25.89x to 22.53x. The decrease happens due to resource contention. Combining all benchmarks together and running them gives improvements from 1.48x to 2.89x. The **High** workload sets, that have long execution times, have

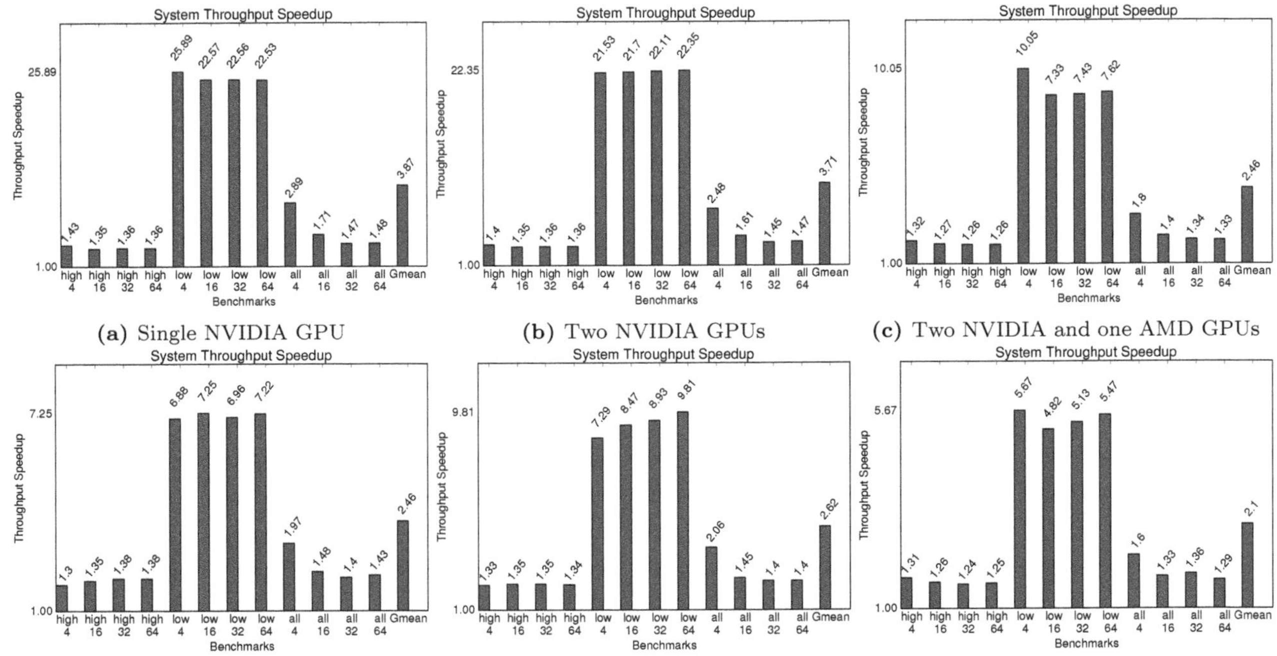

(a) Single NVIDIA GPU (b) Two NVIDIA GPUs (c) Two NVIDIA and one AMD GPUs

(d) One NVIDIA GPU and Intel CPU (e) Two NVIDIA GPUs and Intel CPU (f) Two NVIDIA and one AMD GPUs, Intel CPU

Figure 9: Throughput Speedup Results delivered by PALMOS. Multi-program sets are executed on 6 platform configurations where different number and types of accelerators are available. We consider 3 groups of benchmarks, the **High** Workload, **Low** Workload and **All** benchmarks. Group size varies from 4 to 64 benchmark instances. The baseline is the Standard OpenCL environment. Logarithmic scale is used.

lower performance gains than **Low** workload sets. However, for the **All** workload sets, PALMOS provides significant throughput speedups. Averaged across each scenario we see a significant 3.87x improvement over standard OpenCL.

Two NVIDIA GPUs: Figure 9b gives the throughput speedup results when two NVIDIA GPUs are available. When compared to figure 9a, the speedups obtained are highly consistent. However, the results for **Low** workloads are now reduced and they range from 21.53x to 22.35x. The results for **All** workloads are slightly reduced ranging from 2.48 to 1.47. This happens because (a) the same workloads are now computed on two accelerators and the concurrency reduces the potential performance improvements, (b) some overhead is introduced for using two accelerators. The NUMA aware scheduling reduces that overhead but still many driver and OS operations are centralized. Overall, the average improvement across all the scenarios is 3.71x.

Two NVIDIA and one AMD GPUs: Figure 9c shows the results for two NVIDIA and one AMD GPUs. Here the results follow the trends of the previous configurations but the throughput speedup gains are reduced giving a geomean improvement of 2.46 while **Low** workloads report significant reductions ranging from 10.05 to 7.62x. The reason for the relative reduction is (a) the lower setup cost introduced by AMD OpenCL, (b) the higher overhead of managing and using three accelerators of different vendors and (c) the fact that the same workloads are now computed by three accelerators concurrently. The **Low** workload set of 4 benchmarks reports a higher throughput speedup of 10.05x in comparison to larger **Low** sets because of lower resource contention.

One NVIDIA GPU and Intel CPU: Figure 9d shows the results when one NVIDIA GPU and Intel CPU are available as accelerators. The throughput speedup trends remain the same with the previous configurations but they are now degraded, specially for **Low** workloads which now have throughput speedup ranging from 6.88 to 7.22. The improvement rates are degraded mainly because of (a) the longer execution times on CPU and (b) the reduced setup overhead of Intel OpenCL. The geomean speedup is 2.46x.

Two NVIDIA GPUs and Intel CPU: Figure 9e shows the throughput speedup results given by PALMOS when two NVIDIA GPUs and Intel CPU are available. The throughput speedup results are now higher in comparison with the `One NVIDIA GPU and Intel CPU` configuration. The reason is that there are two NVIDIA GPUs in use (a) that lead to faster executions and (b) have higher setup overheads in contrast to Intel CPU. The geomean improvement is 2.62x.

Two NVIDIA GPUs, one AMD GPU and Intel CPU: Here we make all the accelerators available. The results, shown in figure 9f, follow the same trends as before but the throughput values are further reduced. **Low** workloads now range from 5.67x to 5.47x and the mixed, **All** workloads from 1.6 to 1.29. **High** workloads remain on the same levels. The reason is (a) the overhead of using multiple accelerators of three different vendors, (b) the lower setup overhead of Intel and AMD OpenCL implementations, (c) the slower executions on CPU and (d) the fact that the same workloads are executed concurrently on 4 accelerators. However the geomean throughput speedup, 2.1x, is still significant.

9.3 PALMOS against existing approaches

In this section we evaluate the performance of PALMOS against the default OpenCL environment and an alternative approach [8] which uses message passing for communication

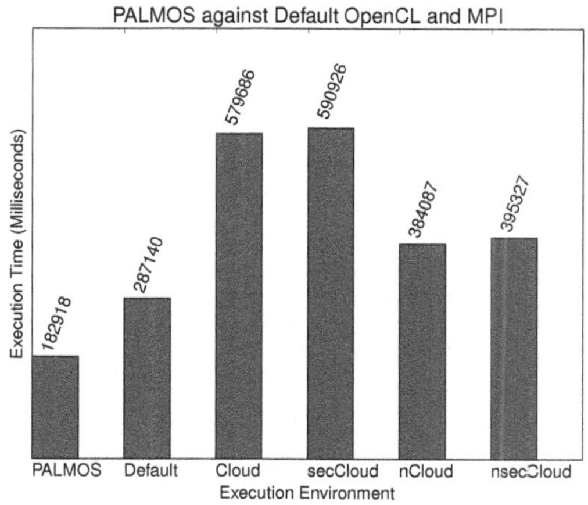

Figure 10: This figure shows the absolute times for the execution of (spmv, histo, spmv, histo) set on PALMOS, Default OpenCL and the 4 versions of Cloud infrastructure.

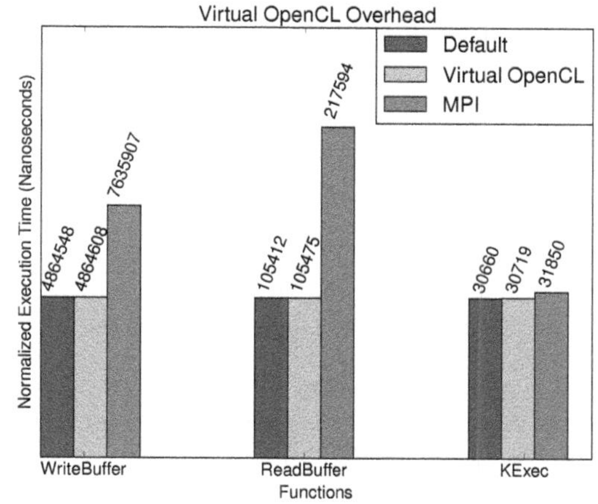

Figure 11: Virtual OpenCL overhead. Comparison against default call convention and RPC via MPI. The results are normalized to Default.

and we refer to it as **Cloud**. We consider four versions of **Cloud**. The first version controls all the accelerators centrally, where there is little application setup overhead. The second, is a secure version called **secCloud**, where a new OpenCL context is created per application The last two versions are NUMA aware versions of Cloud and secCloud, called **nCloud** and **nsecCloud**. As the OpenCL benchmarks have to be modified to use **Cloud**, we perform a smaller evaluation than the previous section. Here, we use one of the NVIDIA GPUs as the accelerator.

Performance Overview: Here, we take a pair of Parboil benchmarks, histo from the **High** workload group and spmv from the **Low** workload group and we create a workload set, (spmv, histo, spmv, histo). We run it on PALMOS, Standard OpenCL, and, once suitably modified, on the four Cloud infrastructures and the results are shown in figure 10. PALMOS outperforms all the other approaches. PALMOS is 57% faster than default OpenCL execution, where the speedup comes from the reduced setup overhead and NUMA awareness. It outperforms Cloud and secCloud by 217% and 223% respectively. The Cloud approaches require extensive data copies across different address spaces, something that PALMOS avoids by using shared memory. Cloud is 7% faster than its secure version, secCloud. The NUMA aware versions, nCloud and nsecCloud are significantly faster. The data placement improves the data copying performance. However, both remain significantly slower.

Virtual OpenCL Performance Analysis: Figure 11 shows the execution times for function calls performed with (a) the default call convention of standard OpenCL, (b) Virtual OpenCL and (c) MPI when executing **spmv**.

Kernel execution, **clEnqueueNDRangeKernel**, as expected, is roughly the same for each scheme. In the case of host-accelerator communication, **clEnqueueWriteBuffer** and **clEnqueueReadBuffer**, Virtual OpenCL introduces negligible overhead. MPI however introduces an overhead of 1.56x and 2.06x as data need to be copied before the actual host-accelerator communication can take place. These two calls consume significant proportion of the application execution and lead to critical execution slowdowns for MPI/message passing based schemes.

10. RELATED WORK

PALMOS is the first secure, user-space virtualization layer for multi-tasking on heterogeneous architectures that enables mixed-vendor sharing, efficient scheduling and improved performance. It requires no modifications or recompilation of the applications, OS or runtime libraries. It significantly improves system throughput and individual application performance. Here, we present related academic work.

A cloud infrastructure that enables GPU access and sharing across multiple cluster nodes is presented in [8]. This design outperforms single node performance but requires code modification, extensive data transfers, as shown in section 9.3 and is vendor specific. VOCL [49] and Libwater[17] unify the management of local and remote accelerators by using OpenCL and MPI. Neither tackles multi-tasking and their evaluation is bound to naive benchmarks. In [26], the authors unify virtually the OpenCL devices and provide a single computational device to application. However, they doe not support multi-tasking. rCUDA[16] enables access to GPUs located on remote cluster nodes. It requires code modifications, it is vendor specific and lacks security control.

In [42][1][18], the authors propose techniques to increase accelerator resource utilization by executing multiple kernels concurrently on a single accelerator. However they require the static merge and modification of applications and no application multi-tasking is considered. [7] presents a "multikernel" OS that targets the management of platforms with heterogeneous memory hierarchies, instruction sets and interconnects. This approach requires the redesign of the software stack, it is not therefore transparent.

The SKMD framework[29] performs collaborative execution of data parallel kernels across multiple asymmetric CPUs and GPUs. An autotuning framework and runtime collaborative scheme of different accelerator types is presented in [43]. In both cases, however, only single applications are considered. Concord [6] is a compiler and runtime framework that enables efficient execution of kernels on integrated GPUs. It enables seamless sharing of pointer containing data structures but again it targets just a single application. RSMV [22] is a CPU-GPU memory management mechanism. It is a region based memory allocator across CPU and GPU distributed memories. It supports kernel-issued, on demand, data fetching and GPU memory swapping into the main memory. However, it supports single application execution exclusively.

TimeGraph [24] is a real-time scheduler that enables GPU sharing across applications and mimics preemption behavior in the absence of hardware support. It is implemented as part of the kernel driver, it is vendor specific and its evaluation is limited to OpenGL graphics benchmarks. In [34], the authors have modified the Linux kernel and intervene in the driver operations for supporting fair sharing of NVIDIA GPUs between multiple applications. This work aims on new driver features and it orthogonal to our work. Our virtualization layer could exploit this driver feature for enhanced accelerator handling and scheduling.

The PALMOS design exploits the following techniques developed for non-heterogeneous systems. [9] presents a two level heap based allocator that provides scalability and performance for multi-threaded applications. NUMA impact on memory allocation performance is discussed in [23]. The work of [10] provides algorithms and template libraries for the construction of custom memory allocators and we use them. [13] tackles the congestion at interconnects and memory controllers of NUMA systems by controlling data traffic. The papers [12] [19][47] demonstrate the efficiency and low level overheard of OS-level virtualization.

11. CONCLUSION

In this paper, we have presented PALMOS, a secure user-space virtualization layer that integratees accelerator resources. It targets heterogeneous systems found in data center nodes and requires mo modification of OS, OpenCL or the application. Our approach reduces application setup overhead, enables inter-vendor accelerator sharing and provides efficient platform aware scheduling. Our evaluation on multiple platforms configurations with workloads ranging from 1 up to 64 applications shows average improvement from 1.29x to 3.87x throughput speedup. We also show that our approach outperforms both vendor accelerator sharing facilities and message passing solutions. Future work will investigate additional scheduling policies, different performance goals and accelerator architectures with hardware preemption.

12. REFERENCES

[1] J. Adriaens, K. Compton, N. S. Kim, and M. Schulte. The case for gpgpu spatial multitasking. HPCA '12.

[2] B. Alpern, J. Auerbach, et al. Pds: A virtual execution environment for software deployment. VEE '05.

[3] AMD. Accelerated parallel processing: Opencl programming guide revision 2.7, 2013.

[4] G. Banga et al. Resource containers: A new facility for resource management in server systems. OSDI '99.

[5] P. Barham, B. Dragovic, et al. Xen and the art of virtualization. SOSP '03.

[6] R. Barik, R. Kaleem, et al. Efficient mapping of irregular c++ applications to integrated gpus. CGO '14.

[7] A. Baumann, P. Barham, et al. The multikernel: A new os architecture for scalable multicore systems. SOSP '09.

[8] M. Becchi et al. A virtual memory based runtime to support multi-tenancy in clusters with gpus. HPDC '12.

[9] E. D. Berger, K. S. McKinley, R. D. Blumofe, and P. R. Wilson. Hoard: A scalable memory allocator for multithreaded applications. *SIGPLAN Not.*, 35(11):117–128, Nov. 2000.

[10] E. D. Berger, B. G. Zorn, and K. S. McKinley. Composing high-performance memory allocators. PLDI '01.

[11] A. D. Birrell and B. J. Nelson. Implementing remote procedure calls. *ACM Trans. Comput. Syst.*, 2(1):39–59, Feb. 1984.

[12] J. A. Colmenares, G. Eads, et al. Tessellation: Refactoring the os around explicit resource containers with continuous adaptation. DAC '13.

[13] M. Dashti et al. Traffic management: A holistic approach to memory placement on numa systems. ASPLOS '13.

[14] C. Delimitrou and C. Kozyrakis. Quasar: Resource-efficient and qos-aware cluster management. ASPLOS '14.

[15] Docker. Docker Project. http://www.docker.com/.

[16] J. Duato, A. J. Pena, F. Silla, R. Mayo, and E. S. Quintana-Ortí. rcuda: Reducing the number of gpu-based accelerators in high performance clusters. HPCS '10.

[17] I. Grasso, S. Pellegrini, B. Cosenza, and T. Fahringer. Libwater: Heterogeneous distributed computing made easy. ICS '13.

[18] M. Guevara, C. Gregg, K. Hazelwood, and K. Skadron. Enabling task parallelism in the cuda scheduler. In *Workshop on Programming Models for Emerging Architectures '09.*

[19] A. Gupta et al. Exploring the performance and mapping of hpc applications to platforms in the cloud. HPDC '12.

[20] S. E. Hallyn and A. G. Morgan. Linux capabilities: Making them work. In *Linux Symposium '08.*

[21] ISO. C standard. Technical report, 1999.

[22] F. Ji, H. Lin, and X. Ma. Rsvm: A region-based software virtual memory for gpu. PACT '13.

[23] P. Kaminski. Numa aware heap memory manager. *AMD Developer Central*, 2009.

[24] S. Kato et al. Timegraph: Gpu scheduling for real-time multi-tasking environments. USENIX ATC '11.

[25] Khronos Group. The opencl specification, version 1.2, '11.

[26] J. Kim, H. Kim, J. H. Lee, and J. Lee. Achieving a single compute device image in opencl for multiple gpus. PPoPP '11.

[27] A. Kivity, Y. Kamay, D. Laor, U. Lublin, and A. Liguori. kvm: the linux virtual machine monitor. Linux Symposium '07.

[28] C. Lattner and V. Adve. Llvm: A compilation framework for lifelong program analysis & transformation. CGO '04.

[29] J. Lee et al. Transparent cpu-gpu collaboration for data-parallel kernels on heterogeneous systems. PACT '13.

[30] Linux Documentation. Linux programmer's manual, 2014.

[31] J. Mars and L. Tang. Whare-map: Heterogeneity in "homogeneous" warehouse-scale computers. ISCA '13.

[32] C. McCurdy and J. Vetter. Memphis: Finding and fixing numa-related performance problems on multi-core platforms. ISPASS '10.

[33] P. B. Menage. Adding generic process containers to the linux kernel. volume 2 of *Linux Symposium*, pages 45–58, 2007.

[34] K. Menychtas, K. Shen, and M. L. Scott. Disengaged scheduling for fair, protected access to fast computational accelerators. ASPLOS '14.

[35] Message Passing Interface Forum. Mpi: A message-passing interface standard, version 2.2. Technical report.

[36] P. Micikevicious. Multi-gpu programming. GTC '12.

[37] NVIDIA. Nvidia kepler gk110 architecture, 2012.

[38] NVIDIA. *CUDA C Programming Guide, Version 6.0.* 2014.

[39] NVIDIA GRID. Nvidia. http://www.nvidia.co.uk/object/grid-vdi-desktop-virtualisation-uk.html.

[40] Open Group and IEEE. Posix.1-2008, 2008.

[41] OpenVZ. Openvz linux containers. http://www.openvz.org/.

[42] S. Pai, M. J. Thazhuthaveetil, and R. Govindarajan. Improving gpgpu concurrency with elastic kernels. ASPLOS '13.

[43] P. M. Phothilimthana, J. Ansel, et al. Portable performance on heterogeneous architectures. ASPLOS '13.

[44] S. Soltesz, H. Pötzl, et al. Container-based operating system virtualization: A scalable, high-performance alternative to hypervisors. EuroSys '07.

[45] K. Spafford, J. S. Meredith, and J. S. Vetter. Quantifying numa and contention effects in multi-gpu systems. GPGPU '11.

[46] J. A. Stratton et al. Parboil: A revised benchmark suite for scientific and commercial throughput computing. *Center for Reliable and High-Performance Computing*, 2012.

[47] Z. Wang et al. Capacity and performance overhead in dynamic resource allocation to virtual containers. IM '07.

[48] A. Whitaker et al. Scale and performance in the denali isolation kernel. *SIGOPS Oper. Syst. Rev.*, 36(SI):195–209, Dec. 2002.

[49] S. Xiao et al. Vocl: An optimized environment for transparent virtualization of graphics processing units. InPar '12.

A Nested Partitioning Algorithm for Adaptive Meshes on Heterogeneous Clusters

Hari Sundar
University of Utah
Salt Lake City, UT 84112
hari@cs.utah.edu

Omar Ghattas
University of Texas at Austin
Austin, TX 78712
omar@ices.utexas.edu

ABSTRACT

In the era of the accelerator, load balancing strategies that are well-understood for traditional homogeneous supercomputers must be re-worked in order to address the problem of distributing work across heterogeneous hardware such that neither the CPU nor the accelerator is left idle. Whereas partitioning for a homogeneous system need only balance node-level workload against single-node performance, partitioning for an accelerator-enabled system requires a nested partitioning scheme that ensures both an optimal intra-node and inter-node load balance. We refer to this as *enclave partitioning*. Our parallelization scheme allows the same shared-memory-level code to be used on both the CPU and the accelerator, and also allows inter-node communication code to be reused during CPU-accelerator communication. This is in contrast to the traditional "offload" model, in which accelerator code can differ significantly from CPU code in both form and programming language. Using a hybrid MPI-OpenMP implementation of the acoustic-elastic wave propagation, we demonstrate the efficacy of the proposed partitioning scheme on a heterogeneous, Intel® Xeon Phi™-accelerated supercomputer (Stampede). With our approach we have realized speedups of up to 5.78x using a 7th order discretization and 6.88x for 15th order discretization relative to a baseline, pure-MPI implementation. We present strong and weak scaling results as well as individual node performance to illustrate the benefits and limits of the accelerator-enabled scientific computing.

Categories and Subject Descriptors

D.1.3 [**Concurrent Programming**]: Distributed programming; C.1.4 [**Parallel Architectures**]: Distributed Architectures

Keywords

accelerator; offload; mic; heterogeneous; partitioning; wave equation; pde; hybrid parallelism;

ICS'15, June 8–11, 2015, Newport Beach, CA, USA.

DOI: http://dx.doi.org/10.1145/2751205.2751246.

1. INTRODUCTION

The trend in modern supercomputing is to move toward systems that realize the bulk of their computational power from accelerators [11]. According to the Nov 2014 version of the top500 list [18], 75 of the clusters on the list (15%) had accelerators and this number has steadily been rising in the last few years. On most of these machines the majority of the flops are available from the accelerator. For example on Stampede at the Texas Advanced Computing Center (TACC), 2.2PetaFlop/s is the peak performance of the base cluster while an additional 7.4PF/s is available from the use of the Intel® Xeon Phi™ accelerator available on its 6400 nodes. Additionally, while the peak performance is usually 3-4 times higher for the accelerator, the total available memory is smaller on the accelerator by a similar factor. The situation is similar for other top machines utilizing accelerators. To make effective use of such machines, application codes need to parallelize across 4 levels; *a)* across distributed memory nodes, *b)* across the CPU and the accelerator, *c)* shared-memory parallelism with the CPU/accelerator, and *d)* vectorization at the finest level. The asymmetry in performance as well as memory at the cpu-accelerator makes this particularly challenging for complex applications.

Load balancing strategies that are well-understood for traditional homogeneous supercomputers must be re-worked in order to address the problem of distributing work across heterogeneous hardware such that neither the CPU nor the accelerator is left idle. A common paradigm for accelerator computing is to offload computationally intensive tasks to the accelerator. In many such cases, the CPU is left relatively idle. Additionally, this requires $\mathcal{O}(n)$ data transfer between the CPU and the accelerator. Given that the accelerators have less memory available, such an approach is inefficient unless the operations being offloaded are of extremely high computational efficiency. Instead, we believe it is preferable to treat the accelerator the same as any other compute node, reducing the data transfer costs to $\mathcal{O}(n^{2/3})$ for 3D problems. This allows programmers to use a Single-Program, Multiple-Data (SPMD) programming paradigm, which is much easier than programming separate logic for the CPU and the accelerator. This is particularly attractive on clusters such as Stampede and Tianhe-2 using the Intel® Xeon Phi™ as the accelerator, as it is based on the `x86` architecture as the CPU. This means that on such clusters, we can have true SPMD code[1].

[1]there are still minor differences, but this statement is for the most part true.

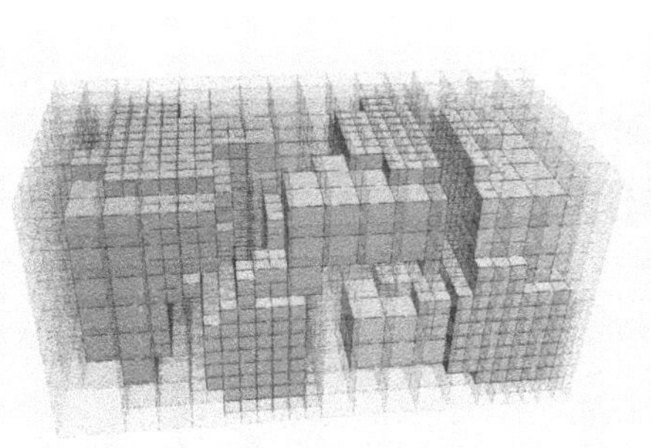

Figure 1: Enclave partition: The computational domain is first partitioned among MPI processes, shown here separated and in different colors. Each MPI process then partitions its subdomain into a set of elements to assign to the CPU (transparent) and a set of elements to assign to the accelerator.

The key ***challenge*** for the equivalent treatment of CPUs and accelerators—besides the differences in performance and memory—is that the communication cost from an accelerator to any other process other than its host node is significantly higher. In this regards, they are not the same as the CPUs and therefore when we divide work across the nodes, and between the CPU and the accelerator, we need to partition such that the accelerators only require data transfers with their hosts. In other words, the task graph for the problem is such that the tasks assigned to any accelerator have data-dependencies only with their host CPUs. *A novel $\mathcal{O}(n)$, node-local partitioning algorithm that facilitates such a data-dependency is the main contribution of this work.* We call this *enclave partitioning* and an example of such a partition is shown in Figure 1. The partitioning improves the overall performance of the system by ensuring proper utilization of both the CPU and the accelerator, and also makes it easier to program for such systems by using a SPMD programming paradigm. Using a hybrid MPI-OpenMP implementation of the acoustic-elastic wave propagation, we demonstrate the efficacy of the proposed partitioning scheme on Stampede. Using our approach, we have realized speedups of up to 5.78x using a 7th order discretization and 6.88x for 15th order discretization relative to a baseline, pure-MPI implementation. We present strong and weak scaling results as well as individual node performance to illustrate the benefits and limits of the coprocessor-accelerated scientific computing. To the best of our knowledge, this is the first work considering such a partition that enables SPMD programming for heterogeneous clusters.

Organization of this paper:.

The rest of this paper is organized as follows. In §2, we present the Seismic wave propagation problem—our test application—as it is important to understand the computational structure of the application to appreciate the algorithmic choices. In §3 we provide a baseline analysis that we performed prior to this work, that led to the development of the current work. In §4, we present the enclave partitioning algorithm and in §5 we discuss the implementation details of our algorithms. Finally, in §6 we present experiments and scalability results in support of enclave partitioning and conclude with directions for future research.

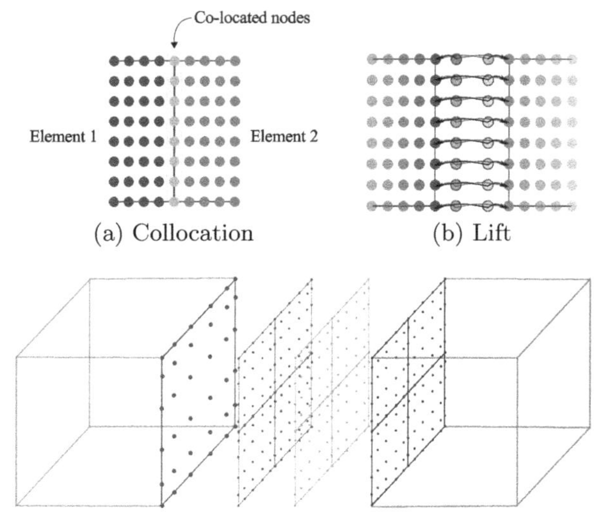

(a) Collocation

(b) Lift

(c) Interpolation to facemesh

Figure 2: (a) Nodes on the faces of adjacent elements are collocated. (b) Fluxes on virtual face nodes get "lifted" back to the elements. (c) Nodes from parent faces are interpolated to four virtual hanging faces on the facemesh.

2. SEISMIC WAVE PROPAGATION

We are primarily concerned with accelerating the solution of the acoustic-elastic wave equations to simulate the propagation of seismic waves in coupled acoustic-elastic media. Our long-term goal is the solution of the global-scale inverse problem of determining the interior structure of the earth using full seismic waveform inversion [20]. Each step of the inverse problem requires a full, explicit forward-in-time solution of the acoustic-elastic wave equations. As such, a moderate speedup in the forward solution translates to a significant speedup in the inverse solution [5].

For isotropic media, seismic wave propagation can be described in velocity-strain form by the first-order system [10]

$$\rho\frac{\partial \mathbf{v}}{\partial t} = \nabla\cdot(\boldsymbol{C}\boldsymbol{E}) + \mathbf{f} = \nabla\cdot(\lambda tr(\boldsymbol{E})\boldsymbol{I} + 2\mu\boldsymbol{E}) + \mathbf{f} \quad (1a)$$

$$\frac{\partial \boldsymbol{E}}{\partial t} = \frac{1}{2}(\nabla\mathbf{v} + \nabla\mathbf{v}^T) \quad (1b)$$

where we make use of the Lamé parameters λ and μ as our material parameters. This formulation allows us to describe wave propagation in an acoustic medium by simply setting μ to zero [20]. To make the system well-posed, we assume initial conditions $\mathbf{v}(\mathbf{x},0) = \mathbf{v}_0(\mathbf{x})$ and $\boldsymbol{E}(\mathbf{x},0) = \boldsymbol{E}_0(\mathbf{x})$ on the problem domain B, and boundary condition $\boldsymbol{S}\mathbf{n} = \mathbf{t}_{bc}$ on the boundary of the domain, ∂B, where we prescribe the traction $\mathbf{t}_{bc}$, $\mathbf{n}$ is the outward unit normal vector at the boundary, and $\boldsymbol{S} = \boldsymbol{C}\boldsymbol{E}$ is the Cauchy stress tensor. At an interface Γ between two elastic media, we impose continuity in the velocity and the traction

$$\mathbf{v}^+ = \mathbf{v}^- \qquad \mathbf{x}\in\Gamma \quad (2a)$$

$$\boldsymbol{S}^+\mathbf{n} = \boldsymbol{S}^-\mathbf{n} \qquad \mathbf{x}\in\Gamma \quad (2b)$$

whereas at an interface between an elastic medium and an acoustic medium or between two acoustic media we impose continuity between the normal component of velocity and the traction

$$\mathbf{n} \cdot \mathbf{v}^{+} = \mathbf{n} \cdot \mathbf{v}^{-} \qquad \mathbf{x} \in \Gamma \tag{3a}$$

$$\boldsymbol{S}^{+}\mathbf{n} = \boldsymbol{S}^{-}\mathbf{n} \qquad \mathbf{x} \in \Gamma \tag{3b}$$

Additional details on the mathematical formulation of the problem can be found in [20].

2.1 Discontinuous Galerkin Method

The discontinuous Galerkin (DG) finite element method is characterized by its use of discontinuous basis functions, which allow the methods to operate on h-adaptive, nonconforming meshes [8]. Global solution continuity is enforced weakly on element boundaries through the use of a numerical flux. This makes most DG operators highly local. In this paper we will present only a cursory examination of the features of DG that are relevant to an optimal implementation on a heterogeneous system. For a more detailed treatment of the solution of the acoustic-elastic wave equations using a DG method, see [20], [13], [4].

Our DG formulation uses an h-adaptive, possibly nonconforming, mesh of hexahedral curvilinear elements, which we require conforms to a 2:1 balance. A 2:1 balance indicates that only 1:1 and 2:1 size relations are allowed between neighboring elements. Following [8], the basis of each element is composed of tensor products of 1-D Lagrange polynomials. Numerical integration points are chosen to coincide with the basis function nodes, which we have chosen to place at the Legendre-Gauss-Lobatto points (again following [8]). Each element, then, can be conceptualized as a collection of nodes. Element face nodes collocate when elements are adjacent to each other (Figure 2a). At the beginning of each iteration, we isolate the nodes on the faces of the elements and copy them to the "facemesh". We call a face that is adjacent to four faces from neighboring elements a "parent face", and the faces of the smaller neighboring elements "hanging faces". When transferring face data to the facemesh, we interpolate the data from a parent face to four corresponding virtual hanging faces in the face mesh. This ensures that neighboring faces always conform to one another in the facemesh (Figure 2c).

The key kernels used in the DG formulation of the acoustic-elastic wave equations are shown in Table 1. The "Locality" column in the table describes the data domain on which each kernel operates. Element- and face-local kernels can operate on each element independently, while face-global kernels require nodal values from multiple neighboring elements. In this sense of the word "global", the only global kernel in our DG formulation is the *Lift* kernel, which applies the fluxes from adjacent faces to the volume nodes of the elements to which they correspond (Figure 2b).

Table 1: Key kernels used in DG solution of acoustic-elastic wave equations.

Kernel	Locality	FLOPS/MOPS
Interpolate $\mathbf{q} \rightarrow \mathbf{qf}$	Face-local	$[0, 4/15(2N+1)]$
Derivatives	Element-local	$3/8(2N+1)$
Numerical *Flux*	Face-local	5.27
Project $\mathbf{qf} \rightarrow \mathbf{q}$	Face-local	$N + 7/4$
Lift flux to volume	Face-global	0.90
Runge-Kutta	Element-local	1.25

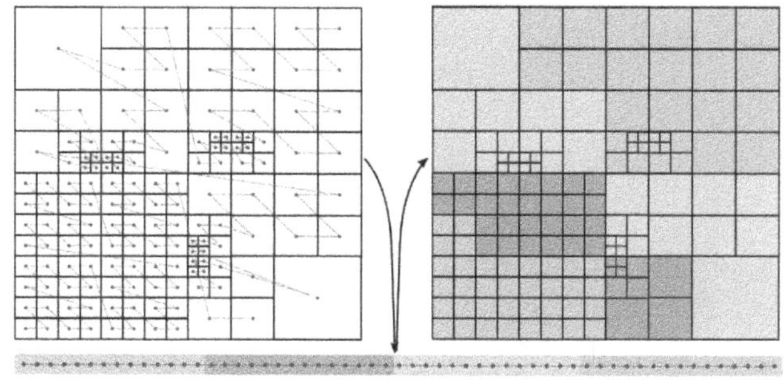

Figure 3: Partitioning between MPI processes is done by segmentation along the Morton curve. The mesh on the left is shown with the space-filling Morton curve shown in blue connecting the elements. Partitioning can be thought of as untangling this curve and laying it out in one dimension, as in the color-coded curve at the bottom of the figure. The colors represent the different processes to which these elements are assigned.

2.2 Adaptive Meshing

In this section, we briefly describe our adaptive meshing framework. Octrees are axis-aligned space partitions in 3D. The root of an octree can be associated with a topologically equivalent 3D domain that can be mapped smoothly to a cube. A forest is a collection of octrees, which are connected conformingly through faces, edges and corners [6]. Such a forest of octrees allows for a two-tier decomposition of geometric domains, where the first tier, the macromesh, is an unstructured mesh of conforming hexahedral elements (possibly with curved boundaries). Recursive octree subdivision then allows for efficient octree-based adaptivity of the mesh in the geometric domain. Localized refinement generally creates non-conforming meshes, which can still be used to represent continuous finite element solutions by incorporating algebraic constraints at the element level (hanging nodes).

The adaptive octree structure can naturally be interpreted to define a recursive space filling curve that traverses all octants in all trees in the so-called Morton- or z-order [12]. This curve provides the basis for indexing and fast partitioning of octants between processes, a fact that we exploit while assigning work across nodes.

3. BASELINE ANALYSIS

We first performed baseline analysis to estimate what changes would be necessary to achieve good performance on a heterogeneous cluster like Stampede. All test runs in this paper are made up of 300 time steps of the solution of a wave propagation through a domain with a material discontinuity in the center of the domain. A time-varying boundary strain is applied at the lowest z-face of the domain, generating compressional waves that travel toward the material discontinuity, at which they are partially reflected and partially refracted according to Snell's law (Figure 4). The mesh was refined according to two Gaussian density functions centered at arbitrarily selected points within the domain. Though meshes with varying numbers of elements were generated by specifying different minimum allowable element sizes, the under-

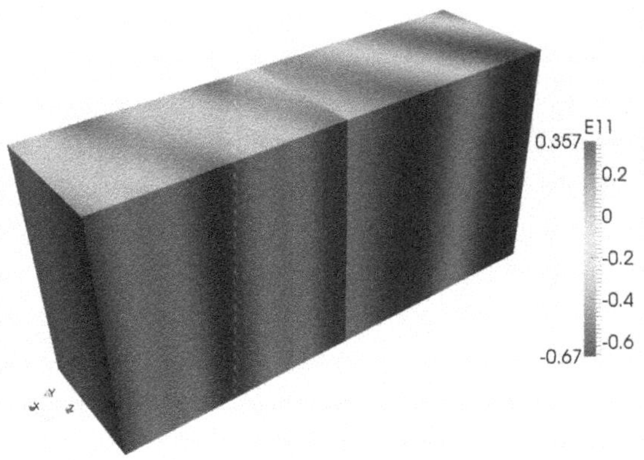

Figure 4: Compressional strain in the x-direction. Our test problem is a time-varying wave propagation through a medium with a central material discontinuity.

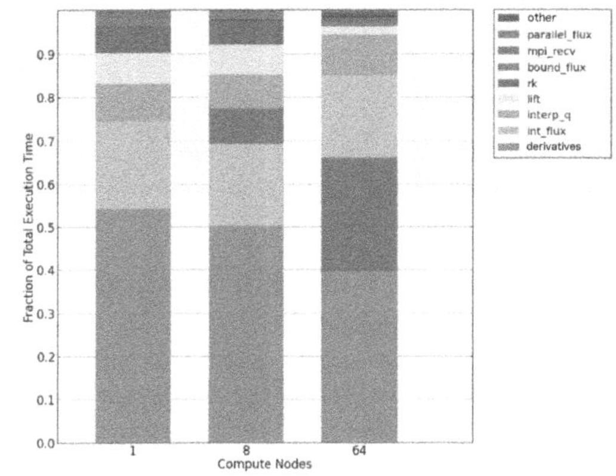

Figure 5: Fraction of execution time for key kernels in the solution of the acoustic-elastic wave propagation problem for a fixed problem size and varying number of compute nodes. All runs were completed using a fixed number of 7th order elements.

lying Gaussian densities were the same for all runs. One such mesh is shown in Figure 1.

The fraction of execution time taken by each of the key kernels discussed in the previous section was measured for the baseline code, the results are shown in Figure 5. As can be seen, the derivatives kernel accounts for almost half the execution time. This would normally point to a task-offloading approach, wherein the derivative computation is offloaded to the Xeon Phi, while the CPU takes care of the rest. Unfortunately, given that the derivatives need to be computed on the volume unknowns, the overall speedup factoring-in the cost of transferring data back and forth to the accelerator was $< 10\%$. Equating this with communication costs normally observed on homogeneous clusters, one can see that a similar setup where the communication is proportional to the surface-area instead of the volume would be highly beneficial. As mentioned earlier, it would have the added benefit of simplifying the programming by allowing us to adopt the SPMD programming paradigm. In the next section, we expand on this idea and introduce our partitioning scheme.

4. PARTITIONING

As previously discussed, in the discontinuous Galerkin finite element method, inter-process communication consists entirely of the transfer of shared element faces. Thus, the partitioning of the global domain into processor-local domains directly controls the amount of communication required. If partitions are created such that the number of faces shared amongst processors is minimized, then communication will also be minimized. Partitioning must take place at two levels—first, the inter-node partitioning is done using the Morton ordering of the elements to ensure load-balance at the node level. For some total number of elements K and compute nodes p, we assign K/p elements to each node with node-i receiving elements $\mathcal{E} = [(i-1)K/p, iK/p]$ according to the Morton order. We assign one MPI process to each compute node, and so each MPI process owns a subdomain of contiguous[2] elements. This domain is then partitioned—locally on each node by the CPU—into two domains such that one domain is an *enclave*[3] within the other. We refer to this as *enclave partitioning*.

This approach differs from the way in which accelerators have traditionally been used. A common paradigm for accelerators computing is to offload whole computationally intensive tasks to the accelerator. For example, in the solution of the acoustic-elastic wave equation, one might offload the *Derivatives* kernel to the accelerator while the CPU computes the *Flux* kernel. While the *Derivatives* kernel is certainly computationally intensive, and maps well to accelerator architectures, the amount of data that must be transferred at each timestep is proportional to the total number of elements K owned by the compute node, times the number of degrees of freedom per element $(N+1)^3$. In contrast, transferring only a subset K_{MIC} of elements to the accelerator and transferring only shared face data, assuming that K_{MIC} is structured such that inter-facial area is minimized, is proportional to $6K_{MIC}^{2/3}(N+1)^2$. The tradeoff is that, although less data is transferred, we must ensure the entire timestep runs optimally on the Xeon Phi^{TM}, rather than just one or two computationally-intensive kernels. As mentioned earlier, this supports the SPMD paradigm, which is a huge advantage when the accelerator and CPU share the same architectural basis, as is the case for Stampede. While this can be an issue with using say GPUs with `x86` CPUs, where it might be easier to take an incremental approach of only porting a single kernel, we believe that the SPMD approach is better and more scalable and maintainable in the long run.

The approach proposed in this paper is to treat the relationship between the host and offload processes in much the same way as the relationship between compute nodes is treated. Once an enclave has been identified within the node's domain, the enclaved domain is assigned to the accelerator and therefore only needs to communicate with the host CPU. Note that due to the nature of the partition, the inter-node communication patterns are identical to the case when no accelerator is used. This is important as we do not pay any penalty for the use of accelerators. Each host ini-

[2]in the Morton order

[3]enclave: a region completely surrounded by a different territory.

tializes its accelerator, then launches an offload process that runs each timestep in parallel with the host. Synchronization is only required once per time step, when the CPU and accelerator exchange their shared face data. At the end of the computation, all of the degrees of freedom computed on the accelerator are transferred back to the host, and so we incur the cost of transferring large datasets only once.

Given the different computational capabilities of the CPU and the accelerator, enclave partitioning has to be able to produce enclaves of different sizes such that the ratio of the number of elements in the enclave to those surrounding it is similar to the relative performance of the accelerator to that of the CPU on the problem(s) of interest. We now explain our algorithm for enclave partitioning.

4.1 Enclave Partitioning

Our goal is to extract a specified number of elements $\mathcal{E}_\phi \subset \mathcal{E}$, where $\mathcal{E}_\phi$ is the set of elements owned by the accelerator and $\mathcal{E}$ is the initial subdomain assigned to a given node. The goal of enclave partitioning is to determine $\mathcal{E}_\phi$ such that it does not share any faces with elements $\notin \mathcal{E}$. We would also like to minimize the number of faces shared between $\mathcal{E}_\phi$ and $\mathcal{E} \setminus \mathcal{E}_\phi$ to minimize the cost of exchanging data between the CPU and the accelerator. It is important to note that it might not be possible in every case to find an enclave of the specified size satisfying these criteria. Specifically, $\mathcal{E}_\phi$ is by definition made up of interior elements, and if the number of elements in $\mathcal{E}$ is small, then it is entirely possible that the number of interior elements is less than requested or even zero. For real applications however, we expect to have significant number of elements in $\mathcal{E}$ such that it will be possible to compute $\mathcal{E}_\phi$.

The algorithm first extracts the boundary elements $\mathcal{E}_b$, i.e., elements that share at least one face with elements $\notin \mathcal{E}$. A simple version of the algorithm can then simply select the specified number of elements from $\mathcal{E} \setminus \mathcal{E}_b$ to belong to $\mathcal{E}_\phi$. This does not however minimize the number of faces shared between $\mathcal{E}_\phi$ and $\mathcal{E} \setminus \mathcal{E}_\phi$. Heuristically, we can minimize the number of shared faces by ensuring that the boundary is largely a smooth face and not made of jagged faces. For our octree-based meshes, this implies selecting sets of elements that are contained within *coarser* octants. Following this heuristic, we construct a coarse interior region, $\mathcal{E}_{coarse}$ by constructing the minimal linear octree between successive elements $\in \mathcal{E}_b$ using Algorithm 1 (see [17] for a detailed discussion). This algorithm runs in $\mathcal{O}(nl)$, where l is the number of levels used in the octree (practically a constant) and n is the number of elements in the boundary.

Initializing $\mathcal{E}_\phi$ with the elements $\in \mathcal{E}$ contained within the "largest" octant in $\mathcal{E}_{coarse}$, we keep adding the "largest" adjacent (next or previous octant in the Morton order) octants till $\mathcal{E}_\phi$ contains the desired number of elements. When we speak of a "large" coarse octant $\mathcal{O}$, we are not referring to the geometric size of the octant, but the number of octants in $\mathcal{E}$ that are overlapped by $\mathcal{O}$. Generating the coarse interior region helps us in two ways. First, it attempts to minimize the effective number of shared faces between the CPU and the Xeon Phi^{TM}. Secondly, while adding additional elements to $\mathcal{E}_\phi$, $\mathcal{E}_{coarse}$ acts as a skip list and speeds up the partitioning.

Determining the size of the enclave.

In order to determine the optimal number of elements to offload to the accelerator, we estimate the accelerator runtime, CPU runtime, and PCI-bus data transfer time for a given set of partition parameters, such as the number of elements on the CPU and the accelerator, the number of faces shared between the CPU and the accelerator, and the order of the elements. We can calculate the number of FLOPs that each key kernel will execute for the given partition parameters, then use measured FLOP rates from each of the kernels (gathered under a variety of partitions and element orders) to estimate the per-timestep runtime of the kernels for the theoretical partition. We select the number of elements to offload by calculating at which point the estimated accelerator runtime plus the PCI-bus data transfer time is equal to the estimated CPU runtime, under the assumption that the global domain is a perfect cube of uniform elements, and that any accelerator subdomain will also be a cube of uniform elements. The resulting number of elements to offload K_{MIC} is then passed as an input to our intra-node partitioning algorithm.

Algorithm 1. *Constructing a minimal linear octree between two octants (sequential)* - `CompleteRegion`

Input: Two octants, a and $b > a$.
Output: R, the minimal octree between a and b.
Work: $\mathcal{O}(n \log n)$, where $n =$ len(R).
Storage: $\mathcal{O}(n)$, where $n =$ len(R).

$W \leftarrow \mathcal{C}(\mathcal{A}_{finest}(a, b))$
for each $w \in W$
  if $(a < w < b)$ AND $(w \notin \{\mathcal{A}(b)\})$
    $R \leftarrow R + w$
  else if $(w \in \{\{\mathcal{A}(a)\}, \{\mathcal{A}(b)\}\})$
    $W \leftarrow W - w + \mathcal{C}(w)$
  end if
end for
Sort(R)

5. IMPLEMENTATION

In this section we describe the parallelization at the two lowermost levels of parallelism shown in Figure ??—shared memory parallelism using OpenMP and vectorization. While several of these optimizations were done to improve the performance on the Intel® Xeon Phi^{TM}, they also helped improve the performance of the code on the CPU. This is another big advantage of the SPMD paradigm.

5.1 Vectorization

Several authors have identified vectorization as a key component in achieving good performance on the Xeon Phi^{TM} [16] [14] [21] [15]. Indeed, the 512-bit wide SIMD vector processing capabilities of the Xeon Phi^{TM} allow for up to 16 DP FLOPS per clock cycle per core (for a fused multiply-add). Code which is not vectorizable, then, suffers a significant performance hit relative to vectorized code. There are several approaches to vectorization, including auto-parallelization by the Intel® compiler, the use of Intel® Cilk^{TM} Plus directives [1], and hand-coding using vector intrinsics or assembly. For each of the key kernels presented in Table 1 we implemented each of these vectorization strategies, though only the results for the *Derivative* kernel will be presented here.

Table 2: FLOP rates in GFLOPS for the CPU and Xeon Phi™ 7th order *Derivate* kernels for various vectorization methods. 16 OpenMP threads were used across the two Xeon™ sockets on the CPU side, and 120 OpenMP threads were used on the Xeon Phi™.

Vectorization	CPU	Xeon Phi™
No vector	53.8	10.9
Compiler	74.7	39.6
Cilk	126.9	161.8
Hand	205.6	159.4

For all other kernels there was no significant performance difference between the three vectorization methods.

The *Derivative* kernel calculates 27 tensor products, producing the partial derivatives of the nine field variables in the three canonical directions. There are three tensor application kernels, one for each canonical direction, and for order N elements the operation of each tensor kernel is analogous to performing $N+1$ matrix-matrix multiplications of size $(N+1)\times(N+1)$. This is the reason that we choose 7th and 15th order elements, to allow the matrices to be 8×8 and 16×16, enabling better vectorization. Though many optimized *dgemm* kernels are available [19], [7], including the Phi-optimized Intel® Math Kernel Library [2], these kernels achieve high performance only for matrices that are relatively large compared to the amount of data available in registers and the L1 cache. Our problem deals with much smaller data structures, however, as for, e.g., 7th order elements, four $(N+1)\times(N+1)$ matrices can fit in the vector registers of a single Xeon Phi™ core. A full examination of our hand-optimized tensor kernels exceeds the scope of this paper, and so we will simply say that our optimization strategy was to minimize loads and stores between registers and the cache, perform all arithmetic operations in the VPU, and amortize loads and stores by reordering instructions such that arithmetic operations could be executed concurrent to memory transfers. For the CPU, we observed a significant speedup over both compiler-vectorized and Cilk™ Plus-vectorized code, as Table 2 shows. On the Xeon Phi™, however, although our vectorized code performs significantly better than unvectorized code, we were not able to produce performance significantly better than the Cilk™ Plus-vectorized code.

Anomalously, the only vectorization method for which we observed higher performance on the Xeon Phi™ than on the CPU was the Cilk™ Plus-vectorized kernel. We expect the Xeon Phi™ to outperform the CPU by a factor of three, and are currently investigating the reasons for the weaker-than-expected performance on the Xeon Phi™.

5.2 Multithreading and Offload

Currently, OpenMP is the method of choice for making full use of the many hardware threads available on the Xeon Phi™ [9]. While MPI libraries are available on the Xeon Phi™, treating the Xeon Phi™ as a distributed memory system would give each core only 134 MB of RAM. When we consider that each Xeon Phi™ core can only issue a vector instruction every other clock cycle, which necessitates the use of at least two hardware threads per core, we see that using MPI to keep the Xeon Phi™ fully scheduled would lead to only 67 MB of RAM per MPI process.

With the decision to use OpenMP on the Xeon Phi™ firmly in place, we are faced with the remaining decisions of how to implement parallelism on the CPU and how to implement communication between the CPU and the Xeon Phi™. The existing codebase we have inherited for the solution of the acoustic-elastic wave equations utilizes pure MPI for interprocess communication and parallelization, spawning one MPI process per core on each compute node. On Stampede this translates to 16 MPI processes per compute node, each process having its own address space, arrays of unknowns, and computational subdomain. At each time step, facial degrees of freedom on faces that fall on inter-processor boundaries are communicated between MPI processes. An obvious option is to maintain this distributed-memory parallelism on the CPU side of the compute nodes and launch a single MPI process on the Xeon Phi™ that then spawns OpenMP threads. This would require an overhaul of our existing MPI scheduling algorithm, however, which assigns a roughly equal amount of work to each MPI process. It would also mean that the computational subdomain owned by the Xeon Phi™ could have a potentially large number of neighboring subdomains, which would lead to a large amount of data being transferred over the PCI bus and subsequently over the InfiniBand network. The worst case data path would be a Xeon Phi™ whose subdomain was neighbored by a subdomain owned by a Xeon Phi™ on another compute node, in which case the shared faces would have to travel across the PCI bus, then between nodes via Infiniband, then back across the PCI bus after arrival at the destination node.

To reduce traffic on the PCI bus and simplify load balancing, then, we choose to assign only one MPI process to the CPU side of each compute node, which then spawns OpenMP threads on the CPU-side to take advantage of the multiple Xeon™ cores. This same MPI process also controls offload to the Xeon Phi™ and MPI communication. We restrict the subdomain assigned to the Xeon Phi™ to a subset of the elements owned by the parent MPI process whose faces do not lie on inter-processor boundaries. This eliminates the need for a reworking of our MPI load balancing algorithm, as each compute node can be given the same amount of work and the partitioning between the CPU and the Xeon Phi™ domains can be done independently and locally on each compute node.

SPMD programming differences.

Though each host MPI process does technically "offload" in the sense that it initiates the execution of the Xeon Phi™ code through offload compiler directives, the behavior of the Xeon Phi™ and the dynamic between the CPU and the Xeon Phi™ is more like that of a distinct compute node. Each Xeon Phi™ owns a set of elements forming a computational subdomain and executes full time steps in the solution of the acoustic-elastic wave equation. The only difference between the CPU and Xeon Phi™ codes lies in the communication phases of each time step. The CPU maintains communication buffers and maps to inter-processor boundary faces for both inter-node MPI communication and intra-node Xeon Phi™ communication, whereas the Xeon Phi™ concerns itself only with faces along the CPU-Xeon Phi™ boundary. CPU-CPU communication is carried out asyn-

Table 3: Key performance characteristics of Stampede compute node.

	Xeon Phi™	2x Xeon E5
Peak DP GFLOPS	1070	346
Peak Bandwidth (GB/s)	320	102.4
Memory (GB)	8 GDDR5	32 DDR3

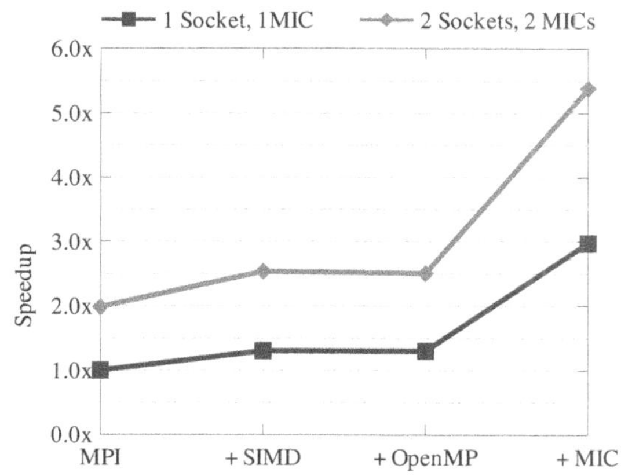

Figure 6: Incremental optimization of 7th order code.

chronously via MPI, while CPU-Xeon Phi™ communication is implemented synchronously through compiler offload directives. Although the Xeon Phi™ is capable of asynchronous computation, and theoretically capable of asynchronous data transfer, we have not observed a significant time difference in data transferred between the CPU and the Xeon Phi™ when using asynchronous offload directives versus synchronous directives. We postulate that this is due to a fixed overhead in the offload runtime that, though possibly amortized by actual asynchronous transfer for larger array sizes, is significant enough for the amount of face data we need to transfer to be very nearly the same as the time required to synchronously transfer that data.

6. RESULTS

We present results in support of the proposed partitioning algorithm in this section. All experiments were carried out on Stampede at the Texas Advanced Computing Center (TACC). Stampede consists of 6400 compute nodes, each of which houses two 8-core Intel® Xeon™ E5 CPUs and up to two 61-core Intel® Xeon Phi™ SE10P accelerators [3]. As table 3 shows, in terms of floating point performance and memory bandwidth the Xeon Phi™ outperforms the CPU by approximately a factor of three. As with most accelerators, the amount of work that can be done by the Xeon Phi™ is constrained by its limited amount of random-access memory. To begin with, the Xeon Phi™ has only 25% as much RAM as is available to its host-node CPUs. Considering the Xeon Phi™'s higher core count the situation becomes worse, as there are approximately 134 MB of RAM for every Xeon Phi™ core, compared to 2 GB of RAM for each CPU core. Thus, the Xeon Phi™ is most effectively used as a large SMP node, programmed using a shared-memory paradigm.

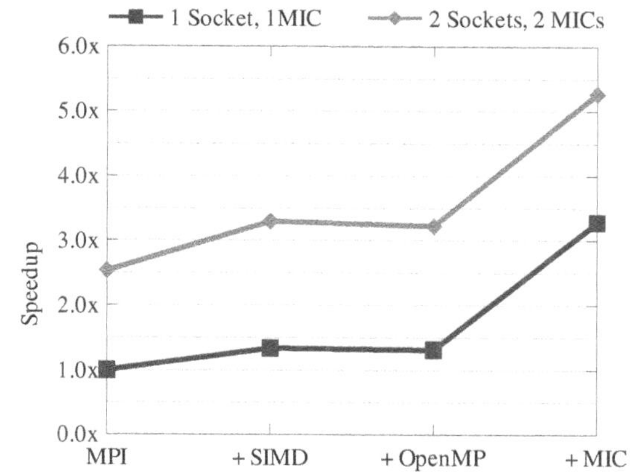

Figure 7: Incremental optimization of 15th order code.

6.1 Single-Node Optimization and Offloading

We first present the results of each step in the transformation from our baseline pure-MPI code to our vectorized, hybrid MPI-OpenMP, coprocessor-accelerated code. Figures 6 and 7 show the speedup realized after each subsequent optimization step relative to the baseline MPI-only code run on a single socket of Stampede. Some compute nodes on Stampede contain two Xeon Phi™. Our code seamlessly handles the utilization of two Xeon Phi™ per compute node by simply scheduling two MPI processes per node, each pinned to a different socket. Each of these MPI processes then spawns 8 OpenMP threads on the 8 cores of their host socket and controls offloading to one of the two available Xeon Phi™. Though we expected a performance hit when moving from pure MPI code to hybrid MPI-OpenMP code, we did not observe any difference in runtime between our OpenMP and pure MPI codes. We took care in our OpenMP implementation to minimize memory sharing amongst threads as much as possible so as to mimic the distributed-memory behavior of MPI processes.

6.2 Partitioning

To measure the consistency of the partitions produced by our partitioning algorithm we examine the distribution of Xeon Phi™ runtimes across a large run. Examining Figure 8 we see that most of the Xeon Phi™ runtimes are within 5% of the mean runtime. We believe this is a very good result and within acceptable bounds given the variable nature of adaptive meshes. While it might be possible to get a more uniform load, the simplicity of the current algorithm makes it very efficient.

6.3 Scaling Results

The difficulty in achieving strong scalability using coprocessor-enabled code is that as the number of compute nodes is increased for a fixed number of elements, the ratio of boundary to interior elements on each node's subdomain also increases. Since only interior elements are assigned to the Xeon Phi™, this means that the percentage of elements eligible for offload to the accelerator decreases as the number of compute nodes increases. At very high compute node counts, the performance of the Phi-accelerated code approaches the performance of the baseline code due to the increased ratio of work

Table 4: **Speedup of optimized, accelerated strong scaling runs relative to baseline MPI.**

Cores	PHIs	7th Order	15th Order
32	4	5.78x	6.88x
64	8	5.46x	4.51x
128	16	4.08x	4.15x
256	32	3.44x	3.44x
512	64	2.75x	2.75x
1024	128	2.33x	1.89x
2048	256	1.57x	

being assigned to the CPU. This behavior is illustrated in Figures 9 and 11.

We observed weak scaling comparable to or better than our baseline pure-MPI code. For weak scaling runs using dual-Phi compute nodes, the size of our experiments were constrained by the available number of compute nodes with two Phis. We present dual-Phi weak scaling for up to as many nodes as were available. Table 4 shows the speedup factor for our vectorized, MPI-OpenMP, Xeon Phi™-enabled code relative to our MPI baseline for the strong scaling runs shown in Figures 9 and 10. The "Cores" column specifies how many CPU-side cores were used in the computation. Baseline computations used one MPI process per core, while accelerated runs used one MPI process per socket, each spawning 8 OpenMP threads to make full use of the available cores. This table illustrates that when compute nodes are given nontrivial workloads, as is the case in the strong scaling runs at low core count, the Xeon Phi™ contributes to a significant speedup.

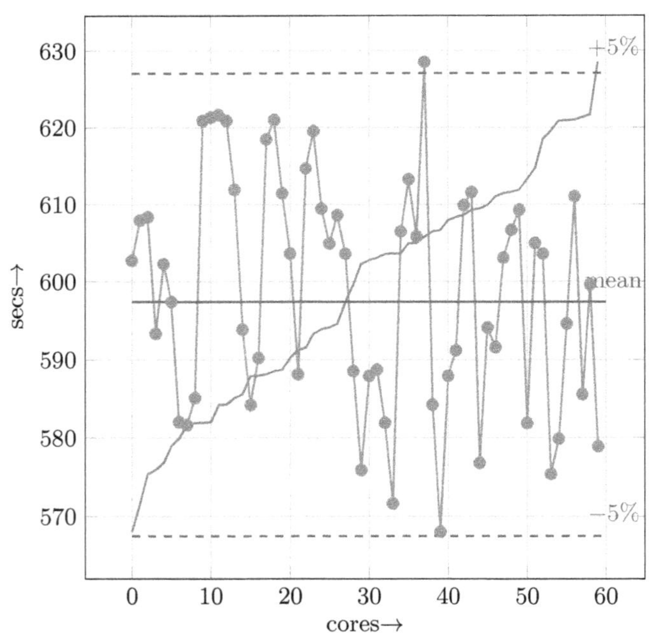

Figure 8: Distribution of Xeon Phi™ runtimes for a 64-node run. The solid blue line indicates the mean runtime, while the dotted lines indicate deviation from the mean. The curve in magenta ignores the core numbers and plots the sorted times, to make it easier to visualize the distribution.

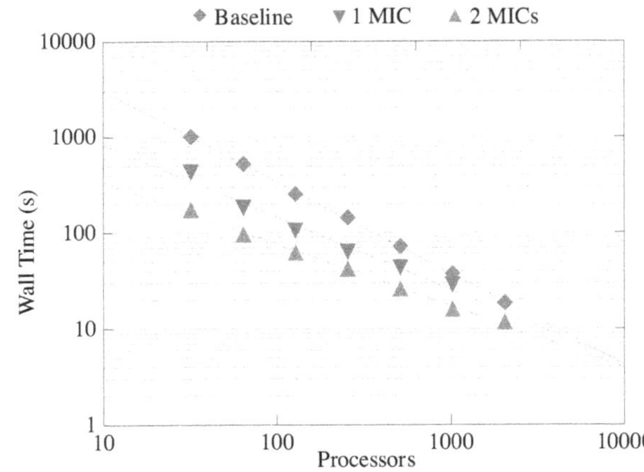

Figure 9: Strong scaling for 93k 7th order elements. Phi-enabled runs assigned 63% of the elements per node to the Xeon Phi™ (s). Baseline runs were original MPI-only code. Number of processors refers to total number of CPU cores used in baseline case, and total number of OpenMP threads used on the host CPU side in Xeon Phi™-accelerated cases.

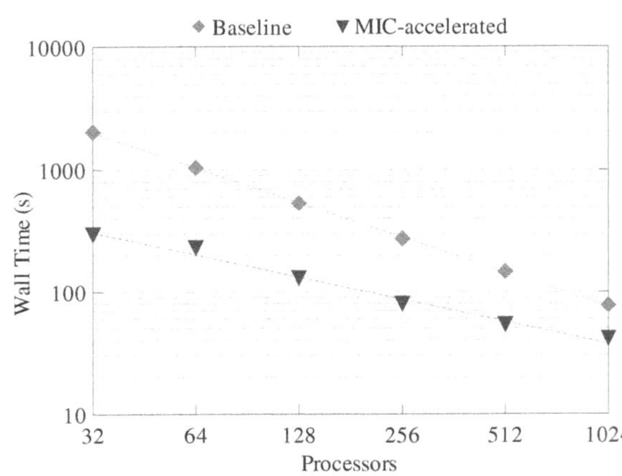

Figure 10: Strong scaling for 17.4k 15th order elements. Phi-enabled runs assigned 66% of the elements per node to the Xeon Phi™ (s). Baseline runs were original MPI-only code. Number of processors refers to total number of CPU cores used. Phi-accelerated runs used 1 Xeon Phi™ for every 8 CPU cores (1 socket).

7. CONCLUSION

In this work we have presented a new partitioning algorithm targeting hybrid codes on heterogeneous clusters. We demonstrated the efficacy of our algorithm using a large-scale seismic wave propagation application on the Stampede Supercomputer. We observed speedups of up to 5.78x for runs using 7th order elements and up to 6.88x for 15th order elements. Our partitioning scheme was able to construct relatively consistent subdomains for the Xeon Phi™. We were able to increase the performance of the baseline MPI code through the use of vector instructions, and were also able to maintain performance when moving from pure MPI

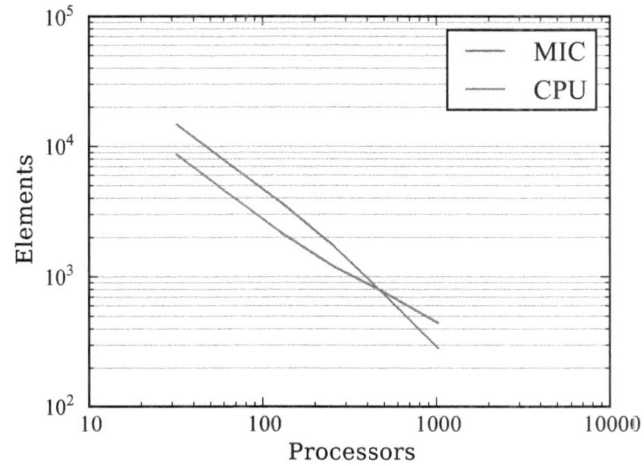

Figure 11: Number of elements assigned to the CPU and Xeon Phi™ in the single-socket strong scaling runs. Number of processors refers to total number of CPU cores used in baseline case, and total number of OpenMP threads used on the host CPU side in Xeon Phi™-accelerated cases.

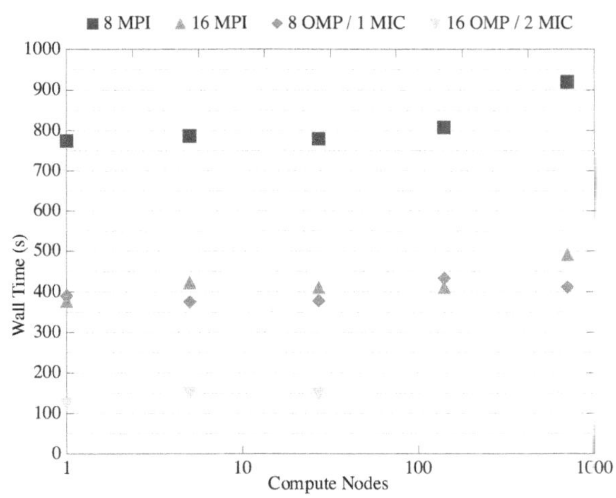

Figure 12: Weak scaling for 7th order elements. Phi-enabled runs completed with 63% of the elements given to the Xeon Phi™ (s). Baseline runs were original MPI-only code. Runs labeled "8 MPI" or "8 OMP" indicate that only one socket per node was used.

to an MPI-OpenMP hybrid. On a system like Stampede where the majority of computational power is delivered by accelerators, we have seen that optimizing code for effective execution on the accelerator can have a dramatic impact on performance. The partitioning scheme also enables the developers to program using a SPMD paradigm, which does not appear straightforward while considering heterogeneous architectures. We believe our work is the first to take such an approach and will make it easier to obtain good performance and scalability on large heterogeneous clusters.

Acknowledgements

We would like to thank Jesse Kelly for contributions to the preliminary version of this project. Support for this work

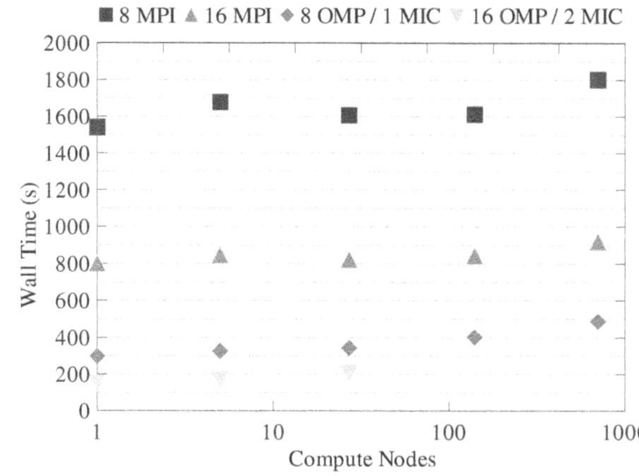

Figure 13: Weak scaling for 15th order elements. Phi-enabled runs completed with 66% of the elements given to the Xeon Phi™ (s). Baseline runs were original MPI-only code. Runs labeled "8 MPI" or "8 OMP" indicate that only one socket per node was used.

was provided through the U.S. National Science Foundation (NSF) grant CMMI-1028889 and through the Scientific Discovery through Advanced Computing (SciDAC) project DE-SC0009286 funded by the U.S. Department of Energy Office of Science, Advanced Scientific Computing Research and Biological and Environmental Research.

8. REFERENCES

[1] Intel Cilk plus, October 2014.
[2] Intel Math Kernel Library, October 2014.
[3] Stampede user guide, October 2014.
[4] J. D. D. Basabe and M. K. Sen. Stability of the high-order finite elements for acoustic or elastic wave propagation with high-order time stepping. *Geophysical Journal International*, 181:577–590, 2010.
[5] T. Bui-Thanh, C. Burstedde, O. Ghattas, J. Martin, G. Stadler, and L. C. Wilcox. Extreme-scale UQ for Bayesian inverse problems governed by PDEs. In *SC12: Proceedings of the International Conference for High Performance Computing, Networking, Storage and Analysis*, 2012.
[6] C. Burstedde, L. C. Wilcox, and O. Ghattas. `p4est`: Scalable algorithms for parallel adaptive mesh refinement on forests of octrees. *SIAM Journal on Scientific Computing*, 33(3):1103–1133, 2011.
[7] K. Goto and R. A. V. D. Geijn. Anatomy of high-performance matrix multiplication. *ACM Transactions on Mathematical Software*, pages 1–25, 2008.
[8] J. S. Hesthaven and T. Warburton. *Nodal Discontinuous Galerkin Methods*, volume XIV of *Texts in Applied Mathematics*. Springer, 2008.
[9] J. Jeffers and J. Reinders. *Intel Xeon Phi Coprocessor High Performance Programming*. Morgan Kaufmann, March 2013.
[10] A. A. Kaufman and A. L. Levshin. *Acoustic and Elastic Wave Fields in Geophysics, III*, volume 39 of

Methods in Geochemistry and Geophysics. Elsevier B.V., 2005.

[11] V. Kindratenko and P. Trancoso. Trends in high-performance computing. *Computing in Science Engineering*, 13(3):92–95, 2011.

[12] G. M. Morton. *A computer oriented geodetic data base and a new technique in file sequencing*. International Business Machines Co., 1966.

[13] B. Riviere and M. F. Wheeler. Discontinuous finite element methods for acoustic and elastic wave problems. In *Current Trends in Scientific Computing: ICM 2002 Beijing Satellite Conference on Scientific Computing, August 15-18, 2002, Xi'an Jiaotong University, Xi'an, China*, volume 329, page 271. American Mathematical Society, 2003.

[14] C. Rosales. Porting to the intel xeon phi: Opportunities and challenges. Technical report, Texas Advanced Computing Center, The University of Texas at Austin, Extreme Scaling Workshop 2013, September 2013.

[15] E. Saule, K. Kaya, and U. V. Catalyurek. Performance Evaluation of Sparse Matrix Multiplication Kernels on Intel Xeon Phi, Feb. 2013.

[16] K. Schulz, R. Ulerich, N. Malaya, P. Bauman, R. Stogner, and C. Simmons. Early experiences porting scientific applications to the many integrated core (mic) platform. Technical report, Texas Advanced Computing Center, The University of Texas at Austin, April 2012.

[17] H. Sundar, R. Sampath, and G. Biros. Bottom-up construction and 2:1 balance refinement of linear octrees in parallel. *SIAM Journal on Scientific Computing*, 30(5):2675–2708, 2008.

[18] Top 500 Supercomputing Sites. `http://www.top500.org/`.

[19] R. C. Whaley, A. Petitet, and J. J. Dongarra. Automated empirical optimization of software and the ATLAS project. *Parallel Computing*, 27(1–2):3–35, 2001. Also available as University of Tennessee LAPACK Working Note #147, UT-CS-00-448, 2000 (`www.netlib.org/lapack/lawns/lawn147.ps`).

[20] L. Wilcox, G. Stadler, C. Burstedde, and O. Ghattas. A high-order discontinuous galerkin method for wave propagation through coupled elastic–acoustic media. *Journal of Computational Physics*, 229(24):9373–9396, 2010.

[21] S. Williams, D. D. Kalamkar, A. Singh, A. M. Deshpande, B. Van Straalen, M. Smelyanskiy, A. Almgren, P. Dubey, J. Shalf, and L. Oliker. Optimization of geometric multigrid for emerging multi- and manycore processors. In *Proceedings of the International Conference on High Performance Computing, Networking, Storage and Analysis*, SC '12, pages 96:1–96:11, Los Alamitos, CA, USA, 2012. IEEE Computer Society Press.

Criticality-Aware Dynamic Task Scheduling for Heterogeneous Architectures

Kallia Chronaki*, Alejandro Rico*, Rosa M. Badia*†,
Eduard Ayguadé*‡, Jesús Labarta*‡, Mateo Valero*‡
*Barcelona Supercomputing Center, Barcelona, Spain
†Artificial Intelligence Research Institute (IIIA) -
Spanish National Research Council (CSIC), Barcelona, Spain
‡Universitat Politècnica de Catalunya - BarcelonaTech, Barcelona, Spain
kallia.chronaki@bsc.es, alejandro.rico@bsc.es, rosa.m.badia@bsc.es,
eduard.ayguade@bsc.es, jesus.labarta@bsc.es, mateo.valero@bsc.es

ABSTRACT

Current and future parallel programming models need to be portable and efficient when moving to heterogeneous multi-core systems. OmpSs is a task-based programming model with dependency tracking and dynamic scheduling. This paper describes the OmpSs approach on scheduling dependent tasks onto the asymmetric cores of a heterogeneous system. The proposed scheduling policy improves performance by prioritizing the newly-created tasks at runtime, detecting the longest path of the dynamic task dependency graph, and assigning critical tasks to fast cores. While previous works use profiling information and are static, this dynamic scheduling approach uses information that is discoverable at runtime which makes it implementable and functional without the need of an oracle or profiling. The evaluation results show that our proposal outperforms a dynamic implementation of Heterogeneous Earliest Finish Time by up to 1.15×, and the default breadth-first OmpSs scheduler by up to 1.3× in an 8-core heterogeneous platform and up to 2.7× in a simulated 128-core chip.

Categories and Subject Descriptors

C.1.3 [**Processor Architectures**]: Heterogeneous systems; C.1.4 [**Processor Architectures**]: Mobile processors; D.1.3 [**Programming Techniques**]: Parallel programming; D.3.2 [**Programming Languages**]: Parallel languages

Keywords

High performance computing; Scheduling; Heterogeneous systems; Task-based programming models

1. INTRODUCTION

The future of high-performance computing is highly restricted by energy efficiency [18]. The use of heterogeneous multi-core architectures is an approach towards increasing energy efficiency [13, 14]. These architectures feature different types of processing cores that are designed to target different performance and power optimization points.

Load balancing and scheduling are two of the main challenges in utilizing such heterogeneous platforms. The use of task-based programming models with dynamic scheduling is an answer to tackle these challenges. Some of these programming models allow the specification of inter-task dependencies that enable automatic scheduling and synchronization by the runtime system. OmpSs [10, 4] is an example of this type of programming models. It maintains a dynamic directed-acyclic graph of tasks with their current state. Whenever a task's dependencies are satisfied, it becomes ready to be scheduled to an available core.

The mapping of ready tasks to different types of cores on a heterogeneous system becomes a challenge when considering the reduction of the total execution time. Some task-based applications expose a complex dependency graph in which tasks in the critical path determine the total application duration. This opens an opportunity to accelerate the overall application by running critical tasks on fast cores. Some previous works [15, 9, 25, 20] tackled this issue using static scheduling over the whole dependency graph to statically map tasks to processors on a heterogeneous system. However, they required the knowledge of profiling information and most of them were evaluated on synthetic randomly-generated task dependency graphs (TDGs).

In this paper, we propose a criticality-aware *dynamic* task scheduler that dynamically assigns critical tasks to fast cores to improve performance in a heterogeneous system with fast and slow cores. Compared to previous proposals, this scheduler is based on information discoverable at runtime, is implementable and works without the need of an oracle or profiling. Furthermore, our evaluation is based on a real heterogeneous multi-core platform with real applications and, therefore, using real TDGs.

The contributions of this paper are the following:

- A novel criticality-aware task scheduler (CATS) that dynamically assigns critical tasks to fast cores in a heterogeneous multi-core. Tasks are defined to be critical if they are part of the longest path in the in-flight dynamic state of the dependency graph. The flexibility and work stealing policy of our scheduler are configurable. Flexibility increases the number of tasks

ICS'15, June 8–11, 2015, Newport Beach, CA, USA.

http://dx.doi.org/10.1145/2751205.2751235.

considered critical. Work stealing may be uni- or bi-directional: only fast cores can steal from slow cores, or slow cores can also steal from fast cores.

- An evaluation of our implementation of CATS in the OmpSs programming model compared to a dynamic implementation of Heterogeneous Earliest Finish Time [25] and the default OmpSs scheduler. We evaluate the effectiveness of CATS on different numbers of cores and shares of fast and slow cores on an Odroid-XU3 development board featuring an eight-core Samsung Exynos 5422 chip with ARM big.LITTLE architecture including four Cortex-A15 and four Cortex-A7 cores. We also evaluate the effectiveness of CATS on different speed ratios between fast and slow cores using simulation of heterogeneous multi-cores with up to 128 cores. The results show that CATS improves overall performance up to 1.3× on the real eight-core platform, and up to 2.7× on a simulated 128-core system.

2. RELATED WORK

The search for efficient task scheduling on multi-core systems has been intensively studied. Most scheduling heuristics target homogeneous multiprocessors, nevertheless there exists an important number of studies in heterogeneous multiprocessors. In this section we give an overview of different categories of schedulers for heterogeneous systems, we explain some details about schedulers targeting specific systems using compute accelerators and explain details of previous works on criticality-aware schedulers.

2.1 Schedulers for Heterogeneous Systems

Previous works on schedulers for heterogeneous systems form four different types of schedulers: listing, clustering, guided-random, and duplication-based schedulers.

Listing schedulers [1, 15, 9, 25, 20] have two scheduling stages. In the first stage, each task is given a priority based on the policy defined in each algorithm. In the second stage, tasks are assigned to processors depending on their priorities. Most criticality-aware schedulers fall in this category, and we discuss them in Section 2.3. The scheduler proposed in this paper is also a list scheduler.

Clustering schedulers [26, 27, 15, 17] first separate tasks into clusters, where each cluster is to be executed on the same processor. During the clustering stage, the algorithm assumes an unlimited number of available processors in the system. If the number of clusters exceeds the number of available cores, the *merging* stage joins multiple clusters so that they match the number of available processors. An example is the Levelized Min Time [17] clustering scheduler. This heuristic clusters tasks that can execute in parallel according to their *level* (i.e. sibling nodes in a graph have the same level), and assigns priorities to the tasks in a cluster according to its execution time, (i.e. tasks with the highest execution time have the highest priority). The task-to processor assignment is done in decreasing order of priority.

Guided-random schedulers [28, 19, 21] randomize their schedules by applying policies influenced by other sciences. Genetic algorithms [28] group tasks into generations and schedule them according to a randomized genetic technique. Chemical reaction algorithms [19] mimic molecular interactions to map tasks to processors. Some of these guided-random approaches [28, 19] are designed for heterogeneous systems. The scheduler by Page et al. [21] enables dynamic scheduling of multiple-sized tasks for heterogeneous systems. However, it does not support dependencies between tasks.

Duplication-based schedulers [5, 29, 2] aim to eliminate communication costs between processors by scheduling tasks and their successors on the same processor. If a task has many successors, it is duplicated and executed in multiple cores prior to its successors so all successor tasks get the data from their predecessors with the lowest communication cost. This scheduling potentially introduces redundant duplications of tasks which may lead to bad schedules. The Heterogeneous Economical Duplication scheduler [2] performs task duplication in an economical manner as it removes the redundant duplicates if they do not affect performance.

These previous works schedule tasks statically and assume the prior knowledge of the task execution times on the different processor types in the heterogeneous system.

2.2 Schedulers for Compute Accelerators

The schedulers in the previous section target the scheduling of generic TDGs on generic heterogeneous architectures. In this section we cover schedulers that target specific systems with compute accelerators. These works are more focused on the scheduling of tasks on the target platform based on the abstractions provided by the corresponding mixture of programming models for the general-purpose processors and the compute accelerators in the system.

Most heterogeneous systems with compute accelerators nowadays combine general-purpose CPUs and GPU compute accelerators. There is a set of programming models providing abstractions to ease the development of applications on these platforms. OmpSs [10, 4] offers this abstraction by allowing multiple implementations of a given task to be executed on different processing units [23]. The scheduler then assigns the execution of a task to the best resource according to its earliest finish time. Another case is StarPU [3], a library that offers runtime heterogeneity support and provides priority schedulers for task-to-processor allocation. AHP [22] is another framework that generates software pipelines for heterogeneous systems and schedules tasks to their earliest executor, based on profiling information gathered prior to runtime.

None of these works, however, take into account the criticality of tasks regarding task dependencies, but they rather focus on the earliest execution time of individual tasks on the processor types in the specific system configuration.

2.3 Criticality-Aware Schedulers

Several previous works propose scheduling heuristics that focus on the critical path in a TDG to reduce total execution time [15, 9, 25, 20]. To identify the tasks in the critical path, most of these works use the concept of *upward rank* and *downward rank*. The upward rank of a task is the maximum sum of computation and communication cost of the tasks in the dependency chains from that task to an exit node in the graph. The downward rank of a task is the maximum sum of computation and communication cost of the tasks in the dependency chain from an entry node in the graph up to that task. Each task has an upward rank and downward rank for each processor type in the heterogeneous system, as the computation and communication costs differ across processor types.

The Heterogeneous Earliest Finish Time (HEFT) algorithm [25] maintains a list of tasks sorted in decreasing order of their upward rank. At each schedule step, HEFT assigns the task with the highest upward rank to the processor that finishes the execution of the task at the earliest possible time. Another work is the Longest Dynamic Critical Path (LDCP) algorithm [9]. LDCP also statically schedules first the task with the highest upward rank on every schedule step. The difference between LDCP and HEFT is that LDCP updates the computation and communication costs on multiple processors of the scheduled task by the computation and communication cost in the processor to which it was assigned.

The Critical-Path-on-a-Processor (CPOP) algorithm [25] also maintains a list of tasks sorted in decreasing order as in HEFT, but in this case it is ordered according to the addition of their *upward rank* and *downward rank*. The tasks with the highest *upward rank* + *downward rank* belong to the critical path. On each step, these tasks are statically assigned to the processor that minimizes the critical-path execution time.

The main weaknesses of these works are that (a) they assume prior knowledge of the computation and communication costs of each individual task on each processor type, (b) they operate statically on the whole dependency graph, so they do not apply to dynamically scheduled applications in which only a partial representation of the dependency graph is available at a given point in time, and (c) most of them use randomly-generated synthetic dependency graphs that are not necessarily representative of the dependencies in real workloads.

3. OMPSS PROGRAMMING MODEL

OmpSs is a task-based programming model that offers a high level abstraction to the implementation of parallel applications for various homogeneous and heterogeneous architectures [10, 4]. It enables the annotation of function declarations with the task directive, which declares a task. Every invocation of a such function creates a task that is executed concurrently with other tasks or parallel loops. OmpSs also supports task dependencies and it uses the StarSs [12] dependency tracking mechanisms. OmpSs is built with the support of the Mercurium compiler, responsible for the translation of the OmpSs annotation clauses to source code, and the Nanos++ runtime system, responsible for the internal creation and execution of the tasks.

Nanos++ is an environment designed to serve as the runtime platform of OmpSs. It provides device support for heterogeneity and includes different plug-ins for implementations of scheduling policies, throttling policies, thread barriers, dependency tracking mechanisms, work-sharing and instrumentation. This design allows to maintain the runtime features by adding or removing plug-ins. Thus, the implementation of a new scheduler, or the support of a new architecture becomes simple.

The implementations of the different scheduling policies in Nanos++ perform various actions on the states of the tasks. A task is *created* if a call to this task is discovered but it is waiting until all its inputs are produced by other previous tasks. When all the input dependencies are satisfied, the task becomes *ready*. The ready tasks of the application at a given point in time are inserted in the *ready queues* as stated by the scheduling policy. Ready queues can be thread-private or shared among multiple threads. When a thread becomes idle, the scheduling policy picks a task from the ready queues for that thread to execute.

The Nanos++ internal data structures support task prioritization. The task priority is an integer field inside the task descriptor that rates the importance of the task. If the scheduling policy supports priorities, the ready queues are implemented as *priority queues*. In a priority queue, tasks are sorted in a decreasing order of their priority. The insertion in a priority queue is always ordered and the removal of a task is always from the head of the queue, i.e., the task with the highest priority. The priority of a task can be either set in user code, by using the *priority* clause, which accepts an integer priority value or expression, or dynamically by the scheduling policy, as is described in the next section.

4. CRITICALITY-AWARE SCHEDULER

The proposed scheduling algorithm generally applies to task-based programming models supporting task dependencies, but for simplicity we explain it in the context of the OmpSs programming model.

The Criticality-Aware Task Scheduler (CATS) uses bottom-level longest-path priorities and consists of three steps:

- *Task prioritization*: when a task is created and added to the TDG, it is assigned a priority and the priority of the rest of tasks in the graph is updated accordingly.
- *Task submission*: when a task becomes *ready*, i.e., all its predecessors finished their execution, it is submitted to a *ready queue*. At this point, the algorithm decides whether the task is considered *critical* or *non critical*. The task is then inserted in the corresponding ready queue: tasks in the *critical ready queue* will be executed by fast cores, and tasks in the *non-critical ready queue* will be executed by slow cores.
- *Task-to-core assignment*: when a core becomes idle, it tries to retrieve a task from its corresponding ready queue to execute it. If the queue is empty, it might try to steal from the other queue depending on the work stealing policy. Currently, we support two work stealing mechanisms: *simple* work stealing, i.e., fast cores can steal from slow cores; and *bi-directional* (*2DS*) work stealing, i.e., both types can steal from the other. The default policy is *simple*.

These steps are performed dynamically and potentially in parallel in different cores. This means that while some tasks are being prioritized, previously created tasks may be submitted, and others assigned to available cores or executed.

To give an overview of the scheduling process, Figure 1 shows a scheme of the operation of CATS. In the TDG on the left, each node represents a task and each edge of the graph represents a dependency between two tasks. The number inside each node is the *bottom level* of the task: the length of the longest path in the dependency chains from this node to a leaf node. The priority of a task is given by its bottom level. The pattern-filled nodes indicate tasks that are considered critical. The number outside each node is the task id and is used in the text to refer to each task. Critical tasks are inserted in the critical queue, and non-critical tasks to the non-critical queue. The insertion is ordered with the highest priorities at the head of the queue and the lowest priorities at the tail. Slow cores retrieve tasks from the

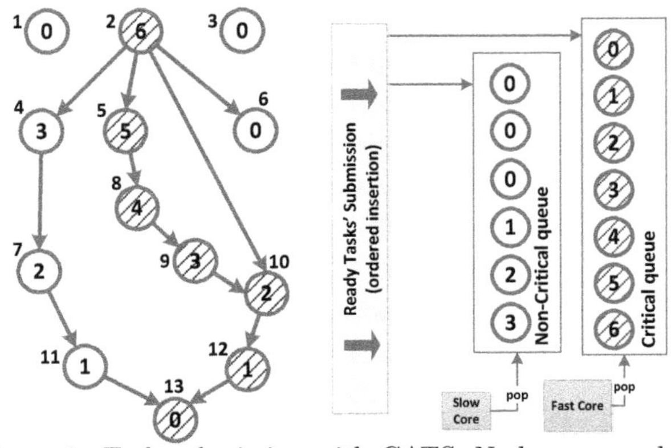

Figure 1: Task submission with CATS. Nodes are marked with the *bottom level* of each task. Pattern-filled nodes mark the critical tasks.

head of the non-critical queue and fast cores from the critical queue. The following sections describe these scheduling steps in more detail.

4.1 Task Prioritization

Each task in the TDG has a list to include its predecessors (*plist*). Every time an edge is added into the TDG on the creation of a new task, the corresponding predecessor of the dependency is added in the *plist* of its successor. For example, in Figure 1, when the dependency between tasks 2 and 5 occurs, the task number 2 is inserted into the *plist* of the task number 5. Thus, the *plist* of task number 5 becomes {2}. Accordingly, the *plist* of task number 10 will be {2, 9} when the edge 9→10 is inserted to the TDG.

The priority given to a task is the *bottom level* of the task. The *bottom level* is computed by traversing the TDG upwards starting from the successor that the currently created edge is pointing to. The priority of this successor is 0 because it is a leaf node of the graph, as it is the last created task. Then, using *plist* for each task, the algorithm navigates to the upper levels of the TDG and updates the priority on each visited node. This way not all the graph is updated, but only the tasks that are predecessors in the paths to the new edge. The algorithm also stops going up through a path, when it finds a priority larger than the one it would be updated to.

Listing 1 shows the algorithm for task prioritization. This function is called on the creation of a new edge with the successor as argument. The algorithm traverses the *plist* of the successor task (line 5) and if the priority of the current predecessor is lower than the bottom level of the successor plus one, it updates the current predecessor's priority to that value (lines 7-8). If the updated predecessor task is ready (i.e., it sits in one of the ready queues), the scheduler reorders the ready queue so it remains ordered considering the updated priority (lines 9-10). Then, the same actions are performed recursively for each predecessor of the *plist* to update all the possible upward paths from the successor.

The terminate conditions for the navigation of the TDG are two: *(a)* if the *plist* of the current task (`currPred`) is empty, so either we reach an entry node or the predecessors of the task have finished execution; or *(b)* if the priority of the current task (`currPred`) remains unchanged, which means that the successor task (`succ`) does not belong to the longest path because its predecessor already has a higher priority (bottom level).

```
1 void prioritize_task(task *succ) {
2  int blev = succ->priority;
3  list plist = plistOf(succ);
4  task *currPred;
5  while( not isEmpty(plist) ) {
6    currPred = plist.next();
7    if(priorityOf(currPred) < blev+1) {
8     currPred->priority = blev+1;
9     if(isReady(currPred))
10     readyQueueOf(currPred)->reorder();
11    prioritize_task(currPred);
12   }
13   else return;
14 }
15}
```

Listing 1: Pseudo-code task prioritization with CATS.

4.2 Task Submission

The purpose of this step is to divide the tasks in two groups: *critical* and *non-critical*. Critical tasks are tasks that belong to the longest path of the dynamic TDG. The longest path is the path of the TDG with the maximum number of tasks (or nodes). Thus, the longest path starts from the task with the maximum bottom level. At runtime, the longest path changes as tasks complete execution and new tasks are created. CATS manages to detect those changes and dynamically decide if the submitted task belongs to the longest path of the TDG.

When a task's dependencies are satisfied, the task becomes ready for execution and is to be inserted in the *ready queues*. Ready queues are priority queues that keep tasks in a decreasing order of task priorities, i.e., the task with the maximum priority resides on the head of the queue. Critical tasks are inserted in the critical queue and non-critical tasks in the non-critical queue. The pattern-filled nodes in Figure 1 represent the critical tasks in that graph.

To determine the criticality of a task, CATS keeps track of the last discovered critical task. Then, for each task that becomes ready, CATS checks the following conditions:

- Whether the priority of the current ready task is higher than the priority of the last discovered critical task (`maxPriority`).
- Whether the current ready task is the highest-priority immediate successor of the last discovered critical task.

In the first case, the algorithm detects new longest paths that may have been created by the application throughout the execution of a prior longest path. In this case, the scheduler can either be *strict* or *flexible*:

- *Strict*: marks as critical tasks with priority higher than the priority of the last critical task.
- *Flexible*: marks as critical tasks with priority higher or equal to the priority of the last critical task.

As a result, the flexible scheduler ends up with more critical tasks than the strict. The flexibility of the scheduler can be set by the programmer through an environment variable.

The task that satisfies the second condition is a task with a lower priority than the maximum but the task belongs to the longest path because it is the highest priority immediate successor of the last detected critical task.

Listing 2 shows a simplified version of the task submission code. The variable `maxPriority` (line 1) is used to store the

```
1 int maxPriority = 1;
2 task *maxPriorityTask = NULL;
3
4 void submit_task(task *t) {
5   if( t->priority >= maxPriority or
6      (t->priority == maxPriority-1 and
7       t ∈ succListOf(maxPriorityTask)) )
8   { //the task is critical
9     critical_queue.push(t);
10    maxPriority = priorityOf(t);
11    maxPriorityTask = t;
12    return;
13 }
14 //the task is non-critical
15 non_critical_queue.push(t);
16}
```

Listing 2: Pseudo-code for task submission with CATS.

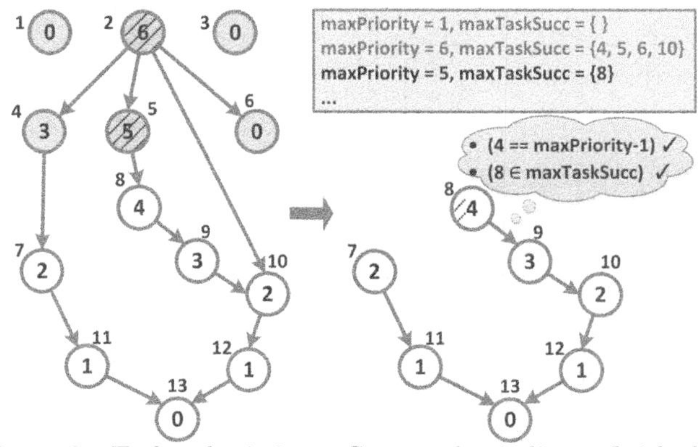

Figure 2: Task submission. Gray nodes indicate finished tasks and pattern-filled nodes indicate critical tasks.

priority of the last critical task, and **maxPriorityTask** (line 2) is used to store the last critical task. Initially, **maxPriority** is set to 1 and **maxPriorityTask** is set to **NULL**. This avoids the scheduling of independent tasks (i.e., tasks with zero priority) to fast processors at the start of the execution. On the first ready task, if its priority is higher (or equal if in flexible mode) than 1 (line 5) , it is considered to be the first task of the longest path. Therefore, it is inserted in the critical queue and the variables **maxPriority** and **maxPriorityTask** are updated accordingly (lines 9-11) to determine correctly the criticality of the next submitted task.

If the priority of the submitted task is equal to **maxPriority - 1**, we check if it also belongs to the successors of the task with the maximum priority (lines 6-7) and therefore to the longest path. If these two conditions are met, the task is determined to be critical, it is inserted in the critical queue and, as before, the variables **maxPriority** and **maxPriorityTask** are updated (lines 9-11). In the rest of the cases the task is not considered critical and it is inserted in the non-critical queue.

Figure 2 shows an example of a TDG during task submission. The gray nodes in the graph are tasks that have finished execution and the pattern-filled nodes are critical tasks. The numbers inside the nodes indicate their priority and the numbers outside the nodes show the task id, which is assigned in task creation order. The variable **maxPriority** corresponds to the priority of the last critical task and the **maxTaskSucc** is the list of the successors of the last critical task, filled with the task ids of the successors. Initially, **maxPriority** is set to 1 and **maxTaskSucc** is empty. When task 2 is about to be submitted, it is inserted in the critical queue because its priority is higher than the maximum, which at the beginning is 1. Then, the value of **maxPriority** is set to 6 (priority of task 2), and the **maxTaskSucc** list is updated with the successors of task 2. At the point where all the gray tasks have finished execution, the values of **maxPriority** and **maxTaskSucc** are updated as shown in Figure 2. For every newly-ready task, the conditions listed before will be evaluated. When task 7 is submitted, it will not be considered as critical because it does not belong to the **maxTaskSucc** list and its priority is not equal to **maxBotlev - 1**. Contrarily, task 8 satisfies both conditions and so the task is inserted in the critical queue.

4.3 Task-to-Core Assignment

Task-to-core assignment takes place dynamically and in parallel to the previous steps. When a core becomes idle, it checks the corresponding ready queue (depending on the core type) to get a task to execute. Fast cores retrieve critical tasks from the critical queue, while slow cores retrieve non-critical tasks from the non-critical queue. Each ready queue is shared among the cores of the same type so there is no need for work stealing among cores of the same type.

If tasks in an application are imbalanced, i.e., the majority are non-critical and only a few tasks are critical, or vice versa, one of the types of processors would be overloaded and the other group would starve for work. This can happen in applications with wide graphs and a large amount of tasks, where the ratio between critical tasks and the total amount of tasks may be small. To leverage the resources, the default work-stealing mechanism for CATS lets fast cores steal work from slow cores whenever the critical queue becomes empty. Also, CATS can be configured to perform *bi-directional work stealing* so slow processors can also steal tasks from the critical queue if the non-critical queue becomes empty. We evaluate these different options and show the results in the next section.

5. EVALUATION

5.1 Methodology

We measure the execution time of four criticality-sensitive applications using CATS, the default OmpSs scheduler and the Heterogeneous Earliest Finish Time scheduler (HEFT) [25] implemented in OmpSs. We evaluate four different CATS configurations based on the options explained in Section 4. The options consist of whether the task submission policy is strict or flexible, and the type of the work stealing mechanism. This results in the following configurations:

- Flexible with simple work stealing (SS FLEX)
- Flexible with bidirectional work stealing (2DS FLEX)
- Strict with simple work stealing (SS STRICT)
- Strict with bidirectional work stealing (2DS STRICT)

The default OmpSs scheduler employs a *breadth-first* policy (BF) [11]. The BF scheduler implements a single first-in-first-out ready queue shared among all threads. When a task is ready, it is inserted in the tail of the ready queue and when a core becomes available, it retrieves a task from the head of the queue. Tasks are ordered according to their ready time: the earliest ready task resides at the head of the queue. Since the ready queue is shared, there is no need for

Table 1: Evaluated benchmarks and relevant characteristics

Application	Problem size	#Tasks	#Task types	Avg task exec. time (μs)	Measured perf. ratio	Critical tasks %
Cholesky factorization	8×8 blocks of 1024×1024 floats	120	4	1 009 786	2.23	17.50
	16×16 blocks of 512×512 floats	816		147 812		5.51
	32×32 blocks of 512×512 floats	5984		147 812		2.60
QR factorization	16×16 blocks of 512×512 doubles	1 496	4	1 225 254	4.26	4.47
Heat diffusion	16×16 blocks of 512×512 doubles	5 124	3	88 689	2.83	4.13
Integral Histogram	8×8 blocks of 512×512 floats	2 048	2	83 055	1.71	7.32

work stealing and the load is balanced automatically. BF does not differentiate among core types and assigns tasks in a first-come-first-served basis.

We implemented a dynamic version of the HEFT scheduler (dHEFT) in the OmpSs programming model. The implementation assumes two different types of cores (big and little) and keeps records of the tasks' execution times in each core. The original HEFT [25] implementation assumes the prior knowledge of the TDG as well as the costs of the tasks. In our case, since the evaluation consists of running real applications, the best way to compare HEFT to our proposal is to keep the scheduling idea of HEFT and transform it from a static to a dynamic scheduler. This means that dHEFT discovers the costs of the tasks at runtime, computes a mean value of the costs for each task-type and parameter-size duple for each type of core, and then finds the core that will finish the task at the earliest possible time. A difference between the static HEFT and dHEFT is the order in which tasks are being submitted. In HEFT tasks are submitted in decreasing order of their upward rank, which is computed statically with the known task costs. Since dHEFT discovers the costs as tasks execute, there is no priority in task submission. In dHEFT tasks are submitted as soon as they become ready.

To find the earliest possible executor, dHEFT maintains one list per core (wlist) including the ready tasks waiting to be executed by that core. When another task becomes ready, dHEFT first checks if there are records of prior execution of this task. If the number of records is sufficient (in our experiments we require a minimum of three records) then the estimated execution time of the task is considered stable. Then, using that estimated execution time, the task is scheduled to the earliest executor by consulting the wlist of all the cores. If the number of records is not sufficient for one of the core types, then the task is scheduled to the earliest executor of this core type to get another record of that task-type and core-type execution time. In all cases, dHEFT updates the history of records on every task execution to adapt for phase changes in the application.

Our test bed comprises a big.LITTLE processor and a simulated heterogeneous system:

5.1.1 ODROID-XU3

The Hardkernel ODROID-XU3 development board has an 8-core Samsung Exynos 5422 chip with an ARM big.LITTLE architecture and 2GB of LPDDR3 RAM at 933MHz. The chip has four Cortex-A15 cores at 2.0GHz and four Cortex-A7 cores at 1.4GHz. The four Cortex-A15 cores form a *cluster* with a shared 2MB L2 cache, and the Cortex-A7 share a 512KB L2 cache. The two *clusters* are coherent, so a single shared memory application can run on both clusters, using up to eight cores simultaneously. In our experiments, we evaluate a set of possible combinations of fast and slow cores varying the total number of cores from two to eight. For the remainder of the paper, we refer to Cortex-A15 cores as *big* and to Cortex-A7 cores as *little*.

5.1.2 Simulation

To evaluate CATS on larger multi-core systems we use the heterogeneous multi-core TaskSim simulator [24]. TaskSim allows the specification of a heterogeneous system with two different types of cores: fast and slow. We can configure the amount of cores of each type and the difference in performance between the different types (performance ratio) in the TaskSim configuration file. In our experiments, we evaluate the effectiveness of CATS on a total of 80 distinct heterogeneous machine configurations. These comprise systems with the total number of cores ranging from 16 to 128, and the number of fast cores ranging from 1 to 16. For all these configurations, we evaluate the following performance ratios between fast and slow cores: 2×, 2.5×, 3×, 3.5× and 4×.

For both real and simulated platforms, each set-up has a given number of *total* and *big* cores. Our metrics are the improvement of CATS over the baseline scheduler, and the speedup over the execution on one *little* core. Equations 1 and 2 show the improvement and speedup calculations.

$$\text{Improv. over BF(total, big)} = \frac{\text{Exec. time BF(total, big)}}{\text{Exec. time CATS(total, big)}} \tag{1}$$

$$\text{Speedup(total, big)} = \frac{\text{Exec. time(1, 0)}}{\text{Exec. time(total, big)}} \tag{2}$$

The execution time in these calculations is the average of 10 executions of the application on each machine set-up.

5.2 Applications

We use four scientific kernels implemented in the OmpSs programming model: Cholesky factorization, QR factorization, Heat diffusion and Integral Histogram. These benchmarks are accessible in the BSC Application Repository [6]. Their different configurations and characteristics are shown in Table 1.

The applications have different sensitiveness depending on the inter-task dependencies that determine the available parallelism and the percentage of critical tasks, shown in the table. The larger proportion of critical tasks, the larger the potential improvement of CATS, as these are tasks that, once accelerated, reduce the application overall execution time. The percentage of critical tasks in Table 1 is from a single-core execution of CATS. Since CATS is dynamic, the tasks considered critical would be different for different configurations, since the algorithm runs on a partial dependency graph, including only the outstanding tasks. However,

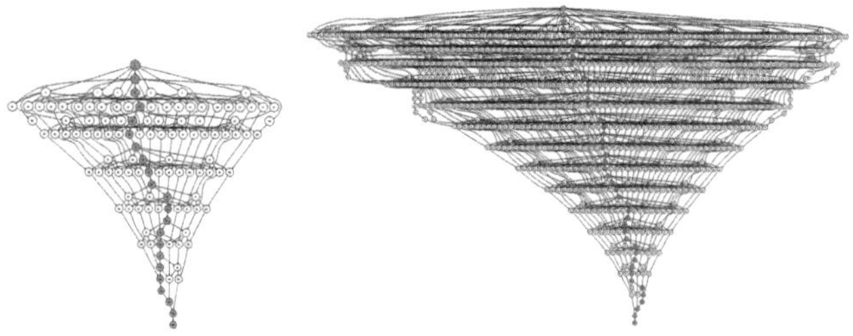

(a) 8×8 blocks (b) 16×16 blocks
Figure 3: Cholesky factorization task dependency graphs.

the single-core figures serve as an estimation of the percentage of critical tasks intrinsic to the overall application, that allows us to reason about the results with respect to this application characteristic.

The performance ratio between big and little cores depends on the application. For example, the difference between the issue rate and throughput of double-precision floating point units of both types of cores is larger than the difference for single-precision floating point instructions. Therefore, applications with heavy double-precision operation get a larger benefit from running on the big cores, than single-precision dominated applications, as shown in Table 1.

The performance ratios in Table 1 are computed for the real machine by comparing the execution time on one little core over the execution time on one big core. Using these performance ratios, we can estimate the ideal speedup over a little core for each application running on all eight cores. Equation 3 is used for the ideal speedup. The ideal speedup considers a fully parallel workload, without any dependencies, overheads or sequential sections, thus unachievable by the dependency-intensive applications in our evaluation.

$$\text{ideal\_speedup}(\text{workload}, 8) = 4 \times \text{perf\_ratio}(\text{workload}) + 4 \quad (3)$$

The average overhead per task for each scheduler is negligible compared to the average task execution time shown in Table 1. Specifically, it is observed that the per-task overhead ranges in the order of tens of microseconds for BF and in the order of hundreds of microseconds for dHEFT and CATS when running on 8 cores. The most time consuming phase of CATS is the task prioritization, in which the TDG is traversed to update the bottom levels of the tasks For dHEFT, the search of the appropriate worker for a task becomes an obstacle in performance. Normally these obstacles in heterogeneous schedulers are paid off by the more effective task execution.

5.2.1 Cholesky Factorization

Cholesky factorization is a dense matrix operation that is used for the efficient solution of linear equations in linear least square systems. The OmpSs implementation of Cholesky blocks the input matrix into square blocks of floats and it then performs the factorization on each block using tasks that call the functions of the Intel MKL library [16].

Figure 3 shows the TDGs for input sizes of (a) 8×8 and (b) 16×16 blocks. Critical tasks are denoted as red nodes. The TDG becomes wider as the number of blocks increases. This reduces the percentage of critical tasks as shown in Table 1. The 8×8 blocks case shows a narrower TDG that makes the application more criticality sensitive than the 16×16 blocks case that exposes more parallelism. We evaluate both configurations to show the impact of scheduling on different criticality sensitiveness of the application configuration.

5.2.2 QR Factorization

QR Factorization is a linear algebra algorithm that is often used to solve the linear least squares problem [8]. We evaluate the performance of a blocked, communication avoiding QR factorization implementation in OmpSs. We use an input matrix of 8192×8192 doubles and a block size of 512×512, that creates 16×16 blocks.

5.2.3 Heat Diffusion

Heat diffusion benchmark uses the Gauss-Seidel method to compute the heat distribution on a matrix A from heat sources represented by x. Heat diffusion implements an iterative solver of the equation that invokes the Gauss-Seidel method until the desired convergence is reached. In the specific implementation [6] the number of iterations can be set as an argument in order to control the workload of the experiments. The code splits the matrix into blocks and creates one task per block for the Gauss-Seidel computation. We use a matrix of 8192×8192 doubles and block size of 512×512. We set the number of iterations to 20.

5.2.4 Integral Histogram

The integral histogram is a method to compute a cumulative histogram for each pixel of an image [7]. The OmpSs implementation performs a blocked cross-weave scan for each block of the image. The horizontal scan processes one image block at a time and transmits the histograms to the block on the right. The vertical scan processes one block and transmits the histograms to the block below the current block. Due to the histograms' transmissions, the application introduces many task dependencies. We evaluate Integral Histogram with an input image of 4096×4096 pixels and block size of 512×512, resulting in an 8×8 blocked matrix.

5.3 Real Environment Evaluation

Figure 4 shows the results from the experiments on the ODROID-XU3. Figure 4a shows the speedup of CATS (SS FLEX), dHEFT and BF when running the applications on all eight cores, as well as the estimated ideal speedup of the platform for each application. Cholesky and Integral Histogram operate on single-precision data, while QR and Heat Diffusion operate on double-precision. Double-precision applications get larger speedups over one little core because they benefit from a larger performance ratio when running on a big core. For all cases, CATS scales better than dHEFT and BF. The shortening of the critical path by running all critical tasks on big cores effectively shortens total execution time when running on all cores.

Figure 4b shows the improvement of the CATS configurations and dHEFT over BF, and the speedup obtained with CATS, dHEFT and BF, for Cholesky on an 8×8 blocked matrix. CATS consistently achieves better performance than dHEFT and BF and the improvement over BF increases as the number of cores is increased. Specifically, the improvement is observed to be up to 30% when running on seven and eight cores.

Figure 4c shows the performance on a 16×16 block input matrix, where the improvement of CATS is smaller and ranges from 2 to 9% and all schedulers perform fairly well.

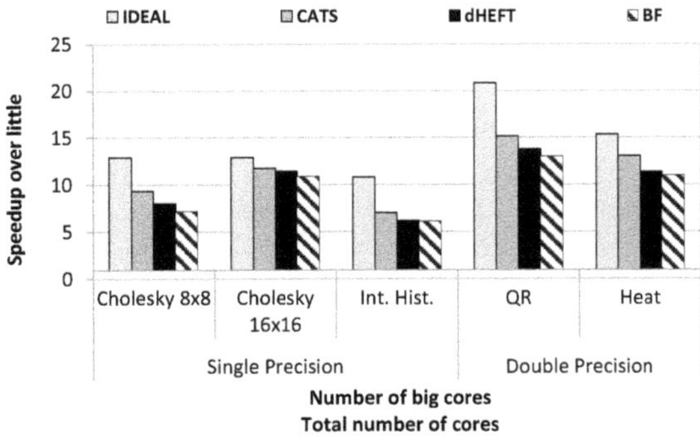

(a) Speedup of CATS, dHEFT and BF on 8 cores compared to the ideal

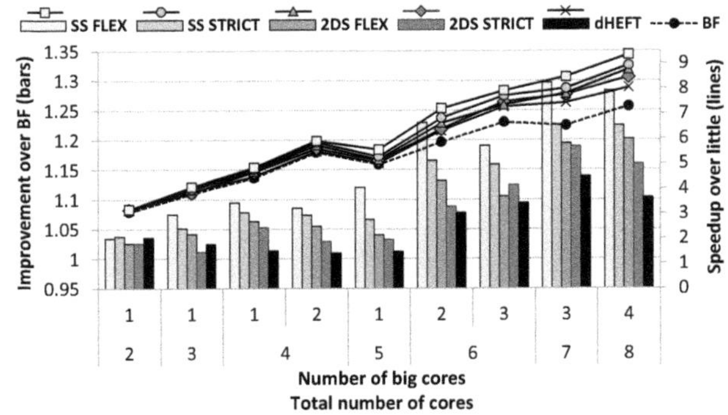

(b) Cholesky 8×8

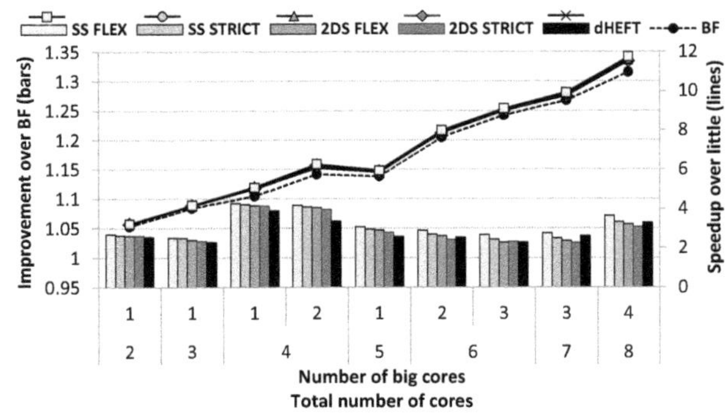

(c) Cholesky 16×16

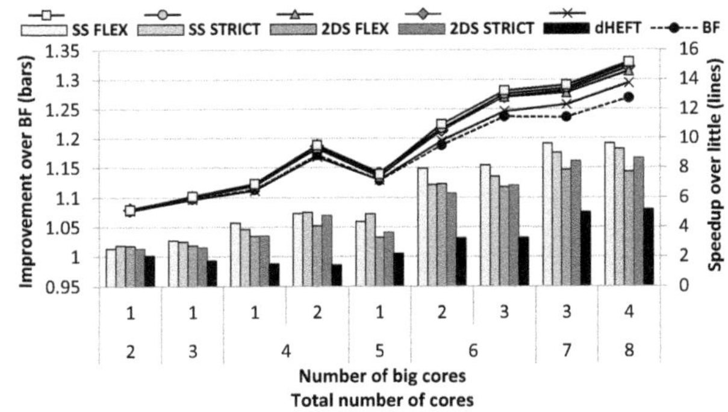

(d) QR

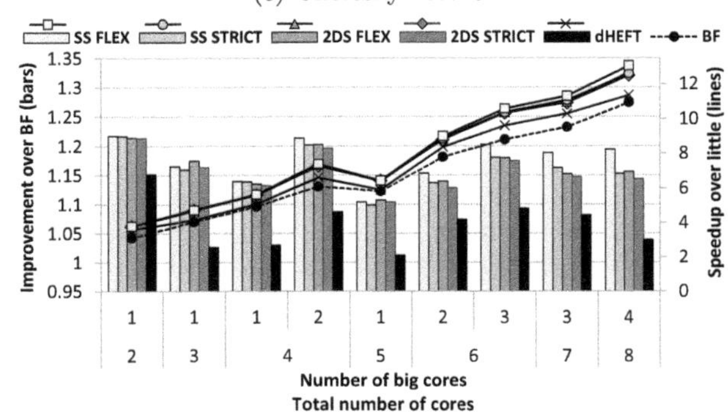

(e) Heat Diffusion

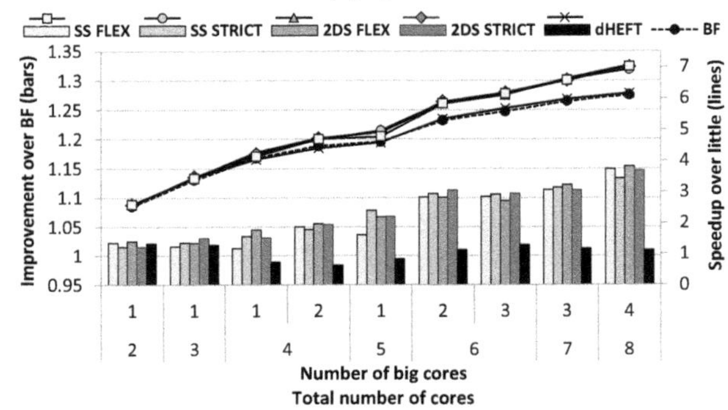

(f) Integral Histogram

Figure 4: Schedulers comparison on ODROID-XU3

In this case the opportunities for enhancement are limited, since, according to Figure 4a, BF performance approaches the ideal speedup. The lower improvement in this case comes from the fact that the application is less sensitive to the critical path. The task graph is wider (as shown in Figure 3) and, accordingly, the percentage of critical tasks is lower. However, CATS still outperforms BF by 7% when using the eight cores in the system and performs as good as dHEFT.

Figure 4d shows the improvement of CATS and dHEFT over BF and their speedup for QR factorization. QR consists of double precision operations which cause the big cores to be 4.26× faster than the little cores. Thus, the ideal speedup of the system for QR is 20.1×. CATS achieves a 15× speedup by shortening the execution of the dynamic longest path in the TDG. Since dHEFT is not focusing on the longest path of the TDG, and it performs some random scheduling at the beginning of the execution in order to determine the task costs, it becomes less effective than CATS but still better than BF as the number of cores increases.

Figure 4e shows the improvement of the different CATS configurations and dHEFT over BF, and the speedup obtained, for heat diffusion. As shown in Table 1 heat diffusion consists of 5124 tasks; 5120 tasks of them are tasks of the same type and parameter size. This limits the effect of dHEFT, that tries to find the earliest executor for each task in comparison to BF in which whenever a core becomes available, it retrieves a task from the ready queue. Thus, dHEFT is better than BF because it uses private ready queues for each core, thing that reduces the congestion of using only one ready queue. CATS consistently improves the scheduling of the asymmetric system from 15% to 22%, since the main criterion of scheduling is the TDG structure. CATS achieves a 13× speedup when using all eight cores, thus getting very close to the ideal 15.3× shown in Figure 4a.

Figure 4f shows the improvement of CATS and dHEFT over BF, and the speedup obtained, for integral histogram. The impact of CATS is again positive for all configurations, since the improvement is at least 5% with the peak be-

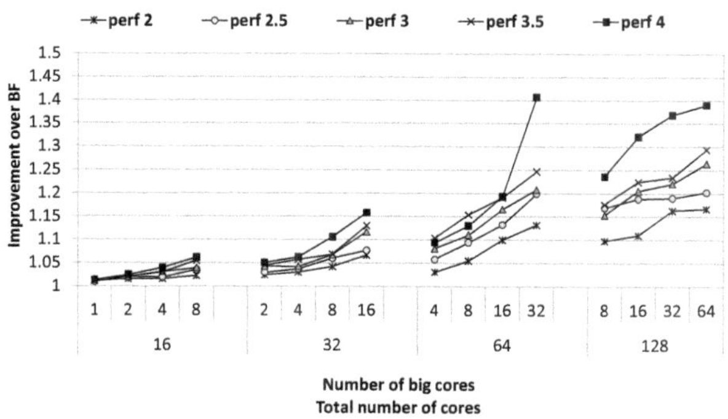

Figure 5: Cholesky 32×32 SS FLEX simulation; perf x is the performance ratio between fast and slow cores

ing 15% for 8 cores. Experiments on larger systems show that the specific application's scalability saturates beyond 16 cores. This is because the intensive dependencies between tasks reduce the available parallelism that is mainly present among the diagonal-placed blocks due to the cross-weave scanning process. Since dHEFT does not take into account the dependencies between tasks, the scheduling of an application with limited parallelism due to dependencies becomes trickier. Moreover, the performance ratio of this single-precision application is 1.7×, so the ideal speedup is limited to 10.8×.

An interesting observation is that for single-precision kernels the improvement of CATS is proportional to the percentage of critical tasks. Integral histogram achieves greater improvements in comparison to Cholesky 16×16 since it schedules immediately more tasks to the fast cores of the system, according to the percentage of the critical tasks on Table 1. On the other hand, QR and heat diffusion show the opposite effect: QR has the largest performance ratio and a larger percentage of critical tasks than heat diffusion. However, heat diffusion shows higher overall improvement over the different configurations. We attribute this to the larger sensitivity of heat diffusion to the critical path, which allows CATS to achieve a large improvement even for a configuration of one big and one little core. The dHEFT scheduler outperforms BF but struggles to handle applications with complex TDG. Applications that consist of multiple instances of the same task type benefit less from dHEFT than applications that process tasks with variable costs, such as Cholesky and QR.

In all cases, the SS FLEX configuration of CATS achieves the best performance, since it produces a decent amount of critical tasks for the big cores, fact that shortens the longest path of the TDG. A smaller amount of critical tasks is produced by the SS STRICT policy, which causes a slight imbalance that is fixed through the work stealing mechanism but with lower effectiveness. The 2DS FLEX configuration, produces the same amount of critical tasks as the SS FLEX, but the bi-directional work stealing allows little cores to steal critical tasks, which lengthens the critical path execution and directly increases overall execution time.

5.4 Simulations

To estimate the impact of CATS on larger systems, we run three of the benchmarks using the TaskSim simulator [24]. Integral Histogram is excluded from the simulated evaluation because it does not scale beyond 16 cores. Also, dHEFT

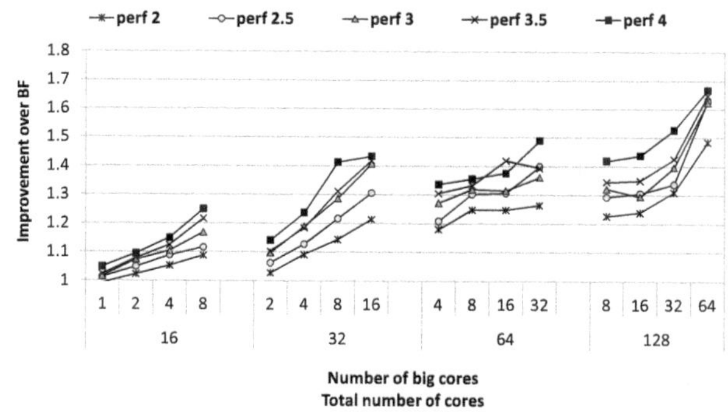

Figure 6: QR SS FLEX simulation; perf x is the performance ratio between fast and slow cores

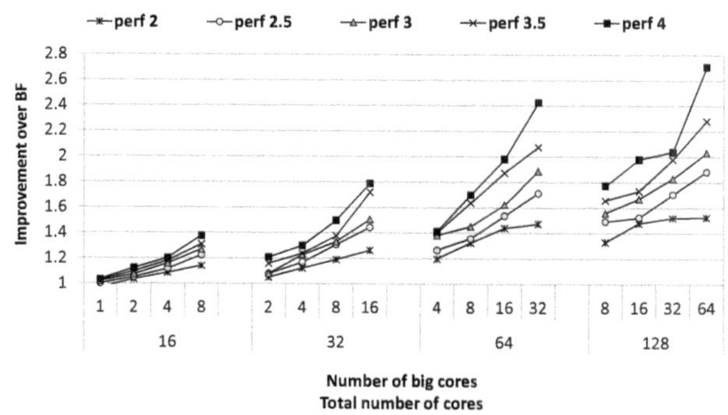

Figure 7: Heat diffusion SS FLEX simulation; perf x is the performance ratio between fast and slow cores

is not included in the simulation experiments because the simulation platform does not support informing task execution costs to the scheduler.

Simulation allows us to evaluate on larger systems and multiple performance ratios. The results contain a fixed scheduling overhead for all configurations, regardless of the dynamic overheads during execution (e.g., work stealing). The error introduced by this assumption is small because, as stated above, the average scheduling overheads in our applications are negligible compared to the average task execution time. For space purposes, we only show simulation results for the best CATS configuration: SS FLEX.

Figures 5, 6 and 7 show the improvement of CATS over BF in systems with multiple performance ratios (*perf x*) for Cholesky, QR and heat diffusion respectively. The impact of CATS is larger for systems with higher performance ratio between fast and slow cores. This makes sense, as a faster execution of the critical path directly shortens overall execution time. In addition, CATS utilises fast cores more effectively than BF, which results in larger improvements with larger number of fast cores. In Figure 5, the improvement for 16 cores is comparatively small. This is because the problem size used in this specific experiment is a matrix of 16384×16384 floats using 512×512 blocks, which creates a 32×32 blocked matrix. This is because the other Cholesky configurations do not scale to 128 cores. The small amount of critical tasks in the 32×32 input, as shown in Table 1, makes the workload less sensitive to critical tasks and limits the improvement of CATS for Cholesky to a maximum of 1.4×, while QR and heat diffusion are improved by factors of 1.6× and 2.7×. Again, heat diffusion gets the largest improvement due to its larger sensitiveness to criticality, as was also shown in the real platform evaluation.

6. CONCLUSION

We introduced the first criticality-aware dynamic scheduling policy for heterogeneous environments. Contrary to previous works on criticality-aware scheduling that use synthetic task graphs and require previous knowledge of profiling information, our proposal works on real platforms with real applications, is implementable and works without the need of an oracle or profiling.

We implemented and evaluated our criticality-aware task scheduler in the runtime system of the OmpSs programming model getting satisfactory results. The implementation shown in this paper will be included in the next stable release of OmpSs. Furthermore, there are no restrictions on applying our policy to other task-based programming models with support for task dependencies.

From our experiments on a real heterogeneous multi-core platform, we found a consistent performance improvement over the default breadth-first scheduling policy and a dynamic implementation of Heterogeneous Earliest Finish Time. The improvement of our proposal, which in most cases ranges from 10 to 20% and reaches up to 30%, is larger as we increase the number of cores. This gives a positive projection for CATS, as it is expected that the number of cores in multicores will increase throughout future generation designs.

From our simulation experiments, we found out that the improvement of CATS increases over the baseline with larger differences of performance among fast and slow cores. We explored performance ratios between two and four times faster fast cores over slow cores, with improvements ranging from 30% to 170%.

In conclusion, this paper shows the potential of a criticality-aware scheduler to speed up dependency-intensive applications and take advantage of the asymmetric compute resources. For future work, we aim to extend the scheduling policy to be adaptive so it can dynamically adjust its flexibility and work stealing policy depending on the application characteristics and availability of resources at runtime.

Acknowledgements

The authors would like to thank Paul Carpenter and Alex Ramirez for their help to improve the quality of this paper. This work has been supported by the grant SEV-2011-00067 of the Severo Ochoa Program, awarded by the Spanish Government, by the Spanish Ministry of Science and Innovation (contracts TIN2012-34557, and CAC2007-00052), by Generalitat de Catalunya (contracts 2014-SGR-1051 and 2014-SGR-1272), and by the Mont-Blanc project (FP7-610402).

7. REFERENCES

[1] T. L. Adam, K. M. Chandy, and J. R. Dickson. A Comparison of List Schedules for Parallel Processing Systems. *Commun. ACM*, 17(12), 1974.

[2] A. Agarwal and P. Kumar. Economical Duplication Based Task Scheduling for Heterogeneous and Homogeneous Computing Systems. IACC 2009, 2009.

[3] C. Augonnet, S. Thibault, R. Namyst, and P.-A. Wacrenier. StarPU: A Unified Platform for Task Scheduling on Heterogeneous Multicore Architectures. *Concurr. Comput. : Pract. Exper.*, 23(2), 2011.

[4] E. Ayguadé, R. Badia, P. Bellens, D. Cabrera, A. Duran, R. Ferrer, M. Gonzàlez, F. Igual, D. Jiménez-González, J. Labarta, L. Martinell, X. Martorell, R. Mayo, J. Pérez, J. Planas, and E. Quintana-Ortí. Extending OpenMP to Survive the Heterogeneous Multi-Core Era. *International Journal of Parallel Programming*, 38(5-6), 2010.

[5] S. Bansal, P. Kumar, and K. Singh. An Improved Duplication Strategy for Scheduling Precedence Constrained Graphs in Multiprocessor Systems. *Parallel and Distributed Systems, IEEE Transactions on*, 14(6), 2003.

[6] Barcelona Supercomputing Center. Barcelona Application Repository. Available online on April 18th, 2014.

[7] P. Bellens, K. Palaniappan, R. Badia, G. Seetharaman, and J. Labarta. Parallel Implementation of the Integral Histogram. In *Advanced Concepts for Intelligent Vision Systems*, volume 6915 of *Lecture Notes in Computer Science*. 2011.

[8] A. Buttari, J. Langou, J. Kurzak, and J. Dongarra. Parallel tiled QR factorization for multicore architectures. Technical report, 2007.

[9] M. Daoud and N. Kharma. Efficient Compile-Time Task Scheduling for Heterogeneous Distributed Computing Systems. ICPADS 2006, 2006.

[10] A. Duran, E. Ayguadé, R. M. Badia, J. Labarta, L. Martinell, X. Martorell, and J. Planas. Ompss: a Proposal for Programming Heterogeneous Multi-Core Architectures. *Parallel Processing Letters*, 21, 2011.

[11] A. Duran, J. Corbalán, and E. Ayguadé. Evaluation of OpenMP Task Scheduling Strategies. IWOMP'08, 2008.

[12] A. Duran, J. M. Perez, E. Ayguadé, R. M. Badia, and J. Labarta. Extending the OpenMP Tasking Model to Allow Dependent Tasks. IWOMP'08, 2008.

[13] A. Fedorova, J. C. Saez, D. Shelepov, and M. Prieto. *Communications of the ACM*, (12).

[14] P. Greenhalgh. big.LITTLE Processing with ARM Cortex-A15 & Cortex-A7. *ARM White Paper*, 2011.

[15] M. Hakem and F. Butelle. Dynamic Critical Path Scheduling Parallel Programs onto Multiprocessors. IPDPS'05, 2005.

[16] Intel Corporation. Reference Manual for Intel Math Kernel Library 11.1 .

[17] M. A. Iverson, F. Özgüner, and G. J. Follen. Parallelizing Existing Applications in a Distributed Heterogeneous Environment. HCW'95, 1995.

[18] P. Kogge, K. Bergman, S. Borkar, D. Campbell, W. Carson, W. Dally, M. Denneau, P. Franzon, W. Harrod, K. Hill, and Others. Exascale Computing Study: Technology Challenges in Achieving Exascale Systems. Technical report, University of Notre Dame, CSE Dept., 2008.

[19] K. Li, Z. Zhang, Y. Xu, B. Gao, and L. He. Chemical Reaction Optimization for Heterogeneous Computing Environments. ISPA, 2012.

[20] C.-H. Liu, C.-F. Li, K.-C. Lai, and C.-C. Wu. A dynamic Critical Path Duplication Task Scheduling Algorithm for Distributed Heterogeneous Computing Systems. volume 1 of *ICPADS 2006*, 2006.

[21] A. Page and T. Naughton. Dynamic Task Scheduling using Genetic Algorithms for Heterogeneous Distributed Computing. In *Parallel and Distributed Processing Symposium, 2005. Proceedings. 19th IEEE International*, 2005.

[22] J. A. Pienaar, S. Chakradhar, and A. Raghunathan. Automatic Generation of Software Pipelines for Heterogeneous Parallel Systems. SC '12, 2012.

[23] J. Planas, R. Badia, E. Ayguade, and J. Labarta. Self-Adaptive OmpSs Tasks in Heterogeneous Environments. IPDPS, 2013.

[24] A. Rico, F. Cabarcas, C. Villavieja, M. Pavlovic, A. Vega, Y. Etsion, A. Ramirez, and M. Valero. On the Simulation of Large-Scale Architectures Using Multiple Application Abstraction Levels. *ACM Trans. Archit. Code Optim.*, 8(4).

[25] H. Topcuoglu, S. Hariri, and M.-Y. Wu. Performance-Effective and Low-Complexity Task Scheduling for Heterogeneous Computing. *IEEE Transactions on Parallel and Distributed Systems*, 13(3), 2002.

[26] M.-Y. Wu and D. Gajski. Hypertool: a Programming Aid for Message-Passing Systems. *Parallel and Distributed Systems, IEEE Transactions on*, 1(3), 1990.

[27] T. Yang and A. Gerasoulis. DSC: Scheduling Parallel Tasks on an Unbounded Number of Processors. *Parallel and Distributed Systems, IEEE Transactions on*, 5(9), 1994.

[28] H. Yu. A Hybrid GA-based Scheduling Algorithm for Heterogeneous Computing Environments. SCIS'07, 2007.

[29] Z. Zong, A. Manzanares, X. Ruan, and X. Qin. EAD and PEBD: Two Energy-Aware Duplication Scheduling Algorithms for Parallel Tasks on Homogeneous Clusters. *Computers, IEEE Transactions on*, 60(3), 2011.

CSR5: An Efficient Storage Format for Cross-Platform Sparse Matrix-Vector Multiplication

Weifeng Liu, Brian Vinter
Niels Bohr Institute, University of Copenhagen
Copenhagen, Denmark
{weifeng.liu, vinter}@nbi.ku.dk

ABSTRACT

Sparse matrix-vector multiplication (SpMV) is a fundamental building block for numerous applications. In this paper, we propose CSR5 (Compressed Sparse Row 5), a new storage format, which offers high-throughput SpMV on various platforms including CPUs, GPUs and Xeon Phi. First, the CSR5 format is insensitive to the sparsity structure of the input matrix. Thus the single format can support an SpMV algorithm that is efficient both for regular matrices and for irregular matrices. Furthermore, we show that the overhead of the format conversion from the CSR to the CSR5 can be as low as the cost of a few SpMV operations.

We compare the CSR5-based SpMV algorithm with 11 state-of-the-art formats and algorithms on four mainstream processors using 14 regular and 10 irregular matrices as a benchmark suite. For the 14 regular matrices in the suite, we achieve comparable or better performance over the previous work. For the 10 irregular matrices, the CSR5 obtains average performance improvement of 17.6%, 28.5%, 173.0% and 293.3% (up to 213.3%, 153.6%, 405.1% and 943.3%) over the best existing work on dual-socket Intel CPUs, an nVidia GPU, an AMD GPU and an Intel Xeon Phi, respectively. For real-world applications such as a solver with only tens of iterations, the CSR5 format can be more practical because of its low-overhead for format conversion.

Categories and Subject Descriptors

G.1.3 [**Numerical Linear Algebra**]: Sparse, structured, and very large systems (direct and iterative methods); G.4 [**Mathematical Software**]: Parallel and vector implementations

General Terms

Algorithms, Experimentation, Performance

ICS'15, June 8–11, 2015, Newport Beach, CA, USA.

ACM 978-1-4503-3559-1/15/06 ...$15.00.
http://dx.doi.org/10.1145/2751205.2751209 .

Keywords

Sparse Matrices, Storage Formats, SpMV, CSR, CSR5, CPU, GPU, Xeon Phi

1. INTRODUCTION

Over the past few decades, sparse matrix-vector multiplication (SpMV) has probably been the most studied sparse BLAS routine because of its importance in many scientific applications. The SpMV operation multiplies a sparse matrix A of size $m \times n$ by a dense vector x of size n and obtains a dense vector y of size m. Its naïve sequential implementation can be very simple, and can be easily parallelized by adding a few pragma directives for the compilers. But to accelerate large-scale computation, parallel SpMV is still required to be hand-optimized with specific data storage formats and algorithms [1, 2, 3, 4, 6, 7, 10, 13, 16, 17, 19, 21, 22, 24, 29, 30, 31, 33, 34].

As a result, a conflict may emerge between the requirements of SpMV and other sparse matrix operations such as preconditioning operations [22] and sparse matrix-matrix multiplication [23]. The reason is that those operations commonly require matrices stored in the basic formats such as the compressed sparse row (CSR). Therefore, when users construct a real-world application, they need to consider a cost of format conversion between the SpMV-oriented formats and the basic formats. Unfortunately, this conversion overhead may offset the benefits of using these specialized formats, in particular when only tens of iterations are needed in a solver.

The conversion cost is mainly from the expensive structure-dependent parameter tuning of a storage format. For example, some block-based formats require finding a good 2D block size [6, 7, 10, 31, 32, 34]. Moreover, some hybrid formats [4, 29] may need completely different partitioning parameters for distinct input matrices.

To avoid the format conversion overhead, a few algorithms have concentrated on accelerating CSR-based SpMV with either row block methods [1, 17] or segmented sum methods [5, 16]. However, each of the two types of methods has its own drawbacks. As for the row block methods, despite their good performance for regular matrices, they may provide very low performance for irregular matrices due to unavoidable load imbalance. In contrast, the segmented sum methods can achieve near perfect load balance, but suffer from high overhead due to more global synchronizations and global memory accesses. Furthermore, none of the above work can avoid an overhead from preprocessing, since certain auxiliary data for the basic CSR format have to be generated for better load balancing [1, 17] or established primitives [5, 16].

Therefore, to be practical, an efficient format must satisfy two criteria: (1) it should limit format conversion cost by avoiding structure-dependent parameter tuning, and (2) it should support fast SpMV for both regular and irregular matrices.

To meet these two criteria, in this paper, we have designed CSR5 (Compressed Sparse Row 5)[1], a new format directly extending the classic CSR format. The CSR5 format leaves one of the three arrays of the CSR format unchanged, stores the other two arrays in an in-place tile-transposed order, and adds two groups of extra auxiliary information. The format conversion from the CSR to the CSR5 merely needs two tuning parameters: one is hardware-dependent and the other is sparsity-dependent (but structure-independent). Because the added two groups of information are usually much shorter than the original three in the CSR format, very limited extra space is required. Furthermore, the CSR5 format is SIMD-friendly and thus can be easily implemented on all mainstream processors with the SIMD units. Because of the structure-independence and the SIMD utilization, the CSR5-based SpMV algorithm can bring stable high throughput for both regular and irregular matrices.

In this paper, we make the following contributions:

- We propose CSR5, an efficient storage format with low conversion cost and high degree of parallelism.
- We present a CSR5-based SpMV algorithm based on a redesigned low-overhead segmented sum algorithm.
- We implement the work on four mainstream devices: CPU, nVidia GPU, AMD GPU and Intel Xeon Phi.
- We evaluate the CSR5 format in both isolated SpMV tests and iteration-based scenarios.

We compare the CSR5 with 11 state-of-the-art formats and algorithms on dual-socket Intel CPUs, an nVidia GPU, an AMD GPU and an Intel Xeon Phi. By using 14 regular and 10 irregular matrices as a benchmark suite, we show that the CSR5 obtains comparable or better performance over the previous work for the regular matrices, and can greatly outperform the prior work for the irregular matrices. As for the 10 irregular matrices, the CSR5 obtains average performance improvement of 17.6%, 28.5%, 173.0% and 293.3% (up to 213.3%, 153.6%, 405.1% and 943.3%) over the second best work on the four platforms, respectively. Moreover, for iteration-based real-world scenarios, the CSR5 format achieves higher speedups because of the fast format conversion. To the best of our knowledge, this is the first time that a single storage format can outperform state-of-the-art work on all four modern multicore and manycore processors.

2. PRELIMINARIES

2.1 The CSR Format

The CSR format for sparse matrices consists of three arrays: (1) `row_ptr` array which saves the start and end pointers of the nonzeros of the rows. It has size $m + 1$, where m is the number of rows of the matrix, (2) `col_idx` array of size nnz stores column indices of the nonzeros, where nnz is the number of nonzeros of the matrix, and (3) `val` array of size nnz stores values of the nonzeros. Figure 1 shows an example.

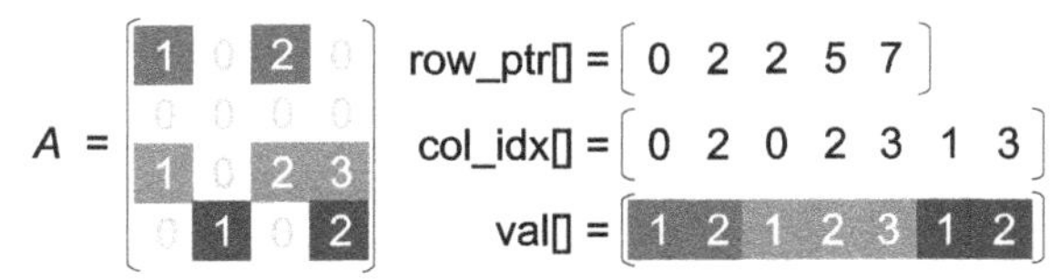

Figure 1: A sparse matrix and its CSR format.

2.2 Parallel Algorithms for CSR-based SpMV

2.2.1 *Row Block Methods*

In a given sparse matrix, rows are independent from each other. Therefore an SpMV operation can be parallelized on decomposed row blocks. A logical processing unit is responsible for a row block and stores dot product results of the matrix rows with the vector x to corresponding locations in the result y. When the SIMD units of a physical processing unit are available, the SIMD reduction sum operation can be utilized for higher efficiency. These two methods are respectively known as the CSR-scalar and the CSR-vector algorithms, and have been implemented on CPUs [33] and GPUs [4, 29]. Algorithm 1 shows a parallel CSR-scalar method.

Algorithm 1 SpMV using the CSR-scalar method.

```
for i = 0 to m − 1 in parallel do
    y[i] ← 0
    for j = row_ptr[i] to row_ptr[i + 1]−1 do
        y[i] ← y[i] + val[j] × x[col_idx[j]]
    end for
end for
```

Despite the good parallelism, exploiting the scalability in modern multi-processors is not trivial for the row block methods. The performance problems mainly come from load imbalance for matrices which consist of rows with uneven lengths. Specifically, if one single row of a matrix is significantly longer than the other rows, only a single core can be fully used while the other cores in the same chip may be completely idle. Although various strategies, such as data streaming [11, 17], memory coalescing [13], data reordering or reconstruction [3, 18, 25], static or dynamic binning [1, 17] and Dynamic Parallelism [1], have been developed, none of those can fundamentally solve the problem of load imbalance, and thus provide relatively low SpMV performance for the CSR format.

2.2.2 *Segmented Sum Methods*

Blelloch et al. [5] pointed out that the segmented sum may be more attractive for the CSR-based SpMV, since it is SIMD friendly and insensitive to the sparsity structure of the input matrix, thus overcoming the shortcomings of the row block methods.

Segmented sum (which is a special case of the backward segmented scan) performs a reduction sum operation for the entries in each segment in an array. A segment has its first

[1] The reason we call the storage format CSR5 is that it has five groups of data, instead of three in the classic CSR.

entry flagged as TRUE and the other entries flagged as FALSE. Algorithm 2 lists a serial segmented sum algorithm. Vectorized parallel segmented sum algorithms can be found in [9, 15, 28].

Algorithm 2 Serial segmented sum operation.

```
function SEGMENTED_SUM(*in, *flag)
    length ← SIZEOF(*in)
    for i = 0 to length − 1 do
        if flag[i] = TRUE then
            j ← i + 1
            while flag[j] = FALSE && j < length do
                in[i] ← in[i] + in[j]
                j ← j + 1
            end while
        else
            in[i] ← 0
        end if
    end for
end function
```

In the SpMV operation, the segmented sum treats each matrix row as a segment and calculates a partial sum for the entry-wise products generated in each row. The SpMV operation using the segmented sum methods consists of four steps: (1) generating an auxiliary bit_flag array of size nnz from the row_ptr array. An entry in bit_flag is flagged as TRUE if its location matches the first nonzero entry of a row, otherwise it is flagged as FALSE, (2) calculating all intermediate entries (i.e., entry-wise products) to an array of size nnz, (3) executing the parallel segmented sum for the array, and (4) collecting all partial sums to the result vector y if a row is not empty. Algorithm 3 lists the pseudocode. Figure 2 illustrates an example using the matrix A plotted in Figure 1.

Algorithm 3 Segmented sum method CSR-based SpMV.

```
MALLOC(*bit_flag, nnz)
MEMSET(*bit_flag, FALSE)
for i = 0 to m − 1 in parallel do                 ▷ Step 1
    bit_flag[row_ptr[i]] ← TRUE
end for
MALLOC(*product, nnz)
for j = 0 to nnz − 1 in parallel do               ▷ Step 2
    product[j] ← val[j] × x[col_idx[j]]
end for
SEGMENTED_SUM(*product, *bit_flag)                ▷ Step 3
for k = 0 to m − 1 in parallel do                 ▷ Step 4
    if row_ptr[k] = row_ptr[k + 1] then
        y[k] ← 0
    else
        y[k] ← product[row_ptr[k]]
    end if
end for
FREE(*bit_flag)
FREE(*product)
```

We can see that once the heaviest workload, i.e., step 3, is parallelized through a fast segmented sum method described in [9, 15, 28], nearly perfect load balance can be expected in all steps of Algorithm 3. However, in this context, the load balanced computation does not mean high performance. Figure 3 shows that the row block method in cuSPARSE v6.5 can significantly outperform the segmented sum method in cuDPP v2.2 [16, 28], while doing SpMV on relatively regular matrices (see Table 2 for the used benchmark suite).

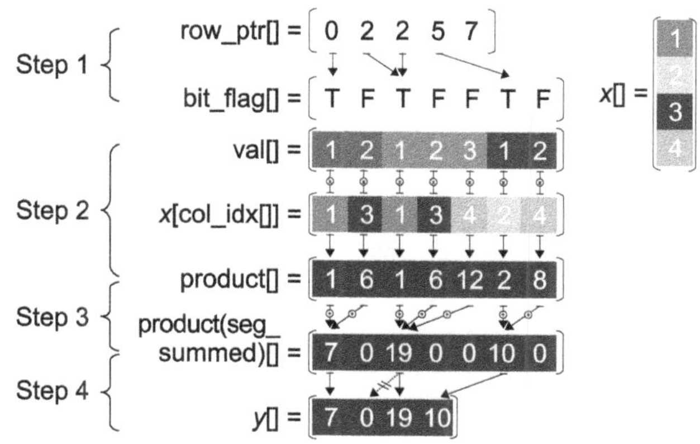

Figure 2: CSR-based SpMV using segmented sum.

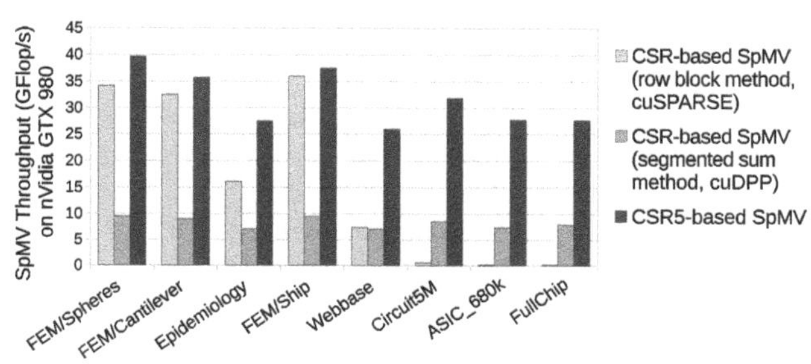

Figure 3: Single precision SpMV performance.

Why is this the case? We can see that the step 1 is a scatter operation and the step 4 is a gather operation, both from the row space of size m. This prevents the two steps from fusing with the steps 2 and 3 in the nonzero entry space of size nnz. In this case, more global synchronizations and global memory accesses may degrade the overall performance. Previous research [4, 29] has found that the segmented sum may be more suitable for the COO (coordinate storage format) based SpMV, since the fully stored row index data can convert the steps 1 and 4 to the nonzero entry space: the bit_flag array can be generated by comparison of neighbor row indices, and the partial sums in the product array can be directly saved to y since their final locations are easily known from the row index array. Further, Yan et al. [34] and Tang et al. [30] reported that some variants of the COO format can also benefit from the segmented sum. However, it is well known that accessing row indices in the COO pattern brings higher off-chip memory pressure, which is just what the CSR format tries to avoid.

In the following, we will show that the CSR5-based SpMV can utilize both the segmented sum for load balance and the compressed row data for better load/store efficiency. In this way, the CSR5-based SpMV can obtain up to 4x speedup (see Figure 3) over the CSR-based SpMV using the segmented sum primitive [28].

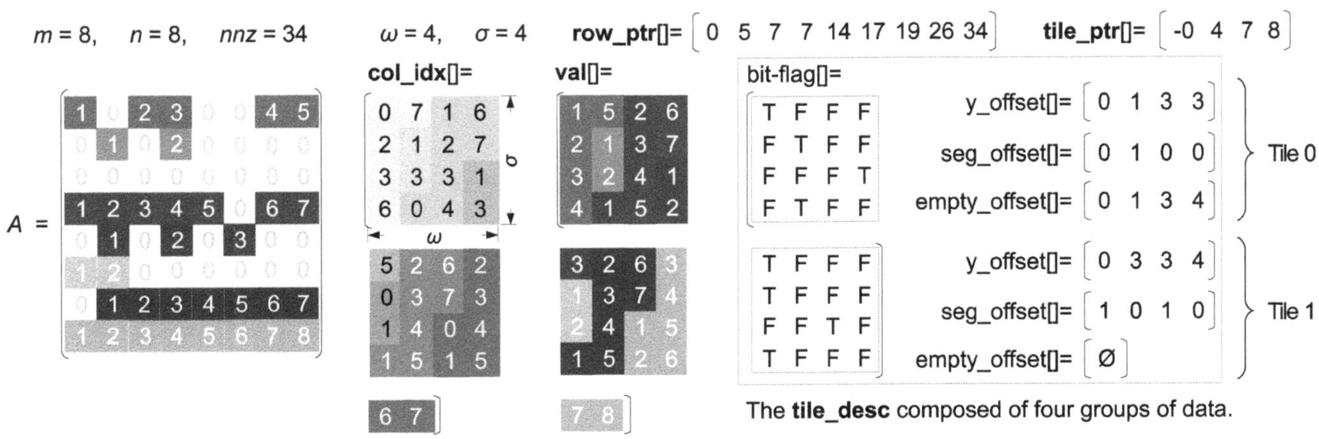

Figure 4: The CSR5 storage format of a sparse matrix A of size 8×8. The five groups of information include `row_ptr`, `tile_ptr`, `col_idx`, `val` and `tile_desc`.

3. THE CSR5 STORAGE FORMAT

3.1 Basic Data Layout

To achieve near-optimal load balance for matrices with any sparsity structures, we first evenly partition all nonzero entries to multiple 2D tiles of the same size. Thus when executing parallel SpMV operation, a compute core can consume one or more 2D tiles, and each SIMD lane of the core can deal with one column of a tile. Then the main skeleton of the CSR5 format is simply a group of 2D tiles. The CSR5 format has two tuning parameters: ω and σ, where ω is a tile's width and σ is its height. In fact, the CSR5 format *only has* these two tuning parameters.

Further, we need extra information to efficiently compute SpMV. For each tile, we introduce a tile pointer `tile_ptr` and a tile descriptor `tile_desc`. Meanwhile, the three arrays, i.e., row pointer `row_ptr`, column index `col_idx` and value `val`, of the classic CSR format are directly integrated. The only difference is that the `col_idx` data and the `val` data in each complete tile are in-place transposed (i.e., from row-major order to column-major order) for coalesced memory access from contiguous SIMD lanes. If the last entries of the matrix do not fill up a complete 2D tile (i.e., $nnz \bmod (\omega\sigma) \neq 0$), they just remain unchanged and discard their `tile_desc`.

In Figure 4, an example matrix A of size 8×8 with 34 nonzero entries is stored in the CSR5 format. When $\omega = 4$ and $\sigma = 4$, the matrix is divided into three tiles including two complete tiles of size 16 and one incomplete tile of size 2. The arrays `col_idx` and `val` in the two complete tiles are stored in tile-level column-major order now. Moreover, only the first two tiles have `tile_desc`, since they are complete.

3.2 Auto-Tuned Parameters ω and σ

Because the computational power of the modern multicore or manycore processors is mainly from the SIMD units, we design an auto-tuning strategy for high SIMD utilization.

First, the tile width ω is set to the size of the SIMD execution unit of the used processor. Then an SIMD unit can consume a 2D tile in σ steps without any explicit synchronization, and the vector registers can be fully utilized. For the double precision SpMV, we always set $\omega = 4$ for CPUs with 256-bit SIMD units, $\omega = 32$ for the nVidia GPUs, $\omega = 64$ for the AMD GPUs, and $\omega = 8$ for Intel Xeon Phi with 512-bit SIMD units. Therefore, ω can be automatically decided once the processor type used is known.

The other parameter σ is decided by a slightly more complex process. For a given processor, we consider its on-chip memory strategy such as cache capacity and prefetching mechanism. If a 2D tile of size $\omega \times \sigma$ can empirically bring better performance than using the other sizes, the σ is simply chosen. We found that the x86 processors fall into this category. For the double precision SpMV on CPUs and Xeon Phi, we always set σ to 16 and 12, respectively.

As for GPUs, the tile height σ further depends on the sparsity of the matrix. Note that the "sparsity" is not equal to "sparsity structure". We define "sparsity" to be the average number of nonzero entries per row (or nnz/row for short). In contrast, "sparsity structure" is much more complex because it includes 2D space layout of all nonzero entries.

On GPUs, we have several performance considerations on mapping the value nnz/row to σ. First, σ should be large enough to expose more thread-level local work and to amortize a basic cost of the segmented sum algorithm. Second, it should not be too large since a larger tile potentially generates more partial sums (i.e., entries to store to y), which bring higher pressure to last level cache write. Moreover, for the matrices with large nnz/row, σ may need to be small. The reason is that once the whole tile is located inside a matrix row (i.e., only one segment is in the tile), the segmented sum converts to a fast reduction sum.

Therefore, for the nnz/row to σ mapping on GPUs, we define three simple bounds: r, s and t. The first bound r is designed to prevent a too small σ. The second bound s is used for preventing a too large σ. But when nnz/row is further larger than the third bound t, σ is set to a small value u. Then we have

$$\sigma = \begin{cases} r & \text{if} \quad nnz/\text{row} \leq r \\ nnz/\text{row} & \text{if} \quad r < nnz/\text{row} \leq s \\ s & \text{if} \quad s < nnz/\text{row} \leq t \\ u & \text{if} \quad t < nnz/\text{row}. \end{cases}$$

The three bounds, r, s and t, and the value u are hardware-dependent, meaning that for a given processor, they can be fixed for use. For example, to execute double precision SpMV on nVidia Maxwell GPUs and AMD GCN GPUs, we always set $<r, s, t, u> = <4, 32, 256, 4>$ and $<4, 7, 256, 4>$, respectively. As for future processors with new architectures, we can obtain the four values through some simple benchmarks during initialization, and then use them for later runs. So the parameter σ can be decided once the very basic information of a matrix and a low-level hardware are known.

Therefore, we can see that the parameter tuning time becomes negligible because ω and σ are easily obtained. This can save a great deal of preprocessing time.

3.3 Tile Pointer Information

The added tile pointer information `tile_ptr` stores the row index of the first matrix row in each tile, indicating the starting position for storing its partial sums to the vector y. By introducing `tile_ptr`, each tile can find its own starting position, allowing tiles to execute in parallel. The size of the `tile_ptr` array is $p + 1$, where $p = \lceil nnz/(\omega\sigma) \rceil$ is the number of tiles in the matrix. For the example in Figure 4, the first entry of Tile 1 is located in the *4th* row of the matrix, and thus 4 is set as its tile pointer. To build the array, we binary search the index of the first nonzero entry of each tile on the `row_ptr` array. Lines 1–4 in Algorithm 4 show this procedure.

Recall that an empty row has exactly the same row pointer information as its first non-empty right neighbor row (see the second row in the matrix A in Figure 1). Thus for the non-empty rows with an empty left neighbor, we need a specific process (which is similar to lines 12–16 in Algorithm 3) to store their partial sums to correct positions in y. To recognize whether the specific process is required, we give a hint to the other parts (i.e., tile descriptor data) of the CSR5 format and the CSR5-based SpMV algorithm. Here we set an entry in `tile_ptr` to its negative value, if its corresponding tile includes any empty rows. Lines 5–12 in Algorithm 4 show this operation.

Algorithm 4 Generating `tile_ptr`.

```
 1: for tid = 0 to p in parallel do
 2:     bnd ← tid × ω × σ
 3:     tile_ptr[tid] ← BINARY_SEARCH(*row_ptr, bnd) −1
 4: end for
 5: for tid = 0 to p − 1 do
 6:     for rid = tile_ptr[tid] to tile_ptr[tid + 1] do
 7:         if row_ptr[rid] = row_ptr[rid + 1] then
 8:             tile_ptr[tid] ← NEGATIVE(tile_ptr[tid])
 9:             break
10:         end if
11:     end for
12: end for
```

If the first tile has any empty rows, we need to store a -0 (negative zero) for it. To record -0, here we use unsigned 32- or 64-bit integer as data type of the `tile_ptr` array. Therefore, we have 1 bit for explicitly storing the sign and 31 or 63 bits for an index. For example, in our design, tile pointer -0 is represented as a binary style '1000 ... 000', and tile pointer 0 is stored as '0000 ... 000'. To the best of our knowledge, the index of 31 or 63 bits is completely compatible to most numerical libraries such as Intel MKL. Moreover, reference implementation of the recent high performance conjugate gradient (HPCG) benchmark [14] also uses 32-bit signed integer for problem dimension no more than 2^{31} and 64-bit signed integer for problem dimension larger than that. Thus it is safe to save 1 bit as the empty row hint and the other 31 or 63 bits as a 'real' row index.

3.4 Tile Descriptor Information

Only having the tile pointer is not enough for a fast SpMV operation. For each tile, we also need four extra hints: (1) `bit_flag` of size $\omega \times \sigma$, which indicates whether an entry is the first nonzero of a matrix row, (2) `y_offset` of size ω used to further let each column know where the starting point to store its local partial sums is, (3) `seg_offset` of size ω used to accelerate the local segmented sum inside a tile, and (4) `empty_offset` of unfixed size (but no longer than $\omega \times \sigma$) constructed to help the partial sums to find correct locations in y if the tile includes any empty rows. The tile descriptor `tile_desc` is defined to denote a combination of the above four groups of data.

Generating `bit_flag` is straightforward. The procedure is very similar to lines 3–5 in Algorithm 3. The main difference is that the bit flags are saved in column-major order, which matches the in-place transposed `col_idx` and `val`. Additionally, the first entry of each tile's `bit_flag` is set to `TRUE` for sealing the first segment from the top and letting 2D tiles to be independent from each other.

The array `y_offset` of size ω is used to help the columns in each tile knowing where the starting points to store their partial sums to y are. In other words, each column has one entry in the array `y_offset` as a starting point offset for all segments in the same column. We save a row index offset (i.e., relative row index) for each column in `y_offset`. Thus for the ith column in the *tid*th tile, by calculating `tile_ptr[`*tid*`] + y_offset[`*i*`]`, the column knows where its own starting position in y is. Thus the columns can work in a high degree of parallelism without waiting for a synchronization. Generating `y_offset` is simple: each column counts the number of `TRUE`s in its previous columns' `bit_flag` array. Consider Tile 1 in Figure 4 as an example: because there are 3 `TRUE`s in the 1st column, the 2nd column's corresponding value in `y_offset` is 3. In addition, since there are in total 4 `TRUE`s in the 1st, 2nd and 3rd columns' `bit_flag`, Tile 1's `y_offset[3]`= 4. Algorithm 5 lists how to generate `y_offset` for a single 2D tile in an SIMD-friendly way.

Algorithm 5 Generating `y_offset` and `seg_offset`.

```
MALLOC(*tmp_bit, ω)
MEMSET(*tmp_bit, FALSE)
for i = 0 to ω − 1 in parallel do
    y_offset[i] ← 0
    for j = 0 to σ − 1 do
        y_offset[i] ← y_offset[i] + bit_flag[i][j]
        tmp_bit[i] ← tmp_bit[i] ∨ bit_flag[i][j]
    end for
    seg_offset[i] ← 1− tmp_bit[i]
end for
EXCLUSIVE_PREFIX_SUM_SCAN(*y_offset)
SEGMENTED_SUM(*seg_offset, *tmp_bit)
FREE(*tmp_bit)
```

The third array `seg_offset` of size ω is used for accelerating a local segmented sum in the workload of each tile. The local segmented sum is an essential step that synchronizes partial sums in a 2D tile (imagine multiple columns in the tile come from the same matrix row). In the previous segmented sum (or segmented scan) method [5, 9, 28,

15], the local segmented sum is complex and not efficient enough. Thus we prepare `seg_offset` as an auxiliary array to facilitate implementation of segmented sum by way of the prefix-sum scan, which is a well optimized fundamental primitive for the SIMD units.

To generate `seg_offset`, we let each column search its right neighbor columns and count the number of contiguous columns without any `TRUE`s in their `bit_flag`. Using Tile 0 in Figure 4 as an example, its 2nd column has one and only one right neighbor column (the 3rd column) without any `TRUE`s in its `bit_flag`. Thus the 2nd column's `seg_offset` value is 1. In contrast, because the other three columns (the 1st, 3rd and 4th) do not have any 'all `FALSE`' right neighbors, their values in `seg_offset` is 0. Algorithm 5 shows how to generate `seg_offset` using an SIMD-friendly method.

Algorithm 6 and Figure 5 show the fast segmented sum using `seg_offset` and an inclusive prefix-sum scan. The principle of this operation is that the prefix-sum scan is essentially an increment operation. Once a segment knows the distance (i.e., offset) between its head and its tail, its partial sum can be deduced from its prefix-sum scan results. Therefore, the more complex segmented sum operation in [5, 9, 28, 15] can be converted to a faster prefix-sum scan operation (line 5) and a few arithmetic operations (lines 6–8).

Algorithm 6 Fast segmented sum using `seg_offset`.

```
1: function FAST_SEGMENTED_SUM(*in, *seg_offset)
2:     length ← SIZEOF(*in)
3:     MALLOC(*tmp, length)
4:     MEMCPY(*tmp, *in)
5:     INCLUSIVE_PREFIX_SUM_SCAN(*in)
6:     for i = 0 to length − 1 in parallel do
7:         in[i] ← in[i+seg_offset[i]] − in[i] + tmp[i]
8:     end for
9:     FREE(*tmp)
10: end function
```

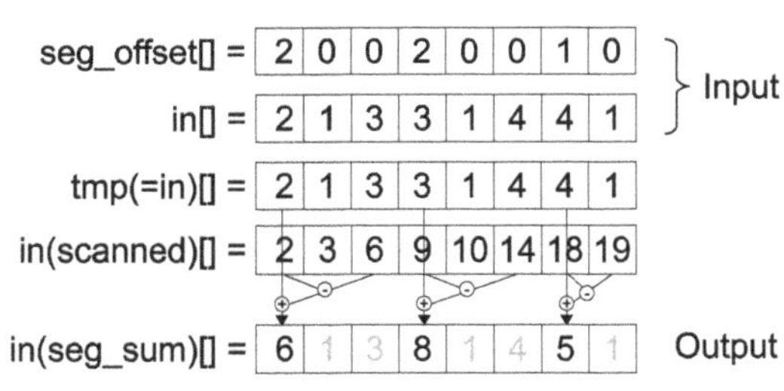

Figure 5: An example of the fast segmented sum.

The last array `empty_offset` occurs when and only when a 2D tile includes any empty rows (i.e., its tile pointer is negative). Because an empty row of a matrix has the same row pointer with its rightmost non-empty neighbor row (recall the second row in the matrix A in Figure 1), `y_offset` will record an incorrect offset for it. We correct for this by storing correct offsets for segments within a tile. Thus the length of `empty_offset` is the number of segments (i.e., the total number of `TRUE`s in `bit_flag`) in a tile. For example, Tile 0 in Figure 4 has 4 entries in its `empty_offset` since its `bit_flag` includes 4 `TRUE`s. Algorithm 7 lists the pseudocode that generates `empty_offset` for a tile that contains at least one empty row.

Algorithm 7 Generating `empty_offset` for the *tid*th tile.

```
length ← REDUCTION_SUM(*bit_flag)
MALLOC(*empty_offset, length)
eid ← 0
for i = 0 to ω − 1 do
    for j = 0 to σ − 1 do
        if bit_flag[i][j] = TRUE then
            ptr ← tid × ω × σ + i × σ + j
            idx ← BINARY_SEARCH(*row_ptr, ptr) −1
            idx ← idx − REMOVE_SIGN(tile_ptr[tid])
            empty_offset[eid] ← idx
            eid ← eid + 1
        end if
    end for
end for
```

3.5 Storage Details

To store the `tile_desc` arrays in a space-efficient way, we find upper bounds to the entries and utilize the bit-field pattern. First, since entries in `y_offset` store offset distances inside a 2D tile, they have an upper bound of $\omega\sigma$. So $\lceil \log_2(\omega\sigma) \rceil$ bits are enough for each entry in `y_offset`. For example, when $\omega = 32$ and $\sigma = 16$, 9 bits are enough for each entry. Second, since `seg_offset` includes offsets less than ω, $\lceil \log_2(\omega) \rceil$ bits are enough for an entry in this array. For example, when $\omega = 32$, 5 bits are enough for each entry. Third, `bit_flag` stores σ 1-bit flags for each column of a 2D tile. When $\sigma = 16$, each column needs 16 bits. So 30 (i.e., $9 + 5 + 16$) bits are enough for each column in the example. Therefore, for a tile, the three arrays can be stored in a compact bit-field composed of ω 32-bit unsigned integers. If the above example matrix has 32-bit integer row index and 64-bit double precision values, only around 2% extra space is required by the three newly added arrays.

The size of `empty_offset` depends on the number of groups of contiguous empty rows, since we only record one offset for the rightmost non-empty row with any number of empty rows as its left neighbors.

3.6 The CSR5 for Other Matrix Operations

Since we in-place transposed the CSR arrays `col_idx` and `val`, a conversion from the CSR5 to the CSR is required for doing other sparse matrix operations using the CSR format. This conversion is simply removing `tile_ptr` and `tile_desc` and transposing `col_idx` and `val` back to row-major order. Thus the conversion can be very fast. Further, since the CSR5 is a superset of the CSR, any entry accesses or slight changes can be done directly in the CSR5 format, without any need to convert it to the CSR format. Additionally, some applications such as finite element methods can directly assemble sparse matrices in the CSR5 format from data sources.

4. THE CSR5-BASED SPMV ALGORITHM

Because all computations of the information (`tile_ptr`, `tile_desc`, `col_idx` and `val`) of 2D tiles are independent of each other, they can execute concurrently. On GPUs, we assign a bunch of threads (i.e., warp in nVidia GPUs or wavefront in AMD GPUs) for each tile. On CPUs and Xeon Phi, we use OpenMP pragma for assigning the tiles to available x86 cores. Furthermore, the columns inside a tile are independent of each other as well. So we assign a thread on GPU cores or an SIMD lane on x86 cores to each column in a tile.

While running the CSR5-based SpMV, each column in a tile can extract information from `bit_flag` and label the segments in its local data to three colors: (1) *red* means a sub-segment unsealed from its top, (2) *green* means a completely sealed segment existed in the middle, and (3) *blue* means a sub-segment unsealed from its bottom. There is an exception that if a column is unsealed both from its top and from its bottom, it is colored to *red*.

Algorithm 8 shows the pseudocode of the CSR5-based SpMV algorithm. Figure 6 plots an example of this procedure. We can see that the green segments can directly save their partial sums to y without any synchronization, since the indices can be calculated by using `tile_ptr` and `y_offset`. In contrast, the red and the blue sub-segments have to further add their partial sums together, since they are not complete segments. For example, the sub-segments B_2, R_2 and R_3 in Figure 6 have contributions to the same row, thus an addition is required. This addition operation needs the fast segmented sum shown in Algorithm 6 and Figure 5. Furthermore, if a tile has any empty rows, the `empty_offset` array is accessed to get correct global indices in y.

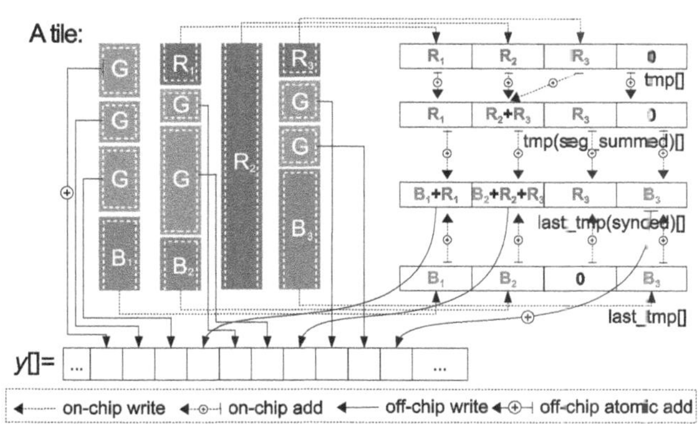

Figure 6: The CSR5-based SpMV in a tile. Partial sums of the green segments are directly stored to y. The red and the blue sub-segments require an extra segmented sum before issuing off-chip write.

Consider the synchronization among the tiles, since the same matrix row can be influenced by multiple 2D tiles running concurrently, the first and the last segments of a tile need to store to y by atomic add (or a global auxiliary array used in device-level reduction, scan or segmented scan [15, 28]). In Figure 6, the atomic add operations are highlighted by arrow lines with plus signs.

For the last entries not in a complete tile (e.g., the last two nonzero entries of the matrix in Figure 4), we execute a conventional CSR-vector method after all of the complete 2D tiles have been consumed. Note that even though the last tile (i.e., the incomplete one) does not have `tile_desc` arrays, it can extract a starting position from `tile_ptr`.

In Algorithm 8, we can see that the main computation (lines 5–21) only contains very basic arithmetic and logic operations that can be easily programmed on all mainstream processors with SIMD units. As the most complex part in our algorithm, the fast segmented sum operation (line 22) only requires a prefix-sum scan, which has been well-studied and can be efficiently implemented by using CUDA, OpenCL or x86 SIMD intrinsics.

Algorithm 8 The CSR5-based SpMV for the *tid*th tile.

```
 1: MALLOC(*tmp, ω)
 2: MEMSET(*tmp, 0)
 3: MALLOC(*last_tmp, ω)
 4: /*use empty_offset[y_offset[i]] instead of
    y_offset[i] for a tile with any empty rows*/
 5: for i = 0 to ω − 1 in parallel do
 6:     sum ← 0
 7:     for j = 0 to σ − 1 do
 8:         ptr ← tid × ω × σ + j × ω + i
 9:         sum ← sum + val[ptr] × x[col_idx[ptr]]
10:         /*check bit_flag[i][j]*/
11:         if /*end of a red sub-segment*/ then
12:             tmp[i − 1] ← sum
13:             sum ← 0
14:         else if /*end of a green segment*/ then
15:             y[tile_ptr[tid] + y_offset[i]] ← sum
16:             y_offset[i] ← y_offset[i] +1
17:             sum ← 0
18:         end if
19:     end for
20:     last_tmp[i] ← sum //end of a blue sub-segment
21: end for
22: FAST_SEGMENTED_SUM(*tmp, *seg_offset)      ▷ Alg. 6
23: for i = 0 to ω − 1 in parallel do
24:     last_tmp[i] ← last_tmp[i] + tmp[i]
25:     y[tile_ptr[tid] + y_offset[i]] ← last_tmp[i]
26: end for
27: FREE(*tmp)
28: FREE(*last_tmp)
```

5. EXPERIMENTAL RESULTS

5.1 Experimental Setup

We evaluate the CSR5-based SpMV and 11 state-of-the-art formats and algorithms on four mainstream platforms: dual-socket Intel CPUs, an nVidia GPU, an AMD GPU and an Intel Xeon Phi. The platforms and participating approaches are shown in Table 1.

Host of the two GPUs is a machine with AMD A10-7850K APU, dual-channel DDR3-1600 memory and 64-bit Ubuntu Linux v14.04 installed. Host of the Xeon Phi is a machine with Intel Xeon E5-2680 v2 CPU, quad-channel DDR3-1600 memory and 64-bit Red Hat Enterprise Linux v6.5 installed. The two GPU platforms use the g++ compiler v4.8.2. The two Intel machines always set the Intel C/C++ complier 15.0.1 as default.

Here we evaluate double precision SpMV. So cuDPP library [16, 28], clSpMV [29] and yaSpMV [34] are not included since they only support single precision floating point as data type. Two recently published methods [20, 30] are not tested since the source code is not available to us yet.

We use OpenCL profiling scheme for timing SpMV on the AMD platform and record wall-clock time on the other three platforms. For all participating formats and algorithms, we evaluate SpMV 10 times (each time contains 1000 runs and records the average) and report the best observed result.

The testbeds	The participating formats and algorithms
Dual-socket Intel Xeon E5-2667 v3 (Haswell, 2×8 cores @ 3.2 GHz, 1.64 SP TFlops, 819.2 DP GFlops, 64 GB GDDR4, ECC-on, 2×68.3 GB/s bandwidth).	(1) The CSR-based SpMV in Intel MKL 11.2 Update 1. (2) BiCSB v1.2 using CSB [7] with bitmasked register block [6]. (3) pOSKI v1.0.0 [8] using OSKI v1.0.1h [31, 32] kernels. (4) The CSR5-based SpMV implemented by using OpenMP and AVX2 intrinsics.
An nVidia GeForce GTX 980 (Maxwell GM204, 2048 CUDA cores @ 1.13 GHz, 4.61 SP TFlops, 144.1 DP GFlops, 4 GB GDDR5, 224 GB/s bandwidth, driver v344.16).	(1) The best CSR-based SpMV [4] from cuSPARSE v6.5 and CUSP v0.4.0 [11]. (2) The best HYB [4] from the above two libraries. (3) BRC [2] with texture cache enabled. (4) ACSR [1] with texture cache enabled. (5) The CSR5-based SpMV implemented by using CUDA v6.5.
An AMD Radeon R9 290X (GCN Hawaii, 2816 Radeon cores @ 1.05 GHz, 5.91 SP TFlops, 739.2 DP GFlops, 4 GB GDDR5, 345.6 GB/s bandwidth, driver v14.41).	(1) The CSR-vector method [4] extracted from CUSP v0.4.0 [11]. (2) The CSR-Adaptive algorithm [17] implemented in ViennaCL v1.6.2 [26]. (3) The CSR5-based SpMV implemented by using OpenCL v1.2.
An Intel Xeon Phi 5110p (Knights Corner, 60 x86 cores @ 1.05 GHz, 2.02 SP TFlops, 1.01 DP TFlops, 8 GB GDDR5, ECC-on, 320 GB/s bandwidth, driver v3.4-1, μOS v2.6.38.8).	(1) The CSR-based SpMV in Intel MKL 11.2 Update 1. (2) The ESB [24] with dynamic scheduling enabled. (3) The CSR5-based SpMV implemented by using OpenMP and MIC-KNC intrinsics.

Table 1: The testbeds and participating formats and algorithms.

5.2 Benchmark Suite

In Table 2, we list 24 sparse matrices as our benchmark suite for all platforms. The first 20 matrices have been widely adopted in previous SpMV research [2, 4, 17, 24, 29, 33, 34]. The other 4 matrices are chosen since they have more diverse sparsity structures. All matrices except *Dense* are downloadable at the University of Florida Sparse Matrix Collection [12].

To achieve a high degree of differentiation, we categorize the 24 matrices in Table 2 into two groups: (1) *regular* group with the upper 14 matrices, (2) *irregular* group with the lower 10 matrices. This classification is mainly based on the minimum, average and maximum lengths of the rows. Matrix *dc2* is a representative of the group of irregular matrices. Its longest single row contains 114K nonzero entries, i.e., 15% nonzero entries of the whole matrix with 117K rows. This sparsity pattern challenges the design of efficient storage format and SpMV algorithm.

Id	Name	*Dimensions*	*nnz*	*nnz* per row (min, avg, max)
r1	Dense	2K×2K	4.0M	2K, 2K, 2K
r2	Protein	36K×36K	4.3M	18, 119, 204
r3	FEM/Spheres	83K×83K	6.0M	1, 72, 81
r4	FEM/Cantilever	62K×62K	4.0M	1, 64, 78
r5	Wind Tunnel	218K×218K	11.6M	2, 53, 180
r6	QCD	49K×49K	1.9M	39, 39, 39
r7	Epidemiology	526K×526K	2.1M	2, 3, 4
r8	FEM/Harbor	47K×47K	2.4M	4, 50, 145
r9	FEM/Ship	141K×141K	7.8M	24, 55, 102
r10	Economics	207K×207K	1.3M	1, 6, 44
r11	FEM/Accelerator	121K×121K	2.6M	0, 21, 81
r12	Circuit	171K×171K	959K	1, 5, 353
r13	Ga41As41H72	268K×268K	18.5M	18, 68, 702
r14	Si41Ge41H72	186K×186K	15.0M	13, 80, 662
i1	Webbase	1M×1M	3.1M	1, 3, 4.7K
i2	LP	4K×1.1M	11.3M	1, 2.6K, 56.2K
i3	Circuit5M	5.6M×5.6M	59.5M	1, 10, 1.29M
i4	eu-2005	863K×863K	19.2M	0, 22, 6.9K
i5	in-2004	1.4M×1.4M	16.9M	0, 12, 7.8K
i6	mip1	66K×66K	10.4M	4, 155, 66.4K
i7	ASIC_680k	683K×683K	3.9M	1, 6, 395K
i8	dc2	117K×117K	766K	1, 7, 114K
i9	FullChip	2.9M×2.9M	26.6M	1, 9, 2.3M
i10	ins2	309K×309K	2.8M	5, 9, 309K

Table 2: The benchmark suite.

5.3 Isolated SpMV Performance

Figure 7 shows double precision SpMV performance of the 14 regular matrices on the four platforms. We can see that, on average, all participating algorithms deliver comparable performance. *On the CPU platform*, Intel MKL obtains the best performance on average and the other 3 methods behave similar. *On the nVidia GPU*, the CSR5 delivers the highest throughput. The ACSR format is slower than the others, because its binning strategy leads to non-coalesced memory access. *On the AMD GPU*, the CSR5 achieves the best performance. Although the dynamic assigning in the CSR-Adaptive method can obtain better scalability than the CSR-vector method, it still cannot achieve near perfect load balance. *On the Xeon Phi*, the CSR5 is slower than Intel MKL and the ESB format. The main reason is that the current generation of Xeon Phi can only issue up to 4 relatively slow threads per core (i.e., up to 4×60 threads in total on the used device), and thus the latency of gathering entries from vector x becomes the main bottleneck. Then reordering or partitioning nonzero entries based on the column index for better cache locality behaves well in the ESB-based SpMV. However, in Section 5.6 we will show that this strategy leads to very high preprocessing cost.

Figure 8 shows double precision SpMV performance of the 10 irregular matrices. We can see that the irregularity can dramatically impact SpMV throughput of some approaches. *On the CPU platform*, the row block method based Intel MKL is now slower than the other methods. The CSR5 outperforms the others because of better SIMD efficiency from the AVX2 intrinsics. *On the nVidia GPU*, the CSR5 brings the best performance because of the near perfect load balance. The other two irregularity-oriented formats, HYB and ACSR, behave well but still suffer from imbalanced work decomposition. Note that the ACSR format is based on Dynamic Parallelism, a technical feature only available on recently released nVidia GPUs. *On the AMD GPU*, the CSR5 greatly outperforms the other two algorithms using the row block methods. Because the minimum work unit of the CSR-Adaptive method is one row, the method delivers degraded

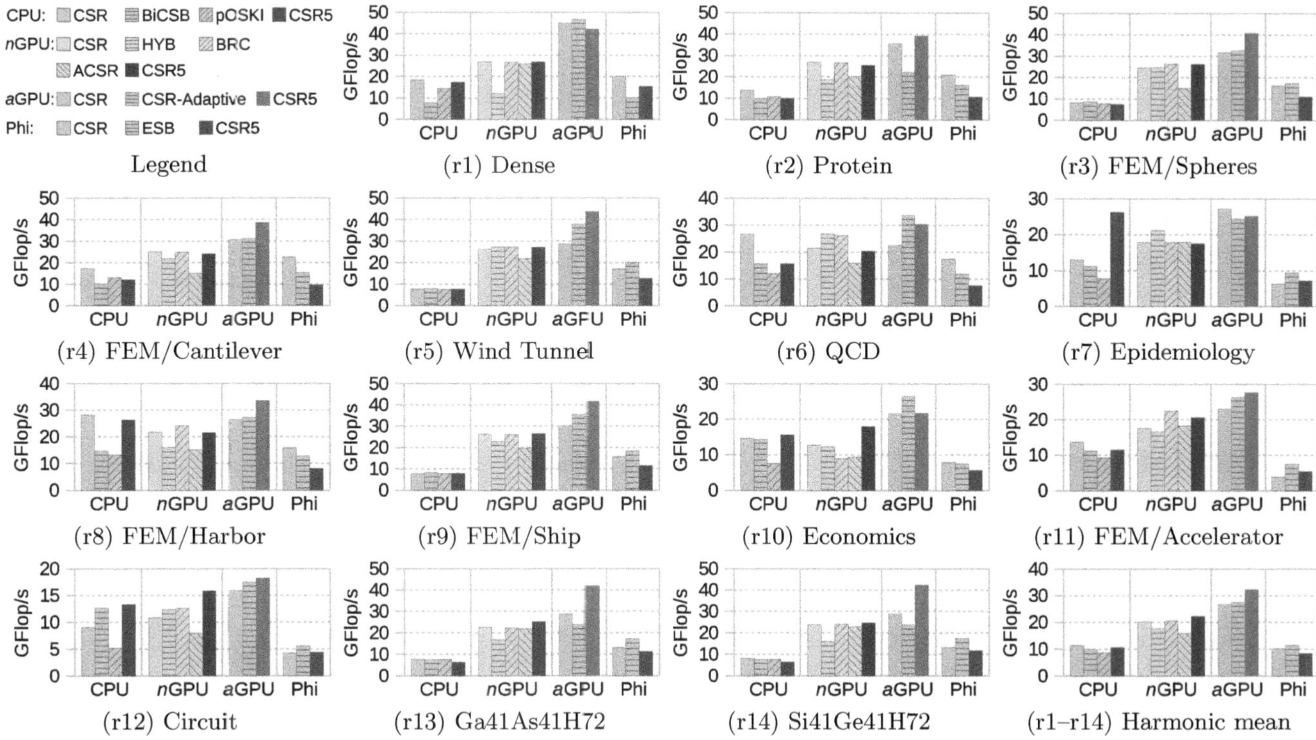

Figure 7: The SpMV performance of the 14 regular matrices. (*n*GPU=nVidia GPU, *a*GPU=AMD GPU)

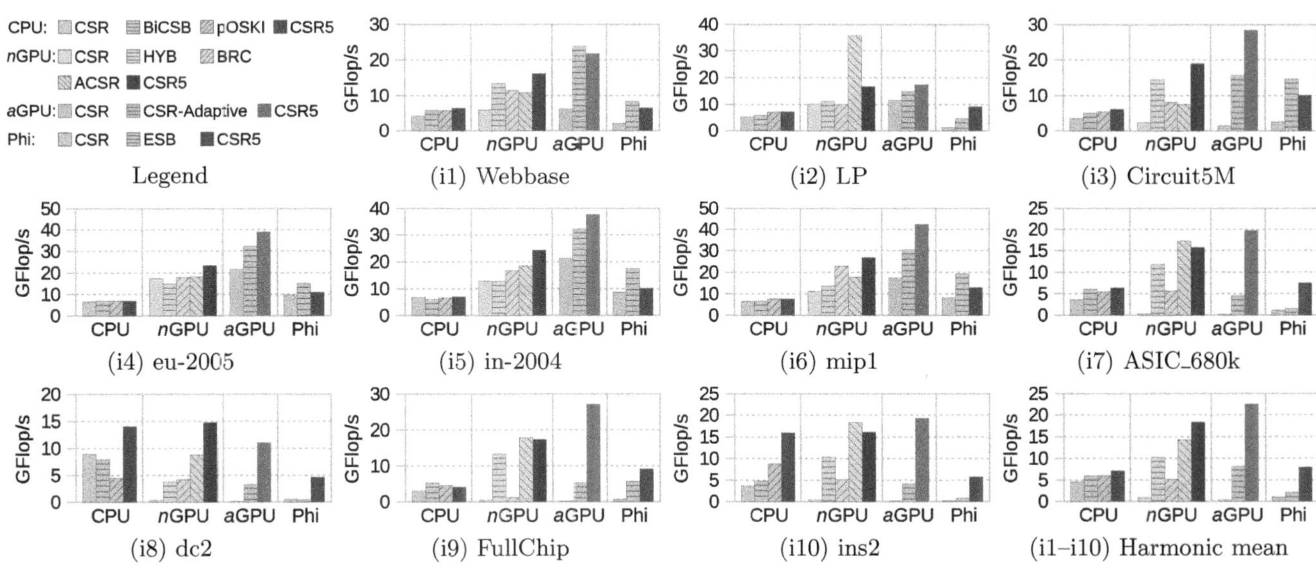

Figure 8: The SpMV performance of the 10 irregular matrices. (*n*GPU=nVidia GPU, *a*GPU=AMD GPU)

performance for matrices with very long rows[2]. *On the Xeon Phi*, the CSR5 can greatly outperform the other two methods in particular when matrices are too irregular to expose cache locality of x by the ESB format. Furthermore, since ESB is designed on top of the ELLPACK format, it cannot obtain the best performance for some irregular matrices.

Overall, the CSR5 achieves better performance (on the two GPU devices) or comparable performance (on the two x86 devices) for the 14 regular matrices. For the 10 irregular matrices, compared to pOSKI, ACSR, CSR-Adaptive and ESB as the second best methods, the CSR5 obtains average performance gain of 17.6%, 28.5%, 173.0% and 293.3% (up to 213.3%, 153.6%, 405.1% and 943.3%), respectively.

[2]Note that we use an implementation of the CSR-Adaptive from the ViennaCL Library. The AMD's version of the CSR-Adaptive, which is not available to us yet, may have slightly different performance.

Benchmark	The 14 regular matrices					The 10 irregular matrices				
Metrics	Preprocessing to SpMV ratio	Speedup of #iter.=50		Speedup of #iter.=500		Preprocessing to SpMV ratio	Speedup of #iter.=50		Speedup of #iter.=500	
		avg	best	avg	best		avg	best	avg	best
CPU-BiCSB	538.01x	0.06x	0.11x	0.35x	0.60x	331.77x	0.13x	0.24x	0.60x	1.07x
CPU-pOSKI	12.30x	0.43x	0.88x	0.57x	0.99x	10.71x	0.62x	1.66x	0.83x	2.43x
CPU-CSR5	**6.14x**	0.52x	0.74x	0.59x	0.96x	**3.69x**	0.91x	**2.37x**	**1.03x**	**2.93x**
*n*GPU-HYB	13.73x	0.73x	0.98x	0.92x	1.21x	28.59x	1.86x	13.61x	2.77x	25.57x
*n*GPU-BRC	151.21x	0.26x	0.31x	0.80x	0.98x	51.85x	1.17x	7.60x	2.49x	15.47x
*n*GPU-ACSR	**1.10x**	0.68x	0.93x	0.72x	1.03x	3.04x	5.05x	41.47x	5.41x	51.95x
*n*GPU-CSR5	3.06x	**1.04x**	**1.34x**	**1.10x**	**1.45x**	**1.99x**	**6.43x**	**48.37x**	**6.77x**	**52.31x**
*a*GPU-CSR-Adaptive	**2.68x**	1.00x	1.33x	1.07x	1.48x	**1.16x**	3.02x	27.88x	3.11x	28.22x
*a*GPU-CSR5	4.99x	**1.04x**	**1.39x**	**1.14x**	**1.51x**	3.10x	**5.72x**	**135.32x**	**6.04x**	**141.94x**
Phi-ESB	922.47x	0.05x	0.15x	0.33x	0.88x	222.19x	0.27x	1.15x	1.30x	2.96x
Phi-CSR5	**11.52x**	0.54x	**1.14x**	0.65x	**1.39x**	**9.45x**	**3.43x**	**18.48x**	**4.10x**	**21.18x**

Table 3: Preprocessing cost and its impact on the iteration-based scenarios.

5.4 Effects of Auto-Tuning

In section 3.2, we discussed a simple auto-tuning scheme for the parameter σ on GPUs. Figure 9 shows its effects (the x axis is the matrix *ids*). We can see that compared to the best performance chosen from a range of $\sigma = 4$ to 48, the auto-tuned σ does not have obvious performance loss. On the nVidia GPU, the performance loss is on average -4.2%. On the AMD GPU, the value is on average -2.5%.

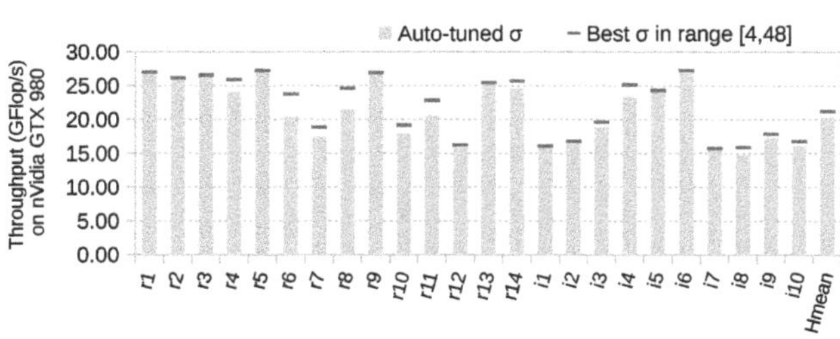

(a) The nVidia GTX 980 GPU.

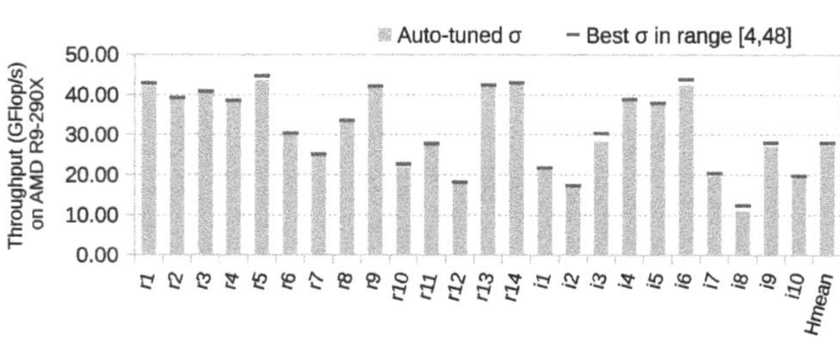

(b) The AMD R9-290X GPU.

Figure 9: Auto-tuning effects on the two GPUs.

5.5 Format Conversion Cost

The format conversion from the CSR to the CSR5 includes four steps: (1) memory allocation, (2) generating `tile_ptr`, (3) generating `tile_desc`, and (4) transposition of `col_idx` and `val` arrays. Figure 10 shows the cost of the four steps for the 24 matrices (the x axis is the matrix *ids*) on the four used platforms. Cost of one single SpMV operation is used for normalizing format conversion cost on each platform. We can see that the conversion cost can be on average as low as the overhead of a few SpMV operations on the two GPUs. On the two x86 platforms, the conversion time is longer (up to cost of around 10–20 SpMV operations). The reason is that the conversion code is manually SIMDized using CUDA or OpenCL on GPUs, but only auto-parallelized by OpenMP on x86 processors.

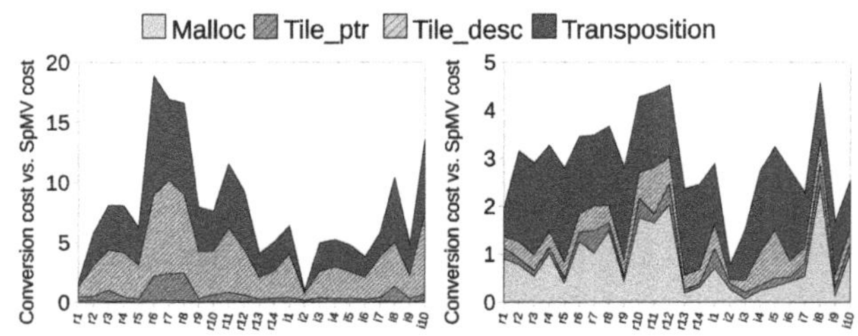

(a) The CPU. (b) The nVidia GPU.

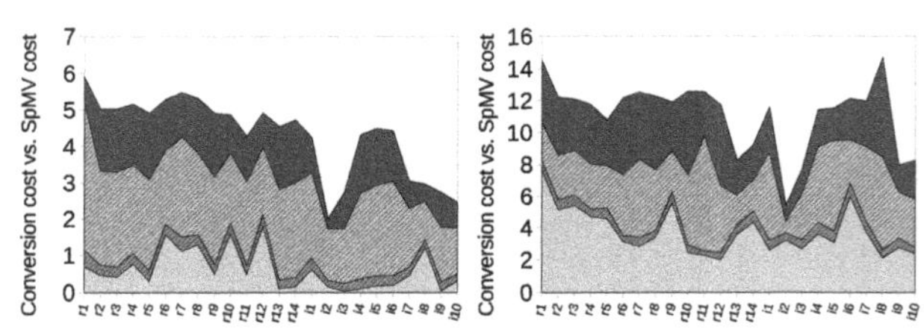

(c) The AMD GPU. (d) The Xeon Phi.

Figure 10: The normalized format conversion cost.

5.6 Iteration-Based Scenarios

Since both the preprocessing (i.e., format conversion from a basic format) time and the SpMV time are important for real-world applications, we have designed an iteration-based benchmark. This benchmark measures the overall performance of a solver with n iterations. We assume the input matrix is already stored in the CSR format. So the overall cost of using the CSR format for the scenarios is nT^{csr}_{spmv}, where T^{csr}_{spmv} is execution time of one CSR-based SpMV operation. For a new format, the overall cost is $T^{new}_{pre} + nT^{new}_{spmv}$, where T^{new}_{pre} is preprocessing time and the T^{new}_{spmv} is one SpMV time using the new format. Thus we can calculate speedup of a new format over the CSR format in the scenarios, through $(nT^{csr}_{spmv})/(T^{new}_{pre} + nT^{new}_{spmv})$.

Table 3 shows the new formats' preprocessing cost (i.e., $T^{new}_{pre}/T^{new}_{spmv}$) and their speedups over the CSR format in the iteration-based scenarios when $n = 50$ and $n = 500$. The emboldened font in the table shows the highest positive speedups on each platform. The compared baseline is the fastest CSR-based SpMV implementation (i.e., Intel MKL, nVidia cuSPARSE/CUSP, CSR-vector from CUSP, and Intel MKL, respectively) on each platform. We can see that because of the very low preprocessing overhead, the CSR5 can further outperform the previous methods when doing 50 iterations and 500 iterations. Although two GPU methods, the ACSR format and the CSR-Adaptive approach, in general have shorter preprocessing time, they suffer from lower SpMV performance and thus cannot obtain the best speedups. On all platforms, the CSR5 always achieves the highest overall speedups. Moreover, the CSR5 is the only format that obtains higher performance than the CSR format when only 50 iterations are required.

6. RELATED WORK

A great deal of work has been published on accelerating the SpMV operation. The **block-based sparse matrix construction** has received most attention [2, 6, 7, 10, 25, 31, 34] because of two main reasons: (1) sparse matrices generated by some real-world problems (e.g., finite element discretization) naturally have the block sub-structures, and (2) off-chip load operations may be decreased by using the block indices instead of the entry indices. However, for many matrices that do not exhibit a natural block structure, trying to extract the block information is time consuming and has limited effects.

On the other hand, the **hybrid formats** [4, 29], such as HYB, have been designed for irregular matrices. However, higher kernel launch overhead and invalidated cache among kernel launches tend to decrease their overall performance. Moreover, it is hard to guarantee that every sub-matrix can saturate the whole device. In addition, some relatively simple operations such as solving triangular systems become complex while the input matrix is stored in two or more separate parts.

The recent **row block methods** showed good performance either for regular matrices [17] or for irregular matrices [1], but not for both. In contrast, the CSR5 can deliver higher throughput both for regular matrices and for irregular matrices.

The **segmented sum methods** have been used in two recently published papers [30, 34] for the SpMV on either GPUs or Xeon Phi. However, both of them need to store the matrix in COO-like formats to utilize the segmented sum. In contrast, the CSR5 format saves useful row index information in a compact way, and thus can be more efficient both for the format conversion and for the SpMV operation.

Sedaghati et al. [27] constructed machine learning classifiers for **automatic selection of the best format** for a given sparse matrix on a target GPU. The CSR5 format described in this work can further simplify such a selection process because it is insensitive to the sparsity structure of the input sparse matrix.

Moreover, to the best of our knowledge, the CSR5 is the only format that supports high throughput **cross-platform SpMV** on CPUs, nVidia GPUs, AMD GPUs and Xeon Phi at the same time. This advantage may simplify the development of scientific software for processors with massive on-chip parallelism.

7. CONCLUSIONS

In this paper, we proposed the CSR5 format for efficient cross-platform SpMV on CPUs, GPUs and Xeon Phi. The format conversion from the CSR to the CSR5 was very fast because of the format's insensitivity to sparsity structure of the input matrix. The CSR5-based SpMV was implemented by a redesigned segmented sum algorithm with higher SIMD utilization compared to the classic methods. The experimental results showed that the CSR5 delivered high throughput both in the isolated SpMV tests and in the iteration-based scenarios.

8. ACKNOWLEDGMENTS

The authors would like to thank James Avery (KU), Huamin Ren (AAU), Wenliang Wang (BOC), Jianbin Fang (NUDT), Joseph L. Greathouse (AMD), Shuai Che (AMD), Ruipeng Li (UMN), Anders Logg (Chalmers and GU), and our anonymous reviewers for their insightful feedback. We thank Klaus Birkelund Jensen (KU), Hans Henrik Happe (KU) and Rune Kildetoft (KU) for access to the Intel Xeon and Xeon Phi machines. We thank Bo Shen (Inspur) for helpful discussion about Xeon Phi programming. We also thank Arash Ashari (OSU), Intel MKL team, Joseph L. Greathouse (AMD) and Mayank Daga (AMD) for sharing source code, libraries or implementation details of their SpMV algorithms with us. Finally, we thank the PPoPP '15 reviewers for their valuable suggestions and comments.

9. REFERENCES

[1] A. Ashari, N. Sedaghati, J. Eisenlohr, S. Parthasarathy, and P. Sadayappan. Fast Sparse Matrix-Vector Multiplication on GPUs for Graph Applications. In *Proceedings of the International Conference for High Performance Computing, Networking, Storage and Analysis*, SC '14, pages 781–792, 2014.

[2] A. Ashari, N. Sedaghati, J. Eisenlohr, and P. Sadayappan. An Efficient Two-Dimensional Blocking Strategy for Sparse Matrix-vector Multiplication on GPUs. In *Proceedings of the 28th ACM International Conference on Supercomputing*, ICS '14, pages 273–282, 2014.

[3] M. M. Baskaran and R. Bordawekar. Optimizing Sparse Matrix-Vector Multiplication on GPUs. Technical Report RC24704, IBM, 2008.

[4] N. Bell and M. Garland. Implementing Sparse Matrix-Vector Multiplication on Throughput-Oriented Processors. In *Proceedings of the Conference on High Performance Computing Networking, Storage and Analysis*, SC '09, pages 18:1–18:11, 2009.

[5] G. E. Blelloch, M. A. Heroux, and M. Zagha. Segmented Operations for Sparse Matrix Computation on Vector Multiprocessors. Technical Report CMU-CS-93-173, Carnegie Mellon University, 1993.

[6] A. Buluç, S. Williams, L. Oliker, and J. Demmel. Reduced-Bandwidth Multithreaded Algorithms for Sparse Matrix-Vector Multiplication. In *Proceedings of the 2011 IEEE International Parallel & Distributed Processing Symposium*, IPDPS '11, pages 721–733, 2011.

[7] A. Buluç, J. T. Fineman, M. Frigo, J. R. Gilbert, and C. E. Leiserson. Parallel Sparse Matrix-Vector and Matrix-Transpose-Vector Multiplication Using Compressed Sparse Blocks. In *Proceedings of the Twenty-first Annual Symposium on Parallelism in*

Algorithms and Architectures, SPAA '09, pages 233–244, 2009.

[8] J.-H. Byun, R. Lin, J. W. Demmel, and K. A. Yelick. pOSKI: Parallel Optimized Sparse Kernel Interface Library. Technical report, University of California, Berkeley, 2012.

[9] S. Chatterjee, G. Blelloch, and M. Zagha. Scan Primitives for Vector Computers. In *Supercomputing '90., Proceedings of*, pages 666–675, 1990.

[10] J. W. Choi, A. Singh, and R. W. Vuduc. Model-Driven Autotuning of Sparse Matrix-Vector Multiply on GPUs. In *Proceedings of the 15th ACM SIGPLAN Symposium on Principles and Practice of Parallel Programming*, PPoPP '10, pages 115–126, 2010.

[11] S. Dalton and N. Bell. *CUSP : A C++ Templated Sparse Matrix Library*, 2014.

[12] T. A. Davis and Y. Hu. The University of Florida Sparse Matrix Collection. *ACM Trans. Math. Softw.*, 38(1):1:1–1:25, 2011.

[13] Y. S. Deng, B. D. Wang, and S. Mu. Taming Irregular EDA Applications on GPUs. In *Proceedings of the 2009 International Conference on Computer-Aided Design*, ICCAD '09, pages 539–546, 2009.

[14] J. Dongarra and M. A. Heroux. Toward a New Metric for Ranking High Performance Computing Systems. Technical Report SAND2013-4744, Sandia National Laboratories, 2013.

[15] Y. Dotsenko, N. K. Govindaraju, P.-P. Sloan, C. Boyd, and J. Manferdelli. Fast Scan Algorithms on Graphics Processors. In *Proceedings of the 22Nd Annual International Conference on Supercomputing*, ICS '08, pages 205–213, 2008.

[16] M. Garland. Sparse Matrix Computations on Manycore GPU's. In *Proceedings of the 45th Annual Design Automation Conference*, DAC '08, pages 2–6, 2008.

[17] J. L. Greathouse and M. Daga. Efficient Sparse Matrix-Vector Multiplication on GPUs using the CSR Storage Format. In *Proceedings of the International Conference for High Performance Computing, Networking, Storage and Analysis*, SC '14, pages 769–780, 2014.

[18] D. Guo and W. Gropp. Adaptive Thread Distributions for SpMV on a GPU. In *Proceedings of the Extreme Scaling Workshop*, pages 2:1–2:5, 2012.

[19] K. Kourtis, G. Goumas, and N. Koziris. Exploiting Compression Opportunities to Improve SpMxV Performance on Shared Memory Systems. *ACM Trans. Archit. Code Optim.*, 7(3):16:1–16:31, 2010.

[20] M. Kreutzer, G. Hager, G. Wellein, H. Fehske, and A. Bishop. A Unified Sparse Matrix Data Format for Efficient General Sparse Matrix-Vector Multiplication on Modern Processors with Wide SIMD Units. *SIAM Journal on Scientific Computing*, 36(5):C401–C423, 2014.

[21] J. Li, G. Tan, M. Chen, and N. Sun. SMAT: An Input Adaptive Auto-Tuner for Sparse Matrix-Vector Multiplication. In *Proceedings of the 34th ACM SIGPLAN Conference on Programming Language Design and Implementation*, PLDI '13, pages 117–126, 2013.

[22] R. Li and Y. Saad. GPU-accelerated preconditioned iterative linear solvers. *The Journal of Supercomputing*, 63(2):443–466, 2013.

[23] W. Liu and B. Vinter. An Efficient GPU General Sparse Matrix-Matrix Multiplication for Irregular Data. In *Proceedings of the 2014 IEEE 28th International Parallel and Distributed Processing Symposium*, IPDPS '14, pages 370–381, 2014.

[24] X. Liu, M. Smelyanskiy, E. Chow, and P. Dubey. Efficient Sparse Matrix-Vector Multiplication on x86-based Many-Core Processors. In *Proceedings of the 27th International ACM Conference on International Conference on Supercomputing*, ICS '13, pages 273–282, 2013.

[25] A. Pinar and M. Heath. Improving Performance of Sparse Matrix-Vector Multiplication. In *Proceedings of the 1999 ACM/IEEE Conference on Supercomputing*, SC '99, 1999.

[26] K. Rupp, F. Rudolf, and J. Weinbub. ViennaCL - A High Level Linear Algebra Library for GPUs and Multi-Core CPUs. In *GPUScA*, pages 51–56, 2010.

[27] N. Sedaghati, T. Mu, L.-N. Pouchet, S. Parthasarathy, and P. Sadayappan. Automatic Selection of Sparse Matrix Representation on GPUs. In *Proceedings of the 29th ACM International Conference on Supercomputing*, ICS '15, 2015.

[28] S. Sengupta, M. Harris, Y. Zhang, and J. D. Owens. Scan Primitives for GPU Computing. In *Proceedings of the 22Nd ACM SIGGRAPH/EUROGRAPHICS Symposium on Graphics Hardware*, GH '07, pages 97–106, 2007.

[29] B.-Y. Su and K. Keutzer. clSpMV: A Cross-Platform OpenCL SpMV Framework on GPUs. In *Proceedings of the 26th ACM International Conference on Supercomputing*, ICS '12, pages 353–364, 2012.

[30] W. T. Tang, R. Zhao, M. Lu, Y. Liang, H. P. Huynh, X. Li, and R. S. M. Goh. Optimizing and Auto-Tuning Scale-Free Sparse Matrix-Vector Multiplication on Intel Xeon Phi. In *Proceedings of the 13th Annual IEEE/ACM International Symposium on Code Generation and Optimization*, CGO '15, pages 136–145, 2015.

[31] R. Vuduc, J. W. Demmel, and K. A. Yelick. OSKI: A Library of Automatically Tuned Sparse Matrix Kernels. *Journal of Physics: Conference Series*, 16(1):521–530, 2005.

[32] R. W. Vuduc. *Automatic Performance Tuning of Sparse Matrix Kernels*. PhD thesis, University of California, Berkeley, dec 2003.

[33] S. Williams, L. Oliker, R. Vuduc, J. Shalf, K. Yelick, and J. Demmel. Optimization of Sparse Matrix-Vector Multiplication on Emerging Multicore Platforms. *Parallel Computing*, 35(3):178–194, 2009.

[34] S. Yan, C. Li, Y. Zhang, and H. Zhou. yaSpMV: Yet Another SpMV Framework on GPUs. In *Proceedings of the 19th ACM SIGPLAN Symposium on Principles and Practice of Parallel Programming*, PPoPP '14,

Optimistic Delinearization of Parametrically Sized Arrays

Tobias Grosser
INRIA/ETH Zurich*
tobias.grosser@inf.ethz.ch

J. Ramanujam
Louisiana State University
ram@cct.lsu.edu

Louis-Noël Pouchet
The Ohio State University
pouchet@osu.edu

P. Sadayappan
The Ohio State University
sadayappan.1@osu.edu

Sebastian Pop
Samsung Austin R&D Center
sebpop@gmail.com

ABSTRACT

A number of legacy codes make use of linearized array references (i.e., references to one-dimensional arrays) to encode accesses to multi-dimensional arrays. This is also true of a number of optimized libraries and the well-known LLVM intermediate representation, which linearize array accesses. In many cases, the only information available is an array base pointer and a single dimensional offset. For problems with parametric array extents, this offset is usually a multivariate polynomial. Compiler analyses such as data dependence analysis are impeded because the standard formulations with integer linear programming (ILP) solvers cannot be used. In this paper, we present an approach to delinearization, i.e., recovering the multi-dimensional nature of accesses to arrays of parametric size. In case of insufficient static information, the developed algorithm produces run-time conditions to validate the recovered multi-dimensional form. The obtained access description enhances the precision of data dependence analysis. Experimental evaluation in the context of the LLVM/Polly system using a number of benchmarks reveals significant performance benefits due to increased precision of dependence analysis and enhanced optimization opportunities that are exploited by the compiler after delinearization.

Categories and Subject Descriptors

D.3.4 [**Programming Languages**]: Processor – Compilers

Keywords

polyhedral analysis, linear memory layout, multi-dimensional arrays

1. INTRODUCTION

Dense multi-dimensional arrays are data structures widely used in programs, such as in scientific, engineering and image processing applications. Multi-dimensional arrays are native constructs in languages such as Java, FORTRAN or C99, but unfortunately not in languages like C++ or C89. Given a dense C99 multi-dimensional array `A[N][N]`, it can be equivalently viewed as a one-dimensional array `Alin[N*N]`: the memory layout of data described by a dense multi-dimensional array corresponds to a linear, consecutive chunk of data that can be viewed as a vector of memory locations. Therefore a particular memory cell reference in the multi-dimensional view, e.g., `A[i][j]` is *linearized* to `Alin[i*N + j]`.

Using a multi-dimensional view usually exposes simpler expressions for the subscript in each dimension (e.g., `i` and `j`) while the linearized view can complicate numerous compiler analyses and optimizations: `i*N + j` is a polynomial. Dependence and dataflow analysis on affine array accesses is a well known compiler technique [3], whereas performing the same analyses on polynomial expressions is significantly more complex and commonly not performed by many compilers. Therefore the ability to recover multi-dimensional array views is important to obtain precise data dependences. Such information enables a wide range of loop optimizations, and is essential for automatic parallelization, including GPGPU off-loading and MPI parallelization. For the latter two, the knowledge of multi-dimensional array views also eases precise memory footprint analyses, as well as the generation of communication code.

With languages not offering native support for multi-dimensional arrays, programmers must use explicitly linearized array index expressions with 1D arrays to encode algorithms that are naturally expressed using multi-dimensional arrays. Even with languages like C99 that provide native support for multi-dimensional arrays, the internal representation of compilers like Clang/LLVM only provides a linearized view of multi-dimensional arrays, for consistency across multiple input languages. Various legacy codes and several modern C++ template libraries also make use of linearized array references to encode accesses to multi-dimensional arrays. Listing 1 shows a function that initializes a sub-array of size $s_0 \times s_1 \times s_2$ located at offset $o_0 \times o_1 \times o_2$ inside a larger array of size $n_0 \times n_1 \times n_2$, implemented with C99 variable length arrays. Looking at the internal LLVM [5] representation after compiling with Clang (Listing 2), it may be seen that all array references have been linearized. LLVM's scalar evolution analysis [10] derives the access to `A` as $A[(n_2(n_1 o_0 + o_1) + o_2) + n_1 n_2 i + j n_2 + k]$. Neither the array dimensionality nor the extent of individual dimensions is preserved.

We use a simple example to illustrate the impact of multi-dimensional array views on compiler optimization. The kernels in Listing 3 copy data from the odd rows of a 2D array to the even rows. The code has been deliberately made inefficient by accessing the data column-wise instead of row-wise. If a compiler can successfully prove the absence of data-dependences in this loop nest, it can interchange the two loops to avoid the inefficient data accesses and obtain significantly better performance. We compile three versions of the code. The first two versions mimic a multi-dimensional

*Finalized at the Dep. of Computer Science, ETH Zurich

ICS'15, June 8–11, 2015, Newport Beach, CA, USA.
ACM 978-1-4503-3559-1/15/06 ...$15.00.
DOI: http://dx.doi.org/10.1145/2751205.2751248.

```
void set_subarray(unsigned n1, unsigned n2,
    unsigned o0, unsigned o1, unsigned o2,
    unsigned s0, unsigned s1, unsigned s2,
    float A[][n1][n2]) {
  for (unsigned i = 0; i < s0; i++)
    for (unsigned j = 0; j < s1; j++)
      for (unsigned k = 0; k < s2; k++)
S:      A[i + o0][j + o1][k + o2] = 1;
}
```

Listing 1: Initialization of sub-array (multi-dimensional)

```
define void @set_subarray(i32 %n1, i32 %n2, i32 %o0, i32 %o1,
  i32 %o2, i32 %s0, i32 %s1, i32 %s2, float* %A) {
  ; for i:
  ;   for j:
  ;     for k:
          %add = add i32 %k, %o2
          %add1 = add i32 %j, %o1
          %add2 = add i32 %i, %o0
          %0 = mul nuw i32 %n1, %n2
          %1 = mul nsw i32 %add2, %0
          %2 = mul nsw i32 %add1, %n2
          %idx1 = add i32 %1, %2
          %idx2 = add i32 %idx1, %add
          %idx3 = getelementptr float, float* %A, i32 %idx2
          store float 1.000000e+00, float* %idx3
  ;     endfor k
  ;   endfor j
  ; endfor i
}
```

Listing 2: Internal representation in Clang/LLVM

array using a macro that yields a linearized access into a single-dimensional array. Version #1 fixes the number of elements in the inner array dimension at compile time ($N = 20000$) whereas #2 uses a symbolic value for the size of the inner array dimension. Version #3 uses C99 variable-length arrays to make the two-dimensional symbolically sized shape explicit to the compiler. If compiled with the Intel icc 15.0 compiler both #1 and #3 are executed in 2 seconds, whereas #2 takes 15 seconds. icc is not able to perform the beneficial loop interchange for #2, but performs it for the other two versions. As loop interchange is clearly beneficial here, icc's inability to perform loop interchange is likely caused by imprecise and overly conservative data dependence information.

```
#define A_2D(o0, o1) A[(o0) * N + (o1)]
void oddEvenCopyLinearized(long N, float *A) {
#ifdef FIXED_SIZE
  N = 20000;
#endif
  for (long i = 0; i < N; i++)
    for (long j = 0; j < N; j++)
      A_2D(2 * j, i) = A_2D(2 * j + 1, i);
}
void oddEvenCopy2DArray(long N, float A[][N]) {
  for (long i = 0; i < N; i++)
    for (long j = 0; j < N; j++)
      A[2 * j][i] = A[2 * j + 1][i];
}
```

Listing 3: Dependence free odd-even copy within an array

In this paper, we address the *delinearization* problem: to infer equivalent multi-dimensional views of linearized arrays. This problem has been previously addressed by the work of Maslov [7] and Cierniak [2], but in a much more restricted context than we do. These previous efforts developed static analysis approaches that guaranteed a compile time solution under restricted scenarios: either produce a delinearized version, or declare infeasibility. In contrast, we significantly broaden the scope of programs that are delinearized, by taking an hybrid static/dynamic approach. Our analysis approach *optimistically* deduces a delinearized form, along with a set of validity conditions to be dynamically checked at runtime. If the runtime check passes, the deduced delinearized form is guaranteed to be equivalent to the linearized input, but if the dynamic check fails, no delinearized form is available. Although the check is dynamic, such an approach allows for conditional code with static program transformations applied to the delinearized form: the runtime check determines whether the statically optimized version using the delinearized form is executed or the unmodified version using the original linearized form is executed. We make the following contributions:

- We develop an effective approach to delinearization, inferring multi-dimensional views of arrays of parametric size; this approach also handles cases where statically proving the correctness of the recovered multi-dimensional view is infeasible.
- We implement and incorporate important parts of the approach into the Polly/LLVM system, thereby increasing the precision of data dependence analysis in Polly.
- We present experimental results demonstrating the benefit of the delinearization approach in enhancing performance optimization.

2. PROBLEM STATEMENT

Given a set of single dimensional array accesses with index expressions that are multivariate polynomials in terms of loop iterators and symbolic program parameters, and a set of corresponding iteration domains, derive an equivalent multi-dimensional view with linear array index expressions.

The view consists of 1) a multi-dimensional array definition (including the number of array dimensions and sizes for all but the outermost dimension), 2) for each original array access expression, a corresponding multi-dimensional array index expression. We impose the following set of conditions on the derived multi-dimensional view:

- **(R1) Affine:** The new access functions are affine in loop parameters and program parameters.
- **(R2) Equivalence:** For each array access, the memory location referenced by the original linearized subscript expression and the memory location obtained from the multi-dimensional view, after lowering it using the derived array sizes for a row-major array layout, are identical for all loop instances within the iteration space.
- **(R3) Within bounds:** The array subscript expressions (for all but the outermost dimension) are within the bounds of the multi-dimensional array, for all iteration instances within the iteration space.

For cases where the multi-dimensional view cannot be statically proven to be equivalent to the input linearized form, we derive a multi-dimensional view and provide a set of conditions under which the view is valid. $R1$ ensures that we can represent the resulting access expressions as affine integer maps. $R2$ ensures that the multi-dimensional form of the array has the same access characteristics as the single dimensional array. $R3$ ensures together with $R2$ that if we define a relation R between the elements of the linearized and the multi-dimensional view of the linearized array such that two elements are related if and only if they map to the same data location, this relation is always bijective. This property is important as it ensures that for each actual memory location there is only a single data location in our model; this is necessary for the correct computation of data dependences.

3. ARRAYS OF PARAMETRIC SIZE

We now present an algorithm to delinearize a 1D array reference in the form of a multivariate polynomial indexing expression into a set of affine indexing functions referencing a multi-dimensional array of shape $A[P_0][P_1]\dots[P_{n-1}]$, $P_i \in \mathcal{P}$ with $\mathcal{P}$ referring to the set of program parameters. We obtain a multi-dimensional array shape with the size of each dimension being defined by a single parameter, with multiple dimensions possibly sharing the same parameter.

3.1 Basic algorithm

We propose a basic algorithm consisting of the following steps:

1. Collect possible array size parameters
2. Derive dimensionality and array size
3. Compute multi-dimensional access functions
4. Derive validity conditions

We first collect information about possible array size parameters, symbolic values unknown at compile time that correspond to the size of an array dimension in the multi-dimensional view. To do this, we expand the given polynomial expression into a sum of products. From this sum, we extract all terms that contain both a loop induction variable and (possibly multiple) parameters. Those terms are interesting as the presence of a term that multiplies a parameter with an induction variable makes the expression non-affine. However, in case a parameter P is an array size parameter, P may be removed from the index expressions during delinearization, so that the original expression is turned into an access with affine subscript expressions. Consequently, we guess that P defines the size of at least one array dimension.

As the second step, we derive the dimensionality and the size of the array. To do this we start from the terms obtained in the previous step and assume all of them form products. In case a term is not a product, we treat it as a product with just a single factor. We remove from each term all factors that are non-parametric. The resulting terms are sorted according to the number of contained factors and we check that the terms with fewer factors symbolically divide the larger terms. If this is true, we assume the results of these symbolic divisions are the sizes of the array dimensions.

As the third step, we extract the access functions of the individual dimensions. We start with the original polynomial expression and first divide it symbolically by the size of the elements accessed. The resulting expression is then divided by the assumed dimension sizes starting with the innermost size. The remainder is the access function of the innermost dimension and the quotient is divided again by the size of the next array dimension. The new remainder is the access function of the second array dimension and the quotient is divided further. If no more dimension sizes are available, the last quotient becomes the access function of the outermost dimension.

As a last step, we derive the validity conditions. Up to this step, the delinearization we propose is an educated guess. It is only valid if $\forall i \in [1, n-1] : 0 \le f_i(\mathbf{i}) < d_i$ holds, with n being the number of array dimensions computed, d_i being the size of dimension i and $f_i(\mathbf{i})$ being the access function of dimension i, which given a vector of loop induction variables and program parameters derives a subscript expression. To check if these conditions hold, we can simplify them taking into account the range of the surrounding loop induction variables. In simple cases this simplification yields $\top$, which means the delinearization has been statically proven to be unconditionally correct. In cases where this is not enough, the remaining conditions need to be emitted as run-time checks.

We illustrate the delinearization algorithm using the sub-array initialization example presented in the introduction, but now start from its single-dimension version (Listing 4). To recover the multi-dimensional nature of the access in statement S, we first expand

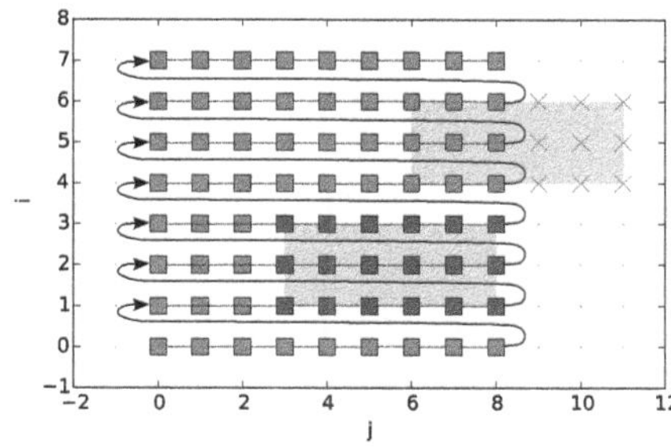

Figure 1: Sub-array accesses for different parameter values

the offset expression $(n_2(n_1o_0 + o_1) + o_2) + n_1n_2i + n_2j + k$ to a sum of products $n_2n_1o_0 + n_2o_1 + o_2 + n_1n_2i + n_2j + k$. Next, all products that involve induction variables are extracted, induction variables are removed and the products are sorted by the number of factors. This yields the set $\{n_1n_2, n_2\}$. As the smaller terms in this set evenly divide the larger ones, we assume a multi-dimensional array of shape `A[][n1][n2]`. We now use the new array shape to derive the individual index expressions. We do this by symbolically dividing the original offset expression by the size of the individual array dimensions, starting from the innermost dimension. As a first step we divide by n_2, which leaves us with a remainder $o_2 + k$, the index expression we assume for the innermost dimension. The quotient of the division is $n_1o_0 + o_1 + n_1i + j$. This quotient is now divided by n_1. The resulting remainder $o_1 + j$ allows us to derive $A[?][j + o_1][?]$ and the resulting quotient $o_0 + i$ allows us to derive $A[o_0 + i][?][?]$. The reconstructed full array access is $A[i + o_0][j + o_1][k + o_2]$.

```
void set_subarray(unsigned n1, unsigned n2,
    unsigned o0, unsigned o1, unsigned o2,
    unsigned s0, unsigned s1, unsigned s2,
    float A[]) {
  for (unsigned i = 0; i < s0; i++)
    for (unsigned j = 0; j < s1; j++)
      for (unsigned k = 0; k < s2; k++)
S:      A[(n2 * (n1 * o0 + o1) + o2)
          + n1 * n2 * i + n2 * j + k] = 1;
}
```

Listing 4: Initialization of sub-array (single-dimensional)

As a last step, we check the correctness of the delinearization by forming the following validity condition:

$$\forall i, j, k : \; 0 \le i < s_0 \wedge 0 \le j < s_1 \wedge 0 \le k < s_2 :$$
$$0 \le k + o_2 < n_2 \wedge 0 \le j + o_1 < n_1 \wedge 0 \le i + o_0$$

Using isl [13], we simplify this condition to $o_1 \le n_1 - s_1 \wedge o_2 \le n_2 - s_2$, exploiting the fact that all parameters are given as unsigned types. As further simplifications are not possible at compile time, the remaining conditions need to be verified at run-time.

Figure 1 illustrates a two dimensional version of this example highlighting two sets of parameter values, one that satisfies the validity condition and one that does not. Both examples work on a 2D data array `A[n0][n1]` with $n_0 = 8 \wedge n_1 = 9$. The first set of parameter values is $o_0 = 1 \wedge o_1 = 3 \wedge s_0 = 3 \wedge s_1 = 6$, which yields $3 \le 9 - 6$ and evaluates to $\top$. The corresponding set of data elements (illustrated in blue) are all within the bounds of the 2D array. However, of the accesses that correspond to the parameter values $o_0 = 4 \wedge o_1 = 6 \wedge s_0 = 3 \wedge s_1 = 6$ (red square) only the left half is within the array bounds. The right half accesses are out-of-bounds. In this case, the out-of-bounds accesses reference memory locations that correspond to the array elements $\{A[i, j] : 5 \le i \le 7 \wedge 0 \le j \le 2\}$ (red squares). This is problematic, as e.g., the data stored to `A[6][9]` affects the values read from `A[7][0]`. This relation is not visible in the delinearized program, which means the corresponding data dependences are not modeled and certain program transformations may be performed incorrectly. When checking the validity conditions we see that $o_1 \leq n_1 - s_1 \Rightarrow 6 \leq 9 - 6 \Rightarrow \bot$, which correctly shows that for this set of parameters we cannot rely on the delinearization.

3.2 Multiple array references

In case the kernel we analyze contains more than one access to the same array (e.g., identified by its base pointer), it is important to ensure that all accesses are properly delinearized using the same assumed array shape. Ensuring this requires only a slight adjustment of the algorithm. In the case of multiple arrays, we extract the terms from all arrays and derive the assumed array size from the combined terms. Using this common array size, we can once again derive the array accesses individually. The validity conditions are also derived individually, but redundant conditions are removed in a subsequent step. In case data accesses reference different arrays, we group the data accesses by the different arrays they access and analyze each group individually assuming the absence of aliasing between accesses to different arrays. To generate the run-time conditions we merge the constraints from the individual arrays, remove redundant constraints and generate a single run-time check to verify the analysis.

3.3 Subscripts containing size parameters

```
float A[][N][M];
for (i = 0; i < L; i++)
  for (j = 0; j < N; j++)
    for (k = 0; k < M; k++)
S1:    A[i][j][k] = ...;           // A[i N M + j M + k]

S2: A[1][1][1] = ...;              // A[N M + M + 1]
S3: A[0][0][M - 1] = ...;          // A[M - 1]
S4: A[0][N - 1][0] = ...;          // A[N M - M]
S5: A[0][N - 1][M - 1] = ...;      // A[N * M - 1]
```

Listing 5: Array sizes in subscripts (multi-dimensional)

Listing 5 shows an example of multi-dimensional array accesses where the subscript expressions contain array size parameters. In case these accesses are linearized (see comments) for an access `A[0][0][M-1]` with array size `A[][N][M]`, the algorithm presented in Section 3 derives the access `A[0][1][-1]`, as it associates multiples of `M` with the second dimension. This delinearization is invalid, as the subscript in the inner dimension becomes negative.

In general, there is always a set of delinearizations that differ in their derived subscript expressions, even though they all compute the same address expression. For the above example, the accesses `A[0][-1][2*M-1]`, `A[0][0][M-1]` and `A[0][1][-1]` all compute the same address expression. In fact, for a given two dimensional access and an arbitrary $k \in \mathbb{N}$ the following holds:

$$\begin{aligned} & A[f_0][f_1] && \text{with } A[\,][s_1] \\ = \; & A[f_0 s_1 + f_1] = A[(f_0 - k)s_1 + (ks_1 + f_1)] && \text{with } A[\,] \\ = \; & A[f_0 - k][ks_1 + f_1] && \text{with } A[\,][s_1] \end{aligned}$$

For d-dimensional accesses and any pair of neighboring dimensions $(t, t+1), t \in [0, d-2]$ the following equality holds for all $k_t \in \mathbb{N}$:

$$\&A[\ldots, f_t, f_{t+1}, \ldots] = \&A[\ldots, f_t - k_t, k_t s_{t+1} + f_{t+1}, \ldots]$$

This means there exists a set of values $k_t, t \in [0, d-2]$ which can be arbitrarily chosen to generate an infinite number of array accesses that all yield the same linearized address expression. However, for a specific set of loop iterators and parameters, not all k_t values ensure array accesses within bounds. We need to find the right values of k_t that avoid out-of-bounds accesses. One idea is to look at the loop bounds and to statically derive the right values of k_t. This is possible as long as the range of the subscript expression is known, but causes problems for accesses such as `A[N * i + N + p]`, which might be modeled as an array access `A[i + 1][p]` to an array of shape `A[][N]` in case $0 \leq p < N$ holds, but which would better be modeled as `A[i][N + p]` in case $-N \leq p < 0$ holds. In general it is not possible to derive an optimal value for k without knowledge about the values p can take. In some cases (e.g., $-10 \leq p < N - 10$) there is not even a single optimal value for k. To still be able to model such cases we can create a piece-wise delinearization that chooses the correct value of k depending on the values of the subscript expressions. For the 2D case, we could be tempted to use a mapping $(f_0, f_1) \rightarrow (f_0 + k, -ks_1 + f_1) \mid \exists k : ks_1 \leq f_1 < (k+1)s_1$, which models all possible values of k. Unfortunately, the product between k and s_1 is non-affine and consequently this map cannot be represented as an affine integer map. However, if we bound k such that $k \in [k_l, k_u]$ with k_l, k_u being known integer values, we can model this map with a finite number of affine pieces.

$$(f_0, f_1) \rightarrow \begin{cases} (f_0 + k_l, -k_l s_1 + f_2) & f_1 < k_l s_1 \\ \vdots & \\ (f_0 + (\text{-}1), \text{-}(\text{-}1)s_1 + f_2) & (\text{-}1)s_1 \leq f_1 < 0 \\ (f_0, f_1) & 0 \leq f_1 < 1s_1 \\ (f_0 + 1, \text{-}(1)s_1 + f_2) & 1s_1 \leq f_1 < 2s_1 \\ \vdots & \\ (f_0 + k_u, -k_u s_1 + f_2) & k_u s_1 \leq f_1 \end{cases}$$

For d-dimensional accesses, we now define a set of maps $M_t, t \in [0, d-2]$, where a map M_t is an identity map with dimension t and $t+1$ modified to use a generalized version of the above mapping. Each M_t approximates a map $(\ldots, f_t, f_{t+1}, \ldots) \rightarrow (\ldots, f_t + k, -k * s_{t+1} + f_{t+1}, \ldots) \mid \exists k : ks_{t+1} \leq f_1 < (k+1)s_{t+1}$ using a finite set of affine pieces. Starting from the highest t, we apply all maps M_t one by one to the delinearized (i.e., the multi-dimensional view) accesses. Using the original algorithm on the example given in Listing 5, we obtain the following set of delinearized accesses: $\{S1(i,j,k) \rightarrow A(i,j,k),\ S2() \rightarrow A(1,1,1),\ S3() \rightarrow A(0,1,-1),\ S4() \rightarrow A(1,-1,0), S5() \rightarrow A(1,0,-1)\}$. After applying a set of maps M_t generated with values $k_{t,l} = 0, k_{t,u} = 0$ chosen to only cover two cases, one with no transformation and one with a single multiple of the problem size parameter added, we obtain the following delinearized accesses:

$$S1(i,j,k) \rightarrow \begin{cases} A(i-1, N+j-1, M+k) & k \leq -1 \wedge j-1 \leq -1 \\ A(i, j-1, M+k) & k \leq -1 \wedge j-1 \geq 0 \\ A(i-1, N+j, k) & k \geq 0 \wedge j \leq -1 \\ A(i,j,k) & k \geq 0 \wedge j \geq 0 \end{cases}$$

$$\begin{aligned} & S2() \rightarrow A(1,1,1), && S3() \rightarrow A(0,0,M-1) \\ & S4() \rightarrow A(0,N-1,0), && S5() \rightarrow A(0,N-1,M-1) \end{aligned}$$

S2, S3, S4 and S5 show directly the correct delinearization. The access function for S1 is now slightly more complicated, but the three additional cases only apply under conditions that are removed when simplifying the access under the constraints implied by the iteration domain of S1. After these simplifications we obtain the mapping $S1(i,j,k) \rightarrow A(i,j,k)$ for $S1$. So the piecewise mappings have all been statically reduced to maps with just a single piece.

3.4 Arrays of size $A[\,][\beta_1 P_1][\beta_2 P_2]$

In certain cases (e.g., resizing of images) we may have array sizes of the form $A[\,][\beta_1 P_1][\beta_2 P_2]$, $P_i \in \mathcal{P}$, $\beta_i \in \mathbb{N}$. Accesses to such arrays would be delinearized to an access $A[\beta_1 f_0][\beta_2 f_1][f_2]$, into an array of size $A[\,][P_1][P_2]$. As f_1 can be in the range $0 \leq f_1 < \beta_1 P_1$, the expression $\beta_2 f_1$ may not fit into the new range. To address this, we can find the *gcd* of the values in each dimension and use it to adjust the array sizes. Specifically, if all subscript expressions in a certain dimension can be divided by a value x, we can divide all of them by x and multiply the size of the next innermost dimension by x. This transformation is always beneficial in the sense that it only increases the chance that the delinearization will be correct. As it reduces the range of the subscript expression, the subscript expression is more likely to fit into the ranges implied by the array size. Similarly, as we increase the size of the inner dimension the corresponding subscript expressions on this dimension are also more likely to fit in.

4. PARAMETER + CONSTANT

We look now at a specific case, where the shape of the array is of the form $A[P_0+\alpha_0]\ldots[P_{n-1}+\alpha_{n-1}]$ with $\forall i \in [0,n-1] : P_i \in \mathcal{P}$, $\alpha_i \in \mathbb{N}$, with P_i being different for different values of i.[1] As an example we show in Listing 6 a simplified 3D stencil computation which computes the average over the elements in a diagonal stencil and which uses a one element border around the actual data elements to avoid the need for special boundary statements.

```
int In[Q+2][R+2][S+2]; int Out[Q+2][R+2][S+2];

for (int i = 1; i <= Q; i++)
  for (int i = 1; i <= R; i++)
    for (int i = 1; i <= S; i++)
      Out[i][j][k] = 0.33f * (In[i][j][k]
        + In[i+1][j+1][k+1] + In[i-1][j-1][k-1]);
```

Listing 6: Dimensions of size $P_i + \alpha_i$ (multi-dimensional)

```
int In[]; int Out[];

for (int i = 1; i <= Q; i++)
  for (int i = 1; i <= R; i++)
    for (int i = 1; i <= S; i++)
      Out[i*R*S+2*i*S+2*i*R+4*i+j*S+j*2+k] =
        0.33f * (In[i*R*S+2*i*S+2*i*R+4*i+j*S+j*2+k]
                 + In[7+2*j+k+2*R+3*S+j*S+
                      R*S+4*i+2*R*i+2*S*i+R*S*i]
                 + In[-7+2*j+k-2*R-3*S+j*S-R*S
                      +4*i+2*R*i+2*S*i+R*S*i]);
```

Listing 7: Dimensions of size $P_i + \alpha_i$ (linearized)

When analyzing the linearized access to `Out`, as visible in Listing 7, two problems become visible. First of all, the previous algorithm fails to guess an array size, as the terms R, S and RS all appear in products that contain induction variables. Our previous approach can consequently not define an order on the parameters that allows it to assign parameters to array dimensions. Assuming we could still derive an array shape (e.g., `Out[][R][S]`), we obtain from the remaining algorithm the access `Out[i][2i + j][4 i + 2 j + k + 2 i R]`. This delinearization is incorrect. As it has been derived according to the wrong array size, it causes out-of-bound accesses and even fails to fully eliminate non-affine terms in the subscript expressions. Before presenting the general approach to delinearize polynomial expressions to d-dimensional array shapes of the form $A[P_0+\alpha_0]\ldots[P_{d-1}+\alpha_{d-1}]$, $P_i \in \mathcal{P}$, $\alpha \in \mathbb{N}$, we present the special case of two and three dimensions.

An access to a two dimensional array $A[f_0(\mathbf{i})][f_1(\mathbf{i})]$ with shape $A[\,][P_1+\alpha_1]$ corresponds to the single dimensional array access $A[f_0(\mathbf{i})(P_1+\alpha_1)+f_1(\mathbf{i})]$, which after expansion becomes the access $A[f_0(\mathbf{i})P_1+f_0(\mathbf{i})\alpha_1+f_1(\mathbf{i})]$. However, it is unlikely that this structure is preserved. The only structure that can be assumed is a sum of terms $g_{\{1\}}(\mathbf{i})P_1+g_{\emptyset}(\mathbf{i})$ where each term contains a different subset of the program parameters. In the general case we write this expression as $\sum_{S\in\wp([0,f-1])}(g_S(\mathbf{i})\prod_{s\in S}P_s)$, where f is the number of parameters, $\wp([0,f-1])$ is the powerset of $[0,f-1]$, the different $g_S(\mathbf{i})$ are expressions in loop induction variables, and the different P_s are program parameters. To delinearize this polynomial expression we need to recover expressions $f_0(\mathbf{i}), f_1(\mathbf{i}), \alpha_1$ as a function of g_x's. As $f_0(\mathbf{i})$ is the only coefficient to P_1, recovering the relation $f_0(\mathbf{i}) = g_{\{1\}}(\mathbf{i})$ is easy. The second equality we can obtain is $g_{\emptyset}(\mathbf{i}) = f_0(\mathbf{i})\alpha_1 + f_1(\mathbf{i})$. With $f_0(\mathbf{i})$ plugged in we obtain $g_{\emptyset}(\mathbf{i}) = g_{\{1\}}(\mathbf{i})\alpha_1 + f_1(\mathbf{i})$, which allows us to express $f_1(\mathbf{i})$ as a function of α_1: $f_1(\mathbf{i}) = g_{\emptyset}(\mathbf{i}) - g_{\{1\}}(\mathbf{i})\alpha_1$. For different values of α_1 we obtain different array sizes and the corresponding delinearizations, which all are lowered to the very same linearized function, perform the same memory accesses and consequently model the program behavior correctly. However, depending on the iteration space boundaries only certain delinearizations ensure the absence of out of bounds accesses. As boundary offsets are commonly small and there is only one value α_1 to verify, it is possible to scan a certain number of α_1 by either statically checking for valid delinearizations or possibly even by generating run-time versioned code for different values of α_1.

Looking at the three dimensional case, we observe that an access $A[f_0(\mathbf{i})][f_1(\mathbf{i})][f_2(\mathbf{i})]$ to an array of shape $A[\,][P_1+\alpha_1][P_2+\alpha_2]$ has, after linearization and expansion, the form:

$$f_0(\mathbf{i})P_1P_2 + f_0(\mathbf{i})P_1\alpha_2 + f_0(\mathbf{i})P_2\alpha_1 + f_0(\mathbf{i})\alpha_1\alpha_2 +$$
$$f_1(\mathbf{i})P_2 + f_1(\mathbf{i})\alpha_2 + f_2(\mathbf{i})$$

It corresponds to the polynomial expression:

$$g_{\{1,2\}}(\mathbf{i})P_1P_2 + g_{\{1\}}(\mathbf{i})P_1 + g_{\{2\}}(\mathbf{i})P_2 + g_{\emptyset}(\mathbf{i})$$

From the single term that contains P_1P_2, the product of all symbolic parameters defining the array sizes, we recover the relation $f_0(\mathbf{i}) = g_{\{1,2\}}(\mathbf{i})$. Assuming P_1 is the outermost parameter, we obtain the value of α_2 from the single term that contains P_1, but not P_2: $g_{\{1\}}(\mathbf{i}) = f_0(\mathbf{i})\alpha_2 \Rightarrow \alpha_2 = g_{\{1\}}(\mathbf{i})/f_0(\mathbf{i}) = g_{\{1\}}(\mathbf{i})/g_{\{1,2\}}(\mathbf{i})$. Looking at the P_2 terms, we obtain the relation $g_{\{2\}}(\mathbf{i}) = f_0(\mathbf{i})\alpha_1 + f_1(\mathbf{i})$. This allows us to derive $f_1(\mathbf{i}) = g_{\{2\}}(\mathbf{i}) - f_0(\mathbf{i})\alpha_1 = g_{\{2\}}(\mathbf{i}) - g_{\{1,2\}}(\mathbf{i})\alpha_1$. Again, an expression containing α_1 as a free variable. To obtain $f_2(\mathbf{i})$ we look at the terms without any parameters. Here we have $g_{\emptyset}(\mathbf{i}) = f_0(\mathbf{i})\alpha_1\alpha_2 + f_1(\mathbf{i})\alpha_2 + f_2(\mathbf{i})$ from which we can derive $f_2(\mathbf{i}) = g_{\emptyset}(\mathbf{i}) - f_0(\mathbf{i})\alpha_1\alpha_2 - f_1(\mathbf{i})\alpha_2 = g_{\emptyset}(\mathbf{i}) - f_0(\mathbf{i})\alpha_1\alpha_2 - (g_{\{2\}}(\mathbf{i}) - f_0(\mathbf{i})\alpha_1)\alpha_2 = g_{\emptyset}(\mathbf{i}) - f_0(\mathbf{i})\alpha_1\alpha_2 - g_{\{2\}}(\mathbf{i})\alpha_2 + f_0(\mathbf{i})\alpha_1\alpha_2 = g_{\emptyset}(\mathbf{i}) - g_{\{2\}}(\mathbf{i})\alpha_2$. As α_1 cancels out, we can unambiguously derive $f_2(\mathbf{i})$. We can conclude that delinearizing to a three-dimensional array shape does not introduce more freedom. Only α_1 remains unknown and different values may need to be explored.

We now present with Algorithm 1 a general algorithm to delinearize polynomial expressions to array shapes of arbitrary dimensionality. We first collect the set of possible array size parameters and then try for each order to find a valid delinearization. To check if a valid delinearization exists, we first compute $f_0(\mathbf{i})$ and use it to try to derive a set of consistent α values. If we succeed, we derive subscript expressions and run-time conditions. In case the run-time condition is not a contradiction, we assume we found a

[1] This does not include shapes such as `A[][N+1][N+1]`

Algorithm 1: Derive a delinearization

Data: A polynomial expression in function of induction variables and parameters, a list of array size parameters
Result: A set of values $\alpha_k, k \in [1, d-1]$, index expressions $f_k, k \in [0, d-1]$ and set of array size parameters $P_k, k \in [1, d-1]$ or an error if no delinearization found.

```
collect possible array sizes parameters;
foreach permutation of array sizes parameters do
    derive f_0;
    alpha = derive alpha values;
    if alpha ≠ [ ] then
        derive subscript expressions;
        derive run-time condition;
        if run-time condition is a contradiction then
            continue;
        else
            return subscript expressions, run-time-condition,
                   array-sizes
return No delinearization found!
```

valid delinearization and finish, otherwise we try the next permutation. To obtain the set of possible array size parameters, we take the expanded version of the polynomial expression and look again for parameters that are multiplied with a loop induction variable.

For the remaining analysis it is necessary to understand the shape of the analyzed polynomial expression. Specifically, we must be able to group them in a manner that each term is the product between a subset of the assumed array size parameters and an expression $g_?(\mathbf{i})$ in loop indexes, non array-size parameters and integer constants:

$$
\begin{aligned}
g_{\emptyset}(\mathbf{i}) + \; & g_{\{1\}}(\mathbf{i})P_1 + g_{\{2\}}(\mathbf{i})P_2 + \cdots + g_{\{d-1\}}(\mathbf{i})P_{d-1} \\
& + g_{\{1,2\}}(\mathbf{i})P_1P_2 + g_{\{1,3\}}(\mathbf{i})P_1P_3 + \cdots + g_{\{2,3\}}(\mathbf{i})P_2P_3 + \ldots \\
& + g_{[1,d-1]}(\mathbf{i})P_1 \ldots P_{d-1} \\
& = \sum_{K \in \mathcal{P}([1,d-1])} \Big(g_K(\mathbf{i}) \prod_{k \in K} P_k \Big)
\end{aligned}
$$

We now want to express the previous polynomial as a d-dimensional access $A[f_0(\mathbf{i})] \ldots [f_{d-1}(\mathbf{i})]$ to an array of size $A[\,][P_1 + \alpha_1] \ldots [P_{d-1} + \alpha_{d-1}]$. To do so, look at how such an array is linearized:

$$
\begin{aligned}
& f_0(\mathbf{i})(P_1 + \alpha_1)(P_2 + \alpha_2) \ldots (P_{d-1} + \alpha_{d-1}) \\
& + f_1(\mathbf{i})(P_2 + \alpha_2) \ldots (P_{d-1} + \alpha_{d-1}) \\
+ \ldots \; & + f_{d-2}(\mathbf{i})(P_{d-1} + \alpha_{d-1}) \\
& + f_{d-1}(\mathbf{i}) \\
& = \sum_{j \in [0,d-1]} \Big(f_j(\mathbf{i}) \prod_{k \in [j+1,d-1]} (P_k + \alpha_k) \Big)
\end{aligned}
$$

and assume this linearized form yields the same access computation as the one-dimensional expression we want to delinearize:

$$
\begin{aligned}
\sum_{K \in \mathcal{P}([1,d-1])} \Big(g_K(\mathbf{i}) \prod_{k \in K} P_k \Big) &= \sum_{j \in [0,d-1]} \Big(f_j(\mathbf{i}) \prod_{k \in [j+1,d-1]} (P_k + \alpha_k) \Big) \\
&= \sum_{j \in [0,d-1]} \sum_{K \in \mathcal{P}([j+1,d-1])} \Big(f_j(\mathbf{i}) \prod_{k \in K} P_k \prod_{k \in [j+1,d-1] \setminus K} \alpha_k \Big)
\end{aligned}
$$

We now equate terms that contain the same set of parameters and, assuming the parameters to be positive, drop the common parameters on both sides. As a result, we obtain $\forall K \in \mathcal{P}([1, d-1])$:

$$
\begin{aligned}
\frac{g_S(\mathbf{i})}{g_T(\mathbf{i})} &= \frac{\sum\limits_{\substack{j \in [0,d-1] \\ \wedge S \subseteq [j+1,d-1]}} \Big(f_j(\mathbf{i}) \prod\limits_{x \in [j+1,d-1] \setminus S} \alpha_x \Big)}{\sum\limits_{\substack{j \in [0,d-1] \\ \wedge T \subseteq [j+1,d-1]}} \Big(f_j(\mathbf{i}) \prod\limits_{x \in [j+1,d-1] \setminus T} \alpha_x \Big)} = \frac{\sum\limits_{\substack{j \in [0,d-1] \\ \wedge S \subseteq [j+1,d-1]}} \Big(f_j(\mathbf{i}) \alpha_k \prod\limits_{x \in [j+1,d-1] \setminus T} \alpha_x \Big)}{\sum\limits_{\substack{j \in [0,d-1] \\ \wedge T \subseteq [j+1,d-1]}} \Big(f_j(\mathbf{i}) \prod\limits_{x \in [j+1,d-1] \setminus T} \alpha_x \Big)} \\
&= \frac{\alpha_k \cdot \sum\limits_{\substack{j \in [0,d-1] \\ \wedge S \subseteq [j+1,d-1]}} \Big(f_j(\mathbf{i}) \prod\limits_{x \in [j+1,d-1] \setminus T} \alpha_x \Big)}{\sum\limits_{\substack{j \in [0,d-1] \\ \wedge T \subseteq [j+1,d-1]}} \Big(f_j(\mathbf{i}) \prod\limits_{x \in [j+1,d-1] \setminus T} \alpha_x \Big)} = \frac{\alpha_k \cdot \sum\limits_{\substack{j \in [0,d-1] \\ \wedge T \subseteq [j+1,d-1]}} \Big(f_j(\mathbf{i}) \prod\limits_{x \in [j+1,d-1] \setminus T} \alpha_x \Big)}{\sum\limits_{\substack{j \in [0,d-1] \\ \wedge T \subseteq [j+1,d-1]}} \Big(f_j(\mathbf{i}) \prod\limits_{x \in [j+1,d-1] \setminus T} \alpha_x \Big)} \\
&= \alpha_k
\end{aligned}
$$

Figure 2: Deriving α_k

$$
g_K(\mathbf{i}) = \sum_{\substack{j \in [0,d-1] \\ \wedge K \subseteq [j+1,d-1]}} \Big(f_j(\mathbf{i}) \prod_{k \in [j+1,d-1] \setminus K} \alpha_k \Big)
$$

Having established this set of equalities, we start to relate our terms $g_?(\mathbf{i})$ to the terms $f_?(\mathbf{i})$ and $\alpha_?$ that we want to derive. We first derive $f_0(\mathbf{i}) = g_{[1,d-1]}(\mathbf{i})$, which can be trivially derived by setting $K = [1, d-1]$ in the previous equation.

Algorithm 2: Derive alpha values

Data: A dimensionality d, a set of expressions $g_s(\mathbf{i})$
Result: A list of values $\alpha_k, k \in [2, d-1]$ or [] in case of inconsistencies

```
foreach k ∈ [2, d-1] do
    if g_[1,d-1] not evenly divides g_[1,d-1]\{k}(i) then
        return [];
    α_k = g_[1,d-1]\{k}(i) / g_[1,d-1](i);
    foreach S ∈ P([2, k-1] \ (∅ ∪ ([1, d-1] \ {k}))) do
        if g_[1,d-1](i) not evenly divides S then
            return [];
        α'_k = g_S(i) / g_[1,d-1](i);
        if α'_k ≠ α_k then
            return [];
return {k → α_k : k ∈ [2, d-1]}
```

We derive the values α_k from the terms $g_{[1,d-1] \setminus \{k\}}(\mathbf{i})$. In the four-dimensional case such terms have the form:

$$
\begin{aligned}
g_{\{2,3,4\}}(\mathbf{i}) &= \alpha_1 f_0(\mathbf{i}) + f_1(\mathbf{i}) \\
g_{\{1,3,4\}}(\mathbf{i}) &= \alpha_2 f_0(\mathbf{i}) && \Rightarrow \alpha_2 = g_{\{1,3,4\}}(\mathbf{i}) / g_{[1,d-1]}(\mathbf{i}) \\
g_{\{1,2,4\}}(\mathbf{i}) &= \alpha_3 f_0(\mathbf{i}) && \Rightarrow \alpha_3 = g_{\{1,2,4\}}(\mathbf{i}) / g_{[1,d-1]}(\mathbf{i}) \\
g_{\{1,2,3\}}(\mathbf{i}) &= \alpha_4 f_0(\mathbf{i}) && \Rightarrow \alpha_4 = g_{\{1,2,3\}}(\mathbf{i}) / g_{[1,d-1]}(\mathbf{i})
\end{aligned}
$$

In general $\alpha_k, k \in [2, d-1]$ is $\alpha_k = g_{[1,d-1] \setminus \{k\}}(\mathbf{i}) / g_{[1,d-1]}(\mathbf{i})$. Similar to the two and three dimensional case, we cannot derive a value for α_1, as we do not know the value of $f_1(\mathbf{i})$. However, for higher dimensional cases we can make an interesting observation. The values of α_k can not just be obtained by the equalities presented above. In fact, there is a larger set of equalities that all need to return the same values α_k for an array view to be a valid delinearization. Specifically, to derive $\alpha_k, k \in [1, d-1]$ we can choose any pair of sets $(S, T), \emptyset \subset S \subseteq [1, k-1] \wedge T = S \cap \{k\}$ which can be used to compute α_k as shown in Figure 2. The following lists the closed form expressions that compute α_2 and α_3 for the 4D case:

$$\alpha_2 = g_{\{1,3\}}(\mathbf{i})/g_{\{1,2,3\}}(\mathbf{i}), \qquad \alpha_3 = g_{\{1\}}(\mathbf{i})/g_{\{1,3\}}(\mathbf{i})$$
$$\alpha_3 = g_{\{2\}}(\mathbf{i})/g_{\{2,3\}}(\mathbf{i}), \qquad \alpha_3 = g_{\{1,2\}}(\mathbf{i})/g_{\{1,2,3\}}(\mathbf{i})$$

We can see that α_3 can be derived in multiple ways. The delinearization is correct only if all yield the same result. By checking all of them and comparing them, we can validate the order of the array size parameters. Algorithm 2 gives the full algorithm used to obtain the different alpha values.

After deriving the different values of α_k, we can now derive the terms $f_j, j \in [2, d-1]$ by looking at the terms $g_{[j+1,d-1]}(\mathbf{i})$ (only interesting terms listed):

$$\begin{aligned}
g_{\{1,\ldots,d-1\}}(\mathbf{i}) &= f_0(\mathbf{i}) \\
g_{\{2,\ldots,d-1\}}(\mathbf{i}) &= \alpha_1 f_0(\mathbf{i}) + f_1(\mathbf{i}) \\
g_{\{3,\ldots,d-1\}}(\mathbf{i}) &= \alpha_1\alpha_2 f_0(\mathbf{i}) + \alpha_2 f_1(\mathbf{i}) + f_2(\mathbf{i}) \\
&= \alpha_2 g_{\{2,\ldots,d-1\}}(\mathbf{i}) + f_2(\mathbf{i}) \\
g_{\{j,\ldots,d-1\}}(\mathbf{i}) &= \alpha_{j-1} g_{\{j-1(\mathbf{i}),\ldots,d-1\}}(\mathbf{i}) + f_{j-1}(\mathbf{i}) \\
g_{\emptyset}(\mathbf{i}) &= \alpha_{d-1} g_{\{d-1\}}(\mathbf{i}) + f_{d-1}(\mathbf{i})
\end{aligned}$$

from which we derive $f_j(\mathbf{i}) = g_{[j+1,d-1]}(\mathbf{i}) - \alpha_j g_{[j,d-1]}(\mathbf{i})$. The general algorithm (Algorithm 3) is straightforward, as it mainly uses the equalities just given to derive the relevant values. As a last step, we obtain the set of necessary run-time conditions. This step is unchanged from Section 3.

Algorithm 3: Derive subscript expressions

Data: A dimensionality d, a set of expressions $g_s(\mathbf{i}), s \in \mathcal{P}([0, d-1])$, a set of values $\alpha_k, k \in [2, d-1]$
Result: A set of expressions $f_k(\mathbf{i}), k \in [0, d-1]$
$f_0(\mathbf{i}) = g_{[1,d-1]}(\mathbf{i})$;
`/* The next line assumes` $\alpha_1 = 0$. `*/`
$f_1(\mathbf{i}) = g_{2,d-1]}(\mathbf{i})$;
foreach $j \in [2, d-1]$ **do**
  $f_j(\mathbf{i}) = g_{[j+1,d-1]}(\mathbf{i}) - \alpha_j g_{[j,d-1]}(\mathbf{i})$
return $\{j \to f_j(\mathbf{i}) : j \in [0, d-1]\}$

5. EVALUATION

Essential parts of the presented approach have been implemented within LLVM and Polly [4]. In our implementation, LLVM's scalar evolution analysis has been used to perform the necessary transformations of index expressions, for example to extract the array size parameter candidates or to perform the division and remainder computations for obtaining subscript expressions. Besides basic delinearization support (Section 3.1), we also implemented support for array size parameters in the index expressions (Section 3.3), as well as support for deriving a unique array shape for a set of accesses (Section 3.2). We also have full support for the generation of run-time conditions that validate the delinearization. For the generation of run-time conditions, we rely on a new AST generator developed as part of isl [13] and use its support to generate AST expressions from user-provided integer sets. This feature allows us to use isl to compute the set of run-time constraints that need to be checked, the AST generator to generate optimal code for them, and Polly's code generation back-end to translate the resulting AST expressions to LLVM IR. One optimization that has shown to be useful for reducing the complexity of run-time conditions is to use isl to remove constraints that are only valid for parameter values for which no memory access is executed. This is obviously valid. In case no data access is executed, we cannot possibly model this access incorrectly. Finally, even though our implementation is reasonable robust, the delinearization problem itself is not always nicely exposed by LLVM. For example, sometimes LLVM can not prove that certain symbols are loop invariant, the use of different integer types causes type casts in subscript expressions or information about the absence of integer wrapping is not available. The manual modifications required to expose the delinearization problems will be stated for each experiment. We generally assume the absence of integer wrapping.

5.1 C99 arrays in PolyBench/C

We tested the implementation of the delinearization on all 30 PolyBench/C 3.2 kernels [11] with the use of C99 variable length arrays enabled (`-DPOLYBENCH_USE_C99_PROTO`). From the 30 kernels, Polly could correctly recover (after removal of ternary conditions and the use of 'long' to avoid spurious casts), the multi-dimensional view of arrays in 28 of them (Figure 3b). Two kernels (ludcmp, fdtd-apml) are currently skipped, due to the array size itself being of the form $N+1$. However, with both of these kernels, using either two dimensional arrays or arrays with different parameters in each size declaration, the approach proposed in Section 4 is applicable and would allow us to extend Polly to handle these cases as well. It is also interesting to note that the PolyBench/C code is written in a way that almost all delinearizations are statically provable. Nevertheless, our delinearization concluded that run-time checks are necessary for six benchmarks (correlation, covariance, 2mm, doitgen, symm, and reg_detect). On looking closer as to why run-time checks are still generated, we understand that for the first five benchmarks in the original PolyBench/C source code certain parameters have been accidentally swapped in the array declarations and loop bounds. This unintentionally changed the semantics of the loop kernels in a way that only if a certain relation between the different parameter holds (e.g., the matrices are square), the execution does not inhibit out-of-bound accesses. The run-time conditions computed directly reflect those conditions and ensure that only in such cases the optimized loop is used. For the last benchmark, reg_detect, a condition $length > 0$ is derived which is required as `S2` will access negative locations in the innermost dimension in case `length` is smaller or equal to zero. This is visible in Listing 8. Even though not foreseen, these examples show the benefits of the approach to delinearization. Not only did it prevent a possible mis-compilation, but it also ensured that we could still optimize it even though there exists a set of parameter values under which this optimization is not correct.

```
    for (j = 0; j <= n - 1; j++)
      for (i = j; i <= n - 1; i++) {
S0:       sum_diff[j][i][0] = ...
          for (cnt = 1; cnt <= length - 1; cnt++)
S1:            sum_diff[j][i][cnt] = ...
S2:         ... = sum_diff[j][i][length - 1];
      }
```

Listing 8: PolyBench/C's reg_detect requires length > 0.

To understand if the more precise access information enables additional compiler transformations we optimized the PolyBench/C test suite with 'clang -O3', 'clang -O3 -polly', and 'clang -O3 -polly -delinearize' and run the resulting binaries single-threaded on an Intel Xeon E5430 CPU. The results in Figure 3a show that delinearization has a very visible impact on performance. Several benchmarks show speedups of 5.0x and beyond, but we also see for trmm and floyd-warshall significant performance reductions due to additional loop transformations that became legal, but that have been poorly chosen by Polly. ludcmp and fdtd-apml, the benchmarks where we do not yet delinearize the kernels, do not show any performance impact. Also, benchmarks with run time checks, e.g., covariance and 2mm, show visible performance changes, which means their run-time check is evaluated to true. There is also a set of kernels that do not see performance changes. In general this is because Polly's current set of optimizations do not affect any of these kernels.

5.2 C++ template libraries – boost::ublas

We also evaluated our approach in the context of C++ template libraries. C++ template libraries are widely used to raise the level of abstraction in programming, but at the same time they make it a lot harder to gather information about the execution of a program via analysis of the source code. In general, heavy inlining is required to remove C++ iterators, virtual method calls as well as other tools of abstraction. Only after these have been removed can a compiler possibly understand the memory access pattern of a program. However, at this point of the compilation, high level information about the original array shapes is not available any more.

For our evaluation we have chosen boost::ublas, a C++ template library for dense, packed, and sparse matrices that uses efficient code generation via expression templates to avoid unnecessary memory and object allocation. For our evaluation, we implemented a simple dgemm kernel in boost::ublas and compiled it in production mode `-DNDEBUG -DBOOST_UBLAS_NDEBUG` and without exceptions to evaluate how different compilers can optimize this code. We considered gcc 4.8.3, icc 15.0 and clang+Polly pre-3.6 (r226126) and run our experiment on an Intel i7-3520M. For Polly we ensured the inliner is run *before* Polly is executed and we manually performed some simple manual LICM to expose the delinearization problem. As visible in Figure 3c, the binaries produced by the different compilers all run in 2.2 seconds. With Polly and our delinearization approach enabled, we achieve a speedup of 1.8x, just by applying some simple cache tiling.

5.3 Julia

We also considered Julia [1], a dynamic high-level language for scientific computing. One specialty of Julia is that it is very easy to write generic code that can be specialized for different data types. We used this feature to evaluate our approach on different data types, again using a gemm kernel as the computational pattern. As with the ublas example, after some simple loop-invariant code motion is performed manually, delinearizing the array accesses yields the expected results, run-time checks are emitted (and required) and the Julia kernel can be optimized with Polly. For matrices of size 1024×1024, Polly's default optimizations (mainly loop tiling) already give speedups from 3.5x–5.0x across all different data types, compared to compilation without delinearization, where Polly is not able to apply any transformation. Even though Julia's performance is still far from a tuned library such as ATLAS, reaching reasonable performance also for data-types that commonly lack specialized blas libraries is valuable. As arrays in Julia are commonly of parametric size, understanding their structure at the IR level is essential to enable a wide range of loop optimizations.

5.4 UTDSP

The UTDSP [6] benchmark evaluates the ability of C compilers to generate efficient code for kernels and applications from the digital signal processing domain. UTDSP provides each kernel in multiple versions, including versions that are specialized for a specific input size by relying on fixed-size multi-dimensional arrays and versions relying on pointer arithmetic, which could conceptually support inputs of varying size. To evaluate the delinearization algorithm, we modified the UTDSP edge detection benchmark to take problem sizes as command line arguments and use these sizes to both dynamically allocate the data arrays and to provide parametric bounds for the computation. In addition, we also replaced a scalar summation variable with a direct summation into the output image to remove spurious scalar dependences that can complicate later optimizations. We also ensured consistent use of 64-bit integer types to avoid complications due to sign-extensions and truncations.

Listing 9 shows the core loop of the UTDSP edge detection kernel used for our evaluation. The loop implements a generic convolution, that is executed three times. First, a Gaussian convolution is performed to smoothen the image; then, both a horizontal and a vertical Sobel filter are applied. When analyzing the kernel with Polly, three interesting compute statements are detected. They have been marked as `S0`, `S1` and `S2`. When recovering the data accesses in these statements without using our delinearization approach, the repeating addition of `NN` into the pointer variables yields access functions that contain products between the parameter `NN` and (virtual) loop induction variables. Such non-affine functions prevent precise dependence analysis and parallelism detection.

Using our delinearization approach, we recognize the variables `output_image`, `input_image` and `kernel` as base pointers of two dimensional array accesses. This allows us to derive the following, possibly multi-dimensional, but always affine access functions:

$$\begin{aligned}
S_0(r,c) &\rightarrow_{\text{write}} \text{output_image}(\text{dead_rows}+r, \text{dead_cols}+c)\\
S_1(r,c,i,j) &\rightarrow_{\text{dead}} \text{output_image}(\text{dead_rows}+r, \text{dead_cols}+c)\\
S_1(r,c,i,j) &\rightarrow_{\text{write}} \text{output_image}(\text{dead_rows}+r, \text{dead_cols}+c)\\
S_1(r,c,i,j) &\rightarrow_{\text{dead}} \text{input_image}(r+i, c+j)\\
S_1(r,c,i,j) &\rightarrow_{\text{dead}} \text{kernel}(i,j)\\
S_2(r,c) &\rightarrow_{\text{dead}} \text{output_image}(\text{dead_rows}+r, \text{dead_cols}+c)\\
S_2(r,c) &\rightarrow_{\text{write}} \text{output_image}(\text{dead_rows}+r, \text{dead_cols}+c)\\
S_2(r,c) &\rightarrow_{\text{dead}} \text{normal_factor}()
\end{aligned}$$

We compiled the kernel with gcc 4.8.3, clang+Polly pre-3.6 (r226126) and icc 15.0. Using the flags `-O3` alone and in combination with automatic parallelization (`-ftree-parallelize-loops=2` (gcc), `-polly-parallel -lgomp` (clang + Polly) or `-parallel` (icc)) we automatically optimized and parallelized the code. Executing the benchmark on an Intel i7-3520M dual core system using an array of size 4096×4096 with a convolution kernel of size 3×3, we obtain the results shown in Figure 3e.

We can see that neither icc nor gcc is able to automatically parallelize the loop. Clang itself does not have any automatic parallelization facilities. However, in combination with Polly and our improved analysis, the loop nest is successfully parallelized and the execution time is reduced by 50%, now outperforming both icc and gcc. When optimizing the code in Listing 9, Polly generates the following run-time check:

$$KK \geq NN+1 \vee (NN \geq KK \wedge KK \geq \text{dead\_cols}+1 \wedge \text{dead\_cols} \geq 0)$$

The first condition under which the delinearization is valid is $KK \geq NN+1$. This is trivially true. If this condition is false, then the loop nest is not entered at all and there is consequently no access that can be out-of-bounds. The second condition verifies the validity of the delinearization in case the loop is actually executed. Theoretically, the source code shown provides enough information to statically prove the validity of the delinearization for all input values. However, LLVM's scalar evolution analysis does not support signed divisions, which prevents Polly from understanding that

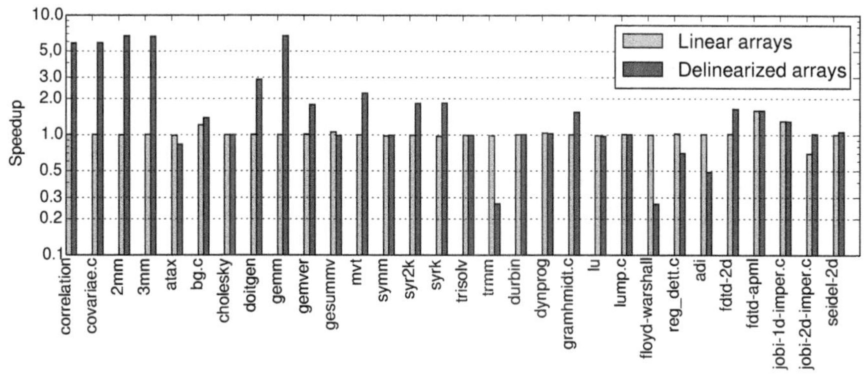

(a) PolyBench/C – Speedup of Polly over 'clang -O3' using linear and delinearized arrays

Name	correlation	covariance	2mm	3mm	atax	bicg	cholesky	doitgen	gemm	gemver	gesummv	mvt	symm	syr2k	syrk
Parameter in subscript	+														
Run-time checks	+	+	+					+					+		
# 3D arrays								2							
# 2D arrays	2	2	5	7	1	1	1	1	3	1	2	1	3	3	2
# 1D arrays	2	1			3	4	13			8	3	4	5		

Name	trisolv	trmm	durbin	dynprog	gramschmidt	lu	ludcmp	floyd-warshall	reg_detect	adi	fdtd-2d	fdtd-apml	jacobi-1d-imper	jacobi-2d-imper	seidel-2d
Parameter in subscript			+	+				+		+					
Run-time checks									+						
# 3D arrays				1					2						
# 2D arrays	1	2	2	2	3	1		1	3	3	3			2	1
# 1D arrays	8		4	4	5						1		2		

(b) PolyBench/C – Statistics about the delinearized array views

Compiler	linear	delin.	Speedup
icc	2.2	-	-
gcc	2.2	-	-
clang	2.2	-	-
Polly	2.2	**1.2**	**1.8x**

(c) Run time [s] of dgemm written in boost::ublas

Type	linear	delin.	Speedup
single float	13	**3**	**4.3x**
double float	14	**3**	**4.6x**
i16	7	**2**	**3.5x**
i32	13	**3**	**4.3x**
i64	15	**3**	**5.0x**
i128	22	**5**	**4.4x**

(d) Run time [s] of different Julia gemm kernels

Compiler	O3	parallel	Speedup
icc	1.4	1.4	1.0x
gcc	1.0	1.0	1.0x
clang	1.4	-	-
Polly	1.4	**0.7**	**2.0x**

(e) Run time [s] of UTDSP edge detection kernel

Compiler	O3	parallel (2/4/8)	Speedup
icc	2.5	2.5/2.5/2.5	1.0x
gcc	2.5	2.5/2.5/2.5	1.0x
clang	2.5	-	-
Polly	2.5	1.6/1.4/1.4	**1.6/1.8/1.8x**

(f) Run time [s] of MATLAB convolution kernel

Figure 3: Experimental Results

dead_cols = KK/2 holds; consequently, there is insufficient static information available to Polly to derive the validity of the delinearization. However, as our approach is optimistic, Polly emits run-time checks that still allow it to optimize the program. The basic validity conditions Polly derives require dead_cols to be positive and strictly smaller than KK, a condition that always holds for dead_cols = KK/2. Overall, we see that for the UTDSP edge detection benchmark our delinearization approach has enabled a complex transformation that showed significant speedups compared to use of competing production quality compilers. Even though shortcomings in LLVM's scalar evolution would have hindered a statically proven delinearization, our optimistic approach enabled us to verify the needed optimization at run-time.

5.5 MATLAB

MATLAB [9] is a high-level language primarily focused on numerical computations, and is widely used for signal and image processing, communications, control systems and computational finance. Besides directly executing the developed programs within MATLAB, MATLAB provides a facility, called MATLAB Coder, that allows the generation of independent C and C++ programs from an algorithm implemented in MATLAB.

To evaluate our work we use a simple convolution kernel implemented in MATLAB. Even though the original MATLAB code consists of a single call to a built-in function, the derived C code consists of more than 100 lines of comment-free auto-generated program code and includes four loop levels that use pointer addressing to model the multi-dimensional arrays. For reasons of brevity we cannot present the full loop nest, but present in Listing 10 the struct definition used to model the multi-dimensional arrays. As we can see, arrays in MATLAB use a manually implemented multi-dimensional array of parametric size, where accesses use a base pointer in combination with a possibly polynomial offset, requiring delinearization to perform precise dependence analysis.

For our evaluation we use the MATLAB generated C code, which is in its structure more complicated than the UTDSP code. Hence, we first perform some simplifications to ensure compilers are able to address the delinearization problem. This includes loop invariant code motion to avoid `Array->size[0]` style loads in the core loop, the removal of one unnecessary maximum computation in the access function, the consistent use of 64 bit integer types and the simplification of an if-condition.

We then compile the canonicalized C code with gcc 4.8.3, icc 15.0 and clang 3.6 pre (+ Polly) using '-O3' as well as automatic parallelization capabilities. The resulting binary, performs a 3x3 convolution on a 4096×4096 floating point matrix repeating it 5 times. The results (median over 5 runs) for running on an 8-core Intel Xeon E5430 CPU are shown in Figure 3f. We can see that if compiled sequentially, there is no performance difference with the different compilers. However, when generating parallel code, our delinearization algorithm has been able to recover the multi-dimensionality of the array and generated relevant run-time checks that allow the verification of the delinearization. Using this information Polly was able to compute precise data-dependences that prove that executing the loop nest in parallel is correct. Parallel execution reduces the execution time of the correlation kernel from 2.5 to 1.4 seconds and yields a 1.6 to 1.8x speedup. Even though we see improving performance due to parallel execution only for

```
dead_rows = KK / 2; dead_cols = KK / 2;
...
row = 0;
output_image_ptr = output_image;
output_image_ptr += (NN * dead_rows);
for (r = 0; r < NN - KK + 1; r++) {
  output_image_offset = output_image_ptr;
  output_image_offset += dead_cols;
  col = 0;
  for (c = 0; c < NN - KK + 1; c++) {
    input_image_ptr = input_image;
    input_image_ptr += (NN * row);
    kernel_ptr = kernel;
S0:    *output_image_offset = 0;
    for (i = 0; i < KK; i++) {
      input_image_offset = input_image_ptr;
      input_image_offset += col;
      kernel_offset = kernel_ptr;
      for (j = 0; j < KK; j++) {
S1:        temp1 = *input_image_offset++;
S1:        temp2 = *kernel_offset++;
S1:        *output_image_offset += temp1 * temp2;
      }
      kernel_ptr += KK; input_image_ptr += NN;
    }
S2:    *output_image_offset =
        ((*output_image_offset)/ normal_factor);
    output_image_offset++; col++;
  }
  output_image_ptr += NN; row++;
}
```

Listing 9: Core loop nest in UTDSP edge detection benchmark

```
struct emxArray_real_T {
    double *data; long *size; long allocatedSize;
    long numDimensions; boolean_T canFreeData;
};
```

Listing 10: MATLAB multi-dimensional array declaration

up to 4-cores, the analysis and transformation capabilities enabled by our delinearization will prove useful for future optimizations.

6. RELATED WORK

There have been previous efforts at delinearization, starting with the work of Maslov [7], who introduced delinearization to speed up dependence analysis for arrays of fixed size and also briefly discussed non-linear references arising from arrays of symbolic size. He required iteration spaces of rectangular shape, along with sufficient information to statically validate the delinearization. Loop induction variables can only appear in at most one dimension of a recovered array access. Maslov contributed a second approach in his work on polynomial constraint simplification [8], where delinearization in the context of triangular iteration spaces and possibly non-rectangular (triangular) arrays is discussed, but most of the other previously mentioned restrictions still apply. Simbürger and Größlinger [12] recently addressed delinearization in the context of Polly. Their approach is specific to dependence analysis and does not recover array sizes or even array subscripts. The use of advanced mathematical tools such as quantifier elimination techniques makes it hard to incorporate their techniques into a production compiler. Cierniak [2] presented a solution independent of dependence analysis, discussed delinearization for non-rectangular arrays and also provided on ideas how to unify the delinearization of multiple subscripts. He did not discuss a symbolic solution and he required each loop index to appear in index expressions of most one array dimension.

7. CONCLUSION

We have developed an approach to recovering a multi-dimensional array view from single-dimensional polynomial array access expressions. Multi-dimensional array shapes with sizes given as individual parameters, parameters times a constant, or parameters plus a constant are handled, with the first two cases also supporting the use of identical parameters for extents along multiple dimensions. Our approach can recover the multi-dimensional view for array accesses even in those cases where we cannot prove the validity statically. Instead, we provide a set of conditions that can be used to verify the validity of the multi-dimensional view at run-time. The approach has been partially implemented in the context of LLVM and Polly and this implementation has been used to evaluate the approach on kernels from Julia, blast::ublas, PolyBench/C, UTDSPs and MATLAB. With our optimistic approach to delinearization, we have been able to recover the multi-dimensional structure of data accesses in all these contexts and we have shown that the resulting increase in dependence analysis precision can *enable* large speedups. We have observed several kernels with more than 5.0x speedup compared to Clang, large improvements compared to the Julia compiler, and 1.8x improvement on the sequential execution of a standard dgemm kernel over icc. The new support for analysis of parametrically sized arrays significantly widens the set of compute kernels for which precise data dependences can be computed, thereby enabling much greater opportunities for application of optimizing transformations.

Acknowledgments

The LLVM community and especially Hal Finkel, Armin Größlinger and Andrew Trick provided important inputs. We received funding from Google Europe (Fellowship of Efficient Computing), Swissuniversities (Platform for Advanced Computing Initiative), the U.S. National Science Foundation (0811457, 0926127, 0926687, 1059417, 1321147 and 1440749), the U.S. Department of Energy (DE-SC0012489) and the Louisiana State University.

8. REFERENCES

[1] J. Bezanson, S. Karpinski, V. B. Shah, and A. Edelman. Julia: A fast dynamic language for technical computing. *CoRR*, abs/1209.5145, 2012.

[2] M. Cierniak and W. Li. Recovering logical data and code structures. Technical report, 1995.

[3] P. Feautrier. Dataflow analysis of array and scalar references. *International Journal of Parallel Programming*, 20(1):23–53, 1991.

[4] T. Grosser, A. Größlinger, and C. Lengauer. Polly – performing polyhedral optimizations on a low-level intermediate representation. *Parallel Processing Letters (PPL)*, 22(04), 2012.

[5] C. Lattner and V. Adve. LLVM: A compilation framework for lifelong program analysis & transformation. In *Int. Symp. on Code Generation and Optimization (CGO)*, 2004.

[6] C. Lee and M. Stoodley. Utdsp benchmark suite, 1998.

[7] V. Maslov. Delinearization: An efficient way to break multiloop dependence equations. *SIGPLAN Not.*, 27(7):152–161, July 1992.

[8] V. Maslov and W. Pugh. Simplifying polynomial constraints over integers to make dependence analysis more precise. In *Int. Conf. on Parallel and Vector Processing*, 1994.

[9] MATLAB. *version 8.4.0150421 (R2014b)*. The MathWorks Inc., Natick, Massachusetts, 2014.

[10] S. Pop, A. Cohen, and G.-A. Silber. Induction variable analysis with delayed abstractions. In *High Performance Embedded Architectures and Compilers*, pages 218–232. Springer, 2005.

[11] L.-N. Pouchet. PolyBench/C 3.2. `http://sourceforge.net/projects/polybench/`.

[12] A. Simbürger and A. Größlinger. On the variety of static control parts in real-world programs: from affine via multi-dimensional to polynomial and just-in-time. In *Proc. of the 4th Inter. Workshop on Polyhedral Compilation Techniques*, Vienna, Austria, Jan. 2014.

[13] S. Verdoolaege. isl: An integer set library for the polyhedral model. In *Mathematical Software (ICMS'10)*, LNCS 6327, 2010.

DASX: Hardware Accelerator for Software Data Structures

Snehasish Kumar, Naveen Vedula, Arrvindh Shriraman and Vijayalakshmi Srinivasan†
School of Computing Science, Simon Fraser University and †IBM Research
{ska124, nvedula, ashriram}@sfu.ca and viji@us.ibm.com

ABSTRACT

Recent research [3, 37, 38] has proposed compute accelerators to address the energy efficiency challenge. While these compute accelerators specialize and improve the compute efficiency, they have tended to rely on address-based load/store memory interfaces that closely resemble a traditional processor core. The address-based load-/store interface is particularly challenging in data-centric applications that tend to access different software data structures. While accelerators optimize the compute section, the address-based interface leads to wasteful instructions and low memory level parallelism (MLP). We study the benefits of raising the abstraction of the memory interface to data structures.

We propose DASX (Data Structure Accelerator), a specialized state machine for data fetch that enables compute accelerators to efficiently access data structure elements in iterative program regions. DASX enables the compute accelerators to employ data structure based memory operations and relieves the compute unit from having to generate addresses for each individual object. DASX exploits knowledge of the program's iteration to i) run ahead of the compute units and gather data objects for the compute unit (i.e., compute unit memory operations do not encounter cache misses) and ii) throttle the fetch rate, adaptively tile the dataset based on the locality characteristics and guarantee cache residency. We demonstrate accelerators for three types of data structures, Vector, Key-Value (Hash) maps, and BTrees. We demonstrate the benefits of DASX on data-centric applications which have varied compute kernels but access few regular data structures. DASX achieves higher energy efficiency by eliminating data structure instructions and enabling energy efficient compute accelerators to efficiently access the data elements. We demonstrate that DASX can achieve 4.4× the performance of a multicore system by discovering more parallelism from the data structure.

1. Introduction

Accelerators are gaining importance as energy-efficient computational units due to the breakdown of Dennard scaling. However, these accelerators continue to rely on traditional load/store interfaces to access data. For example, recent proposals that advocate specialization (e.g., Conservation cores [38] and Dyser [3]), as well as past work in kilo-instruction processors [32] have all had to contend with power hungry load/store units [33]. Even large (e.g., 256 entry) load/store queues can sustain only a few (10s of) cache refills [33] which falls short of the requirements for kernels that stream over large data structures. A promising avenue of research is to improve the efficiency of data accesses via hardware acceleration using techniques such as specialized ISA extensions [40], and customized hardware (e.g., SQL-like language constructs [12] and hash lookups [19]).

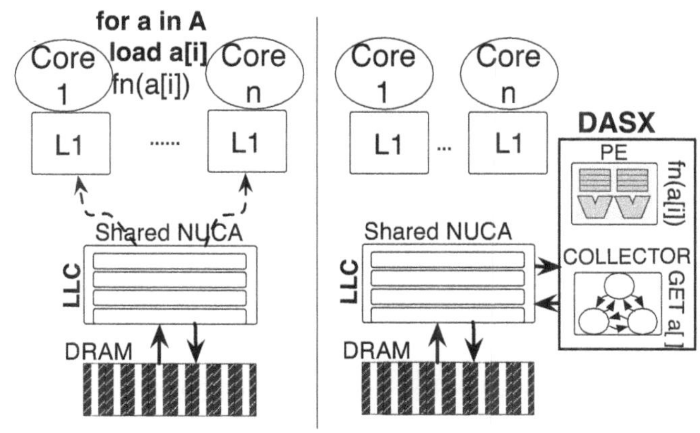

Left: Multicore processor. Right: DASX integrated with the shared LLC (NUCA tiles not shown). In multicore, instruction regions show instructions eliminated by DASX. Broken lines indicate data transfers eliminated by DASX.

Figure 1: DASX Overview. Accelerating an iterative computation on an array.

A key application domain seeking to use compute accelerators are data centric applications that perform iterative computation over large data structures [30]. Unfortunately, the conventional address-based load/store interface does not scale to exploit the available memory bandwidth and expends significant energy on instructions required to fetch the objects from within the data structure. The main benefits of parallelizing datacentric applications come from fetching multiple data objects simultaneously and hiding long memory latencies. Parallelization with threads can increase the number of memory accesses issued and improve the MLP, however as our evaluation shows, increasing MLP (memory-level-parallelism) using the same thread as the compute kernel is energy inefficient.

Our work makes the key observation that by raising the abstraction of the memory interface from addresses to object indices (or keys), we can enable a high performance (i.e., more MLP) and energy efficient data-structure specific memory interface for compute acceler-

ICS'15, June 8–11, 2015, Newport Beach, CA, USA.

DOI: http://dx.doi.org/10.1145/2751205.2751231.

ators. We propose DASX (Data Structure Accelerator), a hardware accelerator that integrates with the LLC and enables energy-efficient iterative computation on data structures (see Figure 1). Supporting iterative computation requires DASX to adapt to the locality requirements of the compute kernel and effectively supply data as the compute kernel streams over the entire dataset. Inspired by the decoupled access-execute paradigm [36], DASX partitions iterative computation on data structures into two regions: the data collection and the compute kernel. Figure 1 illustrates an example of an iterative computation on an array. Since DASX removes the data structure instructions from the compute kernel, it also eliminates complex address generation logic from the compute unit which instead interfaces with memory by issuing loads and stores to object keys (unique identifiers for each object). It uses specialized hardware to translate object keys to memory addresses, and issue the requests.

DASX relies on the observation that the MLP available in data structures is independent of ILP and TLP limitations. DASX employs a novel data structure-specific controller (Collector) to traverse the data structure, mine the MLP, and stage the corresponding cache lines in the LLC until the compute unit consumes the data. In this paper, our compute unit is a PE (processing element) array, a set of light-weight in-order cores that execute data parallel loop iterations. The PEs operate on the data objects in the Obj-Store supplied by the Collector and do *not* generate addresses. DASX is aware of the compute iterations and appropriately tiles the data to fit in the LLC to prevent thrashing. The Collector is aware of the organization of the data structure and runs ahead of the compute kernel so as to prefetch the objects to hide memory latency. Overall, DASX eliminates the instructions required for the data structure accesses (bold instructions in Figure 1), eliminates data structure transfers over the cache hierarchy (broken lines in Figure 1), and runs the compute kernel on the lightweight PE.

We evaluate DASX using a variety of algorithms spanning text processing, machine learning and data analytics, and accelerate three types of data structures: Vector, Hash Table, and a BTree. Relative to a multicore system (2 cores, 4 threads per core), DASX improves performance by 4.4×, reduces core energy consumption by 27× and reduces cache hierarchy energy by 7×. Overall, DASX has the potential to improve the efficiency of language-level data structures and idioms such as *list* and *map* by exploiting the parallelism implicit in the data structures that is often lost in the implementation due to the address-based memory interface of the processor core that requires many instructions to fetch a single object. Our contributions are:

- DASX exposes MLP available in data structures and uses specialized hardware, the Collector, to access data using object keys. Other specialized programmable co-processor [3, 18, 37, 38] approaches can also use the Collector to achieve high MLP and energy efficiency.
- DASX targets iterative computation and leverages data structure-awareness to run far ahead of the compute kernel and prefetches data to improve performance.
- DASX exploits information about compute iterations to guarantee that the data is cache-resident until the kernel finishes processing and efficiently drives the compute kernel based on the presence of data in the cache.

2. Background and Motivation

In this section we discuss the overheads associated with software data structures using *Blackscholes* [5] with unit stride vectors as an example. Figure 2 illustrates the compute kernel from *Blackscholes*.

```
Params: Spot[], strike[], rate[], volatility[], time[], type[]
        are vectors of length nOptions.
compute_d1(),compute_d2() are re-entrant. Loop is data parallel.
for i:= 0 to nOptions do
  d1 = compute_d1(volatility[i],time[i],spot[i],strike[i],rate[i]);
  d2 = compute_d2(volatility[i],time[i]);
  prices[i] = CNF(d1)*spot[i]-CNF(d2)*strike[i] *exp(-rate[i]*time[i])
end for
```

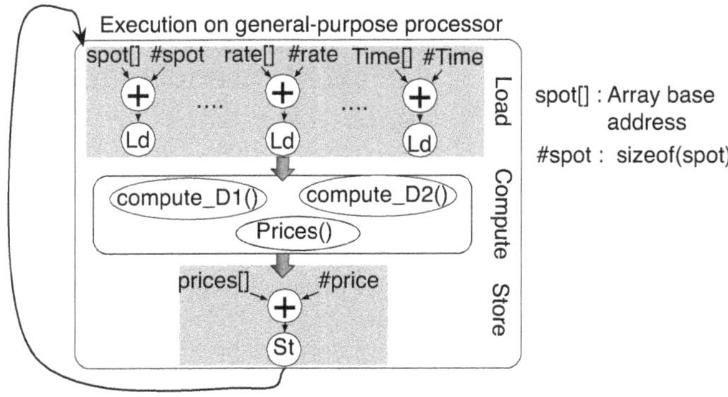

Figure 2: *Blackscholes* [5] Kernel.

The program kernel reads in a list of *"options"* data stored across six C++ STL vectors (`spot[], strike[], rate[], volatility[ time[], and type[]`) and calculates the pricing (`prices[]`). Note that the use of vector data structures gives rise to easily accessible MLP, but the compute kernel itself could include dependencies that limit parallelization and SIMDization. Figure 2 also shows the execution on a typical general-purpose processor. Every iteration requires 6 `add` and 6 `load` instructions (for generating the load slice), and 1 `add` and 1 `store` instruction. As the compute kernel streams over the 6 data structures it is also imperative to ensure that i) the elements are fetched into the cache ahead of the iteration that needs them and ii) the elements continue to reside in the cache until the corresponding iteration finishes processing them. The former requires the processor to aggressively fetch data into the caches while the latter requires the processor to fetch conservatively so as to not thrash the caches. Finally, the memory interface needs to be flexible to enable access to multiple independent data structures (6 read-only data structures and 1 read/write) and possibly multiple elements from the same data structure. The energy inefficiencies of general-purpose processor tend to be more acute with complex key-value based hash tables and pointer- based trees/graphs. Even a simple strided iteration incurs significant address generation overheads.

Benchmark	% Time	% DS Ins.	% INT	% BR	% MEM
Blackscholes	99.7	9	13.3	13.5	26.6
Recomm.	44.6	65.9	26.9	6.4	51.9
2D-Datacube	34.1	14.3	32.8	12.3	54.7
Text Search	64.7	30.9	32.6	14.1	53.1
Hash Table	25.9	34.7	34.1	17.0	48.7
BTree	100	63.7	32.7	15.7	51.5

Table 1: Data structure usage in Data-centric Applications

Table 1 shows the % execution time, % data structure instructions and the breakdown of instructions[1] in the benchmarks. Overall in our application suite, between 25—100% of the time is spent in operations iterating over the data structures. The number of instruc-

[1]We used gcc -O0 optimization to enable us to identify STL library calls in the binary and use pintool to profile. Our performance evaluation builds with -O2.

tions spent on data structures can be significant (up to 66% in *Recommender*) and contribute to dynamic power consumption. In data structures such as *HashTable* and *BTree*, the value of the data element determines the control flow and involves many branches (15.7%-17% of total instructions). Condition checks can constitute up to a 2× overhead in data traversals [27]. Additionally, compute kernels in different applications may exhibit significant diversity in temporal and spatial locality even when accessing the same type of data structure (e.g, vector) which requires the data structure accesses to be carefully managed to ensure optimal cache behaviour. The parallelism available from the data structure can differ from the parallelism available in compute kernel. Consider a reduction operation ($\Sigma_{i=1}^{N} A[i]$), even though the compute region's parallelism is limited, the data structure itself is embarrassingly parallel and exploiting the available MLP will improve overall speedup. To summarize:

- Programs may spend significant time performing iterative computations on data structures. Overall, removing the data structure instructions will improve energy efficiency.
- Even if compute parallelism is limited(e.g. reduction), we can exploit the MLP to reduce the average memory access latency and improve performance. We need to develop scalable energy efficient techniques to extract the available MLP.
- The implementation of the memory interface needs to be flexible and adapt to compute kernels with varied temporal and spatial locality.

3. DASX: Data Structure Accelerator

DASX consists of two components (Figure 3): i) An array of processing elements (PEs), each PE is an in-order core running the compute kernel (§ 3.1) and ii) a data-structure specific refill engine, the Collector (§ 3.2). The PEs only access data elements using data structure based memory operations. The PEs share a common object cache, Obj-Store. The Obj-Store (object-cache) holds the data elements needed to execute and is explicitly managed by the Collector which ensures the data structure memory operations do not miss in the Obj-Store. The Collector translates object keys to address locations and manages data fetches needed by the compute kernel. The PEs do not perform address generation and do not require miss-handling logic. We begin with a description of the data structure memory operations to help the reader understand the design requirements of the Collector.

3.1 Processing Elements

Table 2: Special instructions and registers

Special Registers		
%CUR	contains the compute cursor (the loop trip count)	
%BAR	synchronization barrier across PE array	
Special Instructions		
Type	Instruction	Description
Mem	LD [Key],%R	load key from Obj-Store.
	ST [Key],%R	store key from Obj-Store.
Loop	NEXT	Advance cursor and trigger a refill of the Obj-Store.

The PE array consists of a set of light-weight 32 bit in-order, 4-stage integer/floating-point pipelines. All the execution pipelines share both the front-end instruction buffer (256 entries) and the back-end Obj-Store. The memory operations only access the data in the Obj-Store which is loaded in bulk by the Collector. Each execution pipeline has 32 integer and 32 floating point registers. Within our framework each PE's pipeline runs an instance of the compute kernel; most importantly each PE has its own PC and is capable of taking a different branch path within the iteration. Table 2 shows the special instructions added to support DASX. The load and store operations access data structures using a unique identifier (the key) and the PE's cursor indicates the loop trip count of the compute kernel. All PEs sync up at a barrier after performing the set of iterations statically assigned to the PE array. The PEs do not communicate with each other except via loads/stores to the data structure. The number of execution pipelines depends on the bandwidth of the shared front end and Obj-Store; with the MLP extracted by the Collectors, we find that limited compute parallelism(4—8 PEs) is sufficient (see § 4.5). The key to DASX's performance improvement is the MLP exploitation using the Collector.

Key-based loads and stores (PE↔Memory interface)

DASX raises the abstraction of the memory interface from addresses and the compute PE accesses elements in the data structure through *keys*. The *key* is an index to identify a particular element in the data structure. A unique key value is associated with every element in the data structure. Some of the key values may be implicit (e.g., array index) while others may be explicit (e.g., hash table). The unique identification provides a name space with which the compute units can indicate the load/store slices to the Collector. With containers such as arrays/vectors, *key* refers to the index of the element. For a hash table, *key* refers to the search key and with structures like the BTree, the *key* is a unique integer. All the address generation logic is centralized in the Collector and is data-structure specific. Using keys to access data elements allows DASX to eliminate data structure instruction, specialize the address generation logic to reduce overhead and extract memory level parallelism implicit in the data structure. Further benefits include the ability for DASX to coalesce and amortize the cost of address generation and virtual-to-physical translation for multiple objects in the same data structure. The key-based memory operations access data from the Obj-Store.

Obj-Store

The Obj-Store shared between the PEs serves as a data store for elements from the data structure. The PE accesses the Obj-Store using key-based memory instructions. When starting a set of iterations the Collector performs a bulk refill of the Obj-Store. The Obj-Store does *not* encounter misses and is explicitly managed by the Collector. The main utility of the Obj-Store is to provide a flexible interface to access the data structure elements without requiring the PEs to generate addresses. In addition, the Obj-Store also captures the locality within an iteration and filters small width (4-byte) accesses from the LLC to save energy. Obj-Store is organized as a fully associative decoupled sector-cache [34] with a sector size of 4 bytes (8 sectors/line) [24] and 32 tag entries (Figure 4). The decoupled sector organization provides the following benefits : i) by varying the number of sectors allocated data objects of varying length are supported ii) the small sector sizes (4 bytes) support structures of primitive type (e.g., array of floats), iii) tag overhead is minimized. The tag stores the Collector id dedicated to the data structure and up to 8 adjacent keys. When the compute iteration completes execution, the Obj-Store flushes the dirty objects back to the LLC triggering any required coherence operations. Writebacks use the LLC backpointer in the Obj-Store entry (Figure 4); the backpointer is set when the Collector loads the Obj-Store.

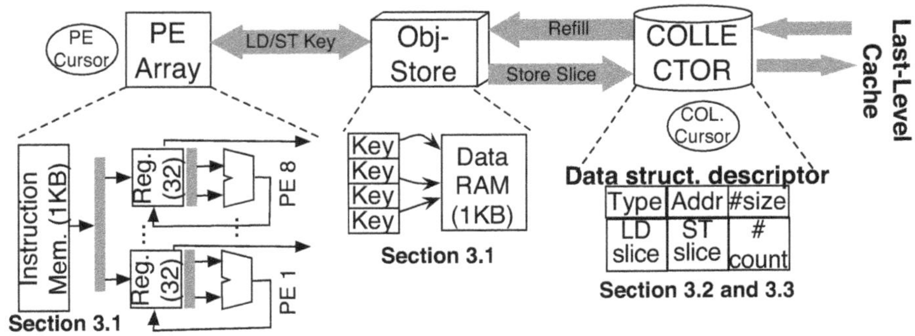

Figure 3: DASX Architecture Overview

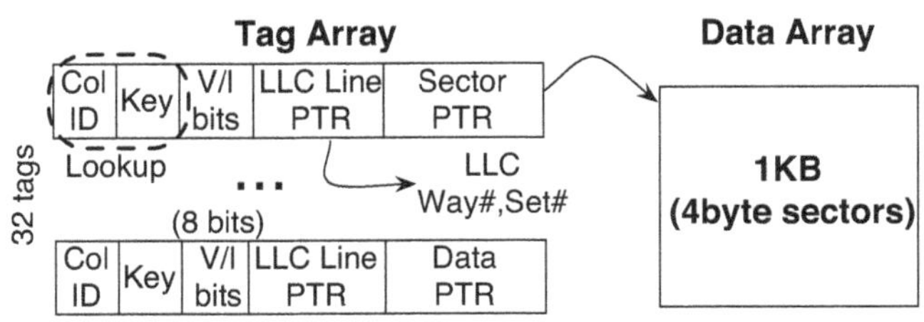

Figure 4: Obj-Store organized as a decoupled sector cache.

3.2 Collector

The Collector is a data-structure specific refill engine. A Collector has three tasks, i) it decodes the load and store slices , ii) translates the object keys to addresses and fetches them into the LLC and iii) it explicitly manages the Obj-Store. The Collector writes back data from the Obj-Store and refills it, setting up the appropriate tags and Obj-Store lines at the beginning of each set of iterations. To supply data objects to the PEs the Collector runs ahead and fetches the cache lines corresponding to the objects and locks the LLC lines until the compute kernel has processed the objects.[2] The accelerators do not need to perform address-generation or miss-handling since the Collector ensures the data is present in the Obj-Store for the duration of the computation. Before we discuss the details of individual Collectors, we illustrate the overall working of DASX with *Blackscholes*.

Illustration: Blackscholes Execution on DASX

In *Blackscholes*, the load slice consists of elements from the vectors spot[], strike[], rate[], volatility[], time[] and type[] while the store slice consists of elements from price[] (see Figure 2); all vectors employ a unit stride. Figure 5 (Left) illustrates the programmer's C++ API for DASX. `new coll(..)` initializes a new Collector and specifies the data structure parameters; specific details of each Collector are discussed in the next section. `group.add(..)` binds Collectors together to run in lock-step fetch elements from different data structures needed by a specific iteration. The need to run Collectors in a synchronized fashion is described in § 3.3. In this example, a Collector is initialized for each vector accessed in the compute kernel.

For this example, we assume 8 PEs and a 1KB Obj-Store. Each iteration requires space for 4×5 (floats) + 1 (char) + 4 (float) = 25 bytes. The 1 KB Obj-Store can hold data for 40 iterations of the *Blackscholes* kernel. The loop is unrolled with each PE executing a single iteration of the compute kernel; PEs sync up after each iteration. A group of iterations processing the data held in the Obj-Store is called a *tile*. The DASX software runtime loads the VEC descriptor for each of the vectors being accessed and invokes DASX by setting the memory mapped control register.

Figure 5 illustrates the steps involved in the execution of *Blackscholes* on DASX. The Collectors issue requests to DRAM (❸) for the first tile while the PEs are stalled. Subsequent DRAM requests overlap with execution of the PEs. The Collectors use some of the ways in each set of the last level cache to prefetch and "lock" (❹) in place, data which will be consumed by the PEs in the future. Locked cache lines may not be selected for replacement. The Collectors load the tile of data into the Obj-Store (❶) and the PEs commence execution of a group of concurrent iterations (❷). For *Blackscholes*, 40 iterations of the original loop consumes all the data in the Obj-Store. The Collectors then write back the dirty data, unlock the cache lines (❺) and initiate a refill (❸) of the Obj-Store. We implement LLC line locking using a logical reference counter (Ref.# in Figure 5). The Ref.# is set to the number of data objects in the LLC line needed by the computation. The Ref.# is zeroed out when the tile of iterations complete execution.

Overall, the key performance determinant is the ability of the Collector to generate addresses and run ahead to fetch the cache lines corresponding to the object keys. The logic required to generate addresses from the object keys is dependent on the type of Collector.

3.3 Types of Collectors

The DASX system evaluated includes three types of Collectors, VEC (vector/array), HASH (hash-table) and BTREE. Each Collector includes a data structure descriptor that contains information to enable the Collector to fetch and stage data independent of the compute kernel.

Vector Collector (VEC)

Figure 6 shows the descriptor that software needs to specify for vectors. The *Keys/Iter.* specifies the per-iteration load slice of the particular vector. For instance, in *Blackscholes* (see Figure 2), each of the vectors are accessed with a unit stride i.e., in the ith iteration accesses the ith element. The *Keys/Iter* is a single entry with offset 0. The descriptor limits the number of vectors accessed per-loop iteration (8 in this paper). The descriptor for spot[] in *Blackscholes* would be: <LD,&spot[0], FLOAT (4 bytes), nOptions (length of vector), [0] (unit stride access) >. The address generation to map data structure *keys* to cache block addresses is simple and shown in Figure 6.

[2] To ensure deadlock-free progress for the CPU cores we ensure that at least one way per set in the LLC remains unlocked.

```
begin blackscholes
   // Initialize collectors
   c_spot = new coll(LD,&spot,FP,#length,0,VEC)
   ...
   c_time = new coll (LD,&time,FP,#length,0,VEC)
   // Run collectors in step.
   group.add (c_spot...c_time);

  // Unroll to # of PEs. Tile based on Obj. Store size.
  start(kernel(),#iterations)
end
```

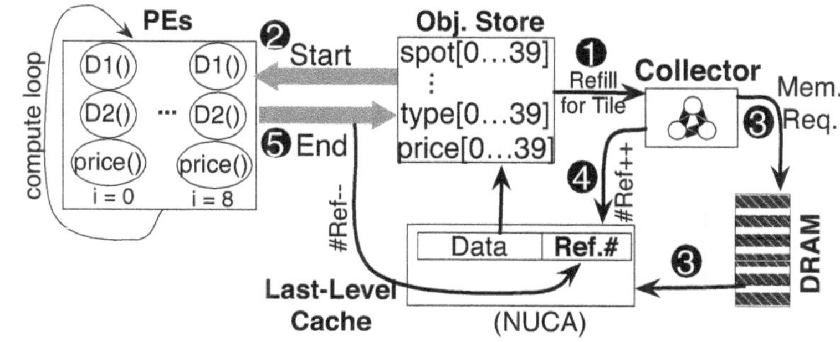

Figure 5: Blackscholes execution on DASX

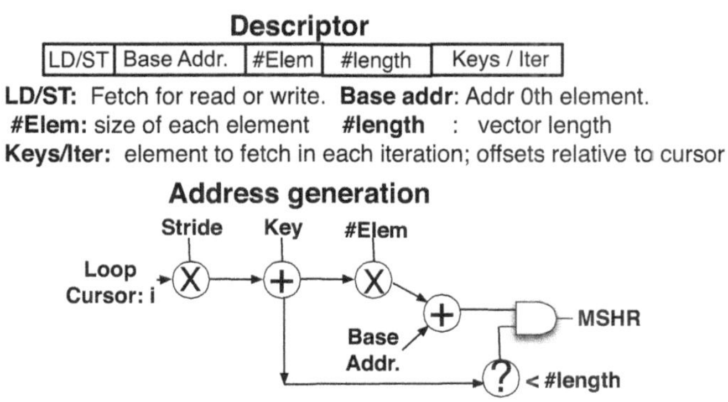

Figure 6: Descriptor for vector Collector

BTree Collector (BTREE)

The BTree is a common data structure widely used in databases; it arranges the key entries in a sorted manner to allow fast searches. Similar to the hash table, we do not accelerate insertions.

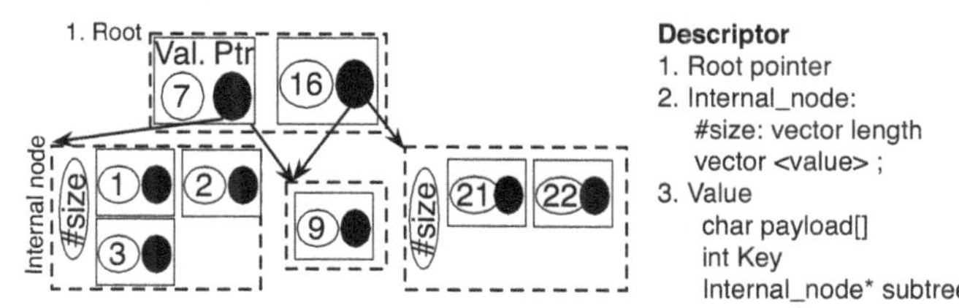

Figure 8: Descriptor for BTree Collector

Our BTree implementation supports keys up to 64 bit length. The key parameters required by the Collector are the root pointer and the description of the internal node. As shown in Figure 8, each sub-tree in the BTree is essentially a vector of value nodes. Each value node contains the key value, the data payload, and a pointer to the sub-tree (if present). When dereferencing each level, the Collector performs a range check and obtains the required sub-tree pointer. There is moderate parallelism in the data structure; the range checks that searches for the key position in the internal node vector can be parallelized.

Hash-Table Collector (HASH)

The hash Collector we study in this work supports only lookups similar to [19]; we use the general purpose processor to perform insertions. We only support a fixed organization for the hash table with fixed-size keys (128bits) and three data slabs 32byte, 64byte, and 128byte.

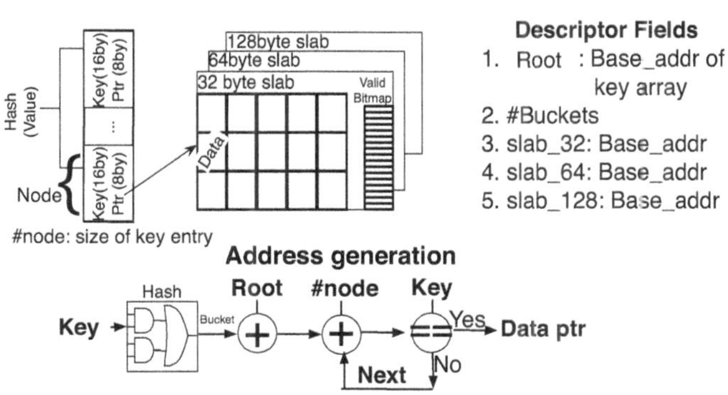

Figure 7: Descriptor for HASH Collector

As shown in Figure 7 the layout consists of a contiguous array for buckets (key-value pairs); the value could be either a 4 byte blob or a pointer to an entry in the data slabs. To search for a single key, the Collector iterates over the bucket array dereferencing each key. To enable better use of the accelerator we typically search for multiple keys simultaneously.

The hash-table also has to perform a comparison between the expected key and the key in the bucket. To amortize the cost of invoking the accelerator we search for multiple keys simultaneously.

Collector overhead

To estimate the overhead of the state machine of the Collector we use Aladdin [35], a pre-RTL power-performance simulator. Aladdin uses an ISA independent dynamic trace to estimate the power,area, and energy for custom hardware. Table 3 shows the overhead for the address generation logic of the individual Collectors. We quantify the data transfer latency and account for the Collector energy in § 4 as part of the energy consumed in the cache hierarchy.

Table 3: Design parameters for Collector state machine

	Area	Latency (cycles)	Energy
VEC	$0.23mm^2$	3	138pJ
HASH	$0.23mm^2$	5	266pJ
BTREE (order 5)	$1mm^2$	20	1242pJ

Obtained using Aladdin [35]. OpenPDK Library 45nm

Handling Corner Cases: Collector Groups

Here, we describe the subtle corner case conditions that affect the overall working of DASX. DASX requires that the data needed by one iteration of the loop be LLC resident before the iteration commences. In our benchmarks, we find that *Hash Table* needs 1, *2D-Datacube*, *Text Search*, *BTree* need to have 2, *Recommender* needs 3 and *Blackscholes* needs 7 lines locked in the LLC for DASX to make progress.

In DASX, a single loop iteration's working set cannot exceed the LLC's set capacity (i.e., bytes/set) lest all the data needed by an iteration map to the same set. Using a victim cache can relax this upper bound. Compiler techniques such as loop fission can also reduce the data footprint of the loop by splitting it into multiple loops. This guarantees that PEs can access data from the Obj-Store using *keys* and eliminates the non-determinism due to memory instructions missing in the cache. However, Figure 9 illustrates the possible deadlock that can occur when an iteration traverses multiple data structures. In *Blackscholes*, each iteration needs to access the element from seven different vectors. When a separate Collector is set up for each of the vectors, they run independent of each other and can issue accesses to the LLC in any order. The example illustrates one such case where the LLC is filled by locked lines for spot[0]..spot[255] and does not have any remaining space for the other vector's elements (e.g., type[0]). However, to even commence iteration 0, DASX requires all the data needed by that iteration i.e., the load slice including spot[0],rate[0],volatility[0],type[0], and time[0] and the store slice including price[0] has to be LLC resident. The deadlock arises because we have locked space in the LLC for data elements needed in a future iteration without ensuring there is space available for the data elements in the current iteration.

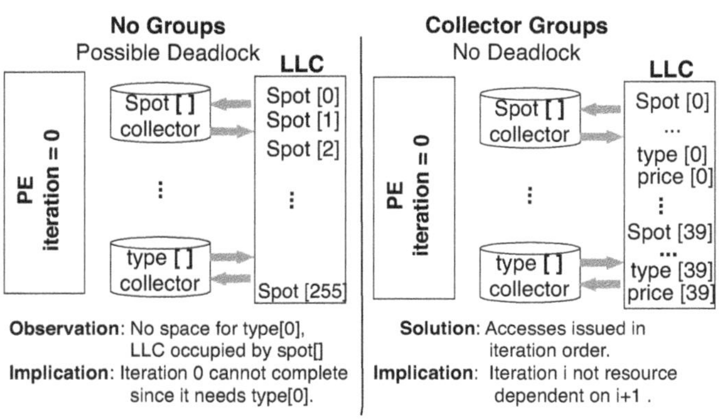

Figure 9: Collector Group. Left: Illustration of possible deadlock in Blackscholes without Collector groups. Right: Collector groups avoiding the deadlock issue.

To resolve the deadlock, we introduce the notion of *Collector group*. In *Blackscholes*, the six Collector (spot[]...type[]) form a Collector group (group() in Figure 2). DASX ensures that the individual Collectors in a group run in lock-step and issue accesses in *iteration order* to the LLC i.e., accesses are issued in the order spot[i]...type[i] before spot[i+1]...type[i+1]. We only require that the LLC allocate space for these elements in- order, the refill requests from DRAM itself can be in any order. Collector groups avoid deadlocks since they guarantee that data needed by every iteration i is allocated space in the LLC before iteration i+1.

4. Evaluation

We perform cycle accurate simulation of DASX with the x86-ISA based out-of-order core[3] modeled using Macsim [1], the cache hierarchy using GEMS [25] and main memory using DRAMsim2 [31]. We added support for DASX's cores into Macsim, and model the state machine of DASX's Collectors faithfully. We model energy using McPAT [22] and use the 45nm technology configuration; our caches are modeled using CACTI [26]. The energy consumption of DASX components are modeled with the templates for the register files, buffers, and ALUs from the Niagara 1 pipeline. Table 4 lists the parameters. The applications include multiple iterative regions and we profile the entire run apart from the initialization phase. We compare DASX against both an OOO (Out-of-Order) core and a multicore (with in-order processors). The baseline DASX system studies 8 PEs with 1KB Obj-Store (in Section 4.5 we vary the number of PEs). We compare the baseline DASX system against a 2C-4T (2core, 4thread-s/core) multicore with the same level of TLP as DASX (in Section 4.5 we compare DASX against 2C-8T and 4C-8T systems).

[3]We assume a 32K I-cache when modeling fetch energy; the performance simulation assumes all accesses hit to ensure fair comparison with DASX's PEs.

Table 4: System parameters

Cores	2 GHz, 4-way OOO, 96 entry ROB, 6 ALU, 2 FPU, INT RF (64 entries), FP RF (64 entries) 32 entry load queue, 32 entry store queue
L1	64K 4-way D-Cache, 3 cycles
LLC	4M shared 16 way, 8 tile NUCA, ring, avg. 20 cycles. Directory MESI coherence
Main Memory	4ch,open-page, DDR2-400, 16GB 32 entry cmd queue,
Energy Params	L1 (100pJ Hit, HP transistors). LLC (230pJ hit, LP transistors) [23] L1-LLC link (6.8pJ/byte [2, 26]), LLC-DRAM (62.5 pJ per byte [15])
Multicore	2C-4T (2 cores, 4 Threads/core), 2C-8T, 4C-8T 2Ghz, In order, FPU, 32K L1 cache per core, 4MB LLC
DASX Components	
	2GHz. 8 PEs, 4 stages in-order at 2 Ghz, 1 FPU and 1 ALU (per PE) INT Reg./ PE : 32 , FP Reg. / PE: 32
	Shared Obj-Store (1KB fully-assoc. sector cache, 32 tags). Shared Instruction buffer (1KB, 256 entries)

4.1 DASX : Performance Evaluation

Result: *DASX improves performance of data-centric applications by 4.4× over 2C-4T. Maximum speedup (Hash Table): 26.8 ×. Minimum speedup (Recommender): 1.3×.*

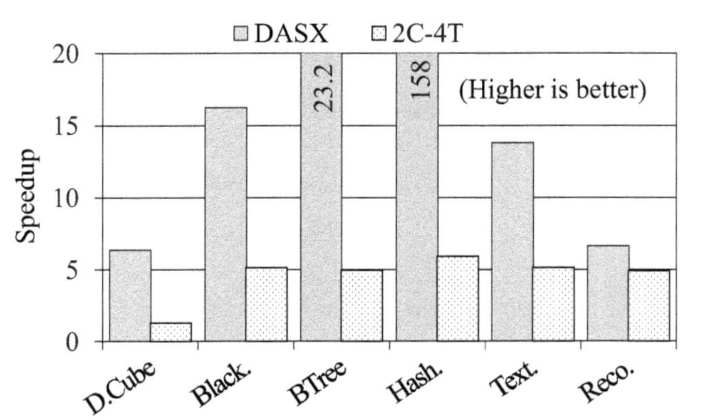

Figure 10: Execution Time (DASX vs 2C-4T). Y-axis: Times reduction in execution cycles over OOO.

We use the 2C-4T multicore to illustrate the benefits that DASX's MLP extraction can provide above the TLP. With *2D-Datacube*, the compute region in the loop body is small (only 21 static instructions); DASX removes the extraneous data structure instructions and mines the MLP implicit in the data structure to achieve a 6.4× performance improvement. 2C-4T suffers from synchronization overheads between the private L1 caches while DASX's simpler cache hierarchy minimizes synchronization overhead. *Blackscholes* includes many (up to 65% of executed instructions) long latency floating point instructions and the OOO processor is hindered by these instructions filling up the ROB before the independent memory instructions can be discovered. While 2C-4T extracts the available TLP (5× speedup) it exploits minimal MLP since the in-order pipeline resources are occupied by the compute instructions. DASX improves performance further (3.2× speedup over 2C-4T) by extracting the MLP without wasting execution resources. In *Text Search* the compute region requires many instructions to compare strings. DASX improves performance over the 2C-4T primarily by discovering MLP beyond the TLP. For *Blackscholes*, the OOO and the multicore also suffer from L1 thrashing due to repeated iterations over the dataset (3MB); DASX moves the compute closer to the LLC and is less susceptible to cache trashing. Similarly, with the *BTree* the working set fits in the large LLC but as lookups iterate over the tree they thrash the L1 leading to poor performance; DASX moves the compute closer to the LLC.

BTree and *Hash Table* highlight the ability of the Collector hardware to discover the MLP implicit in the data structure. With the *BTree* the traversal between tree-levels is sequential and requires pointer chasing; however DASX does parallelize the range search within a tree. Both the OOO and 2C-4T find it challenging to mine the MLP across pointer dereferences and data dependent branches. DASX improves performance by fetching in parallel the data elements for the range search. With the *Hash Table* the Collector eliminates the data structure instructions to check for the matching key; the removal of the LLC-L1 transfers also helps in improving performance.

In the case of *Recommender* the compute region processes a sparse matrix and the loop body execution is predicated on the value of each element in the matrix. With DASX the hardware barrier that we use to coordinate the PEs at the end of a group (8 in this case corresponding to 8PEs) of iterations introduces an inefficiency. We find that for 8% of the iterations, 1 or more PE executes the loop body while the other PEs are stalled at the barrier. An interesting extension to DASX would be to add support for predication checks into the Collector similar to [27], which advocates "triggered instructions" for spatially programmed architectures.

To summarize the benefits of DASX are due to i) the exploitation of data structure knowledge to run ahead and stage data in the LLC, and ii) the leaner cache hierarchy and small Obj-Store to reduce latency of local accesses within an iteration compared to the conventional cores which has to access the L1, and iii) elimination of the data structure access instructions from the iterative region.

4.2 DASX : Energy Evaluation

Result 1: *DASX is able to reduce energy in the PEs between 3.5—20× relative to 2C-4T.*
Result 2: *Data transfer energy is reduced by 4× relative to 2C-4T by eliminating L1-LLC transfers.*
Result 3: *DASX's shallow memory hierarchy helps reduce on-chip cache access energy by 7×.*

Core vs. PEs

Figure11 shows the reduction in dynamic energy. *BTree* and *Hash Table* are not included in Figure 11 as they do not include any work in the compute region and use only the Collector to traverse the data structure. DASX's PEs also use a simple pipeline which requires minimal energy for instruction fetch (1KB I-buffer vs I-cache on OOO/2C-4T) and data fetches from the Obj-Store

In *2D-Datacube* we see a 11× reduction in energy as the data structure instructions (eliminated in DASX) constitute a major part of all the instructions. With *Blackscholes* and *Text Search* which have compute intensive iteration, the primary energy reduction is due to the simpler PE pipeline and reduction in fetch overhead. The main benefit of DASX is being able to reduce execution time by extracting MLP without requiring the PE to sacrifice its energy efficiency.

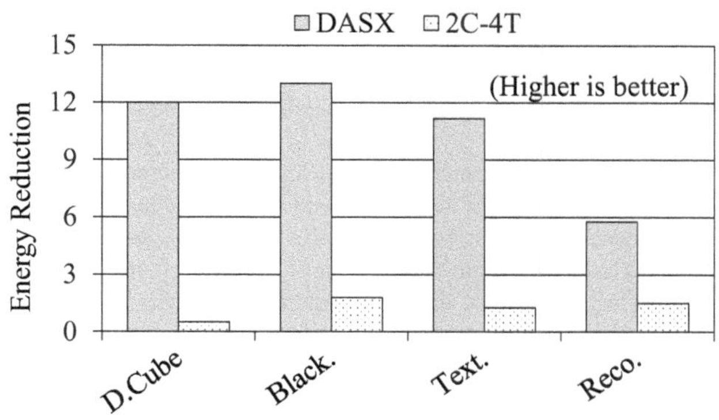

Figure 11: Dynamic energy reduction (Unit: × Times) in PEs vs. 2C-4T (Baseline: OOO core). *BTree* and *Hash Table* do not use the PE.

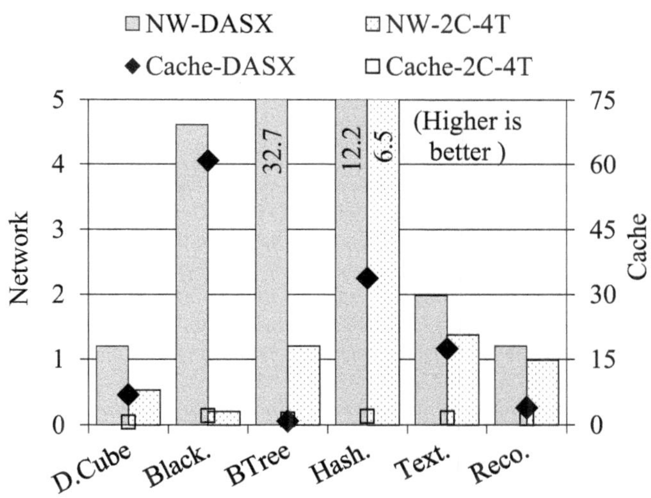

Figure 12: Energy reduction (Unit: ×times). DASX vs 2C-4T normalized to OOO. Left Y-axis: Network energy. Right Y-axis: Cache energy.

Network

Another key benefit of DASX is moving the compute closer to the LLC. Eliminating the L1-LLC transfers result on an average reduction of 3.7× of data transfer energy consumption. For example, *BTree* has low spatial locality which results in compulsory L1 cache misses, but the working set is contained within the LLC. Consequently, DASX achieves 17× reduction in network energy. With *2D-Datacube*, and *Recommender* the data transfer energy is dominated by the LLC-DRAM data transfer energy which is 11× that of LLC-L1 data transfer energy (see Table 4). With applications such as *Hash Table* which exhibit good spatial locality the multicore can exploit TLP to reduce execution time and thereby energy; DASX minimizes LLC-L1 transfers to further reduce energy by 2× compared to the multicore.

Cache

DASX employs a lean memory hierarchy (1KB Obj-Store + 4MB LLC). As the Collector runs ahead of the PEs in DASX and stages the data in the LLC, it requires two accesses to the LLC for each cache line : (1) when the data is fetched from DRAM into the LLC, and (2) when the Obj-Store is refilled. Comparatively, both the OOO and multicore access the LLC only on L1 misses.

Overall, DASX still reduces cache access energy, on average, by 13.6× (Figure12). This reduction comes primarily from two factors, namely, spending less energy in loading data from the Obj-Store relative to the L1 cache and remove stack references by the elimination of register spills due to a larger physical register file shared by the PEs.

We observe that *Blackscholes* and *Hash Table* benefits from the leaner memory hierarchy of DASX and from significant reduction in stack accesses. On the other hand, for *2D-Datacube* and *Recommender* both the OOO and 2C-4T benefit from the spatial locality in the L1 cache, and DASX incurs the additional penalty of accessing the LLC twice for each cache line, thereby limiting the energy savings in the cache. Finally, for *BTree* the higher probability of finding the non-leaf nodes in the L1 cache benefits both the OOO and 2C-4T and consequently limit the cache energy gains observed using DASX.

For all benchmarks apart from *Hash Table* and *BTree*, the energy for the Collector with respect to overall energy consumed was less than 0.25%. For the *Hash Table* and *BTree* benchmark, the Collector accounts for 6% and 4% respectively and when compared with the cache energy consumption for DASX, they represent 16% and 51% respectively. The OOO baseline consumes an order of magnitude higher energy in the cache hierarchy relative to DASX (Figure 12).

4.3 DASX MSHRs

To run ahead of the compute and prefetch far ahead, the Collectors need Miss Status Handling Registers (MSHRs) to keep track of outstanding cache misses. In this section we study the effect of MSHRs on DASX execution time (Figure 13). We found that for *Blackscholes*, which has a compute intensive iteration (many floating point operations), 8 MSHRs (1MSHR/PE) was able to hide the memory latency. With *BTree*, in which each level examines 2 or 3 nodes (we use a binary search within each level to find the next pointer), since we traverse by level and only prefetch within each level, again 8 MSHRs suffice. *Text Search* benchmark builds a heap structure and its size depends on the length of the strings to be compared, these strings can have locations which do not have spatial locality and hence, needed 32 MSHRs. *2d-Datacube* has a small compute region and iterates over a large data set (20Mb) and so requires a lot of MLP, thus 32 MSHRs. Both *Hash Table* and *Recommender* demonstrate high spatial locality and required at most 16 MSHRs.

What about a bigger OOO?

Overall, we find that more ILP $\neq$ more MLP for datacentric applications. We explored a more aggressive OOO to understand the limiting factor to finding more MLP. The instruction window was resized to 256 instructions with 2× the register file and load/store queue entries. Table 5 shows the maximum number of concurrent cache misses sustained and the challenges introduced by a particular data structure. Multicores with TLP help improve MLP but the gains are limited by the ILP of the individual cores.

Collector as Prefetcher

To evaluate the upper bounds of the Collector as a prefetcher, we

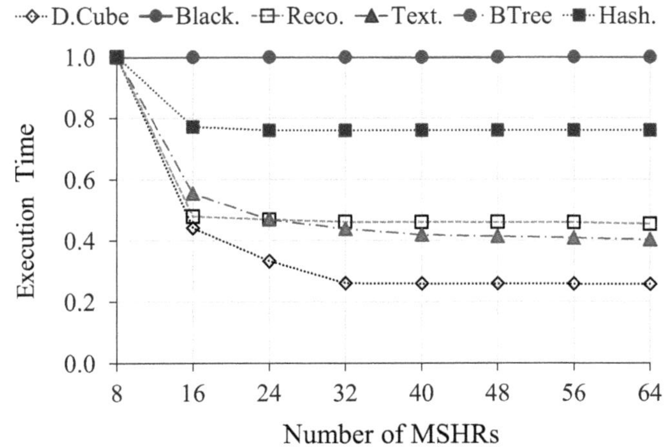

Figure 13: DASX Execution time for 8–64 MSHRs (normalized to 8 MSHRs).

Table 5: Max # of MSHR entries used for a 256 ROB core

Max. Misses	Application	Possible primary cause for limited misses
3	Text Search	Data-dependent branches
4	Hash Table	Data-dependent branches
5	BTree	Pointer chasing. MLP only within tree-level
5	Recommender	ROB filled by compute, waiting on data
6	2D-Datacube	Stalled accesses fill load/store queue
7	Blackscholes	ROB filled by compute, waiting on data

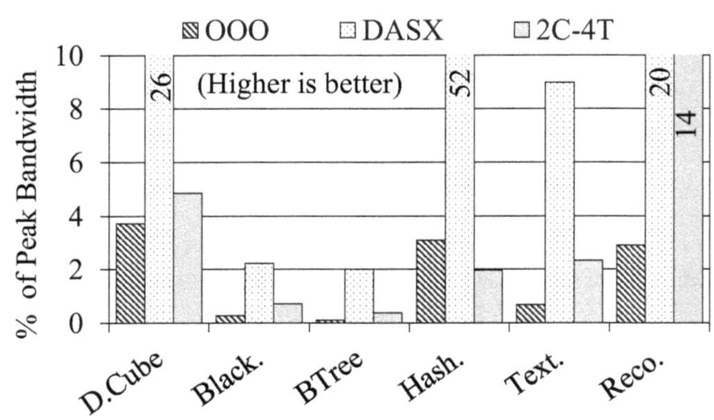

Figure 14: DRAM bandwidth utilization (OOO, 2C-4T and DASX) normalized to peak DRAM bandwidth (6.4GB/s)

modelled a perfect LLC for *Blackscholes*, *Recommender* and *2D-Datacube* and found that maximum performance improvement was 22% for OOO core due to the overheads of the cache hierarchy. Note that any prefetcher is best effort and does not guarantee a timely LLC hit; additionally the core will issue the load instruction anyway (energy overhead). The Collector eliminates these instructions and minimizes energy by using special purpose hardware.

4.4 Memory Bandwidth Utilization

Result: *DASX attains 13.9× increase in off-chip DRAM bandwidth compared to the OOO. Max: 82.4×(*BTree*).*

With data structure specific information DASX is able extract the MLP and issue timely requests to stage the data in the LLC before the PEs consume it. As shown in Figure 14, large increases in DRAM bandwidth utilization are observed for *2D-Datacube*, *BTree* and *Hash Table*. For *Hash Table* DASX is able to approach within 52% of the theoretical peak bandwidth of 6.4GB/s. *Text Search* and *Recom-*

mender both include computationally intensive kernels which lag far behind the Collector. This causes the Collector to fill up the LLC and then wait for the PEs to catch up and free space. The memory fetch rates are essentially limited by the latency of the compute kernels. DRAM bandwidth utilization improves by 3.9× and 1.4× for *Text Search* and *Recommender* respectively, relative to 2C-4T. The increase in bandwidth is observed due to the reduced run time of the kernels. All the DASX accelerated benchmarks access the same amount of data as their baseline counterparts apart from *Text Search* which overflows the LLC and leads to a large number of replacements as it iterates over the dataset repeatedly.

4.5 TLP vs MLP

Result: *Even with 50% lower TLP, (DASX: 4PEs vs 2C-4T) DASX exploits MLP to improve performance by 2.3× and reduce energy by 12.3× (Figure 15).*

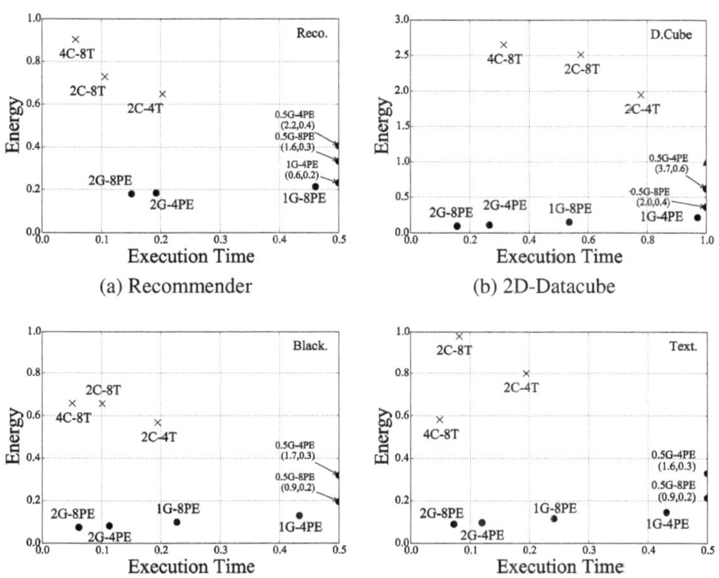

(a) Recommender (b) 2D-Datacube

(c) Blackscholes (d) Text Processing

Figure 15: Energy vs Execution Time plot. Y-Axis: Energy. Lower is better. X-axis: Execution time (scale different for each benchmark). towards origin is better. Baseline : OOO (1,1). × : Multicore systems 2C-4T,2C-8T,4C-8T 2Ghz frequency. • DASX systems: 0.5G,1G,2G - Clock frequency in Ghz.

We compare the energy and performance of a variety of multicore and DASX configurations to understand the benefits of extracting MLP versus TLP. We use parallel versions of each of the benchmarks where the work is partitioned across multiple threads. We varied the PE configuration of DASX between 2—10 and the frequency of the PE (0.5Ghz,1Ghz,2Ghz) to understand the dependence of our workloads on the execution pipeline performance, if the Collector can extract the MLP independent of the compute units. We study three different multicore configurations 2C-4T (2core, 4threads) which has the same level of parallelism as the 8-PE system, 2C-8T (16 threads) and 4C-8T (32 threads); all multicores run at 2Ghz. Figure 15 plots the dynamic energy vs execution time (we only show the 4 PE and 8 PE DASX for brevity).

Overall, we find that DASX extracts MLP in an energy efficient manner and provides both energy and performance benefits over multicores which only exploit TLP. However, even with DASX the performance of compute units is important to ensure that the compute kernel does not limit the performance gains of DASX. When the PE clock is reduced to 0.5Ghz or 1Ghz resulting in increase in execution time of the compute region, the performance loss varies 2–5× compared to the 2C-4T multicore; *2D-Datacube* is an exception since the compute kernel has less work. The multicore performance benefit and energy reduction are limited due to synchronization overheads (*2D-Datacube* performs a reduction). For embarrassingly parallel workloads (*Blackscholes*, *Recommender*, *Text Search* and *Hash Table*), multicores improve performance proportionate to the TLP but have minimal reduction in energy as execution resources are required to maintain the active threads. DASX is able to provide significant benefits with half the compute resources since the Collectors offload the MLP extraction from the compute cores. A 2G-4PE (2Ghz,4PE) DASX improves performance by 1.1–4.6× and reduce energy by 3.6–38× compared to a 2C-4T (8 threads).

Multicore with OOO cores

We used parallel (8 thread) versions of *Blackscholes* and *Recommender* to illustrate the pitfalls of using an OOO multicore to extract MLP. With 8 cores (single thread per OOO core), *Blackscholes* shows a performance improvement of 7.44× with a net increase in energy of 42% vs a single OOO core. With *Recommender* the parallel version demonstrates a 8× speedup with a 24% increase in energy consumption. While the OOO multicore has performance better than DASX (16% and 21% respectively), the energy consumption is far greater than DASX (17× and 7× reduction in energy consumption by DASX).

4.6 Breakdown of performance gains

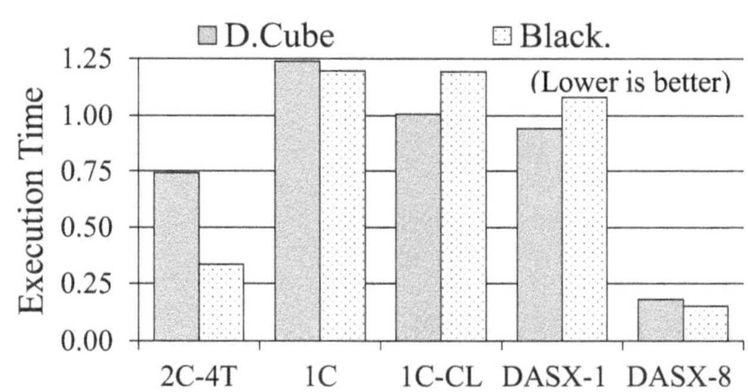

Figure 16: Motivation for Collector and Obj-Store to interface accelerators (PEs) to the memory system. (Lower is better)

To further illustrate the impact of each design decision of the DASX architecture, we conducted the following experiment. Using in-order cores as compute units, we measured the performance while a) varying the number of cores b) placing them near the LLC with only a 1KB L1 c) using a Collector to stage data in to the LLC d) adding an Obj-Store and removing address generation from the cores to form a complete DASX system and e) increasing the number of PEs to exploit loop level parallelism. Figure 16 shows the five configurations in the order they have been described herein. The performance of each configuration, for each benchmark, was normalized to the execution of the benchmark on an OOO core. We illustrate our findings using 2 benchmarks based on their behaviour on an OOO core, i.e memory bound (*2D-Datacube*) and compute bound (*Blackscholes*).

We find that the 2C-4T configuration only improves performance by 25% for the memory bound *2D-Datacube* benchmark. Placing a single in-order core near the LLC (1C configuration) is able to buy back some of the performance drop and is within 24% of the OOO baseline. This illustrates the benefit of computing near memory for data centric iterative workloads. Adding a Collector to ensure all accesses to the LLC are hits (1C-CL configuration) works well for the memory bound workload and a single in-order core is able to match the performance of the OOO baseline. Adding an Obj-Store and removing data structure access instructions from the compute kernel allows DASX-1 to further improve performance by 6% for *2D-Datacube* and 11% for *Blackscholes*. Finally, using 8 PEs in DASX-8 improves performance by 5× for *2D-Datacube* and 7× for *Blackscholes*.

4.7 Area Evaluation

We use McPAT to model the area overhead of the DASX's PEs. To model the DTLB, Obj-Store, and the reference count (Ref.# for locking cache lines), we use CACTI 6. The dominant area overhead in DASX is the FPU macro which is adopted from the Penryn processor in McPAT. Out of the six data-centric applications we investigated, five of them require minimal FPU support; however, we require an FPU per PE for Blackscholes (up to 65% of the compute kernel instructions are floating-point). It may be feasible to share the FPUs between the PEs like Sun-Niagara multicores to reduce the overhead. In comparison, the OOO core occupies 25.701 mm^2.

Table 6: Area Analysis (45nm ITRS HP)

Component	Area (mm^2)
ALUs (1 each)	INT (0.078), FP (2.329), MUL/DIV (0.235)
Reg File (32+32)	0.346
Total (PE)	2.988
Ins. Buffer (256 entries)	0.052
DTLB (64 entries)	0.143
Ref.#	6b/line. 47KB/4MB LLC
DASX w/ FPU (8*PEs)	24.099
w/o FPU	5.46

5. Related Work

Table 7 qualitatively compares DASX's design against existing architectures. We discuss individual designs below.

Specialized Core Extensions

Recently, researchers have proposed specialized compute engines that are closely coupled with the processor [3, 16, 29, 38]. In kernels which operate on large data structures [11] the load/store interface imposes high energy overhead for address generation [33]. The collectors in DASX exploit data structure knowledge to minimize the complexity of the address generation and improve MLP to supply data to compute accelerators. Loop accelerators [14] exploit repeated instruction streams to save fetch energy; DASX focuses on data structures. SIMD extensions reduce per instruction overheads, but are limited by the register width and difficult to apply to value dependent traversals. However, the PEs themselves may be enhanced with SIMD support similar to the GPGPU execution model.

Data structure Appliances

Recent research has focused exclusively on key-value stores [9, 17]. FPGA-Memcached [9] developed an FPGA-based hash-table and TCAM exploited power efficient content-addressable memory [17]. Unfortunately, these systems are challenging to use in general-purpose programs. Key-value stores do not efficiently represent associative containers; an integer array represented in TCAM [17] would require 2× the storage as a software data structure. More recently, HARP [39] developed support for database partitioning. Their memory system includes an application-specific on-chip streaming framework to interface with a custom on-chip computational logic. DASX seeks to accelerate iterative computation that access data structures and exhibit temporal and spatial locality. DASX also develops techniques for tiling the dataset at runtime to fit in the LLC and build a general-purpose memory interfaces to support software compute kernels.

Prior work have proposed using limited capacity hardware data structures [10, 13, 20, 40]. While this enables high performance, the hardware exports a limited interface to software which also needs to provide virtualization support [6]. DASX accelerates software data structures and does not require any specialized storage for the data structures. Since software manages the allocation DASX does not require complex virtualization support. Past work have also focused on CPU instructions for assisting software queues [21, 28].

Hardware walkers, both TLB [4] and more recently hash-table [19] focus on supporting efficient lookups in indexed data structures. While both DASX and hardware walkers exploit semantic information about data structures, DASX targets iterative compute kernels that stream over the entire data structure. DASX permits the compute kernels to be written in software. DASX adaptively tiles the dataset to handle cache contention between multiple data structures in an iteration and adapts to the compute kernel's temporal and spatial locality. While hardware walkers use a narrow queue-like interface to supply data, DASX supports a more flexible general purpose interface to the compute kernel. Programmable memory controllers [7, 8] provide an effective site to embed DASX's data-structure Collectors.

6. Summary

We have focused on exploiting data structure information to provide compute accelerators with energy-efficient interfaces to the memory hierarchy. We developed DASX, a hardware accelerator that integrates with the LLC and supports energy efficient iterative computation on software data structures. DASX exploits information about the computation kernel and actively manages the space in the LLC to ensure that no data fetch is wasted. DASX deploys cache refill engines that are customized for software data structures which increases the MLP, eliminates the penalty of transfers through the cache hierarchy, and removes data structure instructions.

7. References

[1] Macsim : Simulator for heterogeneous architecture - https://code.google.com/p/macsim/.

[2] D. Albonesi, K. A, and S. V. *NSF workshop on emerging technologies for interconnects(WETI)*, 2012.

[3] J. Benson, R. Cofell, C. Frericks, C.-H. Ho, V. Govindaraju, T. Nowatzki, and K. Sankaralingam. Design, integration and implementation of the DySER hardware accelerator into OpenSPARC. *IEEE 18th International Symposium on High Performance Computer Architecture (HPCA), 2012*, pages 1–12, 2012.

[4] R. Bhargava, B. Serebrin, F. Spadini, and S. Manne. Accelerating two-dimensional page walks for virtualized systems. In *PROC of the 13th ASPLOS*, 2008.

[5] C. Bienia, S. Kumar, J. P. Singh, and K. Li. The PARSEC benchmark suite: characterization and architectural implications. In *PROC of the 17th PACT*, 2008.

[6] G. Bloom. Operating System Support for Shared Hardware Data Structures. *GWU Thesis*, pages 1–136, Apr. 2013.

[7] M. N. Bojnordi and E. Ipek. PARDIS: a programmable memory controller for the DDRx interfacing standards. In *ISCA '12: Proceedings of the 39th Annual International Symposium on Computer*

Table 7: DASX vs Existing Approaches

	OOO+SIMD	Decoupled Architecture [36]	HW Prefetching	**DASX (this paper)**
Memory-Level Parallelism	**More MLP (limiting factor listed below)** →			
	Register width	Strands and inter-pipeline queues	Predictor table	MSHRs
Data-Struct. Instructions	Core executes data structure instructions (increases dynamic energy).			No (saves dynamic energy)
Big data-structure support	Limited by L1 cache size and load/store queue interface.		Limited by predictor table	Limited by LLC size
Fixed-latency Loads	No; cache misses	Yes (hardware queue)	No; cache misses	Yes (LLC line locking)
Value-Dependent Traversal	Challenging	Limited by branch prediction.	X (No support)	Efficient. Data structure-specific.

Architecture. ACM, June 2012.

[8] J. Carter, W. Hsieh, L. Stoller, M. Swanson, L. Zhang, E. Brunvand, A. Davis, C.-C. Kuo, R. Kuramkote, M. Parker, L. Schaelicke, and T. Tateyama. Impulse: building a smarter memory controller. In *PROC of the 5th HPCA*, 1999.

[9] S. R. Chalamalasetti, K. Lim, M. Wright, A. AuYoung, P. Ranganathan, and M. Margala. An FPGA memcached appliance, 2013.

[10] R. Chandra and O. Sinnen. Improving application performance with hardware data structures. *Parallel & Distributed Processing, Workshops and Phd Forum (IPDPSW), 2010*, pages 1–4, 2010.

[11] J. Chang, P. Ranganathan, T. Mudge, D. Roberts, M. A. Shah, and K. T. Lim. A limits study of benefits from nanostore-based future data-centric system architectures, 2012.

[12] E. S. Chung, J. D. Davis, and J. Lee. LINQits: big data on little clients. In *PROC of the 40th ISCA*, 2013.

[13] E. S. Chung, J. C. Hoe, and K. Mai. CoRAM: an in-fabric memory architecture for FPGA-based computing. In *PROC of the 19th FPGA*. ACM Request Permissions, Feb. 2011.

[14] N. Clark, A. Hormati, and S. Mahlke. VEAL: Virtualized Execution Accelerator for Loops. In *PROC of the 35th ISCA*, 2008.

[15] B. Dally. Power, programmability, and granularity: The challenges of exascale computing. In *Parallel Distributed Processing Symposium (IPDPS), 2011 IEEE International*, pages 878–878, 2011.

[16] H. Esmaeilzadeh, A. Sampson, and D. Burger. Neural Acceleration for General-Purpose Approximate Programs . *PROC of the 44th MICRO*, 2012.

[17] Q. Guo, X. Guo, Y. Bai, and E. Ipek. A resistive TCAM accelerator for data-intensive computing. In *MICRO-44 '11: Proceedings of the 44th Annual IEEE/ACM International Symposium on Microarchitecture*. ACM Request Permissions, Dec. 2011.

[18] S. Gupta, S. Feng, A. Ansari, S. Mahlke, and D. August. Bundled execution of recurring traces for energy-efficient general purpose processing. In *PROC of the 44th MICRO*, Dec. 2011.

[19] O. Kocberber, B. Grot, J. Picore, B. Falsafi, K. Lim, and P. Ranganathan. Meet the Walkers. *PROC of the 46th MICRO*, pages 1–12, Oct. 2013.

[20] S. Kumar, C. J. Hughes, and A. Nguyen. Carbon: architectural support for fine-grained parallelism on chip multiprocessors. In *PROC of the 34th ISCA*, 2007.

[21] S. Lee, D. Tiwari, Y. Solihin, and J. Tuck. HAQu: Hardware-accelerated queueing for fine-grained threading on a chip multiprocessor. In *HPCA '11: Proceedings of the 2011 IEEE 17th International Symposium on High Performance Computer Architecture*. IEEE Computer Society, Feb. 2011.

[22] S. Li, J. H. Ahn, R. D. Strong, J. B. Brockman, D. M. Tullsen, and N. P. Jouppi. McPAT: an integrated power, area, and timing modeling framework for multicore and manycore architectures. In *PROC of the 42nd MICRO*, 2009.

[23] S. Li, K. Chen, J. H. Ahn, J. B. Brockman, and N. P. Jouppi. CACTI-P: Architecture-level modeling for SRAM-based structures with advanced leakage reduction techniques, 2011.

[24] K. T. Malladi, I. Shaeffer, L. Gopalakrishnan, D. Lo, B. C. Lee, and M. Horowitz. Rethinking dram power modes for energy proportionality. In *Proceedings of the 2012 45th Annual IEEE/ACM International Symposium on Microarchitecture*, pages 131–142. IEEE Computer Society, 2012.

[25] M. M. K. Martin, D. J. Sorin, B. M. Beckmann, M. R. Marty, M. Xu, A. R. Alameldeen, K. E. Moore, M. D. Hill, and D. A. Wood. Multifacet's general execution-driven multiprocessor simulator (gems) toolset. *SIGARCH Comput. Archit. News*, 33(4):92–99, Nov. 2005.

[26] N. Muralimanohar, R. Balasubramonian, and N. Jouppi. Optimizing NUCA Organizations and Wiring Alternatives for Large Caches with CACTI 6.0. In *PROC of the 40th MICRO*, 2007.

[27] A. Parashar, M. Pellauer, M. Adler, B. Ahsan, N. Crago, D. Lustig, V. Pavlov, A. Zhai, M. Gambhir, A. Jaleel, R. Allmon, R. Rayess, S. Maresh, and J. Emer. Triggered instructions: a control paradigm for spatially-programmed architectures. In *PROC of the 40th ISCA*, pages 1–12, Apr. 2013.

[28] Y. M. Patt. Microarchitecture choices (implementation of the VAX). In *PROC of the 22nd annual workshop on microprogramming and microarchitecture*, 1989.

[29] W. Qadeer, R. Hameed, O. Shacham, P. Venkatesan, C. Kozyrakis, and M. Horowitz. Convolution Engine: Balancing Efficiency & Flexibility in Specialized Computing. *PROC of the 40th ISCA*, pages 1–12, Apr. 2013.

[30] P. Ranganathan. From Micro-processors to Nanostores: Rethinking Data-Centric Systems. *Computer*, 44(January):39–48, 2011.

[31] P. Rosenfeld, E. Cooper-Balis, and B. Jacob. Dramsim2: A cycle accurate memory system simulator. *Computer Architecture Letters*, 10(1):16 –19, jan.-june 2011.

[32] K. Sankaralingam, R. Nagarajan, R. McDonald, R. Desikan, S. Drolia, M. S. Govindan, P. Gratz, D. Gulati, H. Hanson, C. Kim, H. Liu, N. Ranganathan, S. Sethumadhavan, S. Sharif, P. Shivakumar, S. W. Keckler, and D. Burger. Distributed Microarchitectural Protocols in the TRIPS Prototype Processor. In *PROC of the 39th MICRO*, 2006.

[33] S. Sethumadhavan, R. McDonald, D. Burger, S. S. W. Keckler, and R. Desikan. Design and Implementation of the TRIPS Primary Memory System. In *International Conference on Computer Design (ICCD), 2006*, pages 470–476, 2006.

[34] A. Seznec. Decoupled sectored caches: conciliating low tag implementation cost. In *PROC of the 21st ISCA*, 1994.

[35] Y. S. Shao, B. Reagen, G.-Y. Wei, and D. Brooks. Aladdin: A pre-rtl, power-performance accelerator simulator enabling large design space exploration of customized architectures. In *Proceeding of the 41st Annual International Symposium on Computer Architecuture*, 2014.

[36] J. E. Smith. Decoupled access/execute computer architectures. In *25 years of International Symposia on Computer Architecture*, 1998.

[37] S. Srinath, B. Ilbeyi, M. Tan, G. Liu, Z. Zhang, and C. Batten. Architectural specialization for inter-iteration loop dependence patterns. In *Intl Symp. on Microarchitecture (MICRO)*, 2014.

[38] G. Venkatesh, J. Sampson, N. Goulding, S. Garcia, V. Bryksin, J. Lugo-Martinez, S. Swanson, and M. B. Taylor. Conservation cores: reducing the energy of mature computations. In *PROC of the 15th ASPLOS*, 2010.

[39] L. Wu, R. J. Barker, M. A. Kim, and K. A. Ross. Navigating Big Data with High-Throughput, Energy-Efficient Data Partitioning .

[40] L. Wu, M. Kim, and S. Edwards. Cache Impacts of Datatype Acceleration. *IEEE Computer Architecture Letters*, 11(1):21–24, Apr. 2012.

Automatic Energy Efficient Parallelization of Uniform Dependence Computations*

Yun Zou
CS Dept., Colorado State University
Colorado, USA
zou@cs.colostate.edu

Sanjay Rajopadhye
CS Dept., Colorado State University
Colorado, USA
Sanjay.Rajopadhye@colostate.edu

ABSTRACT

Energy is now a critical concern in all aspects of computing. We address a class of programs that includes the so-called "stencil computations" that have already been optimized for speed. We target the energy expended in dynamic memory accesses, since most other components of the total energy are usually already reduced when optimizing for speed alone. For a standard shared memory multi-core processor, we seek to *minimize the total number of off-chip memory accesses without sacrificing execution time.* Our strategy uses two-level tiling with multiple pipelined passes. Because of the sophisticated tiling and parallelization, such codes are difficult to write by hand, especially for parametric tile sizes. They are also beyond the capability of current code generators because the schedules used are polynomial functions, more general than multidimensional schedules. We implement a parametric tiled code generator to support this strategy, and also develop a simple quantitative linear regression model for the energy consumed by a program. We experimentally validate our techniques on a set of benchmarks including those from the Polybench suite on two platforms. Our experiments show that about 78% (resp. 80%) of the dynamic memory energy consumption on an 8-core Xeon E5-2650 v2 (resp. 6-core Xeon E5-2620 v2) based machine can be avoided. This leads to a reduction in the total energy of the program by 2% to 14%.

Keywords

energy consumption; automatic parallelization; hierarchical tiling; off-chip memory access; polyhedral model

1. INTRODUCTION

Uniform dependence computations occur frequently in scientific applications, and a representative class is *Stencil Computations.* One of the thirteen Berkeley dwarfs/motifs [32], is "structured mesh computations," which are nothing but stencils. Naive implementations of many of these applications turn out to be memory-bound. Therefore, many authors seek to exploit data locality for these programs [14, 24, 1]. One such technique is called *time tiling* [33, 5, 34, 7, 25, 8, 29, 1], an advanced form of loop tiling [33, 35], which allows the whole computation space to be tiled and executed in a wavefront fashion. We assume, like most of the work in the literature, that *dense* stencil programs are *compute bound* after time tiling. However, due to the intricate structure of time tiled code, writing it by hand is challenging. Automatic code generation, is an attractive solution, and has been an active research topic, and polyhedral compilation is one of the most successful technique. When tile sizes are fixed, tiling can be described as a linear transformation, and purely polyhedral tools work well [3, 5], but there is a growing need to delay the choice of tile sizes, possibly even to run-time, for which, parametric tiled code generation is needed [2, 16, 11, 10]. Parametric tiling is a nonlinear transformation, and is still an active research problem.

Past research on stencil computations mainly focused on performance (i.e., execution time). Because of the *power wall* [4], energy efficiency is an important concern for exascale systems. Furthermore, widespread utilization of high performance computing (HPC) systems results in a dramatic increase in energy consumption [18, 22], and also raises the operating temperature, hurting the reliability and stability of the machine. In this paper, we address the parallelization and automatic compilation of uniform dependence computations for energy efficiency.

Optimizing highly tuned *compute-bound* programs for energy efficiency needs careful consideration. Assuming that the application and its data set fit in main memory, the energy consumed consists of CPU energy and main memory system energy [13], and each of these can be further divided into static energy and dynamic energy. The static energy takes a significant fraction of the total energy consumption (see Figure 1), and since it is proportional to the execution time, the energy-optimal strategy usually also tends to finish the computation as soon as possible. However, for compute bound problems, the execution time is bounded by the amount of computations, so there is limited "energy slack" to optimize for static energy, and any "optimization" that causes even a small slowdown is likely to lose its energy savings. Our **goal** is to *automatically* capture as much of this as possible—to reduce the energy consumption of tuned stencil computations.

*Supported in part by NSF grants CCF-0917319 and CNS-1240991, and by AFOSR grant FA9550-13-1-0064

ICS'15, June 8–11, 2015, Newport Beach, CA, USA.

ACM 978-1-4503-3559-1/15/06 ...$15.00.
DOI: http://dx.doi.org/10.1145/2751205.2751245.

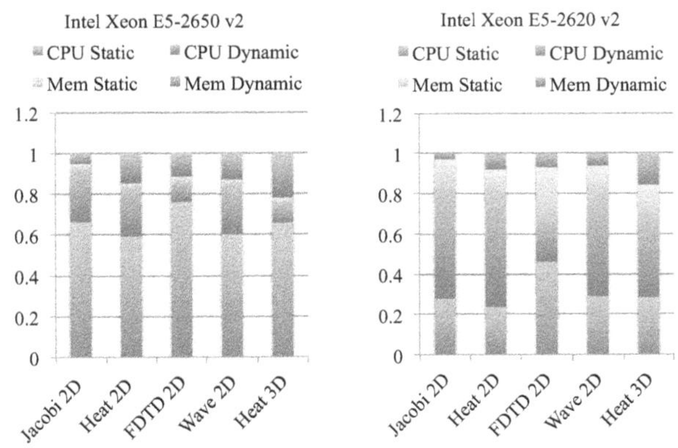

Figure 1: Normalized energy breakdown for stencil benchmarks on Intel Xeon E5-2650 v2 and Intel Xeon E5-2620 v2, based on a simple linear regression model (details are described in Section 5).

The dynamic energy consists primarily of the energy consumed by (on-chip and off-chip) memory accesses, and by arithmetic operations. After performance optimization, the number of computation cannot be reduced, but the energy consumed per cache access is much smaller than that by an off-chip memory access. Therefore, we seek to reduce energy consumption by reducing the off-chip memory accesses, i.e., further improving the cache hit rate. Figure 1 indicates that the dynamic memory energy consumption (purple) only takes up a small portion (3% to 20%) of the total energy. We seek to obtain this energy savings "for free," i.e., with an automatic code generator.

Our strategy uses multi-level tiling associated with *multi-pass* execution [23], originally introduced in the context of systolic arrays. We adapt this strategy to address the last level cache misses on general multi-core processors. Although we highlight it for stencil programs, it is applicable to a larger class—computations described as Systems of Uniform Recurrence Equations [15] that admit a 1D wavefront schedule. Our code generator currently handles only hyper-parallelepiped shaped iteration spaces (structured meshes)—a proper subset of programs that can be analyzed with polyhedral techniques. We target a single shared memory multi-core processor. Our contributions are:

- an energy efficient strategy—flattened multi-pass parallelization (FMPP) for uniform dependence computations, focusing on reducing the number of off-chip memory accesses without sacrificing speed;
- a code generator for FMPP that supports parametric tile sizes for programs with hyper-parallelepiped shaped iteration space, and extends the state of the art in parallel code generation in that it implements *polynomial* rather than *multi-dimensional* schedules;
- evaluation of FMPP on a set of benchmarks, showing that we reclaim most of the *dynamic memory energy*: about 78% (resp. 80%) on a Xeon E5-2650 v2 (resp. Xeon E5-2620 v2) based machine.

2. STENCIL COMPUTATIONS

A stencil computation is a computation that repeatedly updates each point in a d-dimensional grid over T time steps. It therefore has a $(d+1)$-dimensional iteration space. At a time step t, the computation for each point is defined as a function of its neighboring points at either the previous or current time steps. It is called an *n-point stencil* if each update is defined as a function of n neighboring points. The *order* of a stencil is defined as the distance of the farthest grid point in the neighborhood.

Example: Jacobi 1D (J1D) is a first-order 3-point stencil computation that repeatedly updates a 1-dimensional N-element data space over T time steps, and the computation of each point depends on three neighboring points from the previous time step, as described in Equation 1.

$$B_{t,i} = \begin{cases} A_i, \quad t=0 \\ B_{t-1,i}, \quad 0<t\leq T \text{ and } (i=0 \text{ or } i=N) \\ \frac{1}{3}\left(B_{t-1,i-1}+B_{t-1,i}+B_{t-1,i+1}\right), \\ \qquad 0<t\leq T \text{ and } 0<i<N \end{cases} \tag{1}$$

In J1D, updating data point i at time step t requires three values from the previous time step: $(i-1)$, i and $(i+1)$. Due to the dependences between the successive time steps, rectangular cache blocking can not be applied across the time dimension directly. *Time skewing* [7, 34] is a technique that can be used to enable tiling across time dimension. It skews the data space with respect to the time dimension to make all the dependences fall into the first quadrant. Figure 2 shows the tiling result with time skewing. After time skewing, standard *wavefront parallelization* can be applied to parallelize the tiles. All the tiles that are executed at the same time step composite one *wavefront*.

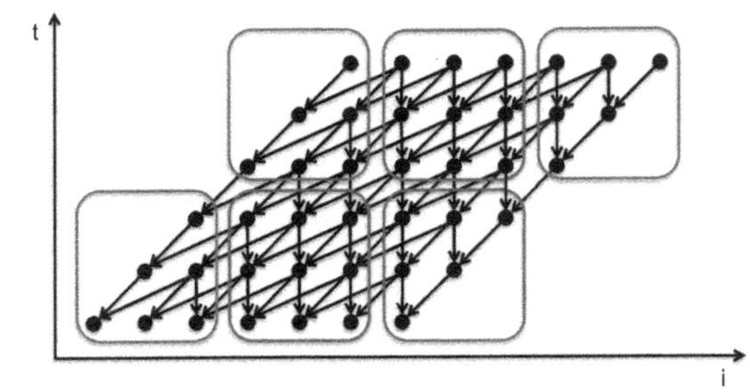

Figure 2: Rectangular tiling for J1D after time skewing ($T=5$, $N=6$). Arrows in the figure show dependences, whose source is a consumer and destination is a producer.

3. FLATTENED MULTI-PASS STRATEGY

We now describe our energy-efficient parallelization strategy called flattened multi-pass parallelization (FMPP). We use the Jacobi 1D as a running example to illustrate our approach and its memory behavior. The main idea is relatively simple, but the challenge arises in automating it.

3.1 Standard Wavefront Parallelization

Figure 3 describes the wavefront parallelization on the tiled iteration space for J1D, where one wavefront (orange dashed line) starts after the previous wavefront is done. The computations in one wavefront require values from the previous wavefront. When the number of values required exceeds the capacity of the last level cache (LLC), each access to the data from the previous wavefront will be a cache miss, leading to an off-chip memory access. This happens when the iteration space is "large enough," and the computation has advanced long enough—the earlier wavefronts have a smaller footprint.

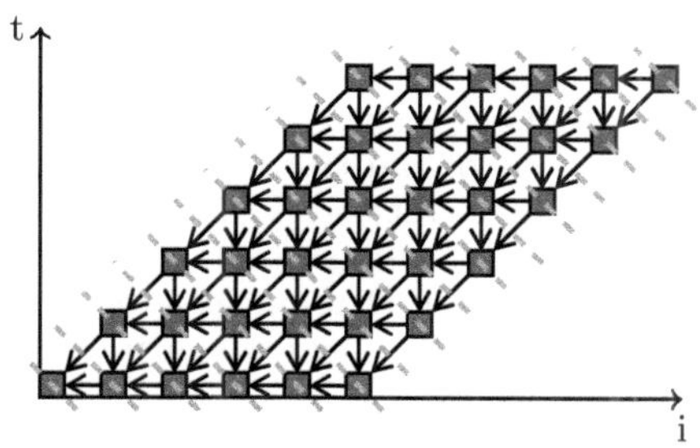

Figure 3: The tiled iteration space and wavefront parallelization for J1D. Each small rectangle represents one tile, and each tile depends on its left tile, bottom tile and lower left tile. Each orange dashed line represents one wavefront.

Let us quantify the off-chip memory accesses for the standard wavefront parallelization of J1D. If the tile size is y along dimension i and x along dimension t, then the total number of tiles N_{tile} is approximately $\frac{T}{x} \times \frac{N+x-1}{y}$. When $N \gg x$, $N_{\text{tile}} \approx \frac{T}{x} \times \frac{N}{y}$. From Figure 2, we can see that one tile requires two columns of values from the left tile, one row from the bottom tile and a single value from the "south-west" tile (we ignore this latter one). Then the number of off-chip accesses of a tile is $(2x + y)$. The total number of off-chip memory access V_{std} of the program is $N_{\text{tile}} \times (2x+y) = \frac{TN(2x+y)}{xy}$. Note that since $\frac{xy}{2x+y}$ is maximized when $2x = y$, and this choice of the tile aspect ratio minimizes V_{std} to $\frac{2TN}{y}$. This is further minimized by making y as large as possible, subject to the capacity constraints of the caches (private) on each core and the degree of parallelism.

3.2 Energy Efficient Parallelization

In the standard wavefront parallelization, there is no data reuse between the successive wavefronts under the worst case. The key idea of our energy efficient Multi-Pass Parallelization (MPP) is to enable data reuse between successive wavefronts.

3.2.1 Multi-Pass Parallelization (MPP) for J1D

To achieve reuse between successive wavefronts, we first tile the iteration space into passes, and then further tile each pass into smaller tiles. The passes are executed sequentially one after another, and standard wavefront parallelization is applied to each pass to enable parallelization. The pass size has to be chosen carefully, so that values produced by each wavefront in one pass fit in the LLC, and note that the values needed from the previous pass will still be misses. This way, we optimize data reuse within one pass. Figure 4 illustrates multi-pass parallelization for the J1D example.

Let the pass height be H, and the tile sizes for the tiles within a pass be x' and y' (the optimal tile sizes for MPP may be different from the optimal ones for the standard wavefront parallelization). Since H is chosen so that there are no cache misses within one pass, the cache misses only occur between passes. Since the computation in one pass requires the last row from the previous pass, the volume, V_{multi}, of off-chip data transfer for J1D with MPP can be estimated as the product of the number of passes and the row size. $V_{\text{multi}} = \frac{T}{H} \times N = \frac{TN}{H}$. Comparing with $V_{\text{std}} = \frac{2TN}{y}$ for the standard wavefront parallelization, and noting that usually $H \gg y$, we expect the multi-pass parallelization to yield significant savings.

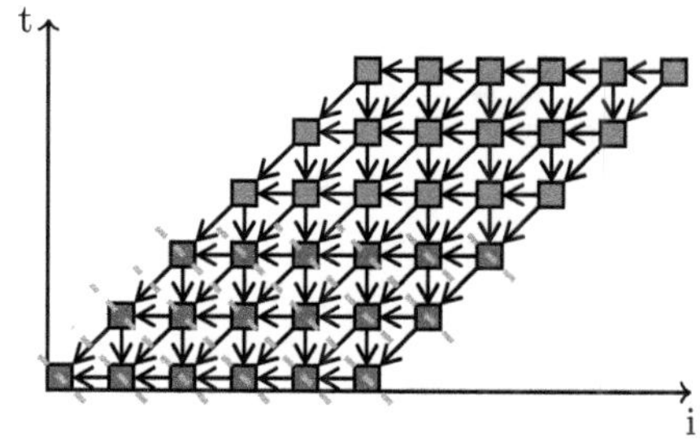

Figure 4: The tiled iteration space and multi-pass parallelization for J1D. Each small rectangle represents one tile, and each tile depends on its left tile, bottom tile and lower left tile. The whole tiled iteration space is separated into two passes (blue and red). Each orange dashed line represents one wavefront.

3.2.2 Higher Dimensional MPP

MPP can be generalized to higher dimensions. For a d-dimensional stencil (i.e., with $d+1$ dimensions in total), we first tile the outer d dimensions into passes, and then, for each pass, perform an inner level tiling on all the dimensions.

As in J1D, when the data space is "large enough." every inter-tile access will cause a cache miss in the standard wavefront parallelization, but in MPP, only those inter-tile accesses that cross a *pass boundary* will cause cache misses.

Consider a 3D program with a regular $T \times N \times M$ iteration space, and assume that rectangular tiling can be applied without time skewing (this is an approximation to get asymptotic bounds). If the tile size for the standard wavefront parallelization is $t \times x \times y$, then the total number of tiles is $N_{\text{tile}} = \frac{T}{t} \times \frac{N}{x} \times \frac{M}{y}$. Assume that one tile requires a faces from its left tile and b faces from the bottom tile and c faces from its front tile, let V_{tile} represent the number of off-chip memory accesses of one tile. Then $V_{\text{tile}} = a \times t \times y + b \times x \times y + c \times t \times x$.

The total number of off-chip memory accesses for the whole program with standard wavefront parallelization is

$$V_{\text{std}} = V_{\text{tile}} \times N_{\text{tile}} = \frac{TNM(aty + bxy + ctx)}{txy} \tag{2}$$

If the pass sizes for the outer two dimensions are H_t and H_x, then the total number of passes N_{pass} for the whole iteration space is $\dfrac{T}{H_t} \times \dfrac{N}{H_x}$. Each pass requires a faces of values from its left pass, b faces from its bottom passes, and no pass is in front of a pass. Therefore,

$$\begin{aligned} V_{\text{multi}} &= N_{\text{pass}} \times (a \times M \times H_t + b \times M \times H_x) \\ &= \frac{TN(aMH_t + bMH_x)}{H_t H_x} \end{aligned} \tag{3}$$

Then, our multi-pass parallelization can achieve better memory performance when $\frac{M(aty+bxy+ctx)}{txy} > \frac{(aMH_t+bMH_x)}{H_t H_x}$, and our experimental results show that this is usually achievable. Of course, our analysis is approximate, and only considers capacity misses. In practice many factors affect memory behavior, such as data access order, conflict misses etc. Sometimes, these factors may have a big impact on the number of cache misses, but can be optimized away with existing techniques.

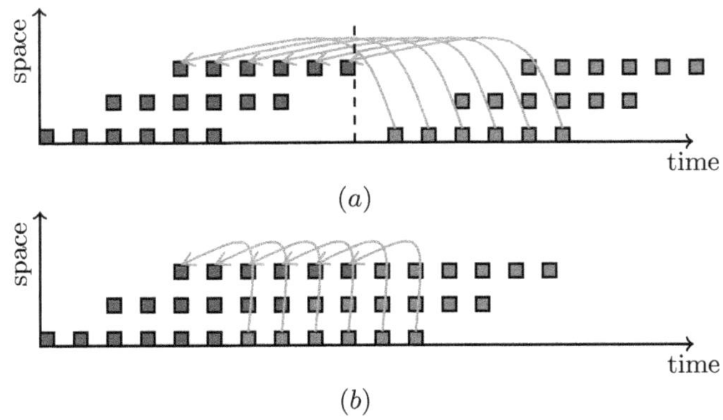

Figure 5: The space-time diagram of the (a) standard, and (b) flattened multi-pass strategy for J1D. The horizontal axis represents the wavefront time step. Note that in the standard scheme, the time stamp is a *multi-dimensional vector*, and in the flattened strategy it is a *quadratic function* of the tile coordinates, pass number and row size.

3.2.3 Flattened Multi-Pass Parallelization (FMPP)

Recall that for our goal of energy-efficiency, it is critical to retain all speed optimizations of the original code, otherwise we risk losing more than the savings we gain from the off-chip accesses. In the standard parallelization of MPP, the computation in one pass starts after the previous pass is complete. As illustrated in Figure 5(a) this introduces idle time between passes due to pipeline flush-fill. This situation will also happen in the standard wavefront parallelization, but only once during the whole computation, whereas it happens for each pass for MPP. It will be exacerbated for higher dimensional cases. Our preliminary experiments showed that the MPP strategy was up to 20% slower than the standard wavefront parallelization, for programs with higher dimensions. The overhead can be eliminated if we remove the gap between two successive passes by overlapping them as shown in Figure 5(b). We call this the *flattened multi-pass parallelization strategy* (FMPP). In this way, the fill-flush overhead will be incurred only once during the whole computation. Although this transformation is intuitively very simple, it raises significant challenges for code generation. Also, note that there may be a limit on how much overlap is allowed, since the inter-pass dependences must be satisfied. We ensure the legality of our code through constraints on tile sizes.

4. FMPP CODE GENERATION

We implemented a parametric tiled code generator for our FMPP strategy by advancing existing code generation techniques [16, 11, 2]. Because of space constraints, we describe here only the generator that produces *sequential* code from perfectly nested loops. Our code generator also parallelizes the code and handles imperfectly nested loops using the approach of DTiler [16]. Currently, our method is only applicable to d-dimensional hyper-parallelepiped shaped iteration spaces, whose bound expressions involve only the outermost loop index and parameters.

4.1 Code structure, challenges and issues

Existing parametric tiled code generators do not support the parallelization schedule we need for FMPP. The main problem is that in all current parametric tiled code generators, the schedule is viewed as a multi-dimensional vector of "time-stamps" under the *lexicographic order*. Therefore, *no event* in a certain dimension of time (i.e., loop) can be executed before *all events* in previous iteration of preceding dimension of time (i.e., an outer loop) are done. This is an **inherent limitation of multidimensional time under lexicographic order**. Our code generator overcomes this by incorporating a *polynomial schedule*.

In order to generate code that executes the tiles in the order as shown in Figure 5(b), the individual passes are "laid out" one after another to create one large pass, called the *flattened space*. First, note that a pass is nothing but a tiling of the outer d loops, leaving the innermost one untiled. Also note that although the original loop nest was fully permutable, the multi-pass strategy introduces inter-pass dependences, and this means that the untiled dimension is no longer permutable with the others. It must therefore be made the outermost loop, and this loop should represent a "symbolic unrolling" over all the passes, of the iterations of the untiled dimension in each pass. Also, for each tile visited in the flattened space, the corresponding iteration points in the original iteration space must be determined, and those computations must be performed. Handling these two tasks raises interesting issues.

Note that symbolic unrolling is a nonlinear transformation, $\mathcal{Z}^{d+1} \rightarrow \mathcal{Z}$, that maps a $(d+1)$-dimensional point in the original space to a single integer in the new outer loop. From this, we need to deduce the original index point (the original pass and tile coordinates). By restricting to hyper-parallelepiped shaped domains, we will show how to obtain simple functions to deduce these inverse mappings as closed form expressions involving the tile size parameters.

Second, dealing with tile loops raises additional complications. For example, for hyper-parallelepiped shaped iteration spaces, although the number of *iterations* of any loop is independent of the values of surrounding loops, the same assertion cannot be made about the loops that visit the tile origins. Furthermore, as we shall see later, we also need to determine the number of tile origins visited in the very first instance of the innermost loop in any given pass, and ensure that this is independent of the specific pass.

In the following section, we will describe our code generation strategy for the sequential flattened multi-pass (FMP) strategy. We first show how to generate code for a 2D parallelogram iteration space with no tiling within each pass, then we generalize it to the 2D iteration space with tiling inside each pass and then to higher dimensional cases.

4.2 2D Space Without Tiling Inside Passes

Figure 6 describes the original multi-pass space and the flattened space for a parallelogram iteration space, and tiling is not applied for each pass. The code we seek to generate is a two dimensional loop nest that enumerates all the iteration points in the flattened space, with the outer one visiting all the points along the flattened *data* dimension i.

4.2.1 Generating The Outer Loop

As shown in Figure 6, the shape of each pass remains a parallelogram, therefore, the number of iteration points in the first row is the same for all the passes, which is the *period* of a pass, denoted by N_{period}. Let n_{pass} be the number of passes. Then, N_{fmp}, the total number of iteration points

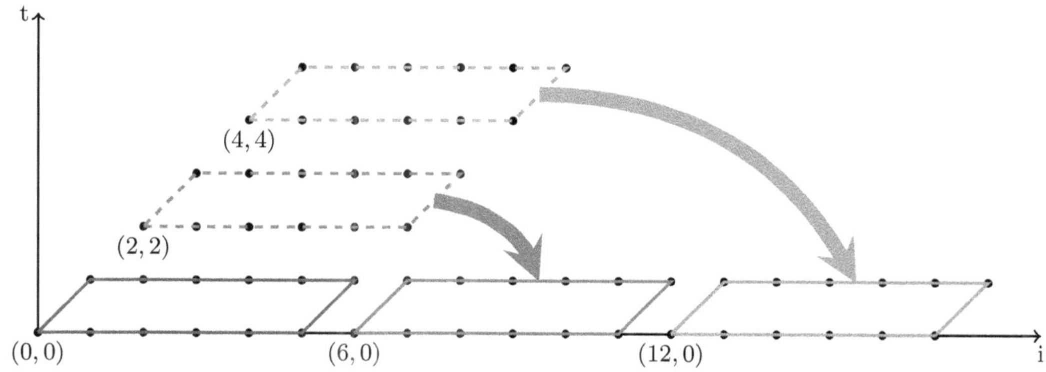

Figure 6: Flattened iteration space for a parallelogram iteration space. The blue box is the first pass for both the original iteration space and flattened space. The red dashed box is the second pass in the original iteration space, and the red solid box is the second in the flattened space. Same for the orange boxes.

along dimension i in the flattened space is the product of the two, plus pipeline fill-flush, which we count as part of the last pass (represented by N_{last}). Then,

$$N_{\text{fmp}} = N_{\text{period}}(n_{\text{pass}} - 1) + N_{\text{last}}$$

For the example in Figure 6, $N_{\text{period}} = 6$, $n_{\text{pass}} = 3$, $N_{\text{last}} = 7$, $N_{\text{fmp}} = 18$. These values can be determined with purely syntactic manipulation of the bound expressions of the loops that iterate over the original multi-pass space. Figure 7(a) describes the loop nest for the original multi-pass space in Figure 6 with parametric problem size and pass size. When the loop nest is fully permutable—this is always true for a tilable program—we can even change the enumeration order for the points in each pass. Figure 7(b) shows a permuted loop nest that is equivalent to the one in Figure 7(a), but the points inside each pass are enumerated along the i dimension first. Since the p loop in Figure 7(a) iterates over the origins of each pass, n_{pass} is the number of iteration points in loop p. Also, the loop i in Figure 7(a) iterates over the points along dimension i for a given t iteration, then N_{period} is equivalent to the number of iteration points in the i loop within the first iteration of the t loop. Similarly, the number of points along dimension i enumerated in the last pass is the number of iteration points for the i loop within the last pass iteration, and the corresponding loop nest is the i loop in Figure 7(b).

For a given loop l, with lower bound lb, upper bound ub and stride s, the number of iteration points in loop l is iters $= \lceil \frac{ub-lb+1}{s} \rceil$, and the last iteration point in loop l is $(\text{iters} - 1) \times s + lb$. For our example, $n_{\text{pass}} = \lceil \frac{5-0+1}{2} \rceil = 3$, $N_{\text{period}} = \lceil \frac{t+5-t+1}{1} \rceil = 6$, the last pass iteration is $p = (3-1)*2+0 = 4$, and $N_{\text{last}} = \left\lceil \frac{\min(p+1,5)+5-p+1}{1} \right\rceil = 7$. After N_{fmp} is computed, the outermost loop of the flattened space can be constructed as a loop that iterates from 0 to N_{fmp} with stride 1.

4.2.2 Generating The Inner Loop

The inner loop for the flattened space enumerates the corresponding points for a visited point along i in the flattened space. Note that the t loop in Figure 7(b) visits the points along t dimension for a given i iteration in the original space, which is exactly the information we need. However, in order to use this information, we need to convert the visited i in the flattened space back to the i values in the original space. For now, let us ignore the points in a pass that overlap with the next pass. Let the ti-th point along the i dimension in the flattened space be the n-th iteration along dimension i within the m-th pass. Then $ti = mN_{\text{period}} + n$, and $0 \leq m < n_{\text{pass}}, 0 \leq n < N_{\text{period}}$. Furthermore, given ti and N_{period}, the m and n can be computed as follows.

$$n = ti \mod N_{\text{period}}$$

$$m = \left\lfloor \frac{ti}{N_{\text{period}}} \right\rfloor$$

Then the corresponding pass origin value and i value in the original space is the m-th iteration value of the p loop and the n-th iteration value of the i loop in Figure 7(b) separately. The t-th iteration point value for a given loop l is $ts + lb$. After the i value in the original multi-pass space is computed, the loop t in Figure 7(b) can be attached to visit the corresponding points along the t dimension.

```
for(p=0; p<=T; p+=h)
  for(t=p; t<=min(p+h-1,T); t++)
    for(i=t; i<=t+M; i++)
        Body(t,i);
                    (a)
```

```
for(p=0; p<=T; p+=h)
  for(i=p; i<=min(p+h-1,T)+M; i++)
    for(t=max(p,i-M);t<=min(i,p+h-1,T);t++)
        Body(t,i);
                    (b)
```

Figure 7: The loop nests for the multi-pass iteration space with the original iteration order (a) and permuted order(b) before flattening. The number of iteration points in each row is M and there are T iterations along the t dimension. h is the pass height.

4.2.3 Handling The Overlapped Part

We handle the overlapped part between passes by checking whether there are points from the current pass and also the previous pass for a visited point along dimension i. Then, the points that are ignored at the current pass will be visited as the points in the previous pass during the execution of next pass. The previous pass information can be deduced easily from the current pass information, for example, the pass number is $m - 1$, and the iteration number along i is

$n + N_{\text{period}}$. Our algorithm generates all those expressions by syntactic manipulations of bound expressions in the loop AST, and the resulting code is shown in Figure 8.

```
n_pass=ceild(T,h);
t=0;  p=t;  N_period=M+t-t;
p=(n_pass-1)*h;  N_last=min(p+h-1,T)+M-p;
N_fmp=(n_pass-1)*N_period+N_last;
for(ti=0; ti<N_fmp; ti++){
 p=(ti/N_period)*h;  i=(ti%N_period)+p;
 if((0<=p<=T) and (p<=i<=min(p+h-1,T)+M))
   for(t=max(p,i-M);t<=min(i,p+h-1,T);t++)
       Body(t,i);

 p=(ti/N_period-1)*h;
 i=ti%N_period+N_period + p;
 if((0<=p<=T) and (p<=i<=min(p+h-1,T)+M))
   for(t=max(p,i-M);t<=min(i,p+h-1,T);t++)
       Body(t,i);
}
```

Figure 8: The final sequential FMP code for the parallelogram with no second level tiling (the function ceild(a, b) returns $\lceil \frac{a}{b} \rceil$).

4.3 Tiling The Passes Of The 2D Space

When tiling is applied to each pass, each point in Figure 6 is replaced with a small tile, and the loops generated visit the tile origins. Note that one important fact that we have used is that N_{period} is the same for all passes. However, this may not be true when the iteration space is tiled. Figure 9 describes the tiled iteration space with $\vec{0}$ as a legal tile origin (an assumption made by most existing tiled code generators) for a parallelogram iteration space whose first iteration point is $(2, 2)$. As shown in Figure 9, although the number of iteration points are the same for each row in each pass, the number of tiles in the first row are different for the first pass and second pass. To resolve this, we align the first tile origin to the first iteration point of the space being tiled, instead of assuming that $\vec{0}$ is a tile origin. Due to the regularity of the iteration space we handle, each pass can be viewed as a shift of the first pass. Now the number of tiles in the first row is the same for all the passes, and the above technique for the flattened space can simply be reused. The tiled loop information is obtained using the existing techniques [16].

4.4 Sequential FMP For Higher Dimensions

The main problem in generalizing to the higher dimensions is how to deduce, from single pass coordinates along the (flattened) pass dimension, the original (non-flattened) pass coordinates. We reuse the same intuition, this time making the number of *passes* the same along each of the outer data dimensions (with possible padding at the boundary). Then, a similar division and modulo technique can be used to convert back to the passes in the original space.

5. EXPERIMENTAL VALIDATION

We evaluated our parallelization strategy using a set of stencil benchmarks. We first describe our experimental setup, then show the comparison between the standard wavefront parallelization and our FMPP strategy, and also evaluate the energy consumption of both strategies based on a linear regression energy model.

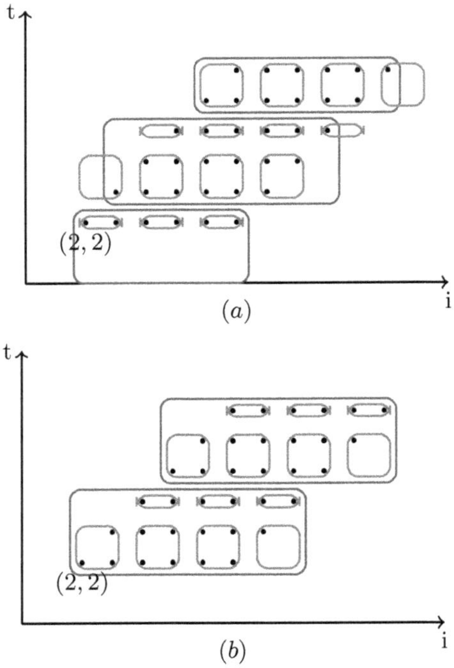

Figure 9: Tiled space for a parallelogram iteration space with the legal tile origin $\vec{0}$ (a) and the first iteration point (b). The first iteration point is $(2, 2)$. Each blue box represents one tile, and each red box is a small tile within a pass.

5.1 Experiment Setup

Our experiments are performed on two platforms: one with an 8-core Intel Xeon E5-2650 v2 with M393B1K70DH0-CK0 DRAM from Samsung, the other with a 6-core Intel Xeon E5-2620 v2 with a HMT41GU7AFR8C-RD DRAM from Hynix Semiconductor. The processors on both platforms have three levels of cache with the LLC shared among all the cores. The LLCs on these platforms are, respectively, 20 MB 20-way associative and 15 MB 20-way associative.

On the Xeon E5-2650 v2 based machine, Fedora 20 is installed and Red Hat 6.6 is installed on the other one. All the programs are compiled using icc 14.0.0 with the optimization flags -03, *-xHost* and *-funroll-loops*. As an estimation of the off-chip memory accesses, the number of LLC misses is measured through PAPI 3.5[31]. Table 1 gives description about the main characteristics of each benchmark. Our benchmark suite includes stencil computations with different number of data dimensions, stencil orders, neighboring points, number of floating point operations per iteration and also different numbers of variables involved.

The best tile size is selected by running an exhaustive search on all the tile sizes that fit into the L2 cache. For our FMPP strategy, the exhaustive search is performed on all the legal tile sizes that fit into the L2 cache, and the pass size is also restricted that the values needed by each wavefront in the pass fit into LLC.

5.2 Efficiency Of Generated Code

In this subsection, we demonstrate the efficiency of the codes generated by our FMPP code generator. We compare the performance of the standard wavefront parallelization codes generated by our code generator with the codes generated from Pluto [5] and Pochoir [30].

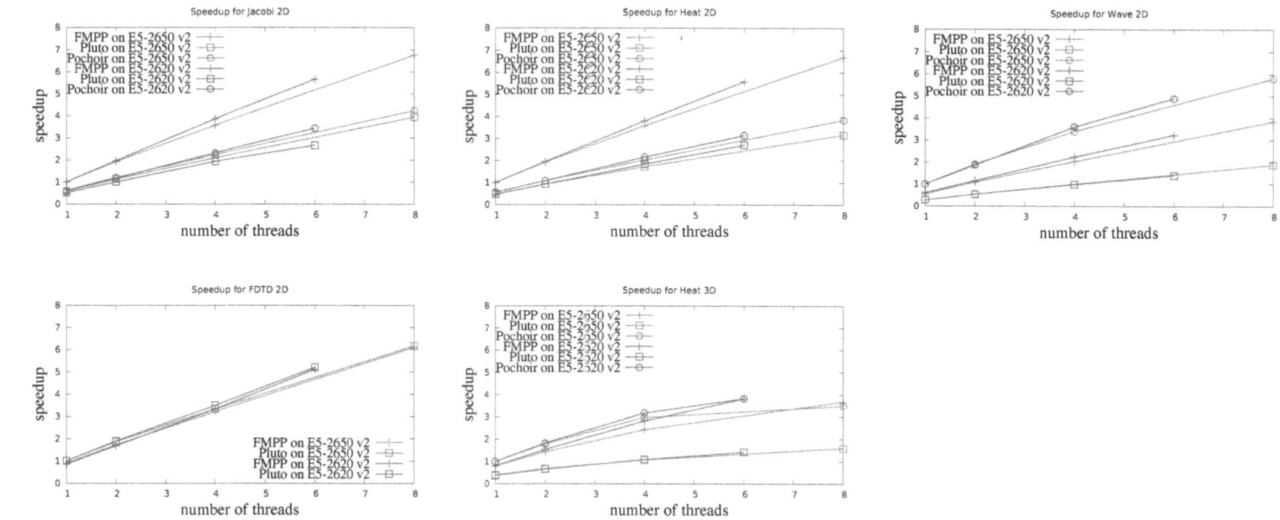

Figure 10: Performance comparison for standard wavefront parallelization from our FMPP code generator with Pluto and Pochoir. There is no performance for Pochoir for FDTD because Pochoir requires the neighboring points are all from the previous time step.

Benchmark	Data D	Order	NP	NV	FPI
Jacobi 2D	2	first	5	1	5
Heat 2D	2	first	5	1	9
FDTD 2D	2	first	5	3	11
Wave 2D	2	third	13	1	13
Heat 3D	3	first	7	1	15

Table 1: Benchmark Details. Data D is the number of dimensions of a data grid, another time dimension is needed. NP stands for neighboring points, it means the number of neighboring points needed for the computation of each point. NV represents the number of variables that have to be computed during the computation. FPI is floating point operations per iteration.

Figure 10 shows the speedup of the codes generated from the three code generators for the benchmarks. The baseline performance is the best single thread performance among all the code generated. We see that the performance of our generated codes is comparable to, often better than, codes generated from existing code generators.

5.3 Efficiency Of Our FMPP Strategy

We evaluate the energy consumption of our benchmark on the Xeon E5-2650 v2 and Xeon E5-2620 v2 based on a simple linear regression energy model.

5.3.1 Energy Model Overview

The energy consumed by an application consists of CPU energy and off-chip memory system energy, each of which can be separated into static and dynamic components.

$$E = E_{\text{cpu}}^{\text{static}} + E_{\text{cpu}}^{\text{dynamic}} + E_{\text{mem}}^{\text{static}} + E_{\text{mem}}^{\text{dynamic}} \quad (4)$$

We model the CPU energy and memory system energy separately. For the memory system energy, the static energy consumed can be computed as $P_{\text{mem}}^{\text{static}} T_{\text{exec}}$, where $P_{\text{mem}}^{\text{static}}$ is the static power of the memory system, and T_{exec} is the total execution time. The dynamic energy consumed by the memory system is proportional to the total number of memory access N_{acc}. Let e_{acc} be the energy consumed per memory access, then $E_{\text{mem}}^{\text{dynamic}} = e_{acc} N_{acc}$. Then the energy consumed by the off-chip memory system E_{mem} can be estimated as follows:

$$E_{\text{mem}} = P_{\text{mem}}^{\text{static}} T_{\text{exec}} + e_{\text{acc}} N_{\text{acc}}$$

The value of $P_{\text{mem}}^{\text{static}}$ and e_{acc} are derived using the DRAM power calculator [21] provided by Micron Technology, Inc. The derived static power for the memory system from Samsung and Hynix Semiconductor are 2.5 W and 8.8 W, and the energy per double memory access are 53.0 nJ and 30.7 nJ. The two platforms used in our experiment have very different internal micro-architectures for DRAM, as indicated from the parameter values derived.

For the CPU energy consumption, we derive a simple energy model using linear regression. The static CPU energy consumption is the static CPU power multiplied by the execution time. Cong et al. [6] observe that dynamic CPU energy consumption is proportional to the number of completed instructions and cache accesses at each level. Since most of the instructions contained in uniform dependence programs are floating point operations (mostly translated to double precision vector instructions) and branch instructions, we further divide the completed instructions into the floating point instructions and branch instructions. In order to derive the linear regression model, we collected hundreds of training data points using a subset of the benchmarks with different problem sizes and tile sizes. Then we collected another hundreds of data points from the other benchmarks to validate the derived model.

The linear regression model is shown in Equation 5.

$$\begin{aligned} E_{\text{cpu}} = \beta_0 + \beta_1 \times \text{DPVec} + \beta_2 \times \text{Branch} + \beta_3 \times \text{L1Acc} \\ + \beta_4 \times \text{L2Acc} + \beta_5 \times \text{L3Acc} + \beta_6 \times T_{\text{exec}} \end{aligned} \quad (5)$$

We collect the double precision vector instructions (DPVec), branch instructions (Branch), L1 data cache access (L1Acc), L2 cache access (L2Acc) and L3 cache access (L3Acc) through PAPI, and measured the energy information through access to Running Average Power Limit (RAPL) sensors (the execution time of the program has to be controlled, so that

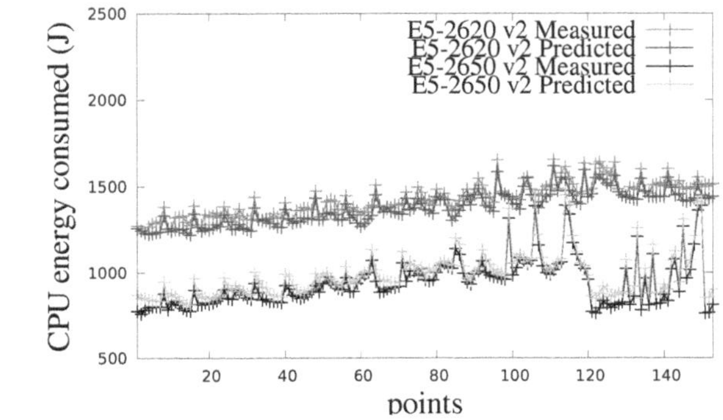

Figure 11: Validation result of our linear regression model for CPU energy.

the RAPL counter does not overflow). Then we build our linear regression model by using the statistical package R. Figure 11 shows the validation result of the energy model. The RMS error for all the validated points is only around 0.3%, this is probably due to the restricted benchmarks that we are using. Building an energy model that handles general programs is out of the scope of this paper.

5.3.2 *Results*

Figures 12 and 13 show the energy consumption for all the benchmarks on the two platforms, normalized to the total energy consumed by the program with standard wavefront parallelization. On the average, dynamic memory energy consumption is about 13% of the total energy on the platform with Xeon E5-2650 v2, and about 7.9% of the total energy consumption on the Xeon E5-2620 v2 based machine. Our FMPP is able to save a significant part of the dynamic memory energy consumption (green part): about 78% of dynamic memory energy consumption on the Xeon E5-2650 v2 and 80% of the dynamic memory energy consumption on Xeon E5-2620 v2. Also, The CPU energy consumption for FMPP does not vary too much compared with the standard wavefront parallelization.

In terms of savings of the total energy consumption, we got an average of 7.9% of total energy consumption saving on the Xeon E5-2650 v2 based machine and an average of 3.4% overall energy savings on the Xeon E5-2620 v2 based machine. We even got up to 14% of energy savings on the platform with Xeon E5-2650 v2 for Heat 2D.

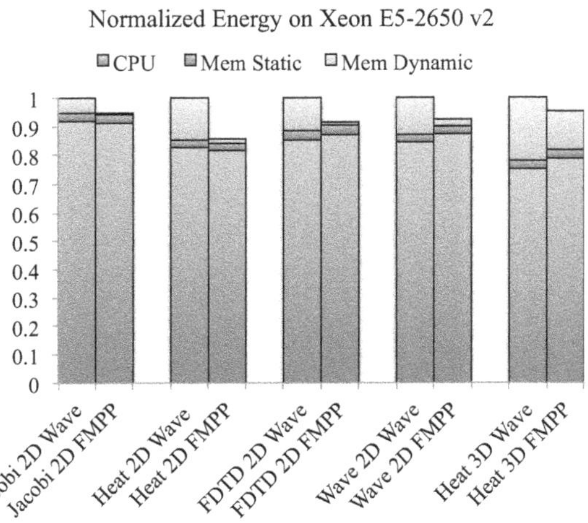

Figure 12: Normalized energy consumption for the standard wavefront parallelization (Wave) and our flattened multi-pass parallelization strategy (FMPP) on Xeon E5-2650 v2.

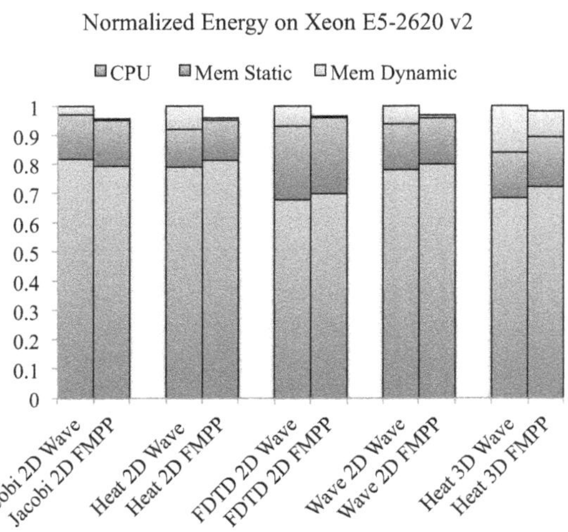

Figure 13: Normalized energy consumption for the standard wavefront parallelization (Wave) and our flattened multi-pass parallelization strategy (FMPP) on Xeon E5-2620 v2.

6. RELATED WORK

The related work deals with two topics, namely tiling and stencils, and tiled code generation.

6.1 Tiling and Stencils

Many authors have worked on applying tiling optimization on stencil computations for both shared and distributed memory or hybrid platforms. On these platforms, *time tiling* (i.e., tiling across multiple time steps) is essential to achieve maximum data reuse.

Time skewing [34, 7] is one of the most important approaches for time tiling. It looks at the dependences in the whole computation space, skews them with respect to the time dimension, then divides it into rectangular tiles. The same effect can also be achieved by hyperplane tiling [12, 5]. Instead of skewing the computation space to make rectangular tiling legal, they are trying to find legal hyperplanes to cut the whole computation space, and it ends up with parallelogram shaped tiles. Due to dependences between tiles, classic 45 degree wavefront parallelization is used to parallelize the program. As we described in section 3, the potential data reuse between successive wavefronts is not exploited when the problem size is "large enough."

Time tiling can also be achieved by using non-rectangular shaped tiles. Strzodka develops a strategy called cache accurate time skewing (CATS) [29]. In CATS, a subset of the program dimensions are tiled to form large tiles with diamond shapes. Grosser et al. [9] presents a hexagonal tiling technique in the context of GPUs. With these techniques, concurrent start can be explored, and the pipeline fill-flush overhead in the classic wavefront parallelization does not occur. However, when the values produced at one parallel time step exceed the LLC, there is no data reuse between successive parallel time steps under the worst condition also. We can easily adapt their method to optimize for LLC misses.

Using the analysis described in Section 3, their strategies would nevertheless perform $\sqrt{P}$ more memory accesses than ours, where P is the number of processors.

Cache-oblivious tiling [25] is another time tiling technique. In cache-oblivious tiling, the whole computation space is recursively divided into small tiles with trapezoid [8, 30] or parallelogram [28] surfaces. The base case of the recursive function is decided based on knowledge or heuristics, and no specific hardware information is needed. The parallel schedule used in cache oblivious tiling is very different from the classic wavefront schedule, the parallelization is enabled whenever independent tiles are obtained during the cut. However, the reuse among parallel tiles is still not explored. There are also some other factors that can impact the efficiency of the cache-oblivious algorithm, e.g., without knowing the cache size, bad choice of base case can be made and it can significantly increase the overall cache misses.

In general, our method is independent of the tile shape or parallelization strategy that are chosen. Our main idea is dividing the iteration space into small passes, so that the data reuse within the whole pass is possible. Within a pass, any existing tiling technique and parallelization strategy for the tiled iteration space can be adapted. The reason why we focused on rectangular tiling and wavefront parallelization is the simplicity of code generation. Similar idea is also used in the wavefront diamond temporal blocking (MWD) strategy developed by Malas et al. [20, 19]. The MWD strategy first applies the diamond tiling technique presented by Strzodka [29], and then applies the classic time tiling and 45 wavefront parallelization within each diamond. The available threads are grouped into groups, and each group is assigned to one diamond, and the diamond size is chosen to fit into the LLC. However, their work comes up with a trade off in performance, which is potentially caused by the pipeline fill-flush overhead of the wavefront parallelization within each diamond. As discussed before, it is necessary to retain the high performance in order to achieve optimal energy.

6.2 Tiled Code Generation

Developing efficient tiled code generator is an active research topic [5, 1, 26, 17, 16, 11, 10, 2]. When tile sizes are fixed, rectangular tiling and hyperplane tiling can be described as a linear transformation, and purely polyhedral code generators [3, 5] are adequate. Fixed sized code generation for other shapes are also tackled by many authors, such as diamond tiling [29, 1], trapezoid tiling [25, 8, 30], hexagonal tiling [9] and etc. Recently, Shrestha [27] presented a multi-hierarchical tiling technique that explores concurrent start for the second level of tiling based on the code generation technique of Pluto. However, when tile sizes are parameterized, tiling becomes a non-linear transformation, and introduces challenges to the code generation problem.

PrimeTile [11], DynTile [10], PTile [2] and DTiler [16] are the most representative parametric tiled code generators developed recently. All of them support multi-level tiling with rectangular tiles, and the algorithms are purely syntactic. DynTile [10] supports the wavefront parallelization through a run-time scheduling technique, while DTiler [16] and PTile [2] compute the 45 degree wavefront schedule statically. However, none of them supports the polynomial schedule that is required in our FMPP strategy.

7. CONCLUSION

We presented an energy-efficient parallelization strategy for dense stencil like programs, on which polyhedral analysis can be used and tiling can be applied. Energy optimization for tuned compute bound codes have very little "energy slack," and we targeted the main contributor—the dynamic memory energy consumption—by minimizing the number of off-chip memory transfers. On both our experimental platforms we were able to reduce this significantly—by over 75%.

We developed a tiled code generator for our parallelization strategy, for which the key challenge was to incorporate schedules that are polynomial, rather than the standard multidimensional ones used in most code generators. This is the first code generator that implements polynomial schedules for parametric tile sizes.

Our experimental results showed that the generated code has performance comparable with, often better than, existing code generators. We achieve, on the average, overall energy savings of 7.9% on the Xeon E5-2650 v2, and 3.4% the Xeon E5-2620 v2. In the best case, we saved 14% of the energy on the Xeon E5-2650 v2.

Our experiments confirm that optimizing energy leads to good performance, but the converse is not necessarily true. Our strategy can be used in many other programming models and architectures—distributed memory codes in MPI, hybrid MPI/OpenMP, accelerators like GPUs, and even FPGAs. It is also interesting and challenging to use different tile shapes within our multi-pass strategy.

8. REFERENCES

[1] V. Bandishti, I. Pananilath, and U. Bondhugula. Tiling Stencil Computations to Maximize Parallelism. In *Proceedings of the International Conference on High Performance Computing, Networking, Storage and Analysis*, SC '12, pages 40:1–40:11, Los Alamitos, CA, USA, 2012.

[2] M. M. Baskaran, A. Hartono, S. Tavarageri, T. Henretty, J. Ramanujam, and P. Sadayappan. Parameterized Tiling Revisited. In *Proceedings of the 8th Annual IEEE/ACM International Symposium on Code Generation and Optimization*, CGO '10, pages 200–209, New York, NY, USA, 2010. ACM.

[3] C. Bastoul. Code Generation in the Polyhedral Model Is Easier Than You Think. In *Proceedings of the 13th International Conference on Parallel Architectures and Compilation Techniques*, PACT '04, pages 7–16, Washington, DC, USA, 2004.

[4] K. Bergman, S. Borkar, D. Campbell, W. Carlson, W. Dally, and et al. ExaScale Computing Study: Technology Challenges in Achieving Exascale Systems Peter Kogge, Editor & Study Lead. 2008.

[5] U. Bondhugula, A. Hartono, J. Ramanujam, and P. Sadayappan. A Practical Automatic Polyhedral Program Optimization System. In *ACM SIGPLAN Conference on Programming Language Design and Implementation (PLDI)*, June 2008.

[6] J. Cong and B. Yuan. Energy-efficient Scheduling on Heterogeneous Multi-core Architectures. In *Proceedings of the 2012 ACM/IEEE International Symposium on Low Power Electronics and Design*, ISLPED '12, pages 345–350, New York, NY, USA, 2012.

[7] D. Wonnacott. Time Skewing for Parallel Computers. In *the 12th International Workshop on Languages and Compilers for Parallel Computing*, LCPC '99, pages 477–480, London, UK, 2000.

[8] M. Frigo and V. Strumpen. Cache Oblivious Stencil Computations. In *International Conference on Supercomputing (ICS), 2005.*, pages 361–366, Cambridge, MA, June 2005.

[9] T. Grosser, A. Cohen, J. Holewinski, P. Sadayappan, and S. Verdoolaege. Hybrid Hexagonal/Classical Tiling for GPUs. In *Proceedings of Annual IEEE/ACM International Symposium on Code Generation and Optimization*, CGO '14, New York, NY, USA, 2014.

[10] A. Hartono, M. Baskaran, J. Ramanujam, and P. Sadayappan. DynTile: Parametric Tiled Loop Generation for Parallel Execution on Multicore Processors. In *Proceedings of 2010 IEEE International Symposium on Parallel Distributed Processing (IPDPS'10)*, pages 1–12, April 2010.

[11] A. Hartono, M. M. Baskaran, C. Bastoul, A. Cohen, S. Krishnamoorthy, B. Norris, J. Ramanujam, and P. Sadayappan. Parametric Multi-level Tiling of Imperfectly Nested Loops. In *Proceedings of the 23rd International Conference on Supercomputing*, ICS '09, pages 147–157, New York, NY, USA, 2009. ACM.

[12] F. Irigoin and R. Triolet. Supernode Partitioning. In *the 15th ACM SIGPLAN-SIGACT symposium on Principles of programming languages*, POPL '88, pages 319–329, New York, NY, USA, 1988.

[13] A. Jaiantilal, Y. Jiang, and S. Mishra. Modeling CPU Energy Consumption for Energy Efficient Scheduling. In *Proceedings of the 1st Workshop on Green Computing*, GCM '10, pages 10–15, New York, NY, USA, 2010.

[14] S. Kamil, C. Chan, L. Oliker, J. Shalf, and S. Williams. An Auto-Tuning Framework for Parallel Multicore Stencil Computations. In *Parallel Distributed Processing (IPDPS), 2010 IEEE International Symposium on*, april 2010.

[15] R. M. Karp, R. E. Miller, and S. Winograd. The Organization of Computations for Uniform Recurrence Equations. *J. ACM*, 14(3), July 1967.

[16] D. Kim. *Parameterized and Multi-Level Tiled Loop Generation.* PhD thesis, Colorado State University, Fort Collins, CO, USA, 2010.

[17] D. Kim, L. Renganarayana, D. Rostron, S. Rajopadhye, and M. M. Strout. Multi-level tiling: m for the price of one. In *Proceedings of the International Conference for High Performance Computing, Networking, Storage, and Analysis (SC)*, November 2007.

[18] J. G. Koomey. Estimating Total Power Consumption by Servers in the U.S. and the World. Technical report, Lawrence Derkley National Laboratory, Feb. 2007.

[19] T. M. Malas, G. Hager, H. Ltaief, and D. E. Keyes. Towards energy efficiency and maximum computational intensity for stencil algorithms using wavefront diamond temporal blocking. *CoRR*, 2014.

[20] T. M. Malas, G. Hager, H. Ltaief, H. Stengel, G. Wellein, and D. E. Keyes. Multicore-Optimized Wavefront Diamond Blocking for Optimizing Stencil Updates. *CoRR*, 2014.

[21] I. Micron Technology. DDR3 SDRAM System-Power Calculator. `http://www.micron.com/products/support/power-calc/`.

[22] L. Minas and B. Ellison. The Problem of Power Consumption in Servers. *Intel Press*, 2009.

[23] D. Moldovan and J. Fortes. Partitioning and Mapping Algorithms into Fixed Size Systolic Arrays. *IEEE Transactions on Computers*, C-35(1):1–12, Jan 1986.

[24] L. Peng, R. Seymour, K. Nomura, R. Kalia, A. Nakano, P. Vashishta, A. Loddoch, M. Netzband, W. Volz, and C. Wong. High-Order Stencil Computations on Multicore Clusters. In *IEEE International Symposium on Parallel Distributed Processing (IPDPS), 2009.*, may 2009.

[25] H. Prokop. Cache-Oblivious Algorithms. Master's thesis, Massachusetts Institute of Technology, Department of Electrical Engineering and Computer Science, 1999.

[26] L. Renganarayanan, D. Kim, S. V. Rajopadhye, and M. M. Strout. Parameterized tiled loops for free. In *PLDI*, pages 405–414, 2007.

[27] S. Shrestha, J. Manzano, A. Marquez, J. Feo, and G. Gao. Jagged Tiling for Intra-tile Parallelism and Fine-Grain Multithreading. In *Proceedings of the 27th International Workshop on Languages and Compilers for Parallel Computing*, LCPC '14, 2014.

[28] R. Strzodka, M. Shaheen, D. Pajak, and H.-P. Seidel. Cache Oblivious Parallelograms in Iterative Stencil Computations. In *24th ACM/SIGARCH International Conference on Supercomputing (ICS)*, pages 49–59, Tsukuba, Japan, June 2010.

[29] R. Strzodka, M. Shaheen, D. Pajak, and H.-P. Seidel. Cache Accurate Time Skewing in Iterative Stencil Computations. In *Proceedings of the International Conference on Parallel Processing (ICPP)*. IEEE Computer Society, Sept. 2011.

[30] Y. Tang, R. A. Chowdhury, B. C. Kuszmaul, C.-K. Luk, and C. E. Leiserson. The Pochoir Stencil Compiler. In *Proceedings of the 23rd ACM symposium on Parallelism in algorithms and architectures*, SPAA '11, New York, NY, USA, 2011. ACM.

[31] K. The University of Tennessee. Performance Application Programming Interface. `http://icl.cs.utk.edu/papi/`.

[32] B. University of California. The Landscape of Parallel Computing Research. http://view.eecs.berkeley.edu.

[33] M. E. Wolf and M. S. Lam. A Data Locality Optimizing Algorithm. In *the ACM SIGPLAN 1991 conference on Programming language design and implementation*, PLDI '91, pages 30–44, New York, NY, USA, 1991. ACM.

[34] D. Wonnacott. Achieving Scalable Locality with Time Skewing. *Int. J. Parallel Program.*, 30(3):181–221, Jun 2002.

[35] J. Xue. *Loop Tiling for Parallelism.* Kluwer Academic Publishers, Norwell, MA, USA, 2000.

ASPaS: A Framework for Automatic SIMDization of Parallel Sorting on x86-based Many-core Processors

Kaixi Hou, Hao Wang, and Wu-chun Feng
Department of Computer Science
Virginia Tech
Blacksburg, VA, 24060
{kaixihou,hwang121,wfeng}@vt.edu

ABSTRACT

Due to the difficulty that modern compilers have in vectorizing applications on vector-extension architectures, programmers resort to manually programming vector registers with intrinsics in order to achieve better performance. However, the continued growth in the width of registers and the evolving library of intrinsics make such manual optimizations tedious and error-prone. Hence, we propose a framework for the *A*utomatic *S*IMDization of *P*arallel *S*orting (*ASPaS*) on x86-based multicore and manycore processors. That is, ASPaS takes any sorting network and a given instruction set architecture (ISA) as inputs and automatically generates vectorized code for that sorting network.

By formalizing the sort function as a sequence of comparators and the transpose and merge functions as sequences of vector-matrix multiplications, ASPaS can map these functions to operations from a selected "pattern pool" that is based on the characteristics of parallel sorting, and then generate the vectorized code with the real ISA intrinsics. The performance evaluation of our ASPaS framework on the Intel Xeon Phi coprocessor illustrates that automatically generated sorting codes from ASPaS can outperform the sorting implementations from STL, Boost, and Intel TBB.

Categories and Subject Descriptors

D.3.4 [**Programming Language**]: Processors—*Code generation, Optimization*

General Terms

Performance

Keywords

sort; merge; transpose; vectorization; SIMD; ISA; MIC; AVX; AVX-512;

ICS'15, June 8 - 11, 2015, Newport Beach/Irvine, CA, USA.

http://dx.doi.org/10.1145/2751205.2751247.

1. INTRODUCTION

To boost performance, modern processors put multiple cores onto a single die rather than increase processor frequency. In addition to this inter-core parallelism, a vector processing unit (VPU) is associated with each core to enable further intra-core parallelism. Execution on a VPU follows a "single instruction, multiple data" (SIMD) paradigm by carrying out the "lock-step" operations over packed data. Although modern compilers can automatically vectorize most regular codes, they often fail to vectorize complex loop patterns due to the lack of accurate compiler analysis and effective compiler transformations [15]. Therefore, the burden falls on programmers' shoulders to implement the vectorization using intrinsics or even assembly code.

Writing efficient SIMD code by hand is a time-consuming and error-prone activity. First, the vectorization of existing (complex) codes requires expert knowledge of the underlying algorithm. Second, the vectorization requires a comprehensive understanding of the SIMD intrinsics. The intrinsics for data management and movement are as important as those for computation because programmers often need to rearrange data in the vector units before sending them to the ALU. However, the flexibility of the data-reordering functions is restricted, since directly supporting an arbitrary permutation is impractical [14]. Consequently, programmers have to resort to a combination of data-reordering functions to attain a desired pattern. Third, the architecture-specific nature of vector instructions, i.e., different processors might support different vector widths and versions of an instruction set architecture (ISA), can cause portability issues. For example, to port Advanced Vector Extensions (AVX) codes to the AVX-512 architecture of the Intel Many Integrated Core (MIC), we either need to identify the instructions with equivalent functionalities or rewrite and tweak the codes using alternative instructions. While library-based optimizations [12] can hide the details of vectorization from the end user, these challenges are still encountered during the design and implementation of the libraries.

To address the above issues with respect to the sorting primitive, we propose a framework called ASPaS, short for Automatic SIMDization of Parallel Sorting, to automatically generate efficient SIMD codes for parallel sorting on x86-based multicore and manycore processors. ASPaS can take any sorting network and a given ISA as inputs and automatically produce vectorized sorting code as the output. The generated code adopts a bottom-up scheme to sort and merge segmented data. Because the vectorized sort function puts partially sorted data in column-major order, AS-

PaS compensates it with the transpose function before the merge stage. Considering the variety of sorting and merging networks[1] [1] that correspond to different sorting algorithms (such as odd-even [3], bitonic [3], Hibbard [11], and Bose-Nelson [4]) and the continuing evolution of the instruction set [7] (such as SSE, AVX, AVX2, and AVX-512), it is imperative to provide such a framework to hide the instruction-level details of sorting and allow programmers to focus on the use of the sorting algorithms instead.

ASPaS consists of four major parts: (1) Sorter, (2) Transposer, (3) Merger, and (4) Code Generator. The *SIMD Sorter* takes a sorting network as input and generates a sequence of comparators for the sort function. The *SIMD Transposer* and *SIMD Merger* formalize the data-reordering operations in the transpose and merge functions as sequences of vector-matrix multiplications. The *SIMD Code Generator* creates an ISA-friendly pattern pool containing the requisite data-comparing and reordering primitives, builds those sequences with primitives, and then maps them to the real ISA intrinsics.

The major contributions of our work include the following. First, we propose the ASPaS framework to automatically generate parallel sorting code using architecture-specific SIMD instructions. Second, using ASPaS, we generate various parallel sorting codes for the combinations of five sorting networks, two merging networks, and three datatypes (integer, float, double) on Intel MIC, and then conduct a series of evaluations. For the one-word type,[2] our SIMD codes can deliver up to 7.7-fold and 5.7-fold speedups over the serial sort and merge, respectively. For the two-word type, the corresponding speedups are 6.3-fold and 3.7-fold, respectively. Compared with other single-threaded sort implementations, including `qsort` and `sort` from STL [19], and `sort` from Boost [24], our SIMD codes deliver a range of speedups from 2.4-fold to 4.3-fold for the one-word type and 1.3-fold to 2.6-fold for the two-word type. We also wrap up our SIMD codes into a multi-threaded version. Compared with `parallel_sort` from Intel TBB [21], ASPaS delivers speedups of up to 2.1-fold and 1.4-fold for the one-word type and the two-word type, respectively.

2. BACKGROUND

This section presents (1) a brief overview of the vector architecture of Intel MIC, (2) a domain-specific language (DSL) to formalize the data-reordering patterns in our framework, and (3) a sorting and merging network.

2.1 Intel MIC Vector Architecture

The MIC coprocessor consists of up to 61 in-order cores, each of which is outfitted with a new vector processing unit (VPU). The VPU state for each thread contains 32 512-bit general registers (zmm0-31), eight 16-bit mask registers (k0-7), and a status register. A 512-bit SIMD ISA is introduced in accordance with the new VPU. However, previous SIMD ISAs, e.g. SSE and AVX, are not supported by the vector architecture of MIC, due to the issues from the wider vector, transcendental instructions, etc. [20].

In MIC, each 512-bit vector is subdivided into four lanes and each lane contains four 32-bit elements. Both of the lanes and elements are ordered as `DCBA`. Fig. 1a shows an example to rearrange data from two vector registers with the masked swizzle instruction. The intrinsics indicate we use the mask `m1` to select elements from either the swizzled vector of `v1` or the vector `v0`, and then store the result to a blended vector `t0`. The behavior of the mask in Intel MIC is non-destructive, in that no element in source `v0` has been changed if the corresponding mask bit is 0.

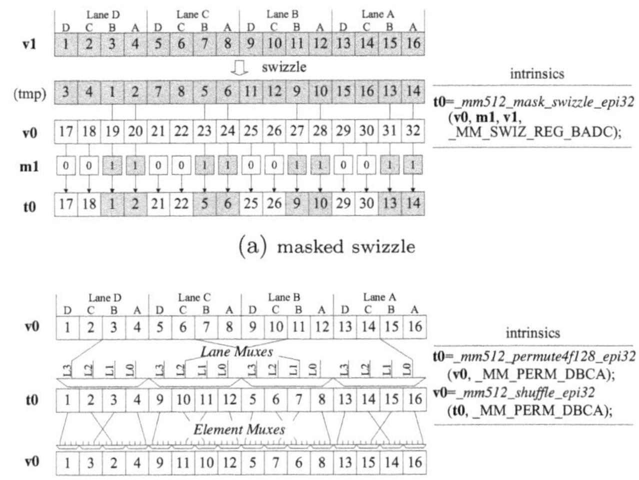

(a) masked swizzle

(b) permute and shuffle

Figure 1: Rearrange data on Intel MIC from: (a) two vector registers with the masked swizzle operation; (b) the same vector register with the permute and shuffle operations

Fig. 1b illustrates an example to rearrange data in the same vector register with the shuffle and permute intrinsics. The permute intrinsic using `_MM_PERM_DBCA` is for inter-lane rearrangement, which exchanges data in lanes `B` and `C`. The shuffle intrinsic with the same parameter is for intra-lane rearrangement to exchange elements at positions `B` and `C` of the same lane. This figure also shows the micro-architecture details [14]. The *Lane Muxes* are used to select desired lanes, and the *Element Muxes* are used to select desired elements in each lane. Because the permute and shuffle intrinsics are executed by different components of the hardware, it is possible to overlap the permute and shuffle intrinsics with a pipeline mode. In the design of ASPaS, we use this characteristic to obtain instruction-level overlapping.

2.2 DSL for Data-Reordering Operations

To better describe the data-reordering operations, we adopt the representation of a domain-specific language (DSL) from [8, 27] but with some modification. In the DSL, the first-order operators are adopted to define operations of basic data-reordering patterns, while the high-order operators connect such basic operations into complex ones. Those operators are described as below.

First-order operators (x is an input vector):

S_2 $(x_0, x_1) \mapsto (min(x_0, x_1), max(x_0, x_1))$. The comparing operator resembles the comparator which accepts two arbitrary values and outputs the sorted data. It can also accept two indexes explicitly written in following parentheses.

A_n $x_i \mapsto x_j, 0 \leqslant i, j < n$, iff $A_{ij} = 1$. A_n represents an arbitrary permutation operators denoted as a permutation matrix which has exactly one "1" in each row and column.

[1]In this paper, we distinguish the sorting network and the merging network.

[2]We use the Integer datatype as the representative of the one-word type, and the Double datatype for the two-word type.

I_n $x_i \mapsto x_i, 0 \leqslant i < n,$. I_n is the identity operator and outputs the data unchanged as its inputs. Essentially, I_n is a diagonal matrix denoted as $I_n = diag(1, 1, \cdots, 1)$.

L_m^{km} $x_{ik+j} \mapsto x_{jm+i}, 0 \leqslant i < m, 0 \leqslant j < k$. L_m^{km} is a special permutation operator, performing a stride-by-m permutation on the input vector of size km.

High-order operators (A, B are two permutation operators):

($\circ$) The composition operator is used to describe a data flow. $A_n \circ B_n$ means a n-element input vector is first processed by A_n and then the result vector is processed by B_n. The product symbol $\prod$ represents the iterative composition.

($\oplus$) The direct sum operator is served to merge two operators. $A_n \oplus B_m$ indicates that the first n elements of the input vector is processed by A_n, while the rest m elements follow B_m.

($\otimes$) The tensor product we used in the paper will appear like $I_m \otimes A_n$, which equals to $A_n \oplus \cdots \oplus A_n$. This means the input vector is divided into m segments, each of which is mapped to A_n.

With the DSL, a sequence of data comparing and reordering patterns can be formalized and implemented by a sequence of vector-matrix multiplications. Note that we only use the DSL to describe the data-comparing and data-reordering patterns instead of creating a new DSL.

2.3 Sorting and Merging Network

The sorting network is designed to sort the input data by using a sequence of comparisons, which are planned out in advance regardless of the value of the input data. The sorting network may depend on the merging network to merge pairs of sorted subarrays. Fig. 2a exhibits the Knuth diagram [1] of two identical bitonic sorting networks. Each 4-key sort network accepts 4 input elements. The paired dots represent the comparators that put the two inputs into the ascending order. After threaded through the wires of the network, these 4 elements are sorted. Fig. 2b is a merging network to merge two sorted 4-key vectors to an entirely sorted 8-key vector. Although sorting and merging networks are usually adopted in the circuit designs, it is also suitable for SIMD implementation thanks to the absence of unpredictable branches.

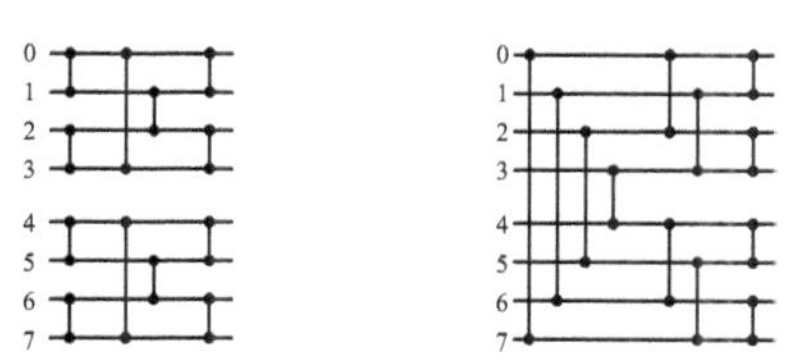

(a) sorting networks (b) merging network

Figure 2: Bitonic sorting and merging networks (a) Two 4-key sorting networks (b) One 8-key merging network

In this paper, the sorting and merging networks are represented by a list of comparators, each of which is denoted as CMP(x, y) that indicates a comparison operation between x-th and y-th elements of the input data.

3. METHODOLOGY

Our parallel sorting adopts a bottom-up approach to sort and merge segmented data, as illustrated in Alg. 1. This algorithm first divides the input data into contiguous segments, each of which size equals to a multiple times of SIMD width. Second, it loads each segment into registers and do the in-register vectorized sorting by calling the functions of `aspas_sort` and `aspas_transpose` (the sort stage in line 3-7). Then, the algorithm will merge successive sorted segments iteratively to generate the final output by calling `aspas_merge` (the merge stage of line 9-13). The functions of `load`, `store`, `aspas_sort`, `aspas_transpose`, and `aspas_merge` will be generated by ASPaS using the ISA-specific intrinsics. Because the `load` and `store` can be translated to the intrinsics once the ISA is given, we focus on other three functions with the prefix `aspas_` in the remaining sections.

Algorithm 1: ASPaS Parallel Sorting Structure

```
   /* w is the SIMD width                                        */
1  Function aspas::sort(Array a)
2      Vector v1, ..., vw;
3      foreach Segment seg in a do
4          // load seg to v1, ..., vw
5          aspas_sort(v1, ..., vw);
6          aspas_transpose(v1, ..., vw);
7          // store v1, ..., vw to seg
8      Array b ← new Array[a.size];
9      for s ←w; s < a.size; s*=2 do
10         for i ←0; i < a.size; i+=2*s do
11             // merge subarrays a + i and a + i + s
12             // to b + i by calling Function aspas::merge()
13         // copy b to a
14     return;
15 Function aspas::merge(Array a, Array b, Array out)
16     Vector v, u;
17     // i0, i1, i2 are offset pointers on a, b, out
18     // load w numbers from a to v
19     // load w numbers from b to u
20     aspas_merge(v, u);
21     // store v to out and update i0, i1, i2
22     while i0 ⩽ a.size and i1 ⩽ b.size do
23         if a[i0]⩽ b[i1] then
24             // load w numbers from a + i0 to v
25         else
26             // load w numbers from b + i1 to v
27         aspas_merge(v, u);
28         // store v to out + i2 and update i0, i1, i2
29     // process the remaining elements in a or b
30     return;
```

Fig. 3 illustrates the structure of the ASPaS framework and the generated `sort` function. Three modules of ASPaS —*SIMD Sorter*, *SIMD Transposer*, and *SIMD Merger* — are responsible for generating the sequences of comparing and data-reordering operations for the corresponding functions. These sequences will be mapped to the real SIMD intrinsics by the module of *SIMD Code Generator*.

3.1 SIMD Sorter

The operations of `aspas_sort` are generated by the *SIMD Sorter*. As shown in Fig. 4, `aspas_sort` loads the n-by-n matrix of data into n vectors and processes them based on the given sorting network, leading to the data sorted along each column of the matrix. Fig. 5 presents an example of a 4-by-4 data matrix going through a 4-key sorting network. Here, each dot represents one vector and each vertical line represents the vectorized comparison on the corresponding vectors. After six comparisons, the original data

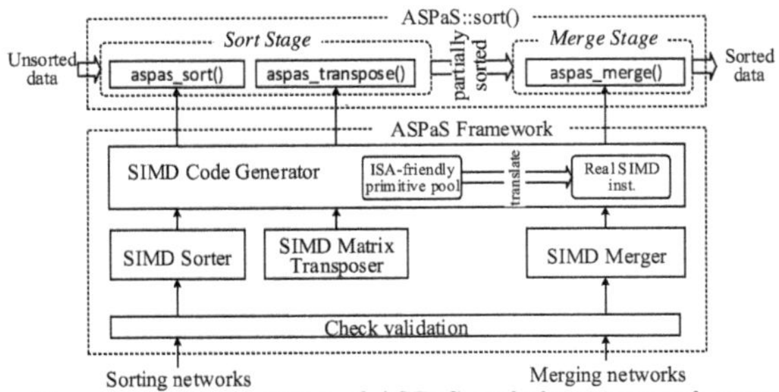

Figure 3: The structure of ASPaS and the generated sort

is sorted in ascending order in each column. Fig. 5 also shows the data dependency among these comparators. For example, CMP(0,1) and CMP(2,4) can be issued simultaneously, while CMP(0,3) can occur only after these two. It is straightforward to achieve three groups of comparators for this sorting network. However, for some sorting networks, we need a careful analysis of the data dependency when grouping the comparators. In the *SIMD Sorter*, we design an optimized grouping mechanism to analyze the input sequence of comparators and organize them into multiple groups. Our mechanism can facilitate the code generation by minimizing the number of groups, and in turn, reduce the code size.

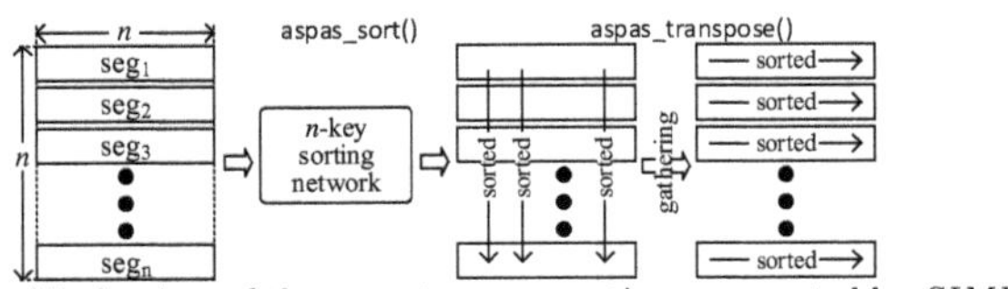

Figure 4: Mechanism of the sort stage: operations generated by *SIMD Sorter* and *SIMD Transposer*

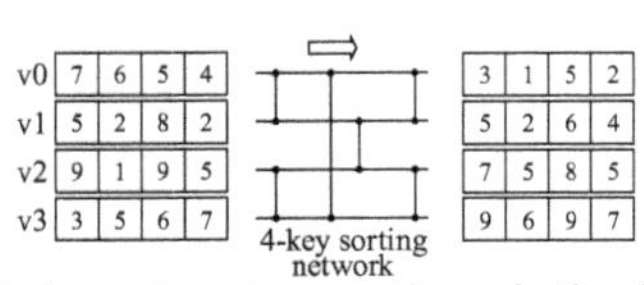

Figure 5: Four 4-element vectors go through the 4-key sorting network. Afterwards data is sorted in each column of the matrix.

Fig. 6 shows the Knuth diagram based on the Bose-Nelson sorting network [4]. The results of the original grouping mechanism and the optimized grouping mechanism are shown in this figure. The original grouping mechanism puts one comparator into the current group if this comparator has no data dependency with all the other operators in the current group; otherwise, a new group is created for this operator. As a result, the comparators are organized as seven groups by this scheme. However, if no data dependency exists among adjacent comparators, changing their order does not matter. Our optimized grouping exploits this feature and optimizes the original grouping. That is, it not only checks the data dependency between the comparators within the current group, but it also checks previous groups in a traceback manner until the data dependency is found or all groups are checked. Then, the comparator is put into the last-found group without any data dependency. By using this scheme, we can reorder $S_2(3,7)$ and $S_2(2,6)$ and place them into the appropriate groups. As a result, the number of groups with the optimized grouping is decreased from seven to six.

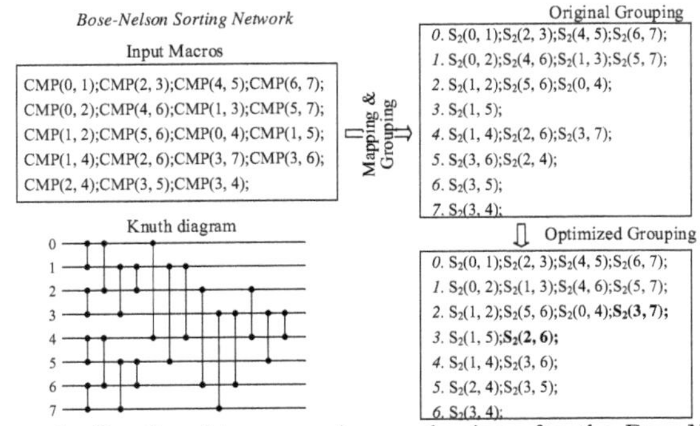

Figure 6: Results of two grouping mechanisms for the Bose-Nelson sorting network. The input is the comparator sequence of the sorting network, and the output is the sequence of grouped S_2 comparison operators of DSL.

To generate the SIMD codes for the **aspas_sort**, we keep two sets of vector variables a and b. Initially, all the loaded vectors are stored in the set a. Then, we move through the groups of the sorting network. For each comparator in the current group, we generate the operations to compare the vector variables, and the results are stored to the set b. For those vectors not used in the current group, we directly copy them to set b. For the next group, we flip the identities of a and b. Therefore, the set b becomes the input, and the results will be stored back to a. This process continues until all groups of the sorting network are gone through. Finally, we obtain all the operations, which will be mapped to the ISA-specific intrinsics (**_mm512_max** and **_mm512_min**) later by the *SIMD Code Generator*. At this point, the data is partially sorted but stored in column-major order.

3.2 SIMD Transposer

As illustrated in Fig. 4, the **aspas_sort** function has scattered the sorted elements in column-major order. The next task is to gather them into the same vectors (i.e., rows). The gathering process corresponds to a matrix transpose. There are two alternative methods to achieve matrix transposition on Intel MIC: one uses the gather/scatter SIMD intrinsics introduced in AVX-512; and the other uses the in-register matrix transpose. The first solution provides a convenient means to handle the scattered data in memory, but with the penalty of high latency from the non-contiguous memory access. The second solution can avoid such a penalty but at the expense of using complicated data-reordering operations. Considering the high latency of the gather/scatter intrinsics and the incompatibility with architectures that do not have gather/scatter intrinsics, we choose the second solution for the *SIMD Transposer*. In order to decouple the binding between the operations of matrix transpose and the real intrinsics with various SIMD widths, we formalize the data-reordering operations using the sequence of the permutation operators. After that, we can hand it over to the *SIMD Code Generator* to generate the efficient SIMD code for the **aspas_transpose** function.

$$\prod_{j=1}^{t-1}(L_2^{2^t} \circ (I_{2^{t-j-1}} \otimes L_{2^j}^{2^{j+1}}) \circ (I_{2^{t-j}} \otimes L_2^{2^j}) \circ L_{2^{t-1}}^{2^t}[v_{index}, v_{index+2^{j-1}}]) \quad (1)$$

Eq. 1 shows the operations performed on the preloaded vectors for the matrix transpose, where w is the SIMD width of the vector units, $t = log(2w)$, and for each j, $index \in \{i \cdot 2^j + n | 0 \leqslant i < \frac{w}{2^j}, 0 \leqslant n < 2^{j-1}\}$, which will create $\frac{w}{2^j} \cdot 2^{j-1} = \frac{w}{2}$ pairs of operand vectors for each preceding sequence of permutation operators. The square brackets wrap these pairs of vectors.

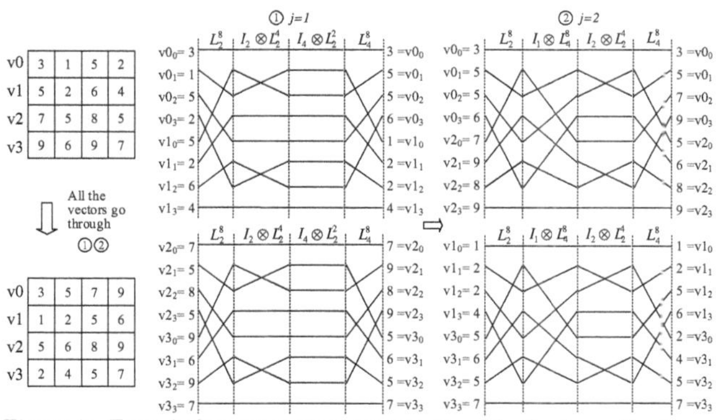

Figure 7: Four 4-element vectors transpose with the formalized permutation operators of DSL.

Fig. 7 illustrates an example with the SIMD width $w = 4$. The elements are preloaded to vectors $v0$, $v1$, $v2$, and $v3$ and have already been sorted vertically. Since $t - 1 = 2$, there are 2 steps denoted as ① and ② in the figure. When $j = 1$, the permutation operators are applied on the pairs $[v0, v1]$ and $[v2, v3]$; and when $j = 2$, the operations are on the pairs $[v0, v2]$ and $[v1, v3]$. The figure shows the values when the vectors go through the two steps accordingly. After that, the matrix is transposed, and the elements are gathered in the same vectors.

3.3 SIMD Merger

After the data is sorted in each segment using the **aspas_sort** and **aspas_transpose**, the **aspas_merge** is used as a kernel function to combine pairs of sorted data into a larger sequence iteratively. This function is generated by *SIMD Merger* based on appropriate merging networks, e.g., odd-even and bitonic networks. Here, we adopt the bitonic merging network for two reasons: (1) the bitonic merging network can be easily extended to any 2^n sized data; and (2) in each comparison step, all elements from the input vectors are processed, leading to symmetric operations on the elements. As a result, it is much easier to vectorize the bitonic merging network than others. From the perspective of the implementation, we have provided two variants of the bitonic merging networks [27], whose data-reordering operations can be formalized, as shown below.

$$\prod_{j=1}^{t}(I_{2^{j-1}} \otimes L_2^{2^{t-j+1}}) \circ (I_{2^{t-1}} \otimes S_2) \circ (I_{2^{j-1}} \otimes L_{2^{t-j}}^{2^{t-j+1}})[v, u] \quad (2)$$

$$\prod_{j=1}^{t} L_2^{2^t} \circ (I_{2^{t-1}} \otimes S_2)[v, u] \quad (3)$$

Similar with Section 3.2, $t = log(2w)$, where w is the SIMD width of the vector units. The vectors v and u represent two sorted sequences (the elements of vector u are inversely stored in advance). In Eq. 2, the data reordering operations are controlled by the variable j and changed in each step, while in Eq. 3, the permutation operators are independent with j, leading to the uniform data reordering patterns in each step. Therefore, we call the pattern in Eq. 2 as the inconsistent and that in Eq. 3 as the consistent. These patterns will be transmitted to *SIMD Code Generator* and generate the **aspas_merge** function. We will present the performance comparison of these two patterns in Section 4.

Figure 8 presents an example of these two variants of bitonic merging networks with the SIMD width $w = 4$.

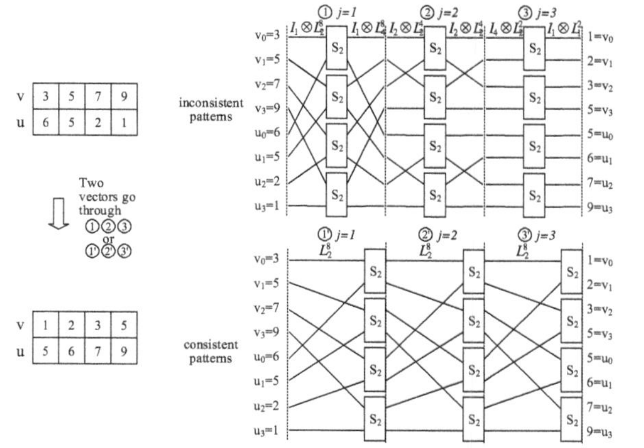

Figure 8: Two formalized variants of bitonic merging networks: the inconsistent pattern and the consistent pattern. All elements in vector v and u are sorted, but inversed in vector u.

As shown, the data-reordering operations derived from the inconsistent pattern are different in each step, while those from the consistent one are identical. Although the data-reordering operations adopted by these two variants are quite different, both of them can successfully achieve the merging functionality within the same number of steps, which is determined by the SIMD width w.

3.4 SIMD Code Generator

This module takes the data comparison operations from *SIMD Sorter* and the data-reordering operations from *SIMD Transposer* and *SIMD Merger* as the input to produce the real vectorized codes. Considering the simplicity of mapping the data comparison operations to real SIMD intrinsics, in this section, we only focus on how to find the most efficient intrinsics sequence to attain the given data-reordering operations. Our method is first to build a primitive pool based on the characteristics of the data-ordering operations, then dynamically build the primitive sequences based on the *matching score* between what we have achieved on the way and the targeting pattern, and finally map the selected primitives to the real intrinsics.

3.4.1 Primitive Pool Building

Different with the previous research, e.g. the automatic Fast Fourier transform (FFT) vectorization [17] using the exhaustive and heuristic search on all possible intrinsics combinations, we first build an ISA-friendly primitive pool to prune the search space. The most notable feature of the data-reordering operations for the transpose and merge is the symmetry: all the operations applied on the first half of the input are equivalent with those on the second half in a mirror style. So, to produce efficient operation sequences, we assume all the components of the sequences are also symmetric. We categorize these components as (1) the primitives for the symmetric permute operations on the same vector and (2) the primitives for the blend operations across two vectors.

Permute Primitives: For Intel MIC, there are 4 32-bit words (e.g. Integer or Float) per lane and 4 lanes in total for each vector register. Although there are $4^4 = 256$ possibilities for either intra-lane or inter-lane permute operations, we only consider those permutations without repetition and thus reduce the possibilities to $4! = 24$. Among them, only

8 symmetric data-reordering patterns will be selected, i.e. DCBA(original order), DBCA, CDAB, BDAC, BADC, CADB, ACBD, and ABCD, in which each letter denotes an element or a lane.

Blend Primitives: To guarantee the elements of the blended vector are from the two input vectors equally and symmetrically, we boil down the numerous mask modifiers to a few pairs of patterns. We define a pair as (0_2^i, $2^i\_2^i$), where $0 \leqslant i < log(w)$ and w is the vector length. Each pattern in the pair represents a 2^{i+1}-bit stream. The first number 0 or 2^i represents the offset of the first 1, and the second number 2^i is the number of consecutive 1s. All the other bits in the bit stream are filled with 0s. The bit streams will be extended to the real masks by duplicating themselves $\frac{w}{2^{i+1}}$ times. For Intel MIC with the w equal to 16, there are 4 pairs of patterns: (0_1, 1_1), (0_2, 2_2), (0_4, 4_4), and (0_8, 8_8). Among them, the pair (0_2, 2_2), where i is equal to 1, represents the bit streams 1100 and 0011. The corresponding masks are $(1100)_4$ and $(0011)_4$.

Now, we can categorize the primitives into 4 types based on permute or blend and intra-lane or inter-lane. Table 1 illustrates the categories and the corresponding operations, where the vector width w is set to 8 (containing 2 lanes) to save the space.

Table 1: Primitive Types

Type	Example (vector_width=8)
intra-lane-permute	ABCDEFGH→BADCFEHG (cdab)
inter-lane-permute	ABCDEFGH→EFGHABCD (--ab)
intra-lane-blend	ABCDEFGH|IJKLMNOP→ABKLEFOP (2_2)
inter-lane-blend	ABCDEFGH|IJKLMNOP→IJKLEFGH (0_4)

ASPaS stores these primitives as the permutation matrices. Since the blend primitives always work over two input vectors, the input can be concatenated as one $2w$ vector and the dimensions of the permutation matrices are expanded to $2w$ by $2w$. In order to unify the format, for the permute primitives, we add an empty vector and specify the primitive operates on the first vector v or the second vector u. Therefore, on MIC, there are 32=8(permute primitives)∗2(intra-lane or inter-lane)∗2(operating on v or u) and 8(4 pairs of the blend primitives) permutation matrices. Fig. 9 illustrates examples of the permutation matrices. The matrix "shuffle_cdab_v" and "shuffle_cdab_u" correspond to the same permute primitive on two halves of the concatenated vector. The matrix "blend_0_1_v" and "blend_1_1_u" correspond to one pair of blend primitives (0_1, 1_1). Finally, 4 sub-pools of permutation matrices are created according to the 4 primitive types.

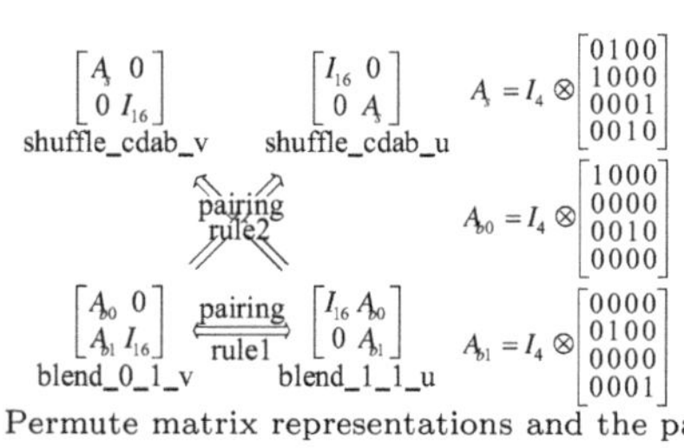

Figure 9: Permute matrix representations and the pairing rules

3.4.2 Sequence Building

ASPaS takes two rules in the sequence building algorithm to facilitate the building process. The rules are based on two observations from the formalized data-reordering operations illustrated in Eq. 1, Eq. 2, and Eq. 3. **Obs.1** The data-reordering operations are always conducted on two input vectors. **Obs.2** The permute operations always accompany the blend operations to keep them symmetric. Fig. 10 shows the data-reordering pattern of a symmetric blend, which is essentially the first step in Fig. 7. Because such an interleaving mode of symmetric blend cannot be directly achieved by the blend primitives, which are limited to pick elements from aligned positions of two input vectors, the associative permute primitives are necessary and coupled with the blend primitives, as the figure shown. Hence, two rules used in the sequence building algorithm are described as below.

Rule 1: when a primitive is selected for one vector v, pair the corresponding primitive for the other vector u. For a permute primitive, the corresponding permute has the totally same pattern; while for a blend primitive, the corresponding blend has the complementary mask, which has already been paired.

Rule 2: when a blend primitive is selected, pair it with the corresponding permute primitive: pair the intra-lane-permute with CDAB pattern for (0_1, 1_1) blend, the intra-lane-permute with BADC for (0_2, 2_2), the inter-lane-permute with CDAB for (0_4, 4_4), and the inter-lane-permute with BADC for (0_8, 8_8).

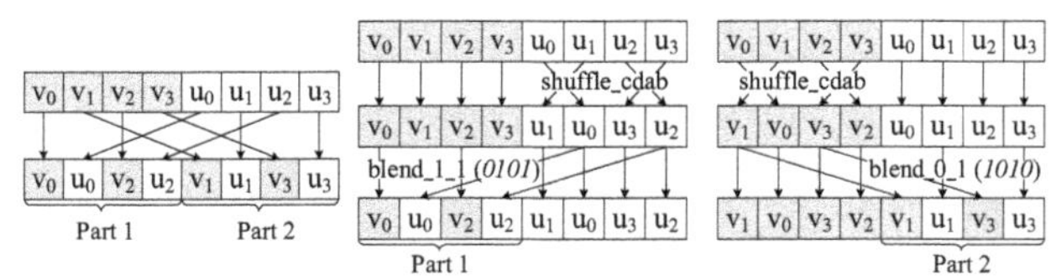

(a) sym-blend (b) sym-blend(details)

Figure 10: Symmetric blend operation and its pairing details

The sequence building algorithm can generate sequences of primitives to implement a given data-reordering pattern for Eq. 1, Eq. 2, and Eq. 3. Two $2w$-sized vectors are used as the input. The vec_{inp} represents the original concatenated vector of v and u and is set to the default offsets (from 1 to $2w$). The vec_{trg} is the target derived by applying the desired data-reordering operators on the vec_{inp}. Our algorithm will select the permutation matrices from the primitive pool, do the vector-matrix multiplications on the vec_{inp}, and check whether the intermediate result vec_{im} approximates the vec_{trg}. We define two types of *matching score* to exhibit how well the vec_{im} matches the vec_{trg}:

l-score lane-level matching score, accumulate by one when the corresponding lanes have exactly same elements (no matter orders).

e-score element-level matching score, increase by one when the element matches its counterpart in the vec_{trg}.

If only considering the 32-bit words with w (vector width) and e (number of elements per lane), the maximum l-score equals to $2w/e$ when all the aligned lanes from two vectors match, while the maximum e-score is $2w$ when all the aligned elements match. With the matching scores, the process of sequence building is transformed to score computations. For example, if we have the input "ABCDEFGH" and the output "HGDCFEBA" (assuming four lanes and two elements per lane), we first search primitives for the inter-lane reordering, e.g, from "ABCDEFGH" to "GHCDEFAB", and then search primitives for the intra-lane reordering, e.g., from "GHCDEFAB" to "HGDCFEBA". By checking the primitives hierarchically, we add those primitives increasing l-score or e-score and approximating to the desired output pattern.

Alg.2 shows the pseudocode of the sequence building algorithm. The input includes the aforementioned vec_{inp} and vec_{trg}. The output $seqs_{\mathsf{ret}}$ is an array to hold selected sequences of primitives, which will be used to generate the real ISA intrinsics later. The $seqs_{\mathsf{cand}}$ is used to store candidate sequences and initialized to contain an empty sequence. First, the algorithm checks the initial vec_{inp} with the vec_{trg} and get the l-score. If it equals to $2w/e$, which means corresponding lanes have matched, we only need to select primitives from "intra-lane-permute" (ln.4) and care about the e-score. Otherwise, we will work on the sub-pools of type 1, 2, or 3 in a round-robin manner. In the while loop, for each sequence in $seqs_{\mathsf{cand}}$, we first calculate the l_score_{old}, and then we will get l_score_{new} by checking primitives one by one from the current type. If the primitive $prim$ comes from the "inter-lane-permute", we produce the paired permute primitive $prim_{\mathsf{prd}}$ based on the Rule 1 (ln.14). If $prim$ is from the blend types, we produce the paired blend primitive $prim_{\mathsf{prd}}$ based on the Rule 1 and then find their paired permute primitives $perm_0$ and $perm_1$ based on the Rule 2 (ln.18-20). The two rules help to form the symmetric operations.

After the selected primitives have been applied, which corresponds to several vector-matrix multiplications, we can get a vec_{upd}, leading to a new l-score l_score_{new} compared to vec_{trg} (ln.25). If the l-score is increased, we add the sequence of the selected primitives to $seqs_{\mathsf{cand}}$. The threshold (ln.7) is a configuration parameter to control the upper bound of how many iterations the algorithm can tolerate, e.g., we set it to 9 in the evaluation so as to find the sequences as many as possible. Finally, we use `PickLaneMatched` to select those sequences that can make l-score equal to $2w/e$, and go to the "intra-lane-permute" selection (ln.32), which can ensure us the complete sequences of primitives.

Now, we can map the sequences from the $seqs_{\mathsf{ret}}$ to the real ISA intrinsics. We have two criteria to pick up the efficient sequences. The first criterion is the length of the sequence. We prefer the shortest one. The second criterion is when multiple shortest solutions exist, we prefer the interleaved style of inter-lane and intra-lane primitives, which could be executed with a pipeline mode on Intel MIC as discussed in Sec.2.1. When the most efficient sequences are collected, we convert them into real intrinsics. For the primitives from "intra-lane-permute" and "inter-lane-permute", we directly map them into vector intrinsics of **_mm512_shuffle** and **_mm512_permute4f128** with corresponding permute parameters. For the primitives of "intra-lane-blend" and "inter-lane-blend", we map them to the masked variants of permute intrinsics **_mm512_mask_shuffle** and **_mm512_mask_permute 4f128**. The masks are from their blend patterns. If the primitive belongs to "intra-lane" and the permute parameter is supported by the swizzle intrinsics, we will use the light-weighted swizzle intrinsics instead.

3.5 Thread-level Parallelism

After generating the intrinsics sequences for the vector comparators and the data-reordering operators in the **aspas_sort**, **aspas_transpose**, and **aspas_merge**, we have the single threaded version of the `aspas::sort` and `aspas::merge` as illustrated in Alg.1. In order to maximize the utilization of the computational resources of Intel MIC, we integrate these two functions with the thread-level parallelism using Pthreads. First, we make each thread work on their own parts of the input data by using the `aspas::sort`. Second, we use half of the threads to merge two neighboring sorted parts into one by iteratively calling the `aspas::merge` until there is only one thread left. In the evaluation, our multi-threaded version refers to this design.

Algorithm 2: Sequence Building Algorithm

```
   Input: vec_inp, vec_trg
   Output: seqs_ret
 1 Sequences seqs_cand ← new Sequences(∅);   // put an null sequence
 2 Int l_score_init ←LaneCmp(vec_inp, vec_trg);
 3 if l_score_init=2w/e then
 4 |  seqs_ret ← InstSelector(seqs_cand,Type[0]);
 5 else
 6 |  i ←1;
 7 |  while not Threshold() do
 8 |  |  ty ←Type[i];
 9 |  |  foreach Sequence seq in seqs_cand do
10 |  |  |  vec_im ←Apply(vec_inp, seq);
11 |  |  |  l_score_old ←LaneCmp(vec_im, vec_trg);
12 |  |  |  foreach Primitive prim in ty do
13 |  |  |  |  if n=1 then
14 |  |  |  |  |  prim_prd ←Pair(prim, RULE1);
15 |  |  |  |  |  vec_upd ←Apply(vec_im, prim + prim_prd);
16 |  |  |  |  |  seq_ext ←prim + prim_prd;
17 |  |  |  |  else
18 |  |  |  |  |  prim_prd ←Pair(prim, RULE1);
19 |  |  |  |  |  perm_0 ←Pair(prim, RULE2);
20 |  |  |  |  |  perm_1 ←Pair(prim_prd, RULE2);
21 |  |  |  |  |  vec_upd0 ←Apply(vec_im, perm_0 + prim);
22 |  |  |  |  |  vec_upd1 ←Apply(vec_im, perm_1 + prim_prd);
23 |  |  |  |  |  vec_upd ←Combine(vec_upd0, vec_upd1);
24 |  |  |  |  |  seq_ext ←perm_0 + prim + perm_1 + prim_prd;
25 |  |  |  |  l_score_new ←LaneCmp(vec_upd, vec_trg);
26 |  |  |  |  if l_score_new > l_score_old then
27 |  |  |  |  |  seqs_buf.add(seq + seq_ext);
28 |  |  seqs_cand.append(seqs_buf);
29 |  |  seqs_buf.clear();
30 |  |  i ←((++i)-1)%3+1;
31 |  seqs_sel ←PickLaneMatchedSeqs(seqs_cand);
32 |  seqs_ret ← InstSelector(seqs_sel,Type[0]);
33 Function InstSelector(Sequences seqs_cand,Type ty)
34 |  foreach Sequence seq in seqs_cand do
35 |  |  vec_im ←Apply(vec_inp, seq);
36 |  |  foreach Primitive prim in ty do
37 |  |  |  prim_prd ←Pair(prim, RULE1);
38 |  |  |  vec_upd ←Apply(vec_im, prim + prim_prd);
39 |  |  |  e_score ←ElemCmp(vec_upd, vec_trg);
40 |  |  |  if e_score=2w then
41 |  |  |  |  seqs_ret.add(seq + prim + prim_prd);
42 |  return seqs_ret;
```

4. PERFORMANCE ANALYSIS

In our evaluation, we use the Integer for the one-word type and the Double for the two-word type. Our experiments are conducted on the Intel Xeon Phi 5110P coprocessor with the codename Knight Corner, which has 60 cores running on 1.05 GHz with 8 GB GDDR5 memory and includes 32 KB L1 cache and 512 KB L2 cache. The compiler is Intel *icpc* 13.0.1, and the compiler options include *-mmic* and *-O3*. We run all experiments using the *native* mode. All the data are generated randomly ranging from 0 to the data size.

4.1 Performance of Different Sorting Networks

In the *sort* stage, ASPaS can accept any type of sorting networks and generate corresponding **aspas_sort** function. We use five sorting networks corresponding to five sorting algorithms, including hibbard[11], odd-even [3], green[10], bose-nelson[4], and bitonic[3]. Fig. 11a illustrates the performance of the **aspas_sort** for five sorting networks over an array with 100 million integers. The data labels also show how many comparators and groups of comparators in each sorting network. Green sort has the best performance that stems from the less comparators and groups, i.e., (60, 10). Although bitonic sort follows a balanced way to compare all elements in each step and is usually considered as the candidate for better performance, it uses more comparators, leading to the relatively weak performance for the *sort* stage. In the remaining experiments, we choose green sort as the sort algorithm for the Integer datatype. For the Double datatype, we choose the second best, i.e., odd-even sort, because green sort cannot take 8 elements as the input.

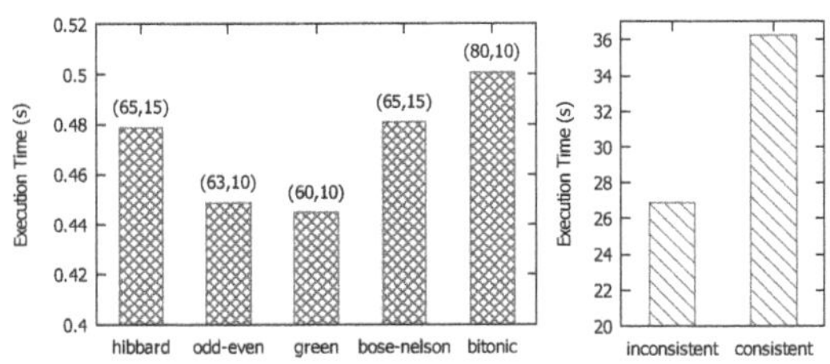

(a) `aspas_sort` (b) `aspas_merge`

Figure 11: Performance comparison of `aspas_sort` and `aspas_merge` for different sorting and merging networks. In (a), the number of comparators and groups are in parenthesis.

In the *merge* stage, ASPaS can solve two variants of bitonic merging networks as shown in Eq.2 and Eq.3 of Sec.3.3. Figure 11b presents the performance comparison for these two variants. The inconsistent merging can outperform the consistent one by 28.6%. Although the consistent merging has uniform data-reordering operations in each step as shown in Fig. 8, the operations are not ISA-friendly and thus requires a longer intrinsic sequence on Intel MIC. Based on Eq.3, the consistent merging uses 5 times of the L_2^{32} data-reordering operations, each of which needs 8 permute/shuffle intrinsics on Intel MIC. In contrast, the inconsistent merging only uses L_2^{32} once and compensate it with much lighter data-reordering operations, including $I_1 \otimes L_{16}^{32} \circ I_2 \otimes L_2^{16}$ and $I_2 \otimes L_8^{16} \circ I_4 \otimes L_2^8$, each of which can be implemented by only 2 intrinsics on Intel MIC. Therefore, we will adopt the inconsistent bitonic merge in the remaining experiments for better performance.

4.2 Vectorization Efficiency

To compare with the auto-vectorized code, we implement a serial sorting based on Alg. 1. Because the serial sorting doesn't store the partially sorted data in a scattered manner, the `aspas_transpose` function has no serial counterpart. We use the Intel compiler option *-vec-* to turn off the vectorization for the serial version and denote it as "no-vec" in the figures. On the other hand, we use the aggressive *pragma simd* and option *-O3* to guide the compiler to generate the vectorized code and denote it as "Comp-vec".

Fig. 12a shows the performance comparison for the *sort* stage with the Integer datatype. Compared with the "no-vec" version without the compiler auto-vectorization, the code generated by ASPaS can get 7.7-fold speedup. Using the Green sorting network, 60 comparators are needed to sort every 16 elements. As a result, for every 16*16 elements, the "no-vec" version needs $16 * 60 = 960$ comparators to partially sort the data. In contrast, the code generated by ASPaS only needs 60 vector comparators, and then uses 4 data-reordering operations (Eq.1) for each pair of vectors in the `aspas_transpose` to transpose the data. In total, the ASPaS code needs $60 + (16/2) * 4 = 92$ vector operations. The theoretical speedup should be $960/92 = 10.4$-fold. The experiment shows we can achieve 74% of the theoretical speedup for the *sort* stage. The figure also shows that the ASPaS code can outperform the "auto-vec" version. Actually, the auto-vectorized code utilizes the gather/scatter instructions to get/put non-contiguous data from/to memory on Intel MIC. However, it cannot mitigate the high latency of non-contiguous memory access. ASPaS can still outperform it by 1.6-fold by using the load/store intrinsics on the contiguous data and the shuffle/permute intrinsics for the transpose in registers.

Fig. 12b presents the performance comparison for the *merge* stage with the Integer datatype. Compared with the "no-vec" version, the ASPaS code can achieve 5.7-fold speedup. Since we use the bitonic merging to merge two sorted 16-element vectors, 80 comparators are needed in the "no-vec" version. In contrast, the ASPaS code only needs 5 comparisons with additional 5 data-reordering operations as shown in Eq.2. This provides a theoretical upper bound of $80/10 = 8$-fold speedup. The results show ASPaS can achieve 71% of the theoretical speedup for the *merge* stage. Note that the "auto-vec" version has the same performance with the "no-vec" version, meaning that even with the most aggressive vectorization pragma, the compiler fails to vectorize the merge code due to the complex data dependency in the loop.

Similarly, we also show the results for the Double datatype in Fig. 12c and Fig. 12d. The ASPaS *sort* and *merge* stages can outperform their counterparts by 6.3-fold and 3.7-fold, respectively.

4.3 Comparison to Sorting from Libraries

We first focus on the single threaded sorting. Since ASPaS uses the similar scheme with the mergesort, we compare the `aspas::sort` with two mergesort variants: top-down and bottom-up. The top-down mergesort recursively splits the input array until the split segments only have one element. Subsequently, the segments are merged together. In contrast, the bottom-up variant directly works on the elements and iteratively merge them into sorted segments. Fig. 13 illustrates the corresponding performance comparison. The `aspas::sort` for Integer datatype can obtain 3.4-fold and 3-fold speedup over the top-down and bottom-up mergesort, respectively; while for Double datatype, the `aspas::sort` can obtain 2.4-fold and 1.9-fold speedup instead.

Note that the speedups of `aspas::sort` over the top-down and bottom-up mergesorts are smaller than what we have reached in Sec.4.2 when compared to the sorting denoted as "no-vec". The "no-vec" sorting is a serial implementation of Alg. 1 using essentially the scheme of a bottom-up mergesort. However, the scheme induces extra comparisons for the ease of vectorization. When merging each pair of two sorted segments, in the case of one-word elements, we fetch w elements into a buffer from each segment and then merge these $2w$ elements using the bitonic merging. After that, we store the first half of merged $2w$ elements back to the result, and load w elements from the segment with the smaller first element into the buffer; and then, the next round of bitonic merge will occur (ln.18-28 in Alg. 1). In contrast, the top-down and bottom-up mergesort keep two pointers, each of which points to the head of its sorted segment, and continuously fetch the smaller element one by one. Therefore, the

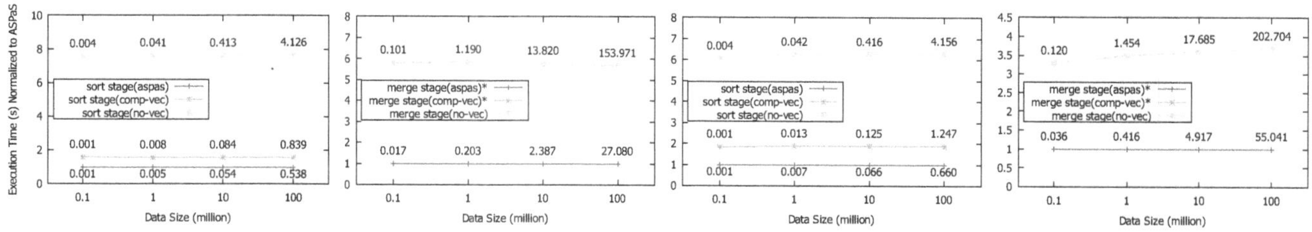

(a) *sort* stage (int) (b) *merge* stage (int) (c) *sort* stage (double) (d) *merge* stage (double)

Figure 12: ASPaS codes vs. *icpc* optimized codes (The sorts asterisked are labeled with the execution time, the same below). In (b) and (d), the lines of "comp-vec" and "no-vec" are overlapped.

comparisons in these two variants are considerably less than what we use in Alg. 1. However, because of the more potential for the vectorization in the scheme of Alg. 1, we observe better performance of **aspas::sort** over the top-down and bottom-up mergesorts.

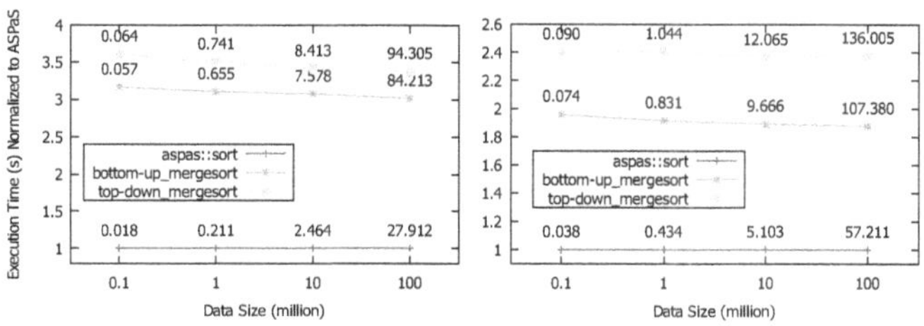

(a) vs. mergesorts (int) (b) vs. mergesorts (double)

Figure 13: **aspas::sort** vs. top-down and bottom-up mergesort

For the single threaded **aspas::sort**, we also compare it with other sorting tools from those widely-used libraries, including the **qsort** and **sort** from STL, **sort** from Boost library, and the **parallel_sort** from Intel TBB (with a single thread). Fig. 14a exhibits that **aspas::sort** for the Integer datatype can achieve up to 4.3-fold speedup over the **qsort**, and up to 2.4-fold speedup over others. For the Double datatype in Fig. 14b, the **aspas::sort** can attain 2.6-fold speedup over the **qsort** and 1.3-fold speedup over others.

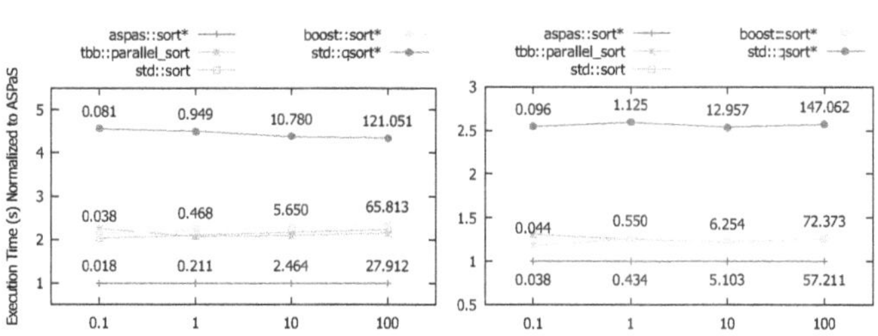

(a) vs. sorting tools (int) (b) vs. sorting tools (double)

Figure 14: **aspas::sort** vs. other sorting tools

Then, we compare our multi-threaded version described in Sec.3.5 with the **parallel_sort** from Intel TBB. We choose a larger dataset from 12.5 million to 200 million integer or double elements. As shown in Fig. 15, our multi-threaded version can outperform the **parallel_sort** by up to 2.1-fold speedup for the Integer datatype and 1.4-fold speedup for the Double datatype. It is worth mentioning that both of these two parallel sort functions can achieve their best performance while using 60 threads and each on a dedicated core.

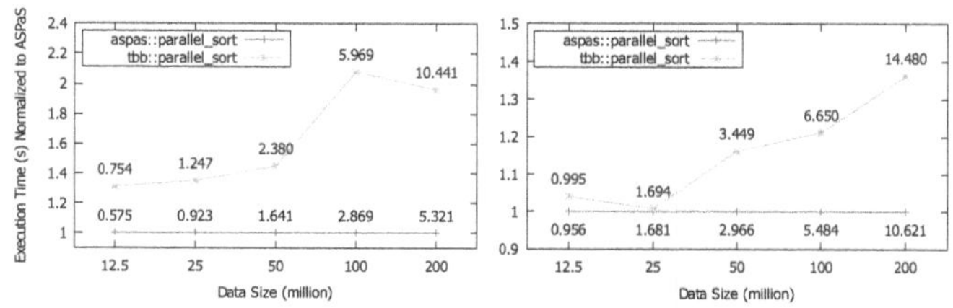

(a) vs. tbb::parallel_sort (int) (b) vs. tbb::parallel_sort (double)

Figure 15: **aspas::parallel_sort** vs. TBB's parallel sort

4.4 Discussion

Merging Networks: Currently, ASPaS supports two variants of bitonic merging networks, because their corresponding permutation operators can symmetrically and completely utilize all elements in each input vector. In contrast, other merging networks, e.g., odd-even network, cannot rearrange all elements and need more masks to hide irrelevant elements in each concurrent step, leading to additional overhead. On the other hand, once those additional data permute and blend primitives for other merging networks are selected out, ASPaS can add them into the primitive pool and generate vectorized merge functions.

Portability: ASPaS can also generate parallel sorting for x86-based multicore processors. We only need to modify one portion in the *SIMD Code Generator*, i.e., how to translate the primitives to the read ISA intrinsics. For the permute primitives, SSE, AVX, and AVX-2 of CPUs also provide the lane-level and element-level permutation intrinsics, such as **_mm256_shuffle** and **_mm256_2f128**. Therefore, these primitives can be also directly mapped to intrinsics. In contrast, for the blend primitives, the behavior of mask on CPUs is quite limited and most intrinsics have no masked variants. Alternatively, we use other intrinsics to emulate similar blend functionalities. For example, on AVX, we use the **_mm256_unpacklo** and **_mm256_unpackhi** intrinsics to implement the intra-lane blend primitives.

5. RELATED WORK

Many sorting algorithms have been modified and optimized to utilize both of the multiple cores and the intra-core parallelism on CPUs, GPU and MIC. Davidson et al.[6] designs a parallel merge sort by increasing the register communication on GPUs. Satish et al.[22, 23] compares and analyzes the radix sort and merge sort on modern accelerators, such as CPUs and GPUs. Chhugani et al.[5] show a SIMD-friendly merge sorting algorithm by using the sorting networks on multicore CPUs. AA-Sort in [13] is a new parallel sorting algorithm for utilizing the SIMD units of multicore CPUs. Their algorithm focuses on taking advantage of SIMD instructions and eliminating the unaligned memory access pattern. HykSort in [25] targets at distributed memory architectures, but on a single node, HykSort also uses SIMD optimized merge sort. For the past work of using the vector resources, developers have to explicitly use the compiler intrinsics to handle the tricky data-reordering operations required by the algorithm. Even with some SIMD-friendly programming compilers (e.g. ISPC [18]), developers still need to refer to the `shuffle()` functions and deal with the corresponding permute parameters.

Some frameworks are proposed to automatically generate application codes to utilize modern parallel architectures. Mint and Physis in [26, 16] can generate effective GPU codes for stencil computations. Benson et al.[2] provides a code generation tool to automatically implement various matrix multiplication algorithms. To facilitate the utilization of the intra-core resources, Huo et al.[12] presents a system with runtime SIMD parallelization with override operators and functions. Operator Language described in [9] is a framework to generate efficient vector load and shuffle instructions to achieve desired data-reordering pattern based on a rewriting system and a search mechanism. McFarlin et al.[17] shows another superoptimizer to conduct a guided search of the shortest sequence of instructions over a large candidate pool. Compared to the past work, the ASPaS uses a pruned ISA-fridendly primitive pools which are derived from the symmetric data-reordering patterns in the parallel sorting.

6. CONCLUSION

In this paper, we propose the ASPaS framework to automatically generate vectorized sorting code for x-86 based multicore and manycore processors. ASPaS can formalize the sorting and merging networks to the sequences of comparing and reordering operators of DSL. Based on the characteristics of such operators, ASPaS first creates an ISA-friendly pool to contain the requisite data comparing and reordering primitives, then builds those sequences with primitives, and finally maps them to the real ISA intrinsics. With ASPaS, we generate various parallel sorting codes on Intel MIC. The performance evaluation illustrates our automatically generated codes can outperform multiple sorting functions from STL, Boost, and Intel TBB. In the future, we will generate sorting codes for multicore architectures, and look for a theoretical model to verify the generated codes can obtain the best performance on the given ISA.

7. ACKNOWLEDGEMENT

This research was supported in part by NSF-BIGDATA program via IIS-1247693. We acknowledge Advanced Research Computing at Virginia Tech for the computational resources.

8. REFERENCES

[1] S. W. Al-Haj Baddar and K. W. Batcher. *Designing Sorting Networks: A New Paradigm*. Springer, 2011.

[2] Austin R. Benson and Grey Ballard. A Framework for Practical Parallel Fast Matrix Multiplication. In *Proc. of the ACM SIGPLAN Symp. on Principles and Practice of Parallel Programming (PPoPP)*, 2015.

[3] K. E. Batcher. Sorting Networks and Their Applications. In *Proc. of ACM Spring Joint Computer Conf.*, 1968.

[4] R. C. Bose and R. J. Nelson. A Sorting Problem. *J. ACM*, 9(2), 1962.

[5] J. Chhugani, A. D. Nguyen, V. W. Lee, W. Macy, M. Hagog, Y.-K. Chen, A. Baransi, S. Kumar, and P. Dubey. Efficient Implementation of Sorting on Multi-core SIMD CPU Architecture. *Proc. of the VLDB Endowment (PVLDB)*, 2008.

[6] A. Davidson, D. Tarjan, M. Garland, and J. Owens. Efficient Parallel Merge Sort for Fixed and Variable Length Keys. In *Innovative Parallel Computing (InPar)*, 2012.

[7] N. Firasta, M. Buxton, P. Jinbo, K. Nasri, and S. Kuo. Intel AVX: New Frontiers in Performance Improvements and Energy Efficiency. White Paper Intel Co, 2008.

[8] F. Franchetti, F. Mesmay, D. Mcfarlin, and M. Püschel. Operator Language: A Program Generation Framework for Fast Kernels. In *Proc. of the IFIP TC 2 Working Conf. on Domain-Specific Languages (DSL)*, 2009.

[9] F. Franchetti and M. Püschel. Generating SIMD Vectorized Permutations. In *Proc. of the Joint Eur. Conf. on Theory and Practice of Software Int'l Conf. on Compiler Construction (CC/ETAPS)*, 2008.

[10] M. W. Green. Some Improvements in Non-adaptive Sorting Algorithms. In *Proc. of the Annual Princeton Conf. on Information Sciences and Systems*, 1972.

[11] T. N. Hibbard. An empirical study of minimal storage sorting. *Commun. ACM*, 6(5), 1963.

[12] X. Huo, B. Ren, and G. Agrawal. A Programming System for Xeon Phis with Runtime SIMD Parallelization. In *Proc. of the ACM Int'l Conf. on Supercomputing (ICS)*, 2014.

[13] H. Inoue, T. Moriyama, H. Komatsu, and T. Nakatani. AA-Sort: A New Parallel Sorting Algorithm for Multi-Core SIMD Processors. In *Proc. of the ACM Int'l Conf. on Parallel Architectures and Compilation Techniques (PACT)*, 2007.

[14] Intel. Intel Xeon Phi Coprocessor System Software Developers Guide, 2012. https://software.intel.com/sites/default/files/article/334766/intel-xeon-phi-systemsoftwaredevelopersguide.pdf.

[15] S. Maleki, Y. Gao, M. Garzaran, T. Wong, and D. Padua. An Evaluation of Vectorizing Compilers. In *Proc. of the ACM Int'l Conf. on Parallel Architectures and Compilation Techniques (PACT)*, 2011.

[16] N. Maruyama, T. Nomura, K. Sato, and S. Matsuoka. Physis: An Implicitly Parallel Programming Model for Stencil Computations on Large-scale GPU-accelerated Supercomputers. In *Proc. of the Int'l Conf. for High Performance Computing, Networking, Storage and Analysis (SC)*, 2011.

[17] D. S. McFarlin, V. Arbatov, F. Franchetti, and M. Püschel. Automatic SIMD Vectorization of Fast Fourier Transforms for the Larrabee and AVX Instruction Sets. In *Proc. of the ACM Int'l Conf. on Supercomputing (ICS)*, 2011.

[18] M. Pharr and W. Mark. ispc: A SPMD compiler for high-performance CPU programming. In *Innovative Parallel Computing (InPar)*, 2012.

[19] P. Plauger, M. Lee, D. Musser, and A. A. Stepanov. *C++ Standard Template Lib.* Prentice Hall PTR, 1st edition, 2000.

[20] R. Rahman. *Intel Xeon Phi Coprocessor Architecture and Tools: The Guide for Application Developers*. Apress, 1st edition, 2013.

[21] J. Reinders. *Intel Threading Building Blocks*. O'Reilly & Associates, Inc., 1st edition, 2007.

[22] N. Satish, M. Harris, and M. Garland. Designing Efficient Sorting Algorithms for Manycore GPUs. In *IEEE Int'l Symp. on Parallel Distributed Processing (IPDPS)*, 2009.

[23] N. Satish, C. Kim, J. Chhugani, A. D. Nguyen, V. W. Lee, D. Kim, and P. Dubey. Fast sort on CPUs and GPUs: a case for bandwidth oblivious SIMD sort. In *Proc. of the ACM SIGMOD Int'l Conf. on Management of Data*, 2010.

[24] B. Schling. *The Boost C++ Libraries*. XML Press, 2011.

[25] H. Sundar, D. Malhotra, and G. Biros. HykSort: A New Variant of Hypercube Quicksort on Distributed Memory Architectures. In *Proc. of the ACM Int'l Conf. on Supercomputing (ICS)*, 2013.

[26] D. Unat, X. Cai, and S. B. Baden. Mint: Realizing CUDA Performance in 3D Stencil Methods with Annotated C. In *Proc. of the ACM Int'l Conf. on Supercomputing (ICS)*, 2011.

[27] M. Zuluaga, P. Milder, and M. Püschel. Computer Generation of Streaming Sorting Networks. In *Proc. of the ACM Design Automation Conf. (DAC)*, 2012.

Optimizing Overlapped Memory Accesses in User-directed Vectorization

Diego Caballero[1,2]
diego.caballero@bsc.es

Sara Royuela[1,2]
sara.royuela@bsc.es

Roger Ferrer[1]
roger.ferrer@bsc.es

Alejandro Duran[3]
alejandro.duran@intel.com

Xavier Martorell[1,2]
xavim@ac.upc.edu

[1]Barcelona Supercomputing Center [2]Universitat Politècnica de Catalunya [3]Intel Corporation Iberia

ABSTRACT

Current processors incorporate wide and powerful vector units whose optimal exploitation is crucial to reach peak performance. However, present autovectorizing compilers fall short of that goal. Exploiting some vector instructions requires aggressive approaches that are not affordable in production compilers. Thus, advanced programmers pursuing the best performance from their applications are compelled to manually vectorize them using low-level SIMD intrinsics.

We propose a user-directed code optimization that targets overlapped vector loads, i.e., vector loads that read scalar elements redundantly from memory. Instead, our optimization loads these elements once and combines them using advanced register-to-register vector instructions. This code is potentially more efficient and it uses advanced vector instructions that compilers do not widely exploit automatically. We also extend the OpenMP* SIMD directives with a new clause called *overlap* that allows users to easily enable and tune this optimization on demand. We implement our proposal for the Intel® Xeon Phi™ coprocessor.

Our evaluation shows up to 29% speed-up over five highly-optimized stencil kernels and workloads from real-world applications. Results also demonstrate how important user hints are to maximize performance.

Categories and Subject Descriptors

D.3.4 [**Programming Languages**]: Processors—*Compilers; Optimization*

General Terms

Performance; Algorithms

Keywords

SIMD, Vectorization, Compiler Optimization, OpenMP, Stencil, Intel Many Integrated Core Architecture

ICS 2015, Newport Beach, California, USA.

http://dx.doi.org/10.1145/2751205.2751224.

1. INTRODUCTION AND MOTIVATION

SIMD instruction sets play a key role in current HPC and general-purpose processors. Their appealing power consumption-to-performance ratio has led to a higher use of these hardware components. A good example of this is the first generation of Intel® Xeon Phi™ processors. These highly-parallel devices, with up to 61 cores and 4 hardware threads per core, yield 1 TeraFLOPS of double precision peak performance at 300W (TDP), where SIMD extensions (Intel® Many Integrated Cores instructions [12]) are crucial [14]. They feature 512-bit vector registers, doubling the previous 256 bits from the Intel® Advanced Vector Extensions. They also add more flexible memory instructions (gathers/scatters), powerful register-to-register instructions for data manipulation (shuffles, permutations and shifts) and masked execution for conditional code, among other features.

However, more powerful SIMD instructions are harder to use. Although a great effort has been made in compilers to enhance their auto-vectorization capabilities [9, 26, 27, 16, 22], production compilers still have strong limitations when dealing with vectorization [24]. They do not implement many state-of-the-art proposals mainly for three reasons: (1) lack of compiler technology (analyses, cost models, idiom recognition and code transformations, among others); (2) aggressive optimizations could be unsafe, degrade performance or prevent other more relevant optimizations; (3) aggressive code transformations could interfere with manual optimizations from programmers.

As a result, advanced programmers pursuing the best performance are compelled to manually vectorize their codes using low-level hardware-specific intrinsics and finely tune them following a trial and error approach. This task is very cumbersome, inefficient and error prone.

In an attempt to reduce these issues and ease SIMD exploitation, programming languages and programming models [18, 11, 25, 23] are introducing SIMD support. In particular, the OpenMP* parallel programming model added SIMD extensions to its release 4.0 [28]. These extensions allow users to instruct the compiler in the vectorization process. Nevertheless, these extensions still leave room for performance improvements. In the example in Figure 1a, we use the new OpenMP SIMD directive to tell the compiler that the outer loop is safely vectorizable. However, groups of vector loads that overlap in memory (Figure 1c) can be optimized using a lower number of non-overlapped vector loads and vector register-to-register instructions (Figure 1d). The manual vectorization of the code and the application of

```
#pragma omp simd aligned(a,b:64)
for(i=0; i <= N-points-1; i++)
{
  float tmp = 0.0f;

  for(j=0; j <= points-1; j++)
    tmp += a[i+j];

  b[i] = tmp / points;
}
```

(a) Scalar code with SIMD directive on the outer loop.

```
for(i=0; i <= N-points-VF; i+=VF)
{
  float_VF tmp = vpromotion_VF(0.0f);

  for(j=0; j <= points-1; j++)
    tmp += unaligned_vload_VF(&a[i+j]);

  tmp = tmp / vpromotion_VF(points);
  aligned_vstore_VF(&b[i], tmp);
}
```

(b) Outer loop vectorized pseudo-code.

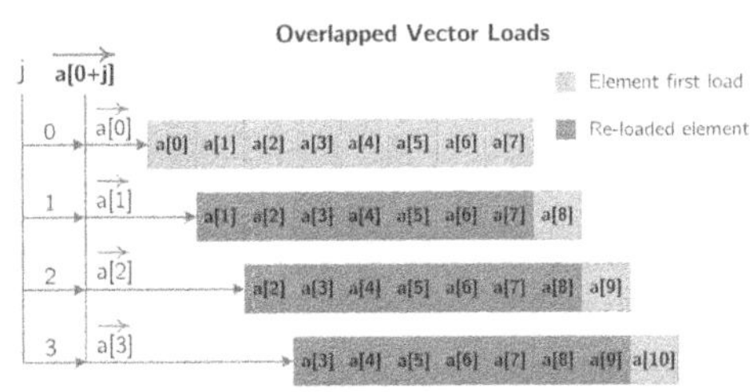

(c) Original overlapped vector loads of the array **a** after outer loop vectorization.

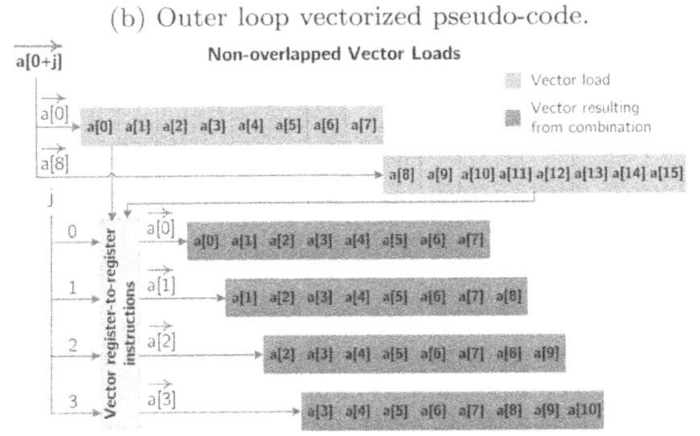

(d) Overlap optimization applied to vector loads of the array **a**.

Figure 1: The Moving Average motivating example. Assuming vectorization factor/length (`VF`) = 8 and `points` = 4.

this optimization outperformed the OpenMP SIMD and the manually vectorized versions by 41% (Intel Xeon Phi coprocessor, 183 threads, `N`=536M, `points`=128)**.

Our goal is to extend OpenMP to optionally enable this vector code optimization which targets groups of vector loads that overlap in memory. This paper makes the following contributions: (1) We introduce a formal framework that describes overlapped vector memory accesses and their properties. (2) We propose a code optimization for overlapped vector loads that works in both inner and outer loop vectorization scenarios. (3) We introduce an extension to the current OpenMP SIMD constructs to allow users to enable the overlap optimization and direct the compiler in its application. (4) We suggest some guidelines and a compiler cost model to assist users to take better advantage of our proposal. (5) We implement our proposal in the Mercurium C/C++ compiler [10] and evaluate it on the Intel Xeon Phi coprocessor using highly-optimized benchmarks from real-world applications. To validate our performance results, we compare them with those from the latest production version of the Intel® C compiler.

2. OVERVIEW

The outer loop in Figure 1a is annotated with an OpenMP SIMD directive. This directive instructs the compiler to vectorize that loop, relaxing constraints that could prevent vectorization (pointer aliasing, data dependencies, cost models, etc.) [18, 28]. Figure 1b shows the code resulting from the outer loop vectorization [27]. Subsequent vector loads on `&a[i+j]` overlap across different stride-one iterations of the innermost loop, as depicted in Figure 1c. For this reason, these vector loads constitute an *overlap group*.

Overlap groups are the key concept of our proposal. We define several properties of these groups, such as the group cardinality (number of vector loads in the group), the number of vector registers to maintain the group and the total number of groups per array. Certain constraints can be established on these *overlap groups'* properties that affect their construction. For conforming groups, the compiler creates and manages a vector register cache. This cache loads elements from memory without overlapping. Then, original vector loads are replaced by vector register-to-register instructions that rebuild the necessary vector operands with data from the register cache (Figure 1d).

Furthermore, we extend the OpenMP SIMD constructs with a new clause called `overlap` to allow users to enable and guide the compiler on which arrays to apply this aggressive vector code optimization. Optionally, the clause can contain extra arguments to finely tune the optimization. These arguments affect the overlap groups' constraints and, therefore, the code transformation algorithm.

The potential benefits of the overlap optimization are:

- Improved use of memory bandwidth: overlapped memory elements are loaded only once.
- Reduced number of unaligned vector loads in SIMD architectures with alignment constraints.
- Reduced number of vector loads and less pressure in the memory units of the architecture.
- Exploitation of advanced SIMD register-to-register instructions.

Moreover, the `overlap` clause gives users different levels of control over a code optimization that the compiler would not be able to apply automatically. In addition, this clause favors the agile benchmarking of different vector versions when looking for the best performance, thus avoiding hand-coded vectorization.

3. OVERLAP RELATIONS AND GROUPS

In this section, we describe a framework to formally introduce the concepts of *overlap group*, *overlapped vector memory load* and other definitions of our proposal. We apply our formalization to the Moving Average example (Figure 1) to offer a practical point of view.

3.1 Preliminaries

We use $a[i]$ to denote a scalar access to the ith element of the array a, and $a[l:u]$ to designate the set of scalar accesses to $a[j]$, $\forall j\ l \leq j \leq u$.

Let K be a scalar loop defined as:

$$K : IV_K = \langle LB_K, UB_K, ST_K, S_K \rangle \quad (1)$$

where IV_K, LB_K, UB_K, ST_K and S_K are the induction variable, the inclusive lower and upper bounds, the step and the scalar statements of K, respectively. Let us assume that the loop has been normalized, i. e., $LB_K = 0$ and $ST_K = 1$, and array accesses have been linearized [17].

We define V as the vectorized version of K following a strip-mining/unroll-and-jam vectorization approach [17, 27], such that:

$$V : IV_V = \langle LB_V, UB_V, ST_V, S_V \rangle \quad (2)$$

where $LB_V = 0$, $ST_V = VF_V$ (vectorization factor, i. e., the number of scalar iterations of K computed within each vector iteration of V), $UB_V = UB_K - VF_V + 1$ and S_V is the set of statements obtained from the vectorization of S_K.

Definition 1. (Stride-one Vector Memory Access). $\overrightarrow{a[e]}$ denotes the *stride-one vector memory access*, henceforth *svma*, of a scalar access $a[e]$ that satisfies that e is of the form $e = IV_K + c$ where c is *invariant* in K. This kind of vector accesses performs the set of scalar memory accesses $a[e : e + VF_V - 1]$ in a vector way.

A *stride-one vector memory load*, denoted *vl*, is an *svma* that reads data from memory. From now on, we limit our description to *vls*, although it can be easily extended to *stride-one vector memory stores*. However, our proposal has limited applicability to stores in real application.

In the Moving Average example, the outer loop in Figure 1a is $K : i = \langle 0, N - points - 1, 1, \{\text{lines } 3 - 10\} \rangle$, the outer loop in Figure 1b is $V : i = \langle 0, N - points - VF, VF, \{\text{lines } 2 - 10\} \rangle$ and `a[i+j]` is a *vl*.

3.2 Overlap Relations

The following definitions are used to establish an equivalence relation among *vls* of each particular array in V.

Definition 2. We say that two *vls* $\overrightarrow{a[e_1]}$ and $\overrightarrow{a[e_2]}$ *overlap*, denoted $\overrightarrow{a[e_1]} \sqcap \overrightarrow{a[e_2]}$, if and only if $a[e_1 : e_1 + VF_V - 1] \cap a[e_2 : e_2 + VF_V - 1] \neq \emptyset$.

Definition 3. We say that two *vls* $\overrightarrow{a[e_1]}$ and $\overrightarrow{a[e_2]}$ are *overlap-related*, denoted $\overrightarrow{a[e_1]} \sqcap^* \overrightarrow{a[e_2]}$, if and only if $\overrightarrow{a[e_1]} \sqcap \overrightarrow{a[e_2]}$ or there exists $\overrightarrow{a[e_3]}$ such that $\overrightarrow{a[e_1]} \sqcap \overrightarrow{a[e_3]}$ and $\overrightarrow{a[e_3]} \sqcap^* \overrightarrow{a[e_2]}$.

It is important to note that some SIMD architectures with alignment constraints need two aligned *vl* instructions to perform one unaligned *vl*. This fact should be considered in those architectures when evaluating whether two *vls* overlap.

3.3 Overlap Groups

We describe several sets of *vls* that are necessary to define the concept of an *overlap group* and its construction.

Given loop V, we define the set of loops $\mathcal{L}_V = \{V\} \cup \{\text{all loops in } S_V\}$. Then, for a loop $L \in \mathcal{L}_V$, we define:

$$A_{L,a} = \{ \text{ all } vls \text{ on the array } a \text{ in the body of } L \ \} \quad (3)$$

Moreover, the set of *vls* on the array a directly nested in the loop L is defined as follows:

$$D_{L,a} = A_{L,a} - \{A_{L',a} \,|\, L' \in \mathcal{L}_L \wedge L' \neq L\} \quad (4)$$

In the Moving Average example, let Lo and Li denote the outer loop and the inner loop from Figure 1b, respectively. Then, $\mathcal{L}_{Lo} = \{Lo, Li\}$ and $\mathcal{L}_{Li} = \{Li\}$. Focusing on the array `a`, $A_{Lo,a}$, $A_{Li,a}$, $D_{Lo,a}$ and $D_{Li,a}$ sets are defined as:

$$A_{Lo,a} = A_{Li,a} = \{ \overrightarrow{\texttt{a[i+j]}} \}$$
$$D_{Lo,a} = A_{Lo,a} - A_{Li,a} = \emptyset \qquad D_{Li,a} = A_{Li,a}$$

Definition 4. (Overlap Group). An *overlap group* $\mathcal{O}_{L,a}$ is an equivalence class of the equivalence relation $\sqcap^*$ on $D_{L,a}$.

The ith overlap group is denoted by $\mathcal{O}_{L,a,i}$. We call $P_{L,a}$ to the quotient set of $D_{L,a}$ by $\sqcap^*$.

Depending on how *vls* overlap in the group, we define the following non-disjoint kinds of overlap groups:

intra: $|\mathcal{O}_{L,a,i}| > 1$, i. e., there exist at least two *vls* in $\mathcal{O}_{L,a,i}$ that *overlap* in the same iteration.

inter: There exist w and w' in $\mathcal{O}_{L,a,i}$ that *overlap* across iterations, i. e., $w \sqcap (w'/IV_L \mapsto IV_L + ST_L)$. Note that w and w' may be the same *vl*.

If the overlap group does not satisfy any of these properties, its kind is *unknown*.

Definition 5. (Overlapped Vector Memory Load). A *vl* in $\mathcal{O}_{L,a,i}$ is an *overlapped vector memory load*, denoted *ovl*, if and only if $\mathcal{O}_{L,a,i}$ is of kind *inter* and/or *intra*.

The length of each overlap group is computed as:

$$\begin{aligned} & length(\mathcal{O}_{L,a,i}) = M - m + 1 \\ \text{where} \quad & \begin{array}{ll} m & = \min \{ \ l \,|\, \forall r \in \mathcal{O}_{L,a,i} \ r = a[l:u] \} \\ M & = \max \{ u \,|\, \forall r \in \mathcal{O}_{L,a,i} \ r = a[l:u] \} \end{array} \end{aligned} \quad (5)$$

Again, in the Moving Average example, we apply the *overlap-related* relation to the only non-empty set, $D_{Li,a}$. It results in one *inter* overlap group $\mathcal{O}_{Li,a,0} = \{ \overrightarrow{\texttt{a[i+j]}} \}$ with $|\mathcal{O}_{Li,a,0}| = 1$ and $length(\mathcal{O}_{Li,a,0}) = VF$.

4. THE OVERLAP PROPOSAL

Our proposal comprises three main parts: (Section 4.1) a code optimization that targets overlapped vector memory loads (*ovls*); (Section 4.2) a proposal to extend OpenMP SIMD constructs to allow users to enable and finely tune this optimization on demand; (Section 4.3) some high-level guidelines to assist users to better exploit our OpenMP extension; (Section 4.4) a simple cost model that can be used by the compiler or a performance tool to give advice to users on the application of the overlap optimization.

4.1 The Overlap Optimization

The overlap optimization is applied to stride-one vector memory loads (*vls*) occurring within the already vectorized loop (V). Figure 2 depicts the implementation phases and their flow. At this point, we assume that basic compiler optimizations (common subexpression elimination, local value numbering, etc. [1, 17]) have already been applied on the input vector code. The high-level steps to apply the overlap optimization are:

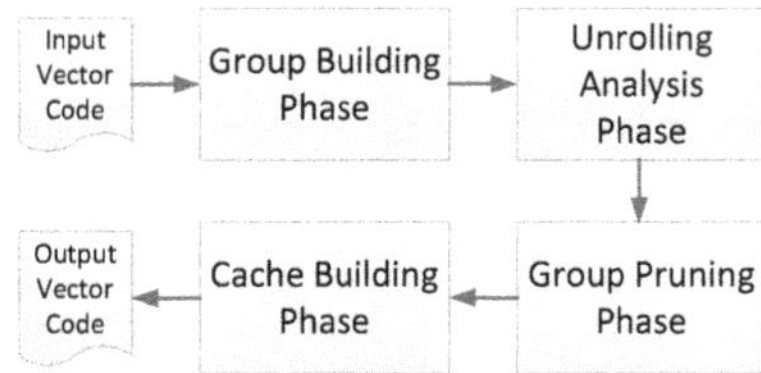

Figure 2: The overlap optimization phases.

- Detecting and building overlap groups in the vectorized code (Group Building Phase, Section 4.1.2).
- Applying loop unrolling to adequate overlap groups properties to user/compiler constraints and vector units of the target architecture. (Unrolling Analysis Phase, Section 4.1.3).
- Pruning overlap groups according to user/compiler constraints (Group Pruning Phase, Section 4.1.4).
- Transforming the code to implement the register cache infrastructure for each overlap group (Cache Building Phase, Section 4.1.5).

As in Section 3, we use the Moving Average example from Figure 1 to illustrate some implementation aspects of the overlap optimization. Figure 5 shows the optimized pseudocode generated for Moving Average, assuming a vectorization factor (*VF*) and vector length (*VL*) equal to 16.

4.1.1 Overlap Group Constraints

We define three constraints on the overlap groups that will affect their construction and the output optimized code:

CARDCONSTR (cardinality): establishes the minimum number of *ovls* that an overlap group must contain. This constraint is useful to discard small groups that will not yield enough performance or that do not have enough data reuse to overcome the overhead of maintaining the vector register cache.

VREGSCONSTR (vector registers): limits the maximum number of vector registers per overlap group. The minimum number allowed is two since vector register-to-register instructions require at least two input vector operands. This constraint is valuable in circumstances where register pressure may lead to registers spilling and, therefore, to a performance penalty.

GROUPSCONSTR (number of groups): limits the maximum number of groups per array. This constraint is useful to limit the number of groups in scenarios with a large number of them. In this situation, the overlap optimization might lead to a performance penalty due to register spilling if it was applied to all groups.

4.1.2 Group Building Phase

In the Group Building Phase, the compiler builds the overlap groups and computes their basic properties (length and cardinality) as explained in Section 3.3. To do so, it constructs the quotient sets $P_{L,a}$ $\forall L \in \mathcal{L}_V, \forall a \; vl \in L$.

In this phase the compiler also computes the number of vector registers necessary to maintain a cache for that group, denoted $VecRegs(\mathcal{O}_{L,a,i})$. The minimum number of vector registers is computed as:

$$VecRegs(\mathcal{O}_{L,a,i}) = \lceil length(\mathcal{O}_{L,a,i}) / VL \rceil \tag{6}$$

where *VL* is the vector length of the target SIMD architecture. However, this minimum number could be tied to unaligned *vls* in architectures with alignment constraints if the first (lowest memory address) *ovl* is unaligned. In this case, using aligned *vls* requires adding an offset from this first memory reference to the first backward aligned address. This could entail one extra register and one extra *vl* over the minimal unaligned approach.

As stated in Section 4.1.1, the minimum number of registers used to maintain an overlap group is two. However, at this point of the optimization, *VecRegs* could be one. When this happens, the Unrolling Analysis Phase (Section 4.1.3) will attempt to increase this value. If it fails to do so, the group will finally be pruned in the Group Pruning Phase (Section 4.1.4).

Afterwards, if *VecRegs* is greater than one, the compiler computes the efficiency of the overlap group, defined as:

$$\eta(\mathcal{O}_{L,a,i}) = \frac{|\mathcal{O}_{L,a,i}|}{(VecRegs(\mathcal{O}_{L,a,i}) - 1) * VL} \tag{7}$$

Efficiency equal to one means that all data loaded into the register cache is optimally reused in the loop body. Values lower than one mean that some data loaded into the register cache is not reused as much as it could be, or even that some elements are not used at all in the loop body. Values greater than one happen when some vector load reads exactly the same data as another vector load from the next iteration (for example, if we have a[i] and a[i+*VL*] in the loop body). The efficiency will be undefined if *VecRegs* is one.

We recall (Section 3.3) that the Moving Average example has one *inter* overlap group $\mathcal{O}_{Li,a,0} = \{ \overrightarrow{\texttt{a[i+j]}} \}$ with $|\mathcal{O}_{Li,a,0}| = 1$ and $length(\mathcal{O}_{Li,a,0}) = VF = 16$. The number of registers is $VecRegs(\mathcal{O}_{Li,a,0}) = 1$, and, therefore, $\eta(\mathcal{O}_{Li,a,0})$ is undefined.

4.1.3 Unrolling Analysis Phase

In the Unrolling Analysis Phase, the compiler analyzes whether loops with overlap groups associated need to be unrolled. Loop unrolling is aimed at:

- making overlap groups satisfy CARDCONSTR (Equation 8) and VREGSCONSTR (Equation 9).
- better fitting the length of each overlap group into the register cache considering the vector length (*VL*) of the target architecture (Equation 10).
- minimizing cache readjusting instructions per loop iteration, mapping original vector loads to the same register cache position across iterations (Equation 10).
- improving the register cache efficiency (η), maximizing the reuse of data loaded into the cache.

Frequently, loop unrolling is indispensable in outer loop vectorization scenarios where *inter* overlap groups are within the innermost loop, as occurs in the Moving Average example. These groups tend to have minimal lengths ($\approx VL$) and cardinalities (≈ 1) that could not satisfy CARDCONSTR and VREGSCONSTR. Innermost loop vectorization scenarios can also benefit from loop unrolling and the reduction of cache management instructions across iterations.

The unroll factor UF of a loop is computed as the lower common multiple of the unroll factor that better fits each overlap group in the loop, denoted $UF_{\mathcal{O}}$. Each $UF_{\mathcal{O}}$ is based on the new cardinality ($|\mathcal{O}_{L,a,i}|_{UF}$), number of vector registers ($VecRegs_{UF}(\mathcal{O}_{L,a,i})$), length ($length_{UF}(\mathcal{O}_{L,a,i})$) and efficiency ($\eta_{UF}(\mathcal{O}_{L,a,i})$) that the group would have after loop unrolling. Starting from $UF_{\mathcal{O}} = 2$, the compiler increments $UF_{\mathcal{O}}$ iteratively to find those values that satisfy the following equations:

$$|\mathcal{O}_{L,a,i}|_{UF} > \text{CARDCONST} \quad (8)$$

$$1 < VecRegs_{UF}(\mathcal{O}_{L,a,i}) \leq \text{VREGSCONST} \quad (9)$$

If no $UF_{\mathcal{O}}$ is found that satisfies Equations 7 and 8, the group will be discarded in the Group Pruning Phase. If more than one value is found that satisfies them, the one that minimizes distance (as defined in Equation 10) and maximizes $\eta_{UF}(\mathcal{O}_{L,a,i})$, in this order or priority, is chosen.

$$dist = (k * VL - ST_L,\ k > 1) - length_{UF}(\mathcal{O}_{L,a,i}) \wedge \\ dist \geq 0 \quad (10)$$

The value of $UF_{\mathcal{O}}$ is also constrained by the number of vector registers available within the loop. Large values of $UF_{\mathcal{O}}$ can increase the register cache size and cause register spilling.

If loop unrolling successfully takes place on the innermost loop in a outer loop vectorization scenario, two consecutive epilogue sections compute the remaining iterations of the unrolled loop:

overlap epilogue: computes up to $(\lceil UF/UF_{EPI} \rceil - 1) * UF_{EPI}$ iterations of the original loop in blocks of UF_{EPI} iterations, where $UF > UF_{EPI} > 1$. This epilogue code still exploits the overlap vector register cache so it must fulfill the overlap group constraints. UF_{EPI} can be the minimum number that satisfies the constraints or be a default value chosen from microbenchmarking experiments, as in our implementation (Section 5.1).

regular epilogue: computes the remaining iterations not covered by the overlap epilogue and the main loop. This epilogue code does not use the overlap vector register cache.

Assuming $VF = VL = 16$, CARDCONSTR $= 4$ and VREGSCONSTR $= 2$, the inner loop in the Moving Average example is unrolled with $UF = 16$ (Figure 5, lines 9 - 21). This value is the minimum number that satisfies Equations 8 – 10, and maximizes efficiency, since:

$$|\mathcal{O}_{Li,a,0}|_{16} = 16 \qquad VecRegs_{16}(\mathcal{O}_{Li,a,0}) = 2$$
$$length_{16}(\mathcal{O}_{Li,a,0}) = 31 \qquad \eta_{16}(\mathcal{O}_{Li,a,0}) = 1$$

The overlap epilogue (Figure 5, lines 24 - 41) is generated with $UF_{EPI} = 4$, which is the minimum number that fulfills CARDCONSTR. It computes up to 12 iterations of the original loop in blocks of 4 iterations. The regular epilogue is shown in lines 44 - 45.

4.1.4 Group Pruning Phase

In the Group Pruning Phase, the compiler processes and prunes overlap groups from the previous phase according to CARDCONSTR, VREGSCONSTR and GROUPSCONSTR, defined in Section 4.1.2. Figure 3 describes the pruning algorithm. It is independently applied to each quotient set $P_{L,a}$ and returns a new set $P'_{L,a}$ with the final overlap groups that have been chosen to receive the overlap optimization.

1: **function** PRUNINGGROUPS($P_{L,a}$)
2: $\quad P'_{L,a} \leftarrow \emptyset$
3: $\quad$ **for all** $\mathcal{O}_{L,a,i} \in P_{L,a}$ **do**
4: $\quad\quad$ **if** NODATADEPENDENCIES($\mathcal{O}_{L,a,i}$) **then**
5: $\quad\quad\quad \mathcal{O}'_{L,a,i} \leftarrow$ APPLYVREGSCONSTR($\mathcal{O}_{L,a,i}$)
6: $\quad\quad\quad$ **if** $|\mathcal{O}'_{L,a,i}| \geq$ CARDCONSTR($\mathcal{O}'_{L,a,i}$) **then**
7: $\quad\quad\quad\quad P'_{L,a} \leftarrow P'_{L,a} \cup \{\mathcal{O}'_{L,a,i}\}$
8: $\quad\quad\quad$ **end if**
9: $\quad\quad$ **end if**
10: $\quad$ **end for**
11: $\quad P'_{L,a} \leftarrow$ APPLYGROUPSCONSTR($P'_{L,a}$)
12: $\quad$ **return** $P'_{L,a}$
13: **end function**

Figure 3: Overlap groups pruning algorithm.

The input overlap groups with data dependencies that could make the overlap optimization unsafe are discarded (Figure 3, line 4). Groups that satisfy dependencies are processed according to constraints on vector registers (Figure 3, line 5) and cardinality (lines 6 - 8).

In APPLYVREGSCONSTR, the compiler decides if the group satisfies VREGSCONSTR. It also determines what will be the final number of vector registers necessary to build the vector register cache for each overlap group. This number depends on the use of aligned or unaligned *vls* (see Section 4.1.2). The compiler will decide the most appropriate approach depending on the register pressure and VREGSCONSTR. It can also decide to discard some *vls* to reduce the number of registers involved in the cache and satisfy VREGSCONSTR. Discarding *vls* might also be useful when one or few *vls* increase that number and reduce the efficiency of the cache.

Regarding the group cardinality, the compiler chooses the overlap group only if its cardinality after the processing of VREGSCONSTR is greater than or equal to the limit imposed by CARDCONSTR (lines 6 - 8).

Once all groups have been processed and pruned according to CARDCONSTR and VREGSCONSTR, the compiler processes the whole set $P'_{L,a}$ to fulfill GROUPSCONSTR (APPLYGROUPSCONSTR). At this point, the compiler will discard some groups if they exceed the limit imposed. Groups with higher efficiency (Equation 7) and lower *VecRegs* (Equation 6), in that order, will be prioritized not to be discarded.

If groups affected by the loop unrolling from the Unrolling Analysis Phase have been pruned at this point, the loop unrolling is undone.

In the Moving Average example, the resulting $\mathcal{O}_{Li,a,0}$ from the Unrolling Analysis Phase has *ovls* without unsafe data dependencies. VREGSCONSTR $= 2$, $VecRegs(\mathcal{O}_{Li,a,0}) = 2$ and the first (lowest memory address) *vl* in the group is aligned after the loop unrolling (Figure 5, comment in line 13). CARDCONSTR $= 4$ is satisfied in the main loop, with $|\mathcal{O}_{Li,a,0}| = 16$. The overlap epilogue also satisfies this constraint since there are 4 *ovls* ($UF_{EPI} = 4$) in each block code (lines 26-29, 32-34 and 37-39). GROUPSCONSTR is not set and has no effect.

4.1.5 Cache Building Phase

The Cache Building Phase creates vector register caches on those loops hosting *ovls*. For each $\mathcal{O}_{L,a,i} \in P'_{L,a}$ resulting

1: **procedure** BUILDGROUPCACHE($\mathcal{O}_{L,a,i}$, L)
2: DECLAREGROUPSYMBOLS($\mathcal{O}_{L,a,i}$, L)
3: ADDGROUPINITSTMTS($\mathcal{O}_{L,a,i}$, L)
4: ADDGROUPPREITERUPDATESTMTS($\mathcal{O}_{L,a,i}$, L)
5: ADDGROUPPOSTITERUPDATESTMTS($\mathcal{O}_{L,a,i}$, L)
6: **for all** $\overrightarrow{a[e_j]} \in \mathcal{O}_{L,a,i}$ **do**
7: $new\_vr2r\_inst \leftarrow$ GETVR2RINSTR($\overrightarrow{a[e_j]}$)
8: REPLACE($\overrightarrow{a[e_j]}$, new_vr2r_inst)
9: **end for**
10: **end procedure**

Figure 4: Cache building algorithm.

from the Group Pruning Phase, the compiler applies the algorithm in Figure 4.

DECLAREGROUPSYMBOLS declares vector symbols that will be used to host the cache data (Figure 5, line 2).

ADDGROUPINITSTMTS inserts the *vl* instructions that initialize the register cache. They will be aligned or unaligned depending on the decision made in the Group Pruning Phase. If $\mathcal{O}_{L,a,i}$ is only of kind *intra*, these statements will be added to the bodies of L and the overlap epilogue. If $\mathcal{O}_{L,a,i}$ is *inter* or both *intra* and *inter*, these statements will precede L. The latter is the case in the Moving Average example (Figure 5, line 6).

ADDGROUPPREITERUPDATESTMTS inserts load instructions in the body of L and the overlap epilogue (Figure 5, lines 11 and 25). They load the new data that will be used in that iteration into the last registers of the cache. They are necessary for both *inter* and *intra* overlap group kinds.

ADDGROUPPOSTITERUPDATESTMTS inserts statements, in the body of L, that shift or readjust data already loaded in the cache (Figure 5, line 20). They rearrange data that will be reused in the next loop iteration to its expected position. Data that will not be reused is overwritten. These statements are required only for *inter* overlap groups.

Once the cache has been settled, the compiler replaces original *vls* in L and in the overlap epilogue code by vector register-to-register instructions (Figure 4, lines 6-9). They rebuild the original vector operands from data in the register cache (for example, lines 13-18 in Figure 5).

4.2 The Overlap Optimization in OpenMP

In the context of the OpenMP SIMD constructs [18, 28], we propose a new clause named **overlap**. This clause instructs the compiler where and how to apply the overlap optimization (Section 4.1). It has the following format:

```
overlap(var_list [: min_group_loads [, max_groups]])
```

where:

- **var_list** is the list of array and/or pointer variables that the overlap optimization will target.
- **min_group_loads** is the minimum number of *ovls* per loop iteration necessary to constitute an overlap group (CARDCONSTR).
- **max_groups** is the maximum number of overlap groups that can be generated for each target variable (GROUPSCONSTR).

The **overlap** clause lets users perform a systematic benchmarking with different overlap groups and constraints that affect the code generated by the overlap optimization. The parameters **min_group_loads** and **max_groups** are optional, independent from each other and must be known at compile time. A value of 0 indicates an undefined parameter. If they are undefined or not specified, their values will be implementation defined. We decided not to expose the control of vector registers to users as they are a low-level hardware component.

The compiler could use heuristics to determine default values for these parameters or fix them by default (see our implementation decisions in Section 5.1), but it is hard to automatically obtain optimal values for them. In addition, the use of the **overlap** clause is necessary to tell the compiler where and over which arrays to apply the optimization to get better performance. Determining this automatically at compile time is even harder due to the number of variables that must be taken into account: selected overlap groups, loop unroll factor, overlap transformation performance/overhead ratio, register and memory unit pressure, and instruction

```
1  for(i=0; i <= N-points-16; i+=16){
2    float16 cache_a_0, cache_a_1;
3    float16 tmp = vpromotion(0.0f);
4
5    // Cache init, j=0
6    cache_a_0 = aligned_vload(&a[i+0]);
7
8    // Unrolled loop (UF=16)
9    for(j=0; j <= points-16; j+=16){
10     // Cache pre-iteration update
11     cache_a_1 = aligned_vload16(&a[i+j+16]);
12     // Rebuild original operands from cache
13     tmp += cache_a_0;//aligned_vload(&a[i+j])
14     tmp += vr2r_op16(//unaligned_vload(&a[i+j+1])
15              cache_a_1, cache_a_0, 1);
16     ...
17     tmp += vr2r_op16(//unaligned_vload(&a[i+j+15])
18              cache_a_1, cache_a_0, 15);
19     // Cache post-iteration update
20     cache_a_0 = cache_a_1;
21   }
22
23   // Overlap Epilogue (UF_EPI=4)
24   if (j <= points-4){ // Block 1
25     cache_a_1 = aligned_vload16(&a[i+j+16]);
26     tmp += cache_a_0_0;
27     tmp += vr2r_op16(cache_a_1,cache_a_0,1);
28     tmp += vr2r_op16(cache_a_1,cache_a_0,2);
29     tmp += vr2r_op16(cache_a_1,cache_a_0,3);
30     j += 4;
31     if (j <= points-4){ // Block 2
32       tmp += vr2r_op16(cache_a_1,cache_a_0,4);
33       ...
34       tmp += vr2r_op16(cache_a_1,cache_a_0,7);
35       j += 4;
36       if (j <= points-4){ // Block 3
37         tmp += vr2r_op16(cache_a_1,cache_a_0,8);
38         ...
39         tmp += vr2r_op16(cache_a_1,cache_a_0,11);
40         j += 4;
41   } } }
42
43   // Regular Epilogue
44   for(; j <= points-1; j++)
45     tmp += unaligned_vload16(&a[i+j]);
46
47   tmp = tmp / vpromotion16(points);
48   aligned_vstore16(&b[i], tmp);
49 }
```

Figure 5: Pseudo-code resulting from the overlap optimization on Moving Average. Assuming $VF = VL = 16$. $\mathtt{vr2r\_op}_{16}$ refers to vector register-to-register instructions.

```
#pragma omp simd aligned(a,b:64) overlap(a:4)
for(i=0; i < N-points; i++){ ... }
```

Figure 6: Example of the **overlap** clause for Figure 1a.

scheduling, among others. These facts support the use of the `overlap` clause and make hints from users indispensable to optimally apply the overlap optimization. User guidelines are described in Section 4.3.

The `overlap` clause must be used in conjunction with SIMD constructs defined in OpenMP, as depicted in Figure 6. Multiple `overlap` clauses can be used to specify a different set of parameters for different variables.

4.3 User Guidelines

In this section, we introduce some hints to guide users on the application of the `overlap` clause, including the whole process of user-directed vectorization with OpenMP. Since OpenMP provides a model for parallel programming, potential users are expected to have a minimum background in parallelism and performance analysis [28]. In addition, some notions in vectorization are also required in order to exploit SIMD extensions in OpenMP and to take advantage of our proposal. For the sake of simplicity, we do not consider other kinds of parallelism besides the data parallelism exploited by the OpenMP `simd` clause.

The first step when applying user-directed vectorization is to choose the most appropriate loop to vectorize. The innermost loop is the traditional option in autovectorizing compilers [17]. However, outer loop vectorization has been proven to yield more performance in some codes when outer loops offer greater data parallelism and data locality than innermost loops [27]. In order to decide the most appropriate loop to be vectorized with the OpenMP's `simd` directive, users may consider the following hints:

- loops that traverse the contiguous memory dimension of data structures in a stride-one fashion are generally better options. They will produce stride-one vector memory accesses (see *svma* in Section 3) instead of gather/scatter access patterns.
- loops with a large trip-count will maximize the number of vector iterations of the loop and will minimize epilogue loop iterations.
- if both the innermost and the outer loops satisfy the previous hints, vectorizing the outer loop is usually the most suitable option, as it will bring vectorization to a larger number of instructions, thus increasing data parallelism.

In some cases, the only way to find the vectorization strategy that offers the best performance is benchmarking the most suitable alternatives. This is one of the greatest benefits of using the OpenMP SIMD extensions, as it is only a matter of moving the `simd` construct from one loop to another.

In the Moving Average example (Figure 1a), the innermost loop traverses the contiguous dimension of the array `a` in a stride-one fashion. However, the outer loop traverses both the array `a` and the array `b` also in a stride-one fashion. In addition, as programmers of the application, we know that the innermost loop trip-count will be considerably smaller than the one from the outer-loop at runtime. Then, according to the third hint, the outer loop is potentially the best candidate for vectorization.

Once the vectorization strategy has been chosen, the second step is to enable the overlap optimization with the `overlap` clause if *ovls* are present in the vectorized code, as described in Section 3.2. Figure 1c shows how *ovls* happen on the array a of the Moving Average example after outer loop vectorization.

The general advice for users pursuing the best performance is to apply the overlap optimization on those arrays with a larger number of *ovls* that are as close as possible to each other. According to the vectorization scenario:

Innermost loop vectorization: *ovls* are close to each other when their indexes only differ in a small constant offset, such as $\overrightarrow{a[i]}$ and $\overrightarrow{a[i+1]}$, where i is the induction variable of the loop. The smaller this offset is, the closer the *ovls* are.

Outer loop vectorization: indexes of *vls* that could overlap across the inner loop iterations typically contain both loops' induction variables, such as $\overrightarrow{a[i+j]}$. The inner loop induction variable with a constant step can be seen as a constant offset and proceed as in the innermost loop scenario. Likewise, arrays could also overlap within the same iteration ($\overrightarrow{a[i+j]}$ and $\overrightarrow{a[i+j+1]}$).

In the outer loop vectorization scenario of the Moving Average example, there are no *ovls* on the array `b` as its index only contains the outer loop induction variable and there is no additional small constant offset. Nonetheless, the array `a` contains both loops' induction variables, so their *vls* will be *ovls*, as described previously.

Again, the only way to know which arrays with *ovls* are the best options to receive the overlap optimization in each particular code is to carry out a trial and error approach. The parameter `min_group_loads` may also help in this process. For example, in an application with several groups of 2 and 4 *ovls*, programmers may run this application twice: one with the parameter unset and another one fixing this parameter to 4. This way, programmers would know if overlap groups with 2 *ovls* increase or decrease performance. In those outer loop vectorization scenarios where discarding groups is not necessary, programmers could use their application knowledge to set `min_group_loads`. For example, in Moving Average, we know that the number of `points` could be small. To exploit the overlap optimization also in the small cases, programmers could find by benchmarking the minimum number that yields the best performance and overcome the overhead of the code transformation.

The parameter `max_groups` can be used in the same way for the same purpose. Thus, programmers could benchmark their application increasing this parameter to find out which value offers the best performance. As vector registers are usually a scarce resource, a large number of groups is generally not recommended.

4.4 Cost Model

We propose a simple cost model that compilers or performance tools can use to give advice to programmers on two aspects: (1) adding the `overlap` clause; (2) setting the specific parameters of the clause. This cost model is based on instruction cycles:

$$\mathcal{C}(\mathcal{O}_{L,a,i}) = overlap\_c(\mathcal{O}_{L,a,i}) - orig\_vls\_c(\mathcal{O}_{L,a,i}) \quad (11)$$

Benchmark	Version	Stencil Kind (Vect. Strategy)	Input Size, Tsteps, Mem. Footprint	Evaluation Key Factors
Moving Average	1D	1D forward (1st outer loop)	536M, 50, 4.0GB	Unknown order at compile time
Convolution	2D	convolution (2nd outer loop)	24000^2, 30, 4.3GB	Unknown order at compile time. `min_group_loads`
Stencil Probe	1D	28th-order star	525M, 200, 3.9GB	Very high-order star
	2D	(1D&3D: innermost loop	22964^2, 50, 3.9GB	stencil. 1D, 2D and 3D
	3D	2D: 1st outer loop)	820^3, 25, 4.1GB	performance comparison
Acoustic Prop.	3D	8th-order star (innermost loop)	928x448x840, 100, 5.5GB	Multi-grid stencil
Cubic Stencil	2nd-order	cubic	832^3, 100, 4.3GB	Cubic stencil evaluation
	4th-order	(innermost loop)	834^3, 20, 4.3GB	with 27 and 125 points

Table 1: Benchmarks Summary.

$overlap\_c(\mathcal{O}_{L,a,i})$ is the number of estimated cycles that are needed to execute the overlap optimization instructions (vector register-to-register instructions, instructions that initialize, load data into and manage the register cache) for the estimated trip count of L. $orig\_vls\_c(\mathcal{O}_{L,a,i})$ is the number of estimated cycles that it takes to execute all the original aligned and unaligned *vls* in the group for the estimated trip count of L.

Values of $\mathcal{C}$ lower than 0 mean that the overlap optimization could run faster than the original code, and it could potentially speed up the execution time. Otherwise, the optimization could degrade the performance.

This cost model does not take into account the weight of the optimized code in the overall number of cycles of the loop, nor memory overheads, such as cache misses or memory units overload, nor register pressure. The latter issue can be tailored by the compiler with Equation 6 and an estimation of the number of vector registers that would be available in that region of the code.

The Intel C compiler 15.0.1 reports the following instruction cycle information for the Intel Xeon Phi coprocessor when generating assembly code: 3 cycles for aligned vector loads, vector register moves and register-to-register instructions (*valignd*), and 6 cycles for unaligned vector loads (2 vector load instructions). We rely on this information to apply the cost model on the Moving Average example. We also assume an estimated $trip\_count_{Li}$ of 200. Then, $orig\_vls\_c(\mathcal{O}_{Li,a,0})$ and $overlap\_c(\mathcal{O}_{Li,a,0})$ are computed as:

$$orig\_vls\_c(\mathcal{O}_{Li,a,0}) = 200 * (1\ vl * 6\ cycles) = 1200\ cycles$$
$$overlap\_c(\mathcal{O}_{Li,a,0}) = init\_stmts\_c + (trip\_count_{Li}/UF) * (pre\_it\_update\_c + r2r\_instr\_c + post\_it\_update\_c)$$

where $init\_stmts\_c$, $pre\_it\_update\_c$, $post\_it\_update\_c$ and $r2r\_instr\_c$ are the number of cycles from the instructions that initialize the register cache (AddGroupInitStmts), manage the cache data (AddGroupPreIterStmts and AddGroupPostIterStmts) and vector register-to-register instructions, respectively (described in Section 4.1.5). Thus, according to Figure 5 ($UF = 16$), the estimated number of cycles of the overlap optimization is:

$$overlap\_c(\mathcal{O}_{Li,a,0}) = (1\ vl + 12.5 * (1\ vl + 15\ r2r\_instr + 1\ register\_move)) * 3\ cycles = 640.5\ cycles$$

Therefore, the cost model turns to be:

$$\mathcal{C}(\mathcal{O}_{Li,a,0}) = 640.5 - 1200 = -559.5\ cycles$$

which suggests that the overlap optimization may improve performance in the Moving Average example.

5. EVALUATION

To measure the performance of the overlap optimization, we implemented our approach in the Mercurium compiler targeting the Intel Xeon Phi coprocessor (Section 5.1). Then, we conducted experiments with OpenMP: first, we finely optimized five well-known kernels used in real-world applications from diverse fields for the Intel Xeon Phi coprocessor (Section 5.4); afterwards, we evaluated the performance of the overlap optimization on these highly-optimized versions of the kernels (Section 5.5).

5.1 Implementation

We implemented our approach in the Mercurium C/C++ Source-to-source Compiler [10] targeting the Intel Xeon Phi coprocessor [14]. Mercurium is a research compiler with support for OpenMP and it has a vectorization infrastructure that generates C/C++ SIMD intrinsics for the Intel MIC instructions [12].

Our implementation uses the *valignd* vector instruction available in the Intel MIC instructions. This instruction shifts scalar elements from two input vector registers and returns the result in a new one. It shifts a fixed number of 32-bit elements that must be known at compile time.

Regarding implementation defined decisions and default values for the overlap algorithm, we set to 4 the default value of the cardinality constraint (CardConstr). This number, far from being optimal, offered some performance improvement and moderate slowdowns in microbenchmarking experiments for this architecture. Constraints on the maximum number of vector registers (VRegsConstr) and the number of groups (GroupsConstr) are set to unlimited by default in our implementation. We always use aligned *vls* to maintain the register cache, unless this results in a higher number of registers than the limit imposed by VRegsConstr. We only apply unrolling to the innermost loop in outer loop vectorization scenarios. We choose the minimum $UF_{\mathcal{O}}$ that satisfies Equations 8 – 10 and maximizes efficiency. UF_{EPI} is set to CardConstr.

5.2 Benchmarks

Our benchmark set contains five kernels from real-world applications using realistic workloads. They cover a wide spectrum of stencil algorithms and vectorization scenarios. Table 1 summarizes their main characteristics.

Moving Average is a low-pass finite impulse response (FIR) filter that is widely used in statistics, economics and signal processing. One of its most popular uses is the smoothing of short-term fluctuations when analyzing long data series. Our benchmark implements the Simple Moving Av-

Bench.	Version	Optimiz.		Input Param.	Threads	Baseline	Speed-up	icc/mcc (time)
Moving Average	1D	AIS,MA, U,SP		4	244	484.74	1.09	1.02
				8		449.10	1.18	1.02
				16		337.06	1.51	1.06
				32		122.02	1.66	1.07
				64		212.68	1.72	1.06
				128		65.86	1.76	1.05
Convol.	2D	AIS,MA, U,SP		3^2	183	276.43	1.10	-
				5^2		135.18	1.53	-
				7^2		78.33	1.60	-
				10^2		41.92	1.67	-
				16^2		12.06	2.58	-
Stencil Probe	1D	AIS, MA, SP,	-	-	122	9683.38	1.10	0.99
					183	10400.45	1.06	1.00
	2D		LB,LI	-	183	1840.77	3.58	1.27
					244	1825.26	3.48	1.12
	3D		LB,LD	-	183	66.61	27.66	2.27
					244	49.65	38.42	2.15
Acoustic Propag.	3D	AIS,MA, SP,LB		-	122	4410.02	1.21	1.00
					183	3790.25	1.49	1.02
Cubic Stencil	2nd order	AIS,MA, SP,LB, LD		-	122	8020.97	1.23	0.96
					183	7675.79	1.35	1.00
	4th order			-	122	1604.78	1.71	1.02
					183	1129.22	2.43	0.98

Table 2: Generic optimizations applied to each benchmark. Absolute performance (in M{elements/pixels}/s) and speed-up over the baseline. Input parameters for Moving Average is number of **points** and for Convolution is filter size.

erage Filter, shown in Figure 1a. We ran experiments for different number of `points`: 4, 8, 16, 32, 64 and 128.

Convolution implements a stencil convolution filter on an image. These kinds of algorithms are widely used in image processing to modify or analyze certain image properties (image blurring, sharpening or edge detection, among others). We used the code of the motivating example from Naishlos et al. [32]. We ran experiments for different filter sizes (3x3, 5x5, 7x7, 10x10 and 16x16).

Stencil Probe [15] is a benchmark based on the Chombo's Heat Equation. It is used to explore the behavior of optimizations in star stencil codes.

We chose the 28th-order 3D version (85 stencil points) proposed by de la Cruz et al. [8]. We extended it to also have 1D (29 stencil points) and 2D (57 stencil points) versions.

Acoustic Propagator computes the acoustic wave propagation in an isotropic non-elastic medium. It solves a Partial Differential Equation (PDE) that involves velocity and two spatial components from previous time steps [4]. Our private algorithm is based on a 8th-order 3D star stencil similar to that published by Intel [13].

Cubic Stencil implements a cubic stencil algorithm where points involved in the neighboring computation form a dense cube around the central point to be updated. We used the 2nd-order 3D cubic stencil code from Datta et al. [7]. We also extended it to have a 4th-order version (125 points).

5.3 Environment and Methodology

We compiled every benchmark with the Intel C compiler 15.0.1 (icc) and the Mercurium Source-to-source C compiler (mcc), both using the Intel OpenMP Runtime Library from the Intel compiler release. Mercurium versions are vectorized with the Mercurium compiler (Section 5.1) and then, the Intel C compiler is used to generate the binary code.

All versions in our experiments, including the baseline, are annotated with OpenMP worksharing and SIMD directives. Memory allocations are aligned to page boundaries (4096 bytes) and pointers are qualified with the `restrict` attribute to maximize compiler optimizations. We also used the following compilation flags: `-fopenmp -O3 -mmic -restrict -ansi-alias`. Both compilers offer similar vectorization performance over baseline codes.

As evaluation metrics, we use the absolute performance in millions of elements or pixels updated per second. We report the speed-up of the highly-optimized versions for the Intel Xeon Phi coprocessor over the OpenMP annotated baseline (Section 5.4), and the speed-up of the overlap optimization over the highly-optimized versions compiled with Mercurium (Section 5.5). We aim to differentiate the improvement of the data reuse of the overlap optimization from the one of other co-lateral transformations in the overlap optimization, such as loop unrolling. Our performance figures are the arithmetic mean of 50 executions.

We ran our benchmarks natively in an Intel Xeon Phi coprocessor C0PRQ-7120 (61 cores @ 1.23 GHz, 16 GB of GDDR Memory)**. We use 122, 183 and 244 threads on a balanced thread affinity policy (2, 3 and 4 threads per core, respectively). We added the compile-time flag `-qopt-threads-per-core=#threads_per_core` to optimize the instruction scheduling depending on the number of threads per core at runtime.

5.4 Generic Optimizations

We applied the following optimizations to our set of benchmarks to improve their performance and scalability in the Intel Xeon Phi coprocessor:

Array Indexes Simplification (AIS): We manually applied common sub-expression elimination and loop-invariant code motion [2, 1] to array indexes.

Loop Unrolling (U): To minimize the impact in the speed-up of the loop unrolling [2, 17] applied by the overlap optimization, we unrolled the same loop in versions without the overlap optimization.

Memory Alignment (MA): We used the OpenMP `align` clause and the `__assume_alined` and `__assume` compiler hints to provide the compiler with information to maximize aligned vector memory accesses and prevent prologue and epilogue loops in the vectorization process [14].

Software Prefetching (SP): We implemented manual software prefetching for L1 and L2 cache levels using the `_mm_prefetch` intrinsic. We performed an extensive exploration to find out the best prefetching distances. Our prefetching strategies include data prefetching among loop iterations and initial prefeching before loops [20]. This approach noticeably outperforms software prefetching automatically generated by the Intel compiler.

Loop Blocking (LB): We applied loop blocking [33, 17] to loops that traverse large multidimensional data structures. We widely explored different block sizes and their scheduling among threads.

Loop Interchange (LI): We applied loop interchange [3, 17] to explore several traversal strategies on grid structures with significant reuse in other dimensions than in the memory contiguous one. If the innermost loop is annotated with the `simd` directive and it is interchanged, initial innermost loop vectorization turns into outer loop vectorization [27].

Loop Distribution (LD): Splitting a single loop body computation into two loops [29, 17] reduced register pressure and memory contention issues in some benchmarks.

Best prefetching distance and best block size explorations were jointly carried out since they affect each other. Table 2 shows which generic optimizations were applied to each benchmark, the absolute performance before optimizing the code (baseline) and the speed-up obtained after it. Both versions were vectorized with the Mercurium compiler. As depicted, generic optimizations yield substantial performance over the baseline, even though the latter is also annotated with OpenMP and is successfully vectorized. These optimizations mainly address memory bandwidth issues. However, loop distribution (LD), which targets register spilling, is critical in some benchmarks, such as in the 3D Stencil Probe (improvement of 27% and 38%).

Whereas Intel and Mercurium compilers yield similar performance on baseline codes, icc/mcc ratio in Table 2 describes how Mercurium vectorization capabilites are on the optimized versions with respect to the last Intel compiler in production. Values close to or greater than one state that Mercurium vectorization is comparable or better than Intel's. This fact increases the confidence in the performance results obtained with Mercurium according to state-of-the-art vectorization techniques. Performance differences are mainly due to Intel compiler problems when vectorizing outer loops. That is the reason why the icc/mcc ratio is not available in Convolution.

5.5 Overlap Optimization Performance

Table 3 summarizes the absolute performance results of the overlap optimization and its speed-up over the highly-optimized version of the benchmarks. Both versions are compiled with Mercurium. The last column of each table depicts the number and kind of overlap groups and the percentage of vector loads affected by the overlap optimization (*ovls*) out of all vector loads per iteration.

Moving Average Filter performance is shown in Table 3a. Because of the outer loop vectorization, the overlap optimization unrolls the innermost loop 16 times and builds a 2-register cache for the single overlap group of the array `a`. An overlap epilogue is also generated with $UF_{EPI} = 4$. The optimized version used as baseline includes the best unroll factor found for every input set. This counteracts performance from the loop unrolling of the overlap optimization.

Results show a gradual performance gain when `points` increases (greater than or equal to 16) and so does the number of *ovls*. This means that this benchmark needs a large group to overcome the register cache overhead.

In **Convolution Filter**, vectorization takes place from the second outer loop (image column traversal). We evaluate how the parameter `min_group_loads` (CARDCONSTR) impacts performance in the overlap optimization. We use the values of the filter size, which are unknown at compile time. These values affect the UF_{EPI} of the overlap epilogue generation (see Section 5.1).

Performance results are summarized in Table 3c. The best configuration for each filter size is highlighted except in filter 3x3, where the overlap optimization only causes a performance slowdown. Speed-up reveals how sensitive the transformation is to the input size and the `min_group_loads` parameter. For the smallest filter sizes, the overlap optimization can obtain a minimal gain (if any) or up to 19% of penalty (size=7, `min_group_loads`=10) depending on the value of `min_group_loads`. For larger filter sizes, the most suitable `min_group_loads` value yields up to 19% of speed-up (size=`min_group_loads`=10), whereas other values lead to up to 18% of slowdown (size=10, `min_group_loads`=16) for the same filter size. This slowdown is higher when the filter size is lower than `min_group_loads` and the overlap code is generated but not executed because CARDCONSTR is not satisfied. Since filter size is unknown at compiler time, the `min_group_loads` parameter is truly important to tune the overlap optimization.

Table 3b gathers results from StencilProbe, Acoustic Propagator and Cubic Stencil. In the three versions of **StencilProbe**, the overlap optimization finds only one overlap group with 29 *ovls*. In the 1D version, all *vls* are *ovls*. The overlap optimization yields a 27% speed-up over the highly optimized version with 122 threads, which greatly outperforms any other version with higher thread configuration. In the 2D version, the overlap optimization obtains a gain of 29% and 24% with 182 and 244 threads, respectively. Even when only 51% of *vls* are optimized, the optimization reduces pressure on the memory system. In the 3D version, the overlap optimization only yields 3% improvement because it only affects 34% of *vls* per iteration. Furthermore, memory bandwidth and computation per updated elements are dramatically high due to the high-order of the stencil.

In **Acoustic Propagator**, however, the overlap optmization only provides a modest improvement of 4-9%. This is due to the different grids involved in the computation (memory bound) and the small number of *ovls* (33%).

In **Cubic Stencil**, unlike in previous star stencil codes, there are multiple overlap groups that affect 100% of *vls*. Even in the 2nd-order version, with only three elements per group, performance results show that the overlap optimization yields an extra 7% of performance over the optimized version. In the 4th-order version, larger overlap groups yield a 12% gain. This demonstrates that the overlap optimization can improve performance under scenarios with high memory and computational requirements if the percentage of *ovls* per loop iteration is high.

6. RELATED WORK

Vectorization has been an active topic in compiler research in the last two decades. Many proposals tackled different well-known issues: alignment constraints [9], interleaved/disjoint data [26], non-temporal stores [20] and outer loop vectorization [27], among others [5]. Even new vectorization strategies were proposed beyond the traditional loop-based vectorization approaches [16, 22].

In this context, inter-register vector shift instructions have been used to improve unaligned vector memory accesses and exploit data reuse in some way [31, 26, 9, 19]. The closest studies to ours are those from Naishlos et al. [26] and Shin et al. [31]. They both proposed a code transformation that involves a vector register cache and vector shift instructions. However, their proposals are limited to certain loop nests where inner-loop vectorization and outer loop unroll-and-jam can jointly be applied.

#points	Melements/s	Speed-up	$\mathcal{O}$s, Kind, (%*ovls*/iteration)
4	528.44	1.00	1 group of 16 *ovls*, inter, (100%)
8	527.07	1.00	
16	522.03	1.03	
32	410.79	1.17	
64	255.97	1.22	
128	144.61	1.25	

(a) Moving Average (244 threads).

Bench.	Ver.	Threads	Melements/s	Speed-up	$\mathcal{O}$s, Kind, (%*ovls*/iteration)	
Stencil Probe	1D	122	13522.11	1.27	1 group of 29 *ovls*,	both, (100%)
		183	12943.67	1.17		
	2D	183	8195.33	1.24		intra, (51%)
		244	8213.63	1.29		
	3D	183	1895.67	1.03		both, (34%)
		244	1960.73	1.03		
Acoustic Propagator	3D	122	5783.41	1.09	1 group of 9 *ovls*, both, (33%)	
		183	5892.36	1.04		
Cubic Stencil	2nd order	122	10570.29	1.07	9 groups of 3,	both, (100%)
		183	11135.66	1.07		
	4th order	122	2877.68	1.05	25 groups of 5,	
		183	3082.98	1.12		

(b) Acoustic Propagator, Cubic Stencil and StencilProbe.

Filter Size	Mpixels/s varying `#min_group_loads` (Speed-up) 3	5	7	10	16	$\mathcal{O}$s, Kind, (%*ovls*/iteration)
3	286.82 (0.94)	286.75 (0.94)	295.69 (0.97)	295.90 (0.97)	296.86 (0.97)	1 group of 16 *ovls*, inter, (100%)
5	208.77 (1.01)	208.80 (1.01)	169.77 (0.82)	169.87 (0.82)	174.30 (0.84)	
7	113.61 (0.91)	113.59 (0.91)	132.17 (1.06)	101.30 (0.81)	104.04 (0.83)	
10	76.07 (1.09)	76.07 (1.09)	68.49 (0.98)	83.65 (1.19)	57.50 (0.82)	
16	34.51 (1.11)	34.50 (1.11)	34.15 (1.10)	34.15 (1.10)	37.16 (1.19)	

(c) Convolution Filter (183 theads, 3 threads/core).

Table 3: Overlap optimization absolute performance (Moving Average, Acoustic Propagator, StencilProbe and Cubic Stencil in Melements/s, Convolution in Mpixels/s) and speed-up results obtained with the Mercurium compiler.

Eichenberger et al. [9] also proposed a vector code transformation mainly focused on vectorizing codes with unaligned memory references in hardware without direct support for them. Although their approach exploits data reuse of the same vector load across iterations, they do not consider groups of overlapped vector loads in a generic way or a vector register cache, as we do.

We present a more generic approach applicable to inner-loop and outer-loop vectorization scenarios where loop unrolling is not always necessary and loop trip-counts can be unknown at compile time. Furthermore, our OpenMP interface allows users to instruct the compiler to apply this aggressive code transformation and finely tune it. This could be a key factor in making this optimization adopted by production compilers. Moreover, we carry out the evaluation on highly-optimized kernels and workloads from real-world applications where the standalone speed-up from our optimization is separately reported from that resulting from other co-lateral optimizations.

On the programmer side, there have been plenty of manual, application specific, code optimization proposals [21, 30, 6]. Lacassagne et al. [21] revisited some high-level transformations targeting SIMD and computer vision algorithms. They considered using several inter-register data manipulation instructions to optimize unaligned vector loads and exploit data reuse, among other things. Satish et al. [30] performed a comparison of codes meticulously optimized at low-level by hand with versions optimized using compiler technology and high-level manual optimization, such as OpenMP thread parallelism, inner and outer loop vectorization, spatial and temporal blocking and data layout transformations. Among their applications, they evaluated simple and small stencil codes. Datta et al. [6] presented a set of optimizations targeting stencil computation: several spacial decomposition strategies, loop unrolling and interchange, padding and software prefetching, among others.

We use similar approaches to optimize our stencil codes. However, we found that some of the proposed solutions were very application specific and they were not applicable or did not result in better performance when dealing with stencil codes with moderate/large order. Consequently, we had to develop and evaluate our own set of optimizations that better fitted each benchmark.

Klemm et al. [18] proposed user-directed vectorization in OpenMP. They introduced a series of new directives and clauses that allow OpenMP's users to describe SIMD parallelism. A refined proposal was firstly incorporated in the 4.0 version of the OpenMP standard [28]. However, it does not include anything similar to our user-directed optimization.

7. CONCLUSIONS AND FUTURE WORK

In this paper, we present an OpenMP user-directed code optimization that targets overlapped vector loads, very common in stencil computation. Independently of the outer or inner loop vectorization scenario, it performs an aggressive code transformation that maximizes data reuse and makes use of advanced SIMD instructions, such as inter-register vector shifts.

We evaluate our proposal on a representative set of different stencil kernels and workloads used in real-world applications. Performance results in the Intel Xeon Phi coprocessor show improvements of up to 29% over previously highly-optimized versions that already exploited OpenMP user-directed vectorization. This gain is significant even in codes with high memory requirements if the number of vector loads affected by the optimization is large. In some cases, the overlap optimization helps to achieve the best benchmark performance with a considerably smaller number of threads than versions not exploiting this optimization. Moreover, results show how the performance of this optimization is highly sensitive to many factors, such as number of overlapped vector loads per group and the characteristics of the surrounding code. Therefore, user guidance and systematic benchmarking is crucial to obtain maximum performance and avoid slowdowns.

As future work, we plan to evaluate our approach on future Intel SIMD extensions. We would also like to improve the cost model and extend our proposal to non-stride-one vector loads with some kind of overlap. In the context of user-directed optimizations, vector permutations would also be a relevant next step.

Acknowledgments

The authors would like to thank to M. Hanzich, A. Farres, J. de la Puente, R. de la Cruz and J.M. Cela, from the CASE department at BSC, for sharing their expertise and applications with us. We would also like to thank to everybody that helped us with the review process of this paper.
This work was supported by Agència de Gestió d'Ajuts Universitaris i de Recerca (FI-DGR, 2014FI_B2 00155), the European Commission (DEEP-ER project, FP7-ICT-610476), the Spanish Ministry of Education (TIN2012-34557) and the Generalitat de Catalunya (MPEXPAR-2014-SGR-1051).
Intel, Xeon, Xeon Phi and Many Integrated Core are trademarks or registered trademarks of Intel Corporation or its subsidiaries in the United States and other countries.
* Other brands and names are the property of their respective owners. ** For more information about performance measurements, go to http://www.intel.com/performance.
System configuration used: Intel Xeon Phi coprocessor with C0 silicon and board version C0PRQ-7120 (61 cores at 1238095 Khz, 16 GB of GDDR Memory at 5.5 GT/sec, 300W TDP), driver v3.4-1, MPSS v3.4 and flash v2.1.02.0390).

8. REFERENCES

[1] A. V. Aho, M. S. Lam, R. Sethi, and J. D. Ullman. *Compilers: Principles, Techniques, and Tools (2nd Ed.).* Addison-Wesley Longman Publishing Co., Inc., 2006.

[2] F. Allen and J. Cocke. A catalogue of optimizing transformations. In *Design and Optimization of Compilers*, pages 1–30, 1972.

[3] J. R. Allen and K. Kennedy. Automatic loop interchange. In *Symp. on Compiler Construction*, pages 233–246, 1984.

[4] M. Araya-Polo, F. Rubio, R. de la Cruz, M. Hanzich, J. M. Cela, and D. P. Scarpazza. 3D seismic imaging through reverse-time migration on homogeneous and heterogeneous multi-core processors. *Sci. Program.*, 17(1-2):185–198, 2009.

[5] A. J. C. Bik. *Software Vectorization Handbook, The: Applying Intel Multimedia Extensions for Maximum Performance.* Intel Press, 2004.

[6] K. Datta, M. Murphy, V. Volkov, S. Williams, J. Carter, L. Oliker, D. Patterson, J. Shalf, and K. Yelick. Stencil computation optimization and auto-tuning on state-of-the-art multicore architectures. In *SC'08*, pages 4:1–4:12.

[7] K. Datta, S. Williams, V. Volkov, J. Carter, L. Oliker, J. Shalf, and K. Yelick. Auto-tuning the 27-point stencil for multicore. In *Proc. of the Workshop on Automatic Performance Tuning*, 2009.

[8] R. de la Cruz and M. Araya-Polo. Algorithm 942: Semi-Stencil. *ACM TOMS*, 40(3):23:1–23:39, Apr. 2014.

[9] A. E. Eichenberger, P. Wu, and K. O'Brien. Vectorization for SIMD Architectures with Alignment Constraints. In *PLDI'04*, pages 82–93.

[10] R. Ferrer, S. Royuela, D. Caballero, A. Duran, X. Martorell, and E. Ayguadé. Mercurium: Design Decisions for a S2S Compiler. *Cetus Users and Compiler Infrastructure Workshop (in PACT'11).* `http://pm.bsc.es/mcxx`.

[11] Intel Corp. Intel® Cilk™ Plus Language Extension Specification Version 1.2.

[12] Intel Corp. Intel® Xeon Phi™ Coprocessor Instruction Set Architecture Reference Manual, September 2012.

[13] Intel Corporation. Experiences in developing Seismic Imaging code for Intel® Xeon Phi™ Coprocessor. `https://software.intel.com/en-us/blogs/2012/10/26/experiences-in-developing-seismic-imaging-code-for-intel-xeon-phi-coprocessor`.

[14] J. Jeffers and J. Reinders. *Intel Xeon Phi Coprocessor High-Performance Programming.* Elsevier Science, 2013.

[15] S. Kamil, P. Husbands, L. Oliker, J. Shalf, and K. Yelick. Impact of modern memory subsystems on cache optimizations for stencil computations. In *MSP'05.*

[16] R. Karrenberg and S. Hack. Whole-function vectorization. In *CGO'11*, pages 141–150.

[17] K. Kennedy and J. R. Allen. *Optimizing Compilers for Modern Architectures: A Dependence-based Approach.* Morgan Kaufmann Publishers Inc., 2002.

[18] M. Klemm, A. Duran, X. Tian, H. Saito, D. Caballero, and X. Martorell. Extending OpenMP with Vector Constructs for Modern Multicore SIMD Architectures. In *IWOMP'12.*

[19] M. Kong, R. Veras, K. Stock, F. Franchetti, L.-N. Pouchet, and P. Sadayappan. When Polyhedral Transformations Meet SIMD Code Generation. In *PLDI'13*, pages 127–138.

[20] R. Krishnaiyer, E. Kultursay, P. Chawla, S. Preis, A. Zvezdin, and H. Saito. Compiler-Based Data Prefetching and Streaming Non-temporal Store Generation for the Intel® Xeon Phi™ Coprocessor. In *IEEE 27th Int. Parallel and Distributed Processing Symposium Workshops PhD Forum*, pages 1575–1586, May 2013.

[21] L. Lacassagne, D. Etiemble, A. Hassan Zahraee, A. Dominguez, and P. Vezolle. High level transforms for SIMD and low-level computer vision algorithms. In *WPMVP'14*, pages 49–56. ACM.

[22] S. Larsen and S. Amarasinghe. Exploiting superword level parallelism with multimedia instruction sets. In *PLDI'00.*

[23] R. Leissa, S. Hack, and I. Wald. Extending a c-like language for portable simd programming. In *PPoPP '12.*

[24] S. Maleki, Y. Gao, M. J. Garzarán, T. Wong, and D. A. Padua. An Evaluation of Vectorizing Compilers. In *PACT'11*, pages 372–382.

[25] J. McCutchan, H. Feng, N. Matsakis, Z. Anderson, and P. Jensen. A simd programming model for dart, javascript,and other dynamically typed scripting languages. In *WPMVP '14*, pages 71–78.

[26] D. Naishlos, M. Biberstein, S. Ben-David, and A. Zaks. Vectorizing for a SIMdD DSP Architecture. In *Proc. of the Int. Conf. on Compilers, Architecture and Synthesis for Embedded Systems*, pages 2–11. ACM, 2003.

[27] D. Nuzman and A. Zaks. Outer-loop Vectorization: Revisited for Short SIMD Architectures. In *PACT'08.*

[28] OpenMP Architecture Review Board. OpenMP Application Program Interface Version 4.0, July 2013.

[29] D. A. Padua and M. J. Wolfe. Advanced compiler optimizations for supercomputers. *Commun. ACM*, 29(12):1184–1201, Dec. 1986.

[30] N. Satish, C. Kim, J. Chhugani, H. Saito, R. Krishnaiyer, M. Smelyanskiy, M. Girkar, and P. Dubey. Can traditional programming bridge the ninja performance gap for parallel computing applications? In *ISCA'12*, pages 440–451.

[31] J. Shin, J. Chame, and M. W. Hall. Compiler-controlled caching in superword register files for multimedia extension architectures. In *PACT'02*, pages 45–55.

[32] K. Trifunovic, D. Nuzman, A. Cohen, A. Zaks, and I. Rosen. Polyhedral-model guided loop-nest auto-vectorization. In *PACT'09*, pages 327–337.

[33] M. Wolfe. Iteration space tiling for memory hierarchies. In *Proc. of the 3th SIAM Conf. on Parallel Processing for Scientific Computing*, pages 357–361, 1989.

COMPASS: A Framework for Automated Performance Modeling and Prediction

Seyong Lee
Oak Ridge National Laboratory
lees2@ornl.gov

Jeremy S. Meredith
Oak Ridge National Laboratory
jsmeredith@ornl.gov

Jeffrey S. Vetter
Oak Ridge National Laboratory
Georgia Institute of Technology
vetter@computer.org

ABSTRACT

Flexible, accurate performance predictions offer numerous benefits such as gaining insight into and optimizing applications and architectures. However, the development and evaluation of such performance predictions has been a major research challenge, due to the architectural complexities. To address this challenge, we have designed and implemented a prototype system, named *COMPASS*, for automated performance model generation and prediction. COMPASS generates a structured performance model from the target application's source code using *automated static analysis*, and then, it evaluates this model using various *performance prediction techniques*. As we demonstrate on several applications, the results of these predictions can be used for a variety of purposes, such as design space exploration, identifying performance tradeoffs for applications, and understanding sensitivities of important parameters. COMPASS can generate these predictions across several types of applications from traditional, sequential CPU applications to GPU-based, heterogeneous, parallel applications. Our empirical evaluation demonstrates a maximum overhead of 4%, flexibility to generate models for 9 applications, speed, ease of creation, and very low relative errors across a diverse set of architectures.

Categories and Subject Descriptors

D.4.8 [**Performance**]: Modeling and prediction

Keywords

automated performance modeling; performance prediction; Aspen modeling language

1. INTRODUCTION

As computer architectures grow more complex in scale, heterogeneous cores and memory, and dynamic behaviors (e.g., DVFS), it becomes increasingly critical to be able to predict performance of applications on these architectures. These predictions can inform design and optimization choices, or runtime decisions. Tools and models for predicting performance must be accurate, flexible, and efficiently evaluated. They must also be easy to create and maintain, and scale to the size of real applications. Once created, these models can answer very important questions including 1) What is the expected runtime of this code segment? 2) What is the best runtime for this code segment across several different architectures? 3) What are the best architectural configuration for a code segment? 4) How much memory does this code segment use during its execution? 5) Is it worth offloading this code segment to a hardware accelerator, given the data movement and coordination overheads?

However, performance prediction is notoriously difficult. First, previous work (cf. section 6) in model development offers a wide range of techniques. Most of them have relied mainly on historical, or profiling data, or models developed using statistical or machine learning (ML) techniques on empirical performance data. While these techniques can be accurate and efficient to evaluate, they lack the flexibility and insight of a parametrized performance model, which has independence from the host platform where it was created, and which may limit its value on different platforms. This situation becomes even more critical as architectures become more complex.

Second, depending on the usage scenario, performance predictions must be efficient to evaluate. Simulation can be far to expensive for many scenarios. For example, if the performance prediction is to be used to assist in runtime decisions for resource selection, the prediction must be evaluated quickly and efficiently not to impact the main application's performance; simulation is not an option.

Finally, the performance models must be easy to create, maintain, and evaluate. Many of the earlier techniques using regression, statistical, or ML techniques to create models fulfill this requirement, but they suffer the earlier problems of not being flexible enough to handle predictions for (future) architectures that are increasingly complex. Ideally, the model and prediction would be generated directly from the source code, so that it would be consistent.

1.1 Contributions

To address these challenges, we have designed and implemented a novel prototype system, named *COMPASS (**C**ode **O**riginated **M**odels of **P**erformance via **A**utomatic **S**ource **S**canning)*, for automated performance model generation and performance prediction. COMPASS is a framework that

ICS 2015, Newport Beach, California, USA
ACM 978-1-4503-3559-1/15/06 ...$15.00.
http://dx.doi.org/10.1145/2751205.2751220.

generates a structured, parametrized performance model by using *automated static analysis* of the target application. This performance model can then be used for a variety of purposes, including predicting performance of the target application on a range of (current and future) target architectures, without access to these systems. We evaluate this system, and show its benefits on several kernels and applications. Specifically, we

1. describe how COMPASS generates an explicit, structured, parametrized performance model directly from the application source code with its automated static analysis;
2. validate the models from COMPASS on 9 applications across several architectures; and,
3. demonstrate the generality of these performance models by showing how they can be used directly to gain insights into application behaviors on diverse architectures from traditional multicore CPUs to heterogeneous GPUs.

2. COMPASS SYSTEM OVERVIEW

COMPASS consists of two main components: 1) a *static-analysis framework*, implemented in Open Accelerator Research Compiler (OpenARC) [9], which analyzes an input program written in C and generates an application performance model in the Aspen performance modeling language and System [15], and 2) *Aspen performance prediction tools*, which digest the generated Aspen models, synthesize symbolic equations representing application characteristics, and derive various performance predictions using these equations.

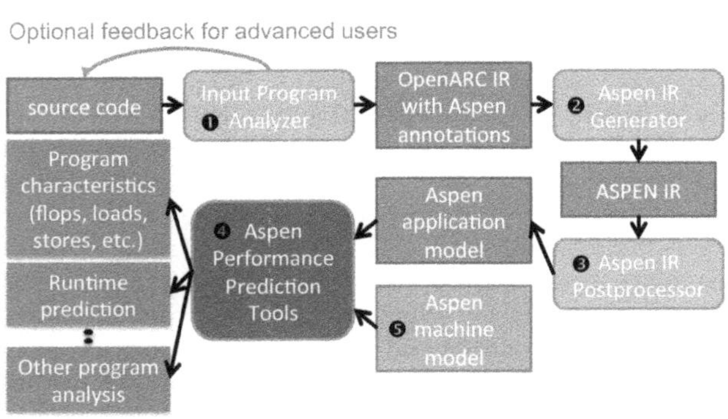

Figure 1: Workflow of the COMPASS Modeling Framework

Importantly, the analysis framework in COMPASS also understands OpenMP/OpenACC directives, which allows it to accurately represent the amount of available parallelism and data movement in a high-level intermediate representation (HLIR), which in turn makes the performance models applicable to a variety of architectures including both CPU and GPU systems.

Figure 1 illustrates the overall workflow of the COMPASS framework. 1) OpenARC (*Input Program Analyzer* in Figure 1) performs a static analysis of the entire program, digesting all source code, OpenMP, OpenACC, and COMPASS directives to generate a HLIR annotated with Aspen attributes. 2) OpenARC performs additional passes (*Aspen IR Generator* in Figure 1) on the HLIR to extract an Aspen IR. Multiple passes may be necessary to complete this step as OpenARC may need to query additional information from HLIR. 3) The Aspen IR postprocessor consumes the Aspen IR to check for errors, perform optimizations, and partition the Aspen kernels into manageable modules. 4) The Aspen performance prediction tools consume the Aspen application model, and then perform any requested queries, convolutions, simulations, or predictions. 5) The Aspen machine model specifies one or more architectural configurations that can be used for the predictions in #4. This machine model can be derived manually or extracted from the target system with benchmarks.

We now describe a motivating example, followed by a brief description of Aspen and OpenARC. We then show how these pieces integrate into the COMPASS system.

2.1 Motivating Example

Although we provide results for 9 applications later, we motivate our discussion of COMPASS with an example input source code for OpenACC Matrix Multiplication (Listing 1), and its respective Aspen performance model (Listing 2).

Listing 1: Input OpenACC Matrix Multiplication Code

```
1  int N = 1024;
2  void matmul(float *a, float *b, float *c){ int i, j, k ;
3  #pragma acc kernels loop gang copyout(a[0:(N*N)]) \
4  copyin(b[0:(N*N)],c[0:(N*N)])
5    for (i=0; i<N; i++){
6  #pragma acc loop worker
7      for (j=0; j<N; j++) { float sum = 0.0 ;
8        for (k=0; k<N; k++) {sum+=b[i*N+k]*c[k*N+j];}
9        a[i*N+j] = sum; }
10   } //end of i loop
11 } //end of matmul()
12 int main() {
13   int i; float *A = (float*) malloc(N*N*sizeof(float));
14   float *B = (float*) malloc(N*N*sizeof(float));
15   float *C = (float*) malloc(N*N*sizeof(float));
16   for (i = 0; i < N*N; i++)
17   { A[i] = 0.0F; B[i] = (float) i; C[i] = 1.0F; }
18 #pragma aspen modelregion label(MM)
19   matmul(A,B,C);
20   free(A); free(B); free(C); return 0;
21 } //end of main()
```

The first (in lines 3 and 6) are standard OpenACC directives — part of the original source code — and they are interpreted by COMPASS in order to understand the available parallelism for each loop and data properties.

The other type of directive (seen line 18) is an example of new *Aspen directives* supported by COMPASS, and in this case, the directive was used to focus the analysis framework on a specific program region. These new Aspen directives contain a rich set of modeling constructs, thus allowing for two-way communication between the static analysis framework and the user; COMPASS can annotate the user's source code to allow the user to see how the generated performance model maps to the input code (*OpenARC IR* annotated with Aspen directives in Fig. 1), and the user can use them to override decisions made in the static analysis. Again, these directives are an optional part of the process; if none are provided, COMPASS will simply generate a performance model for the entire input program. More information about these Aspen directives appears in subsection 3.3.

The automatically generated output Aspen model is shown in Listing 2 This application model can be viewed, analyzed, edited, shared, and reused as with any Aspen model. To make informed predictions about performance on a specific machine, the model evaluation framework must combine the application model with an Abstract Machine Model (AMM) that describes the features and parameters for the target architecture. This AMM can be manually created, or it can be generated from a set of automated benchmark tests.

Listing 2: Output Aspen Performance Model. Note that Aspen *param* variables are parameterizable; the Aspen modeling framework can change their values as necessary.

```
model MM {
  param floatS = 4; param N = 1024
  data A as Array((N*N), floatS)
  data B as Array((N*N), floatS)
  data C as Array((N*N), floatS)
  kernel matmul {
    execute matmul2_intracommIN
    { intracomm [floatS*(N*N)] to C as copyin
      intracomm [floatS*(N*N)] to B as copyin }
    map matmul2 [N] {
      map matmul3 [N] {
        iterate [N] {
          execute matmul5
          { loads [floatS] from B as stride(1)
            loads [floatS] from C; flops [2] as sp, simd }
        } //end of iterate
        execute matmul6 { stores [floatS] to A as stride(1) }
      } // end of map matmul3
    } //end of map matmul2
    execute matmul2_intracommOUT
    { intracomm [floatS*(N*N)] to A as copyout }
  } //end of kernel matmul
  kernel main { matmul() }
} //end of model MM
```

In the following sections, we describe details of the model generation process (section 3) and the model-based performance prediction (section 4).

2.2 Aspen Overview

Aspen (Abstract Scalable Performance Engineering Notation) [15] is a domain-specific language for structured analytical performance modeling, to allow scientists to construct, evaluate, verify, compose, and share models of their applications. Aspen specifies a formal language and methodology that allow modelers to quickly generate representations of their applications as well as abstract machine models. In addition, Aspen includes a suite of analysis tools that consume these models to produce a variety of estimates for computation, communication, data structure sizes, algorithm characteristics, and bounds on expected runtime. Aspen can generate all of these estimates without application source code or low-level architectural information. This ability to cope with high levels of uncertainty distinguishes Aspen from simulators, emulators, and other trace-driven approaches.

A short example of an Aspen kernel is shown in Listing 3. The execute block describes available parallelism (n), and counts and sizes of floating point and memory operations, while traits describe semantic information about operations (such as double precision) or the source and destination of memory traffic. Kernels in Aspen also contain control flow structures, such as iteration or the ability to call other kernels.

2.3 OpenARC

Open Accelerator Research Compiler (OpenARC) [9] is an open source compiler supporting full features of OpenACC specification 1.0 and a subset of 2.0 [12], which allows full research contexts on directive-based GPU computing. Built on top of the Cetus compiler infrastructure [5], OpenARC is equipped with various advanced compile-time analysis

Listing 3: Aspen Kernel Example for 1D FFT

```
kernel 1DFFT {
  execute [n] {
    flops [5 * log2(n)] as dp, complex, simd
    loads [a * max(1, log(n)/log(Z))] of size [wordSize] from fftVol
  }
}
```

and transformation techniques, which provide basic building blocks to easily create more advanced compiler passes. Combined with its very high-level intermediate representation (IR) augmented with a rich set of directives, OpenARC provides a powerful research framework for various source-to-source translation and instrumentation experiments. Within OpenARC, various traceability mechanisms can be implemented to keep the connection between input directive models and output codes/performance, because OpenARC has clear separation between analysis passes and transformation passes, and all compiler passes communicate with each other through annotations. The proposed COMPASS system is built using the OpenARC's annotation-based communication mechanism; by proposing a new set of Aspen directives (explained in subsection 3.3), and using them as both internal and external annotations, COMPASS provides users with an optional, abstract mechanism to guide the overall model generation.

3. AUTOMATED PERFORMANCE MODEL GENERATION

This section explains how the COMPASS system generates the Aspen performance model from the existing input program. This section also describes necessary extensions to the Aspen language and a set of directives proposed to optionally guide the model generation.

3.1 Aspen Language Extension

While control constructs in the base Aspen language [15] are sufficient to express various mathematical algorithms, difference in the synthetic structures of the Aspen language and the general programming languages such as C has necessitated extending the Aspen language with additional control structures, such as *IfBlocks*, *ProbabilityBlocks*, and *ExecuteBlocks*. To better match the Aspen models and the input programs, some Aspen control constructs are redefined (e.g., *Kernel*). Table 1 shows major Aspen control constructs used by COMPASS.

3.2 Automatic Aspen Model Generation

3.2.1 Input Program Analysis

The input program analysis by the static analysis framework (*Input Program Analyser* in Figure 1) starts from an entry function that contains a *model region*, a code region for which to generate Aspen model, which a user may specify either using Aspen directives proposed in subsection 3.3 or using environment variables. If no explicit *model region* was specified, the *main* function becomes the model region. The analysis pass analyzes only those statements and functions reachable from the model region. Other code regions are ignored, except for variable declarations visible to the model region (e.g., global variable declarations and local

Table 1: Aspen Control Constructs (Partial list)

Construct	Description
IterateBlock	a control flow where constructs in the block are repeated specified times with sequential dependence
MapBlock	similar to the IterateBlock except there is no sequential dependence
ExecuteBlock	Aspen's fundamental abstraction for a computation, containing information about operation counts, memory accesses, I/O, and communication
CompoundBlock	control flow where constructs in the block are evaluated sequentially
Kernel	a named CompoundBlock that can be called in multiple places, optionally with arguments
IfBlock	a control flow where constructs in the block are conditionally evaluated
ProbabilityBlock	a CompoundBlock with a probability of evaluation

variable declarations in the entry function). The pass visits each statement and its called functions in a depth-first manner; for each statement, the pass extracts information on the computation (*flops*), memory (*loads*, *stores*, *allocates*, *resizes*, *frees*), and communication (*intra-node communication*, *inter-node communication*).

An *expression analyzer* in the analysis framework calculates the computations/memory accesses/communications in a statement by traversing its expression tree in a bottom-up fashion using a post-order traversal: floating-point operations (*flops*) are calculated by counting each binary/unary operation with float-type operands in the expression tree. If a computation consists of scalar variables and array accesses whose rightmost index expression is affine with respect to the innermost enclosing loop, an *simd* attribute is added to indicate that the computation can be SIMDized. The analyzer also recognizes math functions in the standard C library as floating-point operations if they work on floating-point variables.

For memory access analysis, the analyzer counts each variable access in the expression tree either as load (*loads*) or store (*stores*) operations. The analyzer keeps memory access counters for each distinct variable at the granularity of memory allocation (each data allocated with *malloc()* function has its own counter.). For this, the framework clones user functions if they are called in multiple contexts, as a preprocessing step for this context-sensitive interprocedural analysis pass, and the analyzer keeps track of the original symbol that a pointer variable refers to. If the analyzer fails to resolve pointer aliasing, a new memory access counter is assigned to the pointer variable, which will result in an output Aspen model where multiple Aspen *data* variables refer to the same memory allocation in the input program. However, this will not change the overall memory access statistics since summing up the information of the aliased Aspen *data* variables remains unchanged. Memory access stride information is calculated by analysing the rightmost index expression of an array access; if the rightmost index expression is constant or affine with respect to the innermost enclosing loop, appropriate stride information will be added to the memory access. (See Listing 2 for examples where COMPASS detected strided accesses and SIMD FLOPS.)

Analyzing the memory and communication patterns is possible since the static analysis framework can understand the semantics of the standard C libraries, MPI libraries, and OpenACC/OpenMP directives; for example, if a statement contains a *malloc* function call (e.g., line 13 in Listing 1), the argument of the *malloc* call is used to decide the size of the allocated data. The intra-node communication information is directly extracted from OpenACC data clauses (e.g., *copyin* and *copyout* clauses in line 3 and 4 in Listing 1), and inter-node communications are captured by analyzing MPI communication library calls.

The analysis pass also extracts important control-flow properties such as loop iteration counts and dependency among iterations, and if-conditions. To find loop parallelism, the analyzer exploits existing OpenACC/OpenMP annotations (e.g., OpenACC worksharing clauses such as gang/worker/vector, OpenMP loop construct, etc.); if not existing, the analyzer performs the underlying data-dependence analysis, which performs data-dependence test using the Banerjee-Wolfe inequalities enhanced with symbolic range analysis [5].

Table 2: Mapping of Input Program Structures to Aspen Constructs (Partial list)

Input language constructs	Aspen constructs
Variable/function declaration	
scalar variable declaration	parameter declaration
pointer variable declaration	data declaration
global array declaration	data declaration
function definition	Kernel
Control-flow structure	
function call	Kernel call
if statement	IfBlock
for-loop	IterateBlock or MapBlock
other-type loop	IterateBlock
expression statement	ExecuteBlock
compound statement	CompoundBlock
Statements with explicit Aspen directives	
statement with *ignore* clause	No Aspen construct is generated.
statement with *execute* clause	ExecuteBlock
if statement with if clause	IfBlock whose condition is replaced with that in the if clause
non-if statement with if clause	IfBlock whose body contains Aspen constructs for the attached statement
if statement with probability clause	ProbabilityBlock whose body contains Aspen constructs for the body of the if statement
non-if statement with probability clause	ProbabilityBlock whose body contains Aspen constructs for the attached statement

3.2.2 Aspen Model Generation

To generate the actual Aspen model, the static analysis framework (*Aspen IR Generator* in Fig. 1) visits the analyzed input program again, but in a different traversing order; the framework generates Aspen kernel constructs for called functions before their caller functions in a *call graph* (a directed graph that represents calling relationships between functions in a program). This ordering allows the model generation pass to collapse empty Aspen kernels recursively. Within each function, the generation pass visits each statement in a depth-first order. Translation of each program structure into the Aspen constructs follows the mapping rules in Table 2; 1) scalar variable declarations visible to the model region are translated to Aspen parameter declarations, 2) global array variables and dynamically allocated data are translated to Aspen data declarations, and 3) most of the control-flow structures in the input program are preserved in the output Aspen model by mapping them to the corresponding Aspen constructs.

While creating the Aspen constructs, the pass also performs several correctness checks and optimizations:

1. It detects parameter declarations with missing initial values and data declarations without their dimension/-size information. If found, the pass searches the input program to find the missing information. (e.g., data dimension information may be extracted from OpenACC data clauses.)
2. It detects duplicate parameter and data declarations, which may occur if users put multiple Aspen directives for the same variable, and merge them if not conflicting with each other.
3. It merges consecutive ExecuteBlocks, if applicable.
4. It simplifies IfBlocks/ProbabilityBlocks if their conditions are statically known.
5. Empty Aspen constructs are removed recursively.

The above step stores the generated Aspen constructs as Aspen intermediate representations (Aspen IRs). The generated Aspen IRs require the following postprocessing (*Aspen IR Postprocessor in Fig. 1*) to conform with the current Aspen standard and for better readability:

1. *Remove unused Aspen parameters/data*: Aspen model generation based on the mapping rules in Table 2 may result in many Aspen parameters/data due to many global variables in the included header files, most of which are not used in the model. To remove the unnecessary parameters/data, the pass traverses the Aspen IRs and deletes parameters/data if not used in the Aspen IRs. This step is iterative since deleting a parameter/data may trigger another deletion.
2. *Rename Aspen parameters/data if duplicate names exist*: this is necessary since all parameters and data have global scope in the current Aspen standard while the input C program allows multiple variable scopes.
3. *Rename function-parameter-type variables to the names of the corresponding argument variables*: this is for handling pointer aliasing in the input C program. For example, in Listing 1, variable A in line 13 differs from the variable a in line 2, but these two variables refer to the same memory location (pointer aliasing). If the variable a in the *matmul* function is renamed with the name of the original variable, the generated Aspen constructs for these two variables (A in line 3 and A in line 17 and 21 in Listing 2) will refer to the same Aspen data declaration (line 3 in Listing 2). Multiple aliasing of a formal function parameter due to multiple calling contexts is handled by the user-function cloning mentioned in the previous section. If the pointer aliasing is irresolvable, which may occur if the corresponding function argument expression is too complex to analyze, this renaming will be skipped. (Failing to rename aliased variables does not affect any of performance predictions done in this work, but it may affect the accuracy of future, advanced analyses such as detecting data dependency across Aspen kernel boundaries.)
4. *Rename Aspen parameters/data if their names are reserved keywords in Aspen.*

3.3 Directive-Based, Advanced Aspen Model Generation

Although our static analysis framework as proposed in the previous section can *automatically* extract important program properties, in our experience with COMPASS, we found it necessary to allow users to provide input to the model generation in order to make the resulting models more readable, useful, and concise, and to provide advice where the compiler finds ambiguous situations (*Optional feedback in Fig. 1*). For example, the current Aspen modeling framework enforces that the iteration counts and condition expressions of control structures should consist of only *Aspen parameters* (scalar variables and constants). If those expressions in the input program contain non-scalar variables, the static framework will generate non-conforming Aspen models, necessitating the interaction between the user and the framework to correct the non-conforming models, either by ignoring the troublesome statements or by providing alternative expressions.

As a solution, we have proposed *Aspen directives*, a set of annotations for interactive performance modeling for existing applications. Table 3 shows the types and format of the Aspen directives, which use the syntax common in OpenMP/OpenACC. The *modelregion* directive specifies that the attached code structure is the target region to generate the Aspen model. *Enter modelregion* and *exit modelregion* directives are used together to specify unstructured model region. *Declare* directive describes program variables that will be translated into either *parameters* or *data* in the output Aspen model. *Control* directive is used to describe most of the program properties using the rich set of clauses in Table 5 and also guides the overall model analysis and generation for the attached code structure.

Table 3: Aspen Performance Modeling Directive Format

```
#pragma aspen modelregion [label(name)]
#pragma aspen enter modelregion [label(name)]
#pragma aspen exit modelregion [label(name)]
#pragma aspen declare [clause [,] clause]...]
#pragma aspen control [clause [,] clause]...]
```

Table 4: Aspen Declare Clauses

Clause	Description
param(list)	contains a list of Aspen parameters, where each parameter is in the form of identifier[:expression]
data (list)	contains a list of Aspen data, where each data is in the form of identifier:traits(trait-list)

Primarily, the Aspen directives are *internally* used by the static framework to annotate important properties of the target program (*OpenARC IR* annotated with Aspen directives in Fig. 1), and compiler passes in the framework communicate with each other through these annotations. Users don't have to see these internal annotations, and users need to manually insert some of these directives into the input program only to correct non-conforming behaviors, if existing. The user involvement to correct non-conforming behaviors can be still optional, since the static framework can automatically change the non-conforming expressions to Aspen parameter expressions with compiler-decided initial values. (Note that the Aspen performance modeling framework can change the values of Aspen parameters dynamically depending on modeling purposes; the initial values of Aspen parameters are just *default* values.) However, a rich set of the prescriptive Aspen directives (e.g., *control ignore* and *control execute* in Table 5) allow *advanced users* to control how the static framework analyses and generates a performance model for the input program, in an interactive manner.

For example, the matrix multiplication (MM) code in Listing 1 uses a simple algorithm that requires $O(N^3)$ load operations as shown in the generated Aspen model in Listing 2. If, for instance, the user wants to override the result produced by the static analysis for the *matmul* function in Listing 1 to use the Coppersmith-Winograd algorithm that requires only $O(N^{2.372})$ operations, then the user can create such a new model, without rewriting the *matmul* function, by overriding the COMPASS result with the Aspen *control execute* directive, as shown in Listing 4 (line 2 - 4), facilitating algorithmic exploration.

Table 5: Aspen Control Clauses

Clause	Description
ignore	skips Aspen model generation for the attached statement
execute	does not analyze the attached statement; instead generates Aspen model only with annotated Aspen directives
loop (expression)	contains iteration counts of the attached loop
parallelism (para-arg)	expresses the amount of independent work in the attached statement, in the form of expression[:traits(trait-list)]
if (expr-list)	contains a list of condition expressions
probability (expr-list)	contains a list of the probability expressions
flops (list)	contains a list of Aspen flop resources, in the form of expression[:traits(trait-list)]
loads (list)	contains a list of memory loads, in the form of expression[:from(ID)][:traits(trait-list)]
stores (list)	contains a list of memory stores, in the form of expression[:to(ID)][:traits(trait-list)]
messages (list)	contains a list of internode communications, in the form of expression [:traits(trait-list)]
intracomm (list)	contains a list of intranode transfers, in the form of expression[:traits(trait-list)]
allocates (list)	contains a list of allocated data, in the form of ID:capacity(expression)[:traits(trait-list)]
resizes (list)	contains a list of resized data, in the form of ID:capacity(expression)[:traits(trait-list)]
frees (list)	contains a list of freed data, in the form of ID:capacity(expression)[:traits(trait-list)]
label (name)	contains the label of the attached statement

Listing 4: Input MM Code annotated to use an alternative algorithm

```
1  ...
2  #pragma aspen control execute \
3     flops(N^2.372, traits(sp)) \
4     stores(N*N*floatS:to(A):traits(stride(1))) \
5     loads(N*N*floatS:from(B):traits(stride(1)), ...) \
6     ...
7  void matmul(float * A, float * B, float * C) {
8    ...//the original function body is here.
9  } //end of matmul()
10
11 int main()
12 {
13   ...
14 }
```

4. MODEL-BASED PERFORMANCE PREDICTION

4.1 Analyzing Generated Models with Aspen

Aspen consists of two major components: a library which digests application and machine models, and a set of tools to perform analysis operations on them. One of the basic tools included with Aspen is a resource counter. This tool generates counts of resource usage within each execution block, multiplies them by total nested iteration counts, and returns a total count for the entire program execution for any given resource used in the application model (like FLOPS, loads, and stores). As an analytical tool, Aspen can report these values either numerically or symbolically. Aspen also contains a runtime predictor, which convolves the application model with a machine model. This predictor generates runtimes for each resource usage statement as described by the application model. (For instance, an application model may report that the runtime for n FLOPS is $n/clockspeed$, and that runtime for n double precision FLOPS is $2 * n/clockspeed$.) If the application model contains parallelism, the predictor splits resources and memory bandwidth among the cores, and with given conflicts for each resource in the machine model (e.g., if loads and stores cannot be performed simultaneously), the predictor can determine which resource constrains the runtime of each execution block — e.g., if the block is compute or memory bound. Then, like the resource counter, iteration counts and control flow determine how the runtime of each execution block is combined into a runtime for the entire program.

4.2 COMPASS Extensions to Aspen

For this project, we made several extensions to Aspen. First, we found that the runtime predictor was making some assumptions in the context of hand-coded models, and we made it more flexible to better handle the style of models generated by our system (namely, by allowing some automated grouping of like resources). Second, as COMPASS provides application models which have a direct map to application source code, we extended Aspen with new tools to analyze these generated models as if you were executing the program. Some simple new tools include a basic call stack trace and total memory usage. A more complex tool we generated is a synthetic *gprof* output generator, which uses the call stack tracer to group inclusive and exclusive runtimes for each function, reporting these in both flat and nested call-graph formats. Another new tool is a hardware sensitivity analyzer which will modulate a set of hardware parameters to determine how sensitive an application is to each one. These tools are demonstrated in our evaluation below.

5. EVALUATION

The value of a performance model that is separate both from the compiler and from the application it describes is that it can be applied across parameter ranges and architectures. In this evaluation, we demonstrate that our system can provide useful information both across ranges of application parameters, and across different target architectures. The proposed system was used to automatically generate performance models for various types of applications, ranging from benchmarks (Kernel Benchmarks (JA-

COBI, MATMUL, LAPLACE2D) and Rodinia Benchmarks (BFS, HOTSPOT, KMEANS, LUD, SRAD)) to real HPC applications, with minimal user effort, as shown in Table 8. We validate our approach and evaluate results against all test cases, and due to space constraints present some additional, more detailed evaluation against only the most complex case, the HPC application LULESH (Livermore Unstructured Lagrangian Explicit Shock Hydrodynamics [7]), one of five challenge problems in the DARPA UHPC program and widely studied as an important DOE proxy application.

5.1 Analytical Evaluation

As an analytical modeling framework, Aspen can synthesize various mathematical expressions representing application characteristics. Therefore, the application models generated automatically by COMPASS can be used to explore and analyze application characteristics independent of any given machine architecture. To demonstrate this capability, we can apply tools in the Aspen modeling suite to the automatically generated Aspen output for the tested applications, generating counts of resource usage across various scaling parameters.

An important capability to emphasize is that we can generate *symbolic* equations thanks to this modeling process. For example, MATMUL calculates $A = B \times C$, for matrix A of size $M{\times}N$, matrix B of size $M{\times}P$, and matrix C of size $P{\times}N$. COMPASS reports for this benchmark that the number of floating point operations is $2 * M * N * P$, the number of single precition bytes loaded is $8 * M * N$. and the number of bytes stored is $4 * M * N$. For square matrices of size $N{\times}N$, this simplifies to $2N^3$ FLOPS, $8N^3$ bytes of loads, and $4N^2$ bytes of stores. This is known to those familiar with matrix multiply, but having the symbolic equation is validation that a benchmark is coded properly. Further, most use cases are more complex; for example, LUD loads $N(N - N/2)(4 + 8N/2) + (N - N/2 - 1)(8 + 8N/2)$ bytes.

Results for a full application, like LULESH, are too complex to include here, but the ability to generate them symbolically is useful. They can be *instantly* evaluated and analyzed, even for problem sizes which would not fit on current systems and for which simulation would be infeasible, suitable for assisting various runtime decisions. For example, results for the LULESH application are shown in Table 6. As a hydrodynamics application, we see most parameters scaling with the number of total elements, which itself is proportional to the cube of the number of elements along the edge of the domain (the "Size" parameter in the table). As such, for LULESH, the balance between usage of each resource remains consistent, even up to the petaFLOPS scale.

This information is useful in analyzing constraints on future systems; for example, we know that a system with less than a terabyte of RAM will be unable to contain all the arrays required to solve the 1000^3-element computational domain in LULESH. The use of a standard, composable output model language and format also facilitates exploration; for example, a kernel in the model can be replaced or modified and the application re-analyzed without changing the source code.

5.2 COMPASS Model Validation

As the performance models generated by COMPASS are done on first principles (i.e., static compiler analysis), we must show that the models it generates are valid and match the source code. For the test cases that have known analytical models, like MATMUL ($O(n^3)$ FLOPS, $O(n^3)$ Loads, $O(n^2)$ Stores, etc.), it is easy to validate the generated performance models against the source code, as shown in the previous section. However, only a few test cases have such known resource values; so to generate "ground truth" values against which to measure our predictions, we used PAPI to add measurement of various hardware counters during the run of compiled code. While this method is not foolproof, we compiled code without vectorization, but both with and without optimization, and compared against both versions. This was performed using gcc 4.6.3 on an Intel Xeon E5-2643 system, using the values for PAPI events PAPI_FP_OPS (floating point operations), PAPI_LD_INS and PAPI_SR_INS (load and store instructions, which were then multiplied by floating point width to return the number of bytes).

Table 6: LULESH Resource Usage Example

Size	FLOPS	Loads	Stores	Memory
10	$2.0{\times}10^9$	$7.8{\times}10^9$	$2.5{\times}10^9$	$1.2{\times}10^6$
100	$7.7{\times}10^{12}$	$3.1{\times}10^{13}$	$9.7{\times}10^{12}$	$1.1{\times}10^9$
1000	$6.5{\times}10^{16}$	$2.6{\times}10^{17}$	$8.2{\times}10^{16}$	$1.1{\times}10^{12}$

Table 7: Relative error in model validation across benchmarks of COMPASS prediction versus PAPI measurements of running code. Zero error means that the COMPASS prediction fell between measurements from optimized and unoptimized runs of the code.

Benchmark	FLOPS	Loads	Stores
JACOBI	6%	0%	0%
MATMUL	15%	0%	1%
LAPLACE2D	6%	0%	0%
BFS	0%	11%	0%
HOTSPOT	0%	0%	0%
KMEANS	0%	0%	8%
LUD	7%	0%	2%
SRAD	17%	0%	0%
LULESH	0%	0%	0%

Table 7 shows the results of this validation. Note that most results have an error of zero; this means that the COMPASS prediction fell between measurements from optimized and unoptimized runs of the code, though we note that almost every result tracked most closely against the optimized version. *In no case was the prediction more than 20% from the measured values.*

For strong predictive power, the COMPASS predictions must not only match at a single problem size but must scale identically in response to problem size as the true values. To validate scaling, we ran each test at two different problem sizes and computed the rate at which flops, loads, and stores scaled for both predicted and measured values. This error was vanishingly small, and in most cases, scaling error was within the margin of measurement error. (PAPI results vary slightly from run to run.) For example, loaded bytes in MATMUL in our COMPASS prediction grows by a factor of 8× when problem size doubles, and the measurement for loaded bytes also increased by factor of 8× (±1%).

We examine this phenomenon more closely in our most complex example, LULESH, where we evaluate the FLOPS, load and stored bytes across a range of problem sizes. See Figures 2a, 2b, and 2c for these results. Note that the COM-

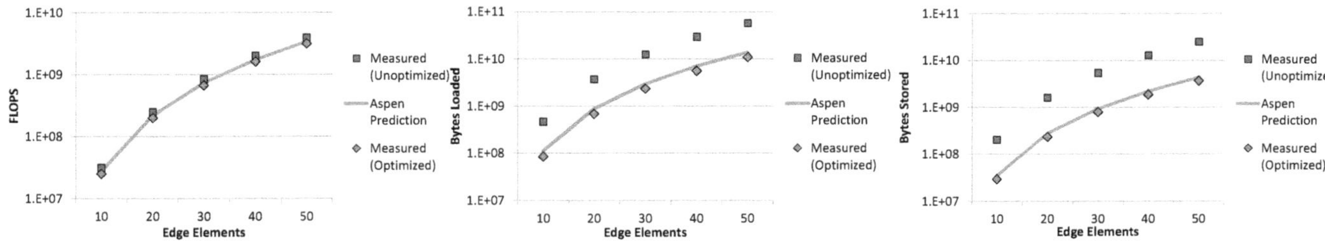

(a) Floating Point Operations (b) Loads in Bytes (c) Stores in Bytes

Figure 2: Predicted Resource Usage of LULESH versus Measured (with and without compiler optimization)

PASS prediction most closely tracks the optimized values, and scales identically with with the hardware measurements.

5.3 COMPASS Annotation Overhead

As described, the generation of performance models from application source code has been largely automated by our analysis framework. To evaluate the user effort involved in practice, we show the number of COMPASS annotations inserted by the user into our test programs for the system to automatically generate output models conforming to the current Aspen standard. Table 8 shows the quantitative results; the average annotation overhead was less than 2%.

We note that many of the annotations we added were trivial. In fact, over half of the annotations merely specify a region of interest or declare parameters to directly expose within the final Aspen model.

Table 8: Aspen Annotations Inserted by Users, where *LOC* means *lines of original code*, *LOA* means *lines of Aspen annotations added by users*, and *Overhead (%) = LOA*100/LOC*.

Benchmark	LOC	LOA	Overhead (%)
JACOBI	241	2	0.8
MATMUL	128	1	0.7
LAPLACE2D	210	7	3.3
BFS	435	16	3.6
HOTSPOT	525	11	2.0
KMEANS	1822	11	0.6
LUD	421	6	1.4
SRAD	550	12	2.1
LULESH	3743	125	3.3

5.4 Advanced Performance Prediction with COMPASS

5.4.1 Exploring Architecture Parameters

Beyond simply using the COMPASS-generated models to generate resource parameters, COMPASS contains a tool which convolves our generated application models with abstract machine models to generate runtime predictions. For this, we created an abstract machine model for a computational node of the Keeneland [18] system, which contains two 6-core Intel Xeon x5660 CPUs, 24GB of DDR3-1066 memory, and Fermi m2090 GPUs connected via PCIe.

This type of analysis can be used to analyze programs without executing them. For example, we created a new Aspen kernel-level profiling tool for COMPASS which generates *gprof*-like output. We ran this tool on LULESH and compared its output to a run of the same problem size on an Intel Xeon CPU. Figure 3 shows that the five most expensive functions as predicted by COMPASS are an exact match for the five most expensive functions as measured by *gprof*. In addition, this tool reports a call graph based on the model alone, with inclusive and exclusive function runtimes.

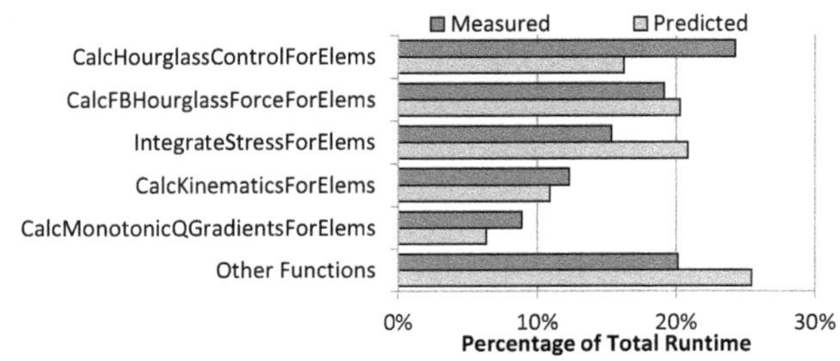

Figure 3: Top 5 functions in LULESH and their percentage of total runtime, as measured by *gprof* and as predicted by COMPASS.

Figure 4 shows predicted performance results of LULESH, both for a CPU-only mode, which uses OpenMP, and in a single-GPU offload mode of operations, across a range of problem sizes, and we plotted these results against actual measurements obtained using OpenARC-generated executables on a Keeneland computational node. The results in the figure show that the predicted runtime of LULESH closely matches its empirically measured runtime. Although we do not (and should not) expect perfect runtime predictions from an analytical system, these results (Figure 4) show good agreement between the measured and predicted runtimes for the target architecture, with similar slopes and absolute run time values. Furthermore, the successful mapping of the runtime onto the GPU shows that COMPASS has accurately assessed the available parallelism within each kernel by properly analyzing the fine-grained parallelism offered by the OpenACC directives.

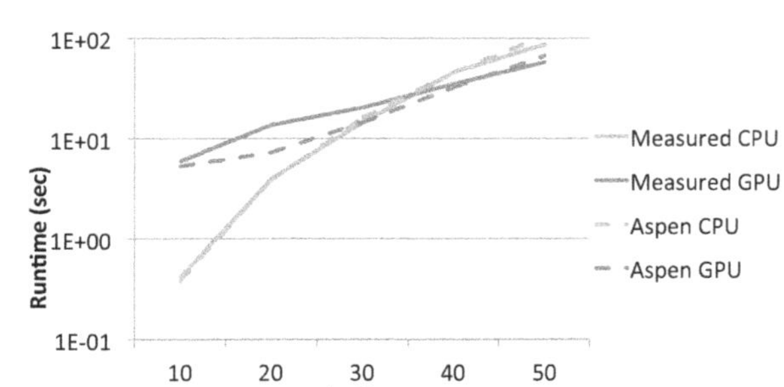

Figure 4: Measured and predicted runtime of the entire LULESH program on CPU and GPU.

5.4.2 *Design Space Exploration*

To explore how our automatically generated application models can inform exploration of current and future architectures, we used COMPASS to explore how the performance of each application kernel varied based on hypothetical changes in future machine parameters when running the code on an NVIDIA Fermi m2090 GPU connected via PCIe.

For example, if we increase the GPU clock by 10% and COMPASS predicts a performance increase of 1.02×, we report the benchmark had a 20% sensitivity to GPU clock-speed. Figure 5 shows the results of this exploration relative to the stock performance of several hardware aspects. We see, for example, that of the benchmarks, KMEANS is most dependent on PCIe bus bandwidth, while MATMUL and LUD show the highest sensitivity to GPU device memory bandwidth.

This type of analytical modeling enabled by COMPASS is particularly useful at an early time horizon in the codesign process where the space of possible application parameters, algorithms, and architectures is too large to search with computationally intensive methods (e.g. cycle-accurate simulation).

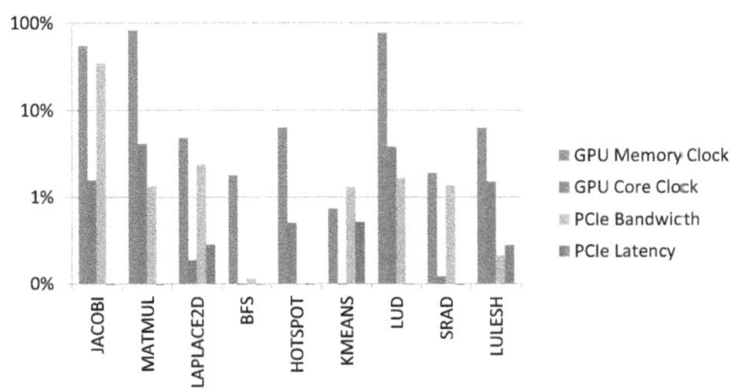

Figure 5: Predicted Sensitivity of Benchmarks to various architectural parameters according to COMPASS.

6. RELATED WORK

Our new technique combines the work of several different research areas to achieve its goal. In particular, we use concepts from performance modeling and from static and runtime analysis. We present related work on each topic separately.

Performance modeling. Performance modeling can be approached in many ways, such as analytical modeling, simulation, and empirical evaluation. In analytical modeling, predictions can be obtained without directly using the application source code. Often created by hand in mathematical equations or spreadsheets, analytical models like BSP [17] and LogP [1, 4] are often evaluated very quickly, but can be hard to extend, modify, and share. Simulation and empirical evaluation both require source code. Simulators such as GEMS [11] and SST [14, 6] vary in accuracy from higher-level functional to cycle-accurate, but generally evaluate each block of code as if it were being executed by the target machine. Though generally more accurate than analytical models, they also execute more slowly. Empirical evaluation, of course, requires source code and hardware similar to (or scaled back from) the target architecture, and can be very accurate, if harder to analyze. Aspen [15] shares traits with analytical approaches. Its ability to more fully capture control flow and flexibility with respect to machine parameters makes it uniquely suited to integration with our systematic, directive approach. We described Aspen in more detail in subsection 2.2.

Analysis-based modeling. Program analysis is a technique that automatically analyzes the behavior of input programs and extract useful program properties to be used for specific goals varying from detecting program errors to optimizing performance. The analysis can be done either at compile time (static analysis, through compiler frameworks like ROSE [13] and Cetus [5]) or at runtime (dynamical analysis, through tools like Intel PIN [10]). A few recent examples use program analysis to drive model generation in a similar vein to our proposed work, but with key differences.

Palm [16] shows a method of using annotations within source code to describe a performance model. In contrast to our proposed method, where the compiler automatically analyzes the source code and user annotations are *optionally* used to control the modeling framework, their technique does not automatically generate performance models from source code. Rather, Palm requires a human to describe the model and its important parameters through annotations; it also fills modeling parameters by sampling or capturing runtime from binaries executing on a specific architecture. While this platform-dependent modeling enables accurate runtime predictions, it provides little ability to explore important application parameters in the absence of a target architecture, or to generate predictions for new architectures. Runtime predictions generated by our system are calculated based on statically analyzed resource usage alone (separately convolved with an abstract machine model), and without foreknowledge of actual runtimes on target architectures.

ExaSAT [3] automatically generates a performance model directly from the source code, and uses it to predict the performance of the target code on various potential hardware platforms. However, ExaSAT is limited to *stencil-specific* analysis that targets specific chip memory hierarchies to ascertain and optimize specific program behaviors, namely memory accesses. In other words, it works only on specific types of loops in the target source code. COMPASS, in contrast, offers to predict the performance of arbitrary code sections in the target program, and optional user annotations allow the ability for programmers to control the scope and granularity of performance modeling.

PEMOGEN [2] is a tool that automatically instruments applications to generate performance models during program execution. If a domain expert provides *critical parameters*, input parameters that influence the runtime of the target application, the PEMOGEN tool automatically instruments the target application to profile the critical parameters and incrementally refines the coefficients of a regression model to reduce prediction errors. However, the proposed online statistical prediction method can work only one target metric at a time (e.g., the absolute execution time), and building a performance model for a specific target metric requires a series of training runs to achieve reasonable accuracy, while our system can generate static performance models without any runtime profiling, and the same model can be used for various analyses/predictions on multiple architectures. Our system can also employ minimal user involvement to guide the overall model generation, but this does not require domain-expert knowledge.

Other approaches [19, 8] to performance modeling have used empirical methods to characterize performance and generate models automatically using statistical inference with regression or machine learning techniques. These techniques can be very effective and automated when considering architectures similar to the original architectures where the model was developed. However, they can lack accuracy on significantly different architectures, and the resulting models and predictions can be difficult to understand or explain. In contrast, Aspen models provides complete transparency in the prediction and modeling process.

7. CONCLUSION

This paper shows the design, implementation, and evaluation of a new technique and prototype system for automated performance model generation and performance prediction. The proposed workflow consists of 1) a static analysis framework to generate parametrized Aspen performance model from the application source code and 2) analysis suite that predicts the performance characteristics of the application using the Aspen model. We have built a prototype system on top of a research compiler framework, called OpenARC; our evaluation using kernels and a DOE proxy application demonstrates that the prototype system can successfully generate structured performance models that can be used for various purposes, from answering basic questions such as predicting resource usages for current and future architectures to complex performance questions such as predicting runtimes under different application and system configurations. The tight yet orthogonal integration of the performance model with the programing system in our framework will facilitate new research opportunities to dive into more advanced and intricate performance questions, such as finding optimal decision points for a performance target with multiple constraints (e.g., whether it is faster to offload a function and pay data transfer costs or to execute the function on the host CPU). Future work includes enabling intelligent runtime systems to make accurate online decisions on these advanced performance questions, which may be possible since the proposed framework can generate lightweight, analytical performance models.

Acknowledgment

This manuscript has been authored by UT-Battelle, LLC under Contract No. DE-AC05-00OR22725 with the U.S. Department of Energy. The United States Government retains and the publisher, by accepting the article for publication, acknowledges that the United States Government retains a non-exclusive, paid-up, irrevocable, world-wide license to publish or reproduce the published form of this manuscript, or allow others to do so, for United States Government purposes. The Department of Energy will provide public access to these results of federally sponsored research in accordance with the DOE Public Access Plan (http://energy.gov/downloads/doe-public-access-plan). This material is based upon work supported by the U.S. Department of Energy, Office of Science, Office of Advanced Scientific Computing Research.

8. REFERENCES

[1] A. Alexandrov, M. F. Ionescu, K. E. Schauser, and C. Scheiman, "LogGP: Incorporating long messages into the LogP model," in *Proceedings of the Seventh Annual ACM Symposium on Parallel Algorithms and Architectures*, ser. SPAA '95, 1995, pp. 95–105.

[2] A. Bhattacharyya and T. Hoefler, "Pemogen: Automatic adaptive performance modeling during program runtime," in *Proceedings of the 23rd International Conference on Parallel Architectures and Compilation*, ser. PACT '14. New York, NY, USA: ACM, 2014, pp. 393–404.

[3] C. Chan, D. Unat *et al.*, "Software design space exploration for exascale combustion co-design," in *Supercomputing*. Springer, 2013, pp. 196–212.

[4] D. Culler, R. Karp *et al.*, "LogP: Towards a realistic model of parallel computation," in *Proceedings of the Fourth ACM SIGPLAN Symposium on Principles and Practice of Parallel Programming*, ser. PPOPP '93, 1993, pp. 1–12.

[5] C. Dave, H. Bae *et al.*, "Cetus: A source-to-source compiler infrastructure for multicores," *IEEE Computer*, vol. 42, no. 12, pp. 36–42, 2009.

[6] C. L. Janssen, H. Adalsteinsson, and J. P. Kenny, "Using simulation to design extremescale applications and architectures: Programming model exploration," *SIGMETRICS Performance Evaluation Review*, vol. 38, no. 4, pp. 4–8, 2011.

[7] I. Karlin, A. Bhatele *et al.*, "LULESH programming model and performance ports overview," Lawrence Livermore National Laboratory (LLNL), Livermore, CA, Tech. Rep. LLNL-TR-608824, 2012.

[8] B. C. Lee and D. M. Brooks, "Accurate and efficient regression modeling for microarchitectural performance and power prediction," in *Proceedings of the 12th international conference on Architectural support for programming languages and operating systems*. San Jose, California, USA: ACM, 2006, pp. 185–194.

[9] S. Lee and J. Vetter, "OpenARC: Open Accelerator Research Compiler for Directive-Based, Efficient Heterogeneous Computing," in *HPDC '14: Proceedings of the ACM Symposium on High-Performance Parallel and Distributed Computing, Short Paper*, June 2014.

[10] C.-K. Luk, R. Cohn *et al.*, "Pin: building customized program analysis tools with dynamic instrumentation," in *Proceedings of the 2005 ACM SIGPLAN conference on Programming language design and implementation*, ser. PLDI '05. New York, NY, USA: ACM, 2005, pp. 190–200.

[11] M. M. K. Martin, D. J. Sorin *et al.*, "Multifacet's general execution-driven multiprocessor simulator (gems) toolset," *SIGARCH Comput. Archit. News*, vol. 33, no. 4, pp. 92–99, Nov. 2005.

[12] OpenACC, "OpenACC: Directives for Accelerators," [Online]. Available: http://www.openacc-standard.org, 2011, (Accessed Jan. 16, 2015).

[13] D. J. Quinlan, "Rose: Compiler support for object-oriented frameworks." *Parallel Processing Letters*, vol. 10, no. 2/3, pp. 215–226, 2000.

[14] A. F. Rodrigues, K. S. Hemmert *et al.*, "The structural simulation toolkit," *SIGMETRICS Performance Evaluation Review*, vol. 38, no. 4, pp. 37–42, 2011.

[15] K. Spafford and J. S. Vetter, "Aspen: A domain specific language for performance modeling," in *SC12: ACM/IEEE International Conference for High Performance Computing, Networking, Storage, and Analysis*, 2012.

[16] N. R. Tallent and A. Hoisie, "Palm: Easing the burden of analytical performance modeling," in *to appear*, 2014.

[17] L. G. Valiant, "A bridging model for parallel computation," *Communications of the ACM*, vol. 33, no. 8, pp. 103–111, 1990.

[18] J. S. Vetter, R. Glassbrook *et al.*, "Keeneland: Bringing heterogeneous GPU computing to the computational science community," *IEEE Computing in Science and Engineering*, vol. 13, no. 5, pp. 90–95, 2011.

[19] W. Wu and B. C. Lee, "Inferred models for dynamic and sparse hardware-software spaces," in *Microarchitecture (MICRO), 2012 45th Annual IEEE/ACM International Symposium on*. IEEE, 2012, pp. 413–424.

Composing Algorithmic Skeletons to Express High-Performance Scientific Applications

Mani Zandifar
Texas A&M University
College Station, Texas 77843
mazaninfardi@cse.tamu.edu

Mustafa Abdul Jabbar
King Abdullah University of Science and Technology
Thuwal, Saudi Arabia
mustafa.abduljabbar@kaust.edu.sa

Alireza Majidi
Texas A&M University
College Station, Texas 77843
majidi@cse.tamu.edu

David Keyes
King Abdullah University of Science and Technology
Thuwal, Saudi Arabia
david.keyes@kaust.edu.sa

Nancy M. Amato
Texas A&M University
College Station, Texas 77843
amato@cse.tamu.edu

Lawrence Rauchwerger
Texas A&M University
College Station, Texas 77843
rwerger@cse.tamu.edu

ABSTRACT

Algorithmic skeletons are high-level representations for parallel programs that hide the underlying parallelism details from program specification. These skeletons are defined in terms of higher-order functions that can be composed to build larger programs. Many skeleton frameworks support efficient implementations for stand-alone skeletons such as `map`, `reduce`, and `zip` for both shared-memory systems and small clusters. However, in these frameworks, expressing complex skeletons that are constructed through composition of fundamental skeletons either requires complete reimplementation or suffers from limited scalability due to required global synchronization. In the STAPL Skeleton Framework, we represent skeletons as parametric data flow graphs and describe composition of skeletons by point-to-point dependencies of their data flow graph representations. As a result, we eliminate the need for reimplementation and global synchronizations in composed skeletons. In this work, we describe the process of translating skeleton-based programs to data flow graphs and define rules for skeleton composition. To show the expressivity and ease of use of our framework, we show skeleton-based representations of the NAS EP, IS, and FT benchmarks. To show reusability and applicability of our framework on real-world applications we show an N-Body application using the FMM (Fast Multipole Method) hierarchical algorithm. Our results show that expressivity can be achieved without loss of performance even in complex real-world applications.

ICS'15, June 8–11, 2015, Newport Beach, CA, USA.

DOI: http://dx.doi.org/10.1145/2751205.2751241.

Categories and Subject Descriptors

D.3.3 [**Programming Languages**]: Language Constructs and Features—*Frameworks*; D.2.13 [**Software Engineering**]: Reusable Software—*Reusable Libraries*

Keywords

algorithmic skeletons, patterns, high-performance computing, distributed systems, data flow programming

1. INTRODUCTION

The increase in availability of high-performance computing systems has made the need for expressive and efficient methods of parallel program specification more evident. Many parallel libraries and frameworks currently provide easier methods for expressing parallel applications [6, 3, 4, 25, 15, 22]. However, most of these studies are tied to specific programming models, and programs expressed using such methods are not reusable in other libraries and frameworks.

Algorithmic skeletons [9], on the other hand, tackle this issue by separating program specification from parallel implementation. These higher-level representations, which are usually defined using polymorphic higher-order functions, represent common interaction patterns prevalent in parallel programs [24]. `map`, `zip`, and `reduce` are examples of these patterns. The functional representation of skeletons provides opportunities for formal analysis and transformations to be applied on parallel programs, regardless of their parallel implementations [24]. Providing efficient parallel implementations for these fundamental skeletons in a skeleton framework can simplify parallel programming. Algorithm developers focus on the computation of an application and leave the parallelism details to be handled by the skeleton framework developers. Moreover, the functional representation of skeletons allows large and complex applications to be composed from these building blocks.

Several skeleton frameworks provide efficient implementations of fundamental skeletons for both shared-memory systems and small clusters [12]. However, in these frameworks, skeleton composition is either not considered at all, requiring reimplementation of composed skeletons, or is a BSP (Bulk Synchronous Parallel) execution of each skeleton in a composition followed by a global synchronization

Operators	elem, repeat, compose
Skeletons	allgather, allreduce, alltoall, allgather, bitreversal, broadcast, butterfly, copy, fft, gather, inner-product, map, reduce, pointer-jumping, reverse-butterfly, tree<k>, zip<k>, zip-reduce<k> reverse-tree<k>, scan, scatter, transpose-2d, transpose-3d, wavefront-2d, wavefront-3d,

Table 1: Provides skeletons and compositional operators.

at each step [18, 20]. Even if these synchronizations do not play a large role in the performance of applications on lower core counts, they can degrade performance at a larger scale.

The STAPL Skeleton Framework resolves these outstanding issues. In this framework, we use parametric data flow graphs as our internal representation of skeletons. This representation allows programs to run efficiently on parallel systems, regardless of their size. We provide efficient implementations for various fundamental skeletons, as listed in Table 1, from which larger programs can be composed. We translate composition of skeletons by point-to-point dependencies between their corresponding data flow graphs. Using point-to-point dependencies, instead of global synchronizations, allows programs written in terms of skeletons to scale better. To show expressivity we present skeleton-based implementation of the NAS EP, IS, and FT benchmarks. An N-Body application using the FMM hierarchical algorithm shows the reusability of skeletons in a real-world application. Our framework can be easily extended either through composition of skeletons or by adding data flow graph representations for new skeletons. Furthermore, our framework can be ported to other libraries with data flow engines.

Our contributions in this paper are as follows:

- a novel representation for skeleton composition as point-to-point dependencies of data flow graphs that avoids global synchronization
- a scalable and extensible skeleton framework that is closed under composition, and respects the formal definition of skeleton composition
- experimental results that show expressivity can be achieved without loss of performance

2. RELATED WORK

Since the the first appearance of skeleton-based programming in [9], several skeleton libraries have been introduced. Some of these libraries support skeleton composition either at the specification level or at the implementation level. Examples are SkeTo [18], Müesli [16], JaSkel [10], SKiPPER [26], and Eden [17].

SkeTo [18] is a C++ skeleton framework implemented on top of MPI that provides parallel skeletons for parallel data structures. SkeTo allows successive invocation of elementary skeletons, but requires global synchronization between skeleton invocations due to the Bulk Synchronization Parallel model it implements. Our framework defines composition in terms of point-to-point dependencies, avoiding global synchronization costs.

Muesli [16] is a C++ skeleton library that is built for both shared and distributed memory, implemented on top of OpenMP and MPI. It provides a variety of task parallel and data parallel skeletons, but the composition of skeletons is restricted. The creation of a new composition requires reimplementation, as it cannot be defined directly from existing skeletons.

JaSkel [10] is a Java skeleton framework that provides `farm`, `pipe` and `heartbeat` skeletons. JaSkel provides separate implementations of each skeleton for shared and distributed memory systems, making it difficult to extend. Moreover, composition of skeletons in this framework requires reimplementation, limiting its generality.

SKiPPER [26] is a skeleton library developed in Caml. SKiPPER allows composition of its limited set of skeletons, e.g., `map`, `reduce`, etc. Theses skeletons are tailored towards vision applications and can work only for shared-memory systems. The compositions in this framework are tailored for specific purposes and cannot be generalized and extended.

Eden [17] is another skeleton framework which is intended to be an extension of Haskell. Similar to other functional languages, Eden allows non-strict functions, demand driven evaluation and monads. Eden provides methods for composing and nesting existing skeletons, and allows new skeletons to be added. The main drawback of Eden is that it cannot compete with high performance computing skeleton frameworks that are developed in languages like C and C++. In our framework we present the same expressivity level as Eden, while preserving performance.

3. THE STAPL SKELETON FRAMEWORK

We have developed the STAPL Skeleton Framework, a C++ skeleton framework, which provides a wide variety of skeletons (Table 1) and allows new skeletons to be composed from these skeletons. In addition, new fundamental skeletons can be quickly created if needed. We provide multiple implementations for many skeletons, such as the `alltoall` and `allreduce` skeletons, allowing tunability of programs.

In our framework, skeletons are represented as parametric data flow graphs that are expanded when input data is provided. Since data flow graphs express available parallelism explicitly, our skeleton implementations can, by definition, run in parallel. This abstraction allows us to hide parallelism details from the specification level of skeletons. In our previous work [29], we showed how these fine-grain representations of skeletons are transformed to coarser-grain data flow graphs to run efficiently on distributes systems. In this work, we focus on skeleton composition and its translation to point-to-point dependencies. We show examples of applications that are composed from many skeletons without requiring global synchronization or reimplementation of the composed skeletons.

To facilitate the composition of data flow graphs, we encapsulate the internal representation of skeletons by defining input and output ports. Ports only expose the external interface of skeletons, as seen in skeletons formal definition, hiding internal complexity. For example, the 1D ports of a `scan` skeleton allows `scan` to be implemented in many ways (Fig. 1(a) and 1(b)), while keeping its external interface unique.

In our framework, skeleton compositions are defined statically, allowing the strong typing system of C++ to ensure the correctness of skeleton compositions. The type inference rules of these operators are given in Table 2.

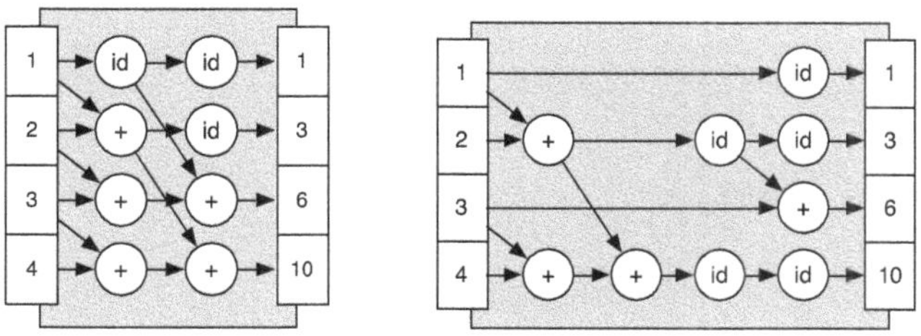

(a) scan using a simultaneous binomial tree. (b) scan using a binomial tree.

Figure 1: Ports of the scan skeleton (prefix sum) hide its internal implementation and expose only its 1D input and output interface. $scan(+)[1,2,3,4] = [1,3,6,10]$.

$$\frac{S : P \rightarrow Q \quad p : P}{S(p) : Q}\ \text{SKELETON} \qquad \frac{S : P \rightarrow Q}{elem_{span}(S) : \{P\} \rightarrow \{Q\}}\ \text{ELEM}$$

$$\frac{size : integer \quad S : P \rightarrow P}{repeat_{size}(S) : P \rightarrow P}\ \text{REPEAT}$$

$$\frac{S_1 : P \rightarrow R \quad S_2 : R \rightarrow Q}{compose(S_1, S_2) : P \rightarrow Q}\ \text{COMPOSE}$$

Table 2: The inference rules for the composition operators.

4. SKELETON COMPOSITION

Since skeletons are defined in terms of higher-order functions, they are by definition composable. Many applications can be expressed as a composition of fundamental skeletons. For example, `map-reduce`, a frequently used skeleton, can easily be expressed as a composition of the `map` and the `reduce` skeletons. Although defining skeletons composition is relatively simple at the specification level, translating them to efficient parallel implementations is not as straightforward. This issue has limited the usability of many skeleton frameworks [12] to very small applications.

In the STAPL Skeleton Framework we use data flow graphs as our internal representation of skeletons. This representation allows composition to be defined in terms of point-to-point dependencies between the data flow graph representation of skeletons. Therefore, we eliminate the need for global synchronizations in algorithms that are defined as compositions of other skeletons, and allow communication and computation to be overlapped.

In this section, we describe the process of generating such data flow graphs from their fine-grain dependence relations using our composition operators: `elem`, `repeat`, and `compose`. The interfaces for these operators are given Table 3.

We use `inner-product` as our example. Formally, this skeleton is defined as a composition of a `zip` and a `reduce` operators ($\texttt{reduce}(+) \circ \texttt{zip}(\times)$). First, we explain how these two fundamental skeletons are created using the `elem` and `repeat` operators from their *parametric dependence relations* which we refer to as *parametric dependencies* for brevity. We then show how these two skeletons are composed to represent the data flow graph representation of the `inner-product` skeleton (Fig. 2).

4.1 Parametric Dependencies

To build data flow graph representations for fundamental skeletons, we use their finest-grain dependence relations, which we refer to as *parametric dependencies*. A parametric dependency defines the relation between input elements of a skeleton and its output as a parametric coordinate mapping and an operation. For example, in a `zip` skeleton with a binary operator, this relation is defined as:

$$\begin{aligned} &zip_{<2>}(\oplus)[a_1 \dots a_n][b_1 \dots b_n] = [a_1 \oplus b_1 \dots, a_n \oplus b_n] \\ &zip\_pd_{<2>}(\oplus) \equiv \{(i,i) \mapsto (i), \oplus\} \end{aligned} \tag{1}$$

In other words, the value of element i of the output of this skeleton is computed by applying the binary $\oplus$ operator on the ith element of each of the inputs. At runtime, parametric dependencies are translated to data flow graph nodes in the execution process.

$$\begin{aligned} S &::= elem < span > (S \mid PD) \\ &\quad \mid repeat(S, size) \\ &\quad \mid compose < portmaps > (S') \\ S' &::= S\ S' \mid \epsilon \end{aligned}$$

Table 3: The grammar for the compositional operators.

4.2 elem

The `elem` operator (Table 3) is an operator that expands a parametric dependency over a subdomain of the given inputs, called the `span`. By default, `span` is defined as the full domain of the inputs. We use a *tree-span* later in this section as an example of a non-default case.

The `elem` operator is used to describe the data flow graph representation of the $\texttt{zip}_{<k>}$ skeleton from its parametric dependency (Fig.2 (a)):

$$zip_{<k>}(\oplus) = elem(zip\_pd_{<k>}(\oplus)) \tag{2}$$

The `map` skeleton, which is a specialization of the $\texttt{zip}_{<k>}$ skeleton with k equals 1, can be expressed similarly.

4.2.1 Ports

As mentioned earlier, ports encapsulate the internal implementation that a skeleton represents and only expose the external interface of a skeleton. For a skeleton implemented using the `elem` operator, we define a default port that allows access to every element in the domain of the given `span`. As can be seen in Fig. 2(a), in a $\texttt{zip}_{<2>}$ skeleton the two input ports (*input-port*$_1$ and *input-port*$_2$), indicate that the `zip` skeleton can accept two inputs with 1D domains. Similarly, its output port allows access to the result of applying multiplication on every pair of input with 1D domains. The values we are showing in Fig. 2 are given for better readability and are not stored in ports.

4.3 repeat

Many data-parallel skeletons, such as `reduce` and `scan`, can be defined as tree-based or multilevel data flow graphs. Our `repeat` operator (Table 3) allows these skeletons to be expressed simply as such. The `repeat` operator successively applies a given skeleton on a given input, a given number of times (determined at runtime) to produce the results.

We use this operator to define the binary-tree representation of the `reduce` skeleton. First, we define the levels of the tree using the `elem` operator and the parametric dependency of the `reduce` skeleton:

$$reduce\_pd(\otimes) \equiv \{((2i, j-1), (2i+1, j-1)) \mapsto (i,j), \otimes\} \tag{3}$$

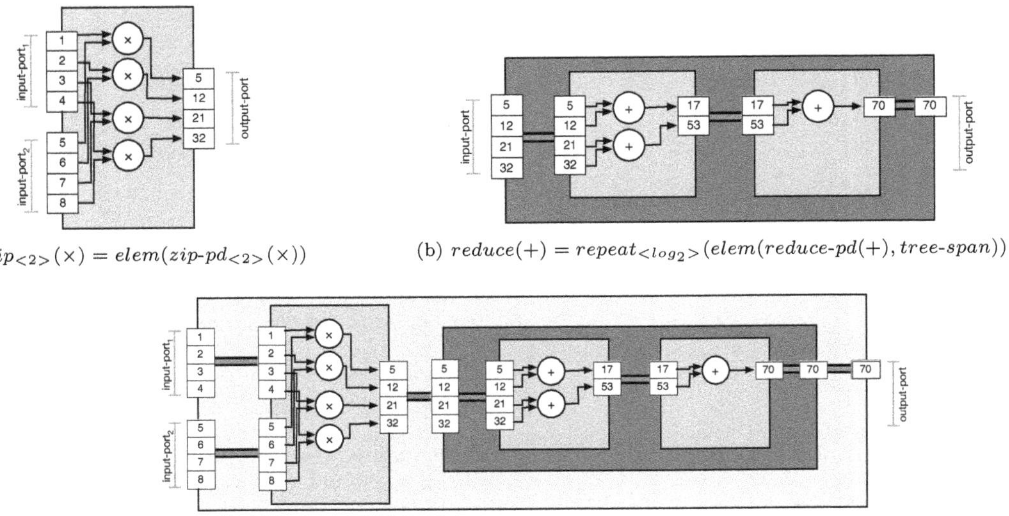

(a) $zip_{<2>}(\times) = elem(zip\text{-}pd_{<2>}(\times))$

(b) $reduce(+) = repeat_{<log_2>}(elem(reduce\text{-}pd(+), tree\text{-}span))$

(c) $inner\text{-}product = compose(zip_{<2>}(\times), reduce(+))$

Figure 2: An example for the composition in the STAPL Skeleton Framework: inner-product.

This parametric dependency says that for every element at index i, we apply the $\otimes$ operator on the two inputs at $2i$ and $2i+1$ from the previous iteration.

Using both the **elem** and the **repeat** operators, we define the data flow graph for the reduce skeleton as:

$$reduce(\otimes) = repeat_{<log_2>}(elem_{<tree_{span}>}(reduce\_pd(\otimes))) \quad (4)$$

The *tree-span* in Eq. 4 is a customized **span** in which its domain is halved at each iteration of the **repeat**(Fig. 2(b)). The log_2 size indicates that the number of iterations for this skeleton is determined by computing log_2 of the input size. Many skeletons listed in Table 1, such as **scan**, **butterfly**, and **broadcast**, are defined in the same way.

4.3.1 Ports

The ports for the data flow graph representation of a skeleton created using the **repeat** skeleton allow access to only the input port of the first iteration and to the output port of the last iteration. As an example, we have shown the input and output ports of a **reduce** skeleton in Fig. 2 (b). In this example, the *input-port* allows access to all elements in the domain of the input, while the $output-port$ only allows access to the final result.

4.4 compose - Functional Composition

In the STAPL Skeleton Framework, we allow skeletons to be composed using the **compose** operator. These compositions can be defined in two ways. In the first method, which we describe here, skeletons are composed using the simple *mathematical* notion of function composition:

$$\begin{aligned} compose(S_1, S_2, \ldots, S_n)\ x &= S_n \circ \ldots \circ S_2 \circ S_1 x \\ &= S_n(\ldots(S_1 x))) \end{aligned} \quad (5)$$

This operator can be used to compose many skeletons, such as the **inner-product** skeleton shown in Fig. 2(c) and the ones listed in [29]. The simplified C++ code required to express these skeletons in our framework is shown in Listing. 1. Each of these skeletons is defined using functions which return the result of composition.

```
auto zip_reduce<2>(*, +) = compose(zip<2>(*), reduce(+))
auto inner_product = compose(zip<2>(*), reduce(+));
auto allreduce(+) = compose(reduce(+), broadcast);
auto fft_dit = compose(bitreversal(), reverse_butterfly(fft_dit_op));
auto fft_dif = compose(butterfly(fft_dif_op), bitreversal());
```

Listing 1: Examples of functional composition.

4.4.1 Ports

The input port for the result of this type of composition is defined as the input port of the first skeleton in the composition. Similarly, the output port is defined as the output port of the last skeleton. As shown in Fig. 2(c), in an **inner-product** skeleton, the two input ports are connected to the input ports of the **zip** skeleton, and the output port is connected to the output port of the **reduce** skeleton.

These port mappings are used in the data flow graph generation phase, explained in Section 5, to define compositions in terms of point-to-point dependencies.

4.5 compose - Arbitrary Composition

Functional composition is very straightforward for defining simple compositions. However, this form of expressing composition becomes less expressive in arbitrary and complex compositions. In functional programming languages this problem is resolved using *let* expressions (*letrec*). A *let* expression simplifies compositions by potentially avoiding repetition and, at the same time, improving readability [23]. In a *let* expression, subexpressions are given names and can be reused; we use a mini-language to express the same type of compositions. The grammar for this mini-language is shown in Table 4.

4.5.1 Ports

We use our mini-language descriptions to define the mappings of the input and output of the skeletons in this type of composition. In Listing 2 we show how the mini-language can be used to express the functional composition used for the **inner-product** skeleton.

Composition :=	*input* = [*Vars*]	
	Stmts	
	output = [*Vars*]	
Stmts ::=	*Vars* = *Vars*[*Vars*] | ϵ	
Vars ::=	*ID Vars* | ϵ	

Table 4: The mini-language grammar used by the compose operator.

The first line after the name in Listing 2 indicates that this skeleton receives two inputs. In the second line, these inputs are passed to the **zip** skeleton. The result of this computation is then passed to the **reduce** skeleton. Finally, the output of the **reduce** skeleton is used as the output of the **inner-product** skeleton. This simple example defines the simple functional composition using our mini-languages and is given here for ease of understandability. In the STAPL Skeleton Framework, we provide generic port-mappings for simple functional compositions of arbitrary size and do not require users to provide port-mappings for such cases.

```
simple-port-mapping:
  input = [in1 in2]
  v1 = zip<2>(*) [in1 in2]
  v2 = reduce(+) [v1]
  output = [v2]

// C++ code for this composition
auto inner_product = compose<portmaps::simple-port-mapping>(
                         zip<2>(*), reduce(+))
```

Listing 2: inner-product composition using the mini-language.

We use the mini-language for complex compositions (such as the **bucket-sort** example in Listing 3) to express the port-mappings. We provide a Python-based tool which translates these descriptions to strongly-typed port-mappings in C++. The generated files can be used in compositions by simply adding the port-mapping name to the **compose** operator (**portmaps::simple-port-mapping** in Listing 2). Our tool also generates a GraphViz [11] dot file for the given composition description. As an example, the graphical representation of the **bucket-sort** skeleton is shown in Fig. 3.

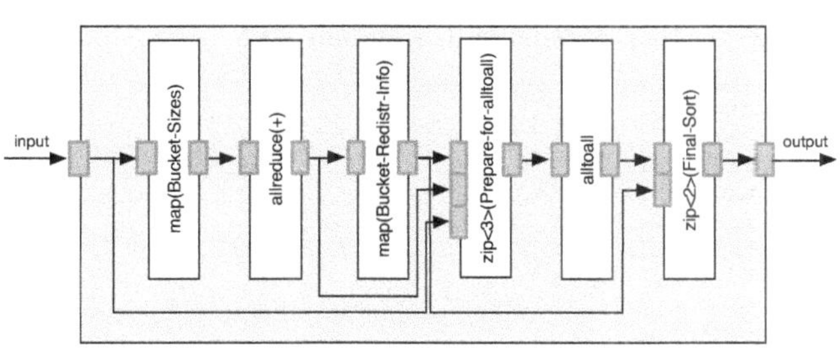

Figure 3: bucket-sort input/output port-mappings.

We use this method of composition in this paper to show the compositions used in our case studies in Section 6. The C++ code for these compositions is similar to the one line listed in Listing 2. Therefore, we omit it in the rest of the examples for better readability.

5. SKELETON EXECUTION

In the previous sections we explained the process of expressing parametric data flow graphs for skeletons. To execute these parametric definition in the STAPL Skeleton Framework, we need to first expand them based on the given inputs and generate data flow nodes for them. These data flow graphs need to be passed to a data flow engine for execution; this process is orchestrated by an entity called the *Skeleton Manager*. Upon the presence of input, the Skeleton Manager starts traversing the expression tree of a skeleton composition in a pre-order, depth-first traversal (Fig. 4). We refer to this step as the *spawning process*. The spawning process populates the data flow graph representation of a skeleton composition to an *execution environment*.

The action taken by the spawning process at each step of traversal varies based on the type of the node visited. For both **compose** and **repeat** nodes, the spawning process spawns children in order. The inputs and output for each child are determined by the given port-mapping. For **repeat** and **compose** in their simple functional composition forms, the input of each child is defined as the output of its preceding child. For the **compose** nodes with arbitrary compositions, these mappings are determined based on the description given in the mini-language description of the composition.

At **elem** nodes, the spawning process is called for all the points in the domain of the **span**. All children of **elem** node have access to the input and output of the **elem** node. Finally, for every parametric dependency reached in the expression tree, a data flow graph node is generated. The parametric dependency issues point-to-point consumption requests to the input port provided. Each port receiving these requests is either mapped to another port, which in turn passes the request on, or is directly defined over a set of tasks, i.e; the output port of an **elem** operator, in which case the dependency definition is finished. The spawning process terminates after all the tasks are generated.

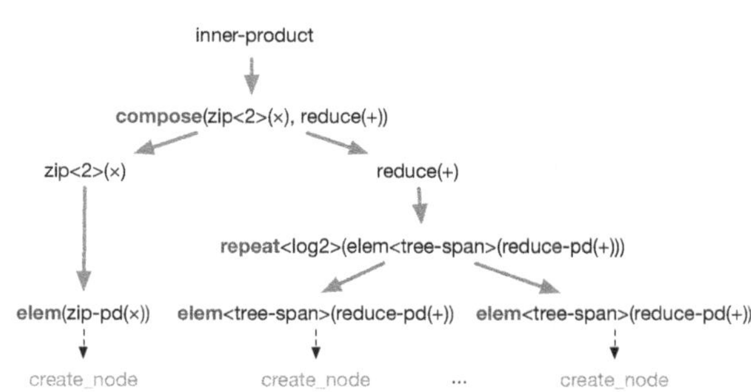

Figure 4: The spawning process of the inner-productskeleton.

We use STAPL PARAGRAPH as the execution environment for our spawning process. STAPL (Standard Template Adaptive Parallel Library) [14, 5, 6, 13, 27] is a parallel library which simplifies parallel programming by providing interfaces similar to the (sequential) ISO C++ standard library (STL) [21]. With the help of the STAPL PARAGRAPH we are able to run our data flow graph representation of skeletons efficiently, even on large scale systems.

In addition to the STAPL PARAGRAPH environment, we can populate our data flow graphs on other execution environments, making our framework potentially portable to other data flow engines. An execution environment defines the meaning of nodes and edges in a data flow graph. Some examples of the execution environments that we provide are: (1) a GraphViz environment which allows the data flow graphs to be stored as GraphViz [11] dot files, (2) a debug environment which prints out the data flow graph specifications to standard output, (3) a graph environment which allows the data flow graphs to be stored in a STAPL parallel graph container [13].

6. CASE STUDIES

In this section, we show examples of using skeleton compositions in various applications. We start from the NAS EP (Embarrassingly Parallel) benchmark, which is defined as a single `map-reduce` skeleton. We show the NAS IS (Integer Sort) benchmark as a more complex example in which we use the `bucket-sort` skeleton. The `bucket-sort` skeleton is composed from many other provided skeletons, which is the first showcase for our composition operators. We then present the skeleton-based implementation of the 3D FFT computation used in the NAS FT (Fourier Transform). In this benchmark we use the `transpose-3D` skeleton, which is also composed from other skeletons. Finally, we show a real-world example, an N-Body application using the FMM algorithm, which uses the `bucket-sort` skeleton, as an example of reusability of skeletons, in addition to several other skeletons.

6.1 NAS Embarrassingly Parallel (EP)

The NAS EP benchmark is designed to evaluate an application with relatively little interprocessor communication. The only communications in this benchmark are the ones used in the pseudo-random number generation in the beginning and the collection of the results in the end. This benchmark determines an upper bound for machine floating point performance. The goal is to tabulate a set of Gaussian random deviates in successive square annuli.

The skeleton-based representation of this benchmark is specified with the `map-reduce` skeleton. The `map` skeleton generates pairs of uniform pseudo-random deviates in the range of $(0, 1)$. The pairs that satisfy the given predicate are summed to compute the global sums and compute the ten counts of deviates in square annuli.

6.2 NAS Integer Sort (IS)

In the NAS IS benchmark, an input with N keys is sorted [2]. The keys are uniformly distributed in memory and are generated using a predefined sequential key generator. The IS benchmark is expressed using the `bucket-sort` skeleton.

```
bucket_sort(bucket-sizes, bucket-redistr-info, final-sort):
  input = [in]
  v1 = map(bucket-sizes) [input]
  v2 = allreduce() [v1]
  v3 = map(bucket-redistr-info) [v2]
  v4 = zip<3>(prepare-for-alltoall) [v3 v2 input]
  v5 = alltoall [v4]
  v6 = zip<2>(final-sort) [v3 v5]
  output = [v6]
```

Listing 3: The NAS IS benchmark defined as a bucket-sort skeleton.

In the `bucket-sort` skeleton (Listing 3), the number of input values in each range are put into buckets. This information is then summed using the `allreduce` skeleton. The summation is used to determine a well-balanced repartitioning scheme for the values in `map`(*bucket-redistr-info*). For this benchmark, we use the partitioning strategy mentioned in the NAS Benchmarks reference manual [2]. Users can provide a customized partitioning strategy to the `bucket-sort` skeleton instead. In the next step, input values are grouped and prepared for a global exchange (`zip<3>`(*prepare-for-alltoall*)). The keys are then redistributed with the help of the `alltoall` skeleton. In the last step, the received values are locally sorted based on the given local sorting method (*final-sort*). We provide several implementations for the `alltoall` skeleton which can be selected by users. Currently, we support four methods for the `alltoall` skeleton; *flat*, *butterfly*, *hybrid*, and *pairwise-exchange*.

6.3 NAS Fourier Transform (FT)

In the NAS FT benchmark, a partial differential equation is solved by using a 3D FFT (Fast Fourier Transform) on a 3D matrix [2]. A 3D FFT algorithm is defined as three steps of applying 1D FFTs on a given matrix across each dimension. In the literature, two methods are generally used for this computation [7]: distributed and transpose-based. In the first method, an efficient distributed 1D FFT is used. Although this method is very expressive, the long-range accesses in the algorithm prevent this method from scaling beyond very small clusters [7]. In the second method, which relies on efficient implementation of the sequential 1D FFT, 1D FFTs are applied across the dimensions for which data is locally available. The matrix is transposed whenever necessary to make the values across a dimension available locally. We use the transpose-based method in our framework due to the lack of scaling in the distributed method (Listing 4).

There are also two methods for matrix partitioning which are used for 3D FFT in the literature [7, 1]: the *slab decomposition*, in which each processor gets a 2D slab of the input, and the *pencil decomposition*, in which each processor gets a pencil (column) of the input. In this paper, we show the expressive skeleton-based representation for the slab decomposition, although the pencil decomposition can be expressed in a similar way. As can be seen in Listing 4, in the forward FFT, we compute 1D FFTs across the x and y axes first, and then transpose the matrix from (x, y, z) to (z, x, y). We use `transpose-3D` for this step. This skeleton is defined in term of the `zip` and `alltoall` skeletons, which is omitted for the sake of brevity. After the matrix is transposed, 1D FFTs are computed across the z dimension. The reverse 3D FFT is defined in a similar way.

```
FFT-3D(forward):
  input = [in]
  v1 = map(cfft1) [in]
  v2 = map(cfft2) [v1]
  v3 = transpose_3d<2,0,1>() [v2]
  v4 = map(cfft1) [v3]
  output = [v4]

FFT-3D(reverse):
  input = [in]
  v1 = map(cfft1) [in]
  v2 = transpose_3d<1,0,2>() [v1]
  v3 = map(cfft1) [v2]
  v4 = map(cfft2) [v3]
  output = [v4]
```

Listing 4: The NAS FFT benchmark.

6.4 Fast Multipole Solver (FMM)

FMM is a fast algorithm designed to allow N-body applications to work at exascale. This algorithm consists of several hierarchical kernels, as shown in Fig. 5: P2M, M2M, M2L, L2L, and L2P [28]. Using a Taylor expansion, the

P2M (particle-to-multipole) kernel propagates the coordinates and potential information into a multipole expansion. The mathematical derivation method used for this step are described in [8]. The next expansion happens at the center of bigger cells using the M2M (multipole-to-multipole) kernel. The M2L (multipole-to-local) kernel then creates a local expansion, out of all multipoles in the tree, based on cell size to distance ratio. The L2L (local-to-local) kernel passes the received information downwards in the tree, until it reaches the particles, for the L2P (local-to-particle) kernel to be applied.

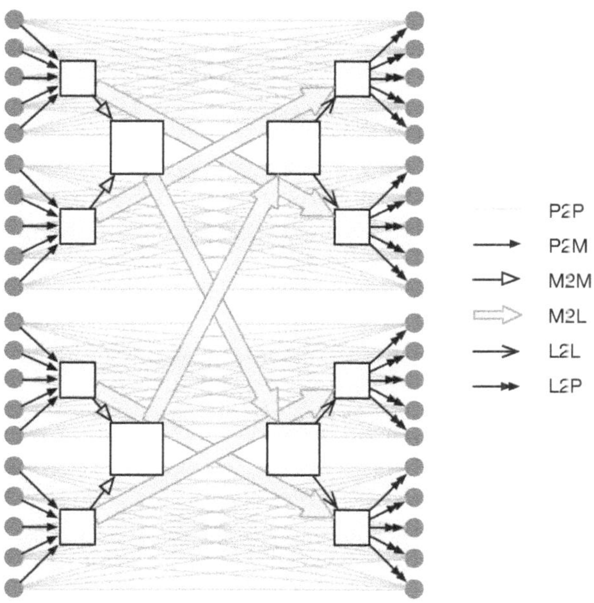

Figure 5: FMM hierarchical kernels.

Using the set of skeletons provided in our framework, we have implemented FMM in terms of skeletons (Listing 5). As we will see in the evaluation section, our implementation not only increases the expressivity of this algorithm, but also improves its overall performance in comparison to the reference implementations. In addition, by providing algorithm selection at user's level (switching between various implementations of **alltoall**, **allreduce**, and **allgather** skeletons in our framework), we allow algorithm developers to adapt their algorithm based on their heuristics. This is an advantage over the MPI implementation of such algorithms.

Moreover, our implementation is reusable for other PDE problems that can be solved using Green's function of the form listed in Eq. 6 (δ represents the Dirac delta function). The Green's function, in these problems, provides a visual interpretation of an impulse response, which is caused by a force or a charge at the center of mass.

$$\pounds G(x, s) = \delta(x - s) \tag{6}$$

To achieve acceptable performance in an N-Body problem, an efficient partitioning scheme should be used. This partitioning scheme has to consider three factors: number of particles per partition, workload, and input distribution. For a uniform distribution, the global geometric ORB (Orthogonal Recursive Bisection) is sufficient for achieving a suitable load-balancing. For a non-uniform distributions the plummer distribution can be used. In both cases, it is important to keep geometrically close points in the same partition, to reduce the intra-node interaction list sizes. Additionally, the previous workload and the amount of communication have to be balanced simultaneously to achieve load-balance across time-steps.

To fine-tune the partitioning algorithm based on the uniformity of input, we use the **bucket-sort** skeleton, listed in the IS benchmark (Listing. 3). Using this skeleton, we sort the splitters for our partitioning selection criteria and determine the physical bounds of each partition by applying an **allreduce** skeleton on the results. We then use the **build-tree** to build an octree at each partition, based on the geometric positions of particles. In the **upward_pass**, we recursively calls the **P2M** kernel for terminal cells or M2M (if a cell is within the multipole acceptance criteria). When octrees are created, we recalculate the bounds and populate them with the help of an **allreduce** skeleton followed by an **allgather** skeleton. Afterwards, to reduce communication in the next steps, we create the Local Essential Trees (LETs) in each partition and make this information available to other partitions using the **alltoall** skeleton. LETs contain a subset of the local tree cells that are required by other partition for their computations. Since the number of LETs required by a partition is inversely proportional to distance, the complexity of this step is $O(log(P))$. Once LETs are received, we combine them to form the global octree. In the **upward_pass** kernel, we invoke the **M2L**, **L2P** and **P2P** kernels on the trees, to calculate potential and acceleration of target particles. Finally, we use the **repeat** operator to calculate the subsequent snapshots. Since particles at boundaries might move across nearby partitions, we do not require a global repartitioning.

```
FMM:
  input = [bodies tree]
  x1 = bucket-sort(selection-citeria) input
  x2 = alltoall [x1]
  x3 = allreduce(<,>) [x2]
  x4 = map(build-tree) [x3]
  repeat
  {
    x5 = map(upward_pass) [x4 x2]
    x6 = allreduce(<,>) [x3 x4]
    x7 = allgather() [x6]
    x8 = alltoall() [x7]
    x9 = map(DTT) [x5]
    x10= map(Traverse and DP) [x5]
  }(max_steps)
  output = [x10]
```

Listing 5: N-Body using the FMM hierarchical algorithm.

7. EVALUATION

We have evaluated our framework on three massively parallel systems: a 24,576 node BG/Q system (VULCAN from LLNL), each node containing a 16-core IBM PowerPC A2 for a total of 393,216 cores; a 5,272 node Cray XC30 supercomputer (PIZ DAINT from CSCS Switzerland), each node containing a hyperthreaded 8-core Intel SandyBridge with 32GB per node, for a total of 42,176 cores (84,352 hyperthreads); and a 1,266 node Cray XC40 supercomputer (a PIZ DAINT extension from CSCS Switzerland), each node containing two 12-core Intel Haswell CPUs, for a toal of 30,144 cores.

7.1 Fundamental Skeletons

To show the efficiency of our fundamental skeletons we show scalability results for the `map`, `reduce`, and `scan` skeletons in Fig. 6, 8, and 7. Our results indicate that these fundamental skeletons can easily scale beyond 100,000 cores. The jump at 64k processes in Fig. 7 is due to the implicit change of algorithms in the MPI implementation of MPI_Scan. As you can see in this figure, the implicit algorithm selection is not always favorable. For this reason, we not only provide default efficient implementations for various fundamental skeletons, but also allow algorithm developers to choose their desired algorithm in their specification.

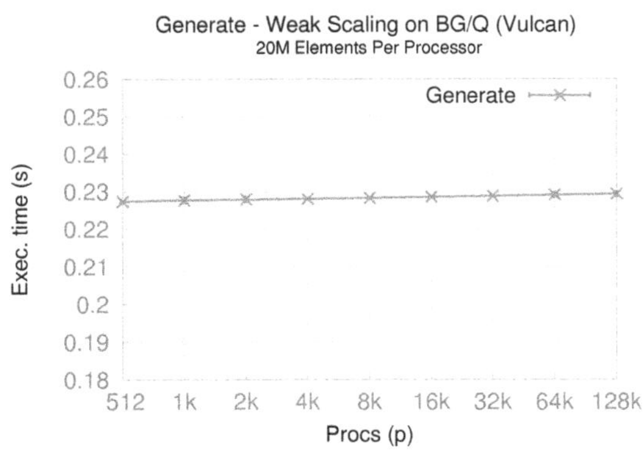

Figure 6: Weak scalability of Generate as an example of *map*.

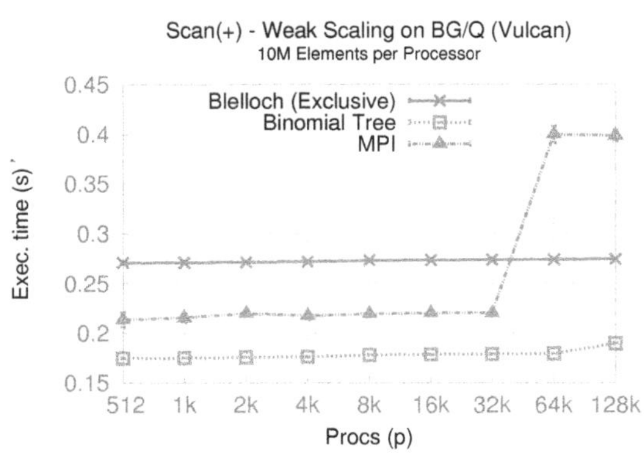

Figure 7: Weak scalability of the various *scan* skeletons vs. a hand-optimized MPI *scan*

7.2 NAS Benchmarks

7.2.1 NAS Embarrassingly Parallel

The EP benchmark shows an example of simple functional composition. This benchmark is expressed as a `map-reduce` skeleton. The `map-reduce` skeleton is in turn composed from our `map` and `reduce` skeletons. The obtained results in Fig. 9 indicate that the simple functional composition in our framework preserves the efficiency of the nested skeletons.

7.2.2 NAS Integer Sort

The IS benchmark shows an example of arbitrary compositions. The results for this benchmark are especially important; they are indicative of the efficiency of arbitrary compositions. Our results for class D of this application (Fig. 10)

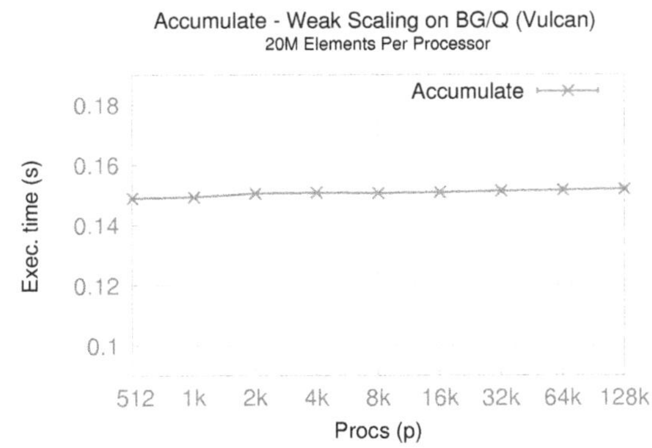

Figure 8: Weak scalability of accumulate(+) as an example of *reduce*.

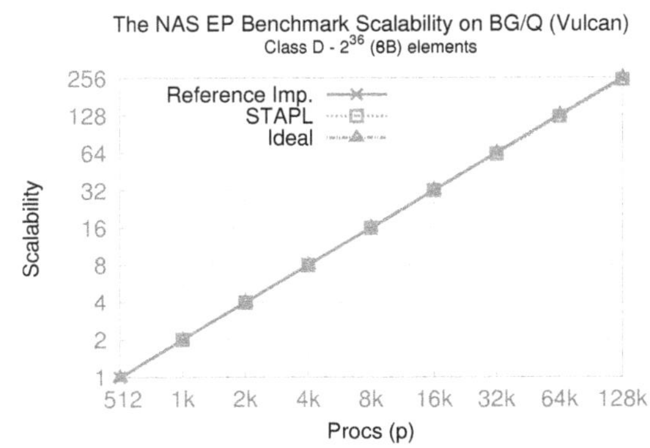

Figure 9: Performance comparison of class D NAS EP benchmark with the reference implementation.

show that our skeleton-based version of this benchmark performs better than the hand-optimized version of this benchmark. The reference MPI IS implementation consists of several blocking MPI calls, such as `alltoall`, and `allreduce`. These constructs require global synchronizations in MPI after each invocation. We avoid these synchronizations by representing the problem in our framework in terms of skeletons. As mentioned earlier, the data flow representation of skeletons, along with the composition operators, can represent the data dependencies between the steps of the problem as point-to-point dependencies of their corresponding data flow graphs. This provides our implementation with better performance than the reference implementation by avoiding global synchronizations (Fig. 10).

7.2.3 NAS Fourier Transform

As shown in Fig. 11, our implementation of the FT benchmark shows comparable performance to the hand-optimized reference implementation (Fig. 11). The FT benchmark stresses the system with interprocessor communication in its 3D matrix transpose, requiring efficient `alltoall` communication. Our overhead is due to the copy-semantics of the STAPL runtime system. The STAPL runtime system requires one copy between the user-level to the MPI level on both sender and receiver side. These extra copies result in only 30-40% overhead in our implementation, as some of the overhead is compensated for by not requiring global synchronizations.

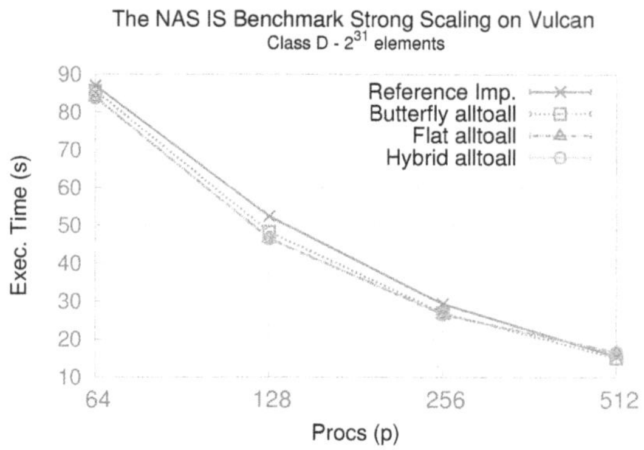

Figure 10: Performance comparison of class D NAS IS benchmark with the reference implementation.

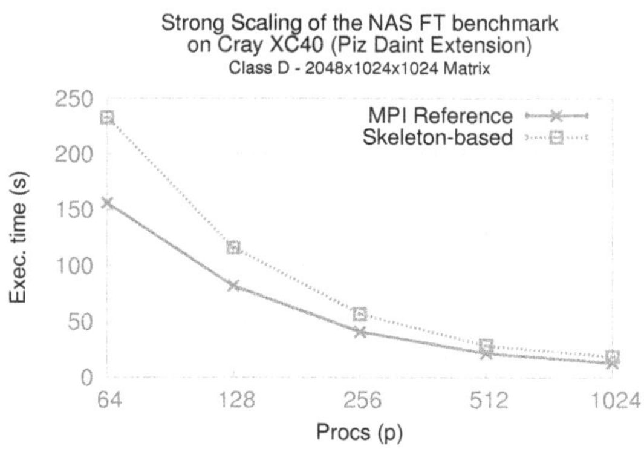

Figure 11: Performance comparison of class D of NAS EP benchmark with the reference implementation.

7.3 Skeleton-based FMM Algorithm

As can be seen in Fig. 12 and 13, our skeleton-based implementation of the FMM algorithm can scale better than the reference implementation. In both versions, we are exploiting distributed memory parallelism; no shared-memory or GPU optimizations are involved. This is attributable to the fact that, for this benchmark, we are making a direct comparison between a hand-optimized MPI implementation, given by Exa-FMM reference code, and a Skeleton-based distributed implementation that internally uses the same serial FMM kernels given by the reference implementation.

In Fig. 12, we show the weak-scaling results for 50k particles per process (100M particles on 2k processes). As can be seen in this figure, the execution time for the reference implementation diverges rapidly from the skeleton-based version, after 32 processes and runs out of memory after 128 processes. This is due to the overhead caused by the global communication of LETs in the reference implementation, using MPI_Alltoall. Our implementation continues to scale up to 2k processes. By replacing global synchronization with point-to-point dependency and using skeletons in our algorithm, we are able to scale by 2 more orders of magnitude than the reference implementation and solve a problem of 10^8 particles.

In Fig. 13, we show the strong scaling results for a problem of 25M particles. In this figure, the scalability of our implementation persists until 256 cores; at this point the theoretical amount of serial work assuming no communication is approximately 0.16s. This is considerably smaller than the actual amount of communication. The reference implementation crashes due of the same memory allocation issue, mentioned earlier, after 8 processes.

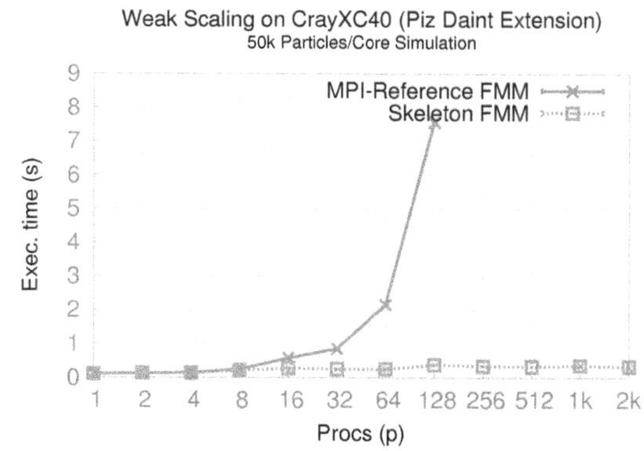

Figure 12: Weak scaling of FMM using MPI vs Skeleton-based Implementations

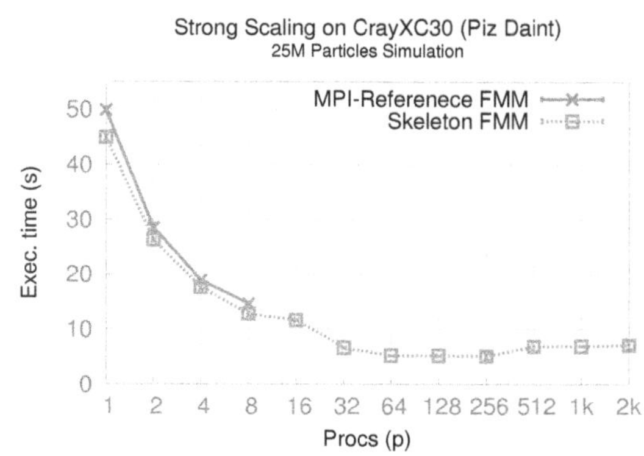

Figure 13: Strong scaling of FMM using MPI vs Skeleton-based Implementations

8. CONCLUSION

In this work, we presented a novel method for representing skeletons and their composition in the STAPL Skeleton Framework. We defined fundamental skeletons from their fine-grain dependence relations, e.g., `map`, `zip`, and `reduce`, and expanded them to form their data flow graph representations. We then composed these skeletons to build more complex real-world applications and benchmarks. With the abstraction that ports provided, we were able to define data dependencies between the skeletons as point-to-point dependencies of their corresponding data flow graphs, allowing programs to scale efficiently beyond 100,000 cores. Our framework addresses many concerns listed in [19] for a parallel programming framework: scalability, portability, extensibility, debuggablity, tunability, and maintainability.

9. ACKNOWLEDGMENTS

This research supported in part by NSF awards CNS-0551685, CCF 0702765, CCF-0833199, CCF-1439145, CCF-1423111, CCF-0830753, IIS-0916053, IIS-0917266, RI-1217991, EFRI-1240483, by NIH NCI R25 CA090301-11, by DOE awards DE-AC02-06CH11357, DE-NA0002376, B575363, by Samsung, IBM, Intel, and by Award KUS-C1-016-04, made by King Abdullah University of Science and Technology (KAUST). This research used resources of the National Energy Research Scientific Computing Center, which is supported by the Office of Science of the U.S. Department of Energy under Contract No. DE-AC02-05CH11231.

10. REFERENCES

[1] R. C. Agarwal, F. G. Gustavson, and M. Zubair. An efficient parallel algorithm for the 3D FFT NAS parallel benchmark. In *Proceedings of the Scalable High-Performance Computing Conf.*, pages 129–133. IEEE, 1994.

[2] D. Bailey and T. H. et al. The NAS Parallel Benchmarks 2.0. Report NAS-95-020, Numerical Aerodynamic Simulation Facility, NASA Ames Research Center, Dec. 1995.

[3] G. Bikshandi, J. Guo, D. Hoeflinger, G. Almasi, B. B. Fraguela, M. J. Garzarán, D. Padua, and C. Von Praun. Programming for parallelism and locality with hierarchically tiled arrays. In *Proceedings of the 11th ACM SIGPLAN symp. on Principles and practice of par. prog.*, pages 48–57. ACM, 2006.

[4] Z. Budimlić, M. Burke, V. Cavé, K. Knobe, G. Lowney, R. Newton, J. Palsberg, D. Peixotto, V. Sarkar, F. Schlimbach, et al. Concurrent collections. *Sci. Prog.*, 18(3):203–217, 2010.

[5] A. Buss, A. Fidel, T. Smith, G. Tanase, N. Thomas, X. Xu, M. Bianco, N. M. Amato, L. Rauchwerger, et al. The STAPL pView. In *Int. Wkshp. on Lang. and Comp. for Par. Comp. (LCPC)*, pages 261–275. Springer, 2011.

[6] A. Buss, Harshvardhan, I. Papadopoulos, O. Pearce, T. Smith, G. Tanase, N. Thomas, X. Xu, M. Bianco, N. M. Amato, and L. Rauchwerger. Stapl: Standard Template Adaptive Parallel Library. In *Proceedings of the 3rd Annual Haifa Experimental Systems Conference*, SYSTOR '10, pages 14:1–14:10, New York, NY, 2010. ACM.

[7] A. Chan, P. Balaji, W. Gropp, and R. Thakur. Communication analysis of parallel 3D FFT for flat cartesian meshes on large Blue Gene systems. In *High Perf. Comp. (HiPC)*, pages 350–364. Springer, 2008.

[8] H. Cheng, L. Greengard, and V. Rokhlin. A fast adaptive multipole algorithm in three dimensions. *Journal of Comp. Physics*, 155(2):468–498, 1999.

[9] M. I. Cole. *Algorithmic skeletons: structured management of parallel computing.* Pitman/MIT, London, 1989.

[10] J. F. Ferreira, J. L. Sobral, and A. J. ProenÃ§a. JaSkel: A Java skeleton-based framework for structured cluster and grid computing. In *in CCGRID, IEEE Computer Society*, pages 301–304, 2006.

[11] E. R. Gansner and S. C. North. An open graph visualization system and its applications to software engineering. *SOFTWARE - PRACTICE AND EXPERIENCE*, 30(11):1203–1233, 2000.

[12] H. González-Vélez and M. Leyton. A survey of algorithmic skeleton frameworks: high-level structured parallel programming enablers. *Software: Practice and Experience*, 40(12):1135–1160, 2010.

[13] A. F. Harshvardhan, N. M. Amato, and L. Rauchwerger. The STAPL Parallel Graph Library. *Languages and Compilers for Parallel Computing, Lecture Notes in Computer Science*, pages 46–60, 2013.

[14] A. F. Harshvardhan, N. M. Amato, and L. Rauchwerger. KLA: A new algorithmic paradigm for parallel graph computations. In *Proc. of the Int. Conf. on Parallel Architectures and Compilation Techniques (PACT)*, 2014.

[15] L. V. Kale and S. Krishnan. CHARM++: A portable concurrent object oriented system based on C++. *SIGPLAN Not.*, 28(10):91–108, 1993.

[16] H. Kuchen and J. Striegnitz. Features from functional programming for a C++ Skeleton library: Research articles. *Concurr. Comput. : Pract. Exper.*, 17(7-8):739–756, June 2005.

[17] R. Loogen, Y. Ortega-mallén, and R. Peña marí. Parallel functional programming in Eden. *J. Funct. Program.*, 15(3):431–475, May 2005.

[18] K. Matsuzaki and H. Iwasaki. A library of constructive skeletons for sequential style of parallel programming. In *Proceedings of the 1st Int. Conf. on Scalable information systems*, page 13. ACM Press, 2006.

[19] M. McCool, J. Reinders, and A. Robison. *Structured parallel programming: patterns for efficient computation.* Elsevier, 2012.

[20] U. Müller-Funk, U. Thonemann, and G. Vossen. The Münster skeleton library Muesli–a comprehensive overview. 2009.

[21] D. Musser, G. Derge, and A. Saini. *STL Tutorial and Reference Guide, 2nd Edition.* Addison-Wesley, 2001.

[22] P. Newton and J. C. Browne. The CODE 2.0 graphical parallel programming language. In *Proceedings of the 6th Int. Conf. on Supercomputing*, pages 167–177. ACM, 1992.

[23] B. C. Pierce. *Types and programming languages.* MIT Press, Cambridge, MA, 2002.

[24] F. Rabhi and S. Gorlatch. *Patterns and skeletons for Parallel and Distributed Computing.* Springer, 2003.

[25] A. D. Robison. Composable parallel patterns with Intel Cilk Plus. *Comp. in Sci. and Eng.*, 15(2):0066–71, 2013.

[26] J. Sérot, J. S, J.-P. DERUTIN, D. GINHAC, and J. pierre D. SKiPPER - a skeleton-based parallel programming environment for real-time image processing applications, 1999.

[27] G. Tanase, A. Buss, A. Fidel, Harshvardhan, I. Papadopoulos, O. Pearce, T. Smith, N. Thomas, X. Xu, N. Mourad, J. Vu, M. Bianco, N. M. Amato, and L. Rauchwerger. The STAPL Parallel Container Framework. *SIGPLAN Not.*, 46(8):235–246, Feb. 2011.

[28] R. Yokota and L. Barba. Comparing the treecode with FMM on GPUs for vortex particle simulations of a leapfrogging vortex ring. *Computers & Fluids*, 45(1):155–161, 2011.

[29] M. Zandifar, N. Thomas, N. M. Amato, and L. Rauchwerger. The STAPL Skeleton Framework. In *Int. Wkshp. on Lang. and Comp. for Par. Comp. (LCPC)*, Hillsboro, OR, 2014.

STAPL-RTS: An Application Driven Runtime System

Ioannis Papadopoulos
ipapadop@cse.tamu.edu
Texas A&M University
College Station, Texas 77843

Nathan Thomas
nthomas@cse.tamu.edu
Texas A&M University
College Station, Texas 77843

Adam Fidel
fidel@cse.tamu.edu
Texas A&M University
College Station, Texas 77843

Nancy M. Amato
amato@cse.tamu.edu
Texas A&M University
College Station, Texas 77843

Lawrence Rauchwerger
rwerger@cse.tamu.edu
Texas A&M University
College Station, Texas 77843

ABSTRACT

Modern HPC systems are growing in complexity, as they move towards deeper memory hierarchies and increasing use of computational heterogeneity via GPUs or other accelerators. When developing applications for these platforms, programmers are faced with two bad choices. On one hand, they can explicitly manage all machine resources, writing programs decorated with low level primitives from multiple APIs (e.g. Hybrid MPI / OpenMP applications). Though seemingly necessary for efficient execution, it is an inherently non-scalable way to write software. Without a *separation of concerns*, only small programs written by expert developers actually achieve this efficiency. Furthermore, the implementations are rigid, difficult to extend, and not portable. Alternatively, users can adopt higher level programming environments to abstract away these concerns. Extensibility and portability, however, often come at the cost of lost performance. The mapping of a user's application onto the system now occurs without the contextual information that was immediately available in the more coupled approach.

In this paper, we describe a framework for the transfer of high level, application semantic knowledge into lower levels of the software stack at an *appropriate level of abstraction*. Using the STAPL library, we demonstrate how this information guides important decisions in the runtime system (STAPL-RTS), such as multi-protocol communication coordination and request aggregation. Through examples, we show how generic programming idioms already known to C++ programmers are used to annotate calls and increase performance.

Categories and Subject Descriptors

D.1.3 [**Programming Techniques**]: Concurrent Programming—*Parallel programming*

ICS'15, June 8–11, 2015, Newport Beach, CA, USA.

DOI: http://dx.doi.org/10.1145/2751205.2751233.

Keywords

Parallel Programming; Data flow; Runtime Systems; Application Driven Optimizations; Distributed Memory; Shared Memory; Remote Method Invocation

1. INTRODUCTION

The current state of the art in high performance computing (HPC) is a distributed memory machine comprised of nodes with accelerators and multiple processor sockets, each with a multi-core chip. Application development for these platforms is usually evolutionary: a scalable, distributed programming model (usually MPI [37]) is used for the initial implementation, with the memory hierarchy largely ignored. To increase performance, the implementation is extended with another library (e.g., OpenMP [30]), with threading for finer grain parallelism and shared memory with explicit synchronization to replace communication between processing elements. Writing such programs decorated with primitives from multiple low level APIs is an inherently non-scalable way to write software. Without a *separation of concerns*, only small programs written by expert developers actually achieve greater efficiency. The implementations are also rigid, difficult to extend, and not portable.

This lack of abstraction clearly detracts from code reuse and program composability. However, developers are often faced with no other choice if they wish to gain even some fraction of the peak performance modern systems offer. Efficiently mapping applications to such architectures requires semantic information that is usually lost when higher level programming models are used.

In this paper, we describe how user-level information is transferred to the runtime system of STAPL [10], a generic library of components for parallel program composition. One of the key design goals of STAPL is portable performance: users must be able to write one version of the code that has good performance on different systems with minimal per-platform effort. The layered component architecture of the library supports this objective, with each component responsible for abstracting some area of concern in parallel programming, such as data distribution, computation specification, work scheduling, and communication. Key to obtaining performance is a *transfer of contextual information* between these components, while still maintaining the proper abstractions necessary for software reuse.

The *STAPL Runtime System* (STAPL-RTS) presents a *unified interface* for both intra-node and inter-node communication to support performance portability. Internally the *mixed-mode* implementation uses both standard shared and distributed memory communication protocols when appropriate. For scalability and correctness, we employ a *distributed Remote Method Invocation* (RMI) model.

Each processing element together with a logical address space forms an isolated computational unit called a *location*. Hence, parameters to RMIs are passed by value, maintaining strict copy semantics with no user-visible sharing. This approach provides safety to the user by guarding against data races. However, as with other features of higher level languages, it can introduce runtime overhead, in this case from excessive copying of large data structures. We show in this paper how *copy elision* (i.e. removing unnecessary copying of objects) can eliminate this performance penalty, via simple annotations inserted by STAPL based on information from higher levels of the software stack.

This paper makes the following contributions:

- **Transfer of application semantics to the runtime.** We employ annotations based on common programming idioms. As STAPL is implemented in C++11 [38], the annotations are similar to C++ standard library interfaces.

- **Copy removal via move semantics and immutable sharing.** To demonstrate application driven optimization, we transparently avoid copies usually incurred when maintaining isolation of computational activities. We employ the commonly known idioms of move semantics [38] and immutable sharing [18], leveraging shared memory for communication between activities whenever possible. STAPL programs are expressed as task dependence graphs, with consumer tasks receiving read-only access to produced values. We use this graph representation to transparently insert annotations whenever possible: tasks with single consumers can direct the runtime to *move* their copy directly to the producer, which it will do if the tasks exist in shared memory. Tasks with multiple consumers can request *immutable references* to the value be transmitted to other locations where these successors exist.

- **Algorithm driven request aggregation.** As another example of application driven runtime optimization, we tune the aggregation of RMIs, an optimization that has been shown to be important for fine-grained asynchronous messaging models [24,33,41]. We create ad-hoc communication channels to efficiently aggregate sequences of RMIs sharing common and constant parameters such as destination and target method. As we will show, the technique can specify custom consistency models for collections of requests that are logically associated with a given computational activity. This technique can have a dramatic effect on application performance, as demonstrated using a common graph traversal algorithm.

2. STAPL OVERVIEW

The *Standard Template Adaptive Parallel Library* (STAPL) [10] is a framework developed in C++ for parallel programming. Both STAPL and the runtime system presented in this paper are libraries, requiring only a C++ compiler (e.g., `gcc`) and established communication libraries such as MPI. An overview of its major components are presented in Figure 1. The library's generic design is based on that of the

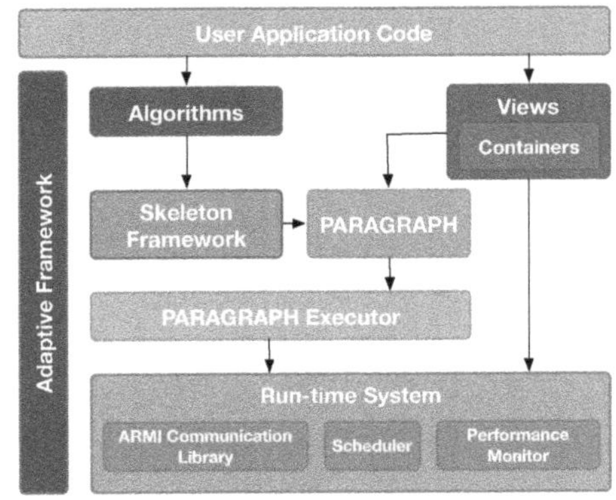

Figure 1: STAPL Components

C++ Standard Template Library (STL) [28], extended and modified for parallel programming.

STAPL provides *parallel algorithms* and *distributed data structures* [20,39] with interfaces similar to the STL. Instead of using iterators, algorithms are written with *views* [9] that decouple the container interfaces from the underlying storage. The *skeletons framework* [43] allows the user to express an application as a composition of parallel patterns.

Algorithmic skeletons are instantiated at runtime as task dependence graphs by the **PARAGRAPH**, STAPL's data flow engine. The **PARAGRAPH** enforces the specified task dependencies and is responsible for the transmission of intermediate values between tasks. When consumer tasks execute on different locations than the producer, the **PARAGRAPH** uses STAPL-RTS primitives for communication. In Section 4.1.1 we discuss how the **PARAGRAPH** annotates these RMI invocations for copy elision, based on information gathered by the program's task dependence graph, without any changes to the program's skeleton specification.

3. THE STAPL RUNTIME SYSTEM

The STAPL-RTS abstracts the platform and its resources, providing a uniform interface for all communication in the library and applications built with it. It provides an SPMD execution model with task parallelism capabilities. Locations only have access to their own address space and communicate with other locations using *Remote Method Invocations* (RMIs) on shared objects. This abstraction of a virtual distributed, parallel machine helps STAPL support general nested parallelism. Similar to the **PARAGRAPH** discussed earlier, containers are distributed objects (i.e., `p_objects`) which use RMIs to read and write elements. In this section, we briefly describe the major components and the interface for RMI invocations. We then describe the STAPL-RTS execution model and discuss design decisions that motivate the application driven optimizations that follow in Section 4.

3.1 Component Overview

The runtime system features a highly modular design, depicted in Figure 2[1], that allows it to be customized and tuned as needed for different platforms. The primary public APIs of STAPL-RTS are briefly described below:

[1]White text signifies components that are user accessible, black text marks components for internal use only.

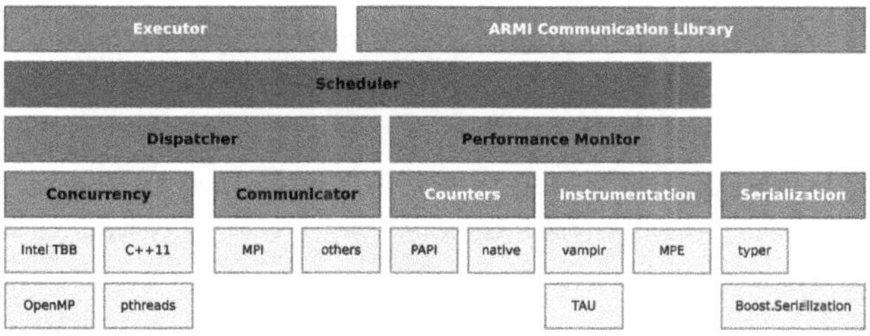

Figure 2: STAPL-RTS components.

ARMI. *Adaptive Remote Method Invocation* (ARMI) [33] provides primitives for registering `p_objects` and invoking RMIs on them. These RMIs allow the asynchronous transfer of both data and work on the system. ARMI also makes use of *future* and *promise* objects [5] to allow the asynchronous return of values from RMIs.

Executor. The EXECUTOR allows the **PARAGRAPH** to schedule runnable tasks for execution with associated scheduling information. It also has work-stealing capabilities [16].

Counters and **Instrumentation**. The STAPL-RTS offers a high-level interface to the native counters available, such as Linux timers or PAPI [2] as well as an *instrumentation* component for tracing and profiling capabilities through the integration of libraries such as TAU [34] and MPE [42].

Serialization. The *serialization* component is used by other components to marshal objects for communication or storage. Packing and unpacking is automatic for simple types, such as empty classes, primitive types and plain old data structures (PODs). For more complex objects, users have to provide a simple definition of the members of each class. It supports integration with other marshaling libraries, such as Boost.Serialization [1].

3.2 The ARMI Interface

An overview of the most commonly used functions from ARMI is presented in Table 1. All primitives are non-blocking, apart from `sync_rmi()`, `rmi_fence()` and `rmi_barrier()`. Primitives provided include standard point-to-point RMIs as well as collective versions for both the case in which all locations participate in the operation and for which a single location initiates the call (one-sided collectives). In Figure 3 we give a simple example of ARMI usage; additional primitives will be discussed as they are used in Section 4.

```
struct A : public p_object {
  int m_value;
  void write(int t) { m_value = t; }
  int read() const { return m_value; }
};

foo(...) {
  A a;
  auto h = a.get_rmi_handle();
  int t = 5;
  async_rmi(1, h, &A::write, t);
  t = 6;
  future<int> f = opaque_rmi(1, h, &A::read);
  int y = f.get();
}
```

Figure 3: Basic Usage of ARMI Primitives.

Primitive	Description
One-Sided Primitives	
void async_rmi(dest, h, f, args ...)	Issues an RMI that calls the function `f` of the `p_object` associated with the `rmi_handle` `h` on location `dest` with the given arguments, ignoring the return value. Synchronization calls or other RMI requests that do not ignore the return value can be used to guarantee its completion.
future<Rtn> opaque_rmi(dest, h, f, args...)	Returns a `future` object for retrieving the return value of the function.
Rtn sync_rmi(dest, h, f, args ...)	Issues the RMI and waits for the return value (blocking primitive).
Collective Primitives	
futures<Rtn> allgather_rmi(h, f, args ...)	The function is called on all locations and the `futures` object is used to retrieve the return values.
future<Rtn> allreduce_rmi(op, h, f, args ...)	The `future` is used to retrieve the reduction of the return values of `f` from each location.
future<Rtn> broadcast_rmi(h, f, args...)	The caller (root) location calls the function and broadcasts the return value to all other locations. Non-root locations have to call `broadcast_rmi(root, f)` to complete the collective operation.
Synchronization Primitives	
void rmi_fence()	Guarantees that all invoked RMI requests have been processed using an algorithm similar to [36].
void rmi_barrier()	Performs a barrier operation.
void p_object::advance_epoch()	Advances the epoch of the `p_object`, as well as the epoch of the location. It can be used for synchronization without communication, avoiding the `rmi_fence()` or `rmi_barrier()` primitives.

Table 1: ARMI Primitives

In Figure 3, function `foo()` is executing on a given location which wishes to communicate with location 1. The shared `p_object` `a` is accessed through a handle `h`, which represents the distributed object with a representative on the destination. The corresponding instance of `a` on location 1 is updated via a call to `A::write()`. Note that pass by value semantics guarantee that the callee sees 5 and not 6. Also, assuming that no other locations send updates to location 1, y will be set to 6 since the ordering of RMI invocations from a single source is enforced by default.

3.3 STAPL-RTS Execution Model

We describe several aspects of the execution model of the STAPL-RTS, motivating design decisions and pinpointing opportunities for application driven optimization.

Execution Environment. A STAPL application is always implicitly parallel and executes on a number of locations. Each location has an isolated, virtual address space which is not directly accessible by other locations. When a location wishes to modify or read a remote location's memory, the work must be expressed via RMIs on distributed `p_objects`, *even if the two locations reside in shared memory.* This design has the following ramifications:

- **Data Races Cannot Occur.** With only one processing element able to directly access memory and RMI atomicity guaranteed by the runtime system, users do not have the ability to create data races as is usually possible in shared memory parallel execution models.

- **Isolation causes copying.** One cost of the added safety is object copying between locations, even if they share a common address space. Maintaining isolation means values returned from RMIs between locations must be copied. We discuss in Section 4.1 how to minimize this overhead when in shared memory.

Asynchronous Communication Primitives. Asynchrony allows us to minimize the effects of high latency by enabling communication and computation overlapping. We further desire to minimize any state associated with the RMI from the initiating location after invoking the non-blocking RMI, allowing the location to proceed with other, potentially unrelated tasks while it awaits any return. Also, in Section 4.1.4 we show how asynchronous RMI return values are handled without requiring blocking, allowing users to move on to another computation while awaiting said value.

RMI Argument Copy Semantics. We enforce pass-by-value semantics for all arguments passed to an RMI. A private copy of any argument passed to a remote function call is presented to the receiver; any mutation on the argument either at the sender or at the receiver will not be visible to the other. Again, if this is done without high level information, the runtime may introduce unnecessary copies to enforce pass-by-value semantics.

Causal RMI Consistency Model. In order to present a coherent model, our RMIs follow a *causal consistency model*. A happened-before relationship is established between RMIs that are invoked from the same source location to the same destination location if they are issued in the same context without requiring extra synchronization. However, these ordering guarantees may be stricter than required by some algorithms, making it a good candidate for application driven optimization in the STAPL-RTS.

4. APPLICATION DRIVEN OPTIMIZATION

We now give examples of how high level information is transferred from STAPL programs into the runtime system to guide optimization. We begin with **PARAGRAPH** directed copy elision between locations in shared memory. We then discuss communication optimization based on RMI aggregation and consistency model tuning. The information is provided at an appropriate level of abstraction (i.e., they need not be aware of how and if STAPL-RTS uses this information) through a well known programming idiom, derived from a standard C++ language feature or library interface.

4.1 Copy Elision in Shared Memory

Copy semantics simplify the reasoning about parallel programs, as they remove potential side-effects. However they can introduce significant runtime overhead. We relax our implementation of copy semantics with assistance from the STAPL **PARAGRAPH**. We describe three RMI annotations that allow STAPL-RTS to remove copies. They include transfer via `move`, return storage specification via `promise` and `future` objects, and the use of shared, immutable data references. We first describe how application contextual information flows to the **PARAGRAPH** to guide copy elision and then discuss the annotations as well as their implementation.

4.1.1 *PARAGRAPH Direction of Copy Elision*

Copy elision annotations are not inserted by STAPL application programmers. Instead the elision is directed by the **PARAGRAPH**, and Figure 4 depicts this process. First an application writer employs an algorithmic skeleton, which the skeleton framework uses to generate a task dependence graph specification. At runtime, this graph is instantiated by the **PARAGRAPH** and mapped onto a set of locations for execution. The **PARAGRAPH** also performs an inspection of the graph to detect where copy elision can be used. In Figure 4 the result of the map operation on location 1 can be transferred (i.e., moved) to the reduction task on location 0, as it is the only consumer of the value. The **PARAGRAPH** uses the following set of rules to identify elision opportunities:

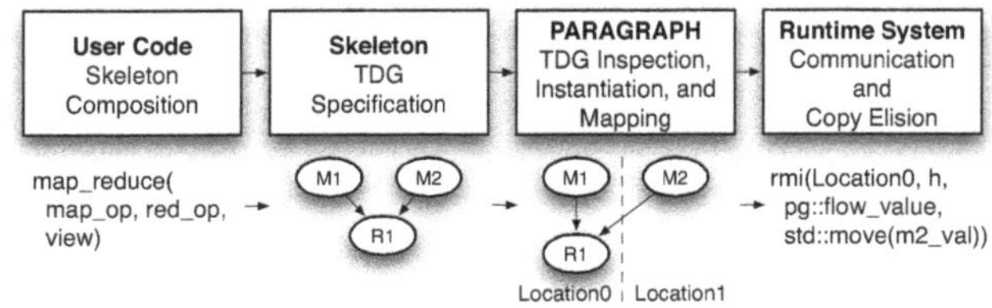

Figure 4: Copy Elision in STAPL.

```
void produce() {
  std::vector<int> v(N);
  ... // populate v
  async_rmi(dest, h, obj::consume, v);
}
```

(a) RMI invocation with copy of `v`.

```
void produce(...) {
  std::vector<int> v(N);
  ... // populate v
  async_rmi(dest, h, obj::consume, std::move(v));
}
```

(b) RMI invocation with move of `v`.

Figure 5: Move Semantics for RMI Arguments

- **`move` annotation**. If a task has single consumer and it is on a remote location (i.e., different than where the task executes), pass the value to `async_rmi` via `std::move`.
- **`immutable_shared` annotation**. If a task has multiple consumers and at least one is on a remote location, use an immutable shared reference. The reference is passed to associated RMIs and also used to service local consumers.
- **No annotation**. If all consumers are on the producer's location, the value is managed locally with no RMIs.

4.1.2 *Using Moves for RMI Parameter Passing*

Consider the code in Figure 5(a) which calls `async_rmi()`. A location executes function `produce()` that creates a vector and sends it to another location via RMI. In this case, the copy of the vector parameter into the runtime is unnecessary. The source location produces the value solely for consumption at the destination location. This is an *object transfer* pattern present in many parallel algorithms (e.g., reductions). This type of value transfer is also desirable in sequential computing. C++11 [38] addresses this problem with language support for *rvalue references* and an associated library function `std::move()`.

The STAPL-RTS supports the direct use of these move semantics with RMI parameter passing, so that the unneces-

```
foo(...) {
  auto t = make_immutable_shared<T>(...);
  async_rmi(1, h, &A::put, t);
  async_rmi(2, h, &A::put, t);
  T const& ref = t.get();
}
```

(a) Example `immutable_shared` usage.

```
t = ...;
async_rmi(1, h, &A::put, immutable(t));
rmi_fence();
t = ...;
```

(b) Example `immutable` usage.

Figure 6: Immutable object sharing in STAPL-RTS.

sary copies can be completely avoided. The trivially modified code in Figure 5(b) has been annotated to express the transfer of v. The parameter is passed without any copying *when the source and destination reside in the same address space* and is presented to `consume_value()` as an rvalue reference, that is as an `std::vector<int>&&`. During execution, the parameter is moved from user space into the runtime, serialization is avoided, and control bits are inserted into the RMI request to forward the rvalue reference to the callee.

4.1.3 *Immutable Object Sharing*

There are times that basic *data transfer* between locations is insufficient. If there is still a local consumer of the value to be transmitted remotely, we can employ *immutable data sharing* to avoid overhead while still preserving copy semantics. This admittedly does not cover all cases (i.e., if the receiver wants to mutate the value, they must still copy it), but when it can be used, it gives similar savings as the zero-copy data transfers discussed in the previous two sections. We currently offer two variations of immutable sharing:

Permanently immutable objects. Values placed in an immutable wrapper via `make_shared_immutable()` are guarded against mutation for the remainder of their lifetime. This STAPL-RTS primitive mimics the behavior of a `std::shared_ptr<const T>` and is used to safely share values between locations in shared memory. When the destination location resides in another address space, a new copy is initialized there to back the immutable wrapper. In each address space, the underlying copy is deleted when the last reference is deleted, using standard reference counting.

Figure 6(a) depicts an example of permanently immutable sharing. Assume that location 1 resides in the same address space as the location executing `foo()`, while location 2 does not. Location 1 shares a copy of `t` with the lifetime managed by STAPL-RTS. When `foo` exits and references on locations 1 are destroyed, the copy is destroyed. Location 2 receives a wrapper to its own copy which is read and subsequently shared, if desired, with other locations.

Temporarily immutable objects. This annotation, demonstrated in Figure 6(b), allows the caller to regain mutability rights of the object after the next synchronization point. Objects are tagged using the `immutable()` function. A reference to such an object can be given to a destination location in shared memory, instead of copying it. Using the `immutable` tag, the caller guarantees that `t` will not be updated until after the `rmi_fence()` collective synchronization call. Afterwards the variable can be safely modified.

```
send_request(...) {
  future<T> f = opaque_rmi(0, h, &A::get_value);
  return f;
}

process_request(T& t, future<T> f) {
  if (f.valid()) {
    t = f.get();
    return true;
  }
  return false;
}

stapl_main(...) {
  T t;
  future<T> f = send_request();
  while (!process_request(t,f))
  { ... // perform other work }
  foo(t); // use t;
}
```

(a) Example `stapl::future` and `stapl::promise` usage.

```
send_request(...) {
   future<T> f1 = opaque_rmi(1, h, &A::get_value)
   f1.then([](future<T> f2) { foo(f2.get()); });
}

stapl_main(...) {
  send_request();
  ... // proceed with other work
};
```

(b) Example `stapl::future::then()` usage.

Figure 7: Asynchronous value retrieval in STAPL-RTS.

4.1.4 *Futures for RMI Return Values*

While the two elision idioms described above adequately address the STAPL-RTS equivalent of *put operations* via parameter passing, for asynchronous *get operations* we draw inspiration from two other C++ STL primitives, `std::future` and `std::promise`. A *future* [5] is a mechanism to retrieve the result of an asynchronous primitive that does not ignore the result of the invoked function, e.g. `opaque_rmi()`. The *promise* is a placeholder for an incoming value, which can be set at the end of complex, multi-hop communication.

While C++ versions are for shared memory, our implementation provides similar semantics transparently in distributed memory without any additional intervention from users. The promise/future provides a standard idiom to facilitate zero copy *gets* and delegate responsibility for receiving the return value from the RMI to code outside the calling context. One example usage is shown Figure 7(a).

This trivial example shows how a return value from an RMI can be handled outside the context of the RMI invocation. A different computational activity can occur while waiting for the internal STAPL-RTS `promise` associated with the `future` to be fulfilled. We also support continuations on future objects through the `future::then()` function [12], an extension that has been proposed for C++17 [19]. Again, we follow the proposed interface, but provide our own implementation that provides a uniform interface for both shared and distributed memory. Together with a lambda expression, this feature is used to refine the previous example as shown in Figure 7(b). In this case, the consuming function of the RMI return value is specified at the RMI call site, and

```
for (int idx = ...)
  async_rmi(dest, handle, A::set_element,
            idx, rand());
```

(a) Default Request Aggregation.

```
auto tunnel = bind(async_rmi, dest, handle,
                   A::set_element, _1, _2);
for (int idx = ...)
  tunnel(idx, rand());
```

(b) Partial Function Evaluation of `async_rmi`.

Figure 8: Application Customized Aggregation in STAPL-RTS.

will be called by STAPL-RTS when the corresponding promise is fulfilled. Other local computation proceeds immediately after the initial RMI request is made.

The **PARAGRAPH** makes use of the `future` and `promise` primitives to easily spawn nested parallel computations from a source location to a set of remote locations. When the nested computation completes, the initiating location asynchronously receives notification of completion from an event handler registered with the STAPL-RTS via `future::then()`.

4.2 Application Driven Request Aggregation

As is usually the case with asynchronous communication models, STAPL encourages fine grain communication. Previous work [24,33,41] has shown aggregating these requests generally leads to overall better performance. In STAPL-RTS, we aggregate multiple RMI requests to the same destination location in the same outgoing buffer. We further enhance this mechanism by implementing *request combining*, a lightweight compression technique for requests that have the same triplet of target `p_object`, function and destination as the previous requests in the buffer. If this triplet is the same, then we need only append the arguments of the request to the aggregation buffer.

Consider the code in Figure 8(a) which updates a sequence of values in a remote object with random values. If the STAPL-RTS were to generate an MPI request for every `async_rmi` invocation in this tight loop, performance would suffer as the overhead of request transmission would greatly outweigh the cost of the requested updates. In this case, however, the STAPL-RTS is free to employ not only basic aggregation but combining as well, without violating the causal consistency guarantee of the execution model.

Note however in this case there is information trivially available to the user that would aid the runtime in this activity. The fact that the object handle, destination location and target method remain constant is immediately clear in the calling context. Using *partial function evaluation*, a common generic programming operation, we can fix one or more arguments of the STAPL-RTS primitives such as `async_rmi`, creating a new function with reduced arity. This new function contains typing information about which parameters have been fixed. To accomplish this, we can use a `bind` function with an interface similar to that of the C++ STL. The operation creates a custom communication channel as shown in Figure 8(b) based solely on algorithm level information. Using this RMI *tunnel* has the following effects:

Relaxed request consistency. Tunnels define a new logical route to destination location with ordering consistency guarantees independent of the default route (the atomicity of all RMIs is maintained). A tunnel defined with only a bound location maintains the same basic causal consistency policy as previously described.

Less runtime overhead and more efficient aggregation. By binding additional arguments during the partial evaluation, we reduce redundancy in the message; only a single copy of the bound parameter is stored in the aggregated message instead of a copy for every RMI. Other optimizations are enabled by different combinations of bound parameters. For example binding both the object handle and target function enables combining at compile time (Section 3.3), eliminating the overhead of runtime detection.

Though not necessary for the example shown in Figure 8(a), dedicated per method tunnels enable greater use of combining in some instances. Consider the case where a small number of non-combinable RMIs are interspersed in an otherwise homogeneous sequence of RMI invocations. By creating a tunnel for the homogeneous requests, the other requests do not interfere with the combining operation.

One use of tunnels in STAPL are in graph traversals, where a vertex *visitor* function passed to the algorithm is repeatedly applied on vertices throughout the `pGraph` data structure. When graph edges cross location boundaries, RMIs are issued to complete the visitation. The algorithm specifies a set of tunnels for these fine grain method invocations through this interface. As we show in Section 5.3, this high level annotation can have a dramatic effect on performance and scalability.

5. EXPERIMENTAL EVALUATION

Our experiments were carried out on three different systems. The code was compiled with maximum optimization levels (`-DNDEBUG -O3`). Each experiment has been repeated 32 times and we present the average along with a 95% confidence interval using the t-distribution.

CRAY-XK7**.** This is our department's Cray XK7m-200 system which consists of twenty-four compute nodes with AMD Opteron 6272 Interlagos 16-core processors at 2.1 GHz. Twelve of the nodes are single socket with 32 GB of memory, and the remaining twelve are dual socket nodes with 64 GB. Our benchmark code has been compiled with `gcc` 4.8.1 and we configured the STAPL-RTS with the OpenMP-based concurrency back-end with each location mapped to one OpenMP thread, pinned to one core.

IBM-BG/Q**.** This is an IBM BG/Q system available at Lawrence Livermore National Laboratory. IBM-BG/Q has 24,576 nodes, with each node populated by a 16-core IBM PowerPC A2 processor clocked at 1.6 GHz and 16 GB of memory. The compiler used was `gcc` 4.7.2, and we used the C++11-thread based multithreaded backend.

X86-CLUSTER**.** This machine is an `x86`-based commodity cluster that consists of 311 nodes with different processor and memory configurations. The slice of the system that we used for our experiments is 128 nodes. Each node has two AMD Opteron 2350 2.5 GHz processors, with each processor having 4 cores, for a total of 8 cores and 32 GB per node. We used `gcc` 4.8.2 and the C++11 thread-backed backend.

5.1 Copy Elision in K-means Clustering

K-means clustering [17] is a widely used data mining algorithm. Given a set of vectors in an n-dimensional space, the algorithm assigns vectors which are similar to one an-

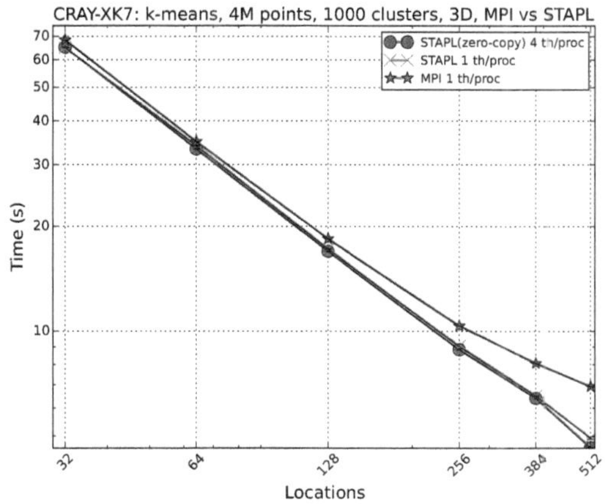

Figure 9: K-means algorithm with 4 M points, 1000 clusters in 3 D space on CRAY-XK7.

other to a specific cluster. The "K" refers to the number of clusters, which is specified by the user, at the start of the algorithm. The "means" refers to the computation for associating the vectors. Each cluster is represented by a single point in the space, which is referred to as a *cluster means* or *cluster centroid*. Dhillon and Modha [15] present a sequential and analogous parallel implementation of k-means. The parallel algorithm is implemented using MPI.

We implemented the Dhillon and Modha MPI version of k-means in C++ and then created a STAPL implementation of the same algorithm. It employs an algorithmic skeleton performing a `map` operation followed by an `all_reduce`. Binary reduction tasks use moves on one of the inputs to colocate data for the operation. The broadcast portion of the allreduce operation uses shared immutability to avoid unnecessary copies during dissemination of new cluster centroids. These optimizations are enabled by the PARAGRAPH using the rules outlined in 4.1.1.

The scalability of the STAPL version (`STAPL 1th/proc`) as shown in Figure 9 surpasses that of the MPI implementation, due to other optimizations besides copy elision. Despite being primarily a computation kernel, the mixed-mode execution with copy elision (`STAPL(zero-copy) 4th/proc`) sees gains of up to 6.2% over the basic STAPL implementation.

5.2 Asynchronous Return Values

RMIs offer additional flexibility compared to MPI for value retrieval. MPI Remote Memory Access (RMA) [27] use is complex, requiring explicit memory registration and synchronizations. RMIs expose a simple, high level interface which allows one to either wait for values or pass them to a continuation via `future::then()`, with data transfer details managed by the STAPL-RTS.

Figure 10 presents the latency of our primitives employing `futures` and `promises` (Section 4.1.4). We compare against one-sided MPI with `MPI_Get()/MPI_Win_flush()`[2] under distributed and shared memory. MPI windows are created through `MPI_Win_create_dynamic()`, as it provides the most flexible form of RMA memory registration for non-trivial applications [7].

[2]This was the best performing combination on our system.

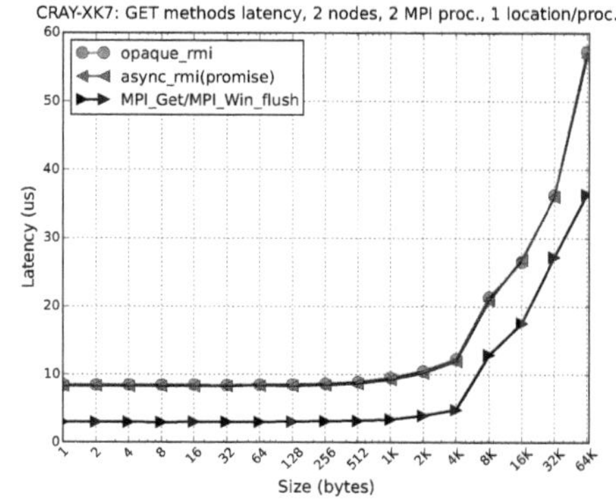

(a) Distributed memory.

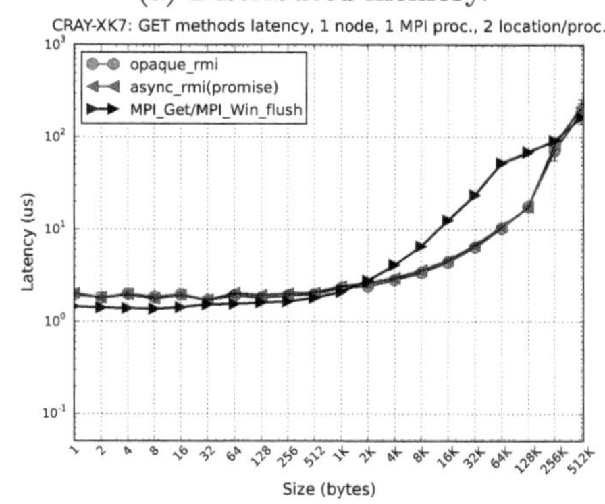

(b) Shared memory (log y-axis).

Figure 10: `opaque_rmi()/async_rmi(promise)` latency against One-Sided MPI.

Both our methods (`opaque_rmi()` and `async_rmi()` with `promise`) have similar latency. They are competitive with MPI in distributed memory. However as the object size increases past 64 KB, serialization begins to noticeably affect perceived latency. In shared memory, especially for medium object sizes (2 KB - 256 KB), we outperform MPI, as we can automatically elide one memory copy that MPI has by performing in-place construction of the object in the receiver's address space. MPI starts to outperform us after 512 KB.

5.3 Custom Aggregation in Graph Algorithms

We evaluate the STAPL-RTS using a parallel connected components (CC) graph algorithm. The algorithm computes the connected components – i.e., the subgraph wherein

```
for (auto&& u : neighbors(v))
  async_rmi(location_of(u), handle,
    Graph::visit<cc_visitor>, cc_visitor(v.id()),
    u);
```

(a) Default Request Aggregation.

```
auto tunnel = bind(async_rmi, _1, handle,
    Graph::visit<cc_visitor>, _2, _3);
for (auto&& u : neighbors(v))
  tunnel(location_of(u), cc_visitor(v.id()), u);
```

(b) Partial Evaluation of `async_rmi`.

Figure 11: Customized Request aggregation for connected components.

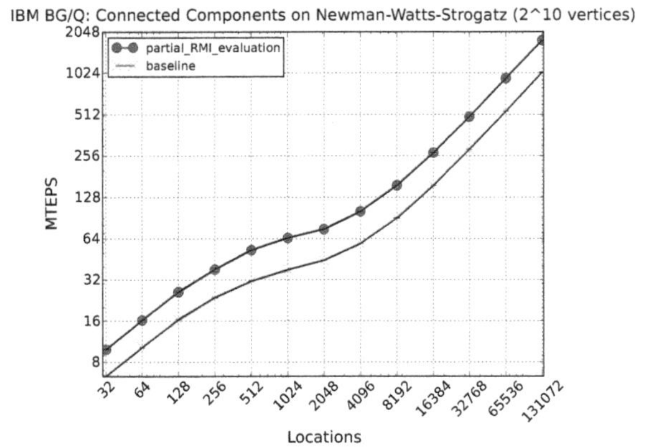

Figure 12: Connected Components on IBM-BG/Q.

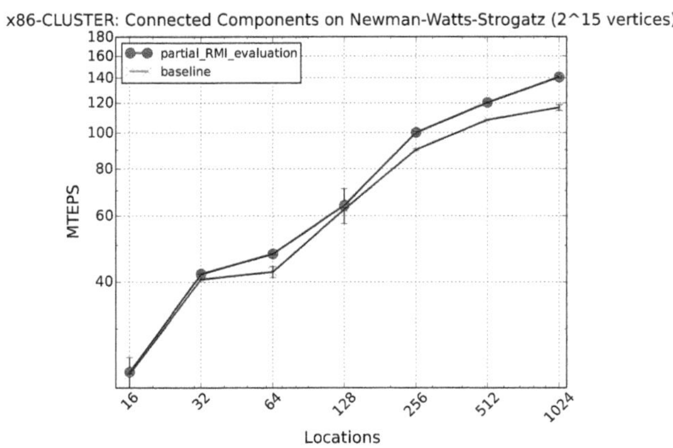

Figure 13: Connected Components on x86-CLUSTER.

any two vertices in the subgraph can be connected through some path – for each vertex, and the ID representing the component is assigned to the vertex. It is a label-propagation algorithm similar to the work presented in [25], wherein nodes set their CC ID to the lowest CC ID of their neighbors iteratively for k rounds. Connected components is widely used to study the connectivity and basic topology of graphs.

In the standard expression of the algorithm, each vertex in parallel visits all other vertices in its neighborhood to propagate its ID as a candidate CC ID. In Figure 11(a), we achieve this by issuing **async_rmis** to the locations of all neighbor vertices to apply the visitation function computing the CC. At the algorithm's level, both the handle of the graph data-structure and the method to apply visitor functions is constant, so we can form a tunnel to aid combining based aggregation of these requests (Figure 11(b)).

Figure 12 evaluates the algorithm's performance in terms of throughput (millions of traversed edges per second or MTEPS), both with and without tunneling on up to 131,072 processors on IBM-BG/Q for a Newman-Watts-Strogatz graph of 2^{10} vertices per core. We see a 1.5× improvement in throughput at lower core counts, which grows to 1.7×, suggesting that tunneling is not only increasing throughput but also improving scalability. Figure 13 shows the performance for the same type of graph with 2^{15} vertices per core on x86-CLUSTER with smaller but still noticeable improvement of about 20% over the approach without tunneling.

6. RELATED WORK

In [23] the authors propose Kanor, a declarative language for writing parallel programs in partitioned address spaces. Users annotate how data flows between address spaces to describe communication. The Kanor source-to-source compiler uses these annotations to do a more informed data-flow analysis and appropriately promote objects to global shared objects in shared memory, achieving zero-copy without explicit synchronization from the user's side, while maintaining the isolation features of distributed memory. The resulting code targets either multithreaded code or MPI code, but not a mix of both. The immutable object support we present is similar to performing the globalization optimization on a variable in Kanor but with the added benefit that it works in mixed-mode as well. A compiler such as Kanor's could easily leverage the immutable object support we offer.

A framework for taking advantage of immutable objects is introduced in [32] for code optimization. The authors describe a set of immutability annotations for Java that can be added to local or member variables. These can be used by the compiler to perform optimizations such as relaxing bounds checking, and load eliminations.

Several papers explore reference and object immutability for type safety reasons, with the potential to enable optimizations using those guarantees. Javari [6] and IGJ [44] extend the Java language with reference and object immutability qualifiers. Using them, they provide *symbolic constants*. While it is mentioned that these qualifiers can enable code optimizations, this opportunity is not explored. The authors of [18] extend the concepts of object and reference immutability to build a type system that offers immutability guarantees for objects, for the purpose of exploiting it in parallel execution. However, the paper does not expand on the performance implications. The presented immutable object support is similar to this work, but our focus is exploiting shared memory, rather than enforcing type safety.

There have been previous attempts to provide a unified communication model. Treadmarks [3] and Intel Cluster OpenMP attempted to expand shared memory models to distributed memory. While novel and popular at the time, such shared memory approaches suffer inherent scalability issues which make them infeasible for large distributed systems. Additionally, it has been suggested that MPI should become aware of shared memory through the use of the RMA functionality [22], but this has yet to be approved in the MPI specification. However, the use of all these primitives must be explicitly set up and managed by the user, making it effectively a multi-protocol approach.

MPI implementations [8, 26] detect intra-node communication and use optimized methods for copying data. While the optimizations take advantage of the node memory hierarchy, data copying is still required between MPI processes.

Hybrid OpenMP+MPI solutions have been used in applications [13, 35] with success. Almost all of these applications have sequences of parallel OpenMP sections followed by sequential sections that perform communication using MPI. The reason for this configuration is that while MPI implementations allow threads to communicate with each other under the **MPI_THREAD_MULTIPLE** mode [27], it has been shown that this negatively affects performance [40].

Habanero-C with MPI (HCMPI) [14] introduces distributed memory communication in Habanero-C. It uses the Habanero task programming model for intra-node computation and synchronization, while introducing new functions based on MPI for the inter-node equivalents. While HCMPI has better performance than MPI or hybrid MPI+OpenMP, it presents two different programming models to the user. Intra-node, HCMPI uses the Habanero-C interface, while inter-node it relies on a MPI-like message passing interface.

HPX [21] supports hybrid-mode, allowing threads to communicate over distributed memory with asynchronous primitives. Future and promise mechanisms are provided for synchronization and data retrieval. The distributed memory communication employs MPI. In shared memory, it allows arguments passed by reference, significantly reducing communication latency. In distributed memory the arguments are copied, exposing a slightly different view to the user depending on the target of the communication primitive.

Charm++ [31] provides support for hybrid mode, either by having multiple threads per node to process messages or by declaring functions threaded and allowing them to block while waiting for a value to arrive. The user has to be aware of the threading capabilities, as data structures that may be accessed by multiple threads have to be properly protected.

Chapel [11] has been designed to specifically fit multicore distributed systems. As such, they offer support for creating tasks asynchronously either on distributed or shared memory. There is not enough information on how Chapel performs in mixed shared and distributed memory applications. However, shared-memory only performance indicates that Chapel may not adequately optimized [29].

Tpetra [4] is a linear algebra package from Trilinos. Tpetra supports hybrid-mode parallelism through Kokkos; communication in distributed memory uses MPI, while shared memory communication and computation employ various Kokkos backends (Pthreads, OpenMP, Intel TBB, CUDA). Tpetra resembles a hybrid MPI+OpenMP system, as Kokkos tasks cannot communicate through distributed memory.

7. CONCLUSION

In this paper, we have demonstrated that application level information can be passed to lower levels of the software stack in a manner that does not break the software encapsulation of the communicating components yet still enables important runtime optimizations. We believe doing so aids the adoption of higher level parallel programming models which help HPC applications achieve greater reuse and portability.

To prove both the viability and utility of the approach, we use the STAPL programming library, extending the interface of its runtime layer so that higher level components can provide contextual information to it. We show that these additional annotations enable important optimizations, including copy elision and custom request aggregation. We believe that the ideas presented have general applicability beyond STAPL, as other libraries can leverage similar information from their internal program representations to drive optimizations in the runtime system.

8. ACKNOWLEDGMENTS

This research is supported in part by NSF awards CNS-0551685, CCF-0702765, CCF-0833199, CCF-1439145, CCF-1423111, CCF-0830753, IIS-0916053, IIS-0917266, EFRI-1240483, RI-1217991, by NIH NCI R25 CA090301-11, by DOE awards DE-AC02-06CH11357, DE-NA0002376, B575363, by Samsung, IBM, Intel, and by Award KUS-C1-016-04, made by King Abdullah University of Science and Technology (KAUST). This research used resources of the National Energy Research Scientific Computing Center, which is supported by the Office of Science of the U.S. Department of Energy under Contract No. DE-AC02-05CH11231.

9. REFERENCES

[1] Boost. http://www.boost.org/.

[2] Performance Application Programming Interface. http://icl.cs.utk.edu/papi/.

[3] C. Amza, A. L. Cox, S. Dwarkadas, P. Keleher, H. Lu, R. Rajamony, W. Yu, and W. Zwaenepoel. Treadmarks: Shared memory computing on networks of workstations. *Computer*, 29(2):18–28, Feb. 1996.

[4] C. G. Baker and M. A. Heroux. Tpetra, and the use of generic programming in scientific computing. *Sci. Program.*, 20(2):115–128, Apr. 2012.

[5] H. C. Baker, Jr. and C. Hewitt. The incremental garbage collection of processes. *SIGPLAN Not.*, 12(8):55–59, Aug. 1977.

[6] A. Birka and M. D. Ernst. A practical type system and language for reference immutability. In *Object-Oriented Prog. Systems, Langs., and Apps. (OOPSLA 2004)*, pages 35–49, Vancouver, BC, Canada, Oct. 2004.

[7] D. Bonachea and J. Duell. Problems with using mpi 1.1 and 2.0 as compilation targets for parallel language implementations. *Int. J. High Perf. Comput. Netw.*, 1(1-3):91–99, Aug. 2004.

[8] D. Buntinas and G. Mercier. Design and evaluation of nemesis, a scalable, low-latency, message-passing communication subsystem. In *Proc. of the Int. Symp. on Cluster Computing and the Grid*, pages 521–530. IEEE Computer Society, 2006.

[9] A. Buss, A. Fidel, Harshvardhan, T. Smith, G. Tanase, N. Thomas, X. Xu, M. Bianco, N. M. Amato, and L. Rauchwerger. The STAPL pView. In *Int. Wkshp. on Langs. and Comps. for Par. Comp. (LCPC)*, Houston, TX, USA, Sept. 2010.

[10] A. Buss, Harshvardhan, I. Papadopoulos, O. Pearce, T. Smith, G. Tanase, N. Thomas, X. Xu, M. Bianco, N. M. Amato, and L. Rauchwerger. STAPL: Standard template adaptive parallel library. In *Proc. Annual Haifa Experimental Systems Conf. (SYSTOR)*, pages 1–10, New York, NY, USA, 2010. ACM.

[11] D. Callahan, B. L. Chamberlain, and H. P. Zima. The cascade high productivity language. In *9th Int. Wkshp. on High-Level Par. Prog. Models and Supportive Environments (HIPS)*, pages 52–60, 2004.

[12] C. Campbell and A. Miller. *A Parallel Programming with Microsoft Visual C++: Design Patterns for Decomposition and Coordination on Multicore Architectures.* Microsoft Press, 1st edition, 2011.

[13] F. Cappello and D. Etiemble. Mpi versus mpi+openmp on ibm sp for the nas benchmarks. In *Proc. of the 2000 ACM/IEEE Conf. on Supercomputing*, SC '00, Washington, DC, USA, 2000. IEEE Computer Society.

[14] S. Chatterjee, S. Tasirlar, Z. Budimlic, V. Cave, M. Chabbi, M. Grossman, V. Sarkar, and Y. Yan. Integrating asynchronous task parallelism with mpi. In

Proc. Int. Par. and Dist. Proc. Symp. (IPDPS), pages 712–725, May 2013.

[15] I. Dhillon and D. Modha. A data-clustering algorithm on distributed memory multiprocessors. In *Large-Scale Par. Data Mining*, volume 1759 of *LNAI*, pages 245–260. Springer-Verlag, 2000.

[16] A. Fidel, S. A. Jacobs, S. Sharma, N. M. Amato, and L. Rauchwerger. Using load balancing to scalably parallelize sampling-based motion planning algorithms. In *Proc. Int. Par. and Dist. Proc. Symp. (IPDPS)*, Phoenix, Arizona, USA, May 2014.

[17] J. Ghosh and A. Liu. K-means. In *The Top Ten Algorithms in Data Mining*. CRC Press, Boca Raton, FL, USA, 2009.

[18] C. S. Gordon, M. J. Parkinson, J. Parsons, A. Bromfield, and J. Duffy. Uniqueness and reference immutability for safe parallelism. In *Proc. of the ACM Int. Conf. on Object Oriented Prog. Systems Langs. and Apps.*, OOPSLA '12, pages 21–40, New York, NY, USA, 2012. ACM.

[19] D. Gregor, B. Stroustrup, J. Widman, and J. Siek. Improvements to std::future<t> and related apis. technical report n3857. *ISO/IEC JTC 1, Information Technology Subcommittee SC 22, Programming Language C++*, 2014.

[20] Harshvardhan, A. Fidel, N. M. Amato, and L. Rauchwerger. The stapl parallel graph library. *In Lecture Notes in Comp. Sci. (LNCS)*, pages 46–60. Springer Berlin Heidelberg, 2012.

[21] T. Heller, H. Kaiser, A. Schäfer, and D. Fey. Using hpx and libgeodecomp for scaling hpc applications on heterogeneous supercomputers. In *Proc. of the Wkshp. on Latest Advances in Scalable Algorithms for Large-Scale Systems*, ScalA '13, pages 1:1–1:8, New York, NY, USA, 2013. ACM.

[22] T. Hoefler, J. Dinan, D. Buntinas, P. Balaji, B. Barrett, R. Brightwell, W. D. Gropp, V. Kale, and R. Thakur. Mpi + mpi: A new hybrid approach to parallel programming with mpi plus shared memory. *Computing*, 95:1121–1136, 2013.

[23] F. Jiao, N. Mahajan, J. Willcock, A. Chauhan, and A. Lumsdaine. Partial globalization of partitioned address spaces for zero-copy communication with shared memory. In *High Perf. Computing (HiPC)*, pages 1–10, Dec 2011.

[24] L. V. Kale and S. Krishnan. Charm++: A portable concurrent object oriented system based on c++. *SIGPLAN Not.*, 28(10):91–108, Oct. 1993.

[25] U. Kang, C. E. Tsourakakis, and C. Faloutsos. Pegasus: A peta-scale graph mining system-implementation and observations, 2009.

[26] S. N. Labs. Portals Message Passing Interface. `http://www.sandia.gov/Portals`.

[27] MPI forum. MPI: A Message-Passing Interface Standard Version 3.0. `http://www.mpi-forum.org/docs/mpi-3.0/mpi30-report.pdf`, 2012.

[28] D. Musser, G. Derge, and A. Saini. *STL Tutorial and Reference Guide, 2nd Edition*. Addison-Wesley, 2001.

[29] S. Nanz, S. West, and K. S. D. Silveira. B.: Benchmarking usability and performance of multicore languages. In *In: ESEM'13. IEEE Computer Society*, 2013.

[30] OpenMP Architecture Review Board. *OpenMP - C and C++ Application Program Interface*, October 1998. Document DN 004-2229-001.

[31] Parallel Programming Laboratory, University of Illinois at Urbana-Champaign. *The Charm++ Programming Language Manual.* Version 6 (Release 1).

[32] I. Pechtchanski and V. Sarkar. Immutability specification and its applications: Research articles. *Concurr. Comput. : Pract. Exper.*, 17(5-6):639–662, Apr. 2005.

[33] S. Saunders and L. Rauchwerger. ARMI: an adaptive, platform independent communication library. In *Proc. of the 9th ACM SIGPLAN Symp. on Principles and Practice of Par. Prog. (PPoPP)*, pages 230–241, San Diego, California, USA, 2003. ACM.

[34] S. S. Shende and A. D. Malony. The tau parallel performance system. *The Int. J. of High Perf. Computing Apps.*, 20:287–331, 2006.

[35] J. Sillero, G. Borrell, J. Jiménez, and R. D. Moser. Hybrid openmp-mpi turbulent boundary layer code over 32k cores. In *Proc. of the 18th European MPI Users' Group Conf. on Recent Advances in the Message Passing Interface*, EuroMPI'11, pages 218–227, Berlin, Heidelberg, 2011. Springer-Verlag.

[36] A. B. Sinha, L. V. Kalé, and B. Ramkumar. A dynamic and adaptive quiescence detection algorithm, 1993.

[37] M. Snir, S. W. Otto, S. Huss-Lederman, D. W. Walker, and J. Dongarra. *MPI: The complete reference*. MIT Press, Cambridge, MA, 1996.

[38] B. Stroustrup. *The C++ Programming Language*. Addison Wesley Professional, 2013.

[39] G. Tanase, A. Buss, A. Fidel, Harshvardhan, I. Papadopoulos, O. Pearce, T. Smith, N. Thomas, X. Xu, N. Mourad, J. Vu, M. Bianco, N. M. Amato, and L. Rauchwerger. The STAPL Parallel Container Framework. In *Proc. ACM SIGPLAN Symp. Prin. Prac. Par. Prog. (PPoPP)*, pages 235–246, San Antonio, Texas, USA, 2011.

[40] R. Thakur and W. D. Gropp. Test suite for evaluating performance of multithreaded mpi communication. *Par. Computing*, 35:608–617, Nov. 2008.

[41] J. J. Willcock, T. Hoefler, N. G. Edmonds, and A. Lumsdaine. Am++: A generalized active message framework. In *Proc. of the 19th Int. Conf. on Par. Architectures and Compilation Techniques*, PACT '10, pages 401–410, New York, NY, USA, 2010. ACM.

[42] C. E. Wu et al. From trace generation to visualization: A performance framework for distributed parallel systems. In *Proc. of SC2000: High Perf. Networking and Computing*, Nov. 2000.

[43] M. Zandifar, N. Thomas, N. M. Amato, and L. Rauchwerger. The STAPL skeleton framework. In *Proc. 27th Int. Wkshp. on Langs. and Comps. for Par. Comp. (LCPC), Hillsboro, OR, US*, 2014.

[44] Y. Zibin, A. Potanin, M. Ali, S. Artzi, A. Kiezun, and M. D. Ernst. Object and reference immutability using java generics. In *Proc. of the the 6th Joint Meeting of the European Soft. Eng. Conf. and the ACM SIGSOFT Symp. on The Foundations of Soft. Eng.*, ESEC-FSE '07, pages 75–84, New York, NY, USA, 2007. ACM.

Author Index

www.ingramcontent.com/pod-product-compliance
Ingram Content Group UK Ltd.
Pitfield, Milton Keynes, MK11 3LW, UK
UKHW051412290926
15471UKWH00009B/1566

9 781450 338691